ColdFusion® MX Bible

Adam Phillip Churvis, Hal Helms,
Charles Arehart, David Churvis

WILEY

Wiley Publishing, Inc.

ColdFusion® MX Bible

Published by
Wiley Publishing, Inc.
909 Third Avenue
New York, NY 10022
www.wiley.com

Library of Congress Number: 2001093600

ISBN: 0-7645-4622-8

Manufactured in the United States of America

10 9 8 7 6 5 4 3 2 1

1B/SQ/QS/QT/IN

Published by Wiley Publishing, Inc., Indianapolis, Indiana
Published simultaneously in Canada

For general information on our other products and services or to obtain technical support, please contact our Customer Care Department within the U.S. at 800-762-2974, outside the U.S. at 317-572-3993 or fax 317-572-4002.

Wiley also publishes its books in a variety of electronic formats. Some content that appears in print may not be available in electronic books.

ColdFusion® MX Bible

About the Authors

Adam Churvis is a database and scalability specialist with more than 20 years of software-industry experience in many languages and database platforms. He is the founder and President of Productivity Enhancement, a full-service consulting, training, and commercial-software development firm, which is entering its 18th year in business and is also the parent company of ColdFusionTraining.com, which provides the most advanced and intensive ColdFusion training in the world. Adam is a member of Team Macromedia and also serves as a current board member and former President of the Atlanta ColdFusion User Group, and he enjoys speaking at other CFUGs as well. He has a wife, whom he worships, three children, three cats, and lots and lots of computers. He can be reached at `adam@ProductivityEnhancement.com`.

Hal Helms is an internationally-known speaker, writer, and trainer on Java, ColdFusion, and best practices in software development. Hal writes the popular "Occasional Newsletter" available at `halhelms.com`, and you can reach him at `hal@techspedition.com`.

Charles Arehart is the founder and CTO of SysteManage, based in Laurel, Maryland. A Macromedia certified advanced developer and instructor, Charles is also a member of Team Macromedia who has logged more than 5 years with ColdFusion and more than 20 years in IT. His monthly "Journeyman" column appears in ColdFusion Developer's Journal, where he's a technical editor. He is a regular speaker at developer conferences, seminars, and user group meetings worldwide, and also provides training and short-term consulting. You can reach him at `carehart@systemanage.com`.

David Churvis is a software-development specialist who got his start in object-oriented programming at the age of eight. He has worked in HyperCard, SuperCard, FutureBasic, CFML, VTML/WIZML, Transact/SQL, PL/SQL, Delphi, C, C++, C#, Java, JSP, JavaScript, VBScript, and DHTML. David is Vice President of Development for Productivity Enhancement and is the chief programmer behind the CommerceBlocks line of modular ColdFusion development tools and LoRCAT, the Load Reduction and Concentration Analysis Tool for ColdFusion.

Credits

Senior Acquisitions Editor
Sharon Cox

Project Editor
Sharon Nash

Technical Editor
Jen and Peter deHaan

Copy Editor
William A. Barton

Editorial Manager
Mary Beth Wakefield

Vice President and Executive Group Publisher
Richard Swadley

Vice President and Executive Publisher
Bob Ipsen

Executive Editorial Director
Mary Bednarek

Project Coordinator
Nancee Reeves

Graphics and Production Specialists
Melissa Auciello-Brogan, Beth Brooks, Jennifer Click, Joyce Haughey, Stephanie D. Jumper, Jeremey Unger

Quality Control Technician
Susan Moritz, Charles Spencer

Permissions Editor
Carmen Krikorian

Media Development Specialist
Travis Silvers

Proofreading and Indexing
TECHBOOKS Production Services

Adam Churvis: This book is dedicated to my uncle, Lionel Bernard Watkins II, and to the Marine Military Academy, for teaching me the most important Code of all. Semper Fidelis, Marines.

Hal Helms: To Stan Cox, whose ideas never fail to inspire me.

Charles Arehart: Begin to weave and God will give you the thread – German Proverb.

David Churvis: I dedicate this book to Anne Granville, Neil Nichols, Pat Greeson, and Ed Coleman, the best schoolteachers I ever had. Thanks for never accepting anything less than my best and thanks for always believing in me.

Preface

ColdFusion has come a long way since its inception. Way back in 1995, Allaire Corporation came out with Version 1 of ColdFusion, and even then, developers loved it and could see its potential. Several versions and one very important merger with Macromedia later, ColdFusion MX has positioned itself as a leading Web-application server, integrating many different Internet technologies, including XML, Web services, and Java.

ColdFusion, at its core, is a server-side scripting environment that enables you to quickly get your sites up and running with much less code than the equivalent ASP, JSP, or PHP application requires but, at the same time, is even more powerful than these other languages. In fact, ColdFusion MX scripts are compiled into Java classes, and those Java classes are executed by an embedded version of JRun, Macromedia's powerful J2EE server.

This book is intended as a comprehensive tour of ColdFusion MX: It's broad enough to give you a feel for everything that ColdFusion MX can do, but it's deep enough that you can use the knowledge that you gain from this book to develop truly powerful ColdFusion applications. Whether you are a beginner or an expert, you should have the ColdFusion MX Bible in your reference library.

How This Book Is Organized

The scope of this book is rather broad and takes a natural progression, starting with a basic introduction, then moving on to using databases and the ColdFusion language itself before discussing more advanced concepts. The last part is the language reference, which has been organized very differently than most other references. There are nine parts to this book.

Part I: Getting Started with ColdFusion MX

The first part of the book incorporates seven chapters relating to the most basic aspects of ColdFusion. After a brief introduction, we provide a tutorial on building (and understanding) your first ColdFusion MX application. The rest of Part I focuses on the basics of the language itself, the underlying technology, and an introduction to using SQL effectively with ColdFusion. The last two chapters in Part I go into more detail about using forms and testing your code.

Part II: Using ColdFusion MX with Databases

ColdFusion would be nearly useless without some kind of database as its backend. Part II starts with a chapter on database design, moves on to a discussion about using databases with ColdFusion, and then spends two whole chapters on effective and advanced database techniques. Even if you think that you know everything about databases, don't skip this part of the book.

Part III: The ColdFusion MX Language

Part III focuses on the ins and outs of the ColdFusion language. The ten chapters in this section move from simple variables to complex variables such as arrays and structures before covering advanced topics such as user-defined functions, custom tags, state management, and exception handling.

Part IV: ColdFusion MX Components, Web Services, and Flash Integration

Part IV covers the new cutting-edge features of ColdFusion MX that can change the way that you write ColdFusion applications forever. The six chapters in Part IV should be read in order, because each builds on the concepts described in the preceding chapter. Part IV starts out with two chapters about understanding and building ColdFusion components and then discusses how and why you should move portions of your existing code to components. The last three chapters discuss Web services, Flash Remoting, and server-side ActionScript.

Part V: Integrating ColdFusion MX with Other Technologies

ColdFusion MX is most powerful if it's extended with other technologies such as Java, COM, and XML. Part V consists of four chapters covering Java objects, JSP, EJB, COM, WDDX and XML, and some of the tags that ColdFusion uses to communicate with external systems. Spend some extra time on Chapter 30, as XML is about to become a big part of your development life.

Part VI: Extending Your ColdFusion MX Applications

Part VI covers additional features that you can use to extend ColdFusion, such as task scheduling, file operations, Verity, and charting, as well as some of the community resources and development tools that help make application development go much faster than normal.

Part VII: ColdFusion MX Development Practices

Sometimes, how you code is as important as the code itself. Part VII covers important topics that are often overlooked, such as code documentation and testing, and also contains a discussion of Fusebox 3 written by none other than the Fusebox master himself, Hal Helms. The part also contains chapters about source-code control, effective use of ColdFusion Studio, and integrating security into your applications.

Part VIII: ColdFusion MX Administration

Part VIII is comparatively short, but it's packed with information about getting the most out of ColdFusion MX by tweaking its server settings. Part VIII is split into two chapters, the first covering all the settings available in ColdFusion Administrator and the second going into more detail about approaching specific settings and sets of options.

Part IX: ColdFusion MX Language Reference

Most language references use the format provided by Macromedia: an alphabetical listing of tags and functions (with tags separated from functions) and a separate list of categories. Part IX turns this model on its ear. Each section of the language (variables, databases, forms, and so on) has its own chapter, and tags and functions are listed together in each chapter.

This way, if you are working on a problem regarding database queries, you see all the tags and functions that are most often used to handle database queries in one place, which means that you nay also see what you've been missing in the language (such as, for example, `CFOBJECTCACHE`).

If you need an alphabetical reference, we also provide a traditional alphabetized listing of all tags and functions with page references, and many tags cross-reference others so that, no matter what you're looking for, you can easily find it.

CD-ROM

The CD-ROM that accompanies this book supplies you with a great deal of additional material including author code listings and samples, many software applications, and a PDF eBook version of the final book. The CD-ROM Appendix at the end of the book gives full details of all these items.

How To Get The Most Out Of This Book

Treat this book as you would a novel and not a cookbook. Most people, on picking up the *ColdFusion MX Bible*, would probably look up the one specific subject that they want to learn about and go directly there. Although this approach is certainly a valid one if you have a specific problem to solve, we recommend that, at some point, you start from the very beginning and work your way all the way through the book. If you are not a beginner, feel free to skip all of Part I but read everything after that.

We recommend this approach even for advanced developers, because many people first starting out in ColdFusion unintentionally pick up some bad habits that remain with them even after they become better developers. The information contained in this book is based on sound development practices born of many years of experience in many different languages and technologies. The first thing that we want to do is help you understand how ColdFusion works and how to get the most out of it, and the second is to make sure that no bad habits come back to haunt you.

What the Icons Mean

Throughout this book, you will find icons in the margins that highlight special or important information. Keep an eye out for the following icons:

A Caution icon indicates a procedure that could cause difficulty or even data loss; pay careful attention to Caution icons to avoid common and not-so-common programming pitfalls.

Cross-Reference icons point to additional information about a topic, which you can find in other sections of the book.

A Note icon highlights interesting or supplementary information and often contains extra bits of technical information about a subject.

Tip icons draw attention to handy suggestions, helpful hints, and useful pieces of advice.

Acknowledgments

We would like to take this opportunity to thank Sharon Cox, our Acquisitions Editor, and Sharon Nash, our Project Editor, for making this project come together and for not making voodoo dolls of us when we missed submission deadlines.

This book would not have achieved its high level of quality without the work diligently performed by its technical editors, Peter and Jen deHaan, and its copy editor, William Barton. If not for their dedicated involvement on these chapters, the end result would have been a book of measurably lower quality. We respectfully request to work with them again on all future Wiley books.

We would also like to thank Alan Preston, Tom Donovan, and Raymond Camden at Macromedia for their excellent technical support and advice during the making of this book.

Thanks also to the CFUG (ColdFusion User Group) and MMUG (Macromedia User Group) leaders who pour lots of unpaid hours into supporting their groups and the new technologies that Macromedia continues to give us. You are the backbone of the Macromedia development community, and the praises that you deserve would fill a book all by themselves.

A special note of thanks to Michael Dinowitz, the father of the ColdFusion community, who has quite literally put his very life into the ColdFusion community. The countless hours that he has given us through developing and maintaining the House of Fusion Web site (`www.houseoffusion.com`) and its critically important mailing lists, the many speaking engagements that he has supported, and the father-like caring that he continues to have for everyone with a development problem can never be sufficiently repaid. This praise is but a small token of what is due this truly admirable man.

Behind every great man is a great woman, and Judith Dinowitz proves this axiom yet again. Judith's tireless efforts running Fusion Authority (www.fusionauthority.com) have resulted in an accurate, up-to-the-minute account of everything ColdFusion on which many readers rely.

And finally, thanks go out to you, the readers of this book, who make writing it all worthwhile.

—Adam Churvis and David Churvis

Thanks to my co-authors and to the indomitable folks at John Wiley & Son who made sure that you're holding this book in your hands.

—*Hal Helms*

I can now appreciate better why so many authors thank their editors. What forbearance, with charm! Our two Sharon's (Nash and Cox) were beacons in the night bringing this ship to port after more than 2 years at sea. Thanks too, of course, to Hal for bringing me on board initially and to Adam for captaining us through the rough seas. Last, and certainly not least, my love and inordinate gratitude to my wife Kim for her very own special patience through it all.

—*Charles Arehart*

Contents at a Glance

Contents

Part III: The ColdFusion MX Language 289

P A R T

I

Getting Started with ColdFusion MX

✦ ✦ ✦ ✦

In This Part

✦ ✦ ✦ ✦

Introducing ColdFusion MX

In This Chapter

The elegant simplicity of the ColdFusion language

Getting started

Extending ColdFusion with other technologies

What's new in MX

Welcome to ColdFusion MX! ColdFusion is one of the easiest-to-use programming languages, yet it can build the most powerful, extensible Web applications in the world. ColdFusion's elegant simplicity is appreciated by both novice programmers who want a fast start on building real-world applications and experienced developers coming from complicated Web technologies such as Active Server Pages.

You may be wondering how much effort learning ColdFusion takes. This really is up to you, because the more time that you spend with ColdFusion, the better you become with it. If you already know a little HTML and you just want to build a simple Web site that presents your collection of antique whistles to the world, you can probably be online with your first application in anywhere from three days to a week. A few more weeks of diligent practice are likely to see you selling your whistles over the Internet, and in a year, who knows . . . ? You may start building WorldWhistleExchange.com!

You need to know surprisingly little before diving into ColdFusion, but the more experience that you have with other programming languages, the better.

If you know a little HTML and you understand how the Internet works, you're good to get started. If you've heavily programmed in a language such as C++ or Java, you're home free, because you're already familiar with solid programming concepts. If you're just beginning your first foray into the world of programming and the Internet, be aware that you need to spend plenty of time going over the basics that we present in Part I of this book.

You should also get involved in your local ColdFusion user group, which is sure to be an excellent resource for learning new techniques. The bottom line is that anyone can learn ColdFusion — it's just a matter of trying.

Why a Tag-Based Language?

ColdFusion is a simple language to learn and use primarily because it employs a *tag-based* syntax, which makes the transition between HTML (the language that your Web browser uses to render content) and CFML (ColdFusion Markup Language, the language that ColdFusion uses to generate that content from dynamic data) within your code very natural. Take, for example, the following HTML listing of companies (no CFML is in this code):

```
<table>
  <tr>
    <td>13</td>
    <td>The Very Big Corporation of America</td>
  </tr>
  <tr>
    <td>14</td>
    <td>Ma's Homemade Pies</td>
  </tr>
  <tr>
    <td>15</td>
    <td>Shecky Records</td>
  </tr>
</table>
```

By using ColdFusion's tag-based syntax, you can easily generate this table dynamically from data stored in your database (the CFML is boldfaced in the following example), as follows:

```
<cfquery name="GetCompanies" datasource="MyDatabase">
SELECT
  CompanyID,
  CompanyName
FROM
  Company
</cfquery>

<table>
  <cfoutput query="GetCompanies">
   <tr>
     <td>#CompanyID#</td>
     <td>#CompanyName#</td>
   </tr>
  </cfoutput>
</table>
```

Basically, ColdFusion performs a *query* against the *MyDatabase* datasource (an object that connects to and communicates with a database) and names the data result set (the data that results from performing the query) *GetCompanies*. Then, for each row in the GetCompanies query, ColdFusion *outputs* the HTML markup used to format an HTML table row containing two table cells. The first table cell contains the value of *CompanyID*, and the second table cell contains the value of *CompanyName* from the current row in the result set.

Because CFML is a tag-based syntax, making the table dynamic is a simple matter of adding some HTML-like tags. Read Chapter 2 to see how simple building applications with a tag-based syntax can be.

ColdFusion Can Be Extended In Many Ways

In addition to being one of the easiest Web-programming languages, ColdFusion is also one of the most easily extensible languages, because it can interface with many different technologies, as shown in the following list:

- ✦ Java objects, which are standalone packages of code written in the Java language
- ✦ Custom tags written in C++ or Java, which are pieces of code to be used only with ColdFusion, but which are written in either C++ or Java

- ✦ Java Server Page (JSP) tag libraries, which are originally built for use within JSP systems
- ✦ Java Server Pages, which are the JSP equivalent of ColdFusion templates
- ✦ Flash Remoting, which enables ColdFusion to easily communicate with Flash movies
- ✦ Web services, which publish portions of a ColdFusion application's functionality for use by other application servers, including non-ColdFusion servers
- ✦ COM (Component Object Model) objects, which are software objects that can communicate with one another on the Microsoft Windows platform
- ✦ CORBA (Common Object Request Broker Architecture) objects, which can communicate with one another over networks and between platforms
- ✦ The operating system (Windows, Unix, and so on), through batch files and executables

Each of these technologies can and do take up entire books by themselves, because they are big topics. ColdFusion, however, makes integrating them with your application a relatively simple matter by using a simple interface—usually just a matter of one or two CFML tags.

For more information about extending ColdFusion, read chapters 17, 18, and 22 through 29.

In addition, refer to *Developing Web Applications with ColdFusion MX* in your ColdFusion MX documentation set to learn about creating CFX custom tags, which are custom tags written in Java or C++ for use in ColdFusion.

What You Need To Get Started

Chapter 2 takes you through the process of creating your first ColdFusion application, but the following list describes what you need before you begin:

- ✦ **A copy of ColdFusion MX Server.** A trial copy is provided on the CD accompanying this book. The trial reverts to a free single-user developer edition after 30 days.
- ✦ **A copy of HomeSite, HomeSite+, Dreamweaver MX, ColdFusion Studio, or another code editor.** You can acquire a trial copy of HomeSite from Macromedia at `www.macromedia.com/software/homesite/`.
- ✦ **Database software.** We provide an Access database for Part I of this book, but if you have Microsoft SQL Server, Oracle, or another Enterprise-level database server, by all means use it after you get past building your first ColdFusion application. Chapters 8, 9, 10, and 11 use Microsoft SQL Server 2000 to explain advanced database concepts, so you should get a trial download of SQL Server from Microsoft.com if you don't already have a copy.

That's all you need to begin developing applications in ColdFusion MX. Follow the installation instructions for ColdFusion MX very carefully and make certain that you heed any warnings during the install process. Our advice is to go very slowly through the installation process and keep your finger off the mouse button so that you don't anxiously click Next before reading important instructions. You shouldn't just "slam through the defaults" in installing ColdFusion MX either, because you have important choices to make regarding your Web-server configuration. For example, ColdFusion MX can install its own standalone web server for development purposes during the installation process, or it can use your currently installed web server, so watch what you're doing.

Good luck!

An Overview of What's New in ColdFusion MX

The MX release of ColdFusion is without doubt the most eagerly anticipated software release in Macromedia's history. Everything—every *single* thing—has been completely rewritten from the ground up, in Java. Not only that, but the ColdFusion software itself now runs on top of JRun, Macromedia's J2EE server engine. You still write your ColdFusion applications in CFML, but behind the scenes, ColdFusion Server translates your CFML into Java source code, compiles it into Java bytecode, and then JRun kicks in and runs the compiled Java byte code. This whole translation-and-compilation process is entirely transparent to you, but the performance gains are very obvious in most cases.

Along with these changes in platform and architecture came big enhancements in the ColdFusion language and some truly powerful new technologies, some of which change the very way that you write ColdFusion applications from now on.

Tag-based user defined functions

ColdFusion MX introduces a new `CFFUNCTION` tag for creating user-defined functions (UDFs) containing CFML tags, which means that you can now declare your own functions that use databases, external systems, or anything else accessible by the ColdFusion language.

Functions declared with `CFFUNCTION` are more formally structured than their CFSCRIPT UDF counterparts. CFFUNCTION formally defines the data type that it returns as the result of the function, and a new child tag—`CFARGUMENT`—formally defines the names and data types of the arguments passed into the function, as well as whether those arguments are required or optional.

The new `CFINVOKE and` `CFINVOKEARGUMENT` tags provide a new way to invoke user-defined functions. Functions can now be invoked through a formally declared interface into the function's arguments, and those arguments can now be declared as either required or optional.

ColdFusion components

ColdFusion components, also known as CFCs, bring some object-like behavior to ColdFusion. (For a basic understanding of objects, read "The Nickel Tour of Objects" in Chapter 22.)

In their simplest implementation, *components* are formal containers for interrelated functions created by using `CFFUNCTION`. By encapsulating all functions related to a specific process or entity in a single component, you take your first step toward thinking in terms of objects rather than in terms of individual pieces of code.

Components can also be implemented as persistent objects that "live" between page requests and contain both user-defined functions and properties (data). ColdFusion components are not true objects, as you find in other languages such as Java or C++, but they do enable some "object-like" capabilities, such as basic inheritance.

Powerful new functionality in ColdFusion MX, such as Web services and Flash Remoting, use ColdFusion components as well.

Flash Remoting services

For anyone who has succeeded in interfacing Flash movies with ColdFusion, MX's new Flash Remoting Services are a true godsend. What used to require a good bit of knowledge in Flash ActionScripting (the language of Flash), plus hours or days of laboring in Flash and ColdFusion MX, now takes only a basic understanding of ActionScript and a few lines of code to link a

Flash movie with ColdFusion. If you're new to ColdFusion, you'll still be amazed at how easy Flash Remoting makes creating Flash movies that use the functionality built into your ColdFusion applications.

Where earlier versions of Flash were basically crude animation tools that could be forced into exchanging data with ColdFusion, Flash Remoting turns the Flash MX authoring environment into a true client-application development environment that is designed from the ground up to work directly with ColdFusion MX. Flash MX applications communicate with ColdFusion by using a new and very efficient binary format named *AMF* (*A*ction *M*essage *F*ormat), which is not only faster but requires only a fraction of the bandwidth previously taken up by XML-based data exchanges.

Flash Remoting enables you to develop applications with truly interactive graphical user interfaces. The best that you could do before Flash Remoting came along was to create an overly complicated DHTML convolution that either cached data locally or made constant page requests from ColdFusion each time that the user touched a form control.

Chapter 26 shows you how to create a basic Flash Remoting interface with interactive controls, but it is not a comprehensive lesson. If you are interested in developing serious Flash MX applications — and we hope that you are — you should also obtain the *Flash MX Action Script Bible,* by Robert Reinhardt and Joey Lott (Wiley Publishing) and digest it thoroughly. I recommend this book not because it comes from the same publisher as this one, but because Robert Reinhardt and Joey Lott have done an excellent treatment of Flash MX that should not be missed.

Web services

A *Web service* exposes a software *component* to *remote* systems in a platform-independent manner, meaning that any application server platform capable of consuming web services can make use of the web services created with ColdFusion MX. ColdFusion MX truly rang the bell with its implementation of Web services: To create a Web service in MX, you simply set the `Access` attribute of a ColdFusion *component* function to `Remote`. No, *really!*

You need to pay attention to a few details, of course, but creating a Web service is a natural extension to ColdFusion's component functionality. Whenever a ColdFusion component is accessed as a Web service, the remote consumer of the Web service receives the result in the native format of the consumer's platform, so .NET consumers receive ColdFusion arrays as .NET arrays, and Java consumers receive them as Java arrays.

Some incompatibilities do exist between certain ColdFusion complex data types and specific consumer platforms, but these hurdles can be cleared by exchanging complex data as XML documents that the consumer may then transform as needed.

One piece of advice: Learn Web services (see Chapter 25), XSLT transformations (see Chapter 30), and how to validate XML documents against DTDs by using COM (see Chapter 29). These skills may sound foreign to you now, but they're soon to be in very high demand, and we want you there to provide the necessary solutions.

Native XML handling

Finally, ColdFusion can handle XML! If you've never heard of it before, XML stands for eXtensible Markup Language, and it provides a way to structure data and encode it with additional information using a plain text format that can be used by most modern application servers and applications. Previously, data interchange with XML was limited to one of the following two options in ColdFusion:

✦ **Use WDDX as an interchange format:** This was a good start, but it was limited because you were locked in to a data-centric flavor of XML. (WDDX is explained in detail in Chapter 30.)

✦ **Use a COM object or third-part custom tag library:** Some good libraries were on the market, but they still are no match for the capability to natively use XML and XML objects.

Now, by using ColdFusion MX, all you need do to create an XML object is use the new `CFXML` tag, as follows:

```
<cfxml variable="XmlObj">
<my-xml-tag>
   <my-child-tag />
</my-xml-tag>
</cfxml>
```

And that's only the beginning of an impressive array of XML handling features; in fact, the only feature missing from ColdFusion's XML implementation is the capability to validate against a DTD or XMLSchema document, which can be easily remedied by using COM. For more information about validating XML with ColdFusion MX, see Chapter 29.

ColdFusion MX also natively handles XSLT transformations, so you can transform structured XML documents into virtually any type of content. MX's XPath capabilities enable you to query an XML object and extract data structures that match search criteria.

After you parse an XML document into an XML object, you can refer to its data elements by using the same ColdFusion syntax used for handling arrays and structures, so your learning curve remains relatively small. Refer to Chapter 30 for a complete discussion of ColdFusion MX's XML handling capabilities.

Simplified security

Does anyone remember Advanced Security? Does anyone want to suffer through that again? ColdFusion MX makes security easier to manage in two ways: *application security* by using the new `CFLOGIN` tag (and its related tags and functions) and the new J2EE-integrated *Sandbox Security*. The following sections briefly describe these two methods of security.

Application security

ColdFusion MX introduces `CFLOGIN`, which solves two problems at once. First, it's easy to use and understand, so it takes less development time than a roll-your-own solution. Second, and perhaps more important, `CFLOGIN` integrates directly with J2EE security, which is a proven security framework that can integrate with other J2EE products. Integrating with J2EE security means that a user can log in to a ColdFusion Web site and have that same login honored by a call to an EJB (Enterprise JavaBean) or a JSP page. This is very powerful stuff.

To learn more about using application security, see Chapter 40.

Sandbox Security

Available only in the Enterprise version of ColdFusion MX (although Professional has a similar feature, named *Resource Security*), Sandbox Security is a great feature for shared hosts or people running a department with multiple applications, because it enables a site administrator to restrict what resources the code on his server can access. The administrator can, for example, restrict the code in one directory from accessing specific tags and datasources, and he can restrict code in another directory from accessing a completely different set of tags and datasources.

To learn more about ColdFusion MX Sandbox Security and how to administer it, see Chapter 44.

Simplified Verity administration

Verity is the name of the company who invented the full-text search technology use by ColdFusion MX, so full-text searching in ColdFusion is commonly referred to as "Verity searching." A full-text search is what you perform on popular search sites like Google and Yahoo, where you can search for a word or phrase, the search engine looks inside collections containing billions of web pages for that word or phrase, and returns a weighted list of results that most likely best fit what you're looking for.

Expansions to the Verity full-text search system have made managing a site that uses Verity easier than ever. You can now obtain a list of all the Verity collections on your server (as well as some extra metadata, such as where they are stored and whether they are K2 Server (a high performance standalone Verity server) collections) by using the CFCOLLECTION tag, as follows:

```
<cfcollection action="LIST" name="GetCollections">
```

ColdFusion MX offers new Verity related functions and still more improvements over earlier versions of ColdFusion, so look at Chapter 32.

Simplified locking

Because ColdFusion MX is now built on Java, you no longer need to worry about data corruption in the shared memory scopes: *Session*, *Application*, and *Server* (see Chapter 12 for more information about scopes). Unfortunately, this fact has been misinterpreted by some to mean "Hey—I don't need to lock my Session variables anymore!" Nothing can be farther from the truth.

You still need to lock shared memory scopes to prevent what are known as *race conditions*, where one piece of code may interfere with another that is also trying to access the same data in shared memory. Race conditions are more prevalent than you may think; all in all, you're most likely to continue to lock shared memory scopes almost as much as you did in earlier versions of ColdFusion.

The new locking rules do enable you to safely read and write "write-once" variables in shared memory scopes without locking. So if you have a Session variable that is created only once during a session, is never destroyed and recreated, is never modified under any conditions whatsoever, and is never `CFSET` a second time—even with the same value that it had previously—you do not need to lock access to it. Refer to Chapter 12 for details on using CFLOCK.

Java Server Pages integration

ColdFusion MX is built on top of the same platform that runs *JSP* (or *J*ava *S*erver *P*ages). You can, therefore, include JSP pages in your application, and you can share variables between ColdFusion and JSP! We can set a Session variable, for example, in `MyCFPage.cfm` as follows:

```
<cfset Session.myvar = 1>
```

And we can then output it on `MyJSPPage.jsp` as follows:

```
<%= session.getAttribute("myvar") %>
```

This example may illustrate only the general principle behind sharing data between the two platforms, but imagine the possibilities. For more information about integrating ColdFusion with Java technologies, see Chapter 28.

Extended graphing capabilities

ColdFusion's integrated charting capabilities received an overhaul in the MX release, so much so that, instead of upgrading the existing ColdFusion 5 `CFGRAPH` tag, Macromedia replaced it with a new `CFCHART` tag. You can now create charts that were totally impossible before, such as the following list describes:

- ✦ Multiple series on a chart
- ✦ 3D charts with full control over the rotation effects
- ✦ New chart types, such as area, pyramid, and scatter charts
- ✦ New point markers
- ✦ PNG output instead of GIF
- ✦ Value rollovers that now work with PNG or JPG formats
- ✦ Improved Flash output
- ✦ Better control over value formats

And these are just *some* of the new features! `CFCHART`'s output is also much more attractive than `CFGRAPH`'s was.

For more information on using `CFCHART` and building chart interfaces, see Chapter 33.

Enhanced query of queries

Introduced with much fanfare in Version 5, *Query of Queries* (or *QoQ* as the feature is sometimes called) was a great idea. It enables you to get data from multiple sources (whether from the database, file structure, or anything that returns a query object to ColdFusion) and combine them into a single result set. The problem was that QoQ was clumsy and couldn't do much.

ColdFusion MX has enhanced its QoQ processor. The SQL used to manipulate QoQ is now a little more natural and less restrictive. You still have no outer join capability, and you still can't alias (provide a different and usually abbreviated name for) the names of tables, but you now don't need to alias the names of columns to retrieve them, and you can now match `NULL`s, which was impossible before.

For more about Query of Queries, see Chapter 11.

Enhanced structured exception handling

Structure exception handling provides a framework within which your code operates, such that, if an error is thrown, it may be interrupted and either handled using alternative code (this is known as an "exception"), or logged and the user politely notified that an error has occurred.

Structured exception handling also received an overhaul in ColdFusion MX—so much so that you can now catch and throw native Java exceptions from your ColdFusion code; in fact, you can even create your own Java exception objects and throw them as well. In addition, more exception information is available if an error is thrown now, and more types of errors can be thrown.

Another excellent exception handling feature is the new CFSCRIPT-based exception handling, which gives you limited try/catch capability within a CFSCRIPT block. Refer to Chapter 21 for a complete discussion of structured exception handling.

Enhanced debugging capabilities

ColdFusion's debugging capabilities were also seriously improved in ColdFusion MX. The debug output is much more in-depth and is now available in a cool new graphical format. You also get a new CFTRACE tag that you can use to watch variables and/or trace execution time.

The traditional debugging capabilities are also improved in ColdFusion MX. CFDUMP now has a much better format, and it no longer puts the names of structure keys in all caps. CFLOG, because most of its attributes are deprecated now, has become simpler to use, because you need only a few attributes to create an effective, detailed log.

For more information about debugging and testing your code, see Chapter 21 and Chapter 42.

Enhanced regular expressions

A *regular expression* is a formula for describing a pattern within a string. String patterns can be very large and complicated, like an email message header, or small and simple, like an email address.

Regular expressions have always been the powerhouse of any string-parsing or data-processing application. ColdFusion 5 and earlier versions had a good implementation of regular expressions, but they suffered because ColdFusion 5 didn't support some important advanced features.

ColdFusion MX has turned this on its ear by introducing some of Perl 5's most advanced regular-expression capabilities, including the following:

- Nonmatching expressions (using ?: in front of a subexpression)
- Positive lookahead (using ?= in front of a subexpression)
- Negative lookahead (using ?! in front of a subexpression)
- Comments in regular expressions (using ?x in front and using ## for a comment)
- Improved buffer operators (which can now work in multiline mode)
- Improved character-set matches

Regular expressions within ColdFusion now offer everything that even the most advanced regular-expression engines do. The only capability missing from ColdFusion's regular expressions is *lookbehind*, a feature so rarely implemented that its omission is understandable.

To learn more about regular expressions, refer to Chapter 16, and also to *Developing Web Applications with ColdFusion MX*, available as part of the ColdFusion MX documentation.

Summary

If you have been exposed to ColdFusion before and are just reading this chapter to find out what's new, you are probably amazed at what MX has to offer. As you've seen in this chapter, the MX release of ColdFusion Server truly vaults it to the Enterprise level with its J2EE-based platform, native XML handling, Web services, and more, as well as its extensibility through other technologies.

If you're just starting in ColdFusion but you've been exposed to other languages, you're going to love ColdFusion MX not only for its simple syntax and ease of use, but also for what's built right into the language. Most other languages use third-party tools for features such as XML, Web services, and charting, but ColdFusion has them all built right in.

And if you're just beginning your Web-development career, ColdFusion is probably the best place to start. It's simple, so it gets you up and running much faster than other languages do. It also has the best developer community of any programming language that we've seen, so getting your questions answered is easy, too.

So why not get started right away? Install the trial version of ColdFusion Server that we included on the companion CD-ROM (just follow the instructions in the installer), turn to Chapter 2, and start building your first ColdFusion application!

✦ ✦ ✦

Writing Your First ColdFusion MX Application

✦ ✦ ✦ ✦

In This Chapter

Understanding how ColdFusion works

Building your first ColdFusion application

Creating forms

Creating, modifying, and deleting data

✦ ✦ ✦ ✦

In this chapter, you're going to build a real-world application in ColdFusion MX. In fact, you'll have the first part of it working in about five to ten minutes!

You're going to create forms to accept user input, validate what the user enters, and put the data into a database. You then get that data back out of the database, change it, and then delete it later. After you build the application, you go back and improve it by adding a few features.

If you are already familiar with earlier versions of ColdFusion and are looking for the new features in ColdFusion MX, see Part IV, "ColdFusion MX Components, Web Services, and Flash Integration." Because the new features in ColdFusion MX are all on an advanced level, putting them in your first ColdFusion MX Application would not make sense.

Your First ColdFusion Application

You learn by doing, and then we go back and explain how ColdFusion worked its magic.

Before you get started, though, you must learn a few terms, set up the database, and create the Web directory that you're going to use.

Some terms

These are some terms that you should know:

- A *template* is a file with a `.cfm` extension. ColdFusion executes these templates and produces HTML that is returned to the user's browser.
- A *page* is what appears in your browser. It is rendered from the HTML that ColdFusion Server sends back to your browser.
- Your browser *requests* a ColdFusion template. ColdFusion processes the template into HTML and sends it to your Web

server, and your Web server *responds* by sending this HTML to your browser, which renders the HTML into the Web page that you see.

What you'll need

You need three things to build your application:

✦ Macromedia ColdFusion MX Server, installed and running.

✦ Macromedia HomeSite or HomeSite+ (or the similar but older ColdFusion Studio editor). You use HomeSite to develop your example application.

✦ A Web browser.

Preparing your Web environment

Create a directory in your Web root (usually `c:\inetpub\wwwroot\`) named `CFMXBible`. Inside this directory, create a subdirectory named `Ch02`. All the templates that you create in this chapter go into this directory.

Copy the file `styles.css` from the CD-ROM provided with this book into the `Ch02` directory after you create that directory. The CD-ROM also contains the finished version of the example application that you create in this chapter.

Setting up the database

We have provided a sample Access database named `CFMXBible.mdb` for you on the accompanying CD-ROM. Follow these steps to set up the database:

1. Copy `CFMXBible.mdb` to the root of your server's C: drive. Notice that you don't place this file inside of the Web root, because if you make the MDB file Web-accessible, anyone can download your MDB file right from their browser. Placing this file outside the Web root offers an extra measure of security.

2. Log in to ColdFusion Administrator, which is the control console for ColdFusion MX. You can go to ColdFusion Administrator through a shortcut in the Macromedia ColdFusion MX group on your server's Start menu, or you can go to ColdFusion Administrator directly by pointing your Web browser to `http://<yourserver>/cfide/administrator` (replacing `<yourserver>` with the name of the server on which you develop your example application).

If you installed the standalone web server with ColdFusion MX, you must add :8500 to your server name, as ColdFusion MX communicates with the standalone web server over port 8500.

3. Click the Data Sources link on the left side of your browser.

4. In the Add New Data Source section that appears, enter **CFMXBibleAccess** in the Data Source Name field; choose Microsoft Access as the driver type; and Click Add.

5. The CF Data Source Name text box should already contain `CFMXBibleAccess`. Enter the path to your MDB file (which should be `C:\CFMXBible.mdb`) in the Database File field, and leave System Database File blank. Leave Use Default Username checked; enter a meaningful description in the Description field; and click Submit.

If you see the message `datasource updated successfully`, you are ready to build your example application. If you don't see this message, the datasource was set up incorrectly. Work through these steps again to resolve your problems before you go any further.

Refer to chapters 43 and 44 for details on using and configuring ColdFusion Administrator.

Planning Program Flow

You can't just sit down and start writing code. All good projects start with a design process.

Think in terms of processes

An application is a collection of processes. The application that you're about to build, for example, among other things, adds new companies and employees to the database. Adding a company is one process in your application, and adding an employee is a second process. The user must also get a list of the companies and employees in the database, update information about a specific company or employee, and delete employees and companies from the database — more processes to consider in designing your application.

Figure 2-1 shows the processes that your application supports.

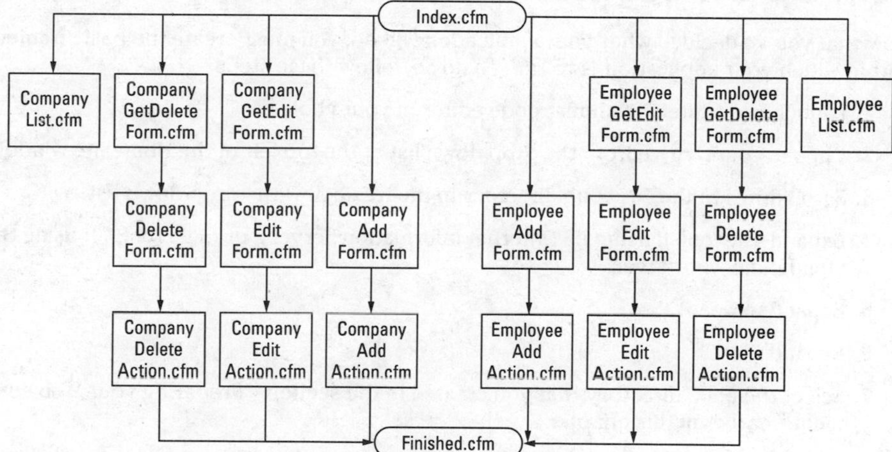

Figure 2-1: Process flowchart for your first ColdFusion MX application.

Real-world process design is quite involved, often employing dedicated process-design tools, but at the very least, you should sketch a flowchart containing all processes that your application should support before you start creating directories, databases, and code.

Think in terms of data

Before you write an application, you should know the structure and nature of the data that your processes use. Will the application manage a store's inventory, blocks of content on a news site, or something completely different?

Your application in this chapter, for example, manages companies and employees. Each company has a name and address, comments about the company, and an identifier, or *key*, that the database uses to keep track of which company is which. (For more information about database concepts, see Part II of this book.)

Employees have a social security number (SSN), which identifies each employee (the employee's key), as well as a name, salary, date of birth, and the identifier, or key, of the company for which each employee works.

Figure 2-2 shows the structure of the data that your application will manage. Chapter 8 explains the notations used in this diagram, but for now, just use it as a conceptual model of the Company and Employee tables and the relationship between them.

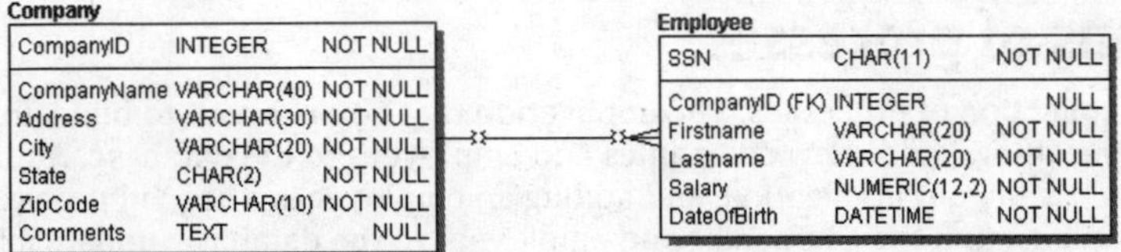

Figure 2-2: Model of employees and companies.

Setting Up the Framework For Your Application

Now that you've decided what your application will do, you must create the basic framework within which your application is to run. To do so, follow these steps:

1. Launch HomeSite or a similar code editor of your choice.
2. Choose your C drive from the drop-down list at the top left of the HomeSite window.
3. Scroll down to the `Inetpub` directory in the tree below the drop-down list.
4. Expand `Inetpub` if using IIS (Internet Information Server), or `CFusionMX` if using the standalone web server.
5. Expand `wwwroot`.
6. Expand `CFMXBible`.
7. Select the `Ch02` directory that you created in the section, "Preparing your Web environment," earlier in this chapter.
8. Choose File ⇨ New Document from the menu.
9. Select everything in the main editing window in HomeSite and press the Delete key to remove any default code.
10. Choose File ⇨ Save from the menu and make sure that you are in the `Ch02` directory (it should appear in the drop-down list above the list of files).
11. Name your new file `Application.cfm` and click Save.

    `Application.cfm` is a special template that ColdFusion automatically executes before each template that you specifically request. It is the backbone of your framework, as you learn in Chapter 19. Make sure that the initial *A* is capitalized in the file name or it will not work on some platforms.

12. Type Listing 2-1 into the editing window and then save the file as Application.cfm.

Listing 2-1: Application.cfm

```
<!--- Give your application a name --->
<cfapplication name="CH02">

<!--- This is the data source your application will use --->
<cfset Request.MainDSN = "CFMXBibleAccess">
```

The `CFAPPLICATION` tag tells ColdFusion Server that all the templates and variables in your application are part of an *application space* named `Ch02` within which all the application's variables and data will be contained, and `Request.MainDSN` contains the name of the datasource that you created earlier in this chapter in the section "Setting up the database."

Adding a Company to the Database

Now that you've set up your application directory and database and created a basic framework, you write code to add a company to the database. You create three templates: a form template, an action template, and a template that displays a message when the action has finished. The form template collects data about the company; the action template puts it into the database and redirects the user to the finished template; and the finished template tells the user that the action was successful.

The terms *template* and *page* are often used interchangeably.

Building the company add form

The first template that you create is the form that collects company data. This form will contain input fields for the company name, address, city, state, and zip code, plus a submit button.

Create a file named `CompanyAddForm.cfm` inside the `Ch02` directory, type the code in Listing 2-2 into the file's editing window, and save the file.

Listing 2-2: CompanyAddForm.cfm

```
<html>
<head>
	<title>ColdFusion MX Bible</title>
	<link rel="stylesheet" href="styles.css">
</head>

<body>

<h1>Add a Company</h1>

<table>
<cfform action="CompanyAddAction.cfm" method="POST">
<tr>
```

Continued

Listing 2-2 *(continued)*

```
            <td>Company Name</td>
            <td>
                <cfinput type="Text"
                    name="CompanyName"
                    message="Please enter a name for this company."
                    required="Yes"
                    size="40"
                    maxlength="40">
            </td>
        </tr>
        <tr>
            <td>Address</td>
            <td>
                <cfinput type="Text"
                    name="Address"
                    message="Please enter this new Company's Address."
                    required="Yes"
                    size="32"
                    maxlength="30">
            </td>
        </tr>
        <tr>
            <td>City</td>
            <td>
                <cfinput type="Text"
                    name="City"
                    message="Please enter a city."
                    required="Yes"
                    size="22"
                    maxlength="20">
            </td>
        </tr>
        <tr>
            <td>State</td>
            <td>
                <cfinput type="Text"
                    name="State"
                    message="Please enter a state."
                    required="Yes"
                    size="3"
                    maxlength="2">
            </td>
        </tr>
        <tr>
            <td>ZIP Code</td>
            <td>
                <cfinput type="Text"
                    name="ZipCode"
                    message="Please enter a valid ZIP Code."
                    validate="zipcode"
                    required="Yes"
```

```
                    size="11"
                    maxlength="10">
        </td>
    </tr>
    <tr>
        <td>Comments</td>
        <td>
            <textarea cols="40" rows="5" name="Comments"></textarea>
        </td>
    </tr>
    <tr>
        <td> </td>
        <td>
            <input type="submit" value="Add to Database">
        </td>
    </tr>
    </cfform>
    </table>

    </body>
    </html>
```

This code is a lot to digest, so we break it down as follows:

- ✦ The TABLE, TR and TD tags define the visual layout of this form. This is plain HTML.
- ✦ CFFORM is the container for the data that the user enters into the form controls, which is passed to the server after the user submits the form.
- ✦ The submit button (INPUT type="submit") submits the form data to the action page, which will take that data and insert it into the database. You build the action page next.

The CFFORM in CompanyAddForm.cfm has two attributes: Method and Action. The form's Method is POST, and its Action is CompanyAddAction.cfm, meaning that when the user clicks Submit, the form data is posted to the CompanyAddAction.cfm template.

Each of the CFINPUT tags has a Type attribute. In this application, the Type is always TEXT, which means that the input field is a single-line text field. Each of the CFINPUT tags has a Name attribute, which is the name of the Form variable that contains the data entered into the field after the form is submitted to the action template.

Building the company add action template

In this section, you create the template that puts your form data into the database. Create a file named CompanyAddAction.cfm inside the Ch02 directory, type the code in Listing 2-3 into the file's editing window, and save the file.

Listing 2-3: CompanyAddAction.cfm

```
<cfquery name="InsertCompany"
    datasource="#Request.MainDSN#">
```

Continued

Listing 2-3 *(continued)*

```
INSERT INTO Company(
     CompanyName,
     Address,
     City,
     State,
     ZipCode,
     Comments
)
VALUES (
     '#Trim(Form.CompanyName)#',
     '#Trim(Form.Address)#',
     '#Trim(Form.City)#',
     '#Trim(Form.State)#',
     '#Trim(Form.ZipCode)#',
     <cfif Len(Trim(Form.Comments)) GT
0>'#Trim(Form.Comments)#'<cfelse>NULL</cfif>
)
</cfquery>

<cflocation url="Finished.cfm?msg=#URLEncodedFormat('#Form.CompanyName#
has been added to the database.')#">
```

`CompanyAddAction.cfm` inserts the new company into the database (the `CFQUERY` call) and then redirects the user to a page that tells him what just happened (the `CFLOCATION` call).

The finished template

Compared to the other two templates that you've already created, `Finished.cfm` is much simpler because it just displays the contents of a variable—in this case, the message that tells the user that he successfully inserted a company into the database. Create a file named `Finished.cfm` inside the `Ch02` directory, type the code in Listing 2-4 into the file's editing window, and save the file.

Listing 2-4: Finished.cfm

```
<cfparam name="URL.msg" default="This page did not receive a message.">

<html>
<head>
     <title>ColdFusion MX Bible</title>
     <link rel="stylesheet" href="styles.css">
</head>

<body>

<h1>Action Finished</h1>

<cfoutput>#URL.msg#</cfoutput>
```

```
</body>
</html>
```

Only two ColdFusion tags are in this file: CFPARAM and CFOUTPUT. The other tags are HTML used for visual layout.

CFPARAM makes sure that a variable exists before attempting to use it. CFPARAM uses two attributes: Name and Default. Name is the variable that you want to ensure exists. If the variable doesn't exist, CFPARAM creates it and assigns it the value specified by Default. If the variable does already exist, then ColdFusion uses its existing value.

CFOUTPUT tells ColdFusion to replace anything between pound signs (such as the #URL.msg# in our example) with the value of the expression — in this case, the message contained in URL.msg.

Now that you've created all three templates in this process, you can take them for a spin! Point your Web browser to http://*<yourserver>*/CFMXBible/Ch02/CompanyAddForm.cfm. Fill in the form with data about a fictitious company and then click the Submit button. If everything works correctly, you see the Finished page, and it tells you that your company was added to the database. If ColdFusion throws an error, compare the code that you've written in this application so far with the respective listings. If all else fails, copy the files from the CD-ROM into the Ch02 directory.

Congratulations! You've finished the first part of your first ColdFusion application! Add a few more companies to the database before proceeding to the next section.

What just happened?

Now take a look at what happened in the company add form, company add action, and finished pages.

CFFORM

After you pointed your Web browser to http://*<yourserver>*/CFMXBible/Ch02/CompanyAddForm.cfm, your browser requested that template, which ColdFusion executed and sent back to your browser. Point your browser back to that same address and choose View ⇨ Source from your browser's menu bar. The HTML that you see is what ColdFusion sent back to your browser after executing the ColdFusion code. If you compare CompanyAddForm.cfm in HomeSite to the HTML that you get from the View ⇨ Source command, you see that they are different.

ColdFusion processes a CFFORM tag into an HTML FORM tag plus a library of JavaScript validation functions. Similarly, ColdFusion processes the CFINPUT tags into HTML INPUT tags that make calls to these JavaScript validation functions. Creating and calling this validation logic manually is difficult and error-prone, so using CFFORM and CFINPUT is a simple way to make the validation logic work correctly with a minimum of fuss.

Defining validation rules for fields

HTML INPUT tags have Size and Maxlength attributes. Size specifies how many characters (on average) are visible in the input field whenever they're displayed in the browser, and Maxlength specifies the maximum number of characters that can go in the input field.

CFINPUT tags can define more than sizes and maximum lengths, as follows:

✦ If `Required = Yes` and the field does not contain any text when the user submits the form, the user receives a JavaScript warning message and the form is not submitted.

✦ `Validate` tells CFINPUT what data format the field can accept.

✦ If the `Required` or `Validate` tests fail, the user sees the `Message` in a JavaScript alert. Make sure that you make the message descriptive of which field failed.

Try submitting the form without entering anything into the required form fields. The page does not submit; instead, it warns you that you must enter a value into the field.

You must have JavaScript enabled in your browser for CFFORM's validation functionality to work correctly.

Inserting data into the database

Now look at `CompanyAddAction.cfm`, which took the company data from `CompanyAddForm.cfm` and created a new company record in the database.

The `CFQUERY` call tells the database to insert a new company into the database. The SQL statement in the `CFQUERY` has two clauses: `INSERT INTO`, which tells the database which table and columns will receive the data, and `VALUES`, which passes the company data to those columns.

`CFQUERY` has two attributes: `Name` and `Datasource`. `Name` tells ColdFusion what to name this query, and `Datasource` tells the ColdFusion how to connect to the database. Notice in the `CFQUERY` call that the `Datasource` is `#Request.MainDSN#`—the variable that you set in `Application.cfm`. `Application.cfm` runs before every request made by your application, so `Request.MainDSN` is already defined when ColdFusion processes this `CFQUERY` tag.

Trim() your strings

Notice that every variable in the `CFQUERY` looks as follows:

```
'#Trim(Form.CompanyName)#'
```

The single quotes treat the data that you submit as a string rather than as a number, which doesn't use single quotes around its value. Inside the single quotes, the expression is surrounded by pound signs, which tell ColdFusion to evaluate the expression.

`Trim()` takes whatever value was passed in to the function and returns that value with all leading and trailing whites pace (spaces, tabs, carriage returns, and so on) removed. Always use `Trim()` around string data before putting it into a database.

In this case, you're trimming the variable `Form.CompanyName`. `Form.` tells ColdFusion to get the variable from the form that was submitted to this template, and `CompanyName` tells ColdFusion the variable (form field) to get.

Using NULL values

The first five variables in `CompanyAddAction.cfm` come from required fields on `CompanyAddForm.cfm`. The sixth variable, `Form.Comments`, however, was not required. What should `CompanyAddAction.cfm` put into the database if the user didn't enter any comments? The template could put an empty string into the database, but a `NULL` value would be more appropriate.

A `NULL` is a special value that means "indeterminate" or "undefined." You want to use `NULL` for the Comments field because the Comments weren't *empty*—they were *not entered*.

To put a `NULL` value into the database, use `NULL` instead of `'#Trim(Form.Comments)#'` in `CFQUERY`, as follows:

```
<cfif Len(Trim(Form.Comments)) GT 0>
'#Trim(Form.Comments)#'
<cfelse>
NULL
</cfif>
```

You build this portion of the SQL statement on-the-fly by using a simple `CFIF` construct. First, you use two ColdFusion functions, `Len()` and `Trim()`, to determine whether the user entered anything into the Comments field. If the length of `Form.Comments` without any surrounding white space is greater than zero, you can put `Form.Comments` directly into the database by using the syntax that you've already learned in "Building the company add action template" earlier in this chapter. If the trimmed length of `Form.Comments` is zero, however, put `NULL` into the database.

Notice the difference between the two syntaxes: If you're putting `Form.Comments` into the database, you use single quotes, pound signs, and a call to `Trim()`. If you're inserting a `NULL` value, however, you use `NULL` by itself without single quotes or pound signs. `NULL` is not a string; it is a special *enumerated constant* in SQL that represents a `NULL` value.

Redirecting the user

`CompanyAddAction.cfm` redirects the user to a different template after inserting a company into the database. If the user clicks the Refresh button after he sees the success message on `Finished.cfm`, ColdFusion executes `Finished.cfm` a second time, but the database is untouched because `Finished.cfm` doesn't make any database calls. Consider what would happen if `CompanyAddAction.cfm` displayed the success message directly instead of redirecting the user. If the user clicked the Refresh button, ColdFusion would execute `CompanyAddAction.cfm` again, which would resubmit the form data and insert the company into the database again.

`CFLOCATION` stops processing the current page and redirects the user to the location specified in its `URL` attribute (`Finished.cfm`). Following is the `CFLOCATION` call in `CompanyAddAction.cfm`:

```
<cflocation url="Finished.cfm?msg=#URLEncodedFormat(
'#Form.CompanyName# has been added to the database.')#">
```

The URL to which the user is redirected is `Finished.cfm`. The question mark tells ColdFusion that everything following it is a parameter or a collection of parameters. Take, for example, the following `URL` parameter:

```
msg=#URLEncodedFormat('#Form.CompanyName# has been added to the
database.')#
```

It is interpreted as follows: The parameter's name is `msg`, meaning that `Finished.cfm` receives a variable named `URL.msg`. The parameter's value is the result of the call to `URLEncodedFormat()`. `URLEncodedFormat()` is a ColdFusion function that takes a string and returns the string with all special characters escaped for safe use in the URL. (*Escaping* a string means that all characters other than letters or numbers are replaced with a special code sequence—for example, a space character becomes `%20`.)

After `Finished.cfm` receives `URL.msg`, ColdFusion converts the escaped string back into plain text so that `Finished.cfm` can display it.

Getting a List of Companies

Now to build a company list. This short exercise requires you to build a single template.

Building the company list

Create a file named `CompanyList.cfm` inside the `Ch02` directory, type the code in Listing 2-5 into the file's editing window, and save the file.

Listing 2-5: CompanyList.cfm

```
<cfquery name="GetCompanies"
    datasource="#Request.MainDSN#">
SELECT
    CompanyID,
    CompanyName,
    Address,
    City,
    State,
    ZipCode,
    Comments
FROM
    Company
ORDER BY
    CompanyName ASC
</cfquery>

<html>
<head>
    <title>ColdFusion MX Bible</title>
    <link rel="stylesheet" href="styles.css">
</head>

<body>

<h1>Company List</h1>

<table>
<tr>
    <td><b>ID</b></td>
    <td><b>Name</b></td>
    <td><b>Address</b></td>
    <td><b>City</b></td>
    <td><b>State</b></td>
    <td><b>ZIP Code</b></td>
</tr>

<cfoutput query="GetCompanies">
<tr>
    <td>#CompanyID#</td>
    <td>#CompanyName#</td>
```

```
        <td>#Address#</td>
        <td>#City#</td>
        <td>#State#</td>
        <td>#ZipCode#</td>
    </tr>
    </cfoutput>

    </table>

    </body>
    </html>
```

Point Your web browser to `http://<yourserver>/CFMXBible/Ch02/CompanyList.cfm`. You should see a list of the companies that you've added to the database, sorted by the company name. If not, or if you throw an error, check your code against Listing 2-5.

Just two ColdFusion tags are at work on this page, and you've seen both of them already. These two tags behave differently, however, in `CompanyList.cfm` than they did in `CompanyAddAction.cfm` and `Finished.cfm`, as the following list describes:

- ✦ In `CompanyAddAction.cfm`, `CFQUERY` told the database to `INSERT` a new company. In `CompanyList.cfm`, `CFQUERY` selects information from the database.
- ✦ In `Finished.cfm`, `CFOUTPUT` evaluated and output a single variable (the `URL.msg` parameter). In `CompanyList.cfm`, `CFOUTPUT` outputs the results of a database query.

Using a SELECT statement

The data that `CFQUERY` requests from the database comes back in a result set, and the `Name` attribute tells ColdFusion what that result set is to be named.

The SQL statement consists of three clauses: `SELECT`, `FROM`, and `ORDER BY`. `SELECT` tells the database which columns to retrieve from the database; `FROM` tells the database which table to retrieve those columns from; and `ORDER BY` tells the database how to sort the results.

Displaying the results of a query

The result set returned from `CFQUERY` contains multiple rows of data, and each row has multiple columns, as shown in Figure 2-3.

query

	ADDRESS	CITY	COMMENTS	COMPANYID	COMPANYNAME	STATE	ZIPCODE
1	5332 Courtland Court	Abilene	The best homemade pies in the business!	14	Ma's Homemade Pies	AL	29574
2	1240 Pierpont Point	Boston	Why wear anything else?	15	Normwelland and Drake Clothing Co.	MA	02134
3	1548 High Point Freeway	New York	We got the best pizzas out there!	16	Pizza Palace	NY	00248
4	5806 Glenn Hollow Lane	Norcross	Sooner or later, you'll be owned by us.	13	The Very Big Corporation of America	GA	30071

Figure 2-3: A query result set containing four rows.

Now look back at Listing 2-5. Inside the `TABLE` tag is a row of header cells. Then inside `<cfoutput query="GetCompanies">` is another row, with each cell containing a variable with the same name as that of a column from the `SELECT` statement.

It would appear that the CFOUTPUT in CompanyList.cfm evaluates variables as the CFOUTPUT in Finished.cfm did. The CFOUTPUT in CompanyList.cfm, however, has a Query attribute, which tells ColdFusion to execute everything between <cfoutput> and </cfoutput> once for each row in the result set, so you end up with one HTML table row for every row in the result set, as shown in Figure 2-4.

Company List

ID	Name	Address	City	State	ZIP Code
14	Ma's Homemade Pies	5332 Courtland Court	Abilene	AL	29574
15	Normwelland and Drake Clothing Co.	1240 Pierpont Point	Boston	MA	02134
16	Pizza Palace	1548 High Point Freeway	New York	NY	00248
13	The Very Big Corporation of America	5806 Glenn Hollow Lane	Norcross	GA	30071

Figure 2-4: CompanyList.cfm.

Modifying a Company in the Database

Now that you can add and list companies, you need to the capability to modify them as well. The edit process is much like the add process, with some additional code.

Choosing a company to edit

Before the user can edit a company record, he needs to retrieve it from the database and load it into a form. In this application, the user chooses a company to edit by entering its CompanyID into one form, submitting it, and editing it in a second form, as shown in Figure 2-5:

Figure 2-5: Process flow for the company edit process.

Create a file named CompanyGetEditForm.cfm inside the Ch02 directory, type the code in Listing 2-6 into the file's editing window, and save the file.

Listing 2-6: CompanyGetEditForm.cfm

```
<html>
<head>
	<title>ColdFusion MX Bible</title>
	<link rel="stylesheet" href="styles.css">
</head>

<body>

<h1>Edit a Company</h1>

<table>
<cfform action="CompanyEditForm.cfm" method="POST">
<tr>
	<td>Company ID</td>
	<td>
		<cfinput type="Text"
			name="CompanyID"
			message="Please enter the Company ID"
			validate="integer"
			required="Yes"
			size="22"
			maxlength="20">
	</td>
</tr>
<tr>
	<td> </td>
	<td>
		<input type="submit" value="Get Company">
	</td>
</tr>
</cfform>
</table>

</body>
</html>
```

The `CFFORM` has a single `CFINPUT` for entering the ID of the company that you want to edit. This form submits its data to the next form that you're going to build, which is where you'll edit the company.

Building the company edit form

The company edit form is much like the company add form, but the edit form must first retrieve the company record from the database and place that data into the form fields.

Create a file named `CompanyEditForm.cfm` inside the `Ch02` directory, type the code in Listing 2-7 into the file's editing window, and save the file.

Listing 2-7: CompanyEditForm.cfm

```
<cfquery name="GetCompany"
    datasource="#Request.MainDSN#">
SELECT
    CompanyName,
    Address,
    City,
    State,
    ZipCode,
    Comments
FROM
    Company
WHERE
    CompanyID = #Val(CompanyID)#
</cfquery>

<html>
<head>
    <title>ColdFusion MX Bible</title>
    <link rel="stylesheet" href="styles.css">
</head>

<body>

<h1>Edit a Company</h1>

<table>
<cfform action="CompanyEditAction.cfm" method="POST">

<cfoutput>
<input type="hidden" name="CompanyID" value="#Val(CompanyID)#">
</cfoutput>

<tr>
    <td>Company Name</td>
    <td>
        <cfinput type="Text"
            name="CompanyName"
            value="#GetCompany.CompanyName#"
            message="Please enter a name for this company."
            required="Yes"
            size="40"
            maxlength="40">
    </td>
</tr>
<tr>
    <td>Address</td>
    <td>
        <cfinput type="Text"
            name="Address"
            value="#GetCompany.Address#"
            message="Please enter this new Company's Address."
```

```
                    required="Yes"
                    size="32"
                    maxlength="30">
          </td>
     </tr>
     <tr>
          <td>City</td>
          <td>
               <cfinput type="Text"
                    name="City"
                    value="#GetCompany.City#"
                    message="Please enter a city."
                    required="Yes"
                    size="22"
                    maxlength="20">
          </td>
     </tr>
     <tr>
          <td>State</td>
          <td>
               <cfinput type="Text"
                    name="State"
                    value="#GetCompany.State#"
                    message="Please enter a state."
                    required="Yes"
                    size="3"
                    maxlength="2">
          </td>
     </tr>
     <tr>
          <td>ZIP Code</td>
          <td>
               <cfinput type="Text"
                    name="ZipCode"
                    value="#GetCompany.ZipCode#"
                    message="Please enter a valid ZIP Code."
                    validate="zipcode"
                    required="Yes"
                    size="11"
                    maxlength="10">
          </td>
     </tr>
     <tr>
          <td>Comments</td>
          <td>
               <textarea cols="40" rows="5"
     name="Comments"><cfoutput>#GetCompany.Comments#</cfoutput></textarea>
          </td>
     </tr>
     <tr>
          <td> </td>
          <td>
```

Continued

Listing 2-7 *(continued)*

```
        <input type="submit" value="Update Database">
    </td>
</tr>

</cfform>
</table>

</body>
</html>
```

The edit form retrieves the company record and populates the form fields with the current data.

Building the company edit action template

The code in `CompanyEditAction.cfm` is like the code in `CompanyAddAction.cfm`, but the edit action updates rather than inserts.

Create a file named `CompanyEditAction.cfm` inside the `Ch02` directory, type the code in Listing 2-8 into the file's editing window, and save the file.

Listing 2-8: CompanyEditAction.cfm

```
<cfquery name="UpdateCompany"
    datasource="#Request.MainDSN#">
UPDATE Company
SET
    CompanyName = '#Trim(Form.CompanyName)#',
    Address = '#Trim(Form.Address)#',
    City = '#Trim(Form.City)#',
    State = '#Trim(Form.State)#',
    ZipCode = '#Trim(Form.ZipCode)#',
    Comments =
  <cfif Len(Trim(Form.Comments)) GT 0>
'#Trim(Form.Comments)#'
  <cfelse>
NULL
  </cfif>
WHERE
    CompanyID = #Val(Form.CompanyID)#
</cfquery>

<cflocation url="Finished.cfm?msg=#URLEncodedFormat('#Form.CompanyName#
has been updated in the database.')#">
```

Now that you've finished these three templates, you can see them in action. Point your Web browser to `http://`*`<yourserver>`*`/CFMXBible/Ch02/CompanyGetEditForm.cfm` and enter a CompanyID. (To get a valid ID, go to the company list and pick a number in the ID column.) Click Submit, and you should see the chosen company's information appear in the form fields on the edit form. Edit the Zip Code and click Submit; then revisit the company list and click your browser's Refresh button. You should see the updated data in the company list. If you don't, compare the files that you've created with their respective listings.

What just happened?

Open `CompanyEditForm.cfm` in HomeSite. Because the edit form is very similar to the add form, compare the two.

The first difference between the edit form and add form is the `CFQUERY` at the beginning of `CompanyEditForm.cfm`. `CompanyEditForm.cfm` calls `CFQUERY` to retrieve the company record that the user wants to edit. This query is like the one in `CompanyList.cfm`, with a few differences. First, `CompanyEditForm.cfm` doesn't include `CompanyID` in the select list, because the chosen company's ID is already available in the `CompanyID` that was sent to this template in the form post. Second, you now find a `WHERE` clause that restricts the result set to include only the company with an ID that matches `CompanyID`. Third, you find no `ORDER BY` clause, because this query returns only a single record.

Using a URL or Form variable

Look at the `WHERE` clause again in the following code:

```
WHERE
    CompanyID - #Val(CompanyID)#
```

`CompanyID` came from the `CompanyGetEditForm.cfm` form post, so it is said to be a part of the *Form scope*, and as such would normally be referenced as `Form.CompanyID`. Likewise, if `CompanyID` had been passed in a hyperlink as a URL parameter, it would be a part of the *URL scope*, and as such would normally be referenced as `URL.CompanyID`.

Notice that in the preceding line of code, we omitted the scope prefix to the `CompanyID` variable. This causes ColdFusion to go "hunting" for the scope that contains the `CompanyID` variable. By using this technique, you can build a flexible template that may receive values from either the URL or a form post. In fact, we will do this later on in the section "Making direct links to the add, view, and delete forms."

Using Val() on your numbers

`Val()` is a ColdFusion function that takes a string and returns the numeric part of that string (for example, `123ABC` would become `123`). If the string does not begin with a number, `Val()` returns zero. `Val()` is very important, especially with `URL` parameters, for the following two reasons:

✦ If the database is expecting a number but the user passes a nonnumeric parameter, `Val()` ensures that the database doesn't throw a syntax error.

✦ `Val()` is a security precaution. If you don't use `Val()`, a hacker could append a malicious query such as `DELETE FROM Customer` onto the end of the `URL` parameter, and the extra query would execute against your database. `Val()` removes all nonnumeric characters, so the malicious query could never touch your database.

Notice also that you don't surround the pound signs with single quotes as you do in `CompanyAddAction.cfm`, because `CompanyID` is a numeric column. Only text strings can be surrounded with single quotes.

Using a hidden form field

Moving further down CompanyEditForm.cfm, you see a plain HTML INPUT tag of Type = "hidden". Hidden form fields are invisible to the user; they pass data to the action page without user intervention.

The hidden INPUT tag has two attributes aside from its Type: Name and Value. Name becomes the name of the Form variable on the action page. Value is what that variable contains. You use a hidden form field here so that CompanyEditAction.cfm knows which company to update in the database. Notice that the value of the hidden form field is CompanyID, which was the CompanyID posted from CompanyGetEditForm.cfm. The hidden INPUT field is the mechanism that passes through CompanyID to CompanyEditAction.cfm.

Prepopulating the contents of the form with what's in the database

The final difference between CompanyEditForm.cfm and CompanyAddForm.cfm is that the edit form's fields are prepopulated with data.

Each of the five CFINPUT tags on CompanyEditForm.cfm has a Value attribute. The Value attribute is the text that the user sees in the input field as he first browses CompanyEditForm.cfm. All the Value attributes look as follows:

```
value="#GetCompany.CompanyName#"
```

Remember that, in CompanyList.cfm, if you output the value of a column in a result set, you just use the column name without the name of the result set preceding it. In CompanyEditForm.cfm, however, your data is not inside a <cfoutput query="GetCompany"> tag, so you must tell ColdFusion where this variable is by preceding the column name with the name of the result set containing it.

The final difference is in the TEXTAREA tag. TEXTAREA doesn't have a Value attribute; the value of the text area is whatever appears between the <textarea> and </textarea> tag pair.

Using an UPDATE statement

Now look at CompanyEditAction.cfm. As in CompanyAddAction.cfm, only two ColdFusion tags are in this template: CFQUERY, which updates the company record in the database; and CFLOCATION, which redirects the user away from the edit action template.

The UPDATE statement on this page uses three SQL clauses: UPDATE, SET, and WHERE. UPDATE tells the database which table to update; SET tells the database the new values to assign to each column in the updated record; and WHERE tells the database which record to update.

Look at the WHERE, clause and you'll see why you used a hidden form field on the company edit form. Remember that the hidden form field contained the CompanyID of the company that you were editing. The WHERE clause tells the database to update the company with the ID that matches CompanyID. This use of the WHERE clause is the same as you saw in the query on CompanyEditForm.cfm in the section "Building the company edit form" — there you restricted what was *returned* from the database, and here you are restricting what is *updated* in the database.

Redirecting the user

After CFQUERY, CompanyEditAction.cfm calls CFLOCATION, which redirects the user to the Finished page. You don't need a separate Finished page for the Edit Action; simply modify URL.msg to describe what happened, as shown in bold:

```
#Form.CompanyName# has been updated in the database.
```

Removing a Company From the Database

Compared to adding and editing companies, deleting a company is a breeze.

As does editing a company, deleting a company requires four templates: one template to choose which company to delete, one template to display the company record so that the user can confirm that he is deleting the correct company, an action page to delete the company from the database, and the Finished page that you have already created.

Choosing a company to delete

Creating the first template is a piece of cake because you've already written it! The Get Delete Form listing is almost exactly the same as the Get Edit Form listing. Create a file named `CompanyGetDeleteForm.cfm` inside the `Ch02` directory, type the code in Listing 2-9 into the file's editing window, and save the file.

Listing 2-9: CompanyGetDeleteForm.cfm

```
<html>
<head>
    <title>ColdFusion MX Bible</title>
    <link rel="stylesheet" href="styles.css">
</head>

<body>

<h1>Delete a Company</h1>

<table>
<cfform action="CompanyDeleteForm.cfm" method="POST">
<tr>
    <td>Company ID</td>
    <td>
        <cfinput type="Text"
            name="CompanyID"
            message="Please enter the Company ID"
            validate="integer"
            required="Yes"
            size="22"
            maxlength="20">
    </td>
</tr>
<tr>
    <td> </td>
    <td>
        <input type="submit" value="Get Company">
    </td>
</tr>
</cfform>
```

Continued

Listing 2-9 *(continued)*

```
</table>

</body>
</html>
```

The only difference between the Get Delete and Get Edit forms is where the user submits them!

Creating the company delete form

The delete form is a template that enables the user to inspect the company record before deciding to delete the company. No editing takes place on this page — the user is just viewing static data.

Create a file named `CompanyDeleteForm.cfm` inside the `Ch02` directory, type the code in Listing 2-10 into the file's editing window, and save the file.

Listing 2-10: CompanyDeleteForm.cfm

```
<cfquery name="GetCompany"
    datasource="#Request.MainDSN#">
SELECT
    CompanyName,
    Address,
    City,
    State,
    ZipCode,
    Comments
FROM
    Company
WHERE
    CompanyID = #Val(CompanyID)#
</cfquery>

<html>
<head>
    <title>ColdFusion MX Bible</title>
    <link rel="stylesheet" href="styles.css">
</head>

<body>

<h1>Delete a Company</h1>

<cfoutput>
<table>
<cfform action="CompanyDeleteAction.cfm" method="POST">
```

```
<input type="hidden" name="CompanyID" value="#Val(CompanyID)#">
<tr>
    <td>Company Name</td>
    <td>#GetCompany.CompanyName#</td>
</tr>

<tr>
    <td>Address</td>
    <td>#GetCompany.Address#</td>
</tr>

<tr>
    <td>City</td>
    <td>#GetCompany.City#</td>
</tr>

<tr>
    <td>State</td>
    <td>#GetCompany.State#</td>
</tr>

<tr>
    <td>ZIP Code</td>
    <td>#GetCompany.ZipCode#</td>
</tr>

<tr>
    <td>Comments</td>
    <td>#GetCompany.Comments#</td>
</tr>

<tr>
    <td> </td>
    <td>
        <input type="submit" value="Delete From Database">
    </td>
</tr>

</cfform>
</table>
</cfoutput>

</body>
</html>
```

The first line of code in the delete form is the same `CFQUERY` used in the edit form; it retrieves the company record from the database.

Confirming the deletion of a company before performing the action

You use CFFORM and a hidden form field because you are submitting the CompanyID to the action page. You don't need any CFINPUT tags because you don't need any user input on this form. All that's left is the Submit button.

Creating the company delete action template

The last template in the company delete process controls the delete action.

Create a file named CompanyDeleteAction.cfm inside the Ch02 directory, type the code in Listing 2-11 into the file's editing window, and save the file.

Listing 2-11: CompanyDeleteAction.cfm

```
<cfquery name="DeleteCompany"
    datasource="#Request.MainDSN#">
DELETE FROM Company
WHERE
    CompanyID = #Val(Form.CompanyID)#
</cfquery>

<cflocation url="Finished.cfm?msg=#URLEncodedFormat('Company ID
#Form.CompanyID# has been deleted from the database.')#">
```

Only two ColdFusion tags are on this page: CFQUERY, which tells the database to delete a row; and CFLOCATION, which redirects the user to the Finished page.

Using a DELETE statement

The CFQUERY in CompanyDeleteAction.cfm uses a DELETE statement with two SQL clauses: DELETE and WHERE. DELETE tells the database the table from which to delete a record, and WHERE tells the database which record to delete.

You can watch the company delete process in action. Point your Web browser to http://<*yourserver*>/CFMXBible/Ch02/CompanyGetDeleteForm.cfm and enter a CompanyID. (To get a valid ID, go to the company list and pick a number from the ID column.) Click Submit to see the chosen company's information. Click Submit again and then go back to the company list. If everything worked, you should no longer see the deleted company in the list. (You may need to click Refresh.)

Adding a New Employee to the Database

You've just created an entire series of company maintenance processes — and now you get to do the same for employees! But the employee processes have a twist: Each employee is related to a company.

Building the employee add form

Start with the add form. Create a file named `EmployeeAddForm.cfm` inside the `Ch02` directory, type the code in Listing 2-12 into the file's editing window, and save the file.

Listing 2-12: EmployeeAddForm.cfm

```
<cfquery name="GetCompanies"
    datasource="#Request.MainDSN#">
SELECT
    CompanyID,
    CompanyName
FROM
    Company
ORDER BY
    CompanyName
</cfquery>

<html>
<head>
    <title>ColdFusion MX Bible</title>
    <link rel="stylesheet" href="styles.css">
</head>

<body>

<h1>Add an Employee</h1>

<table>
<cfform action="EmployeeAddAction.cfm" method="POST">

<tr>
    <td>Company</td>
    <td>
        <cfselect name="CompanyID"
            size="1"
            query="GetCompanies"
            value="CompanyID"
            display="CompanyName"
            required="Yes"
            message="Please select a Company."></cfselect>
    </td>
</tr>

<tr>
    <td>SSN</td>
    <td>
        <cfinput type="Text"
            name="SSN"
            message="Please enter the employee's Social Security
```

Continued

Listing 2-12 *(continued)*

```
Number."
            validate="social_security_number"
            required="Yes"
            size="12"
            maxlength="11">
    </td>
</tr>

<tr>
    <td>First Name</td>
    <td>
        <cfinput type="Text"
            name="Firstname"
            message="Please enter the employee's first name."
            required="Yes"
            size="22"
            maxlength="20">
    </td>
</tr>

<tr>
    <td>Last Name</td>
    <td>
        <cfinput type="Text"
            name="Lastname"
            message="Please enter the employee's last name."
            required="Yes"
            size="22"
            maxlength="20">
    </td>
</tr>

<tr>
    <td>Salary</td>
    <td>
        <cfinput type="Text"
            name="Salary"
            message="Please enter a valid salary."
            validate="float"
            required="Yes"
            size="22"
            maxlength="20">
    </td>
</tr>

<tr>
    <td>DOB</td>
    <td>
        <cfinput type="Text"
            name="DateOfBirth"
```

```
            message="Please enter a valid date of birth in the format
mm/dd/yyyy"
            validate="date"
            required="Yes"
            size="11"
            maxlength="10">
    </td>
</tr>

<tr>
    <td> </td>
    <td>
        <input type="submit" value="Add to Database">
    </td>
</tr>

</cfform>
</table>

</body>
</html>
```

This template is similar to the company add form. You're using Employee table columns instead of Company table columns, but this template still has a `CFFORM` surrounding `CFINPUT` tags. By the way, look at the `Validate` attributes on the `SSN`, `Salary`, and `DateOfBirth` `CFINPUT` tags; `social_security_number`, `float`, and `date` are more ways to validate user input.

The `CFQUERY` call should be somewhat familiar because it's a stripped-down version of the `CFQUERY` from `CompanyList.cfm`. This query is used to populate the `CFSELECT` menu used to choose the company for which this employee works. More on this in the section "What was that CFSELECT tag?" later in this chapter.

Creating the employee add action template

Most of this template should be familiar, but this time you're also going to handle dates. Create a file named `EmployeeAddAction.cfm` inside the `Ch02` directory, type the code in Listing 2-13 into the file's editing window, and save the file.

Listing 2-13: EmployeeAddAction.cfm

```
<cfquery name="InsertEmployee"
    datasource="#Request.MainDSN#">
INSERT INTO Employee(
    SSN,
    CompanyID,
    Firstname,
    Lastname,
    Salary,
    DateOfBirth
```

Continued

Listing 2-13 *(continued)*

```
)
VALUES (
    '#Trim(Form.SSN)#',
    #Val(Form.CompanyID)#,
    '#Trim(Form.Firstname)#',
    '#Trim(Form.Lastname)#',
    #Val(Form.Salary)#,
    #CreateODBCDate(Form.DateOfBirth)#
)
</cfquery>

<cflocation url="Finished.cfm?msg=#URLEncodedFormat('#Form.FirstName#
#Form.Lastname# has been added to the database.')#">
```

The most noticeable differences between `CompanyAddAction.cfm` and `EmployeeAddAction.cfm` are the different table and column names in use. Of course, you remember to use `Trim()` on all strings and use `Val()` on all numbers, but dates are handled differently, as follows:

```
#CreateODBCDate(Form.DateOfBirth)#
```

`CreateODBCDate()` takes a date-formatted string and converts it into a formal date value that the database can understand. Notice that you don't use single quotes because the converted date is not a string value.

Finally, `CFLOCATION` redirects the user to the Finished page, as in all your other action pages.

Now you can add an employee to the database. Point your Web browser to `http://<yourserver>/CFMXBible/Ch02/EmployeeAddForm.cfm`. Fill out the form and click Submit. You should be redirected to the Finished page. If not, compare the files that you've created with their respective listings.

What was that CFSELECT tag?

The only new tag in `EmployeeAddForm.cfm` is `CFSELECT`, which is another ColdFusion form control with extended features — in this case, the capability to populate the select menu by pointing `CFSELECT` to a query. (See the boldfaced code in Listing 2-12, which shows the relationship of the query and its columns to the select menu and its options.)

Every option in a select menu has two parts: the text that appears to the user and the value submitted to the server. In this case, you want the user to choose from a list of company names, but you want the company ID to be submitted to the server.

The list after the following code discusses each of the `CFSELECT` tag's attributes in turn:

```
<cfselect
    name="CompanyID"
    query="GetCompanies"
    display="CompanyName"
    value="CompanyID"
    required="Yes"
    message="Please select a Company.">
</cfselect>
```

✦ *Name* becomes the name of the Form variable on the action page—in this case, Form.CompanyID.

✦ CFSELECT uses the specified *Query* to generate its options.

✦ Each option's text comes from the *Display* column.

✦ Each option's value comes from the *Value* column

✦ If *Required="Yes"*, the user must choose a value before the form can be submitted.

✦ If the user doesn't choose an option and attempts to submit the form, a JavaScript alert box containing this *Message* appears and the form isn't submitted.

Getting a List of Employees

You also need a list of all the employees in the database. The employee list is more complicated than the company list because it shows not only employee information, but also the name of the company each employee works for.

Creating the employee list

Create a file named EmployeeList.cfm inside the Ch02 directory, type the code in Listing 2-14 into the file's editing window, and save the file.

Listing 2-14: EmployeeList.cfm

```
<cfquery name="GetEmployees"
    datasource="#Request.MainDSN#">
SELECT
    c.CompanyName,
    e.SSN,
    e.Firstname,
    e.Lastname,
    e.Salary,
    e.DateOfBirth
FROM
    Employee e INNER JOIN Company c
        ON e.CompanyID = c.CompanyID
ORDER BY
    c.CompanyName,
    e.Lastname,
    e.Firstname
</cfquery>

<html>
<head>
    <title>ColdFusion MX Bible</title>
    <link rel="stylesheet" href="styles.css">
</head>
```

Continued

Listing 2-14 *(continued)*

```
<body>

<h1>Employee List</h1>

<table>
<tr>
    <td><b>Company</b></td>
    <td><b>SSN</b></td>
    <td><b>Name</b></td>
    <td><b>Salary</b></td>
    <td><b>DOB</b></td>
</tr>

<cfoutput query="GetEmployees">
<tr>
    <td>#CompanyName#</td>
    <td>#SSN#</td>
    <td>#Lastname#, #Firstname#</td>
    <td>#Salary#</td>
    <td>#DateFormat(DateOfBirth, "mm/dd/yyyy")#</td>
</tr>
</cfoutput>

</table>

</body>
</html>
```

This file is much like `CompanyList.cfm`, with the difference of the relational query in the `CFQUERY` call and the different column names inside `CFOUTPUT`.

We're going to discuss the employee list further in the section "Making Your Application Better" after you get to see it in action. Point your web browser to `http://<yourserver>/CFMXBible/Ch02/EmployeeList.cfm`. You should see all the employees in the database. If not, compare the files that you've created to their respective listings.

Using DateFormat() to make the date look natural to the user

The `DateFormat()` function around the `DateOfBirth` column in Listing 2-14 returns the employee's birth date reformatted according to a display mask. `DateOfBirth` normally comes back from the database in the following format:

```
2002-01-01 00:00:00.0
```

That format is not very user-friendly. Calling `DateFormat()` with a mask of `"mm/dd/yyyy"` returns the date as follows:

```
01/01/2002
```

This version is, of course, more natural and easy to read.

Modifying an Employee in the Database

When you created the company edit process earlier in the section "Building the company edit action template," it was an expanded version of the company add process. The same is true for the employee edit process.

Choosing an employee to edit

Before the user can edit an employee record, he must enter the SSN of the employee that he wants to edit. `EmployeeGetEditForm.cfm` is nearly identical in behavior to `CompanyGetEditForm.cfm`. Create a file named `EmployeeGetEditForm.cfm` inside the `Ch02` directory, type the code in Listing 2-15 into the file's editing window, and save the file.

Listing 2-15: EmployeeGetEditForm.cfm

```
<html>
<head>
    <title>ColdFusion MX Bible</title>
    <link rel="stylesheet" href="styles.css">
</head>

<body>

<h1>Edit an Employee</h1>

<table>
<cfform action="EmployeeEditForm.cfm" method="POST">
<tr>
    <td>SSN</td>
    <td>
        <cfinput type="Text"
            name="SSN"
            message="Please enter the SSN"
            validate="social_security_number"
            required="Yes"
            size="12"
            maxlength="11">
    </td>
</tr>
<tr>
    <td> </td>
    <td>
        <input type="submit" value="Get Employee">
    </td>
</tr>
</cfform>
</table>

</body>
</html>
```

Building the employee edit form

The employee edit form combines a number of techniques that you've learned so far, such as creating a query to retrieve a record from the database, pre-populating form fields with the data from that record, and so on. Create a file named `EmployeeEditForm.cfm` inside the `Ch02` directory, type the code in Listing 2-16 into the file's editing window, and save the file.

Listing 2-16: EmployeeEditForm.cfm

```
<cfquery name="GetEmployee"
    datasource="#Request.MainDSN#">
SELECT
    CompanyID,
    SSN,
    Firstname,
    Lastname,
    Salary,
    DateOfBirth
FROM
    Employee
WHERE
    SSN = '#Trim(SSN)#'
</cfquery>

<cfquery name="GetCompanies"
    datasource="#Request.MainDSN#">
SELECT
    CompanyID,
    CompanyName
FROM
    Company
ORDER BY
    CompanyName
</cfquery>

<html>
<head>
    <title>ColdFusion MX Bible</title>
    <link rel="stylesheet" href="styles.css">
</head>

<body>

<h1>Edit an Employee</h1>

<table>
<cfform action="EmployeeEditAction.cfm" method="POST">

<cfoutput>
<input type="hidden" name="OldSSN" value="#SSN#">
</cfoutput>
```

```
<tr>
    <td>Company</td>
    <td>
        <cfselect name="CompanyID"
            size="1"
            selected="#GetEmployee.CompanyID#"
            message="Please select a Company."
            query="GetCompanies"
            value="CompanyID"
            display="CompanyName"
            required="Yes"></cfselect>
    </td>
</tr>
<tr>
    <td>SSN</td>
    <td>
        <cfinput type="Text"
            name="SSN"
            value="#GetEmployee.SSN#"
            message="Please enter the employee's Social Security
Number."
            validate="social_security_number"
            required="Yes"
            size="12"
            maxlength="11">
    </td>
</tr>
<tr>
    <td>First Name</td>
    <td>
        <cfinput type="Text"
            name="Firstname"
            value="#GetEmployee.Firstname#"
            message="Please enter the employee's first name."
            required="Yes"
            size="22"
            maxlength="20">
    </td>
</tr>
<tr>
    <td>Last Name</td>
    <td>
        <cfinput type="Text"
            name="Lastname"
            value="#GetEmployee.Lastname#"
            message="Please enter the employee's last name."
            required="Yes"
            size="22"
            maxlength="20">
    </td>
</tr>
<tr>
```

Continued

Listing 2-16 *(continued)*

```
    <td>Salary</td>
    <td>
        <cfinput type="Text"
            name="Salary"
            value="#GetEmployee.Salary#"
            message="Please enter a valid salary."
            validate="float"
            required="Yes"
            size="22"
            maxlength="20">
    </td>
</tr>
<tr>
    <td>DOB</td>
    <td>
        <cfinput type="Text"
            name="DateOfBirth"
            value="#DateFormat(GetEmployee.DateOfBirth, 'mm/dd/yyyy')#"
            message="Please enter a valid date of birth in the format
mm/dd/yyyy"
            validate="date"
            required="Yes"
            size="11"
            maxlength="10">
    </td>
</tr>
<tr>
    <td> </td>
    <td>
        <input type="submit" value="Update Database">
    </td>
</tr>
</cfform>
</table>

</body>
</html>
```

Two calls to `CFQUERY` are on this page. `GetEmployee` populates the employee edit form with the employee record, and `GetCompanies` populates the `CFSELECT` menu with the list of companies.

As you move down the template, you should see the `CFFORM` tag and then a hidden form field named `OldSSN`. Remember that, on the company edit form, the `CompanyID` wasn't editable, so you could just pass the ID through to the action page. On the employee edit form, however, you must pass both the current `SSN` value (in the `OldSSN` hidden form field) and the new `SSN` value (in the `SSN CFINPUT`) to the action page.

We need both the old and new values of `SSN` because changing its value requires you to use the old value (what's currently in the database) in the action template's `WHERE` clause and the new value (what the user has changed) in its `SET` clause.

As in CompanyEditForm.cfm, each CFINPUT tag in this template has a Value attribute that populates the form field with the value retrieved from the query.

CFSELECT's Selected attribute tells ColdFusion which item to select in the select menu as the form is initially displayed to the user.

Creating the employee edit action template

After the employee edit form, the employee edit action template is a welcome reprieve. Create a file named EmployeeEditAction.cfm inside the Ch02 directory, type the code in Listing 2-17 into the file's editing window, and save the file.

Listing 2-17: EmployeeEditAction.cfm

```
<cfquery name="UpdateEmployee"
    datasource="#Request.MainDSN#">
UPDATE Employee
SET
    SSN = '#Trim(Form.SSN)#',
    CompanyID = #Val(Form.CompanyID)#,
    Firstname = '#Trim(Form.Firstname)#',
    Lastname = '#Trim(Form.Lastname)#',
    Salary = #Val(Form.Salary)#,
    DateOfBirth = #CreateODBCDate(Form.DateOfBirth)#
WHERE
    SSN = '#Trim(Form.OldSSN)#'
</cfquery>

<cflocation url="Finished.cfm?msg=#URLEncodedFormat('#Form.FirstName#
#Form.Lastname# has been updated in the database.')#">
```

Point your Web browser to http://*<yourserver>*/CFMXBible/Ch02/EmployeeGetEditForm.cfm. Enter the SSN of an employee currently in the database and click Submit. To get a valid SSN pick one from the employee list. Change a few values on the edit form and click Submit. Then go back to the employee list and make sure that the employee record was changed. (You may need to click Refresh.) If everything doesn't work perfectly, check the files that you created against their respective listings.

Removing an Employee From the Database

The user must have the capability to remove employees from the database. The employee delete process is a simple combination of techniques that you have already learned, such as retrieving a record from the database, displaying that record in a template, and so on.

Choosing an employee to delete

The first page in this process is nearly identical to the employee get edit form. Create a file named EmployeeGetDeleteForm.cfm inside the Ch02 directory, type the code in Listing 2-18 into the file's editing window, and save the file.

Listing 2-18: EmployeeGetDeleteForm.cfm

```
<html>
<head>
    <title>ColdFusion MX Bible</title>
    <link rel="stylesheet" href="styles.css">
</head>

<body>

<h1>Delete an Employee</h1>

<table>
<cfform action="EmployeeDeleteForm.cfm" method="POST">
<tr>
    <td>SSN</td>
    <td>
        <cfinput type="Text"
            name="SSN"
            message="Please enter the SSN"
            validate="social_security_number"
            required="Yes"
            size="12"
            maxlength="11">
    </td>
</tr>
<tr>
    <td> </td>
    <td>
        <input type="submit" value="Get Employee">
    </td>
</tr>
</cfform>
</table>

</body>
</html>
```

The only difference between the get delete form and the get edit form is where each one posts: the get edit form posts to EmployeeEditForm.cfm, whereas the get delete form posts to employeeDeleteForm.cfm.

Building the employee delete form

No new concepts are presented in this template—just new combinations of what you've already learned so far in this chapter.

Create a file named `EmployeeDeleteForm.cfm` inside the `Ch02` directory, type the code in Listing 2-19 into the file's editing window, and save the file.

Listing 2-19: EmployeeDeleteForm.cfm

```
<cfquery name="GetEmployee"
    datasource="#Request.MainDSN#">
SELECT
    c.CompanyName,
    e.SSN,
    e.Firstname,
    e.Lastname,
    e.Salary,
    e.DateOfBirth
FROM
    Employee e INNER JOIN Company c
        ON e.CompanyID = c.CompanyID
WHERE
    e.SSN = '#Trim(SSN)#'
</cfquery>

<html>
<head>
    <title>ColdFusion MX Bible</title>
    <link rel="stylesheet" href="styles.css">
</head>

<body>

<h1>Delete an Employee</h1>

<cfoutput>
<table>
<cfform action="EmployeeDeleteAction.cfm" method="POST">

<input type="hidden" name="SSN" value="#SSN#">

<tr>
    <td>Company</td>
    <td>#GetEmployee.CompanyName#</td>
</tr>

<tr>
    <td>SSN</td>
    <td>#GetEmployee.SSN#</td>
</tr>

<tr>
    <td>First Name</td>
    <td>#GetEmployee.Firstname#</td>
</tr>

<tr>
    <td>Last Name</td>
```

Continued

Listing 2-19 *(continued)*

```
        <td>#GetEmployee.Lastname#</td>
    </tr>

    <tr>
        <td>Salary</td>
        <td>#GetEmployee.Salary#</td>
    </tr>

    <tr>
        <td>DOB</td>
        <td>#DateFormat(GetEmployee.DateOfBirth, 'mm/dd/yyyy')#</td>
    </tr>

    <tr>
        <td> </td>
        <td>
            <input type="submit" value="Delete from Database">
        </td>
    </tr>

    </cfform>
    </table>
    </cfoutput>

    </body>
    </html>
```

The GetEmployee query looks like the query on EmployeeList.cfm with a WHERE clause to restrict the result set to a single record. The inner join enables the company name to appear on the delete form. You don't need the INNER JOIN on the edit form because the company name came from a separate query (GetCompanies).

Creating the employee delete action template

Create a file named EmployeeDeleteAction.cfm inside the Ch02 directory, type the code in Listing 2-20 into the file's editing window, and save the file.

Listing 2-20: EmployeeDeleteAction.cfm

```
<cfquery name="DeleteEmployee"
    datasource="#Request.MainDSN#">
DELETE FROM Employee
WHERE
    SSN = '#Trim(Form.SSN)#'
</cfquery>
```

```
<cflocation url="Finished.cfm?msg=#URLEncodedFormat('Employee
#Form.SSN# has been deleted from the database.')#">
```

The `CFQUERY` deletes the employee from the database, and the `CFLOCATION` redirects the user.

Now that you've finished the employee delete process, take it for a spin. Point your Web browser to `http://<yourserver>/CFMXBible/Ch02/EmployeeGetDeleteForm.cfm`. Enter the `SSN` of an employee currently in the database, and click Submit. Look at the employee information, and Click Submit. Then go back to the employee list and make sure that the employee record was removed. (You may need to click Refresh.)

Creating a Launch Pad

The way things that stand right now, to operate this application, you must manually enter the names of eight different templates. Instead, you can create a "launch pad" to make the application a little easier to use.

Create a file named `index.cfm` inside the `Ch02` directory, type the code in Listing 2-21 into the file's editing window, and save the file.

Listing 2-21: The launch pad

```
<html>
<head>
    <title>ColdFusion MX Bible</title>
    <link rel="stylesheet" href="styles.css">
</head>

<body>

<h1>Companies</h1>

<a href="CompanyList.cfm">List Companies</a><br>
<a href="CompanyAddForm.cfm">Add a Company</a><br>
<a href="CompanyGetEditForm.cfm">Edit a Company</a><br>
<a href="CompanyGetDeleteForm.cfm">Delete a Company</a>

<h2>Employees</h2>

<a href="EmployeeList.cfm">List Employees</a><br>
<a href="EmployeeAddForm.cfm">Add an Employee</a><br>
<a href="EmployeeGetEditForm.cfm">Edit an Employee</a><br>
<a href="EmployeeGetDeleteForm.cfm">Delete an Employee</a>

</body>
</html>
```

No ColdFusion tags are in this template — just hyperlinks pointing to each process's starting template. Point your Web browser to `http://`*`<yourserver>`*`/CFMXBible/Ch02/index.cfm` and click away!

Making Your Application Better

You now have a fully functioning application, but you can do a number of things to make it work better.

Creating a footer at the bottom of every page

You can easily give the application a way to get back to the launch pad no matter where you are. You *could*, of course, open up every template and add a link at the bottom, but that's time-consuming — and what if you forget a template? A better option is to use a special template named `OnRequestEnd.cfm` that ColdFusion automatically executes after the end of every request (just as ColdFusion executes `Application.cfm` at the beginning of every request). `OnRequestEnd.cfm` must be capitalized exactly as shown for it to function on all platforms.

Create a file named `OnRequestEnd.cfm` inside the `Ch02` directory, type the code in Listing 2-22 into the file's editing window, and save the file.

Listing 2-22: OnRequestEnd.cfm

```
<p><a href="index.cfm">Home</a></p>
```

Try it out by going to any page in your application. You should see the `Home` link at the bottom of the page.

Showing a company's employees

A nice touch would be if the company list had a direct link to the employee list so that the user could view all employees of a selected company. Of course, you would still want to be able to view the employees of all the companies at once if the user goes directly to the employee list.

To accomplish this new functionality, you must modify two templates. First, you modify `CompanyList.cfm` so that it contains a link to `EmployeeList.cfm`, passing the company ID in the URL. You pass the CompanyID so that `EmployeeList.cfm` can know the company from which to select employees. Listing 2-23 shows the modifications to make to `CompanyList.cfm`, with the additions in boldface.

Listing 2-23: CompanyList.cfm, adding a link to the employee list

```
...
<table>
<tr>
	<td><b>ID</b></td>
	<td><b>Name</b></td>
	<td><b>Address</b></td>
```

```
        <td><b>City</b></td>
        <td><b>State</b></td>
        <td><b>ZIP Code</b></td>
        <td> </td>
    </tr>
    <cfoutput query="GetCompanies">
    <tr>
        <td>#CompanyID#</td>
        <td>#CompanyName#</td>
        <td>#Address#</td>
        <td>#City#</td>
        <td>#State#</td>
        <td>#ZipCode#</td>
        <td><a
    href="EmployeeList.cfm?CompanyID=#CompanyID#">Employees</a></td>
    </tr>
    </cfoutput>
    </table>
    ...
```

After the user clicks the Employees link, he goes to the employee list page, which receives the CompanyID in a URL parameter named URL.CompanyID. You don't need Val() here because CompanyID comes directly from a numeric database column with no user intervention, so #CompanyID# is absolutely guaranteed to be a number.

Now turn your attention to EmployeeList.cfm. Listing 2-24 shows the modifications made to EmployeeList.cfm, with the additions in boldface.

Listing 2-24: EmployeeList.cfm, adding a filter by CompanyID

```
<cfquery name="GetEmployees"
    datasource="#Request.MainDSN#">
SELECT
    c.CompanyName,
    e.SSN,
    e.Firstname,
    e.Lastname,
    e.Salary,
    e.DateOfBirth
FROM
    Employee e INNER JOIN Company c
        ON e.CompanyID = c.CompanyID
<cfif IsDefined("URL.CompanyID")>
WHERE
    e.CompanyID = #Val(URL.CompanyID)#
</cfif>
ORDER BY
    c.CompanyName,
    e.Lastname,
    e.Firstname
</cfquery>
...
```

You're adding an additional section to the `CFQUERY`, but notice that the new section is inside a `CFIF` test. Remember that you can dynamically construct an SQL statement by using this method. By the way, you do need `Val()` here because the user could have modified `URL.CompanyID` by playing with the URL.

Go to the launch pad and click `Company List`. Click any of the links named `Employees` and you see only those employees who work for that company.

Making direct links to the add, view, and delete forms

Say that you want to modify or delete a company. Right now, you need to remember the company's ID, go back to the launch pad, click `Company Edit`, and enter the company ID, all just to get to the edit form. Wouldn't you rather click a company in the list and go directly to the edit form?

Listing 2-25 shows in bold the modifications to make to `CompanyList.cfm` to accomplish this task.

Listing 2-25: CompanyList.cfm, adding links to add, edit, and delete forms

```
...
<table>
<tr>
    <td><b>ID</b></td>
    <td><b>Name</b></td>
    <td><b>Address</b></td>
    <td><b>City</b></td>
    <td><b>State</b></td>
    <td><b>ZIP Code</b></td>
    <td> </td>
</tr>
<cfoutput query="GetCompanies">
<tr>
    <td>#CompanyID#</td>
    <td>#CompanyName#</td>
    <td>#Address#</td>
    <td>#City#</td>
    <td>#State#</td>
    <td>#ZipCode#</td>
    <td>
        <a href="EmployeeList.cfm?CompanyID=#CompanyID#">Employees</a>
        <a href="CompanyAddForm.cfm">Add</a>
        <a href="CompanyEditForm.cfm?CompanyID=#CompanyID#">Edit</a>
        <a
href="CompanyDeleteForm.cfm?CompanyID=#CompanyID#">Delete</a>
    </td>
</tr>
</cfoutput>
</table>
...
```

Now you can go to the company list and click a link to go directly to the Add, Edit, or Delete Form.

Now that you've seen how to link from `CompanyList.cfm` to `CompanyEditForm.cfm` and `CompanyDeleteForm.cfm`, you can do the same with `EmployeeList.cfm`. Listing 2-26 shows the modifications to make to `EmployeeList.cfm` in bold.

Listing 2-26: **EmployeeList.cfm, adding links to add, edit, and delete forms**

```
...
<table>
<tr>
    <td><b>Company</b></td>
    <td><b>SSN</b></td>
    <td><b>Name</b></td>
    <td><b>Salary</b></td>
    <td><b>DOB</b></td>
    <td> </td>
</tr>

<cfoutput query="GetEmployees">
<tr>
    <td>#CompanyName#</td>
    <td>#SSN#</td>
    <td>#Lastname#, #Firstname#</td>
    <td>#Salary#</td>
    <td>#DateFormat(DateOfBirth, "mm/dd/yyyy")#</td>
    <td>
        <a href="EmployeeAddForm.cfm">Add</a>
        <a
href="EmployeeEditForm.cfm?SSN=#URLEncodedFormat(Trim(SSN))#">Edit</a>
        <a
href="EmployeeDeleteForm.cfm?SSN=#URLEncodedFormat(Trim(SSN))#">Delete<
/a>
    </td>
</tr>
</cfoutput>

</table>
...
```

You use `Trim()` on the `SSN` to make sure that it has no trailing spaces, and you use `URLEncodedFormat()` to make sure that the `SSN` is URL-safe. You didn't need `URLEncodedFormat()` in the company list because `CompanyID` is an integer, and integers are always URL-safe.

You can now go to the employee list and click the `Edit` or `Delete` link to go directly to the edit or delete form.

Redirecting the user back to the company list

The fact that you must go back to the launch pad and then back to the company list every time that you add, edit, or delete a company, all for the sake of a message that really doesn't tell you much of anything, is annoying. A much better situation would be that the action page redirects you back to the list page, not even passing a message (because you can safely assume that, if no error occurred, the company or employee was successfully inserted, updated, or deleted in the database).

Edit the `CFLOCATION` tags in `CompanyAddAction.cfm`, `CompanyEditAction.cfm`, and `CompanyDeleteAction.cfm` to the following:

```
<cflocation url="CompanyList.cfm">
```

Then change the `CFLOCATION` calls in `EmployeeAddAction.cfm`, `EmployeeEditAction.cfm`, and `EmployeeDeleteAction.cfm` to the following:

```
<cflocation url="EmployeeList.cfm">
```

Test your changes by going to any of these form pages and clicking Submit. They should all take you back to their respective list.

Sending a welcome e-mail to a new employee

After you add a new employee to the list, the capability to send that employee an e-mail welcoming him to the new company would be nice. You use `CFMAIL` to send out an e-mail message. For the purposes of this example, assume that all employees have an e-mail address in the style *first.last@somewhere*.com.

Listing 2-27 shows in bold the modifications to make to `EmployeeAddAction.cfm` so it will send a welcome message to the new user.

Listing 2-27: EmployeeAddAction.cfm, adding a call to CFMAIL

```
<cfquery name="InsertEmployee"
    datasource="#Request.MainDSN#">
...
</cfquery>

<cfmail to="#Form.Firstname#.#Form.Lastname#@somewhere.com"
        from="admin@somwhere.com"
        subject="Welcome to your new company!">
Welcome to your new company, #Form.Firstname# #Form.Lastname#!
</cfmail>

<cflocation url="EmployeeList.cfm">
```

`CFMAIL` has three attributes: `From`, `To`, and `Subject`. `From` tells ColdFusion where this e-mail is coming from; `To` tells ColdFusion where to send the message; and `Subject` is what appears in the Subject line. The content between `<cfmail>` and `</cfmail>` becomes the body of the message.

You may not have the capability to execute this modification unless you have a default mail server set up in ColdFusion Administrator. For information on using ColdFusion Administrator, see Part VIII of this book.

Even if you do have a correctly configured mail server, you should take care not to send a bunch of useless e-mails all over the Internet!

Setting a cookie in the employee list

Go to the company list and drill down to the employees of a single company. Click `Add Employee` and add a new employee to the database. After ColdFusion takes you back to the employee list, you see all the employees in the database instead of just the employees for the original company.

A *cookie* is a variable stored locally on a user's machine. You can use a cookie to extend the drill-down from the company list to the employee list such that, after the user adds an employee to the database after drilling down and returns to the list, he still sees only the employees of the original company and not all employees in the database.

Listing 2-28 shows in bold the modifications to `EmployeeList.cfm` to set and use a cookie.

Listing 2-28: EmployeeList.cfm, adding a cookie to store the CompanyID

```
<cfif IsDefined("URL.CompanyID")>
    <cfcookie name="CompanyID" value="#URL.CompanyID#">
</cfif>

<cfquery name="GetEmployees"
    datasource="#Request.MainDSN#">
SELECT
    c.CompanyName,
    e.SSN,
    e.Firstname,
    e.Lastname,
    e.Salary,
    e.DateOfBirth
FROM
    Employee e INNER JOIN Company c
        ON e.CompanyID = c.CompanyID
<cfif IsDefined("Cookie.CompanyID")>
WHERE
    e.CompanyID = #Val(Cookie.CompanyID)#
</cfif>
ORDER BY
    c.CompanyName,
    e.Lastname,
    e.Firstname
</cfquery>
...
```

If URL.CompanyID is defined, CFCOOKIE creates a cookie on your computer that stores URL.CompanyID. CFCOOKIE has a Name attribute, which specifies the name of the cookie variable, and a Value attribute, which specifies the value that is stored in the cookie.

Now look at the CFQUERY statement. Notice how URL.CompanyID has changed to Cookie.CompanyID. You set a cookie variable by using the CFCOOKIE tag, but you read a cookie variable by using the Cookie. prefix.

The next time that you drill down to a company's employees and then perform some action, you see the employee list filtered by the same company after the action page redirects.

The problem now is that even if you go back to the launch pad and click the employee list, you still get only the employees of the most recently listed company.

The first thing that you must do is modify the link in index.cfm to tell the employee list to show all employees, as the code in Listing 2-29 does.

Listing 2-29: **The modified employee list link in index.cfm**

```
<html>
<head>
    <title>ColdFusion MX Bible</title>
    <link rel="stylesheet" href="styles.css">
</head>

<body>

<h1>Companies</h1>

<a href="CompanyList.cfm">List Companies</a><br>
<a href="CompanyAddForm.cfm">Add a Company</a><br>
<a href="CompanyGetEditForm.cfm">Edit a Company</a><br>
<a href="CompanyGetDeleteForm.cfm">Delete a Company</a>

<h2>Employees</h2>

<a href="EmployeeList.cfm?ShowAll=1">List Employees</a><br>
<a href="EmployeeAddForm.cfm">Add an Employee</a><br>
<a href="EmployeeGetEditForm.cfm">Edit an Employee</a><br>
<a href="EmployeeGetDeleteForm.cfm">Delete an Employee</a>

</body>
</html>
```

Next, you must modify the employee list to take the ShowAll parameter into account, as in Listing 2-30.

Listing 2-30: **Modifying EmployeeList.cfm to delete the CompanyID cookie**

```
<cfif IsDefined("URL.CompanyID")>
    <cfcookie name="CompanyID" value="#URL.CompanyID#">
```

```
</cfif>

<cfif IsDefined("URL.ShowAll")>
    <cfcookie name="CompanyID" expires="NOW">
</cfif>

<cfquery name="GetEmployees"
    datasource="#Request.MainDSN#">
    . . .
    <cfif IsDefined("Cookie.CompanyID") AND
Len(Trim(Cookie.CompanyID))>
    WHERE
        e.CompanyID = #Val(Cookie.CompanyID)#
    </cfif>
    . . .
</cfquery>
...
```

Now, if `URL.ShowAll` is defined as you execute `EmployeeList.cfm`, the `CompanyID` cookie is deleted from the user's browser and all employees in the database are displayed. Deleting a cookie from the user's browser sets its corresponding value in ColdFusion to a blank string rather than deleting it, so in essence Cookie.CompanyID still exists, but its value is a blank string. For this reason we must test the length of the trimmed value of `Cookie.CompanyID` as well as its value to see if it is valid. If we don't add the `Len(Trim(Cookie.CompanyID))` test to account for a blank cookie value, the query includes the `WHERE` clause and as a result returns no matching employees because `Val(Cookie.CompanyID)` is zero.

Extending Your Application by Using a Custom Tag

Custom tags are reusable, developer-authored extensions to the ColdFusion language. The custom tag that you create in the following sections displays today's date in a familiar format.

Writing the custom tag

Create a file named `TodaysDate.cfm` inside the `Ch02` directory, type the code in Listing 2-31 into the file's editing window, and save the file.

Listing 2-31: TodaysDate.cfm

```
<cfoutput>#DateFormat(Now(), "ddd, mmm d, yyyy")#</cfoutput>
```

`Now()` returns the current date and time, and `DateFormat()` reformats the date. It's not much now, but you add to it in the section "Extending the custom tag with attributes".

Calling the custom tag

To call your custom tag, open `index.cfm`, add the following code to the top of the template, and save the file:

```
<p><cf_TodaysDate></p>
```

A custom tag is called by appending `CF_` to the name of the tag file, without the `.cfm` extension. Point your browser to `index.cfm` and make sure that today's date now appears at the top of the file in an easy-to-read format. Calling the custom tag runs `TodaysDate.cfm`.

Extending the custom tag with attributes

`CF_TodaysDate` in its current state doesn't do much. The capability to specify the format in which the date should be presented, as follows, would be nice:

```
<cf_TodaysDate Format="American">
```

`Format` is an attribute to this custom tag. Listing 2-32 shows how to use the `Format` attribute in the custom tag. Make the changes shown in bold in Listing 2-32 to your `TodaysDate.cfm` custom tag.

Listing 2-32: TodaysDate.cfm, adding the Attributes variable

```
<cfswitch expression="#Attributes.Format#">
<cfcase value="Long">
    <cfset FormatMask = "ddd, mmm d, yyyy">
</cfcase>
<cfcase value="American">
    <cfset FormatMask = "mm/dd/yyyy">
</cfcase>
<cfcase value="European">
    <cfset FormatMask = "dd/mm/yyyy">
</cfcase>
<cfcase value="Military">
    <cfset FormatMask = "ddmmmyyyy">
</cfcase>
<cfdefaultcase>
    <cfset FormatMask = "mm/dd/yyyy">
</cfdefaultcase>
</cfswitch>

<cfoutput>#DateFormat(Now(), FormatMask)#</cfoutput>
```

`CFSWITCH` evaluates the content of its `Expression` argument and checks it against the `Value` attribute of each of its `CFCASE` statements. As soon as a match is found between `Expression` and `Value`, the matching `CFCASE` block is executed. If no `CFCASE` tags match, the `CFDEFAULTCASE` is executed.

`Attributes.Format` contains the value of the `Format` attribute that was passed to `CF_TodaysDate` (in this case, `American`), and `FormatMask` contains the date mask that the custom tag uses inside the `DateFormat()` function.

To test the new custom tag, modify `index.cfm` so that the call to `<cf_TodaysDate>` looks as follows:

```
<p><cf_TodaysDate Format="American"></p>
```

Run `index.cfm` again. Now try calling `cf_TodaysDate` using `Format="Military"`.

Congratulations!

You've written your first ColdFusion application! This is no small feat, and some of the techniques in this chapter are a little advanced. You've written an entire maintenance application for two entities in a database, created a total of 22 templates, and even made some pretty hefty modifications to your application to make it better. You should be very proud of yourself!

Of course, this application is by no means complete. You have seen a few of ColdFusion's features, but you've only scratched the surface. A real-world application would probably use the extra features described in the following list:

- ✦ To keep things simple, you created a datasource and used a single variable `Request.MainDSN` to reference it. In a real application, you would not specify the username and password in ColdFusion Administrator (see chapters 43 and 44); in `Application.cfm`, you would `CFSET` two more variables, `Request.Username` and `Request.Password`, and then specify the username and password to be used in all your `CFQUERY` calls.
- ✦ A real application would have used structured exception handling to catch such errors as a user trying to delete a company with existing employees or adding the same employee twice.
- ✦ A real application would have some type of graphical treatment and a much more well-developed navigation system.
- ✦ Real applications are usually much more complex than our two-table maintenance system.

Still, this was an impressive entry into the world of ColdFusion MX. You can only get better from this point forward! Read the rest of this book to learn the more advanced real-world principles and techniques that you need to know to create large, complex applications.

Summary

In this chapter, you build an application that manages a simple database of companies and employees. You also modify your application and extend the ColdFusion language itself by creating a custom tag.

In the next chapter, you learn how to use the ColdFusion language in more detail

✦ ✦ ✦

CHAPTER 3

Using ColdFusion MX Tags and Functions

✦ ✦ ✦ ✦

In This Chapter

Building expressions in ColdFusion

Creating expressions by using variables, operators, functions, and literals

Understanding pound signs

Using CFOUTPUT

Using ColdFusion and HTML comments

Many developers have difficulty understanding the rules of ColdFusion syntax, possibly because everyone writes ColdFusion code in a different way. And finding a rulebook for writing ColdFusion can prove a rare experience for a developer.

This chapter explains the correct way to use expressions in ColdFusion. It tells you where to and where not to use pound signs and gives you the rules for using ColdFusion tags and functions. The chapter ends with a discussion of code comments.

ColdFusion Expressions

Expressions are everywhere in ColdFusion. Anything between pound signs is an expression in ColdFusion. Anything inside a CFSET or CFIF tag is an expression. Simply put, anything in ColdFusion that can be *evaluated* (i.e., "resolved into a value") is an expression. Expressions can come in many different forms; the following four are just a small sampling:

```
#myVar#
#Val(1 + 1)#
<cfset aVar = ArrayNew(1)>
<cfif aVar[1] EQ "A"></cfif>
```

You can have many types of expressions, but only the following four elements can make up any expression:

- ✦ **Variables:** Variables are everywhere in ColdFusion.
- ✦ **Operators:** Operators are symbols such as + or –, and comparisons such as GTE, LT, NOT, or MOD.
- ✦ **Functions:** Any function can be part of an expression. Functions are always followed by a pair of enclosing parentheses.
- ✦ **Literals:** A literal is a string or number used as part of an expression. Take, for example, the following expression:

  ```
  #DateFormat(aDateVariable, "mm/dd/yyyy")#
  ```

  The mm/dd/yyyy in the preceding expression is a literal. Similarly, consider the following expression:

```
#Val(0)#
```

Here, the zero is a literal.

Based on these rules, you can deconstruct some expressions. Take the following expression:

```
#DateFormat(aDateVariable, "mm/dd/yyyy")#
```

It has three parts: a function call (`DateFormat()`), a variable (`aDateVariable`), and a string literal (`mm/dd/yyyy`). Now consider the following expression:

```
<cfset aVar = Val(anotherVar) + 1>
```

It has six parts: a variable (`aVar`), an operator (=), a function call (`Val()`), another variable (`anotherVar`), another operator (+), and a numeric literal (1).

The following expression, however, is a trick on your eyes:

```
<cfif NOT(firstVariable GTE secondVariable)>
```

`NOT` looks as though it is a function, and `firstVariable GTE secondVariable` appears to be an argument to that function. This evaluation, however, is not correct. `NOT` is actually a ColdFusion operator, and the parentheses tell ColdFusion to evaluate `firstVariable GTE secondVariable` first and then to use the `NOT` operator on the result. The `NOT` operator takes a true/false expression and flips it — `true` becomes `false` and vice-versa. A better way to write this expression as is follows:

```
<cfif firstVariable LT secondVariable>
```

This version avoids any confusion on the part of the reader.

Using operators

Now that you've seen how to construct ColdFusion expressions, take a look at the operators that ColdFusion uses.

Arithmetic operators

Arithmetic operators work with numbers. If ColdFusion can't convert both operands (the items on either side of the operator) to numbers, ColdFusion throws an error.

Basic operators (+, -, /, *)

Plus, minus, divide, and multiply are the four *basic* math operations. In division, the right-hand operand cannot be zero. Use of these operators is straightforward:

```
1 + 1 returns 2
10 - 1 returns 9
10 / 5 returns 2
4 * 2 returns 8
```

Sign operators (+ and -)

Whenever the *sign* operators appear in front of a number, as in the following examples, they indicate the number's sign:

```
+1 + 5 returns 6 (positive 1 plus 5)
-1 + 7 returns 6 (negative 1 plus 7)
```

Modulo division (MOD)

The *modulo* operator (MOD) divides the first operand by the second operand and returns the remainder. The second operand cannot be zero. Like other operators, MOD is positioned between its operands:

```
10 MOD 3 returns 1 (10/3 is 3 with remainder 1)
15 MOD 8 returns 7 (15/8 is 1 with remainder 7)
15 MOD 5 returns 0 (15/5 is 3 with remainder 0)
5 MOD 7 returns 5 (5/7 is 0 with remainder 5)
```

Integer division (\)

The *integer division* operator (\) divides the first operand by the second and returns the result, discarding the remainder. The second operand cannot be zero. Integer division is as straightforward as when you used it in grade school:

```
10 \ 3 returns 3 (10/3 is 3 with remainder 1)
15 \ 8 returns 1 (15/8 is 1 with remainder 7)
15 \ 5 returns 3 (15/5 is 3 with remainder 0)
5 \ 7 returns 0 (5/7 is 0 with remainder 5)
```

Exponent operator (^)

The *exponent* operator (^) returns the first operand raised to the power of the second operand:

```
2 ^ 3 returns 8 (2 to the third power is 8)
5 ^ 5 returns 3125 (5 to the fifth power is 3125)
8 ^ 2 returns 64 (8 squared is 64)
```

Comparison operators

Comparison operators compare two values and always return a boolean result (TRUE or FALSE). You have eight comparison operators; six of them have optional notational. IS, for example, can also be written as EQ or EQUAL. Contrary to popular belief, no difference—performance, type compatibility, case sensitivity, or otherwise—exists between an operator and any of its shorthand versions.

Comparison operators can take operands of any data type, but be aware that, if the data types are not the same, ColdFusion attempts to convert the operands into compatible types, possibly with unexpected results. The rules for these conversions are explained for each operator in the following sections.

Equality (IS, EQ, EQUAL)

The *equality* comparison operator compares two values and returns TRUE if they are the same and FALSE if they are different. A popular belief is that IS is for strings and EQ is for numbers, but this concept is not true. IS and EQ are equivalent in every way. The operands can be of different types—for example, a string can be compared to a number, as in the third and fourth examples that follow:

```
1 EQ 1 returns TRUE
10 IS 0 returns FALSE
"1" EQUAL 1 returns TRUE
"one" IS 1 returns FALSE
```

Inequality (IS NOT, NEQ, NOT EQUAL)

The *NOT* comparison operator compares two values and returns TRUE if they are different and FALSE if they are the same:

```
1 NEQ 1 returns FALSE
10 IS NOT 0 returns TRUE
"1" NOT EQUAL 1 returns FALSE
"one" IS NOT 1 returns TRUE
```

GREATER THAN, GT

The *GREATER THAN* comparison operator compares two values and returns TRUE if the first is greater than (for numbers), or alphabetically after (for strings), the second. ColdFusion attempts to convert both operands to numbers before doing the comparison. If either operand cannot be converted to a number, ColdFusion compares both operands as strings:

```
2 GREATER THAN 1 returns TRUE
2 GREATER THAN 2 returns FALSE
2 GT 3 returns FALSE
2 GT "1" returns TRUE ("1" can be converted to a number)
2 GT "one" returns FALSE ("2" sorts before "one" alphabetically)
"two" GT "ten" returns TRUE ("two" sorts after "ten")
```

LESS THAN, LT

The *LESS THAN* comparison operator compares two values and returns TRUE if the first is less than (for numbers), or alphabetically before (for strings), the second. Conversion rules are the same as for GREATER THAN:

```
2 LESS THAN 1 returns FALSE
2 LESS THAN 2 returns FALSE
2 LT 3 returns TRUE
2 LT "1" returns FALSE ("1" can be converted to a number)
2 LT "one" returns TRUE ("2" sorts before "one" alphabetically)
"two" LT "ten" returns FALSE ("two" sorts after "ten")
```

GREATER THAN OR EQUAL TO, GTE or GE

This comparison operator compares two values and returns TRUE if the first is greater than (for numbers), or alphabetically after (for strings), the second or if both operands are equal. Conversion rules are the same as for GREATER THAN.

```
2 GREATER THAN OR EQUAL TO 1 returns TRUE
2 GREATER THAN OR EQUAL TO 2 returns TRUE
2 GTE 3 returns FALSE
2 GE "1" returns TRUE ("1" can be converted to a number)
2 GTE "one" returns FALSE ("2" sorts before "one" alphabetically)
"two" GE "ten" returns TRUE ("two" sorts after "ten")
```

LESS THAN OR EQUAL TO, LTE or LE

This comparison operator compares two values and returns TRUE if the first is less than (for numbers), or alphabetically before (for strings), the second, or if both operands are equal. Conversion rules are the same as for LESS THAN:

```
2 LESS THAN OR EQUAL 1 returns FALSE
2 LESS THAN OR EQUAL 2 returns TRUE
2 LTE 3 returns TRUE
2 LE "1" returns FALSE ("1" can be converted to a number)
```

```
2 LTE "one" returns TRUE ("2" sorts before "one" alphabetically)
"two" LE "ten" returns FALSE ("two" sorts after "ten")
```

CONTAINS

The *contains* comparison operator compares two values and returns TRUE if the second operand is contained within the first and FALSE otherwise. This operator converts both operands to strings before comparing them:

```
"Cold Fusion" CONTAINS "Cold" returns TRUE
"ColdFusion" CONTAINS "Cold" returns TRUE
"Cold Fusion" CONTAINS "ColdF" returns FALSE
"ColdFusion" CONTAINS "Hot" returns FALSE
```

DOES NOT CONTAIN

This comparison operator compares two values and returns FALSE if the second operand is contained within the first and TRUE otherwise. This operator converts both operands to strings before comparing them:

```
"Cold Fusion" DOES NOT CONTAIN "Cold" returns FALSE
"ColdFusion" DOES NOT CONTAIN "Cold" returns FALSE
"Cold Fusion" DOES NOT CONTAIN "ColdF" returns TRUE
"ColdFusion" DOES NOT CONTAIN "Hot" returns TRUE
```

Boolean operators

Boolean operators always return either TRUE or FALSE. And all operands of a boolean operator are boolean values themselves. If an operand is not TRUE or FALSE, ColdFusion uses the following three rules to convert the operand to a boolean value:

- ✦ If the operand is a number, ColdFusion converts zero to FALSE and all other numbers, negative and positive alike, to TRUE.
- ✦ If the operand is the string Yes or true, ColdFusion converts it to the boolean value TRUE. If the operand is the string No or false, ColdFusion converts it to FALSE. Any other string argument throws an error (unless it can be converted to a number).
- ✦ If the operand is a date, ColdFusion throws an error.

You have the following six boolean operators in ColdFusion:

- ✦ *Inversion* (NOT) is the simplest boolean operator, because it has only one operand. It reverses the truth-case of its operand. (TRUE becomes FALSE and FALSE becomes TRUE):

  ```
  NOT TRUE returns FALSE
  NOT FALSE returns TRUE
  ```

  Don't confuse NOT by itself with NOT as part of another operator (such as IS NOT or NOT EQUAL).

- ✦ *And* (AND) returns TRUE if both operands are TRUE, as follows:

  ```
  TRUE AND TRUE returns TRUE
  TRUE AND FALSE returns FALSE
  FALSE AND TRUE returns FALSE
  FALSE AND FALSE returns FALSE
  ```

- ✦ *Or* (OR) returns TRUE if either operand, or both, are TRUE, as follows:

  ```
  TRUE OR TRUE returns TRUE
  ```

```
TRUE OR FALSE returns TRUE
FALSE OR TRUE returns TRUE
FALSE OR FALSE returns FALSE
```

✦ *Exclusive OR* (`XOR`) returns `TRUE` if either operand, but not both, are `TRUE`, as follows:

```
TRUE XOR TRUE returns FALSE
TRUE XOR FALSE returns TRUE
FALSE XOR TRUE returns TRUE
FALSE XOR FALSE returns FALSE
```

✦ *Logical Equivalence* (`EQV`) returns `TRUE` if both operands are the same (`EQV` being the logical opposite of the `XOR` operator), as follows:

```
TRUE EQV TRUE returns TRUE
TRUE EQV FALSE returns FALSE
FALSE EQV TRUE returns FALSE
FALSE EQV FALSE returns TRUE
```

`EQV` is similar to `EQ` in that both compare two operands and return `TRUE` if the operands are the same. The difference is that `EQ` converts both operands to numbers or strings before comparing them, but `EQV` attempts to convert both operands to booleans before comparing them and throws an error if it cannot.

✦ *Implication* (`IMP`) returns `FALSE` only if the first operand is `TRUE` and the second operand is `FALSE`, as follows:

```
TRUE IMP TRUE returns TRUE
TRUE IMP FALSE returns FALSE
FALSE IMP TRUE returns TRUE
FALSE IMP FALSE returns TRUE
```

The Implication operator has little relevance to ColdFusion development. `IMP` was included in the ColdFusion language for the sake of completeness.

Concatenation operator

The *concatenation* operator (`&`) takes two strings, puts them together, and returns the result, as in the following examples:

```
"string A" & "string B" returns "string AstringB"
"This is my" & " string" returns "This is my string"
```

If you want a space between the two strings, you must specifically put the space in one of the concatenated strings, as occurs in the second of the preceding examples but not the first.

Assignment operator

The *assignment* operator (`=`) is valid only within a `CFSET` tag. This operator takes the value of the expression on the right-hand side of the = sign and puts that value into the variable on the left hand side of the = sign. Take, for example, the following line of code:

```
<cfset aVar = anotherVar + 1>
```

The preceding line of code sets `aVar` to the current value of `anotherVar` plus one.

Using function calls

A function takes one or more arguments and returns a single value. For a list of all ColdFusion functions, see the "Alphabetical Listing of Functions" in Chapter 45.

A typical function call looks as follows:

```
Trim(myVar)
```

`Trim()` is a ColdFusion function that takes a string and returns that string with all leading and trailing white space removed.

Some functions take no arguments. `Now()`, for example, doesn't need any arguments, because it always returns the current date and time.

Some functions take multiple arguments. `Max()`, for example, takes two arguments, as follows, and returns whichever argument is higher:

```
Max(thisVar, thatVar)
```

Pound Signs

Writing an application in ColdFusion without encountering pound signs is nearly impossible. Unfortunately, some of the rules for where and where not to use them are a bit confusing. In this section, you see where and, more important, where not to use pound signs in your ColdFusion code.

Where and where not to use pound signs

The most important guideline for pound sign usage is that, if you don't need pound signs, don't use them. Take, for example, the following expression:

```
<cfif #varA# GT #varB#>
    <cfset #myVar# = #Trim("#thisVar##thatVar#")#>
</cfif>
```

This example may seem an unreadable section of code, but snippets such as this one are prevalent in the ColdFusion world. The good news is that reducing the pound signs in any expression is easy because pound signs are often unnecessary. The unreadable section that we show here can be reworked as follows:

```
<cfif varA GT varB>
    <cfset myVar = Trim(thisVar & thatVar)>
</cfif>
```

Hard to believe, but all those pound signs were unnecessary. The following section tells you why.

The six rules of pound sign usage

If you use the following six rules as your guide to using pound signs, your code is sure to be easy to understand and maintain:

1. Use pound signs inside tag attributes. Consider, for example, the following call to CFLOOP:

   ```
   <cfloop from="#varA#" to="#varB#" index="i">
   ```

   This call is telling ColdFusion, "Evaluate the variables varA and varB and place their values in the from and to attributes, respectively." The i doesn't have pound signs surrounding it because you are not evaluating its contents; you are telling ColdFusion, "Create a local variable named i if it doesn't already exist and use this variable to contain the value of the loop index while the template executes." You know how to interpret such things by understanding exactly what each tag and function does. Reading the Language Reference (Part IX) at the end of this book is a good start.

2. Use pound signs if you are in clear text between the opening and closing tags of any ColdFusion tag, as in the following example:

   ```
   <cfif varA GT varB>
           #varA# is greater than #varB#
   </cfif>
   ```

   Don't use pound signs inside the CFIF tag itself but do use pound signs between <cfif> and </cfif>.

3. Use pound signs around variables inside of strings in ColdFusion expressions, as in the following example:

   ```
   <cfset aVar = "My name is #First# #Last#.">
   ```

   You use pound signs in this case, even though you are inside a CFSET tag, because you want ColdFusion to evaluate FirstName and LastName inside of the string.

4. Don't use pound signs around variables or functions inside of CFIF or CFSET tags, unless you are inside of a string. Take, for example, the following snippet:

   ```
   <cfif #varA# GT #varB#>
           <cfset #myVar# = #Trim("#thisVar##thatVar#")#>
   </cfif>
   ```

   You can reduce it as follows:

   ```
   <cfif varA GT varB>
           <cfset myVar = Trim("#thisVar##thatVar#")>
   </cfif>
   ```

   You can remove the pound signs around varA and varB because they occur inside a CFIF tag, and you can remove the pound signs around myVar and the call to Trim() because they occur inside a CFSET. The remaining pound signs stay because you must use pound signs in string expressions.

5. If a variable or function call is inside a string in a ColdFusion expression, but that string contains only variables and/or function calls, you should rewrite the expression so that you don't use pound signs. Take, for example, the following expression:

   ```
   <cfset myVar = Trim("#thisVar##thatVar#")>
   ```

   This expression calls Trim(), passing thisVar and thatVar concatenated together into one string. The expression would be more readable, however, if it used the string concatenation operator (&), as in the following example:

   ```
   <cfset myVar = Trim(thisVar & thatVar)>
   ```

The second snippet is more readable than the first because no pound signs are in the way. *Always* use the concatenation operator any time that variables and/or function calls are the only content of a string expression.

6. Never use pound signs around the arguments to a ColdFusion function. The following snippet, for example, generates a ColdFusion error:

   ```
   <cfset aVar = Val(#myVar#)>
   ```

   You can resolve this problem by putting `#myVar#` inside of quotes, as follows:

   ```
   <cfset aVar = Val("#myVar#")>
   ```

   But the more readable way is to remove the pound signs entirely, as follows:

   ```
   <cfset aVar = Val(myVar)>
   ```

Nested pound signs

You should understand the rules for nesting a pair of pound signs within another pair of pound signs, because most nesting is unnecessary. Take, for example, the following expression:

```
<cfoutput>#Trim("  This is my #FName# #LName#.  ")#</cfoutput>
```

This expression calls the `Trim()` function inside `CFOUTPUT`, so it needs pound signs around `Trim()`. The argument to `Trim()`, however, is a string that itself contains variables in pound signs. The good news is that this kind of construct is perfectly legal. Do, however, make a point of getting rid of nested pound signs wherever possible. Always, for example, rewrite constructions such as the following:

```
<cfoutput>#Trim("#myVar#")#</cfoutput>
```

You can rewrite this example as follows:

```
<cfoutput>#Trim(myVar)#</cfoutput>
```

Knowing where and where not to use CFOUTPUT

Many people use `CFOUTPUT` entirely too often. The following snippet, for example, is a common mistake that may people make:

```
<cfoutput>
<cfquery ...>
SELECT * FROM Company
WHERE CompanyID = #Val(URL.CompanyID)#
</cfquery>
</cfoutput>
```

You don't need `CFOUTPUT` around a `CFQUERY` call, because `CFQUERY` automatically resolves any variables inside of its tag body. You don't need `CFOUTPUT` around a call to `CFMAIL` for exactly the same reason. Be aware, however, that `CFQUERY` and `CFMAIL` are the only ColdFusion tags that automatically resolve variable references inside their tag bodies.

The following snippet is another mistake that many people make:

```
<cfoutput>
<cfset aVar = "This is my #FirstName# #LastName#.">
</cfoutput>
```

You don't need CFOUTPUT around the CFSET tag (or any other ColdFusion tag for that matter), because ColdFusion automatically evaluates all variables inside ColdFusion tags. Remember that inside a tag and in between an opening and a closing tag are two different things: inside a tag, a variable is automatically evaluated; between opening and closing tags, a variable is considered content.

What about the following passage — where are CFOUTPUT tags needed?

```
<cfset fromVar = 1>
<cfset toVar = 10>
<cfloop from="#fromVar#" to="#toVar#" index="i">
    #i#
</cfloop>
```

The only place that CFOUTPUT is needed is around #i#, as the following shows:

```
<cfset fromVar = 1>
<cfset toVar = 10>
<cfloop from="#fromVar#" to="#toVar#" index="i">
    <cfoutput>#i#</cfoutput>
</cfloop>
```

#fromVar# and #toVar# are already taken care of because they are inside a ColdFusion tag.

What about the following snippet:

```
<cfset hVar = 100>
<cfset wVar = 300>
<img src="image.gif" width="#hVar#" height="#wVar#">
```

You need CFOUTPUT tags around the IMG tag, as follows:

```
<cfset hVar = 100>
<cfset wVar = 300>
<cfoutput>
<img src="image.gif" width="#hVar#" height="#wVar#">
</cfoutput>
```

This example may seem confusing because you just saw that you don't need CFOUTPUT to evaluate variables inside a ColdFusion tag, but remember that IMG is not a ColdFusion tag — it's an HTML tag. If the tag name begins with CF, you don't need CFOUTPUT to evaluate variables within the tag; if the tag name doesn't begin with CF, you do need CFOUTPUT.

How to escape pound signs

Sometimes a pound sign is just a pound sign (our apologies to Sigmund Freud). If you want to display a pound sign, you must escape it with another pound sign. For example, look at the following statement:

```
<cfset aString = "Please enter your Customer #">
```

In this case, you want to display a pound sign. Because the pound sign is inside a string, ColdFusion expects a variable to follow the pound sign. If ColdFusion sees no variable name following the pound sign, it throws an error. What you need to do is *escape* the pound sign by doubling it, as follows:

```
<cfset aString = "Please enter your Customer ##">
```

Now, whenever ColdFusion sees the two pound signs together, it evaluates the pair as the string #. For another example, look at the following BODY tag:

```
<body bgcolor="#FFFFFF">
This is my content.
</body>
```

What if you surround the BODY tag with a CFOUTPUT because you want to evaluate a variable, as follows:

```
<cfoutput>
<body bgcolor="#FFFFFF">
This is my #aVar#.
</body>
</cfoutput>
```

ColdFusion throws an error, because ColdFusion sees the pound sign in front of FFFFFF and expects a variable. The body tag would have been correctly written as follows:

```
<cfoutput>
<body bgcolor="##FFFFFF">
This is my #aVar#.
</body>
</cfoutput>
```

What if the color were a variable as well? The snippet would look as follows:

```
<cfset theBGColor = "FFFFFF">
<cfoutput>
<body bgcolor="###theBGColor#">
This is my #aVar#.
</body>
</cfoutput>
```

The snippet still shows the two escaped pound signs to represent the pound sign in front of the bgcolor value, and theBGColor is surrounded with pound signs as is any other variable.

Using CFOUTPUT blocks of code

One question that people frequently ask is, "If I have a large block of text with a few variable references inside, which is better: putting one CFOUTPUT around the entire text block or putting CFOUTPUTs around each variable?"

CFOUTPUT tells ColdFusion, "Watch this block of text for any pound signs." A watched block of text is processed more slowly than an unwatched block of text. As soon as ColdFusion encounters a pound sign within a CFOUTPUT block, it evaluates the expression between that pound sign and the next pound sign.

But can you have too many CFOUTPUT tags? The overhead for a given CFOUTPUT block is small, but that small amount of overhead can add up if you have a large number of CFOUTPUT blocks. If many variables are in a given section of text, using one CFOUTPUT around the entire section may be better than using multiple CFOUTPUT tags.

Ultimately, the only way to answer this question is to do a formal load test by using software such as e-TEST Suite from Empirix. The difference between one CFOUTPUT versus many CFOUTPUTs may seem small, but if you slam an application with dozens or hundreds of simultaneous users, this difference is greatly compounded.

How to Use Tags

ColdFusion uses two types of tags: *empty* and *paired*.

A tag such as CFSET, for example, doesn't need a closing tag, because CFSET can exist on its own. A tag such as CFIF, however, must have a closing tag, because CFIF would be meaningless without one, because it must enclose the code to be executed if the test evaluates to True.

Empty tags

Empty tags have no closing tag. The following are all empty tags:

```
<cfset aVar = anotherVariable>
<cfparam name="URL.aParam" default="defaultVal">
<cfinput name="CompanyName" size="20" maxlength="30">
```

Paired tags

A *paired tag* has both an opening and a closing tag. The following are all paired-tag calls:

```
<cfif aVar GT anotherVariable>...</cfif>
<cfloop from="1" to="10" index="i">...</cfloop>
<cfform name="MyForm" method="post">...</cfform>
```

Tags are either empty or paired, but sometimes this status depends on how they are called. CFHTTP, for example, can be called without an ending tag if it passes no parameters, but if parameters are sent, an ending tag is needed to enclose them.

Shorthand closing syntax

Some tags, although they require a closing tag, have no content between their opening and closing tags. The following call to CFTRANSACTION, for example, is rather common:

```
<cftransaction action="COMMIT"></cftransaction>
```

ColdFusion throws an error if you leave off the ending tag, but writing out the entire ending tag is annoying (not to mention ugly). You can use the following short cut if you need the ending tag but don't have any content between the opening and closing tags:

```
<cftransaction action="COMMIT"/>
```

You see in Chapter 18 how this shorthand syntax is used.

Comments

There are two types of comments you can include within your CFML: ColdFusion comments and HTML comments. A ColdFusion comment looks as follows:

```
<!--- This is a ColdFusion comment. --->
```

ColdFusion finds all blocks of text and code that begin with <!--- and end with ---> and removes them from what gets sent to the user's browser.

An HTML comment looks as follows:

```
<!-- This is an HTML comment. -->
```

HTML comments are not stripped out by ColdFusion and are returned to the user's browser.

The differences between HTML and CFML comments are as follows:

- CFML comments use *three* hyphens at the beginning and end, whereas HTML comments use only two.
- Any ColdFusion tags inside a CFML comment are not executed; CFML tags inside of an HTML comment are executed.
- Content inside a CFML comment is not delivered to the user's browser, but content inside an HTML comment is. Neither content shows in the user's browser, but the user can view source on a page and see an HTML comment, whereas the CFML comment is stripped out before it is sent to your browser.

Summary

In this chapter, you learn the rules for using the ColdFusion language. You learn how operators and expressions work, and you learn the correct usage guidelines for pound signs. You then learn the rules for using tags — whether they are empty or closed — as well as the shorthand syntax for closing a content-less tag. Finally, you learn the differences between CFML and HTML comments.

In the next chapter, you learn about the differences between the server and the client (your browser), what happens where, and how the two can and cannot communicate with each other.

✦ ✦ ✦

Understanding Servers and Clients

✦ ✦ ✦ ✦

In This Chapter

Learning the difference between a client and a server

Understanding when ColdFusion executes code

Learning how CFML interacts with JavaScript

✦ ✦ ✦ ✦

One concept that many ColdFusion developers take for granted is the relationship and differences between a client (your Web browser) and a server (ColdFusion). In this chapter, you learn what clients and servers are, how they interact, and how they don't.

You might be surprised at how many developers remain confused about the interactions that are possible and impossible between ColdFusion (a server technology) and JavaScript (a client technology) — even after developing ColdFusion applications for a year or two.

The key to understanding what is and is not possible with clients and servers is visualizing a few key examples of how they can work together. This chapter will show you such examples.

What Is a Server, and What Is a Client?

A *client* sends a request to a *server*, which responds by serving data back to the client.

As you browse a ColdFusion template, your Web browser (the client) requests the template from ColdFusion (the server). ColdFusion executes the template and serves the resulting HTML back to your browser client. Figure 4-1 shows the relationship between server and client.

What happens on the client is inherently disconnected from what happens on the server. Every time that the browser wants data from the server, the browser must make a new request. On the other hand, the server cannot request data from the browser (client).

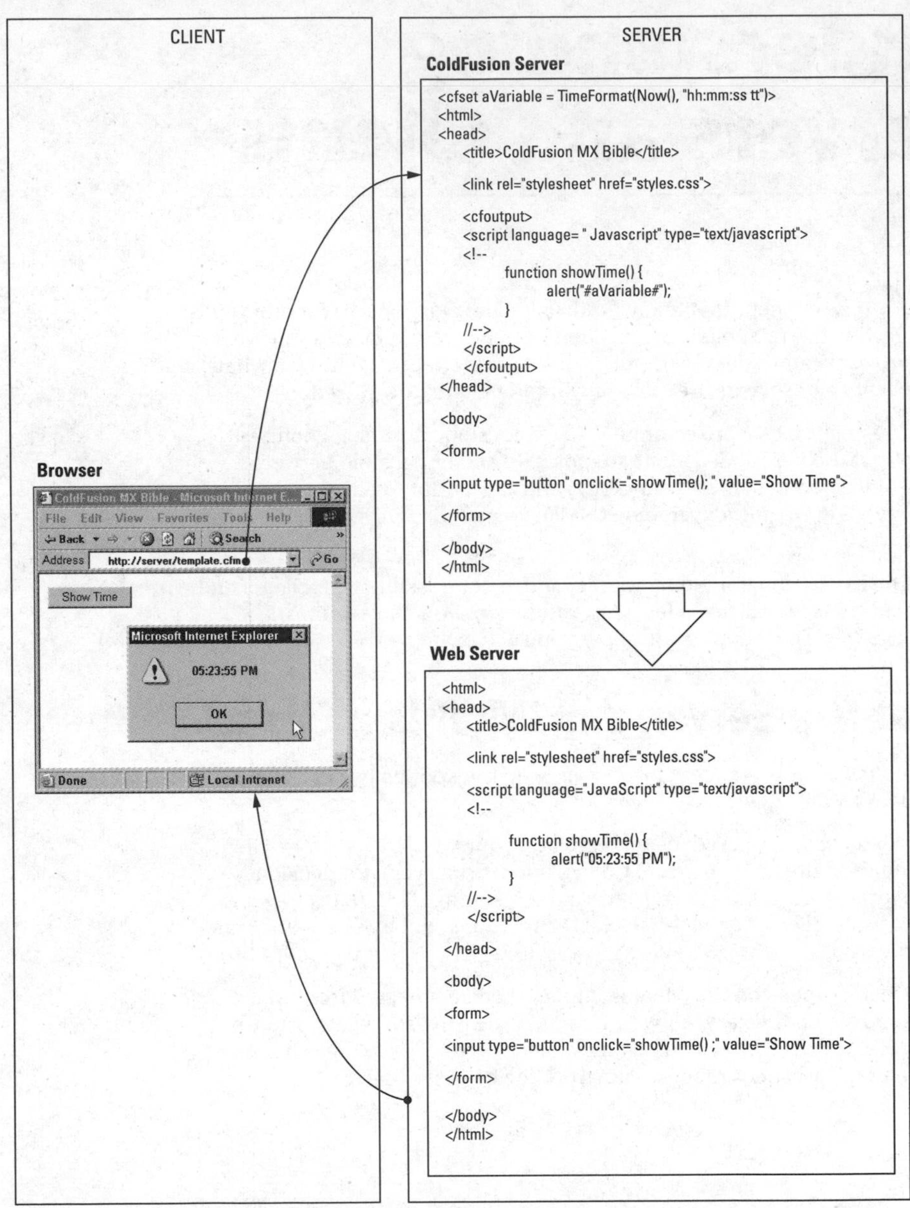

Figure 4-1: A client computer sends a request to a server computer, which responds by serving data back to the client.

CFML and JavaScript

Normally, the separation between the client and the server is transparent to a ColdFusion developer. The separation becomes apparent if you try to make JavaScript and CFML work together.

The interaction between CFML and JavaScript is confusing to many developers. CFML is a language processed entirely on the server, and its results are sent to the client (browser). JavaScript is a language processed entirely in the client (browser).

Listing 4-1 shows a ColdFusion template containing a block of JavaScript shown in bold.

Listing 4-1: Interweaved CFML and JavaScript

```
<html>
<head>
    <title>ColdFusion MX Bible</title>

    <link rel="stylesheet" href="styles.css">
</head>

<body>

<script language="JavaScript" type="text/javascript">
<!--
    aJavaScriptVariable = "this value";
    alert(aJavaScriptVariable);
//-->
</script>

<br>

<cfset aVariable = "some value">
<cfset anotherVariable = "some other value">

<cfoutput>
    #aVariable#<br>
    #anotherVariable#<br>
</cfoutput>

</body>
</html>
```

In case you are unfamiliar with JavaScript, the `SCRIPT` tag surrounds a block of JavaScript code (in bold) in the preceding listing. The JavaScript in Listing 4-1 sets a JavaScript variable and then displays the value of that variable in a pop-up alert box.

Which is executed first: the CFML statements or the JavaScript statements?

Because CFML is executed on the server, the `CFSET` and `CFOUTPUT` statements execute first, producing the HTML that is sent to the browser. Listing 4-2 shows the HTML that your browser receives.

Listing 4-2: The HTML produced from Listing 4-1

```
<html>
<head>
    <title>ColdFusion MX Bible</title>

    <link rel="stylesheet" href="styles.css">
</head>

<body>

<script language="JavaScript" type="text/javascript">
<!--
    aJavaScriptVariable = "this value";
    alert(aJavaScriptVariable);
//-->
</script>

<br>

    some value<br>
    some other value<br>

</body>
</html>
```

The `SCRIPT` block is left untouched, because JavaScript is executed in the client (browser). After the browser receives the HTML in Listing 4-2 from ColdFusion Server, it executes the JavaScript on the Web page, popping up `this value` in the alert box before displaying `some value` and `some other value` on the Web page.

Integrating CFML and JavaScript

What if you wanted the alert box to use the value of a ColdFusion variable instead of a JavaScript variable? Listing 4-3 sets a ColdFusion variable to the current time and passes the variable to JavaScript.

Listing 4-3: JavaScript using a variable set in ColdFusion

```
<cfset aVariable = TimeFormat(Now(), "hh:mm:ss tt")>

<html>
<head>
    <title>ColdFusion MX Bible</title>

    <link rel="stylesheet" href="styles.css">

    <cfoutput>
    <script language="JavaScript" type="text/javascript">
```

```
    <!--
        function showTime() {
            alert("#aVariable#");
        }
    //-->
    </script>
    </cfoutput>
</head>

<body>

<form>

<input type="button" onclick="showTime();" value="Show Time">

</form>

</body>
</html>
```

Clicking the Show Time button displays a JavaScript message box containing the time that the page was requested. But if you keep clicking the button, notice that the time doesn't change. The reason is that the time was calculated on the server and became part of the generated HTML. Listing 4-4 shows the HTML and JavaScript that the browser receives from the server.

Listing 4-4: The HTML produced from Listing 4-3

```
<html>
<head>
    <title>ColdFusion MX Bible</title>

    <link rel="stylesheet" href="styles.css">


    <script language="JavaScript" type="text/javascript">
    <!--
        function showTime() {
            alert("05:23:55 PM");
        }
    //-->
    </script>

</head>

<body>

<form>
```

Continued

Listing 4-4 *(continued)*

```
<input type="button" onclick="showTime();" value="Show Time">
</form>

</body>
</html>
```

ColdFusion evaluates `aVariable` before sending the HTML to the client.

JavaScript can use ColdFusion variables because ColdFusion can generate JavaScript, but ColdFusion cannot use JavaScript variables because JavaScript executes on the client after ColdFusion executes on the server.

Summary

In this chapter, you learn that what happens on the server is disconnected from what happens in the client. ColdFusion Server can generate JavaScript code and variables that get executed on the client, but JavaScript can't interact with ColdFusion Server because the browser executes JavaScript well after ColdFusion server has completed the client's request.

✦ ✦ ✦

Learning a Little SQL

✦ ✦ ✦ ✦

In This Chapter

What is a relational database?

Selecting relational result sets

Modifying data

Using SQL with ColdFusion

✦ ✦ ✦ ✦

We cover basic single-table queries, basic relational queries, inserts, updates, and deletes in this chapter, and we cover much more complicated SQL in Chapter 9. Even if you've been using SQL for quite a long time, we would suggest that you spend a few minutes to carefully read through this chapter, as it contains new ways of describing how SQL works and helps you visualize what happens internally as your SQL statements are processed, all of which can only add to your understanding of how to better write SQL statements. We also assume in Chapter 9 that you already understand the visualization concepts discussed here, so please do take the time to read this chapter in its entirety.

An Overview of Relational Databases

Simply put, a *relational database* is a body of related data stored in tables. Sometimes you learn best by jumping right in and thrashing around a bit. That we're going over queries that join multiple tables before we formally cover basic `SELECT` statements from a single table may seem a little strange, but this approach gives you a very quick understanding of exactly what a relational database is. For now, just take on faith whatever you don't understand; we cover the details in the section "An Overview of Structured Query Language."

If you want to follow along with these exercises, do one of the following:

✦ Set up the Access database named `Chapter5.mdb` on your ColdFusion Server and configure a datasource for it named `Chapter5`. The database is located on the companion CD-ROM, and it is prepopulated with data. See Chapter 2 if you need a refresher on creating a datasource for ColdFusion.

✦ Create a database named `Chapter5` on your Microsoft SQL Server and configure a datasource for it named `Chapter5`. Run the script `Chapter5DDL.sql` against the `Chapter5` database to create its tables and then run the script `Chapter5Data.sql` against it to populate those tables with data.

The script `Chapter5Data.sql` can be run repeatedly against the SQL Server database to reset its data back to its original state.

After you understand and practice the basics here, your next stop on the database trail is Chapter 8. In the meantime, here's the Nickel Tour.

A *relational database* consists of one or more tables containing data, where the data in one table may relate to data in one or more of the other tables. Tables are *related* by sharing key values between their rows, and these related tables are *joined* together in `SELECT` statements to produce relational result sets.

A database containing two tables, Company and Employee, for example, may look something like what is shown in Figure 5-1.

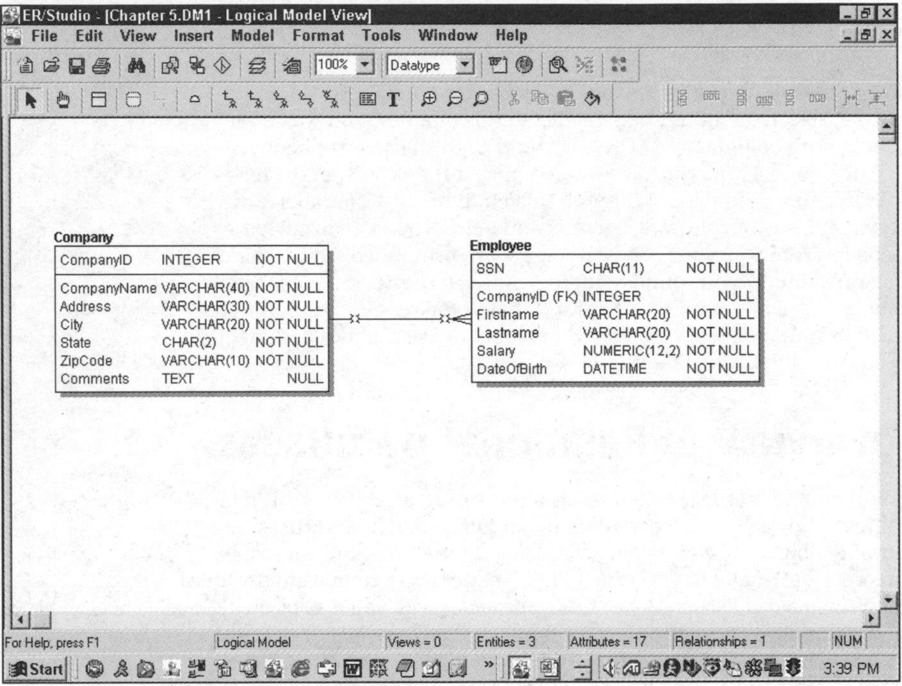

Figure 5-1: An example of two related tables.

For now, don't worry about the notation being used — that is all explained in Chapter 8 — just look at how the data itself is related.

The data contained in these two tables may look something like what is shown in Figure 5-2.

As you can see from the matching values of CompanyID between the two tables, some employees are related to one company, and some to another. Visualizing these rows as slightly separated into their own related groups, as shown in Figure 5-3, sometimes helps.

Company Table:

CompanyID	CompanyName	Address	City	State	ZipCode	Comments
1	ABC Company, Inc.	1234 Main Street	Atlanta	GA	30303	The first company ever kn...
2	The Very Big Corporation of America	One Corporate Boulevard	Norcross	GA	30071	Sooner or later, you'll b...
3	Star Trek Fan Club	1701 Getalife Lane	Orlando	FL	32801	It's not so bad living in...
4	Ye Olde Poodle Accessory Shoppe	45 Mangrum Road	Tucson	AZ	85701	Frilly hair bow specialis...
5	Azure Productions	1087 Veritas Way	Duluth	GA	30096	Light and sound productio...
6	Angry Clown Entertainment	5565 W. Canton Street	Duluth	GA	30097	Let Rankles the Clown bot...
7	Bob's Motorcycle Restoration	477 Reston Avenue	Casper	WY	82604	Harley and Indian special...
8	Developers Anonymous	12 Recovery Way	Winter Haven	FL	33880-3453	Repeat: "I am a good pers...
9	Hamazon.com	9041 Trebuchet Lane	Cracklin	AR	72201	Buy your pork products on...
10	The Stan Cox Society	1234 Tweeble Lane	Barneyville	NJ	01234	Formerly known as "Friend...

Employee Table:

CompanyID	SSN	Firstname	Lastname	Salary	DateOfBirth
1	223-45-6789	Billy	Sanders	33500.00	1967-02-01
1	234-56-7890	Oksal	Kayashunu	23750.00	1953-04-19
1	345-67-8901	Randsford	Worthington	117539.15	1949-07-15
2	456-78-9012	Dave	Johnson	51600.00	1969-03-11
2	567-89-0123	Bethany	Silverberg	76328.94	1973-02-27
2	678-90-1234	Susan	Kokilas	43711.83	1980-06-09
2	789-01-2345	Allen	Davidow	65000.00	1980-07-07
2	890-12-3456	Valerie	Feuilliette	39950.00	1975-05-25
3	901-23-4567	Timmy	Williger	11250.75	1982-10-27
3	012-34-5678	Kevin	Littleman	13650.00	1966-08-18
5	134-56-7890	Arel	Abromovitz	123456.78	1963-06-07
5	245-67-8901	Virgil	Huckster	23750.00	1977-12-28
5	356-78-9012	Natasha	Romanova	79315.95	1976-12-03
6	467-89-0123	Dirk	Thor	5000.00	1978-05-14
6	578-90-1234	Adam	Churvis	9500.00	1961-04-09
8	689-01-2345	Barney	Thickglasses	125000.00	1980-01-23
8	801-23-4567	Stanley	Mernal	115750.00	1975-10-11
8	912-34-5678	Judy	Harbinger	135500.00	1970-08-27
8	023-45-6789	Larry	Nerdsworth	132900.00	1977-09-24
8	098-76-5432	Wayne	Derby	154950.00	1965-03-04
9	987-65-4321	Billy Bob	Tucker	75985.50	1959-08-14
10	765-43-2109	Vernal	Gumby	7012.48	1966-07-11
10	654-32-1098	Lance	Lester	5412.91	1970-11-06
10	543-21-0987	Davey	Mango	4981.33	1960-10-22

Figure 5-2: Sample data contained in the two related tables.

CompanyID	CompanyName	Address	City	State	ZipCode	Comments
1	ABC Company, Inc.	1234 Main Street	Atlanta	GA	30303	The first company ever kn...

CompanyID	SSN	Firstname	Lastname	Salary	DateOfBirth
1	223-45-6789	Billy	Sanders	33500.00	1967-02-01
1	234-56-7890	Oksal	Kayashunu	23750.00	1953-04-19
1	345-67-8901	Randsford	Worthington	117539.15	1949-07-15

CompanyID	CompanyName	Address	City	State	ZipCode	Comments
2	The Very Big Corporation of America	One Corporate Boulevard	Norcross	GA	30071	Sooner or later, you'll b...

CompanyID	SSN	Firstname	Lastname	Salary	DateOfBirth
2	456-78-9012	Dave	Johnson	51600.00	1969-03-11
2	567-89-0123	Bethany	Silverberg	76328.94	1973-02-27
2	678-90-1234	Susan	Kokilas	43711.83	1980-06-09
2	789-01-2345	Allen	Davidow	65000.00	1980-07-07
2	890-12-3456	Valerie	Feuilliette	39950.00	1975-05-25

CompanyID	CompanyName	Address	City	State	ZipCode	Comments
3	Star Trek Fan Club	1701 Getalife Lane	Orlando	FL	32801	It's not so bad living in...

CompanyID	SSN	Firstname	Lastname	Salary	DateOfBirth
3	901-23-4567	Timmy	Williger	11250.75	1982-10-27
3	012-34-5678	Kevin	Littleman	13650.00	1966-08-18

■ ■ ■

Figure 5-3: Visualizing related data separated into groups.

Okay, now to take a look at how this visualization works in the real world. Most likely, you've seen reports that look something like Figure 5-4:

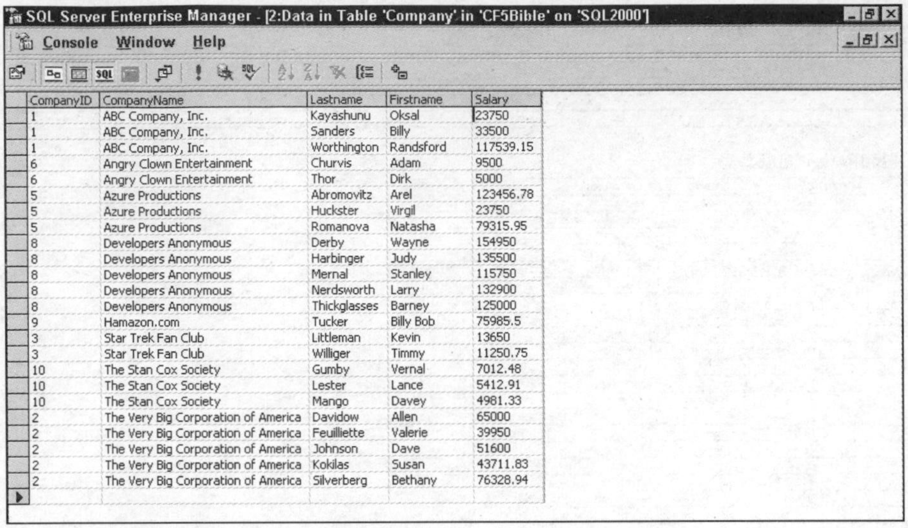

SQL Server Enterprise Manager - [2:Data in Table 'Company' in 'CF5Bible' on 'SQL2000']

Console Window Help

CompanyID	CompanyName	Lastname	Firstname	Salary
1	ABC Company, Inc.	Kayashunu	Oksal	23750
1	ABC Company, Inc.	Sanders	Billy	33500
1	ABC Company, Inc.	Worthington	Randsford	117539.15
6	Angry Clown Entertainment	Churvis	Adam	9500
6	Angry Clown Entertainment	Thor	Dirk	5000
5	Azure Productions	Abromovitz	Arel	123456.78
5	Azure Productions	Huckster	Virgil	23750
5	Azure Productions	Romanova	Natasha	79315.95
8	Developers Anonymous	Derby	Wayne	154950
8	Developers Anonymous	Harbinger	Judy	135500
8	Developers Anonymous	Mernal	Stanley	115750
8	Developers Anonymous	Nerdsworth	Larry	132900
8	Developers Anonymous	Thickglasses	Barney	125000
9	Hamazon.com	Tucker	Billy Bob	75985.5
3	Star Trek Fan Club	Littleman	Kevin	13650
3	Star Trek Fan Club	Williger	Timmy	11250.75
10	The Stan Cox Society	Gumby	Vernal	7012.48
10	The Stan Cox Society	Lester	Lance	5412.91
10	The Stan Cox Society	Mango	Davey	4981.33
2	The Very Big Corporation of America	Davidow	Allen	65000
2	The Very Big Corporation of America	Feuilliette	Valerie	39950
2	The Very Big Corporation of America	Johnson	Dave	51600
2	The Very Big Corporation of America	Kokilas	Susan	43711.83
2	The Very Big Corporation of America	Silverberg	Bethany	76328.94

Figure 5-4: A sample report of related data.

Notice how the report in Figure 5-4 repeats the company data for each employee? We asked the database server to produce this report with the simple piece of SQL code in Listing 5-1.

Listing 5-1: The SQL that produced the sample relational report shown in Figure 5-3

```
SELECT
    Company.CompanyID,
    Company.CompanyName,
    Employee.Lastname,
    Employee.Firstname,
    Employee.Salary
FROM
    Company,
    Employee
WHERE
    Company.CompanyID = Employee.CompanyID
ORDER BY
    Company.CompanyName,
    Employee.Lastname,
    Employee.Firstname
```

In plain English, this SQL code is asking the database server to do the following:

"Look in both the Company and Employee tables, and for every row that matches by the value in each table's CompanyID column, return the values stored in the Company table's CompanyID and CompanyName columns and the values stored in the Employee table's Lastname, Firstname, and Salary columns, sorted by CompanyName, Lastname, and Firstname."

We cover the different types of relational joins and the syntax used to create them in Chapter 9, but for now, you probably get the basic idea that we "joined" these two tables together by using the following clause:

```
WHERE Company.CompanyID = Employee.CompanyID
```

This was the condition used to give us only those rows from both tables where the CompanyID values in the Company table equaled the CompanyID values in the Employee table. This syntax is simple to understand, and for this reason, most people learn SQL by writing their joins in the `WHERE` clauses, but you can (and should) use a more modern and flexible syntax, known as SQL-92, that to produce relational queries. Listing 5-2 shows how our earlier SQL statement looks expressed in SQL-92 syntax.

Listing 5-2: Listing 5-1 expressed in SQL-92 syntax

```
SELECT
    Company.CompanyID,
    Company.CompanyName,
    Employee.Lastname,
    Employee.Firstname,
    Employee.Salary
FROM
    Company INNER JOIN Employee
  ON Company.CompanyID = Employee.CompanyID
ORDER BY
    Company.CompanyName,
    Employee.Lastname,
    Employee.Firstname
```

The code changes very little and is still understandable—especially after you learn the differences between the different types of joins (*inner joins*, *left outer joins*, and so on). But you gain quite a lot by using SQL-92 syntax, such as the capability to easily change join types and the capability to easily and accurately describe even the most complicated multitable result sets. You should get in the habit of writing your statements that contain relational joins by using SQL-92 syntax if your database supports it.

Now that you have a basic overview of what the "relational" part of a relational database is and the basics of how to perform a query against it, you can move on to an overview of the SQL language itself.

An Overview of Structured Query Language (SQL)

SQL, or *S*tructured *Q*uery *L*anguage, is a common language for querying and manipulating data. As have all standards, SQL has gone through a number of revisions to take advantage of new functionality and to incorporate better methods. Some database server products support the very latest standards, but most don't. The standard that we explain here is the SQL-92 Standard, which is currently in use—at least to some extent—by the majority of database products on the market as of this writing.

If your database product doesn't support the SQL-92 join syntax (most notably, Oracle 8i doesn't), it instead supports some manner of encoding special character sequences into the `WHERE` clause to create different types of joins. If so, substitute the appropriate `WHERE` clause for the type of join that you want to perform.

SELECT Statements

You use `SELECT` statements to query the database and return a set of results. Listing 5-3, for example, returns the `CompanyID`, `CompanyName`, `Address`, `City`, `State`, and `ZipCode` columns of all rows in the Company table:

Listing 5-3: A simple `SELECT` statement

```
SELECT
    CompanyID,
    CompanyName,
    Address,
    City,
    State,
    ZipCode
FROM
    Company
```

Figure 5-5 shows what that result set from this listing looks like.

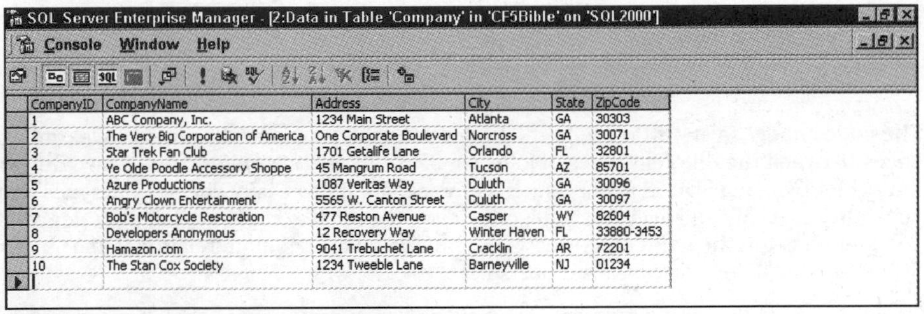

SQL Server Enterprise Manager - [2:Data in Table 'Company' in 'CF5Bible' on 'SQL2000']

Console Window Help

CompanyID	CompanyName	Address	City	State	ZipCode
1	ABC Company, Inc.	1234 Main Street	Atlanta	GA	30303
2	The Very Big Corporation of America	One Corporate Boulevard	Norcross	GA	30071
3	Star Trek Fan Club	1701 Getalife Lane	Orlando	FL	32801
4	Ye Olde Poodle Accessory Shoppe	45 Mangrum Road	Tucson	AZ	85701
5	Azure Productions	1087 Veritas Way	Duluth	GA	30096
6	Angry Clown Entertainment	5565 W. Canton Street	Duluth	GA	30097
7	Bob's Motorcycle Restoration	477 Reston Avenue	Casper	WY	82604
8	Developers Anonymous	12 Recovery Way	Winter Haven	FL	33880-3453
9	Hamazon.com	9041 Trebuchet Lane	Cracklin	AR	72201
10	The Stan Cox Society	1234 Tweeble Lane	Barneyville	NJ	01234

Figure 5-5: The result set from Listing 5-3.

The most important step toward writing perfect `SELECT` statements is *visualizing* the true nature of the result set that you want returned to you. We cover visualization in more depth in Chapter 9, but for now, you should start with our first and most basic premise, as follows:

All SQL query results are in the form of a single table of rows and columns.

This statement holds true for every query regardless of whether the query concerns a single table or multiple joined tables, whether or not grouping or aggregate functions are used, or anything else. Even if the result set consists of a single value, it is still a table with a single column containing one row of data.

This reality is in sharp contrast to the way that many people visualize a relational result set. Many envision their result set structured like the output from a report writer such as Crystal Reports, with headings, subtotals, grand totals, and so on. It is this incorrect visualization that often leads developers down the wrong road toward incorrectly written SQL statements that attempt to group and aggregate values in ways that approximate the printed report but that the database cannot process. Perhaps you've at some point received an error back from your database similar to the following:

```
Column 'Company.CompanyID' is invalid in the select list because it is
not contained in either an aggregate function or the GROUP BY clause.
```

If so, it is because you wrote an SQL statement that attempted to produce an impossible result set. We discuss what is and isn't possible with `SELECT` statements that use `GROUP BY`, `HAVING`, `DISTINCT`, and aggregate functions later on, in Chapter 9, but for now, we concentrate on writing a few more basic `SELECT` statements.

Listing 5-3 seems simple enough, but what if you want only those columns for the one company with a CompanyID of 10? For that, you need to add a `WHERE` clause to the SQL statement, as shown in Listing 5-4.

Listing 5-4: Adding a `WHERE` clause to the `SELECT` statement returns only those rows that satisfy its criterion

```
SELECT
    CompanyID,
    CompanyName,
    Address,
    City,
    State,
    ZipCode
FROM
    Company
WHERE
    CompanyID = 10
```

This `WHERE` clause filters out all rows in the Company table except the one with a CompanyID that equals 10. Figure 5-6 shows the result.

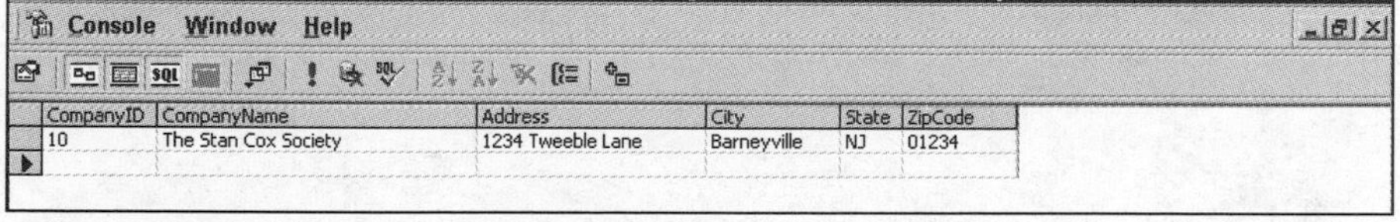

SQL Server Enterprise Manager - [2:Data in Table 'Company' in 'CF5Bible' on 'SQL2000']

Console Window Help

CompanyID	CompanyName	Address	City	State	ZipCode
10	The Stan Cox Society	1234 Tweeble Lane	Barneyville	NJ	01234

Figure 5-6: The result set from Listing 5-4.

If you use a string value as a criterion for a `WHERE` clause, you must surround the string with single quotes, as shown in Listing 5-5.

Listing 5-5: Using a string as a criterion in the WHERE clause

```
SELECT
    CompanyID,
    CompanyName,
    Address,
    City,
    State,
    ZipCode
FROM
    Company
WHERE
    State = 'GA'
```

Listing 5-5 returns a result set containing all rows of the Company table with a State value of `'GA'`, as shown in Figure 5-7.

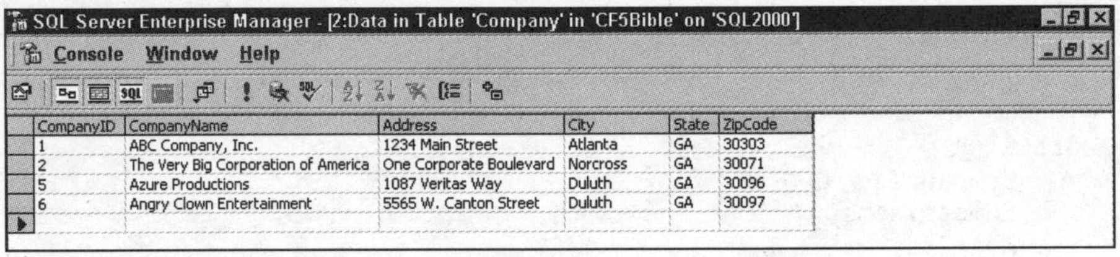

CompanyID	CompanyName	Address	City	State	ZipCode
1	ABC Company, Inc.	1234 Main Street	Atlanta	GA	30303
2	The Very Big Corporation of America	One Corporate Boulevard	Norcross	GA	30071
5	Azure Productions	1087 Veritas Way	Duluth	GA	30096
6	Angry Clown Entertainment	5565 W. Canton Street	Duluth	GA	30097

Figure 5-7: The result set from Listing 5-5.

Those single quotes around the State value aren't just for show; if we didn't use them in Listing 5-5, the database server would throw an error.

If you want to use more than one criterion in your `WHERE` clause, you simply separate each criterion with `AND`, as shown in Listing 5-6.

Listing 5-6: Using multiple criteria in the WHERE clause

```
SELECT
    CompanyID,
    CompanyName,
    Address,
    City,
    State,
    ZipCode
FROM
    Company
WHERE
    State = 'GA' AND
    CompanyName LIKE 'A%'
```

Listing 5-6 returns only those rows in the Company table with a State value of Georgia ('GA') and a company name that begins with A, as shown in Figure 5-8.

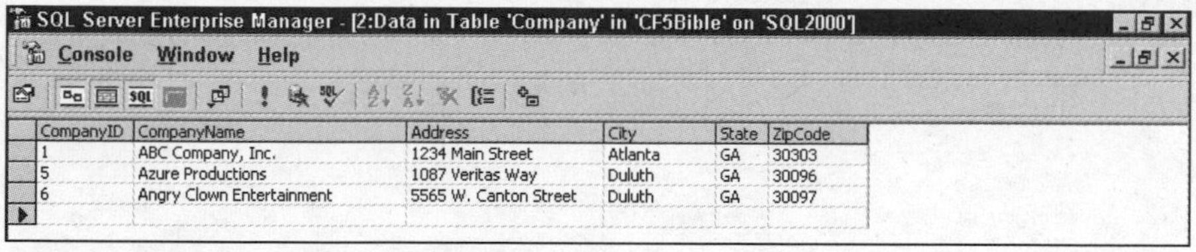

SQL Server Enterprise Manager - [2:Data in Table 'Company' in 'CF5Bible' on 'SQL2000']

Console Window Help

CompanyID	CompanyName	Address	City	State	ZipCode
1	ABC Company, Inc.	1234 Main Street	Atlanta	GA	30303
5	Azure Productions	1087 Veritas Way	Duluth	GA	30096
6	Angry Clown Entertainment	5565 W. Canton Street	Duluth	GA	30097

Figure 5-8: The result set from Listing 5-6.

As you can probably imagine, if you want to return rows where the State is 'GA' *or* the CompanyName began with A, you would replace the AND in the WHERE clause with an OR.

Now that you're getting the hang of it, try sorting the result set from this statement in zip-code order. You can do so by adding an ORDER BY clause, as shown in Listing 5-7.

Listing 5-7: Adding an ORDER BY clause to sort the result set

```
SELECT
    CompanyID,
    CompanyName,
    Address,
    City,
    State,
    ZipCode
FROM
    Company
WHERE
    State = 'GA' AND
    CompanyName LIKE 'A%'
ORDER BY
    ZipCode
```

Sorting is simply a matter of adding an ORDER BY clause and specifying the column on which to perform the sort. The results are as shown in Figure 5-9.

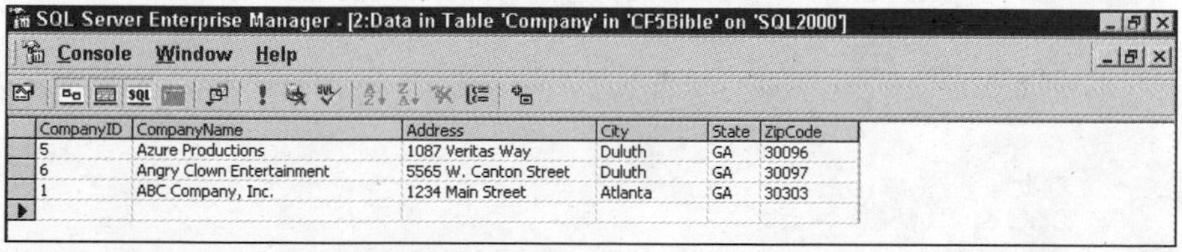

SQL Server Enterprise Manager - [2:Data in Table 'Company' in 'CF5Bible' on 'SQL2000']

Console Window Help

CompanyID	CompanyName	Address	City	State	ZipCode
5	Azure Productions	1087 Veritas Way	Duluth	GA	30096
6	Angry Clown Entertainment	5565 W. Canton Street	Duluth	GA	30097
1	ABC Company, Inc.	1234 Main Street	Atlanta	GA	30303

Figure 5-9: The result set from Listing 5-7.

If you want to sort in descending zip-code order, you simply add the DESC qualifier, as shown in Listing 5-8.

Listing 5-8: Specifying a sort in descending order

```
SELECT
    CompanyID,
    CompanyName,
    Address,
    City,
    State,
    ZipCode
FROM
    Company
WHERE
    State = 'GA' AND
    CompanyName LIKE 'A%'
ORDER BY
    ZipCode DESC
```

The result of executing Listing 5-8 is as shown in Figure 5-10.

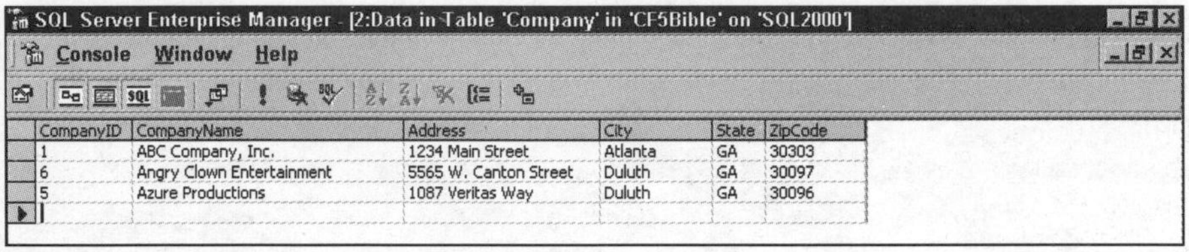

SQL Server Enterprise Manager - [2:Data in Table 'Company' in 'CF5Bible' on 'SQL2000']

Console Window Help

CompanyID	CompanyName	Address	City	State	ZipCode
1	ABC Company, Inc.	1234 Main Street	Atlanta	GA	30303
6	Angry Clown Entertainment	5565 W. Canton Street	Duluth	GA	30097
5	Azure Productions	1087 Veritas Way	Duluth	GA	30096

Figure 5-10: The result set from Listing 5-8.

If the DESC qualifier isn't specified, your database server assumes that you want to sort in ascending order. The qualifier for sorting in ascending order is ASC, so add it to your statement if you would be more comfortable explicitly specifying it. Personally, we explicitly specify all our qualifiers because doing so gets us in the good habit of thinking more precisely about our code.

If you want to sort by more than one column, just add the additional sorting columns separated by commas, as shown in Listing 5-9.

Listing 5-9: Specifying multiple sort orders

```
SELECT
    CompanyID,
    CompanyName,
    Address,
    City,
    State,
    ZipCode
FROM
    Company
WHERE
    State = 'GA' AND
```

```
        CompanyName LIKE 'A%'
    ORDER BY
        City DESC,
        ZipCode DESC
```

Listing 5-9 first sorts the retrieved rows in descending city order and then within each city in descending zip-code order, as shown in Figure 5-11.

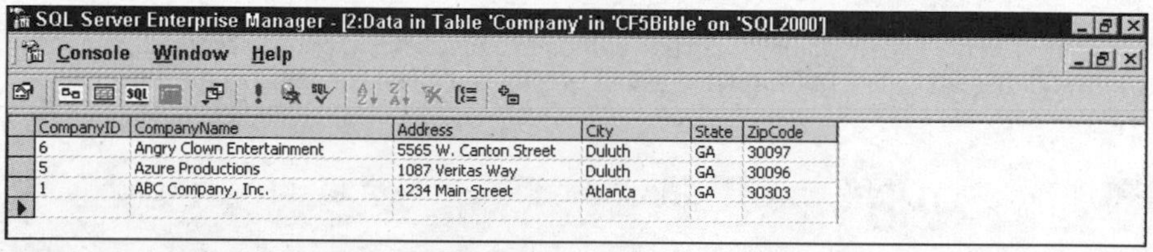

SQL Server Enterprise Manager - [2:Data in Table 'Company' in 'CF5Bible' on 'SQL2000']

Console Window Help

CompanyID	CompanyName	Address	City	State	ZipCode
6	Angry Clown Entertainment	5565 W. Canton Street	Duluth	GA	30097
5	Azure Productions	1087 Veritas Way	Duluth	GA	30096
1	ABC Company, Inc.	1234 Main Street	Atlanta	GA	30303

Figure 5-11: The result set from Listing 5-9.

Now you get into a very useful technique known as *aliasing*, which enables you to assign a *pseudonym* (literally, a "false name") to table and column names. Sometimes, aliasing is a simple convenience for making cryptic column names more readable in the client application (that is, ColdFusion), but at other times, aliasing becomes absolutely necessary for using a query's result set in the client application, as you see in Listings 5-10 and 5-11, and in Chapters 9 and 11.

Start with Listing 5-10, which assigns pseudonyms to the `CompanyID`, `CompanyName`, and `ZipCode` columns.

Listing 5-10: Using pseudonyms to provide aliases for columns

```
SELECT
    CompanyID AS CompNum,
    CompanyName AS Name,
    Address,
    City,
    State,
    ZipCode AS Zip
FROM
    Company
WHERE
    State = 'GA' AND
    CompanyName LIKE 'A%'
ORDER BY
    ZipCode DESC
```

After the result set from Listing 5-10 is returned to ColdFusion, the column names are no longer referred to by their original column names but rather by the pseudonyms assigned to them, as shown in Figure 5-12.

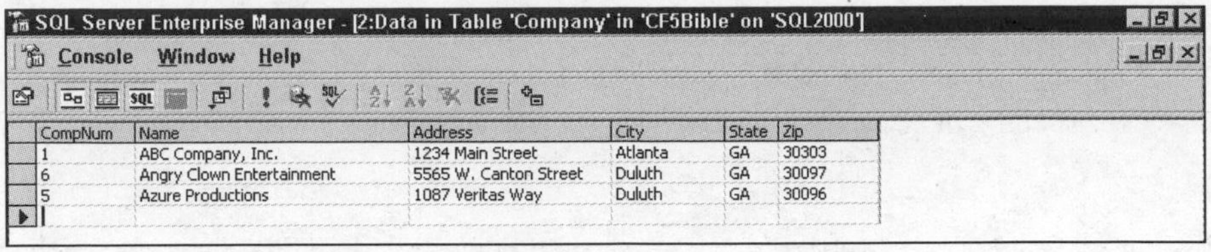

SQL Server Enterprise Manager - [2:Data in Table 'Company' in 'CF5Bible' on 'SQL2000']

Console Window Help

CompNum	Name	Address	City	State	Zip
1	ABC Company, Inc.	1234 Main Street	Atlanta	GA	30303
6	Angry Clown Entertainment	5565 W. Canton Street	Duluth	GA	30097
5	Azure Productions	1087 Veritas Way	Duluth	GA	30096

Figure 5-12: The result set from Listing 5-10.

In other words, if you execute Listing 5-10 via a `CFQUERY` call that names the result `OutputListing510`, the `CFOUTPUT` that you use to display the result set looks something like that in Listing 5-11. Revisit Chapter 2 if you need a refresher on using `CFQUERY`.

Listing 5-11: **Referring to aliased columns in a `CFOUTPUT` call**

```
<cfoutput query="OutputListing510">
<tr>
    <td>#CompNum#</td>
    <td>#Name#</td>
    <td>#Address#</td>
    <td>#City#</td>
    <td>#State#</td>
    <td>#Zip#</td>
</tr>
</cfoutput>
```

As we mentioned in the section “SELECT Statements,” you can alias table names, too. Notice how much easier Listing 5-2 is to read and write after you use pseudonyms, as shown in Listing 5-12.

Listing 5-12: **Abbreviating Listing 5-2 by assigning pseudonyms**

```
SELECT
    c.CompanyID,
    c.CompanyName,
    e.Lastname,
    e.Firstname,
    e.Salary
FROM
    Company AS c INNER JOIN Employee AS e
        ON c.CompanyID = e.CompanyID
ORDER BY
    c.CompanyName,
    e.Lastname,
    e.Firstname
```

By the way, the use of `AS` is not absolutely necessary, and in fact, you most often do not see `AS` used in aliasing table names. There is no special reason for this convention; this seems to be the most popular convention. Listing 5-13 shows the more common method for assigning aliases to table names.

Listing 5-13: Short-form aliasing

```
SELECT
    c.CompanyID,
    c.CompanyName,
    e.Lastname,
    e.Firstname,
    e.Salary
FROM
    Company c INNER JOIN Employee e
        ON c.CompanyID = e.CompanyID
ORDER BY
    c.CompanyName,
    e.Lastname,
    e.Firstname
```

Listing 5-13 shows the way that you typically see table names aliased. As a side note, you don't need to use AS in aliasing column names either; eliminating them entirely is perfectly acceptable. The common practice, however, is to use AS in aliasing column names but not use AS in aliasing tables names.

Go ahead and practice a good number of different SELECT statements on your own databases to become comfortable with them and make sure that you practice at least a few relational SELECT statements by using SQL-92 syntax and pseudonyms so that you are prepared for the more complicated SELECT statements that you encounter later on in your development career.

After you're finished experimenting, and after you've finished working through chapters 6 through 8, make sure that you thoroughly read Chapter 9 so that you can gain a full understanding of the intricacies of complicated SELECT statements that contain GROUP BY, HAVING, and DISTINCT clauses, aggregate functions, and relational joins.

The following sections show you how to manipulate the data in your database by using INSERT, UPDATE, and DELETE statements.

INSERT Statements

Data is inserted into tables by using INSERT statements. Listing 5-14 shows a typical INSERT statement

Listing 5-14: A simple INSERT statement

```
INSERT INTO Company (
    CompanyName,
    Address,
    City,
```

Continued

Listing 5-14 *(continued)*

```
        State,
        ZipCode
    )
    VALUES (
        'Fast Like Bunny',
        '99 Mulberry Lane',
        'Reston',
        'VA',
        '20194'
    )
```

Listing 5-14 inserts a single row into the Company table with the values shown in the listing. As you can see, the values must be specified in the same order that the columns are listed; this is the only way that your database knows which values go into which columns.

The word `INTO` is optional and has no effect on the execution of your code. It simply makes your code more naturally English-like and, therefore, easier to read. `INSERT Company` is identical to `INSERT INTO Company` as far as SQL is concerned.

Now insert another row—this time into the Employee table—by using the code in Listing 5-15.

Listing 5-15: Inserting a row into the Employee table

```
INSERT INTO Employee (
    CompanyID,
    SSN,
    Firstname,
    Lastname,
    Salary,
    DateOfBirth
)
VALUES (
    10,
    '123-45-6789',
    'Stan',
    'Cox',
    11325.00,
    '04/01/1967'
)
```

The `INSERT` statement in Listing 5-15 is very similar to that in Listing 5-14, except that this time, two of the values that you are passing are numeric, and as you can see, they are not surrounded by single quotes. If you surround a numeric value with single quotes, the database throws an error because the data types between the value and the column designed to contain it do not match.

You may also notice that one of the values is a date. Dates are often difficult and error-prone to manipulate in a database, mainly because every database treats date processing differently.

In these listings, we are assuming that you are using Microsoft SQL Server 2000, which takes a string value in the form of a date and automatically converts or "casts" the string value into an actual date value. Oracle does the same thing, but only if Oracle's default date format matches the format of the value. Microsoft Access requires you to either delimit such a string value by using pound symbols (separate from those used by ColdFusion) or to supply a true ODBC date value by using ColdFusion's `CreateODBCDateTime()` function.

To execute this `INSERT` from a ColdFusion `CFQUERY` call, you simply wrap the `CFQUERY` call around the `INSERT` statement, as shown in Listing 5-16.

Listing 5-16: Executing an `INSERT` statement from a `CFQUERY` call

```
<cfquery name="InsertEmployee" datasource="Chapter5">
INSERT INTO Employee (
    CompanyID,
    SSN,
    Firstname,
    Lastname,
    Salary,
    DateOfBirth
)
VALUES (
    10,
    '123-45-6789',
    'Stan',
    'Cox',
    11325.00,
    '04/01/1967'
)
</cfquery>
```

Sure, this approach works, but most likely, you don't hard-code values into your ColdFusion templates. Instead, you probably feed values dynamically from forms and other ColdFusion variables. Notice in Listing 5-17 that the rules pertaining to single quotes apply to ColdFusion variables the same as they do for hard-coded values.

Listing 5-17: Executing an `INSERT` statement from a `CFQUERY` call by using ColdFusion variables

```
<cfquery name="InsertEmployee" datasource="Chapter5">
INSERT INTO Employee (
    CompanyID,
    SSN,
    Firstname,
    Lastname,
    Salary,
    DateOfBirth
```

Continued

Listing 5-17 *(continued)*

```
)
VALUES (
     #Val(Form.CompanyID)#,
     '#Trim(Form.SSN)#',
     '#Trim(Form.Firstname)#',
     '#Trim(Form.Lastname)#',
     #Val(Form.Salary)#,
     '#Trim(Form.DateOfBirth)#'
)
</cfquery>
```

Tip

Always use `Trim()` on string values to remove trailing spaces and Val() on numeric values to ensure that data of compatible types are received by the database. You also want to set the `MAXLENGTH` attributes of string form fields to the lengths of the table columns for which they are destined. These techniques go a long way toward preventing the majority of database errors, so use them everywhere that your Web application touches your database.

So far in these listings, you've seen how to insert individual rows into tables by using values acquired outside the database—such as form variables entered by the user and client variables managed by ColdFusion. Although this use of the `INSERT` statement is by far the most common, you can also insert data into a table by using data from one or more other tables.

In Listing 5-18, you insert some of the columns from some of the rows in the Employee table into a table named Temp. Figure 5-13 shows the structures of the three tables.

The `INSERT` statement in Listing 5-18 inserts into the Temp table all the employees with last names beginning with `M` or other letters later in the alphabet.

Listing 5-18: Using `INSERT` to populate one table from the data in another

```
INSERT INTO Temp (
     SSN,
     Firstname,
     Lastname
)
SELECT
     SSN,
     Firstname,
     Lastname
FROM
     Employee
WHERE
     Lastname >= 'M'
```

If you execute Listing 5-18 against an empty Temp table, Figure 5-14 shows what that Temp table contains as a result.

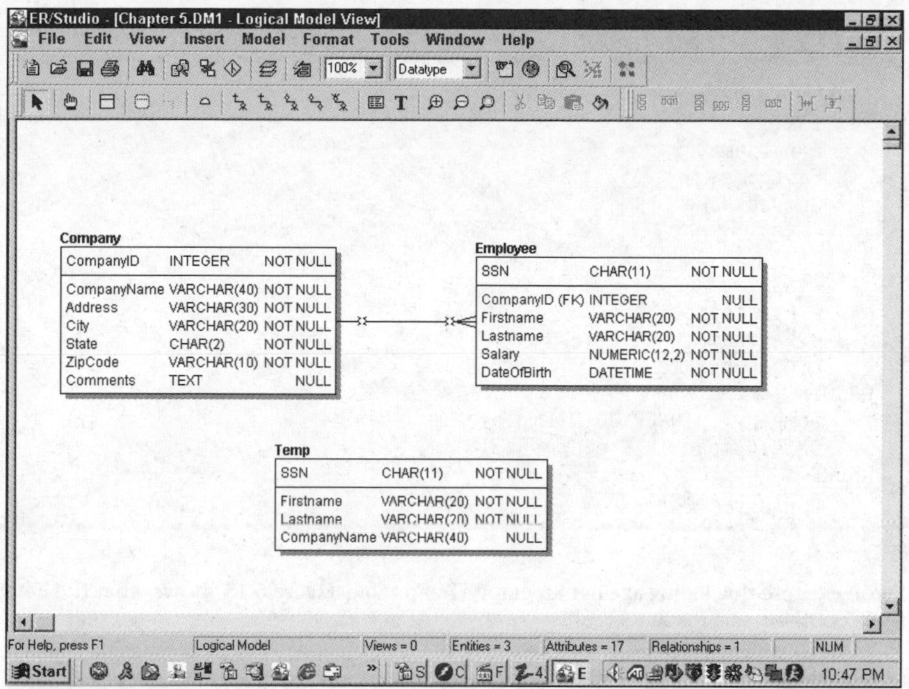

Figure 5-13: The Company, Employee, and Temp tables.

SQL Server Enterprise Manager - [2:Data in Table 'Company' in 'CF5Bible' on 'SQL2000']

Console Window Help

SSN	Firstname	Lastname	CompanyName
223-45-6789	Billy	Sanders	<NULL>
345-67-8901	Randsford	Worthington	<NULL>
567-89-0123	Bethany	Silverberg	<NULL>
901-23-4567	Timmy	Williger	<NULL>
356-78-9012	Natasha	Romanova	<NULL>
467-89-0123	Dirk	Thor	<NULL>
689-01-2345	Barney	Thickglasses	<NULL>
801-23-4567	Stanley	Mernal	<NULL>
023-45-6789	Larry	Nerdsworth	<NULL>
987-65-4321	Billy Bob	Tucker	<NULL>
543-21-0987	Davey	Mango	<NULL>

Figure 5-14: Result of executing Listing 5-18 on an empty Temp table.

Think of the `SELECT` clause of Listing 5-18 as if it were a direct replacement for the `VALUES` portion of a typical `INSERT` statement. Instead of the single row of values specified by the `VALUES` clause, the `SELECT` clause specifies an entire *set* of rows, resulting in that set of rows being inserted into the destination table.

Remember what we said about all `SELECT` statements resulting in a single table—even relational result sets? You can use this to your advantage in populating a table, as we do in the preceding example. To insert all employees of companies in Georgia into the Temp table, for example, you would execute Listing 5-19.

Listing 5-19: Populating a table from a relational query

```
INSERT INTO Temp (
    SSN,
    Firstname,
    Lastname,
    CompanyName
)
SELECT
    e.SSN,
    e.Firstname,
    e.Lastname,
    c.CompanyName
FROM
    Company c INNER JOIN Employee e
    ON c.CompanyID = e.CompanyID
WHERE
    c.State = 'GA'
```

If you execute this listing against an empty Temp table, Figure 5-15 shows what the Temp table contains as a result.

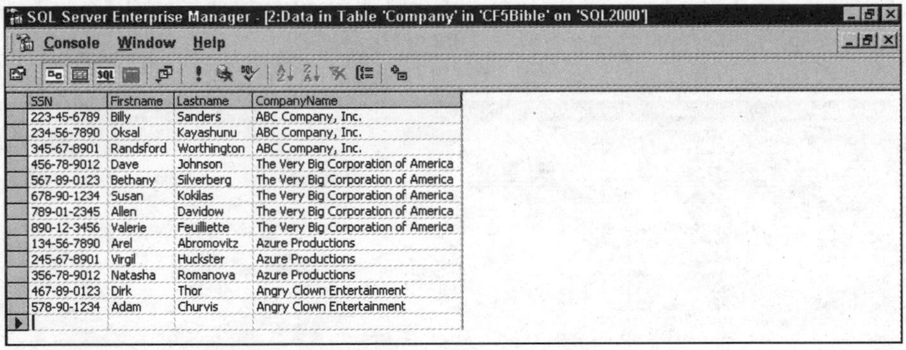

SQL Server Enterprise Manager - [2:Data in Table 'Company' in 'CF5Bible' on 'SQL2000']

Console Window Help

SSN	Firstname	Lastname	CompanyName
223-45-6789	Billy	Sanders	ABC Company, Inc.
234-56-7890	Oksal	Kayashunu	ABC Company, Inc.
345-67-8901	Randsford	Worthington	ABC Company, Inc.
456-78-9012	Dave	Johnson	The Very Big Corporation of America
567-89-0123	Bethany	Silverberg	The Very Big Corporation of America
678-90-1234	Susan	Kokilas	The Very Big Corporation of America
789-01-2345	Allen	Davidow	The Very Big Corporation of America
890-12-3456	Valerie	Feuilliette	The Very Big Corporation of America
134-56-7890	Arel	Abromovitz	Azure Productions
245-67-8901	Virgil	Huckster	Azure Productions
356-78-9012	Natasha	Romanova	Azure Productions
467-89-0123	Dirk	Thor	Angry Clown Entertainment
578-90-1234	Adam	Churvis	Angry Clown Entertainment

Figure 5-15: Result of executing Listing 5-19 on an empty Temp table.

After you understand how to insert data into tables by using SQL, you can move on to updating data that is already in the database, as the following section describes.

UPDATE Statements

Data already present in tables is modified by using `UPDATE` statements. The basic form of an `UPDATE` statement sets one or more columns of a set of rows in a single table to specified values. The set of rows is defined by the criteria specified in the `UPDATE` statement's `WHERE` clause. You must be very careful to specify exactly which row or rows you want to update, or you can permanently modify the wrong data. If you forget to include the `WHERE` clause, you update all the rows in the table to the new values, so be careful.

Now try executing a simple UPDATE statement. The Stan Cox Society has a CompanyID (its unique key) value of 10. If the Stan Cox Society moves from its current address to its new address in Chicago, you update its row in the Company table by using the UPDATE statement in Listing 5-20.

Listing 5-20: A simple UPDATE statement

```
UPDATE
    Company
SET
    Address = 'One WebGenius Drive',
    City    = 'Chicago',
    State   = 'IL',
    ZipCode = '60035'
WHERE
    CompanyID = 10
```

The UPDATE clause specifies the one table being updated; the SET clause pairs specified values with the columns for which they are destined; and the WHERE clause specifies the set of rows to be updated. Remember that even a single row in a result set is indeed an entire table of rows and columns; that particular table just so happens to contain only one row.

After you embed Listing 5-20 in a CFQUERY call, you need to "scrub" the values supplied to the table columns to prevent throwing database errors, as shown in Listing 5-21.

Listing 5-21: Embedding an UPDATE statement in a CFQUERY call

```
<cfquery name="UpdateCompany" datasource="Chapter5">
UPDATE
    Company
SET
    Address = '#Trim(Form.Address)#',
    City    = '#Trim(Form.City)#',
    State   = '#Trim(Form.State)#',
    ZipCode = '#Trim(Form.ZipCode)#'
WHERE
    CompanyID = #Val(Form.CompanyID)#
</cfquery>
```

If you omit one or more columns from your UPDATE statement, the values currently in those columns are not changed.

In the following section, you look at the process of deleting data from your database.

DELETE Statements

You delete data from tables by using DELETE statements. The basic form of a DELETE statement specifies a set of rows to be deleted from a single table. The set of rows is defined by the criteria specified in the DELETE statement's WHERE clause. As in using the UPDATE statement, you must be very careful to specify exactly which row or rows that you want to delete, or you can permanently delete the wrong data. If you forget to include the WHERE clause, you delete all the rows in the table, so be careful.

Use Listing 5-22 to delete an employee who's been playing Quake during business hours.

Listing 5-22: A basic DELETE statement

```
DELETE FROM
    Employee
WHERE
    SSN = '123-45-6789'
```

As you can see, basic DELETEs are the simplest SQL statements, because you specify only the table and the criteria that determine the set of data to be deleted.

Notice how we said "the *set* of data to be deleted." Visualizing the DELETE statement operating over a predefined set of data, rather than as some algorithm moving through a table, deleting individual rows that match the criteria of a WHERE clause or a relational join, can help you understand just how DELETE works.

In Listing 5-22, the WHERE clause is what predefines the set of data to be deleted. In effect, the WHERE clause produces its own "intermediate" result set, which is a single table of rows and columns, as are all result sets (even if that table contains only a single row). This intermediate result set is that on which the DELETE statement operates, resulting in that set of data getting deleted from the Employee table.

This example may seem a roundabout way of explaining the DELETE statement, but as you see in the following example, such visualization becomes absolutely necessary if your DELETE statement becomes more complex.

So now is a good time to state the following as our second premise:

Each step in processing an SQL statement results in a set of data—either an intermediate result set or the final result set—that is in the form of a single table containing rows and columns.

Now you get to see how such visualizing helps you handle more complex delete statements.

Similar to the INSERT statement's INTO, the FROM that lies between DELETE and the table name is superfluous; it is there only to make the DELETE statement more naturally English-like.

DELETE statements become more complicated if the set to be deleted is determined by a relational result set. (Although this feature is currently supported only by SQL Server and Sybase Adaptive Server, it serves as a good teaching example for understanding how SQL works with data in sets rather than in individual rows.) If you want to delete the employees of all companies in Florida, for example, you can replace the WHERE clause with a relational join, as in Listing 5-23.

Listing 5-23: Deleting from a table based on a relational result set

```
DELETE FROM
    Employee
FROM Employee e INNER JOIN Company c
ON e.CompanyID = c.CompanyID
WHERE
    c.State = 'FL'
```

This example is a little confusing at first, until you break it down and look at each part separately.

The first thing that you do is remove the superfluous `FROM` word. You have two `FROM` clauses in this relational `DELETE` statement, so you keep only the one that is absolutely needed in Listing 5-24.

Listing 5-24: Understanding a relational `DELETE`

```
DELETE
    Employee
FROM Employee e INNER JOIN Company c
ON e.CompanyID = c.CompanyID
WHERE
    c.State = 'FL'
```

This listing may seem a meaningless step at first, but it directs your attention not to the Employee table itself but to the relational result set defined by the `FROM` and `WHERE` clauses. Think of it as deleting the Employee rows from the relational result set. This isn't technically true, of course, but bear with us for a moment and you see why we want you to think of it this way.

In a basic `DELETE` statement, you delete directly from the table that stores the data; a simple `WHERE` clause is all that you need to specify the result set to be deleted, and, as in all result sets, the `WHERE` clause defines a single table of rows.

But if you're dealing with a relational delete, the result set to be deleted spans more than the one table that stores the data to be deleted. Fear not, however, because a simple `JOIN` between the tables again reduces the `FROM` clause's result set back down to a single table: the relational result set shown in Figure 5-16.

The result set in Figure 5-16 is then filtered by the `WHERE` clause to let through only those rows where the State is Florida. The final result of the `FROM` clause—the result set that is used to determine which rows in the Employee table are actually deleted—is then fed to the `DELETE` clause as the set of rows to be deleted, thereby resulting in the result set shown in Figure 5-17.

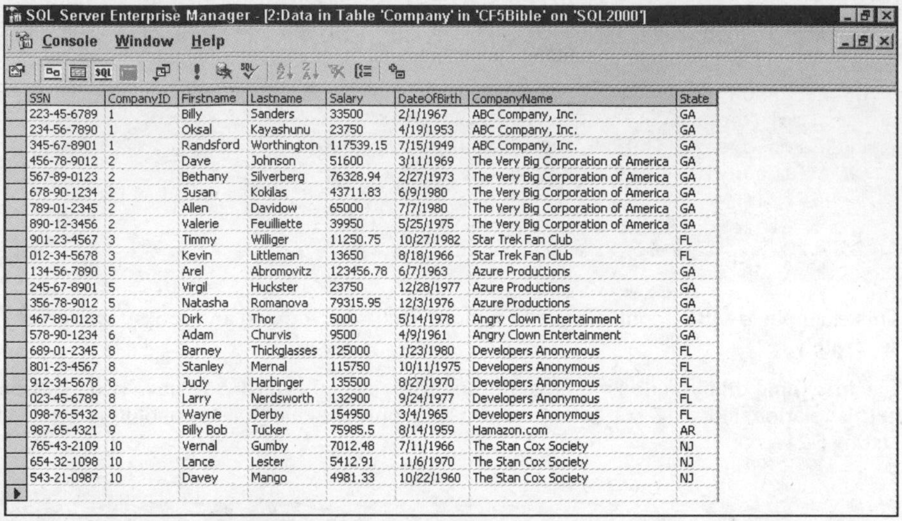

SQL Server Enterprise Manager - [2:Data in Table 'Company' in 'CF5Bible' on 'SQL2000']

Console Window Help

SSN	CompanyID	Firstname	Lastname	Salary	DateOfBirth	CompanyName	State
223-45-6789	1	Billy	Sanders	33500	2/1/1967	ABC Company, Inc.	GA
234-56-7890	1	Oksal	Kayashunu	23750	4/19/1953	ABC Company, Inc.	GA
345-67-8901	1	Randsford	Worthington	117539.15	7/15/1949	ABC Company, Inc.	GA
456-78-9012	2	Dave	Johnson	51600	3/11/1969	The Very Big Corporation of America	GA
567-89-0123	2	Bethany	Silverberg	76328.94	2/27/1973	The Very Big Corporation of America	GA
678-90-1234	2	Susan	Kokilas	43711.83	6/9/1980	The Very Big Corporation of America	GA
789-01-2345	2	Allen	Davidow	65000	7/7/1980	The Very Big Corporation of America	GA
890-12-3456	2	Valerie	Feuilliette	39950	5/25/1975	The Very Big Corporation of America	GA
901-23-4567	3	Timmy	Williger	11250.75	10/27/1982	Star Trek Fan Club	FL
012-34-5678	3	Kevin	Littleman	13650	8/18/1966	Star Trek Fan Club	FL
134-56-7890	5	Arel	Abromovitz	123456.78	6/7/1963	Azure Productions	GA
245-67-8901	5	Virgil	Huckster	23750	12/28/1977	Azure Productions	GA
356-78-9012	5	Natasha	Romanova	79315.95	12/3/1976	Azure Productions	GA
467-89-0123	6	Dirk	Thor	5000	5/14/1978	Angry Clown Entertainment	GA
578-90-1234	6	Adam	Churvis	9500	4/9/1961	Angry Clown Entertainment	GA
689-01-2345	8	Barney	Thickglasses	125000	1/23/1980	Developers Anonymous	FL
801-23-4567	8	Stanley	Mernal	115750	10/11/1975	Developers Anonymous	FL
912-34-5678	8	Judy	Harbinger	135500	8/27/1970	Developers Anonymous	FL
023-45-6789	8	Larry	Nerdsworth	132900	9/24/1977	Developers Anonymous	FL
098-76-5432	8	Wayne	Derby	154950	3/4/1965	Developers Anonymous	FL
987-65-4321	9	Billy Bob	Tucker	75985.5	8/14/1959	Hamazon.com	AR
765-43-2109	10	Vernal	Gumby	7012.48	7/11/1966	The Stan Cox Society	NJ
654-32-1098	10	Lance	Lester	5412.91	11/6/1970	The Stan Cox Society	NJ
543-21-0987	10	Davey	Mango	4981.33	10/22/1960	The Stan Cox Society	NJ

Figure 5-16: Visualizing the relational result set.

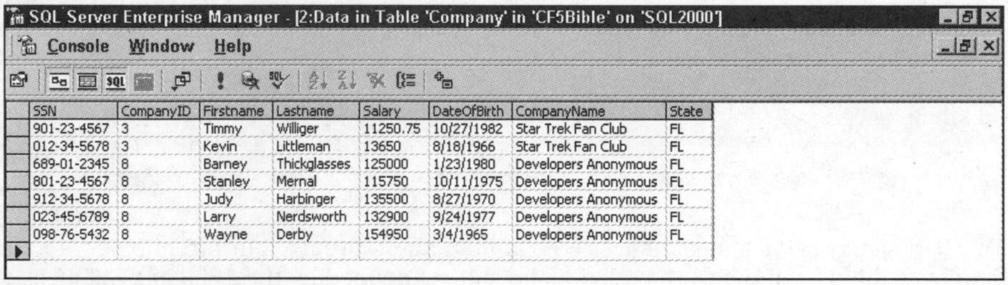

SQL Server Enterprise Manager - [2:Data in Table 'Company' in 'CF5Bible' on 'SQL2000']

Console Window Help

SSN	CompanyID	Firstname	Lastname	Salary	DateOfBirth	CompanyName	State
901-23-4567	3	Timmy	Williger	11250.75	10/27/1982	Star Trek Fan Club	FL
012-34-5678	3	Kevin	Littleman	13650	8/18/1966	Star Trek Fan Club	FL
689-01-2345	8	Barney	Thickglasses	125000	1/23/1980	Developers Anonymous	FL
801-23-4567	8	Stanley	Mernal	115750	10/11/1975	Developers Anonymous	FL
912-34-5678	8	Judy	Harbinger	135500	8/27/1970	Developers Anonymous	FL
023-45-6789	8	Larry	Nerdsworth	132900	9/24/1977	Developers Anonymous	FL
098-76-5432	8	Wayne	Derby	154950	3/4/1965	Developers Anonymous	FL

Figure 5-17: Visualizing the relational result set after the `WHERE` clause has been applied.

But wait a minute! You're not deleting from this relational result set; you're deleting from the Employee table itself. How does this relational result set tell the `DELETE` clause which rows to delete in the Employee table?

SQL looks at the constituent parts that make up that relational result set, and it sees that those rows came from both the Employee and Company tables. It then finds the actual rows from the Employee table that made up the relational result set and uses those as the set of rows to be deleted from the Employee table. Figure 5-18 should help you conceptualize this process.

Pretty cool, huh? This same technique can be used (in databases that support this technique) to specify multiple rows to be modified by using an `UPDATE` statement.

If your database server doesn't support updating and deleting by using references to relational result sets, you can use the *subquery* technique shown in Listing 5-25 instead. A subquery is a query within another query.

Relational Set That Indicates Employee Rows To Be Deleted:

SSN	CompanyID	Firstname	Lastname	Salary	DateOfBirth	CompanyName	State
901-23-4567	3	Timmy	Williger	11250.75	10/27/1982	Star Trek Fan Club	FL
012-34-5678	3	Kevin	Littleman	13650	8/18/1966	Star Trek Fan Club	FL
689-01-2345	8	Barney	Thickglasses	125000	1/23/1980	Developers Anonymous	FL
801-23-4567	8	Stanley	Mernal	115750	10/11/1975	Developers Anonymous	FL
912-34-5678	8	Judy	Harbinger	135500	8/27/1970	Developers Anonymous	FL
023-45-6789	8	Larry	Nerdsworth	132900	9/24/1977	Developers Anonymous	FL
098-76-5432	8	Wayne	Derby	154950	3/4/1965	Developers Anonymous	FL

Employee Table:

CompanyID	SSN	Firstname	Lastname	Salary	DateOfBirth
1	223-45-6789	Billy	Sanders	33500.00	1967-02-01
1	234-56-7890	Oksal	Kayashunu	23750.00	1953-04-19
1	345-67-8901	Randsford	Worthington	117539.15	1949-07-15
2	456-78-9012	Dave	Johnson	51600.00	1969-03-11
2	567-89-0123	Bethany	Silverberg	76328.94	1973-02-27
2	678-90-1234	Susan	Kokilas	43711.83	1980-06-09
2	789-01-2345	Allen	Davidow	65000.00	1980-07-07
2	890-12-3456	Valerie	Feuilliette	39950.00	1975-05-25
3	901-23-4567	*Timmy*	*Williger*	*11250.75*	*1982-10-27*
3	012-34-5678	*Kevin*	*Littleman*	*13650.00*	*1966-08-18*
5	134-56-7890	Arel	Abromovitz	123456.78	1963-06-07
5	245-67-8901	Virgil	Huckster	23750.00	1977-12-28
5	356-78-9012	Natasha	Romanova	79315.95	1976-12-03
6	467-89-0123	Dirk	Thor	5000.00	1978-05-14
6	578-90-1234	Adam	Churvis	9500.00	1961-04-09
8	689-01-2345	*Barney*	*Thickglasses*	*125000.00*	*1980-01-23*
8	801-23-4567	*Stanley*	*Mernal*	*115750.00*	*1975-10-11*
8	912-34-5678	*Judy*	*Harbinger*	*135500.00*	*1970-08-27*
8	023-45-6789	*Larry*	*Nerdsworth*	*132900.00*	*1977-09-24*
8	098-76-5432	*Wayne*	*Derby*	*154950.00*	*1965-03-04*
9	987-65-4321	Billy Bob	Tucker	75985.50	1959-08-14
10	765-43-2109	Vernal	Gumby	7012.48	1966-07-11
10	654-32-1098	Lance	Lester	5412.91	1970-11-06
10	543-21-0987	Davey	Mango	4981.33	1960-10-22

Figure 5-18: Visualizing how SQL finds the rows to be deleted from the Employee table.

Listing 5-25: **Deleting by using a subquery**

```
DELETE FROM
    Employee
WHERE CompanyID IN (
    SELECT
        CompanyID
    FROM
        Company
    WHERE
        State = 'FL'
)
```

As in the days of Algebra I in junior high school, you can resolve Listing 5-25 from the inside out. Look at the `SELECT` statement inside the parentheses: This statement is your *subquery*, so named because it is a query "beneath" the main query statement. The intermediate result set from this subquery looks as shown in Figure 5-19.

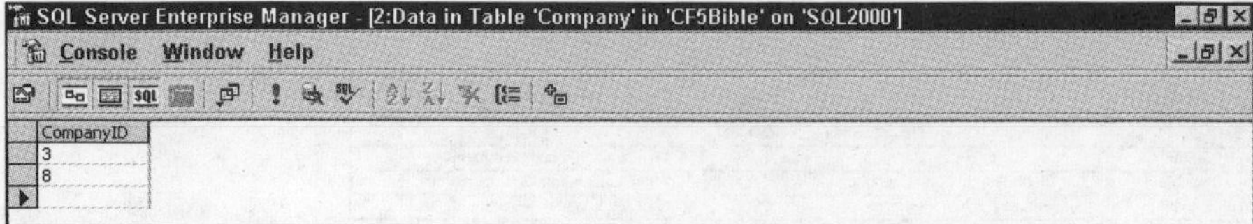

Figure 5-19: The intermediate result set of the subquery in Listing 5-25.

This is the set or "list" of CompanyIDs that is used as the argument of the DELETE clause. "Delete Employee rows with CompanyID values that appear in this list" is basically what Listing 5-25 is telling your database server to do. Figure 5-20 may help you conceptualize this process.

CompanyID
3
8

CompanyID	SSN	Firstname	Lastname	Salary	DateOfBirth
1	223-45-6789	Billy	Sanders	33500.00	1967-02-01
1	234-56-7890	Oksal	Kayashunu	23750.00	1953-04-19
1	345-67-8901	Randsford	Worthington	117539.15	1949-07-15
2	456-78-9012	Dave	Johnson	51600.00	1969-03-11
2	567-89-0123	Bethany	Silverberg	76328.94	1973-02-27
2	678-90-1234	Susan	Kokilas	43711.83	1980-06-09
2	789-01-2345	Allen	Davidow	65000.00	1980-07-07
2	890-12-3456	Valerie	Feuilliette	39950.00	1975-05-25
3	*901-23-4567*	*Timmy*	*Williger*	*11250.75*	*1982-10-27*
3	*012-34-5678*	*Kevin*	*Littleman*	*13650.00*	*1966-08-18*
5	134-56-7890	Arel	Abromovitz	123456.78	1963-06-07
5	245-67-8901	Virgil	Huckster	23750.00	1977-12-28
5	356-78-9012	Natasha	Romanova	79315.95	1976-12-03
6	467-89-0123	Dirk	Thor	5000.00	1978-05-14
6	578-90-1234	Adam	Churvis	9500.00	1961-04-09
8	*689-01-2345*	*Barney*	*Thickglasses*	*125000.00*	*1980-01-23*
8	*801-23-4567*	*Stanley*	*Mernal*	*115750.00*	*1975-10-11*
8	*912-34-5678*	*Judy*	*Harbinger*	*135500.00*	*1970-08-27*
8	*023-45-6789*	*Larry*	*Nerdsworth*	*132900.00*	*1977-09-24*
8	*098-76-5432*	*Wayne*	*Derby*	*154950.00*	*1965-03-04*
9	987-65-4321	Billy Bob	Tucker	75985.50	1959-08-14
10	765-43-2109	Vernal	Gumby	7012.48	1966-07-11
10	654-32-1098	Lance	Lester	5412.91	1970-11-06
10	543-21-0987	Davey	Mango	4981.33	1960-10-22

Figure 5-20: The concept of deleting via a subquery.

The subquery technique in Listing 5-25 may seem simpler code than its equivalent relational join, but it is much slower on large data sets. So if your database supports deleting by using references to relational result sets, use the relational result set technique instead.

Summary

In this chapter you learned not only the basics of writing SQL but also a few advanced topics, like joining multiple tables and performing relational updates.

Now ask yourself: Did you think as you started this chapter that you could so quickly understand and write SQL statements of this complexity? If you understand all the concepts to this point, you should pat yourself on the back: Well done!

Remember that not what you know isn't what's important but how you visualize. To "know" is to memorize how to do a specific thing, but if you visualize, you gain an understanding of behavior patterns, and from these patterns, you can not only interpolate and extrapolate a tremendous amount of practical knowledge, but you can also learn specific techniques faster as well.

✦ ✦ ✦

Using ColdFusion Forms

In This Chapter

Validating data on both the client and the server

Using CFINPUT

Using HTML form controls

Using graphical user interface controls

ColdFusion forms extend normal HTML forms by adding a client-side validation framework that is easy to implement. No faster way is available to develop intelligent forms for your ColdFusion application.

Implementing Client-Side Validation

One of the biggest oversights that ColdFusion developers make is not to validate data before it leaves the form. If you are expecting the user to enter a date, make sure that he enters a date. If a value can't be left blank, make sure that the user enters a value before submitting the form. Thankfully, ColdFusion's built-in client-side validation is easy to implement.

This section is an introduction to using client-side validation with CFFORM. For more in-depth coverage, see Chapter 20 of this book, which also covers other forms of data validation with ColdFusion.

By simply using CFFORM in place of the normal HTML FORM tag, you tell ColdFusion to create the entire validation framework for you. Then, by using ColdFusion form control tags in place of normal HTML form control tags, you tell ColdFusion to use that framework. Take, for example, the following code:

```
<cfform action="dummy.cfm" method="POST"
name="testForm">
Nickname: 
<cfinput type="Text"
    name="Nickname"
    message="You must enter your Extreme
Snowboarding nickname."
    required="Yes"
    size="40"
    maxlength="40"><br>

Age: 
<cfinput type="Text"
    name="Age"
    range="7,70"
    message="Bummer, dude! Your age makes you
ineligible for Extreme Snowboarding!"
    validate="integer"
```

```
        required="Yes"
        size="12"
        maxlength="4"><br>

    <input type="submit">
    </cfform>
```

This code produces the following output in your browser (although we took some liberties with tabs and returns to collapse the height — but the code itself is unchanged):

```
<SCRIPT LANGUAGE="JavaScript" TYPE="text/javascript"
SRC="/CFIDE/scripts/cfform.js"></SCRIPT>
<SCRIPT LANGUAGE="JavaScript" TYPE="text/javascript">
<!--
function  _CF_checktestForm(_CF_this) {
    if  (!_CF_hasValue(_CF_this.Nickname, "TEXT" ))    {
        if  (!_CF_onError(_CF_this, _CF_this.Nickname,
_CF_this.Nickname.value, "You must enter your Extreme Snowboarding
nickname.")) {
            return false;
        }
    }
    if  (!_CF_hasValue(_CF_this.Age, "TEXT" )) {
        if  (!_CF_onError(_CF_this, _CF_this.Age, _CF_this.Age.value,
"Bummer, dude! Your age makes you ineligible for Extreme
Snowboarding!")) {
            return false;
        }
    }
    if  ((!_CF_checkrange(_CF_this.Age.value, 7, 70))) {
        if  (!_CF_onError(_CF_this, _CF_this.Age, _CF_this.Age.value,
"Bummer, dude! Your age makes you ineligible for Extreme
Snowboarding!")) {
            return false;
        }
    }
    if  (!_CF_checkinteger(_CF_this.Age.value)) {
        if  (!_CF_onError(_CF_this, _CF_this.Age, _CF_this.Age.value,
"Bummer, dude! Your age makes you ineligible for Extreme
Snowboarding!")) {
            return false;
        }
    }
    return true;
}
//-->
</SCRIPT>

<FORM NAME="testForm" ACTION="dummy.cfm" METHOD="POST" onSubmit="return
_CF_checktestForm(this)">
Nickname: 
<INPUT TYPE="Text" NAME="Nickname" SIZE="40" MAXLENGTH="40"><br>

Age: 
<INPUT TYPE="Text" NAME="Age" SIZE="12" MAXLENGTH="4"><br>
```

```
<input type="submit">
</FORM>
```

After this form is submitted, the JavaScript function `_CF_checktestForm()` is called before anything else can happen. Each ColdFusion form control is tested according to its validation attributes. The Age field, for example, is tested to determine whether it contains a value, whether that value is an integer, and whether that integer is between 7 and 70. If any of these tests fail, the validation message `Bummer, dude! Your age makes you ineligible for Extreme Snowboarding!` appears in a JavaScript alert box via the `_CF_onError()` function inside the external JavaScript file `cfform.js`, and the form is not submitted. If all form data passes the validation tests, the form is submitted to its action template.

Caution Client-side validation like this will not work if the user turns off JavaScript in his browser.

Using CFINPUT

The example in the preceding section uses `CFINPUT` tags, so you already know how to use this tag. Following are the data formats that `CFINPUT` can validate:

- **`date`:** A date in the standard U.S. format *mm/dd/yyyy*.
- **`eurodate`:** A date in the standard European format *dd/mm/yyyy*.
- **`time`:** A valid time in the format *hh:mm:ss*.
- **`float`:** A floating-point number.
- **`integer`:** A whole number.
- **`telephone`:** A valid U.S. telephone number in the format *###-###-####*, where the hyphens can be replaced with spaces, and the first digits of the first and second group cannot be zero.
- **`zipcode`:** A valid U.S. zip code, either five or nine digits in the format *#####-####*, where the hyphen can be replaced with a space.
- **`creditcard`:** Strips all blanks and dashes from the card number and uses the standard mod 10 algorithm to validate the card number.
- **`social_security_number`:** A valid social security number in the format *###-##-####*, where the hyphens can be replaced by spaces.
- **`regular_expression`:** If the other possible values don't fit your need, you can give your own validation pattern in the form of a JavaScript regular expression.

Where you cannot use CFINPUT

Just as `CFINPUT` does, the `INPUT` tag has a `Type` attribute that tells which type of control the `INPUT` tag represents. The types of `INPUT` controls described in the following sections cannot be duplicated by `CFINPUT`:

Hidden form fields

You see in Chapter 2 that you can use hidden form fields to pass data to the server without the user needing to enter or even see the data. A hidden form field looks as follows:

```
<cfoutput>
```

```
<input type="hidden" name="CompanyID" value="#URL.CompanyID#">
</cfoutput>
```

This control passes the `URL.CompanyID` to the action page without the user's intervention.

Submit buttons

The *Submit button* is a simple version of the `INPUT` tag because it doesn't need a `Name` attribute. It looks as follows:

```
<input type="submit" value="Update Database">
```

No `form` variable is created for this Submit button, because we don't give the `INPUT` tag a name. The `Value` attribute contains the text that appears on the button

Reset buttons

The *Reset button* is another type of `INPUT` tag. Its code looks much like that of the Submit button, as follows:

```
<input type="reset" value="Reset Form">
```

After the user clicks a Reset button, all the controls on the form are reset to the state they were in at the time that the user first came to the form.

Action buttons

Submit and Reset buttons aren't the only kinds of button that you can have on your form. A more generalized type of button that can call a JavaScript function is the *action button*, and its code looks as follows:

```
<input type="button" value="Call a Function" onclick="doSomething();">
```

The `Type` is now `button`, but the `value` serves the same purpose that it does for the Submit and Reset buttons. The `onClick` attribute tells the browser which JavaScript function to call after the user clicks the button.

File browsers

Some forms can upload a file to the server. This is where the *file-browser control* comes in. The following code creates such a control:

```
<input type="file" name="FileToUpload">
```

The `file INPUT` type creates a file-browser control similar to the one shown in Figure 6-1.

After the user clicks the Browse button, he gets the Choose File dialog that he can use to select any file on his machine. He chooses a file, and after the form is submitted, the file is sent to the server for processing.

A snafu occurs if you use the `file INPUT` type — one that catches even experienced ColdFusion developers off guard. Whenever you're using the `file INPUT` type, *always* add the following attribute and value to your `FORM` or `CFFORM` tag:

```
<cfform ... enctype="multipart/form-data">
```

If you forget this attribute, the upload *does not work*.

To process the submitted file on the server, use the `CFFILE Upload` action. For information on `CFFILE`, see Chapter 60.

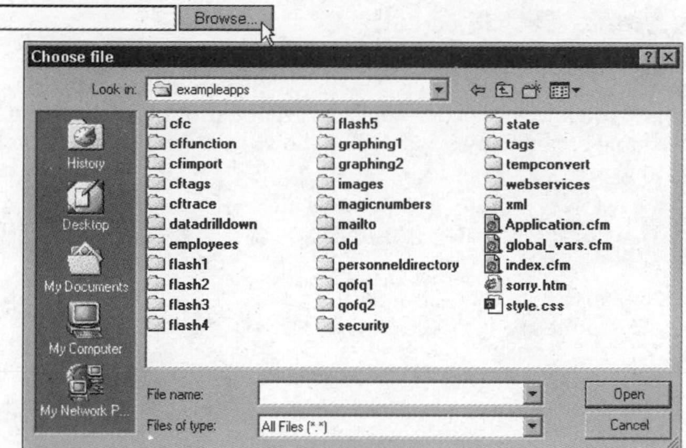

Figure 6-1: A file-browser control created by using `INPUT TYPE="File"`.

Text areas

A *text area* is a large, multiline input field in which the user can enter several lines of text. To put a text area on a form, use the `TEXTAREA` tag as follows:

```
<textarea name="Comments" rows="5" cols="40"></textarea>
```

As do the `INPUT` and `CFINPUT` tags, `TEXTAREA` has a `Name` attribute, which becomes the name of the form variable on the action page. `TEXTAREA`, however, does not have a `Size` or `Maxlength` attribute—instead, `Rows` and `Cols` attributes specify the size of the text area. `TEXTAREA` has no `Value` attribute. Everything between the `<textarea>` and `</textarea>` tags is the initial value of the text area as the form first appears, and the content of the text area is its value after the form is submitted.

Using CFSELECT

`CFINPUT` is useful for information such as a person's name or age, where the user can enter free-form data, but if the user has only a few choices, such as which company he works for or in which state he lives, giving the user a list of options, from which he can choose only one, makes more sense. You use `CFSELECT` to give the user a select menu containing a list of options.

Explicitly specifying options

The following code produces a select menu with three options:

```
<cfselect name="Rating" size="1" required="yes">
    <option value="3" selected>Good</option>
    <option value="2">Mediocre</option>
    <option value="1">Bad</option>
</cfselect>
```

The name of the select menu is `Rating`, meaning that, after the form is submitted, the action page receives a form variable named `Form.Rating`. The user sees three options in the drop-down list: Good, Mediocre, and Bad; Good is selected by default because the `selected` qualifier is added to that option. `Form.Rating` contains `3`, `2`, or `1`, corresponding to the option that the user chooses, and this is the value that is contained in `Form.Rating` after it is received by the action template.

Populating options from a CFQUERY call

Say that you want a list from which a user may choose the company for which an employee works. You could manually code all the option tags, one for each company, but that's a hassle—and what happens if you add or delete a company? A better option is to populate the CFSELECT's options from a table of companies. Listing 6-1 shows what you do in Chapter 2.

Listing 6-1: Populating a select menu's options from a CFQUERY

```
<cfquery name="GetCompanies"
        datasource="#Request.MainDSN#">
SELECT
    CompanyID,
    CompanyName
FROM
    Company
ORDER BY
    CompanyName
</cfquery>

<cfselect name="CompanyID"
          size="1"
          query="GetCompanies"
          value="CompanyID"
          display="CompanyName"
          required="Yes"
          message="Please select a Company."></cfselect>
```

The CFQUERY call returns the companies from the database as a result set named GetCompanies, and CFSELECT uses the GetCompanies result set to generate one OPTION tag for every record in the result set, using the columns specified in the Value and Display attributes to populate the value and display text of each OPTION tag.

Using check boxes and radio buttons

Check boxes are simple on/off toggle controls that can exist either on their own or in a group of multiple check boxes, any number of which can be selected at once. *Radio buttons* always exist in groups of two or more, and only one button in a group can be selected at any given time.

Creating single check boxes

The following CFINPUT tag creates a check-box control in the user's browser:

```
<cfinput type="Checkbox" name="IsVolunteer" value="1">
```

The CFINPUT creates a check box named IsVolunteer. The value of the check box is 1, so if the box is selected as the user submits the form, the value of Form.IsVolunteer is 1. If the check box isn't selected as the user submits the form, no form variable corresponding to the checkbox is created. If the action template expects this variable to exist, but it doesn't, it throws an error.

To prevent this problem, add a CFPARAM tag to the action template, as follows:

```
<cfparam name="Form.IsVolunteer" default="0">
```

Now, as the form is submitted, Form.IsVolunteer contains 1 if the IsVolunteer check box is selected and zero if the check box isn't selected.

Creating groups of check boxes

Check boxes work well by themselves for simple on/off values, where each check box represents a single attribute of some thing. Suppose, however, that you have a group of related check boxes, as shown in Figure 6-2.

Which clubs does this employee belong to?
☐ United Way
☐ Baseball Team
☐ Employee Wellness Committee

Figure 6-2: A group of related check boxes.

In this case, you can't use a single check box by itself to represent the multiple choices made by the user. Each choice is an option that can co-exist with the other options, so this group of check boxes really represents a single multivalued attribute of some thing rather than a collection of individual attributes.

Check boxes belonging to the same group are implemented by assigning them all the same name attribute, as follows:

```
<cfinput type="checkbox" name="IsMemberOf" value="UnitedWay"> United
Way<br>
<cfinput type="checkbox" name="IsMemberOf" value="BaseballTeam">
Baseball Team<br>
<cfinput type="checkbox" name="IsMemberOf" value="Wellness"> Employee
Wellness Committee
```

Notice that all three check boxes are named IsMemberOf, so if any of the check boxes are selected, Form.IsMemberOf is present on the action page. If none of the checkboxes are selected, however, Form.IsMemberOf does not exist, so you must use CFPARAM to give it a default value, as follows:

```
<cfparam name="Form.IsMemberOf" default="">
```

But what does Form.IsMemberOf contain? With only a single check box, Form.IsVolunteer contains 1 if the check box is selected, but now that you have multiple check boxes, all of the values of the selected boxes are put together, with commas in between each value. In other words, if you select United Way and Employee Wellness Committee, Form.IsMemberOf contains UnitedWay,Wellness.

Using radio buttons

Radio buttons are a cross between a single check box and a group of check boxes. On the one hand, radio buttons always occur in groups of two or more buttons with the same name, as does a group of multiple check boxes. On the other hand, because only one button in a group of radio buttons can be selected at any given time, a single value is submitted to the server. To make the situation even stranger, if the user chooses none of the options in a radio button group, the form variable doesn't exist at all on the action page—the same thing that happens with check boxes.

Say that company policy changes, and now an employee may be a member of only one company club at a time. You would change the group of check boxes into a group of radio buttons, as follows:

```
<cfinput type="radio" name="IsMemberOf" value="UnitedWay" checked>
United Way<br>
<cfinput type="radio" name="IsMemberOf" value="BaseballTeam"> Baseball
Team<br>
<cfinput type="radio" name="IsMemberOf" value="Wellness"> Employee
Wellness Committee
```

The result of this code would look like what is shown in Figure 6-3.

United Way
Baseball Team
Employee Wellness Committee

Figure 6-3: A group of radio buttons.

Notice that `Type="checkbox"` is now `Type="radio"`. In addition, the first radio button is initially selected. (Note that if you hadn't made this first option initially selected, you would run the risk of passing nothing to the action page as mentioned earlier.) Always select the first radio button in a group of radio buttons so that the corresponding form variable always exists, even if the user doesn't make a selection.

Implementing Server-Side Validation

Client-side validation does not work if the user turns off JavaScript in his browser. You must account for this possibility by putting even more data validation in your ColdFusion code. Say, for example, that you had a field in your application where the user could enter his age, as follows:

```
<cfinput
    type="text"
    name="Age"
    validate="integer"
    required="yes">
```

Naturally, you would expect that the user could enter only a number for his age, and the `Validate="integer"` in the CFINPUT makes sure of it. The problem is that, if the user turns off JavaScript, he can enter a letter and submit the form. To safeguard against this possibility, put the following code in your action page:

```
<cfif NOT IsNumeric(Form.Age)>
    <!--- CFLOCATION back to form page or display message here --->
</cfif>
```

`IsDate()` and `IsNumericDate()` are also useful functions for this type of validation.

Other forms of server-side validation include testing for specific ranges of values, specific enumerated values, and whether a value was submitted (as opposed to an empty field or a field containing only spaces). All this testing may seem a lot of extra work, but if you don't implement server-side validation to supplement the client-side validation, you run the real risk of exposing your code and database to bad data, and the consequences can be extreme.

Graphical User Interface Widgets

CFINPUT and INPUT are great for basic form controls, but at times you need a special control that is not available as part of a standard HTML form. Fortunately, ColdFusion provides you with a few advanced graphical user-interface controls, or *widgets*, that extend the functionality of standard forms.

CFSLIDER

CFSLIDER creates a slider control that varies a numeric value. Following is a typical call to CFSLIDER:

```
<cfslider name="Salary"
          label="Salary: %value%"
          range="0, 100000"
          scale="1000"
          height="50"
          width="300"
          lookandfeel="METAL">
```

Figure 6-4 shows what the slider control looks like.

Figure 6-4: A slider control produced by using CFSLIDER.

After this slider control is submitted, the value of Form.Salary contains the value that the user selected by sliding the control from left to right.

A slider can have tick marks at major and minor intervals, display a label to show the current value of the slider, have a specific look and feel, and have fonts and colors associated with its text and background.

As do the other form-INPUT tags, CFSLIDER has a Name attribute that becomes the name of the form variable on the action page. The Label appears in the slider control area; the %value% marker shows where in the label the current value appears. Range takes two numbers separated by commas that represent the minimum and maximum values of the slider control. Scale is the interval at which the slider button stops — in this case, all the salaries must be in multiples of 1,000.

The tag also includes a Height and Width attribute to specify the size of the slider control and a LookAndFeel attribute, which tells the Java applet what graphical treatment to use in drawing the slider control. We use the METAL look and feel here because we happen to like how it looks; WINDOWS and MOTIF are the other two available values for LookAndFeel.

The CFSLIDER tag has additional attributes. See Chapter 51 for a listing of CFSLIDER's attributes.

With all the advantages posed by the CFSLIDER tag, you may be surprised to find out that CFSLIDER isn't very useful for creating Web applications, as the following list explains:

✦ Typically, a slider control accompanies some immediate change in the user's environment; for example, changing a volume slider sets the computer's speaker volume to a new level. In a Web application, however, the user must submit the form containing the slider control to the server, which then takes the slider control's position and does something with it.

✦ CFSLIDER is slow to load, so the user must wait quite a while for a control that would probably be better served by a simple CFINPUT with range validation.

✦ As do all graphical user-interface widgets, CFSLIDER requires Java on the client computer.

✦ Graphical user-interface widgets work fairly well in Internet Explorer for Windows but often create problems for Netscape and Macintosh users.

CFTEXTINPUT

CFTEXTINPUT implements a text-input field (as does CFINPUT) by using a Java applet.

You have no reason whatsoever to use CFTEXTINPUT. It performs the same purpose as <cfinput type="text"> but with an unacceptable increase in overhead. The only attributes of CFTEXTINPUT that aren't part of CFINPUT involve font and background styling and colors, all of which can be accomplished by using style sheets. If you must use CFTEXTINPUT, refer to Chapter 51.

CFTREE

CFTREE creates a tree control similar to the one shown in Figure 6-5.

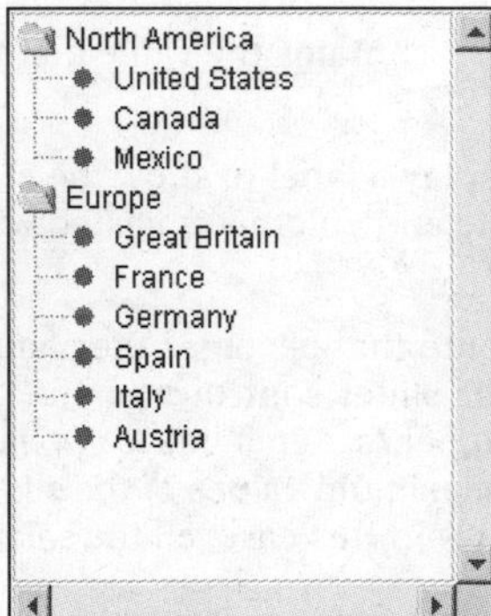

Figure 6-5: A tree control created by using CFTREE and CFTREEITEM.

CFTREE is slightly more complicated than CFSLIDER because, in addition to configuring the tree control by using CFTREE, you must also specify the tree items by using CFTREEITEM, as shown in Listing 6-2.

Listing 6-2: The code that produced the tree control shown in Figure 6-5

```
<cftree name="EmployeeLocation"
        height="250"
        width="200"
        lookandfeel="METAL">
    <cftreeitem value="1" display="North America">
    <cftreeitem value="2" display="United States" parent="1">
    <cftreeitem value="3" display="Canada" parent="1">
    <cftreeitem value="4" display="Mexico" parent="1">

    <cftreeitem value="5" display="Europe">
    <cftreeitem value="6" display="Great Britain" parent="5">
    <cftreeitem value="7" display="France" parent="5">
    <cftreeitem value="8" display="Germany" parent="5">
    <cftreeitem value="9" display="Spain" parent="5">
    <cftreeitem value="10" display="Italy" parent="5">
    <cftreeitem value="11" display="Austria" parent="5">
</cftree>
```

As do all other form controls, `CFTREE` has a `Name` that becomes the name of the form variable on the action template.

Inside `CFTREE` are the `CFTREEITEM` tags that specify the items in the tree. Each `CFTREEITEM` tag has a `Value` and a `Display`, which act just as their equivalents in the `CFSELECT` tag do: If the user chooses North America in the tree control, as shown in Figure 6-5, `Form.EmployeeLocation` contains 1.

The second `CFTREEITEM` tag in Listing 6-2 also has a `Parent` attribute. `Parent` tells the `CFTREEITEM` to relate itself to the `CFTREEITEM` with a `Value` that matches `Parent`—in other words, the tree item for North America.

CFTREE also has a `Height`, `Width`, and `LookAndFeel` as does `CFSLIDER`. `CFTREE` has a rather large number of attributes. See Chapter 51 for complete details.

Populating a CFTREE control from a query

Suppose that you add to the Employee table a `ManagerID` column that holds the `EmployeeID` of an Employee's manager. You can `SELECT` the data from the `Employee` table in a `CFQUERY`, `loop` over the query with `CFLOOP`, and put out `CFTREEITEM` tags, but doing so is somewhat tedious to program. Wouldn't just pointing `CFTREE` to a query result set and having `CFTREE` do all the rest be better?

First, get all the employees from the database by using the following code:

```
<cfquery name="GetEmployees"
         datasource="TreeTest">
SELECT
    EmployeeID AS ItemID,
    ManagerID AS ParentItemID,
    FirstName + ' ' + LastName AS Description
```

```
FROM
    Employee
ORDER BY
    FirstName + ' ' + LastName
</cfquery>
```

This query has some new syntax. First, notice that, instead of just selecting EmployeeID and ManagerID, the query selects EmployeeID AS ItemID and ManagerID AS ParentItemID. The query aliases these columns so that, although the database sees them as EmployeeID and ManagerID, ColdFusion sees them as ItemID and ParentItemID. And instead of selecting FirstName or LastName individually, the query selects the concatenation of FirstName + ' ' + LastName. The expression is aliased so that the employee name is available to ColdFusion as the Description column of the GetEmployees result set.

ColdFusion must make the data presentable to the CFTREE or it does not work correctly. CFTREE requires that data used to populate the tree control be in the same order that you used them in manually specifying each CFTREEITEM tag in the section "CFTREE," earlier in this chapter, and for this purpose, you use a third-party custom tag named CFX_Make_Tree, as follows:

```
<cfx_make_tree query="#GetEmployees#">
```

CFX_MAKE_TREE is a CFX tag written in C++ that is freely available from the Macromedia Developer's Exchange. Go to http://devex.macromedia.com and search for CFX_MAKE_TREE.

After ColdFusion sorts the tree data by using CFX_Make_Tree, you call CFTREE and CFTREEITEM, pointing them to the sorted result set returned from CFX_Make_Tree, as follows:

```
<cftree name="EmployeeID"
        height="250"
        width="200"
        lookandfeel="METAL">

    <cfloop query="GetEmployees">
    <cftreeitem value="#ItemID#"
                display="#Description#"
                parent="#ParentItemID#">
    </cfloop>

</cftree>
```

Notice that this code loops over the query to create a CFTREEITEM for each row in the query result set.

CFGRID

CFGRID creates a grid of data, much as a spreadsheet does. CFGRID can be used in a number of different ways. The simplest is where the user can do nothing other than view the data in the grid. You can also enable the user to select a cell, column, or row and pass the selected values to the action page. CFGRID can also enable the user to edit values in the grid control and submit the modified data to the action page.

In this section, we are going to cover only data-driven calls to CFGRID, because that is by far the most common way that CFGRID is used. For information on manually defining rows and columns in a CFGRID control, see the discussions of CFGRIDCOLUMN and CFGRIDROW in Chapter 51.

Using CFGRID to browse data

The simplest form of CFGRID is one in which the user simply browses data, as follows:

```
<cfquery name="GetEmployees"
datasource="CFMXBible">
SELECT
    SSN,
    FirstName,
    LastName,
    Salary
FROM
    Employee
ORDER BY SSN
</cfquery>

<cfgrid name="EmployeeData"
        height="200"
        width="400"
        query="GetEmployees"
        selectmode="BROWSE"
        autowidth="true">
</cfgrid>
```

You call CFQUERY to get employee data from the database; then you point CFGRID to the query result set. The SelectMode is BROWSE, meaning that the user can do nothing more than browse these results and that nothing is submitted to the action page to represent this grid control.

Enabling the user to select a single cell in a CFGRID control

Suppose that you change the SelectMode attribute as follows:

```
<cfgrid name="EmployeeData"
        height="200"
        width="400"
        query="GetEmployees"
        selectmode="SINGLE"
        autowidth="true">
</cfgrid>
```

CFGRID is the same as in the previous section, except that it now enables the user to select a single cell in the grid. After the user submits the form, the selected cell's value is passed to the action page in a variable named Form.EmployeeData.<selectedcolumnname>, with the name of the selected column replacing <selectedcolumnname>.

You rarely have any reason to use the SINGLE SelectMode.

Enabling the user to select a column in a CFGRID control

Change the SelectMode again, as follows:

```
<cfgrid name="EmployeeData"
        height="200"
        width="400"
```

```
            query="GetEmployees"
            selectmode="COLUMN"
            autowidth="true">
</cfgrid>
```

Now, whenever the user attempts to select a cell, the CFGRID control selects the entire column containing that cell. After the user submits the form, the selected column's values are passed to the action page in a variable named Form.EmployeeData.<selectedcolumnname>, with the name of the selected column replacing <selectedcolumnname>. The cell values are strung together in row order into a comma-delimited list.

Enabling the user to select a row in a CFGRID control

Again, change the SelectMode, this time as follows:

```
<cfgrid name="EmployeeData"
            height="200"
            width="400"
            query="GetEmployees"
            selectmode="ROW"
            autowidth="true">
</cfgrid>
```

Now CFGRID enables the user to select an entire row in the grid control. After the user submits the form, the values of all the selected cells are submitted to the action page in multiple variables named Form.EmployeeData.<columnname>, with the name of the grid columns replacing <columnname>.

Enabling the user to edit content in a CFGRID control

Change the SelectMode one last time, as follows:

```
<cfgrid name="EmployeeData"
            height="200"
            width="400"
            query="GetEmployees"
            selectmode="EDIT"
            autowidth="true">
</cfgrid>
```

Now, after the user clicks cells, he can edit their values. After he submits the form, all changes made to the grid data are submitted to the server.

The actual contents of what is submitted are complicated, but luckily, ColdFusion provides you with a tag named CFGRIDUPDATE that makes all the necessary database changes. Here's an example of using CFGRIDUPDATE on the action template to which the form containing the EmployeeData grid was submitted:

```
<cfgridupdate grid="EmployeeData"
datasource="CFMXBible"
tablename="Employee">
```

All you need to do is tell CFGRIDUPDATE the name of the CFGRID control that was submitted, the datasource, and the name of the table that you want to update. Everything else is handled automatically. CFGRIDUPDATE has additional attributes; see Chapter 51 for more information.

The Caveats of Using CFFORM

With all the benefits of `CFFORM` that you see in this chapter, you may be surprised to know that you *shouldn't* use `CFFORM` unless you really need to, for the following reasons:

- ✦ `CFINPUT` validation requires some overhead to generate the validation framework.
- ✦ The graphical user interface controls — `CFSLIDER`, `CFTEXTINPUT`, `CFTREE`, and `CFGRID` — all require the user to have Java installed on his machine, which also requires overhead.
- ✦ Sometimes you experience problems making the graphical user-interface controls work in an environment other than Internet Explorer for Windows.

Carefully consider your user base before forcing `CFFORM` controls on them. Although these controls may be fine in the controlled environment of an intranet, the general public is often quick to abandon you if problems rear their ugly heads.

Summary

In this chapter, you learn how to use `CFFORM` and its many form controls to enable the user to enter data. You learn how to use `CFINPUT` to perform client-side validation and avoid overburdening your Web server, and you also learn to implement server-side validation as well. You learn how to use `CFSELECT` drop-down lists to restrict a user's choices and that you must revert to using `INPUT` instead of `CFINPUT` to create certain controls. Finally, you learn how to implement the graphical user-interface widgets that ColdFusion provides to make your life easier.

✦ ✦ ✦

CHAPTER 7

Testing Your Code

In This Chapter

Using test harnesses to unit-test your code

Testing your application as a whole

Debugging your code

Rigorous testing is often overlooked to the peril of a development project. Testing can be an aggravating process, but it doesn't need to be. In this chapter, you learn how to create a realistic testing plan to make sure that your code works under all conditions, and then you learn useful debugging techniques to help you find out why your code is breaking.

Testing an application involves two phases: *development testing* and *application testing*. Development testing ensures that individual snippets of your code work correctly. Application testing verifies the functionality of the entire application as a whole.

Development Testing

Development testing uses *test harnesses* to execute single templates in isolation from the rest of your application. These harnesses can test to determine whether the template works correctly and also how well it responds to bad input and exception conditions.

Test harnesses

A test harness is a standalone module of code that establishes an environment within which other code may be tested. For example, consider the `CFQUERY` call in Listing 7-1.

Listing 7-1: `UpdateDatabase.cfm`

```
<cfquery name="UpdateDatabase"
         datasource="#Request.MainDSN#">
UPDATE Employee
SET
    FirstName = '#Form.FirstName#',
    LastName = '#Form.LastName#'
WHERE
    SSN = '#Form.SSN#'
</cfquery>
```

Listing 7-1 receives three `Form` variables and uses them to update the database. To make sure that this template works before you build a form for it, you should build a test harness to execute the template in a controlled manner.

The test harness for a database update action template should do the following four things:

✦ Supply all data inputs that are needed by the CFQUERY call.

✦ Call the update template being tested.

✦ Retrieve the updated data from the database.

✦ Display the updated data to ensure that the update worked.

Listing 7-2 shows the test harness that we created to test UpdateDatabase.cfm from Listing 7-1.

Listing 7-2: test_UpdateDatabase.cfm

```
<cfset Form.FirstName = "John">
<cfset Form.LastName = "Doe">
<cfset Form.SSN = "123-45-6789">

<cfinclude template="UpdateDatabase.cfm">

<cfquery name="GetEmployee"
         datasource="#Request.MainDSN#">
SELECT *
FROM Employee
WHERE SSN = '#Form.SSN#'
</cfquery>

<cfdump var="#GetEmployee#">
```

If you go to test_UpdateDatabase.cfm in your Web browser, the first thing that the template does is to set three Form variables: FirstName, LastName, and SSN. Notice that these are the same three Form variables that Listing 7-1 expects.

After setting the Form variables, the test harness calls UpdateDatabase.cfm, which performs an UPDATE via CFQUERY. After calling UpdateDatabase.cfm, the test harness must show you that the template worked, so the harness selects the modified record and outputs it via CFDUMP.

CFDUMP is a very useful tool during testing in particular and development in general, because it generates a visual representation of any variable you pass to it. This is particularly useful for visualizing complex structure and query objects. See the section "Using CFDUMP" in this chapter for details.

Unit testing with bad data

In Listing 7-2, all the test data is valid. Part of your unit testing, however, should include testing against bad data. What does your query do if you pass letters instead of numbers or 40 characters into a field that expects 30? Run your test harnesses multiple times with different inputs each time to make sure that your template handles bad data gracefully.

Structured exception handling

Structured exception handling catches errors thrown by ColdFusion and elegantly handles them as exceptions to the normal execution of your application. Consider the following block of code:

```
<cftry>
    <cfquery name="UpdateDatabase"
             datasource="#Request.MainDSN#">
    UPDATE Employee
    SET
        FirstName = '#Form.FirstName#',
        LastName = '#Form.LastName#'
    WHERE
        SSN = '#Form.SSN#'
    </cfquery>

<cfcatch type="Any">
    <!--- Alternate code to handle this error --->
</cfcatch>
</cftry>
```

CFTRY tells ColdFusion to watch for errors in the code that it encloses, and CFCATCH tells ColdFusion what to do if any type of error occurs.

Comment out your exception-handling code as follows during unit testing so that your code throws raw errors:

```
<!--- <cftry> --->

    <cfquery name="UpdateDatabase"
             datasource="#Request.MainDSN#">
    UPDATE Employee
    SET
        FirstName = '#Form.FirstName#',
        LastName = '#Form.LastName#'
    WHERE
        SSN = '#Form.SSN#'
    </cfquery>

<!---
    <cfcatch type="Any">
        <!--- Alternate code to handle this error --->
    </cfcatch>
    </cftry>
--->
```

This way, if an error is thrown, you see its error number in your browser. The example just shown handles all errors of all types in the same way, but production-quality exception handling precisely catches errors and handles each one according to its specific needs.

Application testing

Application testing is more involved than development testing, as it encompasses the entire application rather than individual templates. The following sections show you how to create and use test cases to test your code and also show you some common problems to test for.

How to test your application

Before you begin application testing, you need a plan. Imagine that your software was just released and is perfect in every way. Now walk backward from that point of perfection to where your software is now; the path in front of you describes your testing plan, and each step along that path is a *test case*.

The best way to explain test cases is to walk through the process of creating them. To illustrate, we use the example application from Chapter 2.

To create test cases, use a tool such as Microsoft Word that has an outlining feature and set the automatic heading numbering style to 1.1.1. Create level-one headings that correspond to the major areas of your application, which in this case are Companies and Employees.

Create level-two headings for each process, such as company list, company add, company edit, and company delete, with similar entries under the employee heading.

Now you concentrate on the company add form, which contains fields for the company name, zip code, phone number, and other data. Some of your test cases may be as follows:

- ✦ Attempt to create a company with a zip code in an invalid format.
- ✦ Attempt to create a company with letters in the phone-number field.
- ✦ Attempt to create a company without a company name.
- ✦ Attempt to create a company that already exists in the database.
- ✦ Attempt to create a company and then click the Back button and resubmit the form.
- ✦ Attempt to create a company in the same zip code as an existing company.

These are only a fraction of the test cases that you should have—and all just for the company add form. After you first start writing test cases, you may expect to have 20 test cases total, but those 20 quickly turn into 120. Notice, too, that *each of these test cases forms a complete command* that a human can carry out. This is important because you must eventually produce a series of discrete instructions for a tester to follow.

After you flesh out the outline to an excruciating level of detail, invest in a few packs of 3" x 5" ruled index cards and two index-card boxes of different colors. Designate one box as the Good Box and the other as the Bad Box. Next, transcribe all the test cases from your outline onto the index cards, one per card, and include the outline heading number (for example, 2.1.3) on each card.

Now you have one card for each test case. Shuffle them. One key to good testing is to never fall into a particular pattern during testing, so reshuffle them every time that you retest your application.

Now you're ready to start testing your application. Pick up the top card from your stack of test cases and do what it says to do. (This why each test case is a complete command for a user to execute.) If the test succeeds, place the card in the Good Box. If the test fails, place the card in the Bad Box.

At the end of your run through the test cases, fix everything in the Bad Box by correcting and retesting the code that failed. Then take all the cards from both boxes, shuffle them, and test the application all over again. This process may seem strange, but we explain why you must completely retest in the section, "Regression testing," later in the chapter.

The rest of this chapter goes into more detail about what your test cases are and shows ways to resolve any errors that are uncovered.

Testing your application with bad data

In the section "Unit testing with bad data," earlier in this chapter, you test individual snippets of code against bad data; in this section, you create test cases to ensure that your entire application can flawlessly handle bad data.

The hardest part about creating "bad-data" test cases is remembering to test every field in your application in every possible way. Such testing may seem tedious or even needlessly redundant at times, but it is very necessary. This section presents five possible test cases for every field in your application. (We say "possible" test cases. because not all of them apply to every field.)

✦ **Attempt to submit a form with nothing in a required field**. An error with this type of test case can be hard to spot. If this test case fails but no error occurs, check the contents of the database to determine whether any erroneous `NULL` or blank values made it into the database. You may need to add check constraints to your database tables to guard against this possibility. See Chapter 8 for details on check constraints.

✦ **Attempt to submit a form with letters in a numeric field.** One of the following three things can happen if this test case fails:

   a. If the action template performs its validation logic correctly, the user is gracefully told that he made an error.

   b. If the action template uses `Val()` around the string argument to a `CFQUERY`, a zero is inserted into the database.

   c. If neither of the preceding is true and the database is correctly designed, the database throws a syntax error.

   Always watch carefully for any response that seems out of the ordinary.

✦ **Attempt to put more characters in a field than the database column enables.** If your form fields use the `Maxlength` attribute correctly, this test case never fails. Pay extra attention to text areas because they have no `Maxlength` attribute; use server-side validation for text areas.

✦ **Attempt to enter a number outside a column's range.** Try, for example, to enter ridiculously large or small values into numeric fields to see how your application responds. A well-written application does not throw an error if the user enters an out-of-range number but politely notifies him of his mistake instead.

✦ **If a page expects URL parameters, attempt to modify its URL to pass faulty data.** Try changing the value of an existing parameter or try removing parameters completely. A failure of this type of test case usually results in a ColdFusion error but should instead recover gracefully if a URL parameter doesn't exist or is out of range.

After you make sure that your application handles all possible bad data correctly, you next want to concentrate on problems that can be created by misusing the browser.

Browser woes

Much of your testing has nothing to do with how ColdFusion Server works but rather with how the browser and its user interact with your application. The following sections show you how to account for these browser issues in your testing regiment.

Using the Back button

Anyone who's developed with ColdFusion for any significant amount of time can tell you that the Back button presents a problem. If the user clicks the Back button, he interrupts some part of your application's specially designed process and repeats part of that process. This can be bad news if the process is very rigidly designed.

Many people post messages to various ColdFusion developers' lists asking, "How do I get rid of the Back button?" You can't, so you must learn how to take it into account. No clear-cut list of rules for what to do about the Back button is available — you must first make sure that you are following good coding practices and then just fix Back-button problems if they come up.

That's not to say that no guidelines exist on how to avoid Back-button problems. Following are a couple test cases that you can use:

- ✦ If you are expecting that a client or session variable exists (or doesn't already exist) as you execute a page, use `IsDefined()` to test for the variable's existence and reroute the user if the conditions that you expect are not present.
- ✦ Make sure that variable values coming into a page are appropriate. If you have a ten-page process (such as a wizard), for example, and the value of a variable varies depending on which page just executed, make sure that any page in the process can handle whatever value may come into the page.

The majority of your testing for "Back-button shenanigans" must be on the server: Web pages are typically cached on the client computer, so the two submittals in a Submit-Back-Submit sequence look exactly the same to the action page to which the form is submitted. Instead of trying to directly test for a second-page submission in your action page, test instead for some variable value set by the submission directly before the variable is set, as shown in Listing 7-3.

Listing 7-3: Redirecting the user on a Submit-Back-Submit sequence

```
<cfif IsDefined("Client.formSubmitted")>
    <cflocation url="OtherPage.cfm">
</cfif>
<cfset Client.formSubmitted = "Yes">

<cfif IsDefined("Client.someValue")>
    <cfset Client.someValue = Client.someValue + 1>
<cfelse>
    <cfset Client.someValue = 1>
</cfif>
<cflocation url="OtherPage.cfm">
```

If you use the method in Listing 7-3, `Client.someValue` never gets set higher than `1`. Of course, your action page does substantially more than set the value of a variable, but the principle is the same: Prevent work from being duplicated by doing a server-side check for a second submission.

Using the Refresh button

Watch out for clicking Refresh on a page that performs an action on data, either in memory or in the database. If you don't redirect the user away from an action page after the action has finished, then clicking Refresh will run the action a second time. This will most likely cause you problems, such as duplicate records being inserted into your database.

Remember from Chapter 2 that all action pages use CFLOCATION to redirect the user away from the action page, so if the user clicks Refresh, the action page doesn't re-update the database. If your application must not redirect the user away from an action page, you can use Listing 7-4 to disregard the action-page code on a Refresh.

Listing 7-4: Disregarding action-page code on a Refresh

```
<cfparam name="Client.someValue" default="1">
<cfif NOT IsDefined("Client.formSubmitted")>
    <!--- Action page code goes here: --->
    <cfset Client.someValue = Client.someValue + 1>
</cfif>
<cfset Client.formSubmitted = "Yes">
```

Also test how Refresh affects form pages. Sometimes forms are prepopulated according to code that runs at the beginning of the form template, and this code may be affected by a Refresh.

Browser settings

If your application breaks, *don't blame the browser settings!* This sort of thing happens often: You test your code, find a problem, make a change, and it still doesn't work. You spend an hour tracking the problem down, and then you discover that you never refreshed the form, or you find out that you needed to delete your temporary Internet files.

Automatically blaming the browser settings for your problem is a waste of time. Most users have no idea what their browser settings are, let alone how to change them. So if you require a specific browser setting so that a user can use your site, you are setting your application up for a big failure.

Of course, in some cases, you can require the user to turn on certain settings. If your site requires JavaScript, expecting the user to have JavaScript turned on in his browser is reasonable (especially because JavaScript is on by default), but you cannot *assume* that it is turned on; you must still test your application with JavaScript turned off. The same is true for testing both with cookies enabled and cookies disabled.

You can never, under any circumstance, however, require the user to change his cache setting. By the same token, you cannot assume the user hasn't changed his browser cache setting to a different behavior. In essence, you must thoroughly test your application under all possible browser settings to ensure that it doesn't fail under any circumstances.

Empty-nest testing

During development, you typically create test data that lingers in your database and never gets deleted, and your code sometimes assumes the presence of this "comfort" data. *Empty-nest testing* tests your application against an exact copy of your database with all data removed, which brings out errors you don't find during development and shows where your application incorrectly relies on hard-coded data.

During empty nest testing, you of course find that certain database records are necessary, such as a user record describing the master administrative user and the records describing the roles that he requires to function, but the majority of your application should work correctly with no data in your database.

You should ask yourself a few questions during this process to determine whether your application passes the test — among them, the following:

✦ **Does ColdFusion throw an error?** No excuse is possible for your site to throw an error during empty nest testing. If your application requires data, test for the data before attempting to use it and notify the user if he cannot proceed until such data is created.

✦ **Is the user ever left with nowhere to go?** Many data-driven sites have their navigation based on database records. Always make sure that the user can take his next step, even if it's to create missing data.

✦ **Is the user ever confused?** If your application displays a listing of the data in the database and no data is there to list, tell the user so that he's not confused and wondering what happened to the data or when it may appear. (*Dang,* that server sure is awfully slow . . .)

These three questions are appropriate to all forms of testing, but these issues come up more frequently during empty-nest testing than at any other time.

Regression testing

Regression testing, which determines whether fixes or changes to software introduce new errors, is the most aggravating part of the testing process. You test your application, find an error, and fix it. But now you must test the entire application all over again!

Web applications often involve many interconnected layers of functionality. Something that changes in one process often has far-reaching implications that may not be readily apparent. It's like the age-old "butterfly paradox," in which a butterfly flapping its wings in China *shouldn't* have any effect on a hurricane in the Atlantic Ocean, but it *could.*

That's not to say that you should fully regression test as soon as you make the slightest fix to part of your application. Test your application, fixing problems as they come up. After you are finished, run all the way through your test cases again.

Load testing

Load testing verifies how your application behaves (or misbehaves) under a heavy multi-user load. Not only is load testing the only way to predict how well your application will fare during peak use hours, it also often uncovers functional problems you wouldn't otherwise find.

Your application works well if you're the only person using it, and it also works well if you perform what we like to call *MBJJ testing* (Me, Billy, and Jimmy Joe), which some people sadly mistake for multi-user testing. (It isn't — not even a little bit.)

But does your application work well if 100 users are hitting your site at the same moment? How about just five *truly* simultaneous users? Only formal *load testing* can answer these questions.

You need production-scale test data to run a proper load test. If the database supporting your ColdFusion application will eventually contain 650,000 customers, 1 million sales orders, 6 million order items, and so on, then a load test against a data set any smaller than that would be meaningless because it would not truly simulate actual production conditions. You can quickly and easily generate accurate test data by using DataFactory from Quest Software (a trial version is included on the companion CD-ROM).

You will, of course, also need a commercial-grade load-testing tool—our favorite load-testing tool is e-TEST Suite from Empirix—and the experience to use it. If you don't have the time, budget, or experience to correctly load-test your application, you can always hire an outside firm such as ProductivityEnhancement.com to test it for you (shameless plug), but rest assured that a problem caused by 100 users logged-in at the same time can also rear its ugly head with just two *truly* simultaneous users that make requests at the exact same nanosecond from different worker threads.

Ever wonder why your application seems to temporarily hang sometimes, or why using a Session variable throws an error, or why your users are forcibly logged out for no apparent reason? Formal load-testing uncovers problems that you never find otherwise, because the code and database that cause those problems are *technically* okay on paper; they just aren't correctly engineered together as a unit for a multi-user environment. If your application and database pass a proper regimen of realistic load tests, then most likely they are properly engineered.

Debugging Your Code

During the testing process, you may throw errors that don't have readily apparent causes. If simply examining your code doesn't uncover the causes of those errors, you must employ a few special techniques to debug your code, as the following sections describe.

Debug settings

The simplest debugging involves setting certain debugging options within ColdFusion Administrator. To enable these options, log in to ColdFusion Administrator and select the Enable Debugging check box in the Debugging Settings section. Then select the options that you need, as the following list describes:

- **Report Execution Times:** This option is useful if your application takes an unusually long time to execute. Unfortunately, turning on debugging in the first place can sometimes increase execution time. If a request that normally takes only a few milliseconds to execute suddenly takes much more time than normal with debugging on, don't be alarmed; if your request reverts to its normal execution time with this option turned off, your code is okay.
- **Database Activity:** This option shows you all the query and stored procedure calls that ran during a request. Turn on this option if you have dynamically generated SQL statements in a `CFQUERY` and you want to see the actual SQL statement sent to the database.
- **Variables:** Turn on this option to see all the `Form`, `URL`, and `CGI` variables sent into a request. You can list other variable types as well.

Using CFDUMP

CFDUMP is a valuable debugging tool. By using CFDUMP, you get a visualization of any variable of any type, so it really comes in handy for debugging problems involving structures, arrays, and other complex objects.

Say, for example, that you have the following query:

```
<cfquery name="GetEmployees"
         datasource="#Request.MainDSN#">
SELECT
    SSN,
    FirstName,
    LastName,
    Salary
FROM
    Employee
ORDER BY SSN
</cfquery>
```

You must ensure that this query returns the correct data before you attempt to use that data elsewhere in your application. To inspect the entire result set, call CFDUMP as follows:

```
<cfdump var="#GetEmployees#">
```

The output is as shown in Figure 7-1.

query				
	FIRSTNAME	LASTNAME	SALARY	SSN
1	David	Churvis	72000	123-45-6789
2	Skip	Hartley	183000	124-20-3005
3	John	Doe	92300	183-25-3005
4	Elton	Goldfarb	83750	832-04-3958
5	Mabel	Johnson	29000	853-40-1954
6	Penny	Johnson	29000	853-40-1955
7	Mary Sue	Johnson	14000	853-72-0192
8	Harold	Bloomstead	129000	931-15-3512

Figure 7-1: CFDUMP used to output the result of a CFQUERY call.

Sometimes you want to stop a page as soon as you call CFDUMP so that you can immediately see the results of a particular query and not go any further in your code until you're sure that the query result is correct. To stop page execution after the CFDUMP call, use the CFABORT tag as follows:

```
<cfdump var="#GetEmployees#">
<cfabort>
```

The integrated debugger

One of HomeSite+'s coolest features would be its integrated debugger . . . if you could get it to work reliably. Unfortunately at the time of this writing, the integrated debugger lingers somewhere between unreliable and impossible to use.

We look forward to Macromedia's much anticipated fix for the integrated debugger, which would enable you to step through the lines of your ColdFusion code as they happen, inspect the contents of variables, and determine where problems exist in your ColdFusion application. One can only hope. . . .

Summary

Testing is the part of development that every developer hates. Everyone likes to think that his code is perfect, but as you've seen in this chapter, many errors can creep in without your realizing it. Even if you do a good job coding your application, load testing can still uncover serious multi-user problems. No matter how well you code an application, testing almost always discovers errors in your code or in its underlying engineering, and if you don't find your errors, some user is sure to.

In this chapter, you learn how to unit-test your code by using test harnesses, why browser settings must never affect your application design, how to test your application against bad data, and some useful techniques for debugging. Later on, in Chapter 42, you learn even more about perfecting your code, but the following chapter covers another crucial topic: *databases!*

Using ColdFusion MX with Databases

P A R T

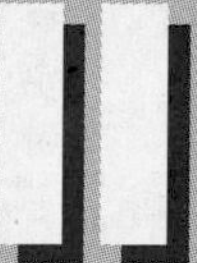

✦ ✦ ✦ ✦

In This Part

✦ ✦ ✦ ✦

Database Design Issues

In This Chapter

Understanding relational-database design

Determining which type of relationship is the right one to use

Enforcing referential integrity

Understanding Normalization and denormalization

Refining your design by using defaults and check constraints

Understanding and using indexes

Most database developers learn by the seat of their pants and, as a result, never learn the underlying concepts necessary to design a truly robust, scalable database that can support an entire enterprise. This chapter gets you started down the right path toward true database *engineering* and can help you replace misconceptions and bad habits with solid engineering concepts and design techniques. If you diligently follow the lessons in this chapter, your databases — and the ColdFusion applications supporting them — are sure to see an immediate and marked increase in performance, maintainability, and adaptability.

We don't cover any history about who invented what and why or when, because that's not going to make a difference to your database or the ColdFusion applications that it supports. Instead, we dive right in and show you how to create a correct relational database design to support your ColdFusion applications.

Relational Database Basics

If you haven't already read Chapter 5, please take a few minutes to go back and read it now. Even if you're an old salt at SQL, that chapter presents some new ways of visualizing how SQL works with relational databases that can help you better understand this chapter in much more depth.

What is a "relational database?"

If you needed to define a relational database in a single phrase, you could say that it involves "a place for everything, and everything in its place." *Everything*, in this case, is the collection of *entities*, or real-world objects, that your application uses and manipulates, and *places* are the database tables that store them.

Entities

If you begin your database-engineering project by considering real-world objects for what they are and how they behave throughout their life cycles, you gain a better insight into the details of how your software must work. The same cannot be said if you are simultaneously considering table definitions, data types, and more as you try to conceptualize your database. Figure 8-1 is a top-level view of the entities that we use in the database model in this chapter.

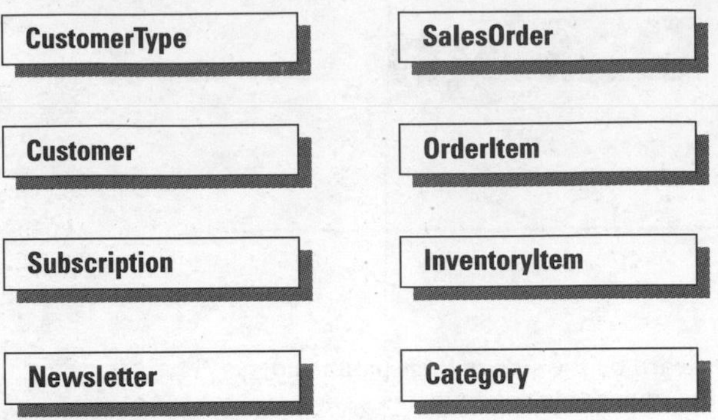

Figure 8-1: Concentrate first on defining which entities are used by your business processes.

Attributes

The model of an entity consists of the name of that entity, the *attributes* that describe it, and other behaviors that we discuss. The model defines how each of those entities is structured — like a mold from which multiple objects of that type can be manufactured. Figure 8-2 shows this data model expanded to display the attributes of each entity.

Keys

Each individual "object" is considered an *instance* of that entity. But after you manufacture all these similarly structured instances, how do you tell one from the other? The same way that you do any individual thing in nature: by using one or more *key* attributes that best describe it.

Each instance of an entity must be uniquely identified by a *primary key*, without which that instance cannot be referenced or operated on. This primary key value is what your software uses to retrieve, update, and delete this instance. Figure 8-3 further expands the data model by displaying above the dividing line those attributes that serve as keys for the entities that they describe.

This is what we've done:

✦ SalesOrder, InventoryItem, and OrderItem all have attributes that initially seem like natural choices for keys, so we choose them.

✦ None of the Customer entity's attributes can be used to uniquely describe each customer instance, so we add a CustomerNumber attribute to act as its key.

✦ The Category, Newsletter, and CustomerType entities have only single attributes that describe them, so we add an attribute to act as the key for each of these entities.

✦ We didn't add a key attribute to the Subscription entity because it is a special case, in that it is identified not by a value of its own, but through its relationships with other entities, as you will see.

Relationships

To refine our discussion of keys, we need to consider the *relationships* between the entities in our diagram. When we created these entities, we already had a basic idea of how they related to one another. For instance:

- A Customer is a specific CustomerType,
- A SalesOrder has multiple OrderItems,
- A SalesOrder can be for a specific Customer, or it may be for a general sale, and
- A Customer may have Subscriptions to one or more Newsletters.

Different types of relationships are possible, as you see later on in the section "Types of relationships," but all of them work through the same basic mechanism: by sharing key values between entities.

If you declare a relationship between two entities, you contribute — or *migrate* — a copy of the primary key from one entity to its related entity. The entity that contributes a copy of its primary key is known as the *parent entity*, and the entity to which this key is migrated is known as the *child entity*. The copy of the primary key that is migrated to the child entity, as shown in Figure 8-4, it is known as a *foreign key* in the child entity.

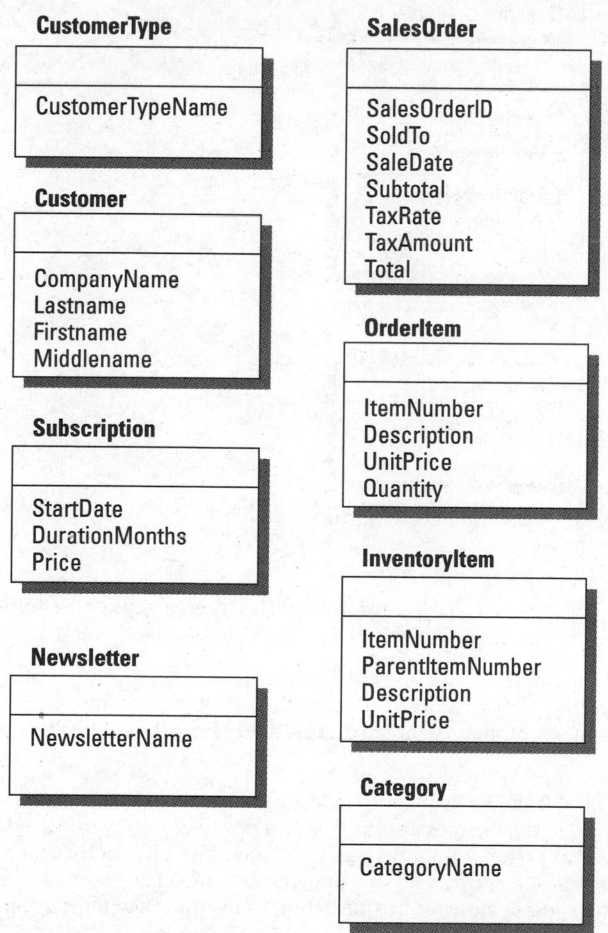

Figure 8-2: Add to each entity the attributes that describe it.

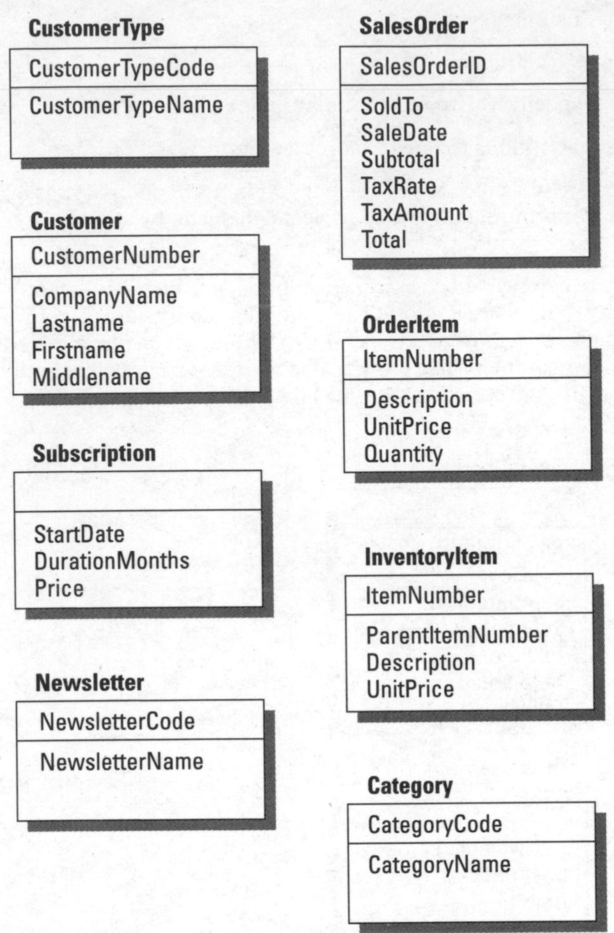

Figure 8-3: An entity's primary key is the attribute or group of attributes that uniquely identifies it.

Notice how Subscription now has a primary key consisting of the foreign keys contributed from its relationships with the Customer and Newsletter entities? Keep this in mind as we discuss relationship types a little later in this chapter.

What you see in this figure is a *Logical Data Model* (or *LDM*) that, as its name suggests, shows how the logical entities in your database are structured and how they relate to one another.

Notice how we developed the LDM from the ground up in layers. We started by considering only which entities were involved in the business processes and not how they were structured. This distinction may seem trivial at first, but it forces you to concentrate on exactly which entities your database manipulates and stores, and this may not be obvious on some larger database models because of the sheer number of business processes that they must support.

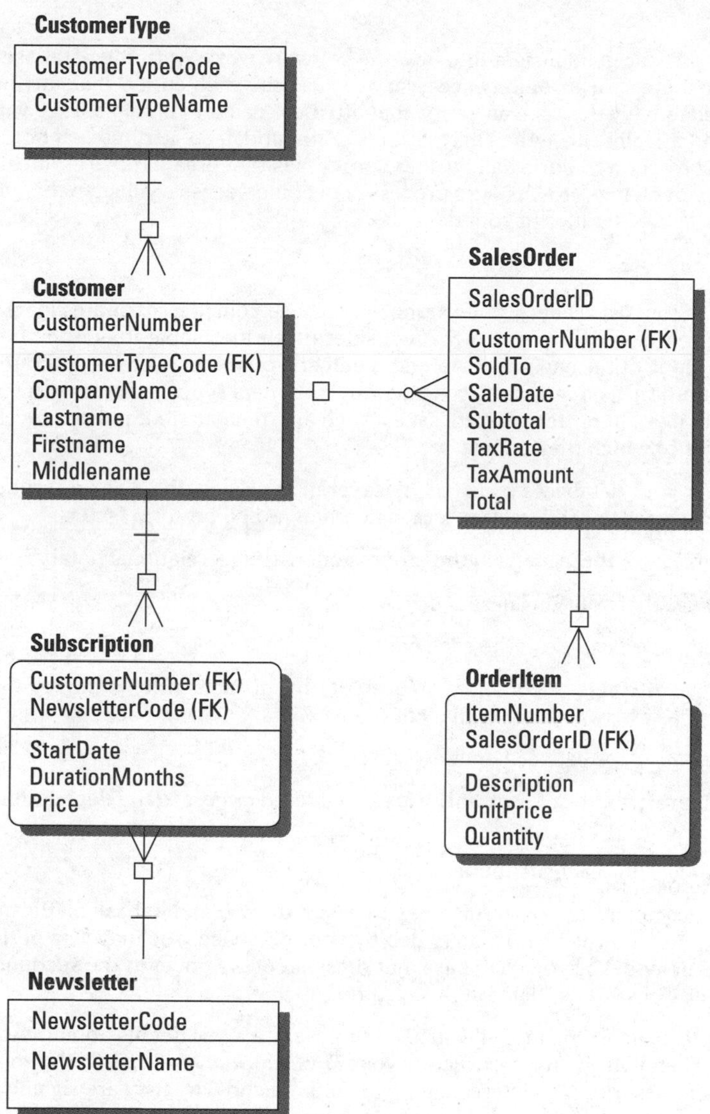

Figure 8-4: A relationship migrates a copy of the parent's primary key to the child entity as its foreign key.

Next, we layered in the attributes that describe each of these entities and then decided which attributes should be used as their keys. From there, we declared relationships between the entities so that we could visualize the interaction between them. We get a better feel for how the software must accommodate these entities once relationships are declared, and we start to think forward to the user interface for creating and editing them.

Critical values

Something else that gives us good insight into how the software works with the database is identifying which attributes are absolutely necessary to describe each entity. If an attribute must be present to effectively describe an entity, that attribute cannot contain a `NULL` value. NULL values have wider significance than may first come to mind; if an attribute cannot be `NULL`, its value must be acquired during all business processes that create those entities. You may find that significant changes to business processes become necessary just so that you can create correctly defined entities in your database.

Data types

It may seem backward to most readers, but waiting until last to consider attributes' data types makes perfect sense. In the same way that considering entities separately from their structure in the beginning of the engineering process helped you to concentrate without distraction, waiting until the last minute to consider attribute data types prevents you from being distracted from more important design issues, such as which attributes are critical to describing the entities to which they belong.

If you always engineer your databases by using this layered approach, the Web applications that they support are easier to code, require less maintenance, and perform faster.

To recap, you want to follow these steps in the process of creating a relational database:

1. Define the *entities* that your business processes use.
2. Determine which *attributes* describe each entity.
3. Determine which attribute or combination of attributes of each entity is the *key* that uniquely identifies every *instance* of that entity.
4. Declare the *relationships* between entities.
5. Determine which attributes of each entity are considered *critical* to the description of that entity.
6. Define the *data type* for each attribute.

The preceding six steps are always performed regardless of the target database platform (SQL Server, Oracle, etc.) on which you plan to deploy your database. You may also perform two additional steps in modeling your database, but these steps we cover in the sections "Defaults" and "Check Constraints," later in this chapter.

After you have a basic, logical data model, you need to describe a few details about how its relationships work. Then you go about extracting your *Physical Data Model*, or *PDM*, from the logical data model and describe the differences between them and why they are significant. The following sections detail how to go about these processes.

Describing relationships

Relationships are described by four attributes: cardinality, identification, optionality, and degree. These attributes are combined to create specific relationship types, as you will see in the section "Types of relationships."

Cardinality

Cardinality describes the quantitative dimension of the relationship as viewed from the parent table's perspective. The relationship between the CustomerType and Customer tables, for example, is a *one-to-many* relationship, meaning that from the standpoint of the CustomerType parent table, *one* CustomerType row can be related to *many* Customer rows.

Figure 8-5 shows the "crows foot" notation typically used to describe a one-to-many relationship. The end of the relationship line with many lines (the "crows foot") is connected to the "many" table, and the other end is connected to the "one" table. The zero above the crows foot denotes that there may also be zero children related to the parent, and the numeral one crossing the other end of the relationship line denotes that there must be one parent related to each child. To be perfectly accurate, this is known as a "one to zero or more" relationship.

By contrast, the relationship between the InventoryItem and Category entities is a *nonspecific relationship* (commonly referred to as a *many-to-many relationship)*, because you have no specific rules regarding the relationship between these two entities. You may have one inventory item that is related to multiple categories, a category with no related inventory items, or an inventory item with no category related to it at all.

The notation used in Figure 8-6 uses the same symbols and terminology used in Figure 8-5, but this time both tables are connected by "zero or more" symbols. This makes perfect sense when you consider the previous description: "You may have one inventory item that is related to multiple categories, a category with no related inventory items, or an inventory item with no category related to it at all."

Notice in Figure 8-6 that nonspecific relationships do not contribute foreign keys between tables. You see why later on in the section "Creating your physical data model" as you generate a physical data model from this logical data model.

One-to-one relationships are also possible, where one row in the parent table is related to one and only one row in the child table. One-to-one relationships are less common than one-to-many and many-to-many relationships and can manifest themselves in more than one way in the physical data model. The related table might be implemented through an identifying relationship whose migrated foreign key also acts as the complete primary key of the inheriting table, or the related table may even be eliminated entirely in favor of migrating its attributes to the other table in the relationship. One-to-one relationships are an advanced design topic that is beyond the scope of this book.

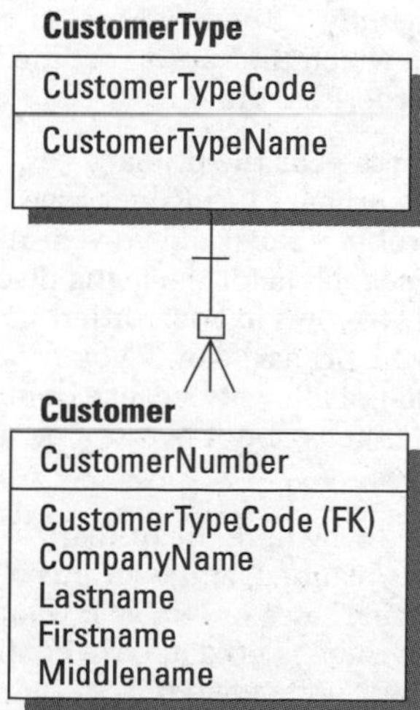

Figure 8-5: A typical one-to-many relationship.

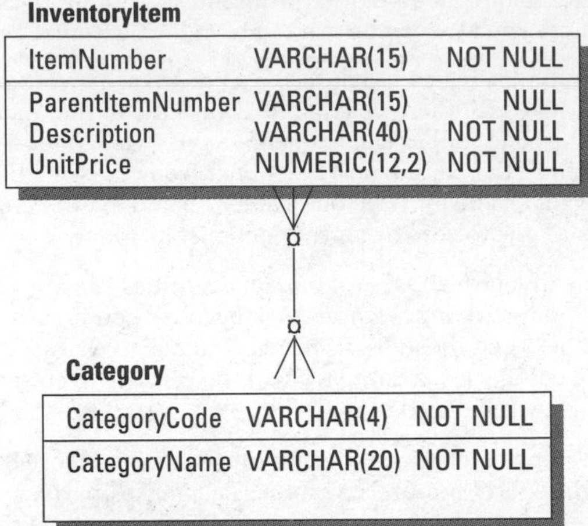

Figure 8-6: A nonspecific relationship, sometimes referred to as a "many-to-many" relationship.

Identification

Identification describes how the relationship contributes to the capability of each row in the child table to be uniquely *identified* among all other rows in the child table. Take, for example, the one-to-many relationship between CustomerType and Customer. Notice the foreign key `Customer.CustomerTypeCode` contributed by the relationship between the two tables? This foreign key doesn't help to identify one row in the Customer table from any other row in the Customer table; the `CustomerNumber` value alone uniquely identifies each row in the Customer table without needing any help from any other column in the Customer table. Because this relationship doesn't contribute anything to the uniqueness of rows in the Customer (child) table, it is considered a *nonidentifying relationship*.

Now consider the relationship between the SalesOrder and OrderItem tables. Every row in the OrderItem table requires two pieces of data to uniquely identify it: the ItemNumber of the item being sold and the SalesOrderID of the sales order on which the sale is recorded. Together, these two values make up the primary key for the OrderItem table.

If you don't use the combination of `SalesOrderID` and `ItemNumber` as the primary key, business would be a disaster, as shown in Figure 8-7 where the primary key values are boldfaced. Say that you sell three different toys: flying discs, rubber balls, and yo-yos. Your first sales order is for two yo-yos and a rubber ball, and your second is for ten flying discs. You cannot have a third sales order, because you now have three rows in your OrderItem table, each one containing a unique value for `ItemNumber` as the primary key. If you try to add another yoyo, rubber ball, or flying disc, the database will not allow it because doing so would enable duplicate primary key values. Clearly, `ItemNumber` cannot by itself be the primary key for the OrderItem table.

If we add `SalesOrderID` to the primary key, as shown in Figure 8-8 where the primary key values now include the `SalesOrderID`, everything can work as planned, and your business can sell as many flying discs, rubber balls, and yo-yos on as many sales orders as it wants. When you sell another two dozen yoyos on a later sales order, there is no database conflict because the primary key consists of *the combination* of the `ItemNumber` and the `SalesOrderID`.

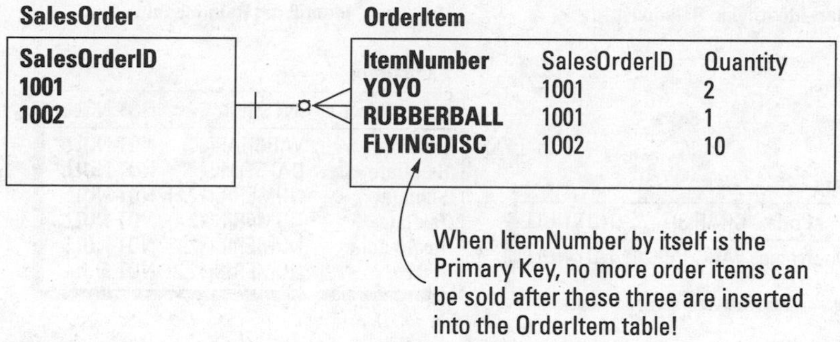

Figure 8-7: The problem of an incorrectly defined primary key.

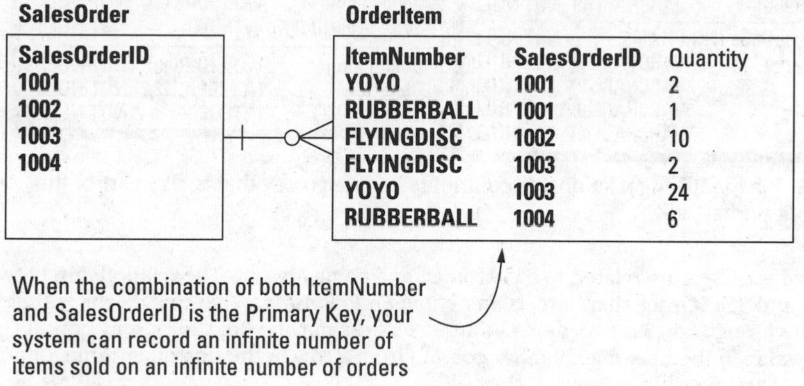

Figure 8-8: The solution is provided by an identifying relationship.

Because the relationship between the SalesOrder and OrderItem tables contributed something (the foreign key `OrderItem.SalesOrderID`) that is used to uniquely *identify* each row in the OrderItem table, it is considered an *identifying relationship*, as shown in Figure 8-9. In other words, if a foreign key in a table is also part of the primary key for that same table, the relationship that contributed the foreign key is an identifying relationship.

Optionality

Optionality describes whether a relationship *must* exist between *all* rows in the child table and one or more rows in the parent table. Take, for example, the Customer and SalesOrder entities and the relationship between them, as shown in Figure 8-10. Say that you use a common database to store sales transactions from both your physical storefront and your Web site. Storefront sales orders are for walk-in sales, for which you don't need to gather customer information, but online sales are handled differently. The user enters the information necessary to ship his online order during the checkout process. If the purchaser is new to your Web site, you want to automatically create a customer record for him and then relate the sales order to this newly created customer. If the purchaser is a returning customer who has logged in, you want to retrieve his customer record and automatically fill his customer information in the entry form that appears during the checkout process.

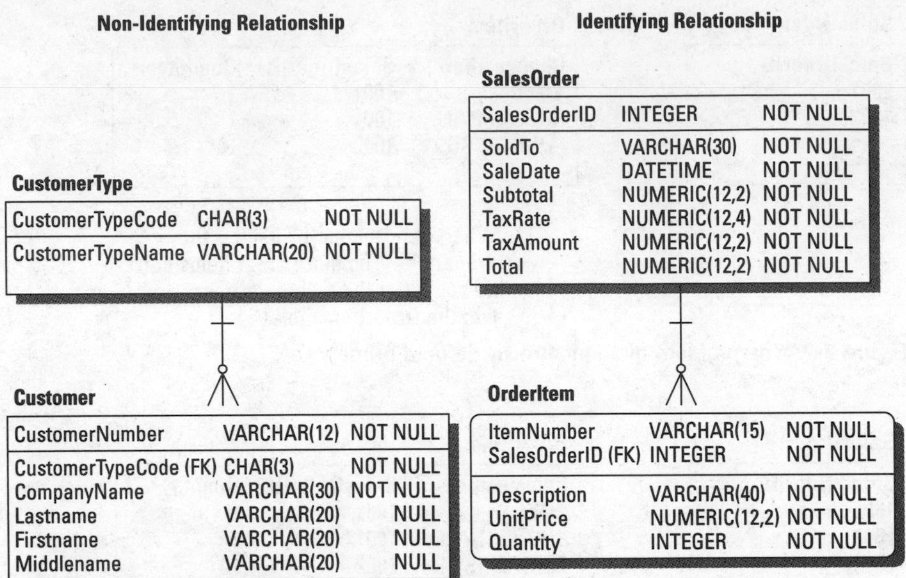

Figure 8-9: An identifying relationship contributes a foreign key that is also part of the child entity's primary key.

So some sales orders are related to a customer, and some are not. The relationship between Customer and SalesOrder, therefore, is an *optional relationship*. What this means is that the value of the foreign key `SalesOrder.CustomerNumber` may be `NULL`, or it may contain a matching value in the CustomerNumber column from a row in the Customer table, but no other values are possible.

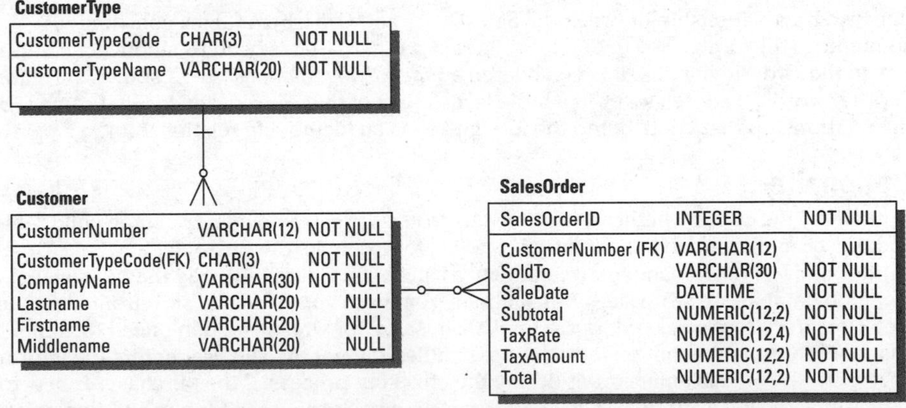

Figure 8-10: By allowing `NULL` values in the foreign key, an optional relationship enables instances of the child entity to either have related parent instances or not have them at all.

The relationship between the CustomerType and Customer tables is a different story, as shown in Figure 8-11. Every customer *must* be of a specific customer type, so every value in `Customer.CustomerTypeCode` *must* match an existing value in `CustomerType.CustomerTypeCode`. The relationship between the CustomerType and Customer tables, therefore, is a *mandatory relationship*. For this reason, the value of `Customer.CustomerTypeCode` cannot be `NULL`.

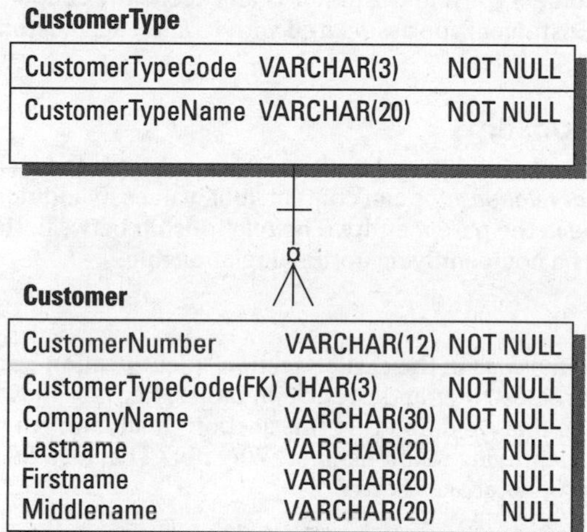

Figure 8-11: In a mandatory relationship, every child instance must have a parent instance to which it is related.

Contrast and compare the Nullability of the foreign-key columns in the Customer and SalesOrder tables. If a foreign key is Nullable, the relationship that contributed it is an optional relationship. If a foreign key disallows NULL values, the relationship that contributed it is a mandatory relationship

Degree

Finally, degree describes whether the relationship is between two tables, which is most common, or between a table and itself. Figure 8-12 illustrates the difference. A relationship between two tables is known as a *binary relationship*, because it relates two elements. The majority of relationships in your databases are binary relationships. A *unary relationship* relates a table to itself to represent a hierarchy, such as an inventory item that is itself composed of other inventory items. Unary relationships are also known as both *recursive relationships* and *reflexive relationships*.

Types of Relationships

The four attributes of a relationship can be combined to produce specific types of relationships. The majority of your database relationships will be one of the following four types:

- ✦ Nonidentifying mandatory relationships.
- ✦ Nonidentifying optional relationships

✦ Identifying relationships

✦ Nonspecific relationships

Nonidentifying mandatory relationships

This relationship is by far the most common that you use. *Nonidentifying mandatory relationships* are used whenever a child must have one and only one parent to which it is related. The relationship between CustomerType and Customer is an excellent example, because every Customer must have a CustomerType associated with it, and each customer may be of only one type.

Non-identifying optional relationships

The only difference between this type of relationship and its mandatory cousin is the fact that the foreign key in *non-identifying optional relationships* can contain NULL values in addition to values that match the primary key value in the parent entity. The relationship between the Customer and SalesOrder tables typifies a nonidentifying optional relationship.

Identifying relationships

We've already discussed *identifying relationships* in the earlier section "Identification"; an example is the relationship between the SalesOrder and OrderItem tables. Perhaps, however, illustrating a point here may help. Notice that we didn't title this section "Mandatory identifying relationships" or "Optional identifying relationships." Why not? The answer may help you understand the general nature of databases better.

A foreign key can be NULL if it is contributed by an optional relationship, but no part of any primary key can *ever* be NULL under any circumstances whatsoever. Because an identifying relationship makes the foreign key also a part of the primary key, that foreign key can never be NULL. If a foreign key cannot be NULL, it must be contributed by a mandatory relationship. In other words, all identifying relationships are mandatory.

Nonspecific relationships

We've also discussed *nonspecific relationships* in the earlier section "Cardinality," but another explanation of why no *mandatory* or *optional* is attached to the name of this relationship type is appropriate here.

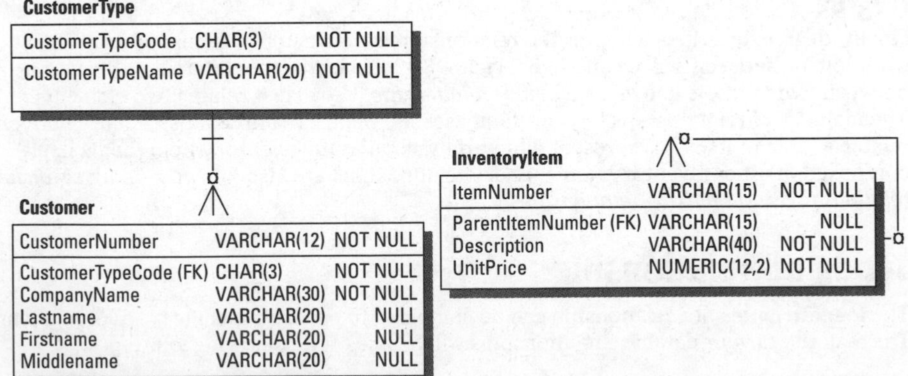

Figure 8-12: CustomerType-Customer is a binary relationship; InventoryItem-InventoryItem is a unary relationship.

Look at Figure 8-6 and notice that the relationship between the InventoryItem and Category entities doesn't contribute any foreign keys. This lack of keys means that we have *neither* a mandatory *nor* an optional relationship — in other words, the relationship is *nonspecific* in its optionality.

Furthermore, because you may have one inventory item that is related to multiple categories, a category with no related inventory items, or an inventory item with no category related to it at all, the cardinality of this relationship is also nonspecific. And because no foreign keys are present to either include or not include in a primary key, the identification of the relationship is nonspecific, too.

Because *nonspecific* refers not only to the cardinality of the relationship, but also to the identification and optionality referring to this relationship as a *nonspecific relationship* is more correct than calling it a *many-to-many relationship*, as it is most often referred to.

When to not create a relationship between tables

Having a solid understanding of database relationships is just as important as knowing when not to create them. Just because you *can* relate two entities doesn't mean that you should.

Take, for example, the InventoryItem and OrderItem entities in Figure 8-3. To create an OrderItem, an application looks up the value of ItemNumber in InventoryItem, copies its `Description` and `UnitPrice` values into memory, and then creates an OrderItem by using these values (along with the `ItemNumber` and `SalesOrderID` values, of course). This process is the correct way to create an OrderItem.

Declaring a relationship between the InventoryItem and OrderItem tables, as shown in Figure 8-13, is tempting, yet incorrect.

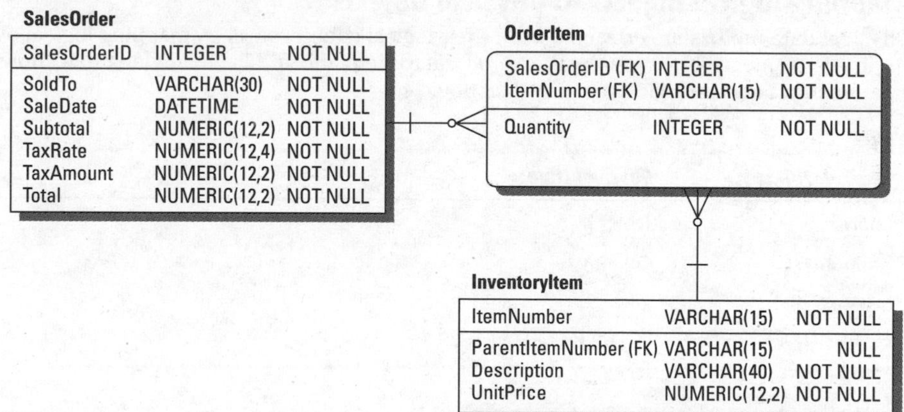

Figure 8-13: This relationship does not persevere over time, so it is an incorrect relationship and, therefore, should not be created.

Why is this relationship an incorrect one? Because a correct relationship perseveres over time, and this one doesn't. The sale of an OrderItem is a legal transaction that occurs at a specific point in time and, as such, must be stored in the database by using the specific values that described the transaction at that point in time; these values must never change because of outside events.

But eventually, `InventoryItem.UnitPrice` does change because of outside influences such as inflation, changes in cost, and so on, and after it does, the relationship between InventoryItem and OrderItem can serve only to corrupt the integrity of the transaction stored in the database.

Imagine recording a sale in the tables shown in Figure 8-13 and then running a sales report on `OrderItem.Quantity` xx `InventoryItem.UnitPrice`. One week later, the prices of inventory items change, and the same sales report is run again — but this time, the results are all incorrect because they no longer report on the facts of the sale at the moment in time that the sale was made. Instead, the report shows the current unit price for inventory items that were sold some time in the past at a different price, so this information is of no value at all.

Always ask yourself before you declare a relationship in your database whether facts stored in the resulting data structure are certain to persevere over time or whether, at some point, some future set of conditions may make the relationship represent nonfactual data. Create a relationship between tables only if you're certain it is permanent under all possible conditions. Otherwise, copy values between tables so that they preserve their values at that time.

Creating your physical data model

A database exists as a logical data model only until it is deployed on a specific database platform. Although all relational database platforms are basically similar, every database platform has its distinct capabilities and restrictions. So your database's physical model on Microsoft SQL Server is at least somewhat different from its physical model on Oracle 9i. In other words, a database has only one logical model and one physical model for every database platform on which it is deployed.

Mapping logical objects to physical objects

Physical data models are extracted from their logical counterparts by mapping logical objects to physical objects supported by the target database platform. The following table shows the relationship between logical and physical objects:

Logical Object	***Physical Object***
Entity	Table
Attribute	Column
Instance	Row
Relationship	Shared Key Pair

In many cases, your physical data model almost mirrors your logical data model because entities typically map directly to the tables that store them. Exceptions to this rule are logical data models that contain nonspecific relationships and entity subtypes. Although entity subtypes are an advanced topic, beyond the scope of this book, we do have a nonspecific relationship in Figure 8-14 that must be resolved into a physical database structure.

Remember that the physical mechanism used to relate a child to its parent is the sharing of key values: The child's foreign key matches the parent's primary key. A nonspecific relationship doesn't migrate keys, so something must change between the structure of the logical data model and the physical data model extracted from it. To store these shared keys you must create a separate table — a table with no *entity* counterpart — as shown in Figure 8-14.

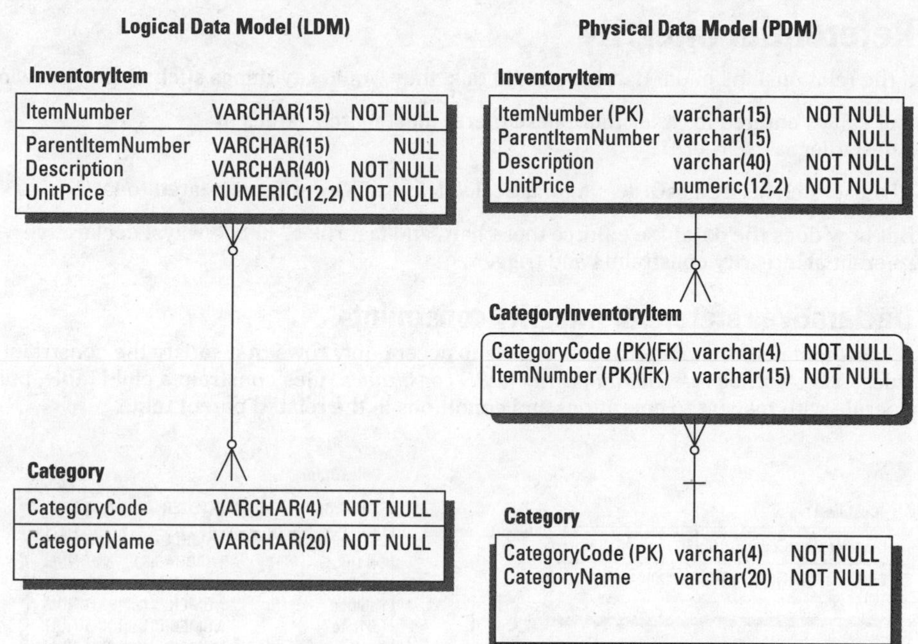

Figure 8-14: Comparison of the logical and physical models of a nonspecific relationship.

Now you can represent related categories and inventory items simply by storing their shared keys in the newly created CategoryInventoryItem table. In other words, for every category to which a particular inventory item belongs, you create a row in the CategoryInventoryItem table that contains foreign keys to both that InventoryItem row and the related Category row. So if that inventory item is related to three categories, three rows in the CategoryInventoryItem table all contain the same foreign key to that InventoryItem row, but each row contains a different foreign key—one for each related Category row.

No real-world entity is called a *CategoryInventoryItem*; this table exists in the physical realm only to store the keys shared by the Category and InventoryItem entities. Therefore, CategoryInventoryItem is a physical table, but it has no corresponding logical entity.

Mapping data types

Data types must also be mapped between the logical and physical data models. The data types that you specify for the attributes in your logical data model may not be directly supported in the target database platform, so each must be mapped to its closest possible supported type. The `Datetime` data type, for example, is directly supported by SQL Server 2000 but not by Oracle 9i, which maps `Datetime` to the `DATE` data type.

Figure 8-15 shows the logical data model for a database, followed by two physical data models extracted from it. The first physical model, shown in Figure 8-16, is targeted to the SQL Server database platform, and the second, shown in Figure 8-17, is targeted to the Oracle 9i database platform. (Notice the data-type mapping differences.)

See also the data description language (DDL) in Listing 8-1 that represents this physical data model.

See also the DDL in Listing 8-2 that represents this physical data model.

Referential integrity

If the relationships in our database could talk, they would say things such as the following:

"All values entered in OrderItem.SalesOrderID must match values in SalesOrder.SalesOrderID."

"If a user deletes a SalesOrder, automatically delete all OrderItems related to it."

But how does the database enforce these hard-and-fast rules? In two ways: declarative referential integrity constraints and triggers.

Declarative referential integrity constraints

A *constraint* restricts or constrains a table to accept only rows that satisfy the constraint's rules. A *declarative referential integrity (DRI) constraint's* rules constrain a child table, but they operate with respect to operations and conditions in the related parent table.

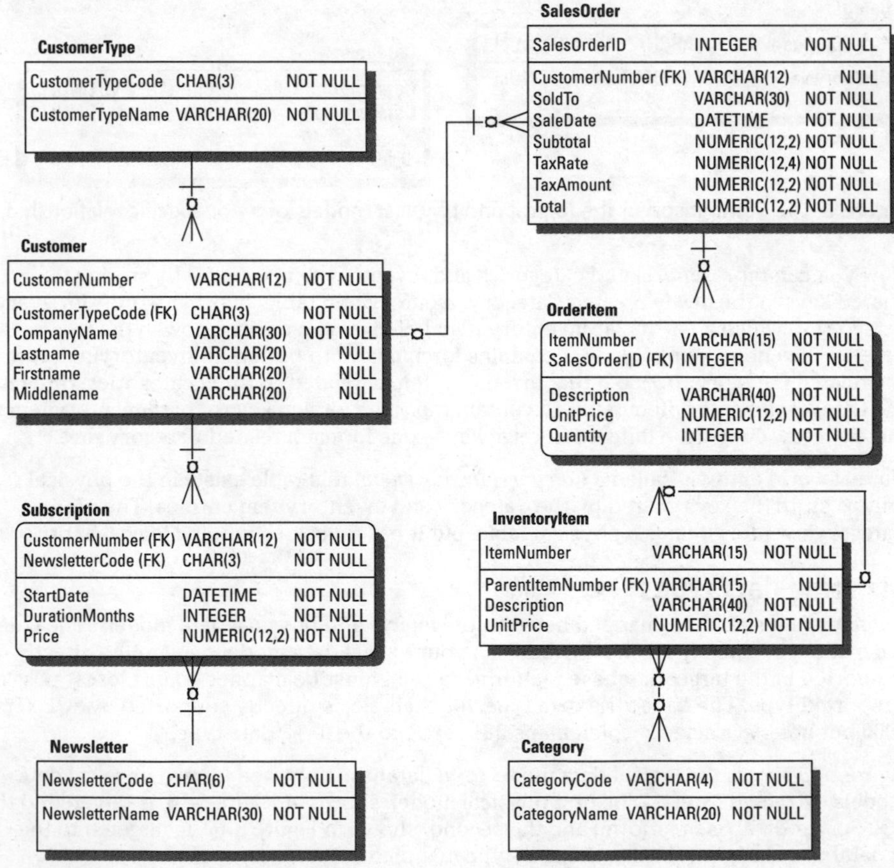

Figure 8-15: The logical model of an example database.

Take, for example, the following statements:

"All values entered in OrderItem.SalesOrderID must match values in SalesOrder.SalesOrderID."

"If a user deletes a SalesOrder, automatically delete all OrderItems related to it."

If you formalize them as a DRI constraint the statements become the following code:

```
ALTER TABLE OrderItem
ADD CONSTRAINT FK__OrderItem_SalesOrder
FOREIGN KEY (SalesOrderID)
REFERENCES SalesOrder(SalesOrderID)
ON DELETE CASCADE
```

Why is this statement called a *declarative referential integrity constraint*? Because it declares the table's referential integrity behavior as part of the table definition itself, as opposed to implementing such behavior as a separate piece of executable computer code.

We now break down this DRI constraint and look at what each phrase means, starting with the following:

```
ALTER TABLE OrderItem
ADD CONSTRAINT FK__OrderItem_SalesOrder
```

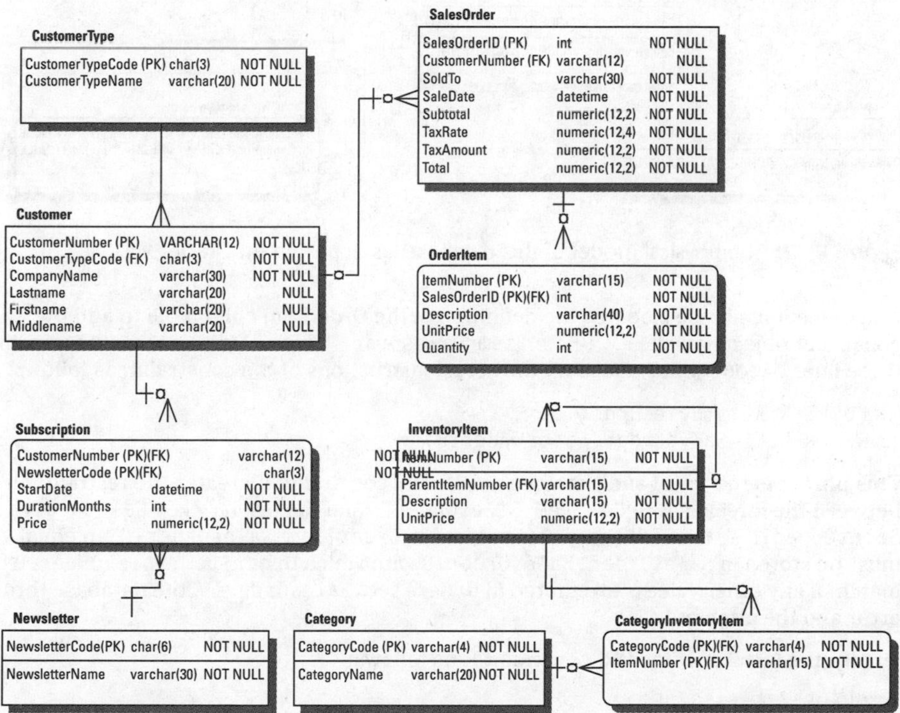

Figure 8-16: The physical model of this database, as deployed on Microsoft SQL Server 2000.

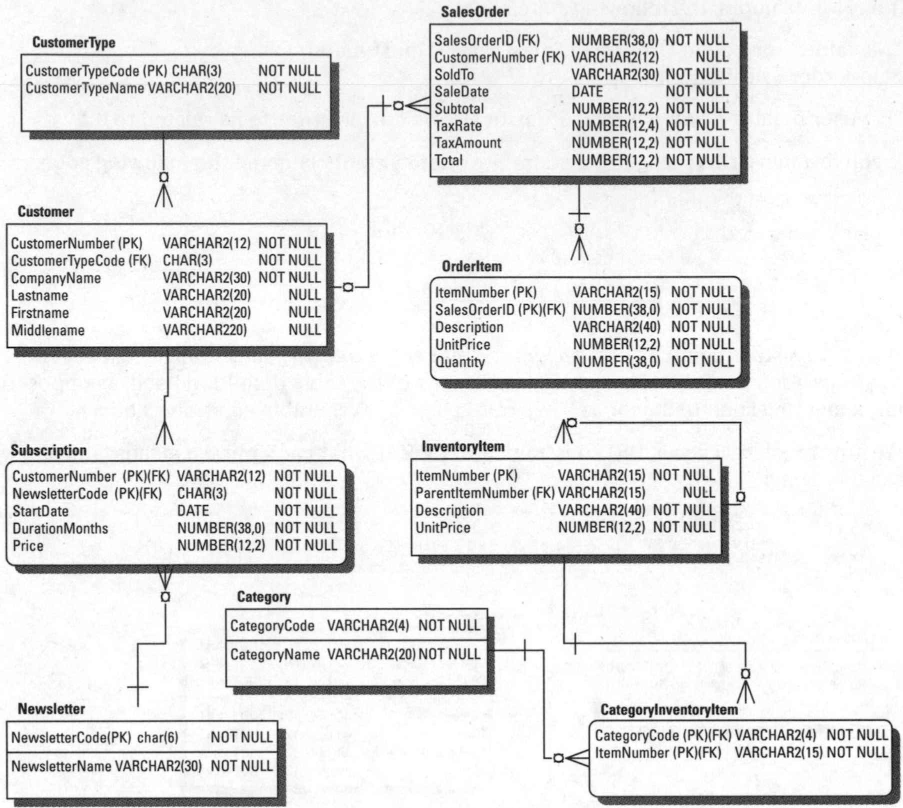

Figure 8-17: The physical model of this database, as deployed on Oracle 9i.

The preceding phrase modifies the definition of the OrderItem child table to add the constraint object named `FK__OrderItem_SalesOrder`. This object contains the remaining three lines of code, which make up the actual instructions of the constraint, as follows:

```
FOREIGN KEY (SalesOrderID)
REFERENCES SalesOrder(SalesOrderID)
```

This phrase is the "meat and potatoes" of the DRI constraint. It creates the restriction between the foreign key `OrderItem.SalesOrderID` and the primary key `SalesOrder.SalesOrderID` so that, for every value stored in `OrderItem.SalesOrderID`, an equal value must be stored in `SalesOrder.SalesOrderID` with which `OrderItem.SalesOrderID` can match. If any other value is attempted in `OrderItem.SalesOrderID`, the database throws an error and the attempt fails.

Finally, the last line of the DRI constraint is as follows:

```
ON DELETE CASCADE
```

This line instructs the database to first delete all OrderItem rows related to a SalesOrder row that is about to be deleted. Without the `ON DELETE CASCADE` clause in this DRI constraint, attempting to delete a SalesOrder row with related OrderItem rows would throw an error, and no changes would be made to either table's contents.

The first four lines of constraint code are standard DRI syntax supported by most database platforms. Some database platforms, such as SQL Server 2000 and Oracle 9i, support the `ON DELETE CASCADE` extension to the basic DRI syntax to facilitate these *cascading deletes*. For database platforms that do not support cascading deletes in DRI constraints, the cascading delete behavior must be implemented by using a separate piece of code that automatically executes whenever a user attempts to delete a SalesOrder row. Such a piece of automatically executing code is called a *trigger*.

Triggers

Although we thoroughly discuss triggers in Chapter 11, we need to cover the basics of what they are and how they work here so that you can contrast and compare them to DRI constraints.

First of all, why are they called *triggers*? The answer is that the execution of one is "triggered" by a database event (`INSERT`, `UPDATE`, or `DELETE`). A trigger is attached to a specific table and is instructed to automatically execute whenever one or more specific database events take place on that table.

You can place just about any SQL code that you want into a trigger, including code that modifies the contents of other tables.

Take, for example, the following clause:

```
ON DELETE CASCADE
```

In the DRI constraint mentioned in the section "Declarative referential integrity constraints." If implemented as a trigger, the preceding clause becomes the following code:

```
CREATE TRIGGER tD_SalesOrder ON SalesOrder
FOR DELETE AS
BEGIN
    DECLARE
        @Rows      int

    SELECT @Rows = @@rowcount
    IF @Rows = 0
        RETURN

    DELETE OrderItem
        FROM OrderItem ch, deleted
        WHERE ch.SalesOrderID = deleted.SalesOrderID
END
```

Now to break down what's happening in this code.

First, start with the trigger header. This header both creates the trigger and attaches it to a specific table and also specifies the event or events that fires it, as follows:

```
CREATE TRIGGER tD_SalesOrder ON SalesOrder
FOR DELETE AS
```

In other words, you're creating a trigger on the SalesOrder table named `tD_SalesOrder`, and you're instructing it to execute every time that a `DELETE` event occurs on the SalesOrder table. So far, so good. Now look at the body of the trigger—the part that actually executes—as follows:

```
BEGIN
    DECLARE
        @Rows       int

    SELECT @Rows = @@rowcount
    IF @Rows = 0
        RETURN
```

You start the code block with `BEGIN` and then immediately declare a local variable of type `Integer` named `@Rows`. This variable holds the count of rows in the SalesOrder table affected by the `DELETE` event. The global variable `@@rowcount` is controlled by the database server; it always contains the count of rows affected in the table most recently modified by the currently executing code, which in this case is the SalesOrder table. So `SELECT @Rows = @@rowcount` places the count of rows deleted from the SalesOrder table into the local variable that you just declared. If the number of rows affected is zero, the trigger code gracefully exits by using the `RETURN` statement, and nothing further happens. If this `RETURN` test doesn't exist in the trigger code, the rest of the trigger code executes, and you don't want that to happen because you'd be executing the code that should only run if there are related child rows.

Now to the part of the trigger that actually performs the cascading delete, as follows:

```
    DELETE OrderItem
        FROM OrderItem ch, deleted
        WHERE ch.SalesOrderID = deleted.SalesOrderID
END
```

This *relational delete* deletes those rows in the OrderItem table that are related to all rows in the Deleted pseudotable—in essence, all OrderItem rows related to the SalesOrder rows deleted. (We talk in detail about the Deleted pseudotable in Chapter 11, but for now, just think of it as consisting of all the rows deleted from the SalesOrder table.)

Finally, you close the body of the trigger by using `END`.

Triggers have very different capabilities on the various database platforms. The trigger that we just discussed, for example, operates on the SQL Server 2000 platform, which defines an *event* at the statement level—meaning that this trigger fires once for each `DELETE` *statement* executed on the table, no matter how many rows are affected by that statement. By comparison, Oracle triggers can operate at either the statement level, as in SQL Server, or at the *row level*, such that the trigger code executes once for each individual row that is affected by the statement.

Another distinction between database platforms is *when* they can fire triggers. SQL Server fires triggers *after* the event takes place and all values are modified by the statement (but before they are committed to disk); Oracle enables you to define a trigger to execute either before *or* after the event takes place. Other distinctions also exist.

So when do you implement referential integrity by using DRI constraints and when do you use triggers? Well, a DRI constraint is almost always faster to execute than the equivalent operation implemented in a trigger—and they certainly are simpler to code—but you may sometimes need more complex logic to be involved, and for that, you need to use triggers. (More about this topic in Chapter 11.)

Normalization

Remember this line from the section "What is a relational database?" earlier in this chapter: "A place for everything, and everything in its place"? The process of making "a place for everything" in your database is called *normalization,* and it is probably the single most important aspect of database design. Put another way, normalization is the process of structuring data to fit the formal definition of a relational database.

The layered approach that we recommend that you use to design your databases helps you create inherently normalized database models from the very beginning, but you often inherit a database with a very bad data structure. This section gives you the basics of how to normalize a bad database structure into a good one.

You begin with a very bad design that places everything into one big entity, as shown in Figure 8-18. The example here is a database that tracks puppies and the tricks that they can perform.

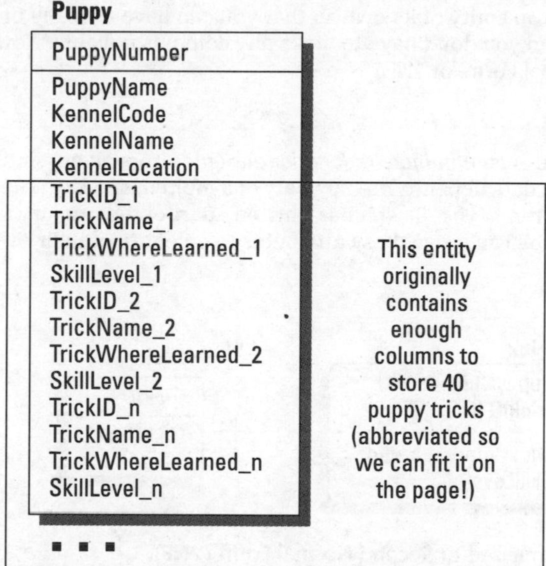

Figure 8-18: The badly mistaken idea that one entity fits all.

Your first clue that the database shouldn't be structured as a single entity is that huge section of repeating attributes (TrickName_1, TrickName_2, etc.), but how do you go about normalizing it? You normalize a database by modifying it through increasing degrees of normalization known as *normal forms.*

First Normal Form (1NF)

To achieve *First Normal Form*, you must *eliminate all repeating groups* of attributes from your entities, as shown in Figure 8-19. A repeating group of attributes is fairly easy to spot, such as the group of `TrickID_N`, `TrickName_N`, `TrickWhereLearned_N`, and `SkillLevel_N`, where N goes from 1 to 40. When you build all those repeating groups into a single entity, you invariably leave one or more of them empty, which not only requires that you leave most or all of their attributes nullable but also leaves a lot of empty space in the physical tables produced from your design. Both of these practices constitute bad database design.

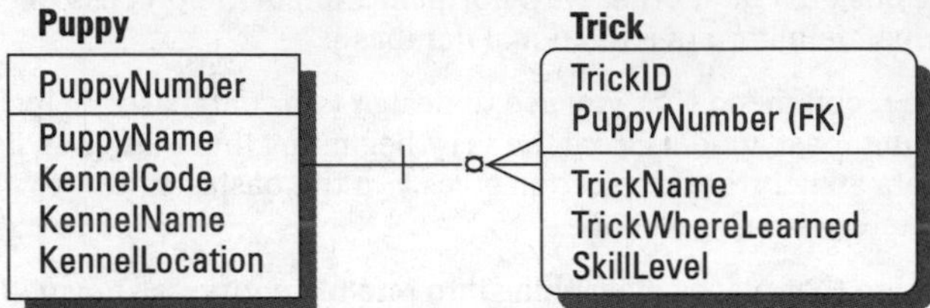

Figure 8-19: The original entity normalized to First Normal Form (1NF).

You move this repeating group into an entity of its own so that you can have as many or as few of these groups as you need, and you don't have to make any columns nullable. Now your database is said to be in First Normal Form, or 1NF.

Second Normal Form (2NF)

To achieve *Second Normal Form*, we must *eliminate redundant attributes* from all our entities, as shown in Figure 8-20. Redundant data depends on only part of a multivalued key. The name of a trick, for example, depends on the `TrickID`, which is only one part of the primary key of the `Trick` entity. This means that you can move these attributes to an entity of their own, as you see in the figure.

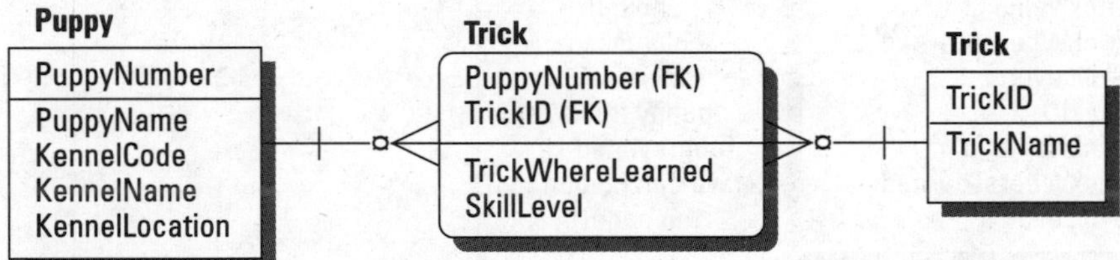

Figure 8-20: The original entity normalized to Second Normal Form (2NF).

Now your database is said to be in Second Normal Form, or 2NF.

Third Normal Form (3NF)

To achieve *Third Normal Form*, we must *remove all attributes that are not dependent on the keys* of each entity, as shown in Figure 8-21. None of the Kennel data, for example, depends on the key of the Puppy table in any way; the entire collection of Kennel attributes is redundantly stored in each row of the Puppy table. You can split the Kennel attributes into a separate entity because none of them depend on the value of the Puppy entity's key.

Now your database is said to be in Third Normal Form, or 3NF.

Further degrees of normalization are possible, but they are beyond the scope of this book. If you normalize your database designs to Third Normal Form, you are typically normalizing far enough.

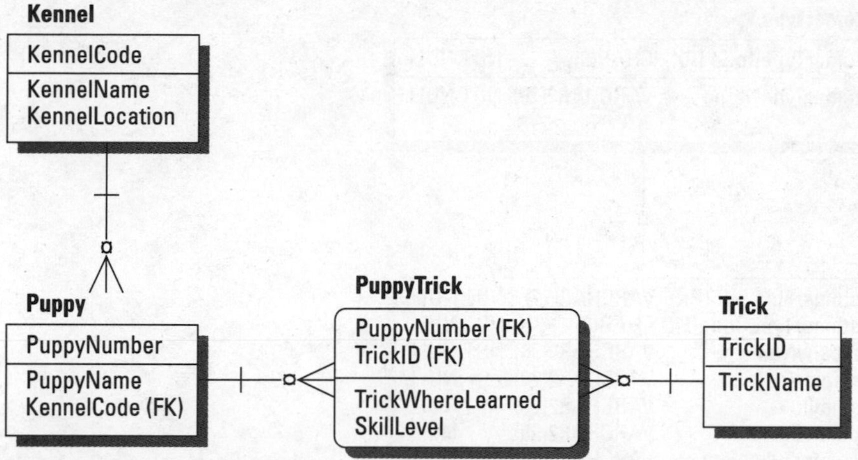

Figure 8-21: The original entity normalized to Third Normal Form (3NF).

Denormalization

Where normalization is the process of structuring data to fit the formal definition of a relational database, *denormalization* is the process of introducing controlled redundancy into your normalized database for specific performance enhancement reasons. The more that you denormalize your database structure, the less it fits the formal definition of a relational database, and the less its data can take advantage of relational database features and functionality. For this reason, you should denormalize only if you have absolutely compelling reasons to do so (such as unbearably slow relational selects)—and even then only as little as possible.

Normalization takes place in the logical data model; denormalization takes place in the physical data model for a specific database platform and uses performance-enhancement techniques best suited to that platform.

The most common denormalization technique is to redundantly store ancestor columns in a child table. If you don't want to perform a relational join every time that you want a report of customers and their customer type, for example, you can redundantly store `CustomerTypeName` in the Customer table, as shown in Figure 8-22.

Now you can return the value of `CustomerTypeName` directly from the Customer table, which saves the database from needing to perform a costly relational join and thereby increases reporting performance.

The downside to denormalization is that, because the denormalized portion of the database no longer conforms to the formal definition of a relational database, you must implement hand-crafted code to automatically handle editing changes migrating from `CustomerType.CustomerTypeName` to `Customer.CustomerTypeName`. You also must implement code that performs an initial copy of `CustomerType.CustomerTypeName` to `Customer.CustomerTypeName` after the Customer row is first inserted. Such code would be implemented as triggers so that these operations occur automatically. The more that you denormalize, the more code you must write to maintain this nonrelational, migrated data, so denormalize sparingly.

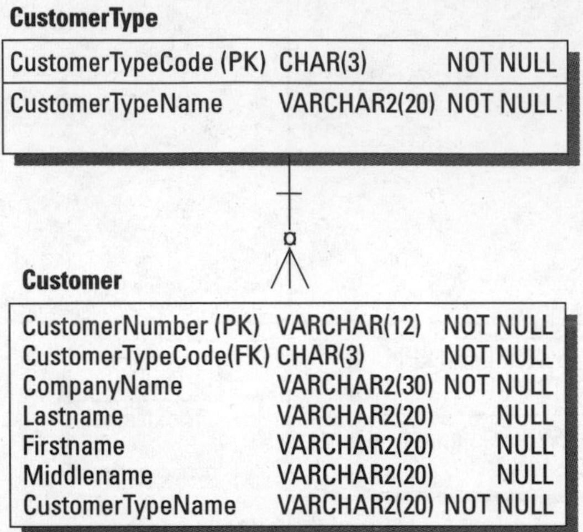

Figure 8-22: Denormalization by redundantly storing ancestor values in a child entity.

Defaults

Many times you want to automatically supply default values to rows inserted into a table—for example, the current date and time of a sale, or a status value that represents some beginning point in a business process. This behavior is implemented by using *defaults*

Defaults are defined on specific table columns, and they tell your database, "If this column isn't included in the INSERT statement for this table, go ahead and automatically enter this default value. If the INSERT statement *does* include this column, use whatever value was supplied for it."

Here's how a default declaration looks in the table definition:

```
CREATE TABLE SalesOrder(
SalesOrderID      int           IDENTITY(1,1),
CustomerNumber    varchar(12)   NULL,
SaleDate          datetime      DEFAULT GetDate() NOT NULL,
<more column definitions>
CONSTRAINT PK_SalesOrder PRIMARY KEY NONCLUSTERED (SalesOrderID))
```

You'll notice throughout this book that we occasionally boldface portions of code. This is a simple yet effective mechanism for helping you "see the forest for the trees" as we discuss a topic. For example, highlighting the DEFAULT phrase in a block of code while discussing defaults helps you quickly acquire the most applicable part of the code without being distracted by the rest during discussion.

This default declaration automatically places the result of SQL Server's GetDate() function—the current date and time—into the SaleDate column as long as the SaleDate column is not a part of the INSERT statement. If the SaleDate column *is* part of the INSERT statement, the value supplied by the statement will be used.

Check constraints

Now we come to one of the most useful yet underutilized features of databases: the capability to restrict or *constrain* the values that can go in table columns. Why is this capability important? Because your database must diligently safeguard against receiving incorrect data, and the database cannot rely on its client applications for this safeguard.

A *check constraint* is a declaration that only certain data may be stored in a database column. Like all declarations, check constraints are made in the DDL (Data Description Language) of your database.

If you want to restrict `OrderItem.Quantity` to accept only values great than zero, for example, you may think that simply coding this behavior in the ColdFusion application that inserts and updates this value during the online shopping process is sufficient. Although that approach may seem a fitting solution, think about some of the other places where you would need to implement that same code, as follows:

- Administrative processes that enable a manager to manually adjust values.
- Processes outside the realm of your ColdFusion application, such as a batch-processing utility or a Visual Basic application that access the same data.
- Additional processes added by another developer at some time in the future.

As you can see, keeping track of everywhere `OrderItem.Quantity` may be inserted or updated quickly becomes impossible. So why not centralize that code right there in the database itself, as follows:

```
CREATE TABLE OrderItem(
ItemNumber      varchar(15)        NOT NULL,
SalesOrderID    int                NOT NULL,
Description     varchar(40)        NOT NULL,
UnitPrice       numeric(12, 2)     NOT NULL,
Quantity        int                DEFAULT 1 NOT NULL
                CHECK (Quantity > 0),
CONSTRAINT PK_OrderItem PRIMARY KEY NONCLUSTERED
(ItemNumber,SalesOrderID))
```

With this check constraint in place, if any process attempts to insert either zero or a negative number into `OrderItem.Quantity`, the database throws an error and the attempted insert or update fails.

Another very useful application of check constraints is preventing empty values. Some database platforms, such as Oracle 8i, consider an empty string a `NULL` value, and as such, the string would be blocked from a column declared `NOT NULL`. But most platforms, such as SQL Server, consider an empty string exactly that: a string with a value of no characters. So SQL Server would permit an empty string to be inserted or updated in a column declared as `NOT NULL` because, to that platform, the empty string *isn't* `NULL`.

So for a database deployed on SQL Server, we like to declare a check constraint for every `CHAR` and `VARCHAR` column declared as `NOT NULL`, as the following example shows:

```
CREATE TABLE CustomerType(
CustomerTypeCode    char(3)           NOT NULL
                CHECK (DataLength(RTrim(CustomerTypeCode)) > 0),
CustomerTypeName    varchar(20)       NOT NULL
                CHECK (DataLength(RTrim(CustomerTypeName)) > 0),
CONSTRAINT PK_CustomerType PRIMARY KEY NONCLUSTERED (CustomerTypeCode))
```

If, for some reason, the user has JavaScript turned off in his Web browser, and the ColdFusion application doesn't perform server-side validation of the submitted form, an empty form field submits an empty string to the database. Each check constraint shown in the preceding examples trims the value of all trailing spaces and then tests whether the result is greater than zero characters long. If the value passes the test, it can go into that column; if not, the database throws an error, and the insert or update operation fails.

Always look for places to declare check constraints on your table columns. Check constraints not only help bulletproof your data integrity, but they are also ultra fast and, therefore, highly scalable —plus they do not add significant overhead to your database.

Creating a Scalable Database

Before asking the question "What makes a database scalable," you need to ask a more basic question: "What does *scalable* mean?"

In the most basic terms, *scalable* means the capability of a database to proportionately accommodate an increasing number of simultaneous transactions without choking. No matter how fast your database server machine's drives and CPUs are or how much RAM it has, the database itself still hits a brick wall of performance if it is not correctly engineered.

The design of your database has an infinitely greater effect on the performance of your ColdFusion application than the design of the queries that execute on that database. How can you create high-performance queries on poorly structured data?

If you diligently apply all the guidelines and techniques discussed in previous sections of this chapter, you are well on your way to building a highly scalable database. In fact, if all you do is apply to your database design what you've learned so far in this chapter, you're likely to end up with a well-engineered database that can be deployed "as is" and even scale to a reasonable number of simultaneous transactions.

But if you're reading this section, you're probably not satisfied with anything less than top performance, and for that, you need to address indexing.

Index design

What is an *index*, and why is it important to database scalability? The answer is probably somewhere near your fingertips! Pick up another book nearby and turn to the index in the back. Scan through the index looking for a topic that is familiar to you. After you find its entry in the index, run your finger across to the first page number listed for that topic; commit the page number to memory and then quickly flip over to that page in the book. Your database does virtually the same thing whenever it uses an index.

If your book didn't have an index, you'd need to read through every page of the book to find all the places where that topic was mentioned, reading each passage as you go. You'd need to expend all that energy to do something that would take but a few seconds if an index were available. If your boss requested that you retrieve this information for her, she would probably pass out from lack of food and water waiting for the result!

Just as with you, the less effort that your database takes to perform a task, the more tasks it can perform within a given time—and *that's* the real key to scalability. And a correctly engineered collection of indexes can help.

Book indexes are in alphabetical order, based on topic. Although a book has only one index, database tables may have multiple indexes built from them to assist in quickly referencing the data in various ways. The Company table, for example, may have one index based on CompanyName to facilitate retrieving and ordering its rows in alphabetical name order and another index on ZipCode to facilitate searches by zip code.

The following sections look a little deeper into how indexes work.

Your first index

You build an index on a table as follows:

```
CREATE INDEX IDX_CompanyName ON Customer(CompanyName)
```

The resulting index object created in your database is an ordered set of rows containing just the `CompanyName` column values from the Customer table and pointers to the rows from which the CompanyName values were extracted. Now the database server can use this `IDX_CompanyName` index to instantly locate customers through its `CompanyName` values and then select the matching rows from the Customer table by using the row pointers in the index. Without this index, the database server would need to scan through the entire Customer table to find the matching rows for the following query:

```
SELECT
   CustomerNumber,
Firstname,
Lastname
FROM
   Customer
WHERE
   CompanyName LIKE 'M%'
```

Indexes can be built on multiple columns. Your telephone white-pages directory, for example, is indexed in last-name, first-name, middle-initial order.

Before you get too deep in the options available for building indexes, take a look in the following section at what makes indexes tick.

Indexes under the covers

If those page numbers in the index of your book are "pointers" to the actual pages that contain the content that you want to read, the index is really just a big list of pointers all linked together in alphabetical order. As you first approach the index, you really don't start at the first page of the index, do you? If the topic you seek is *Objects*, you probably start about halfway through the index and then look where you are. If the earliest index entry that you see is *Mandelbrot* and the latest entry is *Mathematics*, you know right away to grab a few index pages all at once and page farther into the index. You repeat this process, back and forth, grabbing fewer and fewer pages as you go, until you find the index page containing your topic's entry. Then you scan down that page to find the first pointer to the actual page in the book on which that topic appears. After you have the pointer from the index, you immediately go to that page in the book — and there you are!

Database indexes are structurally more efficient than paper-book indexes, because they facilitate the process of traversing the index to rapidly find the index pages containing the pointers to your data. Figure 8-23 shows conceptually how a database index appears.

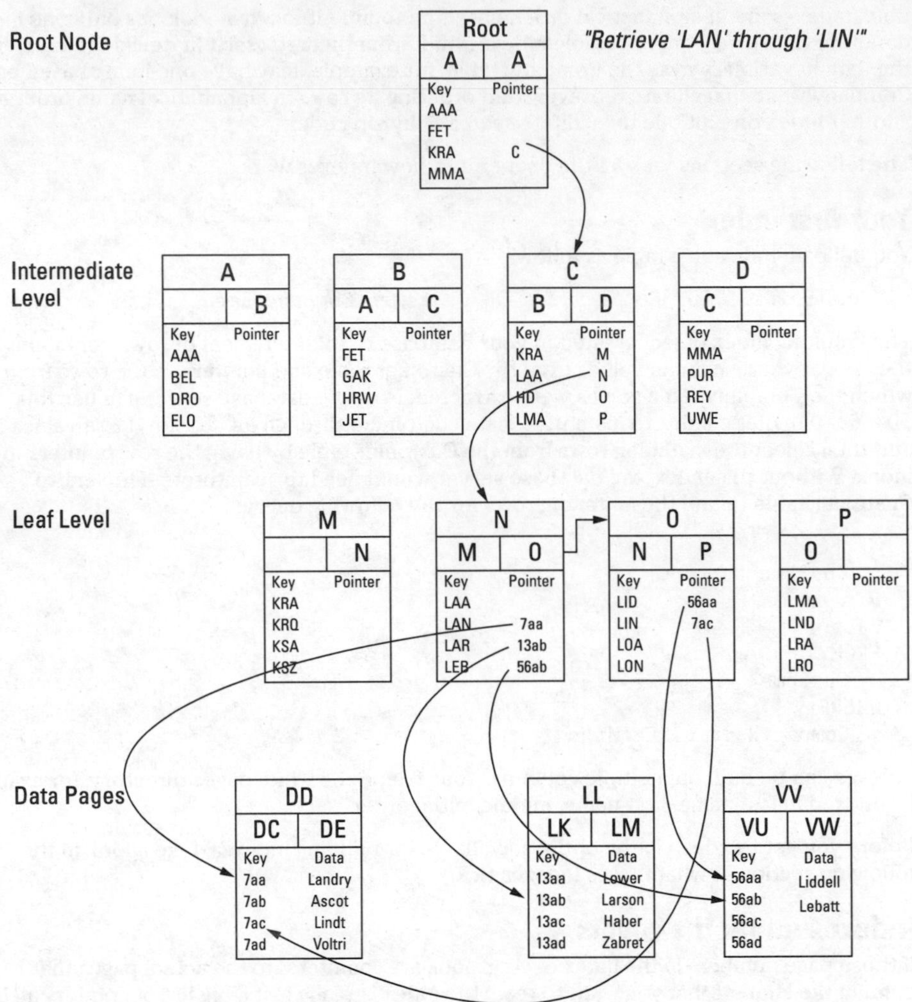

Figure 8-23: Conceptualization of an index and how it is traversed to quickly find the values sought.

The index consists of levels of *nodes*, starting with the root node level and ending with the leaf node level, with possibly one or more intermediate levels in between. Each node above the leaf level stores rows containing the key values that you're seeking and corresponding pointers to the index nodes on the next level down, where the search should continue. After the first index node on the *leaf level* is found, its rows are scanned to find the key values that you're seeking, and their corresponding pointers are used to look up the actual data from the database table.

A few technical facts are important to keep in mind here: First, indexes are separate database objects that are constantly synchronized with the underlying database tables on which they are built. Every time that you insert, update, or delete a row in a table, each index on that table must be modified at the same time. So although indexes can greatly speed data retrieval, they can equally bog down transactions that modify data. For this reason and many others, your decisions regarding which indexes to create should be made very carefully.

Second, tables and indexes are concepts understood by the database server only. The operating system has no concept of "rows" or "keys" at all and instead stores both tables and indexes in evenly sized *data pages*. (SQL Server 2000, for example, uses data pages that are 8K in size.) Whenever your database server requests index or table data from the operating system, the operating system obliges by returning data pages from which the database server can extract what it wants. If a database table's rows are very small in size, many rows fit on a single data page; if the rows are very large, the opposite is true. Indexes store only the table column values on which they are built, along with the pointer to the actual data pages. So their row sizes are typically very small, which means that many of them fit on a single data page. Neither the operating system nor the database server can operate over a partial data page; all reading from and writing to the database is performed on whole data pages.

Third, data pages are linked together in a *page chain*, which makes quickly scanning and retrieving a continuous range of values from multiple data pages possible. The address of both the preceding and following data pages in the chain are stored in the header of each data page. This addressing strategy is important, because these thousands or millions of individual data pages are scattered all across your database server's hard drive. You may think of database table data as being in one concise spot on disk, but it isn't.

Fourth, after you send a query to the database server, it breaks down and analyzes your query to determine which index it should choose to satisfy your request for data as quickly as possible. If the database server cannot find an index that can help speed the query, it performs a *table scan* that reads through the entire table, which is much like the earlier example of reading through a book without an index to find what you're looking for.

Nonclustered indexes

The index that we describe in the preceding section is called a *nonclustered index*. Although most database platforms have a limit on the number of nonclustered indexes that you can create on a table, you're unlikely to ever go anywhere near that limit (more than 200 on many platforms).

To create a nonclustered index on `Customer.CompanyName`, the syntax is as follows:

```
CREATE NONCLUSTERED INDEX IDX_CompanyName
ON Customer(CompanyName)
```

You do not need to specify `NONCLUSTERED` in creating a nonclustered index on most database platforms, because that is typically the default index type. Most indexes are nonclustered.

Clustered indexes

When you execute a database query that uses a non-clustered index to lookup the data you request, the index gives the query processor a list of pointers to the requested data. These pointers are then used to perform lookups that retrieve the actual data from the tables in which it is stored. But what if you could eliminate the need to perform a separate table lookup operation and just have the index return the actual data itself—wouldn't that speed retrieval? Yes, it would, and clustered indexes do just that.

A *clustered index* works similar to a nonclustered index, except that the leaf nodes of the clustered index contain the actual table data rather than pointers to that data. So when the database uses a clustered index, its query processor gets back the data that you requested, right out of the index.

Because the actual table data is stored in the physical order of the clustered index, only one clustered index can be on a table. Your database server heavily favors using a clustered index to satisfy retrieval requests because of its added performance benefit. Because of this preference and because only one clustered index can be chosen on a table, choosing which keys to use to create a clustered index is important. Consider choosing a key column that is often used to retrieve large numbers of rows over a continuous range of values.

To create a clustered index on `Subscription.StartDate`, the syntax is as follows:

```
CREATE CLUSTERED INDEX IDX_StartDate
ON Subscription(StartDate)
```

One way to envision a clustered index is to think of the alphabetical thumb tabs on the side of a large dictionary. To immediately go to the first entries for *M*, you just open the dictionary at the M tab—and there you are. Just as in a clustered index, the data is in the same physical order as the index.

Covering indexes

Consider now a telephone-directory database with the names sorted in typical last-name, first-name, middle-name order. You want to create one index on these three columns to facilitate retrieving and sorting names, as follows:

```
CREATE NONCLUSTERED INDEX IDX_ContactName
ON Customer(Lastname,Firstname,Middlename)
```

Now say that you need a quick listing of the first and last names of every *Smith* in the database. Try the following query:

```
SELECT Lastname, Firstname
FROM Customer
WHERE Lastname = 'SMITH'
```

Guess what? This query never even touches the database table. Why? Because it doesn't need to—everything requested by the query can be satisfied by the index itself, because it contains all the data your query needs!

Remember that an index is a separate database object that is constantly synchronized with its underlying database table. The index values being synchronized by the database engine are the key columns on which the index is built, which means that complete, up-to-date copies of these columns are stored in the index itself. You are searching and reporting just the key columns in the index, and because the index alone can give you everything that you're requesting, why should the database engine bother performing additional lookups of all these values from the underlying database table?

Because the index alone *covers* your entire request for data, the index is known as a *covering index*, and the query that utilized this covering index is known as a *covered query*.

Unique indexes

Consider the CustomerType table in Figure 8-15 and how it is used in your supporting ColdFusion application. Most likely, the CustomerType is implemented as a select menu on the Customer entry and edit forms, where `CustomerTypeCode` is the value of the select menu and `CustomerTypeName` is the displayed text for each option. People often overlook the need for a mechanism built into the database itself that guarantees the uniqueness of `CustomerTypeName`. Failure to include such a mechanism may result in two identical `CustomerTypeName` values appearing in the select menu. Which one represents which `CustomerTypeCode`? The user doesn't know, and at this point, the ColdFusion application is essentially broken with respect to inserting and updating customers.

The easy way to solve this problem is by creating a unique index on CustomerTypeName, as follows:

```
CREATE UNIQUE INDEX AK_CustomerType
ON CustomerType(CustomerTypeName)
```

This code prevents more than one row in the CustomerType table from having a given value of CustomerTypeName. An attempt to create a duplicate value causes the database to throw an error and the insert or update operation to fail.

CustomerTypeCode is the primary key of the CustomerType table, but after you create a unique index on CustomerTypeName, that column becomes an *alternate key* for the CustomerType table. In other words, its value is unique, like that of the primary key, but it is not the primary method used to uniquely identify rows in the CustomerType table. Primary keys often turn out to be the values used by software to uniquely identify rows in tables, while alternate keys are the values used by humans to uniquely identify rows in tables.

Knowing when to create an index and when not to

So indexes are useful. You're probably thinking that you should create all kinds of indexes for your existing databases. Just look through all your queries and, wherever columns are mentioned in WHERE or ORDER BY clauses, create an index on those columns, right? Wrong.

Always remember the heavy transactional overhead that indexes levy on your database. Similar to how medicine is doled out, indexes should be prescribed only for specific "illnesses" — and then only in the minimum feasible amount. Indiscriminate index building, as can indiscriminate medication, can sometimes kill the patient.

The method that we use is to define indexes is as follows:

1. Declare primary key constraints in the table definitions; this declaration automatically creates indexes on the primary keys, as follows:

   ```
   CONSTRAINT PK_SalesOrder PRIMARY KEY NONCLUSTERED (SalesOrderID)
   ```

2. Define unique indexes on alternate keys. This step is typically where the majority of my initial indexing ends, but steps 3 and 4 are often warranted. Even if you don't perform steps 3 and 4, proceed to step 5.

3. Define clustered indexes on tables that contain a large number of rows and in which we can clearly identify columns over which we're likely to perform large-range searches.

4. Define nonclustered indexes on tables that contain a large number of rows and in which we can clearly identify nonkey columns used in ad-hoc relational joins. (Whenever a database joins on nonkey columns, indexes on the join columns can increase performance quite a bit.) Stop creating indexes at this point.

5. Populate the database with test data of the approximate scale that it must handle during production; set up and run a trace by using our database-profiling tool; and then run a battery of stress tests that mimic the queries (both reads and transactions that modify data) that are typically going to be executed by our ColdFusion application. After the stress test and profile trace run together for a while, we stop everything and run the resulting trace data through the Index Tuning Wizard (built into SQL Server 2000). If the Wizard suggests that we build additional indexes, we do. Then we run the whole battery of tests over again and watch for performance hits on transactions that modify data. (Remember the overhead that indexes levy on transactions that modify data.)

As you can see, we take a fairly minimalist approach to initial indexing; then we let analysis tools suggest the rest. Nine times out of ten, this technique gives us the best possible performance for our databases. The remaining ten percent of the time, indexing is just a matter of observing and tweaking.

Index maintenance

One final note: Regularly rebuild your indexes to maintain database performance. Failure to do so can make you wish that you'd never heard of indexes in the first place. Indexes are typically rebuilt by first dropping and then recreating them. For example, the following code snippet rebuilds the IDX_ContactName index from scratch:

```
DROP INDEX IDX_ContactName
CREATE NONCLUSTERED INDEX IDX_ContactName
ON Customer(Lastname,Firstname,Middlename)
```

As data is inserted, updated, and deleted, two things happen. First, "holes" appear in your indexes where data is deleted or key values are updated and, therefore, move to different positions in the index. Second, if you insert new index entries into an index's data page that is already full, that data page must split into two separate data pages to make room for the new entry, and the whole index B-tree structure must be rebalanced. This splitting and rebalancing operation is very costly—so much so that if your indexes get old enough before rebuilding them, you can actually hear the disk laboring more and more as new mass inserts are performed.

Be careful in rebuilding indexes on key values; you can't just drop these indexes and rebuild them, because they are central to table definitions. Consult your database platform's documentation for instructions on rebuilding indexes "in place" without dropping them first.

We are not covering myriad details about indexes here, because they are outside the scope of this book; index design and maintenance can easily fill a book by itself. If you are really serious about scalable database design, you should read further on the subject of index design and maintenance.

Data Description Language (DDL)

When you execute a select, insert, update, or delete, you are employing *Data Manipulation Language*, or DML. When you do something to the structure of the database itself, you are employing *Data Description Language* or DDL.

Listing 8-1 contains the DDL that builds the database shown in the physical data model in Figure 8-16. Listing 8-2 contains the DDL that builds the database shown in the physical data model in Figure 8-17. Carefully study the details and apply the same techniques to your own database designs.

Listing 8-1: Data description language targeted to the Microsoft SQL Server 2000 database platform

```
CREATE TABLE Category(
    CategoryCode     varchar(4)       NOT NULL
        CHECK (DataLength(RTrim(CategoryCode)) > 0),
    CategoryName     varchar(20)      NOT NULL
        CHECK (DataLength(RTrim(CategoryName)) > 0),
    CONSTRAINT PK_Category PRIMARY KEY NONCLUSTERED (CategoryCode)
```

```
)
go

CREATE TABLE CategoryInventoryItem(
    CategoryCode    varchar(4)     NOT NULL,
    ItemNumber      varchar(15)    NOT NULL,
    CONSTRAINT PK_CategoryInventoryItem PRIMARY KEY NONCLUSTERED
(CategoryCode,ItemNumber)
)
go

CREATE TABLE Customer(
    CustomerNumber       varchar(12)    NOT NULL
        CHECK (DataLength(RTrim(CustomerNumber)) > 0),
    CustomerTypeCode     char(3)        NOT NULL,
    CompanyName          varchar(30)    NOT NULL
        CHECK (DataLength(RTrim(CompanyName)) > 0),
    Lastname             varchar(20)    NULL,
    Firstname            varchar(20)    NULL,
    Middlename           varchar(20)    NULL,
    CONSTRAINT PK_Customer PRIMARY KEY NONCLUSTERED (CustomerNumber)
)
go

CREATE TABLE CustomerType(
    CustomerTypeCode     char(3)        NOT NULL
                         CHECK (DataLength(RTrim(CustomerTypeCode)) >
0),
    CustomerTypeName     varchar(20)    NOT NULL
                         CHECK (DataLength(RTrim(CustomerTypeName)) >
0),
    CONSTRAINT PK_CustomerType PRIMARY KEY NONCLUSTERED
(CustomerTypeCode)
)
go

CREATE TABLE InventoryItem(
    ItemNumber           varchar(15)       NOT NULL
                         CHECK (DataLength(RTrim(ItemNumber)) > 0),
    ParentItemNumber     varchar(15)       NULL,
    Description          varchar(40)       NOT NULL
                         CHECK (DataLength(RTrim(Description)) > 0),
    UnitPrice            numeric(12, 2)    NOT NULL
                         CHECK (UnitPrice > 0),
    CONSTRAINT PK_InventoryItem PRIMARY KEY NONCLUSTERED (ItemNumber)
)
go

CREATE TABLE Newsletter(
    NewsletterCode    char(6)        NOT NULL
                      CHECK (DataLength(RTrim(NewsletterCode)) > 0),
    NewsletterName    varchar(30)    NOT NULL
```

Continued

Listing 8-1 *(continued)*

```
                  CHECK (DataLength(RTrim(NewsletterName)) > 0),
    CONSTRAINT PK_Newsletter PRIMARY KEY NONCLUSTERED (NewsletterCode)
)
go

CREATE TABLE OrderItem(
    ItemNumber      varchar(15)       NOT NULL
        CHECK (DataLength(RTrim(ItemNumber)) > 0),
    SalesOrderID    int               NOT NULL,
    Description     varchar(40)       NOT NULL
        CHECK (DataLength(RTrim(Description)) > 0),
    UnitPrice       numeric(12, 2)    NOT NULL
        CHECK (UnitPrice > 0),
    Quantity        int               DEFAULT 1 NOT NULL
        CHECK (Quantity > 0),
    CONSTRAINT PK_OrderItem PRIMARY KEY NONCLUSTERED
(ItemNumber,SalesOrderID)
)
go

CREATE TABLE SalesOrder(
    SalesOrderID      int               IDENTITY(1,1),
    CustomerNumber    varchar(12)       NULL,
    SoldTo            varchar(30)       NOT NULL
        CHECK (DataLength(RTrim(SoldTo)) > 0),
    SaleDate          datetime          DEFAULT GetDate() NOT NULL,
    Subtotal          numeric(12, 2)    DEFAULT 0 NOT NULL,
    TaxRate           numeric(12, 4)    DEFAULT 0 NOT NULL
        CHECK (TaxRate >= 0),
    TaxAmount         numeric(12, 2)    DEFAULT 0 NOT NULL
        CHECK (TaxAmount >= 0),
    Total             numeric(12, 2)    DEFAULT 0 NOT NULL
        CHECK (Total >= 0),
    CONSTRAINT PK_SalesOrder PRIMARY KEY NONCLUSTERED (SalesOrderID)
)
go

CREATE TABLE Subscription(
    CustomerNumber    varchar(12)       NOT NULL,
    NewsletterCode    char(6)           NOT NULL,
    StartDate         datetime          NOT NULL,
    DurationMonths    int               DEFAULT 12 NOT NULL
        CHECK (DurationMonths > 0),
    Price             numeric(12, 2)    NOT NULL
        CHECK (Price >= 0),
    CONSTRAINT PK_Subscription PRIMARY KEY NONCLUSTERED
(CustomerNumber,NewsletterCode)
)
```

```
go

CREATE UNIQUE INDEX AK_category ON Category(CategoryName)
go

CREATE INDEX IDX_ciiCategoryCode ON CategoryInventoryItem(CategoryCode)
go

CREATE INDEX IDX_ciiItemNumber ON CategoryInventoryItem(ItemNumber)
go

CREATE INDEX IDX_CompanyName ON Customer(CompanyName)
go

CREATE INDEX IDX_ContactName ON Customer(Lastname,Firstname,Middlename)
go

CREATE UNIQUE INDEX AK_CustomerType ON CustomerType(CustomerTypeName)
go

CREATE UNIQUE INDEX AK_InventoryItem ON InventoryItem(Description)
go

CREATE UNIQUE INDEX AK_Newsletter ON Newsletter(NewsletterName)
go

CREATE CLUSTERED INDEX IDX_SaleDate ON SalesOrder(SaleDate)
go

CREATE CLUSTERED INDEX IDX_StartDate ON Subscription(StartDate)
go

ALTER TABLE CategoryInventoryItem
    ADD CONSTRAINT FK__CategoryInventoryItem_Category
    FOREIGN KEY (CategoryCode)
    REFERENCES Category(CategoryCode)
go

ALTER TABLE CategoryInventoryItem
    ADD CONSTRAINT FK__CategoryInventoryItem_InventoryItem
    FOREIGN KEY (ItemNumber)
    REFERENCES InventoryItem(ItemNumber)
go

ALTER TABLE Customer
    ADD CONSTRAINT FK__Customer_CustomerType
    FOREIGN KEY (CustomerTypeCode)
    REFERENCES CustomerType(CustomerTypeCode)
go

ALTER TABLE InventoryItem
```

Continued

Listing 8-1 *(continued)*

```
    ADD CONSTRAINT FK__InventoryItem_InventoryItem
    FOREIGN KEY (ParentItemNumber)
    REFERENCES InventoryItem(ItemNumber)
go

ALTER TABLE OrderItem
    ADD CONSTRAINT FK__OrderItem_SalesOrder
    FOREIGN KEY (SalesOrderID)
    REFERENCES SalesOrder(SalesOrderID) ON DELETE CASCADE
go

ALTER TABLE SalesOrder
    ADD CONSTRAINT FK__SalesOrder_Customer
    FOREIGN KEY (CustomerNumber)
    REFERENCES Customer(CustomerNumber)
go

ALTER TABLE Subscription
    ADD CONSTRAINT FK__Subscription_Customer
    FOREIGN KEY (CustomerNumber)
    REFERENCES Customer(CustomerNumber) ON DELETE CASCADE
go

ALTER TABLE Subscription
    ADD CONSTRAINT FK__Subscription_Newsletter
    FOREIGN KEY (NewsletterCode)
    REFERENCES Newsletter(NewsletterCode)
Go
```

Listing 8-2: Data description language targeted to the Oracle 9i database platform

```
CREATE TABLE Category(
    CategoryCode    VARCHAR2(4)     NOT NULL,
    CategoryName    VARCHAR2(20)    NOT NULL,
    CHECK (Length(RTrim(CategoryCode)) > 0),
    CHECK (Length(RTrim(CategoryName)) > 0),
    CONSTRAINT PK_Category PRIMARY KEY (CategoryCode)
)
;

CREATE TABLE CategoryInventoryItem(
    CategoryCode    VARCHAR2(4)     NOT NULL,
    ItemNumber      VARCHAR2(15)    NOT NULL,
    CONSTRAINT PK_CategoryInventoryItem PRIMARY KEY
(CategoryCode,ItemNumber)
)
```

```
;

CREATE TABLE Customer(
    CustomerNumber      VARCHAR2(12)    NOT NULL,
    CustomerTypeCode    CHAR(3)         NOT NULL,
    CompanyName         VARCHAR2(30)    NOT NULL,
    Lastname            VARCHAR2(20),
    Firstname           VARCHAR2(20),
    Middlename          VARCHAR2(20),
    CHECK (Length(RTrim(CustomerNumber)) > 0),
    CHECK (Length(RTrim(CompanyName)) > 0),
    CONSTRAINT PK_Customer PRIMARY KEY (CustomerNumber)
)
;

CREATE TABLE CustomerType(
    CustomerTypeCode    CHAR(3)         NOT NULL,
    CustomerTypeName    VARCHAR2(20)    NOT NULL,
    CHECK (Length(RTrim(CustomerTypeCode)) > 0),
    CHECK (Length(RTrim(CustomerTypeName)) > 0),
    CONSTRAINT PK_CustomerType PRIMARY KEY (CustomerTypeCode)
)
;

CREATE TABLE InventoryItem(
    ItemNumber          VARCHAR2(15)     NOT NULL,
    ParentItemNumber    VARCHAR2(15),
    Description         VARCHAR2(40)     NOT NULL,
    UnitPrice           NUMBER(12, 2)    NOT NULL,
    CHECK (Length(RTrim(ItemNumber)) > 0),
    CHECK (Length(RTrim(Description)) > 0),
    CHECK (UnitPrice > 0),
    CONSTRAINT PK_InventoryItem PRIMARY KEY (ItemNumber)
)
;

CREATE TABLE Newsletter(
    NewsletterCode    CHAR(6)          NOT NULL,
    NewsletterName    VARCHAR2(30)     NOT NULL,
    CHECK (Length(RTrim(NewsletterCode)) > 0),
    CHECK (Length(RTrim(NewsletterName)) > 0),
    CONSTRAINT PK_Newsletter PRIMARY KEY (NewsletterCode)
)
;

CREATE TABLE OrderItem(
    ItemNumber      VARCHAR2(15)      NOT NULL,
    SalesOrderID    NUMBER(38, 0)     NOT NULL,
    Description     VARCHAR2(40)      NOT NULL,
    UnitPrice       NUMBER(12, 2)     NOT NULL,
    Quantity        NUMBER(38, 0)     DEFAULT 1 NOT NULL,
```

Continued

Listing 8-2 *(continued)*

```
    CHECK (Length(RTrim(ItemNumber)) > 0),
    CHECK (Length(RTrim(Description)) > 0),
    CHECK (UnitPrice > 0),
    CHECK (Quantity > 0),
    CONSTRAINT PK_OrderItem PRIMARY KEY (ItemNumber,SalesOrderID)
)
;

CREATE TABLE SalesOrder(
    SalesOrderID        NUMBER(38, 0)     NOT NULL,
    CustomerNumber      VARCHAR2(12),
    SoldTo              VARCHAR2(30)      NOT NULL,
    SaleDate            DATE              DEFAULT SYSDATE NOT NULL,
    Subtotal            NUMBER(12, 2)     DEFAULT 0 NOT NULL,
    TaxRate             NUMBER(12, 4)     DEFAULT 0 NOT NULL,
    TaxAmount           NUMBER(12, 2)     DEFAULT 0 NOT NULL,
    Total               NUMBER(12, 2)     DEFAULT 0 NOT NULL,
    CHECK (TaxRate >= 0),
    CHECK (TaxAmount >= 0),
    CHECK (Total >= 0),
    CHECK (Length(RTrim(SoldTo)) > 0),
    CONSTRAINT PK_SalesOrder PRIMARY KEY (SalesOrderID)
)
;

CREATE TABLE Subscription(
    CustomerNumber      VARCHAR2(12)      NOT NULL,
    NewsletterCode      CHAR(6)           NOT NULL,
    StartDate           DATE              NOT NULL,
    DurationMonths      NUMBER(38, 0)     DEFAULT 12 NOT NULL,
    Price               NUMBER(12, 2)     NOT NULL,
    CHECK (DurationMonths > 0),
    CHECK (Price >= 0),
    CONSTRAINT PK_Subscription PRIMARY KEY
(CustomerNumber,NewsletterCode)
)
;

CREATE UNIQUE INDEX AK_category ON Category(CategoryName)
;

CREATE INDEX IDX_cci_CategoryCode ON
CategoryInventoryItem(CategoryCode)
;

CREATE INDEX IDX_cci_ItemNumber ON CategoryInventoryItem(ItemNumber)
;

CREATE INDEX IDX_CompanyName ON Customer(CompanyName)
```

```
;

CREATE INDEX IDX_ContactName ON Customer(Lastname,Firstname,Middlename)
;

CREATE UNIQUE INDEX AK_CustomerType ON CustomerType(CustomerTypeName)
;

CREATE UNIQUE INDEX AK_InventoryItem ON InventoryItem(Description)
;

CREATE UNIQUE INDEX AK_Newsletter ON Newsletter(NewsletterName)
;

CREATE INDEX IDX_SaleDate ON SalesOrder(SaleDate)
;

CREATE INDEX IDX_StartDate ON Subscription(StartDate)
;

ALTER TABLE CategoryInventoryItem ADD CONSTRAINT
FK__c_CategoryInventoryItem
    FOREIGN KEY (CategoryCode)
    REFERENCES Category(CategoryCode)
;

ALTER TABLE CategoryInventoryItem ADD CONSTRAINT
FK__i_CategoryInventoryItem
    FOREIGN KEY (ItemNumber)
    REFERENCES InventoryItem(ItemNumber)
;

ALTER TABLE Customer ADD CONSTRAINT FK__Customer_CustomerType
    FOREIGN KEY (CustomerTypeCode)
    REFERENCES CustomerType(CustomerTypeCode)
;

ALTER TABLE InventoryItem ADD CONSTRAINT FK__ii_InventoryItem
    FOREIGN KEY (ParentItemNumber)
    REFERENCES InventoryItem(ItemNumber)
;

ALTER TABLE OrderItem ADD CONSTRAINT FK__OrderItem_SalesOrder
    FOREIGN KEY (SalesOrderID)
    REFERENCES SalesOrder(SalesOrderID) ON DELETE CASCADE
;

ALTER TABLE SalesOrder ADD CONSTRAINT FK__SalesOrder_Customer
    FOREIGN KEY (CustomerNumber)
    REFERENCES Customer(CustomerNumber)
```

Continued

Listing 8-2 *(continued)*

```
;

ALTER TABLE Subscription ADD CONSTRAINT FK__Subscription_Customer
    FOREIGN KEY (CustomerNumber)
    REFERENCES Customer(CustomerNumber) ON DELETE CASCADE
;

ALTER TABLE Subscription ADD CONSTRAINT FK__Subscription_Newsletter
    FOREIGN KEY (NewsletterCode)
    REFERENCES Newsletter(NewsletterCode)
;
```

Don't try to get OLAP out of an OLTP database

The databases that you typically create for ColdFusion applications store the results of database transactions, such as entering sales orders and updating inventories. Such a database is called an *OnLine Transaction Processing*, or *OLTP*, database.

OnLine Analytical Processing, or *OLAP*, uses a multidimensional view of data, aggregated from individual transactions to provide business managers with analytical results. Transactional data in an OLTP database has the wrong structure for OLAP: Where an OLTP database is highly normalized and lightly indexed, the data warehouse used for OLAP is highly *de*normalized and heavily indexed. A data warehouse can afford to have as many indexes as necessary for fast retrieval because no inserts or updates are in the data warehouse.

If a manager wants to analyze the business value of his transactions and make decisions based on them, he shouldn't perform this analysis on the same OLTP database that stores his transactional data. Such analyses are complex affairs, requiring a heavy processing load and special software tools. To attempt such a thing by using complex relational queries and subqueries at the same time that users are creating transactions in the same database is unthinkable in light of the performance slowdown levied against the transactional users. (But, unfortunately, managers request such capabilities from their development staff every day.)

Although data warehousing and OLAP are beyond the scope of this book (each subject easily capable of filling its own very large book), virtually *no* data analysis should be performed on the same database that stores your live transactional data. This includes complicated relational queries that produce complex financial reports. Instead, extract copies of your transactions to a separate database, transform them into a data structure that is as close as possible to the report you want, and then report on this warehoused data.

Our favorite tool for extracting and transforming data is the *Data Transformation Services (DTS)* tool built into SQL Server 2000. You can create an entire package of individual database transformations between multiple databases and database servers of all kinds and then schedule the package to automatically execute on a specific schedule. If your boss or client requests heavy analysis of transactional data, use the DTS tool to create a separate database on a separate server and perform your analyses there.

Summary

In this chapter, you learn important details about the relationships between database tables and how to apply these relationships to real world data modeling.

You typically end up with correctly normalized data by following the "layered" data modeling approach that you learn in this chapter, but if the world throws a poorly normalized database your way, you can use the data-normalization steps that we also discuss to give it the correct structure.

Remember to always define column defaults and constraints where possible in your tables, as such definitions prevent invalid data from entering your database. Pay special attention to preventing zero-length strings from entering `NOT NULL` columns by checking the length of trimmed values, because Web forms submit empty fields as zero-length strings that actually pass the `NOT NULL` test.

You also learn some important details about indexes that can help you visualize how they work internally, which guide you on how and when they should be applied in your database. Careful index design and regular maintenance keeps your database running quickly and smoothly.

Finally, don't try to produce analysis or complicated reports from transactional data; instead, transform transactional data into summary data, store it in a separate database, and produce reports from this database.

Chapter 9 can further help you visualize how an SQL statement is processed, which also helps you write error-free SQL. You learn easy-to-follow rules for writing statements containing `GROUP BY`, `HAVING`, and `DISTINCT` clauses and aggregate functions, which are commonly misunderstood and misused.

✦ ✦ ✦

Putting Databases to Work

In This Chapter

Visualizing complicated relational result sets

Understanding what your database can and cannot do

Leveraging database exceptions in your application

Knowing how and when to cache queries

This chapter can help you better understand complicated SQL containing multitable joins, group-related clauses, and aggregate functions — by far the most problematic topics for most database developers. You also learn the correct way to handle database exceptions and incorporate them as actual functionality in your ColdFusion application. You learn, too, how to increase performance by caching queries in memory for fast access.

You can memorize SQL clauses and Bachus-Naur forms until you're blue in the face, but you still end up playing "ready-fire-aim" trying to write complicated SQL that actually works — unless you have a clear picture of exactly how SQL processes statements. Your first step in clearly visualizing SQL is to understand the nature of relational result sets.

Note

The code in this chapter is not supported by Access, so if you want to follow along with the listings in this chapter, run the files Chapter9DDL.sql and Chapter9Data.sql on a new SQL Server 2000 database, and setup a data source named CFMXBible that connects to this new database. This new database contains additional data and tables to help illustrate the various types of joins and the results that they produce.

Understanding All Relational Result Sets

We added *All* to the title of this section for an important reason that was already stated in Chapter 5:

***All** SQL query results are in the form of a single table of rows and columns.*

Whether the result is from the query of a single table or a complicated relational query involving 15 tables doesn't matter — *all* query results are in the form of a single table of rows and columns.

Consider Listing 9-1, which produces a relational query result that, like all query results, is in the form of a single table.

Listing 9-1: A SELECT statement that produces a relational query result

```
SELECT
    c.CompanyID,
    c.CompanyName,
    e.Lastname,
    e.Firstname,
    e.Salary
FROM
    Company c INNER JOIN Employee e
        ON c.CompanyID = e.CompanyID
```

Listing 9-1 is conceptualized in Figure 9-1. Notice that the result of joining these two tables results in a single table.

What's this? Isn't this one of those Venn diagrams? Remember when Mr. Suber, your junior high school math teacher, told you that you really would use them one day in the real world, and you balked? Time to call him up and apologize!

An `INNER JOIN` is the intersection of the two data sets contained in the two tables being joined, as shown in Figure 9-1.

Why is this conceptualization critical to writing flawless SQL? Because we now can easily visualize any type of join between two tables, as shown in Figure 9-2:

Considering Figure 9-2, we can now easily describe what is really happening with each of these types of `JOIN`s.

An `INNER JOIN` result consists of the columns selected from both tables, but it contains only those rows that match the `JOIN` key values (specified in the `ON` clause) in both joined tables, as you can see from Listing 9-1 and Figure 9-1.

A `LEFT OUTER JOIN` result consists of the columns selected from both tables, and it contains all the rows in the left-side table regardless of whether any of them match the `JOIN` key values in the right-side table. The query columns selected from the left-side table contain data from that table. For each row in the query result, if a `JOIN` key value from the left-side table matches a `JOIN` key value from the right-side table, the query columns selected from the right-side table contain column data from that table; if not, those columns contain nulls.

Listing 9-2 is Listing 9-1 modified to produce a `LEFT OUTER JOIN`, and Figure 9-3 displays the query result.

Listing 9-2: An example of a LEFT OUTER JOIN

```
SELECT
    c.CompanyID,
    c.CompanyName,
    e.Lastname,
    e.Firstname,
    e.Salary
FROM
    Company c LEFT OUTER JOIN Employee e
        ON c.CompanyID = e.CompanyID
```

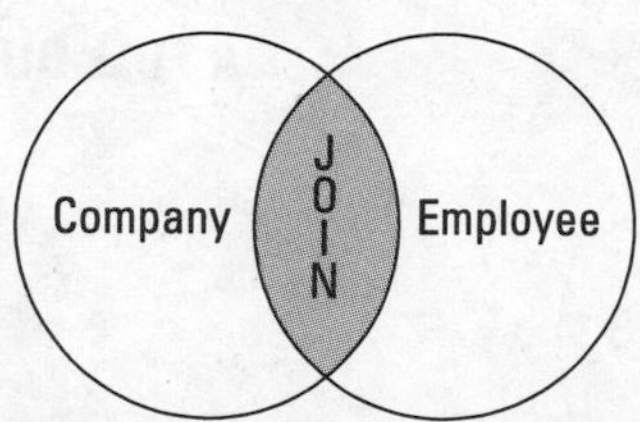

CompanyID	CompanyName	Lastname	Firstname	Salary
1	ABC Company Inc.	Sanders	Billy	33500.00
1	ABC Company Inc.	Kayashunu	Oksal	23750.00
1	ABC Company Inc.	Worthington	Randsford	117539.15
2	The Very Big Corporation of America	Johnson	Dave	51600.00
2	The Very Big Corporation of America	Silverberg	Bethany	76328.94
2	The Very Big Corporation of America	Kokilas	Susan	43711.83
2	The Very Big Corporation of America	Davidow	Allen	65000.00
2	The Very Big Corporation of America	Feuilliette	Valerie	39950.00
3	Star Trek Fan Club	Williger	Timmy	11250.75
3	Star Trek Fan Club	Littleman	Kevin	13650.00
5	Azure Productions	Abromovitz	Arel	123456.78
5	Azure Productions	Huckster	Virgil	23750.00
5	Azure Productions	Romanova	Natasha	79315.95
6	Angry Clown Entertainment	Thor	Dirk	5000.00
6	Angry Clown Entertainment	Churvis	Adam	9500.00
8	Developers Anonymous	Thickglasses	Barney	125000.00
8	Developers Anonymous	Mernal	Stanley	115750.00
8	Developers Anonymous	Harbinger	Judy	135500.00
8	Developers Anonymous	Nerdsworth	Larry	132900.00
8	Developers Anonymous	Derby	Wayne	154950.00
9	Hamazon.com	Tucker	Billy Bob	75985.50
10	The Stan Cox Society	Gumby	Vernal	7012.48
10	The Stan Cox Society	Lester	Lance	5412.91
10	The Stan Cox Society	Mango	Davey	4981.33

Figure 9-1: The result of an `INNER JOIN`.

A `RIGHT OUTER JOIN` result consists of the columns `select`ed from both tables, and it contains all the rows in the right-side table regardless of whether any of them match the `JOIN` key values in the left-side table. The query columns `select`ed from the right-side table contain data from that table. For each row in the query result, if a `JOIN` key value from the right-side table matches a `JOIN` key value from the left-side table, the query columns `select`ed from the left-side table contain column data from that table; if not, those columns contain `null`s.

Listing 9-3 is Listing 9-2 modified to produce a `RIGHT OUTER JOIN`, and Figure 9-4 displays the query result.

A `FULL OUTER JOIN` result consists of the columns `select`ed from both tables, and it contains all the rows from both tables regardless of whether any of them match their `JOIN` key values. For each query result row extracted from the left-side table, if the `JOIN` key value from the left-side table has no match in the right-side table, that query result row contains `null`s in the columns `select`ed from the right-side table. Similarly, in a query result row extracted from the right-side table, if the `JOIN` key value from the right-side table has no match in the left-side table, that query result row contains nulls in the columns `select`ed from the left-side table. If a query result row's `JOIN` key values match between the left- and right-side tables, the data from both tables is contained in that query result row.

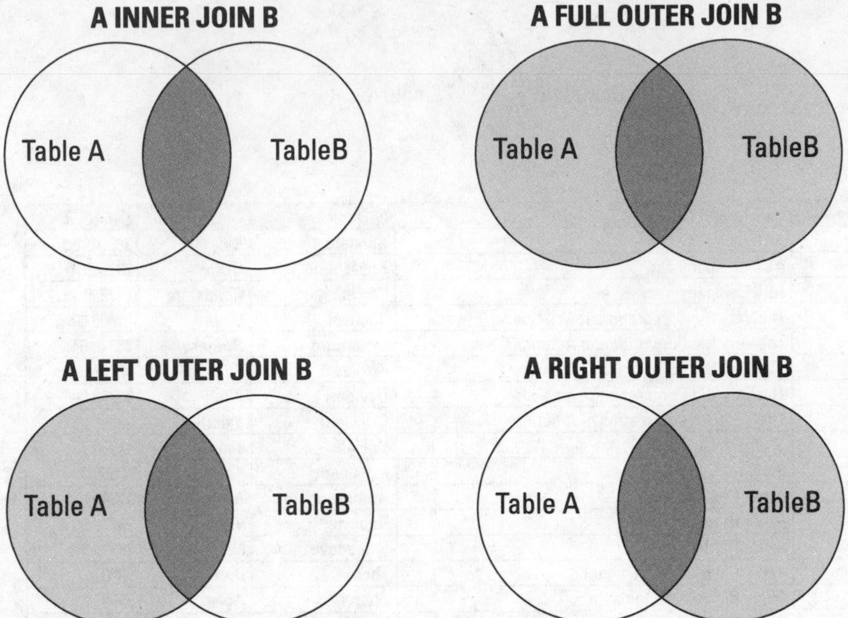

Figure 9-2: The various types of `JOINs` represented as Venn diagrams.

CompanyID	CompanyName	Lastname	Firstname	Salary
1	ABC Company, Inc.	Sanders	Billy	33500.00
1	ABC Company, Inc.	Kayashunu	Oksal	23750.00
1	ABC Company, Inc.	Worthington	Randsford	117539.15
2	The Very Big Corporation of America	Johnson	Dave	51600.00
2	The Very Big Corporation of America	Silverberg	Bethany	76328.94
2	The Very Big Corporation of America	Kokilas	Susan	43711.83
2	The Very Big Corporation of America	Davidow	Allen	65000.00
2	The Very Big Corporation of America	Feuilliette	Valerie	39950.00
3	Star Trek Fan Club	Williger	Timmy	11250.75
3	Star Trek Fan Club	Littleman	Kevin	13650.00
4	Ye Olde Poodle Accessory Shoppe	NULL	NULL	NULL
5	Azure Productions	Abromovitz	Arel	123456.78
5	Azure Productions	Huckster	Virgil	23750.00
5	Azure Productions	Romanova	Natasha	79315.95
6	Angry Clown Entertainment	Thor	Dirk	5000.00
6	Angry Clown Entertainment	Churvis	Adam	9500.00
7	Bob's Motorcycle Restoration	NULL	NULL	NULL
8	Developers Anonymous	Thickglasses	Barney	125000.00
8	Developers Anonymous	Mernal	Stanley	115750.00
8	Developers Anonymous	Harbinger	Judy	135500.00
8	Developers Anonymous	Nerdsworth	Larry	132900.00
8	Developers Anonymous	Derby	Wayne	154950.00
9	Hamazon.com	Tucker	Billy Bob	75985.50
10	The Stan Cox Society	Gumby	Vernal	7012.48
10	The Stan Cox Society	Lester	Lance	5412.91
10	The Stan Cox Society	Mango	Davey	4981.33
101	Sample Data Company	NULL	NULL	NULL
102	TurboBunny Systems	NULL	NULL	NULL

Figure 9-3: The query result of executing Listing 9-2.

Listing 9-3: An example of a RIGHT OUTER JOIN

```
SELECT
    c.CompanyID,
    c.CompanyName,
    e.Lastname,
    e.Firstname,
    e.Salary
FROM
    Company c RIGHT OUTER JOIN Employee e
        ON c.CompanyID = e.CompanyID
```

CompanyID	CompanyName	Lastname	Firstname	Salary
1	ABC Company, Inc.	Sanders	Billy	33500.00
1	ABC Company, Inc.	Kayashunu	Oksal	23750.00
1	ABC Company, Inc.	Worthington	Randsford	117539.15
2	The Very Big Corporation of America	Johnson	Dave	51600.00
2	The Very Big Corporation of America	Silverberg	Bethany	76328.94
2	The Very Big Corporation of America	Kokilas	Susan	43711.83
2	The Very Big Corporation of America	Davidow	Allen	65000.00
2	The Very Big Corporation of America	Feuilliette	Valerie	39950.00
3	Star Trek Fan Club	Williger	Timmy	11250.75
3	Star Trek Fan Club	Littleman	Kevin	13650.00
5	Azure Productions	Abromovitz	Arel	123456.78
5	Azure Productions	Huckster	Virgil	23750.00
5	Azure Productions	Romanova	Natasha	79315.95
6	Angry Clown Entertainment	Thor	Dirk	5000.00
6	Angry Clown Entertainment	Churvis	Adam	9500.00
8	Developers Anonymous	Thickglasses	Barney	125000.00
8	Developers Anonymous	Mernal	Stanley	115750.00
8	Developers Anonymous	Harbinger	Judy	135500.00
8	Developers Anonymous	Nerdsworth	Larry	132900.00
8	Developers Anonymous	Derby	Wayne	154950.00
9	Hamazon.com	Tucker	Billy Bob	75985.50
10	The Stan Cox Society	Gumby	Vernal	7012.48
10	The Stan Cox Society	Lester	Lance	5412.91
10	The Stan Cox Society	Mango	Davey	4981.33
NULL	NULL	Haymen	Turk	61530.00
NULL	NULL	Rodriguez	Kiki	335799.75
NULL	NULL	Castling	David	97650.00

Figure 9-4: The query result of executing Listing 9-3.

Listing 9-4 is Listing 9-3 modified to produce a `FULL OUTER JOIN`, and Figure 9-5 displays the query result.

Listing 9-4: An example of a FULL OUTER JOIN

```
SELECT
    c.CompanyID,
    c.CompanyName,
    e.Lastname,
    e.Firstname,
    e.Salary
FROM
    Company c FULL OUTER JOIN Employee e
        ON c.CompanyID = e.CompanyID
```

CompanyID	CompanyName	Lastname	Firstname	Salary
1	ABC Company, Inc.	Sanders	Billy	33500.00
1	ABC Company, Inc.	Kayashunu	Oksal	23750.00
1	ABC Company, Inc.	Worthington	Randsford	117539.15
2	The Very Big Corporation of America	Johnson	Dave	51600.00
2	The Very Big Corporation of America	Silverberg	Bethany	76328.94
2	The Very Big Corporation of America	Kokilas	Susan	43711.83
2	The Very Big Corporation of America	Davidow	Allen	65000.00
2	The Very Big Corporation of America	Feuilliette	Valerie	39950.00
3	Star Trek Fan Club	Williger	Timmy	11250.75
3	Star Trek Fan Club	Littleman	Kevin	13650.00
5	Azure Productions	Abromovitz	Arel	123456.78
5	Azure Productions	Huckster	Virgil	23750.00
5	Azure Productions	Romanova	Natasha	79315.95
6	Angry Clown Entertainment	Thor	Dirk	5000.00
6	Angry Clown Entertainment	Churvis	Adam	9500.00
8	Developers Anonymous	Thickglasses	Barney	125000.00
8	Developers Anonymous	Mernal	Stanley	115750.00
8	Developers Anonymous	Harbinger	Judy	135500.00
8	Developers Anonymous	Nerdsworth	Larry	132900.00
8	Developers Anonymous	Derby	Wayne	154950.00
9	Hamazon.com	Tucker	Billy Bob	75985.50
10	The Stan Cox Society	Gumby	Vernal	7012.48
10	The Stan Cox Society	Lester	Lance	5412.91
10	The Stan Cox Society	Mango	Davey	4981.33
NULL	NULL	Haymen	Turk	61530.00
NULL	NULL	Rodriguez	Kiki	335799.75
NULL	NULL	Castling	David	97650.00
7	Bob's Motorcycle Restoration	NULL	NULL	NULL
4	Ye Olde Poodle Accessory Shoppe	NULL	NULL	NULL
101	Sample Data Company	NULL	NULL	NULL
102	TurboBunny Systems	NULL	NULL	NULL

Figure 9-5: The query result of executing Listing 9-4.

JOIN direction

A common question is, "What is the difference between a *LEFT* OUTER JOIN and a *RIGHT* OUTER JOIN?" The answer is simple: A *LEFT* OUTER JOIN joins to the entire data set in the table named on the left side of the JOIN operator (typically an equal sign), and a *RIGHT* OUTER JOIN joins to the entire data set in the table named on the right side of the JOIN operator.

In other words, Listing 9-3—a RIGHT OUTER JOIN—places the *Employee* table on the *right* side of the JOIN operator (ON Company.CompanyID = *Employee*.CompanyID), so all rows from the Employee table appear in the query result.

Multiple table joins

Okay, you can now precisely visualize the various types of joins and are more comfortable with the SQL syntax that creates them. That's great! But in the real world, you often deal with joining more than two tables together in a single relational query. How are you going to write the complicated SQL to join seven related tables and get it right the first time, every time?

Actually, it's a piece of cake. In fact, writing a query that performs a combination of INNER, LEFT OUTER, RIGHT OUTER, and FULL OUTER joins between 15 tables is really no harder to write than a query containing a single INNER JOIN between two tables. The trick's all in how you visualize it!

Remember Figure 9-1, where you conceptualize an INNER JOIN between two tables? Say that you want to join to a third table—the Dependant table—as shown in Listing 9-5.

Listing 9-5: Joining three tables

```
SELECT
    c.CompanyID,
    c.CompanyName,
    e.Lastname,
    e.Firstname,
    e.Salary,
    d.FullName,
    d.Relationship
FROM
    Company c INNER JOIN Employee e
        ON c.CompanyID = e.CompanyID
    INNER JOIN Dependant d
        ON e.SSN = d.SSN
```

The trick to visualizing the joining of these three tables is to decompose the process into multiple joins between *pairs* of tables. You may remember from Chapter 8 that a relationship between two tables is called a *bi*nary relationship because it relates *two* tables. You may also remember, from the beginning of this chapter, that we restate the fact that all query results are in the form of a single table.

But what is a query result? Certainly, a *query result* is the data returned from your database server to ColdFusion as the result of a `CFQUERY` call, but the *intermediate work product* of an SQL statement in process is a query result, too.

Conceptually, each step in processing an SQL statement produces an internal, intermediate work product in the form of a single table. This intermediate work product is fed to the next step in the process, which in turn transforms it into its own intermediate work product in the form of another table. This continues until the SQL statement finishes processing steps; the final result is, again, a single table. In fact, the only difference between an intermediate work product and a final query result is the fact that you don't have any more steps to process in the latter.

So if you think of the intermediate work product of the first `JOIN` (between Company and Employee) as one table, and you think of the second `JOIN` as joining this "table" to the Dependant table, your `FROM` clause looks something like what's shown in Figure 9-6.

In a nutshell, the joining of the Company and Employee tables produces an intermediate "table" that is then joined to the Dependant table, which in turn produces another table that is the final query result.

Hey, wait a minute! Doesn't this mean that, no matter how many complicated joins appear in a query, you can still decompose the whole mess into an easy-to-understand series of simple two-table joins? You bet!

In fact, no such thing as a "three-table join" or a "multiple-table join" really exists, because all joins are between just two tables. Even a self-join between a table and itself is conceptually a join between two tables; the table is actually joined to an "image" of itself.

So, joining *N* tables is really a series of *N*-1 simple two-table joins. Think of it that way, and you never experience another problem creating even the most complicated joins ever again.

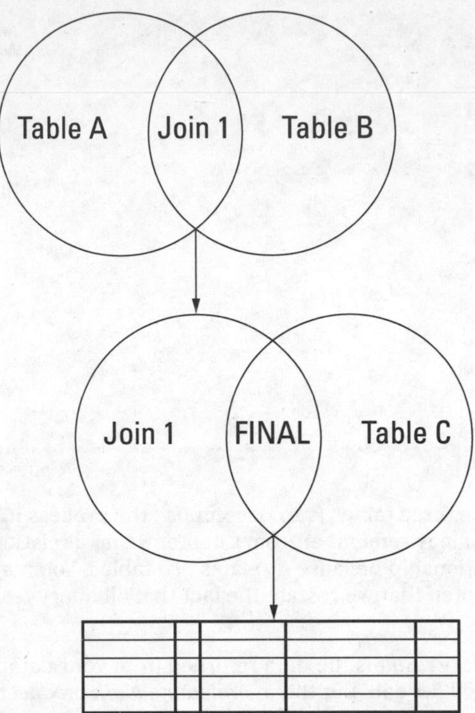

Figure 9-6: Visualizing the joining of three tables.

One final piece of advice: Use the exact SQL code indenting format that we use throughout this chapter, and you have significantly fewer problems writing perfect SQL the first time through. We mean don't even deviate from our format one iota. Do everything—capitalization, tabbing, aliasing, putting each column in the `SELECT` clause on a line by itself, and so on—just as we've done in the listings for this chapter. Trust us—it works. The SQL code formatting technique we use really helps you visually separate each clause so you can see the statement as a collection of logical operations, rather than a haphazardly-typed string of code.

In the following sections, you get to tackle once and for all an even more confusing matter: grouping and aggregate functions.

How to Visualize What is Possible and Impossible Within an SQL Statement

Take a look at the following error message:

```
Column 'e.Firstname' is invalid in the select list because it is not
contained in either an aggregate function or the GROUP BY clause.
```

How many times have you seen something like this? You go back and edit your SQL and give it another try, but it either fails again or doesn't give you what you're looking for. So you give it another try. . . .

Sound familiar? If you follow what we say after you finish reading this chapter, you never encounter this problem again.

SQL's processing order of precedence

To understand exactly what you can and cannot do with SQL, you must first understand the order in which SQL processes the clauses of an SQL statement. You can use Listing 9-6 as an example of the order that SQL follows.

Listing 9-6: An example query for discovering how SQL processes statements

```
SELECT
    c.CompanyName,
    e.LastName + ', ' + e.FirstName AS EmployeeName,
    e.Salary,
    count(*) as NumDependants
FROM
    Company c INNER JOIN Employee e
        ON c.CompanyID = e.CompanyID
    INNER JOIN Dependant d
        ON e.SSN = d.SSN
WHERE
    e.DateOfBirth < '01/01/82'
GROUP BY
    c.CompanyName,
    e.LastName,
    e.FirstName,
    e.Salary
HAVING
    Count(*) >= 2
ORDER BY
    EmployeeName ASC
```

The following sections show you how SQL processes Listing 9-6, step-by-step.

Step 1: The FROM clause

Before SQL can do anything with data, it must *get* that data, so the `FROM` clause is the first to be processed in the statement. The intermediate work product of the `FROM` clause of Listing 9-6 is shown in Figure 9-7.

Remember that the result of the `FROM` clause is a single set of data in the form of a simple table, regardless of how many tables are joined together in the `FROM` clause. Refer to the section "Understanding All Relational Result Sets," earlier in this chapter, for the details of how `JOIN`s are processed in the `FROM` clause.

Step 2: The WHERE clause

The intermediate work product of the `FROM` clause is then "fed" to the `WHERE` clause, which further processes this set of data.

All columns from all joined tables ▸

SSN	CompanyID	Firstname	Lastname	Salary	DateOfBirth	CompanyID	CompanyName
467-89-0123	6	Dirk	Thor	5000.00	1978-05-14 00:00:00.000	6	Angry Clown Entertainment
901-23-4567	3	Timmy	Williger	11250.75	1982-10-27 00:00:00.000	3	Star Trek Fan Club
890-12-3456	2	Valerie	Feuilliette	39950.00	1975-05-25 00:00:00.000	2	The Very Big Corporation of
789-01-2345	2	Allen	Davidow	65000.00	1980-07-07 00:00:00.000	2	The Very Big Corporation of
578-90-1234	6	Adam	Churvis	9500.00	1961-04-09 00:00:00.000	6	Angry Clown Entertainment
890-12-3456	2	Valerie	Feuilliette	39950.00	1975-05-25 00:00:00.000	2	The Very Big Corporation of
223-45-6789	1	Billy	Sanders	33500.00	1967-02-01 00:00:00.000	1	ABC Company, Inc.
356-78-9012	5	Natasha	Romanova	79315.95	1976-12-03 00:00:00.000	5	Azure Productions
901-23-4567	3	Timmy	Williger	11250.75	1982-10-27 00:00:00.000	3	Star Trek Fan Club
234-56-7890	1	Oksal	Kayashunu	23750.00	1953-04-19 00:00:00.000	1	ABC Company, Inc.
356-78-9012	5	Natasha	Romanova	79315.95	1976-12-03 00:00:00.000	5	Azure Productions
654-32-1098	10	Lance	Lester	5412.91	1970-11-06 00:00:00.000	10	The Stan Cox Society
578-90-1234	6	Adam	Churvis	9500.00	1961-04-09 00:00:00.000	6	Angry Clown Entertainment
789-01-2345	2	Allen	Davidow	65000.00	1980-07-07 00:00:00.000	2	The Very Big Corporation of
678-90-1234	2	Susan	Kokilas	43711.83	1980-06-09 00:00:00.000	2	The Very Big Corporation of
567-89-0123	2	Bethany	Silverberg	76328.94	1973-02-27 00:00:00.000	2	The Very Big Corporation of
789-01-2345	2	Allen	Davidow	65000.00	1980-07-07 00:00:00.000	2	The Very Big Corporation of

Figure 9-7: The intermediate work product of the `FROM` clause of Listing 9-6.

The purpose of the `WHERE` clause is to select rows that satisfy a specific criterion or criteria. Only those rows in the intermediate work product of the `FROM` clause that satisfy the `WHERE` clause criteria can pass to the next clause in SQL's processing order of precedence.

The intermediate work product of the `WHERE` clause of Listing 9-6 is shown in Figure 9-8.

All columns from all joined tables ▸

SSN	CompanyID	Firstname	Lastname	Salary	DateOfBirth	CompanyID	CompanyName
467-89-0123	6	Dirk	Thor	5000.00	1978-05-14 00:00:00.000	6	Angry Clown Entertainment
890-12-3456	2	Valerie	Feuilliette	39950.00	1975-05-25 00:00:00.000	2	The Very Big Corporation of
789-01-2345	2	Allen	Davidow	65000.00	1980-07-07 00:00:00.000	2	The Very Big Corporation of
578-90-1234	6	Adam	Churvis	9500.00	1961-04-09 00:00:00.000	6	Angry Clown Entertainment
890-12-3456	2	Valerie	Feuilliette	39950.00	1975-05-25 00:00:00.000	2	The Very Big Corporation of
223-45-6789	1	Billy	Sanders	33500.00	1967-02-01 00:00:00.000	1	ABC Company, Inc.
356-78-9012	5	Natasha	Romanova	79315.95	1976-12-03 00:00:00.000	5	Azure Productions
234-56-7890	1	Oksal	Kayashunu	23750.00	1953-04-19 00:00:00.000	1	ABC Company, Inc.
356-78-9012	5	Natasha	Romanova	79315.95	1976-12-03 00:00:00.000	5	Azure Productions
654-32-1098	10	Lance	Lester	5412.91	1970-11-06 00:00:00.000	10	The Stan Cox Society
578-90-1234	6	Adam	Churvis	9500.00	1961-04-09 00:00:00.000	6	Angry Clown Entertainment
789-01-2345	2	Allen	Davidow	65000.00	1980-07-07 00:00:00.000	2	The Very Big Corporation of
678-90-1234	2	Susan	Kokilas	43711.83	1980-06-09 00:00:00.000	2	The Very Big Corporation of
567-89-0123	2	Bethany	Silverberg	76328.94	1973-02-27 00:00:00.000	2	The Very Big Corporation of
789-01-2345	2	Allen	Davidow	65000.00	1980-07-07 00:00:00.000	2	The Very Big Corporation of

Figure 9-8: The intermediate work product of the `WHERE` clause of Listing 9-6.

If an SQL statement doesn't contain a `WHERE` clause, the intermediate work product of the `FROM` clause instead passes to the next clause in the statement.

Step 3: The GROUP BY clause

The intermediate work product then passes to the `GROUP BY` clause, if one is present in the statement.

The purpose of the `GROUP BY` clause is to group together rows in the intermediate work product based on homogenous values in the columns that define the group.

In other words, if a statement groups by the CompanyName column, all rows containing the same value as CompanyName belong to the same group after the `GROUP BY` clause finishes processing. Similarly, if a statement groups by the LastName and FirstName columns, all rows containing the same *combination* of LastName and FirstName values belong to the same group after the `GROUP BY` clause is finished processing.

But what do we mean by *groups*? If the result of every clause of an SQL statement is a simple table, where do these groups fit in the table that results from a `GROUP BY` clause?

Actually, each group becomes a single row of the intermediate work product of the `GROUP BY` clause, and each group's constituent rows are like separate little invisible tables turned sideways and sitting behind each group, as shown in Figure 9-9.

This "invisible third dimension" to the intermediate work product of the `GROUP BY` clause is available to the `HAVING` clause and aggregate functions, as you learn in the section "Step 4: The HAVING clause," later in this chapter. The invisible third dimension is an internal working structure for these purposes only and is never returned as part of a final query result set.

So the intermediate work product of the `GROUP BY` clause of Listing 9-6 is as shown in Figure 9-10.

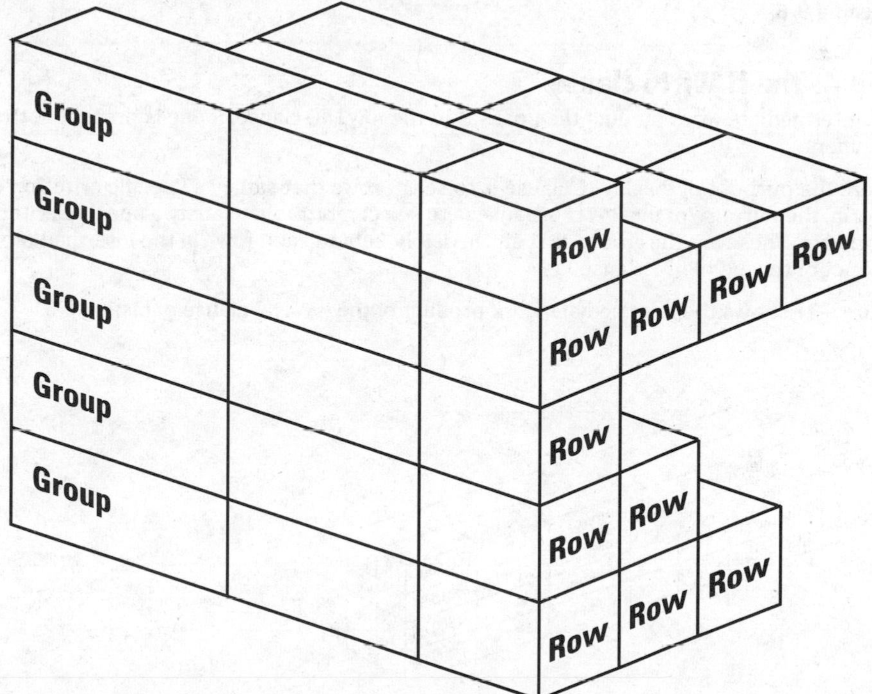

Figure 9-9: Visualizing the result of a `GROUP BY` clause.

If an SQL statement doesn't contain a `GROUP BY` clause, the intermediate work product instead passes to the next clause in the statement.

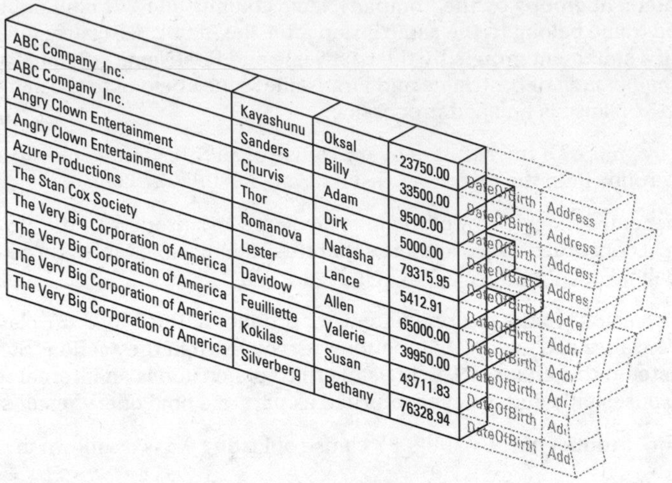

Figure 9-10: The intermediate work product of the `GROUP BY` clause of Listing 9-6.

Step 4: The HAVING clause

The intermediate work product then passes to the `HAVING` clause, if one is present in the statement.

Where the purpose of the `WHERE` clause is to select rows that satisfy a specific criterion or criteria, the purpose of the `HAVING` clause is to select *groups* that satisfy a specific criterion or criteria. These are the groups that sit "invisibly behind each row" in the intermediate work product of the `GROUP BY` clause.

Figure 9-11 shows the intermediate work product of the `HAVING` clause of Listing 9-6.

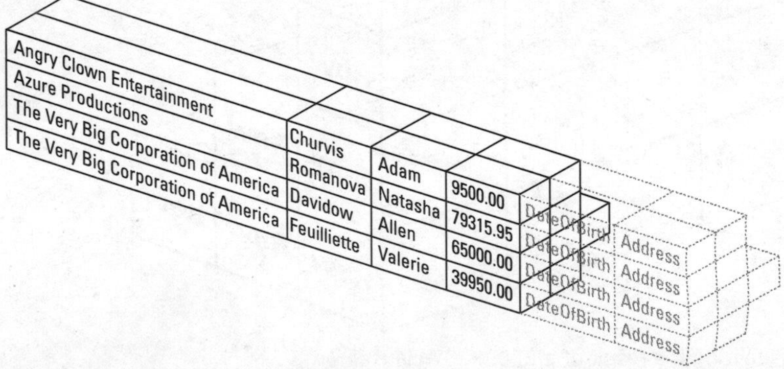

Figure 9-11: The intermediate work product of the `HAVING` clause of Listing 9-6.

Notice how few rows remain in the intermediate work product of the HAVING clause? That's because the criterion of the HAVING clause selects only those groups containing two or more elements — in other words, Employees with two or more Dependants.

If an SQL statement doesn't contain a HAVING clause, the intermediate work product instead passes to the next clause in the statement.

Step 5: The SELECT clause

The intermediate work product then passes to the SELECT clause, which selects from all the columns in the intermediate work product those columns that are part of the final query result.

Figure 9-12 shows the intermediate work product of the SELECT clause of Listing 9-6.

CompanyName	EmployeeName	Salary	NumDependants
Angry Clown Entertainment	Churvis, Adam	9500.00	2
Azure Productions	Romanova, Natasha	79315.95	2
The Very Big Corporation of America	Davidow, Allen	65000.00	3
The Very Big Corporation of America	Feuilliette, Valerie	39950.00	2

Figure 9-12: The intermediate work product of the SELECT clause of Listing 9-6.

Step 6: The ORDER BY clause

The intermediate work product then passes to the ORDER BY clause, which sorts all the columns in the intermediate work product according to the columns and directions specified in the clause.

Figure 9-13 shows the final query result as produced by the ORDER BY clause of Listing 9-6.

CompanyName	EmployeeName	Salary	NumDependants
Angry Clown Entertainment	Churvis, Adam	9500.00	2
The Very Big Corporation of America	Davidow, Allen	65000.00	3
The Very Big Corporation of America	Feuilliette, Valerie	39950.00	2
Azure Productions	Romanova, Natasha	79315.95	2

Figure 9-13: The final query result as produced by the ORDER BY clause of Listing 9-6.

And that's that! Not exactly the way that you envisioned SQL working, eh? Who ever thought that the SELECT clause was one of the last things to be processed? But it makes sense if you see it all laid out as here, doesn't it? In fact, the processing order of precedence that you read here and in the preceding sections solves a few mysteries that you may be wondering about.

You can refer to table-name aliases, for example, anywhere in an SQL statement, but if you try to use a column-name alias in the WHERE, GROUP BY, or HAVING clauses, an error is thrown. This is because table-name aliases are defined in the FROM clause which is processed first, so aliases defined there can be referenced by all the clauses that follow. Column-name aliases, however, are defined in the SELECT clause, which is processed next-to-last, so the only clause that can reference a column name alias is the ORDER BY clause, which is the only clause processed after the SELECT clause.

After you understand how SQL processes statements, you have a much easier time learning how and when to use the more complicated aspects of SQL, as the following sections show you.

How and when to use GROUP BY, HAVING, and DISTINCT

After learning how SQL works internally, you can better learn how to put the more complicated aspects of it to use.

The difference between GROUP BY and DISTINCT

First we need to clarify the difference between `GROUP BY` and `DISTINCT`. Quite a bit of confusion exists over these two clauses, because they often produce the same query results but for very different reasons. In fact, `GROUP BY` and `DISTINCT` are not related in any way whatsoever.

As mentioned earlier in the section "Step 3: The GROUP BY clause," the `GROUP BY` clause produces as its intermediate work product a table of rows representing each group, and a sort of "invisible third dimension" lies behind each row, containing the constituent rows that make up that group. The constituent rows "sitting behind" each group contain the exact same values in each of the columns specified in the `GROUP BY` clause; all columns not specified in the `GROUP BY` clause can have different values in these constituent rows.

By comparison, `DISTINCT` looks at each row produced by the `SELECT` clause and simply discards all duplicate rows so that each row in the final query result is unique (or *distinct*). `DISTINCT` looks at the *combination* of all columns in the `SELECT` clause to determine whether one row is identical to another.

If the `GROUP BY` clause of a statement contains all the same columns contained in the `SELECT` clause, the final query result is the same as a similar statement that doesn't contain a `GROUP BY` clause, but instead contains a `DISTINCT` clause. Because every column in the `SELECT` clause is also specified in the `GROUP BY` clause, the group is defined as any distinct *combination* of those columns, so the final query result contains all such unique combinations because of this grouping mechanism. On the other hand, `DISTINCT` simply discards all but the first occurrence of each unique combination of the columns in the `SELECT` clause.

The two results are the same but for very different reasons. If you are not fully aware of these reasons, you ultimately write incorrect SQL in your application. Read the following sections to gain more insight into how the `GROUP BY` clause works with `HAVING` and aggregate functions—something `DISTINCT` cannot do.

Visualizing how the HAVING clause works

As shown in Listing 9-6, you can use the `HAVING` clause to find out how many Employees have two or more dependants. But how does the SQL statement determine this fact? The `HAVING` clause criterion in the listing is simply as follows:

```
HAVING Count(*) >= 2
```

Who said anything about Dependants here? No one; it is implied.

You see, whenever you create a group, that "invisible third dimension" of constituent rows for that group contains one row for each element in that group. Because you group by the columns that you `SELECT` from the Company and Employee tables, one constituent row for each Dependant is joined in the `FROM` clause.

So the `HAVING` clause performs its calculations and functions on the "invisible third dimension" of constituent rows "sitting behind" each group. Take, therefore, the following line of code:

```
HAVING Count(*) >= 2
```

Using that code in a listing is like saying the following:

For each group `HAVING` *at least two constituent rows sitting behind it.*

Another way to visualize the `HAVING` clause is to think of it as a `WHERE` clause that operates on those constituent rows sitting behind each group. Take a look at Listing 9-7 and its result set in Figure 9-14.

Listing 9-7: **An example without a HAVING clause**

```
SELECT
    e.LastName + ', ' + e.FirstName AS EmployeeName,
    count(*) as NumDependantsAdded13OrOlder
FROM
    Employee e INNER JOIN Dependant d
        ON e.SSN = d.SSN
GROUP BY
    e.LastName,
    e.FirstName
ORDER BY
    EmployeeName ASC
```

EmployeeName	NumDependantsAdded13OrOlder
Churvis, Adam	2
Davidow, Allen	3
Feuilliette, Valerie	2
Haymen, Turk	1
Kayashunu, Oksal	1
Kokilas, Susan	1
Lester, Lance	1
Rodriguez, Kiki	2
Romanova, Natasha	2
Sanders, Billy	1
Silverberg, Bethany	1
Thor, Dirk	1
Williger, Timmy	2

Figure 9-14: The result set from Listing 9-7.

Now you can add a `HAVING` clause as shown in Listing 9-8 so that you retrieve only Employees whose youngest Dependant was added to the database after the age of 13. The result set of Listing 9-8 is shown in Figure 9-15.

Listing 9-8: **An example without a HAVING clause**

```
SELECT
    e.LastName + ', ' + e.FirstName AS EmployeeName,
    count(*) as NumDependantsAdded13OrOlder
FROM
    Employee e INNER JOIN Dependant d
```

Continued

Listing 9-8 (continued)

```
        ON e.SSN = d.SSN
GROUP BY
    e.LastName,
    e.FirstName
HAVING
    Min(d.Age) > 13
ORDER BY
    EmployeeName ASC
```

EmployeeName	NumDependantsAdded13OrOlder
Churvis, Adam	2
Feuilliette, Valerie	2
Haymen, Turk	1
Rodriguez, Kiki	2
Romanova, Natasha	2
Silverberg, Bethany	1
Williger, Timmy	2

Figure 9-15: The result set from Listing 9-8.

Remember that the preceding explanations are conceptualizations, not definitions. We are using terms such as "invisible third dimension," "constituent rows," and "sitting behind" very loosely to help you visualize what is happening behind the scenes, because without this visualization, your coding is likely to be a "ready-fire-aim" affair that doesn't give you what you want.

When you can and cannot use aggregate functions

To *aggregate* means to gather multiple elements into a whole. An *aggregate function* operates on a set of rows and returns a single value representing the aggregate of those rows. For instance, Avg(Salary) returns the average salary of the selected employee rows, so Avg() is considered an aggregate function. Aggregate functions are also known as *set functions* because they operate over a set of data.

The best way to determine when you can and cannot use aggregate functions is to carefully listen to the English language version of the question (that is, the *query*) that you are asking the database. "What is the average salary of all Employees born after July 4, 1975?" is, for example, a straightforward, well-formed question, so it easily fits into an SQL statement, as the following code shows:

```
SELECT
    Avg(Salary)
FROM
    Employee
WHERE
    DateOfBirth > '07/04/1975'
```

But what about "What is the name of every Employee and the average salary of all Employees born after July 4, 1975?" Is this a valid question? Actually, it is two separate questions that are unnaturally "smushed" together. The following query that would attempt to answer this question is equally unnatural and would, therefore, throw an error:

```
SELECT
   LastName + ', ' + FirstName AS EmployeeName,
   Avg(Salary)
FROM
   Employee
WHERE
   DateOfBirth > '07/04/1975'
```

How can you retrieve both individual employees and the average of all employees as a single query result set? You can't! These are two different sets of data with two totally different dimensions, and one has absolutely nothing at all to do with the other. The fact that both questions are about Employees makes no difference.

As do all functions, the `Avg()` function returns a single value—in this case, the average of the values in the Salary column for the *set* of data described by the `WHERE` clause. That's *one* value, meaning that it appears exactly *one* time in the final query result. In other words, it has a dimension of one row by one column.

On the other hand, consider the column defined by the following code:

```
LastName + ', ' + FirstName AS EmployeeName
```

EmployeeName is not a function, nor does it operate over a set of data. As you would expect, this query column definition returns one value for each row in the data described by the `WHERE` clause. In other words, it has a dimension of *N* rows by one column.

Clearly, the averaging function cannot co-exist with the column display in the same SQL statement because they are of different dimensions. These same rules of operation hold for all aggregate functions, such as `Min()`, `Max()`, `Sum()`, and so on.

The rules change if GROUP BY is present

If `GROUP BY` is present in an SQL statement, the set of data over which a set function operates changes from the one entire data set described by the statement to each separate set of *constituent rows sitting behind each group*. Do you see why that visualization is so useful? By showing that invisible third dimension, you can now visualize the result of the set function for each set or group of rows in the result set.

If you want to find the average age at which the Dependants of each Employee were recorded in the database, for example, you would execute the following query:

```
SELECT
   e.LastName + ', ' + e.FirstName AS EmployeeName,
   Avg(d.Age) as AverageAge
FROM
   Employee e INNER JOIN Dependant d
         ON e.SSN = d.SSN
GROUP BY
   e.LastName,
   e.FirstName
```

And the result would be as follows:

```
EmployeeName           AverageAge
Churvis, Adam          55
Davidow, Allen         30
Silverberg, Bethany    15
Sanders, Billy         10
```

```
Thor, Dirk          NULL
Rodriguez, Kiki           17
Lester, Lance             1
Romanova, Natasha 38
Kayashunu, Oksal  10
Kokilas, Susan            2
Williger, Timmy           38
Haymen, Turk              16
Feuilliette, Valerie      59
```

This time, the `GROUP BY` clause tells the `Avg()` function to operate over each employee's "group" of Dependants rather over than the entire data set all at once.

But why can you display the function result and the query columns together in the same query? Because the dimension of the `Avg()` function's results is exactly the same as that of the other query columns in the `SELECT` clause. The `Avg()` function returns a single value for every group, as do the column definitions in the `SELECT` clause.

We hope that these visualizations of how SQL works internally helps you write SQL statements that don't throw errors because you're trying to do the impossible but that give you the results that you're looking for.

Structured Exception Handling

Notice how the title of this section is "Structured *exception* handling" rather than "Structured error handling." The difference may seem casual, but it really points to a new way of thinking about your code, as follows:

Errors are good.

What?! The infidel speaks blasphemy! No, not really. Let us explain.

So far in this book, you've learned how to design databases that plug up all the little holes that you may have had in your previous database designs so that only purified data goes into your tables and referential integrity is indeed preserved under all possible circumstances. And in Chapters 10 and 11, you build database methods directly into your database by using triggers and stored procedures so that only intended users and applications can execute specific operations.

This extra "tightness" inherently causes many more errors to be thrown by your database whenever incorrect operations are attempted. If you've followed along so far, you now know, for example, that you should define alternate keys on unique columns that are not primary keys, such as a user's e-mail address.

Once you have an alternate key defined on the e-mail address column, you can safely try to insert the user no matter what e-mail address that he gives. If a duplicate e-mail address is already in the database, an *exception* is thrown. But this exception is no longer considered an *error*, because you are going to programmatically utilize it in your ColdFusion code to inform the user of the specific problem that he is facing and perhaps also route him to the next logical step in resolving his problem. Now that's good programming!

Previously, if someone attempted to add more than one user with the same e-mail address, you probably had some ColdFusion code attempt to find any users with the same e-mail address. And if `RecordCount` was greater than zero, you told the user "No go."

Listing 9-9 shows an example of structured exception handling in action. It's going to catch exceptions where the database throws an error because of an alternate key violation and then handle those exceptions by sending the user to an alternative registration page that informs him of the problem and enables him either to log in by using his existing e-mail address and password or to e-mail his forgotten password to himself.

Listing 9-9: Handling the exception of an existing e-mail address

```
<cftry>
<cfquery name="AddUser"
    datasource="CFMXBible">
INSERT INTO AppUser (
    Email,
    FirstName,
    LastName,
    Password
    )
VALUES (
    'adam@productivityenhancement.com',
    'Adam',
    'Churvis',
    'licorice'
    )
</cfquery>

<cfcatch type="Database">
    <!--- Duplicate alternate key, when implemented as unique index ---
>
    <cfif CFCATCH.NativeErrorCode EQ "2601">
        <cflocation
url="AlternateRegistrationMethod.cfm?msg=#URLEncodedFormat('Your email
address is already in our database.')#">
    <cfelse>
        <cflocation url="Error.cfm?msg=#URLEncodedFormat('An
unspecified database error occurred attempting to add a user to our
database.')#">
    </cfif>
</cfcatch>
</cftry>

<cflocation url="Finished.cfm?msg=#URLEncodedFormat('The user was
successfully added to the database.')#">
```

So database error 2601 is an error from the database's perspective but an exception from your ColdFusion application's point of view, and you can easily handle it.

Listing 9-10 is a `CFTRY` construct for `CFQUERY` and `CFSTOREDPROC` calls to SQL Server 2000 that catches the most common database errors so that you can handle them as exceptions in your application. It is also on the CD-ROM that accompanies this book. I find wrapping Listing 9-10 (with a little editing) around all my `CFQUERY` calls that modify data very useful so that I can redirect the user whenever an exception occurs.

To discover the NativeErrorCode values for your database, create a template that throws the error you're investigating, wrap the offending code in a CFTRY block, and CFDUMP Var="#CFCATCH#" inside a CFCATCH Type="Any" block. The CFDUMP will display a key named NativeErrorCode whose value is what you're looking for.

Listing 9-10: Universal structured exception-handling code for SQL Server 2000

```
<cftry>

<!--- Your database query or stored procedure call goes here --->

<cfcatch type="Database">
    <cfswitch expression="#CFCATCH.NativeErrorCode#">
    <cfcase value="2627">
        <!--- Duplicate Primary/Alternate Key, implemented as
constraint object --->
        <cflocation
url="#Request.URLRoot#/admin/Error.cfm?msg=#URLEncodedFormat('That
<tablename> already exists.  Please hit your back button and change the
<pkcolumn> for this <tablename>')#">
    </cfcase>
    <cfcase value="2601">
        <!--- Duplicate Alternate Key, implemented as a unique index --
->
        <cflocation
url="#Request.URLRoot#/admin/Error.cfm?msg=#URLEncodedFormat('That
<tablename> already exists.  Please hit your back button and change the
<akcolumn> for this <tablename>')#">
    </cfcase>
    <cfcase value="547">
        <!--- Foreign Key or Check Constraint --->
        <cfif FindNoCase("FOREIGN KEY", CFCATCH.Detail)>
            <cflocation
url="#Request.URLRoot#/admin/Error.cfm?msg=#URLEncodedFormat('That
<tablename> could not be deleted because one or more <childtable>
records are still attached to this <tablename>.  Please delete any
<childtables> attached to this <tablename> and try again.')#">
        <cfelse>
            <cflocation
url="#Request.URLRoot#/admin/Error.cfm?msg=#URLEncodedFormat('The data
you tried to insert into the database is invalid.')#">
        </cfif>
    </cfcase>
    <cfcase value="168,220,244,248,232,8115">
        <!--- Numeric Overflow --->
        <cflocation
url="#Request.URLRoot#/admin/Error.cfm?msg=#URLEncodedFormat('A numeric
value you entered was too large for the database to accept.')#">
    </cfcase>
```

```
        <cfdefaultcase>
            <!--- Custom errors thrown using RAISERROR in the 50000+ range
--->
            <cfif CFCATCH.NativeErrorCode GT 50000>
                <!--- User-defined message from a trigger --->
                <cfset Detail = ListLast(CFCATCH.Detail, "]")>
                <cfset Detail = ListFirst(Detail, Chr(60))>
                <cflocation
url="#Request.URLRoot#/admin/Error.cfm?msg=#URLEncodedFormat(Detail)#">
            <cfelse>
                <!--- Any other error --->
                <cfrethrow>
            </cfif>
        </cfdefaultcase>
        </cfswitch>
    </cfcatch>
    </cftry>
```

Deliberately throwing and handling exceptions is a new way of coding for many ColdFusion developers, but it is truly a best practice that we encourage you to incorporate into your code.

Query Caching

Query caching places the results of a database query into ColdFusion Server's memory where it can be instantly retrieved without querying the database. Query caching is one of the most useful tools for enhancing performance in your ColdFusion applications; unfortunately, it is also one of the least used. A few caveats are involved in query caching, but all in all, it is a very straightforward technique to employ.

You should consider caching only queries that fit the following criteria:

- ✦ The query has a significant allowable latency. In other words, the data in the result set doesn't change often and is, therefore, stable over a significant length of time.
- ✦ The query is universal in scope, such that all users of your application can utilize exactly the same query result.
- ✦ The query requires significant resources to process.

Another way to look at it is as follows:

- ✦ The latency gives you *permission* to use caching.
- ✦ The universality of scope makes caching *possible*.
- ✦ The processing requirements make caching *necessary*.

Whenever you cache a query, you place a copy of it in memory and instruct ColdFusion MX to retrieve the memory-based version of that query for a specified length of time.

For example, Listing 9-11 shows a CFQUERY that caches its result set for 12 hours, after which another call to CFQUERY retrieves data directly from the database and caches that new result set in memory.

Listing 9-11: A CFQUERY call that caches its result set for 12 hours

```
<cfquery name="CacheFor12Hours"
    datasource="CFMXBible"
    cachedwithin="#CreateTimeSpan(0,12,0,0)#">
SELECT
    LastName + ', ' + FirstName AS UserName
FROM
    AppUser
ORDER BY
    UserName ASC
</cfquery>

<cfoutput query="CacheFor12Hours">
#UserName#<br>
</cfoutput>
```

Listing 9-12 shows a `CFQUERY` that caches its result set after 1 a.m. on July 4, 2002; before this time, a call to `CFQUERY` retrieves its data directly from the database.

Listing 9-12: A CFQUERY call that starts to cache after 1 a.m. on July 4, 2002

```
<cfquery name="CacheAfterDate"
         datasource="CFMXBible"
         cachedafter="07/04/2002 1:00:00">
SELECT
    LastName + ', ' + FirstName AS UserName
FROM
    AppUser
ORDER BY
    UserName ASC
</cfquery>

<cfoutput query="CacheAfterDate">
#UserName#<br>
</cfoutput>
```

`CachedWithin` is the more commonly used of the two available caching attributes. `CachedAfter` has very few practical uses; it is mainly used to wait until a specified time when new data becomes available to your database from some external process and then to cache the new data.

Good candidates for caching queries are as follows:

- ✦ The online-store catalog pages that display the thumbnails and descriptions of the categories of items sold.
- ✦ The online-store catalog pages that display each specific category's items.
- ✦ The list of items on sale in an online store.

✦ Select menus that are dynamically populated with infrequently changed data, such as the names of department managers.

Take a look at your current applications and see whether you can find opportunities for query caching. Just make sure that you ask your clients how latent the data produced by each query can realistically be before you cache it.

Watch your memory!

Don't forget where a cached query resides: in memory. If you don't have enough physical memory to easily handle all your cached queries, your operating system pages memory out to disk, and the performance gains that you hoped for are greatly diminished.

Chapter 44 shows you how to configure ColdFusion MX to handle a specific number of cached queries.

You can't use CFQUERYPARAM

`CFQUERYPARAM` creates what are called *bind parameters* in your query that bind to structures in your database through the database driver. If your query is cached, you have no database structure to which anything can bind after the `CFQUERY` call is made. This is one reason why you can't use `CFQUERYPARAM` with cached queries.

The other reason is one of internal identification. ColdFusion MX identifies a cached query in memory by its signature, which is the textual version of the SQL code itself. After ColdFusion MX receives a `CFQUERY` call with a `CACHEDWITHIN` or a `CACHEDAFTER` clause specifying a time value within the caching period, it looks in memory for a query object using the same SQL statement. If the statement requested is identical in every way to the version in memory, the memory-based version of that query's result set is returned to ColdFusion, and the database is bypassed entirely.

Bind parameters obfuscate those portions of the SQL code that are likely to change between queries—namely, the ColdFusion variables that are directly resolved into plain text by ColdFusion's interpretation engine if `CFQUERYPARAM` isn't present. So comparing an SQL statement containing a `CFQUERYPARAM` tag against a plain-text SQL statement is impossible, because you have no way to tell whether anything inside the query's `CFQUERYPARAM` has changed.

Caching stored procedures

`CFSTOREDPROC` does not enable you to cache a result set produced by a stored procedure. But you can cache it if you call your stored procedure by using a special syntax within `CFQUERY`, as shown in Listing 9-13.

Listing 9-13: Caching a stored procedure result set by using CFQUERY

```
<cfquery name="CacheFor12Hours"
        datasource="CFMXBible"
        cachedwithin="#CreateTimeSpan(0,12,0,0)#">

        {CALL sp_GetCompanies('GA')}

</cfquery>

<cfoutput query="CacheFor12Hours">
#CompanyName#, #ZipCode#<br>
</cfoutput>
```

Listing 9-13 calls the stored procedure `sp_GetCompanies`. You build `sp_GetCompanies` in Chapter 10.

This technique works only for stored procedures returning a single result set. If your stored procedure returns more than one result set, you must forego query caching and call your stored procedure by using `CFSTOREDPROC`.

Summary

In this chapter, you've learned how to understand and, most importantly, visualize how SQL is processed internally, including joins, grouping, and aggregate functions. You've also learned how to leverage structured exception handling for routing ColdFusion application behavior based on database errors thrown when a user attempts a forbidden action. Finally, you learned how to improve the performance of your ColdFusion application by caching database result sets in memory.

I sincerely hope this chapter has helped you better understand SQL as a descriptive language through the visualization examples that we've given. You can memorize syntax until you're blue in the face, but just as in any professional endeavor, if you can't "feel it," you can't perfect it.

Always visualize relational result sets as a series of simple two-table joins and your types of joins as Venn diagrams. If you picture the intermediate work product of each clause of your SQL statement as it is produced and then fed to the next clause in the processing order of precedence, you can never get lost again.

Similarly, listen to the English-language version of your SQL statement and ask yourself whether it makes sense. Are you asking for two different things of different dimensions in the same statement? If so, your statement always fails because the question isn't possible to answer.

Remember that `GROUP BY` conceptually produces an invisible third dimension containing the constituent rows that make up each group and that aggregate functions operate over each individual group rather than the entire set of data.

If you design your database by using all of the principles taught in the earlier chapters, plus what you learn in Chapters 10 and 11, you can expect your database to throw errors whenever users attempt to violate the rules that you built into it. Knowing where to catch these database errors in your application and how to handle them simply as exceptions to normal workflow makes your ColdFusion code smaller, easier to write, and more manageable.

Finally, find the places where data doesn't need to be "live" all the time, but can lag for a few hours or days before being refreshed, and turn these segments into cached queries.

✦ ✦ ✦

Using Advanced Database Techniques

In This Chapter

Getting a handle on transactions

Using views for easier development and security

Learning the ins and outs of stored procedures

Understanding Oracle stored procedures

Using stored procedures

Chapter 10 takes you beyond merely querying tables. Here and in Chapter 11, you learn the principles and techniques that really make a database perform to its fullest potential.

Because of the scope of this book, the topics in this chapter can be touched on only summarily. To fully understand them requires many hours of in-depth reading outside this book. My goal is to teach you the basics, give you a solid understanding of how they are correctly used with ColdFusion applications, and encourage you to read further in books that treat these topics with the depth and detail they deserve. For the internal mechanics of SQL Server 2000, we recommend *Inside Microsoft SQL Server 2000* by Kalen Delaney (Microsoft Press). For writing stored procedures and triggers in Transact/SQL, the language used by SQL Server 2000, we recommend *Advanced Transact-SQL for SQL Server 2000*.

These techniques apply mostly to full-fledged database *servers* and not to desktop databases such as Microsoft Access. Desktop databases do not have the advanced features such as stored procedures and triggers that are covered in this chapter.

This chapter is intended to be run on SQL Server 2000 only, except where Oracle 9i techniques are addressed.

If you want to follow along with this chapter, look in the SQL2000 and Oracle9i subdirectories of the Chapter 10 directory on the CD-ROM accompanying this book and carefully follow the installation instructions in their `README.TXT` files.

Transactions

This section covers *transactions*, why they are very important to solid database design, multiuser concerns that you must consider in designing transactions, and how transactions are controlled.

Understanding transactions

A *transaction* is an *indivisible action* (also known as an *atomic action*, a *least unit of work*, or a *single unit of work*). No matter how many individual data manipulations occur within the transaction, it's all or nothing: If all the individual manipulations execute correctly, the transaction is successful; if any one of the individual manipulations fail, the entire transaction fails.

The most common example of a transaction involves the ATM at your bank. If you request $20 from the machine, it should both give you a twenty-dollar bill *and* remove $20 from the balance in your account. Both actions must occur for the transaction to be valid. If only one of them occurs, someone's going to be pretty upset!

Now look at a database transaction. Listing 10-1 creates an order item on a sales order and also removes the amount ordered from the AvailableToSell column of the InventoryItem table.

Listing 10-1: A simple transaction using CFTRANSACTION

```
<cftransaction>

<cfquery name="InsertOrderItem"
        datasource="CFMXBible">
    INSERT INTO OrderItem (
        SalesOrderID,
        ItemNumber,
        Description,
        UnitPrice,
        Quantity
        )
    VALUES (
        1,
        'CAS30-BLK',
        '30-Minute Cassette, Black Case',
        1.05,
        10
        )
</cfquery>

<cfquery name="UpdateInventory"
        datasource="CFMXBible">
    UPDATE
        InventoryItem
    SET
        AvailableToSell = AvailableToSell - 10
    WHERE
        ItemNumber = 'CAS30-BLK'
</cfquery>

</cftransaction>
```

(In Chapter 11, you learn the reasons why this function should be implemented as a trigger, but for now, just concentrate on the transaction.)

Everything between the opening and closing CFTRANSACTION tags is considered a single transaction. For this transaction to succeed, both the insert into the OrderItem table and the update of the InventoryItem table must succeed. That's the whole idea of a transaction: all or nothing. If both queries are successful, the transaction commits, and the effects of both queries are written to the database. If either query fails, the entire transaction is *rolled back* as if nothing ever happened.

Where to control a transaction

In the example in the preceding section, ColdFusion supplies the commands to control the beginning and end of the transaction, but in many cases, such control is handled at the database server itself using native database commands. So where should you control a transaction?

The simple answer to this question is always "At the database server, if you possibly can." The reason for this answer is the database's capability to control its transactions by using native commands and capabilities instead of relying on the database driver's capability to communicate transactional control to the database.

Some database drivers do not have the capability to pass transactional control commands to your database, so in these cases, you need to encapsulate all transactional controls within a stored procedure on the database and simply call it from ColdFusion. Some other drivers can communicate only a subset of the database's available transactional control commands and are, therefore, not as capable a solution.

Look now at a transaction that is controlled within the stored procedure itself. Listing 10-2 is the equivalent of Listing 10-1, except that the transaction is controlled within the stored procedure rather than in ColdFusion.

Listing 10-2: Adapting Listing 10-1 for transactional control within the database rather than in ColdFusion

```
BEGIN TRANSACTION

INSERT INTO OrderItem (
    SalesOrderID,
    ItemNumber,
    Description,
    UnitPrice,
    Quantity
    )
VALUES (
    1,
    'CAS30-BLK',
    '30-Minute Cassette, Black Case',
    1.05,
    10
    )

IF @@ERROR != 0
    BEGIN
```

Continued

Listing 10-2 *(continued)*

```
        RAISERROR 50001 'The OrderItem could not be inserted.'
        ROLLBACK TRANSACTION
        RETURN
        END

    UPDATE
        InventoryItem
    SET
        AvailableToSell = AvailableToSell - 10
    WHERE
        ItemNumber = 'CAS30-BLK'

    IF @@ERROR != 0
        BEGIN
        RAISERROR 50002 'The InventoryItem could not be updated.'
        ROLLBACK TRANSACTION
        RETURN
        END

    COMMIT TRANSACTION
```

The syntax is a little different, but the principles are very similar, aren't they? It's really just a matter of learning both methods for implementing transactions and then controlling them as close to the database server as your application enables you to do so.

A good example of when you *need* to control a transaction within ColdFusion is whenever you are passing multiple rows of data from ColdFusion to the database server, and you want to encapsulate all those queries into a single transaction. Listing 10-3 illustrates this example.

Listing 10-3: Inserting multiple rows within a single transaction

```
<cftransaction>
<cfloop index="i" from="1" to="#ArrayLen(arItemNumber)#">
    <cfquery name="InsertOrderItems"
datasource="CFMXBible">
  INSERT INTO OrderItem (
    SalesOrderID,
    ItemNumber,
    Description,
    UnitPrice,
    Quantity
    )
  VALUES (
    #Val(arSalesOrderID[i])#,
    '#Trim(arItemNumber[i])#',
    '#Trim(arDescription[i])#',
    #Val(arUnitPrice[i])#,
    #Val(arQuantity[i])#
```

```
    )
    </cfquery>
</cfloop>
</cftransaction>
```

You currently have no easy and effective way to directly send multidimensional data from ColdFusion to a database server in a single statement. Until such a method exists, you must loop over ColdFusion arrays or structures and call CFQUERY once for each unit of data to be stored in the database.

CFTRANSACTION and exception handling

The default behavior of the CFTRANSACTION tag is such that if you do not explicitly command it to commit or rollback, it does so implicitly for you. This is the technique shown in Listings 10-1 and 10-3. Many ColdFusion developers are used to coding that way, but if you rely on the implicit behavior that CFTRANSACTION automatically commits and rolls back for you, stop doing so right now. In our own tests, ColdFusion MX slows to a crawl if CFTRANSACTION tags are not explicitly coded with BEGIN, COMMIT, and ROLLBACK commands.

To make sure that you are committing only if everything works correctly and rolling back only if it doesn't, you should be very aware of CFTRANSACTION's behavior with respect to exception handling and also how to correctly nest CFTRANSACTION and CFTRY tags.

The best practice for coding CFTRANSACTION is as follows:

1. CFSET a flag variable TRUE.
2. Begin a CFTRANSACTION.
3. Open a CFTRY block.
4. Code any database queries you need.
5. Test for exceptions with CFCATCH blocks as necessary.
6. Within any and all CFCATCH blocks that would indicate a failure of any part of the transaction, CFSET the flag FALSE.
7. Close the CFTRY block.
8. Test the flag: Commit the transaction if TRUE and roll it back if FALSE.
9. Close the CFTRANSACTION.

Listing 10-4 rewrites Listing 10-1 to incorporate CFTRANSACTION best practices.

Listing 10-4: Combining CFTRANSACTION with CFTRY and CFCATCH

```
<cfset OKtoCommit = TRUE>
<cftransaction action="BEGIN">
<cftry>
<cfquery name="InsertOrderItem"
        datasource="CFMXBible">
    INSERT INTO OrderItem (
```

Continued

Listing 10-4 *(continued)*

```
            SalesOrderID,
            ItemNumber,
            Description,
            UnitPrice,
            Quantity
            )
        VALUES (
            1,
            'CAS30-BLK',
            '30-Minute Cassette, Black Case',
            1.05,
            10
            )
    </cfquery>
    <!--- If an error occurs after the first query,
    control immediately falls to CFCATCH --->

    <cfquery name="UpdateInventory"
            datasource="CFMXBible">
        UPDATE
            InventoryItem
        SET
            AvailableToSell = AvailableToSell - 10
        WHERE
            ItemNumber = 'CAS30-BLK'
    </cfquery>

        <cfcatch type="Any">
            <cfset OKtoCommit = FALSE>
        </cfcatch>
    </cftry>

    <cfif OKtoCommit>
        <cftransaction action="COMMIT"/>
    <cfelse>
        <cftransaction action="ROLLBACK"/>
    </cfif>

    </cftransaction>
```

As soon as any one of the queries throws an exception, program flow falls immediately to the applicable CFCATCH block, which then takes control and sets the OKtoCommit flag to FALSE. This circumvents any attempts to execute any other queries in the transaction. After the CFTRY block, the flag is tested and the entire transaction is either committed to disk or rolled back as if nothing ever happened.

If you're upgrading from an earlier version of ColdFusion Server, go right now and run the Find command on all your code for CFTRANSACTION, inspect your code, and determine whether you need to shore up your CFTRANSACTION tags.

Transaction isolation

Transaction isolation is one of the most misunderstood concepts of transactions, possibly because it forces you to think in terms of multiple users executing various multitable transactions over time, and that isn't easy. If you don't quite get it at first, that's okay—don't be so hard on yourself.

Transaction isolation is the degree to which the effects of one *transaction* are *isolated* from those of other transactions that are also trying to execute at the same time. Isolating the effects of one transaction from those of another is controlled through the database server's data-locking mechanisms, and these are, in turn, controlled through the `SET TRANSACTION ISOLATION LEVEL` command.

Transaction isolation is a balancing act between *concurrency* and *consistency*. In other words, "how many people can bang on it at once" versus "how accurate is the data at any given point in time." At one extreme, you can have everyone accessing data simultaneously (high concurrency) but at the cost of them working with data that may still be undergoing change as they access it (low consistency). At the other extreme, you can have each transaction absolutely separated from every other transaction such that everything appears to have been performed on a single-user machine (high consistency) but at the cost of considerably slowing down multi-user access (low concurrency).

The key to a high performance database is executing each transaction with the minimum amount of locking possible to enable sufficiently consistent data. Doing so enables your database to operate with the highest possibly concurrency while affording it the data consistency that it requires.

All in all, you have the following four levels of transaction isolation:

- Read Uncommitted
- Read Committed
- Repeatable Read
- Serializable

Various database servers have various degrees of support for transaction isolation: Some support all four levels, some support none, and most serious database products support only two or three, so carefully read the documentation for both your database product and its driver before you attempt to set a transaction's isolation level.

The following sections describe what each of these levels mean.

Read Uncommitted

Read Uncommitted is the least-used level of isolation, because it is the least safe of all. Remember that all data operations (selects, inserts, updates, deletes) take place in the database server's RAM and not on its disk. After data is requested, the database engine first looks for it in RAM—the data is possibly already there from another user's request—and if the data isn't there, it retrieves the necessary data from disk and loads it into RAM for use. If the data is being modified, after the database server sees that its operations in RAM are successful, it becomes "committed" to writing such modifications to disk, where they become permanent changes.

Between the time that data is being modified in RAM and the time that the database server is committed to writing such modifications to disk, the data is said to be in an *uncommitted* state. If you set the isolation level to Read Uncommitted and then perform a query of data that is in the process of being updated by another user, the result set contains data exactly as it appears with the other user's modifications at that moment — even if those modifications have not yet been written to disk. If the original transaction rolls back, its modifications never really existed, and therefore the second transaction's read of its uncommitted data was "dirty." This is what the term *dirty read* means.

Read Uncommitted can perform dirty reads because it has nothing at all to do with locks of any kind. At this level of isolation, locks are neither set by a transaction nor are they honored if set by another transaction. If you query the database to give you a set of data, it returns to you whatever values are in that data set at the very moment that it is requested, regardless of anything else that's going on at the time.

Read Uncommitted has the highest concurrency and the lowest consistency. It is set as follows:

```
SET TRANSACTION ISOLATION LEVEL READ UNCOMMITTED
go
BEGIN TRANSACTION
. . .
```

Note Oracle doesn't support the Read Uncommitted isolation level.

Read Committed

If you take one step up in the consistency department, you take one corresponding step down in the concurrency department, and you end up at the *Read Committed* isolation level. The difference between Read Uncommitted and Read Committed is that Read Committed sees only data that has been *committed* to being written out to disk — in other words, locks placed on the data modified by the first user's transaction are honored by the second user's transaction, so data read by the second transaction is "clean" rather than "dirty."

Although Read Committed doesn't permit dirty reads, it does permit what are called *nonrepeatable reads*, which can also become a problem. If you have a transaction that reads a set of data, performs some operation, and then reads the same set of data, for example, another user's transaction could have modified your set of data in between the two times that it was read, thereby causing the second read to appear different from the first. In other words, the read was *nonrepeatable*.

Read Committed is the default level of isolation for most database products and offers a good combination of concurrency and consistency for most applications. It is set as follows:

```
SET TRANSACTION ISOLATION LEVEL READ COMMITTED
go
BEGIN TRANSACTION
. . .
```

Repeatable Read

If your isolation level is set to *Repeatable Read*, no one else's transactions can affect the consistency between one read of a data set at the beginning of the transaction and another read toward its end. By *data set*, we are talking about *exactly the same collection* of rows — not the results of a repeat of the `SELECT` statement that produced those rows.

You see, a repeat of the `SELECT` statement may return rows that satisfy the `WHERE` clause that were inserted mid-transaction by another user. Such newly inserted rows are called *phantom rows* and are permitted under the Repeatable Read isolation level, because Repeatable Read preserves only the *exact* collection of rows originally read at the beginning of the transaction.

Repeatable Read involves more locks on data across transactions, so although it increases data consistency, concurrency takes a performance hit. It is set as follows:

```
SET TRANSACTION ISOLATION LEVEL REPEATABLE READ
go
BEGIN TRANSACTION
. . .
```

Oracle doesn't support the Repeatable Read isolation level.

Serializable

Now you come to the most isolated level of all. *Serializable* means that all transactions operate as if they were executed *in series*, or one after the other. In other words, the Serializable isolation level reduces your big, expensive, multi-user database server to a single-user machine so that the effects of one user's operations are totally unaffected by those of others. That's because each user, in effect, hogs the entire database while he is using it and doesn't give it up until he finishes.

The Serializable isolation level is the only one that prevents phantom rows, but you should ask yourself whether your transactions really care about this. As you can imagine, the Serializable level inflicts a serious and sometimes deadly hit to the multi-user performance of your system and, as such, should be used only if you have an absolutely compelling reason for it.

The Serializable isolation level is set as follows:

```
SET TRANSACTION ISOLATION LEVEL SERIALIZABLE
go
BEGIN TRANSACTION
. . .
```

The big picture of transaction isolation

Having a chart that plots isolation level against behavior may be useful, so check out the following table.

Transaction isolation levels versus behaviors

Isolation Level	*Dirty Read*	*Nonrepeatable Read*	*Phantom*
Read Uncommitted	X	X	X
Read Committed		X	X
Repeatable Read			X
Serializable			

With all this about transaction isolation level said, how do you choose the appropriate isolation level for your transactions? By carefully studying the code in your transactions and considering their minimum consistency needs with respect to every other possible transaction that could be occurring simultaneously in the system. It's not a simple task, but the following list gives you the basics:

1. Start with your default transaction isolation level set to Read Committed.
2. Examine your first transaction's code for the tables that it reads from and writes to.
3. If you don't care whether the data being read is dirty, if the transaction's modifications could take place anyway despite other concurrently running transactions, and if no further tests require a higher level of isolation, you can reduce the isolation level to Read Uncommitted for that transaction.
4. If you read from the same table twice during the same transaction and whether the first and second reads are different makes a difference to you, increase your isolation level to Repeatable Read on that transaction.
5. If you have any transactions that must not see others rows that are inserted while your transaction is executing, increase the isolation level of that transaction to Serializable.
6. Examine the rest of the transactions in your system by using this technique.

Remember that you must individually consider each of your transactions in parallel with all other database operations that could possibly occur at the same time with multiple users—doing so is what makes fine-tuning transaction isolation such a difficult task.

By the way, many developers just go as far as Step 1 and leave it at that. But if you're going to use your database in a high-transaction throughput system, it serves you well to take the hours necessary to carefully analyze your transactions for their optimum isolation level and dial them in accordingly.

Views

As we state in Chapter 9, no matter how many tables a relational join traverses, regardless of whether it contains a `GROUP BY` clause (or anything else for that matter), all query result sets manifest themselves as one or more rows that contain an identical collection of one or more columns. So, in a way, query results are virtual tables based on underlying physical tables of data.

Now imagine if you could take a query statement and define it as a formal database object that could be accessed just as a table can. Well, you can—that is what is called a *view*. Listing 10-5 defines a database view.

Listing 10-5: Defining a database view

```
CREATE VIEW vwEmployee
AS
SELECT
    SSN,
    CompanyID,
    Firstname,
    Lastname,
    DateOfBirth
FROM
    Employee
```

The boldfaced code in Listing 10-5 is just a standard `SELECT` statement; the rest of the listing simply encapsulates that `SELECT` statement as a formal, reusable database object — a *view* — with a formal name. Now, whenever you want to see all employees without their salaries, you can simply perform the following:

```
SELECT * FROM vwEmployee
```

Similarly, you can perform more elaborate queries on a view, as if it was a table, as follows:

```
SELECT
    SSN,
    Firstname + ' ' + Lastname AS Fullname,
    DateOfBirth
FROM
    vwEmployee
WHERE
    DateOfBirth > '01/01/1960'
ORDER BY
    DateOfBirth DESC
```

In fact, views can be filtered, sorted, and joined just as any physical table can.

Horizontal and vertical masking

Views typically hide elements of data so that what is returned exposes only the data that is needed. The elements being hid can be specific columns of a table, rows in that table that do not satisfy a `WHERE` clause, or a combination of both. Basically, a view *masks* unneeded data from your application.

These masks can be either *vertical* or *horizontal*. A *vertical mask* shields specific columns of a table from returning and is simply the defined collection of underlying table columns that your view contains. A *horizontal mask* shields specific rows of a table from returning and is simply the `WHERE` clause that supplies the filtering criteria for the view.

You can combine both vertical and horizontal masking in the same view. Listing 10-6, for example, returns only the `SalesOrderID`, `SaleDate`, and `OrderTotal` columns of only those sales orders with a `Status` of `20`.

Listing 10-6: A view that combines both vertical and horizontal masking

```
CREATE VIEW vwFinishedSalesOrder
AS
SELECT
    SalesOrderID,
    SaleDate,
    Total
FROM
    SalesOrder
WHERE
    Status = 20
```

Relational views

Views don't stop at a single table. In fact, views are often used to simplify complicated relational joins across multiple tables so that the application developer doesn't need to concern himself with such complexities and can instead concentrate on simply displaying relevant data. Listing 10-7 defines such a relational view.

Listing 10-7: Defining a view across multiple joined tables

```
CREATE VIEW vwEmployeeCompany
AS
SELECT
    e.SSN,
    e.Firstname + ' ' + e.Lastname AS Fullname,
    e.DateOfBirth,
    c.CompanyName
FROM
    Employee e INNER JOIN Company c
    ON e.CompanyID = c.CompanyID
```

The ColdFusion developer now can select all employees born earlier than 1960, hide the salary column, and display the name of the company for which each works, all by simply doing the following:

```
SELECT * FROM vwEmployeeCompany
```

Similarly, suppose that you tried to perform a `SELECT` against this view that included the `Salary` column, as follows:

```
SELECT
    SSN,
    Fullname,
    DateOfBirth,
    CompanyName
FROM
    VwEmployeeCompany
WHERE
    Salary > 100000
```

It would fail, because although the Salary column is a part of the underlying Employee table, it is not a part of the `vwEmployeeCompany` view being queried.

Precompiling queries

So why define views at all? Why not just `CFINCLUDE` a common `CFQUERY` call wherever that query is needed? Isn't that just as good?

No, it isn't. Not by a long shot. You see, if you send a query to your database server, the server goes through the complexities and processing expense of parsing the syntax with which the query is defined, optimizing the query for best performance, and compiling an execution plan. This very expensive process is what happens almost every time that you send a plain query to your database — just so that it can run the query!

If you define a view, your database performs the same parse/optimize/compile process on the query for which the view is defined. If you call the view, the database server knows that an appropriate execution plan already exists and executes it directly, thereby eliminating virtually all the overhead necessary to execute the query and, in the bargain, increasing performance.

You realize the biggest increases in performance by defining views on very complex relational queries, because these queries are the most difficult and time-consuming to parse and optimize.

Enhancing security

Another benefit that views afford you is the capability to lock down security on your database. Because a view is a formal database object, you can grant user and group privileges to it just as you would a table or a stored procedure. If fact, to denying direct access to physical tables and granting them only on views and stored procedures is a good practice overall — that way, you are absolutely certain that ColdFusion developers touch only the data that you want them to access.

Caveats

Views are great for easily selecting only that data that you want to access, but they can also be used to insert and update data. This can be both a help and a hindrance, depending on the view.

Suppose that your view is a simple, single-table view containing all the `NOT NULL` columns of a table, as shown in Figure 10-1.

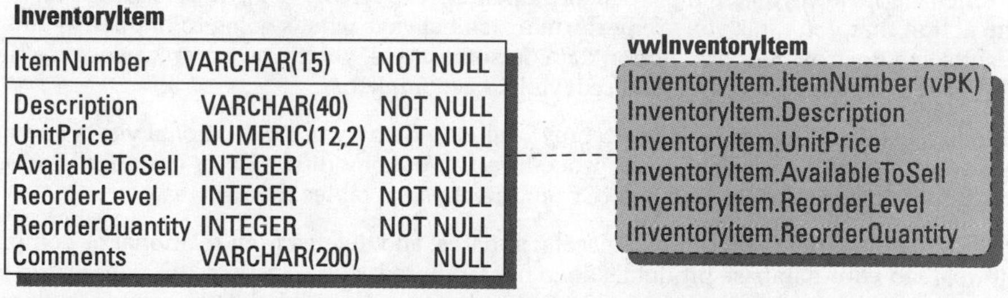

InventoryItem

ItemNumber	VARCHAR(15)	NOT NULL
Description	VARCHAR(40)	NOT NULL
UnitPrice	NUMERIC(12,2)	NOT NULL
AvailableToSell	INTEGER	NOT NULL
ReorderLevel	INTEGER	NOT NULL
ReorderQuantity	INTEGER	NOT NULL
Comments	VARCHAR(200)	NULL

vwInventoryItem

InventoryItem.ItemNumber (vPK)
InventoryItem.Description
InventoryItem.UnitPrice
InventoryItem.AvailableToSell
InventoryItem.ReorderLevel
InventoryItem.ReorderQuantity

Figure 10-1: A simple view containing all critical columns of a single table.

In such a case, you can easily insert and update data through this view, as shown in Listing 10-8.

Listing 10-8: Examples of inserting and updating through a simple view

```
INSERT INTO vwInventoryItem (
	ItemNumber,
	Description,
	UnitPrice,
	AvailableToSell
	)
VALUES (
	'CAS30-BLK',
```

Continued

Listing 10-8 *(continued)*

```
    '30-Minute Cassette, Black Case',
    1.05,
    100
    )

UPDATE
    vwInventoryItem
SET
    Description          = '30-Minute Cassette, Black Case',
    UnitPrice            = 1.25,
    AvailableToSell      = 90
WHERE
    ItemNumber           = 'CAS30-BLK'
```

But if the view does not contain all the critical (that is, NOT NULL) columns from its underlying table, you cannot insert new rows into the underlying table through that view, because you cannot supply all the data necessary to create a valid row in that table. The exception to this rule are NOT NULL columns for which default values are defined; these columns are automatically assigned their default values on insert if they're not part of the view. You can update existing rows through such a view as long as you are setting the values only of those columns defined in the view—but that's it.

Problems appear if you attempt to insert, update, or delete by using relational views, because the action that you think you are performing isn't always what's going to happen—and the results can destroy your production data. In some cases, you throw an error because the database can't figure out what you're trying to accomplish.

Our suggestion is that you never attempt to modify data by using relational views and instead define specific views and/or stored procedures for data modification or have application developers insert, update, and delete from the physical tables themselves.

If you are interested in performing inserts, updates, and deletes from relational or complicated views, read your database product's documentation regarding "Instead-Of Triggers," which replace the code in the triggering statement with code of your own. Although we do touch on Instead-Of Triggers in Chapter 11, a discussion of using them to resolve relational view data modification problems is beyond the scope of this book.

Stored Procedures

After you first learned ColdFusion, you performed every call to your database by using a CFQUERY call. CFQUERY is simple and straightforward, so it is popular with developers who just want to get the job done, but another method is more scalable and flexible for manipulating your data: *stored procedures*.

What is a stored procedure?

At its most basic level, a stored procedure takes the SQL logic that you would normally write into a CFQUERY call and stores it directly in the database server. This may not sound like a big deal, and it may not even seem that useful at first, but the added efficiency of stored procedures can spell a huge performance gain for your ColdFusion applications.

Whenever ColdFusion Server sends a CFQUERY call to your database server, the SQL logic in that CFQUERY call is pulled apart, or *parsed*, and translated into internal machine language instructions that your database server can directly understand; then these instructions are put through a process that determines the most efficient methods for executing them against the database. After the most efficient methods are decided on, they are assembled into an execution plan that is compiled and executed against the database. With some exceptions, this process happens every time that you send a CFQUERY call to your database server. That's a lot of work to do just to get ready to execute your SQL logic.

A stored procedure eliminates the need to repeat such drudgery every time that it is executed because it stores the compiled execution plan on the database server, where it can be called directly by an outside program—such as your ColdFusion application.

And after this procedure is placed into the server's memory, it remains there until it is pushed out by some other process that needs to run. So if you have sufficient memory, your stored procedure most likely stays cached in memory; this means that your database server doesn't even need to retrieve the stored procedure object from disk to execute it, resulting in the fastest possible execution of SQL logic.

Nice theory, but you need to take a look at the nuts and bolts of how it's done. Listing 10-9 shows a typical CFQUERY call.

Listing 10-9: A typical CFQUERY call

```
<cfquery name="GetCompanies"
         datasource="CFMXBible">
    SELECT
        CompanyName,
        ZipCode
    FROM
        Company
    WHERE
        State = '#Trim(FORM.State)#'
    ORDER BY
        ZipCode ASC
</cfquery>
```

To create a stored procedure in Microsoft SQL Server from the SQL logic inside this CFQUERY call, you add the following code (Listing 10-10) and execute it against the database server (by using Query Analyzer or some other batch processing utility).

Listing 10-10: Creating a stored procedure from the SQL inside Listing 10-9

```
CREATE PROCEDURE sp_GetCompanies (
    @State CHAR(2)
)
AS
SELECT
```

Continued

Listing 10-10 *(continued)*

```
    CompanyName,
    ZipCode
FROM
    Company
WHERE
    State = @State
ORDER BY
    ZipCode ASC

RETURN
```

After you execute Listing 10-10 against the database, you have a precompiled stored procedure object, `sp_GetCompanies`, that you can call from your ColdFusion application.

To call this stored procedure from ColdFusion, you use a `CFSTOREDPROC` tag in place of the `CFQUERY` tag, and you supply the parameter used by the `WHERE` clause through the `CFPROCPARAM` tag. This process is shown in Listing 10-11.

Listing 10-11: Calling the stored procedure created in Listing 10-10

```
<cfstoredproc procedure="sp_GetCompanies"
    datasource="CFMXBible">

    <cfprocparam type="In"
        cfsqltype="CF_SQL_CHAR"
        dbvarname="@State"
        value="#Trim(FORM.State)#"
        maxlength="2"
        null="No">

    <cfprocresult name="GetCompanies" resultset="1">

</cfstoredproc>
```

The database server receives this parameter from the `CFPROCPARAM` tags and supplies it to the stored procedure.

You may also notice that, in Listing 10-12, you have a third tag involved named `CFPROCRESULT`. `CFPROCRESULT` binds the result set returned from the stored procedure to a named ColdFusion query object that can be `CFOUTPUT` just as the result of running your original `CFQUERY` call can in Listing 10-9.

Listing 10-12: Stored procedure result sets are identical to CFQUERY result sets

```
<table cellspacing="2" cellpadding="2" border="1">
<tr>
    <td>Company Name</td>
    <td>Zip Code</td>
</tr>
<cfoutput query="GetCompanies">
<tr>
    <td>#CompanyName#</td>
    <td>#ZipCode#</td>
</tr>
</cfoutput>
</table>
```

Listing 10-12 is a very simple stored procedure that takes a single *input parameter* and returns a single result set. Listing 10-13 is a stored procedure that takes two input parameters and returns two result sets. See the section "Input parameters" for more details.

Listing 10-13: A stored procedure that returns two result sets

```
CREATE PROCEDURE sp_GetCompaniesEmployees (
    @State Char(2),
    @Name Char(1)
)
AS
BEGIN
    SELECT
        CompanyName,
        ZipCode
    FROM
        Company
    WHERE
        State = @State
    ORDER BY
        ZipCode ASC

    SELECT
        Firstname,
        Lastname
    FROM
        Employee
    WHERE
        Lastname LIKE @Name + '%'
    ORDER BY
        Lastname ASC,
        Firstname ASC
END
```

Listing 10-13 is an easy extension of Listing 10-10. You just add another input parameter and another result set. Whenever multiple parameters are sent to a stored procedure, they are sent in the order that they appear within the `CFSTOREDPROC` tag. Listing 10-14 shows how you call Listing 10-13 from ColdFusion.

Listing 10-14: Calling the stored procedure from Listing 10-13

```
<cfstoredproc procedure="sp_GetCompaniesEmployees"
    datasource="CFMXBible">

    <cfprocparam type="In"
        cfsqltype="CF_SQL_CHAR"
        dbvarname="@State"
        value="#Trim(FORM.State)#"
        maxlength="2"
        null="No">

    <cfprocparam type="In"
        cfsqltype="CF_SQL_CHAR"
        dbvarname="@Name"
        value="#Trim(FORM.Name)#"
        maxlength="1"
        null="No">

    <cfprocresult name="GetCompanies" resultset="1">

    <cfprocresult name="GetEmployees" resultset="2">

</cfstoredproc>
```

Again, Listing 10-14 is an easy extension of what you've already done in Listing 10-11: You just supply another input parameter and return a second result set that you can use as you can any other ColdFusion query object, as shown in Listing 10-15.

Listing 10-15: Using multiple result sets from a stored procedure.

```
<h1>Companies</h1>
<table cellspacing="2" cellpadding="2" border="1">
<tr>
    <td><b>Company Name</b></td>
    <td><b>Zip Code</b></td>
</tr>
<cfoutput query="GetCompanies">
<tr>
    <td>#CompanyName#</td>
    <td>#ZipCode#</td>
</tr>
</cfoutput>
</table>
```

```
<h1>Employees</h1>
<table cellspacing="2" cellpadding="2" border="1">
<tr>
    <td><b>Firstname</b></td>
    <td><b>Lastname</b></td>
</tr>
<cfoutput query="GetEmployees">
<tr>
    <td>#Firstname#</td>
    <td>#Lastname#</td>
</tr>
</cfoutput>
</table>
```

That's the big picture of stored procedures. The following sections delve into the details.

The three components of calling a stored procedure

As you saw earlier in the section "What is a stored procedure?" the following three tags are associated with calling a stored procedure:

1. CFSTOREDPROC, which specifies the stored procedure being called.
2. CFPROCPARAM, which enables the flow of parameters between ColdFusion and the stored procedure.
3. CFPROCRESULT, which enables ColdFusion to use result sets returned from the stored procedure.

We cover each of these in detail by using stored procedures written for SQL Server 2000, because it is a good platform for learning stored procedures. After you're familiar with how stored procedures are implemented in SQL Server 2000, we follow up by showing how sp_GetCompaniesEmployees is adapted to run on the Oracle 9i platform so that you can see the critical differences between them — and you see *plenty*.

CFSTOREDPROC

To make ColdFusion call a stored procedure and use any result sets it returns, you must tell the CFSTOREDPROC tag the following four things:

✦ What database contains the stored procedure.

✦ The name of the stored procedure to be executed.

✦ How big the database server should make the blocks of data that it returns to ColdFusion Server.

✦ Whether you want ColdFusion to have access to the stored procedure's Return Code.

Now take a look at the following typical example of database connection parameters in the CFSTOREDPROC tag:

```
<cfstoredproc procedure="sp_SomeStoredProcedure"
    datasource="CFMXBible"
    blockfactor="10"
    returncode="Yes">
```

After you are pointing to the right datasource, you specify the name of the stored procedure to execute through the procedure parameter, as follows:

```
<cfstoredproc procedure="sp_SomeStoredProcedure"
    datasource="CFMXBible"
    blockfactor="10"
    returncode="Yes">
```

You may need to prefix the stored procedure object with the owner's name, followed by a period.

BLOCKFACTOR controls how many rows at a time are returned from the database server to ColdFusion server. The range of values is from 1 to 100. Most developers never touch the BLOCKFACTOR parameter, because its default value of 1 is perfectly serviceable in most cases.

If you increase the value of BLOCKFACTOR, you increase the size of each block of data transmitted between your database server and ColdFusion server and similarly decrease the number of fetches required to service the stored procedure request. This sounds pretty enticing, because fewer fetches mean less time wasted in mechanical overhead, and processing larger blocks of data is more efficient than processing smaller blocks of data, but you face a tradeoff if you do so.

First, depending on the size of the individual rows returned from your stored procedure, you may run into memory issues with a large BLOCKFACTOR value. Your application may also suffer under heavy multi-user load with a large BLOCKFACTOR value. The optimum BLOCKFACTOR value is the largest setting that your application can consistently handle, considering memory constraints and multi-user load under production conditions. The following, for instance, code shows how to specify 10 rows at a time to be fetched from the database:

```
<cfstoredproc procedure="sp_SomeStoredProcedure"
    datasource="CFMXBible"
    blockfactor="10"
    returncode="Yes">
```

If you have a good load-testing tool, such as Empirix e-TEST Suite, start your stored procedure with a BLOCKFACTOR of 1, perform load tests on the section of your application that makes use of the stored procedure, and then increase BLOCKFACTOR in increments of 10 between each load test until your Performance Per User graph begins to plateau.

Finally, you can control whether your stored procedure passes its Return Code back to ColdFusion server by using the following code:

```
<cfstoredproc procedure="sp_SomeStoredProcedure"
    datasource="CFMXBible"
    blockfactor="10"
    returncode="Yes">
```

The Return Code is programmatically set within the stored procedure so that it can be used to communicate any number of things, such as the status of the stored procedure's execution, whether one option is taken as opposed to another, and so on.

Although it is called a Return Code — which is exactly what it is — it is referred to by ColdFusion server as a *Status Code* — specifically, CFSTOREDPROC.StatusCode. See the section "Using the Return Code," later in this chapter, to see how you can increase the flexibility of your ColdFusion apps.

CFPROCPARAM

After you have your call from ColdFusion to your stored procedure established, you need to establish the interface between your ColdFusion variables and the arguments used by your stored procedure.

Understand first, however, that not all stored procedures take arguments. Listing 10-16, for example, creates a stored procedure that simply lists all companies in Georgia.

Listing 10-16: A simple stored procedure

```
CREATE PROCEDURE sp_GetGeorgiaCompanies
AS
SELECT
    CompanyName,
    ZipCode
FROM
    Company
WHERE
    State = 'GA'
ORDER BY
    ZipCode ASC

RETURN
```

Now all that you need to do is to call the stored procedure, as shown in Listing 10-17.

Listing 10-17: Call the simple stored procedure

```
<cfstoredproc procedure="sp_GetGeorgiaCompanies"
    datasource="CFMXBible">

    <cfprocresult name="GetGeorgiaCompanies" resultset="1">

</cfstoredproc>
```

Input parameters

Listing 10-16 doesn't require any values to be passed to it, but most stored procedures require one or more *input parameters* to be supplied by ColdFusion. An input parameter is a value that is passed to a function or procedure. If you adapt Listing 10-16 to use an input parameter in place of the hard coded `GA` value, for example, you end up with Listing 10-18 (which is identical to Listing 10-10).

Listing 10-18: Adapting sp_GetGeorgiaCompanies to accept an argument

```
CREATE PROCEDURE sp_GetCompanies (
    @State CHAR(2)
)
AS
SELECT
```

Continued

Listing 10-18 *(continued)*

```
        CompanyName,
        ZipCode
    FROM
        Company
    WHERE
        State = @State
    ORDER BY
        ZipCode ASC

    RETURN
```

The code in Listing 10-19 used to call the new stored procedure in Listing 10-18 is almost identical to the stored procedure call in Listing 10-17, except for adding a single CFPROCPARAM tag to supply the state abbreviation to the stored procedure. You should recognize this call as the same call in Listing 10-11.

Listing 10-19: Calling sp_GetCompanies from ColdFusion

```
<cfstoredproc procedure="sp_GetCompanies"
    datasource="CFMXBible">

    <cfprocparam type="In"
        cfsqltype="CF_SQL_CHAR"
        dbvarname="@State"
        value="#Trim(FORM.State)#"
        maxlength="2"
        null="No">

    <cfprocresult name="GetCompanies" resultset="1">

</cfstoredproc>
```

Here's a basic breakdown of what you're seeing. ColdFusion takes the value from the input form that posted to this template and supplies that value to the stored procedure through CFPROCPARAM's VALUE attribute. The value is formally defined as being of the database's CHAR data type by specifying CFSQLTYPE="CF_SQL_CHAR", and its maximum length is limited to 2 via the MAXLENGTH attribute.

If the parameter had been a NUMERIC data type, SCALE would be used to specify the number of decimal places to which the number is accurate. MAXLENGTH is used to specify the overall length of string data types, but in some cases, MAXLENGTH can also be used to limit the size of a numeric parameter being fed to a stored procedure and, thereby, prevent out-of-range errors from being thrown, as shown in Figure 10-2.

Because you are not supplying this stored procedure parameter as a NULL value, you specify NULL="No". If you had wanted to supply a NULL value in this stored procedure parameter, you would have specified NULL="Yes", and the VALUE attribute of the CFPROCPARAM tag would have been ignored.

The TYPE attribute specifies whether the parameter is being supplied to the stored procedure, received from the stored procedure, or both. In this case, you are just supplying the parameter to the stored procedure, so the value of the TYPE attribute is IN—it is being sent from ColdFusion *in*to the stored procedure.

```
<cfstoredproc procedure="sp_GetCompanies"
 datasource="CFMXBible">

 <cfprocparam type="In"
   cfsqltype="CF_SQL_CHAR"
   dbvarname="@State"
   value="#Trim(FORM.State)#"
   maxlength="2"
   null="No">

 <cfprocresult name="GetCompanies"
   resultset="1">

<cfstoredproc>
```

```
CREATE PROCEDURE sp_GetCompanies(
 @State CHAR(2)
)
AS

SELECT
 CompanyName,
 ZipCode
FROM
 Company
WHERE
 State = @State
ORDER BY
 ZipCode ASC

RETURN
```

Figure 10-2: Visualizing the communication between ColdFusion input parameters and their corresponding stored procedure parameters.

And that's basically how you pass parameters from ColdFusion to a stored procedure. Just think of it as a more formal way to supply ColdFusion values to a query, where the strings supplied by ColdFusion are formally bound to specific data types native to your database server and are given specific size limits within which to fit.

After you know how to pass individual ColdFusion values to a stored procedure by using input parameters, you can move on to passing individual values from a stored procedure back to ColdFusion server by using output parameters.

Output parameters

You're probably used to receiving values back from stored procedures as multirow result sets, but how should you handle receiving values that are not associated with table rows? For that situation, you use *output parameters* that, unlike input parameters that send values from ColdFusion to stored procedures, receive values *from* stored procedures and bind them to ColdFusion variables so that they can be used by ColdFusion applications.

Listing 10-20 shows a stored procedure that calculates the average salary of all employees and returns the result as a single output parameter:

Listing 10-20: A stored procedure that returns a single value in an output parameter

```
CREATE PROCEDURE sp_GetAvgSalary (
    @AverageSalary Numeric(12,2) OUTPUT
)
AS
```

Continued

Listing 10-20 *(continued)*

```
SELECT
    @AverageSalary = Avg(Salary)
FROM
    Employee

RETURN
```

The OUTPUT qualifier next to a parameter is what instructs the stored procedure to expose that parameter to the calling program (in this case, your ColdFusion application) after it has finished executing.

Listing 10-21 shows the ColdFusion code that executes the stored procedure in Listing 10-20 and displays the output parameter.

Listing 10-21: Calling the stored procedure from Listing 10-20 and displaying the output parameter that it returns

```
<cfstoredproc procedure="sp_GetAvgSalary"
    datasource="CFMXBible">

    <cfprocparam type="Out"
        cfsqltype="CF_SQL_NUMERIC"
        variable="AverageSalary"
        dbvarname="@AverageSalary"
        scale="2"
        null="No">

</cfstoredproc>

<cfoutput>#AverageSalary#</cfoutput>
```

The output parameter is exposed in ColdFusion as a simple local variable that is not associated with the stored procedure that created it. It is as if you had created the local variable by using a simple CFSET call.

You are not restricted to only one output parameter; you can have as many output parameters as you want. Figure 10-3 shows what the communications between ColdFusion and the stored procedure look like.

InOut parameters

An *InOut parameter* can be sent to a stored procedure containing one value and then returned to the calling program containing a different value. Say, for example, that you have a stored procedure that receives a gift certificate coupon code and an amount due (for a sales order, inventory item, or any other monetary amount), and if the gift certificate if still valid, the Amount Due value is decreased by the amount of the certificate and is returned in the same parameter to the calling ColdFusion template. If the coupon doesn't exist (@@ROWCOUNT != 1), then the Amount Due remains unchanged. Listing 10-22 contains a perfect application of an InOut parameter.

Listing 10-22: Calling a stored procedure that contains an InOut parameter

```
CREATE PROCEDURE sp_GetAmountDue (
    @CouponCode          Varchar(16),
    @AmountDue           Numeric(12,2) OUTPUT
)
AS
DECLARE
    @Redeemed          Bit,
    @PercentDiscount     Numeric(12,2)

SELECT
    @Redeemed          = Redeemed,
    @PercentDiscount     = PercentDiscount
FROM
    Coupon
WHERE
    CouponCode = @CouponCode

IF (@@ROWCOUNT != 1)
    BEGIN
    RETURN    -- Coupon doesn't exist; no price change
    END

IF (@Redeemed = 1)
    BEGIN
    RETURN    -- Coupon already redeemed; no price change
    END
ELSE
    BEGIN
    SELECT @AmountDue = @AmountDue * (1 - @PercentDiscount / 100)
    END

RETURN
```

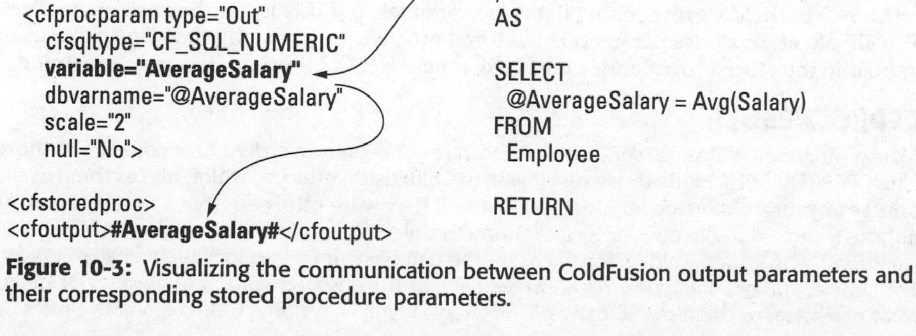

```
<cfstoredproc procedure="sp_GetAvgSalary"
 datasource="CFMXBible">

 <cfprocparam type="Out"
  cfsqltype="CF_SQL_NUMERIC"
  variable="AverageSalary"
  dbvarname="@AverageSalary"
  scale="2"
  null="No">

<cfstoredproc>
<cfoutput>#AverageSalary#</cfoutput>
```

```
CREATE PROCEDURE sp_GetAvgSalary(
 @AverageSalary Numeric(12,2) OUTPUT
)
AS

SELECT
 @AverageSalary = Avg(Salary)
FROM
 Employee

RETURN
```

Figure 10-3: Visualizing the communication between ColdFusion output parameters and their corresponding stored procedure parameters.

Listing 10-23 shows the ColdFusion code that executes the stored procedure and then displays the InOut parameter.

Listing 10-23: Calling the stored procedure from Listing 10-22 and displaying the InOut parameter

```
<cfstoredproc procedure="sp_GetAmountDue"
    datasource="CFMXBible">

    <cfprocparam type="In"
        cfsqltype="CF_SQL_VARCHAR"
        dbvarname="@CouponCode"
        value="#Trim(FORM.CouponCode)#"
        maxlength="16"
        null="No">

    <cfprocparam type="InOut"
        cfsqltype="CF_SQL_NUMERIC"
        dbvarname="@AmountDue"
        value="#Val(FORM.AmountDue)#"
        variable="AmountDue"
        scale="2"
        null="No">

</cfstoredproc>
```

Figure 10-4 shows a conceptual diagram of how InOut parameters communicate with stored procedures.

Although both SQL Server and Oracle support `InOut` type `CFPROCPARAM`s, only Oracle supports `IN OUT` qualifiers in the stored procedure definition itself. To use `InOut` parameters with SQL Server stored procedures, specify `InOut` as the `CFPROCPARAM` type and use the `OUTPUT` qualifier next to the names of the parameters in the stored procedure itself. For Oracle stored procedures, specify `InOut` as the `CFPROCPARAM` type and use the `IN OUT` qualifier next to the names of the parameters in the stored procedure itself.

Passing parameters by position rather than by name

Various documentation has mentioned that parameters may be passed to stored procedures in any order and that the binding that you specify by using `DBVARNAME` correctly maps `Value` attributes to their corresponding database variables, but this is not the case in practice. You should always pass parameters to stored procedures in exactly the same order as they appear in the stored procedure's interface; otherwise, ColdFusion throws an exception.

CFPROCRESULT

Many, but not all, database servers can return result sets from stored procedures. For those that can, `CFPROCRESULT` binds those result sets to ColdFusion queries, which makes them available for use in your ColdFusion applications just as if they were returned from a `CFQUERY` call. And although some database servers can return multiple result sets from a single `CFSTOREDPROC` call, the driver with which ColdFusion accesses the database must support such a capability as well. For Oracle, you need a *Type 4 JDBC Driver*, such as the one that ships standard with ColdFusion MX Enterprise, or the free OIC driver from Oracle if you're running ColdFusion MX Professional.

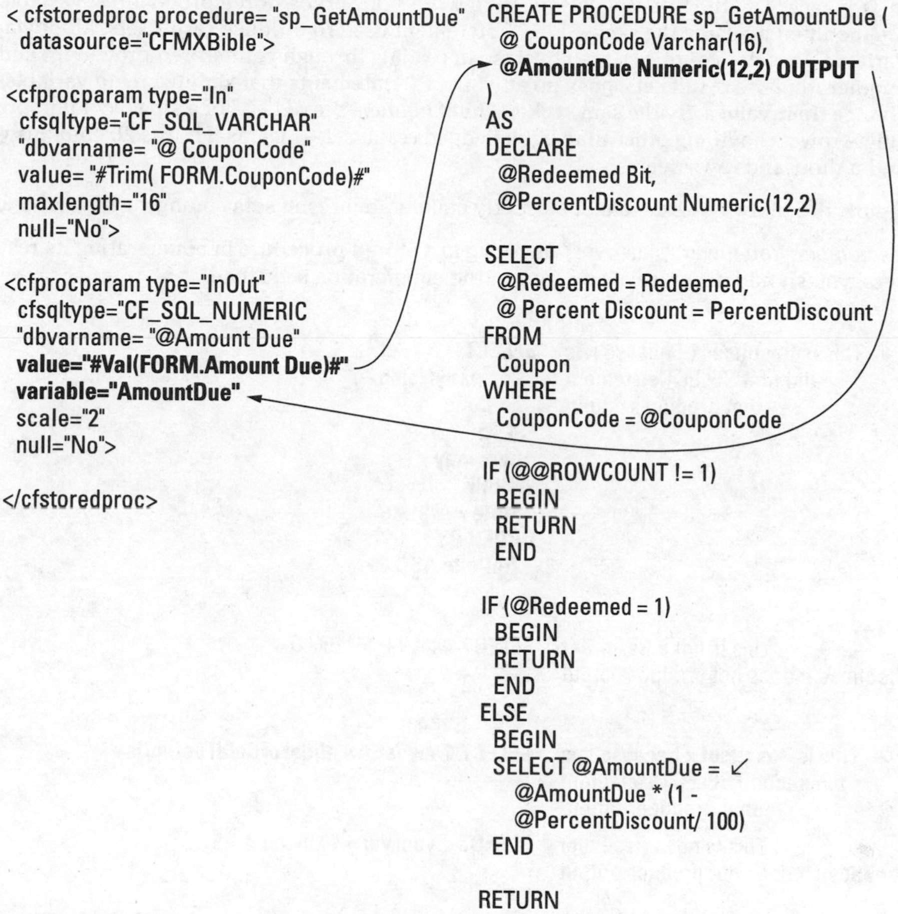

```
< cfstoredproc procedure= "sp_GetAmountDue"
 datasource="CFMXBible">

<cfprocparam type="In"
 cfsqltype="CF_SQL_VARCHAR"
 "dbvarname= "@ CouponCode"
 value= "#Trim( FORM.CouponCode)#"
 maxlength="16"
 null="No">

<cfprocparam type="InOut"
 cfsqltype="CF_SQL_NUMERIC
 "dbvarname= "@Amount Due"
 value="#Val(FORM.Amount Due)#"
 variable="AmountDue"
 scale="2"
 null="No">

</cfstoredproc>
```

```
CREATE PROCEDURE sp_GetAmountDue (
 @ CouponCode Varchar(16),
 @AmountDue Numeric(12,2) OUTPUT
)
AS
DECLARE
 @Redeemed Bit,
 @PercentDiscount Numeric(12,2)

SELECT
 @Redeemed = Redeemed,
 @ Percent Discount = PercentDiscount
FROM
 Coupon
WHERE
 CouponCode = @CouponCode

IF (@@ROWCOUNT != 1)
 BEGIN
 RETURN
 END

IF (@Redeemed = 1)
 BEGIN
 RETURN
 END
ELSE
 BEGIN
 SELECT @AmountDue = ↙
   @AmountDue * (1 -
   @PercentDiscount/ 100)
 END

RETURN
```

Figure 10-4: Visualizing the communication between ColdFusion InOut parameters and their corresponding stored procedure parameters.

Look back for a moment at Listing 10-17. You expected back only one result set from this stored procedure, and you bound that result set to a ColdFusion query object named `GetGeorgiaCompanies` by using the following `CFPROCRESULT` tag:

```
<cfprocresult name="GetGeorgiaCompanies" resultset="1">
```

This tag is instructing ColdFusion Server to take the first result set returned from the stored procedure and bind it to a ColdFusion query object named `GetGeorgiaCompanies`. After this tag executes, your ColdFusion application can use that `GetGeorgiaCompanies` query object just as if it came from a `CFQUERY` call.

`CFPROCRESULT` binds result sets to ColdFusion query objects in the order in which they are created within the stored procedure. Mapping result sets in the stored procedure to query objects in ColdFusion may seem an obvious and trivial task — just number them in the order they appear, top to bottom — but this task can become confusing unless you follow the rules, as follows.

In Transact/SQL, the SQL language used to write SQL Server stored procedures, variables are modified by using the same SELECT statement used to produce result sets. Modifying a variable does not count as a result set, so in reading through your stored procedure and enumerating the result sets, pass up any SELECT statements that simply create variables or change their values. By the same token, don't confuse the SELECT of a single column from a single row as anything other than a full-fledged result set — just as if it was 20 columns wide and a thousand rows deep.

Figure 10-5 shows an example of correctly enumerated result sets among variable operations.

Remember: You never "skip over" anything in a stored procedure in enumerating its result sets; you should never leave any gaps in the enumeration sequence.

This is **Resultset 1** because it is the first SELECT statement that produces output	**SELECT** **CompanyName,** **ZipCode** **FROM** **Company** **WHERE** **State = @State** **ORDER BY** **ZipCode ASC**
This is not a ResultSet because it does not produce output	SELECT @myVar = 125000
This is **Resultset 2** because it is the second SELECT statement that produces output	**SELECT @myVar AS aliasForColdFusionUse**
This is not a Resultset because it does not produce output	SELECT @yourVar = @myVar * 1.5
This is **Resultset 3** because it is the third SELECT statement that produces output	**SELECT** **Firstname,** **Lastname** **FROM** **Employee** **WHERE** **Salary > @yourVar**

Figure 10-5: If a SELECT statement produces output, it is an enumerated result set, regardless of its dimensions.

Oracle stored procedures and packages

In this section, you adapt Listing 10-13 to produce exactly the same results in Oracle. As you soon see, the differences are significant.

Oracle has some amazing capabilities and is a very complex product to master. Oracle enables you to create stored procedures, for example, but it also enables you to create stored *functions* that, as do all functions, return single values to the programs that call them. Oracle even enables you to bundle together collections of stored procedures, stored functions, and user-defined data types into *packages*, which are another type of database object that can be called from an outside application such as ColdFusion. Some of these complexities become apparent if you write Oracle stored procedures that must return multiple result sets.

Every time that you execute a query on an Oracle database, a workspace in memory called a *cursor* is created that contains the data result set. This data is a static constant, like a simple string or number, except that it is multivalued. Just as you can place a simple string or number value into a variable and then reference that variable by its name later on in your code, you can do the same thing with a cursor by placing it into a *cursor variable*. Cursor variables have the data type `REF CURSOR`, so named because it holds a *reference* (or pointer) to the original *cursor* in memory.

By passing this cursor variable back to ColdFusion server, ColdFusion can gain access to the Oracle result set *referred* to by the cursor variable. Finally, by including a call to `CFPROCRESULT`, you can bind that cursor to a standard ColdFusion query object and make use of it in your ColdFusion applications. By using this method through the Type 4 JDBC Oracle database driver available in ColdFusion MX Enterprise or Oracle's free OIC database driver in conjunction with ColdFusion MX Professional, Oracle can return multiple result sets from Oracle packages, as in Listing 10-24.

Listing 10-24: Returning multiple result sets through an Oracle package

```
CREATE OR REPLACE PACKAGE pkg_CompaniesEmployees AS

   TYPE recCompany IS RECORD (
      vCompanyName      Company.CompanyName%TYPE,
      vZipCode          Company.ZipCode%TYPE
   );

   TYPE recEmployee IS RECORD (
      vLastname          Employee.Lastname%TYPE,
      vFirstname          Employee.Firstname%TYPE
   );

   TYPE curCompanies IS REF CURSOR RETURN recCompany;

   TYPE curEmployees IS REF CURSOR RETURN recEmployee;

   PROCEDURE sp_GetCompaniesEmployees (
      vState IN Char,
      vName IN Char,
      rsCompanies OUT curCompanies,
      rsEmployees OUT curEmployees
   );

END pkg_CompaniesEmployees;
```

Continued

Listing 10-24 *(continued)*

```
/

CREATE OR REPLACE PACKAGE BODY pkg_CompaniesEmployees AS

    PROCEDURE sp_GetCompaniesEmployees (
        vState IN Char,
        vName IN Char,
        rsCompanies OUT curCompanies,
        rsEmployees OUT curEmployees
    )
    AS
    BEGIN

        OPEN rsCompanies FOR
        SELECT
            CompanyName,
            ZipCode
        FROM
            Company
        WHERE
            State = sp_GetCompaniesEmployees.vState
        ORDER BY
            ZipCode ASC;

        OPEN rsEmployees FOR
        SELECT
            Firstname,
            Lastname
        FROM
            Employee
        WHERE
            Lastname LIKE sp_GetCompaniesEmployees.vName || '%'
        ORDER BY
            Lastname ASC,
            Firstname ASC;

    END sp_GetCompaniesEmployees;

END pkg_CompaniesEmployees;
/
```

The following sections take this listing step-by-step so that you can get a solid understanding of what's going on.

The package header

First, an Oracle package is just what its name implies: a big package or *container* for individual components — in this case, four user-defined data types and a stored procedure. A package has two parts: a *header*, where user-defined data types and the interfaces into any stored procedures and functions contained in the package are defined, and the *body*, where the stored procedures and functions themselves are programmed. So the first task in creating an Oracle package is to define its interface, which you do by using the following section of code:

```
CREATE OR REPLACE PACKAGE pkg_CompaniesEmployees AS

    TYPE recCompany IS RECORD (
        vCompanyName        Company.CompanyName%TYPE,
        vZipCode        Company.ZipCode%TYPE
    );

    TYPE recEmployee IS RECORD (
        vLastname        Employee.Lastname%TYPE,
        vFirstname        Employee.Firstname%TYPE
    );

    TYPE curCompanies IS REF CURSOR RETURN recCompany;

    TYPE curEmployees IS REF CURSOR RETURN recEmployee;

    PROCEDURE sp_GetCompaniesEmployees (
        vState IN Char,
        vName IN Char,
        rsCompanies OUT curCompanies,
        rsEmployees OUT curEmployees
    );

END pkg_CompaniesEmployees;
/
```

But to see exactly what the header must contain, you need to look ahead — in the body of the Oracle package — to the actual cursor that contains the first query result set, as follows:

```
OPEN rsCompanies FOR
SELECT
    CompanyName,
    ZipCode
FROM
    Company
WHERE
    State = sp_GetCompaniesEmployees.vState
ORDER BY
    ZipCode ASC;
```

Every row retrieved into this cursor contains two columns from the Company table: CompanyName and ZipCode; which define the *dimension* of the cursor variable that references this cursor.

Next, you need a data type that is of this dimension. Fortunately, Oracle has the capability to create complex user-defined data types called *records* (similar to ColdFusion structures, which you can read about in Chapter 15). You take advantage of this capability and create a `RECORD` data type named `recCompany` that holds the CompanyName and ZipCode columns of each row retrieved from the Company table, as follows:

```
TYPE recCompany IS RECORD (
    vCompanyName        Company.CompanyName%TYPE,
    vZipCode        Company.ZipCode%TYPE
);
```

The constituent parts of the recCompany data type must also have their data types defined. Appending %TYPE to a data element returns its data type, so the preceding record definition is equivalent to the following code:

```
TYPE recCompany IS RECORD (
    vCompanyName        VARCHAR2(40),
    vZipCode        VARCHAR2(10)
);
```

After you have a data type of the same dimension as the rows to be contained by the cursor, you can define a cursor variable to refer to the cursor, as follows:

```
TYPE curCompanies IS REF CURSOR RETURN recCompany;
```

What this TYPE definition is saying is, *"Define a cursor variable named curCompanies that returns rows that have the same dimension as the recCompany data type."*

You repeat the same programming for the second cursor variable—curEmployees—and you're ready to move on to the package header's interface into the stored procedure.

The interface of the stored procedure that returns your two result sets is similar to the stored procedures that you created in the section "InOut parameters," earlier in this chapter, in that it contains parameters of specific data types. You declare two input parameters that are used in the WHERE clauses of your two queries, plus you declare two output parameters of the REF CURSOR data types that you defined in the section "Oracle stored procedures and packages," as follows:

```
rsCompanies OUT curCompanies,
rsEmployees OUT curEmployees
```

The entire code block that defines the interface into the stored procedure is as follows:

```
PROCEDURE sp_GetCompaniesEmployees (
    vState IN Char,
    vName IN Char,
    rsCompanies OUT curCompanies,
    rsEmployees OUT curEmployees
);
```

It defines the *interface* of the sp_GetCompaniesEmployees stored procedure.

Finally, you have the following code:

```
END pkg_CompaniesEmployees;
/
```

It concludes the formal definition of the interface into the pkg_CompaniesEmployee Oracle package.

The package body

After the package header is defined, you move on to defining the package body, which contains the actual executable code.

Everything coded between the following lines becomes the *body* of the Oracle package with the header that you define in the preceding section:

```
CREATE OR REPLACE PACKAGE BODY pkg_CompaniesEmployees AS
    . . .
END pkg_CompaniesEmployees;
/
```

If the interface for a stored procedure or function is defined in the package header, that stored procedure or function must be programmed in the package body, and the interface in the body must exactly match its counterpart in the package header.

So you start by programming the actual sp_GetCompaniesEmployees stored procedure, as follows:

```
PROCEDURE sp_GetCompaniesEmployees (
    vState IN Char,
    vName IN Char,
    rsCompanies OUT curCompanies,
    rsEmployees OUT curEmployees
)
AS
BEGIN

    OPEN rsCompanies FOR
    SELECT
        CompanyName,
        ZipCode
    FROM
        Company
    WHERE
        State = sp_GetCompaniesEmployees.vState
    ORDER BY
        ZipCode ASC;

    OPEN rsEmployees FOR
    SELECT
        Firstname,
        Lastname
    FROM
        Employee
    WHERE
        Lastname LIKE sp_GetCompaniesEmployees.vName || '%'
    ORDER BY
        Lastname ASC,
        Firstname ASC;

END sp_GetCompaniesEmployees;
```

We've already covered the interface into the stored procedure in the section "The package header," so you now need to look at what the procedure's going to do after it executes.

The first thing that sp_GetCompaniesEmployees does is open a cursor named rsCompanies. As defined in the interface, rsCompanies is an output parameter of the data type curCompanies, and curCompanies is a REF CURSOR data type with the same dimensions as a row of the query that the cursor contains.

The input parameter vState is used in the WHERE clause to filter the rows returned by the query and placed into the cursor, and the ORDER BY clause sorts the result set in ascending ZipCode order. At this point our cursor contains the static data returned from the query, and our cursor variable named rsEmployees contains a reference to this cursor.

After the first cursor is created, the second cursor — `rsEmployees` — is created the same way. The input parameter used to filter its result set is concatenated by using the percent character `%` so that you can perform a pattern search for everything that begins with the character passed in the input parameter `vName`, as follows:

```
OPEN rsEmployees FOR
SELECT
    Firstname,
    Lastname
FROM
    Employee
WHERE
    Lastname LIKE sp_GetCompaniesEmployees.vName || '%'
ORDER BY
    Lastname ASC,
    Firstname ASC;
```

(Oracle uses a pair of pipe characters, `||`, as a concatenation operator; many other databases use +, and ColdFusion uses an ampersand, `&`, as a concatenation operator.)

Finally, the definition of the stored procedure is terminated by using an `END` clause, as follows:

```
END sp_GetCompaniesEmployees;
```

And there you have it! Oracle stored procedures take more effort to develop, but after you understand the principles behind them and develop a few examples, they quickly become old hat.

Calling an Oracle stored procedure

After you understand how the package and its stored procedure works, you can call it from ColdFusion by using the code in Listing 10-25.

Listing 10-25: Calling sp_GetCompaniesEmployees from ColdFusion

```
<cfstoredproc
procedure="pkg_CompaniesEmployees.sp_GetCompaniesEmployees"
        datasource="CFMXBible">

    <cfprocparam type="In"
        cfsqltype="CF_SQL_VARCHAR"
        dbvarname="vState"
        value="GA"
        null="No">

    <cfprocparam type="In"
        cfsqltype="CF_SQL_VARCHAR"
        dbvarname="vName"
        value="M"
        null="No">

    <cfprocresult name="GetCompanies" resultset="1">
    <cfprocresult name="GetEmployees" resultset="2">
</cfstoredproc>
```

This listing may seem a little confusing at first, but we can explain it.

The name of the stored procedure that you're calling is sp_GetCompaniesEmployees, which is contained within the Oracle package pkg_CompaniesEmployees. You employ the familiar dot notation used in most languages for accessing subordinate elements (for example, Parent.Child) to call sp_GetCompaniesEmployees, as follows:

```
<cfstoredproc
        procedure="pkg_CompaniesEmployees.sp_GetCompaniesEmployees"
        datasource=" CFMXBible">
```

Now take a look at the following two input parameters:

```
    <cfprocparam type="In"
        cfsqltype="CF_SQL_VARCHAR"
        dbvarname="vState"
        value="GA"
        null="No">

    <cfprocparam type="In"
        cfsqltype="CF_SQL_VARCHAR"
        dbvarname="vName"
        value="M"
        null="No">
```

You may have noticed that these parameters are defined as CF_SQL_VARCHAR, even though they match up with CHAR data types in the Oracle stored procedure. This is done to circumvent a problem that sometimes crops up if you try to send CF_SQL_CHAR input parameters into an Oracle stored procedure that also uses CHAR data types, in that they often fail to produce expected results. The way around this problem is to still use the CHAR data types in your Oracle stored procedure but specify the input parameters in your CFPROCPARAM tags as CF_SQL_VARCHAR.

And there you have it! If you want to make use of the two result sets in ColdFusion, you do so as if they were two regular query objects returned from two separate CFQUERY calls, as in Listing 10-26.

Listing 10-26: Using multiple result sets from an Oracle stored procedure

```
<h1>Companies</h1>
<table cellspacing="2" cellpadding="2" border="1">
<tr>
    <td><b>Company Name</b></td>
    <td><b>Zip Code</b></td>
</tr>
<cfoutput query="GetCompanies">
<tr>
    <td>#CompanyName#</td>
    <td>#ZipCode#</td>
</tr>
</cfoutput>
```

Continued

Listing 10-26 *(continued)*

```
</table>

<h1>Employees</h1>
<table cellspacing="2" cellpadding="2" border="1">
<tr>
    <td><b>Firstname</b></td>
    <td><b>Lastname</b></td>
</tr>
<cfoutput query="GetEmployees">
<tr>
    <td>#Firstname#</td>
    <td>#Lastname#</td>
</tr>
</cfoutput>
</table>
```

In fact, you may notice that Listing 10-26 is identical to Listing 10-14, which calls an SQL Server stored procedure that returns these same result sets. You find no difference at all in the way that different database platforms' result sets are used.

The preceding example was a simple one containing only two user-defined data types and one stored procedure, but a single Oracle package can contain many stored procedures, functions, and user-defined data types. Oracle packages are one of the platform's most powerful features, and their capabilities go far beyond what is mentioned here. If you are interested in leveraging the power of Oracle packages then head for your local bookstore.

Using multiple result sets from Oracle stored procedures in ColdFusion 5 requires an unusual treatment of the `CFSTOREDPROC` call. If you are still using ColdFusion 5 and want to make use of multiple result sets in Oracle stored procedures, please e-mail us at adam@ProductivityEnhancement.com, and we'll send you detailed instructions.

Important notes about Oracle stored procedures

You need to keep in mind a few special considerations in writing Oracle stored procedures. The following sections don't give you a comprehensive list, by any means; they provide only a short list of the notes that we have found most useful over the years.

Strongly typing cursor variables to compile before runtime

Strongly typing your cursor variables is important, as follows:

```
TYPE curCompanies IS REF CURSOR RETURN recCompany;
```

If a cursor variable is *strongly typed* (i.e., its data dimension is explicitly declared), Oracle can catalog the definition of this data type and *at compile time* perform a compatibility match between the data type and any record or table row that either uses or is used by the cursor. Suppose that the `REF CURSOR` is *weakly typed* (i.e., its data dimension is *not* explicitly declared), as follows:

```
TYPE curCompanies IS REF CURSOR;
```

The cursor variable in this example can reference any cursor of any column structure. This flexibility comes at a price, however, because Oracle must check this *weakly typed* cursor variable for compatibility *at runtime* with each statement that can potentially throw an incompatibility error. Such runtime checking takes time and, therefore, slows down stored procedure operation.

Weakly typed cursor variables have their place in advanced Oracle programming, but if you don't absolutely need them, don't use them.

Abstracting type definitions by using %TYPE to make maintenance easier

In the section "Oracle stored procedures and packages," earlier in this chapter, we said that appending `%TYPE` to the end of a data element returns the data type of that element This is the preferred method for typing data in Oracle stored procedures, because it abstracts the data type and ties it to whatever the current data element's data type is, as in the following example:

```
DECLARE vCompanyName Company.CompanyName%TYPE;
```

This code declares the variable `vCompanyName` as the same data type as that in the CompanyName column of the Company table. So if you change the CompanyName column from a `VARCHAR2(40)` to a `VARCHAR2(65)`, the `vCompanyName` variable follows suit and is declared as a `VARCHAR2(65)` data type as well.

This way, you can change the data type of a table column or a variable, and unless the operations on the resulting declared variable are incompatible with the data type, everything continues to work swimmingly.

Qualifying variables by using long form notation

Most stored procedures make use of parameters and local variables that eventually hand off their values to table columns for storage. A common (although ill-advised) practice is to name these variables the same as their corresponding table columns for simplicity sake and ease of reading. If you insist on using this practice, you should refer to your variables by using *qualified* (or *long-form*) *notation* to avoid misinterpretation, as in the following example:

```
/*
This refers to the CompanyName column of the Company table:
*/
Company.CompanyName

/*
This refers to a variable declared in the stored procedure sp_Test:
*/
Sp_Test.CompanyName
```

We like to qualify our variables in Oracle, regardless of how they're named. We got into this habit after years of working with other languages (even ColdFusion) that can become confused and throw errors because of naming ambiguities. Really, your best bet is to name your variables slightly differently from their table-column counterparts. *Hungarian notation* or simply prefixing a `v` are both useful methods of uniquely naming variables from their table-column counterparts.

Unrestricted parameters

Unlike SQL Server, Oracle does not permit restrictions on parameter size in the interfaces to its stored procedures. The following example is a stored procedure, as written for both SQL Server and Oracle:

```
/* As written for SQL Server */
CREATE PROCEDURE sp_GetEmployees (
    vFirstname Varchar(20),
```

```
    vLastname Varchar(20)
)
AS
BEGIN
    Return
END

/* As written for Oracle */
CREATE OR REPLACE PROCEDURE sp_GetEmployees (
    vFirstname IN Varchar2,
    vLastname IN Varchar2
)
IS
BEGIN
    Return;
END sp_GetEmployees;
/
```

As long as the incoming parameter is of the `Varchar2` data type (which is identical to other platforms' `Varchar` data type), it can go into the Oracle stored procedure. If it is of an incorrect size for the stored procedure to handle, the stored procedure throws an exception.

Practical things that you can do in using stored procedures

By now, you probably see the benefits of using stored procedures versus standard `CFQUERY` calls, but what are some of the truly practical uses of stored procedures? The following sections take a look at these practical uses.

These examples are written for SQL Server, but they can, of course, be adapted for use on Oracle and other platforms.

Intelligently inserting or updating by using a single stored procedure

There are a number of choices for handling a situation where a user submits a form containing data that is destined for storage in the database, but you don't know whether that person is inserting a new row or updating a row that already exists. One method is to perform a query on the key for that row, check `QueryName.RecordCount` to see whether the row is found, and then either insert or update based on the result. Another method is to attempt the insert via `CFQUERY`, catch the primary key constraint violation that is thrown if the row already exists via `CFCATCH`, and then re-attempt the operation as an update via `CFQUERY`. Both of these methods are very slow, however, and require multiple requests between ColdFusion Server and your database server.

The best way to accomplish this task is to create a single stored procedure that you can call, regardless of whether you're inserting or updating, as shown in Listing 10-27.

Listing 10-27: A stored procedure that intelligently inserts or updates

```
CREATE PROCEDURE sp_InsertUpdateCoupon (
    @CouponCode         Varchar(16),
    @PercentDiscount    Numeric(12,2),
```

```
    @Redeemed           Bit
)
AS
UPDATE
    Coupon
SET
    PercentDiscount     = @PercentDiscount,
    Redeemed            = @Redeemed
WHERE
    CouponCode          = @CouponCode

IF(@@ROWCOUNT > 0)
    BEGIN
    RETURN 10
    END

INSERT INTO Coupon (
    CouponCode,
    PercentDiscount,
    Redeemed
    )
VALUES (
    @CouponCode,
    @PercentDiscount,
    @Redeemed
    )

IF (@@ERROR != 0)
    BEGIN
    RETURN -10
    END

RETURN 20
```

Here's how Listing 10-27 works. Every time that you execute an SQL statement on SQL Server, a global variable named `@@ROWCOUNT` is automatically updated to contain the number of rows that are affected by the most recent SQL statement. If you attempt to update a table row that doesn't exist, `@@ROWCOUNT` contains `0` after such an attempt. If the row that you intended to update does exist, `@@ROWCOUNT` contains 1 because one row is affected by the `UPDATE` statement.

So you use this fact to your advantage and simply check the value of `@@ROWCOUNT` immediately after attempting the update. If `@@ROWCOUNT` is `0`, the row doesn't exist yet, and you must create it by using an `INSERT` statement.

Statistically, such a system updates more often than it inserts, so in most cases — all except the first time that it is executed, in fact — this stored procedure performs only half its code and then return to the ColdFusion template that called it. This technique is a very practical use of stored procedures, is very scalable, and enables you to reuse a large part of your ColdFusion code. Just create a single ColdFusion template containing the `CFSTOREDPROC` call to this procedure and `CFINCLUDE` it wherever you need to insert or update those table rows, as shown in Listing 10-28.

Listing 10-28: Reusable ColdFusion code that both inserts and updates

```
<cfstoredproc procedure="sp_InsertUpdateCoupon"
    datasource="CFMXBible"
    returncode="Yes">

    <cfprocparam type="In"
        cfsqltype="CF_SQL_VARCHAR"
        dbvarname="@CouponCode"
        value="#Trim(CouponCode)#"
        maxlength="16"
        null="No">

    <cfprocparam type="In"
        cfsqltype="CF_SQL_NUMERIC"
        dbvarname="@PercentDiscount"
        value="#Val(FORM.PercentDiscount)#"
        scale="2"
        null="No">

    <cfprocparam type="In"
        cfsqltype="CF_SQL_BIT"
        dbvarname="@Redeemed"
        value="#Val(FORM.Redeemed)#"
        null="No">

</cfstoredproc>
```

One thing to remember is that the intelligent `INSERT/UPDATE` stored procedure technique works only if you know the value of your row's key in advance.

Using the return code

Look back at Listing 10-27. Notice how it adds a numeric value after the two `Return` statements, whereas in the section "CFSTOREDPROC," earlier in this chapter, not all `Return` statements were followed by values. Adding a signed integer value after a `Return` statement sends that value to the outside program that called it (in this case, ColdFusion Server).

After your stored procedure is programmed to send the value back to ColdFusion Server, you open a pipeline to it by adding `ReturnCode="Yes"` to your `CFSTOREDPROC` call and access its value by using the variable `CFSTOREDPROC.StatusCode`.

Listing 10-29—which is a modification of Listing 10-28—displays the appropriate message to the user based on what actually happens in the database.

Listing 10-29: Routing ColdFusion application flow by using the Return Code.

```
<cfstoredproc procedure="sp_InsertUpdateCoupon"
    datasource="CFMXBible"
    returncode="Yes">
```

```
      <cfprocparam type="In"
         cfsqltype="CF_SQL_VARCHAR"
         dbvarname="@CouponCode"
         value="#Trim(CouponCode)#"
         maxlength="16"
         null="No">

      <cfprocparam type="In"
         cfsqltype="CF_SQL_NUMERIC"
         dbvarname="@PercentDiscount"
         value="#Val(FORM.PercentDiscount)#"
         scale="2"
         null="No">

      <cfprocparam type="In"
         cfsqltype="CF_SQL_BIT"
         dbvarname="@Redeemed"
         value="#Val(FORM.Redeemed)#"
         null="No">
   </cfstoredproc>

   <cfswitch expression="#Val(CFSTOREDPROC.StatusCode)#">
      <cfcase value="10">
         <cflocation url="CouponUpdated.cfm" addtoken="Yes">
      </cfcase>

      <cfcase value="20">
         <cflocation url="CouponInserted.cfm" addtoken="Yes">
      </cfcase>

      <cfcase value="-10">
         <cflocation url="CouponFailed.cfm" addtoken="Yes">
      </cfcase>
   </cfswitch>
```

Now your ColdFusion application can route program flow based on what happens inside the stored procedure, whether ColdFusion is controlling a complicated data-entry wizard or telling the user what he has just accomplished.

During the design phase, we carefully define and document each and every Return Code that is used by our application. Following are the guidelines that we use to set the values of our Return Codes:

- ✦ Zero indicates an error-free operation.
- ✦ Positive values in the 1 through 49,999 range indicate the resulting status of the operation according to the application's business rules. If an application manages mortgages, for example, and the successful completion of a stored procedure advances the status of a mortgage from Approved (where the enumerated value of Approved is 50) to Closed (where the enumerated value of Closed is 60), we may use the Return Code to contain the enumerated value of the resulting status of the operation.

- Positive values in the 50,000 through 99,999 range indicate a noncritical warning condition, such as "Sales order entered, but inventory is getting low."
- Negative values typically indicate a critical condition according to the application's business rules, such as "Sales order entered, but with negative inventory levels."
- We increment return codes by ten. If a change to the system introduces a new return code that should logically go between those already present, we have room for up to nine of them between each existing Return Code.
- If the Return Code indicates a change in status, we assign return codes to increase numerically as the status progresses through its life cycle.

An important point to remember is that we are talking about *Return Codes* here—not error codes. Return codes are user-defined values that communicate the general status of what happens inside a procedure and can be defined and used entirely at the developer's discretion. *Error codes*—both system-defined and user-defined—communicate an error condition that is thrown inside a procedure and cannot be used for any other purpose.

Reusing stored procedure code

In the same way that you can create custom tags from fragments of ColdFusion code and then call those custom tags from other ColdFusion templates, you can do virtually the same thing with stored procedures. Stored procedures can call other stored procedures much the same way that they are called from ColdFusion but without the tag-based interface.

Say, for example, that you have a stored procedure, `sp_GetInventoryItem`, that retrieves an InventoryItem row based on the `ItemNumber` value passed. You use `sp_GetInventoryItem` throughout your e-commerce application to get product information as users browse the catalog, and you also use it to retrieve inventory items for administrative work. Now you want to incorporate `sp_GetInventoryItem` with another stored procedure—`sp_DiscountItem`—that discounts the price of an item based on whether the user enters a valid discount coupon code at the beginning of his shopping session. You can repeat the code to retrieve the inventory item and perform the discount in each stored procedure that requires such a function, or you can make code maintenance easier by breaking out examples of common code into their own procedures and calling them where needed, as shown in Listing 10-30.

Listing 10-30: Calling stored procedures from other stored procedures

```
-- This procedure will be called by sp_DiscountItem
CREATE PROCEDURE sp_GetInventoryItem (
    @giiItemNumber          Varchar(15),
    @giiDescription          Varchar(40) OUTPUT,
    @giiUnitPrice              Numeric(12,2) OUTPUT,
    @giiAvailableToSell           Integer OUTPUT,
    @giiComments              Varchar(200) OUTPUT
)
AS
SELECT
    @giiDescription          = Description,
    @giiUnitPrice              = UnitPrice,
    @giiAvailableToSell        = AvailableToSell,
    @giiComments             = Comments
FROM
    InventoryItem
WHERE
```

```
    ItemNumber              = @giiItemNumber

RETURN
go

-- This procedure will also be called by sp_DiscountItem
CREATE PROCEDURE sp_GetAmountDue (
    @CouponCode         Varchar(16),
    @AmountDue          Numeric(12,2) OUTPUT
)
AS
DECLARE
    @Redeemed           Bit,
    @PercentDiscount    Numeric(12,2)

SELECT
    @Redeemed           = Redeemed,
    @PercentDiscount    = PercentDiscount
FROM
    Coupon
WHERE
    CouponCode = @CouponCode

IF (@@ROWCOUNT != 1)
    BEGIN
    RETURN      -- Coupon doesn't exist; no price change
    END

IF (@Redeemed = 1)
    BEGIN
    RETURN      -- Coupon already redeemed; no price change
    END
ELSE
    BEGIN
    SELECT @AmountDue = @AmountDue * (1 - @PercentDiscount / 100)
    END

RETURN
go

-- This is the parent procedure that is called
CREATE PROCEDURE sp_DiscountItem (
    @diCouponCode           Varchar(16),
    @diItemNumber           Varchar(15),
    @diDescription      Varchar(40) OUTPUT,
    @diUnitPrice            Numeric(12,2) OUTPUT,
    @diAvailableToSell      Integer OUTPUT,
    @diComments             Varchar(200) OUTPUT
)
AS

EXEC sp_GetInventoryItem (
```

Continued

Listing 10-30 *(continued)*

```
        @giiItemNumber       = @diItemNumber,
        @giiDescription       = @diDescription OUTPUT,
        @giiUnitPrice           = @diUnitPrice OUTPUT,
        @giiAvailableToSell      = @diAvailableToSell OUTPUT,
        @giiComments          = @diComments OUTPUT
    )

    EXEC sp_GetAmountDue (
        @CouponCode          = @diCouponCode ,
        @AmountDue           = @diUnitPrice OUTPUT
    )

    RETURN
    go
```

The first time that we ever coded such a thing, our heads nearly split wide open from confusion! Which parameter is the input to which output, and how does this one pass back to that one and so on?

Well, we finally figured out a way to explain one procedure by using `OUTPUT` parameters that call another in a way that makes sense. On the CD-ROM accompanying this book, you find an Adobe Acrobat file named `Output Parameter Tracing.pdf`, which contains the preceding listing repeated once for each step in the parameter passing process, along with a diagram for each step and an explanation in plain English of what is happening in each step. We follow one of these `OUTPUT` parameters — the `UnitPrice` — on its complete journey through all the stored procedures that use it and show how values are acquired and passed between parameters.

We highly suggest that you take a few moments to open that document and follow each step of the process. To really leverage stored procedures in your ColdFusion applications, you need to fully understand this complicated topic. We have repeated the plain English description of each step in the following numbered list, but having the diagram at hand as you read them really helps.

The process all starts with the procedure `sp_DiscountItem` that is called from ColdFusion as follows:

1. `sp_DiscountItem` is the first stored procedure called. The `@diUnitPrice` output parameter starts off with a `NULL` value; at this point, `@diUnitPrice` is just an "empty bucket" to receive a value back from `sp_DiscountItem` after it finishes executing and then return that value to the client application. `OUTPUT` tells `sp_DiscountItem`, *"If you do anything to the value of `@diUnitPrice` during your execution, `OUTPUT` its new value* back into `@diUnitPrice` *so that the new value can be used by whatever application or procedure called you."* If `@diUnitPrice` didn't have the `OUTPUT` qualifier, it would remain `NULL` after `sp_DiscountItem` finished executing.

2. `@diUnitPrice` is the value fed to the `@giiItemUnitPrice OUTPUT` parameter of the call to `sp_GetInventoryItem`. Right now, it is still just a `NULL` value.

3. `@giiUnitPrice` initializes with the `NULL` value supplied by `@diUnitPrice` and is now ready to call `sp_GetInventoryItem`.

4. sp_GetInventoryItem is now called with @giiUnitPrice as an OUTPUT parameter. It still contains a NULL value. It's only job at this point is to provide an empty bucket into which sp_GetInventoryItem may place a value.

5. After sp_GetInventoryItem executes, it selects the column value of InventoryItem.UnitPrice into the OUTPUT parameter @giiUnitPrice.

6. @giiUnitPrice now contains the unit price retrieved from the inventory item rather than a NULL value.

7. Because @giiUnitPrice is an OUTPUT parameter in sp_GetInventoryItem, its new value is OUTPUT *back into @giiUnitPrice inside sp_DiscountItem*, which just called sp_GetInventoryItem.

8. This new value of @giiUnitPrice is further OUTPUT *back into the @diUnitPrice parameter* that originally fed the NULL value to @giiUnitPrice, ***because @diUnitPrice has the OUTPUT qualifier in the call to** sp_GetInventoryItem*. Now @diUnitPrice contains the same value returned from sp_GetInventoryItem.

9. You now have the undiscounted unit price value from the inventory item record stored in @diUnitPrice, and you can feed this value to sp_GetAmountDue for a possible price reduction.

10. @AmountDue is initialized with the value stored in @diUnitPrice and is now ready to call sp_GetAmountDue.

11. sp_GetAmountDue is now called with @AmountDue as an OUTPUT parameter. It currently contains the unit price value returned from the inventory item record.

12. sp_GetAmountDue may or may not modify the value stored in @AmountDue, but if it does, the modified value is restored in @AmountDue.

13. Because @AmountDue is an OUTPUT parameter in sp_GetAmountDue, its new value is OUTPUT back into @AmountDue inside sp_DiscountItem, which just called sp_GetAmountDue.

14. This new value of @AmountDue is further OUTPUT back into the @diUnitPrice parameter that originally fed the unmodified unit price value to @AmountDue, because @diUnitPrice has the OUTPUT qualifier in the call to sp_GetAmountDue. Now @diUnitPrice contains the (possibly) modified unit price value returned from sp_GetAmountDue.

15. Because @diUnitPrice is an OUTPUT parameter in sp_DiscountItem, @diUnitPrice can OUTPUT its final, possibly modified value to the ColdFusion application that called it in the first place.

We know that this process sounds complicated — and it is — but that's just the way that it goes. Some things in software development are rather complicated, and this is one of them. Go over the PDF document a few times, and it should start to become clear. Better yet, experiment with a couple examples of your own and trudge through the complexity until you get it.

All things considered, having one stored procedure call another is much better than executing one stored procedure from ColdFusion, coming back to ColdFusion, running another stored procedure from ColdFusion, and so on. Remember that, every time that you establish a separate connection between ColdFusion Server and your database server, you create overhead and decrease the performance of your ColdFusion application.

Encapsulating complex business logic in a single call

You can combine Input, Output, and InOut parameters, call multiple stored procedures, and return multiple result sets from a single stored procedure call. If you have a very complicated routine, implement it as multiple stored procedures that are called from a single stored procedure that is, in turn, called by ColdFusion, as shown in the preceding section.

Always look for ways to encapsulate large amounts of data work in stored procedures. As you engineer your ColdFusion applications in this way, pay close attention to the transactional model that you build around the inserts, updates, and deletes that modify your data. Refer to the section "Transactions," earlier in this chapter for details.

Security

Just as are views, stored procedures are formally defined database objects and, as such, can have user and group privileges granted to them. By denying developers direct access to physical tables and, instead, granting them access only to views for selecting data and stored procedures for modifying data, you eliminate all inadvertent ColdFusion developer mistakes that could corrupt or destroy production data.

If you analyze your ColdFusion application in terms of the business processes that it supports, break down those processes into specific tasks and transactions, and encapsulate those transactions into stored procedures, you reduce ColdFusion development down to its purest essential: feeding user data to business transactions.

In Chapter 11, we look at another type of stored procedure known as a *trigger*, which automatically fires based on database events.

Summary

In this chapter you've learned how to create and use stored procedures and views, and also how to understand, configure, and use transactions.

Programmers often design and develop databases as if they are single-user systems and discover the flaws of such thinking only after it is too late. Understanding the exact nature of transactions and how to control the isolation between them is crucial to deploying database systems that effectively handle real-world traffic.

Stored procedures may seem a little foreign and difficult at first, but learning and using them in your everyday code is well worth your time. By encapsulating complex business logic into single calls that are executed directly on the database server, you not only make code management simpler and easier, but you also gain an important performance enhancement.

Stored procedures that return multiple result sets may seem daunting if Oracle is your database server of choice, but after you understand the unique mechanisms that Oracle uses to reference result sets and how ColdFusion interfaces with these mechanisms, you should have no problem implementing them.

Combining your new knowledge of transactions and stored procedures helps you produce secure, maintainable code that performs well under heavy multi-user loads. Take a close look at your existing code and you most likely find a number of opportunities where stored procedures can improve the performance and robustness of your applications.

✦ ✦ ✦

CHAPTER 11

More Advanced Database Techniques

In This Chapter

Understanding triggers

Implementing complex referential integrity via triggers

Using triggers to automate database transactions

Understanding practical uses for query of queries

Data binding by using CFQUERYPARAM

In Chapter 11, you're going to expand on your newfound knowledge of stored procedures, as described in Chapter 10, and create a whole new kind of stored procedure called a *trigger*, which executes automatically whenever specific database events occur.

We show you in this chapter how to implement fancy referential integrity rules that cannot be implemented in any other way, and we contrast and compare the similarities and differences between triggers in SQL Server and Oracle.

After we're done with triggers, we cover the effective use of ColdFusion MX's enhanced *query of queries* (*QoQ*) feature. Finally, we end the chapter by covering data binding by using `CFQUERYPARAM` to specify your `CFQUERY` parameters.

Triggers

A *trigger* is a stored procedure that is executed (or *triggered*) automatically every time that a specific database event occurs. You cannot instruct a trigger to execute through user actions or ColdFusion code, and a stored procedure cannot instruct a trigger to execute. A trigger executes only if its triggering event occurs on the table to which it is attached. Listing 11-1 shows a typical trigger.

Listing 11-1: A trigger attached to the Insert event on the OrderItem table.

```
CREATE TRIGGER tI_OrderItem
ON OrderItem
AFTER Insert
AS
BEGIN

DECLARE
  @iQuantity INTEGER,
  @sItemNumber VARCHAR(15)
```

Continued

Listing 11-1 (continued)

```
SELECT
  @iQuantity = Quantity,
  @sItemNumber = ItemNumber
FROM
  Inserted

UPDATE
  InventoryItem
SET
  AvailableToSell = AvailableToSell - @iQuantity
WHERE
  ItemNumber = @sItemNumber
END
```

Listing 11-1 is actually flawed. Can you spot the flaw? We correct it by using two different methods in the section "Affecting Single and Multiple Rows," later in this chapter.

As you can probably tell from the bold text, this trigger executes immediately after an INSERT statement executes against the OrderItem table. In this case, the trigger subtracts the quantity ordered from the AvailableToSell column of the InventoryItem table. No matter what ColdFusion template, Excel macro, Visual Basic module, or Query Analyzer batch inserts rows into the OrderItem table, this trigger code executes automatically after the INSERT statement concludes.

This is an important design consideration and a best practice for designing multitiered systems such as ColdFusion applications. By placing critical business logic in a trigger, you never need to worry about whether every client application accessing your database server executes the code necessary to preserve your business rules.

If you didn't place this code in a trigger, for example, but instead relied on your ColdFusion application code to perform this same database operation, you would be at constant risk of forgetting to duplicate this code everywhere that an INSERT is performed against the OrderItem table. To make things even worst, consider things outside your realm, such as Visual Basic applications or even the occasional DBA (database administrator) working in an SQL batch utility.

So how can you ensure that your business rules are preserved everywhere and that InventoryItem.AvailableToSell is always updated in tandem with inserts into OrderItem.Quantity? You can't — unless you put that code in an Insert Trigger on the InventoryItem table.

Triggers and implicit transactions

A trigger is considered an integral part of the underlying SQL statement that triggers it. If the SQL statement fails, the trigger must not execute, because the triggering event never really happened. Similarly, if the trigger code fails to complete execution for any reason, both the trigger *and* the SQL statement that triggered it must be rolled back. Because the trigger is considered part of the underlying SQL statement that triggers it, the *entire* set of statements didn't complete execution, so *everything* must be rolled back as if *nothing* ever happened.

In other words, a trigger and the SQL statement that triggers it are parts of an *implicit transaction*, meaning that *both* the SQL statement and the trigger must successfully execute or both are rolled back. Remember that a transaction is a single unit of work: If all the instructions inside a transaction execute flawlessly, the transaction succeeds; if any single instruction inside a transaction fails, all the instructions inside the transaction are rolled back, and the entire transaction fails.

This transaction is called an *implicit* transaction because the fact that it is a transaction is *implied* by its very nature rather than it being *explicitly* declared as a transaction by programming statements to that effect. Now take a look at why both a trigger and the statement that triggers it must be part of the same transaction.

To prevent nasty things from happening to your data, your database server performs a number of checks on the operations that you throw at it before it accepts them as valid and enables them to insert, modify, or delete data. To make operations as fast as possible, your database server performs the easiest and fastest checks before it tries the more difficult and slower checks. This makes sense, because as soon as your database server performs a check that fails, it can totally disregard all the other checks and return an error as quickly as possible.

The first checks that your server performs are *data-type checks*, which are the very simplest and, therefore, the fastest. If you attempt to place a string into a numeric column, for example, the data-type check on that column fails, and the database server can stop processing at that point and return an error message. The server doesn't need to waste precious CPU time processing the other checks, because it already knows that the SQL statement must not proceed.

The next checks to be performed are the *check constraints* placed on the individual columns, such as a range check that permits only values between zero and 100. (These constraints are covered in more detail in Chapter 8.) After these simple checks pass muster, next come the *referential-integrity constraint checks* (also covered in Chapter 8). After all checks have succeeded, the database server clears the way for the SQL statement to be processed.

If your trigger is defined to execute *before* the triggering SQL statement is executed (and some database products enable you to do so), the trigger code executes at this point in the sequence, and then the SQL statement runs. If your trigger is defined to execute *after* the triggering SQL statement is executed, the SQL statement runs first, and *then* the trigger code executes.

Now ask yourself: Why would you want to execute any part of a trigger if the underlying SQL statement that triggered it failed? Well, because the triggering event never really happened (it failed), the failure of the trigger code to execute seems a logical outcome as well. What if the triggering SQL statement succeeds, but the trigger code that it fires fails? Wouldn't you want to keep the effects of the triggering SQL statement and just handle the failed trigger in some other way?

The answer becomes clear if you consider the fact that a trigger is a *database object* and, as such, is a formally defined part of the database design itself. Because a trigger is defined to execute whenever its triggering event occurs, you would be working against the very design of the database by enabling the effects of an SQL statement to be committed to disk without also demanding that the effects of the trigger that it was supposed to fire be committed as well. For this reason, both the trigger and any SQL statement that triggers it are considered part of the same transaction. If any part of either the trigger code or the underlying SQL statement that triggers it fails, the entire sequence of events is rolled back as a single unit of work, and your data looks as if nothing ever happened.

Remember that the trigger is an *implicit* transaction because the fact that it is a transaction is *implied* by the nature of how the trigger is used, and that an *explicit* transaction is *explicitly* declared through programming statements? A trigger is considered an implicit transaction for another reason: You couldn't make it an explicit transaction even if you tried. Where would you put the explicit statements that define the boundaries of the transaction?

In a Before Trigger, your `BEGIN TRANSACTION` would appear at the top of the trigger code, but where would the `COMMIT TRANSACTION` statement go? It would need to come at the end of whatever SQL statement triggers the trigger, but you have no control over those statements. (They could come from anywhere.) Similarly, in an After Trigger, your `BEGIN TRANSACTION` statement would need to appear at the top of the SQL statement that triggers the trigger, and your `COMMIT TRANSACTION` would need to appear at the end of the trigger itself. You can't do either of these things, so the fact that the `BEGIN TRANSACTION` and `COMMIT TRANSACTION` statements just sort of "magically happen" in the places that we are mentioning is *implied*.

Finally, although you don't physically see the `BEGIN TRANSACTION` and `COMMIT TRANSACTION` statements in a trigger, you can explicitly place a `ROLLBACK TRANSACTION` statement in a trigger anywhere that your code needs one. As you can probably tell from this discussion of triggers and implicit transactions, if a trigger processes a `ROLLBACK TRANSACTION` statement, both the trigger and the SQL statement that triggered it are rolled back as part of the same implicit transaction.

Sick to death of transactions by now? So are we. Time to move on to the next topic: combining triggers with DRI constraints.

Where DRI constraints alone just don't do

In Chapter 8, we cover declarative referential integrity (DRI), and how the database enforces it by using DRI constraints. But what happens if your database's referential integrity is more complicated than *"Unless a corresponding value to this foreign key is in the parent table's primary-key column, do not permit this row to be inserted or updated in this table"*? The answer is to handle your complex referential integrity checking via triggers or a combination of triggers and DRI constraints.

Because DRI constraints can perform only relatively straightforward operations, they cannot enforce complex business rules. Triggers, however, can contain almost any data operations that you want (although you have both technical and practical restrictions to incorporating logic in triggers — consult your database product's documentation on triggers), so you should implement any complex business rules that your system requires as triggers. But does this mean that you should abandon DRI constraints as soon as the need for complex business rules arise? The answer is "No — but you may need to."

As we've said, DRI constraints are fairly easy for your database to perform and, therefore, execute quickly. DRI constraints are executed before any triggers are executed, so if the DRI constraint fails, the entire SQL statement is rolled back, and the trigger never gets a chance to execute. So the guidelines for DRI constraints and triggers are as follows:

- ✦ Implement as DRI constraints all referential integrity rules that *cannot* conflict with any business rules that may affect referential integrity. In other words, if any triggers contain logic that relies on one or more *key* values in an outside table, there should be no DRI constraint between the table on which the trigger is declared and that outside table.
- ✦ Implement as triggers those referential integrity rules that are conditional or that *may* conflict with any business rules that may affect referential integrity.

Say, for example, that you have a WholesaleOrder table that is related to your Customer table, but this relation is valid only if `Customer.CustomerType` equals `W`. In this case, you would keep the DRI constraint that ensured that the WholesaleOrder row had a valid parent row in the Customer table, but you would also add an Insert and Update Trigger to the

WholesaleOrder table that tested Customer.CustomerType for a value of W and that, if this business rule failed the test, would perform a rollback.

Listing 11-2 shows the DRI constraint and trigger mentioned in the preceding paragraph.

Listing 11-2: Implementing referential integrity via a combination of DRI constraint and a trigger

```
/*
This foreign key constraint prevents a wholesale order from being
entered for a nonexistent customer.
*/
ALTER TABLE WholesaleOrder ADD CONSTRAINT FK__WholesaleOrder_Customer
    FOREIGN KEY (CustomerNumber)
    REFERENCES Customer(CustomerNumber)
go

/*
This insert and update trigger prevents a wholesale order from being
entered for an existing customer that is not a wholesale customer.
*/
CREATE TRIGGER tIU_WholesaleOrder
ON WholesaleOrder
AFTER INSERT, UPDATE
AS
BEGIN
IF (@@ROWCOUNT = 0)
    BEGIN
    RETURN
    END

IF (@@ROWCOUNT > 1)
    BEGIN
    RAISERROR 50001 'You cannot enter more than one wholesale order at
a time.'
    ROLLBACK TRANSACTION
    RETURN
    END

IF ((SELECT
        Count(*)
    FROM
        Customer c INNER JOIN Inserted i
        ON c.CustomerNumber = i.CustomerNumber
    WHERE
        c.CustomerType = 'W') != 1)
    BEGIN
    RAISERROR 50002 'You cannot enter a wholesale order for a
nonwholesale customer.'
    ROLLBACK TRANSACTION
```

Continued

Listing 11-2 *(continued)*

```
    RETURN
    END

END
go
```

As another example, suppose that you had a PricingFactors table that contained pricing factors (discounts) for your e-commerce site. These factors are very flexible in that they may be related to a specific customer, a specific inventory item, or a specific pairing of customer and item (for example, if a customer purchases a particularly heavy volume of a specific item on a regular basis, he is given a special discount to keep his business). The business rules for determining which type of relationship exists for a pricing factor are simple and straightforward, but they are determined through logic at runtime rather than at design time. In this case, you cannot implement any of the referential integrity rules related to the PricingFactors table via DRI constraints, because whether a relationship exists between one table and another is determined by business logic. If you set up DRI constraints between the PricingFactors table and the Customer and InventoryItem tables, at least one of these constraints would always fail (the constraint is *logical* rather than *declarative*), and nothing could ever be inserted or updated in the PricingFactors table! Instead, you must implement *only as triggers* all referential integrity rules that are related to the PricingFactors table.

Listing 11-3 shows this trigger. (We've removed all business logic not related to referential integrity for the sake of clarity.)

Listing 11-3: **Implementing referential integrity solely through a trigger**

```
Create TRIGGER tIU_PricingFactor ON PricingFactors
FOR INSERT, UPDATE
AS
BEGIN

IF (@@ROWCOUNT != 1)
    BEGIN
    RAISERROR 50010 'You cannot enter more than one pricing factor at a
time.'
    ROLLBACK TRANSACTION
    RETURN
    END

DECLARE
    @ItemNumber         varchar(15),
    @CustomerNumber     varchar(12),
    @Factor         numeric(12,4)

SELECT
```

```
    @ItemNumber         = ItemNumber,
    @CustomerNumber     = CustomerNumber,
    @Factor         = Factor
FROM
    inserted

/*
Ensure a significant value for the Primary Key
*/
IF (Len(RTrim(@ItemNumber)) + Len(RTrim(@CustomerNumber))) = 0
    BEGIN
    RAISERROR 50020 'The Primary Key cannot be empty'
    ROLLBACK TRANSACTION
    RETURN
    END

/*
Ensure referential integrity with "inherently related" tables
InventoryItem and Customer
*/
IF Len(RTrim(@ItemNumber)) > 0
BEGIN
  IF (SELECT COUNT(*)
        FROM InventoryItem p, inserted
        WHERE p.ItemNumber = inserted.ItemNumber) = 0
    BEGIN
        RAISERROR 50030 'The InventoryItem item related to this Pricing
Factor does not exist'
        ROLLBACK TRANSACTION
        RETURN
    END
END

IF Len(RTrim(@CustomerNumber)) > 0
BEGIN
  IF (SELECT COUNT(*)
        FROM Customer p, inserted
        WHERE p.CustomerNumber = inserted.CustomerNumber) = 0
    BEGIN
        RAISERROR 50040 'The Customer related to this Pricing Factor
does not exist'
        ROLLBACK TRANSACTION
        RETURN
    END
END

/*
Perform other business logic here. . .
*/
END
```

Getting the database to do the work for you

As you see in Listing 11-1, which automatically adjusts `InventoryItem.AvailableToSell` whenever a new OrderItem row is inserted, triggers can handle business logic that you'd normally think of implementing in ColdFusion, and they handle it with absolute reliability. This is only one small example, however. If you look at your business processes, you're likely to find quite a lot of business tasks that are *triggered* by the successful completion of one or more previous tasks. Does this get you thinking about triggers?

It should. Why wait for a human being to realize that a task can be started and then take action if the database already knows it and can do much (or all) the same thing? Why not use a trigger to handle such things?

Say, for example, your business logic specifies that a tech support call must be assigned to the least-busy support technician after a tech support call has escalated to "Intervention" status, which is enumerated as the value 40.

Figure 11-1 shows the tables and relationship involved in this scenario. Notice that this relationship is optional (the relationship line attached to the SupportTechnician parent table shows a 0).

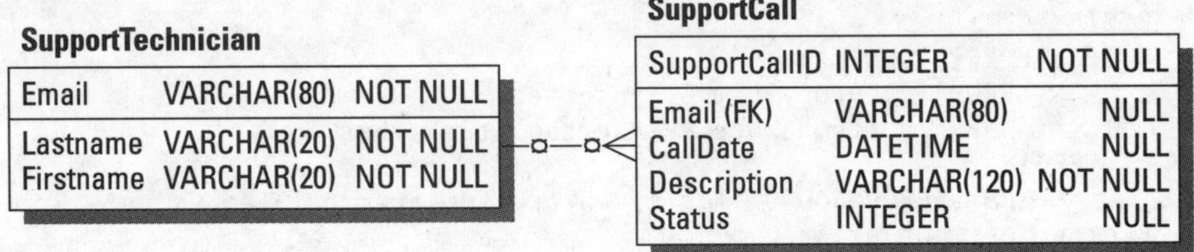

Figure 11-1: The two tables involved in a support call assignment scenario.

Listing 11-4 shows how to implement the assignment logic as a trigger.

Listing 11-4: Implementing workflow via a trigger

```
CREATE TRIGGER tIU_SupportCall
ON SupportCall
AFTER INSERT, UPDATE
AS
BEGIN
IF (UPDATE(Status))
    BEGIN
    UPDATE
        SupportCall
    SET
        Email = (
            SELECT TOP 1
                st.Email
            FROM
                SupportTechnician st LEFT OUTER JOIN SupportCall sc
                ON st.Email = sc.Email
                AND sc.Status = 40
```

```
                GROUP BY
                    St.Email,
                    ISNULL(sc.Email, '')
                ORDER BY
                    COUNT(*) ASC,
                    ISNULL(sc.Email, '') ASC
                )
        FROM
            SupportCall sc INNER JOIN Inserted i
            ON sc.SupportCallID = i.SupportCallID
        WHERE
            i.Status = 40 AND
            sc.Email IS NULL
        END
    END
```

How does the user take advantage of this trigger? Simply by choosing Intervention (which has a value of 40) from the Status select menu on the ColdFusion app's Tech Support Call form and then clicking the Submit button. The `CFQUERY` call in the form's action page needs only to update that call record's Status value to 40 for the trigger in Listing 11-4 to fire automatically, at which point the call is assigned to the support technician with the fewest open calls assigned to him. Thinking ahead, you may build a simple list interface that automatically selects all open support calls assigned to a support technician after he logs into the system.

If you use this technique, your ColdFusion development work is reduced to only a few lines of very simple code, and your database can support any type of client application written in any computer language—with all your business logic always remaining intact.

Pretty cool, huh?

The trigger logic shown in Listing 11-4 is rather involved and uses grouping, a subquery, relational updating, and unusual extensions to SQL-92 join syntax to accomplish everything in a single statement. If such complexity seems beyond your current capabilities at this time, we encourage you to learn these techniques, as they pay you back manifold if you put them to use in your development.

If you're going to develop robust, trigger-based business applications, pay particular attention to your database server's documentation regarding recursive and nested triggers, because the wrong settings can destroy your data.

A *recursive trigger* performs or causes to be performed an operation on the table to which it is attached. That operation fires the trigger again. You have two types of recursion: *direct* and *indirect*.

A *directly recursive trigger* executes an operation on the very same table to which is attached. That operation causes the triggering event to fire, which in turn causes the trigger to fire again.

An *indirectly recursive trigger* executes an operation on another table, and the trigger on that other table, in turn, executes an operation on the table to which the first trigger is attached. That operation causes the first trigger to fire again.

A *nested trigger* is a trigger that was fired by an event caused by another trigger. If a trigger on the OrderItem table updates the InventoryItem table, for example, and a trigger on the InventoryItem table updates the ReorderItem table, the trigger on the InventoryItem table is a nested trigger. SQL Server can nest triggers up to 32 levels deep.

All recursive triggers are nested triggers, but the reverse is not true. Make sure that you fully understand your database server's configuration controls regarding the behavior (or allowance) of recursive and nested triggers before you modify the default settings. Sometimes these settings affect an entire database server — not just a single database on that server. And keep in mind that, if you are going to deploy on an ISP's shared database server, you most likely must settle for operating under the default settings. So make your engineering decisions early but only after consulting in detail with your ISP.

Affecting single and multiple rows

You need to be especially aware that, in some database products, such as SQL Server 2000, a trigger fires *once* for each *statement* and not once for each *row* affected by a statement. We can't tell you how many times we've seen developers make critical coding mistakes based on the very wrong assumption that their trigger code executes once for each row affected by the statement rather than just once for the entire statement.

Even Oracle, which enables you to define triggers that fire once for each row affected by a statement, can still have problems modifying data correctly, as you see later in the section "Mutating and constraining tables."

You have several ways around this problem in SQL Server 2000. The following sections take a look at these workarounds.

Single row restriction

If your application is designed such that you never need to insert more than a single row at a time into a table, you can simply place a restriction on that table to that effect by adding the code in Listing 11-5 to its insert trigger.

Listing 11-5: Placing a single-row insert restriction on a table

```
IF (@@ROWCOUNT != 1)
    BEGIN
    RAISERROR 50010 'You cannot enter more than one row at a time.'
    ROLLBACK TRANSACTION
    RETURN
    END
```

Of course, you can also place such restrictions on `UPDATE` and `DELETE` operations, but always ask yourself twice whether you can really enforce such a restriction and still keep your application operating smoothly.

Listing 11-4, for example, is really designed to fire once for each row affected by a statement, but if you put a single-row restriction in that trigger, it prevents Listing 11-1 from executing across multiple rows. Leaving the single-row restriction off Listing 11-4 would cause it to assign all support calls affected by the triggering statement to the one tech-support person who has the least calls assigned to him at the time that the statement executes. That is acceptable because the system would never have such a function to insert multiple support calls in a single statement because support calls occur one at a time rather than in batches — and even if it did, assigning support calls in such a way would still sufficiently serve your business rules.

Single-row restrictions are the easiest but least useful method of ensuring that statement-level trigger code executes once for every row (in this case, the only row) that's affected by the triggering SQL statement. In many cases, updating multiple rows by joining them with a pseudotable is better than using a single-row restriction, as you see in the following section.

Updating multiple rows by joining the pseudotable

Whenever you insert one or more rows into a table, SQL Server creates a *pseudotable* in memory that it names `Inserted`. This pseudotable has the identical structure of the actual table into which the data was inserted, and it contains the exact contents of what you inserted into that table.

Similarly, whenever you delete one or more rows from a table, SQL Server creates a pseudotable in memory that it names `Deleted`. This pseudotable has the identical structure of the actual table from which the data was deleted, and it contains the exact contents of the deleted rows.

If you update one or more rows in a table, SQL Server creates both the `Inserted` and `Deleted` pseudotables. The *`Deleted`* pseudotable contains the rows affected by the `UPDATE` statement, and these rows reflect the data values that existed *before* the update occurred. The *`Inserted`* pseudotable contains these same rows but with the data values that existed *after* the update occurred.

Technically, both the `Inserted` and `Deleted` pseudotables are always created, regardless of which table event occurs. If the event is an `INSERT`, the `Deleted` pseudotable contains zero rows; similarly, if the event is a `DELETE`, the `Inserted` pseudotable also contains zero rows. These facts are often used to advantage in triggers that execute for a combination of table events. A trigger that executes for the `INSERT`, `UPDATE`, and `DELETE` table events, for example, can always execute two blocks of code—one that affects data joined to the `Inserted` pseudotable and another block that affects data joined to the `Deleted` pseudotables—without worry that the wrong data is affected, because any data set joined to an empty set produces another empty set. In other words, on a `INSERT`, any code that's designed to affect data joined to the `Deleted` pseudotable does not affect any data, because zero rows are in the `Deleted` pseudotable. You will see an example of this in Listing 11-7 later on in this section.

A pseudotable lives only as long as its underlying trigger executes; then it is automatically destroyed and purged from memory. While it lives, however, a pseudotable can be used by the trigger to do just about anything that a regular table can do. You can even join pseudotables with real tables.

This capability comes in handy if you want to apply the trigger code to all rows affected by an update. Take, for example, the trigger code in Listing 11-6.

Listing 11-6: An incorrectly designed trigger

```
CREATE TRIGGER tU_OrderItem
ON OrderItem
AFTER Update
AS
BEGIN
/* Declare variables for use by the trigger */
DECLARE
  @iOldQuantity INTEGER,  @iNewQuantity INTEGER,
  @sOldItemNumber VARCHAR(15),
```

Continued

Listing 11-6 *(continued)*

```
   @sNewItemNumber VARCHAR(15)

/* Get the old ordered quantity and item number */
SELECT
   @iOldQuantity = Quantity,
   @sOldItemNumber = ItemNumber
FROM
   Deleted

/* Get the new ordered quantity and item number */
SELECT
   @iNewQuantity = Quantity,
   @sNewItemNumber = ItemNumber
FROM
   Inserted

/*
Update the old item number to put the former
ordered quantity back into inventory
*/
UPDATE
   InventoryItem
SET
   AvailableToSell = AvailableToSell + @iOldQuantity
WHERE
   ItemNumber = @sOldItemNumber
/*
Update the new item number (it might have changed)
to remove the new ordered quantity from inventory
*/
UPDATE
   InventoryItem
SET
   AvailableToSell = AvailableToSell - @iOldQuantity
WHERE
   ItemNumber = @sNewItemNumber
END
```

This trigger code executes only once and uses only the values from the first row in the `Deleted` pseudotable, in turn causing only one row in the InventoryItem table to be updated. Consider, however, the trigger code in Listing 11-7.

Listing 11-7: Modifying all rows affected by the triggering SQL statement by joining a pseudotable

```
CREATE TRIGGER tU_OrderItem
ON OrderItem
```

```
AFTER Update
AS
BEGIN
/* Put the old ordered quantity back into inventory */
UPDATE
  InventoryItem
SET
  AvailableToSell = AvailableToSell + d.Quantity
FROM
  Deleted d INNER JOIN InventoryItem ii
  ON d.ItemNumber = ii.ItemNumber

/* Remove the new ordered quantity from inventory
   Remember: the item number may have changed! */
UPDATE
  InventoryItem
SET
  AvailableToSell = AvailableToSell - i.Quantity
FROM
  Inserted i INNER JOIN InventoryItem ii
  ON i.ItemNumber = ii.ItemNumber
END
```

This trigger code updates all InventoryItem rows that correspond to the OrderItem rows being updated—even if the ItemNumber key changes value. By joining the `Inserted` and `Deleted` pseudotables with the InventoryItem table, you can perform the necessary calculations to increase and decrease each inventory item by the old and new quantities ordered, respectively. The code is also much less cumbersome if written correctly.

In actual practice, you would probably do three things differently. First, you would have three separate triggers to accomplish this task—one each for the `INSERT`, `UPDATE`, and `DELETE` events—and each would contain the specific logic for adjusting the inventory level according to the database event that occurred. Second, you would place logic in your `UPDATE` trigger to prevent changing the ItemNumber from its original value. Third, you would consolidate the two `UPDATE` queries in the trigger into one query joining the InventoryItem table and both pseudotables, as in Listing 11-8.

Listing 11-8: Modifying the `UPDATE`-trigger to take advantage of a nonmodifiable key

```
CREATE TRIGGER tU_OrderItem
ON OrderItem
AFTER Update
AS
BEGIN
IF (UPDATE(ItemNumber))
    BEGIN
    RAISERROR 50010 'You cannot change the Item Number.'
    ROLLBACK TRANSACTION
```

Continued

Listing 11-8 *(continued)*

```
    RETURN
    END

    UPDATE
      InventoryItem
    SET
      AvailableToSell = ii.AvailableToSell + d.Quantity - i.Quantity
    FROM
      Inserted i INNER JOIN InventoryItem ii
      ON i.ItemNumber = ii.ItemNumber
      INNER JOIN Deleted d
          ON d.ItemNumber = ii.ItemNumber
END
```

The last resort: cursors

Imagine retrieving a bunch of rows into a separate place in memory and then fetching those rows one at a time, looking at the column values in each row and possibly performing some operation based on the values in each row. This is the life of a cursor.

Cursors are a last resort because they are cumbersome, slow, and resource intensive, and they destroy the scalability of your database if used on high-transaction throughput areas of your database. Cursors are often used where they shouldn't be, either as substitutes for good SQL code or to work around poorly designed databases.

At times, however, a cursor is the only practical solution to your problem. Say, for example, that you have a stored procedure named `sp_ArchiveCall` that is used in many places throughout your database, including the Insert trigger shown in Listing 11-9.

Listing 11-9: Modifying all rows affected by the triggering SQL statement by scrolling over a cursor

```
CREATE PROCEDURE sp_ArchiveCall (
    @SupportCallID    Integer
)
AS
BEGIN
UPDATE
    SupportCall
SET
    Status = 60
WHERE
    SupportCallID = @SupportCallID
END
go

CREATE TRIGGER tI_SupportCallArchive
ON SupportCallArchive
AFTER INSERT
```

```
AS
BEGIN
DECLARE
    @SupportCallID    Integer

DECLARE curClosedCalls CURSOR FOR
SELECT
    SupportCallID
FROM
    Inserted

OPEN curClosedCalls
FETCH NEXT FROM curClosedCalls INTO @SupportCallID

WHILE @@FETCH_STATUS = 0
    BEGIN
    EXECUTE sp_ArchiveCall @SupportCallID
    FETCH NEXT FROM curClosedCalls INTO @SupportCallID
    END

CLOSE curClosedCalls
DEALLOCATE curClosedCalls

END
go
```

You use a cursor here because you must call the stored procedure once for *every row affected* by the statement, and the only way to do so is to place the stored procedure call within each retrieval or *fetch* of a cursor row.

Please treat all cursors with fear and loathing. They are bad, and you'd better have a defensible excuse for using them — or your source-code peer review is likely to embarrass you terribly.

Instead-Of triggers

And now for something completely different: *Instead-Of Triggers*.

That's an accurate intro to the subject, because Instead-Of triggers enable you to do something completely different from the intended database operation. In essence, an Instead-Of trigger interrupts the SQL statement that fired it and says, *"Instead of doing that, do this."*

Why would you want to do such a thing? Because sometimes you simply need to.

Take, for example, the situation in which you want to transform physical deletes into logical deletes. You have critical table rows that users occasionally want to delete, but you need to hold onto them until some other business processes that need them run to conclusion. Instead of actually deleting the rows after the user performs a `DELETE`, you want to set a Status column to `50` (Closed status) for each row that the user tries to delete. You perform the physical delete later on in some administrative function after all your other business processes have exhausted their need for those rows and they are correctly archived (see Listing 11-9). In the meantime, you filter the rows used in front-end business processes by Status `< 50` so that the "deleted" rows don't appear.

Listing 11-10 shows the Instead-Of trigger that you'd create to implement this process.

Listing 11-10: Transforming physical deletes into logical deletes via an Instead-Of trigger

```
CREATE TRIGGER tIOD_SupportCall
ON SupportCall
INSTEAD OF DELETE
AS
BEGIN
UPDATE
    SupportCall
SET
    Status = 50
FROM
    SupportCall sc INNER JOIN Deleted d
    ON sc.SupportCallID = d.SupportCallID
END
```

Now, every time that someone performs a DELETE against this table, the rows stay in place but their Status column is set to 50. As you see in Listing 11-9, archiving these rows sets their Status column to 60, meaning that they are ready to physically delete. To physically delete these rows, you create a simple stored procedure, such as the one in Listing 11-11.

Listing 11-11: Physically deleting the rows set to `Status = 60`

```
CREATE PROCEDURE sp_PhysicallyDeleteSupportCalls
AS
BEGIN TRANSACTION

-- Disabling the Instead-Of trigger will allow normal DELETEs
ALTER TABLE SupportCall DISABLE TRIGGER tIOD_SupportCall

IF (@@ERROR != 0)
    BEGIN
    RAISERROR 50010 'An error occurred attempting to disable
tIOD_SupportCall.'
    ROLLBACK TRANSACTION
    RETURN
    END

/* Physically delete with an exclusive table lock so no one
   modifies the table while the Instead-Of trigger is disabled. */
DELETE FROM
    SupportCall
WITH
    (TABLOCKX)
WHERE
    Status = 60

ALTER TABLE SupportCall ENABLE TRIGGER tIOD_SupportCall
```

```
IF (@@ERROR != 0)
    BEGIN
    RAISERROR 50020 'An error occurred attempting to enable
tIOD_SupportCall.'
    ROLLBACK TRANSACTION
    RETURN
    END

COMMIT TRANSACTION
```

That's a pretty cool use of an Instead-Of trigger on a table, but Instead-Of triggers are mainly intended for use on views. As you may remember from Chapter 10, views can be used to update the physical tables on which they are built, but some views are structured in such ways that inserting and updating is either impossible or would give unintended results. If you have a relational view that joins multiple tables, for example, exactly how would an update to that view be accomplished? Typically, such an update would be possible only through an Instead-Of trigger.

Unfortunately, such a discussion is beyond the scope of this book, but if you make heavy use of relational views and want to tighten down the security on physical tables, you want to read more about them in some of the books that we recommend in Chapter 10 of this book.

Oracle triggers

Oh, boy—are you in for a treat! Oracle has the most complete set of triggers of any database product in the world. Where SQL Server has statement-level After and Instead-Of triggers, Oracle has 14 different types of triggers, as the following list shows:

- ✦ Before Insert, statement-level
- ✦ Before Insert, row-level
- ✦ Before Update, statement-level
- ✦ Before Update, row-level
- ✦ Before Delete, statement-level
- ✦ Before Delete, row-level
- ✦ After Insert, statement-level
- ✦ After Insert, row-level
- ✦ After Update, statement-level
- ✦ After Update, row-level
- ✦ After Delete, statement-level
- ✦ After Delete, row-level
- ✦ Instead-Of, statement-level
- ✦ Instead-Of, row-level

What's more, Oracle triggers have more granular control over when they are fired. You can. for example, create an Oracle Update trigger that fires only after one or more specific columns are updated or if specific conditions exist — not just every time that an update occurs.

Pseudorows versus pseudotables

Remember pseudotables from the section "Updating multiple rows by joining the pseudotable," earlier in this chapter? Oracle doesn't have pseudotables; instead, it has *pseudorows*.

As you can imagine, a pseudorow is like a single row of a pseudotable.

Other similarities exist between pseudotables and pseudorows. Whenever you perform an update in SQL Server, you create two pseudotables for the Update Trigger to use: `Deleted` and `Inserted`, where `Deleted` contains the old pre-update values and `Inserted` contains the new post-update values. After you perform an update in Oracle, you create two pseudorows for the row-level Update Trigger: `Old` and `New`, where `Old` contains the old pre-update values and `New` contains the new post-update values.

The reason why Oracle uses pseudorows instead of pseudotables is because Oracle permits row-level triggers that fire once for every row affected by the triggering SQL statement. Programming by using pseudorows is actually much easier than programming by using pseudotables, because you have direct access to the values of their columns via bind variables, as in Listing 11-12. Boldfaced code denotes the major changes between Listing 11-7 and Listing 11-12.

Listing 11-12: Adapting Listing 11-7 as an Oracle row-level Update Trigger

```
CREATE TRIGGER tU_OrderItem
AFTER Update of Quantity ON OrderItem
For Each Row
BEGIN
/* Put the old ordered quantity back into inventory */
UPDATE
  InventoryItem
SET
  AvailableToSell = AvailableToSell + :old.Quantity
WHERE
  ItemNumber = :old.ItemNumber

/* Remove the new ordered quantity from inventory
   Remember: the item number may have changed! */
UPDATE
  InventoryItem
SET
  AvailableToSell = AvailableToSell - :new.Quantity
WHERE
  ItemNumber = :new.ItemNumber
END;
```

Because of Oracle's powerful capability to define row-level triggers, you can simplify your trigger code even more. The `:old` and `:new` values are available via the pseudorows affected by the `UPDATE` statement, so you can use them directly in your trigger code without declaring variables or joining tables. And this trigger fires only if the Quantity column is part of the UPDATE statement and not just every time that the OrderItem table is updated.

Mutating and constraining tables

Developers new to Oracle are often stumped by *mutating table errors* that occur after implementing seemingly well-written triggers, such as the following:

```
ORA-04091: table USERNAME.TABLENAME is mutating, trigger/function may
not see it.
```

Really understanding the nature of what is going wrong whenever these errors occur is important, because if you don't, you spend a lot of time spinning your debugging wheels.

A table is said to be *mutating* if its contents are changing via an INSERT, UPDATE, or DELETE statement or a DELETE CASCADE is performed between related tables. If a trigger attempts to read or modify information in a table *while* it is mutating, the preceding error occurs. This makes sense, because to try such a thing is like trying to hit a moving target: Until the data has a stable value, it is of no use to the trigger that wants to read or modify it.

Take the example of a row-level trigger shown in Listing 11-13, which attempts to read the number of rows in the table to which it is attached.

Listing 11-13: A row-level trigger unsuccessfully attempting to read from the table to which it is attached

```
CREATE OR REPLACE TRIGGER tDAR_CompanyCount
AFTER DELETE ON Company
FOR EACH ROW
DECLARE
    nRowCount INTEGER;
BEGIN
    SELECT COUNT(*) INTO nRowCount FROM Company;
END;
```

Now run the following SQL statement against the Company table:

```
DELETE FROM Company WHERE State = 'GA'
```

This trigger isn't a good practical example (because the trigger doesn't do anything useful), but it's a great teaching example because you can plainly see that the trigger attempts to use information that is currently being modified. As *each row* is deleted by the DELETE statement, the table is *still mutating* because it hasn't yet finished deleting all the rows targeted by the DELETE statement.

How can a row count be made while rows are still being deleted? The number of rows is *mutating* at the same time that a request for the count of those rows is being requested, so the mutating table error occurs.

On the other hand, say that you change the trigger in Listing 11-13 from a row-level trigger to the statement-level trigger shown in Listing 11-14.

Listing 11-14: A statement-level trigger that can read from the table to which it is attached

```
CREATE OR REPLACE TRIGGER tDAR_CompanyCount
AFTER DELETE ON Company
DECLARE
    nRowCount INTEGER;
BEGIN
    SELECT COUNT(*) INTO nRowCount FROM Company;
END;
```

Now *this* trigger works, because the trigger code executes after *the entire statement* has processed. Don't confuse the fact that the trigger works with the fact that it is an After trigger; a Before statement-level trigger would also work. The issue is whether the trigger executes once for the entire SQL statement versus once *for each row* affected by SQL statement: If the trigger is for each row, the triggering SQL statement can still be mutating the table while the trigger is attempting to work with it, and such an action is not permitted.

An exception to the mutating table rule occurs for `INSERT` statements that are designed to insert only a single row into a table—in other words, not an `Insert into ... Select` that can insert multiple rows in a single statement. A row-level Insert Trigger that can insert only a single row does *not* raise the mutating table exception if you attempt to select against the table on which that trigger was defined.

Another reason why you may receive mutating table errors is if your trigger attempts to read from or modify primary, unique, or foreign key columns of tables related through foreign key constraints. Such related tables are considered *constraining tables* because they constrain the data that can be inserted or modified in the table to which the trigger is attached.

If you place a row-level Insert Trigger on a parent table that attempts to insert a record into a related child table, for example, a foreign-key lookup must be performed against the parent table to see whether the child record can indeed be inserted by using its foreign key value. This procedure also raises the mutating table error, because the trigger that fires for *each row* of the parent table is attempting an action that causes a lookup on *the entire parent table* while it is still changing from the effects of the SQL statement.

Mutating and constraining tables is an advanced topic that is beyond the scope of this book, but it is covered thoroughly in some of the more advanced Oracle books on the market. We cover just enough here to make you aware of the potential problems they can cause, and to spur you onto further reading on your own.

Practical things that you can do by using triggers

The following sections give examples based on SQL Server triggers, because SQL Server is an easier platform on which to teach than any other, but these examples can also be adapted for use on other platforms.

Return identity values

SQL Server takes whatever output is placed in the output buffer and sends it back to the calling application as a result set. This feature is what makes ColdFusion access to SQL Server result sets so easy: Perform a `SELECT` just about anywhere in SQL Server, and it becomes a result set.

Listing 11-15 uses this feature to return the newly inserted Identity column value from an Insert trigger.

Listing 11-15: An Insert Trigger that returns the Identity column value

```
CREATE TRIGGER tI_SalesOrder
ON SalesOrder
AFTER INSERT
AS
BEGIN
    SELECT SalesOrderID FROM Inserted
END
```

One very important thing about this trigger is that it is useful only if you insert a single sales order in your SQL statement. Remember that this is a statement-level trigger, so it fires only once for the entire SQL statement that triggers it. Most systems insert sales orders one at a time, and the only time that you typically need the value of an Identity column is if you insert a sales order and then want to add line items to that sales order and, therefore, must have the foreign key (the Identity value).

Automatic reordering

Earlier in the section "Updating multiple rows by joining the pseudotable," we show how inventory levels can be automatically adjusted by placing Insert, Update, and Delete Triggers on the OrderItem table. But what happens if the inventory gets low? You can use *nested triggers* to automatically handle reordering from your vendors, too! Remember from the section "Getting the database to do the work for you," earlier in this chapter, that we said that you can nest triggers up to 32 levels deep? Well, we don't quite use that many levels of depth, but we can use three levels of nesting very effectively by placing the Update trigger in Listing 11-16 on the InventoryItem table.

Listing 11-16: A nested Update trigger on the InventoryItem table

```
CREATE TRIGGER tU_InventoryItem
ON InventoryItem
AFTER UPDATE
AS
BEGIN
DECLARE
    @ItemNumber            Varchar(15),
    @AvailableToSell    Integer,
    @ReorderLevel        Integer,
    @ReorderQuantity    Integer

DECLARE curUpdatedInventoryItems CURSOR FOR
SELECT
    ItemNumber,
    AvailableToSell,
```

Continued

Listing 11-16 *(continued)*

```
        ReorderLevel,
        ReorderQuantity
    FROM
        Inserted
    FOR READ ONLY

    OPEN curUpdatedInventoryItems
    FETCH NEXT FROM curUpdatedInventoryItems INTO
        @ItemNumber,
        @AvailableToSell,
        @ReorderLevel,
        @ReorderQuantity

    WHILE (@@FETCH_STATUS = 0)
        BEGIN
        IF (@AvailableToSell <= @ReorderLevel)
            BEGIN
            EXEC sp_ReorderItem @ItemNumber, @ReorderQuantity
            END

        FETCH NEXT FROM curUpdatedInventoryItems INTO
            @ItemNumber,
            @AvailableToSell,
            @ReorderLevel,
            @ReorderQuantity
        END

    CLOSE curUpdatedInventoryItems
    DEALLOCATE curUpdatedInventoryItems
    END
```

Here's the chain of events: An OrderItem row is inserted, which fires the Insert trigger on that table. The Insert trigger updates the InventoryItem row corresponding to that OrderItem, which fires the Update trigger on the InventoryItem table that checks whether the current `AvailableToSell` value is at or below the `ReorderLevel` value. If it is, the trigger calls a stored procedure that inserts a `ReorderItem` row related to the currently open reorder.

Of course, this example is highly simplified for illustrative purposes, but you get the idea of how nested triggers are very useful and practical.

Enforcing complex business rules

Because a trigger is fired according to well-defined database events, it is the perfect mechanism for implementing business rules. Because business rules must be followed at all times within a system, they are always followed if they execute alongside modifications to your data, and this means that you need to use triggers.

You can call stored procedures from triggers to leverage their usefulness. If you have a routine that must be performed against your data under both user control and every time that certain database events occur, just place that logic inside a stored procedure and call it from both your

ColdFusion application and the triggers that must execute it. Just remember that all parameters that you pass to called stored procedures must come from data available within the trigger.

Eliminating the Need for Post-Processing Data Within ColdFusion

Your database server is very highly optimized for manipulating data, but ColdFusion Server isn't. Your database server can evaluate an enumerated value much faster than ColdFusion Server can. You should always, therefore, try to execute evaluation logic on your database server and have it return the finished results to ColdFusion for direct display to the user.

Say, for example, that you have a ColdFusion query object that contains a Status column of enumerated values, where 0 equates to Open, 10 equates to In Process, 20 equates to Suggested Solution, and so on. The common way to handle this is to loop over the query in ColdFusion, test the Status column's value, and display the English string corresponding to the numeric value, as in Listing 11-17.

Listing 11-17: Evaluating column values in ColdFusion

```
<cfquery name="GetSupportCalls"
        datasource="#Request.MainDSN#">
SELECT
        SupportCallID,
        Status,
        Description
FROM
        SupportCall
ORDER BY
        Status ASC
</cfquery>

<h1>Support Calls</h1>

<table cellspacing="2" cellpadding="2" border="1">
<tr>
    <td><b>Call #</b></td>
    <td><b>Status</b></td>
    <td><b>Description</b></td>
</tr>
<cfoutput>
<cfloop query="GetSupportCalls">
<tr bgcolor="<cfif GetSupportCalls.Status EQ
0>Lime<cfelse>White</cfif>">
    <td align="Right">#SupportCallID#</td>
    <td>
    <cfswitch expression="#GetSupportCalls.Status#">
        <cfcase value="0">
            Opened
```

Continued

Listing 11-17 *(continued)*

```
          </cfcase>
          <cfcase value="10">
              In Process
          </cfcase>
          <cfcase value="20">
              Suggested Solution
          </cfcase>
          <cfcase value="30">
              Customer Closed
          </cfcase>
          <cfcase value="40">
              Escalated
          </cfcase>
          <cfcase value="50">
              Admin Closed
          </cfcase>
          <cfcase value="60">
              Archived
          </cfcase>
      </cfswitch>
      </td>
      <td>#Description#</td>
  </tr>
  </cfloop>
  </cfoutput>
  </table>
```

The best practice is to handle such evaluations at the database server and then return the finished results to ColdFusion for simple display by using CFOUTPUT, as in Listing 11-18.

Listing 11-18: Evaluating column values at the database server

```
<cfquery name="GetSupportCalls"
        datasource="#Request.MainDSN#">
    SELECT
        SupportCallID,
        CASE Status
            WHEN 0 THEN 'Opened'
            WHEN 10 THEN 'In Process'
            WHEN 20 THEN 'Suggested Solution'
            WHEN 30 THEN 'Customer Closed'
            WHEN 40 THEN 'Escalated'
            WHEN 50 THEN 'Admin Closed'
            WHEN 60 THEN 'Archived'
        END AS DisplayStatus,
        CASE Status
            WHEN 0 THEN 'Lime'
            ELSE 'White'
```

```
          END AS Bgcolor,
          Description
     FROM
          SupportCall
     ORDER BY
          Status ASC
</cfquery>

<h1>Support Calls</h1>

<table cellspacing="2" cellpadding="2" border="1">
<tr>
     <td><b>Call #</b></td>
     <td><b>Status</b></td>
     <td><b>Description</b></td>
</tr>
<cfoutput query="GetSupportCalls">
<tr bgcolor="#Bgcolor#">
     <td align="Right">#SupportCallID#</td>
     <td>#DisplayStatus#</td>
     <td>#Description#</td>
</tr>
</cfoutput>
</table>
```

Why is this a best practice? Because the database server can perform this evaluation many times faster than ColdFusion Server can.

This same technique can be used for a number of different evaluations and not just with `CASE` expressions. Take a close look at your existing applications to see whether you can find places where you can put this useful technique to work and measure the performance metrics before and after. You're likely to be pleasantly surprised!

Effective Use of ColdFusion MX's Enhanced Query of Queries

After Ben Forta announced the new Query of Queries (QoQ) feature in ColdFusion 5 at the 2000 Developer's Conference, the crowd went absolutely wild! What a truly cool feature — and how useful it was going to be! The problem is that Query of Queries is way too easily misused and even abused.

We first need to explain the difference between what happens inside ColdFusion Server and what happens inside your database server as each handles a query.

Your database server is a highly optimized data manipulation machine designed to do one thing really well and very fast: handle data. ColdFusion Server is an interpretation engine for parsing and processing a wide range of CFML requests via HTTP. In Version 5, ColdFusion added an internal library of database routines that enable ColdFusion query objects to be treated as ODBC table objects and that also enable certain SQL statements to be executed against them. Because the query objects look and act just as tables do to ColdFusion, they can be queried just as tables can by using the same methods (at least in theory). With ColdFusion MX, this library was enhanced slightly, but the underlying QoQ mechanism is still the same.

Now think about the internal differences for just a moment. On one side, you have a small library of routines that expose query objects as tables and enable basic row and column manipulation. No indexes to greatly speed queries, no sophisticated low-level data-handling algorithms — just the most basic capabilities. On the other side, you have a screamer of an optimized data-manipulation machine that can do dataset gymnastics.

QoQ becomes truly useful whenever you can't do everything that you need to do in the database itself. You see an example of this type of situation in the following section.

QoQ is also useful if the original database query is very complicated and resource intensive, executes over a very large dataset in the database, produces a relatively small result set, and subsequent queries are subsets or mutations of the result set. An example of this situation is shown in the section, "Getting multi-dimensional results," later in this chapter.

Performing relational joins between ColdFusion query objects

Only in a very few instances does using QoQ outperform the simple task of going back to the data server for a fresh query from scratch. QoQ was not designed to circumvent the database server; it was mainly meant to expand the capabilities of single ColdFusion queries by enabling them to be joined with other queries and data sources and then querying them as a consolidated "table."

Expanding `CFDIRECTORY`'s capabilities is an excellent example for the effective use of QoQ. Say, for example, that you have a collection of files that are uploaded to a common directory and that you also have a database containing descriptions and comments regarding those files. One party handles creating and uploading files, and another party enters descriptions for them in the database. This is an ongoing process, and no real synchronization occurs between the time that files are uploaded and the time that their descriptions get entered into the database. The application must display a list containing only those files for which descriptions have also been added in the database.

In Listing 11-19, a `CFDIRECTORY` call returns a ColdFusion query object containing a list of all files and subdirectories in the directory that's listed, and a `CFQUERY` call returns a list of all descriptions from an Access database. By using QoQ, you can inner join the ColdFusion query object containing the directory listing with the database query containing descriptions. (The file name makes an excellent key value, because it is guaranteed to be unique by the filing system.) The result is a consolidated listing of only those files that are already uploaded and that contain corresponding descriptions in the database.

Listing 11-19: Code for joining two ColdFusion `query` objects

```
<!---
Create a query object containing the contents of the download directory
--->
<cfdirectory action="LIST"
        directory="C:\Inetpub\wwwroot\cfmxbible\download"
        name="dirContents">

<!---
Create a query object containing all descriptions entered for all
files, whether they are currently in the download directory or not.
--->
```

```
<cfquery name="fileInfo"
        datasource="#Request.MainDSN#">
    SELECT
        Filename,
        Description,
        Rating
    FROM
        DownloadableFile
</cfquery>

<!---
Create a relational query for only files that have matching
descriptions in the database.
--->
<cfquery name="downloadableFiles"
        dbtype="Query">
    SELECT
        dirContents.Size AS Size,
        dirContents.DateLastModified AS DateLastModified,
        fileInfo.Filename AS Filename,
        fileInfo.Description AS Description,
        fileInfo.Rating AS Rating
    FROM
        dirContents, fileInfo
    WHERE
        dirContents.Name = fileInfo.Filename
</cfquery>
```

Notice the boldface text that specifies *Query* as the data source—that's what tells ColdFusion Server to match table names in the SQL statement with internal `query` objects rather than external data tables.

Figure 11-2 shows a conceptual drawing of the two datasets contained in these two queries and the single dataset resulting from the `INNER JOIN` between them.

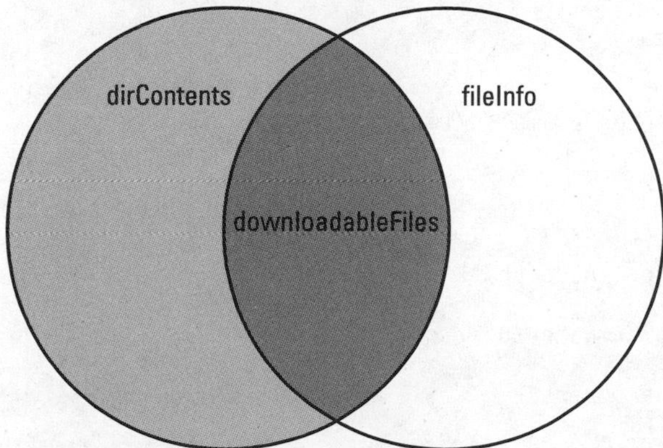

Figure 11-2: The intermediate and final results of joining two query objects.

This type of operation is what QoQ was made for! Before QoQ, you didn't have a simple way to do this kind of thing.

You can also use this technique to join multiple, disparate data sources. If you have a comma-delimited text file, Access database tables, and Oracle database tables that you want to join together, just create ColdFusion queries from them and join them by using the same QoQ technique shown in the preceding listing.

Now to take a look at an example of querying an existing `query` object.

Querying a query object

Because ColdFusion MX treats `query` objects as if they were database tables, you can perform a query on another ColdFusion query, as shown in Listing 11-20

Listing 11-20: **Querying a ColdFusion query**

```
<cfquery name="baseQuery"
         datasource="#Request.MainDSN#">
SELECT
    CustomerNumber,
    CompanyName
FROM
    Customer
</cfquery>

<cfquery name="secondaryQuery"
         dbtype="Query">
SELECT
    CompanyName AS Custname
FROM
    baseQuery
WHERE
    CompanyName LIKE 'A%'
</cfquery>


<html>
<head>
    <title>Query of Queries Example</title>
</head>

<body>

<table cellspacing="2" cellpadding="2" border="0">
<tr>
    <td nowrap><b>Customer Name</b></td>
</tr>
<cfoutput query="secondaryQuery">
<tr>
    <td>#Custname#</td>
</tr>
```

```
</cfoutput>
</table>

</body>
</html>
```

Notice that you don't specify a datasource if dbtype="Query". Instead, you just refer to the names of the queries as if they were table names, and ColdFusion Server knows to access its own queries rather than look in a specific datasource for tables.

Caveats and restrictions

As useful as QoQ is in certain circumstances, you need to consider a few caveats and restrictions in using it, as the following list describes:

- OUTER JOINs are not supported.
- SQL-92 JOIN syntax (for example, Table1 INNER JOIN Table2 ON Key1 = Key2) is not supported
- Table-name aliases are not supported, which means that you must always fully qualify table names in relational JOINs.
- If an aggregate function is retrieved as one of the columns in your result set, that function cannot be used in GROUP BY or HAVING clauses.
- Because QoQ text matches are case-sensitive, you must compare a functionally converted value of a column against the matching criterion to ensure positive matches (for example, WHERE Upper(LastName) LIKE 'SMI%').
- ODBC-formatted dates and times are not supported.

QoQ also has a couple "enhancements" over what was available in ColdFusion 5, as the following list describes:

- If an aggregate function is aliased, the alias must be used in the GROUP BY and HAVING clauses rather than the function itself. This behavior is counter to logical SQL statement processing, as the SELECT clause where aliases are defined is internally processed *after* the GROUP BY and HAVING clauses, so don't try to use the same flawed syntax with your normal database queries.
- The LIKE conditional works more like a normal database LIKE conditional, which supports search patterns containing wildcard characters.

So a typical relational join with QoQ performs an INNER JOIN in the WHERE clause and uses long-form table naming, as the following example shows:

```
SELECT
    Customer.CompanyName AS CompanyName,
    SalesOrder.SalesOrderID AS SalesOrderID,
    SalesOrder.SaleDate AS SaleDate,
    SalesOrder.OrderTotal AS OrderTotal
FROM
    Customer, SalesOrder
WHERE
    Customer.CustomerNumber = SalesOrder.CustomerNumber
```

You may also notice that we aliased the column names in this example to be the same as their original names. If we didn't do so in ColdFusion 5, an error would be thrown in trying to resolve the variable name. If instead of providing an alias, we fully resolved the column as `TableName.ColumnName` in the `CFOUTPUT`, ColdFusion 5 would incorrectly interpreted this syntax as *`QueryName`*`.ColumnName` and instead would repeat the value in the first row of the table for each row of the output. You prevent all such problems by simply providing an alias for each column name in a query join. This problem with fully resolved column names was fixed with ColdFusion MX, but you should still alias your columns for both ease of programming and backward compatibility.

So, now that you know how to query a query . . . *don't!* At least, not unless you *truly* need to.

Always remember that QoQ is a low-performance feature that's not designed for serious query work. If you're thinking that you can gain performance by making one big database server query and then using QoQ to extract data from the resulting ColdFusion query, think again. Why are you averse to going back to the database server for a fresh query instead of extracting a subset of your existing ColdFusion query? Take our advice: Turn on your performance metrics and load-test the system both ways. Do so and you clearly see the difference in performance. Most of the time, going back to the database server for a fresh query wins.

Don't be tempted to post-process data

The same admonition about evaluating and otherwise post-processing ColdFusion query results within `CFLOOP`s holds just as true for QoQ. You want to return results from your database server in the exact format in which they are displayed, if at all possible. Under most circumstances, if you can program the data to look the way that you want in ColdFusion, you can probably also do the same thing directly in the database by using SQL (or whatever extensions to SQL that your database server gives you).

Getting multi-dimensional results

One technique for which QoQ is useful is the ad-hoc display of various dimensions of a single dataset. If you have a chart that you want to plot from various columns of the same result set, for example, QoQ is the perfect solution: You have already queried the database for the exact rows that you need, so no further return trips to the database are necessary. All QoQ does is change which columns are targeted for plotting against the X and Y axes, as shown in Listing 11-21. Note that we omit explicit `Session` scope locking for the sake of clarity, but your production code should diligently lock `Session` variables.

Listing 11-21: Plotting specific dimensions of a single dataset

```
<!--- Uncomment the following line to rerun the base query --->
<!--- <cfset Session.GetStatistics = ""> --->

<cfparam name="FORM.MetricType" default="Volume">
<cfparam name="FORM.YearNumber" default="2001">

<h1>Base Query</h1>

<cfif NOT IsDefined('Session.GetStatistics') OR NOT
IsQuery(Session.GetStatistics)>
The base query was executed<BR>
```

```
<cfquery name="Session.GetStatistics"
  datasource="#Request.MainDSN#">
    SELECT
      YearNumber,
      MonthNumber,
      CASE MonthNumber
        WHEN 1 THEN 'January'
        WHEN 2 THEN 'February'
        WHEN 3 THEN 'March'
        WHEN 4 THEN 'April'
        WHEN 5 THEN 'May'
        WHEN 6 THEN 'June'
        WHEN 7 THEN 'July'
        WHEN 8 THEN 'August'
        WHEN 9 THEN 'September'
        WHEN 10 THEN 'October'
        WHEN 11 THEN 'November'
        WHEN 12 THEN 'December'
      END
        AS MonthName,
      Volume,
      AverageXA,
      MinimumXA,
      MaximumXA
    FROM
      MonthlyStatistic
</cfquery>
<cfelse>
The base query was <b>not</b> executed<BR>
</cfif>

<cfquery name="QoQ"
  dbtype="Query">
    SELECT
      MonthNumber,
      MonthName,
      <cfswitch expression="#Trim(FORM.MetricType)#">
        <cfcase value="Volume">
          Volume AS MetricValue
        </cfcase>
        <cfcase value="AverageXA">
          AverageXA AS MetricValue
        </cfcase>
        <cfcase value="MinimumXA">
          MinimumXA AS MetricValue
        </cfcase>
        <cfcase value="MaximumXA">
          MaximumXA AS MetricValue
        </cfcase>
      </cfswitch>
    FROM
      Session.GetStatistics
```

Continued

Listing 11-21 *(continued)*

```
    WHERE
      YearNumber = #Val(FORM.YearNumber)#
    ORDER BY
      MonthNumber ASC
</cfquery>

<table cellspacing="0" cellpadding="0" border="0">
<tr>
  <td valign="Bottom"><b>Month</b></td>
  <td align="Right" valign="Bottom">  <b>Volume</b></td>
  <td align="Right"
valign="Bottom">  <b>Average<BR>  Transaction</b></
td>
  <td align="Right"
valign="Bottom">  <b>Minimum<BR>  Transaction</b></
td>
  <td align="Right"
valign="Bottom">  <b>Maximum<BR>  Transaction</b></
td>
</tr>
<cfoutput query="Session.GetStatistics">
<tr bgcolor="###Iif(Session.GetStatistics.CurrentRow MOD 2,
DE('EAEAFF'), DE('FFFFFF'))#">
  <td>#MonthName#</td>
  <td align="Right">  #NumberFormat(Volume,
"999,999,999,999.99")#</td>
  <td align="Right">  #NumberFormat(AverageXA,
"999,999,999,999.99")#</td>
  <td align="Right">  #NumberFormat(MinimumXA,
"999,999,999,999.99")#</td>
  <td align="Right">  #NumberFormat(MaximumXA,
"999,999,999,999.99")#</td>
</tr>
</cfoutput>
</table>

<h1>Choose the Metric to Graph:</h1>

<form action="Listing11-21.cfm" method="post" name="GraphForm">

Metric: 
<select name="MetricType" size="1">
    <option value="Volume" <cfif FORM.MetricType EQ
"Volume">SELECTED</cfif>>Volume</option>
    <option value="AverageXA" <cfif FORM.MetricType EQ
"AverageXA">SELECTED</cfif>>Average Transaction</option>
    <option value="MinimumXA" <cfif FORM.MetricType EQ
"MinimumXA">SELECTED</cfif>>Minimum Transaction</option>
    <option value="MaximumXA" <cfif FORM.MetricType EQ
"MaximumXA">SELECTED</cfif>>Maximum Transaction</option>
</select>  
```

```
Year: 
<select name="YearNumber" size="1">
    <option value="2001" <cfif FORM.YearNumber EQ
"2001">SELECTED</cfif>>2001</option>
    <option value="2002" <cfif FORM.YearNumber EQ
"2002">SELECTED</cfif>>2002</option>
    <option value="2003" <cfif FORM.YearNumber EQ
"2003">SELECTED</cfif>>2003</option>
</select>  

<input type="submit">
</form>

<cfchart
        format="flash"
        chartheight="400"
        chartwidth="600"
        scalefrom="0"
        seriesplacement="default"
        foregroundcolor="Black"
        font="Arial"
        fontsize="8"
        showborder="yes"
        labelformat="number"
        show3d="yes"
        rotated="no"
        tipstyle="mouseOver"
        pieslicestyle="sliced">

    <cfchartseries
        type="bar"
        query="QoQ"
        itemcolumn="MonthName"
        valuecolumn="MetricValue"
        seriescolor="##FF0000"
        paintstyle="plain">
    </cfchartseries>
</cfchart>
```

The reasons why multi-dimensional charting is such a great application of the QoQ feature are as follows:

✦ No matter which dimensions are chosen, they all originate from the same small set of rows retrieved from the database, so QoQ eliminates the need to requery the database.

✦ The result set that QoQ operates over is very small, so the lack of indexes or query optimization is of little hindrance to performance.

✦ In cases where the result set must be resorted according to the data dimensions plotted, the QoQ feature makes this task practical.

If fact, these are good criteria to use in determining whether your application should use QoQ versus requerying the database.

Leveraging QoQ by using query caching

QoQ and query caching work together beautifully. Combining the capability to cache a query with the capability to requery that same query can make for a nicely scalable solution, as long as the result set you're requerying isn't extremely large.

You may remember from Chapter 9 that the CACHEDWITHIN attribute of the CFQUERY tag is what prevents ColdFusion from returning to the database every time that it needs the base query from which QoQ makes its detailed queries.

Whenever you build an action page that enables users to requery existing ColdFusion queries, you should cache the base query from which QoQ works or you overburden your database server with a redundant base query each time that the action page is run.

This technique works best if the base query results in a relatively small selection of rows from the database tables queried. If you are caching a 10,000-row database query and then querying those 10,000 rows by using QoQ, stop and think whether you would be better off requerying the database each time so that you can take full advantage of all the query optimization features that your database server offers. Better yet, formally load-test both methods and have the metrics decide for you.

Although you can use QoQ in many more ways than those described in this chapter, overtaxing such an underpowered feature is most likely not a good idea. If you are in doubt as to whether to use QoQ in a specific part of your application if other querying techniques are available to you, perform a formal load test by using both techniques and pay special attention to the RAM usage meter as the test runs. If 100 virtual users simultaneously slamming QoQ's pegs your RAM usage, while alternative query techniques don't, implementing QoQ in that part of your application is probably asking for trouble.

On the other hand, if QoQ is your only possible solution, the only thing that you can do is to try to limit the total amount of data manipulated in a QoQ call, which in turn limits the amount of RAM needed to handle that data.

Data Binding

Suppose that you specify dynamic values in your CFQUERY calls as follows:

```
<cfquery name="GetSalesOrders"
        datasource="#Request.MainDSN#">
    SELECT
        SalesOrderID,
        SaleDate,
        TaxRate,
        TaxAmount,
        Total
    FROM
        SalesOrder
    WHERE
        SaleDate >= '#AfterDate#'
    AND    Total >= #Amount#
</cfquery>
```

If you do so, you are sending a complete query to your database for parsing and execution. The parser must determine whether the dynamic values from ColdFusion used to feed columns of the database tables and used in the WHERE clause are compatible with data types and data-size restrictions (for example, trying to feed 42 characters to a VARCHAR(40) column). If a value is fed to a table column can be directly converted to the data type of that column, the database server performs the conversion before the statement processes. This checking and conversion process takes time and, therefore, potentially slows execution.

CFQUERYPARAM

Remember from Chapter 10 how CFPROCPARAM formally data-types and -sizes the parameters sent to database stored procedures? Well, you can do the same thing with a CFQUERY call by using CFQUERYPARAM to formalize its parameters, as shown in Listing 11-22.

Listing 11-22: Formally declaring the data types and sizes of CFQUERY parameters by using CFQUERYPARAM

```
<cfquery name="GetSalesOrders"
        datasource="#Request.MainDSN#">
    SELECT
        SalesOrderID,
        SaleDate,
        TaxRate,
        TaxAmount,
        Total
    FROM
        SalesOrder
    WHERE
        SaleDate >= <cfqueryparam value="#AfterDate#"
                    cfsqltype="CF_SQL_TIMESTAMP">
    AND     Total >= <cfqueryparam value="#Amount#"
                    cfsqltype="CF_SQL_NUMERIC"
                    maxlength="12"
                    scale="2">
</cfquery>
```

Okay, fine—but why should you care? This technique seems a lot of extra work for nothing, so why not just continue to feed ColdFusion values to CFQUERY calls without using CFQUERY-PARAM? The answer is hidden behind the scenes..

Whenever ColdFusion sees a CFQUERYPARAM tag nested inside a CFQUERY call, it sends your query to the database server with what are essentially variables in place of the actual values normally supplied by ColdFusion and then follows them with the values of those variables. These *bind variables* (a.k.a. *bind parameters*) are strongly data typed and sized to match the corresponding data types and sizes of the database's columns. So the entire data-type and -size checking process and the entire data-type conversion process can be completely circumvented, and this circumvention speeds query execution.

Bind parameters also more easily enable your database server to recognize queries that are essentially the same as ones that have previously executed and to react to such queries by reusing existing query execution plans instead of taking the time to compile new ones. As the database server's query optimizer examines the current query for similarities to previously executed queries, it sees commonly named variables instead of dissimilar hard values, so it makes the obvious decision to reuse an existing execution plan for this seemingly "same" query.

Your query optimizer can usually spot similarities between very simple queries by using hard-coded values. But as the complexity of your query increases, the more difficulty the query optimizer experiences in spotting similarities between that query and ones that were executed before it. At some point, the optimizer just gives up and compiles a new execution plan.

CFQUERYPARAM's capability to circumvent all data typing, sizing, and conversion, combined with its capability to enable your database server's query optimizer to reuse existing query execution plans, greatly increases the performance of your database queries.

Caveats

If you're experiencing problems in getting your CFQUERY calls to work with CFQUERYPARAM tags, follow these guidelines toward resolution:

- ✦ If you get an `out of range` error, try adding the MAXLENGTH attribute to your CFQUERYPARAM tag for any noninteger numeric values. An example is shown in Listing 11-22 for the Amount parameter. If the numeric data type fed to the query is a NUMERIC(12,2), for example, use MAXLENGTH="12" and SCALE="2".
- ✦ If you get a `driver not capable; optional feature not implemented` error, make sure that you're not using the CF_SQL_DATE enumerated data type with a database that doesn't directly support the DATE data type. SQL Server 2000 doesn't support the DATE data type, for example, but supports the DATETIME data type instead. Because no CF_SQL_DATETIME enumerated data type is available, you must use the CF_SQL_TIMESTAMP enumerated data type instead. An example of this substitution is also shown in Listing 11-22 for the AfterDate parameter.
- ✦ If you're having problems getting CF_SQL_CHAR data types to work, try the same CFQUERYPARAM tag by using CF_SQL_VARCHAR with the same MAXLENGTH dimension as the database column it searches against.
- ✦ In some versions of ColdFusion Studio, the CFQUERYPARAM tag editor has a bug, where it doesn't honor your setting for Null="No" but instead insists on writing your CFQUERYPARAM tag by using Null="Yes" no matter what you do. Make sure that you carefully inspect all your CFQUERYPARAM tags for the correct NULL attribute settings and manually edit them if necessary. If you are familiar with VTML (Visual Tools Markup Language), you may want to take a moment to fix this bug in the CFQUERYPARAM.VTM file that controls this tag editor.

If you continue to experience problems, start with a plain CFQUERY call containing no CFQUERYPARAM tags and then replace and debug one CFQUERYPARAM tag at a time until they are all successfully implemented.

The extra time that implementing data binding by using CFQUERYPARAM takes pays you back manifold in faster database response times and increased application performance.

Summary

In this chapter you've learned when, why, and how to implement triggers of all types, and you've seen how triggers on SQL Server 2000 differ from those on Oracle 9i. You've also learned when to make the switch from DRI constraints to triggers for implementing referential integrity, and when to use both methods together. You've also learned how to make your database server rather than having ColdFusion Server do the hard work for you, and why this is a best practice. You also learned about query of queries and when they should and shouldn't be used, and you learned how to implement effective data binding in your database queries.

If you haven't started implementing triggers in your database designs, now's the time to start. You need to move the referential integrity rules out of your ColdFusion application and put them directly in the database where they belong. The same goes for all the code that you always execute whenever certain data transactions occur: Implement such code as triggers or it is not bound to your data, and manipulation of your data outside of ColdFusion may cause it to become "out of whack" or corrupted.

The new Query of Queries feature is a useful technique in some circumstances, but you shouldn't use it as a substitute for writing the correct SQL, and you must never use it to requery huge query objects in memory—if you do so, you destroy performance. Try to use QoQ only if nothing else can do—such as whenever you're working with nondatabase `query` objects—or working with reasonably sized cached queries.

And, finally, start using `CFQUERYPARAM` in your noncached `CFQUERY` calls to both improve performance and ensure correct data typing of the parameters sent from ColdFusion to your database.

✦ ✦ ✦

The ColdFusion MX Language

P A R T

✦ ✦ ✦ ✦

In This Part

✦ ✦ ✦ ✦

CHAPTER 12

Understanding ColdFusion Variables

✦ ✦ ✦ ✦

In This Chapter

Understanding the difference between local and global variables

Nonpersistent variable scopes

Persisting variables between requests

✦ ✦ ✦ ✦

ColdFusion developers tend to take variables for granted. A *variable* is, of course, a named container for data, but that is a simplistic definition that doesn't take into account the number of types of variables and each type's strengths and weaknesses.

Some variables live longer than others. Some variables can be seen by only one user, but other variables can be seen by any user of an application. This chapter explains the differences between different types of variables and shows you how to use each type.

What Is Meant By Scope?

A *variable* is a named container for data. However, different variables have different origins, life spans, timeouts, and storage locations, and the collection of these properties together is known the *scope* of the variable. For instance, a variable that is specific to a single client is in the *`Client`* scope. Likewise, a variable that exists for all applications on the entire server is in the *`Server`* scope. The rest of this chapter will describe all of ColdFusion's scopes in detail.

In addition to its scope, a variable is also said to be *local* or *global*. A variable is *local* when the template that created the variable is the only template that can use the variable. A variable is *global* when the variable can be accessed beyond the template that created it.

Figure 12-1 shows ColdFusion's variable scopes, arranged by whether they are *local or global* (how many templates can see the variables in each scope) and how *persistent* variables in each scope are (how long variables in each scope live). We explain scope and persistence in greater detail throughout this chapter.

Note that a *`Client`-scoped variable*, a *variable in the `Client` scope*, and a *`Client` variable* all refer to the same thing; they are just three ways to describe a variable that lives in the `Client` scope.

Scope Versus Persistence

	Non-Persistent (Do not exist past a single request)	**Persistent** (Exist across multiple requests)
Local (Seen only by a single template and its CFINCLUDEd templates)	**Variables** **Attributes** **Caller** **Arguments** **This**[1]	(Ask yourself: Why is this cell empty?)
Global (Seen by all templates)	**Request** **CGI** **Form** **URL**	**Server** **Application** **Session** **Client**[2] **Cookie**[3]

1. If a component is instantiated in the Session scope, its This-scoped variables will persist for the lifetime of the session, but this fact does not make the This scope itself a persistent scope

2. Stored in a server disk structure: either the Registry or a database

3. Stored in a client disk structure

Figure 12-1: The big picture of variable scope versus persistence.

Local Variables

A *local variable* can be seen only by a single template and any of its included templates. After the request for the template that originally set a local variable finishes, the variable disappears.

The Variables scope

Local variables that are not specifically reserved for use with custom tags are part of the `Variables` scope. Take, for example, the following statement:

```
<cfset aVariable = "some value">
```

That statement is the same as this statement:

```
<cfset Variables.aVariable = "some value">
```

Using the prefix `Variables.` is optional in many cases, but as you will see later in this section, prefixing all variables with their scope names to prevent ColdFusion Server from using the wrong variable is a best practice.

Consider, for example, the following code:

```
<cfset Form.myVar = 1>
<cfset myVar = 3>
```

You may be thinking that Form.myVar would still be 1, and that you now have a local variable named myVar with a value of 3, but this is not the case. The second CFSET statement changed the value of the Form variable rather than creating a new local variable, because ColdFusion automatically guesses that you are attempting to change the Form variable.

This feature is commonly called *scope hunting*, and although it sometimes makes coding easier for beginning programmers, this feature can have the unintended results shown in the preceding code if you're not careful. Scope hunting was intended to be used constructively and not as a crutch for sloppy programming. If an action template may receive a value either from a form post or a URL parameter, for example, eliminating the prefix from the reference to that variable on the action template would cause ColdFusion Server to go looking for it in every scope. After ColdFusion finds a variable of that name, it uses the value of the found variable and stops looking in the remaining scopes.

Suppose, however, that you used the following snippet:

```
<cfset Form.myVar = 1>
<cfset Variables.myVar = 3>
```

No confusion would be possible, because you are explicitly stating that you are setting a local variable named myVar *in the Variables scope.*

So if you're sure as to precisely which scope contains your variable, specify the scope name as the prefix to that variable both in setting it and then, later on, in referring to it.

The Attributes scope

After you pass an attribute to a custom tag (as we do with Chapter 2's cf_TodaysDate custom tag), the attribute becomes available in the custom tag within the *Attributes* scope.

The Attributes scope is completely separate from the Variables scope within the custom tag. Attributes is a separate scope, because if data in a calling template is not separated from data in the called template, a collision may occur, where data in the calling template is overwritten by data in the called template. For information on custom tags and the terms *calling template* and *called template*, see Chapter 18.

In other words, the following two variables within a custom tag are completely separate from one another:

```
<cfoutput>
    Attributes-scoped variable: #Attributes.myVar#<br>
    Variables-scoped variable:  #Variables.myVar#
</cfoutput>
```

You can manually define Attributes-scoped variables as follows:

```
<cfset Attributes.FirstName = "Lisa">
```

Or you can pass them to custom tags as attributes, as follows:

```
<cf_myCustomTag FirstName="Lisa">
```

This is about all that you need to know until you start really working heavily with custom tags in Chapter 18, so we now move on to the Attributes scope's kissing cousin, the Caller scope.

The Caller scope

The Caller scope is used within custom tags to set or read variables in the calling template. This is the mechanism that custom tags use to, in a way, return values to the templates that call them. If the Caller-scoped variable does not exist in the calling template at the moment that the custom tag sets its value, ColdFusion automatically creates the Caller variable in the calling template.

Like Attributes-scoped variables, Caller-scoped variables are nonpersistent, so they disappear as soon as the current request finishes executing. (You get the whole story later on in Chapter 18.)

Global Variables

A local variable can be seen only by the template that creates it, as well as by any of the creating template's included templates. On the other hand, any template within a request—including templates that are custom tags and templates that are components—can see a global variable. Nonpersistent global variables live only as long as the current request; persistent global variables, such as Session variables, live longer than a single request.

Nonpersistent global variables

Nonpersistent global variables live for a single request, but all templates within a request, whether they are called by using CFINCLUDE, CFMODULE, or CFINVOKE, have access to these variables.

The Request scope

Request-scoped variables are nonpersistent global variables. You saw a Request variable in the example application in Chapter 2, as follows:

```
<cfset Request.MainDSN = "CFMXBible">
```

We set MainDSN as a Request variable because we want MainDSN to be available to any CFQUERY call regardless of whether the call to CFQUERY is in the main page, a custom tag, or component call.

You should use Request variables for simple application settings—such as the name of the DSN used by the application and the username and password that the DSN uses—so that custom tags and components can access those settings.

The Form scope

If a form is submitted to ColdFusion by using the POST method, all the fields in that form become variables in the Form scope. Suppose, for example, that you click the Submit button on the following form:

```
<form action="ActionPage.cfm" method="post">
    <input type="text" name="FirstName">
    <input type="text" name="LastName">
    <input type="submit">
</form>
```

ActionPage.cfm receives two variables named Form.FirstName and Form.LastName that contain whatever the user enters in the form fields. (For information on creating form fields, see Chapter 6.)

In addition to the Form-scoped variables created from form fields, ColdFusion also provides a variable named Form.FieldNames that contains a list of all the names of the form fields passed to a page. In the example earlier in this section, Form.FieldNames would contain the following elements:

```
FIRSTNAME,LASTNAME
```

Form variables are global variables, because any template in a request — whether it's a custom tag, component, or included page — can access them. Form variables are nonpersistent because they disappear after the request in which they are created finishes executing.

The URL scope

Form variables pass form data through the HTTP request header (the part that you don't see) to the template named in the Action attribute of the FORM tag. This is not the only way to pass information to a ColdFusion template; you can also use *URL variables*, which pass parameters directly in the URL. We could pass FirstName and LastName to ActionPage.cfm, for example, by doing the following:

```
http://myserver/ActionPage.cfm?FirstName=John&LastName=Doe
```

In this case, ActionPage.cfm would have two variables named URL.FirstName and URL.LastName, with values of John and Doe respectively.

One thing about URL variables is that you can't use some special characters in URLs. The following URL, for example, would be illegal because it contains commas:

```
http://myserver/MyPage.cfm?MyParam=This,That,TheOther
```

You must *escape* the commas by replacing them with a special code, as follows (shown in bold):

```
http://myserver/MyPage.cfm?MyParam=This%2CThat%2CTheOther
```

ColdFusion sees %2C and replaces it with a comma. You have a number of these escape sequences that you can use to replace certain characters, a few of which are as follows:

- **comma (,):** %2C
- **semicolon (;):** %3B
- **plus (+):** %2B
- **equals (=):** %3D
- **percent sign (%):** %25
- **period (.):** %2E
- **space ( ):** %20 or + (both are valid escape sequences for a space)

The ColdFusion Documentation claims that spaces are replaced with plus signs (+). This does not appear to be the case, as repeated tests have shown that URLEncodedFormat() replaces spaces with %20 instead of a plus sign. Both %20 and a plus sign are valid escape sequences for a space, but ColdFusion only uses the first one when you call URLEncodedFormat().

Many more of these escape sequences exist. Luckily, ColdFusion can manage these sequences for you through the use of URLEncodedFormat(), as follows:

```
<cfset MyVar = "I, John Doe, am me.">
<a href="page.cfm?Param=#URLEncodedFormat(MyVar)#">Next</a>
```

After you click the link to the next page, the URL is converted to the following:

```
http://127.0.0.1/page.cfm?Param=I%2C%20John%20Doe%2C%20am%20me%2E
```

You may notice that all the commas and spaces and the period are replaced with their escape sequences. Notice also that, in some places, you find two escapements in a row; a comma followed by a space is encoded as `%2C%20`.

ColdFusion automatically decodes these sequences for you. After `page.cfm` reads `URL.Param`, the latter doesn't contain `I%2C%20John%20Doe%2C%20am%20me%2E`; it contains `I, John Doe, am me`. If, however, you do ever need to decode an encoded URL parameter, use `URLDecode()`; this function reverses the results of calling `URLEncodedFormat()`.

Calling `URLEncodedFormat()` on `I, John Doe, am me.`, for example, returns the following:

```
I%2C%20John%20Doe%2C%20am%20me%2E
```

If we want, we can "unescape" the escaped string by calling `URLDecode()`, as follows:

```
<cfoutput>#URLDecode("I%2C%20John%20Doe%2C%20am%20me%2E")#</cfoutput>
```

The preceding code produces the following:

```
I, John Doe, am me.
```

`URL` variables, as are `Form` variables, are global and nonpersistent, meaning that any template in a request can access them, but they disappear after the current request finishes executing.

The CGI scope

`CGI` variables describe the current request's environment. `CGI.SCRIPT_NAME`, for example, contains the path of the currently executing request. `CGI.SERVER_NAME` contains the name of the current server. Many different `CGI` variables exist; see your ColdFusion documentation for a list.

One thing about the `CGI` scope that is different from other ColdFusion variable scopes is that you can always assume that any CGI variable exists, even if it's not one of the standard variables. This is because ColdFusion automatically creates any variable with a `CGI.` in front of it, giving it a blank value if it doesn't already exist when you try to use it. In other words, don't use `IsDefined("CGI.variable")`—use `Len(Trim(CGI.variable))` instead.

You can't assign a value to a `CGI` variable; doing so causes an error. (`CGI` variables are *read-only*; they can be read from but never modified.) You can, however, read a `CGI` variable from any template in a request—custom tag templates, components, or otherwise.

Persistent global variables

`Request`-, `Form`-, `URL`-, and `CGI`-scoped variables are all nonpersistent variables, meaning that they do not last beyond a single request. The variables in this section, however, are *persistent*, meaning that they last beyond a single request and are, therefore, available to other templates that execute in later requests.

Different persistent variable types serve different purposes. The following sections highlight the differences so that you can choose which type to use.

The Cookie scope

A *cookie* is a global variable stored locally on a user's machine. Because the cookie is stored on the user's machine rather than in memory on the ColdFusion Server machine, the cookie doesn't go away after the current request is finished, which means that it is also a persistent variable. Rather, a cookie is given a specific expiration date, and the browser sends the cookie to ColdFusion for every request until the cookie expires.

Unlike what happens with other variable types, you don't set cookies by using the `CFSET` tag. Instead, you use the `CFCOOKIE` tag:

```
<cfcookie
     name="myVar"
     value="some value">
```

`CFCOOKIE` tells ColdFusion Server to send a command through the HTTP response header to the user's browser, instructing it to create the `Cookie` variable. To read the `myVar` cookie, you reference it as `Cookie.myVar`, as the following code shows:

```
<cfoutput>#Cookie.myVar#</cfoutput>
```

If the cookie does not exist, ColdFusion throws an error.

Cookie expiration dates

`Cookie.myVar` was not given an expiration date in the preceding section, so it disappears after the user closes his browser. To give the cookie an expiration date, you must specify the `expires` attribute in the `CFCOOKIE` tag, as follows:

```
<cfcookie
     name="myVar"
     value="some value"
     expires="10">
```

In this code, `10` is the number of days that the cookie exists before the browser deletes it. The `expires` attribute is usually a number of days, but it can also be an actual date (although this is rarely used). Or it can be the constants `NOW` or `NEVER`. `NOW` tells `CFCOOKIE` to delete the cookie from the user's browser, and `NEVER` tells the `CFCOOKIE` to never expire.

What do I use cookie variables for?

A user can turn off cookies in his browser, making cookies useless. If a user's browser does not have cookies enabled, `CFCOOKIE` does not throw an error, but the cookie is never set.

Cookies are best used for small pieces of data that are not necessary for a site to function. Whenever a user logs in to your Web site, for example, you could set a cookie storing his user ID. The next time that the user comes to your site, you can look up his record by that user ID. Amazon.com does this—whenever you return to the site, the user ID stored in a cookie on your machine is used to pull up your first name, welcome you to the site, and display any new recommendations based on your purchase history. If the cookie doesn't exist, the site doesn't break—you just need to log in to see your recommendations.

Domain cookies

For security reasons, the only server that can access a cookie is the one that originally set it. The problem is that, in a clustered environment, a user's session can move between multiple servers in a cluster—meaning that a cookie set on one server isn't accessible to another server in the cluster, rendering it pretty much useless, because in a clustered environment, you have no guarantee that the user will go to the same server from one request to the next. See Chapter 19 for information on clustering.

To get around this single-server restriction, you can set a *domain cookie* so that any server in the cluster can access it. To set a domain cookie, use the following syntax:

```
<cfcookie
    name="myVar"
    value="some value"
    domain=".somewhere.com">
```

The `domain` attribute tells the cookie to make itself available for every server in the given domain. Notice that the specified domain must be the same as the domain setting the cookie or the cookie is not set.

Restricting cookies to a specific path

Sometimes, if you host multiple applications under a single domain, you may want to separate cookies out by different directories. Say, for example, that you have the following three applications under your central domain:

```
www.mydomain.com
    consumer
    admin
    extranet
```

You probably wouldn't want cookies from the `consumer` directory interfering with cookies from the `extranet` directory. You can make a cookie that you set in the consumer directory available only to other templates in the `consumer` directory by using the `path` attribute of `CFCOOKIE`, as follows:

```
<cfcookie
    name="myVar"
    value="some value"
    path="/consumer/">
```

If the template's path (not including the server name) does not begin with the `consumer` directory, the browser does not send the cookie for the given request. To make a cookie apply to all paths, omit the `path` attribute or set it to `"/"`, as follows:

```
<cfcookie
    name="myVar"
    value="some value"
    path="/">
```

Securing cookies

One thing that you can do to increase the security of cookies stored on the user's machine is to restrict a particular cookie to SSL (Secure Sockets Layer) requests. This setting means that the cookie is sent back to the server during a request only if the request is using SSL. To enable this behavior, add `secure="Yes"` to the `CFCOOKIE` tag, as follows:

```
<cfcookie
    name="myVar"
    value="some value"
    secure="Yes">
```

The Client scope

Variables in the *`Client`* scope are also persistent global variables, but they are stored on ColdFusion Server rather than on the client machine. Client variables are tied to a specific user's browser, so each user can have a different value for `Client.myVar`. For ColdFusion to identify a browser's specific set of Client variables from one request to the next, the browser must send its "ID card" to ColdFusion Server with each request. This ID card is the combination of two values named CFID and CFTOKEN, which are issued to the browser by ColdFusion Server after the browser makes its first request. Chapter 19 describes this binding mechanism; for this chapter, you can assume that it "just works."

How long do Client variables last?

ColdFusion periodically purges client variables according to the timeout specified in ColdFusion Administrator. The default timeout is 90 days, but you can set it down to as short as one day. If ColdFusion does not process a request with a given CFID and CFTOKEN within the specified timeout, ColdFusion deletes the Client variables and the CFID and CFTOKEN from the client store.

Chapter 19 shows you a technique for manually timing out Client variables before ColdFusion's purge cycle.

Deleting a Client variable

To delete a Client variable, use the DeleteClientVariable() function, as follows:

```
<cfset result = DeleteClientVariable("myVar")>
```

The name of the variable is in a string and does not show Client. in front. Deleting a Client variable in effect "unsets" it; the variable no longer exists, and IsDefined() returns false if called with the name of the deleted variable.

The Session scope

Session variables are persistent global variables that are stored in ColdFusion Server's RAM and are bound to a user's browser with the same CFID and CFTOKEN mechanism that is used to bind Client variables to a user's browser. Following are a few differences between Session and Client variables:

- ✦ Session variables can store complex objects such as arrays and structures, but Client variables are limited to simple strings, numbers, and dates. For information about arrays and structures, see Chapters 14 and 15.
- ✦ Session variables require the use of CFLOCK, but Client variables don't. (More on this in "Using CFLOCK with Session, Application, and Server variables" later in this chapter.)
- ✦ Session variables are shorter-lived than Client variables.
- ✦ If the ColdFusion service or the server machine restarts, Session variables are lost, but Client variables are spared because they are stored on disk.
- ✦ Session variables technically have no size limit, whereas Client variables are limited to 32K in size.

How long do Session variables live?

Session variables time out on a more granular scale than client variables do. The lifetime of a Session variable can be specified down to the second, whereas the lifetime of a Client variable is specified in days. To specify a Session timeout, you can use the default session timeout in ColdFusion Administrator, or you can use the sessiontimeout attribute of CFAPPLICATION, as follows:

```
<cfapplication
    ...
    sessiontimeout="#CreateTimeSpan(0,0,20,0)#">
```

CreateTimeSpan() takes four arguments, corresponding to number of days, hours, minutes, and seconds to include in the time span. The example CFAPPLICATION tag sets the Session timeout to 20 minutes, meaning that if a user goes more than 20 minutes without making a request in this application, all his Session variables are deleted.

Deleting Session variables

ColdFusion automatically deletes a user's Session variables if his time between requests exceeds the Session timeout, but at times, you may want to manually delete a Session variable. To delete a specific Session variable, use the `StructDelete()` function, as follows:

```
<cfset result = StructDelete(Session, "myVar")>
```

To delete all of a user's Session variables at once, use the following technique:

```
<cfapplication
    ...
    sessiontimeout="#CreateTimeSpan(0,0,0,0)#">
```

This code tells ColdFusion Server to time out the entire application for the current user, which successfully deletes all Session variables for that user.

After repeated tests, it appears that using `CFAPPLICATION` with zero for the SessionTimeout no longer works in ColdFusion MX; instead of expiring the session, the `CFAPPLICATION` appears to do nothing. This method did work in earlier versions of ColdFusion Server, however. If you need to expire a session prematurely, consider looping over the Session structure and deleting its keys rather than using `CFAPPLICATION`. (Looping over a structure and deleting structure keys are described in Chapter 15.)

Also, do not use `StructClear()` on the `Session` scope. Doing so deletes `Session.CFID` and `Session.CFTOKEN`, which causes unexpected errors. See Macromedia TechNote 14143 for more information on `StructClear()` and expiring a session.

Keep in mind that, because Session variables are stored in memory, you must have enough memory to handle the Session variables for all users within the timeout period. So if you're expecting hundreds or thousands of simultaneous users, don't go creating huge complex Session variables for each user and expect the system to handle your application gracefully. If you do, you soon find your application slowing down, because ColdFusion must constantly cache memory to disk.

The Application scope

Variables in the `Session` and `Client` scopes are persistent global variables tied to individual users, but variables in the *`Application`* scope are persistent global variables accessible by all users of a specific application. In other words, `Session.FirstName` may contain different values for each user of an application, but `Application.appStatus` contains a single value for all users of that application.

Application variables are typically set in `Application.cfm` inside a `CFIF` test as follows:

```
<cfif NOT IsDefined("Application.myVar")>
    <!--- Work to calculate Application.myVar --->
    . . .
    <cfset Application.myVar = "some value">
</cfif>
```

This snippet sets `Application.myVar` only if it doesn't already exist.

Reserve the Application scope for "universal" values that require effort to calculate, such as a list of flagged words derived from a `CFQUERY` call. You wouldn't put such a list in the Request scope (described in the section of that name, earlier in this chapter) because it would need to be recalculated for each request from each user. Placing this list in the Application scope enables it to be persisted between requests.

The Server scope

Where `Application.myVar` can have one value in one application and a different value in another application, *`Server`*-scoped variables are set for *all* applications hosted by a ColdFusion Server, so all users of all applications on a server see the same value. Server variables are rarely used in actual practice because so few settings apply to all applications at the same time.

One reason why Server variables should not be used unless truly necessary is that they create performance bottlenecks if many applications constantly modify them, because Server variables must be locked whenever your code is modifying their values, as you will see in the next section.

Server variables can be created by a simple `CFSET` in any ColdFusion code anywhere, but they are destroyed if ColdFusion Server is restarted.

Using CFLOCK with Session, Application, and Server variables

`Session`, `Application`, and `Server` variables are stored in ColdFusion Server's memory space and are known as *shared-memory variables* because multiple users may attempt to access them simultaneously. Having two requests attempt to write to the same memory space at the same time is possible (and quite common), which can cause the `Session`, `Application`, or `Server` variable to become corrupted.

To prevent this problem, ColdFusion provides a locking mechanism to synchronize code that writes to and reads from shared memory variables. By wrapping code that writes to `Session`, `Application`, or `Server` variables with a `CFLOCK` tag that is assigned a specific name, ColdFusion ensures that such code is synchronized with all other code that's wrapped in a `CFLOCK` tag of the same name, regardless of the template or application in which that code is run, as shown in the following example:

```
<cflock name="Session_LoggedInUserID"
        type="EXCLUSIVE"
        timeout="10"
        throwOnTimeOut="Yes">
    <cfset Session.LoggedInUserID = 1>
</cflock>
```

This example ensures that any other code wrapped in a `CFLOCK` tag that's named `Session_LoggedInUserID` cannot run while this snippet runs, because among all such code, this snippet has the *exclusive* right to execute. On the other hand, consider the following example:

```
<cflock name="Session_LoggedInUserID"
        type="READONLY"
        timeout="10"
        throwOnTimeOut="Yes">
    <cfset Variables.myVar = Session.LoggedInUserID>
</cflock>
```

This example ensures that any other code wrapped in a `CFLOCK` tag that's named `Session_LoggedInUserID` *may* run while this snippet runs, as long as all the `Session_LoggedInUserID` locks are *not exclusive* locks.

This way, two requests attempting to access the same variable don't accidentally collide, because `CFLOCK` with a `type` of `EXCLUSIVE` makes sure that only one request can execute at a time. In these examples, we named the CFLOCK tag the same as the variable name, replacing periods with underscores. Naming the CFLOCK this way means that we can individually lock single variables without locking an entire scope.

By adding the timeout and thrownOnTimeOut attributes to the CFLOCK tag, we're telling ColdFusion, "If you can't acquire the lock within ten seconds, throw an error and halt execution." That way, we can catch and handle the error as an exception and either alert the user, try again, or take some other action.

CFLOCK's scope attribute

Many ColdFusion programmers just learning about CFLOCK see the scope attribute and like its simplicity, as the following example shows:

```
<cflock scope="Session" type="EXCLUSIVE">
     <cfset Session.LoggedInUserID = 1>
</cflock>
```

If you use the scope attribute rather than the name attribute to synchronize your code, you create an inherently tighter bottleneck through which your CFLOCKed code must pass, because all code that uses a particular scope must synchronize with all other code that uses that scope. Hence, it must wait for all locks to end before a new EXCLUSIVE lock can be acquired and data can be modified.

The scoped-lock problem gets worse as you set more and more shared-memory variables. Session-scoped locks synchronize code executed by a particular user, so only the code executed by that one user must synchronize with other similarly-scoped code executed by that same user. Application-scoped locks, however, must synchronize all code from all users of that one application using the same scoped lock.

Now imagine the performance bottleneck created by the Server-scope-locked code in all applications running on the same server — especially if values are CFSET in each application's Application.cfm template!

By intelligently planning all access to shared resources on ColdFusion Server and carefully crafting a set of named locks to synchronize access to those resources, you can greatly speed the safe execution of large applications. As the size of your codebase that accesses shared resources grows linearly, the speed with which that code may safely execute slows exponentially if you use scoped locks rather than named locks.

Why don't I need CFLOCK with client variables?

Session, Application, and Server variables are stored in memory and shared by multiple users, so access to them must be synchronized to prevent collision. Client variables are stored in a disk structure in either the Windows Registry, a database, or in a disk structure (cookie) on the client's machine. Access to these disk structures is inherently locked by the operating system (in the case of the Registry), the database server, or the host machine (in the case of a cookie), so no CFLOCK synchronization of the code that attempts to access and manipulate these structures is necessary.

Nesting calls to CFLOCK

Beware of nesting one call to CFLOCK inside another. Never, for example, do the following:

```
<cflock scope="SESSION" type="READONLY" timeout="60">
     . . .
     <cflock scope="SESSION" type="EXCLUSIVE" timeout="60">
          . . .
```

```
    </cflock>
    . . .
</cflock>
```

Spotting the error in this code may be difficult. The problem is that the code acquires a *read-only* lock of the Session scope and then attempts to acquire an *exclusive* lock of the same scope while it is still locked. This snippet of code leads to a condition called a *deadlock*, where your code is trying to acquire a second lock on a resource that it's already locked.

The best way to avoid deadlock conditions is to do the following:

1. Put your calls to CFLOCK around only that code that absolutely must be synchronized with other code.
2. Never attempt to acquire a second lock on a scope while that scope is already locked.
3. Release locks in the reverse order in which they are acquired.

Take, for example, the following code:

```
<cflock scope="SESSION" type="EXCLUSIVE" timeout="60">
  . . .
  <cflock scope="APPLICATION" type="EXCLUSIVE" timeout="60">
    . . .
    <cflock scope="SERVER" type="EXCLUSIVE" timeout="60">
      . . .
    </cflock>
  </cflock>
</cflock>
```

This use of nested locks is valid here because you never attempt to acquire a second lock of the same scope until the first is released, and you also lock *and release* the smaller scopes before acquiring locks on the larger scopes.

Testing for Variables

One of the more often-used tags in ColdFusion is CFPARAM, which lets you do three things:

✦ Ensure that a variable exists,

✦ Give a variable a default if the variable doesn't exist, or

✦ Ensure that a variable is of a given type.

The following snippet ensures that a variable named Form.MyFormField exists:

```
<cfparam name="Form.MyFormField">
```

When ColdFusion executes the preceding line, ColdFusion looks for a variable named Form.MyFormField. If the variable exists, ColdFusion will continue on with the next line of code. If Form.MyFormField does not exist, however, ColdFusion will throw an error. You will see in Chapter 18 how this helps ensure that custom tags are always used correctly.

There are times when you may not want to throw an error if a variable doesn't exist. If Form.MyFormField were a checkbox, for example, you wouldn't want to throw an error of Form.MyFormField didn't exist; rather, you'd want to automatically create Form.MyForm Field and give it a default of zero. (See Chapter 6 for information on using checkboxes in form fields.) The following snippet shows how to give Form.MyFormField a default:

```
<cfparam name="Form.MyFormField" default="0">
```

Adding the default attribute tells ColdFusion to assign the default if Form.MyFormField doesn't already exist.

CFPARAM will also allow you to check the type of an incoming variable, as in the following snippet:

```
<cfparam name="Form.MyFormField" type="numeric">
```

The preceding line checks to see that Form.MyFormField exists, and also that it is a numeric value. If, for instance, the user had entered ABC into the form field, the preceding line of code would throw an error.

Note that you can combine the type and default attributes together, as in the next snippet:

```
<cfparam name="Form.MyFormField" type="numeric" default="0">
```

The preceding line checks that Form.MyFormField exists, and if it does not, assigns the variable a value of zero. If the variable is not numeric, ColdFusion will throw an error.

In addition to CFPARAM, ColdFusion provides a function named IsDefined() that lets you specifically check whether a variable is defined or not. For instance, the following snippet puts out a different message depending on whether or not Form.MyFormField is defined:

```
<cfif IsDefined("Form.MyFormField")>
    The form variable is defined.
<cfelse>
    The form variable is not defined.
</cfif>
```

IsDefined() will not throw an error or give a default value if the variable doesn't exist; the function simply returns true or false.

Summary

In this chapter, you learn about the differences between local and global variables, as well as the meaning and significance of variable persistence and how it affects your choice of which variable scopes to use in your code.

Always carefully enforce the rules regarding synchronization of code that accesses shared variable scopes. And, if you can, carefully craft a collection of named locks to synchronize your code rather than relying on the easier-to-code yet less granular scoped locks. Keep in mind that locking a large scope creates an equally large potential for performance bottlenecks.

The rest of Part III expands on the concepts that you learn in this chapter. The next chapter focuses on *flow control*—or how to make your application do different things, depending on conditions in your application.

✦ ✦ ✦

CHAPTER 13

Constructing Flow Control

In This Chapter

Conditional flow constructs

Looping constructs

Including code from external templates

Redirecting the user

If your program did the same thing regardless of how it was called, it wouldn't be very useful. A real application responds to different situations by calling different code, which is the essence of *flow control*. In this chapter, you learn how to use conditional and loop logic to construct efficient flow control for your application. You also learn how to redirect the user to a different template and how to include code from external templates.

If/ElseIf/Else Constructs

An *If construct* consists of a *condition* and a *dependent statement*. ColdFusion evaluates the condition to determine whether it is `True` or `False`. If the condition is true, ColdFusion executes the dependent statement. Take, for example, the following code:

```
<cfif myVar GREATER THAN myOtherVar>
    <cfoutput>#myVar#</cfoutput>
</cfif>
```

In the preceding If construct, ColdFusion tests to see whether `myVar` is greater than `myOtherVar`. If the test result is `True`, ColdFusion outputs the value of `myVar`; if the test result is False, ColdFusion doesn't do anything.

You can make ColdFusion execute alternative code if the condition tests False, as follows:

```
<cfif myVar GREATER THAN myOtherVar>
    <cfoutput>#myVar#</cfoutput>
<cfelse>
    <cfoutput>#myOtherVar#</cfoutput>
</cfif>
```

We've extended the original If construct to include a `CFELSE` tag. Now, if `myVar` is not greater than `myOtherVar`, ColdFusion outputs `myOtherVar`.

You can extend `CFIF` even further by adding additional conditions with `CFELSEIF`, as follows:

```
<cfif myVar GREATER THAN myOtherVar>
    <cfoutput>#myVar#</cfoutput>
<cfelseif myVar EQUAL myOtherVar>
    <cfoutput>#myVar + myOtherVar#</cfoutput>
```

```
<cfelse>
    <cfoutput>#myOtherVar#</cfoutput>
</cfif>
```

Now, if myVar is equal to myOtherVar, ColdFusion adds the two together and outputs the result. Notice that the CFELSE statement now executes only if both the CFIF and CFELSEIF conditions are False.

You can add as many CFELSEIF conditions as you want to a CFIF tag, but if you have more than two or three based on different results from the same conditional test, you should consider using a Switch construct instead.

Switch/Case Constructs

A Switch construct evaluates a single expression against multiple test values and then executes the block of code associated with the test value that matches.

Consider the following snippet of code:

```
<cfif myVar EQ 1>
    One
<cfelseif myVar EQ 2>
    Two
<cfelseif myVar EQ 3>
    Three
</cfif>
```

This snippet evaluates myVar three times, checking each time to determine whether myVar is a certain value. This code is better written by using a CFSWITCH block:

```
<cfswitch expression="#myVar#">
<cfcase value=1>
    One
</cfcase>
<cfcase value=2>
    Two
</cfcase>
<cfcase value=3>
    Three
</cfcase>
</cfswitch>
```

Both snippets do the same thing, but the CFSWITCH construct is more efficient because it evaluates myVar once rather than three times. ColdFusion executes CFSWITCH statements more efficiently than it does CFIF statements, because CFIF evaluates each condition until it finds one that's true, while CFSWITCH simply chooses the CFCASE block with the matching value.

CFCASE values must be constant; in other words, the following construction is illegal:

```
<cfswitch expression="#myVar#">
...
<cfcase value="#1+1#">
    Two
</cfcase>
...
</cfswitch>
```

This code would throw an error because variables and expressions are not permitted in CFCASE's value attribute.

In the code below, CFDEFAULTCASE is the Switch construct's equivalent to CFELSE, as the following example shows:

```
<cfswitch expression="#myVar#">
<cfcase value=1>
    One
</cfcase>
<cfcase value=2>
    Two
</cfcase>
<cfcase value=3>
    Three
</cfcase>
<cfdefaultcase>
    Some other number
</cfdefaultcase>
</cfswitch>
```

If none of the CFCASE values match the expression in CFSWITCH, ColdFusion executes the CFDEFAULTCASE block.

Even with the benefits provided by CFSWITCH, at times you must still use CFIF logic. Take, for example, the following code block:

```
<cfif myVar GREATER THAN myOtherVar>
    <cfoutput>#myVar#</cfoutput>
<cfelseif myVar EQUAL myOtherVar>
    <cfoutput>#myVar + myOtherVar#</cfoutput>
<cfelse>
    <cfoutput>#myOtherVar#</cfoutput>
</cfif>
```

This code cannot be converted to CFSWITCH because this CFIF construct contains multiple tests rather than a single test with a single expression. CFSWITCH uses its single expression as a "lookup key" to find the matching CFCASE to execute.

Loop Constructs

Loops repeat the same section of code multiple times. CFML has the following five different kinds of loops:

✦ *Index loops* (also known as *For loops*), which loop a specified number of times.

✦ *Conditional loops*, which loop as long as a condition tests True.

✦ *Query loops*, which loop over each row in a query.

✦ *List loops*, which loop over each element in a list.

✦ *Structure loops*, which loop over each top-level key in a structure.

Each is discussed in the following sections. We start with the index loop.

Looping a specified number of times

The simplest type of loop loops from a specific starting point to a specific ending point — for example, from one to ten. This type of loop is called an *index loop* and is shown in Listing 13-1.

Listing 13-1: A simple index loop

```
This is code before the loop.<br>

<cfloop from="1" to="10" index="i">
    <cfoutput>
        #i#<br>
    </cfoutput>
</cfloop>

This is code after the loop.<br>
```

The example loops from one to ten, outputting each number in order. That snippet produces the output shown in Figure 13-1.

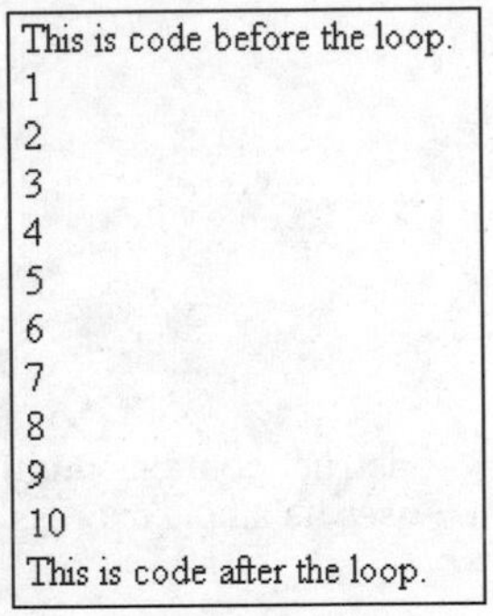

This is code before the loop.
1
2
3
4
5
6
7
8
9
10
This is code after the loop.

Figure 13-1: The output from Listing 13-1.

Everything between <cfloop> and </cfloop> is the *body* of the loop. The body is executed once for each loop, and the loop index is incremented by 1 after each execution of the loop's body.

So what exactly does index="i" mean? The *index* of a loop is a counter containing the number of the current loop iteration. In other words, for the first time through the loop, i would contain 1. The next time through, i would contain 2 and so on. After i reaches 10, the loop is executed one last time. You can see this sequence of events occurring in Figure 13-1.

This type of loop has one additional attribute. If we wanted to loop backwards from 10 to 1, we would include the step attribute, as in Listing 13-2.

Listing 13-2: A reverse index loop

```
This is code before the loop.<br>

<cfloop from="10" to="1" step="-1" index="i">
    <cfoutput>
        #i#<br>
    </cfoutput>
</cfloop>

This is code after the loop.<br>
```

Running Listing 13-2 produces the output shown in Figure 13-2.

```
This is code before the loop.
10
9
8
7
6
5
4
3
2
1
This is code after the loop.
```

Figure 13-2: The output from Listing 13-2.

Looping while a condition is true

An index loop is appropriate if you know the number of loops in advance. You can, however, also loop an indefinite number of times while a given condition is true, as shown in Listing 13-3.

Listing 13-3: A conditional loop

```
<cfset bLoop = TRUE>
<cfloop condition="bLoop EQ TRUE">
    This is one iteration through the loop.<br>
    <cfif RandRange(1, 10) EQ 10>
        <cfset bLoop = FALSE>
    </cfif>
</cfloop>
```

`RandRange(1,10)` returns a random number between 1 and 10. Listing 13-3 keeps looping while `bLoop` is `TRUE`, and after `RandRange()` returns 10, we set `bLoop` to `FALSE`. If the loop attempts to execute again, the condition tests `FALSE`, and execution halts before the loops executes.

Looping over a query

CFLOOP can also loop over a query, as shown in Listing 13-4. Remember that when looping over queries, you don't surround the query object name with pound signs.

Listing 13-4: A query loop

```
<cfquery name="GetEmployees"
         datasource="#Request.MainDSN#">
SELECT
    CompanyName
FROM
    Company
</cfquery>

<cfoutput>
<cfloop query="GetEmployees">
    #CompanyName#<br>
</cfloop>
</cfoutput>
```

The CFLOOP in Listing 13-4 loops over each row present in the GetEmployees query object and outputs each company name in the query. This type of loop is similar to a CFOUTPUT statement, except that CFLOOP can be nested inside of another CFOUTPUT (something that you cannot do with CFOUTPUT alone).

Looping over a list

CFLOOP can also loop over a list of items, as shown in Listing 13-5. Unlike query objects, you *do* surround the list name with pound signs.

Listing 13-5: A list loop

```
<cfset myList = "this,that,the other">

<cfoutput>
<cfloop list="#myList#" index="theItem">
    #theItem#<br>
</cfloop>
</cfoutput>
```

This type of loop iterates over each element in a list and executes a block of code once for each element. Each time that the loop iterates, index contains the value of the current element.

List loops are discussed in detail in Chapter 14.

Looping over a structure

Structures are complex objects that store collections of key-value pairs. You can loop over a structure with `CFLOOP` by using the `collection` loop syntax shown in Listing 13-6.

Listing 13-6: A collection loop

```
<cfset myStruct = StructNew()>
<cfset myStruct.keyA = "value A">
<cfset myStruct.keyB = "value B">
<cfset myStruct.keyC = "value C">

<cfoutput>
<cfloop collection="#myStruct#" item="theKey">
  #theKey#: #myStruct[theKey]#
</cfloop>
</cfoutput>
```

Collection is another term for *structure* in most computer languages, and it is the term used for such objects in COM. Hence, the name of the attribute.

`item` contains the name of the current key each time that the loop iterates. Only top-level keys are considered in the loop, so if the structure being looped over has nested structures, the keys from those nested structures do not populate `item`. To loop over a nested structure, you must pass its dot path to the `collection` attribute.

For more information on structures and looping over structures, see Chapter 15.

Breaking out of a loop

Sometimes, you may want to end a loop prematurely. In Listing 13-7, for example, ColdFusion ends the index loop prematurely if a particular random number comes up.

Listing 13-7: Breaking out of a loop

```
<cfoutput>
<cfloop from="1" to="10" index="i">
    #i#<br>

    <cfif RandRange(1,10) EQ 10>
        <cfbreak>
    </cfif>
</cfloop>
</cfoutput>
```

The `CFBREAK` in Listing 13-7 prematurely breaks out of the `CFLOOP`. If, during the normal course of this loop, `RandRange()` returns `10`, `CFBREAK` ends the loop before `i` reaches `10`.

Another technique that often accompanies `CFBREAK` is the *infinite loop*, as shown in Listing 13-8.

Listing 13-8: An infinite loop

```
<cfloop condition="TRUE">
    This is one iteration through the loop.<br>
    <cfif RandRange(1, 10) EQ 10>
        <cfbreak>
    </cfif>
</cfloop>
```

Listing 13-8 does the same thing as Listing 13-3, but in less code. The `condition="TRUE"` attribute of `CFLOOP` means that the loop executes forever, but `CFBREAK` instructs the loop to terminate if `RandRange()` returns `10`.

Just make *absolutely sure* that your code eventually reaches the break condition if you choose to code by using the infinite-loop technique. (Just the term alone is enough to make us shudder!)

Including One Template's Code in Another

Some elements of your site may be common to many pages, such as a standard header or footer. By using `CFINCLUDE`, you can have one template that contains the header or footer code and then include that template in another, as shown in Listing 13-9.

Listing 13-9: Including a header and footer template in another template

```
<cfinclude template="header.cfm">

This is the main page content.

<cfinclude template="footer.cfm">
```

Before ColdFusion outputs `This is the main page content.`, it pulls the code from `header.cfm` and `footer.cfm` into the current template. The header code, therefore, appears *before* the text `This is the main page content.`, and the footer code appears after it.

You can also use variables in the included source, as the following example shows:

```
<cfinclude template="#Client.Theme#/header.cfm">
```

Paths to included templates are relative; the included files in Listing 13-9 would need to exist in the same directory as the template that called them. To include a file in a parent directory, use the following syntax:

```
<cfinclude template="../template.cfm">
```

The two dots tell ColdFusion to go up a level in the directory structure to find a file. You cannot use a disk path for the `template` attribute of `CFINCLUDE`.

You can also include a file based on a *directory mapping*, as follows:

```
<cfinclude template="/template.cfm">
```

Whenever the template path begins with a slash, ColdFusion uses the directory mappings defined in ColdFusion Administrator to locate the template. Our server has two directory mappings defined, as shown in Figure 13-3.

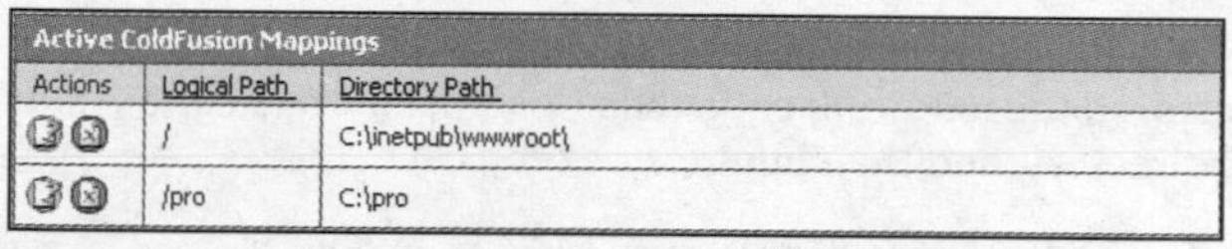

Active ColdFusion Mappings

Actions	Logical Path	Directory Path
	/	C:\inetpub\wwwroot\
	/pro	C:\pro

Figure 13-3: The directory mappings defined for our ColdFusion Server.

Our directory mappings show that / maps to `C:\inetpub\wwwroot\` and `/pro/` maps to `C:\pro\`. Suppose, therefore, that we call the following:

```
<cfinclude template="/template.cfm">
```

ColdFusion includes the file `C:\inetpub\wwwroot\template.cfm` because / maps to the Web root. Suppose now that, on the other hand, we call the following instead:

```
<cfinclude template="/pro/template.cfm">
```

ColdFusion includes `C:\pro\template.cfm` because `/pro/` maps to `C:\pro`. Your path can also add directories after the mapping, as in the following example:

```
<cfinclude template="/myIncludes/template.cfm">
```

No mapping exists for `myIncludes`, so ColdFusion includes `C:\inetpub\wwwroot\myIncludes\template.cfm`.

To help solidify these ideas, take a look at a few more examples. Our directory structure looks as follows:

```
C:
    pro
    inetpub
        wwwroot
            includes
            commonfiles
```

We're inside `C:\inetpub\wwwroot\commonfiles\mypage.cfm`.

The following line includes `C:\inetpub\wwwroot\commonfiles\myotherpage.cfm`, which tells ColdFusion to look for `myotherpage.cfm` in the same directory as the current template:

```
<cfinclude template="myotherpage.cfm">
```

The following line includes `C:\inetpub\wwwroot\index.cfm`, which tells ColdFusion to move up one directory and look for `index.cfm`:

```
<cfinclude template="../index.cfm">
```

The following line includes C:\inetpub\wwwroot\includes\myinclude.cfm, which tells ColdFusion to move up one directory, move into the includes subdirectory at that level, and then look for myinclude.cfm:

```
<cfinclude template="../includes/myinclude.cfm">
```

The following line includes C:\pro\mytemplate.cfm. /pro/ is defined as a mapping in ColdFusion Administrator, so the following code tells ColdFusion to look in the /pro/ mapping and hunt for mytemplate.cfm:

```
<cfinclude template="/pro/mytemplate.cfm">
```

The following line includes C:\inetpub\wwwroot\commonfiles\mytemplate.cfm. No /commonfiles/ mapping exists, so the following code tells ColdFusion to use the / mapping, look in the commonfiles subdirectory, and then hunt for mytemplate.cfm:

```
<cfinclude template="/commonfiles/mytemplate.cfm">
```

The following line includes C:\inetpub\wwwroot\includes\myinclude.cfm, which tells ColdFusion to move up two directories (into C:\Inetpub), move into the wwwroot subdirectory, move into the includes subdirectory, and then look for myinclude.cfm:

```
<cfinclude template="../../wwwroot/includes/myinclude.cfm">
```

Good planning of directory structure ahead of time and applying a root mapping to your application makes your CFINCLUDEs easy to code.

Redirecting the User to a Different Location

In the example application in Chapter 2, you use CFLOCATION to redirect the user after a database action Listing 13-10 shows an example of such a redirect.

Listing 13-10: Redirecting the user with CFLOCATION

```
<cfquery name="DeleteCompany"
    datasource="#Request.MainDSN#">
DELETE FROM Company
WHERE
    CompanyID = #Val(Form.CompanyID)#
</cfquery>

<cflocation url="CompanyList.cfm" addtoken="Yes">
```

CFLOCATION takes two attributes: url and addtoken. url specifies where you want to redirect the user, and addtoken tells ColdFusion whether to append CFID and CFTOKEN to the URL. CFID and CFTOKEN are two values that uniquely identify a user's session.

The important thing to remember about CFLOCATION is that it creates a separate request on the server, which means that none of the nonpersistent variables referenced before the CFLOCATION tag are accessible in the destination template. If you want to pass variables to the destination page, add them to the end of CFLOCATION's url attribute as key-value pairs.

Remember to never send secure data (such as credit card numbers) through the URL, as this information is typically collected in Web-server logs.

Stopping a Page's Execution

Use `CFABORT` to halt a request at a specific point in processing and send the output created up to that point back to the user's browser. `CFABORT` has an optional attribute, `showerror`, as shown in the following line:

```
<cfabort showerror="This is my error message.">
```

Calling `CFABORT` with the `showerror` attribute stops processing the page and also throws an error. The `showerror` attribute is rarely used anymore; `CFTHROW` is the preferred method of throwing user-defined errors. See Chapter 21 for more information.

Summary

In this chapter you've learned the various flow control constructs and techniques available in ColdFusion and how to use them effectively. You have available only a few types of flow control — `If` constructs, Switch constructs, Loop constructs, inclusions, redirections, and aborts — but they appear throughout almost every ColdFusion application, so you must master them if you are to become a proficient developer.

After you finish this chapter, take a little while with Chapter 49 in the Language Reference (Part IX) at the back of the book and start memorizing the exact syntax of these most often-used ColdFusion tags.

✦ ✦ ✦

Creating Lists and Arrays

CHAPTER 14

✦ ✦ ✦ ✦

In This Chapter

Understanding the difference between lists and arrays

Knowing when to use a list versus an array

Delimiting and qualifying lists

Converting lists to arrays and vice versa

L*ists* and *arrays* are two types of variables that store multiple values. Although they are similar to one another in this respect, lists and arrays are not interchangeable, and each is suited to a specific purpose in your application.

Using Lists

A *list* is just a simple string variable with formally defined delimiters between each value or "element." The default delimiter character is a comma, but almost any character can be specified as a list delimiter. All of the following lines, for example, are lists:

```
a,b,c
1:2:3:4
A;B;C
```

These lists contain *elements* (such as `a`, `b`, and `c` in the first list) and *delimiters* (what separates the elements from each other). A delimiter can be anything; the second list uses colons, and the third list uses semicolons. We tend to speak of lists in terms of what delimits them; for example, we would call the first list a *comma-delimited list.*

Creating a list

Because a list is just a string with delimiters, you create it just as you would any other variable, as the following example shows:

```
<cfset myList = "a,b,c">
```

`myList` has three elements (`a`, `b`, and `c`) and two delimiters (the commas). Commas are simply the most common list delimiter.

A list can use multiple delimiters, however, such as is shown in the following example:

```
<cfset myList = "a,b;c">
```

You see in the section "Finding an item in a list," later in this chapter, how to use lists with multiple delimiters.

Adding an item to a list

The simplest way to add an item to a list is to use the `ListAppend()` function, as follows:

```
<cfset myList = "a,b,c">
<cfset myList = ListAppend(myList, "d")>
```

After calling `ListAppend()`, `myList` would contain `"a,b,c,d"`. The question, however, is how `ListAppend()` knows to use a comma as the delimiter for the new element. As things turn out, all ColdFusion functions beginning with `List` have an optional argument for the list delimiter, as follows:

```
<cfset myList = "a,b,c">
<cfset myList = ListAppend(myList, "d", ",")>
```

If you leave the third argument out of your calls to list functions, ColdFusion assumes that the delimiter character is a comma. If the list in this example used a semicolon as the delimiter, it would look as follows:

```
<cfset myList = "a;b;c">
<cfset myList = ListAppend(myList, "d", ";")>
```

`ListAppend()` adds an element to the end of a list. Conversely, `ListPrepend()` adds an element to the *beginning* of a list, as in the following code:

```
<cfset myList = "a,b,c">
<cfset myList = ListPrepend(myList, "d")>
```

`myList` now contains `"d,a,b,c"`.

If you want to insert a new element in the middle of the list rather than at the beginning or end, use `ListInsertAt()`, as follows:

```
<cfset myList = "a,b,c">
<cfset myList = ListInsertAt(myList, 2, "d")>
```

This snippet inserts `d` as the new second item in the list and moves everything that was previously in positions two through the end of the list down one position, so `myList` now contains `"a,d,b,c"`. Notice that `ListInsertAt()` takes three attributes if you leave out the delimiter: the original list, the position at which to insert a new item, and the new item to insert.

Deleting an item from a list

Deleting an item from a list is as simple as inserting it, as the following example shows:

```
<cfset myList = "a,b,c,d">
<cfset myList = ListDeleteAt(myList, 2)>
```

That call to `ListDeleteAt()` removes the second item from the list, so `myList` now contains `"a,c,d"`. To use a delimiter other than the comma, you need to add a third argument to the function call, as follows:

```
<cfset myList = "a;b;c;d">
<cfset myList = ListDeleteAt(myList, 2, ";")>
```

`myList` now contains `"a;c;d"`.

Finding an item in a list

Now that you know how to add and remove items from a list, you can look at how to search existing lists to find a particular item. Say, for example, that you wanted to find `apple` in the following list:

```
<cfset myList = "pear,apple,orange,banana">
```

You use `ListFind()` to locate the position of `apple` in `myList`, as follows:

```
<cfset pos = ListFind(myList, "apple")>
```

`pos` would contain 2, because `apple` is the second item in the list. Suppose, however, that you use the following instead:

```
<cfset pos = ListFind(myList, "tangerine")>
```

`pos` would contain 0, since `tangerine` does not exist in `myList`.

What if `myList` contained mixed-case items, as follows:

```
<cfset myList = "Pear,Apple,Orange,Banana">
```

Calling `ListFind(myList, "apple")` would return 0 this time, because `ListFind()` is a case-sensitive match. To find a list item regardless of its case, call `ListFindNoCase()`, as follows:

```
<cfset pos = ListFindNoCase(myList, "apple")>
```

Now `pos` would contain 2 again because `ListFindNoCase()` performs a case-insensitive match.

You can also match a substring of a list item. Take, for example, the following code:

```
<cfset pos = ListContains(myList, "ple")>
```

Here, `pos` would return 2, because `apple` is the first list item that contains the substring `ple`. As is `ListFind()`, ListContains() is case-sensitive, but a case-insensitive version also is available, as follows:

```
<cfset pos = ListContainsNoCase(myList, "ple")>
```

This code would match `Apple`, `apple`, and `apPLe`.

Suppose, however, that your list contains multiple delimiters, as follows:

```
<cfset myList = "pear,apple:orange;banana">
```

In this version of `myList`, commas, semicolons, and colons can all be delimiters, so to call `ListFind()` on this function, you must use the extra delimiter argument, as follows:

```
<cfset pos = ListFind(myList, "apple", ":;,")>
```

Notice that the extra argument contains more than one delimiter, so ColdFusion treats any of these characters as delimiters.

Getting an item from a list by the item's index

You haven't seen it for a while (well, at least not since the beginning of the preceding section), so you may need to take another look at the example list, as follows:

```
<cfset myList = "pear,apple,orange,banana">
```

`ListGetAt()` retrieves the item at a particular position in a list:

```
<cfset item = ListGetAt(myList, 2)>
```

In that example, `item` would contain `apple`, because that is the second item in the list.

The following code is a shortcut to retrieving the first and last items in a list:

```
<cfset firstItem = ListFirst(myList)>
<cfset lastItem = ListLast(myList)>
```

In this example, `firstItem` would contain `pear`, and `lastItem` would contain `banana`.

You also have a function to get every list item except the first, as follows:

```
<cfset subList = ListRest(myList)>
```

After calling `ListRest()`, `subList` would contain `apple,orange,banana`. `ListRest()` is useful for "peeling off" the first values of a list inside a list loop and then setting the list to the remaining items.

GetToken() vs. ListGetAt()

You learn in the preceding sections about `ListGetAt()`, which retrieves the item at a specific index in a list. Another function, called `GetToken()`,does the same thing, as the following example shows:

```
<cfset myList = "pear,apple,orange,banana">
<cfset item = GetToken(myList, 2, ",")>
```

`GetToken()` returns `apple`, the second item in the list. Notice, however, that we use the delimiter argument even though the delimiter is a comma. `GetToken()` uses spaces, tabs, and newlines, instead of commas, as the default delimiter.

The advantage to using `GetToken()` is that `GetToken()` doesn't throw an error if the index is outside the bounds of the list. Try, for example, calling the following:

```
<cfset item = ListGetAt(myList, 5)>
```

This call would cause ColdFusion to throw an error because there only four elements are in `myList`. Try, however, calling `GetToken()` instead, as follows:

```
<cfset item = GetToken(myList, 5, ",")>
```

This call would simply return an empty string and not throw an error.

You should usually use `ListGetAt()` because its syntax is simpler and it is easier to read. If you don't know for sure how many elements may be in a list, however, use `GetToken()` to avoid throwing an error and then test the return value for an empty string to determine whether it was successful.

Getting the length of a list

To get the number of elements in a list, you can use `ListLen()`, as follows:

```
<cfset numElements = ListLen(myList)>
```

Calling `ListLen()` on `myList` returns `4`.

You can also get the number of elements with a specific value by using `ListValueCount()`, as follows:

```
<cfset myOtherList = "apple,apple,orange,pear">
<cfset numApples = ListValueCount(myOtherList, "apple")>
```

ListValueCount() would return 2, because two occurrences of apple are in myOtherList. Notice that ListValueCount() is case-sensitive. To ignore case, use ListValueCountNoCase(), as follows:

```
<cfset myOtherList = "apple,Apple,Orange,Pear">
<cfset numApples = ListValueCountNoCase(myOtherList, "apple")>
```

Looping over a list

One version of CFLOOP loops over a list, as the following code shows:

```
<cfoutput>
<cfloop list="#myList#" index="theElement">
    #theElement#<br>
</cfloop>
</cfoutput>
```

This version of CFLOOP executes once for each element in a list, storing the current element in the variable specified in the Index attribute. Notice that the value of the list attribute is enclosed in pound signs.

Choosing a list's delimiters

In this chapter, we've mostly used commas as our list delimiters. We do so because commas are the default list delimiter, as well as what the majority of people use. However, you can't always use commas for your list delimiters. Say, for example, that you have the following three items:

```
my element
another element
yet another, I'm afraid
```

The last item has a comma in it, so you can't use commas as a delimiter. To show you why, the following example puts those three items together into a comma-delimited list:

```
<cfset myList = "my element,another element,yet another, I'm afraid">
```

If you put the three items together into a single comma-delimited list, ColdFusion sees the comma in the third item as another delimiter rather than as part of the item value. As such, you'd run into problems calling the following:

```
<cfoutput>#ListLen(myList, ",")#</cfoutput>
```

This call returns 4 instead of the 3 that you'd expect. The problem can be solved if you use a semicolon as a delimiter, as follows:

```
<cfset myList = "my element;another element;yet another, I'm afraid">
<cfoutput>#ListLen(myList, ";")#</cfoutput>
```

Now you're treating the semicolon as the delimiter, so ListLen() returns 3.

Always consider every possible character that the list data may contain in choosing a delimiter. Table 14-1 shows some common delimiters and some good applications for each one.

Table 14-1: Common List Delimiters

Symbol	*Applications*
comma (,)	A good general purpose delimiter. Usually appropriate if you're creating a list of numbers (but make sure that you are not using commas in the numbers) or a list of short codes from a database lookup table.
semicolon (;)	A good substitute for the comma if the list data contains commas.
vertical pipe (|)	Usually best used with data that contains multiple special characters. This is also a native field delimiter if you're importing some text files. It shouldn't be used with some product descriptions, however, because product descriptions sometimes contain pipe characters.
tilde (~)	Best for processing lists that may contain user input. This character is very rarely used by itself. Can be easily confused with a dash, however, so be careful to comment your code.
space ( )	Can be used in combination with other punctuation to search text if you're looking for certain words.
period (.)	Combine the period with the question mark and exclamation point to parse a list of sentences. Rarely used in ColdFusion programming.

If you can't use any of these characters, you may consider using an array to store your data instead of a list, because arrays don't use delimiters. You learn about arrays in the section "Using Arrays," later in this chapter.

Dealing with empty elements

Empty elements are elements within a list that contain no value. To see how to deal with them, take the following list:

```
<cfset myList = "apple,pear,,orange,banana,">
```

How many elements are in `myList`? You'd think six, but ColdFusion's list functions see only four because ColdFusion counts empty list elements — such as the one between `pear` and `orange` and the empty element at the end of the list — as nonexistent. If you need an empty element, you must put spaces in the list, as in the following example:

```
<cfset myList = "apple,pear, ,orange,banana, ">
```

A good practice is to avoid empty elements if possible. ColdFusion's list-processing functions work differently than do the list-processing functions in most other languages and could present a portability issue.

Changing a list's delimiters

What if you suddenly needed to use a semicolon as your list delimiter instead of a comma? You would use `ListChangeDelims()` as follows:

```
<cfset myList = ListChangeDelims(myList, ";", ",")>
```

myList now contains "apple;pear;orange;banana". The interesting thing about ListChangeDelims() is that it automatically removes empty elements. Take, for example, the following list:

```
<cfset myList = "apple,pear,,orange,banana,">
```

ListChangeDelims() would return "apple;pear;orange;banana". Using ListChangeDelims(), therefore, is also a good way to remove empty elements even if you're not changing delimiters, as follows:

```
<cfset myList = ListChangeDelims(myList, ",", ",")>
```

Sorting list elements

The lists that we've been using in the preceding sections have all been in random order. If you need items in a list to be in a particular order, you can use ListSort(), as follows:

```
<cfset myList = ListSort(myList, "text", "asc")>
```

After calling ListSort(), myList would contain the following:

```
apple,banana,orange,pear
```

As does ListChangeDelims(), ListSort() removes empty elements.

The second argument to ListSort() is the type of sort to perform. This argument can take any of the following three values:

- Numeric: Sorts the list numerically. If any list element cannot be converted to a number, ColdFusion throws an error.
- Text: Sorts the list alphabetically but is case sensitive. Try calling ListSort() on the following list:

  ```
  Pear, apple, Banana, peach
  ```

  This call would return the following:

  ```
  Banana, Pear, apple, peach
  ```

  A case-sensitive sort always returns uppercase letters before lowercase letters; as such, any words in all capital letters would sort before any initial-capped words. Just the fact that a letter is uppercase is enough to guarantee that the letter will come before any lowercase letter.
- Textnocase: Sorts the list alphabetically, ignoring case. Calling ListSort() on the preceding list would return the following:

  ```
  apple, Banana, peach, Pear
  ```

The third argument to ListSort() can be asc or desc depending on whether you want an ascending or descending sort.

Qualifying list elements

Suppose that you had the following list:

```
pear, orange, lemon, citron
```

But suppose, too, that you wanted to use it in a query such as the following:

```
SELECT *
FROM Fruit
WHERE FruitName IN ('pear','orange','lemon','citron')
```

You couldn't just use it as follows:

```
SELECT *
FROM Fruit
WHERE FruitName IN (#myList#)
```

That's because `myList` doesn't have single quotes around its items, and the database would throw an error when it tried to execute the query. Before using `myList` in a query, you must *qualify* the list elements by surrounding them with single quotes. ColdFusion offers a function named `ListQualify()` to do just that, as the following example shows:

```
SELECT *
FROM Fruit
WHERE FruitName IN (#ListQualify(myList, "'")#)
```

The second attribute describes the qualifier—in this case, a single quote.

Using Arrays

Arrays, as do lists, store multiple values under a single name and have a library of functions built around them. Unlike lists, however, arrays store data in separate *compartments* and not just as a delimited string.

Where lists are simple variables (that is, they are just simple strings with formally defined delimiters), arrays are *complex variables*, meaning that they may contain more than a single value and create programmatically addressable compartments for those values.

An array is an ordered stack of data, as shown in Figure 14-1.

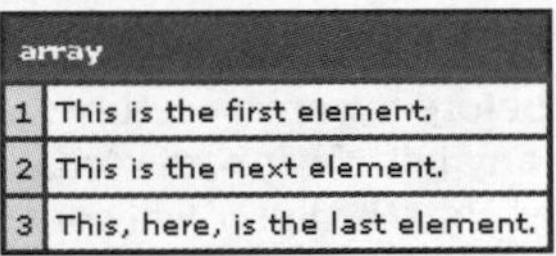

Figure 14-1: A visualization of an array.

Creating an array

Unlike a list, which is a simple string variable, an array is a special type of object that is created by calling a function named `ArrayNew()`, as follows:

```
<cfset myArray = ArrayNew(1)>
```

`ArrayNew()` creates a new, one-dimensional array object and assigns it to the variable myArray.

An array can have up to three dimensions. A *one-dimensional array* creates a stack of elements such as that shown in Figure 14-1. A *two-dimensional array* is like a grid of elements, such as that shown in Figure 14-2.

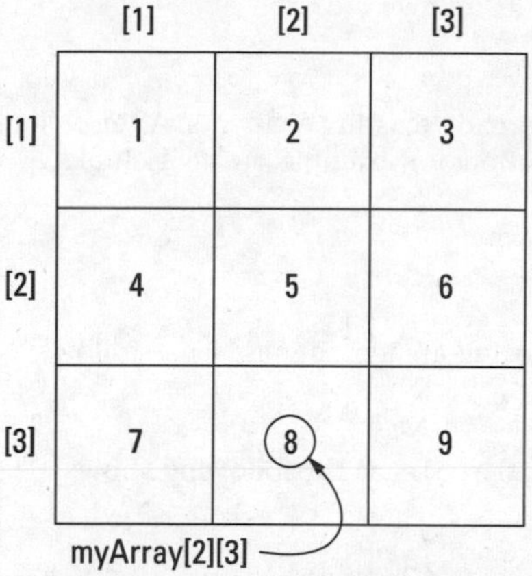

	[1]	[2]	[3]
[1]	1	2	3
[2]	4	5	6
[3]	7	8	9

myArray[2][3]

Figure 14-2: A two-dimensional array.

As you can probably guess, a *three-dimensional array* is like a cube of elements.

Multidimensional arrays are rarely useful unless you're doing matrix mathematics (which no one should be doing in ColdFusion anyway). Chapter 15 is about *structures*, which give you a much better way to implement what most people use multidimensional arrays for. The rest of this chapter deals only with one-dimensional arrays.

Referring to an array element

You refer to an array element through positional notation, as follows:

```
<cfoutput>#myArray[2]#</cfoutput>
```

This snippet outputs the second element in the array. The index of an array (the number between the square brackets) can also be a variable containing a numeric value.

Mentioning that arrays begin counting at `1` may seem redundant, but in most computer languages — such as JavaScript — arrays begin at element `0`. Keep this fact in mind if you ever populate a JavaScript array by using ColdFusion array elements.

Adding an item to an array

To add an element to the end of an array, use `ArrayAppend()`, as follows:

```
<cfset myArray = ArrayNew(1)>
<cfset ArrayAppend(myArray, "apple")>
```

Notice the difference between `ListAppend()` and `ArrayAppend()` in the following examples:

```
<cfset myList = ListAppend(myList, "apple")>
<cfset ArrayAppend(myArray, "apple")>
```

`ListAppend()` does not modify the original list; instead, it returns the original list with the new element appended. `ArrayAppend()`, however, modifies the original array. The only thing that `ArrayAppend()` ever returns is `TRUE`, so you don't even need to store the return value.

ColdFusion also has an ArrayPrepend() function, as follows:

```
<cfset ArrayPrepend(myArray, "peach")>
```

You can also insert a new array element between already existing elements. After calling ArrayNew() and ArrayAppend() earlier in this section, for example, myArray looks as follows:

```
1: peach
2: apple
```

You can insert a new element between the two by using ArrayInsertAt() as follows:

```
<cfset ArrayInsertAt(myArray, 2, "lemon")>
```

myArray now has a new element between peach and apple, as the following shows:

```
1: peach
2: lemon
3: apple
```

You can also create array elements by directly assigning a value to a position, as follows:

```
<cfset myArray[4] = "blueberry">
```

Now myArray has a fourth element, as you can see in the following result:

```
1: peach
2: lemon
3: apple
4: blueberry
```

You can also skip elements, as follows:

```
<cfset myArray[6] = "pomegranate">
```

This code leads to another array element in myArray, as shown in the following:

```
1: peach
2: lemon
3: apple
4: blueberry
5: <no element>
6: pomegranate
```

Notice that no element lies at position 5 in myArray. This result doesn't mean that the element is blank; it simply doesn't exist. The difference between *blank* and *nonexistent* is sometimes hard to understand, but it boils down to this: Attempting to use myArray[5] when the fifth element doesn't exist will throw an error, whereas if the fifth element is blank, myArray[5] will return a blank string.

Deleting an item from an array

You can delete an item from an array by using ArrayDeleteAt(), as follows:

```
<cfset ArrayDeleteAt(myArray, 6)>
```

That line deletes the sixth item from the array that we describe in the preceding section. Notice that the new length of the array is now five, even though the fifth element is undefined.

If you need to quickly delete all the elements of an array, use ArrayClear(), as follows:

```
<cfset ArrayClear(myArray)>
```

After you call ArrayClear(), the array has no elements remaining.

Getting information about an array

Following is an easy way to find out whether an array has any elements:

```
<cfif ArrayIsEmpty(myArray)>
    This array is empty.
<cfelse>
    This array has at least one element.
</cfif>
```

To find the specific number of elements in an array, use ArrayLen(), as follows:

```
<cfset numElements = ArrayLen(myArray)>
```

Both ArrayLen() and ArrayIsEmpty() count undefined elements, so be careful because you usually don't account for undefined elements in the rest of your code.

Finding an item in an array

Finding an item in a list is a simple matter of calling ListFind() or ListFindNoCase(). You have, however, no array-based equivalent to ListFind(). Instead, you must use a loop, as follows:

```
<cfloop from="1" to="#ArrayLen(myArray)#" index="i">
    <cfif myArray[i] EQ "apple">
        <cfbreak>
    </cfif>
</cfloop>
```

After this loop is finished, i contains the array index that contains "apple"—in this case, 3.

Using aggregate functions

An *aggregate* function takes an array containing numbers as an argument and returns a single value representing some characteristic of those numbers. ColdFusion arrays have four aggregate functions, and they are all shown in Listing 14-1. Note that the aggregate functions are shown in bold, and that each of them take a single argument: the array containing the data to be aggregated.

Listing 14-1: Using aggregate functions

```
<cfset myNumericArray = ArrayNew(1)>
<cfset myNumericArray[1] = 1>
<cfset myNumericArray[2] = 7.5>
<cfset myNumericArray[3] = 5>
<cfset myNumericArray[4] = 8>
<cfset myNumericArray[5] = 2>
```

Continued

Listing 14-1 (continued)

```
<cfset myNumericArray[6] = 10>
<cfset myNumericArray[7] = 0>
<cfset myNumericArray[8] = 1.5>

<pre>
<cfoutput>
Sum of array elements:       #ArraySum(myNumericArray)#
Smallest array element:      #ArrayMin(myNumericArray)#
Largest array element:       #ArrayMax(myNumericArray)#
Average of array elements: #ArrayAvg(myNumericArray)#
</cfoutput>
</pre>
```

Listing 14-1 produces the output shown in Figure 14-3.

```
Sum of array elements:      35
Smallest array element:     0
Largest array element:      10
Average of array elements: 4.375
```

Figure 14-3: Array aggregates.

If any elements in an array cannot be converted to a number, ColdFusion throws an error if you attempt to use an aggregate function.

Swapping elements in an array

Another feature arrays have that lists don't is the capability to easily swap elements. Suppose that `myArray` looks as follows:

```
1: peach
2: lemon
3: apple
4: blueberry
```

To swap the first and third elements, you would use `ArraySwap()`, as follows:

```
<cfset ArraySwap(myArray, 1, 3)>
```

`myArray` would then look as follows:

```
1: apple
2: lemon
3: peach
4: blueberry
```

Sorting array elements

As with lists, you can easily sort an array by using `ArraySort()`, as follows:

```
<cfset ArraySort(myArray, "text", "asc")>
```

After you call ArraySort(), myArray would contain the following:

```
1: apple
2: blueberry
3: lemon
4: peach
```

If any undefined elements are in the array as you attempt to use ArraySort(), ColdFusion throws an error.

As for ListSort(), the second argument to ArraySort() describes the type of sort that you want to perform. This argument can take the following three values:

✦ Numeric: Sorts the array numerically. If any array element cannot be converted to a number, ColdFusion throws an error.

✦ Text: Sorts the array alphabetically but is case sensitive. Suppose that you call ArraySort() on the following array:

```
1: Pear
2: blueberry
3: Apple
4: peach
```

This call would return the following result:

```
1: Apple
2: Pear
3: blueberry
4: peach
```

✦ Textnocase: Sorts the array alphabetically, ignoring case. Calling ArraySort() on the preceding array would return the following result:

```
1: Apple
2: blueberry
3: peach
4: Pear
```

The third argument to ArraySort() can be asc or desc, depending on whether you want an ascending or descending sort.

Resizing an array

Whenever you add an element to an array, you're allocating memory in ColdFusion Server. Sometimes, however, not enough memory is available in the array's current location; if this happens, the entire array must be reallocated and moved. This operation can be very costly in terms of CPU time and memory usage if you have more than a few elements in your array.

For efficiency's sake, if you know the number of elements that an array is to contain before you start adding them, you can use ArrayResize() to pre-allocate the space that you need, as follows:

```
<cfset ArrayResize(myArray, 500)>
```

For maximum efficiency in your code, call ArrayResize() immediately after ArrayNew().

Converting Between Lists and Arrays

Lists offer certain features that arrays don't, such as the capability to easily find an element. But you can also do some things easily with arrays that are difficult with lists, such as finding an average. For this reason, you often find yourself using a list when you need the functionality of an array and vice-versa. To get around this conundrum, you can convert a list to an array—or an array to a list—by using the `ListToArray()` and `ArrayToList()` functions, as follows:

```
<cfset myNewArray = ListToArray(myList)>
<cfset myNewList = ArrayToList(myArray)>
```

These functions can be memory-intensive for large lists and arrays, so use these two functions only if you really need them.

If your array contains complex values, ArrayToList() throws an error.

Also note that when you convert a list to an array using ListToArray (), ColdFusion removes empty elements from the array, but the converse is not true. ArrayToList () preserves any empty elements in the array, possibly throwing off code that requires both to be synchronized.

Choosing Between Lists and Arrays

After you know how to use lists and arrays, you need to decide what to *do* with them. Both expose much of the same functionality, so which is better for what purpose?

Think of lists more as multivalued strings than as actual complex data types. Lists are good for storing sets of data in which you may need to find items quickly. Arrays are better suited for highly ordered sets of data, especially if you must coordinate the contents of two arrays. Remember, too, that arrays are the only effective way to use aggregate functions.

You must, however, use lists if you must store data in a Client variable. You cannot use an array for this purpose, because Client variables can't store complex data. You can, however, convert the array to a list and then store the list in a Client variable.

As we mention in the section "Choosing a list's delimiters," earlier in this chapter, if you can't guarantee that any particular delimiter is going to appear in the list items, you should use an array to store the data instead. An array separates its values from one another by keeping each value in its own compartment rather than stringing them all together.

Summary

Arrays and lists are powerful tools if applied correctly. Each has its pros and cons, but in most cases, you can convert one to the other so that its specific set of functions can be used. In this chapter you learned how to effectively use both arrays and lists, and also how to choose between the two.

Lists are simple variables that contain multiple values separated by delimiters, and they are useful where you don't need use aggregate functions on their values. Arrays are complex variables that contain multiple values in programmatically addressable compartments, and they are useful where aggregate functions are needed.

The next chapter expands on this one to show the most powerful, complex object type in ColdFusion: the structure. Make sure that you understand all the concepts in this chapter before moving on to the next, because it shows you how to nest arrays inside structures — and vice-versa!

✦ ✦ ✦

Working with Structures

✦ ✦ ✦ ✦

In This Chapter

Understanding structures

Manipulating structure keys

Visualizing complex structures

The various notations used in referencing structures

Structure copying caveats and solutions

This chapter discusses structures, which are the most complex and most useful of the complex data types. You learn what structures are, how to use them, and when to use them.

What is a Structure?

Simply put, a *structure* is a container for other variables. Structures are like arrays in that they contain programmatically addressable elements, but structures *name* each element rather than simply assigning them numeric positions. Graphically, a structure looks as shown in Figure 15-1.

struct	
hisElement	his value
myElement	my value
yourElement	your value

Figure 15-1: A graphical representation of a structure.

Notice that each element in a structure has a name. Always remember that each element in an *array* has a *number*, while *structure* elements have *names*. You see how naming each element is useful throughout the chapter.

Creating a Structure

As are arrays, structures are complex objects with a specific initialization function, as the following example shows:

```
<cfset myStruct = StructNew()>
```

`StructNew()` doesn't take any arguments, because structures do not have a simple dimension. As you will see in the section "Nested Structures" later in this chapter, structures may have arbitrarily complex dimensions.

If `myStruct` currently contains a value, `StructNew()`destroys the old value and replaces it with an empty structure.

Adding an Element to a Structure

An *element* in a structure consists of a *key* and a *value*. The key is the name of the element, and the value is what the element contains. Think of the package as if each element were a variable and the structure a named container of those variables.

You can add an element to a structure in multiple ways, all of which we discuss in the following sections.

StructInsert() vs. StructUpdate()

One way to add an element to a structure is by using StructInsert(), as follows:

```
<cfset success = StructInsert(myStruct, "FavoriteFruit", "apple",
"TRUE")>
```

The return value of StructInsert() is TRUE if the operation is successful; if unsuccessful, the function call throws an error.

After the preceding call to StructInsert(), myStruct would look as follows:

```
FavoriteFruit: apple
```

The first argument to StructInsert() is the structure that you are inserting a key into. The second argument to StructInsert() is the name of the new key, and the third argument is the new key's value. The fourth argument tells ColdFusion whether to permit the overwriting of an already existing key: If it is FALSE and the key already exists, ColdFusion throws an error. Note that the fourth argument defaults to FALSE if omitted.

To modify an element that's already in the structure, you can use StructUpdate(), as follows:

```
<cfset success = StructUpdate(myStruct, "FavoriteFruit", "pineapple")>
```

StructUpdate() throws an error if the specified key doesn't already exist in the structure. After you use StructUpdate(), myStruct looks as follows:

```
FavoriteFruit: pineapple
```

We usually use StructInsert() by passing TRUE for the fourth parameter, because that way, you don't need to know whether the specified key already exists before creating it.

Using dot notation

StructInsert and StructUpdate() are unwieldy. Take, for example, the following statement:

```
<cfset success = StructInsert(myStruct, "SweetestFruit", "peach",
"TRUE")>
```

Now compare it to the following:

```
<cfset myStruct.SweetestFruit = "peach">
```

The second version is simpler and easier to read, and it does the same thing. The only drawback to using dot notation is that you can't embed special characters in the name of the key, as you can by using StructInsert(), as shown in the following snippet:

```
<cfset success = StructInsert(myStruct, "Biggest Fruit", "watermelon",
"TRUE")>
<cfset myStruct.Biggest Fruit = "watermelon">
```

Notice that the second CFSET statement would cause a syntax error. You also can't use dot notation to create a key name that is a number, as follows:

```
<cfset myStruct.3182 = "some value">
```

This statement throws an error. You can use StructInsert() or StructUpdate() to create this key.

Another problem with dot notation is that it does not preserve the case of the key. Suppose that you do the following:

```
<cfset someStruct.SomeKey = 1>
```

Here, someStruct contains a key named SOMEKEY, because ColdFusion converts all key names created by using dot notation to uppercase. It is unclear why this occurs, but the good news is that the uppercase keys will rarely affect your code because ColdFusion doesn't consider case when looking up a key name.

Using associative array notation

You have yet another syntax that you can use for creating a structure key, as the following example shows:

```
<cfset myStruct["NotARealFruit"] = "zucchini">
```

That syntax is equivalent to the following:

```
<cfset myStruct.NotARealFruit = "zucchini">
```

This new syntax is called *associative-array* notation. For an explanation, look at Figure 15-2.

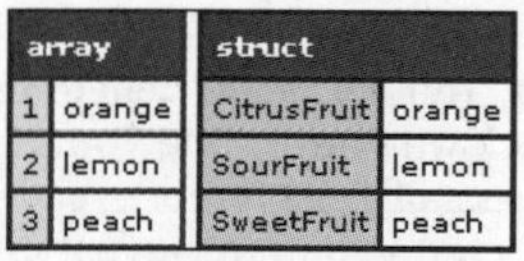

array		struct	
1	orange	CitrusFruit	orange
2	lemon	SourFruit	lemon
3	peach	SweetFruit	peach

Figure 15-2: Side-by-side comparison of an array and a structure.

Notice that the structure readout in the figure looks almost like two arrays sandwiched together—one array containing the element names and the other containing the element values. These two "arrays" are associated with one another so that referring to an element in one array retrieves the element in the other array. (Note, however, that the names and values are not actually arrays; it's just convenient to use arrays as a comparison.)

The first advantage to this notation is that you can now embed special characters in the key name, as follows:

```
<cfset myStruct["3182"] = "some value">
<cfset myStruct["Coolest Fruit"] = "cherry">
```

Another advantage is that associative-array notation preserves the case of the key name. This syntax truly is the best of both worlds—it's as easy to use as dot notation but as flexible as StructInsert(). Given the choice between dot notation and associative-array notation, the latter is usually your best bet for creating structure keys.

The real advantage to using an associative array, however, is the capability to use dynamic key names, as shown in the following example:

```
<cfset myKeyName = "Sourest Fruit">
<cfset myStruct[myKeyName] = "lemon">
```

After that last call, `myStruct` would look as follows:

```
FavoriteFruit: pineapple
SweetestFruit: peach
Biggest Fruit: watermelon
NotARealFruit: zucchini
Coolest Fruit: cherry
Sourest Fruit: lemon
```

Notice that, instead of storing `lemon` in an element named `myKeyName`, ColdFusion evaluates `myKeyName` and stores `lemon` in an element named `Sourest Fruit`.

Retrieving an Element From a Structure

You have two ways to retrieve an element from a structure. The simplest is to use dot notation or associative-array notation, as follows:

```
<cfoutput>
    #myStruct.NotARealFruit#<br>
    #myStruct["Coolest Fruit"]#
</cfoutput>
```

If you'd rather use a function, use `StructFind()` as follows:

```
<cfoutput>
    #StructFind(myStruct, "NotARealFruit")#<br>
    #StructFind(myStruct, "Coolest Fruit")#
</cfoutput>
```

Both syntaxes throw an error if the specified key does not exist. You derive no benefit from one or the other syntax, because both do the same thing, so pick whichever one you that like and use it. Using associative-array or dot notation, however, is usually much more readable. Notice that you can set an element by using associative-array notation and retrieve it by using dot notation; this is what we usually do, as the following example shows:

```
<cfset myStruct["TangiestFruit"] = "orange">
<cfoutput>#myStruct.TangiestFruit#</cfoutput>
```

We set elements by using associative-array notation to preserve the case of the key, but we retrieve the element by using dot notation because it's typically more readable. Remember, however, that you aren't required to use only one syntax — use whichever syntax best fits the situation.

Removing an Element From a Structure

You delete a key from a structure by using `StructDelete()`, as follows:

```
<cfset success = StructDelete(myStruct, "Coolest Fruit")>
```

After you call `StructDelete()`, `myStruct` looks as follows:

```
FavoriteFruit: pineapple
SweetestFruit: peach
Biggest Fruit: watermelon
NotARealFruit: zucchini
Sourest Fruit: lemon
TangiestFruit: orange
```

`Coolest Fruit` is gone. Notice that you never have undefined keys in a structure, which is another way that structures are different from arrays.

To quickly remove all elements from a structure, use `StructClear()`, as follows:

```
<cfset success = StructClear(myStruct)>
```

After you call `StructClear`, `myStruct` still exists, but it contains no elements.

Getting Information About a Structure

`StructIsEmpty()` tells you whether any elements are in a given structure, as the following example shows:

```
<cfif StructIsEmpty(myStruct)>
```

To get a specific count of how many top-level (that is, nonnested) elements are in a structure, use `StructCount()`, as follows:

```
<cfoutput>#StructCount(myStruct)#</cfoutput>
```

To tell whether a given variable contains a structure, use `IsStruct()`, as follows:

```
<cfif IsStruct(myStruct)>
```

`IsStruct` returns `TRUE` if the passed variable is a structure and `FALSE` if it does not.

Looping Over a Structure

One form of `CFLOOP` enables you to loop over the keys in a structure, as the following example shows:

```
<cfoutput>
<cfloop collection="#myStruct#" item="theItem">
    The value of the #theItem# key is #myStruct[theItem]#.<br>
</cfloop>
</cfoutput>
```

The `collection` attribute tells ColdFusion which structure to loop over, and the `item` attribute is what ColdFusion names the variable that contains the key name. ColdFusion loops over every element in the structure and puts the key's *name* in `theItem` each time that the loop iterates.

If you don't need to loop over the structure but you need a list or array containing the structure's keys, use `StructKeyList()` or `StructKeyArray()`, as follows:

```
<cfset keyList = StructKeyList(myStruct)>
<cfset keyArray = StructKeyArray(myStruct)>
```

`StructKeyList()` takes an optional second parameter describing the delimiter to use for the list. The following line of code, for example, creates a semicolon-delimited list containing the names of the top-level keys in `myStruct`:

```
<cfset keyList = StructKeyList(myStruct, ";")>
```

Nested Structures

So far you've created keys containing simple string values, but the most powerful feature of structures is their capability to *nest* inside another structure. Nesting enables you to create hierarchical data structures that closely resemble real-world data models.

The simple structure that we created earlier looks like what's shown in Figure 15-3.

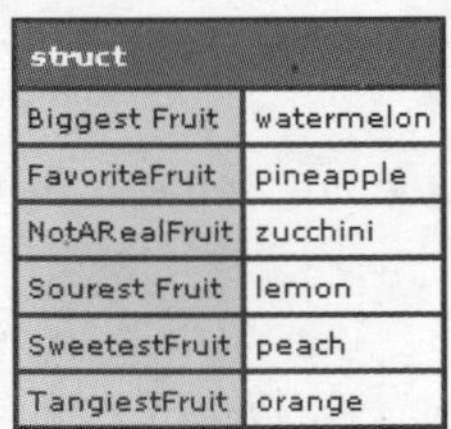

Figure 15-3: A simple structure.

A nested structure would look like what's shown in Figure 15-4.

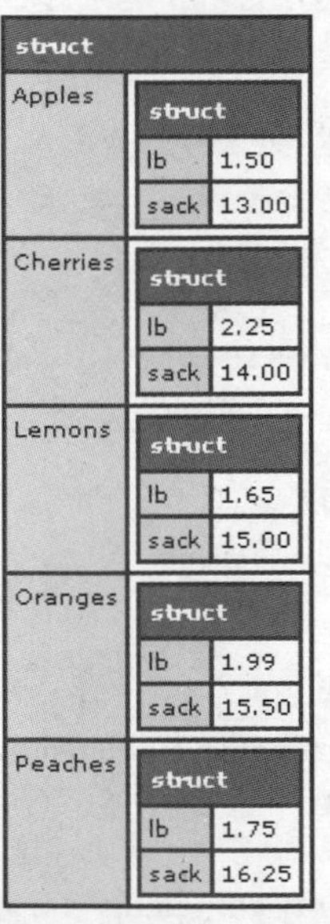

Figure 15-4: Structures nested inside one another.

Notice that in Figure 15-4, smaller structures are nested inside the enclosing structure.

Creating a nested structure may seem complicated, but it really is quite simple. In the following example, you create a new key named `FruitCosts` in `myStruct` that contains a substructure that, in turn, contains the names of fruits and their respective costs:

```
<cfset myStruct["FruitCosts"] = StructNew()>
<cfset myStruct.FruitCosts["Oranges"] = 1.99>
<cfset myStruct.FruitCosts["Apples"] = 1.50>
<cfset myStruct.FruitCosts["Peaches"] = 1.75>
```

Now `myStruct` looks like what's shown in Figure 15-5.

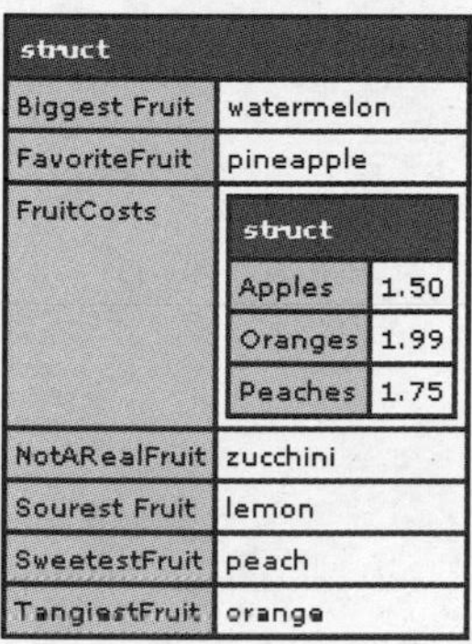

Figure 15-5: A substructure inside `myStruct`.

Structures can be nested many levels deep in any configuration.

You can also use associative-array notation to create nested structures, as follows:

```
<cfset myStruct["FruitCosts"] = StructNew()>
<cfset myStruct["FruitCosts"]["Oranges"] = 1.99>
<cfset myStruct["FruitCosts"]]"Apples"] = 1.50>
<cfset myStruct["FruitCosts"]["Peaches"] = 1.75>
```

Our personal preference is to use dot notation for every nesting level except the final one, as in the following example:

```
<cfset myStruct["FruitCosts"] = StructNew()>
<cfset myStruct.FruitCosts["Oranges"] = 1.99>
<cfset myStruct.FruitCosts]"Apples"] = 1.50>
<cfset myStruct.FruitCosts["Peaches"] = 1.75>
```

Just make sure that you don't have any special characters or spaces in your key names — or have key names made entirely of numbers — in the dot-path portion of your notation.

Complex nesting

After you understand the general concept of nesting structures, you can delve a little deeper into more complex nesting schemes, where one complex variable is nested within another.

You can, for example, also nest arrays inside of structures, as follows:

```
<cfset myStruct["FruitArray"] = ArrayNew(1)>
<cfset myStruct.FruitArray[1] = "orange">
<cfset myStruct.FruitArray[2] = "lemon">
<cfset myStruct.FruitArray[3] = "pineapple">
```

After you add the array, `myStruct` looks like what's shown in Figure 15-6.

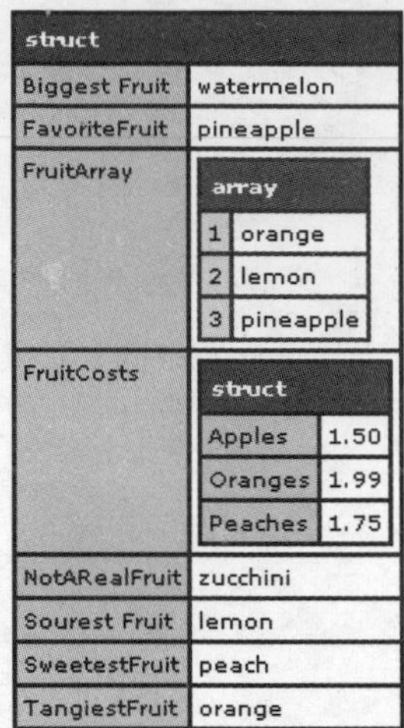

Figure 15-6: An array nested inside `myStruct`.

Structures can be nested any number of levels deep. In addition, array elements can contain structures, as the following example shows:

```
<cfset myArray = ArrayNew(1)>
<cfset myArray[1] = StructNew()>
<cfset myArray[1]["MyTestKey"] = "my value">

<cfoutput>
#myArray[1].MyTestKey#
</cfoutput>
```

Structures become truly useful if you use them as containers for complex data that models the real world. You can create a shopping cart by using a structure, for example, as shown in Listing 15-1.

Listing 15-1: **Creating a shopping cart in a structure**

```
<cfset myCart = StructNew()>
<cfset myCart.cartID = CreateUUID()>
<cfset myCart.saleDate = Now()>
<cfset myCart.arItemNumber = ArrayNew(1)>
<cfset myCart.arItemName = ArrayNew(1)>
<cfset myCart.arQuantity = ArrayNew(1)>
<cfset myCart.arUnitPrice = ArrayNew(1)>
<cfset myCart.arExtended = ArrayNew(1)>
<cfset myCart.subtotal = 0>
<cfset myCart.salesTaxRate = 4.0000>
<cfset myCart.salesTaxAmount = 0>
<cfset myCart.shippingAmount = 0>
<cfset myCart.total = 0>
```

Later on, after your shopping cart contains line items in its arrays, you can easily produce familiar values, as the following list describes:

✦ The subtotal is simply `ArraySum(myCart.arExtended)`,.

✦ The sales-tax amount is simply `(myCart.salesTaxRate * myCart.subtotal)`.

✦ The total is `(myCart.subtotal + myCart.salesTaxAmount + myCart.shippingAmount)`.

You face no limits on how much information that your structure can store, nor do you have any limits as to how complex it can be. The only thing that you must watch out for is making your structure *too* complicated for your needs. You can usually keep track of what goes where quite easily if you make the format of your structures emulate the real-world data that you are storing.

How dot notation automatically creates a nested structure

Until now, you've created structures only by using `StructNew()`. You can also create structures just by using dot notation, as follows:

```
<cfset aNewStruct.SomeKey.SomeValue = 1>
```

That line creates a structure named `aNewStruct` with a substructure named `SomeKey` that has an element named `SomeValue` with a value of 1. You can visualize it as what's shown in Figure 15-7.

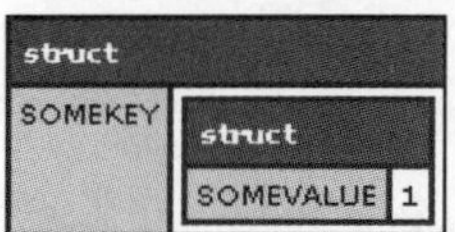

Figure 15-7: A structure created by using dot notation.

Notice that, in the figure, the names of all newly created structures and keys are all uppercase, regardless of the capitalization that you use in the code.

As convenient as this method may seem, it does have a drawback. Consider the following snippet:

```
<cfset aNewStruct = StructNew()>
<cfset aNewStruct.myKey = 2>
<cfset aNewStruct.yourKey = 3>
```

After running the preceding snippet, two new keys, named `myKey` and `yourKey`, are created, and `aNewStruct` looks as shown in Figure 15-8.

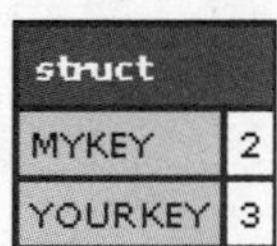

Figure 15-8: aNewStruct.

Suppose that you now attempt to call the following snippet to create a nested structure named myKey:

```
<cfset aNewStruct.myKey.subKey = 4>
```

If the previous line had worked, it would have overwritten the previous simple value of myKey with a *substructure* named myKey, and aNewStruct would look as shown in Figure 15-9.

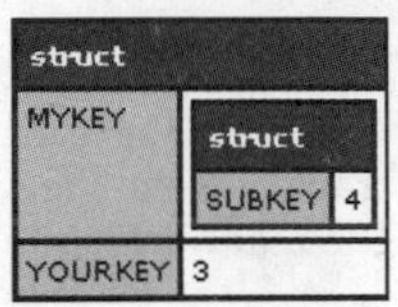

Figure 15-9: aNewStruct **with a nested substructure.**

Fortunately, however, attempting to overwrite a simple key with a substructure throws an error in ColdFusion MX.

You do face a limitation in creating structure keys by using this method. ColdFusion MX can create nested structures only up to three levels deep in a single call, as in this example:

```
<cfset a = StructNew()>
<cfset a.b.c.d = "some value">
```

Attempting to create a key more than three levels deep gives you unexpected results. ColdFusion ignores all but the last three keys. Running the following code, for example, outputs "some value":

```
<cfset a = StructNew()>
<cfset a.b.c.d.e.f.g = "some value">
<cfoutput>
#a.e.f.g#
</cfoutput>
```

You can, however, create structures nested as deeply as you want as long as you don't attempt to go more than three levels deeper than currently exists.

Sorting a Structure

Sometimes data is useful only if it is sorted in a specific order. Although this is easy to do with tabular data in a database, sorting data in a structure takes a little more understanding and effort.

Say that you have a structure containing the prices per pound of different fruits, as following:

```
<cfset FruitCosts = StructNew()>
<cfset FruitCosts["Oranges"] = 1.99>
<cfset FruitCosts["Apples"] = 1.50>
<cfset FruitCosts["Peaches"] = 1.75>
<cfset FruitCosts["Cherries"] = 2.25>
<cfset FruitCosts["Lemons"] = 1.65>
```

You can loop over these prices and output them by using the code in Listing 15-2.

Listing 15-2: Looping over a structure of fruit prices

```
<cfoutput>
<cfloop collection="#FruitCosts#" item="Fruit">
    #Fruit#: #FruitCosts[Fruit]# / lb.<br>
</cfloop>
</cfoutput>
```

Listing 15-2 would produce the output shown in Figure 15-10.

```
Peaches: 1.75 / lb.
Oranges: 1.99 / lb.
Cherries: 2.25 / lb.
Lemons: 1.65 / lb.
Apples: 1.50 / lb.
```

Figure 15-10: The output of Listing 15-2.

The problem here is that structures don't have any kind of inherent order. Structure keys are stored in an internal order that only ColdFusion Server understands, and if you loop over the structure, that's the order that you see. The order in which you insert the keys doesn't even matter.

`StructSort()` returns an array of key names sorted by their values (*not* their key names). Listing 15-3 uses `StructSort()` to put the fruit costs out in order.

Listing 15-3: Ordering the structure before looping

```
<cfset keyArray = StructSort(FruitCosts, "numeric", "asc")>

<cfoutput>
<cfloop from="1" to="#ArrayLen(keyArray)#" index="i">
    #keyArray[i]#: #FruitCosts[keyArray[i]]# / lb.<br>
</cfloop>
</cfoutput>
```

Listing 15-3 produces the output shown in Figure 15-11.

```
Apples: 1.50 / lb.
Lemons: 1.65 / lb.
Peaches: 1.75 / lb.
Oranges: 1.99 / lb.
Cherries: 2.25 / lb.
```

Figure 15-11: The output of Listing 15-3.

The biggest difference between Listings 15-2 and 15-3 is the approach that each takes to looping over the structure. In Listing 15-2, we just use a standard collection loop, relying on whatever order ColdFusion stored the structure in. In Listing 15-3, we call `StructSort()` first, which returns an array of key names that look as follows:

```
1: Apples
2: Lemons
3: Peaches
4: Oranges
5: Cherries
```

These elements still may not seem to be in any particular order, but look at the following prices associated with each element (although the values in parentheses are not actually part of the array):

```
1: Apples   (1.50)
2: Lemons   (1.65)
3: Peaches  (1.75)
4: Oranges  (1.99)
5: Cherries (2.25)
```

Although the key names appear in the array, the values remain back in the structure.

After calling `StructSort()`, Listing 15-3 loops through `keyArray`, which contains the sorted key names. During this loop, `keyArray[i]` contains the current key name, which can in turn be used to supply the key name to the `FruitCosts` structure. If you follow the ColdFusion processing engine along step-by-step, the resolution of this reference is as follows:

```
Step 1:    #FruitCosts[keyArray[i]]#
Step 2:    #FruitCosts[keyArray[1]]#
Step 3:    #FruitCosts["Apples"]#
Result:    1.50
```

But what if you want to sort by a key in a nested structure? We've modified the `FruitCosts` structure from earlier in the chapter by using the following code:

```
<cfset FruitCosts = StructNew()>
<cfset FruitCosts["Oranges"] = StructNew()>
<cfset FruitCosts["Oranges"]["lb"] = 1.99>
<cfset FruitCosts["Oranges"]["sack"] = 15.50>
<cfset FruitCosts["Apples"] = StructNew()>
<cfset FruitCosts["Apples"]["lb"] = 1.50>
<cfset FruitCosts["Apples"]["sack"] = 13.00>
<cfset FruitCosts["Peaches"] = StructNew()>
<cfset FruitCosts["Peaches"]["lb"] = 1.75>
<cfset FruitCosts["Peaches"]["sack"] = 16.25>
<cfset FruitCosts["Cherries"] = StructNew()>
<cfset FruitCosts["Cherries"]["lb"] = 2.25>
<cfset FruitCosts["Cherries"]["sack"] = 14.00>
<cfset FruitCosts["Lemons"] = StructNew()>
<cfset FruitCosts["Lemons"]["lb"] = 1.65>
<cfset FruitCosts["Lemons"]["sack"] = 15.00>
```

Each element in the `FruitCosts` structure is a substructure containing two keys: `"lb"` (price per pound) and `"sack"` (price per sack). To help you visualize this structure, look at Figure 15-12.

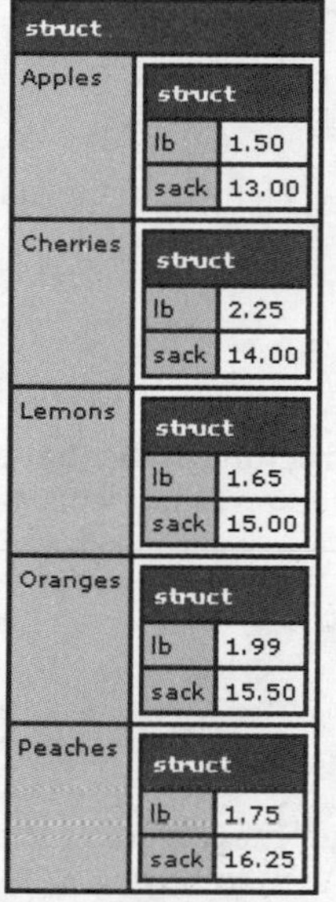

Figure 15-12: A structure with fruit prices by the pound and by the sack.

So now that you have this set of nested structures, how do you sort by price per pound? A fourth attribute of `StructSort()` describes a dot path to the sort value, as shown in Listing 15-4.

Listing 15-4: Sorting by a nested key

```
<cfset keyArray = StructSort(FruitCosts, "numeric", "asc", "lb")>

<cfoutput>
<cfloop from="1" to="#ArrayLen(keyArray)#" index="i">
   #keyArray[i]#: #FruitCosts[keyArray[i]].lb# / lb.<br>
</cfloop>
</cfoutput>
```

The good thing about this method is that you can very easily switch to sorting by price per sack, as shown in Listing 15-5.

Listing 15-5: Sorting by a different nested key

```
<cfset keyArray = StructSort(FruitCosts, "numeric", "asc", "sack")>

<cfoutput>
<cfloop from="1" to="#ArrayLen(keyArray)#" index="i">
   #keyArray[i]#: #FruitCosts[keyArray[i]].sack# / sack.<br>
</cfloop>
</cfoutput>
```

You can sort by a key any number of levels deep by adding elements to the dot path:

```
<cfset keyArray = StructSort(FruitCosts, "numeric", "asc",
"sack.10lb.fresh")>
```

Be aware that, if the specified subkey doesn't exist for every top-level element in the main structure, ColdFusion throws an error.

Copying a Structure

Now you come to one of the most confusing parts of dealing with structures: What happens after you copy a structure and then start modifying the copy? The answer is not what you may think, so pay close attention to the details.

Consider the following snippet:

```
<cfset myVar = 1>
<cfset yourVar = myVar>
<cfset myVar = 2>
```

In these three lines, you have two *simple* variables: `myVar`, containing `1`, and `yourVar`, containing `2`. If you set `yourVar` equal to `myVar`, you make a copy of `myVar`, so setting `myVar` to a different value doesn't affect `yourVar`. This is true for almost every variable type in ColdFusion—assigning one variable to another makes a copy and then divorces the two variables so that making a change in one doesn't make a change in the other.

Structures, however, are the one variable type where such simple copying doesn't apply. Say that you call the following snippet, which creates a structure named `myStruct`, populates it with a couple values, and then copies `myStruct` into a new structure named `yourStruct`:

```
<cfset myStruct = StructNew()>
<cfset myStruct["aKey"] = 1>
<cfset myStruct["bKey"] = 2>
<cfset yourStruct = myStruct>
<cfset myStruct["aKey"] = 3>
```

You would expect to end up with `myStruct.aKey` equal to `3` and `yourStruct.aKey` still equal to the original value of `1`, but Figure 15-13 shows what *really* happens.

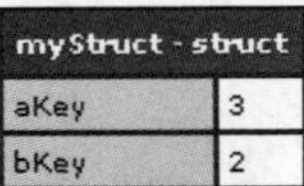

Figure 15-13: Two structures after attempting to copy and modify one.

What's going on here? Both structures show the same value for `aKey` even though you changed it only in `myStruct`. This happens because of the way that you attempted to copy `myStruct`, as follows:

```
<cfset yourStruct = myStruct>
```

Unlike any other ColdFusion data type, structures are accessed by *reference* and not by *value*. If you access a variable by value, the variable *is* the actual value. If you access a variable by reference, the variable is a *pointer* to the value, which is stored somewhere else in memory.

Suppose that you call the following:

```
<cfset yourStruct = myStruct>
```

You aren't copying the *value*—you're copying the *reference*. `yourStruct`, therefore, is now pointing to the same object as `myStruct`, so changing something about `myStruct` changes `yourStruct` as well—because they're really the same structure. In fact, the opposite holds true as well: Changing the value of `yourStruct.aKey` changes the value of `myStruct.aKey` to the same value.

If you want to copy `myStruct` to `yourStruct` so that the values in each structure are no longer linked to one another, use `StructCopy()`, as follows:

```
<cfset yourStruct = StructCopy(myStruct)>
```

Now, making a modification to `myStruct` doesn't affect the contents of `yourStruct`.

Well, *not exactly*. Things get a little confusing here, so hold on tight . . .

Say that you change the contents of `myStruct` to include a nested structure, as follows:

```
<cfset myStruct = StructNew()>
<cfset myStruct["aKey"] = 1>
<cfset myStruct["bKey"] = 2>
<cfset myStruct["aSubStruct"] = StructNew()>
<cfset myStruct.aSubStruct["subKey"] = 4>
<cfset yourStruct = StructCopy(myStruct)>
<cfset myStruct["aKey"] = 3>
<cfset myStruct.aSubStruct["subKey"] = 3>
```

You would expect that, because you copied the structure by using `StructCopy()` instead of just copying the reference, modifying `myStruct.aKey` wouldn't affect `yourStruct.aKey`, and you are correct. The change to `myStruct.aSubStruct.subKey`, however, *does* modify `yourStruct's` value. This situation is shown in Figure 15-14.

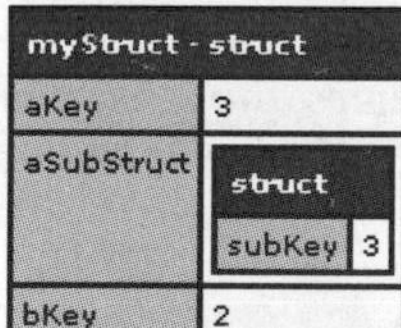

Figure 15-14: Copying structures by using `StructCopy()`.

This result happens because of how StructCopy() copies a structure's members. As the code copied myStruct to yourStruct, it copied aKey and bKey by value. (Remember that this means that aKey and bKey refer to actual values in both structures.) StructCopy(), however, still copies nested structures by reference, meaning that it copies the pointer to the structure rather than the actual structure itself. As such, both myStruct.aSubStruct and yourStruct.aSubStruct still point to the same structure after a StructCopy().

To *completely* divorce myStruct and all its substructures from yourStruct and all its substructures, you must use Duplicate(), as follows:

```
<cfset myStruct = StructNew()>
<cfset myStruct["aKey"] = 1>
<cfset myStruct["bKey"] = 2>
<cfset myStruct["aSubStruct"] = StructNew()>
<cfset myStruct.aSubStruct["subKey"] = 4>
<cfset yourStruct = Duplicate(myStruct)>
<cfset myStruct["aKey"] = 3>
<cfset myStruct.aSubStruct["subKey"] = 3>
```

Now all keys in both myStruct and yourStruct are completely separate, regardless of whether they contain simple values or nested structures, as shown in Figure 15-15.

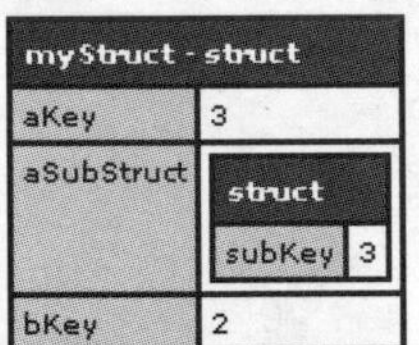

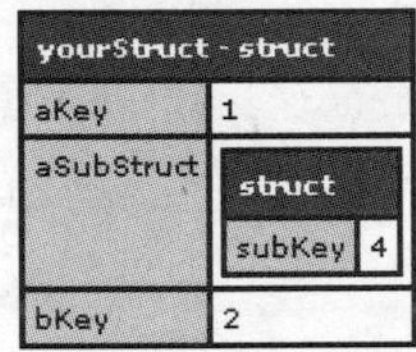

Figure 15-15: Using Duplicate() to make a "deep copy."

Nine times out of ten, you use Duplicate() to copy a structure. At times, the other two methods can prove useful, but those times are rare and typically very advanced. Just be aware of exactly what your code does in duplicating a structure.

Using Variable Scopes as Structures

You may not realize it, but you were using structures as far back as Chapter 2! You may remember the following code from that chapter:

```
<cfquery name="DeleteCompany"
    datasource="#Request.MainDSN#">
DELETE FROM Company
WHERE
    CompanyID = #Val(Form.CompanyID)#
</cfquery>
```

```
<cflocation url="Finished.cfm?msg=#URLEncodedFormat('Company ID
#Form.CompanyID# has been deleted from the database.')#" addtoken="No">
```

`Form.CompanyID` is actually an element in a structure! All the ColdFusion variable scopes are actually structures: `Form`, `URL`, `Client`, and so on. This may not seem very interesting until you think about what you can do with structures. You can get a list of all of a request's form variables by using `StructKeyList()`. You can delete a local variable by using `StructDelete()`. You can even sort all of a request's incoming URL variables by value by using `StructSort()`.

You should, however, never do one thing with a variable scope: Never call `StructClear()` on the Session scope. Calling `StructClear()` on the Session scope clears the `CFID`, `CFTOKEN`, and `URLToken` variables, possibly causing problems within ColdFusion server. Refer to Macromedia TechNote 14143 in the Macromedia KnowledgeBase for more information on this issue.

Other Structure Operations

The techniques that you learn in the preceding sections of this chapter are all useful, and you're likely to use most if not all of them at some point in your development career. The techniques in this section are advanced, but that's not to say that you shouldn't learn them. You may eventually run into a situation where these techniques are just what the doctor ordered.

Merging two structures

If you have two related structures, you may decide to group them together. You can create a *superstructure*, which simply sets the two structures as subkeys of a larger one. You can also take the keys from one structure and transplant them into the other.

The simplest technique is to create a superstructure. Consider the following snippet:

```
<cfset myStruct = StructNew()>
<cfset myStruct["myKey"] = 1>
<cfset myStruct["myOtherKey"] = 2>
<cfset yourStruct = StructNew()>
<cfset yourStruct["yourKey"] = 3>
<cfset yourStruct["yourOtherKey"] = 4>
<cfset ourStruct = StructNew()>
<cfset ourStruct["myStuff"] = myStruct>
<cfset ourStruct["yourStuff"] = yourStruct>
```

`ourStruct` has grouped together the contents of `myStruct` and `yourStruct`. `ourStruct` looks like what's shown in Figure 15-16.

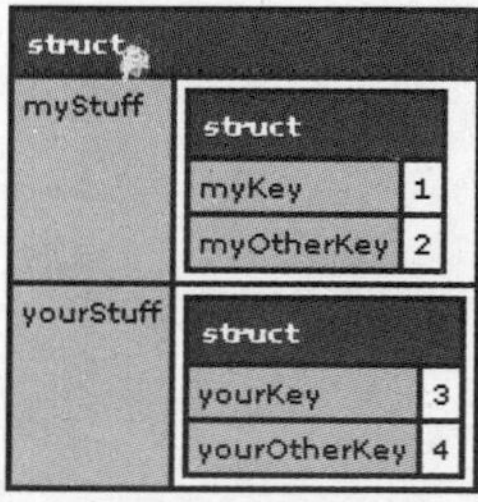

Figure 15-16: `ourStruct` as a superstructure.

Another option is to roll the keys from one structure into another by using `StructAppend()`, as follows:

```
<cfset myStruct = StructNew()>
<cfset myStruct["myKey"] = 1>
<cfset myStruct["myOtherKey"] = 2>
<cfset yourStruct = StructNew()>
<cfset yourStruct["yourKey"] = 3>
<cfset yourStruct["yourOtherKey"] = 4>
<cfset StructAppend(myStruct, yourStruct)>
```

`myStruct` now contains the keys from `yourStruct`, as shown in Figure 15-17.

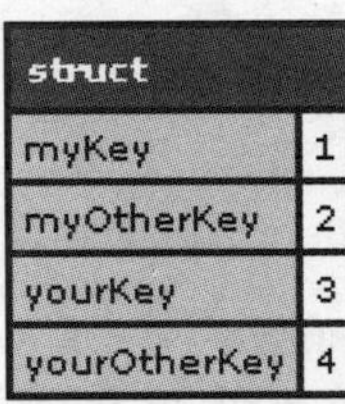

Figure 15-17: `myStruct` **after you call** `StructAppend()`.

Finding a key or value deep in a nested substructure

Two functions enable you to search for a key or value within a structure. `StructFindKey()` and `StructFindValue()` return an array with elements that are structures describing the matched key or value.

Consider the following call to the `FruitCosts` array from the section "[name section]," earlier in this chapter:

```
<cfset resultsArray = StructFindKey(FruitCosts, "lb", "ALL")>
```

`resultsArray` would look as shown in Figure 15-18:.

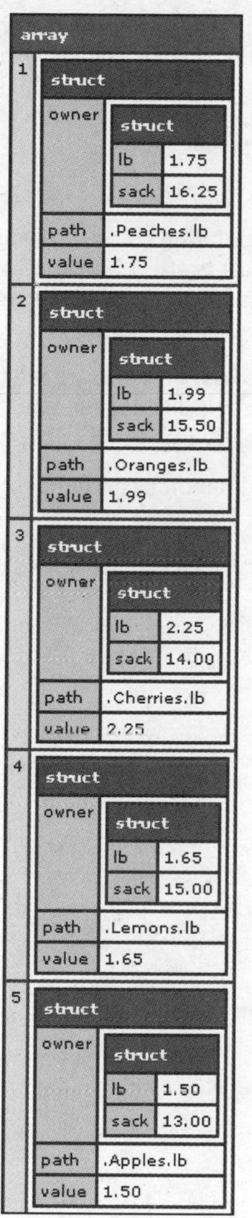

Figure 15-18: The results of calling `StructFindKey()` to find all prices per pound.

In the figure, `value` is the value of the found key; `owner` is a reference to the structure that "owns" the found key; and `path` is the dot path to the found key. `StructFindValue()` returns the same results, but it searches by the value of the key rather than by the name of the key.

Summary

We can think of no way to simplify the details of creating and manipulating structures any more than how we've described them in this chapter, and the subject is still a hard one to master. Go back and read the stuff that's still a bit hazy, and by all means, play with the example code that we discussed in the chapter.

Structures are widely regarded as the most difficult feature of ColdFusion, but they are the basis for some of the best programming techniques in ColdFusion. In this chapter, you learned what you can do with structures and how to use them effectively.

The next chapter covers `CFSCRIPT`, which enables you to use ColdFusion as an efficient scripting language.

✦ ✦ ✦

CHAPTER 16

Scripting ColdFusion with CFSCRIPT

In This Chapter

The differences between tag-based ColdFusion syntax and scripting syntax

Setting variables by using CFSCRIPT

Flow control by using scripting syntax

One of the great things about ColdFusion is its easy-to-use, tag-based syntax. Having the capability to intersperse CFML and HTML tags without needing to open and close script blocks or needing to remember what syntax you're currently working in is a wonderful thing.

At times, however, using a scriptable syntax would be nice—for example, if you're doing heavy data processing on a page. As nice as CFML's tag-based syntax is, number crunching is best expressed in script.

CFSCRIPT is a server-side scripting language that works with CFML to give you the best of both worlds: an elegant, tag-based syntax whenever you need it and a flexible scripting syntax if you don't.

User-defined functions are discussed in Chapter 17. We do not include them in this chapter because of ColdFusion MX's capability to define UDFs by using either CFSCRIPT or CFML syntax. This chapter describes the basics of CFSCRIPT.

What is CFSCRIPT?

Essentially, CFSCRIPT is an instruction to the ColdFusion processing engine to treat a block of code as scripting-based syntax rather than as tag-based syntax. Why mess with a perfectly good thing (CFML) by adding another complication (scripting)? Because the latter is easier to code and faster to process.

Consider the following snippet, for example, which loops from 1 to 10, adding each index to a running total:

```
<cfset TheSum = 0>
<cfloop from="1" to="10" index="i">
    <cfset TheSum = TheSum + i>
</cfloop>
```

Following is the same code expressed in CFSCRIPT's scripting syntax:

```
<cfscript>
TheSum = 0;
for(i = 1; i LTE 10; i = i + 1) {
```

```
    TheSum = TheSum + 1;
}
</cfscript>
```

CFSCRIPT doesn't support the ++ syntax for incrementing a variable that may be familiar to you if you have experience with Java, JavaScript, or C++.

Look familiar? If you're having JavaScript *déjà vu*, that's normal, because CFSCRIPT is almost identical to JavaScript. CFSCRIPT blocks mostly instantiate variables and perform calculations, but they can produce output, too. Consider, for example, the following extension of the preceding code snippet:

```
<cfset TheSum = 0>
<cfloop from="1" to="10" index="i">
    <cfset TheSum = TheSum + i>
</cfloop>

<cfoutput>#TheSum#</cfoutput>
```

Normally, anything that isn't part of a CFML tag is output to the page. CFSCRIPT, however, uses a function named `WriteOutput()` for page output, as the following example shows:

```
<cfscript>
TheSum = 0;
for(i = 1; i LTE 10; i = i + 1) {
    TheSum = TheSum + 1;
}

WriteOutput(TheSum);
</cfscript>
```

Think of `WriteOutput()` as the server-side equivalent of JavaScript's client-side `document.write()` method.

The difference between `WriteOutput()` and `document.write()` shows the different mindset of CFSCRIPT as compared to CFML. Rather than the text just "being there," as it is in CFML, CFSCRIPT must be directed to output the text.

Notice the use of semicolons, which terminate CFSCRIPT statements. CFSCRIPT is less forgiving than JavaScript with respect to semicolon termination; forget one, and ColdFusion throws an error.

Another thing that you need to get used to in CFSCRIPT is the use of curly braces. Curly braces surround blocks of CFSCRIPT code similar to the way that opening and closing tags surround blocks of CFML code, but their use is actually more critical. A simple `if` construct in CFSCRIPT looks as follows:

```
<cfscript>
    if(this EQ that)
      doThis();
    else
      doThat();
</cfscript>
```

The preceding snippet runs error free, but suppose that you need to add another statement after `doThis()`, as in the following example:

```
<cfscript>
```

```
    if(this EQ that)
      doThis();
      doSomeOtherThingToo();
    else
      doThat();
</cfscript>
```

ColdFusion throws an error, because it sees an `else` clause without a corresponding `if` clause. This happens because the `doSomeOtherThingToo()` statement is considered the continuation of statements *after* the `if` statement finishes executing the `doThis()` statement. For CFSCRIPT to execute both statements when the `if` tests `TRUE`, you must enclose them within curly braces as follows:

```
<cfscript>
    if(this EQ that) {
      doThis();
      doSomeOtherThingToo();
    } else
      doThat();
</cfscript>
```

In fact, a best practice is to *always* include the curly braces, regardless of whether you need them or not, as in the following example:

```
<cfscript>
    if(this EQ that) {
      doThis();
      doSomeOtherThingToo();
    } else {
      doThat();
    }
</cfscript>
```

Why? Because you never know when you're going to add another statement to an existing `if` test. We can't tell you how many times that we threw errors in the early days by adding a second statement to an existing, unenclosed `if` construct, simply because we didn't pay attention to the enclosure mechanism. If you always enclose, you never throw errors. The same holds true for any language that requires such enclosure.

How to use CFSCRIPT

All CFSCRIPT code is contained between `CFSCRIPT` tags, as shown in the following example:

```
... Regular CFML code goes here ...

<cfscript>
... CFSCRIPT code goes here
</cfscript>

... Regular CFML code goes here ...
```

Notice that the content of a `CFSCRIPT` block must be a complete statement. You *cannot*, for example, do the following:

```
<cfscript>
if(myVar GT yourVar) {
```

```
</cfscript>

My text goes here.

<cfscript>
}
</cfscript>
```

That type of construction is valid in some other scripting languages, but not in CFSCRIPT. CFSCRIPT operations must be self-contained in a single code block, as follows:

```
<cfscript>
if(myVar GT yourVar) {
    WriteOutput("My text goes here.");
}
</cfscript>
```

You can have several CFSCRIPT blocks in a single ColdFusion template, but each CFSCRIPT block must be a self-standing block of executable code.

Setting variables in CFSCRIPT

The simplest operation in CFSCRIPT is setting a variable, as follows:

```
<cfscript>
myVar = 1;
</cfscript>
```

Setting a variable in CFSCRIPT requires no CFSET tag, and the statement ends with a semicolon. You can now use myVar just as you would any other ColdFusion variable. Notice that you can share any variable between CFSCRIPT and regular CFML, as follows:

```
<cfset myVar = 1>

<cfscript>
    myVar = myVar + 1;
    yourVar = 3;
</cfscript>

<cfoutput>#yourVar + myVar#</cfoutput>
```

You are not limited to setting and reading variables in the Variables scope, either. Any variable that you can set by using tag-based CFML can also be set by using CFSCRIPT's scripting syntax.

If constructs in CFSCRIPT

The if construct in CFSCRIPT works exactly the same as its CFML counterpart, CFIF. ColdFusion evaluates a condition and executes a dependant statement based on whether the condition is true or false.

Compare the following CFML and CFSCRIPT if constructs:

✦ CFML:

```
<cfif myVar GT yourVar>
```

```
    ... execute if true ...
</cfif>
```

✦ CFSCRIPT:

```
if(myVar GT yourVar) {
    ... execute if true ...
}
```

CFSCRIPT also has an equivalent to CFELSE, as the following example shows:

```
if(myVar GT yourVar) {
    ... execute if true ...
}
else {
    ... execute if false ...
}
```

You also find an equivalent to CFELSEIF in CFSCRIPT, as follows:

```
if(myVar GT yourVar) {
    ... execute if true ...
}
else if (myVar EQ yourVar) {
    ... execute if true ...
}
else {
    ... execute if all conditions false ...
}
```

Switch constructs in CFSCRIPT

CFSCRIPT has an equivalent to CFSWITCH, but you find some important differences. Take, for example, the following CFSWITCH statement:

```
<cfswitch expression="#myVar#">
<cfcase value="1">
    ... Execute if myVar equals 1 ...
</cfcase>
<cfcase value="2,3">
    ... Execute if myVar equals 2 or 3 ...
</cfcase>
<cfdefaultcase>
    ... Execute if no other case executes ...
</cfdefaultcase>
</cfswitch>
```

Now compare it to its CFSCRIPT counterpart, as follows:

```
switch(myVar) {
    case 1:
        ... Execute if myVar equals 1 ...
        break;

    case 2:
    case 3:
```

```
        ... Execute if myVar equals 2 or 3 ...
        break;

    default:
    ... Execute if no other case executes ...
}
```

These snippets are very different, but they do the same thing. Both evaluate `myVar` and then execute whichever `case` statement matches. If none of the statements match, ColdFusion executes the default section.

Look at the differences in syntax between the tag-based and script-based versions. Rather than each case being in its own enclosed in a paired tag (`<CFCASE></CFCASE>`), each `case` declaration (for example, `case 1:`) is followed by dependent statements and terminated by a `break` statement. Without that `break` statement, the `case` declaration remains open, so execution of that case's dependent statements continues.

The use of explicit `break` statements in CFSCRIPT emulates `CFCASE`'s capability to use a comma-delimited list of match values. If myVar equals either `2` or `3` in the preceding snippet, for example, the same dependent statements are executed until a `break` is reached.

Looping constructs in CFSCRIPT

Looping constructs in CFSCRIPT are rather different from those in CFML. You have the following five types of CFML loops:

- *Index loops* (also known as *For loops*), which loop a specified number of times.
- *Conditional loops*, which loop as long as a condition tests true.
- *Query loops*, which loop over each row in a query.
- *List loops*, which loop over each element in a list.
- *Structure loops*, which loop over each top-level key in a structure.

You have only the following four types of CFSCRIPT loops:

1. *For loops*, which loop a specified number of times.
2. *While loops*, which loop as long as a condition tests true.
3. *Do-While loops*, which loop at least once and then continue looping as long as a condition tests true.
4. *Structure loops*, which loop over each top-level key in a structure.

CFSCRIPT's While loop is the direct equivalent of CFML's Conditional loop, but CFML has no direct equivalent to the CFSCRIPT Do-While loop.

The following sections look at each of these four types of loops.

Looping a set number of times

The For loop is akin to `CFLOOP` using the `from`, `to`, `index`, and `step` attributes. In CFSCRIPT it is structured like this:

```
for(indexVar = 1; indexVar LTE 10; indexVar = indexVar + 1) {
    ... body of loop ...
}
```

One of the disorienting things about CFSCRIPT is its lack of attribute names. Whereas in CFML, you can clearly identity the `index` variable, `step` increment, and other attributes of the loop, you now must positionally deconstruct the syntax in CFSCRIPT. Doing so is easier than you think, however. The following code snippet uses `CFLOOP` attribute names in CFSCRIPT syntax to help you compare them to one another:

```
from = 1;
to = 10;
step = 1;
for(index = from; index LTE to; index = index + step) {
    ... body of loop ...
}
```

The CFSCRIPT version initializes the `index` variable with the first loop count, loops while the `index` variable is less than or equal to the last loop count, and each time that the loop executes, it increments `index` by one.

Looping while a condition is true

You have two different types of conditional loop in CFSCRIPT. The first is a While loop, as shown in the following example:

```
bLoop = TRUE;
while(bLoop EQ TRUE) {
    WriteOutput("This is one iteration through the loop.<br>");
    if(RandRange(1, 10) EQ 10) {
        bLoop = FALSE;
    }
}
```

The other type is a Do-While loop, as shown in the following code:

```
do {
    WriteOutput("This is one iteration through the loop.<br>");
    if(RandRange(1, 10) EQ 10) {
        bLoop = FALSE;
    }
    else {
        bLoop = TRUE;
    }
} while(bLoop EQ TRUE);
```

These two loops are both conditional loops, but they work differently. The While loop evaluates its condition *before* executing the body of the loop, meaning that, if the condition is false before the loop begins, the loop never executes.

Conversely, the Do-While loop evaluates its condition *after* the loop body, meaning that the loop body always executes at least once.

Looping over a structure

Another type of loop that CFSCRIPT carries over from CFML is the Structure loop, which loops over the top-level keys in a structure and looks as follows in CFML:

```
<cfloop collection="#myStruct#" item="theKey">
    <cfoutput>#theKey#: #myStruct[theKey]#<br></cfoutput>
</cfloop>
```

The CFSCRIPT version is similar, as the following example shows:

```
for(theKey in myStruct) {
    WriteOutput("#theKey#: #myStruct[theKey]#<br>");
}
```

Breaking out of a loop

CFSCRIPT also has an equivalent to CFBREAK, as the following example shows:

```
for(i = 1; i LTE 10; i = i + 1) {
    if(RandRange(1,10) EQ 10) {
        break;
    }
    WriteOutput("#i#<br>");
}
```

In this example, ColdFusion normally ends the loop after iterating ten times. If `RandRange()` ever returns `10` during the execution of this loop, however, the `break` statement ends the loop prematurely, immediately skipping past the end of the loop.

Skipping an iteration of a loop

CFSCRIPT's `continue` statement instructs ColdFusion to skip the rest of the current loop iteration and immediately begin the next iteration of the loop, as shown in the following example:

```
for(i = 1; i LTE 10; i = i + 1) {
    if(RandRange(1,10) EQ 10) {
        continue;
    }
    WriteOutput("#i#<br>");
}
```

In this example, whenever ColdFusion calculates a random value equal to `10`, it skips the `WriteOutput()` statement and instead skips to the beginning of the next iteration of the loop, if any iterations remain.

Comments in CFSCRIPT

You cannot use CFML comments within a `CFSCRIPT` block. Instead, you must use one of the `CFSCRIPT` comment types, as follows:

```
<cfscript>
// This is a single-line comment before some code.
myVar = 1;
```

```
/*
This is a multi-line comment.
Both of these lines are commented.
*/
</cfscript>
```

Single-line comments begin with two forward slashes — the entire line after the slash marks is commented out, meaning that any code in that line does not execute.

Multiline comments are surrounded by `/*` and `*/` — everything in between those two marks is a comment. You cannot nest multiline comments inside one another, but you can nest a single-line comment inside a multiline comment.

Advantages of CFSCRIPT

CFSCRIPT has the following two primary advantages:

- ✦ It is often more understandable to use CFSCRIPT than CFML in processing data, because CFSCRIPT's procedural syntax is often clearer than that of CFML.
- ✦ You get a healthy performance gain form using CFSCRIPT. CFML is basically an XML-based language and, as such, must be parsed by an XML parser and executed by an interpreter, and both operations are relatively slow. CFSCRIPT requires only a single XML-based tag pair to be parsed, after which its contents — essentially a simple list of preparsed commands — are passed to the processing engine all at once.

Sometimes entire pages of code are written in CFSCRIPT. The best practice is to analyze your templates to determine whether you can group together large blocks of code that don't require CFML tags and then write that code as a single CFSCRIPT block. Sometimes you must interweave CFSCRIPT blocks with CFML, in which case you should try to minimize the number of CFSCRIPT blocks that you create in a single template.

Summary

In this chapter, you learn that CFSCRIPT is a powerful addition to the ColdFusion language and is useful for use in large blocks of code that do not require the use of tag-based CFML. The syntax is much simpler than that of tag-based CFML for variable assignments and function calls, and although the syntax for flow-control constructs like `if`, `switch`, and the various loops may seem difficult to grasp at first, your payoff is faster execution of more efficient code.

✦ ✦ ✦

CHAPTER 17

Building User-Defined Functions

✦ ✦ ✦ ✦

In This Chapter

Understanding user-defined functions (UDFs)

Building UDFs by using CFSCRIPT

Building UDFs by using CFFUNCTION

Working with function arguments

Choosing a function invocation method

Planning function libraries

✦ ✦ ✦ ✦

ColdFusion has more than 250 functions in its language. It has string-manipulation functions, array functions, structure functions, and many other types of functions. Even with this wide variety of functions, however sometimes you may want to define your own function that does things that the built-in ColdFusion functions can't.

This chapter does not describe how to use CFSCRIPT—only how to use CFSCRIPT in conjunction with user-defined functions. CFSCRIPT itself is discussed as a separate subject in Chapter 16.

Building UDFs by Using CFSCRIPT

A *user-defined function*, or *UDF*, can be built in CFSCRIPT, CFML, or a combination of the two. The following sections describe how to build UDFs by using CFSCRIPT. CFSCRIPT UDFs are very natural because they mimic function creation in JavaScript, Java, and many other programming languages which you may already be familiar with.

UDF structure

In general, *functions* receive one or more arguments and return a single result. Some functions (such as ColdFusion's `Now()` function) do not take arguments, but almost all functions do return a result.

A basic UDF built by using CFSCRIPT looks as follows:

```
<cfscript>
function GetCurrentTime() {
    return TimeFormat(Now(), "h:mm:ss tt");
}
</cfscript>
```

The only four things required for every function are the `function` keyword, the name of the function, the parentheses after the name, and the curly braces around the body of the function. Although the `return` statement is technically optional, `return` is what makes a function truly useful, as this statement represents the result returned to the code that calls the function. We call the function that we just created as we would any built-in ColdFusion function, as follows:

```
<cfoutput>#GetCurrentTime()#</cfoutput>
```

We can expand my function by defining a local variable, as follows:

```
function GetCurrentTime() {
    var szTime = TimeFormat(Now(), "h:mm:ss tt");

    return szTime;
}
```

More on the var keyword in the following section. We can also add code to our function between the variable declaration and the return statement, as follows:

```
function GetCurrentTime() {
    var szTime = TimeFormat(Now(), "h:mm:ss tt");

    szTime = ReplaceNoCase(szTime, "am", "in the morning");
    szTime = ReplaceNoCase(szTime, "pm", "in the evening");

    return szTime;
}
```

This UDF is a very simple example that doesn't take any arguments. You learn how to build UDFs that take arguments in the section "Defining function arguments," a little later on in this chapter.

The var keyword

Now to take a look at var in more detail. var declares a variable that's local to a function. If we didn't use var, for example, we could do the following:

```
<cfscript>
function myFn() {
    myVar = 1;
    return TRUE;
}
</cfscript>

<cfoutput>
#myFn()#
#myVar#
</cfoutput>
```

After you call myFn(), myVar is available to code outside the function. That's because any variable defined inside CFSCRIPT is also available to CFML. This is very sloppy programming because you could be inadvertently creating or overwriting variables you weren't intending to affect.

To keep myVar local to myFn() such that it can't leak outside the function, use var, as follows:

```
<cfscript>
function myFn() {
    var myVar = 1;
    return TRUE;
}
</cfscript>
```

Now, attempting to use `myVar` outside `myFn()` throws an error, which is exactly what you want it to do.

All variables created by using `var` must be initialized; ColdFusion throws an error if they are not. And notice, too, that you cannot place the `var` keyword anywhere other than at the very top of a function declaration.

The return keyword

Functions return a single value, as the following example shows:

```
function myFn() {
    return TimeFormat(Now(), "h:mm:ss tt");
}
```

As soon as CFSCRIPT encounters a `return` statement, ColdFusion stops executing the function and returns the value following the `return` keyword to the calling code.

You can also conditionally return different values based on different circumstances, as in the following code:

```
function myFn() {
    if(IsDefined("Client.myVar")) {
        return Client.myVar;
    } else {
        return TimeFormat(Now(), "h:mm:ss tt");
    }
}
```

Every control path in a function must return a value or you get inconsistent results. A best practice, therefore, is to define a default `return` value and use only one `return` statement in your function declaration, as follows:

```
function myFn() {
    var result = TimeFormat(Now(), "h:mm:ss tt");
    if(IsDefined("Client.myVar")) {
        result = Client.myVar;
    }
    return result;
}
```

Defining function arguments

Most functions take one or more *arguments*, as the following example shows:

```
<cfscript>
function add2(firstNumber, secondNumber) {
    return firstNumber + secondNumber;
}
</cfscript>

<cfoutput>
#add2(1,2)#
</cfoutput>
```

The argument names are defined in a list inside the parentheses after the function declaration. You see more advanced uses of arguments in the section "Using the Arguments Collection," later in this chapter.

The preceding example used *positional arguments*, meaning that the first argument in the function call was passed to the first argument in the function, the second in the call became the second in the function, and so on. You can also name the arguments in the call if you want to pass them in a different order, as follows:

```
<cfoutput>
#add2(secondNumber=2,firstNumber=1)#
</cfoutput>
```

This syntax is not widely used because it is slightly harder to read; it can help you, however, if you don't remember the order of a function's parameters. If any of a function call's arguments are named, however, all the arguments must be named.

Calling one function from another

Functions can be called anywhere within a ColdFusion template, even from within another ColdFusion function. Take the following example:

```
<cfscript>
function myFn(myNum, yourNum) {
    return myNum * yourNum;
}

function myOtherFn() {
    var num1 = RandRange(1,10);
    var num2 = RandRange(1,10);

    return myFn(num1, num2);
}
</cfscript>
```

Calling functions recursively

A function can also call itself. We wrote the following function, for example, to calculate the factorial of a number (a *factorial* will be defined in a moment):

```
<cfscript>
function Factorial(myNum) {
    if(myNum EQ 1) {
        return 1;
    }
    else {
    return myNum * Factorial(myNum - 1);
}
}
</cfscript>

<cfoutput>#Factorial(6)#</cfoutput>
```

The *factorial* of 6, for example, is 6 x 5 x 4 x 3 x 2 x 1, or 720. To calculate the factorial, we return the number passed to the function, multiplied by the next smaller factorial (because the 6 factorial can also be represented as 6 x 5 factorial).

You must be careful in creating recursive functions to make sure that you have a *stop condition*. In our case, we stop the recursion whenever `myNum` is `1`. If you don't build a stop condition into your logic, you put the request into an infinite loop.

Passing structures to functions

In Chapter 15, we show you that structures are accessed by reference, whereas other variables are referenced by value. The same applies to passing variables to a function. If you pass a number to a function, the function has a local copy of that number, and any modifications that functions makes to the number are not repeated outside the function call.

Structures are passed to a function by reference, however, so any modifications that the function makes to the structure parameter can be seen outside the function call.

Building UDFs by Using CFFUNCTION

The chief drawback to building UDFs by using CFSCRIPT is that you can't use ColdFusion tags in them. If you need to do a database call while in a CFSCRIPT block, you must exit the `CFSCRIPT` block and use a ColdFusion tag, so that tag cannot be included in the CFSCRIPT function definition.

In MX, you can also define functions by using the `CFFUNCTION` tag, which *does* enable you to use virtually any CFML tag in the declaration of a function. Following is the CFML version of `GetCurrentTime()` from the section "UDF structure," earlier in the chapter:

```
<cffunction name="GetCurrentTime" returntype="string">
    <cfset var szTime = TimeFormat(Now(), "h:mm:ss tt")>

    <cfreturn szTime>
</cffunction>
```

The CFFUNCTION version of this UDF is very similar to its CFSCRIPT counterpart: You give the function a name by using `CFFUNCTION`; you return a value by using `CFRETURN`; and you handle all the business logic in between.

The var keyword

Use of the `var` keyword in a CFFUNCTION function is identical to its use in a CFSCRIPT function. All local variables must be defined before any function code is executed, and all local variables must be initialized.

CFRETURN

The only difference between the `CFRETURN` tag and CFSCRIPT's `return` keyword is the syntax. Both return a single value.

However, `CFFUNCTION` has an optional `returntype` attribute, which specifies the type of data that the function must return. If `CFRETURN` does not return a value of the specified type, ColdFusion throws an error.

Defining function arguments

The main difference between CFFUNCTION and CFSCRIPT functions is how arguments are defined. CFSCRIPT just places argument names in an ordered list after the function name, but CFFUNCTION more clearly defines its arguments by using the CFARGUMENT tag:

```
<cffunction name="add2" returntype="numeric">
    <cfargument name="firstNumber" type="numeric">
    <cfargument name="secondNumber" type="numeric">

    <cfreturn firstNumber + secondNumber>
</cffunction>
```

You can still pass arguments to CFFUNCTION-declared UDFs positionally and without naming them, just as you would with CFSCRIPT UDFs. If you do, CFFUNCTION matches arguments in the order that they are passed to each declaration of arguments in the UDF.

Similarly, you can pass named arguments in an order that's different from that in which they are declared in CFFUNCTION, just as you can with CFSCRIPT UDFs.

Required arguments

One benefit to writing UDFs by using the new CFFUNCTION syntax is the capability to specify which arguments are required and which are optional — something that you cannot do with CFSCRIPT UDFs.

If we want the firstNumber argument to be required, for example, we write the UDF as follows:

```
<cffunction name="add2" returntype="numeric">
    <cfargument name="firstNumber" type="numeric" required="Yes">
    <cfargument name="secondNumber" type="numeric">

    <cfreturn firstNumber + secondNumber>
</cffunction>
```

If you leave the required attribute off a CFARGUMENT, it defaults to an optional argument (required="No").

Choosing Between CFSCRIPT and CFFUNCTION

In this chapter, you've learned about two different ways to create functions in ColdFusion, but which one should you choose?

The easiest answer is to use CFSCRIPT unless you must call a CFML tag. Because CFFUNCTION can call any tag, including CFQUERY or CFSTOREDPROC, it's the only option for doing database work in a UDF. On the other hand, if all you're doing is processing variables, you can use CFSCRIPT's simpler syntax.

What's more, you can call one type of function from the other. Following is an example with one of each type of function showing a valid way for the two to interact:

```
<cffunction name="GetEmployeesFromDB" returntype="Query">
    <cfset var GetEmployees = "">
    <cfquery name="GetEmployees"
            datasource="CFMXBible">
```

```
        SELECT Salary, SSN
        FROM Employee
        </cfquery>

        <cfreturn GetEmployees>
    </cffunction>

    <cfscript>
    function GetSalaries() {
        var qEmp = GetEmployeesFromDB();

        TheMax = ArrayMax(qEmp["Salary"]);
        TheMin = ArrayMin(qEmp["Salary"]);
        TheSum = ArraySum(qEmp["Salary"]);

        return qEmp;
    }
    </cfscript>

    <cfdump var="#GetSalaries()#">
    <cfoutput>
    Max: #TheMax#<br>
    Min: #TheMin#<br>
    Sum: #TheSum#
    </cfoutput>
```

This example gets all the salaries and social security numbers of all the employees in the database and returns the query object as well as some aggregate values. The aggregate values can be calculated in CFSCRIPT, but `GetSalaries()` must call a function written by using `CFFUNCTION` to get the salaries from the database.

Note that in the preceding example we seem to violate our own guideline by setting variables without using `var`, but here it's actually valid. Because we're *expecting* that the calling code will use `TheMax`, `TheMin`, and `TheSum`, it's OK to set these without using `var`. Do note, however, that it is very rare that this technique is valid. In fact, some would argue that instead of setting TheMax, TheMin, and TheSum, we should have created a structure to contain all three values and returned the single structure.

Using the Arguments Collection

Typically, you individually reference each argument passed to a function by its name, as follows:

```
<cffunction name="UseNamedArgs" returntype="numeric">
    <cfargument name="arg1" type="numeric" required="yes">
    <cfargument name="arg2" type="numeric" required="yes">
    <cfset var result = Arguments.arg1 + Arguments.arg2>
    <cfreturn result>
</cffunction>
```

But referring to arguments by their names isn't the only method that you can use to access argument values.

Whenever you pass arguments to a function, ColdFusion creates an object named Arguments that contains this collection of arguments. We say *collection* rather than structure or array because Arguments is different from any other ColdFusion object: It can behave as either a structure *or* an array under certain circumstances.

If your arguments are named in either the declaration of the function or as the function is called, a structure named Arguments that contains keys named for those arguments is created, and you can CFDUMP this structure to inspect it. Calling the preceding snippet, for example, creates an Arguments structure containing two keys named arg1 and arg2, and their values are equal to those passed for each argument.

Suppose, however, that you don't name your arguments in the declaration of the function or as it is called, as is the case with the following example:

```
<cffunction name="UseUnnamedArgs" returntype="numeric">
    <cfset var result = ArrayLen(Arguments)>
    <cfreturn result>
</cffunction>

<cfoutput>#UseUnnamedArgs(5,11)#</cfoutput>
```

In this case, ColdFusion creates an Arguments object that cannot be inspected with CFDUMP (and you can't even loop over it using a Collection loop) but *can* be used the same as an array. So you can reference the individual arguments as Arguments[1], Arguments[2], and so on, and you can also use ArraySum(Arguments), ArrayMin(Arguments), and so on.

Following is an example of when you'd use Arguments as an array:

```
<cfscript>
function SumUnnamedArgs() {
    return ArraySum(Arguments);
}
</cfscript>

<cfoutput>
#SumUnnamedArgs(1,6,4,22,8,5,3)#
#SumUnnamedArgs(8,3,4,2)#
</cfoutput>
```

Because you don't know how many arguments are passed in to the function, you can just use the Arguments array to use all of them without names.

Calling a function by Using CFINVOKE

In the preceding sections, you've called functions only by using a syntax such as SumArgs(8,3,4,2). You can, however, also call functions by using two CFML tags: CFINVOKE and CFINVOKEARGUMENT. The following code, for example, is a function that we used in the section "Defining function arguments," earlier in the chapter:

```
<cfscript>
function add2(firstNumber, secondNumber) {
    return firstNumber + secondNumber;
}
</cfscript>
```

Following is how we would call that function by using the standard syntax:

```
<cfoutput>#add2(1,2)#</cfoutput>
```

If we call that function by using CFINVOKE, it looks as follows:

```
<cfinvoke method="add2" returnvariable="theSum">
    <cfinvokeargument name="firstNumber" value="7">
    <cfinvokeargument name="secondNumber" value="3">
</cfinvoke>

<cfoutput>#theSum#</cfoutput>
```

Notice that, in using CFINVOKE, we specify the name of the variable in the calling template into which the result of the function is returned. This is necessary because we are not simply outputting an inline function call: Some container must be there for the result that is external to the tag-based function invocation code.

CFINVOKEARGUMENT also enables you to conditionally include or modify arguments, because it is a tag-based construction, as the following example shows:

```
<cfinvoke method="add2" returnvariable="theSum">
    <cfinvokeargument name="firstNumber" value="7">
    <cfif secNum GT 100>
        <cfinvokeargument name="secondNumber" value="100">
    <cfelse>
        <cfinvokeargument name="secondNumber" value="#secNum#">
    </cfif>
</cfinvoke>

<cfoutput>#theSum#</cfoutput>
```

Note that when using CFINVOKEARGUMENT, you must always provide a name for every parameter, so you can't use positional notation with CFINVOKEARGUMENT.

You have another option for calling a function by using CFINVOKE. You can put the function's arguments into a structure named argumentcollection and pass the structure to CFINVOKE, as follows:

```
<cfset myStruct = StructNew()>
<cfset myStruct["firstNumber"] = 7>
<cfset myStruct["secondNumber"] = 3>

<cfinvoke method="SumArgs" returnvariable="theSum"
argumentcollection="#myStruct#">
```

All the keys in myStruct become the arguments to the SumArgs() function; in essence, myStruct becomes the function's Arguments collection.

The advantage to this method is that you can assemble the arguments into the structure well before the function is called and then just pass the single structure to the function. The disadvantage is that you must always use named notation; you can have no unnamed arguments.

You have yet another option for calling CFINVOKE. The arguments to the function can be passed as extra attributes to CFINVOKE, as follows:

```
<cfinvoke method="SumArgs" returnvariable="theSum" firstNumber="7"
secondNumber="3">
```

This method is not as flexible as the others, because it must always use named notation, and you can't dynamically pass parameters. But if you are familiar with using custom tags, the technique should be familiar to you. The best suggestion is to use whichever syntax you're familiar with. Table 17-1 summarizes the strengths and weaknesses of each function call's syntax.

Table 17-1: Pros and Cons of Different Function-Invocation Syntaxes

Syntax	*Named Arguments?*	*Positional Arguments?*	*Dynamic Arguments?*
`SumArgs(7,3)`	Yes	Yes	No
`CFINVOKEARGUMENT`	Yes	No	Yes
`argumentcollection`	Yes	No	Yes
As attributes of `CFINVOKE`	Yes	No	No

Caution You face one caveat in using `CFINVOKE`. Attempting to pass `argumentcollection` and separate argument attributes at the same time causes `CFINVOKE` to ignore the `argumentcollection`, causing some of your function's arguments to be undefined. Strangely enough, changing `argumentcollection` to `attributecollection` corrects the problem. This has been verified by Macromedia and may be changed in the future, so don't rely on this behavior.

Specialized functions

Not all functions must return a value. The function in the following code, for example, converts all the values in an array to uppercase:

```
<cfscript>
function UCaseArray(arArray) {
    for(i = 1; i LTE ArrayLen(arArray); i = i + 1) {
        arArray[i] = UCase(arArray[i]);
    }

    return arArray;
}
</cfscript>


<cfset myArray = ArrayNew(1)>
<cfset myArray[1] = "My String">
<cfset myArray[2] = "Your String">
<cfset myArray[3] = "Our String">
<cfscript>
myArray = UCaseArray(myArray);
</cfscript>

<cfdump var="#myArray#">
```

In this case, we needed to return myArray because we had modified the elements in a copy of the original array. If we write the function to modify the keys of a structure, however, we don't need to return a value, as the following example shows:

```
<cfscript>
function UCaseStruct(myStruct) {
    for(item in myStruct) {
        myStruct[item] = UCase(myStruct[item]);
    }

    return;
}
</cfscript>

<cfset myStruct["Mine"] = "My String">
<cfset myStruct["Yours"] = "Your String">
<cfset myStruct["Ours"] = "Our String">

<cfscript>
UCaseStruct(myStruct);
</cfscript>

<cfdump var="#myStruct#">
```

Because the structure is passed by reference, we can just modify the values in the original structure, and we don't need to return anything, because referencing the same structure after the function is called yields the newly modified key values. This is not the case in ColdFusion 5, however, where all functions must return a value.

Where to Put Your UDFs

UDFs can be separately placed in each template that requires them, but this isn't exactly efficient coding. A better technique is to place related UDFs in a single template by themselves and then CFINCLUDE that template wherever one or more of its functions are needed.

Building a library of related functions is a better practice than placing all UDFs in a single template, as ColdFusion must still process these functions as they are included, and this process takes time. Including a library containing 127 UDFs when you need to use only one of them doesn't make sense.

A much better practice is to have one UDF library template for each category of UDFs, so you may create a library template named StringUDFs.cfm that contains all UDFs related to string manipulation and another library template named FinancialUDFs.cfm that contains all financially-oriented UDFs. This way, you create a healthy balance between ease of code maintenance and time wasted processing unneeded UDFs.

Summary

User-defined functions enable you to extend ColdFusion's built-in library of functions with your own. If you use the new CFFUNCTION syntax, your functions can do anything from simple string or number operations to database calls. You see how truly useful functions are as you learn about components in Chapter 22, but you can probably already imagine good uses for them in your existing code. To get a scope of the sheer number of custom functions already available to you, visit www.cflib.org.

In this chapter you learned how to create functions with both CFSCRIPT and CFFUNCTION. You also learned how to call functions with positional and named notation, and you learned about some of the caveats that occur when you use CFINVOKE and CFINVOKEARGUMENT.

The next chapter teaches you about custom tags, which are another way to extend ColdFusion's built-in functionality. Pay attention to the ways in which custom tags and UDFs are different; although they both extend ColdFusion, they serve different purposes and should not be thought of as interchangeable.

✦ ✦ ✦

CHAPTER 18

Writing Custom Tags

✦ ✦ ✦ ✦

In This Chapter

What is a custom tag?

Custom tags versus CFINCLUDE

Custom tags versus user-defined functions

Paired custom tags

Families of nested custom tags

Organizing and accessing your custom tags

Using CFIMPORT with custom tags

✦ ✦ ✦ ✦

The preceding chapter described user-defined functions, which enable you to extend ColdFusion's library of built-in functions with your own. Custom tags are similar in that they enable you to extend ColdFusion's library of built-in *tags* with your own. This chapter shows you how to use every aspect of custom tags and also shows you how to choose between a custom tag and a user-defined function.

Writing Custom Tags

Listing 18-1 shows a simple list of Employee names in a given company.

Listing 18-1: EmployeeList.cfm

```
<cfquery name="GetEmployees"
         datasource="#Request.MainDSN#">
SELECT
    SSN,
    FirstName,
    LastName
FROM
    Employee
WHERE
    CompanyID = #Val(URL.CompanyID)#
</cfquery>

<table>
<cfoutput query="GetEmployees">
<tr>
    <td>#SSN#</td>
    <td>#FirstName# #LastName#</td>
</tr>
</cfoutput>
</table>
```

You can go directly to EmployeeList.cfm, passing CompanyID in the URL, and you get a list of employees that work for the given company.

But what if you want to use this list as part of another page? You *could* copy and paste the code, but what happens if you want to make a change to all places the list is used?

The first thing that most people do is CFINCLUDE the employee list, as follows:

```
<cfinclude template="EmployeeList.cfm">
```

You can also turn the employee list into a custom tag by replacing the calls to CFINCLUDE with the following code:

```
<cf_EmployeeList>
```

You've just written your first custom tag! Whenever ColdFusion encounters the custom tag call, it runs EmployeeList.cfm as if it were a part of the current request. As things stand right now, the only difference between the CFINCLUDE and the custom tag call is the syntax.

The only problem is that, as the custom tag stands now, you must pass the CompanyID in the URL to *every page that calls the custom tag*, which can be annoying. You can modify EmployeeList.cfm to use a tag attribute instead of a URL parameter, as shown in Listing 18-2.

Listing 18-2: EmployeeList.cfm, using an attribute for the CompanyID parameter

```
<!---
Calling CFPARAM without a Default tells ColdFusion to throw an error if
the parameter doesn't exist. Attributes.CompanyID comes from a
CompanyID attribute passed in the call to the custom tag.
--->
<cfparam name="Attributes.CompanyID">

<cfquery name="GetEmployees"
         datasource="#Request.MainDSN#">
SELECT
    EmployeeID,
    FirstName,
    LastName
FROM
    Employee
WHERE
    CompanyID = #Val(Attributes.CompanyID)#
</cfquery>

<table>
<cfoutput query="GetEmployees">
<tr>
    <td>#EmployeeID#</td>
    <td>#FirstName# #LastName#</td>
</tr>
</cfoutput>
</table>
```

Now, you can call the employee list in two different ways. If the company ID comes from a URL parameter, you can call the employee list as follows:

```
<cf_EmployeeList CompanyID="#URL.CompanyID#">
```

But if you have a special interface for a single company, you can pass a specific ID to the tag, as follows:

```
<cf_EmployeeList CompanyID="4">
```

The best part about using a custom tag for this employee list is that you can change the custom tag's output in one place and have the change propagate to everywhere in the application that uses the tag.

Using a custom tag versus using a CFINCLUDE

In Chapter 13, you learn that `CFINCLUDE` *includes* another template in the current one and executes its code. But what exactly is the difference between *including* a template by using `CFINCLUDE` and `calling` a custom tag?

If you include a template by using `CFINCLUDE`, doing so is almost as if the code from the included page were just copied and pasted into the calling page. Any variables in the calling page are also available in the included page. The included page, therefore, can overwrite variables on the calling page, and no clear interface exists between the two.

If you call a custom tag, the variables in the calling page and the variables in the custom tag are defined in separate variable spaces, and if you use tag attributes, a clearly defined interface exists between the calling page and the custom tag. Figure 18-1 shows the difference between calling a page by using `CFINCLUDE` and calling it as a custom tag.

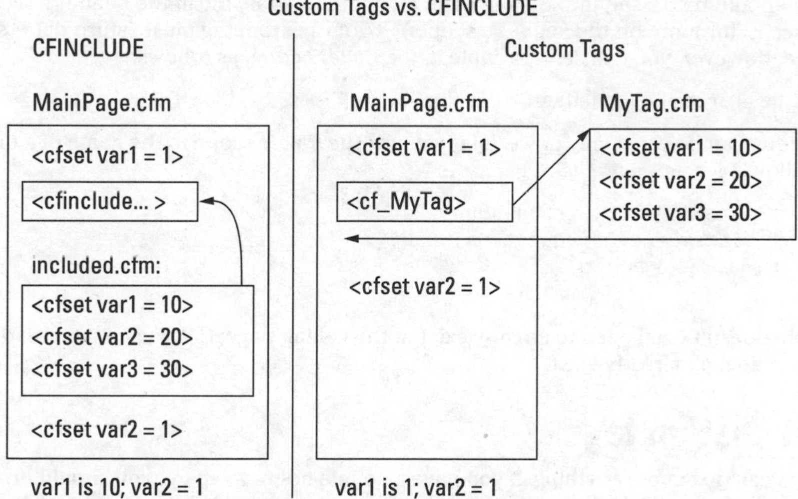

Figure 18-1: The difference between `CFINCLUDE` and a custom tag.

As you can see in the figure, the `CFSET` statements in the included page overwrite `var1` in the calling page, and the second `CFSET` in the calling page overwrites `var2` as set in the included page. On the other hand, none of the `CFSET` statements in the custom tag interfere with code on the calling page.

Using the Caller scope

You see in Listing 18-2 how to pass data from a calling page to a custom tag by using the `Attributes` scope; in this section, we show you how to return data from the custom tag back to the calling page.

All of the calling page's variables are available in the `Caller` *scope*, as shown in Listing 18-3, which shows a calling page, and Listing 18-4, which shows the custom that tag it calls.

Listing 18-3: `MyCallingPage.cfm`

```
<cfset myVar = 1>
<cf_MyCustomTag>
```

Listing 18-4: `MyCustomTag.cfm`

```
<cfoutput>#Caller.myVar#</cfoutput>
```

Usually, a custom tag should not read variables in the Caller scope; any data needed by the custom tag should be passed into the tag as an attribute or available in the `Request` scope. (See Chapter 12 for more on the `Request` scope.) If your custom tag must return data to the calling page, however, you can set a variable in the Caller scope, as follows:

```
<cfset Caller.myReturnedVar = "some value">
```

This technique can be especially powerful if you use the Caller scope in the name of a query, as in the following example:

```
<cfquery name="Caller.ReturnedQuery"
         datasource="#Request.MainDSN#">
...
</cfquery>
```

The variable doesn't even need to already exist in the calling page; ColdFusion automatically creates it if it doesn't already exist.

Uses of custom tags

Custom tags can do almost anything. If you have a couple hours to spare, you should browse the Macromedia Developer's Exchange at `http://devex.macromedia.com` to see what kinds of custom tags the developer community has created. Typically, custom tags create a kind of standalone *widget* on a page, similar to the employee list in Listing 18-2, earlier in this chapter. We can place the List widget anywhere on our page just by calling the custom tag as follows:

```
<html>
<head>
    <title>My Application</title>
</head>
```

```
<body>

<table>
<tr>
    <td>This is some page content.</td>
    <td><cf_EmployeeList CompanyID="#Client.CompanyID#"></td>
</tr>
</table>

</body>
</html>
```

Generally speaking, a custom tag should be some kind of user-interface widget. If your custom tag does not show user interface but, instead, does some kind of action that returns a result, you should consider migrating the custom tag into a user-defined function.

How custom tags have changed

Back in the days of ColdFusion 4, custom tags were the only way to extend CFML. You would, for example, sometimes find a custom tag such as `CF_AddTwo` (a fictional example), which includes the following:

```
<cfparam name="Attributes.FirstNumber">
<cfparam name="Attributes.SecondNumber">

<cfset Caller.TheSum = Attributes.FirstNumber +
Attributes.SecondNumber>
```

This was before the introduction of UDFs in ColdFusion 5. Now you can write `AddTwo` as a user-defined function (UDF), as follows:

```
function AddTwo(firstNumber, secondNumber) {
    return firstNumber + secondNumber;
}
```

Not only is it much easier to understand, but the UDF is also much more efficient. The only problem was that, in CF5, you couldn't use CFML tags in your user-defined functions, so you were still limited to using a custom tag if you needed to do database work.

ColdFusion MX adds the CFML function capability that you see in Chapter 17. Now you can call ColdFusion tags from your function, making functions much more powerful.

Modifying Content by Using Paired Custom Tags

You see how to pass attributes into custom tags. If you had a tag that took a single attribute, for example, you could call it as follows:

```
<cf_MyTag MyAttribute="some value">
```

But what if instead of passing `"some value"` to the custom tag, you want to pass the entire Gettysburg Address? Passing all that content in an attribute just isn't feasible. Instead, you can use a *paired tag*, as follows:

```
<cf_MyTag>
Four Score and Seven Years ago, our fathers...
</cf_MyTag>
```

Whenever ColdFusion sees a paired tag, it executes the tag once in `Start` mode, executes anything between the opening and closing tags, and then executes the custom tag again in `End` mode. This process may seem overly complicated, but perfect reasoning lies behind it, as you see throughout the rest of this chapter.

To see how paired tags are processed, look at Listing 18-5, which calls a paired custom tag, and Listing 18-6, the custom tag itself.

Listing 18-5: `MyCallingPage.cfm`, calling a paired tag

```
<cf_MyCustomTag>
This is the content between the tags.<br>
</cf_MyCustomTag>
```

Listing 18-6: `MyCustomTag.cfm`, differentiating between start and end modes

```
<cfif ThisTag.ExecutionMode EQ "Start">
    This is the Start mode of the custom tag.<br>
<cfelse>
    This is the End mode of the custom tag.<br>
</cfif>
```

Running Listing 18-6 produces the output shown in Figure 18-2.

This is the Start mode of the custom tag.
This is the content between the tags.
This is the End mode of the custom tag.

Figure 18-2: Calling a paired custom tag.

`MyCustomTag.cfm` can tell the difference between being in Start mode and End mode by testing the value of `ThisTag.ExecutionMode`, as shown in Listings 18-7 and 18-8.

Listing 18-7: `MyCallingPage.cfm`, passing attributes to a paired tag

```
<cf_MyCustomTag myAttr="MyValue">
This is the content between the tags.<br>
</cf_MyCustomTag>
```

Listing 18-8: `MyCustomTag.cfm`, using passed attributes in both Start and End modes

```
<cfif ThisTag.ExecutionMode EQ "Start">
    This is the Start mode of the custom tag. The value of myAttr is:
    <cfoutput>#Attributes.myAttr#</cfoutput><br>
<cfelse>
    This is the End mode of the custom tag. The value of myAttr is:
    <cfoutput>#Attributes.myAttr#</cfoutput><br>
</cfif>
```

Calling Listing 18-8 produces the output shown in Figure 18-3.

```
This is the Start mode of the custom tag. The value of myAttr is: MyValue
This is the content between the tags.
This is the End mode of the custom tag. The value of myAttr is: MyValue
```

Figure 18-3: Passing attributes to a paired custom tag.

The End mode has access to all the tag's attributes, even though you pass them only to the opening tag. In fact, most of your paired tag processing takes place in End mode, as you see throughout the rest of this chapter.

Getting content between the opening and closing tags

The most powerful feature of paired tags is their capability to gain access to and modify the content between the opening and closing tags. This content is available to the End mode as `ThisTag.GeneratedContent`, as shown in Listing 18-9.

Listing 18-9: `MyCustomTag.cfm`, using the content between the opening and closing tags

```
<cfif ThisTag.ExecutionMode EQ "Start">
    This is the Start mode of the custom tag.<br>
<cfelse>
    This is the End mode of the custom tag.<br>
    This was the content between the opening and closing tags:
    <cfoutput>#ThisTag.GeneratedContent#</cfoutput><br>
</cfif>
```

Calling Listing 18-9 produces the output shown in Figure 18-4.

```
This is the Start mode of the custom tag.
This is the content between the tags.
This is the End mode of the custom tag.
This was the content between the opening and closing tags: This is the content between the tags.
```

Figure 18-4: Outputting `ThisTag.GeneratedContent` in End mode.

Notice in the figure that the content between the opening and closing tags appears twice. If you want to make the content appear only after the end tag, you can clear the generated content, as shown in Listing 18-10.

Listing 18-10: `MyCustomTag.cfm`, clearing the content between the opening and closing tags

```
<cfif ThisTag.ExecutionMode EQ "Start">
    This is the Start mode of the custom tag.<br>
<cfelse>
    This is the End mode of the custom tag.<br>
    This was the content between the opening and closing tags:
    <cfoutput>#ThisTag.GeneratedContent#</cfoutput>
    <cfset ThisTag.GeneratedContent = "">
</cfif>
```

The preceding code may seem strange; after all, isn't the content between the tags generated *before* the end tag executes? It is a bit counter-intuitive, but it makes more sense after you start using paired tags in your own development.

What can or should a paired tag do?

In the section "Uses of custom tags," earlier in the chapter, we mention that simple, non-paired custom tags are best used for creating user interface widgets. Paired custom tags are different. Rather than creating widgets, paired tags are best suited to modifying, enhancing, or processing page content.

Listing 18-11 shows a custom tag that surrounds a block of text with a border, then truncates the text to the first 300 characters.

Listing 18-11: `FormatQuote.cfm`

```
<cfif ThisTag.ExecutionMode EQ "Start">
    <div style="border: 1px solid black;">
<cfelse>
    </div>

    <cfset ThisTag.GeneratedContent = Left(ThisTag.GeneratedContent,
300)>
</cfif>
```

The preceding code is a simple example, but it shows what paired tags are best used for: surrounding content with HTML and/or modifying the content in some way.

Listing 18-11 also shows an effective division of labor between the Start and End modes. The Start mode puts out the beginning of the HTML that surrounds the generated content, and the End mode puts out the ending HTML. In addition, the End mode modifies the tag's generated content.

The End mode almost always does more than the Start mode. In fact, in some custom tags, the Start mode does nothing. Usually this happens if the custom tag merely modifies the generated content rather than adding surrounding HTML.

How paired tags are executed

The hardest thing to understand about paired custom tags is the sequence of events in executing a paired custom tag. Commit the following sequence to memory, because it can save you hours of frustration:

1. The opening tag is executed. During this phase, the value of `ThisTag.ExecutionMode` equals `Start`. Use this phase to initialize any variables needed by your custom tag or to output text or HTML that should appear before any generated content.
2. The code between the opening and closing tags is executed, and any output is saved in a variable called `ThisTag.GeneratedContent`. Nothing is output to the page yet.
3. The ending tag is executed. During this phase, the value of `ThisTag.ExecutionMode` equals `End`, and the custom tag has access to all tag attributes as well as `ThisTag.GeneratedContent`. Keep in mind that nothing is output to the page yet.
4. After the ending tag is finished, `ThisTag.GeneratedContent` is output to the page. Then any content generated inside the ending tag (such as closing HTML markup tags) is output to the page. This is how the End mode can modify the generated content even though the content is already finished.

There is also a variable named `ThisTag.HasEndTag` that contains either `TRUE` or `FALSE` depending on whether or not a given tag has an ending tag. Consider checking this value in the `Start` mode to ensure that the developer doesn't forget the ending tag.

Creating tag families

One of the more powerful features of custom tags is the capability to create your own *families* of related tags. As an example, consider `CFFUNCTION` and `CFARGUMENT`. `CFFUNCTION` defines a user-defined function, and `CFARGUMENT` supplements `CFFUNCTION` by adding necessary functionality. The same idea applies to custom tag families. Listing 18-12 shows a family of related tags.

Listing 18-12: `TagCall.cfm`

```
<cf_OutputTable TableName="Employee" HeaderRowColor="EAFFFF">
    <cf_OutputColumn ColumnName="SSN" Label="SSN">
    <cf_OutputColumn ColumnName="FirstName" Label="First Name">
    <cf_OutputColumn ColumnName="LastName" Label="Last Name">
</cf_OutputTable>
```

`CF_OutputTable` queries the database and outputs a list of employees, making the header row a light blue color, and `CF_OutputColumn` describes the columns to be output to the page, as well as the columns' header labels. In this example, `CF_OutputTable` is a *parent* of `CF_OutputColumn`.

This is a good example of a tag family. A table is the natural parent of a column; `CF_OutputTable` thus becomes a natural parent for `CF_OutputColumn`. This is the crux of creating a family of custom tags. Don't try to enforce a hierarchy where one doesn't naturally exist; rather, consider only natural parent-child relationships as candidates for custom tag families.

The following sections builds these two tags from start to finish; the finished examples are available on the accompanying CD-ROM.

Associating a child tag with its parent

The most important thing to understand about nested tags is how parent and child tags communicate. A parent tag can gain access to a child tag's data, but that access is not automatic; a child must *associate* itself with the parent via `CFASSOCIATE`.

`CFASSOCIATE` saves a copy of the child tag's attributes inside the parent tag. The parent tag can then access these attributes during its End mode. `OutputColumn.cfm`, shown in Listing 18-13, outputs the header row for every column in the table by using the `Label` attribute that is passed into it.

Listing 18-13: `OutputColumn.cfm`

```
<cfparam name="Attributes.ColumnName">
<cfparam name="Attributes.Label" default="#Attributes.ColumnName#">

<cfassociate basetag="CF_OUTPUTTABLE">

<cfoutput>
<th>#Attributes.ColumnName#</th>
</cfoutput>
```

The `CFASSOCIATE` tag in Listing 18-13 tells ColdFusion to save `Attributes.ColumnName` inside of `CF_OutputTable`.

This leads us to the question of how these attributes are stored. Every call to `CFASSOCIATE` makes a new entry into an array named `ThisTag.AssocAttribs` in the parent tag. `OutputTable.cfm`'s End mode sees `ThisTag.AssocAttribs` as shown in Figure 18-5.

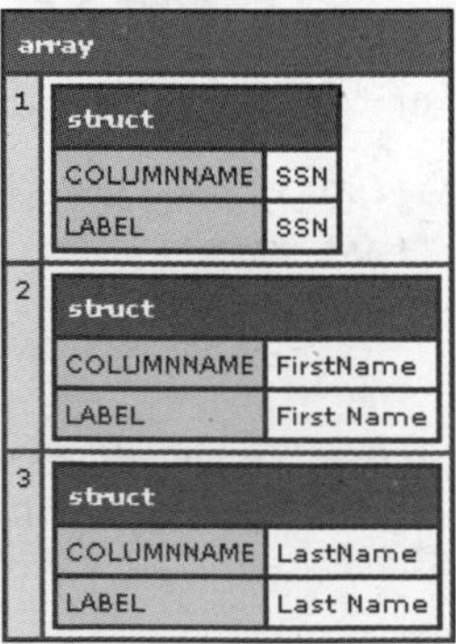

Figure 18-5: `ThisTag.AssocAttribs`, as seen by the End mode of `OutputTable.cfm`.

ThisTag.AssocAttribs is an array in which each element is a structure containing all the attributes of every child tag created by using CFASSOCIATE.

This is contrary to the ColdFusion Language Reference, which states that ThisTag.AssocAttribs is a structure rather than an array. ThisTag.AssocAttribs is indeed an array and cannot be used as a structure.

You can name this array a different name if you want by using the DataCollection attribute, as follows:

```
<cfassociate basetag="CF_MYTAG" datacollection="MySubTags">
```

You may want to do this if you have multiple child tags and want to keep each one's data separated as it is passed back to the parent tag. A child called CF_OutputColumn, for example, may store its attributes in an array called ThisTag.Columns, but another child called CF_OutputExpression may store its attributes in an array called ThisTag.Expressions.

Listing 18-14 shows how OutputTable.cfm uses ThisTag.AssocAttribs.

Listing 18-14: OutputTable.cfm

```
<cfparam name="Attributes.TableName">

<cfif ThisTag.ExecutionMode EQ "Start">

    <!--- I am in Start mode, so the only thing I can do is put out the
beginning table tag and the opening table row tag for the header row. I
won't know what columns are in use in this example until I enter the
End mode. --->
    <table>
    <tr>
<cfelse>
    <!--- I am now in End mode, so I now know all of the columns I'll
be selecting and outputting. --->

    <!--- The start mode opened the header row with a TR tag, so I have
to close it here. --->
    </tr>

    <!--- I dynamically build this query based on the contents of
ThisTag.AssocAttribs. --->
    <cfquery name="GetData"
            datasource="#Request.MainDSN#">
    SELECT
        <cfloop
            from="1"
            to="#ArrayLen(ThisTag.AssocAttribs)#"
            index="i">
        #ThisTag.AssocAttribs[i].ColumnName#
        <cfif i LT ArrayLen(ThisTag.AssocAttribs)>,</cfif>
        </cfloop>
```

Continued

Listing 18-14 *(continued)*

```
    FROM
        #Attributes.TableName#
    </cfquery>

    <cfoutput query="GetData">
    <tr>
        <!--- I output one table cell for each column in this
particular row of GetData. You will see how to simplify this later in
the chapter. --->
        <cfloop
            from="1"
            to="#ArrayLen(ThisTag.AssocAttribs)#"
            index="i">
        <td>
        #GetData[ThisTag.AssocAttribs[i].ColumnName][CurrentRow]#
        </td>
        </cfloop>
    </tr>
    </cfoutput>

    <!--- I now close the table --->
    </table>
</cfif>
```

Remember that `ThisTag.AssocAttribs` contains one element for every column in this query. We refer to each tag's `ColumnName` attribute by referring to each array element's `ColumnName` member.

Getting the parent to communicate with its child

You see in the preceding section how a parent tag accesses its associated child tags' data; in this section and the following one, you're going to see how a child tag accesses data from its parent tag.

In Listing 18-12, we pass an attribute to `CF_OutputTable` named `HeaderRowColor`. We output the header rows, however, inside each call to `CF_OutputColumn`. Listing 18-15 shows the modifications necessary to `OutputColumn.cfm` to make use of this parent attribute.

Listing 18-15: `OutputColumn.cfm`, using the `HeaderRowColor` attribute from the parent tag

```
<cfparam name="Attributes.ColumnName">
<cfparam name="Attributes.Label" default="#Attributes.ColumnName#">

<cfassociate basetag="CF_OUTPUTTABLE">

<cfset ParentData = GetBaseTagData("CF_OUTPUTTABLE")>
```

```
<cfoutput>
<td bgcolor="#ParentData.Attributes.HeaderRowColor#">
    <b>#Attributes.ColumnName#</b>
</td>
</cfoutput>
```

We call `GetBaseTagData()`, which returns a structure containing all variables defined in the parent tag, including any attributes. Then we reference `ParentData.Attributes.HeaderRowColor`, which gets the value of `Attributes.HeaderRowColor` that is passed into the parent tag.

And that's really all that using nested tags involves. The process may seem very complicated at first, but after you understand the mechanisms for communicating data between parent and child and between child and parent, you find a world of solutions waiting for you in nested custom tags. Play around with them to get comfortable; this truly is one of the coolest features of ColdFusion.

The difference between GetBaseTagData() and the Caller scope

A final note before we sign-off nested custom tags: Figure 18-6 describes the difference between the Caller scope and the structure returned from `GetBaseTagData()`. These two are often confused in people's minds, but they are very different. You rarely have any reason at all to use the Caller scope in a nested tag.

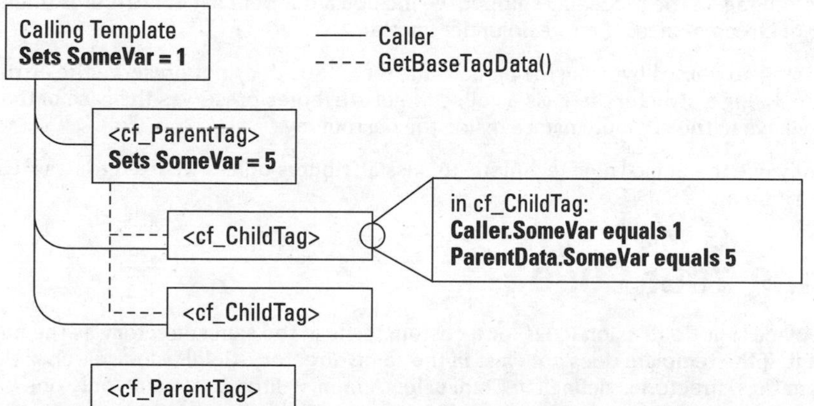

Figure 18-6: The difference between the Caller scope and `GetBaseTagData()`.

Notice that two totally separate values for `myVar` are set in the Caller scope versus `myVar` as set in the parent data. Keep this idea at the forefront of your mind in developing nested tags.

Passing Attributes

In the preceding sections of this chapter, you've seen us pass attributes in only one way: by defining them in the tag call as follows:

```
<cf_MyTag MyAttr="value">
```

You have another way, however, to pass `MyAttr` to `MyTag.cfm`, as the following example shows:

```
<cfset myStruct = StructNew()>
<cfset myStruct["MyAttr"]>
<cf_MyTag AttributeCollection="#myStruct#">
```

If you pass a structure in the `AttributeCollection` attribute of a custom tag, all the elements in that structure become attributes of the custom tag. You derive the following two benefits from using `AttributeCollection`:

✦ You can more easily pass dynamic sets of attributes into a custom tag, because you can use code as follows:

```
<cfset attrStruct = StructNew()>
<cfset attrStruct["Attr1"] = "value">
<cfset attrStruct["Attr2"] = "value2">

<cfif IsDefined("URL.CompanyID")>
    <cfset attrStruct["CompanyID"] = URL.CompanyID>
</cfif>


<cf_MyTag AttributeCollection="#attrStruct#">
```

A dynamic set is one where you don't know exactly what attributes are passed into the custom tag. In the preceding snippet, we include a different set of attributes under one set of circumstances than we do under another.

✦ Passing attributes by using the name-value technique does not preserve the attributes' case. Using a structure to pass a collection of attributes preserves the case of the structure keys in the attribute names inside the custom tag.

We typically use the name-value technique to pass attributes unless we need to pass dynamic sets of attributes.

Organizing Your Code

The first place that ColdFusion looks for a custom tag is in the same directory as the page that calls it. If the template does not exist in the same directory, ColdFusion searches through the custom-tags directories defined in ColdFusion Administrator. By default, only one is there — `C:\CFusionMX\CustomTags`. In addition to searching all the defined custom-tags directories, ColdFusion Server searches recursively through all subdirectories of the defined custom-tags directories.

As you can imagine, this searching takes time — time that you'd rather ColdFusion spend on executing your code rather than looking for it. `CFMODULE` enables you to tell ColdFusion exactly where the custom tag is and circumvent the searching process altogether, as follows:

```
<cf_MyTag>
<cfmodule template="MyTag.cfm">
```

CFMODULE points ColdFusion directly to the custom tag that you want to call. The best part is that, by using CFMODULE, you can call tags you couldn't using the CF_ syntax. You can, for example, point CFMODULE to a relative path, as in the following example:

```
<cfmodule template="../CustomTags/MyTag.cfm">
```

You can also point CFMODULE to a directory mapping created in ColdFusion Administrator, as follows:

```
<cfmodule template="/MyMapping/MyTag.cfm">
```

If your tag exists in one of the shared custom-tags directories declared in ColdFusion Administrator, you can use the name attribute instead of template, as follows:

```
<cfmodule name="MyTag">
```

If you are using a paired tag, you use </cfmodule> to close the tag pair, as follows:

```
<cfmodule template="MyTag.cfm">
Content between tags
</cfmodule>
```

A best practice is to have a single CustomTags directory at the root of your application directory and point all of your calls to CFMODULE there. Every template in your application, therefore, can access the tag library that you create for your application.

One caveat exists when using nested tags with CFMODULE. Try to spot the error in the following nested-tag hierarchy

```
<cfmodule template="OutputTable.cfm" TableName="Employee"
HeaderRowColor="EAFFFF">
    <cfmodule template="OutputColumn.cfm" ColumnName="SSN" Label="SSN">
    <cfmodule template="OutputColumn.cfm" ColumnName="FirstName"
Label="First Name">
    <cfmodule template="OutputColumn.cfm" ColumnName="LastName"
Label="Last Name">
</cfmodule>
```

It may not be immediately apparent, but the problem is with that ending CFMODULE: Which tag is it closing? Is it closing the call to OutputTable.cfm, or is it closing the last call to OutputColumn.cfm? ColdFusion Server would interpret it as closing OutputColumn.cfm, thus running the wrong template twice.

The way around this problem is to use the following shorthand closing syntax for the subtags, as shown in Chapter 3:

```
<cfmodule template="OutputTable.cfm" TableName="Employee"
HeaderRowColor="EAFFFF">
    <cfmodule template="OutputColumn.cfm" ColumnName="SSN"
Label="SSN"/>
    <cfmodule template="OutputColumn.cfm" ColumnName="FirstName"
Label="First Name"/>
    <cfmodule template="OutputColumn.cfm" ColumnName="LastName"
Label="Last Name"/>
</cfmodule>
```

But that's not all! Now that you're closing the subtags, all of them run twice. Now you must move all the code in OutputColumn.cfm into a CFIF test, as shown in Listing 18-16.

Listing 18-16: OutputColumn.cfm, taking into account the dual execution due to the shorthand closing syntax

```
<cfparam name="Attributes.ColumnName">
<cfparam name="Attributes.Label" default="#Attributes.ColumnName#">

<cfif ThisTag.ExecutionMode EQ "End">
    <cfassociate basetag="CF_OUTPUTTABLE">

    <cfset ParentData = GetBaseTagData("CF_OUTPUTTABLE")>

    <cfoutput>
    <td bgcolor="#ParentData.Attributes.HeaderRowColor#">
        <b>#Attributes.ColumnName#</b>
    </td>
    </cfoutput>
</cfif>
```

Using CFMODULE to call your custom tags may seem a lot of extra work, but in the long run, the increase in execution speed is well worth it.

Using the Request Scope

Variables within custom tags exist in their own variable space, and the only way to share data back and forth between the calling page and the custom tag is by using the Attributes and Caller scopes.

Request variables are available to all templates in a request, including custom tags, and are the best way to give custom tags access to global variables such as Request.MainDSN, Request.Username, and Request.Password.

You should generally restrict your use of Request-scope variables in your custom tags to global constants such as these. All other data needed by a custom tag should be passed to it via attributes.

Recursively Calling a Custom Tag

As can functions, custom tags can be called recursively. This is rare, however, and usually on an advanced scale, because recursion in custom tags is used differently than in user-defined functions. Because UDFs are more suited to making calculations, you find more numeric recursion in UDFs. On the other hand, recursion in custom tags is best suited for such procedures as recursing over structures or directory hierarchies, where the purpose is page output rather than returning single results from each recursive call.

Listing 18-17 shows a custom tag that takes a directory path and returns a listing of all the files and subfolders of that path. It uses recursion to list the contents of subdirectories as well.

Listing 18-17: ListDir.cfm

```
<cfparam name="Attributes.Directory">

<cfoutput>
#Attributes.Directory#\<br>
</cfoutput>

<cfdirectory action="LIST"
             directory="#Attributes.Directory#"
             name="GetFiles">

<cfloop query="GetFiles">
    <cfif GetFiles.Type EQ "Dir">
        <cfif GetFiles.Name NEQ "." AND GetFiles.Name NEQ "..">
            <cf_ListDir
directory="#Attributes.Directory#\#GetFiles.Name#">
        </cfif>
    <cfelse>
        <cfoutput>
        #Attributes.Directory#\#GetFiles.Name#<br>
        </cfoutput>
    </cfif>
</cfloop>
```

Note The `CFIF` test for `"GetFiles.Name NEQ "." AND GetFiles.Name NEQ "..""` is not necessary in ColdFusion MX, because MX no longer returns these values. We kept the test in this listing for backward compatibility with ColdFusion 5.

`ListDir.cfm` uses `CFDIRECTORY` to get all of the files and subfolders of the directory passed to the tag. It then loops over the list of files and directories and outputs every file that it finds. Whenever the loop encounters a directory, `ListDir.cfm` calls itself recursively, passing the name of the new directory. We called `ListDir.cfm` on our systems by using the following:

```
<cf_ListDir Directory="C:\inetpub\wwwroot\BibleExample">
```

Calling this tag produces what's shown in Figure 18-7.

```
C:\inetpub\wwwroot\BibleExample\
C:\inetpub\wwwroot\BibleExample\Application.cfm
C:\inetpub\wwwroot\BibleExample\Ch04\
C:\inetpub\wwwroot\BibleExample\Ch04\Listing 4-1.cfm
C:\inetpub\wwwroot\BibleExample\Ch04\Listing 4-3.cfm
C:\inetpub\wwwroot\BibleExample\Ch18\
C:\inetpub\wwwroot\BibleExample\Ch18\FirstOutputColumn.cfm
C:\inetpub\wwwroot\BibleExample\Ch18\FirstOutputTable.cfm
C:\inetpub\wwwroot\BibleExample\Ch18\index.cfm
C:\inetpub\wwwroot\BibleExample\Ch18\OutputColumn.cfm
C:\inetpub\wwwroot\BibleExample\Ch18\OutputTable.cfm
C:\inetpub\wwwroot\BibleExample\Ch33\
C:\inetpub\wwwroot\BibleExample\Ch33\Application.cfm
C:\inetpub\wwwroot\BibleExample\Ch33\Ch33.mdb
C:\inetpub\wwwroot\BibleExample\Ch33\index.cfm
C:\inetpub\wwwroot\BibleExample\Ch33\styles.css
```

Figure 18-7: Results of calling `ListDir.cfm`.

Exiting a Tag Before It is Finished

Chapter 13 mentions `CFABORT` as a way to immediately stop a request's execution. Inside a custom tag, you rarely want to end an entire request, but you may want to end the execution of the tag and return to the calling page.

A call to `CFEXIT` looks as follows:

```
<cfexit method="ExitTag">
```

You have the following three possible values for `method`:

- ✦ `ExitTag`: Resumes execution after the closing tag.
- ✦ `ExitTemplate`: Resumes execution after either the opening or closing tag, depending on where it's called.
- ✦ `Loop`: Re-executes the body of the custom tag.

Using the ExitTag method

`ExitTag` stops the current tag, meaning that execution continues after the closing tag (or the opening tag if you have no closing tag). Listings 18-18 and 18-19 show a custom tag and its calling page.

Listing 18-18: `MyTagCall.cfm`

```
<cf_MyTag>
This is the tag content.
</cf_MyTag>
This is content after the closing tag.
```

Listing 18-19: MyTag.cfm

```
<cfif ThisTag.ExecutionMode EQ "Start">
    This is the opening tag content.
    <cfexit method="ExitTag">
    This is content after the CFEXIT call.
<cfelse>
    This is the closing tag content.
</cfif>
```

Running `MyTagCall.cfm` produces the following:

```
This is the opening tag content.
This is content after the closing tag.
```

Calling `CFEXIT` immediately skips past the closing tag, so ColdFusion skips all the extra output in the tag and calling page.

Using the ExitTemplate method

`ExitTemplate` is similar to `ExitTag`; in fact, it's different only if you call it in the Start mode. Instead of exiting the *tag*, `ExitTag` skips past the end of the current *template*; in other words, calling `ExitTemplate` in the Start mode immediately begins executing the tag body. On the other hand, calling `ExitTemplate` in the End mode immediately ends the custom tag. Listing 18-20 modifies listing 18-19 to show this in action.

Listing 18-20: MyTag.cfm

```
<cfif ThisTag.ExecutionMode EQ "Start">
    This is the opening tag content.
    <cfexit method="ExitTemplate">
    This is content after the CFEXIT call.
<cfelse>
    This is the closing tag content.
</cfif>
```

Calling Listing 18-18 now shows the following output:

```
This is the opening tag content.
This is the tag content.
This is the closing tag content.
This is content after the closing tag.
```

`ExitTemplate` skips the end of the Start mode, but continues execution at the beginning of the body.

Using the Loop method

Loop is very different from ExitTag and ExitTemplate because Loop executes code that's already run. Rather than skipping past part of the tag, Loop re-executes the body of the custom tag. As such, it can be called only in the End mode of the custom tag.

Loop is used much less often than ExitTag or ExitTemplate and is almost exclusively used with nested tags. To demonstrate this method, you modify OutputTable and OutputColumn from Listings 18-14 and 18-15, earlier in the chapter.

The changes to these two tags require a change in the tag's architecture. In Listings 18-14 and 18-15, OutputTable.cfm did most of the work, and OutputColumn.cfm just defined the columns to select from the database and output the header row for the listing. The modifications that you're going to make in the following listings make OutputTable.cfm get the data from the database, but the work of outputting the data mostly falls on OutputColumn.cfm, which is a better division of labor.

Listings 18-21 and 18-22 show the modifications to OutputTable.cfm and OutputColumn.cfm.

Listing 18-21: OutputTable.cfm, modified to use CFEXIT Loop

```
<cfparam name="Attributes.TableName">

<cfif ThisTag.ExecutionMode EQ "Start">
    <table>
    <tr>

    <!--- Request.RowNumber contains the current row index of the
query. I start this value at zero, meaning that OutputColumn should put
out the header row. --->
    <cfset Request.RowNumber = 0>
<cfelse>

    <!--- The first thing I need to do in the closing tag is put out
the ending TR for the current row. --->
    </tr>

    <!--- I only want to perform the query once, so I check to see that
it was the header row that was just output. --->
    <cfif Request.RowNumber EQ 0>
        <!--- I dynamically build this query based on the contents of
ThisTag.AssocAttribs. --->
        <cfquery name="Request.GetData"
                datasource="#Request.MainDSN#">
        SELECT
            <cfloop
                from="1"
                to="#ArrayLen(ThisTag.AssocAttribs)#"
                index="i">
            #ThisTag.AssocAttribs[i].ColumnName#
            <cfif i LT ArrayLen(ThisTag.AssocAttribs)>,</cfif>
            </cfloop>
```

```
        FROM
            #Attributes.TableName#
        </cfquery>
    </cfif>

    <!--- I increment the current row number --->
    <cfset Request.RowNumber = Request.RowNumber + 1>

    <!--- If the new row number is still within the query's record
count, I begin a new table row and use CFEXIT Loop to re-execute the
body of the custom tag, meaning that the calls to CF_OutputColumn will
be re-run. --->
    <cfif Request.RowNumber LTE Request.GetData.RecordCount>
        <tr>
        <cfexit method="Loop">
    </cfif>

    </table>
</cfif>
```

Listing 18-22: `OutputColumn.cfm`, modified to output all the rows of the `Request.GetData` query

```
<cfparam name="Attributes.ColumnName">
<cfparam name="Attributes.Label" default="#Attributes.ColumnName#">

<cfassociate basetag="CF_OUTPUTTABLE">

<cfset ParentData = GetBaseTagData("CF_OUTPUTTABLE"))>

<!--- I must check to see which row to output. If Request.RowNumber is
zero, the query hasn't been run yet, so I output the header row.
Otherwise, I put out the value of the current cell in the
Request.GetData query. --->
<cfoutput>
<cfif Request.RowNumber EQ 0>
    <td bgcolor="#ParentData.Attributes.HeaderRowColor#">
        <b>#Attributes.Label#</b>
    </td>
<cfelse>
    <td>
        #Request.GetData[Attributes.ColumnName][Request.RowNumber]#
    </td>
</cfif>
</cfoutput>
```

Notice how these listings are using `Request` variables? You use `Request` variables to communicate back and forth between the parent tag's End mode and the nested child tags, which is another acceptable use of them. You can also do this by using `CFASSOCIATE` and `GetBaseTagData()`, but doing so would be more complicated.

Using the New CFIMPORT tag

ColdFusion MX gives you yet another way to call a custom tag. Instead of calling a tag by using `CF_` or `CFMODULE`, you can use `CFIMPORT` to *import* a library (meaning *directory*) of custom tags and use your own prefix, as in the following example:

```
<cfimport taglib="/CustomTags" prefix="MyTags">

<MyTags:MyCustomTag MyAttribute="some value">
```

This example calls `CFIMPORT`, which tells ColdFusion that every custom tag in the `/CustomTags` directory can be called by prefixing the name with `"MyTag:"` and then giving the name of the tag file without the extension. Think of `"MyTag:"` as a substitute for `CF_`. Attributes are passed in the same manner as with the standard custom-tag syntax.

You can still use paired tags with the custom prefixes as well, as follows:

```
<MyTags:FormatQuote>
This is the tag's body.
</MyTags:FormatQuote>
```

One caveat about `CFIMPORT` is that it defines custom prefixes only *for the template that calls CFIMPORT* and not for any included pages or custom tags. You also can't call `CFIMPORT` in `Application.cfm` and have the call propagate to all of your templates. You must call `CFIMPORT` on every page where you want to use a custom prefix.

You may be wondering why you would want to use this new syntax; after all, the earlier syntax works, and you don't have this business about calling `CFIMPORT` on every page where you want to use a custom tag. `CFIMPORT`, however, is not just for ColdFusion custom tags; in fact, its original purpose was to enable you to call JSP tag extensions from ColdFusion code. Getting used to using custom prefixes may be a good idea, because a number of markup language technologies use tag prefixes, and this use may become more standardized in the future.

Another benefit of tag prefixes is that they are the best of both worlds between `CFMODULE` and `CF_`. As does `CFMODULE`, they give you the capability to pinpoint the exact directory where the custom tags are located, but they give the simplicity of calling a tag by using `CF_` because you don't need to pass the tag path with every call. What's more, you don't need to use the shortcut tag-ending notation in using nested tags as you do in using `CFMODULE`.

Summary

In this chapter you learned how to use basic, paired, and nested custom tags, as well as how to pass attributes to custom tags using both name/value pairs and AttributeCollection. You also learned how to modify a page's generated content with paired tags, and you learned how to pass data back and forth between parent tags and child tags using nested tags.

Custom tags may seem simple at first: They enable you to extend the ColdFusion language with your own code, and they also enable you to use a familiar, tag-based syntax. Custom tags, however, involve much more than meets the eye. Paired custom tags and nested custom tags add levels of complexity that may seem daunting, but their capabilities are more than worth the challenge.

The techniques that you learn in this chapter run the gamut from basic custom tags to complex nested custom tags that use `CFEXIT` to loop over the tag body. You learn the different ways to pass attributes to a custom tag, and you also learn about all the different variable scopes that come into play in using a custom tag.

CHAPTER

Maintaining State

In This Chapter

Understanding *state* and *session*

Reviewing the various mechanisms that bind a browser to data from its previous requests

Storing Client variables

Exploring J2EE Session Management caveats

Building your application framework

You've probably used Client and Session variables before without giving them much thought. But have you ever considered how ColdFusion can tell one user's session from another? What about the mechanism that ColdFusion uses to bind the user's browser to the Client and Session variables stored in ColdFusion Server? This chapter answers all these questions about maintaining state—and more.

What is State Management?

State means remembering data from earlier requests. In other words, after a user clicks a link to go from Page A to Page B, Page B can *remember* Page A's data if state is maintained.

If state is "remembering data from earlier requests," a *session* is the period of time over which the server reminds a user's requests of data from his earlier requests. This session lasts as long as the user continuously uses the application—meaning that the user never takes longer between requests than a specified timeout. (More about session timeouts in the section, "Expiring a session after it times out," later in this chapter.)

State management is the mechanism by which ColdFusion binds a given user's browser to the data to be persisted across his requests. In a nutshell, the browser sends a unique ID to the server with each request that it makes, and the server uses that ID to retrieve the data associated with that browser's current and previous requests.

You may be wondering what this "browser ID" is. The format of the ID is explained in the section "Identifying a session by using `CFID` and `CFTOKEN`," later in this chapter, but for now, think of it as similar to a FedEx account number. The first time that you call FedEx to ship a package, the person whom you speak to asks you for your FedEx account number. If you don't have one, the person issues one to you. From that point forward, you give that account number to FedEx every time that you call to ship a package, and the person to whom you speak retrieves your account information based on the number that you provide.

In this analogy, you are the browser, FedEx is ColdFusion Server, and your account number is the browser ID. The key point to remember is that ColdFusion Server is the issuing authority of that ID—not you or your browser.

How ColdFusion Manages State

State management consists of two parts: identifying a session based on the browser ID and expiring the session after too much time passes between requests from a given user.

Identifying a session by using CFID and CFTOKEN

If you have used CFLOCATION before, you may have noticed that ColdFusion adds two URL parameters to the end of the URL that you specify in the tag. The *combination* of CFID and CFTOKEN together form the *browser ID* that we mention in the preceding section.

You may be wondering why ColdFusion uses two numbers instead of a single ID value. It's a precaution that makes guessing the complete browser ID harder for someone. CFID is a monotonically increasing number, so the first session on the server gets CFID 1, the next session gets CFID 2, and so on. You can probably imagine that if you were CFID number 1472, guessing that the session before you was CFID 1471 wouldn't be too hard, and impersonating session 1471 and possibly gaining access to private data would be easy for you.

That's where CFTOKEN comes in. CFTOKEN is an eight-digit random number that ColdFusion generates along with CFID and CFTOKEN. You can't predict the CFTOKEN as you can the CFID, so it adds an extra measure of security.

Ways of persisting CFID and CFTOKEN between requests

So how exactly are these CFID and CFTOKEN values persisted from request to request? In the following two ways:

- ✦ You can store CFID and CFTOKEN in a cookie on the user's browser. This cookie is sent back to ColdFusion with every request.
- ✦ You can pass CFID and CFTOKEN in the URL of every request. This overrides any value that may also be stored in a cookie.

All you need to do to set a cookie for CFID and CFTOKEN is set an attribute in your CF APPLICATION tag, as follows:

```
<cfapplication
    ...
    setclientcookies="Yes">
```

ColdFusion handles the setting and retrieving of CFID and CFTOKEN.

The problem with this automatic handling of CFID and CFTOKEN is that it requires that the user have cookies enabled. If the user has disabled cookies, you can't set client variables and make them last for more than one request — because ColdFusion can't see the cookie, it assumes that the user has not visited the site before and assigns a new CFID and CFTOKEN with each request.

If you want to set client variables even if users have cookies disabled, you must pass CFID and CFTOKEN as URL parameters in every URL in your site so that ColdFusion can see who you are, as the following code shows:

```
<a href="page.cfm?CFID=#Client.CFID#&CFTOKEN=#Client.CFID#">
```

Luckily, ColdFusion provides a shorter syntax, as follows:

```
<a href="page.cfm?#Client.URLToken#">
```

You also have a new syntax in ColdFusion MX that automatically chooses whether the page needs the URLToken appended to the end, as follows:

```
<a href="#URLSessionFormat('page.cfm')#">
```

If the user has cookies enabled, URLSessionFormat () returns the URL unmodified. If cookies are disabled, URLSessionFormat() automatically appends the CFID and CFTOKEN to the URL.

You do face certain issues in using URLSessionFormat() with J2EE sessions enabled. See the section "Using URLSessionFormat() with J2EE sessions enabled," later in this chapter, for more info.

In addition to hyperlinks, form posts also need the URLToken, as follows:

```
<form action="action.cfm?#Client.URLToken#" method="POST">
```

A form that uses the GET method, however, must CFID and CFTOKEN in hidden form fields, as follows:

```
<form action="action.cfm" method="GET">
<input type="hidden" name="CFID" value="#Client.CFID#">
<input type="hidden" name="CFTOKEN" value="#Client.CFTOKEN#">
</form>
```

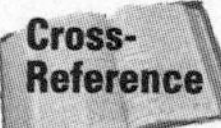

Hidden form fields, as well as forms in general, are discussed in Chapter 6.

The last method of passing CFID and CFTOKEN from one page to the next is somewhat hidden. CFLOCATION has a parameter named addtoken that defaults to Yes. If addtoken is Yes, CFLOCATION will append the CFID and CFTOKEN to the end of a URL, as in the following example:

```
<cflocation url="finished.cfm" addtoken="Yes">
```

By specifying addtoken="Yes", we told ColdFusion to redirect the user to the following URL:

```
finished.cfm?CFID=12345&CFTOKEN=12345678
```

Of course, ColdFusion would use the actual values of CFID and CFTOKEN when redirecting. Note that if you have not turned on Client variables in your CFAPPLICATION tag, addtoken="Yes" does nothing.

Using a UUID for CFTOKEN

Following are typical values for CFID and CFTOKEN:

```
CFID:     594
CFTOKEN: 15660220
```

As you can see, both values are relatively short. Anyone can access the session by using these CFID and CFTOKEN values by adding them to the URL, as follows:

```
http://server/template.cfm?CFID=594&CFTOKEN=15660220
```

Because the CFTOKEN value is a simple integer, this setup is rather insecure. You can, however, give the CFTOKEN an impossible-to-guess UUID (*U*niversally *U*nique *ID*entifier) value as shown in the following example:

```
CFID:     1606
CFTOKEN: 5dbd2148f73730cf-520DAB22-4762-3D9E-F63219AD42A329EC
```

To use a UUID for the CFTOKEN, choose Use UUID for CFTOKEN under the Settings section of ColdFusion Administrator. Notice that all users who currently have short CFTOKENs continue to have shortened CFTOKENs, but all new sessions have the UUID CFTOKEN values.

Expiring a session after it times out

In Chapter 12, you learn that session variables time out after a certain amount of time of the user's session remaining idle. Usually, that timeout is measured in minutes or hours. Client variables also time out after a period of inactivity, but the timeout for client variables is normally measured in days. (The default setting is 90, and it can be set as low as 1.)

You also learn in Chapter 12 that Client variables are typically better than Session variables because of the lack of locking constraints on Client variables, but giving up the Session scope's short, easy-to-use automatic timeout mechanism is difficult. Luckily, you have a way to time out Client variables before their normal, long-term purging period.

All you need to do is add the following snippet to your Application.cfm:

```
<cfif Now() - Client.LastVisit GT CreateTimeSpan(0,0,20,0)>
    <cfloop collection="#Client#" item="szVar">
        <cfif NOT
ListFindNoCase("cfid,cftoken,urltoken,lastvisit,hitcount,timecreated",
szVar)>
            <cfset StructDelete(Client, szVar)>
        </cfif>
    </cfloop>
</cfif>
```

That snippet gives all the Client variables in your application a 20-minute timeout, deleting only those Client variables that need to be timed out. To change the timeout, modify the parameters of CreateTimeSpan().

Storing Client Variables

Chapter 12 discusses Session and Client variables in detail, but the issue of exactly how Client variables are stored is outside the scope of that chapter. You may remember that Session variables are stored in memory, whereas Client variables are stored in a disk structure. The internal structure of the Session variables in memory is unimportant, but the options for storing Client variables deserve some discussion.

By default, ColdFusion stores Client variables in the Windows Registry. Figure 19-1 shows the format in which Client variables are stored:

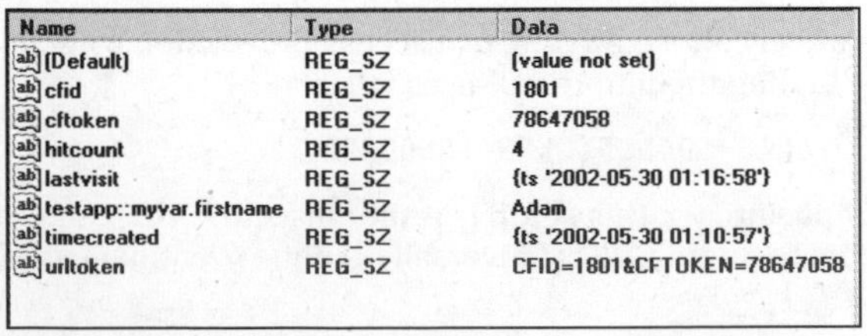

Name	Type	Data
(Default)	REG_SZ	(value not set)
cfid	REG_SZ	1801
cftoken	REG_SZ	78647058
hitcount	REG_SZ	4
lastvisit	REG_SZ	{ts '2002-05-30 01:16:58'}
testapp::myvar.firstname	REG_SZ	Adam
timecreated	REG_SZ	{ts '2002-05-30 01:10:57'}
urltoken	REG_SZ	CFID=1801&CFTOKEN=78647058

Figure 19-1: How Client variables are stored in the Windows Registry.

As you can see in the figure, all the Client variables assigned to a given session are stored under a key that takes its name from the CFID and CFTOKEN of a given session. The problem is that the Windows Registry was never intended as a high-speed data-storage and -retrieval system, and large numbers of consecutive accesses can affect a server's performance.

A better option is to store Client variables on a database server. This is slightly more involved than storing data in the Registry. You must first set up the database as one that ColdFusion can use for Client-variable storage. To do so, follow these steps:

1. In ColdFusion Administrator, set up a ColdFusion datasource in which to store client variables. (It should be an actual database server, such as Microsoft SQL Server or Oracle and not a file-based product such as Microsoft Access.)
2. Go to the Client Variables section of ColdFusion Administrator, choose the datasource that you just created, and click Add.
3. Give the datasource a meaningful description, leave all the check boxes in their default positions, and click Submit. Modify the check-box settings only if you're absolutely sure that you need to.

After following those steps, your database now contains two new tables: CDATA and CGLOBAL. CDATA contains the client variable data, and CGLOBAL contains global information for each session, such as the hit count and time of last visit.

To start using the Client variables database, you can do one of the following two things:

- ✦ Set the datasource as the default Client-variable storage option in ColdFusion Administrator. This is a good idea because none of your code must change to support it. This is not a good idea, however, if you run multiple Web sites with multiple Client-variable databases, because you may inadvertently store variables in the wrong place.
- ✦ Use the CFAPPLICATION tag as follows:

  ```
  <cfapplication
      ... clientstorage="MyDataSourceName">
  ```

  This is a better option in general, as it gives you more granular control over where your client variables are stored.

How ColdFusion Can Use J2EE to Maintain Sessions

In the section "Identifying a session by using CFID and CFTOKEN," earlier in this chapter, we describe CFID and CFTOKEN and how they're used. CFID and CFTOKEN are ColdFusion's native method of maintaining state. In ColdFusion MX, however, you have a new option: If you need to integrate your application with JSP or J2EE applications, you can use *J2EE session management*, which is the J2EE-standard mechanism for maintaining state. Instead of two values for CFID and CFTOKEN, J2EE session management issues a single JSESSIONID value that is highly random.

JSESSIONID works in much the same way that CFID and CFTOKEN do. If a request is made that has no JSESSIONID attached, ColdFusion generates a new JSESSIONID and stores it in a nonpersistent cookie on the user's browser. If the browser doesn't support cookies, you can pass JSESSIONID in the URL (with the restriction that it *must* be all uppercase), and ColdFusion uses the JSESSIONID from the URL to identify a user's session.

Notice that enabling J2EE Session Management now splits the state-management mechanism for Session and Client. Session variables now use JSESSIONID to identify the user's session, but Client variables still use CFID and CFTOKEN, because Client variables are not interoperable with JSP, as Session variables are. With J2EE session management enabled, CFML can share its Request, Session, and Application scopes with JSP and J2EE Servlet applications. You can't share Client variables with these non-ColdFusion applications, however, because J2EE doesn't use them.

To enable J2EE session management, log in to ColdFusion Administrator and go into the Memory Variables section. Select the Use J2EE Session Variables checkbox and click Submit. Restart both ColdFusion server and your Web server after enabling this option.

In the section "Ways of persisting CFID and CFTOKEN between requests," earlier in this chapter, we mention URLSessionFormat(), which automatically appends the CFID and CFTOKEN to a page's URL only if needed. You can also use URLSessionFormat() to add JSESSIONID to the URL if necessary. You do face a problem, however, in using URLSessionFormat() while J2EE sessions are enabled.

Normally, URLSessionFormat() creates a URL as follows:

```
http://127.0.0.1/page.cfm?CFID=2136&CFTOKEN=25334417
```

If J2EE sessions are enabled (and Client variables are disabled — more on this later in this section), however, URLSessionFormat() instead creates a URL similar to the following example:

```
http://127.0.0.1/page.cfm;JSESSIONID=8030379221028482598796
```

Notice that, instead of a question mark as in the first example, a semicolon introduces JSESSIONID. The semicolon is part of the J2EE Servlet standard, but Microsoft's Internet Information Server and Apache Web Server *may* not recognize the semicolon as valid. As such, attempting to use the URL from URLSessionFormat() if J2EE sessions are enabled may lead to a 404 File Not Found error if running against these incompatible Web servers.

Adding Client variables to the mix complicates the problem even more, as the following example shows:

```
http://127.0.0.1/page.cfm;JSESSIONID=8030990701028482815171?CFID=2148&C
FTOKEN=76305005&jsessionid=8030990701028482815171
```

Notice that the semicolon is still there before JSESSIONID but that the normal question mark that introduces the query string is appended *after* the JSESSIONID. Notice, too, that JSESSIONID is included twice, but the second version is lowercase, in violation of the J2EE standard. (However, because JSESSIONID appears in uppercase, ColdFusion knows what to do; it's just confusing to see.)

The best solution is to use URLSessionFormat() if your Web server supports a semicolon as the character that delimits the URL from its parameters; if not, append Session.URLToken to the page URL, as follows:

```
<a href="page.cfm?#UCase(Session.URLToken)#">...</a>
```

Why do we use UCase()? Unfortunately, the JSESSIONID parameter that's part of Session.URLToken is included as a lowercase parameter; J2EE, however, requires that JSESSIONID be included as uppercase. If you don't include the call to UCase(), state is not maintained between requests.

Building a Framework

One important detail of ColdFusion development that is often sadly overlooked is the application framework, which boils down to two parts: effective use of Application.cfm, OnRequestEnd.cfm, and the CFAPPLICATION tag.

Using Application.cfm and OnRequestEnd.cfm

One file that will exist in almost every ColdFusion application is Application.cfm. ColdFusion executes this file before every page request, making Application.cfm an excellent place to set variables that every page request can use, such as the name of your datasource, the database username and password, and other global constants. In addition, ColdFusion will also execute a template named OnRequestEnd.cfm *after* every page request, making OnRequestEnd.cfm an ideal place to put footer code for your site.

When you request a ColdFusion template, the first thing ColdFusion does is look for Application.cfm in the directory that contains the template you requested. If ColdFusion finds Application.cfm, the search stops and ColdFusion executes Application.cfm. If there is not an Application.cfm in the current directory, ColdFusion searches each directory in the requested template's path until ColdFusion finds a file named Application.cfm. For example, if you requested c:\inetpub\wwwroot\mydirectory\mytemplate.cfm, ColdFusion would search for Application.cfm in the following directories in this order:

```
c:\inetpub\wwwroot\mydirectory\
c:\inetpub\wwwroot\
c:\inetpub\
c:\
```

If ColdFusion doesn't find an Application.cfm anywhere in the requested template's directory hierarchy, ColdFusion simply executes the requested template.

When the requested template finishes, ColdFusion looks *in the same directory where it found Application.cfm* for a file named OnRequestEnd.cfm. If ColdFusion doesn't find OnRequestEnd.cfm in the same place as Application.cfm, ColdFusion simply ends the request. OnRequestEnd.cfm doesn't follow the same directory traversal process that Application.cfm does.

The problem is knowing where to put Application.cfm and OnRequestEnd.cfm. Some applications put an Application.cfm in every single directory in the application, whereas others don't include Application.cfm at all. The best practice lies somewhere in between these two extremes; I usually have only one Application.cfm at the root of the directory structure for my entire application. I will, however, add an Application.cfm anywhere that it's absolutely necessary, but I'm very careful to add an Application.cfm only where I have a compelling reason to do so.

What CFAPPLICATION does

CFAPPLICATION is the cornerstone of ColdFusion's application framework. Without CFAPPLICATION, you wouldn't be able to set Client, Session, or Application variables, and you wouldn't be able to maintain state because CFAPPLICATION is ColdFusion's mechanism for handling CFID and CFTOKEN. The state management aspects of CFAPPLICATION were mentioned in earlier sections of this chapter, but one attribute of CFAPPLICATION that is unfortunately often overlooked is the name attribute:

```
<cfapplication
    name="MyApp">
```

The name attribute of CFAPPLICATION partitions Application, Session, and Client variables into separate *application spaces*. If you call CFAPPLICATION with a name of MyApp in one request and a name of YourApp in another request, neither request will share the other's Application, Session, or Client variables because the two requests are in different application spaces.

The point is that all the CFAPPLICATION tags in your entire application should always reference the same application name. Some developers try to split the application into different parts, but don't do this. Splitting a single application into multiple application spaces backfires every time because the developer will invariably forget that templates in one application space use different Session variables than templates in another application space. Keep it simple and use only one application name for every request in your application.

Summary

In this chapter you learned how ColdFusion manages state using CFID, CFTOKEN, and possibly JSESSIONID. You also learned the different ways of persisting these values from one request to the next. Finally, you learned how Application.cfm and OnRequestEnd.cfm are found and included in every request, and how CFAPPLICATION creates the space for your application's variables.

State management encompasses a number of concepts that ColdFusion developers unfortunately tend to ignore. Most developers have an intrinsic understanding of state management (or at least think that they do), but that understanding often has flaws, and the new curve balls thrown by ColdFusion MX can certainly strain even the most seasoned ColdFusion developer's mastery of state management. The key to mastering state management is understanding the exact nature of the mechanism that binds a browser to data from its previous requests and the various caveats involved.

Form Validation

CHAPTER 20

✦ ✦ ✦ ✦

In This Chapter

When and why to use validation

Automatic validation on the server by using hidden form fields

Automatic validation on the client by using CFFORM and JavaScript

Hand-coded validation on the client by using JavaScript

qForms: A third-party solution for validation

Hand-coded validation on the server by using CFML

✦ ✦ ✦ ✦

You can't do much ColdFusion development before you begin creating forms that ask users for their input. An important question, however, is whether users are providing their input in the form that you're expecting? In this chapter, we introduce *form validation*, describing what it is and telling you when and why you need it and how to do it.

By *form validation*, we mean ensuring that the user's input meets some expected criteria. This can prove vital if the form's input is used to perform database updates. If the input values violate the database integrity or exceed a table column's size, for example, the update fails. You also want to prevent users from entering data that doesn't make sense — for example, trying to submit a login form without providing a user ID and password. Then comes the matter of validating any user ID and password that they do enter.

Each of these examples represents a type of form validation, and many more are possible. In this chapter, we explore several kinds of validations that you may want to perform, which should help you see why this is important; we also show you how to do it.

We show you two major types of validation: those that can occur on the client (primarily with JavaScript) and those that can occur on the server (within ColdFusion). And for each of these validation types, we show how ColdFusion provides mechanisms that can automate the validation process.

Still, such automatic processes aren't sufficient at times, and you need to hand-code a custom solution, either in the client or on the server. We show you how to do that as well and even describe some available third-party solutions, already coded for you.

Form validation is a very important — and too often overlooked — dimension to add to your arsenal as a Web-application developer.

When and Why to Use Validation

Even if you're an experienced ColdFusion developer, perhaps you've not carefully considered all aspects of form validation. Before skipping past this chapter because you "already know" about CF's form validation features, know that we're talking about more than just those features in this chapter. In particular, we cover some aspects of validation that may not be obvious just from knowing only about those CF features. Certain aspects of validation also may not be obvious, such as validating to ensure that the user hasn't skipped your form.

Before we discuss how to write forms and action pages to support validation, we first need to talk about the kinds of validations that you may want to perform. If you haven't given this subject careful thought, you may be surprised by the many possibilities that exist.

Don't let these discussions of JavaScript scare you off,either, because ColdFusion has mechansisms for creating that JavaScript code automatically.

And even if you're an experienced Web-application developer already familiar with the idea of validating your forms by using JavaScript, consider this fact: Some forms of validation simply can't be done on the client. Furthermore, if you think only in terms of validating *the form* rather than the *form data* passed to the server, you may run into problems that you're not anticipating and handling.

Some problems arise because the user comes to your form's action page without first going through the form. He may do so innocently (such as by having bookmarked the action page or simply typing in its URL). But some users may do so intentionally, even subversively, trying to avoid your form and pass in data to be processed by the action page. If you're validating only by using the form-based (client-side) processes that we introduce, you're leaving yourself exposed not only to errors, but also to possible exploitation.

You need to think carefully about what sort of problems can be created by a user providing unexpected input (or bypassing your form entirely). Some problems may be introduced simply by the user's mistake. Although a first line of defense is to simply take care in wording how your form prompts the user for input, you do need to be prepared in case a user's input either innocently or intentionally provides unexpected input. That's the role of form validation.

The following sections show you some actual validation code that you can use to prevent such situations.

Automatic Validation on the Server by Using Hidden Form Fields

ColdFusion was designed from the start as a Web-application development environment. As such, form validation was recognized early on as a fundamental need for most applications. Although, as you see later, you can perform any kind of validation on the server by using hand-coded programming, ColdFusion's creators recognized that certain basic validations would be very easy to automate, and they created a simple mechanism to perform those most basic validations.

As nifty as this automatic server-side validation may seem, it has its deficits. It's probably more trouble than it's worth. We address these problems later in this section. But because you may encounter it, it's worth understanding. And for small forms, its benefits may outweigh its deficits.

It's a simple idea, really. It enables you to place information on the form that identifies which form fields are to be validated and what validation should be done for each field. The validation then takes place automatically.

Say that you have a form field such as the following:

```
<input type="text" name="username">
```

This field prompts the user to enter his username, naturally, and may be used on a login screen, as shown in Figure 20-1. In such an application, you really need to require the user to enter a username; otherwise, the user can't log in. So this is a good opportunity for a "required" validation. Although we show a more effective client-side validation for this in the section "Adding validation by using CFINPUT," later in this chapter, you first need to see how to do it by using automatic server-side processing.

Figure 20-1: A sample login screen.

The hidden field "directive"

The way that this automatic server-side validation works is that you place a *hidden field* (as discussed in Chapter 6) on the form. This hidden field has the same name as the field to be validated, adding one of several predefined validation directives. In the example in the preceding section, to make the username required input, you would use the following code:

```
<input type="hidden" name="username_required">
```

Notice the validation directive, `required`, which is appended to the form's field name, with an underscore connecting them. This states that the field with the name `username` requires a value to be entered. That's all that you need to do. (You see later that you could use several other such directives.) The code for the form, with this added field (and one for a password as well), is as follows:

```
<form action="login_action.cfm" method="post">
   Enter your username and password:<br>
   Username: <input type="text" name="username"><br>
   <input type="Hidden" name="username_required">
   Password: <input type="text" name="password"><br>
   <input type="hidden" name="password_required">
   <input type="submit" value="Login">
</form>
```

Where you place the hidden field doesn't matter, as long as it's within the form containing the field to be validated.

Adding this hidden field makes no change at all to the appearance of the form that's displayed to the user, as shown in Figure 20-1. Hidden fields are just that—hidden.

If you use this specially formatted hidden field in the form, after it's submitted (if, of course, the action page for the form is a ColdFusion template), the username and password are validated to ensure that a value is entered in each field. Here is where ColdFusion performs its magic.

As we explain in a moment, for this validation to take place, the action page for the form must be a ColdFusion template, and more importantly, it must already exist. If you try to submit this form without an existing action page (in our case, `login_action.cfm`), you don't get a validation error but instead a `file not found` error.

Create a blank template called `login_action.cfm`. It need have no code in it at all. Of course, you add code to it later to perform the check to actually authenticate the user's login attempt. We explain why it must exist and be a ColdFusion template for the validation to take place.

Assuming that the action page has been created, if the user fails to provide a value, he receives the error shown in Figure 20-2.

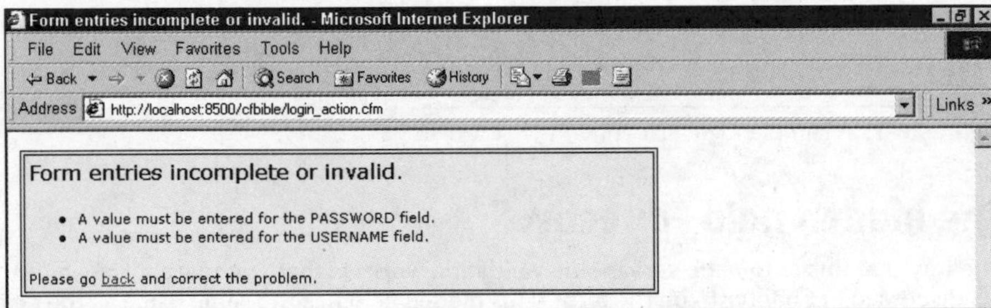

Figure 20-2: The validation error message for a "required" field.

Notice a couple important things: First, all you did was add a hidden field to the form. And you need to be clear on this fact: HTML has no native support for using a hidden field to perform validation this way. As far as the form is concerned, it's just another hidden field on the form. This really is a bit of magic that ColdFusion is performing.

Developers familiar with ColdFusion 5 and previous releases may notice that the look and feel of the validation error message has changed slightly, with the gray box surrounding the message and the available hyperlink to go `back` to the previous page. And the order that the messages appears is no longer the order in which they were defined.

What's going on, really?

So how does all this work? Well, look closely at the browser's URL line in Figure 20-2. Notice that it's the name of the action page. So this validation is really coming from the processing of the action page. That's why the action page must exist. But recall that, in our example, the action page is basically an empty file.

So where did all that text for the error message come from? That's the automatic aspect of this form of validation! ColdFusion created it for you. Simply because you sent a form field with a name that ended in `_required`, ColdFusion stepped in before processing the action page (if indeed any code was in the action-page template) and performed the validation for you.

That's why we say that the action page for the form must be a ColdFusion template.

Experienced developers may wonder why a CF template acting as an action page to this sort of validation can execute if it's empty (because we've not yet provided any code). Normally, CF would complain if you try to execute a template with zero length content, because the template's code isn't really executed if the validation fails. CF performs the validation before evaluating the action-page template itself, and if the validation triggers the validation error message, the rest of the action page is never evaluated. It could even have a compilation error in it, and CF wouldn't flag it as long as the validation message is triggered first!

The fact that all this validation magic happens with just a single hidden form field for each field that you're validating is pretty impressive. But in practice, certain aspects of the result may not be entirely satisfactory.

You need to get back to the validation error message that was automatically formatted for you. It tells the user what's wrong (for example, `A value must be entered for the USERNAME field`). Are you entirely happy with that result? And how about that simple black-on-white message display? Finally, it tells users to `Please go back and correct the problem`. Is that a good thing to recommend? We look at each of these issues in the following sections.

Improving the error message

Recall that the validation error message in Figure 20-2 read, `A value must be entered for the USERNAME field`. That happened automatically, and ColdFusion simply used the name of the form field that was being validated. It did uppercase the entire field name for us (we just used `username`), and the on-screen prompt does simply ask for USERNAME.

Although it's not really about validation per se, consider that some users may be confused by a prompt on-screen requesting their *Username*. Most computer people recognize that as a prompt for the user's authentication identifier, often called a *username* or *userid*. A user may possibly enter his real name (**bob** or **bob smith**) rather than what you were expecting (perhaps **bsmith**?). This raises the issues of usability and human factors that are beyond the scope of this discussion, but at a minimum, consider prompting users for their Login or LoginID.

Consider, too, that if you're developing an application from scratch, you may have better ways to uniquely identify a user than to force him to create and remember a contrived username. Perhaps the user's e-mail address would suffice, or an employee number if that's commonly known by all users of a corporate application. Of course, if this is leveraging the username of an enterprise security domain (see Chapter 40), prompting for that username or userid, however, it's known in that environment may make perfect sense.

But what if the form field name was something more obscure, such as *uname*? Users don't normally see form-field names (they see only the prompts you offer), and you may want to add this validation capability to an existing application where the developer wasn't as concerned about making the form-field name more descriptive. You certainly don't want to change the name of the form field just so that this validation message is more understandable, because then you would need to change all the variable names on the action page as well.

More important, maybe you'd simply rather have a friendlier tone to the error message, such as `Please provide your username`.

The good news is that you can solve both these problems, simply by providing an alternative message in the `value` attribute of the hidden field, as in the following example:

```
<input type="hidden" name="username_required"

value="Please provide your username.">
```

Now, as the form is validated, if the username is not provided, the user will receive our custom error message instead of ColdFusion's default error message.

There is a bug in ColdFusion MX where the custom error messages for required form fields are being ignored. This is a known issue with Macromedia and is scheduled to be fixed in their upcoming ColdFusion MX Updater 2, which should be available for download by the time this book is published.

Although the string provided for the `value` attribute can just be any wording that you want displayed, putting additional HTML within the string is also acceptable. Because it's simply passed through to the browser, you could, for example, use `<b>` or `<strong>` tags to add some more formatting to your error messages.

Improving the page appearance

Okay, so the `value` attribute enables you to improve the wording of the error message, as you learn in the preceding section, but what about the overall appearance of the screen in which it's offered? How does this message affect the overall appearance of your colorful application, with its pastel-blue body background and suitable text colors, to suddenly appear on-screen with its black Times Roman text on a white background?

And what about your site's navigational toolbar? If a user has questions about the error that appears, how can he find your Contact Us page? Users don't even see your standard footer with a link to the Webmaster. Suddenly, this nifty automatic tool doesn't look as useful as it did at first glance.

Indeed, many developers have simply abandoned it for this very reason. It's a problem that can be solved, however, at least to a greater degree than leaving the page in this plain black-on-white format. You can control the entire layout of the page (color, font, and so on) by using normal HTML tags. You can even place your navigational toolbars and other features right on the page.

The solution is to add to your code `CFERROR type="validation"`, which enables you to designate an error handling template of your own creation to format the appearance of just these validation errors. (It's still not a perfect solution, however, as we discuss in Chapter 21.)

The problem with backing up in the browser

The last of the three problems identified in the section above regarding the use of this automatic server-side validation may be the worst of all, and for many, it's reason enough to not even recommend the use of server-side automatic validation. The problem is that the process requires the user to "use the back button on your Web browser to return to the previous page and correct the listed problems." Is that a good thing to recommend? Probably not.

In some instances, doing so causes the information that was entered on the form to be lost! Imagine the frustration of a user spending a good bit of time filling out a registration form that's asking for several pieces of data. S/he submits it, is told that it contains an error (maybe just one mistake), and the user hits the Back button only to find that the form is cleared!

And you can do absolutely nothing about this problem. It's generally related to browser caching issues that aren't easily controlled.

You may be thinking that this isn't that big a deal anyway, because failing the required validation means that the user didn't enter anything for the required field in the first place, but consider that you may be asking for several fields of data, of which only one fails the validation. The issue isn't that serious if the prompt is just for username and password. But in a more complex form, it could indeed become a major problem. Just be sensitive to the challenge. Fortunately, alternatives exist in the client-side validation that we discuss later.

For now, you do have other kinds of validations that you can perform by using this automatic server-side validation. After you understand how the process works in general, you need to learn about the other directives, which we discuss in the following sections.

Other automatic server-side validations available

Besides the `_required` validation, several more provide some of the simple validations that we list in the section "Validating the format of input data," earlier in this chapter. Table 20-1 lists all the available validation directives.

Table 20-1: Automatic ColdFusion Server-Side Validations

Directive	*Description*
`_required`	Verifies that the user enters some value (for a text field), selects at least one check box (for a group of check-box fields), selects at least one button (in a radio-button group), or selects at least one option in a multiple-select control.†
`_integer`	Verifies that the user enters a number. If the user enters a floating-point value (with a decimal point), it is rounded to an integer.
`_float`	Verifies that the user enters a number. Does not do any rounding of floating-point values.
`_range`	Verifies that the numeric value entered is within boundaries specified in the `VALUE` attribute (see the following list).
`_date`	Verifies that a date is entered and also converts the date value into the correct ODBC date format. Accepts most common date forms – for example, 9/1/98 and Sept. 9, 1998.
`_eurodate`	Verifies that a date is entered in a standard European date format and converts into the correct ODBC date format.
`_time`	Verifies that a time is correctly entered and converts the time to the correct ODBC time format.

† Remember that a nonmultiple select control is always selected, so a required validation has no meaning for such a control.

As straightforward as these options may appear, you need to be aware of certain issues for most of them. Many of these issues revolve around the fact that, in addition to merely validating the data entered, the validation process also changes the data in some cases before it passes on to the action page—and in ways that may not be obvious nor expected, as the following list describes:

✦ `_integer`: If the number entered by the user contains commas or dollar signs, these characters are removed for the validation and are not passed to the action page. The documentation also says that it rounds the number entered if it includes decimal values, but in fact, it simply truncates them.

✦ `_float`: Removes commas and dollar signs the same way that `_integer` does, but also converts the number (as presented on the action page) so that it has six places after the decimal, filled with zeros.

✦ `_range`: Expects the range of values to be specified in the `value` attribute as `min=`*xxx* `max=`*yyy*, separated by a space. It also treats numbers the same as `_float` does (permitting decimal values and converting the number so that it has six places right of decimal, as well as removing commas and dollar signs).

  `_range` can also specify just one boundary. (But it must place a space after the number, as in `min=5 `. It can't state `min=5` with no space, at least prior to Version 5, as doing so would cause a severe bug.) Finally, because the range is specified in the `VALUE` attribute, you can't offer a customized message for a failed range validation.

✦ `_date`: Accepts a wide range of formats, such as 12/2/01, 12/2/2001, and even 12-2-01, 12/2, December 2, Dec 2, and so on. More important, it converts the date entered to an ODBC date format: 12/13/01 becomes `{d '2001-12-13'}`. This is fine if you're storing the value in an ODBC database (because it saves you the need to convert the date to that format), but if it's needed for display on an action page (or stored in a non-ODBC database), you need to convert it. Be aware of the `DateFormat()` function, which is available for use to convert the new version back to a regular date format. If the year is left off a date, this directive assumes the current year. If only a single number is entered, however (perhaps in intending a date in the current month), it doesn't work at all. This single number is rejected as an invalid date.

  `_date` does accepts European-format dates (day before month), if it's the only way that the date could possibly be valid: 13/12/01, therefore, is accepted and becomes `{d '2013-12-01'}`. Even so, using the `_eurodate` option is preferable to using just `_date` if your users are entering their dates in the European format. Oddly, if the value entered is either not a valid date (13/13/13) or not a date at all (*x*), the default message for both is simply: `The value entered for the` *`formfield`* `field ('`*`value`*`') is not correctly formatted`. Doesn't really convey that it needs to be a date, much less a valid one. This suggests that you really should provide a custom message.

✦ `_eurodate`: Shares all the facets of `_date`. The only difference is that the default format expected is the European order of day, followed by month (and then, optionally, year).

✦ `_time`: As does `_date`, this directive not only validates the time but also converts it to an ODBC time format: 1:12 becomes `{t '01:12:00'}`. As with `_date`, this conversion is fine if you're storing the data in an ODBC database (as it saves you the need to convert it to that format), but if it's needed for display on an action page (or is stored in a non-ODBC database), you need to convert it back by using the available `TimeFormat()` function.

_time accepts a/am/a.m. and p/pm/p.m. for a period designation. If the designation is left off, it assumes am. You also can enter just an hour and a period designator, such as 10am, which assumes that hour (10:00:00). If only a single number is entered without a period designator, however, perhaps because the user is intending to mean a time in the morning, that value is rejected as an invalid time. Strangely, if a date is entered, it accepts it, but coverts it to the value {t '00:00:00'}, meaning midnight. (Such a result may be logical but is not likely expected by most developers.)

A few other general issues apply to one or more of these server-side validations, as the following list describes:

✦ As demonstrated in the examples earlier in the chapter, where we were validating both the username and password fields, you can, of course, validate more than one field at a time in a form. You simply add a hidden-field tag for each field that you want to validate. The error message displayed reflects all the validation errors that occur.

✦ You can also specify more than one validation per field. To indicate that an Age field is both required and must be an integer, for example, you simply create two hidden-field tags named age_required and age_integer, respectively.

✦ Adding a validation rule to a field does not make it a required field. You need to add a separate _required hidden field if you want to ensure user entry.

✦ You may be worried about the effect on server-side processing time if it's always performing this validation. Any time lost is negligible, really, compared to more important performance-draining facets. (See Chapter 42 for examples.)

You do face one unfortunate issue, however, that you must always remain aware of: CF action pages always look at a form to determine whether it contains fields ending with the suffixes in Table 20-1. Furthermore, it then removes those fields from the list of form fields used in the database update tags CFINSERT and CFUPDATE.

This could cause a problem if you have such a field in your database as Joined_Date (meaning the date that a user joined your service). CF would see any form field containing that name (Joined_Date) as a validation for a "joined" field. Worse, because it would then remove that Joined_Date field before processing CFINSERT or CFUPDATE, you may find that the column is never inserted/updated.

Again, just be aware of the issue. It's often a source of very difficult-to-resolve bugs.

So that's a quick rundown of the automatic server-side validation. It's a feature that has its plusses and minuses. But an overriding concern should be that, because server-side validation forces the user to backup to correct any errors, it really should not be used if the form asks the user for more than a couple input fields. (And you see later that hand-coded server-side validation is used for other purposes entirely.)

Instead, if you need to validate several form fields, you can provide a much better user experience by using client-side validation, and the automatic features in CF make this quite easy to do, even if you don't know JavaScript.

Automatic Validation on the Client by Using CFForm and JavaScript

By *client-side validation*, we refer here to validation that takes place on the user's browser as it's processing the form, meaning that the page is not passed to the ColdFusion server to be processed (as happens with automatic server-side validation, as described in the preceding sections). Instead, the user sees a pop-up JavaScript message that indicates the problem (see Figure 20-3).

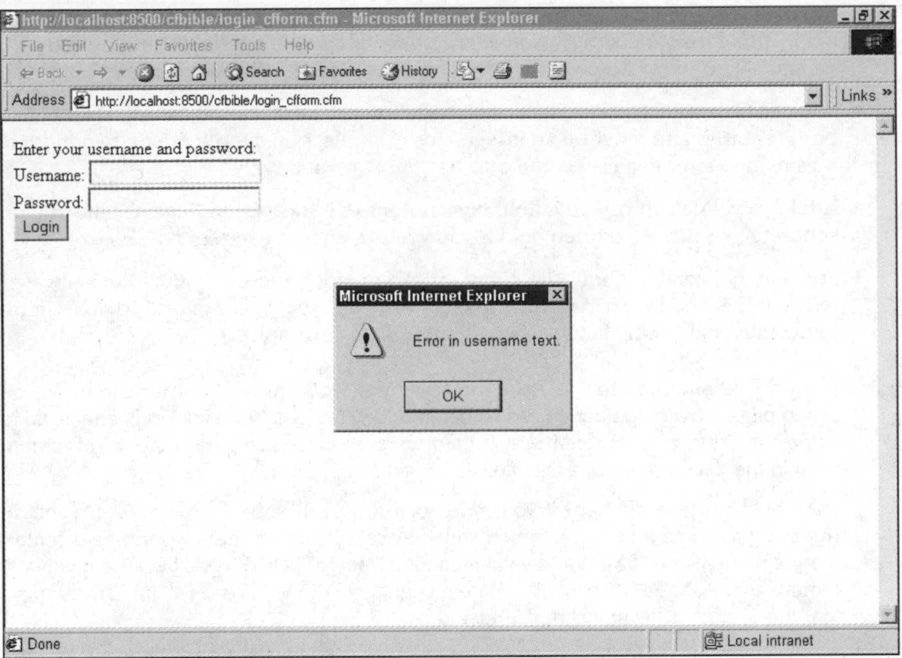

Figure 20-3: Validation message as a JavaScript pop-up.

The user can press the OK button and correct the problem immediately, without needing to back up to correct it (with the attendant problems that action can cause, as explained in the section "The problem with backing up the browser," earlier in this chapter).

But does this JavaScript pop-up concept scare you? Are you perhaps not familiar with JavaScript? Or worried about cross-browser script-support issues?

The great thing about CF's automatic client-side validation capability is that *it* creates the JavaScript for you to perform this validation and pop-up such messages. You, the programmer, don't need to understand or code any JavaScript at all. And the JavaScript that's created works even in older browser versions.

Introducing CFFORM

So how do you get the goods? You just need to make a couple minor changes to the form. Indeed, the first thing to do is to change the `FORM` tag itself to a `CFFORM` tag (and also change the closing /FORM tag to a closing /CFFORM tag). This tells ColdFusion that you are creating a form that leverages the validation capabilities that we're discussing here.

Note

CFFORM can also be used to introduce some enhanced interface features such as CFGRID, CFTREE, and others. These Java applet-based features are beyond the scope of this chapter's discussion about validation and are discussed further in Chapter 51. And although we also discuss a CFSELECT tag that does add some validation capabilities, the CFSELECT tag can be used without any validation to easily create drop-down lists (SELECT lists) based on ColdFusion Query results. Again, see Chapter 51 for more information.

The CFFORM tag is an interesting tag, compared to most other tags. It's clearly intended to be a replacement for the HTML FORM tag, but it adds extra functionality that was not part of the HTML specification. How can this work? How can CF cause a browser to do something that it (theoretically) can't do?

Well, what happens is that the ColdFusion turns the CFFORM tag back into a regular FORM tag, and then it also adds to the page the JavaScript code that's needed to perform whatever validation you've requested. And how do you request validation?

You have two kinds of tags for which you can add JavaScript validation, CFINPUT and CFSELECT. As does the CFFORM tag, these correspond directly to their INPUT and SELECT counterparts. So the first step in turning the login form at the beginning of the chapter into one that uses CF's built-in JavaScript validation is to simply change the FORM tag pair and INPUT tags into CFFORM tag pairs and CFINPUT tags, as follows:

```
<cfform action="login_action.cfm" method="post">
  Enter your username and password:<br>
  Username: <cfinput type="text" name="username"><br>
  <input type="hidden" name="username_required">
  Password: <cfinput type="text" name="password"><br>
  <input type="hidden" name="password_required">
  <input type="submit" value="Login">
</cfform>
```

If you look closely, you may notice that we've left in the hidden-field validation from the earlier example (in the section "The hidden field 'directive'," earlier in this chapter. Having both client- and server-side validation in a single form is perfectly fine. If for any reason the browser doesn't support the JavaScript to process the client-side validation that ColdFusion generates, the hidden-field validation can be there to back it up as the form is processed on the server.

Although you can keep the hidden fields in place within a CFFORM, you *must not* change the INPUT tags for those hidden fields to CFINPUT tags. Only INPUT tags that are not type="hidden" can be used with CFINPUT (including the type values "text", "checkbox", "radio", and "password".)

As this page is processed, what's sent to the browser is still the same form that appears in Figure 20-1. It really doesn't appear any differently at all. ColdFusion changes the CFFORM into a FORM tag and the CFINPUT into corresponding INPUT tags and adds some JavaScript code to perform any requested validation. But, of course, if you haven't yet requested any validation, to using the CFFORM and CFINPUT tags is not logical. As you step toward understanding the feature, however, understanding this characteristic is useful.

Adding validation by using CFINPUT

Just as with the automatic server-side (hidden-field) validation that we discuss, CFINPUT can be used to indicate either that a field is a required one (meaning that the user must enter a value), and/or it can indicate some particular kind of validation. Indeed, it not only shares most of the same validation types (_date, _time, _integer, _float, and so on), but it also adds additional validations (such as credit card, telephone, and more). We discuss those in a moment.

First, take a look at an example of adding required validation by using CFINPUT. It's different from the hidden-field approach, and yet it's more straightforward. Instead of adding a new field to the form, you simply add a new attribute-value pair to the tag. Indeed, for required validation, it's simply a matter of adding required="yes", as in the following example:

```
<cfinput type="text" name="username" required="yes">
```

In the example below, we would change both this field and the CFINPUT tag for the password prompt, giving us the following:

```
<cfform action="login_action.cfm" method="post">
   Enter your username and password:<br>
   Username: <cfinput type="text" name="username"
required="yes"><br>
   <input type="hidden" name="username_required">
   Password: <cfinput type="text" name="password"
required="yes"><br>
   <input type="hidden" name="password_required">
   <input type="submit" value="Login">
</cfform>
```

Notice that, because the space available [where?], the CFINPUT tags are each split across two lines in the preceding example. The required attribute is specified within the CFINPUT tag.

If this form is processed and submitted with no value entered for a username, the result is the JavaScript pop-up message shown back in Figure 20-3.

As a CF developer, you shouldn't worry about the JavaScript that's created, but if it interests you, simply use the View ➪ Source or View ➪ Page Source command from your browser's menu bar to display the generated HTML from your page. Whereas CF5 and earlier versions generated perhaps as many as 50 lines of JavaScript code that appeared at the top of the generated HTML, CF MX uses an embedded JavaScript file (using a <script src> tag for those familiar with it), which results in a less verbose script.

Improving the error message

As is the case with the hidden-field examples, you may also have noticed that the wording of the pop-up error message shown in Figure 20-3 may not be that helpful. Indeed, it's an even less friendly Error in username text. That's perhaps too terse. You can easily improve on it, which is as simple to do as adding the required validation itself (and, again, more straightforward than the hidden-field approach).

You can simply add a message attribute with a value that you want shown to the user. You can, for example, change the CFINPUT tag to the following:

```
<cfinput type="text" name="username" required="yes" message="Please
provide your username.">
```

Suppose that, in the example, we change this (and the password prompt) to reflect appropriate new wording. Then, if the user submits the form without providing a value in the Username field, the improved message shown in Figure 20-4 is shown.

That's better. Unlike with hidden-field validation, however, where you see both the username and password validation messages if both are left off, the JavaScript code that ColdFusion creates for `CFFORM` JavaScript validation (such as in the preceding example, enabled with `CFINPUT`) shows only one message at a time.

Some may find this outcome less desirable, but it's a limitation that's not easily avoided. We discuss some possibilities in a moment. For now, just be aware of the behavior. At least one big improvement is that the user remains on the form while addressing these validation issues, as opposed to what happens in server-side validation, where they need to use the Back button to return to the form (and risk losing form data).

You may also recall that the wording of the error message in the `value` attribute in the hidden-field approach can include HTML tags (such as `<b>` or `<strong>`) to help the formatting. Because the wording in the `message` attribute of `CFINPUT` is simply passed fore processing as a JavaScript pop-up message, it definitely *cannot* contain HTML tags. They are not processed. Indeed, the tags themselves would just appear as part of the message. Don't use HTML in the messages that you indicate for this type of client-side validation.

On the other hand, something that you can do to perhaps improve the appearance of these messages is to add JavaScript string-control characters. The `\n` character, for example, indicates that you want to show a line break or split the message into two lines. The message=`"This is line1\nThis is line 2"`, for example, displays two lines within the JavaScript pop-up message. This can be handy for improving the formatting.

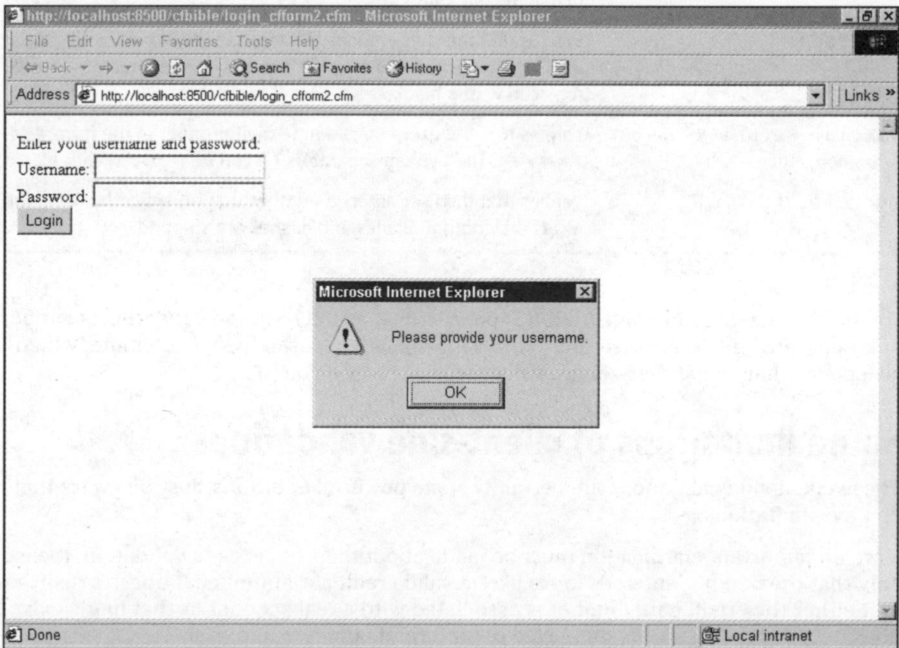

Figure 20-4: An improved JavaScript validation message.

Other automatic server-side validations available

As we mention in the section "Other automatic server-side validations available," earlier in this chapter, you have several other forms of validation that you can use besides _required. The means of specifying these CFINPUT is also easier than the hidden-field approach. Just as the CFINPUT adds a new message attribute to make that easy to specify, it also adds a validate attribute to make the data-type validations easy to apply.

To add validation to ensure that the user enters a valid date, for example, you add validate="date" to your CFINPUT tag. Table 20-2 provides a list of all the possible validations that you can use.

Table 20-2: Automatic ColdFusion Client-Side Validations

Directive	*Description*
integer	Verifies that the user enters a number without decimal points.
float	Verifies that the user enters a number, with or without decimal points.
date	Verifies that the user enters a date in the format *mm/dd/yyyy*.
eurodate	Verifies that the user enters a valid European date in the format *dd/mm/yyyy*.
time	Verifies that the user enters a time in the format *hh:mm:ss*.
telephone	Verifies that the user enters a telephone number. Telephone data must be entered as ###-###-####. The hyphen separator (-) can be replaced with a blank. The area code and exchange must begin with a digit between 1 and 9.
zipcode	Verifies that the user enters a U.S. zip code of either five digits, or nine digits in the form #####-####. The hyphen separator (-) can be replaced with a blank.
social_security_number	Verifies that the user enters a nine-digit number in the form ###-##-####. The hyphen separators (-) can be replaced with blanks.
creditcard	Verifies that the user enters a number that is verified by using the Luhn Mod10 algorithm. Blanks and dashes are stripped.

You may notice that no range option is offered. Just as the required validation is supported by a separate required attribute, CFINPUT also has a separate range attribute, which accepts a minimum and maximum value, separated by a comma.

Some limitations of client-side validations

These client-side validations are certainly some powerful additions. Just be aware that they do have limitations.

First, an important clarification must be made about the creditcard validation. It ensures only that the number entered "looks like" a valid credit card number. It doesn't really ensure that either the credit card number is associated with a real account or that funds exist! But it does do more than look for some kind of pattern of numbers and dashes.

Indeed, the number is validated against an algorithm (called the `Luhn Mod 10` algorithm) which is used to create all valid credit card numbers. The goal of that algorithm is to help with this very sort of validation check: If a number can't pass this check, it obviously can't be a real credit card—and, therefore, it saves the merchant (you) and the processing service the effort of trying to make a charge on a number that can't possibly be valid.

Note To determine whether a credit card number offered is indeed a valid account with funds, you would need to pass the credit card number to a card-processing service. Several such services are available for Web merchants. That subject, however, is beyond the scope of this chapter.

Another challenge is that the `telephone`, `zipcode`, and `social_security_number` validations are very U.S.-centric. Postal codes in other countries often use a combination of letters and numbers. And their phone numbers almost certainly may vary from the format expected in the description in the preceding table. With this `zipcode` validation in place, for example, users with postal codes that include characters or aren't in five-digit or five+four-digit format couldn't pass the validation. You could lose a customer! The only way to solve this problem is not to do any validation for such data or possibly use hand-coded client- or server-side validation, if appropriate, as we discuss in the section "Validating CFINPUT by using regular expressions," later in this chapter.

Even within the U.S., however, the facts that the telephone validation requires users to enter an area code and that they can't use parentheses around the area code may also cause confusion and hassle for unexpecting users. You must provide clarification of the expected format in the prompt that you show on-screen, in the error message that you offer them, or in both.

A new alternative solution for solving these problems exists, where the built-in validations aren't quite as flexible as you need. The following section discusses this new CF 5 feature.

One other issue to be aware of is that the `_required` validation doesn't work correctly if a blank value (literally, a blank space) is entered. In other words, this passes the validation, so be aware of that. You may want to solve this by keeping the automatic server-side `_required` validation in place (which doesn't permit a space to pass). You can also solve the problem by using either hand-coded client- or server-side validation, as we discuss in the section "Validating CFINPUT by using regular expressions," later in this chapter.

Finally, consider how the hidden-field validation process converts certain data values entered, in addition to validating them (such as the `_integer` validation's rounding off of decimal values and the `_date` validation's converting the value to an ODBC date format). The `CFINPUT` validation, on the other hand, does *not* perform any such conversions. Data is passed to the action page just as it's entered, assuming that it passes the validation.

Validating CFINPUT by using regular expressions

We mention a couple of examples below where the built-in validations are a little too restrictive in that they expect input to follow a predefined pattern that may not quite meet your needs. Wouldn't you like to just tell ColdFusion what sort of validation pattern you expect the input to follow?

Of course, if you want to hand-code your own JavaScript (which we cover in the section "Hand-coded Validation on the Client by Using JavaScript," later in this chapter), you can certainly do that. The process of describing a pattern with which to match a string often involves using something called *regular expressions*. This is a language of its own that is supported in many languages, including JavaScript and CFML.

But what if you want to use regular expressions without understanding how to hand-code JavaScript? The good news is that, as of CF 5, you *can* now create a JavaScript regular expression validation in `CFINPUT`. You don't need to code any JavaScript; just indicate the appropriate regular expression (`regexp`). By using the new ColdFusion option `validate="regular_expression"`, you provide the `regexp` in a `pattern="regexp_string"` attribute.

You can, for example, permit a more flexible specification of an expected phone number, indicating that you'd be willing to accept either an area code or not, with parentheses surrounding it or not, with the area code separated from the rest of the number by a space or not, and with a space or a dash or nothing between the exchange (the next three numbers) and the last four numbers. Without explaining how the regular expression works, we offer the following lines of code to provide the desired pattern and validation:

```
<cfform action="actionpage.cfm">
Phone: <cfinput type="text" name="phone"
validate="regular_expression"
pattern="^(\(?[1-9]\d{2}\)?)?\s?[1-9]\d{2}[\s\-]?\d{4}$"
message="Phone is improperly formatted">
<input type="submit">
</cfform>
```

This code also ensures that the first number of the area code and exchange does not start with `0`, which is another current requirement for U.S. phone numbers. Admittedly, this is a very U.S.-centric validation. It does serve as a good launching point for validation of other phone number patterns.

Before leaving this subject, perhaps you noticed that neither the automatic client- nor server-side validations provide support for checking e-mail addresses. This regular-expression approach can also be used to check e-mails. Here's a code sample for that purpose:

```
<cfform action="actionpage.cfm">
Email: <cfinput type="text" name="email"
validate="regular_expression"
pattern="^([_a-z0-9-]+(\.[_a-z0-9-]+)*@[a-z0-9-]+(\.[a-z0-9-]+)*\.(([a-
z]{2,3})|(aero|coop|info|museum|name)))?$"
message="Email is improperly formatted">
<input type="submit">
</cfform>
```

This does a little more than some may expect. Yes, it does look for an address in the generally expected format of *`someone@somedomain.sometld`*, so `carehart@systemanage.com` would work while `carehart@systemanagecom` would not. Some aspects, however, may surprise some of you.

The code doesn't catch the e-mail address, for example, if the user types `carehart@systemanage.co` (leaving off the `m` in `.com`). The pattern permits two- or three-character top-level domain (TLD) names (to allow for international domains such as `.ca` and `.au`.) And those who look closely at the pattern may be surprised to see the list of other possible TLD values: `.aero`, `.coop`, `.info`, `.museum`, `.name`. These are the newer top-level domain names that were created recently by the Internic. Still others are possible, but they're either two or three characters (such as `.tv`).

CFSELECT validation

The preceding sections on CFFORM and automatic client-side validation have focused on CFINPUT. That's not the only tag, however, that can be used inside CFFORM to perform JavaScript validation. Just as CFINPUT is a replacement for the INPUT tag, the available CFSELECT tag is an alternative that enables you to add validation to a SELECT control (a drop-down list). The only available validation is the required attribute (as used in CFINPUT). As we mention in our discussion of automatic server-side validation, using required validation for a CFSELECT that's not also using the multiple attribute doesn't make much sense. Otherwise, a value is always selected and the validation can never fail to pass.

Alternative JavaScript processing

You should be aware of a means by which to cause alternative processing of the errors that arise from validation failures on CFINPUT and CFSELECT by using the onerror attribute. This attribute names a JavaScript function that you can write to process the validation error.

The CFINPUT tag also offers an onvalidate attribute, which can be used to perform alternative validation detection (in which case, the validate attribute is ignored).

The CFFORM tag itself also offers an alternative onsubmit attribute, which can name a JavaScript function that is processed after the validation passes but before the form is finally submitted to the action page.

Hand-Coded Validation on the Client by Using JavaScript

Although the automatic client-side validation provided by ColdFusion is very simple to use, we've identified a few limitations. Still other forms of validation are available that you may want to perform that are not supported either by HTML forms or by CFFORM. In such cases, you must hand-code that validation. You can do the validation either on the client (in JavaScript) or on the server (in CFML). Admittedly, coding JavaScript isn't a trivial matter, and understanding it fully is beyond the scope of this book.

To learn more about JavaScript, you can check out a couple excellent resources. One is *The JavaScript Bible* by Danny Goodman, from Wiley (formerly IDG Books Worldwide, Inc.). Another is *JavaScript: The Definitive Guide*, by David Flanagan, from O'Reilly. For a simpler introduction to incorporating JavaScript into your ColdFusion pages, see the June 2000 CFDJ article, "Getting Focus(ed) – And a Quick JavaScript Overview," by Charlie Arehart.

Although we have no room to explain JavaScript coding in depth, at least a few ideas are worth considering here. The first is also very easy to add without much JavaScript knowledge.

Testing the length of a TEXTAREA field

Have you ever wanted to limit the length of data that someone can enter in a field created by the HTML TEXTAREA tag? As opposed to the INPUT tag, which permits only a single line of data to be entered, the TEXTAREA tag enables users to input long, multi-paragraph text.

But what if the input of that TEXTAREA is passed (in the action page) to a SQL INSERT or UPDATE statement that places that data into a database with column definitions of a limited length? If you don't test to ensure that the user's data fits in that specified size, the INSERT or UPDATE fails.

Unfortunately, whereas the INPUT tag has a maxlength attribute, in HTML, you have no way to limit the length of a TEXTAREA field.

This is a surprisingly easy test to add, however, if you know the appropriate JavaScript. Again, we have no space to explain this procedure in detail, but assume that you have a TEXTAREA field such as the following:

```
<textarea name="description" rows="10" cols="50"
   wrap="virtual">
</textarea>
```

To add a test for length, you have a couple of choices, but perhaps the simplest to explain is to leverage the available onchange attribute. This attribute can be used to specify some JavaScript (right inside the value of the attribute) that is executed whenever the user changes the value of the TEXTAREA field. This is an appropriate solution to our problem.

To add the test for length, you simply need to know the JavaScript code for referring to the value of the field and for testing its length against some maximum number. Even without knowing JavaScript, you can easily use this as a model. To add a test to the preceding example, change the example as follows:

```
<textarea name="description" rows="10" cols="50"
   wrap="virtual"
   ONCHANGE="if (this.value.length > 2000) {
   alert('Description must be limited to 2000 chars.')};">
</textarea>
```

This code will display a JavaScript alert box when the user types over 2,000 characters. You can easily add this code to your own examples. Just copy the entire onchange attribute and its value, changing the length value (2000 in the preceding example) to whatever maximum that you want.

Of course, the message should be changed as well to reflect whatever on-screen prompt the field has for the user. You'd change the string inside the quotes after alert. (Just be careful not to split the string over multiple lines. JavaScript does not permit strings to be split that way.

Other hand-coded client-side validations that you may consider

Some other validations where you may consider using this approach are also possible. Some of them may take more effort to understand the JavaScript to make them happen. Again, contact either of the excellent books that we point out in the preceding Note to learn more about applying the language this way. You may, for example, consider testing the following:

✦ Whether the two values entered for a password and password confirmation field are the same.

✦ Whether, in a SELECT control, a choice was made other than a Select One option that may have been placed at the top of the list to guide the user. (Something that could prevent submission or force assignment of some default value.)

✦ Whether a date entered is in the past or future, as you want it.

Consider carefully other possibilities that may exist in your application to test for.

The possibilities expand if you also consider that, with ColdFusion generating the HTML (and JavaScript) that's sent to the browser, you can also create validations on the client that are based on comparisons with data that's sent from the server. This is an interesting, but clearly intermediate, challenge.

Of course, many of these examples of testing can be performed on the server side as well. But performing validation on the client can be so much more effective in providing a good experience for a user.

qForms: A Third-Party Solution for Validation

Before we conclude this chapter with a section on server-side validation in CFML, however, you need to know about one other form of client-side validation. It's not a built-in feature of ColdFusion, but it is something written by a member of the ColdFusion community, Dan Switzer of PengoWorks. Best of all, it's free (and open source).

We're referring to *qForms*, which is available at the PengoWorks Web site, at `www.pengoworks.com/index.cfm?action=qForms`, and which is also on the CD accompanying this book. The very simple installation process not only provides the tool, but also excellent examples and documentation. Just run through the examples to see the sort of things that are possible.

We have no room to explain the use of qForms in detail, but know that it can perform many useful tasks in processing forms, including more effective error messaging. Just by adding a few lines of simple JavaScript and pointing to a provided Cascading Stylesheet file, qForms can perform many of the same validations (indeed, more) but adds more power and finesse to the process.

In addition to providing a JavaScript pop-up such as the one that CF MX offers, for example, qForms can also provide color-coded indications of the specific fields on the page that are in error. The included examples easily demonstrate this. Other features include the option to perform validations on leaving each field (rather than on submitting the form).

qForms can also permit different parts of the form to be validated based on other data entered on the form, can enable you to change `SELECT` values based on choices made in another `SELECT` control, and lots more—again, all for free!

Hand-Coded Validation on the Server by Using CFML

The final form of validation that we cover in this chapter is hand-coded validation that takes place on the server—in other words, coding CFML to perform validation, such as on a form's action page. This type of validation is an important alternative for several reasons, including the following:

✦ It enables you to perform additional validations (which are not available otherwise).

✦ It enables you to performing data processing/integrity checks.

✦ It enables you to back up client-side validation.

Performing additional validations

Occasionally, the built-in automatic validations (client- and server-side) of ColdFusion may fail to meet some need that you have. In that case, if you must code a manual solution, you are probably more comfortable coding in CFML than in JavaScript.

If you following the explanations elsewhere in this book about how to perform conditional tests, how to process form fields, and how to use certain important functions, this type of validation is pretty straightforward. Indeed, Chapter 6 shows the basics of validating form input to perform SQL processing.

Just be aware that having the user perform validation on the client clearly has value (and, indeed, value in terms of reduced processing resources on your server).

Performing data processing/integrity checks

You may perform still other forms of validation in your form action page by using CFML. Again, some of these are covered in other chapters and may not be thought of strictly as validation, although to a degree they really are. These include such procedures as the following:

- ✦ Checking a username/password combination on logging in.
- ✦ Validating that the quantity on hand for an order is still available (before processing an order from a form submission).
- ✦ Ensuring that expected URL, Session, or other variables exist on the page before proceeding.
- ✦ Checking any URL or `FORM` variable values used as input to SQL clauses to ensure that no strings other than those expected are processed. (See the `CFQUERYPARAM` tag in chapter 52.)

Some other validations of form entries may relate more to the relationship between one entry on the form and another. You may, for example, want to validate that the following situations are true:

- ✦ If one check box is selected, another other can't be selected.
- ✦ If one `SELECT` option is chosen, some other field can't be (or must be) chosen.

The section "qForms: A Third-Party Solution for Validation," earlier in this chapter, shows that it has features to perform that sort of validation on the client, but you may want to back that processing up on the server in case the browser doesn't support JavaScript. Indeed, this leads to the last reason to consider some sort of hand-coded server-side validation.

Backing up client-side validation

For all the power and effectiveness of client-side validation, it can possibly be bypassed.

The browser may not support JavaScript, for example, or it may not support the particular JavaScript that you (or ColdFusion) provides. Maybe you don't think that you need to worry about old browsers such as that.

Something that may surprise many, however, is that some organizations (and individuals) choose to disable JavaScript support in their browsers because of security concerns. If they disable it, whatever nifty validation you've got on the client (whether hand-coded or automatic) doesn't matter. The validation can't take place. In such a case, the capability to perform server-side validation becomes especially important.

Indeed, this suggests very strongly that performing hand-coded server-side validation to back up whatever client-side validation you may be performing is in your interest.

Of course, one may argue that the automatic server-side validation that we discuss at the beginning of the chapter, should serve as an adequate backup for that sort of situation. But can you think of why that may still not be enough? When may your form's action page be executed without the form being processed at all?

What if the user bookmarks the action page (or types in its URL) to visit it directly? Or what if he uses something such as CFHTTP, which we discuss in Chapter 31 and is available on other application servers with similar capabilities?

Such a user could intentionally try to process your form's action page by sending a real form posting but not really executing your form. In that case, the user could also remove any client-side validation or hidden-field validation that you placed there. In these days of security concerns and hacking, you need to take such issues into consideration.

Even if such an effort isn't with the intent to do harm, if the client-side validations that you have in place are intended to prevent database errors because of invalid input. Recall the `TEXTAREA` maxlength test from the section "Testing the length of a TEXTAREA field," earlier in this chapter: If validation wasn't performed on the client (and backed up on the server), the user may experience unexpected database errors.

Summary

In this chapter, we describe two major forms of validation — those that take place on the client (in JavaScript) and those that take place on the server (in CFML). We also show you that ColdFusion MX includes mechanisms to automatically handle both forms of validation. The *hidden-field* capability offers automatic server-side validation (although, of course, the specification is sent to the client but is processed on the server). It enables you to test for certain expected data types and string formats, but the appearance of the error message and the need for the user to press the Back button to correct mistakes (and possibly lose data because of browser caching features) make this type of validation less desirable for all but the simplest forms.

Client-side validation, by using JavaScript, offers several advantages. The nice thing about `CFFORM` and its associated `CFINPUT` and `CFSELECT` tags is that they cause CF MX to automatically build JavaScript for you. They also add validations for things such as credit cards, telephone numbers, and zip codes. These last two follow only U.S. formats, however, and have some other limitations, so we explain how the new CF 5 feature of supporting *regular-expression* patterns in `CFINPUT` gives you much more freedom and capability (at the cost of learning how to write regular expressions).

Creating such validations on your own leads naturally to a discussion of performing your own hand-coded client- and server-side validation. In each case, the cost is simply the effort of creating the language constructs and algorithms (in JavaScript or CFML, respectively) to perform the needed validation. Finally, you learn that you may want to back up the client-side validation by using server-side validation, even though such a course may seem redundant, to support those situations in which the client-side validation is bypassed either because of lack of JavaScript support in the browser or by intentional (or unintentional) bypassing of the form.

✦ ✦ ✦

Handling Exceptions

In This Chapter

Understanding the structured exception handling framework

Handling errors as exceptions to normal execution

Rethrowing caught exceptions as errors

Throwing custom errors

Designing a collection of error handling templates

The site-wide error handler

Exception handling boils down to a single question: "What do you do if something occurs out of the ordinary?" If your database throws an error because you input bad data, exception handling determines how your system reacts. If CFHTTP throws an error because it can't connect to a remote system, exception handling enables you to gracefully recover. No ColdFusion application is complete without at least some plan for how to handle exceptions.

This chapter shows you the many things that you can do with exception handling, as well as how to pull these techniques together into a consolidated framework that enables your application to gracefully recover from almost any error.

What Is Structured Exception Handling?

If an error occurs in your ColdFusion code, it normally stops page execution and outputs the standard ColdFusion error page, which shows what happened and where, as shown in Figure 21-1.

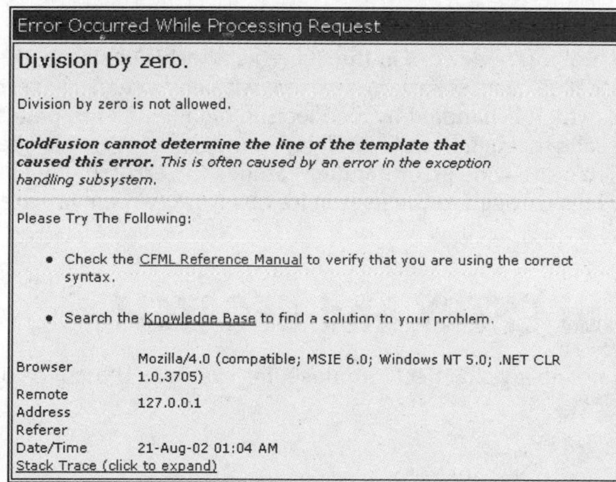

Figure 21-1: The standard ColdFusion error page.

Structured exception handling enables you to *catch* the error before the user sees it and do something different, depending on the circumstances of the error.

Whenever something goes wrong in your application, it throws an *error*. You can choose to leave this error as is so that the user can see it, or you can catch the error and handle it yourself. You catch errors so that you can handle them as *exceptions* to the normal execution of a request. This is the essence of exception handling.

The *structured* part of structured exception handling refers to the natural structure of ColdFusion's exception framework, as shown in Figure 21-2.

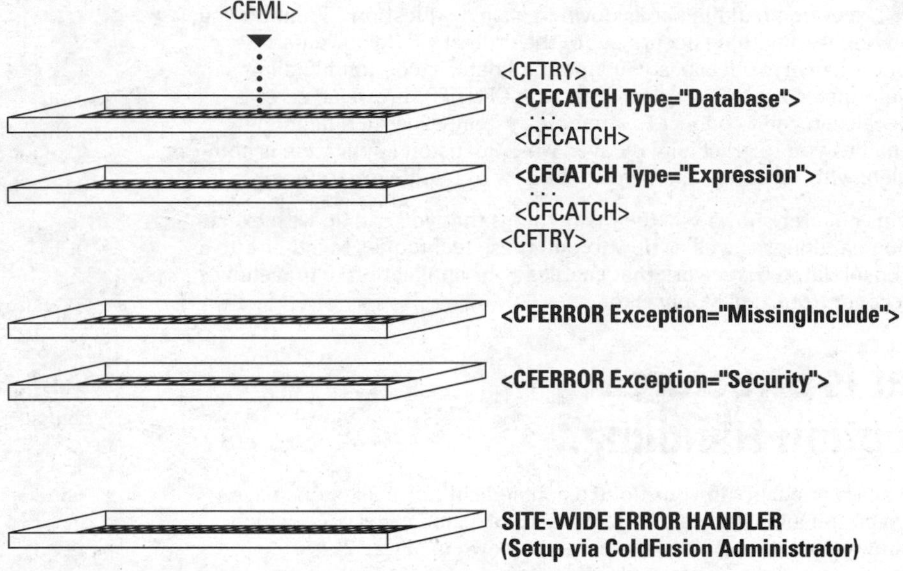

Figure 21-2: ColdFusion's structured exception handling model.

Notice that we depict the error-handling framework in the figure as a series of sieves, in which the top level of sieves (`CFCATCH`) catches *expected* errors, with any *unexpected* errors "falling through" to the next level, which is handled by a collection of `CFERROR` templates that handle specific errors. If an error falls through the `CFERROR` layer, or if no `CFERROR` is specified to handle the error, ColdFusion's site-wide error handler catches the error. If you have no site-wide error handler, the error falls through to the user in its raw form (which you are probably all too familiar with, eh?).

Catching an Error with CFTRY and CFCATCH

Structured exception handling is not always in effect. Suppose, for example, that an error occurs with the following code:

```
<cfquery name="MyQuery"
        datasource="#Request.MainDSN#">
...
</cfquery>
```

The error is not caught, because structured exception handling is not yet in effect, and the user sees the standard error message. Before you can catch the error, you must tell ColdFusion to try to catch an error:

```
<cftry>
<cfquery name="MyQuery"
         datasource="#Request.MainDSN#">
...
</cfquery>

<cfcatch type="Any">
    <!--- Handle the error --->
</cfcatch>
</cftry>
```

CFTRY tells ColdFusion to watch the enclosed block of code for errors, and CFCATCH tells ColdFusion what to do if an error occurs. CFCATCH type="Any" tells ColdFusion that any error causes execution to pass to the code within that specific CFCATCH block.

Types of catch handlers

CFCATCH takes a single attribute named type, which specifies the type of error that is caught. If you want to catch only database errors, for example, you can use the following code:

```
<cftry>
<cfquery name="MyQuery"
         datasource="#Request.MainDSN#">
...
</cfquery>

<cfcatch type="Database">
    <!--- Only database errors cause this code to be run --->
</cfcatch>
</cftry>
```

If you use this CFTRY/CFCATCH construct, all database errors are caught and handled by the code within the CFCATCH tag pair, and all nondatabase errors fall through to the next level in your application's structured exception-handling framework.

ColdFusion's built-in exception types are as described in Table 21-1.

Table 21-1: Basic ColdFusion Exception Types

Name	*Description*
Application	Usually thrown as a custom error, but also catches errors arising from attempting to call a component that does not exist or from calling a component method if the user does not have the correct roles for the method.
Database	Catches any error thrown by a database call. Does not catch errors related to missing ColdFusion variables used in a CFQUERY; only those errors thrown *by the database* cause this error type. Database is the most common error type.

Continued

Table 21-1: *(continued)*

Name	*Description*
`Security`	Catches errors arising from Sandbox Security violations. Does not catch errors from `CFLOGIN` or its related tags and functions. Sandbox Security is defined by using ColdFusion Administrator; see Chapter 44 for more information.
`Object`	Catches errors arising from invalid calls to COM, CORBA, or Java objects. Errors that occur while calling component or Web service objects throw the `Application` type.
`MissingInclude`	Catches any error from a `CFINCLUDE` or `CFMODULE` call where the specified template does not exist or cannot be found. Calling a custom tag with `CF_` or the `name` attribute of `CFMODULE` does not throw this error, but throws an `Expression` error instead. (In ColdFusion 5, a missing custom tag threw an error of type `UNKNOWN`, which no longer exists in ColdFusion MX.)
`Template`	The difference between `MissingInclude` errors and `Template` errors is sometimes difficult to understand because they appear to be the same thing. A `Template CFCATCH` block also catches a `MissingInclude` error. The `Template` type is actually an internal error type used by the ColdFusion page compiler, and `MissingInclude` is a subset of the `Template` type. The only way to catch a `Template` error that is not also a `MissingInclude` is to `CFINCLUDE` a page that contains a compile-time error. See the sidebar "Why can't I catch certain errors?," later in this chapter, for more information.
`Expression`	Catches any error from an invalid expression, including divide-by-zero errors. Also catches errors from trying to use a variable that doesn't exist. Also catches missing template errors if you're using `CF_` or the `Name` attribute of `CFMODULE`.
`Lock`	Catches errors from `CFLOCK`; either the lock cannot be created or the lock timed out. Note that `CFLOCK` only throws an error if its `ThrowOnTimeout` attribute is set to `Yes`.
`SearchEngine`	Catches any errors occurring with the `CFSEARCH`, `CFINDEX`, or `CFCOLLECTION` tags. ColdFusion 5 did not have a `SearchEngine` type; it used type `UNKNOWN`.
`Any`	Catches any ColdFusion error, regardless of source.

In addition to the basic ColdFusion types in Table 21-1, you have a large number of very specific advanced exception types.

- `COM.Allaire.ColdFusion.CFEXECUTE.OutputError`
- `COM.Allaire.ColdFusion.CFEXECUTE.Timeout`
- `COM.Allaire.ColdFusion.FileException`
- `COM.Allaire.ColdFusion.HTTPAccepted`
- `COM.Allaire.ColdFusion.HTTPAuthFailure`
- `COM.Allaire.ColdFusion.HTTPBadGateway`
- `COM.Allaire.ColdFusion.HTTPBadRequest`
- `COM.Allaire.ColdFusion.HTTPCFHTTPRequestEntityTooLarge`

- COM.Allaire.ColdFusion.HTTPCGIValueNotPassed
- COM.Allaire.ColdFusion.HTTPConflict
- COM.Allaire.ColdFusion.HTTPConnectionTimeout
- COM.Allaire.ColdFusion.HTTPContentLengthRequired
- COM.Allaire.ColdFusion.HTTPContinue
- COM.Allaire.ColdFusion.HTTPCookieValueNotPassed
- COM.Allaire.ColdFusion.HTTPCreated
- COM.Allaire.ColdFusion.HTTPFailure
- COM.Allaire.ColdFusion.HTTPFileInvalidPath
- COM.Allaire.ColdFusion.HTTPFileNotFound
- COM.Allaire.ColdFusion.HTTPFileNotPassed
- COM.Allaire.ColdFusion.HTTPFileNotRenderable
- COM.Allaire.ColdFusion.HTTPForbidden
- COM.Allaire.ColdFusion.HTTPGatewayTimeout
- COM.Allaire.ColdFusion.HTTPGone
- COM.Allaire.ColdFusion.HTTPMethodNotAllowed
- COM.Allaire.ColdFusion.HTTPMovedPermanently
- COM.Allaire.ColdFusion.HTTPMovedTemporarily
- COM.Allaire.ColdFusion.HTTPMultipleChoices
- COM.Allaire.ColdFusion.HTTPNoContent
- COM.Allaire.ColdFusion.HTTPNonAuthoritativeInfo
- COM.Allaire.ColdFusion.HTTPNotAcceptable
- COM.Allaire.ColdFusion.HTTPNotFound
- COM.Allaire.ColdFusion.HTTPNotImplemented
- COM.Allaire.ColdFusion.HTTPNotModified
- COM.Allaire.ColdFusion.HTTPPartialContent
- COM.Allaire.ColdFusion.HTTPPaymentRequired
- COM.Allaire.ColdFusion.HTTPPreconditionFailed
- COM.Allaire.ColdFusion.HTTPProxyAuthenticationRequired
- COM.Allaire.ColdFusion.HTTPRequestURITooLarge
- COM.Allaire.ColdFusion.HTTPResetContent
- COM.Allaire.ColdFusion.HTTPSeeOther
- COM.Allaire.ColdFusion.HTTPServerError
- COM.Allaire.ColdFusion.HTTPServiceUnavailable

- COM.Allaire.ColdFusion.HTTPSwitchingProtocols
- COM.Allaire.ColdFusion.HTTPUnsupportedMediaType
- COM.Allaire.ColdFusion.HTTPUrlValueNotPassed
- COM.Allaire.ColdFusion.HTTPUseProxy
- COM.Allaire.ColdFusion.HTTPVersionNotSupported
- COM.Allaire.ColdFusion.POPAuthFailure
- COM.Allaire.ColdFusion.POPConnectionFailure
- COM.Allaire.ColdFusion.POPDeleteError
- COM.Allaire.ColdFusion.Request.Timeout
- COM.Allaire.ColdFusion.SERVLETJRunError

By specifying an advanced exception type as the argument to CFCATCH's type attribute, you can catch and handle very specific errors that occur outside the boundaries of ColdFusion Server.

The point of having this many error types is that your structured exception handling can granularly respond to each type in a specific way. You could, for example, have an exception handler that catches two different types and handles them two different ways, as follows:

```
<cftry>
... Code to execute goes here ...

<cfcatch type="Database">
   A database error occurred.
</cfcatch>
<cfcatch type="Expression">
   An expression error occurred
</cfcatch>
</cftry>
```

The preceding example catches either a Database error or an Expression error and outputs a different message depending on which one. If the error is not a Database or Expression error, the error is not caught and the user sees the standard message output.

CFCATCH type="Any" cannot catch one kind of error. Specifically, type="Any" catches any error deriving from the Java class java.lang.Exception. type="Any" does not, however, catch errors deriving from java.lang.Throwable. To catch these errors, you must define a special CFCATCH, as follows:

```
<cftry>
...
<cfcatch type="java.lang.Throwable">
...
</cfcatch>
</cftry>
```

You rarely encounter this type because none of the standard ColdFusion features throw this type of error.

Why Can't I Catch Certain Errors?

You may be surprised to learn that that you can't catch certain errors at all. The following code, for example, throws an error regardless of the CFTRY surrounding the bad code:

```
<cftry>
<cfset>

<cfcatch type="Any">
An error occurred!
</cfcatch>
</cftry>
```

The CFSET has no content, so ColdFusion throws an error stating, `Invalid CFML Construct Found on line 9 at column 7`. This result may seem strange, however, because you have a CFTRY and `CFCATCH type="Any"`. The problem here is that the bad CFSET created a *compile-time error*, which can't be caught with CFCATCH. CFCATCH can catch only a *run-time error*, which occurs during the execution of the template. In the case of the preceding snippet, ColdFusion couldn't successfully parse and compile the page, so the exception handling didn't take effect.

If you were to CFINCLUDE a page with a compile-time error, the calling page could catch a Template type error. This is rare, and you should be careful not to rely on exception handling to catch compile-time errors.

What can I do if an error occurs?

The short answer is anything! You can handle an error any way that you see fit, from ignoring it completely to examining it in fine detail, to rerouting the user to an alternative template. You usually do one of two things, however. Either redirect the user to a different page or display a user-friendly message telling him what happened.

You can follow either of two philosophies in redirecting the user. The first is to have a specific error page for each error that can occur and redirect the user to that specific page, as in the following example:

```
<cftry>
...
<cfcatch type="Database">
    <cflocation url="dberror.cfm">
</cfcatch>
</cftry>
```

The downside to this approach is that you can't tell exactly what happened and why. A better option is redirect the user to an error page, but pass the error message in the URL, as follows:

```
<cftry>
...
<cfcatch type="Database">
    <cflocation
url="error.cfm?msg=#URLEncodedFormat(CFCATCH.Message)#">
</cfcatch>
</cftry>
```

This code passes a detailed error message in a URL parameter to the error page.

Another option is to directly display some type of message rather than redirecting the user, as follows:

```
<cftry>
...
<cfcatch type="Database">
    A database error occurred.
    <cfabort>
</cfcatch>
</cftry>
```

You may notice that the preceding code adds a CFABORT after the message; you don't want the errored page to continue execution after an error occurs.

A final option that is rarely used is to ignore the error. This is usually appropriate only if you are expecting an error to occur, but it doesn't matter to you whether the error occurs or not, as the following code shows:

```
<cftry>
...
<cfcatch type="Database">
    <!--- Ignore this error --->
</cfcatch>
</cftry>
```

If you're ignoring an error, adding a comment to the CFCATCH block is usually a good idea so that you're not confused if you go back and read your code later. And be aware that ignoring an error can prove dangerous, because you may end up inadvertently catching a more serious error than the one you were expecting. At least logging the error by using CFLOG may be a good idea, even if you plan to ignore it, as in the following example:

```
<cftry>
...
<cfcatch type="Database">
    <!--- Ignore this error, but log it in case there is a legitimate
error --->
    <cflog log="Application" text="#CFCATCH.Message#">
</cfcatch>
</cftry>
```

This way, you can review the specific error in the log file.

Using CFCATCH variables

Whenever you catch an error, you can find out what happened by using any of a family of CFCATCH variables, as described in Table 21-2.

Table 21-2: CFCATCH Variables

Variable	*Description*
CFCATCH.Type	The type of error thrown (such as Application, Database, or Security).
CFCATCH.Message	A diagnostic message. Usually short and usually the most important part of the error.

Variable	Description
CFCATCH.Detail	More detail about the nature of the error and where it occurred. Can contain HTML formatting.
CFCATCH.TagContext	An array of structures detailing what threw the error. Can be useful but usually better to rely on the Detail.
CFCATCH.NativeErrorCode	Exists only for type="Database". Describes the database driver's native error code for the error that occurred.
CFCATCH.SQLState	Exists only for type="Database". Primarily used with ODBC applications and should not be relied on.
CFCATCH.ErrNumber	Exists only for type="Expression". Internal error number provided by ColdFusion. Do not rely on this member being present, as some Expression-type errors do not create this key.
CFCATCH.MissingFileName	Exists only for type="MissingInclude" and type= "Template". Name of the file that ColdFusion could not locate.
CFCATCH.LockName	Exists only for type="Lock". The name of the lock that failed. Do not rely on this member if you are using a scope lock.
CFCATCH.LockOperation	Exists only for type="Lock". Can be Timeout, CreateMutex, or Unknown. This member has shown some erratic behavior; it is best not to rely on this key.
CFCATCH.ErrorCode	Exists only for errors thrown with CFTHROW. A developer-defined error code.
CFCATCH.ExtendedInfo	Exists only for errors thrown with CFTHROW. Developer-defined extended error information.

As described in Table 21-2, not all the CFCATCH variables are guaranteed to exist at all times. You can be relatively certain, however, that Type, Message, Detail, and TagContext exist for all errors.

Making decisions by using the CFCATCH variables

Now that you know what the CFCATCH variables are, what do you do with them? Typically, the only three variables that you ever need be concerned with are CFCATCH.Message, CFCATCH.Detail, and CFCATCH.NativeErrorCode. CFCATCH.Message and CFCATCH.Detail may contain valuable information, and CFCATCH.NativeErrorCode can be used with database errors to determine exactly what went wrong.

Say, for example, that you had a query that inserted a new e-mail address into your database, as follows:

```
<cfquery name="InsertUser"
         datasource="#Request.MainDSN#">
INSERT INTO Tickler(
    Email
)
VALUES (
    '#Form.Email#'
)
</cfquery>
```

Assume also that you used good database design and placed a unique index on the e-mail address to turn the e-mail into an alternate key. Now say that you attempt to insert an e-mail address that is already in the database. If you're using Microsoft SQL Server, you throw an error message that looks like what's shown in Figure 21-3.

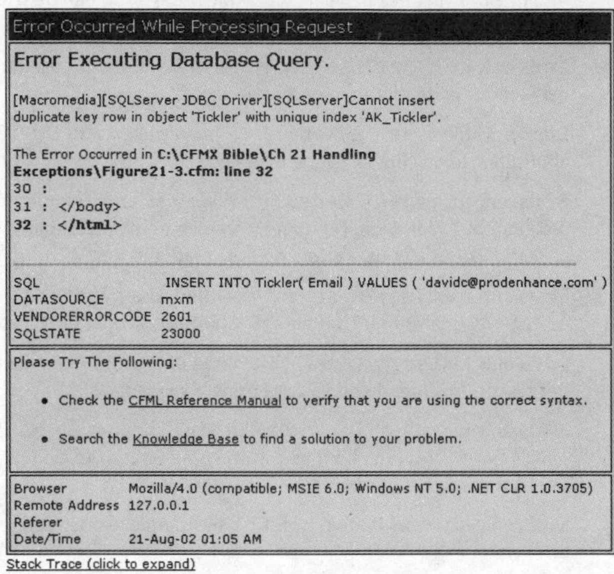

Figure 21-3: An error message thrown from the database on a duplicate alternate key error.

As you can see, that error is actually rather descriptive to you, the developer. The average user, on the other hand, would see that and start to sweat, thinking that he'd broken the Internet! The good news is that you don't need to rely on the error message to tell the user what happened, because you can intercept the error by using `CFCATCH`. The first thing that you can do is add a `CFCATCH` to give the user a friendlier-looking message, as follows:

```
<cftry>
    <cfquery name="InsertUser"
             datasource="#Request.MainDSN#">
    INSERT INTO Tickler(
        Email
    )
    VALUES (
        '#Form.Email#'
    )
    </cfquery>

    <cfcatch type="Database">
    <!--- For a database error, CFCATCH.Detail is the most descriptive
CFCATCH member. --->
    <cfoutput>#CFCATCH.Detail#</cfoutput>
    </cfcatch>
</cftry>
```

Now, running the problematic query returns the output shown in Figure 21-4.

[Macromedia][SQLServer JDBC Driver][SQLServer] Cannot insert duplicate key row in object 'Tickler' with unique index 'AK_Tickler'.

Figure 21-4: The error message filtered through CFCATCH.

Now most of the scary-looking diagnostics are gone, but the message itself is not exactly appealing. The question is how to make the error message less scary and, at the same time, more informative to the average user.

You can't just parse apart the message because the user would still have no concept of what happened. You *can*, however, put out a custom message based on the error number returned from SQL Server. If you look at Figure 21-3 again, you see a VENDORERRORCODE, with a value of 2601, which is SQL Server's native error code for a UNIQUE constraint violation.

You need to test for native error code 2601, therefore, and display a custom message, as follows:

```
<cfquery name="InsertUser"
        datasource="#Request.MainDSN#">
    INSERT INTO Tickler(
        Email
    )
    VALUES (
        '#Form.Email#'
    )
    </cfquery>

    <cfcatch type="Database">
        <cfif CFCATCH.NativeErrorCode EQ 2601>
            A duplicate record was encountered.
        </cfif>
    </cfcatch>
</cftry>
```

The following section shows you what to do if the native error code is *not* 2601.

Rethrowing an error you don't want to handle as an exception

Look back at the last snippet of code in the preceding section and notice how it displays a custom error message based on the native error code, telling the user what happened. The only problem is that it doesn't do anything for any other type of error.

Unfortunately, it really *can't* do anything useful, because any error other than the unique constraint violation is likely to be more serious than anything you'd want to handle programmatically. Your application needs to handle the 2601 error as an exception, but *rethrow* any database error that is not the expected alternate key violation, as the following code shows:

```
<cftry>
<cfquery name="MyQuery"
        datasource="#Request.MainDSN#">
...
</cfquery>

<cfcatch type="Database">
    <!--- 2601 is SQL Server's native code for a duplicate primary key
violation. --->
    <cfif CFCATCH.NativeErrorCode EQ 2601>
        A duplicate record was encountered.
    <cfelse>
        <cfrethrow>
    </cfif>
</cfcatch>
</cftry>
```

CFRETHROW tells ColdFusion that, even though CFCATCH caught the error, CFCATCH couldn't handle the error as an exception, so the error must be *rethrown* to the next level down on your exception-handling framework. (Think back to the sieve metaphor from Figure 21-2 — you're forcing an error to fall through to the CFERROR level of sieves.)

Throwing a custom error

In the preceding sections, we've concentrated on catching and handling exceptions thrown by ColdFusion or some external system; now you're going to take a look at throwing errors of your own.

You can use CFTHROW to throw any custom error type, which can be very descriptive in some cases. Take, for example, the following code:

```
<cftry>

<cfthrow message="An error occurred." type="MyError">

<cfcatch type="MyError">
    <!--- Handle the error --->
</cfcatch>
</cftry>
```

The custom type of error can also include dots in its name, as follows:

```
<cftry>

<cfthrow message="An error occurred." type="MyError.MySubType">

<cfcatch type="MyError.MySubType">
    <!--- Handle the error --->
</cfcatch>
</cftry>
```

The advantage to using dots in the exception type is that you can match the error by pattern, as in the following example:

```
<cftry>

<cfthrow message="An error occurred." type="MyError.MySubType">

<cfcatch type="MyError">
    <!--- Handle the error - notice that this CFCATCH will catch the
thrown error since MyError will match the pattern from
MyError.MySubType --->
</cfcatch>
</cftry>
```

CFTRY chooses the catch handler that best matches the CFTHROW type, as the following example shows:

```
<cftry>

<cfthrow message="An error occurred."
type="MyError.MySubType.MyOtherSubtype">

<cfcatch type="MyError.MySubType.YourOtherSubtype">
    <!--- This CFCATCH will not execute because the last part of the
type does not match --->
</cfcatch>

<cfcatch type="MyError.MySubType">
    <!--- This CFCATCH is the best match for the thrown type --->
</cfcatch>

<cfcatch type="MyError">
    <!--- This CFCATCH does not execute because a more specific handler
superceded it. --->
</cfcatch>
</cftry>
```

Throwing and catching Java exceptions

Java objects throw exceptions in a slightly different way than ColdFusion does. Java exceptions are handled as follows:

```
<cfobject type="JAVA" action="Create" name="myObject" class="myClass">

<cftry>
<cfset myVar = myObject.CauseException()>

<cfcatch type="Any">
    <cfset exception = GetException(myObject)>

    <cfoutput>
    #exception.toString()#
    </cfoutput>
</cfcatch>
</cftry>
```

GetException() retrieves the most recent exception that occurred for myObject. Exception.toString() gets a message that you can display to the user.

Using try and catch in CFSCRIPT

CFSCRIPT also contains a limited ability to perform exception handling. Instead of using CFTRY and CFCATCH, you would use the try and catch keywords in a CFSCRIPT block, as follows:

```
<cfscript>
try {
    oExcel = CreateObject("COM", "Excel.Application");
}
catch(Any exception) {
    WriteOutput("An error occurred while instantiating a COM object.
COM returned the following error message: #exception.Message#);
}
</cfscript>
```

If Excel is not installed on the ColdFusion Server that executes the preceding example, CreateObject() will throw an error that will then be caught by the catch block.

Notice the difference between the CFCATCH syntax and the catch syntax. Inside CFSCRIPT, you specify the catch keyword, followed by the exception type, followed by the name of the *exception object*. The exception object is the equivalent of the CFCATCH structure you used in the section "Using CFCATCH variables," earlier in this chapter.

Unfortunately, CFSCRIPT's exception handling is limited because there is no way to throw a custom error, and there is no way to rethrow an error once you've caught it.

Using CFERROR

CFTRY and CFCATCH are useful for specific errors that occur in targeted sections of code. You can, however, also catch any error that occurs in your application and pass control to a generalized error handler page by using the CFERROR tag.

CFERROR is usually placed inside Application.cfm. A typical call looks as follows:

```
<cferror type="EXCEPTION" template="error.cfm" exception="Any">
```

That call to CFERROR tells ColdFusion that, if any uncaught exception of any type occurs in your application, it should redirect the user to error.cfm. This is similar to a CFCATCH type="Any" that redirects the user to an error page, but CFERROR covers all code in your application rather than just a single targeted block.

This approach has its advantages, because you can now give a user-friendly error page to the user regardless of where the error may have occurred. The disadvantage to using CFERROR by itself is that diagnosing the error is much more difficult, because you can't pinpoint the location as easily. Your best course is to use CFTRY and CFERROR together — putting CFTRY in specific areas of your code and then relying on CFERROR for unexpected errors that cannot be handled as exceptions.

Whenever CFERROR encounters an error, it passes page execution to the template specified in the Template attribute. The error page has access to information about the error as well as all the content generated up to the point that the error occurred.

A good idea is to use the error template to e-mail the site administrator, sending him all the error information, and then to output a user-friendly error message that integrates with the regular graphical treatment for your site. Listing 21-1 shows a well-written error page.

Listing 21-1: A Well-Written Error Template

```
<!--- Email the site administrator --->
<cfmail to="admin@site.com"
        from="site@site.com"
        subject="An error occurred">
An error occurred while processing the template
#Error.TagContext[1].Template# at line #Error.TagContext[1].Line#.  The
diagnostic information is below:

Error Type:
#Error.RootCause.Type#

Referer:
#Error.HTTPReferer#

Error Message:
#Error.RootCause.Message#

Error Detail:
#Error.Rootcause.Detail#
</cfmail>

<!--- Tell the user an error occurred.  If this site had a graphical
treatment, we would also include the code for that here. --->

An error occurred during your request.  Please try again.
```

The CFERROR example that we show you at the beginning of this section has an exception attribute. CFERROR's exception attribute is similar to CFCATCH's type attribute: It tells ColdFusion which type of exception affects the CFERROR tag. Suppose, for example, that you have the following calls to CFERROR:

```
<cferror type="EXCEPTION" template="dberr.cfm" exception="Database">
<cferror type="EXCEPTION" template="anyerr.cfm" exception="Any">
```

Any time an uncaught database error occurs, ColdFusion redirects the user to dberr.cfm. Any other type of uncaught error redirects the user to anyerr.cfm.

The reason that you want to have specific error templates for specific exception types is that each one exposes different information. (Refer to Table 21-2, earlier in this chapter, for details.)

The type Attribute of CFERROR

Until Version 4.01 of ColdFusion Server, you had only two types of CFERROR: Request and Validate. The error templates associated with those CFERROR types could not include any ColdFusion code, because any error occurring in the error template would throw the server into an infinite loop. ColdFusion 4.5 introduced two new types, Exception and Monitor. Monitor was a great idea; it enabled you to run code for any error that occurred, regardless of whether it was caught. The only problem is that it would occasionally cause errors worse than what was originally thrown, and it has now been deprecated in ColdFusion MX. That leaves you with the final type, Exception, which is the only one that you should use from now on. Unlike CFERROR's Request and Validate types, the Exception type can use CFML in the error-handling template.

Using the Site-Wide Error Handler

Suppose that your error isn't caught by CFTRY and CFCATCH. CFERROR doesn't catch it either. What's your last resort before the user sees a scary, raw error message? The *site-wide error handler.*

The site-wide error handler template works like a CFERROR for the entire server, with some differences.

The site-wide error handler can use ColdFusion tags just as the CFERROR template (with type="EXCEPTION") can. It doesn't, however, have access to any of the error variables. (This is in conflict with the documentation, but tests have confirmed that you can't use the Error scope in the site-wide error handler.) As such, you can e-mail the Administrator to tell him that *an* error occurred, but you can't tell him *which* error occurred.

The site-wide error handler should be a last resort; ideally it would never be called in the lifetime of an application, because CFERROR should catch any unexpected errors. This means that your site-wide handler should create a log entry and e-mail the administrator every time that the site-wide handler is called, because a call to the site-wide handler could indicate a serious problem with your application or with ColdFusion Server in general.

Using the Log Files

ColdFusion logs all the errors that occur in your application. You can get a history of all the errors in your application by viewing the log files and seeing what happened when.

The log files are stored inside the *cf_root*\logs\ directory. The log file that you should be most concerned with is Application.log, which contains the errors that occur in your application. You can track an error by looking at the log files and finding the record.

Even errors that are caught with CFCATCH or CFERROR are stored in Application.log, so you can see exactly what happened even if CFCATCH obscures the error.

You can also write your own messages to the log files by using CFLOG as follows:

```
<cflog text="My Message" file="MyLog">
```

That writes a message to a file called MyLog.log inside the cf_root\logs\ directory. This can be very useful for certain problematic situations in which you want to log a specific error. Do not log every error that occurs because doing so unnecessarily burdens the server.

Summary

ColdFusion offers a wide range of exception handling techniques, from CFTRY and CFCATCH to the all-encompassing site-wide error handler. Each technique can be powerful by itself, but only when these three are intelligently integrated do you reach the full potential of ColdFusion's exception handling framework.

In this chapter you learn about the different ways to use ColdFusion's exception-handling framework and how the different pieces work together. You also learn about the many types of errors that can be thrown and caught with CFCATCH and CFERROR, and you even learn how to create your own custom error types that you can use for your own purposes.

✦ ✦ ✦

PART

IV

ColdFusion MX Components, Web Services, and Flash Integration

✦ ✦ ✦ ✦

In This Part

✦ ✦ ✦ ✦

CHAPTER 22

Understanding ColdFusion MX Components

✦ ✦ ✦ ✦

In This Chapter

Using components to separate logic from presentation

Structuring components

Invoking component functions in various ways

Understanding both static and persistent components

Implementing advanced component techniques

✦ ✦ ✦ ✦

Components are perhaps the most eagerly anticipated new feature of ColdFusion MX — and for good reason. Components not only offer a new and better way to write ColdFusion code, but they also enable ColdFusion to expose its functionality to the outside world through Web services and also make developing Flash MX applications a snap.

Components bring a more object-like approach to ColdFusion, so be prepared to learn some new coding techniques. In fact, if ColdFusion is your first and only language, this object-like approach to ColdFusion programming may seem very odd and cumbersome at first, but if you stay with us through this chapter, you see a faster and more logical way to write maintainable applications.

This chapter assumes that you have read about and are familiar with creating user-defined functions by using `CFFUNCTION`, `CFARGUMENT`, and `CFRETURN` tags. If not, start by reading Chapter 17.

As you may remember from the database-related chapters (8, 9, 10 and 11) in this book, we like to teach you how to build things in "layers," where we show you only the most critically relevant elements necessary to focus on the specific topic at hand and then layer on more complexity, bit by bit, until the entire subject is covered. This technique really helps to communicate complex topics, and ColdFusion components is certainly one such topic. We're using this same layered technique here, so make sure that you read the entire chapter, in order, from beginning to end or you may come away from it with misconceptions and incomplete code.

What Is a Component?

At its most basic, a *component* is a collection of *related user-defined functions* (refer to Chapter 17 for more about user-defined functions). This is the simplest and probably the most common use of components, so we use this definition for our teaching example in the beginning of this chapter.

If you design it by using a few advanced principles, a component can represent a unique instance of an *entity*—for example, a specific company—that persists in your application and has both *properties* (data pertaining to that specific company) and *methods* (functions that the company may perform, such as updating itself in the database). More on persistent components in the section "Persistent components," later in this chapter.

When referring to both components and objects, the terms *function* and *method* are interchangeable. We use each term where it seems to make the most sense or fit best with the surrounding discussion.

Chapter 23 takes you step by step through the process of creating two real-world components, but you need a simple example in the meantime to help explain things, so we start you out in the following sections with a basic component that simply groups together the functions related to working with a company.

A simple example

You know from experience that just about every entity in our database requires basic *CRUD* (*C*reate, *R*ead, *U*pdate, and *D*elete) functionality and also probably requires some kind of listing capability, so you start out by creating the shell of the component that contains these functions. The name of the component is *Company*, so you create a file named `Company.cfc` that contains the first layer of the shell, as follows:

```
<cfcomponent>
    <cffunction name="GetCompany"></cffunction>
    <cffunction name="ListCompanies"></cffunction>
    <cffunction name="CreateCompany"></cffunction>
    <cffunction name="UpdateCompany"></cffunction>
    <cffunction name="DeleteCompany"></cffunction>
</cfcomponent>
```

Without any explanation at all, you can already tell that the preceding is a *component* containing five functions named `GetCompany`, `ListCompanies`, `CreateCompany`, `UpdateCompany`, and `DeleteCompany`—and we bet that you can guess what each of these functions is going to do! The only thing that requires any explanation is the new extension, `.cfc`, which specifies the file as a *C*old*F*usion *c*omponent.

So far, so good. Now to give the first function, `GetCompany()`, an interface so it can be invoked. The next layer of the shell specifies what is *returned* from the `GetCompany()` function—a query contained in a variable named `companyRec`, as follows:

```
<cfcomponent>
    <cffunction name="GetCompany" returntype="query">

        <cfreturn companyRec>
    </cffunction>

    <cffunction name="ListCompanies"></cffunction>
    <cffunction name="CreateCompany"></cffunction>
    <cffunction name="UpdateCompany"></cffunction>
    <cffunction name="DeleteCompany"></cffunction>
</cfcomponent>
```

But you need to know which company record to retrieve, so you must supply an argument containing the CompanyID, as follows:

```
<cfcomponent>
    <cffunction name="GetCompany" returntype="query">
        <cfargument name="CompanyID" type="numeric" required="yes">

        <cfreturn companyRec>
    </cffunction>

    <cffunction name="ListCompanies"></cffunction>
    <cffunction name="CreateCompany"></cffunction>
    <cffunction name="UpdateCompany"></cffunction>
    <cffunction name="DeleteCompany"></cffunction>
</cfcomponent>
```

Now you have a complete input/output interface, so you can add the business logic that does the actual work, as follows:

```
<cfcomponent>
    <cffunction name="GetCompany" returntype="query">
        <cfargument name="CompanyID" type="numeric" required="yes">

        <cfquery name="companyRec"
            datasource="#Request.MainDSN#">
            SELECT
            CompanyID,
            CompanyName,
            Address,
            City,
            State,
            ZipCode,
            Comments
            FROM
            Company
            WHERE
            CompanyID = #Arguments.CompanyID#
        </cfquery>

        <cfreturn companyRec>
    </cffunction>

    <cffunction name="ListCompanies"></cffunction>
    <cffunction name="CreateCompany"></cffunction>
    <cffunction name="UpdateCompany"></cffunction>
    <cffunction name="DeleteCompany"></cffunction>
</cfcomponent>
```

At this point, you have a ColdFusion component containing one working function and shells for four more functions that you complete a little later in this section.

But how do you call the GetCompany() function inside this component? You may remember from Chapter 17 that you can call a *local* function inside a ColdFusion template as follows:

```
<cfinvoke
    method="GetCompany"
    returnvariable="returnVar">
        <cfinvokeargument name="CompanyID" value="10">
</cfinvoke>
```

Calling a function in a component requires only one additional attribute, as follows:

```
<cfinvoke
    component="Company"
    method="GetCompany"
    returnvariable="returnVar">
        <cfinvokeargument name="CompanyID" value="10">
</cfinvoke>
```

If you specify `component="Company"` in the `CFINVOKE` tag, ColdFusion does the following:

1. Finds the file `Company.cfc`.
2. Invokes the function named in the `Method` attribute.
3. Creates a local variable in the calling page with the name specified in the `ReturnVariable` attribute and the contents of what was returned by `CFRETURN`.

Listing 22-1, for example, produces the result shown in Figure 22-1. (Notice how `ReturnVariable` makes the connection with `Query` between the `CFINVOKE` and `CFOUTPUT` tags.)

Listing 22-1: Invoking a component function and displaying the result

```
<cfinvoke
    component="Company"
    method="GetCompany"
    returnvariable="returnVar">
        <cfinvokeargument name="CompanyID" value="10">
</cfinvoke>

<table cellspacing="2" cellpadding="2" border="1">
<cfoutput query="returnVar">
<tr>
    <td><b>CompanyID</b></td>
    <td>#CompanyID#</td>
</tr>
<tr>
    <td><b>CompanyName</b></td>
    <td>#CompanyName#</td>
</tr>
<tr>
    <td><b>Address</b></td>
    <td>#Address#</td>
</tr>
<tr>
```

```
    <td><b>City</b></td>
    <td>#City#</td>
</tr>
<tr>
    <td><b>State</b></td>
    <td>#State#</td>
</tr>
<tr>
    <td><b>ZipCode</b></td>
    <td>#ZipCode#</td>
</tr>
<tr>
    <td><b>Comments</b></td>
    <td>#Comments#</td>
</tr>
</cfoutput>
</table>
```

CompanyID	10
CompanyName	The Stan Cox Society
Address	1234 Tweeble Lane
City	Barneyville
State	NJ
ZipCode	01234
Comments	Formerly known as "Friends of Stan Cox"

Figure 22-1: The resulting output from Listing 22-1.

After you flesh out the rest of the `Company` component's functions, you end up with Listing 22-2.

Listing 22-2: The completed Company component

```
<cfcomponent>
    <cffunction name="GetCompany" returntype="query">
        <cfargument name="CompanyID" type="numeric" required="yes">

        <cfquery name="companyRec" datasource="#Request.MainDSN#">
            SELECT
                CompanyID,
                CompanyName,
                Address,
                City,
                State,
                ZipCode,
                Comments
```

Continued

Listing 22-2 *(continued)*

```
            FROM
                Company
            WHERE
                CompanyID = #Arguments.CompanyID#
        </cfquery>

        <cfreturn companyRec>
    </cffunction>

    <cffunction name="ListCompanies" returntype="query">
        <cfargument name="CompanyFilter" type="string" required="no">

        <cfquery name="companyRecs" datasource="#Request.MainDSN#">
            SELECT
                CompanyID,
                CompanyName,
                Address,
                City,
                State,
                ZipCode,
                Comments
            FROM
                Company
            <cfif IsDefined('Arguments.CompanyFilter')>
            WHERE
                CompanyName LIKE '#Trim(Arguments.CompanyFilter)#%'
            </cfif>
            ORDER BY
                CompanyName
        </cfquery>

        <cfreturn companyRecs>
    </cffunction>

    <!--- Void functions are explained later in this chapter in the
section "Void functions" --->
    <cffunction name="CreateCompany" returntype="void">
        <cfargument name="CompanyName" type="string" required="Yes">
        <cfargument name="Address" type="string" required="Yes">
        <cfargument name="City" type="string" required="Yes">
        <cfargument name="State" type="string" required="Yes">
        <cfargument name="ZipCode" type="string" required="Yes">
        <cfargument name="Comments" type="string" required="Yes">

        <cfquery name="insCompany" datasource="#Request.MainDSN#">
            INSERT INTO Company(
                CompanyName,
                Address,
                City,
                State,
                ZipCode,
```

```
                Comments
            )
            VALUES (
                '#Trim(Arguments.CompanyName)#',
                '#Trim(Arguments.Address)#',
                '#Trim(Arguments.City)#',
                '#Trim(Arguments.State)#',
                '#Trim(Arguments.ZipCode)#',
                '#Trim(Arguments.Comments)#'
            )
        </cfquery>

        <cfreturn>
    </cffunction>

    <cffunction name="UpdateCompany" returntype="void">
        <cfargument name="CompanyID" type="numeric" required="Yes">
        <cfargument name="CompanyName" type="string" required="Yes">
        <cfargument name="Address" type="string" required="Yes">
        <cfargument name="City" type="string" required="Yes">
        <cfargument name="State" type="string" required="Yes">
        <cfargument name="ZipCode" type="string" required="Yes">
        <cfargument name="Comments" type="string" required="Yes">

        <cfquery name="updCompany" datasource="#Request.MainDSN#">
            UPDATE
                Company
            SET
                CompanyName = '#Trim(Arguments.CompanyName)#',
                Address = '#Trim(Arguments.Address)#',
                City = '#Trim(Arguments.City)#',
                State = '#Trim(Arguments.State)#',
                ZipCode = '#Trim(Arguments.ZipCode)#',
                Comments = '#Trim(Arguments.Comments)#'
            WHERE
                CompanyID = #Arguments.CompanyID#
        </cfquery>

        <cfreturn>
    </cffunction>

    <cffunction name="DeleteCompany" returntype="void">
        <cfargument name="CompanyID" type="numeric" required="Yes">

        <cfquery name="delCompany" datasource="#Request.MainDSN#">
            DELETE
                Company
            WHERE
                CompanyID = #Arguments.CompanyID#
        </cfquery>

        <cfreturn>
    </cffunction>
</cfcomponent>
```

By now, you probably get the basic idea that, at its most basic level, a component is like a container for related functions, and invoking component functions is much like invoking local functions except that you must also specify the name of the component that contains the function.

So . . . big deal? *You bet!* Even the most basic use of the simplest components changes your approach to ColdFusion development, because you're now completely separating logic from presentation; you're exposing logic as a set of simple, yet formal function calls available to any part of your application (even remote applications, as you see in Chapters 25 and 26); and you're encapsulating the functions related to a single entity into a single component.

And if you think components are just a substitute for a bunch of `CFINCLUDE`s, keep reading. .

Separating logic from presentation

The need to separate logic from presentation is more important now than it has ever been for a number of reasons, as outlined in the following list:

- ✦ The ever-increasing array of handheld devices and their widely varying display formats.
- ✦ The renewed interest in syndicated content that must form-fit various Web layouts.
- ✦ The trend away from delivering plain-text streams and HTML and toward delivering generalized XML, XHTML, WML, and other "pivot" formats (i.e, formats that acts as intermediate steps in a data conversion process) that are further processed into finished content on target devices.
- ✦ The desire to easily expand very large corporate applications while minimizing new errors or anomalies into the software.
- ✦ The headlong rush into delivering better, faster Web applications through Flash MX Remoting technology.

By encapsulating into a single component all the functionality related to an entity and then simply calling on that component whenever data is needed to be retrieved, updated, deleted, and so on, you build applications that help achieve the goals of targeting common functionality to multiple display formats and building Enterprise-scale applications that are straightforward to develop and easy to maintain.

Another benefit of such encapsulation is the focus that it naturally places on good design. If you've developed in earlier versions of ColdFusion, think for a moment how you approached pre-MX ColdFusion application design. Data was the stuff that you shoved into and pulled out of databases for the sole purpose of accomplishing some task spread out across a number of individual browser pages. Sure, you had `CFINCLUDE` and custom tags, and you could create snippets of reusable code if you were keen enough to spot duplicated code, but all your logic was still thinly spread out across multiple templates located who-knows-where.

If you take the opposite approach and gather together all the functionality related to an entity into a single component, you begin to "think like the entity" and ask yourself, "What does a company need to do?" After the obvious partial answer of "Create, read, update, delete, and list," you begin to uncover a few specialized needs such as "calculate the annual sales of the company" and "tell me how many people are employed by this company"—all of which can be incorporated into that one `Company` component.

Before you even know what you've done, you've built a centralized source from which to request all operations and data related to companies, regardless of how the data is supplied to or requested from that source. Now, all you need to do is call this functionality and display the results.

Get used to passing messages

So things are a little different from earlier versions of ColdFusion, eh? Now you have a formal input interface requiring data of specific types and a formal output interface returning data of a specific type — as you learn in Chapter 17, as you first start building user-defined functions by using the new `CFFUNCTION` tag. Now everything is done through messages: one message containing arguments going in and one message containing the single result variable coming out. This technique may seem a little odd at first, but this is precisely how object-oriented languages work.

The Nickel Tour of objects

Your telephone is an *object*; it is a specific *instance* of the general *class* of telephones. As do all other instances of the class telephones, your telephone has all the general *properties* of a telephone: a receiver to which you can listen, a transmitter into which you can speak, a control for dialing someone's number, and so on. Any phone can also be expected to support a set of functions, or *methods*: picking up the receiver, dialing a number, ringing, hanging up, and so on.

Note This Nickel Tour uses a fictional object-oriented syntax for teaching purposes. It's similar to a simplified form of Java that doesn't require formal data typing or other complications.

That telephone *object* that you hold in your hand is the combination of all the *properties* that describe it and the *methods* that it can perform. In the physical world, your telephone was manufactured in a factory. In the object-oriented world, your telephone is conceptually manufactured as follows:

```
yourTelephone = new Telephone();
```

Now you have an object named `yourTelephone` that is an *instance* of the class `Telephone`. In object-oriented terms, you have just *instantiated* a `Telephone` object named `yourTelephone`. `yourTelephone` contains all the properties and methods that any new `Telephone` would have because it was manufactured in the `Telephone` "factory" (that is, instantiated from the `Telephone` class).

In the physical world, you pick up your telephone's receiver and dial a number with your finger. In the object-oriented world, you tell your telephone to pick up its own receiver and then you tell your telephone to dial the number for you, conceptually, as follows:

```
yourTelephone.OffHook();
yourTelephone.DialNumber('1-770-446-8866');
```

Your friend Stan Cox has a telephone, too, as follows:

```
stansTelephone = new Telephone();
```

But Stan isn't calling Productivity Enhancement as you are; he's trying to find a hot date with a woman who shares his main interest in life, as the following example indicates:

```
stansTelephone.OffHook();
stansTelephone.DialNumber('1-900-4CF-CHIX');
```

Clearly, your telephone and Stan's telephone can do the same kinds of things because they are both objects of the `Telephone` class, but each telephone might do the same thing in a different way (such as dial a different number) because each is a separate, distinct *instance* of a `Telephone`. Your instance of a `Telephone` is named `yourTelephone`, and Stan's instance of a `Telephone` is named `stansTelephone`. Each instance is a complete, standalone copy of all the properties and methods that any `Telephone` has.

Not all telephones are exactly alike

Stan's telephone is similar to most other telephones, but his probably has a few functions that a public telephone doesn't have, and his probably doesn't have some of the functions of Larry Ellison's telephone (such as Oracle-based speed dial).

Stan was so enamored with his date that he has asked the factory to invent a Stan-specific telephone with a special speed-dial function, as the following code describes:

```
class StanPhone extends Telephone {
    SpeedDial(theNumber) {
      this.OffHook();
      if (theNumber == '1') {
          this.DialNumber('1-900-4CF-CHIX');
      }
    }
}
```

And Stan wants the factory to manufacture one of these phones for him, as follows:

```
stansnewTelephone = new StanPhone();
```

Now, whenever Stan wants to talk with a beautiful, intelligent ColdFusion programmer of the female persuasion, all he must do is the following:

```
stansnewTelephone.SpeedDial ('1');
```

Stan's very special telephone *extends* the capabilities of a normal telephone with an additional method named `SpeedDial()`, which in turn makes use of the methods available to any telephone (`OffHook()` and `DialNumber()`).

Notice the prefix `this` used in the preceding code example to call the inherited methods `OffHook()` and `DialNumber()`. If you guessed that `this` refers to *this instance*, you're right. Because the `StanPhone` class simply *extends* the `Telephone` class, all the methods available to the `Telephone` class are automatically a part of the `StanPhone` class and, as such, are available in all instances of the StanPhone class.

Sometimes you don't need a telephone at all

The *methods* that we've discussed so far operate on a specific *instance* of an object. Dialing a number on `stansnewTelephone`, for example, just dials it on that one instance of a telephone. If `stansnewTelephone` didn't exist, you couldn't dial a number from it. These methods are known as *instance methods*.

Some methods don't operate on a specific instance of an object, but instead operate with respect to the entire *class* of objects. If Stan called the telephone manufacturer and asked how many telephones had been manufactured to date, for example, the manufacturer may ask itself the following:

```
telephonesManufacturedToDate = Telephone.GetCount();
```

The `GetCount()` function in this code queries the manufacturer's database and totals the number of telephones manufactured in all production runs to the present date.

These methods are known as *class methods* because they operate on the entire class of objects and not on just a single instance of an object.

So there you have the Nickel Tour of objects—just enough terminology and explanation so that you can make sense of a discussion of ColdFusion components and understand at least a little bit of the discussions comparing CFCs to true objects. If you want more—and you *know* that you do—learn Java. Your career is sure to thank you.

Components are similar to objects

Listing 22-2 encapsulates into a single component all the functionality related to a company. Every time that you need to do something to or get something from a company, you invoke one of the `Company` component's functions and pass in the `CompanyID` used to identify the target company; then your functions go out and manipulate that company's data in the database.

None of these functions do anything with data associated with the component itself; all these functions directly manipulate the database without any regard to the concept of an *instance*. In other words, these component functions are the equivalent of *class methods* in traditional object-oriented terms.

To create component functions that are the equivalent of *instance methods*, an instance of the component needs data or *properties* directly associated with it, and these instance methods must work with the properties rather than directly with the database. If an instance of a component is created, it contains a scope named `This`, which is the rough equivalent of the `this` prefix that we mention in the section "Not all telephones are exactly alike," a little earlier in this chapter, in that `This` refers in this case to *This instance*. (The difference in the capitalization of `This` is due to the difference in syntax between ColdFusion and Java, which I used in the Nickel Tour.)

So suppose that, inside your component, you set a variable in the `This` scope, as follows:

```
<cfset This.CompanyName = "Productivity Enhancement">
```

In this code, you create a property for *This instance* of the `Company` component. And suppose that you then create a component function named `GetCompanyName()` that simply returns that property, as follows:

```
<cffunction name="GetCompanyName" ReturnType="String">
   <cfreturn This.CompanyName>
</cffunction>
```

You've now given the caller what it wants directly from the *properties* of an *instance* of the component. In other words, `GetCompanyName()` is an *instance method* rather than a *class method.*

Before you can set a component property, you must get the data from somewhere—typically from a database query—and this query requires processing overhead. So setting component properties becomes practical only if those properties are going to persist longer than a single component-function call—otherwise, you may just as well manipulate the database each time that a function is called.

We get into the details of designing effective persistent components and instance methods in the section "Persistent components," a little later in this chapter; then you build one step by step in Chapter 23. But for starters, we show you in the following sections how to create an instance of a component that persists longer than a single function call.

Invoking a Component Function

If you invoke a component function by using the CFINVOKE tag, ColdFusion creates an instance of that component and calls the function named in the Method attribute. In essence, ColdFusion instantiates an object of the class of that component, but the name of that object is invisible to you. (It's internally referenced by ColdFusion Server.) If you use CFINVOKE to call three of a component's functions in a single ColdFusion template, as shown in Listing 22-3, ColdFusion Server creates three separate instances of that component to give you what you want, and that's not very efficient.

Listing 22-3: Repetitively instantiating a component

```
<cfinvoke
        component="Company"
        method="GetCompany"
        returnvariable="companyRecord1">
    <cfinvokeargument name="CompanyID" value="8">
</cfinvoke>

<cfinvoke
        component="Company"
        method="GetCompany"
        returnvariable="companyRecord2">
    <cfinvokeargument name="CompanyID" value="9">
</cfinvoke>

<cfinvoke
        component="Company"
        method="GetCompany"
        returnvariable="companyRecord3">
    <cfinvokeargument name="CompanyID" value="10">
</cfinvoke>
```

The correct way to call a component's functions multiple times from a single template is to separately instantiate an object with a formal name and then call the functions of that one instance as you need them. Listing 22-4 shows this principle in action. Notice that the component attribute of the CFINVOKE tag references an *instance* of the component rather than the component itself.

Listing 22-4: Instantiating a component and repetitively invoking its methods

```
<cfobject name="myCompany" component="Company">

<cfinvoke
        component="#myCompany#"
        method="GetCompany"
        returnvariable="companyRecord1">
```

```
    <cfinvokeargument name="CompanyID" value="8">
</cfinvoke>

<cfinvoke
        component="#myCompany#"
        method="GetCompany"
        returnvariable="companyRecord2">
    <cfinvokeargument name="CompanyID" value="9">
</cfinvoke>

<cfinvoke
        component="#myCompany#"
        method="GetCompany"
        returnvariable="companyRecord3">
    <cfinvokeargument name="CompanyID" value="10">
</cfinvoke>
```

You can pass arguments to component functions by incorporating them directly into the CFINVOKE tag. This is the same technique shown in Chapter 17.

You create a single instance of the `Company` component that persists for as long as the current page request lasts; then you simply call the functions of that one instance as many times as you need. After the current page request ends, ColdFusion automatically destroys the instance that you create. (In the following section, you learn how to make your component instances live longer.)

Using the `CFOBJECT` tag isn't the only way to instantiate an object. The `CreateObject()` function returns an object as well. The following three lines of code, for example, produce the same results:

```
<cfobject name="myCompany" component="Company">
<cfset myCompany = CreateObject("Component", "Company")>
<cfscript>myCompany = CreateObject("Component", "Company");</cfscript>
```

Similarly, using `CFINVOKE` isn't the only way to invoke a component function. After you create an instance of a component, you can call its methods by using simple dot notation. Listing 22-5, for example, returns the list of companies produced by the `ListCompanies` function to a variable named `listOfCompanies`.

Listing 22-5: **Invoking a component function by using dot notation**

```
<cfscript>
    myCompany = CreateObject("Component", "Company");
    listOfCompanies = myCompany.ListCompanies('A');
</cfscript>
<cfdump var="#listOfCompanies#">
```

In fact, Listing 22-5 is probably the most popular way of working with component functions for ColdFusion developers who are versed in object-oriented languages, as the syntax is very close to the way that both Java and C++ instantiate objects and call their methods.

You can directly access component functions via forms and URLs, but the results are basically worthless. Instead of defining a return value to pass from your function to the function call that invokes it, you must push displayable content directly out of the body of the function, as shown in Listing 22-6.

Listing 22-6: Using direct function output instead of a return value

```
<cffunction name="OutputTest" output="yes">

    <cfquery name="companyRecs" datasource="#Request.MainDSN#">
        SELECT
            CompanyID,
            CompanyName,
            Address,
            City,
            State,
            ZipCode,
            Comments
        FROM
            Company
        ORDER BY
            CompanyName
    </cfquery>

    <cfoutput query="companyRecs">
    <p><b>#CompanyName#</b>:<br>#Comments#</p>
    </cfoutput>

</cffunction>
```

This kind of coding is nasty stuff, folks. Don't do it. The real power of content-producing functions, whether they are local to a template or encapsulated within a component, comes from returning content contained in a complex variable of a specific data type and then merging the content with presentation code. Separating logic from presentation (and, by extension, data from presentation) should be your mantra.

If you absolutely must create a function that directly outputs content, remove the `ReturnType` attribute from the `CFFUNCTION` tag and add `Output="Yes"`. Never have both a return type and direct output in the same function.

The `Output` attribute actually has the following three states:

- ✦ `Output="Yes"` treats the entire function as if it were inside a `CFOUTPUT` tag pair.
- ✦ `Output="No"` treats the entire function as if it were inside a `CFSILENT` tag pair.
- ✦ Eliminating the `Output` attribute entirely enables explicit `CFOUTPUT` tags inside the function to leak output to the caller.

We haven't been explicit about the `Output` attribute yet because this is a learning chapter, and we want to eliminate as much extraneous code as possible so that you can focus your concentration on specific topics. Chapter 23, on the other hand, is a *doing chapter*, where you start actually building these little monsters, so starting in that chapter, we explicitly specify `Output="No"` for all component functions, which is a best practice.

Persistent Components

In the preceding sections of this chapter, you learn how to create a named instance of a component, you find out about the basics of instance properties in a component's `This` scope, and you learn the differences between class methods and instance methods. Now to put these theories into action!

The instance of the component that you create in Listing 22-5 persists only as long as the page request and then ColdFusion Server automatically destroys it. If you want to work with a persistent component past a single page request, you simply must create it in a persistent scope that lives longer than one request, as shown in Listing 22-7.

Listing 22-7: Persisting an instance of a component in a long-lived scope

```
<cfscript>
    Session.myCompany = CreateObject("Component", "Company");
    listOfCompanies = Session.myCompany.ListCompanies('A');
</cfscript>
<cfdump var="#listOfCompanies#">
```

Listing 22-7 is just Listing 22-5 modified to create the instance of the `Company` component in the Session scope rather than in the Variables (local) scope. Now this instance persists as long as the user's session does, which means that its properties do, too.

This means that you can execute one ColdFusion template that creates an instance of the `Company` component, go have a cup of coffee, execute a second ColdFusion template that invokes a function of that component, go place a bid on eBay, execute a third ColdFusion template that invokes another function of that component, and so on, until you pause longer than your session timeout permits and the instance is destroyed. This is why we refer to `Company` as a *long-lived* persistent component.

Components can also be persisted in the Application scope as well. Just remember that all users of your application use the same instance of your component, so locking becomes even more critical and performance bottlenecks potentially become more of a concern if your component manipulates properties in its `This` scope.

We bet that, right now, you're thinking, "I'm clustering my application, which means that I don't use Session variables anywhere, so I'm going to persist my component instance by serializing it with WDDX (see Chapter 30 for details) and storing it in the Client scope." That's a clever idea, but unfortunately, it doesn't work. If you serialize a component instance, the properties in the `This` scope serialize just fine, but you lose all your functions, so on deserialization, all you get back are the properties.

Why use a persistent component?

Why use a persistent component? Good question! Why create an "object-wannabe" that carries its own data (properties) around with it? A few practical applications of persistent components do exist, but one in particular clearly stands out.

As you may remember from Chapter 8, if an attribute must be present to effectively describe an entity, that attribute cannot contain a `NULL` value. You can never, therefore, insert a partial record into a database table. If one or more of these non-`NULL` values must be calculated from currently unavailable values, or if the value is discovered or created late in some user task, you need a temporary staging area to store your partial data, and a persistent component's properties fit the bill nicely for this purpose.

So one good application for a long-lived persistent component is a wizard that collects data throughout a complicated process and then calls component functions that insert or update the component's properties into the database after you collect sufficient data to form each entity completely.

You begin to build a partial Company wizard in the next section, to see the basics of how a persistent component can be useful; then you complete the wizard in Chapter 23 to see how you'd deploy it as a complete solution.

The elements of a persistent component

The following list describes what you need to create a persistent component that makes use of its properties:

- ✦ A granular locking mechanism bound to the component.
- ✦ An `Initialization()` function that creates the component's properties.
- ✦ A `GetEntity()` function that retrieves data from the database.
- ✦ A `FlushEntityToDatabase()` function that sends data to the database.

The names of the preceding functions are only generalizations. You may name your functions anything you want.

Some developers also create specific component functions to formally set and get specific properties or collections of properties. We discuss these "setters and getters" in the section "Using setters and getters," a little later in this chapter.

A granular locking mechanism bound to the component

First, because your component persists in a shared memory scope (Session or Application), you need to pay attention to locking. As we mention in Chapter 12, locking an entire scope creates a bottleneck through which all requests to that scope's variables must pass.

To prevent such bottlenecks, we use *named locks* with *persistent components*. We use the `CreateUUID()` function to generate our lock name—which ensures that our lock name is unique from any other lock name—and we bind our lock name to the component itself by storing it in a component property, as follows:

```
This.lockName = CreateUUID();
```

But where should we execute this line of code? We need our lock name to become available as soon as we create an instance of the component, but we must execute this code only once to prevent our lock name from changing, as we must refer to the lock name in calls to the component.

Fortunately, an initialization area inside every component serves this purpose. Any code that you place between the `CFCOMPONENT` tag and the first `CFFUNCTION` tag executes only once if an instance of the component is created through either `CFOBJECT` or `CreateObject()` or through a direct call to an uninstantiated component from `CFINVOKE`.

So we place our lock-naming code in the component's initialization area, as follows:

```
<cfcomponent>
    <cfscript>
        This.lockName = CreateUUID();
    </cfscript>

    <cffunction . . . >
</cfcomponent>
```

We explain why and where to use locks with persistent components in the section "Where to apply locking," just a bit later in this chapter, but for now, we're going to move on to the other parts that make up a persistent component.

An initialization() function that creates the component's properties

After a persistent component is first instantiated, it should contain all the properties that it's ever to have during its lifecycle. The values of these properties, of course, change as you add and modify data in the tasks that make use of the component, but they must start off with some value—typically an empty string or zero, depending on the property's data type.

In this wizard example, you initialize these properties by using an `InitCompany()` function, as follows:

```
<cfcomponent>
    <cfscript>
        This.lockName = CreateUUID();
        InitCompany();
    </cfscript>

    <cffunction name="InitCompany" returntype="void">

        <cfscript>
            This.companyID = 0;
            This.companyName = "";
            This.address = "";
            This.city = "";
            This.state = "";
            This.zipCode = "";
            This.comments = "";
        </cfscript>

        <cfreturn>
    </cffunction>

    <cffunction . . . >
</cfcomponent>
```

You're going to come back after you complete the next section and expand this function, but for now, you should get the basic idea of how to initialize persistent component properties from this example.

A GetEntity() function that retrieves data from the database

The initialization function that you create in the preceding section initializes the component properties to a "blank canvas" ready to be painted with new values, but sometimes you're going to edit an existing collection of data rather than create new data, so you're going to need a way to get that data from your most common external source, the database. The following example shows you how to do so:

```
<cffunction name="GetCompany" returntype="query">
    <cfargument name="CompanyID" type="numeric" required="yes">

    <cfquery name="companyRec" datasource="#Request.MainDSN#">
        SELECT
            CompanyID,
            CompanyName,
            Address,
            City,
            State,
            ZipCode,
            Comments
        FROM
            Company
        WHERE
            CompanyID = #Arguments.CompanyID#
    </cfquery>

    <cfreturn companyRec>
</cffunction>
```

The preceding code is the same `GetCompany()` function from Listing 22-2. You can call this function from outside the component, but you can also call it from within the component as a simple function call. Technically, if you want to initialize your component properties with data from a specific `Company` record, you can do so as follows:

```
<cfscript>
    This.lockName = CreateUUID();
    InitCompany(10);
</cfscript>

<cffunction name="InitCompany" returntype="void">
    <cfargument name="companyID" type="numeric" required="Yes">

    <cfscript>
        CompanyInitRec = GetCompany(Arguments.companyID);
        This.companyID = CompanyInitRec.companyID;
        This.companyName = CompanyInitRec.companyName;
        This.address = CompanyInitRec.address;
        This.city = CompanyInitRec.city;
        This.state = CompanyInitRec.state;
        This.zipCode = CompanyInitRec.zipCode;
        This.comments = CompanyInitRec.comments;
    </cfscript>

    <cfreturn>
</cffunction>
```

But this method doesn't serve you well at all, because it hard-codes CompanyID 10 into the initialization function. Passing an argument to the initialization area of a component is impossible, so you can call InitCompany() only from within the component initialization area.

The trick is to create an initialization function that takes an optional argument containing a CompanyID and then set an additional property that describes whether the component is initialized with empty values or data from a database record, as follows:

```
<cfscript>
    This.lockName = CreateUUID();
    InitCompany();
</cfscript>

<cffunction name="InitCompany" returntype="void">
    <cfargument name="companyID" type="numeric" required="no">

    <cfscript>
        if (IsDefined('Arguments.companyID')) {
            CompanyInitRec = GetCompany(Arguments.companyID);
            This.companyID = CompanyInitRec.companyID;
            This.companyName = CompanyInitRec.companyName;
            This.address = CompanyInitRec.address;
            This.city = CompanyInitRec.city;
            This.state = CompanyInitRec.state;
            This.zipCode = CompanyInitRec.zipCode;
            This.comments = CompanyInitRec.comments;
            This.isNewCompany = FALSE;
        } else {
            This.companyID = 0;
            This.companyName = "";
            This.address = "";
            This.city = "";
            This.state = "";
            This.zipCode = "";
            This.comments = "";
            This.isNewCompany = TRUE;
        }
    </cfscript>

    <cfreturn>
</cffunction>
```

After an instance of the component is first created, the initialization area executes InitCompany() with no arguments, so the component properties are all initialized to a "blank canvas" of empty strings and a companyID of 0. If you want to edit an existing company in your wizard, you simply call this same InitCompany() function and pass the CompanyID of the company record that you want to acquire, and your component properties get initialized to the values stored in the database.

The other important thing that you do is to create an additional property named isNewCompany that indicates whether the component instance currently represents a new company to be created in the database or an existing company to be updated in the database. The following section shows how the isNewCompany property is used.

A FlushEntityToDatabase() function that sends data to the database

Your component's properties eventually must find their way to the database so that they can persist longer than the timeout of the Session or Application scope into which the component is instantiated. For this purpose, you create a function that either inserts or updates the record in the database, depending on whether the properties represent a new or an existing record, as the following example shows:

```
<cffunction name="FlushCompanyToDatabase" returntype="void">
    <cfif This.isNewCompany>
        <cfquery name="insCompany" datasource="#Request.MainDSN#">
            INSERT INTO Company(
                CompanyName,
                Address,
                City,
                State,
                ZipCode,
                Comments
            )
            VALUES (
                '#Trim(This.companyName)#',
                '#Trim(This.address)#',
                '#Trim(This.city)#',
                '#Trim(This.state)#',
                '#Trim(This.zipCode)#',
                '#Trim(This.comments)#'
            )
        </cfquery>
    <cfelse>
        <cfquery name="updCompany" datasource="#Request.MainDSN#">
            UPDATE
                Company
            SET
                CompanyName = '#Trim(This.companyName)#',
                Address = '#Trim(This.address)#',
                City = '#Trim(This.city)#',
                State = '#Trim(This.state)#',
                ZipCode = '#Trim(This.zipCode)#',
                Comments = '#Trim(This.comments)#'
            WHERE
                CompanyID = #This.companyID#
        </cfquery>
    </cfif>

    <cfreturn>
</cffunction>
```

Notice that the meat and potatoes of this function are taken from the two previous `CreateCompany()` and `UpdateCompany()` component functions. Because the instance of the component is "self-aware" of its own state, you need call only a single function and have the instance decide for itself how to persist the component's properties in the database.

Where to apply locking

If you've been highly suspicious of the persistent component in the preceding sections, you're on the ball! If you're going to persist this component in the Session scope, where does the locking go? The complete answer is, "Anywhere that you access the `This` scope after initialization."

Because you no longer need to worry about data corruption in shared-memory scopes, you now must concern yourself only with preventing *race conditions*, where two pieces of code attempt to access the same shared-memory variables at the same moment. During initialization of a component instance into the Session or Application scope, nothing except the single line of code that creates the object (the `CFOBJECT` tag or the `CreateObject()` function) can possibly access that object, so locking is not needed to set `This.lockName`, nor is it needed if `InitCompany()` is called from the initialization area of the component, so you can eliminate the use of `CFLOCK` there.

You do, however, need to lock the portions of the `InitCompany()` function that access the `This` scope during all later calls, and because such code is inside a `CFSCRIPT` tag pair, you must lock the entire `CFSCRIPT` block. And because this access modifies the `This` scope rather than simply reading it, the lock needs to be an exclusive one, as in the following example:

```
<cflock name="#This.lockName#"
        timeout="10"
        throwontimeout="Yes"
        type="EXCLUSIVE">
    <cfscript>
        if (IsDefined('Arguments.companyID')) {
            CompanyInitRec = GetCompany(Arguments.companyID);
            This.companyID = CompanyInitRec.companyID;
            This.companyName = CompanyInitRec.companyName;
            This.address = CompanyInitRec.address;
            This.city = CompanyInitRec.city;
            This.state = CompanyInitRec.state;
            This.zipCode = CompanyInitRec.zipCode;
            This.comments = CompanyInitRec.comments;
            This.isNewCompany = FALSE;
        } else {
            This.companyID = 0;
            This.companyName = "";
            This.address = "";
            This.city = "";
            This.state = "";
            This.zipCode = "";
            This.comments = "";
            This.isNewCompany = TRUE;
        }
    </cfscript>
</cflock>
```

`This.lockName` is guaranteed to contain a universally unique value, which means that you acquire a granular lock inside this instance of your component without blocking access to any other code in your application that doesn't use this same instance of the component. The only other function in your persistent component that requires locking is the `FlushCompanyToDatabase()` function, because it reads from the `This` scope, as the following example shows:

```
<cffunction name="FlushCompanyToDatabase" returntype="void">
    <cflock name="#This.lockName#"
            timeout="10"
            throwontimeout="Yes"
            type="READONLY">
        <cfif This.isNewCompany>
            <cfquery name="insCompany"
                    datasource="#Request.MainDSN#">
                INSERT INTO Company(
                    CompanyName,
                    Address,
                    City,
                    State,
                    ZipCode,
                    Comments
                )
                VALUES (
                    '#Trim(This.companyName)#',
                    '#Trim(This.address)#',
                    '#Trim(This.city)#',
                    '#Trim(This.state)#',
                    '#Trim(This.zipCode)#',
                    '#Trim(This.comments)#'
                )
            </cfquery>
        <cfelse>
            <cfquery name="updCompany"
                    datasource="#Request.MainDSN#">
                UPDATE
                    Company
                SET
                    CompanyName = '#Trim(This.companyName)#',
                    Address = '#Trim(This.address)#',
                    City = '#Trim(This.city)#',
                    State = '#Trim(This.state)#',
                    ZipCode = '#Trim(This.zipCode)#',
                    Comments = '#Trim(This.comments)#'
                WHERE
                    CompanyID = #This.companyID#
            </cfquery>
        </cfif>
    </cflock>

    <cfreturn>
</cffunction>
```

Notice that you need only a `ReadOnly` lock here because your are reading only from the `This` scope.

Now that your locking problems are solved, you can tackle another prevalent problem: *function variable leakage*.

Preventing function variable leakage: the Var scope

If you declare a local variable in the standard fashion inside a function, that variable "leaks out" of the function and can be accessed and modified by code outside the function itself. This isn't just a quibbling little piece of trivia, because such behavior can inadvertently modify values outside your function.

We discuss this problem in Chapter 17 but it bears repeating here because the problem follows user-defined functions whenever they are placed inside components. If you have multiple functions in your component that use the same variable names (a very common and expected occurrence), this variable leakage causes you no end of problems.

Solve this problem by creating a *function variable declaration block* immediately after the last CFARGUMENT tag in your function and then declaring the initial values of the variables that should live only inside your function, as follows:

```
<cfset Var aVar = "">
<cfset Var anotherVar = "">
<cfset Var yetAnotherVar = "">
```

The Var keyword places the declared variable into the Var scope, which is a special scope that lives only inside user-defined functions. By declaring function-only variables in the Var scope, you absolutely guarantee that your variables don't leak outside the function.

Declaring a variable in the Var scope can take place only before any logic is performed by the function, which is why you must always place your function variable declaration block immediately after the final CFARGUMENT tag in your function. In fact, ColdFusion is so strict about this rule that you can't even use a CFSCRIPT block to perform simplified multiple Var declarations inside a CFFUNCTION tag, as the opening CFSCRIPT tag is considered to be a line of logic, so it violates the rule that Var declarations must come first.

Because of the placement restrictions of the function variable declaration block, you don't always know the final value of all Var-scoped variables after they are declared. In this case, just initialize the variable with an empty string (as shown in the example in the preceding section). Then later, whenever you want to assign the final value to the variable, just treat the variable as if it is a local variable. We can use this technique in the InitCompany() function to prevent the variable containing the query object from leaking outside the function, as the following example shows:

```
<cfargument name="companyID" type="numeric" required="no">
<cfset Var CompanyInitRec = "">

<cflock name="#This.lockName#"
        timeout="10"
        throwontimeout="Yes"
        type="EXCLUSIVE">
    <cfscript>
        if (IsDefined('Arguments.companyID')) {
            CompanyInitRec = GetCompany(Arguments.companyID);
            This.companyID = CompanyInitRec.companyID;
            This.companyName = CompanyInitRec.companyName;
            This.address = CompanyInitRec.address;
            This.city = CompanyInitRec.city;
            This.state = CompanyInitRec.state;
            This.zipCode = CompanyInitRec.zipCode;
            This.comments = CompanyInitRec.comments;
            This.isNewCompany = FALSE;
```

```
        } else {
            This.companyID = 0;
            This.companyName = "";
            This.address = "";
            This.city = "";
            This.state = "";
            This.zipCode = "";
            This.comments = "";
            This.isNewCompany = TRUE;
        }
    </cfscript>
</cflock>
```

After you assign a value to a local variable named CompanyInitRec within a function, ColdFusion automatically goes "scope hunting" for a variable named CompanyInitRec within the Var scope and, if it finds that variable, assigns the value to the Var-scoped CompanyInitRec. If no such Var-scoped variable of the same name exists, ColdFusion creates a local variable of that name that leaks outside the function.

In fact, for every query you create inside a function, whether via CFQUERY or CFPROCRESULT, you should first CFSET a Var-scoped variable of the same name as the query to an empty string. This will prevent your queries from leaking out of the functions that create them. We didn't use this practice until now in this chapter in order to isolate you from details while you were getting a basic understanding of components.

Now you know that the core functionality makes a persistent component useful. And now that you have a persistent component, you can play with it.

Working with component properties

To begin learning how to work with component properties, persist an instance of your new PersistentCompany.cfc component in the Session scope, as follows:

```
<cfscript>
    Session.myCompany = CreateObject("Component", "PersistentCompany");
</cfscript>
```

At this point, all properties of Session.myCompany are empty strings and zeros. If you want to re-initialize Session.myCompany with the company that has a CompanyID = 10, you can call the InitCompany() function as follows:

```
<cfscript>
    Session.myCompany.InitCompany(10);
</cfscript>
```

Reading and modifying component properties directly

Now the properties of Session.myCompany contain data from the Company record that has a CompanyID = 10. So you can directly output the company name persisting in the instance as follows:

```
<cflock name="#Session.myCompany.lockName#"
        timeout="10"
        throwontimeout="Yes"
        type="READONLY">

    <cfoutput>#Session.myCompany.companyName#</cfoutput>

</cflock>
```

(Remember that the `This.` inside the component instance correlates to `Session.myCompany.` outside the component instance).

Hey—doesn't this locking look a little weird? Or at least very inconsistent? Well it may look that way, but it's perfectly legitimate. Let us explain.

You don't need to lock the instantiation of the component, even though it is being instantiated in the Session scope, because no race condition can possibly exist during instantiation.

You also don't need to lock the call to `Session.myCompany.InitCompany(10)` because the `InitCompany()` function handles its own locking.

But now you come to what appears to be a conundrum: How do you acquire a named lock where the name of the lock itself is in the Session scope? Doesn't `Session.myCompany.lockName` need to be locked before it is accessed?

The answer is "no" because `This.lockName` (that is, `Session.myCompany.lockName`) is never written to more than once throughout the entire life cycle of the component's `This` scope (or the Session scope that, in turn, contains it). If `This.lockName` is, in essence, a *write-once constant*, no race condition can ever occur, so no locking is needed.

If `This.lockName` can ever be rewritten, even with the same value that it already contained, you would need to lock it on every read. The decision to lock is based on whether the variable is written to memory only once or multiple times during its scope's life cycle and not whether its value changes from one writing to the next.

You *do* need to `ReadOnly` lock access to `Session.myCompany.companyName` on outputting it, however, because it may be read while another piece of code attempts to modify its value.

Similarly, you must *exclusively* lock any direct writes to the instance's `This` scope (via `Session.myCompany`), as follows:

```
<cflock name="#Session.myCompany.lockName#"
        timeout="10"
        throwontimeout="Yes"
        type="EXCLUSIVE">

    <cfset Session.myCompany.CompanyName = "Stan's Fans">

</cflock>
```

Using setters and getters

Our preference is to directly set and get instance properties by using the techniques shown in the preceding section. They are quick, easy, sure, and perfectly legitimate techniques—as long as you pay careful attention to locking requirements.

Another technique is often favored by developers who come from the object-oriented world, where a whole slew of specific granular component functions are created for the sole purpose of setting and getting instance properties.

So, for example, you don't want to do the following:

```
<cflock name="#Session.myCompany.lockName#"
        timeout="10"
        throwontimeout="Yes"
        type="READONLY">

    <cfoutput>
        #Session.myCompany.city#,
```

```
            #Session.myCompany.state#
            #Session.myCompany.zipCode#<br>
        </cfoutput>

    </cflock>
```

Instead, you can create getter functions inside your component as follows:

```
    <cffunction name="GetCity"
            returntype="string"
            output="No">

        <cflock name="#This.lockName#"
                timeout="10"
                throwontimeout="Yes"
                type="READONLY">

            <cfreturn This.city>

        </cflock>
    </cffunction>

    <cffunction name="GetState"
            returntype="string"
            output="No">

        <cflock name="#This.lockName#"
                timeout="10"
                throwontimeout="Yes"
                type="READONLY">

            <cfreturn This.state>

        </cflock>
    </cffunction>

    <cffunction name="GetZipCode"
            returntype="string"
            output="No">

        <cflock name="#This.lockName#"
                timeout="10"
                throwontimeout="Yes"
                type="READONLY">

            <cfreturn This.zipCode>

        </cflock>
    </cffunction>
```

And you can call these getter functions as follows:

```
    <cfoutput>
        #Session.myCompany.GetCity()#,
        #Session.myCompany.GetState()#
```

```
    #Session.myCompany.GetZipCode()#<br>
</cfoutput>
```

Notice that you don't need to lock your calls to the getter functions, because all locking is handled by the functions themselves.

Setters are the flip-sides of getters in that they set property values rather than get and return them. If you are going to create setter functions, make sure that you acquire an `Exclusive` lock on the code inside the functions that modify the `This` scope, as in the following example:

```
<cffunction name="SetCity"
        returntype="void"
        output="No">

    <cfargument name="city" type="string" required="yes">

    <cflock name="#This.lockName#"
            timeout="10"
            throwontimeout="Yes"
            type="EXCLUSIVE">

        <cfset This.city = Arguments.city>

        <cfreturn>
    </cflock>
</cffunction>

<cffunction name="SetState"
        returntype="void"
        output="No">

    <cfargument name="state" type="string" required="yes">

    <cflock name="#This.lockName#"
            timeout="10"
            throwontimeout="Yes"
            type="EXCLUSIVE">

        <cfset This.state = Arguments.state>

        <cfreturn>
    </cflock>
</cffunction>

<cffunction name="SetZipCode"
        returntype="void"
        output="No">

    <cfargument name="zipCode" type="string" required="yes">

    <cflock name="#This.lockName#"
            timeout="10"
            throwontimeout="Yes"
```

```
            type="EXCLUSIVE">

        <cfset This.zipCode = Arguments.zipCode>

        <cfreturn>
    </cflock>
</cffunction>
```

Because your locking is handled by the setters themselves, you can safely call them as follows:

```
<cfoutput>
    #Session.myCompany.SetCity("Norcross")#,
    #Session.myCompany.SetState("GA")#
    #Session.myCompany.SetZipCode("30071")#<br>
</cfoutput>
```

A definite benefit of using correctly designed setters and getters is the capability to simply call them without worrying about locking them — or anything else, for that matter. If you're working with novice developers, you may want to consider foregoing direct property manipulation in favor of employing setters and getters.

Just don't bow down to the self-appointed "object gods" who try to convince you that you must employ setters and getters for absolutely everything that accesses the `This` scope. The technique that you choose to employ is entirely up to you.

Security

Components centralize business logic rather than leaving it distributed among various templates and directories, and with this change in code location comes a necessary change in the mechanism used to restrict code access.

ColdFusion MX has a new mechanism for authenticating and authorizing users that is very straightforward and easy to use. Based on user roles and requiring just a few simple tags and functions (`CFLOGINUSER`, `IsUserInRole()`, `CFLOGOUT`, and so on), the new security mechanism creates an *ID badge* from a user name and a list of roles in which the user has been granted membership; it then stores that ID badge in a nonpersistent cookie. Each browser request presents this ID badge to ColdFusion Server, which uses it to determine whether the user making the request is authenticated (that is, he is who he says he is) and authorized (that is, he has membership in a role that is authorized to access that part of the application).

Chapter 40 contains an excellent discussion of exactly how ColdFusion MX's security framework functions and how to build a working user login system for your own applications. If you're not already familiar with all of MX's security-related tags and functions, take a few minutes to read Chapter 40 before proceeding so that you can get more out of the following discussion.

Restricting access at the component level doesn't make sense because a component may contain many different functions. So ColdFusion MX restricts access at the function level instead. Preventing unauthorized access to a function is as simple as adding the `Roles` attribute to the `CFFUNCTION` tag, as in the following example:

```
<cffunction name="DeleteCompany"
        returntype="void"
        output="No"
```

```
        roles="ADMIN,CLERK">

    <cfargument name="CompanyID"
            type="numeric"
            required="Yes">

    <cfquery name="delCompany"
            datasource="#Request.MainDSN#">
        DELETE
            Company
        WHERE
            CompanyID = #Arguments.CompanyID#
    </cfquery>

    <cfreturn>
</cffunction>
```

By adding `roles="ADMIN,CLERK"` to the `DeleteCompany()` function, ColdFusion Server now checks every call to `DeleteCompany()` for the correct authorization. If the user making the request is both authenticated (logged in) and authorized (is a member of either the `ADMIN` or `CLERK` role), the function executes; if the user is not authorized, the request throws an error.

If the `roles` attribute is omitted from the `CFFUNCTION` tag, any user may access that function, provided that some other security mechanism doesn't prevent him from calling the function.

Access Levels

Whereas component-function security grants access to *users*, setting the access level of a component function grants access to *software*. Access levels apply only to component functions.

You have the following four access levels:

- **Public:** This degree of access is the default access level for a component function. Public access enables the function to be invoked by another local component or ColdFusion template but not from an external source such as Flash Remoting Services or consumed as a Web service.
- **Private:** This level of access "hides" the component function from everything outside the component that contains it so that it can be invoked only from other functions within the same component.
- **Package:** This level of access restricts a component function to invocation by function, either from within the same component or from within another component in the same package. Component packages are discussed in the section "Advanced Component Concepts," later in this chapter.
- **Remote:** This level of access enables a component function to be invoked from any local or remote system. This is the access level that you must choose to make a component function available as a Web service or to Flash Remoting applications.

Use a combination of tight security and restrictive access levels to diligently restrict all component functions to only those users and software that must have authorization.

Advanced Component Concepts

We like to "tell the story" of components, where we start with the simplest concepts and build up the topic with easily digestible layers of additional complexity. This teaching method works really well for components, because they are such a radical departure from traditional ColdFusion development concepts, and they offer lots of new concepts to master.

We've delayed talking about advanced concepts until the very end of this chapter, mainly because they are not absolutely critical to understanding and developing 90 percent of the components that you're likely to ever build. You *could* probably work until retirement building ColdFusion components and never need to employ any of the concepts in the following sections, but if you do take the time to understand and use them where warranted, your code takes on a more "natural" feel. And the more naturally that your code conforms to good design principles, the easier it is for others to understand and maintain it.

Void functions

In traditional terms, a *function* returns a single result to its caller. Code that simply goes out and does something to something else without returning a result is commonly known as a *procedure*. In ColdFusion terms, a *tag* is a procedure, and a *function* is . . . well, a function.

The line between these two became somewhat blurred with the introduction of object-oriented languages, because the properties of an object are also known as *data members*, and the object's methods are also known as *member functions*. In fact, they're known as member functions even if they do not return a value; no such thing as a "member procedure" exists.

Suddenly, "functions" didn't need to return results to their callers. To distinguish between "normal" functions and these new-style functions that don't return values, the term *void function* was coined. Basically, a void function is just a function that doesn't return a result.

In the following code snippet, you call a getter that returns a string containing a zip code and then call a setter that sets the zip code to a new value:

```
<cfscript>
    theZipCode = Session.myCompany.GetZipCode();
    Session.myCompany.SetZipCode(theZipCode & "-1234");
</cfscript>
```

You may remember that `SetZipCode()` is a void function (as almost all setter functions are), so it doesn't return a value. To invoke a void function, you simply call it directly rather than set a variable to its return value, as shown in the first line of the preceding script.

Some developers have an aversion to void functions and instead substitute traditional functions that return `True` on success or `False` on failure, but this is not a sound design, because to implement such code, you must internally handle errors as exceptions and then produce a viable return value as a proxy for a genuine error. This technique goes against the concepts of sound exception handling. An error that doesn't describe an expected alternative (that is, *exception*-al) path of execution is indeed an error that should either be rethrown from within a `CFTRY` block or fall through your exception-handling framework to be caught by an error-handling template. (See Chapter 21 for a detailed explanation.)

Don't be afraid to implement void functions. If your function doesn't need to return a value, it is indeed a void function. If your void function throws an error, your exception-handling framework can handle it.

Packages

Whereas components aggregate related functions into a single unit, *packages* aggregate related components into an even larger unit. A package contains components that are designed to work together as a complete library of functions with a general common purpose.

Say, for example, that you have two components named Comp.cfc and Emp.cfc that handle employee bonus calculations, and you want them to be part of the CalcBonus package.

Creating a component package is rather simple—just follow these basic steps:

1. Create a directory (or hierarchy of directories) that is addressable by ColdFusion Server.
2. Place your components in that directory (or throughout your hierarchy of directories).
3. Set the access levels of your component functions to reflect the manner in which they are to be called.

A common practice is to create a hierarchy of directories under your Web root, where the path is the reverse of the domain name, as follows:

```
C:\inetpub\wwwroot\com\herdomain\calcbonus\
C:\inetpub\wwwroot\com\hisdomain\calcbonus\
C:\inetpub\wwwroot\com\mydomain\corp\
C:\inetpub\wwwroot\com\mydomain\corp\partners\
C:\inetpub\wwwroot\com\mydomain\corp\transfers\
C:\inetpub\wwwroot\com\mydomain\utils\
```

The following code prevents naming collisions between multiple domains on the same server:

```
C:\inetpub\wwwroot\com\herdomain\calcbonus\Comp.cfc
C:\inetpub\wwwroot\com\herdomain\calcbonus\Emp.cfc
C:\inetpub\wwwroot\com\hisdomain\calcbonus\CompanyCalc.cfc
C:\inetpub\wwwroot\com\hisdomain\calcbonus\Emp.cfc
```

The resulting ColdFusion notational equivalents to these disk paths are as follows:

```
com.herdomain.calcbonus.Comp
com.herdomain.calcbonus.Emp
com.hisdomain.calcbonus.CompanyCalc
com.hisdomain.calcbonus.Emp
```

Instantiating herdomain.com's calcbonus package components is, therefore, as simple as using the code shown in the following example:

```
<cfscript>
    employeeServices = CreateObject("Component",
"com.herdomain.calcbonus.Emp");
</cfscript>
```

The only difference that's shown so far between using a component in a package and using a standalone component is in the dot path, but the *real* difference lies inside the components themselves, where access levels are established. Listings 22-8 and 22-9 show the Comp.cfc and Emp.cfc components of the calcbonus package. The CFSETs of This-scoped variables are discussed in the following section on inheritance, but for now, pay special attention to the functions' access levels.

Listing 22-8: The Comp.cfc component of the CalcBonus package

```
<cfcomponent>
    <cfset This.compProperty = "Original Comp">

    <cffunction name="SizeOfCompany"
        access="package"
        returntype="numeric">

        <cfargument name="CompanyID"
            type="numeric"
            required="yes">

        <cfquery name="GetNumEmployees"
                datasource="#Request.MainDSN#">
            SELECT
                COUNT(*) AS NumEmployees
            FROM
                Employee
            WHERE
                CompanyID = #Val(Arguments.CompanyID)#
        </cfquery>

        <cfreturn GetNumEmployees.NumEmployees>
    </cffunction>
</cfcomponent>
```

Listing 22-9: The Emp.cfc component of the CalcBonus package

```
<cfcomponent>
    <cfset This.empProperty = "Original Emp">

    <cffunction name="XmasBonus"
        access="private"
        returntype="numeric">

        <cfargument name="SSN"
            type="string"
            required="yes">

        <cfquery name="GetCompany"
                datasource="#Request.MainDSN#">
            SELECT
                CompanyID
            FROM
                Employee
            WHERE
                SSN = '#Trim(Arguments.SSN)#'
```

```
        </cfquery>

        <cfif GetCompany.RecordCount EQ 1>
            <cfinvoke component="Comp"
                    method="SizeOfCompany"
                    returnvariable="returnVar"
                    CompanyID="#GetCompany.CompanyID#">
            <cfreturn returnVar * 10>
        <cfelse>
            <cfreturn 0>
        </cfif>
    </cffunction>

    <cffunction name="Bonus"
            access="public"
            returntype="numeric">

        <cfargument name="SSN"
            type="string"
            required="yes">

        <cfquery name="GetSalary"
                datasource="#Request.MainDSN#">
            SELECT
                Salary
            FROM
                Employee
            WHERE
                SSN = '#Trim(Arguments.SSN)#'
        </cfquery>

        <cfreturn (Val(GetSalary.Salary) * 0.05) +
XmasBonus(Arguments.SSN)>
    </cffunction>
</cfcomponent>
```

All that you need to do to calculate the bonus for the employee whose SSN is 012-34-5678 is the following:

```
<cfoutput>#employeeServices.Bonus("012-34-5678")#</cfoutput>
```

This package shows a good example of how Public-, Private-, and Package-access types work together. Following is the chain of events, in order:

1. The `Bonus()` function — a *Public*-access function because you must be able to call it from anywhere within the ColdFusion application — is called with the argument `"012-34-5678"`, which represents the SSN of the employee whose bonus is being calculated.
2. A query retrieves the employee's salary from the database, multiplies this value by 5 percent, and adds the product to the result of the `XmasBonus()` function, as follows:
    a. `XmasBonus()` — a *Private*-access function because it needs to be accessed only from within the `Emp` component — in turn invokes `Comp.SizeOfCompany()`, passing the SSN of the employee whose bonus is being calculated.

   b. `Comp.SizeOfCompany()` — a *Package*-access function because it needs to be accessed only by functions in both its own component and the `Emp` component — returns to `XmasBonus()` the number of people working at the employee's employer.

   c. `XmasBonus()` returns to `Bonus()` the number of employees multiplied by 10.

3. `Bonus()` returns the final calculation of the employee's bonus to the calling template.

During your design phase, don't stop after you figure out which functions are going to be declared within which components. Go the extra mile to see how your functions may call each other *between* components and restrict access to them as "close to the vest" as possible. Place the results in a logically named hierarchy of ColdFusion-accessible directories, and — *voila!* — you've just created a very useful component package.

Inheritance

We've said much regarding the theory of *ColdFusion component inheritance*, and frankly, much of it is seriously overblown. Inheritance shares its name with the object-oriented world, but that's about all that it shares. CFC inheritance can be easily summed up with the following three simple statements:

✦ One component can inherit from or *extend* another, after which the inheriting component can make use of its ancestor's properties and methods.

✦ If the inheriting component declares its own methods named *differently* from those in its ancestor, *both* the ancestor's methods and the inheriting component's methods can be called through the inheriting component. The same holds true for declaring properties by using names that do not match their ancestor's.

✦ If the inheriting component declares its own methods named *the same* as those in its ancestor, the inheriting component's methods *override* the ancestor's methods with the same name, as if the ancestor's methods are *hidden*. The same holds true for declaring properties by using names that match their ancestor's.

Just keep these three simple principles in mind as you proceed through the following sections and don't think that inheritance is any more complicated than this. Inheritance has a few applications in real-world ColdFusion development, but you're likely to find that they are rare. Nevertheless, you should understand inheritance so that you can spot places in your application where it may be warranted.

Extending inherited functions and properties

You can use the package that you create in Listings 22-8 and 22-9 to learn about extending components. Although we didn't discuss it earlier, we created a property in the `Emp` component named `empProperty`, as follows:

```
<cfset This.empProperty = "Original Emp">
```

Creating a variable in the `This` scope of the `Emp` component makes that variable a *property* of that component.

Remember that all code in a component's initialization area is executed once as an instance of the component is first created, which means that the `empProperty` property is automatically created and initialized to the value `Original Emp` as each instance of the Emp component is created. You can change the value of This.empProperty after it is initialized, and each instance of the Emp component may contain its own value of empProperty.

If you inherit or *extend* a component, the functions and properties of the ancestor are, in essence, copied into the inheritor, where they can be called and used just as if they were a part of the inheritor.

So, if you create a component named Manager that extends the Emp component, as shown in Listing 22-10, the Manager component also contains a property named empProperty. Manager *extends* Emp, so Manager *inherits* Emp's properties and functions.

Listing 22-10: The Manager component extends Emp with ManagerBonus()

```
<cfcomponent extends="com.herdomain.calcbonus.Emp">
    <cfset This.managersOwnProperty = "Just for us Managers">

    <cffunction name="ManagerBonus"
            access="public"
            returntype="numeric">

        <cfargument name="SSN"
            type="string"
            required="yes">

        <cfreturn Bonus(Arguments.SSN) * 1.15>
    </cffunction>
</cfcomponent>
```

Notice also that the preceding code declares a property directly in Manager, named managersOwnProperty. Manager inherits Emp's properties, but the process is a one-way street, so managersOwnProperty is available only in the Manager component and, not in the Emp component.

The same principles of inheritance that work for component properties also work for component functions.

The Emp component contains a Bonus() function that calculates the bonuses of nonmanagerial employees, but managers make an additional 15 percent bonus. To calculate manager bonuses, you *extend* Manager's functionality by declaring a function named ManagerBonus(), as shown in Listing 22-10. To retrieve the normal bonus for an employee, ManagerBonus() must call the Bonus() function that is declared in the Emp component. But Manager *extends* Emp, so Bonus() is available as one of Manager's own functions; all ManagerBonus() must do is return Bonus() multiplied by 1.15, as follows:

```
<cfreturn Bonus(Arguments.SSN) * 1.15>
```

Listing 22-11 shows inheritance in action. Notice how the properties and functions of both Emp and Manager are directly accessible from Manager.

Listing 22-11: Accessing Manager's functions and properties

```
<cfscript>
    managerServices = CreateObject("Component",
"com.herdomain.calcbonus.Manager");
</cfscript>

<cfoutput>
    <p>These are all accessed through the Manager component only:</p>

    <p>Manager Bonus:
        <b>#managerServices.ManagerBonus("012-34-5678")#</b><br>

    managersOwnProperty:
        <b>#managerServices.managersOwnProperty#</b></p>

    <p>Standard Bonus:
        <b>#managerServices.Bonus("012-34-5678")#</b><br>

    empProperty:
        <b>#managerServices.empProperty#</b></p>
</cfoutput>
```

The result of executing Listing 22-11 is shown in Figure 22-2.

These are all accessed through the Manager component only:

Manager Bonus: **807.875**
managersOwnProperty: **Just for us Managers**

Standard Bonus: **702.5**
empProperty: **Original Emp**

Figure 22-2: The result of executing Listing 22-11.

Everything that you've done so far is known as *extending* because you leave all the functionality of the ancestor component unmodified and *extend* it only by adding new functions and properties. In the object-oriented world, this technique is known as *specialization*: A manager is a specialized employee who does the same basic things plus a few more. To use a couple more object-oriented terms, a manager is a *subtype* of an employee, and the employee is the *supertype* of the manager.

Don't get hung up on these terms; we mention them here only so that you can follow along in the inevitable discussions that you hear in comparing components to objects.

Overriding inherited functions and properties

"And now for something completely different . . ." — Monty Python

Overriding replaces inherited properties and functions with something completely different from what was inherited. To override a function or property, simply declare a function or property of the same name in the inheritor component. It's as simple as that.

Listing 22-12 shows overriding in action. The company that manufactured Stan Cox's telephone — Fooster — turns out to be scamming everyone. Through creative trading contracts with various "hot-talk" services and bundling service options with Fooster's Model ADHCC (AutoDial Hot ColdFusion Chicks) Telephone, Fooster alleged nonexistent profits that made its stock price soar sky-high and attract investors. The money started pouring in, so the company had to find something to do with it. The answer: employee bonuses.

Listing 22-12: The Fooster component overrides Bonus()

```
<cfcomponent extends="com.herdomain.calcbonus.Emp">
    <cfset This.empProperty = "Fooster Override Emp">
    <cfset This.foostersOwnProperty = "Just for Fooster">

    <cffunction name="Bonus"
        access="public"
        returntype="numeric">

        <cfargument name="SSN"
            type="string"
            required="yes">

        <cfreturn XmasBonus(Arguments.SSN) + 113000000>
    </cffunction>
</cfcomponent>
```

So if you are a Fooster employee, your total annual bonus is your Christmas bonus plus 113 million dollars. *Sweet!*

By declaring its own `Bonus()` function, the `Fooster` component overrides the `Bonus()` function inherited from the `Employee` component, but the inherited `XmasBonus()` function is still available because *it* wasn't overridden. Listing 22-13 shows Fooster's bonus system in action.

Listing 22-13: Calling Fooster's Bonus() function.

```
<cfscript>
    embezzlerServices = CreateObject("Component",
"com.herdomain.calcbonus.Fooster");
</cfscript>

<cfoutput>
    <p>These are all accessed through the Fooster component only:</p>

    <p>Standard Bonus, Fooster-style:
        <b>#embezzlerServices.Bonus("012-34-5678")#</b><br>

    empProperty:
        <b>#embezzlerServices.empProperty#</b><br>

    foostersOwnProperty:
        <b>#embezzlerServices.foostersOwnProperty#</b></p>
</cfoutput>
```

The result of executing Listing 22-13 is shown in Figure 22-3.

These are all accessed through the Fooster component only:

Standard Bonus, Fooster-style: **113000000**
empProperty: **Fooster Override Emp**
foostersOwnProperty: **Just for Fooster**

Figure 22-3: The result of executing Listing 22-13.

Do you see how straightforward ColdFusion component inheritance is? The rules are simple: Ancestor functions and properties are available in the inheritor unless overridden.

These examples are, by necessity, very brief. Real-world implementations of component overriding are the result of very careful component planning and design, because they must take into consideration the complete set of behaviors of each component type and its extended subtypes. Try to do that with some category of things in nature, like aircraft or guns, and you quickly see how this is not a trivial matter.

Summary

You've learned quite a lot about components in this chapter. Not only did you see one being built from the ground up, you followed the very structure of how they are built so you could get a better feel for how to use them. You learned how component functions are often referred to as methods, how methods can be either class methods or instance methods depending on how the component that declares them is used, and how these principles are similar to object oriented development.

You've also learned how to create component packages and how to declare a component with unique behavior by inheriting an existing component and overriding some of its methods. You also learned how to apply role-based security to component methods to prevent unauthorized access.

You've probably already heard a lot of talk about how ColdFusion components are similar to objects in object-oriented programming languages, but although some similarities do exist, the two are very different. In short, don't try too hard to make ColdFusion components act the same as objects, and don't labor for hours on end creating elaborate coding schemes so that your components are forced into a bad ballet where they must dance and act like real objects in Java or C++, because you're only going to end up spending a lot of time being sorely disappointed. Components are *not* objects; they're not even surrogates. They're object wannabes.

So don't be afraid to break certain "object rules," because they're not component rules. The only components rules are the ones that *you* define for your applications. If you decide to directly set or get a persistent component property rather than call a component function to do the same thing, the worst that you get are a few whiny tongue lashings from overly excitable discussion-list members.

This chapter covers only what you need to understand the basics of components. If we start weighing you down with more details before you build some for yourself, we may lose you. So in the Chapter 23, you build a couple components; then you finish up with the details that we purposefully omit from this chapter, including component documentation, metadata, and the many caveats that you encounter in implementing component-based applications.

After you finish reading the next chapter and building its components, you should have a solid understanding of both the theory and practice of designing and implementing components, and you should understand how critical engineering decisions affect the overall strength of your application.

✦ ✦ ✦

Building Your First ColdFusion Components

In This Chapter

Building components by using both class methods and instance methods

Using components in your applications

Understanding MVC architecture

Working around component caveats

Documenting components

In this chapter, you're going to build a simple application based on two ColdFusion components, or CFCs: one that handles companies and another that handles its employees. The `Company` component declares only class methods, so persisting longer than a single page request has no practical purpose, but the `Employee` component is designed to collect data submitted from multiple forms and, therefore, must persist between page requests.

A component may contain both *instance methods* and *class methods*, but instance methods become truly useful only within the context of a long-lived persistent component. Don't think of a component as either a class (static) component or an instance component, because such behavior is attributed to a component's methods and not the component itself.

Chapter 23 is an exercise in building two components based on the principles and techniques taught in Chapter 22, so this chapter may not mean much to you unless you've already read and fully understand Chapter 22.

The Application That You're Going to Build

You're going to build in this chapter a component-based wizard that collects data about employees and then either inserts or updates those employees in the database. This application shows you the elements and techniques involved in building an effective component-based system, but we purposefully remove all exception handling and validation so that you can easily see exactly how ColdFusion reacts to any mistakes in your code.

You should follow along with the "building in layers" approach that we're taking and enter your code the same way rather than just jumping to the finished listing. The first layer is a sort of "50,000-foot view" of the component, and successive layers focus in closer on more and more details, so you can get a true feel for the component as a whole rather than as just a bunch of lines of code that you type in.

After you're finished with this chapter, we invite you to experiment with what you've built. Modify it and see how ColdFusion reacts. Add some validation and an exception-handling framework to see how your wizard would operate in a production environment.

You want to start with a clean slate. Execute against your CFMXBible database the file `RefreshCh23Data.sql` in the Chapter 23 directory of the companion CD-ROM to replace everything in your Company, Employee, and Dependant tables with fresh data. That way, your results match the figures in this chapter and you don't think that something's wrong.

This wizard enables the user to add and enter employees. The first three wizard pages are used to enter data, and the fourth page is for viewing the employee data before it is committed to the database. On first thought, you may visualize the wizard's application flow to look something like what you see in Figure 23-1. (The heavy lines denote the main path of application flow.)

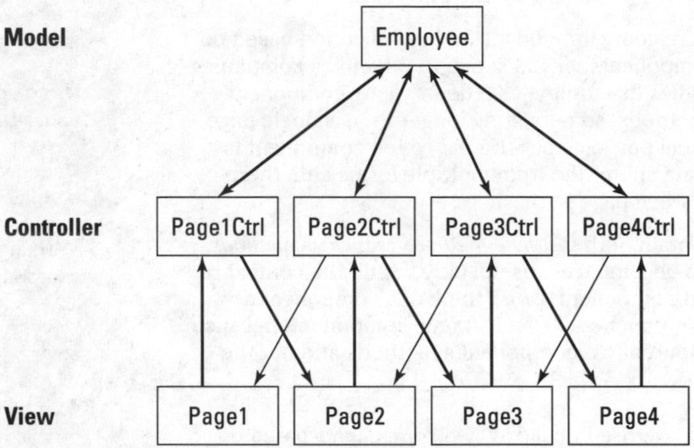

Figure 23-1: Initial concept of application flow.

Before you continue, however, you must first consider all possible interactions with other entities. Because employees require employers, you need to consider *companies* as well, so your flowchart expands to Figure 23-2.

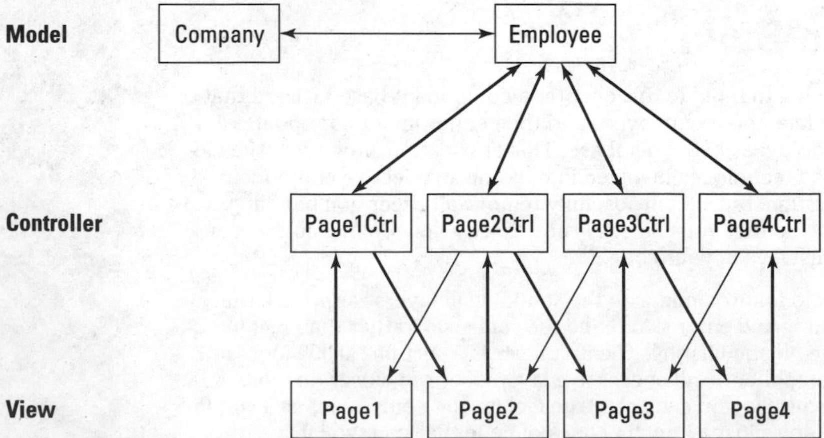

Figure 23-2: Taking interaction with the Company component into consideration.

Another consideration that can help you flesh out your application flow is the *base of operations* where the user starts his tasks and where he returns after those tasks are complete. A common mechanism for such a base of operations is a list of the entities that you can manipulate, as shown in Figure 23-3:

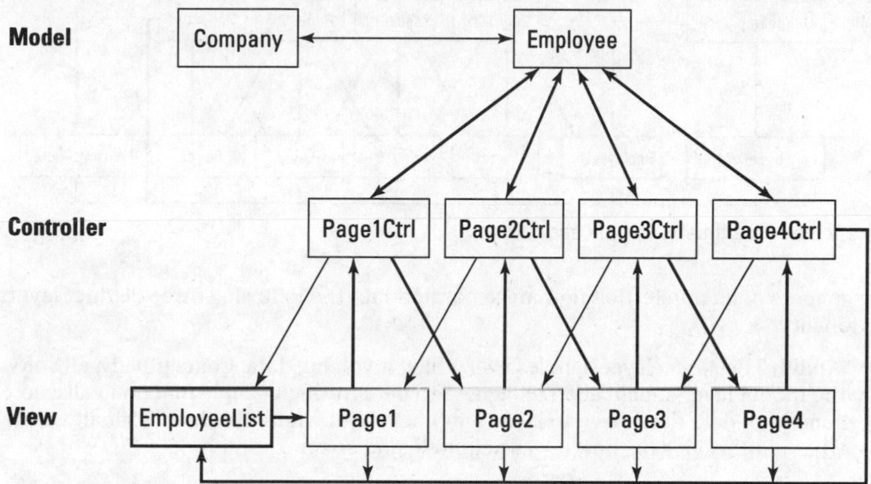

Figure 23-3: Adding a base of operations to the application flow.

At this point, you look through your flowchart to determine whether you've neglected to consider any features in your application. We noticed, for example, that we currently have no interface for *deleting* an existing employee, so we add that feature to our application flow, as shown in Figure 23-4.

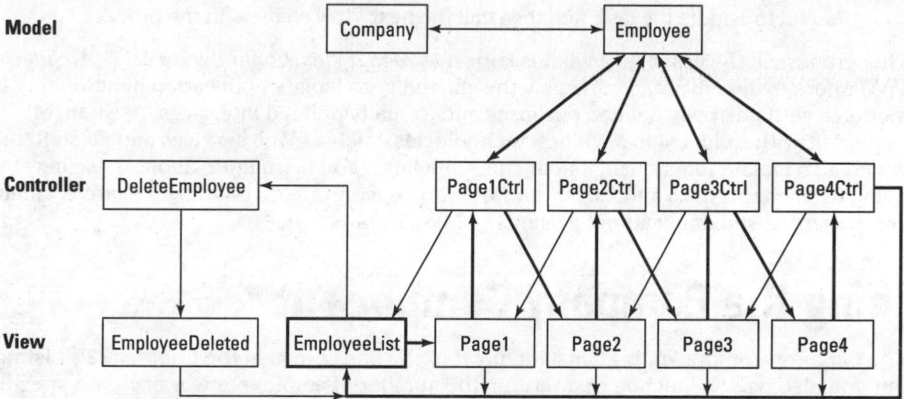

Figure 23-4: Adding a delete feature to the application flow.

And finally, the user needs a way to "jump ship" if he wants to delete his wizard entirely, so you'll add a WizardDeleted process, as shown in Figure 23-5.

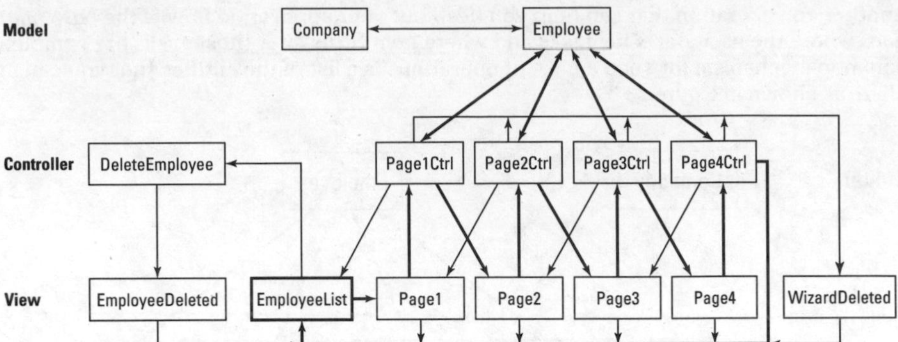

Figure 23-5: The finished application flow.

The elements of an application flow are separated into the following three distinct layers of functionality:

- **Model:** The *Model* layer handles everything involving data. Conceptually, all software in the model layer should abstract access to data through simple function calls, so consumers of data don't need to know anything about where the data originally came from, what platform it's on, how it was acquired, and so on.
- **View:** The *View* layer displays data to the user, collects data from the user, and is responsible for the entire human interface with the application in general. Elements in the View layer request data from and send data to an intermediary known as the Controller layer.
- **Controller:** The *Controller* layer is responsible for determining what a View element wants, acquiring it from the Model, and then calling another View element to display a result or provide the user with a next step in a process. Similarly, the Controller may also receive data from a View element, determine what to do with it, call the appropriate method in the Model to handle the task, and then call the next View element in the process.

This process is the essence of what is known as *Model-View-Controller*, or *MVC, Architecture*. MVC offers many advantages, namely the capability to isolate application functionality into modules with narrowly defined purposes and formally defined interfaces. As such, MVC is a perfect fit with ColdFusion MX's new technologies, such as Web services and Flash Remoting, which also isolate functionality along the same lines. You learn more about these new technologies in chapters 25 and 26, but for now you concentrate on building a relatively simple component-based application by using the MVC architecture.

Building the Company Component

The `Company` component is almost identical to the one shown in the Chapter 22's Listing 22-2, but you also need a function that returns the number of employees working for a specific company. You build this component up a little faster than you did in Chapter 22, but you still use the layered approach. You begin by declaring the functions that you need in Listing 23-1.

Listing 23-1: The first layer: Declaring Company functions and their return types

```
<cfcomponent>
    <!--- GetCompany() [class method] --->
    <cffunction name="GetCompany" returntype="query">
    </cffunction>

    <!--- ListCompanies() [class method] --->
    <cffunction name="ListCompanies" returntype="query">
    </cffunction>

    <!--- CreateCompany() [class method] --->
    <cffunction name="CreateCompany" returntype="void">
    </cffunction>

    <!--- UpdateCompany() [class method] --->
    <cffunction name="UpdateCompany" returntype="void">
    </cffunction>

    <!--- DeleteCompany() [class method] --->
    <cffunction name="DeleteCompany" returntype="void">
    </cffunction>

    <!--- SizeOfCompany() [class method] --->
    <cffunction name="SizeOfCompany" returntype="numeric">
    </cffunction>
</cfcomponent>
```

As you can see from this listing, we like to document the names of our functions (methods) before each is declared, and we include information on whether it is a class method or an instance method. We also begin our first pass by declaring both the function's name and the data type that is returned to the caller.

After declaring all the functions that you need in your `Company` component, you start building out their interfaces with arguments and returns in Listing 23-2. Notice that you start out with only the names and data types of the arguments at this point.

Listing 23-2: The second layer: Declaring Company arguments and returns

```
<cfcomponent>
    <!--- GetCompany() [class method] --->
    <cffunction name="GetCompany" returntype="query">
        <cfargument name="CompanyID" type="numeric">
        <cfreturn companyRec>
    </cffunction>

    <!--- ListCompanies() [class method] --->
```

Continued

Listing 23-2 *(continued)*

```
    <cffunction name="ListCompanies" returntype="query">
        <cfargument name="CompanyFilter" type="string">
        <cfreturn companyRecs>
    </cffunction>

    <!--- CreateCompany() [class method] --->
    <cffunction name="CreateCompany" returntype="void">
        <cfargument name="CompanyName" type="string">
        <cfargument name="Address" type="string">
        <cfargument name="City" type="string">
        <cfargument name="State" type="string">
        <cfargument name="ZipCode" type="string">
        <cfargument name="Comments" type="string">
        <cfreturn>
    </cffunction>

    <!--- UpdateCompany() [class method] --->
    <cffunction name="UpdateCompany" returntype="void">
        <cfargument name="CompanyID" type="numeric">
        <cfargument name="CompanyName" type="string">
        <cfargument name="Address" type="string">
        <cfargument name="City" type="string">
        <cfargument name="State" type="string">
        <cfargument name="ZipCode" type="string">
        <cfargument name="Comments" type="string">
        <cfreturn>
    </cffunction>

    <!--- DeleteCompany() [class method] --->
    <cffunction name="DeleteCompany" returntype="void">
        <cfargument name="CompanyID" type="numeric">
        <cfreturn>
    </cffunction>

    <!--- SizeOfCompany() [class method] --->
    <cffunction name="SizeOfCompany" returntype="numeric">
        <cfargument name="CompanyID" type="numeric">
        <cfreturn GetNumEmployees.NumEmployees>
    </cffunction>
</cfcomponent>
```

You now know what's coming into your methods and what's going back out of them (if anything), so at this point, you're ready to start building business logic in Listing 23-3.

Listing 23-3: The third layer: Adding Company business logic

```
<cfcomponent>
    <!--- GetCompany() [class method] --->
    <cffunction name="GetCompany" returntype="query">
        <cfargument name="CompanyID" type="numeric">

        <cfset Var companyRec = "">

        <cfquery name="companyRec"
                datasource="#Request.MainDSN#">
            SELECT
                CompanyID,
                CompanyName,
                Address,
                City,
                State,
                ZipCode,
                Comments
            FROM
                Company
            WHERE
                CompanyID = #Arguments.CompanyID#
        </cfquery>

        <cfreturn companyRec>
    </cffunction>

    <!--- ListCompanies() [class method] --->
    <cffunction name="ListCompanies" returntype="query">
        <cfargument name="CompanyFilter" type="string">

        <cfset Var companyRecs = "">

        <cfquery name="companyRecs"
                datasource="#Request.MainDSN#">
            SELECT
                CompanyID,
                CompanyName,
                Address,
                City,
                State,
                ZipCode,
                Comments
            FROM
                Company
            <cfif IsDefined('Arguments.CompanyFilter')>
            WHERE
```

Continued

Listing 23-3 *(continued)*

```
            CompanyName LIKE '#Trim(Arguments.CompanyFilter)#%'
        </cfif>
        ORDER BY
            CompanyName
    </cfquery>

    <cfreturn companyRecs>
</cffunction>

<!--- CreateCompany() [class method] --->
<cffunction name="CreateCompany" returntype="void">
    <cfargument name="CompanyName" type="string">
    <cfargument name="Address" type="string">
    <cfargument name="City" type="string">
    <cfargument name="State" type="string">
    <cfargument name="ZipCode" type="string">
    <cfargument name="Comments" type="string">

    <cfset Var insCompany = "">

    <cfquery name="insCompany"
            datasource="#Request.MainDSN#">
        INSERT INTO Company(
            CompanyName,
            Address,
            City,
            State,
            ZipCode,
            Comments
        )
        VALUES (
            '#Trim(Arguments.CompanyName)#',
            '#Trim(Arguments.Address)#',
            '#Trim(Arguments.City)#',
            '#Trim(Arguments.State)#',
            '#Trim(Arguments.ZipCode)#',
            '#Trim(Arguments.Comments)#'
        )
    </cfquery>

    <cfreturn>
</cffunction>

<!--- UpdateCompany() [class method] --->
<cffunction name="UpdateCompany" returntype="void">
    <cfargument name="CompanyID" type="numeric">
    <cfargument name="CompanyName" type="string">
    <cfargument name="Address" type="string">
    <cfargument name="City" type="string">
    <cfargument name="State" type="string">
```

```
    <cfargument name="ZipCode" type="string">
    <cfargument name="Comments" type="string">

    <cfset Var updCompany = "">

    <cfquery name="updCompany"
            datasource="#Request.MainDSN#">
        UPDATE
            Company
        SET
            CompanyName = '#Trim(Arguments.CompanyName)#',
            Address = '#Trim(Arguments.Address)#',
            City = '#Trim(Arguments.City)#',
            State = '#Trim(Arguments.State)#',
            ZipCode = '#Trim(Arguments.ZipCode)#',
            Comments = '#Trim(Arguments.Comments)#'
        WHERE
            CompanyID = #Arguments.CompanyID#
    </cfquery>

    <cfreturn>
</cffunction>

<!--- DeleteCompany() [class method] --->
<cffunction name="DeleteCompany" returntype="void">
    <cfargument name="CompanyID" type="numeric">

    <cfset Var delCompany = "">

    <cfquery name="delCompany"
            datasource="#Request.MainDSN#">
        DELETE
            Company
        WHERE
            CompanyID = #Arguments.CompanyID#
    </cfquery>

    <cfreturn>
</cffunction>

<!--- SizeOfCompany() [class method] --->
<cffunction name="SizeOfCompany" returntype="numeric">
    <cfargument name="CompanyID" type="numeric">

    <cfset Var GetNumEmployees = "">

    <cfquery name="GetNumEmployees"
            datasource="#Request.MainDSN#">
        SELECT
            COUNT(*) AS NumEmployees
        FROM
            Employee
```

Continued

Listing 23-3 *(continued)*

```
            WHERE
                CompanyID = #Val(Arguments.CompanyID)#
        </cfquery>

        <cfreturn GetNumEmployees.NumEmployees>
    </cffunction>
</cfcomponent>
```

The new `SizeOfCompany()` method returns an integer representing the number of employees who work for a specified company. You must set the `access` type of the `SizeOfCompany()` method to `package` because it is called by the `Employee` component only, as you see later on in the section "Building the Employee Component." You should already be familiar with the other component methods from Chapter 22, so we don't need to explain them here.

The only things left to add to this component's methods are their `access` and `output` settings, and you also need to specify whether arguments are required. The finished `Company` component is shown in Listing 23-4.

Listing 23-4: The finished Company component

```
<cfcomponent>
    <!--- GetCompany() [class method] --->
    <cffunction name="GetCompany"
            access="public"
            returntype="query"
            output="No">

        <cfargument name="CompanyID"
            type="numeric"
            required="yes">

        <cfset Var companyRec = "">

        <cfquery name="companyRec"
                datasource="#Request.MainDSN#">
            SELECT
                CompanyID,
                CompanyName,
                Address,
                City,
                State,
                ZipCode,
                Comments
            FROM
                Company
            WHERE
                CompanyID = #Arguments.CompanyID#
```

```
    </cfquery>

    <cfreturn companyRec>
</cffunction>

<!--- ListCompanies() [class method] --->
<cffunction name="ListCompanies"
        access="public"
        returntype="query"
        output="No">

    <cfargument name="CompanyFilter"
        type="string"
        required="no">

    <cfset Var companyRecs = "">

    <cfquery name="companyRecs"
            datasource="#Request.MainDSN#">
        SELECT
            CompanyID,
            CompanyName,
            Address,
            City,
            State,
            ZipCode,
            Comments
        FROM
            Company
        <cfif IsDefined('Arguments.CompanyFilter')>
        WHERE
            CompanyName LIKE '#Trim(Arguments.CompanyFilter)#%'
        </cfif>
        ORDER BY
            CompanyName
    </cfquery>

    <cfreturn companyRecs>
</cffunction>

<!--- CreateCompany() [class method] --->
<cffunction name="CreateCompany"
        access="public"
        returntype="void"
        output="No">

    <cfargument name="CompanyName"
        type="string"
        required="Yes">

    <cfargument name="Address"
        type="string"
```

Continued

Listing 23-4 *(continued)*

```
        required="Yes">

    <cfargument name="City"
        type="string"
        required="Yes">

    <cfargument name="State"
        type="string"
        required="Yes">

    <cfargument name="ZipCode"
        type="string"
        required="Yes">

    <cfargument name="Comments"
        type="string"
        required="Yes">

    <cfset Var insCompany = "">

    <cfquery name="insCompany"
            datasource="#Request.MainDSN#">
        INSERT INTO Company(
            CompanyName,
            Address,
            City,
            State,
            ZipCode,
            Comments
        )
        VALUES (
            '#Trim(Arguments.CompanyName)#',
            '#Trim(Arguments.Address)#',
            '#Trim(Arguments.City)#',
            '#Trim(Arguments.State)#',
            '#Trim(Arguments.ZipCode)#',
            '#Trim(Arguments.Comments)#'
        )
    </cfquery>
    <cfreturn>
</cffunction>

<!--- UpdateCompany() [class method] --->
<cffunction name="UpdateCompany"
        access="public"
        returntype="void"
        output="No">

    <cfargument name="CompanyID"
        type="numeric"
```

```
            required="Yes">

        <cfargument name="CompanyName"
            type="string"
            required="Yes">

        <cfargument name="Address"
            type="string"
            required="Yes">

        <cfargument name="City"
            type="string"
            required="Yes">

        <cfargument name="State"
            type="string"
            required="Yes">

        <cfargument name="ZipCode"
            type="string"
            required="Yes">

        <cfargument name="Comments"
            type="string"
            required="Yes">

        <cfset Var updCompany = "">

        <cfquery name="updCompany"
                datasource="#Request.MainDSN#">
            UPDATE
                Company
            SET
                CompanyName = '#Trim(Arguments.CompanyName)#',
                Address = '#Trim(Arguments.Address)#',
                City = '#Trim(Arguments.City)#',
                State = '#Trim(Arguments.State)#',
                ZipCode = '#Trim(Arguments.ZipCode)#',
                Comments = '#Trim(Arguments.Comments)#'
            WHERE
                CompanyID = #Arguments.CompanyID#
        </cfquery>
        <cfreturn>
    </cffunction>

    <!--- DeleteCompany() [class method] --->
    <cffunction name="DeleteCompany"
            access="public"
            returntype="void"
            output="No">

        <cfargument name="CompanyID"
```

Continued

Listing 23-4 *(continued)*

```
        type="numeric"
        required="Yes">

    <cfset Var delCompany = "">

    <cfquery name="delCompany"
            datasource="#Request.MainDSN#">
        DELETE
            Company
        WHERE
            CompanyID = #Arguments.CompanyID#
    </cfquery>

    <cfreturn>
</cffunction>

<!--- SizeOfCompany() [class method] --->
<cffunction name="SizeOfCompany"
        access="package"
        returntype="numeric"
        output="No">

    <cfargument name="CompanyID"
        type="numeric"
        required="yes">

    <cfset Var GetNumEmployees = "">

    <cfquery name="GetNumEmployees"
            datasource="#Request.MainDSN#">
        SELECT
            COUNT(*) AS NumEmployees
        FROM
            Employee
        WHERE
            CompanyID = #Val(Arguments.CompanyID)#
    </cfquery>

    <cfreturn GetNumEmployees.NumEmployees>
</cffunction>
</cfcomponent>
```

Because the `Company` component declares class methods only, instantiating it in a long-lived scope makes no practical sense, so you have no use for the `This` scope, and locking is unnecessary.

The `Company` component is straightforward and easy to build because it's just a formal collection of standard database functions. The `Employee` component that you build next is a little more complicated because it is designed for use as a persistent instance that carries its own data with it rather than calling the database each time that the application needs data, as the `Company` component does.

Building the Employee Component

The Employee component is designed to persist between page requests and carry with it data pertaining to a specific employee. If the component's data pertains to a new employee, it originates from user input; otherwise, it originates from the database.

As an instance of Employee is created, its initialization method declares the instance's properties with empty or zeroed values. If the user wants to add a new employee, he enters data into a form and sends it (through the Controller) to that instance, and its properties are set to those new values. The instance persists its properties (the new values) throughout its lifespan.

If the user wants to edit an existing employee, the initialization method is called a second time with an optional argument that is the key value of that employee. The initialization method first retrieves the employee's data from the database, and then it sets the property's values to those retrieved from the database, which again persists its properties throughout its lifespan.

Whether the user is adding a new employee or editing an existing one, a single function named FlushEmployeeToDatabase() flushes the instance's properties to the database for permanent storage after the adding or editing task is complete.

As is typical of almost any entity-centric component, this Employee component declares a list method, a method for getting a specific employee's record from the database, a method for deleting a specific employee from the database, and methods for calculating employee bonuses. And, because you want to go the extra mile, you're going to declare a full compliment of setter and getter functions.

The following list provides a brief description of each method and what it does:

✦ **InitEmployee()** is a class method that returns nothing, so it is a void function (see Chapter 22). Its purpose is to initialize the properties of the current instance of the Employee component. InitEmployee() takes an optional argument of an employee's SSN, which, if passed, causes the method to retrieve that employee's record from the database and initialize properties with its data.

The SSN retrieved from the database is used to instantiate two SSN properties, one of which is designated as the "key" SSN. This is necessary, as the user may edit the value of the employee's SSN, and you need the original SSN value as the predicate to the WHERE clause of the UPDATE statement in the FlushEmployeeToDatabase() method, which we describe a little later in this list.

✦ **GetEmployee()** is a class method that returns a query data type containing a single employee. GetEmployee() is called only from inside the component by InitEmployee() as the optional SSN argument is passed, so GetEmployee() is a private method.

✦ **FlushEmployeeToDatabase()** is an instance method that returns nothing, so it is a void function. Its purpose is to either insert the current instance's properties into the database if the properties represent a new employee or update an existing employee's record if his properties are being edited.

✦ **DeleteEmployee()** is a class method that returns nothing, so it is a void function. It makes sense to design DeleteEmployee() as a class method rather than an instance method because your application may need to delete an employee other than the current one, and first initializing an instance of the Employee component with an existing employee's data just so that you can delete it doesn't make sense.

- `ListEmployees()` is a class method that returns a query data type containing the list of employees that match any filter criteria passed to the method. This method declares two optional arguments representing the first few characters of the employers' names and/or employees' last names. If one or more of these criteria are specified, `ListEmployees()` uses them to filter the list of employees returned. A list of employees can't possibly have anything to do with the current instance's `Employee` properties, so designing `ListEmployees()` as an instance method makes no sense, and, therefore, it is designed as a class method.
- `GetEmployeeSSN()` is an instance method that returns a string data type. It is a getter function that simply returns `This.SSN`.
- `GetEmployeeCompanyID()` is an instance method that returns a numeric data type. It is a getter function that simply returns `This.CompanyID`.
- `GetEmployeeCompanyName()` is an instance method that returns a string data type. It is a getter function that simply returns `This.CompanyName`.
- `GetEmployeeFirstname()` is an instance method that returns a string data type. It is a getter function that simply returns `This. Firstname`.
- `GetEmployeeLastname()` is an instance method that returns a string data type. It is a getter function that simply returns `This.Lastname`.
- `GetEmployeeFullname()` is an instance method that returns a string data type. It is a getter function that returns the concatenation of `This.Firstname`, a space character, and `This.Lastname`. Creating an entire method that performs such a simple task may seem strange, but this is a common practice in object-oriented systems.
- `GetEmployeeSalary()` is an instance method that returns a numeric data type. It is a getter function that simply returns `This.Salary`.
- `GetEmployeeDateOfBirth()` is an instance method that returns a date data type. It is a getter function that simply returns `This.DateOfBirth`.
- `SetEmployeeSSN()` is an instance method that returns nothing, so it is a void function. It is a setter function that simply sets `This.SSN`.
- `SetEmployeeCompanyID()` is an instance method that returns nothing, so it is a void function. It is a setter function that not only sets `This.CompanyID`, but also sets `This.CompanyName`. This is an important principle to follow: If your entity-based component persists properties related to a foreign entity (as `Company` is within `Employee`), you should have only one setter function related to that foreign entity, and it must be based on that foreign entity's key. The single foreign setter function must set all properties in the component that are related to the foreign entity. In this case, `SetCompanyID()` must also set `This.CompanyName` at the same time, hence the invocation of `Company.GetCompany()` from within `SetEmployeeCompanyID()`.
- `SetEmployeeFirstname()` is an instance method that returns nothing, so it is a void function. It is a setter function that simply sets `This.Firstname`.
- `SetEmployeeLastname()` is an instance method that returns nothing, so it is a void function. It is a setter function that simply sets `This.Lastname`.
- `SetEmployeeSalary()` is an instance method that returns nothing, so it is a void function. It is a setter function that simply sets `This.Salary`.
- `SetEmployeeDateOfBirth()` is an instance method that returns nothing, so it is a void function. It is a setter function that simply set `This.DateOfBirth`.

✦ `XmasBonus()` is an instance method that returns a numeric data type containing the current employee's Christmas bonus. `XmasBonus()` is a private method, because it is accessed only from other methods declared within the `Employee` component.

✦ `Bonus()` is an instance method that returns a numeric data type containing the current employee's total annual bonus, of which `XmasBonus()` is a part.

This time, we move you a little faster through the design process, and you start by declaring both the functions and their I/O interfaces at the same time, as shown in Listing 23-5. Make sure that you type the comments exactly as shown in the listing, including whether each function is a class method or an instance method.

Listing 23-5: Declaring Employee functions and their I/O interfaces

```
<cfcomponent>
    <!--- Initialization Area --->
    <cfscript>
        InitEmployee();
    </cfscript>

    <!--- InitEmployee() [class method] --->
    <cffunction name="InitEmployee" returntype="void">
        <cfargument name="SSN" type="string">
        <cfreturn>
    </cffunction>

    <!--- GetEmployee() [class method] --->
    <cffunction name="GetEmployee" returntype="query">
        <cfargument name="SSN" type="string">
        <cfreturn employeeRec>
    </cffunction>

    <!--- FlushEmployeeToDatabase() [instance method] --->
    <cffunction name="FlushEmployeeToDatabase" returntype="void">
        <cfreturn>
    </cffunction>

    <!--- DeleteEmployee() [class method] --->
    <cffunction name="DeleteEmployee" returntype="void">
        <cfargument name="SSN" type="string">
        <cfreturn>
    </cffunction>

    <!--- ListEmployees() [class method] --->
    <cffunction name="ListEmployees" returntype="query">
        <cfargument name="EmployeeFilter" type="string">
        <cfargument name="CompanyFilter" type="string">
        <cfreturn employeeRecs>
    </cffunction>

    <!--- GetEmployeeSSN() [instance method] --->
```

Continued

Listing 23-5 *(continued)*

```
<cffunction name="GetEmployeeSSN" returntype="string">
    <cfreturn This.ssn>
</cffunction>

<!--- GetEmployeeCompanyID() [instance method] --->
<cffunction name="GetEmployeeCompanyID" returntype="numeric">
    <cfreturn This.companyID>
</cffunction>

<!--- GetEmployeeCompanyName() [instance method] --->
<cffunction name="GetEmployeeCompanyName" returntype="string">
    <cfreturn This.companyName>
</cffunction>

<!--- GetEmployeeFirstname() [instance method] --->
<cffunction name="GetEmployeeFirstname" returntype="string">
    <cfreturn This.firstname>
</cffunction>

<!--- GetEmployeeLastname() [instance method] --->
<cffunction name="GetEmployeeLastname" returntype="string">
    <cfreturn This.lastname>
</cffunction>

<!--- GetEmployeeFullname() [instance method] --->
<cffunction name="GetEmployeeFullname" returntype="string">
    <cfreturn This.firstname & ' ' & This.lastname>
</cffunction>

<!--- GetEmployeeSalary() [instance method] --->
<cffunction name="GetEmployeeSalary" returntype="numeric">
    <cfreturn This.salary>
</cffunction>

<!--- GetEmployeeDateOfBirth() [instance method] --->
<cffunction name="GetEmployeeDateOfBirth" returntype="date">
    <cfreturn This.dateOfBirth>
</cffunction>

<!--- SetEmployeeSSN() [instance method] --->
<cffunction name="SetEmployeeSSN" returntype="void">
    <cfargument name="SSN" type="string">
    <cfreturn>
</cffunction>

<!--- SetEmployeeCompanyID() [instance method] --->
<cffunction name="SetEmployeeCompanyID" returntype="void">
    <cfargument name="CompanyID" type="string">
```

```
        <cfreturn>
    </cffunction>

    <!--- SetEmployeeFirstname() [instance method] --->
    <cffunction name="SetEmployeeFirstname" returntype="void">
        <cfargument name="Firstname" type="string">
        <cfreturn>
    </cffunction>

    <!--- SetEmployeeLastname() [instance method] --->
    <cffunction name="SetEmployeeLastname" returntype="void">
        <cfargument name="Lastname" type="string">
        <cfreturn>
    </cffunction>

    <!--- SetEmployeeSalary() [instance method] --->
    <cffunction name="SetEmployeeSalary" returntype="void">
        <cfargument name="Salary" type="numeric">
        <cfreturn>
    </cffunction>

    <!--- SetEmployeeDateOfBirth() [instance method] --->
    <cffunction name="SetEmployeeDateOfBirth" returntype="void">
        <cfargument name="DateOfBirth" type="date">
        <cfreturn>
    </cffunction>

    <!--- XmasBonus() [instance method] --->
    <cffunction name="XmasBonus" returntype="numeric">
        <cfreturn returnVar * 10>
    </cffunction>

    <!--- Bonus() [instance method] --->
    <cffunction name="Bonus" returntype="numeric">
        <cfreturn (Val(This.Salary) * 0.05) + XmasBonus()>
    </cffunction>
</cfcomponent>
```

Do you get a feel for how this component behaves? If, later on, as you're designing your own components, the first layer doesn't make perfect sense, go back to your functional requirements document and make sure that you have all of the following:

✦ A matching method for everything that your component must do.

✦ A matching argument for every data input that each method requires. (Concern yourself with optional arguments later.)

✦ A return type for each method that matches how it is consumed by its caller.

If you go farther into development before you have these steps completed and a resulting component "shell" that is straightforward and obvious, you end up with only "spaghetti code" and debugging nightmares.

After you have laid the foundation for your component, you can add the business logic, as shown in Listing 23-6.

Listing 23-6: Adding Employee business logic

```
<cfcomponent>
    <!--- Initialization Area --->
    <cfscript>
        InitEmployee();
    </cfscript>

    <!--- InitEmployee() [class method] --->
    <cffunction name="InitEmployee" returntype="void">
        <cfargument name="SSN" type="string">

        <cfset Var EmployeeInitRec = "">
        <cfscript>
            if (IsDefined('Arguments.ssn')) {
                EmployeeInitRec = GetEmployee(Arguments.SSN);
                This.keySSN = EmployeeInitRec.SSN;
                This.ssn = EmployeeInitRec.SSN;
                This.companyID = EmployeeInitRec.CompanyID;
                This.companyName = EmployeeInitRec.CompanyName;
                This.firstname = EmployeeInitRec.Firstname;
                This.lastname = EmployeeInitRec.Lastname;
                This.salary = EmployeeInitRec.Salary;
                This.dateOfBirth = EmployeeInitRec.DateOfBirth;
                This.isNewEmployee = FALSE;
            } else {
                This.keySSN = "";
                This.ssn = "";
                This.companyID = 0;
                This.companyName = "";
                This.firstname = "";
                This.lastname = "";
                This.salary = 0;
                This.dateOfBirth = "12/30/1899";
                This.isNewEmployee = TRUE;
            }
        </cfscript>

        <cfreturn>
    </cffunction>

    <!--- GetEmployee() [class method] --->
    <cffunction name="GetEmployee" returntype="query">
        <cfargument name="SSN" type="string">

        <cfset Var employeeRec = "">
        <cfquery name="employeeRec"
                datasource="#Request.MainDSN#">
            SELECT
                e.SSN,
                e.CompanyID,
                e.Firstname,
                e.Lastname,
```

```
                e.Salary,
                e.DateOfBirth,
                c.CompanyName
            FROM
                Employee e INNER JOIN Company c
                    ON e.CompanyID = c.CompanyID
            WHERE
                e.SSN = '#Arguments.SSN#'
        </cfquery>

        <cfreturn employeeRec>
    </cffunction>

    <!--- FlushEmployeeToDatabase() [instance method] --->
    <cffunction name="FlushEmployeeToDatabase" returntype="void">

        <cfset Var insEmployee = "">
        <cfset Var updEmployee = "">
        <cfif This.isNewEmployee>
            <cfquery name="insEmployee"
                    datasource="#Request.MainDSN#">
                INSERT INTO Employee(
                    SSN,
                    CompanyID,
                    Firstname,
                    Lastname,
                    Salary,
                    DateOfBirth
                )
                VALUES (
                    '#Trim(This.SSN)#',
                    #Val(This.CompanyID)#,
                    '#Trim(This.Firstname)#',
                    '#Trim(This.Lastname)#',
                    #Val(This.Salary)#,
                    '#Trim(This.DateOfBirth)#'
                )
            </cfquery>
        <cfelse>
            <cfquery name="updEmployee"
                    datasource="#Request.MainDSN#">
                UPDATE
                    Employee
                SET
                    SSN = '#Trim(This.SSN)#',
                    CompanyID = #Val(This.CompanyID)#,
                    Firstname = '#Trim(This.Firstname)#',
                    Lastname = '#Trim(This.Lastname)#',
                    Salary = #Val(This.Salary)#,
                    DateOfBirth = '#Trim(This.DateOfBirth)#'
                WHERE
                    SSN = '#This.keySSN#'
```

Continued

Listing 23-6 *(continued)*

```
            </cfquery>
        </cfif>

        <cfreturn>
    </cffunction>

    <!--- DeleteEmployee() [class method] --->
    <cffunction name="DeleteEmployee" returntype="void">
        <cfargument name="SSN" type="string">

        <cfset Var delEmployee = "">
        <cfquery name="delEmployee"
                datasource="#Request.MainDSN#">
            DELETE
                Employee
            WHERE
                SSN = '#Arguments.SSN#'
        </cfquery>

        <cfreturn>
    </cffunction>

    <!--- ListEmployees() [class method] --->
    <cffunction name="ListEmployees" returntype="query">
        <cfargument name="EmployeeFilter" type="string">
        <cfargument name="CompanyFilter" type="string">

        <cfset Var employeeRecs = "">
        <cfquery name="employeeRecs"
                datasource="#Request.MainDSN#">
            SELECT
                c.CompanyName,
                e.CompanyID,
                e.SSN,
                e.Firstname,
                e.Lastname,
                e.Salary,
                e.DateOfBirth,
                (SELECT Count(*) FROM Dependant d WHERE d.ssn = e.ssn)
AS NumDependants
            FROM
                Company c INNER JOIN Employee e
                    ON c.CompanyID = e.CompanyID
            WHERE
                1 = 1
            <cfif IsDefined('Arguments.CompanyFilter')>
                AND c.CompanyName LIKE
'#Trim(Arguments.CompanyFilter)#%'
            </cfif>
            <cfif IsDefined('Arguments.EmployeeFilter')>
```

```
            AND e.Lastname LIKE '#Trim(Arguments.EmployeeFilter)#%'
        </cfif>
        ORDER BY
            e.Lastname ASC,
            e.Firstname ASC
    </cfquery>

    <cfreturn employeeRecs>
</cffunction>

<!--- GetEmployeeSSN() [instance method] --->
<cffunction name="GetEmployeeSSN" returntype="string">
    <cfreturn This.ssn>
</cffunction>

<!--- GetEmployeeCompanyID() [instance method] --->
<cffunction name="GetEmployeeCompanyID" returntype="numeric">
    <cfreturn This.companyID>
</cffunction>

<!--- GetEmployeeCompanyName() [instance method] --->
<cffunction name="GetEmployeeCompanyName" returntype="string">
    <cfreturn This.companyName>
</cffunction>

<!--- GetEmployeeFirstname() [instance method] --->
<cffunction name="GetEmployeeFirstname" returntype="string">
    <cfreturn This.firstname>
</cffunction>

<!--- GetEmployeeLastname() [instance method] --->
<cffunction name="GetEmployeeLastname" returntype="string">
    <cfreturn This.lastname>
</cffunction>

<!--- GetEmployeeFullname() [instance method] --->
<cffunction name="GetEmployeeFullname" returntype="string">
    <cfreturn This.firstname & ' ' & This.lastname>
</cffunction>

<!--- GetEmployeeSalary() [instance method] --->
<cffunction name="GetEmployeeSalary" returntype="numeric">
    <cfreturn This.salary>
</cffunction>

<!--- GetEmployeeDateOfBirth() [instance method] --->
<cffunction name="GetEmployeeDateOfBirth" returntype="date">
    <cfreturn This.dateOfBirth>
</cffunction>

<!--- SetEmployeeSSN() [instance method] --->
<cffunction name="SetEmployeeSSN" returntype="void">
```

Continued

Listing 23-6 *(continued)*

```
    <cfargument name="SSN" type="string">

    <cfset This.ssn = Arguments.SSN>

    <cfreturn>
</cffunction>

<!--- SetEmployeeCompanyID() [instance method] --->
<cffunction name="SetEmployeeCompanyID" returntype="void">
    <cfargument name="CompanyID" type="string">

    <cfset Var companyRec = "">
    <cfset This.companyID = Arguments.CompanyID>
    <cfinvoke component="Company"
        method="GetCompany"
        returnvariable="companyRec"
        CompanyID="#This.companyID#">
    <cfset This.companyName = companyRec.companyName[1]>

    <cfreturn>
</cffunction>

<!--- SetEmployeeFirstname() [instance method] --->
<cffunction name="SetEmployeeFirstname" returntype="void">
    <cfargument name="Firstname" type="string">

    <cfset This.firstname = Arguments.Firstname>

    <cfreturn>
</cffunction>

<!--- SetEmployeeLastname() [instance method] --->
<cffunction name="SetEmployeeLastname" returntype="void">
    <cfargument name="Lastname" type="string">

    <cfset This.lastname = Arguments.Lastname>

    <cfreturn>
</cffunction>

<!--- SetEmployeeSalary() [instance method] --->
<cffunction name="SetEmployeeSalary" returntype="void">
    <cfargument name="Salary" type="numeric">

    <cfset This.salary = Arguments.Salary>

    <cfreturn>
```

```
    </cffunction>

    <!--- SetEmployeeDateOfBirth() [instance method] --->
    <cffunction name="SetEmployeeDateOfBirth" returntype="void">
        <cfargument name="DateOfBirth" type="date">

        <cfset This.dateOfBirth = Arguments.DateOfBirth>

        <cfreturn>
    </cffunction>

    <!--- XmasBonus() [instance method] --->
    <cffunction name="XmasBonus"
            access="private"
            returntype="numeric"
            output="No">

        <cfset Var returnVar = 0>
        <cfinvoke component="Company"
            method="SizeOfCompany"
            returnvariable="returnVar"
            CompanyID="#This.CompanyID#">

        <cfreturn returnVar * 10>
    </cffunction>

    <!--- Bonus() [instance method] --->
    <cffunction name="Bonus"
            access="public"
            returntype="numeric"
            output="No">

        <cfreturn (Val(This.Salary) * 0.05) + XmasBonus()>

    </cffunction>
</cfcomponent>
```

By using this “building-in-layers” technique, you can start testing basic component functionality much sooner in the development phase. You can test the `Employee` component right now, for example, and determine whether everything works without the encumbrances of security authorization, access types, argument requirements, and so on.

And because you eliminate as many details as possible until the last feasible moment, you avoid going into “debug paralysis” from hunting down lots of little annoyances. Remember that, as you linearly add complexities, you exponentially add difficulties.

Now you’re ready to finish up your `Employee` component. In actual practice, we always add locking mechanisms in one layer and the remaining function and argument attributes in another, but the publisher understandably has a page count within which we must stay so we’re moving you along a little faster than normal and having you add both layers at the same time to complete your `Employee` component in Listing 23-7.

Listing 23-7: The finished Employee component

```
<cfcomponent>
    <!--- Initialization Area --->
    <cfscript>
        This.lockName = CreateUUID();
        InitEmployee();
    </cfscript>

    <!--- InitEmployee() [class method] --->
    <cffunction name="InitEmployee"
            access="public"
            returntype="void"
            output="No">

        <cfargument name="SSN"
                type="string"
                required="no">

        <cfset Var EmployeeInitRec = "">
        <cflock name="#This.lockName#"
                timeout="10"
                throwontimeout="Yes"
                type="EXCLUSIVE">
            <cfscript>
                if (IsDefined('Arguments.ssn')) {
                    EmployeeInitRec = GetEmployee(Arguments.SSN);
                    This.keySSN = EmployeeInitRec.SSN;
                    This.ssn = EmployeeInitRec.SSN;
                    This.companyID = EmployeeInitRec.CompanyID;
                    This.companyName = EmployeeInitRec.CompanyName;
                    This.firstname = EmployeeInitRec.Firstname;
                    This.lastname = EmployeeInitRec.Lastname;
                    This.salary = EmployeeInitRec.Salary;
                    This.dateOfBirth = EmployeeInitRec.DateOfBirth;
                    This.isNewEmployee = FALSE;
                } else {
                    This.keySSN = "";
                    This.ssn = "";
                    This.companyID = 0;
                    This.companyName = "";
                    This.firstname = "";
                    This.lastname = "";
                    This.salary = 0;
                    This.dateOfBirth = "12/30/1899";
                    This.isNewEmployee = TRUE;
                }
            </cfscript>
        </cflock>

        <cfreturn>
    </cffunction>
```

```
<!--- GetEmployee() [class method] --->
<cffunction name="GetEmployee"
      access="private"
      returntype="query"
      output="No">

    <cfargument name="SSN"
          type="string"
          required="yes">

    <cfset Var employeeRec = "">
    <cfquery name="employeeRec"
          datasource="#Request.MainDSN#">
        SELECT
            e.SSN,
            e.CompanyID,
            e.Firstname,
            e.Lastname,
            e.Salary,
            e.DateOfBirth,
            c.CompanyName
        FROM
            Employee e INNER JOIN Company c
                ON e.CompanyID = c.CompanyID
        WHERE
            e.SSN = '#Arguments.SSN#'
    </cfquery>


    <cfreturn employeeRec>
</cffunction>

<!--- FlushEmployeeToDatabase() [instance method] --->
<cffunction name="FlushEmployeeToDatabase"
      access="public"
      returntype="void"
      output="No"
      roles="CLERK">

    <cfset Var insEmployee = "">
    <cfset Var updEmployee = "">
    <cflock name="#This.lockName#"
          timeout="10"
          throwontimeout="Yes"
          type="READONLY">

        <cfif This.isNewEmployee>
            <cfquery name="insEmployee"
                  datasource="#Request.MainDSN#">
                INSERT INTO Employee(
                    SSN,
```

Continued

Listing 23-7 *(continued)*

```
                    CompanyID,
                    Firstname,
                    Lastname,
                    Salary,
                    DateOfBirth
                )
                VALUES (
                    '#Trim(This.SSN)#',
                    #Val(This.CompanyID)#,
                    '#Trim(This.Firstname)#',
                    '#Trim(This.Lastname)#',
                    #Val(This.Salary)#,
                    '#Trim(This.DateOfBirth)#'
                )
            </cfquery>
        <cfelse>
            <cfquery name="updEmployee"
                    datasource="#Request.MainDSN#">
                UPDATE
                    Employee
                SET
                    SSN = '#Trim(This.SSN)#',
                    CompanyID = #Val(This.CompanyID)#,
                    Firstname = '#Trim(This.Firstname)#',
                    Lastname = '#Trim(This.Lastname)#',
                    Salary = #Val(This.Salary)#,
                    DateOfBirth = '#Trim(This.DateOfBirth)#'
                WHERE
                    SSN = '#This.keySSN#'
            </cfquery>
        </cfif>
    </cflock>

    <cfreturn>
</cffunction>

<!--- DeleteEmployee() [class method] --->
<cffunction name="DeleteEmployee"
        access="public"
        returntype="void"
        output="No"
        roles="ADMIN,CLERK">

    <cfargument name="SSN"
            type="string"
            required="Yes">

    <cfset Var delEmployee = "">
    <cfquery name="delEmployee"
            datasource="#Request.MainDSN#">
        DELETE
```

```
                Employee
            WHERE
                SSN = '#Arguments.SSN#'
        </cfquery>

        <cfreturn>
    </cffunction>

    <!--- ListEmployees() [class method] --->
    <cffunction name="ListEmployees"
            access="public"
            returntype="query"
            output="No">

        <cfargument name="EmployeeFilter"
                type="string"
                required="no">

        <cfargument name="CompanyFilter"
                type="string"
                required="no">

        <cfset Var employeeRecs = "">
        <cfquery name="employeeRecs"
                datasource="#Request.MainDSN#">
            SELECT
                c.CompanyName,
                e.CompanyID,
                e.SSN,
                e.Firstname,
                e.Lastname,
                e.Salary,
                e.DateOfBirth,
                (SELECT Count(*) FROM Dependant d WHERE d.ssn = e.ssn)
AS NumDependants
            FROM
                Company c INNER JOIN Employee e
                    ON c.CompanyID = e.CompanyID
            WHERE
                1 = 1
            <cfif IsDefined('Arguments.CompanyFilter')>
                AND c.CompanyName LIKE
'#Trim(Arguments.CompanyFilter)#%'
            </cfif>
            <cfif IsDefined('Arguments.EmployeeFilter')>
                AND e.Lastname LIKE '#Trim(Arguments.EmployeeFilter)#%'
            </cfif>
            ORDER BY
                e.Lastname ASC,
                e.Firstname ASC
        </cfquery>
```

Continued

Listing 23-7 *(continued)*

```
    <cfreturn employeeRecs>
</cffunction>

<!--- GetEmployeeSSN() [instance method] --->
<cffunction name="GetEmployeeSSN"
        access="public"
        returntype="string"
        output="No">

    <cflock name="#This.lockName#"
            timeout="10"
            throwontimeout="Yes"
            type="READONLY">

        <cfreturn This.ssn>

    </cflock>
</cffunction>

<!--- GetEmployeeCompanyID() [instance method] --->
<cffunction name="GetEmployeeCompanyID"
        access="public"
        returntype="numeric"
        output="No">

    <cflock name="#This.lockName#"
            timeout="10"
            throwontimeout="Yes"
            type="READONLY">

        <cfreturn This.companyID>

    </cflock>
</cffunction>

<!--- GetEmployeeCompanyName() [instance method] --->
<cffunction name="GetEmployeeCompanyName"
        access="public"
        returntype="string"
        output="No">

    <cflock name="#This.lockName#"
            timeout="10"
            throwontimeout="Yes"
            type="READONLY">

        <cfreturn This.companyName>

    </cflock>
```

```
</cffunction>

<!--- GetEmployeeFirstname() [instance method] --->
<cffunction name="GetEmployeeFirstname"
        access="public"
        returntype="string"
        output="No">

    <cflock name="#This.lockName#"
            timeout="10"
            throwontimeout="Yes"
            type="READONLY">

        <cfreturn This.firstname>

    </cflock>
</cffunction>

<!--- GetEmployeeLastname() [instance method] --->
<cffunction name="GetEmployeeLastname"
        access="public"
        returntype="string"
        output="No">

    <cflock name="#This.lockName#"
            timeout="10"
            throwontimeout="Yes"
            type="READONLY">

        <cfreturn This.lastname>

    </cflock>
</cffunction>

<!--- GetEmployeeFullname() [instance method] --->
<cffunction name="GetEmployeeFullname"
        access="public"
        returntype="string"
        output="No">

    <cflock name="#This.lockName#"
            timeout="10"
            throwontimeout="Yes"
            type="READONLY">

        <cfreturn This.firstname & ' ' & This.lastname>

    </cflock>
</cffunction>

<!--- GetEmployeeSalary() [instance method] --->
<cffunction name="GetEmployeeSalary"
```

Continued

Listing 23-7 *(continued)*

```
        access="public"
        returntype="numeric"
        output="No">

    <cflock name="#This.lockName#"
        timeout="10"
        throwontimeout="Yes"
        type="READONLY">

        <cfreturn This.salary>

    </cflock>
</cffunction>

<!--- GetEmployeeDateOfBirth() [instance method] --->
<cffunction name="GetEmployeeDateOfBirth"
        access="public"
        returntype="date"
        output="No">

    <cflock name="#This.lockName#"
        timeout="10"
        throwontimeout="Yes"
        type="READONLY">

        <cfreturn This.dateOfBirth>

    </cflock>
</cffunction>

<!--- SetEmployeeSSN() [instance method] --->
<cffunction name="SetEmployeeSSN"
        access="public"
        returntype="void"
        output="No">

    <cfargument name="SSN"
        type="string"
        required="yes">

    <cflock name="#This.lockName#"
        timeout="10"
        throwontimeout="Yes"
        type="EXCLUSIVE">

        <cfset This.ssn = Arguments.SSN>

        <cfreturn>
    </cflock>
```

```
</cffunction>

<!--- SetEmployeeCompanyID() [instance method] --->
<cffunction name="SetEmployeeCompanyID"
        access="public"
        returntype="void"
        output="No">

    <cfargument name="CompanyID"
        type="string"
        required="yes">

    <cfset Var companyRec = "">
    <cflock name="#This.lockName#"
            timeout="10"
            throwontimeout="Yes"
            type="EXCLUSIVE">

        <cfset This.companyID = Arguments.CompanyID>
        <cfinvoke component="Company"
            method="GetCompany"
            returnvariable="companyRec"
            CompanyID="#This.companyID#">
        <cfset This.companyName = companyRec.companyName[1]>

        <cfreturn>
    </cflock>
</cffunction>

<!--- SetEmployeeFirstname() [instance method] --->
<cffunction name="SetEmployeeFirstname"
        access="public"
        returntype="void"
        output="No">

    <cfargument name="Firstname"
        type="string"
        required="yes">

    <cflock name="#This.lockName#"
            timeout="10"
            throwontimeout="Yes"
            type="EXCLUSIVE">

        <cfset This.firstname = Arguments.Firstname>

        <cfreturn>
    </cflock>
</cffunction>

<!--- SetEmployeeLastname() [instance method] --->
<cffunction name="SetEmployeeLastname"
```

Continued

Listing 23-7 *(continued)*

```
          access="public"
          returntype="void"
          output="No">

     <cfargument name="Lastname"
          type="string"
          required="yes">

     <cflock name="#This.lockName#"
               timeout="10"
               throwontimeout="Yes"
               type="EXCLUSIVE">

          <cfset This.lastname = Arguments.Lastname>

          <cfreturn>
     </cflock>
</cffunction>

<!--- SetEmployeeSalary() [instance method] --->
<cffunction name="SetEmployeeSalary"
          access="public"
          returntype="void"
          output="No">

     <cfargument name="Salary"
          type="numeric"
          required="yes">

     <cflock name="#This.lockName#"
               timeout="10"
               throwontimeout="Yes"
               type="EXCLUSIVE">

          <cfset This.salary = Arguments.Salary>

          <cfreturn>
     </cflock>
</cffunction>

<!--- SetEmployeeDateOfBirth() [instance method] --->
<cffunction name="SetEmployeeDateOfBirth"
          access="public"
          returntype="void"
          output="No">

     <cfargument name="DateOfBirth"
          type="date"
```

```
        required="yes">

    <cflock name="#This.lockName#"
        timeout="10"
        throwontimeout="Yes"
        type="EXCLUSIVE">

        <cfset This.dateOfBirth = Arguments.DateOfBirth>

        <cfreturn>
    </cflock>
  </cffunction>

    <!--- XmasBonus() [instance method] --->
  <cffunction name="XmasBonus"
        access="private"
        returntype="numeric"
        output="No">

    <cfset Var returnVar = 0>
    <cflock name="#This.lockName#"
        timeout="10"
        throwontimeout="Yes"
        type="READONLY">

        <cfinvoke component="Company"
            method="SizeOfCompany"
            returnvariable="returnVar"
            CompanyID="#This.CompanyID#">

        <cfreturn returnVar * 10>
    </cflock>
  </cffunction>

  <!--- Bonus() [instance method] --->
  <cffunction name="Bonus"
        access="public"
        returntype="numeric"
        output="No">

    <cflock name="#This.lockName#"
        timeout="10"
        throwontimeout="Yes"
        type="READONLY">

        <cfreturn (Val(This.Salary) * 0.05) + XmasBonus()>

    </cflock>
  </cffunction>
</cfcomponent>
```

The following list discusses these last details of Listing 23-7 in a little more detail:

✦ `Output="No"` is added to every method because none of your methods produce direct output. We never author functions that produce direct output and, instead, prefer the formal return of a result. Because `Output="No"` is the functional equivalent of wrapping a function's logic with a pair of `CFSILENT` tags, you absolutely prevent any output from leaking out of your method — even white space.

✦ `Date` properties should be initialized with actual date values rather than empty strings; otherwise, you throw validation errors in attempting to return those properties from a function with a `Returntype="Date"`.

✦ `Returntype="Date"` honors the time component of `Datetime` values. Don't confuse this with the `Date` datatype of some database platforms that either strip times from `Datetime` values or reject them entirely.

✦ The `Roles` attribute is included in the `FlushEmployeeToDatabase()` and `DeleteEmployee()` methods so that you can experiment with user authorization after you've built the completed application. Just play with the `CFLOGINUSER` tag at the top of Listing 23-8 to see how ColdFusion MX reacts to calling functions that you are not authorized to execute. You may even try implementing a structured exception-handling framework for this application. One warning, however: `CFCATCH Type="Security"` has nothing to do with user authorization, so don't try to use it as such. User authorization errors are `Type="Application"`.

✦ The `EmployeeFilter` and `CompanyFilter` arguments of the `ListEmployees()` method are optional, so you must check to determine whether they are defined before attempting to use them. Later on, you find an easy way of passing only those arguments that you actually use, in Listing 23-8. Notice, too, that we name these two arguments differently from the properties to which they correspond, because naming them `Lastname` and `CompanyName` would be confusing to a maintenance developer who may reasonably expect complete values to be passed rather than just the beginning portions.

✦ `WHERE 1 = 1` avoids complicated logic for handling `AND` conditions in the presence of zero, one, or more predicates to the `WHERE` clause of the `SELECT` statement in the `ListCompanies()` method. Notice that, by starting the `WHERE` clause this way, you simply prepend all filter conditions with `AND` to make the `WHERE` clause work no matter how many filter conditions exist.

✦ **Getters and setters should always be locked** to safely synchronize access to persistent properties. Getters should always be `ReadOnly` locked, and setters should always be exclusively locked.

This statement may seem in conflict with recent misinformation being spread about the new locking rules in ColdFusion MX. The only change in MX is that you can no longer create or retrieve *corrupted* data from shared memory scopes (Server, Application, and Session), but everything else remains exactly the same as it was in ColdFusion 5. Whenever you are told that "you need to lock only to prevent race conditions," please understand that this is the very same reason you were locking before.

The best way for us to describe how and why to handle locking is to use a safety analogy. Imagine that a certain handgun model (analogous to earlier versions of ColdFusion) has a design flaw where it may accidentally fire if jostled with its safety lock disengaged, so the manufacturer warns, "If you wave this handgun around wildly while it is loaded and the safety lock is disengaged, the handgun may accidentally fire." Later, the manufacturer fixes the design flaw so that jostling the loaded handgun with the safety lock disengaged no longer causes it to accidentally fire. This fix *does not* mean that you should throw caution to the wind and start wildly waving the newly fixed loaded handgun around the room, because some other event may come into conflict with your actions and cause the very same results. You may think that the area is free of other people, for example, but one may run into you when you least expect it and cause your finger to accidentally hit the trigger.

You may think that your component's getter function doesn't conflict with a corresponding setter function under the specific environment that you have planned for your application, but what happens if you or someone else changes things later on? Do you really want to hunt down and fix all those blocks of unlocked (read that as *unsynchronized*) code, or would you rather take a few moments during initial development to lock code that *may* be involved in a race condition under some strange (but possible) condition in your application? Keep in mind Murphy's Law and you're not likely to wind up sorry.

✦ **Setters are void functions** because nothing of value can be returned from setting a property. Don't design your setters to return `True` on success and `False` on failure; just let such an error be thrown and catch it with your structured exception-handling framework. Remember that a setter failure is a true *error* and not an *exception*.

✦ **Compare this chapter's `XmasBonus()` and `Bonus()` functions** with those from Chapter 22, and you see one area where instance methods have an advantage. The following example shows the `Bonus()` function implemented as an instance method:

```
<!--- Bonus() [instance method] --->
<cffunction name="Bonus"
        access="public"
        returntype="numeric"
        output="No">

    <cfreturn (Val(This.Salary) * 0.05) + XmasBonus()>
</cffunction>
```

Compare the simplicity of the preceding example, with the `Bonus()` function implemented as a class method, as shown in Listing 22-9 from the Chapter 22:

```
<cffunction name="Bonus"
        access="public"
        returntype="numeric">

    <cfargument name="SSN"
        type="string"
        required="yes">

    <cfquery name="GetSalary"
            datasource="#Request.MainDSN#">
        SELECT
            Salary
        FROM
            Employee
        WHERE
            SSN = '#Trim(Arguments.SSN)#'
    </cfquery>

    <cfreturn (Val(GetSalary.Salary) * 0.05) +
XmasBonus(Arguments.SSN)>
</cffunction>
```

The instance method works directly from existing properties, whereas the class method must always retrieve its data from the database because it doesn't use properties.

The two components that you've just finished building are the entire Model layer of the MVC architecture on which this sample application is built. This is a significant change in the way that you design ColdFusion applications, wouldn't you say? No more hunting for a dozen or so included templates, custom tags, and so on. Everything is conveniently organized into two collections of entity-centric functions, so you have one place to go for everything that you need.

Using Your New Components

Next you learn how to make use of these components in the real world. You start by building the View layer of the MVC architecture, and then you connect the Model and View layers with the Controller layer and take this baby for a spin!

Building the View layer

The View layer encompasses all interface elements of your application, whether they're human interface elements or interfaces to other systems.

Your View elements consist of the wizard pages shown in the View layer of Figure 23-5. Because all tasks begin and end in the employee list, you start by building that View element first. Create a template named `EmployeeList.cfm` containing the code shown in Listing 23-8

Listing 23-8: **EmployeeList.cfm**

```
<cflogout>
<cflogin>
    <cfloginuser name="username" password="pw" roles="ADMIN,CLERK">
</cflogin>

<cfscript>
    Session.employeeWizard = CreateObject("Component", "Employee");
    urlParams = StructNew();
    if (IsDefined('URL.CompanyFilter') AND Len(URL.CompanyFilter) GT 0)
{
        urlParams.CompanyFilter = URL.CompanyFilter;
    }
    if (IsDefined('URL.EmployeeFilter') AND Len(URL.EmployeeFilter) GT
0) {
        urlParams.EmployeeFilter = URL.EmployeeFilter;
    }
    employeeList =
Session.employeeWizard.ListEmployees(ArgumentCollection=urlParams);
</cfscript>

<html>
<head>
    <title>Persistent Component Example</title>
    <LINK REL="StyleSheet" HREF="styles.css" type="text/css">
</head>

<body>

<form>
```

```
<table cellspacing="2" cellpadding="2" border="0">
<tr>
    <td valign="bottom">
        <b>Company begins with:</b><br>
        <input type="text" name="CompanyFilter" size="20"
maxlength="6">
    </td>
    <td valign="bottom">
        <b>Last name begins with:</b><br>
        <input type="text" name="EmployeeFilter" size="20"
maxlength="6">
    </td>
    <td valign="bottom">
        <input type="submit" value="Display">
    </td>
</tr>
</table>
</form>

<table cellspacing="0" cellpadding="0" border="0">
<tr>
    <th>Company Name</th>
    <th>Employee Name</th>
    <th>SSN</th>
    <th>Dep.</th>
    <th> </th>
</tr>
<cfoutput query="employeeList">
<tr bgcolor="#IIF(employeeList.CurrentRow MOD 2, DE('EFEFEF'),
DE('FFFFFF'))#">
    <td>#CompanyName#</td>
    <td><a href="Page1.cfm?ssn=#ssn#">#Lastname#, #Firstname#</a></td>
    <td>#SSN#</td>
    <td>#NumDependants#</td>
    <td><a href="DeleteEmployee.cfm?ssn=#ssn#">[Delete]</a></td>
</tr>
</cfoutput>
<tr>
    <td colspan="3"><a href="Page1.cfm?newemp=1"><b>Add a New
Employee</b></a></td>
</tr>
</table>

</body>
</html>
```

`EmployeeList.cfm` is a form containing two fields named `CompanyFilter` and `EmployeeFilter`. This form posts to itself by using the `GET` method, so the form fields are passed in the URL as parameters. The user can do any of the following:

- Leave both fields empty to display all employees from all companies.
- Enter the first few characters of a company name to display only employees from companies with names that begin with those characters.

✦ Enter the first few characters of a last name to display only employees whose last names begin with those characters.

✦ Enter characters into both fields to filter the list by both company name and employee last name.

Because you don't know whether you have zero, one, or two arguments to pass (based on which parameters are present in the URL), you use the `ArgumentCollection` method of passing arguments to the `ListEmployees()` function. If you pass a parameter named `ArgumentCollection` containing a structure of simple key-value pairs to a function, ColdFusion MX decomposes the structure into individual arguments and passes them to the function instead.

So you create an empty structure, and then you test for the existence of each possible URL parameter (`URL.CompanyFilter` and `URL.EmployeeFilter`). For each existing URL parameter, you create a key-value pair in the structure; then you assign the structure to `ArgumentCollection` as it is passed to the `ListEmployees()` function, and ColdFusion does the rest. The resulting list is shown in Figure 23-6.

Company begins with: **Last name begins with:** Display

Company Name	Employee Name	SSN	Dep.	
Azure Productions	Abromovitz, Arel	134-56-7890	0	[Delete]
Angry Clown Entertainment	Churvis, Adam	578-90-1234	2	[Delete]
The Very Big Corporation of America	Davidow, Allen	789-01-2345	3	[Delete]
Developers Anonymous	Derby, Wayne	098-76-5432	0	[Delete]
The Very Big Corporation of America	Feuilliette, Valerie	890-12-3456	2	[Delete]
The Stan Cox Society	Gumby, Vernal	765-43-2109	0	[Delete]
Developers Anonymous	Harbinger, Judy	912-34-5678	0	[Delete]
Azure Productions	Huckster, Virgil	245-67-8901	0	[Delete]
The Very Big Corporation of America	Johnson, Dave	456-78-9012	0	[Delete]
ABC Company, Inc.	Kayashunu, Oksal	234-56-7890	1	[Delete]
The Very Big Corporation of America	Kokilas, Susan	678-90-1234	1	[Delete]
The Stan Cox Society	Lester, Lance	654-32-1098	1	[Delete]
Star Trek Fan Club	Littleman, Kevin	012-34-5678	0	[Delete]
The Stan Cox Society	Mango, Davey	543-21-0987	0	[Delete]
Developers Anonymous	Mernal, Stanley	801-23-4567	0	[Delete]
Developers Anonymous	Nerdsworth, Larry	023-45-6789	0	[Delete]
Azure Productions	Romanova, Natasha	356-78-9012	2	[Delete]
ABC Company, Inc.	Sanders, Billy	223-45-6789	1	[Delete]
The Very Big Corporation of America	Silverberg, Bethany	567-89-0123	1	[Delete]
Developers Anonymous	Thickglasses, Barney	689-01-2345	0	[Delete]
Angry Clown Entertainment	Thor, Dirk	467-89-0123	1	[Delete]
Hamazon.com	Tucker, Billy Bob	987-65-4321	0	[Delete]
Star Trek Fan Club	Williger, Timmy	901-23-4567	2	[Delete]
ABC Company, Inc.	Worthington, Randsford	345-67-8901	0	[Delete]

Add a New Employee

Figure 23-6: The employee list, where everything starts and ends.

The first page in the data-entry or editing process is always `Page1.cfm`, which you build next. So create a template named `Page1.cfm` and enter into it the code from Listing 23-9.

Listing 23-9: **Page1.cfm**

```
<cfscript>
    if (IsDefined('URL.ssn')) {
        Session.employeeWizard.InitEmployee(URL.ssn);
    } else if (IsDefined('URL.newemp')) {
        Session.employeeWizard.InitEmployee();
    }
</cfscript>

<html>
```

```
<head>
    <title>Persistent Component Example</title>
    <LINK REL="StyleSheet" HREF="styles.css" type="text/css">
</head>

<body>
<h1>Persistent Component-Based Wizard</h1>
<h2>Employee Name &amp; SSN</h2>

<cfoutput>
<form action="Page1Ctrl.cfm" method="post">

<table cellspacing="0" cellpadding="0" border="0">
<tr>
    <th>SSN</th>
    <td><input type="text" name="SSN"
value="#Session.employeeWizard.GetEmployeeSSN()#" maxlength="11"></td>
</tr>
<tr>
    <th>First Name</th>
    <td><input type="text" name="Firstname"
value="#Session.employeeWizard.GetEmployeeFirstname()#"
maxlength="20"></td>
</tr>
<tr>
    <th>Last Name</th>
    <td><input type="text" name="Lastname"
value="#Session.employeeWizard.GetEmployeeLastname()#"
maxlength="20"></td>
</tr>
</table>

<cf_NavButtons mode="Start">
</form>
</cfoutput>

</body>
</html>
```

Now to follow the code from top to bottom.

If a social security number is passed in the URL, the `InitEmployee()` method is called, using social security number as its optional argument, which, as may you remember from the section "Building the Employee Component," earlier in this chapter, causes `InitEmployee()` to re-initialize its properties with data from the employee record keyed to that SSN. If `URL.newemp` is present, `InitEmployee()` is called with no argument, and the properties are re-initialized with empty and zeroed values.

This form submits to a Controller element named `Page1Ctrl.cfm`, which we discuss later in the section "Building the Controller layer," but for now, just think of it as the action page that causes the component's properties to be updated with the values entered into the fields on this form.

The form-field values are populated via `getter` functions declared in the `Employee` component. If you're creating a new employee, the properties contain only empty and zeroed values and, therefore, so do the form fields. If you're editing an existing employee, the properties and form fields contain data retrieved from the database.

The `cf_NavButtons` custom tag contains both `Previous` and `Next` Submit buttons and a Cancel button. We discuss them in detail later in the section "Building the Controller layer." Page one of your wizard is shown in Figure 23-7.

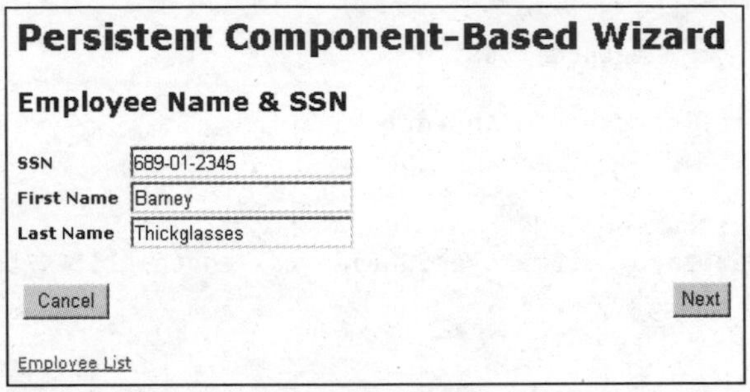

Figure 23-7: Page 1 of your wizard.

Now you create a template named `Page2.cfm` and enter the code from Listing 23-10.

Listing 23-10: **Page2.cfm**

```
<cfinvoke
    component="Company"
    method="ListCompanies"
    returnvariable="companyList">

<cfscript>
    currentCompanyID = Session.employeeWizard.GetEmployeeCompanyID();
</cfscript>

<html>
<head>
    <title>Persistent Component Example</title>
    <LINK REL="StyleSheet" HREF="styles.css" type="text/css">
</head>

<body>
<h1>Persistent Component-Based Wizard</h1>
<h2>Employer</h2>

<form action="Page2Ctrl.cfm" method="post">

<table cellspacing="0" cellpadding="0" border="0">
<cfoutput>
<tr>
    <th>SSN</th>
```

```
        <td>#Session.employeeWizard.GetEmployeeSSN()#</td>
    </tr>
    <tr>
        <th>First Name</th>
        <td>#Session.employeeWizard.GetEmployeeFirstname()#</td>
    </tr>
    <tr>
        <th>Last Name</th>
        <td>#Session.employeeWizard.GetEmployeeLastname()#</td>
    </tr>
    </cfoutput>
    <tr>
        <th>Employer</th>
        <td>
            <select name="CompanyID" size="1">
                <cfoutput query="companyList">
                    <option value="#CompanyID#"
                        <cfif currentCompanyID EQ
companyList.CompanyID>SELECTED</cfif>>#CompanyName#</option>
                </cfoutput>
            </select>
        </td>
    </tr>
    </table>

    <cf_NavButtons>
    </form>

    </body>
    </html>
```

Page two repeats the component's property values as entered in page one, plus it enables the user to choose an employer for the current employee through a drop-down list that is dynamically populated from the `ListCompanies` method of the `Company` component. The current company ID is retrieved by using the getter function `GetEmployeeCompanyID()`, and it is used to test for which company should be preselected (if any) in the drop-down list, as shown in Figure 23-8.

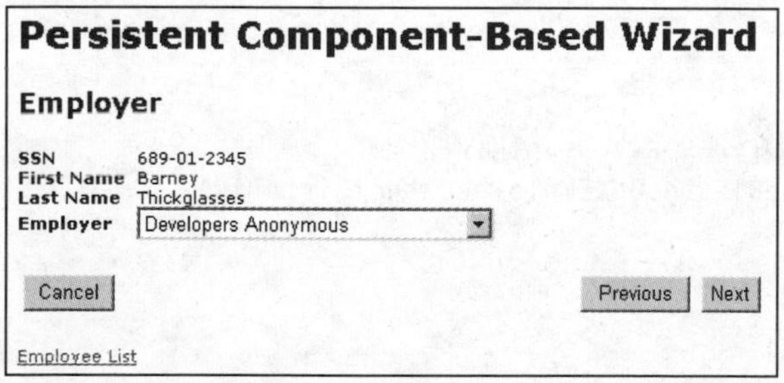

Figure 23-8: Page 2 of your wizard.

Create next a template named `Page3.cfm` containing the code from Listing 23-11.

Listing 23-11: Page3.cfm

```
<html>
<head>
    <title>Persistent Component Example</title>
    <LINK REL="StyleSheet" HREF="styles.css" type="text/css">
</head>

<body>
<h1>Persistent Component-Based Wizard</h1>
<h2>Salary &amp; Date of Birth</h2>

<cfoutput>
<form action="Page3Ctrl.cfm" method="post">

<table cellspacing="0" cellpadding="0" border="0">
<tr>
    <th>SSN</th>
    <td>#Session.employeeWizard.GetEmployeeSSN()#</td>
</tr>
<tr>
    <th>First Name</th>
    <td>#Session.employeeWizard.GetEmployeeFirstname()#</td>
</tr>
<tr>
    <th>Last Name</th>
    <td>#Session.employeeWizard.GetEmployeeLastname()#</td>
</tr>
<tr>
    <th>Employer</th>
    <td>#Session.employeeWizard.GetEmployeeCompanyName()#</td>
</tr>
<tr>
    <th>Salary</th>
    <td><input type="text" name="Salary"
value="#Session.employeeWizard.GetEmployeeSalary()#"
maxlength="20"></td>
</tr>
<tr>
    <th>Date of Birth</th>
    <td><input type="text" name="DateOfBirth"
value="#Session.employeeWizard.GetEmployeeDateOfBirth()#"
maxlength="30"></td>
</tr>
</table>

<cf_NavButtons>
```

```
</form>
</cfoutput>

</body>
</html>
```

Nothing special here — just two more form fields to submit, as shown in Figure 23-9.

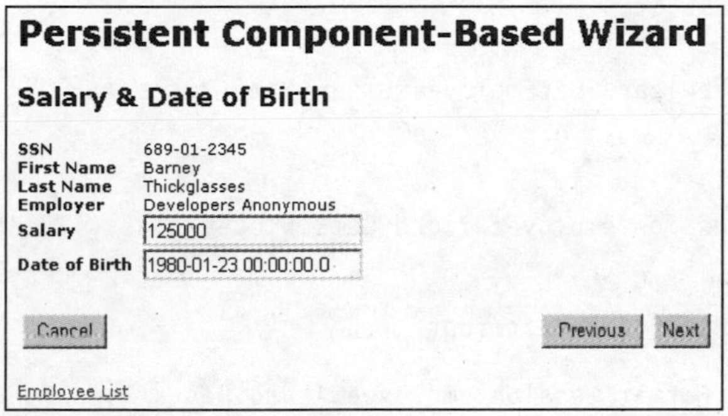

Figure 23-9: Page 3 of your wizard.

The final wizard page is mainly to verify what you have entered and to see the annual bonus that the employee earns before you commit the employee's properties to the database.

Create a template named `Page4.cfm` containing the code from Listing 23-12.

Listing 23-12: Page4.cfm

```
<html>
<head>
	<title>Persistent Component Example</title>
	<LINK REL="StyleSheet" HREF="styles.css" type="text/css">
</head>

<body>
<h1>Persistent Component-Based Wizard</h1>
<h2>Please Verify</h2>

<cfoutput>
<form action="Page4Ctrl.cfm" method="post">

<table cellspacing="0" cellpadding="0" border="0">
<tr>
	<th>SSN</th>
	<td>#Session.employeeWizard.GetEmployeeSSN()#</td>
</tr>
<tr>
```

Continued

Listing 23-12 *(continued)*

```
    <th>First Name</th>
    <td>#Session.employeeWizard.GetEmployeeFirstname()#</td>
</tr>
<tr>
    <th>Last Name</th>
    <td>#Session.employeeWizard.GetEmployeeLastname()#</td>
</tr>
<tr>
    <th>Employer</th>
    <td>#Session.employeeWizard.GetEmployeeCompanyName()#</td>
</tr>
<tr>
    <th>Salary</th>
    <td>#DollarFormat(Session.employeeWizard.GetEmployeeSalary())#</td>
</tr>
<tr>
    <th><font color="##008000">Bonus</font></th>
    <td><font
color="##008000">#DollarFormat(Session.employeeWizard.Bonus())#</font><
/td>
</tr>
<tr>
    <th>Date of Birth</th>
    <td>#DateFormat(Session.employeeWizard.GetEmployeeDateOfBirth(),
"mmmm d, yyyy")#</td>
</tr>
</table>

<cf_NavButtons mode="Finish">
</form>
</cfoutput>

</body>
</html>
```

You may have just passed it up without a second thought, but look again at how simple it is to display the current employee's annual bonus, as shown in Figure 23-10. Just a simple method call without even needing to pass an argument identifying the employee!

Two more View elements are in your application. `EmployeeDeleted.cfm` is a simple display page that appears after an `Employee` component instance is deleted, and `WizardDeleted.cfm` is a similar page that is displayed after the wizard itself is deleted. Their purpose is simply to inform the user that his actions were successful.

As you can see, building wizard pages based on long-lived persistent components is rather easy after you get the pattern down.

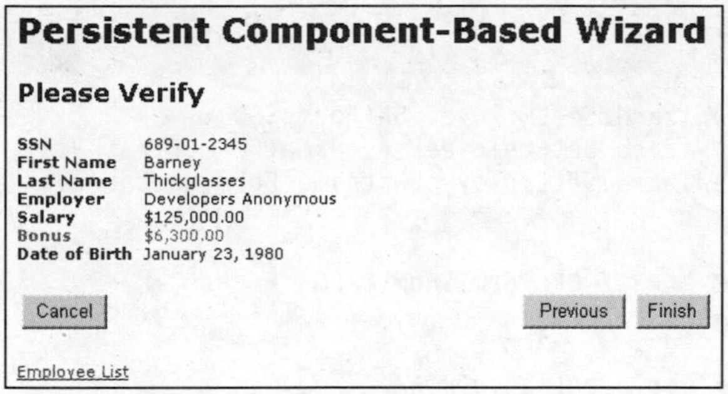

Persistent Component-Based Wizard

Please Verify

SSN	689-01-2345
First Name	Barney
Last Name	Thickglasses
Employer	Developers Anonymous
Salary	$125,000.00
Bonus	$6,300.00
Date of Birth	January 23, 1980

Cancel Previous Finish

Employee List

Figure 23-10: Page 4 of your wizard.

Building the Controller layer

Next you build the Controller elements that tie the View and Model layers together. The purpose of the Controller layer is to determine which data the submitting View element wants, acquire that data, and then call the appropriate View element responsible for either displaying the results or providing the user with the next step in a process.

We have organized your example application in a very straightforward manner: the View element `Page1.cfm` submits to the Controller element `Page1Ctrl.cfm`; `Page2.cfm` submits to `Page2Ctrl.cfm`, and so on.

The Controller elements are all almost identical to one another as well. The first thing that a Controller does is check for a form submission and relocate to the employee list if no submission was made. Next, if the Cancel button was clicked, the Controller deletes the wizard by deleting the key in the Session structure that contains it; then it relocates to the `WizardDeleted.cfm` page to inform the user that the deletion was successful.

Next, the Controller calls the setter methods responsible for updating the component's properties. Finally, the Controller determines which Submit button was clicked and relocates to the appropriate View element.

This pattern is followed exactly in Listings 23-13, 23-14, and 23-15, which contain the code for the Controllers `Page1Ctrl.cfm`, `Page2Ctrl.cfm`, and `Page3Ctrl.cfm`, respectively. Take a few moments to create the templates named in these listings.

Listing 23-13: Page1Ctrl.cfm

```
<cfif NOT IsDefined("Form.Submit")>
    <cflocation url="EmployeeList.cfm">
</cfif>

<cfif Form.Submit EQ "Cancel">
    <cfset success = StructDelete(Session, "employeeWizard")>
    <cflocation url="WizardDeleted.cfm">
<cfelse>

    <cfscript>
```

Continued

Listing 23-13 *(continued)*

```
        Session.employeeWizard.SetEmployeeSSN(Form.SSN);
        Session.employeeWizard.SetEmployeeFirstname(Form.Firstname);
        Session.employeeWizard.SetEmployeeLastname(Form.Lastname);
    </cfscript>

    <cfif Form.Submit EQ "Next" OR Form.Submit EQ "Finish">
        <cflocation url="Page2.cfm">
    <cfelse>
        <cflocation url="EmployeeList.cfm">
    </cfif>

</cfif>
```

Listing 23-14: Page2Ctrl.cfm

```
<cfif NOT IsDefined("Form.Submit")>
    <cflocation url="EmployeeList.cfm">
</cfif>

<cfif Form.Submit EQ "Cancel">
    <cfset success = StructDelete(Session, "employeeWizard")>
    <cflocation url="WizardDeleted.cfm">
<cfelse>

    <cfscript>
        Session.employeeWizard.SetEmployeeCompanyID(Form.CompanyID);
    </cfscript>

    <cfif Form.Submit EQ "Next" OR Form.Submit EQ "Finish">
        <cflocation url="Page3.cfm">
    <cfelse>
        <cflocation url="Page1.cfm">
    </cfif>

</cfif>
```

Listing 23-15: Page3Ctrl.cfm

```
<cfif NOT IsDefined("Form.Submit")>
    <cflocation url="EmployeeList.cfm">
</cfif>

<cfif Form.Submit EQ "Cancel">
    <cfset success = StructDelete(Session, "employeeWizard")>
```

```
    <cflocation url="WizardDeleted.cfm">
<cfelse>

    <cfscript>
        Session.employeeWizard.SetEmployeeSalary(Form.Salary);

Session.employeeWizard.SetEmployeeDateOfBirth(Form.DateOfBirth);
    </cfscript>

    <cfif Form.Submit EQ "Next" OR Form.Submit EQ "Finish">
        <cflocation url="Page4.cfm">
    <cfelse>
        <cflocation url="Page2.cfm">
    </cfif>

</cfif>
```

The Controller for `Page4.cfm`, as shown in Listing 23-16, is different because, instead of setting properties, it flushes the current properties to the database.

Listing 23-16: Page4Ctrl.cfm

```
<cfif NOT IsDefined("Form.Submit")>
    <cflocation url="EmployeeList.cfm">
</cfif>

<cfif Form.Submit EQ "Cancel">
    <cfset success = StructDelete(Session, "employeeWizard")>
    <cflocation url="WizardDeleted.cfm">
<cfelse>

    <cfscript>
        Session.employeeWizard.FlushEmployeeToDatabase();
    </cfscript>

    <cfif Form.Submit EQ "Next" OR Form.Submit EQ "Finish">
        <cflocation url="EmployeeList.cfm">
    <cfelse>
        <cflocation url="Page3.cfm">
    </cfif>

</cfif>
```

After flushing the `Employee` properties to the database, `Page4Ctrl.cfm` relocates back to the base of operations: `EmployeeList.cfm`.

Deleting an employee is handled through the `DeleteEmployee.cfm` Controller, as shown in Listing 23-17.

Listing 23-17: DeleteEmployee.cfm

```
<cfif IsDefined('URL.ssn')>
    <cfscript>
        Session.employeeWizard.InitEmployee(URL.ssn);
        fullname = Session.employeeWizard.GetEmployeeFullname();
        Session.employeeWizard.DeleteEmployee(URL.ssn);
        success = StructDelete(Session, "employeeWizard");
</cfscript>
    <cflocation
url="EmployeeDeleted.cfm?fullname=#URLEncodedFormat(fullname)#">
<cfelse>
    <cflocation url="EmployeeList.cfm">
</cfif>
```

If you want to pass the full name of the employee being deleted to the `EmployeeDeleted.cfm` display page, you first need to acquire the employee from the database. The `GetEmployee()` method is a private method, so you can't call it directly, but you *can* re-invoke the `InitEmployee()` method with the SSN passed in the URL and then call the `GetEmployeeFullname()` method to accomplish what you want.

Supporting files

You just need to cover the remaining supporting files, and then you're ready to rock and roll. You gain no new knowledge by creating these supporting files, so we've included them for you on the companion CD-ROM. Just copy them to your project directory.

Application.cfm

Other than turning on Session variables and defining the datasource to be used, the only significant thing that `Application.cfm` does is call `<cflogin />` for every page request, which is necessary for preventing errors whenever you're testing authorization for component functions. (This appears to be a bug in MX.) Please refer to Chapter 40 for details on implementing user authentication and authorization using ColdFusion MX's new `CFLOGIN` and related tags.

OnRequestEnd.cfm

`OnRequestEnd.cfm` is a convenient place to put a link back to the employee list for every page in the application, and it's also where you dump the current state of the `Employee` component instance so that you can watch it work from page to page.

NavButtons.cfm

`NavButtons` is a custom tag that displays the wizard navigation buttons. It has three modes: `Start`, which displays the Next button and hides the Previous button; `InProcess`, which displays both the Previous and Next buttons; and `Finish`, which changes the label of the Next button to Finish.

Styles.css

You include a simple external style sheet so that the wizard doesn't look nasty.

Exercising (and exorcising) the application that you just built

Now you're ready to rock! Open `EmployeeList.cfm` in your browser and play around a little. If you screw things up terribly, just rerun `RefreshCh23Data.sql` and start over. If your software throws errors, recheck your code against the listings in this chapter and try again. No shortcuts — you gotta grok the box!

After you have everything up and running, click an existing employee and inspect the visual representation of the wizard instance at the bottom of your browser, as shown in Figure 23-11. You can collapse items by clicking their labels on the left.

component Employee

LASTNAME	Thickglasses
COMPANYID	8
ISNEWEMPLOYEE	FALSE
FIRSTNAME	Barney
SSN	689-01-2345
DATEOFBIRTH	1980-01-23 00:00:00.0
COMPANYNAME	Developers Anonymous
LOCKNAME	B15C017A-B0D0-019C-D7BFF5326BBA6B11
KEYSSN	689-01-2345
SALARY	125000
LISTEMPLOYEES	function ListEmployees
FLUSHEMPLOYEETODATABASE	

function ListEmployees — *Arguments:*

Name	Required	Type	Default
EmployeeFilter	Optional	string	
CompanyFilter	Optional	string	

Return Type: query
Roles:
Access: public
Output: No

Figure 23-11: Visualizing your Employee component instance.

We also want you to modify the Roles attribute of the `CFLOGINUSER` tag at the top of `EmployeeList.cfm`. Following are the related lines of code:

```
<cflogout>
<cflogin>
    <cfloginuser name="username" password="pw" roles="ADMIN,CLERK">
</cflogin>
```

Every time that `EmployeeList.cfm` is called, it logs the user out and then logs him back in again with the `CFLOGINUSER` tag. By editing the `Roles` attribute, you can modify the roles in which the user has been granted membership and see how the `FlushEmployeeToDatabase()` and `DeleteEmployee()` methods react as you try to invoke them. This should give you a feel for how component functions work with MX's new security model.

So play until your heart's content and you get a feel for the component-based application that you just built. After you're happy with the results, make a copy of the entire application in a separate directory and start modifying the code to do things a little differently. The best way to learn is by muddling through the code and seeing what works and what doesn't.

Caveats and Warnings

Before you put this chapter away, you need to know some important warnings and learn a few workarounds for various caveats involved with building components.

Variable leakage

Bugs in ColdFusion MX permit variables to "leak" outside the code bodies that declare them. These are not just "nice-to-fix" curiosities; if you don't solve them all, your variables may mysteriously change values on you.

The Variables scope

Never explicitly declare variables with the `Variables` prefix inside a function or a component, as they can leak into calling page. This is a documented bug.

The Var scope

As we mention in Chapter 22, if you declare a local variable in the standard fashion inside a function, that variable "leaks out" of the function and can be accessed and modified by code outside the function itself. If you have multiple functions in your component that use the same variable names, this leakage can make your components malfunction.

The `Var` keyword places the declared variable into the `Var` scope, which is a special scope that lives only inside user-defined functions. By declaring function-only variables in the `Var` scope, you absolutely guarantee that your variables don't leak outside the function.

The This scope

Component properties are stored in the `This` scope inside the component, but `This` is a public scope, so it can be both read and modified by code outside the component. `This`-scoped variables (properties) are exposed in a `CFDUMP` of the component instance, which is very convenient for visualizing and debugging behavior, but if you want to create "properties" that are truly local to the component, you must forego using the `This` scope in favor of what is sometimes called the *Unnamed* scope.

The Unnamed scope

By eliminating an explicit prefix from variables declared inside a component, you make those variables private to the entire component, and these variables persist for the life of the component.

If you `CFSET` a variable named `myVar` in the Unnamed scope within a component function and then `CFSET myVar` inside a different function within the same component, you are setting the same variable, as it pertains to the entire component and not just the function in which it is declared.

The setter and getter functions in Listing 23-18 treat variables in the Unnamed scope as local "properties," even though they don't show up in a `CFDUMP` of the component instance.

Listing 23-18: Setter and getter functions that manipulate local "properties"

```
<!--- SetMyName() [instance method] --->
<cffunction name="SetMyName"
        access="public"
        returntype="void"
        output="No">

    <cfargument name="MyName"
        type="string"
        required="yes">

    <cflock name="#This.lockName#"
            timeout="10"
            throwontimeout="Yes"
            type="EXCLUSIVE">

        <cfset myName = Arguments.MyName>

        <cfreturn>
    </cflock>
</cffunction>

<!--- GetMyName() [instance method] --->
<cffunction name="GetMyName"
        access="public"
        returntype="string"
        output="No">

    <cflock name="#This.lockName#"
            timeout="10"
            throwontimeout="Yes"
            type="READONLY">

        <cfreturn myName>

    </cflock>
</cffunction>
```

Our personal preference is to use `This`-scoped properties and just be very careful about our coding because we like the capability to inspect all aspects of our components as they execute, but the choice of which scope to use for your component properties is entirely up to you.

Function-name collision

You may notice that we don't have a function named `Delete()` in the `Company` component and another function named `Delete()` in the `Employee` component. In fact, we always name our component functions uniquely, regardless of which component declares them, to avoid having one function name collide (read that *conflict*) with another if both are consumed by the same software.

This collision problem mainly applies to Flash Remoting, which we cover later in Chapter 26, but because collision involves components, we wanted to at least generally cover it here. Just keep the principle of uniquely naming your component functions in mind for now, and you see how it makes your life easier in Chapter 26.

CFINCLUDE and the Arguments scope

We bet that one of the very first things that you thought of doing after you saw the structure of a component was to use `CFINCLUDE`s inside the bodies of your functions to move business logic into separate templates so that you could both call them separately and collapse the component for easier reading.

That problem is that this approach doesn't work. The Arguments scope is not seen by the code inside the included templates, so your logic fails. You must place all your logic inside your component functions directly.

J2EE clustering caveats

If you employ J2EE clustering of your application servers, you can store Session variables in a shared location so that all your servers can use them. Before you jump for joy thinking that you can share long-lived components that persist in the Session scope between all the servers in your cluster, you should know that this approach doesn't work either.

J2EE Session variables stored in a shared location can contain only simple values, much as Client variables do. Although you can serialize complex variables into simple variables by using WDDX, if you serialize an instance of a component, WDDX strips away all the component methods and leaves only the component properties intact after you later deserialize the instance.

Synchronizing component properties by using datastores

After you retrieve data from a database, place a copy of that data in the properties of an instance of a component, and then persist that instance over a long period of time, you run the risk of corrupting the integrity of your database data.

Developers sometimes forget that they are not creating single-user applications and that other users may very well manipulate data at the same time that you are. The longer that you wait between retrieving and updating data from a database, the higher is the probability that another user may modify or delete that same data before you do.

Implementing long-lived persistent components in high-transactional processes within your application is probably not a good idea for this very reason, unless you are creating new data.

Documenting Components

The remainder of this chapter is optional, as nothing that you implement from this section has any effect whatsoever on the functionality of your components. The sole purpose of documenting components is to expose such documentation to the ColdFusion *Component Browser*, which is a useful tool that displays every detail about a component and its constituent parts in a graphical format.

Documenting your components enables developers who want to consume them discover the following information:

- ✦ What a component does.
- ✦ How a component is used.
- ✦ What each property of a component represents.
- ✦ The data type of each property.
- ✦ Whether a property is required.
- ✦ What each component method (function) does.
- ✦ How each component method is used.
- ✦ What each function argument represents.
- ✦ How each function argument is used.

Most of this documentation is handled through additional attributes to the tags that you've already used in this chapter, but one additional tag—CFPROPERTY—is introduced here for the sole purpose of documenting the properties of a component. CFPROPERTY, however, is a completely benign tag. For all the information that you can provide regarding a property, CFPROPERTY does absolutely nothing other than expose property documentation to the ColdFusion Component Browser. CFPROPERTY doesn't set properties; if you want to set a property, use either CFSET or an assignment operator with CFSCRIPT to set a variable in the This scope. CFPROPERTY's Default and Required parameters do nothing either, except publish themselves as metadata for the Component Browser.

Listing 23-19 shows an abbreviated component that doesn't expose any documentation to the ColdFusion Component Browser.

Listing 23-19: An abbreviated undocumented component

```
<cfcomponent>
    <!--- Initialization Area --->
    <cfscript>
        This.lockName = CreateUUID();
        InitEmployee();
    </cfscript>

    <!--- InitEmployee() [class method] --->
    <cffunction name="InitEmployee"
            access="public"
            returntype="void"
            output="No">

        <cfargument name="SSN"
                type="string"
```

Continued

Listing 23-19 *(continued)*

```
                    required="no">

            <cfset Var EmployeeInitRec = "">

            <cflock name="#This.lockName#"
                    timeout="10"
                    throwontimeout="Yes"
                    type="EXCLUSIVE">
                <cfscript>
                    if (IsDefined('Arguments.ssn')) {
                        EmployeeInitRec = GetEmployee(Arguments.SSN);
                        This.keySSN = EmployeeInitRec.SSN;
                        This.ssn = EmployeeInitRec.SSN;
                        This.companyID = EmployeeInitRec.CompanyID;
                        This.companyName = EmployeeInitRec.CompanyName;
                        This.firstname = EmployeeInitRec.Firstname;
                        This.lastname = EmployeeInitRec.Lastname;
                        This.salary = EmployeeInitRec.Salary;
                        This.dateOfBirth = EmployeeInitRec.DateOfBirth;
                        This.isNewEmployee = FALSE;
                    } else {
                        This.keySSN = "";
                        This.ssn = "";
                        This.companyID = 0;
                        This.companyName = "";
                        This.firstname = "";
                        This.lastname = "";
                        This.salary = 0;
                        This.dateOfBirth = "12/30/1899";
                        This.isNewEmployee = TRUE;
                    }
                </cfscript>
            </cflock>

            <cfreturn>
        </cffunction>
    </cfcomponent>
```

Figure 23-12 shows how Listing 23-19 looks in the CFC Browser.

Figure 23-12 doesn't give you any useful information. If you want other developers to dive right in and start using the components that you've written, you must document those components with enough information to guide them. Listing 23-20 shows the code from Listing 23-19 with a full compliment of documentation added.

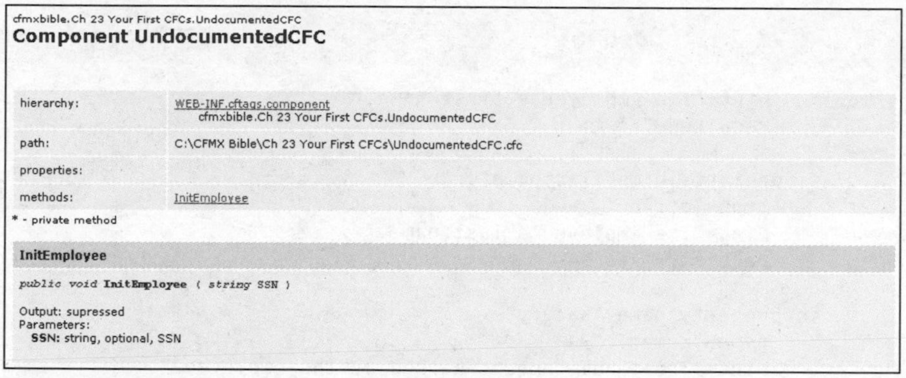

cfmxbible.Ch 23 Your First CFCs.UndocumentedCFC
Component UndocumentedCFC

hierarchy:	WEB-INF.cftags.component cfmxbible.Ch 23 Your First CFCs.UndocumentedCFC
path:	C:\CFMX Bible\Ch 23 Your First CFCs\UndocumentedCFC.cfc
properties:	
methods:	InitEmployee

* - private method

InitEmployee

public void **InitEmployee** (*string* SSN)

Output: supressed
Parameters:
SSN: string, optional, SSN

Figure 23-12: Exploring an undocumented component.

Listing 23-20: **Listing 23-19 with full documentation added**

```
<cfcomponent
    displayname="Documented CF Component"
    hint="I created this abbreviated version of the Employee component
(it contains the InitEmployee() method only) for the sole purpose of
showing you how to document all aspects of components.">

    <cfproperty name="keySSN"
        type="string"
        hint="The original value of  employee's SSN.  It is used as the
predicate of the WHERE clause of the UPDATE statement when flushing
properties to the database."
        required="Yes">

    <cfproperty name="ssn"
        type="string"
        hint="The current value of the  employee's SSN.  This is the
value that will be stored in the database."
        required="Yes">

    <cfproperty name="companyID"
        type="numeric"
        hint="The foreign key of the employee's employer (company)."
        required="Yes">

    <cfproperty name="companyName"
        type="string"
        hint="The name of the employee's employer (company)."
        required="Yes">

    <cfproperty name="firstname"
        type="string"
```

Continued

Listing 23-20 *(continued)*

```
		hint="The employee's first name."
		required="Yes">

	<cfproperty name="lastname"
		type="string"
		hint="The employee's last name."
		required="Yes">

	<cfproperty name="salary"
		type="numeric"
		hint="The annual amount earned by the employee."
		required="Yes">

	<cfproperty name="dateOfBirth"
		type="date"
		hint="The employee's birthday."
		required="Yes">

	<cfproperty name="isNewEmployee"
		type="date"
		hint="True when a new employee is being created; False when an
existing employee is being edited."
		required="Yes">

	<cfproperty name="fictionalOptionalProperty"
		type="numeric"
		hint="This fictional property was included only so I could have
an example of an optional property that has a default value declared
for it."
		required="No"
		default="0">

	<!--- Initialization Area --->
	<cfscript>
		This.lockName = CreateUUID();
		InitEmployee();
	</cfscript>

	<!--- InitEmployee() [class method] --->
	<cffunction name="InitEmployee"
			access="public"
			returntype="void"
			output="No"
			displayname="Initialize Employee"
			hint="Called during instantiation without the optional SSN
argument to initialize empty and zeroed properties.  Called with SSN to
intialize from values in the database.">
```

```
        <cfargument name="SSN"
                type="string"
                required="no"
                displayname="Social Security Number"
                hint="The key used to retrieve an employee record from
the database.">

        <cfset Var EmployeeInitRec = "">

        <cflock name="#This.lockName#"
                timeout="10"
                throwontimeout="Yes"
                type="EXCLUSIVE">
            <cfscript>
                if (IsDefined('Arguments.ssn')) {
                    EmployeeInitRec = GetEmployee(Arguments.SSN);
                    This.keySSN = EmployeeInitRec.SSN;
                    This.ssn = EmployeeInitRec.SSN;
                    This.companyID = EmployeeInitRec.CompanyID;
                    This.companyName = EmployeeInitRec.CompanyName;
                    This.firstname = EmployeeInitRec.Firstname;
                    This.lastname = EmployeeInitRec.Lastname;
                    This.salary = EmployeeInitRec.Salary;
                    This.dateOfBirth = EmployeeInitRec.DateOfBirth;
                    This.isNewEmployee = FALSE;
                } else {
                    This.keySSN = "";
                    This.ssn = "";
                    This.companyID = 0;
                    This.companyName = "";
                    This.firstname = "";
                    This.lastname = "";
                    This.salary = 0;
                    This.dateOfBirth = "12/30/1899";
                    This.isNewEmployee = TRUE;
                }
            </cfscript>
        </cflock>

        <cfreturn>
    </cffunction>
</cfcomponent>
```

That's a lot of lines of code just for the purpose of documentation, but take a look at what it gets you! Figure 23-13 shows the rich information that you publish if you document everything in your components.

cfmxbible.Ch 23 Your First CFCs.DocumentedCFC

Component DocumentedCFC (Documented CF Component)

I created this abbreviated version of the Employee component (it contains the InitEmployee() method only) for the sole purpose of showing you how to document all aspects of components.

hierarchy:	WEB-INF.cftags.component cfmxbible.Ch 23 Your First CFCs.DocumentedCFC
path:	C:\CFMX Bible\Ch 23 Your First CFCs\DocumentedCFC.cfc
properties:	companyID, companyName, dateOfBirth, fictionalOptionalProperty, firstname, isNewEmployee, keySSN, lastname, salary, ssn
methods:	InitEmployee

* - private method

Property	Hint	Type	Req.	Implemented In	Default Value
companyID	The foreign key of the employee's employer (company).	numeric	Yes	DocumentedCFC	-
companyName	The name of the employee's employer (company).	string	Yes	DocumentedCFC	-
dateOfBirth	The employee's birthday.	date	Yes	DocumentedCFC	-
fictionalOptionalProperty	This fictional property was included only so I could have an example of an optional property that has a default value declared for it.	numeric	No	DocumentedCFC	0
firstname	The employee's first name.	string	Yes	DocumentedCFC	-
isNewEmployee	True when a new employee is being created; False when an existing employee is being edited.	date	Yes	DocumentedCFC	-
keySSN	The original value of employee's SSN. It is used as the predicate of the WHERE clause of the UPDATE statement when flushing properties to the database.	string	Yes	DocumentedCFC	-
lastname	The employee's last name.	string	Yes	DocumentedCFC	-
salary	The annual amount earned by the employee.	numeric	Yes	DocumentedCFC	-
ssn	The current value of the employee's SSN. This is the value that will be stored in the database.	string	Yes	DocumentedCFC	-

InitEmployee (Initialize Employee)

public void **InitEmployee** (*string* SSN)

Called during instantiation without the optional SSN argument to initialize empty and zeroed properties. Called with SSN to intialize from values in the database.

Output: supressed
Parameters:
SSN: string, optional, Social Security Number - The key used to retrieve an employee record from the database.

Figure 23-13: Exploring a well-documented component.

Now imagine how easy consuming a component would be if the whole thing were documented like the one shown in Listing 23-20. Sure, you'd have hundreds of lines of code on your hands, but you wouldn't need to read through it all — that's what the CFC Browser is for.

You may notice as you begin to diligently document your components that many documentation-related attributes are missing from both the ColdFusion Language Reference (Part IX) and the tag editors of the tags to which you want to add documentation. Don't worry about these oversights; if you use Listing 23-20 as your guide, your components are sufficiently documented, using all possible attributes.

Component metadata

Metadata is "data about data" that enables you to better understand the data itself. A component's metadata consists of the descriptions of its properties, methods, arguments, and data about the physical component file itself. Although you can always directly CFDUMP an instance of a component to visualize its properties and functions, you can't write software to programmatically inspect and interface with your component through the results of a

CFDUMP. The GetMetaData() function, however, enables you to do just that; it returns a structure of key-value pairs containing all the metadata for a component.

The code in Listing 23-21, for example, produces a structure containing the metadata.

Listing 23-21: Producing component metadata

```
<cfobject name="myDocumentedCFC" component="DocumentedCFC">
<cfset cfcMetaData = GetMetaData(myDocumentedCFC)>
<cfdump var="#cfcMetaData#">
```

A CFDUMP of the Employee component's metadata (not the component itself) is shown in Figure 23-14.

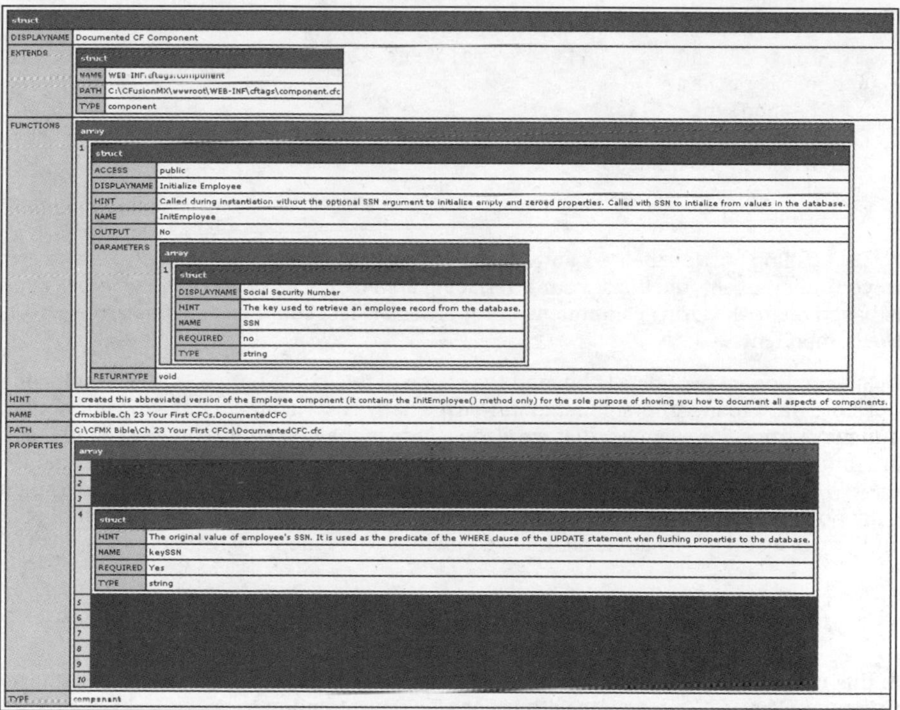

Figure 23-14: The metadata of the component in Listing 23-21.

By using GetMetaData(), you can write an application that iterates through metadata keys, interprets the contents, and programmatically interfaces with and uses the component. Such functionality isn't easy to produce by using standard metadata elements alone; if you want to create such a programmatically derived interface for your components (or the components produced by other members of your team), you probably need more detailed metadata that is specifically implemented for the purpose. That's where custom metadata comes in.

Specifying your own custom metadata

If you add any nonstandard attributes to the CFCOMPONENT, CFPROPERTY, CFFUNCTION, or CFARGUMENT tags, they publish as component metadata that can be retrieved by the GetMetaData() function. This can be very useful for building a programmatically derived interface into components used by your company—especially if you have control over company-wide metadata specifications and can dictate the metadata to be published for all components that your applications use.

Say, for example, that you want to specify whether a component function is a class method or an instance method so that you can programmatically determine the manner in which it is to be used. You can accomplish this task by adding a MethodType attribute to your component functions, as follows:

```
<cffunction name="ListEmployees"
     access="public"
     returntype="query"
     output="No"
     displayname="List Employees"
     hint="Produces a list of employees, optionally filtered by company
and/or last name"
     MethodType="Class"
ColumnsExposed="CompanyName,CompanyID,SSN,Firstname,Lastname,Salary,.Da
teOfBirth,NumDependants">
. . .
</cffunction>
```

By first calling GetMetaData() and then checking the values of the MethodType keys related to your component functions, your interfacing application can determine whether a function is based on its declaring component's properties or data supplied from a source external to the component.

Using component metadata is beyond the scope of this book, but you should still look for possible ways to incorporate metadata—especially custom metadata—in your applications. You may notice, for example, that we also include in the preceding code a second custom attribute named ColumnsExposed. If you establish that all component methods that produce query result sets must have a ColumnsExposed metadata attribute, you can programmatically poll metadata, look for the ColumnsExposed attribute, loop through its list of columns, and create an on-the-fly an HTML table containing that function's result set.

Summary

In this chapter you took what you learned from Chapter 22 and applied it to creating and using your first CFCs, complete with proper locking, attention to scope leakage, and so on. You also learned how to document your components with metadata that is viewable from the Component Browser. Organize what you've learned in this chapter through a few simple axioms for excellent component design:

✦ **Always build your components in layers.**

Whether you do so slowly through many layers or rapidly through only two or three, you have the best chance of visualizing the big picture of your application's functionality, which in turn starts you thinking about how individual components may integrate as cohesive packages. As an added bonus, after you are finished building the first layer of all your components, you have also defined the interface to your application's Model layer. This is significant because, after the Model layer's interface is defined, you can move on to laying the foundations of your View and Controller layers. We always like to complete this "50,000-foot view" of our application before we go any farther so that we can feel comfortable that we have a component method for every function that our application must support, and that we are implementing interfaces into every one of these functions.

✦ **Carefully consider whether your component functions are instance methods or class methods.**

If you gain something from persisting an instance of a component in a long-lived scope, your component has certainly declared at least one instance method, but don't let that dictate the rest of that component's methods. Don't think of an entire component as either instance-based or class-based (also known as *static*), because no such thing exists in reality. Each component function may be declared as either a class method or an instance method, as your needs dictate.

✦ **Pay careful attention to variable leakage as if it may destroy your components and the templates that call them.**

As an added precaution, don't use the same variable names everywhere. If you follow our suggestions and give your variables rather long and obvious names, you are less likely to use two variables of different meaning that happen to have the same name.

✦ **Pay special attention to locking.**

Please don't make the mistake of throwing caution to the wind because you heard someone say that locking isn't necessary anymore, because in many cases, locking is just as necessary as it was in earlier versions. If your component declares instance methods and you intend to persist instances of your component in long-lived scopes, your component should declare a publicly accessible property containing a lock named uniquely for that instance alone, and all access to that instance's data should be synchronized by using that named lock.

✦ **Finally, always document your components by using available metadata attributes of the** `CFCOMPONENT`, `CFPROPERTY`, `CFFUNCTION`, **and** `CFARGUMENT` **tags.**

They don't add functionality to your application, but they enable your development team to rapidly understand and implement your components through use of the ColdFusion Component Browser.

Get used to designing your applications around ColdFusion components by using MVC architecture, and your application build time is shorter, your code is more straightforward and easier to understand, and extending your application is relatively simple—even if you're extending it to remote systems, as you discover in the next few chapters.

✦ ✦ ✦

CHAPTER 24

Migrating Custom Tags and UDFs to Components

✦ ✦ ✦ ✦

In This Chapter

Knowing when to implement reusable code as a custom tag, an included template, a UDF, or a component

Migrating existing code to a components

✦ ✦ ✦ ✦

So far in this book, you've seen entirely new ways of implementing reusable ColdFusion code, so by now, you're probably wondering which approach to take. The waters have also been muddied by misguided discussions on popular ColdFusion mailing lists that suggest things such as "custom tags are obsolete now that components are here" or "you shouldn't implement collections of UDFs as included libraries but should always implement these as components instead." These statements are patently false.

You have the following four primary means of implementing reusable code:

- ✦ Included templates
- ✦ Custom tags
- ✦ Included libraries of user-defined functions
- ✦ Components

Each technique is perfectly valid in ColdFusion MX, but now that you have more options than before, more criteria are involved in making the most appropriate choice, and so the decision is a bit more difficult to make.

If you follow our logic for choosing the most appropriate method for implementing reusable code, your applications use the most powerful principles of ColdFusion technology to their maximum benefit—and yours.

Choosing an Implementation Method

Before you go through this decision process, stop and ask yourself, "Do I really need to change anything that is already working?" You probably don't. The old adage "If it ain't broke, don't fix it" still rings true, but we would amend it a little by adding, "If it doesn't need to do anything *more* than it already does, don't change it." If you suddenly need to make the output of a custom tag available to a remote .NET server, for example, a custom tag just doesn't do the trick anymore.

You may notice that, with few exceptions, we don't make definitive statements such as "Always do this." Wherever an answer isn't clear-cut, we try to steer your decision in a direction.

Visualize the decision process this way: Imagine a large circle where, at 90-degree intervals around the circumference, each of the four methods of reuse are placed in the same order as shown in the introduction to this chapter, and shown again in Figure 24-1.

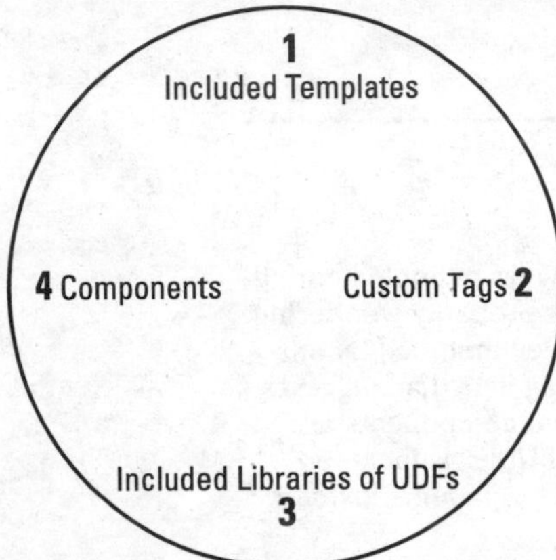

Figure 24-1: Visualizing which reusable code technique to implement.

For each reusable piece of code, walk to the center of the circle and ask yourself each of the qualifying questions in the following section. If your answer to a question results in a recommendation for a specific method, take a step toward that method—the bigger the recommendation, the bigger the step. If an answer disqualifies a method, take no further steps toward it regardless of any further recommendations.

After you answer all the questions in the following section, the method closest to you is the one that you should choose to implement that piece of code. Of course, this is an empirical process that is open to wide interpretation, but it really does help give you some initial guidance.

Qualifying Questions

For each piece of code that can potentially be reused, ask yourself the following questions:

- ✦ **Does the code require parameters or arguments?** If so, you should formalize an interface that requires the necessary parameters or arguments to be passed into the code. This disqualifies included templates as an implementation method.
- ✦ **If the code stands alone, is it a specialized routine?** If the code doesn't require any arguments or parameters and it produces specialized output, such as a list of current news items, it would work well as a included template containing all database calls and formatted output.

✦ **Is the code closely bound to an entity or a clearly defined business process?** Well-designed components encompass all the functionality required of the entities or business processes that they support, so if the code in question also falls under this category, it should most likely be included in the same component that declares the remaining functionality for that entity or process. If you don't include it, the component's functionality is incomplete.

✦ **Does the code need to directly modify data local to the caller?** Be careful with your answer to this question. Directly modifying data local to the caller is done through a custom tag setting a value in the Caller scope, which either creates or overwrites a local variable in the calling template. This can almost always be replaced by returning data from a user-defined function to the caller and then locally setting values in the caller based on the data returned to it.

If you have a compelling reason to *directly* modify data local to the caller, you must use a custom tag. Again, this is rare.

✦ **Does the code simply return one or more data values?** A function can return one (and only one) value, but that value can be a complex variable such as a structure containing multiple key-value pairs. So in essence, you can return multiple data values this way. If you're returning only raw data to the caller, your code is a strong candidate for implementation as a user-defined function.

✦ **Does the code produce formatted content?** You find a distinct difference between returning data and outputting formatted content. *Returned data* are granular items that can be rearranged, used in calculations, formatted, and repurposed in any way that you see fit. *Formatted content* is a cohesive chunk of visual information that acts as a single unit and is typically not used in calculations.

If your code produces formatted output based on input parameters or arguments, it is a strong candidate for implementation as a custom tag.

✦ **Does the code need to be completely isolated from the caller?** If you want to ensure that variables manipulated in the reusable code do not conflict with variables of the same names in their callers, you cannot use included templates to implement the code.

✦ **How is the output of the code to be consumed?** If the code's output is to be consumed by a remote server or if the output is to be consumed by Flash MX applications via Flash Remoting, you must implement the reusable code as a component with `Access="Remote"`.

✦ **Must users be authorized to use the code?** If you must restrict access to the reusable code to a specific set of MX security roles, you either need to implement the code as a component or you need to wrap the custom tag's internal code with `CFLOGIN` and the necessary code to log the user in. Choose one of these methods.

✦ **Are the data services portions of a custom tag closely bound to an entity or a clearly defined business process?** Just because a reusable piece of code has a display element to it doesn't mean that all of it must be relegated to a custom tag. Consider moving the portions of the custom tag that require data services (`SELECT`, `UPDATE`, and so on) to component functions and calling them from within the custom tag.

Migrating User-Defined Functions to Components

If you find that, after answering the qualifying questions, some of your existing functions are best implemented as functions declared within components, follow these steps:

1. Start by identifying the entities and business processes that are to be supported by the functions that qualify for implementation as components. Create a component file named for each entity or process.
2. As a temporary step, translate all `CFSCRIPT`-based UDFs to `CFFUNCTION`-based UDFs. Use the same function and argument names, specify their `ReturnType` attributes, and leave the new functions in the same locations as their previous versions.
3. As you translate each function, fully regression-test it to make sure that the function still executes correctly. This process ensures that, as you take the next step in the migration process, you introduce as few new problems as possible.
4. Add all qualifying functions to their respective component files and wrap the collection of functions with a single `CFCOMPONENT` tag pair.
5. Determine the user roles to which each new function must be restricted and then add the `roles` attribute to each restricted function.
6. Set the appropriate access level required by each function by adding the `access` attribute.
7. If you are so inclined, add metadata documentation attributes to the `CFCOMPONENT`, `CFFUNCTION`, `CFARGUMENT`, and `CFPROPERTY` tags.
8. If the component is not to be persisted longer than a single page request, place the instantiation call in all templates that require the component. Now prefix all former local function calls with *`instanceName`*.
9. If an instance of the component is to be persisted in the Application scope, it most likely declares class methods only. Wrap its instantiation call in an `IsDefined()` test for existence of the instance and then place this snippet in your `Application.cfm` templates. Now prefix all former local function calls with `Application.instanceName`.
10. If an instance of the component is to be persisted in the Session scope, it most likely declares at least some instance methods, so you need to add to the component the appropriate `InitEntity()`, `GetEntity()`, and `FlushEntityToDatabase()` functions and to assign a unique lock name. (See Chapter 22 for details on implementing long-lived persistent components.) After this procedure is done, place the instantiation call in your template that begins the process requiring the component. Now prefix all former local function calls with `Session.instanceName`.
11. Regression-test the application and fix any problems.

Migrating Custom Tags to Components

If you find that, after answering the qualifying questions, some of your existing custom tags are best implemented as functions declared within components, follow these steps:

1. For a custom tag to be a true candidate for having all of its code migrated to a component function, the tag's primary purpose must be to set local variables back in the calling template. Count the number of values set in the caller by the custom tag and then migrate the business logic of the custom tag to a user-defined function.

If the number of values set is only one, make the `Returntype` of the UDF the same as that value's data type. If more than one value is set in the caller, make the `Returntype` of the UDF a `Struct` and add `<cfset Var returnStruct = StructNew()>` as the first line of business logic in the function. Now modify the code to manipulate key-value pairs in `returnStruct` rather than individual variables.

2. Back in the caller, call the new component function in place of the previous custom tag and then reference the returned structures key-value pairs rather than the original local variables that used to be set by the custom tag.

3. If the data manipulation logic of a custom tag is a standalone routine, combining both data logic and display markup together in the custom tag is perfectly feasible. If, however, the data manipulation portions of a custom tag are closely bound to an entity or a clearly defined business process, you should separate the code for those data services from the custom tag, migrate the code to a function declared within the component that supports that entity or business process, and leave the display element in the custom tag.

   You have good reasons for doing this. A component should contain *all* the functionality necessary to completely support an entity or business process's data, and separating logic from display markup is a best practice, so this "custom tag plus component function" approach is viable.

Summary

ColdFusion MX was designed from the very beginning to make maximum reuse of code in ways that simply can't be handled by the custom tags and user-defined functions of earlier versions.

Yes, components are a very powerful addition to the ColdFusion arsenal, but they are not the panacea for all that ails your application. Included templates, custom tags, and user-defined functions are just as viable as they were in earlier versions of ColdFusion; you just have more choices in MX, and some of these choices are better choices.

By thoughtfully answering the qualifying questions posed in this chapter, you are guided toward the most appropriate technique for implementing your reusable code.

✦ ✦ ✦

CHAPTER 25

Building Web Services with ColdFusion MX

✦ ✦ ✦ ✦

In This Chapter

Building and testing a Web service

Creating a custom tag for your Web service

Designing around Web-service restrictions and caveats

✦ ✦ ✦ ✦

The power of ColdFusion components can now be extended to any system anywhere on the Internet, regardless of its platform or whether it runs ColdFusion. This is accomplished through the power of Web services, and you can find no easier way to publish or consume Web services than with ColdFusion MX.

By using Web services, you can syndicate news content from your Web site to other sites that want to display it, provide a job quotation service through another Web site, or do anything else that you'd normally do on your own site for your own customers.

This chapter assumes that you have already read Chapters 22 and 23, have built the components in Chapter 23, and fully understand how to build and use ColdFusion MX components, as they are the underlying mechanism for publishing Web services. You might find it useful to also read Chapter 30 if you want to follow the XML-related code in this chapter in detail.

What Is a Web Service?

A *Web service* is a remotely consumable software component that is published on the Web through a universal interface. Web services provide the way to extend your system — component by component — to other servers throughout the world, regardless of whether they run ColdFusion MX or not. The truly brilliant thing about Web services is their capability to automatically translate, or *cast*, most data types between ColdFusion MX and the remote systems that consume them, so an array returned from ColdFusion is also seen as an array by its .NET consumer, a date is seen as a date, and so on.

This commonality between platforms is provided through Web services' universal interface, known as *WSDL*, or *Web Services Description Language*. By publishing its XML-formatted WSDL specifications document, a Web service becomes *self-describing* to any Web service consumer. The description of a Web service includes its available methods (functions), the input/output interface to those methods, and the data types of the arguments and return values passed through that interface, so it is a complete functional specification of everything needed to make full use of the Web service.

Where WSDL provides a full specification of a Web service through an XML-structured document, *SOAP*, or *Simple Object Access* Protocol, provides an XML-structured protocol for making requests of Web services and receiving their results. WSDL and SOAP are the two technologies necessary to publish and consume Web services.

But you don't want to get bogged down with background discussions or details that don't apply to your real-world use of Web services. You want to build and use them instead.

Publishing Your First Web Service

A Web service can return any type of data as its result, and through the miracle of WSDL, that data can typically be used natively within the consuming platform. We say "typically" because, although ColdFusion MX has no problem consuming any data type from any ColdFusion MX-published Web service, WSDL sometimes has a problem casting ColdFusion query and structure objects to foreign platforms. This limitation, combined with the universal popularity of XML as an information-exchange medium, has made XML a very popular output format for Web services on all platforms, and ColdFusion MX is no exception.

The Web service that you're going to build publishes a dynamically generated XML document containing your company's trading partners who are located within a specific geographical area, based on the first few numbers of a zip code. These trading partners are stored in your sample database's Company table. An example of the XML document looks as follows (with indents and line breaks added for clarity):

```
<companies>
    <company id="7">
        <name>Bob&apos;s Motorcycle Restoration</name>
        <street>477 Reston Avenue</street>
        <city>Casper</city>
        <state>WY</state>
        <zip>82604</zip>
        <comments>Harley and Indian specialists.</comments>
    </company>
    <company id="4">
        <name>Ye Olde Poodle Accessory Shoppe</name>
        <street>45 Mangrum Road</street>
        <city>Tucson</city>
        <state>AZ</state>
        <zip>85701</zip>
        <comments>Frilly hair bow specialists.</comments>
    </company>
</companies>
```

The Web service takes one argument, which is a string containing the first few numbers of the zip-code area in which the consumer wants to look for one of your trading partners.

Building the component functions

This Web service in the preceding section contains only one method, but in the real world, a Web service may contain many methods. Create a file named `WebService.cfc` inside the `com` directory of your Web root (which you create in the component packages section of Chapter 22) and enter the code shown in Listing 25-1.

Listing 25-1: Component that serves the Web service

```
<cfcomponent>
    <cffunction name="ListPartners"
        access="remote"
        returntype="string"
        output="no">

        <cfargument name="zipFilter"
            type="string"
            required="yes">

        <cfset Var xmlDoc = "">
        <cfset Var partnerList = "">
        <cfquery name="partnerList"
            datasource="#Request.MainDSN#">
            SELECT
                CompanyID,
                CompanyName,
                Address,
                City,
                State,
                ZipCode,
                Comments
            FROM
                Company
            WHERE
                ZipCode LIKE '#Arguments.zipFilter#%'
            ORDER BY
                CompanyName ASC
        </cfquery>

        <cfsavecontent variable="xmlDoc">
            <companies>
            <cfoutput query="partnerList">
                <company id="#CompanyID#">
                    <name>#XMLFormat(CompanyName)#</name>
                    <street>#XMLFormat(Address)#</street>
                    <city>#XMLFormat(City)#</city>
                    <state>#XMLFormat(State)#</state>
                    <zip>#XMLFormat(ZipCode)#</zip>
                    <comments>#XMLFormat(Comments)#</comments>
                </company>
            </cfoutput>
            </companies>
        </cfsavecontent>

        <cfreturn xmlDoc>
    </cffunction>
</cfcomponent>
```

The important points to consider in Listing 25-1 are as follows:

✦ `access="remote"` is required to make a component method accessible to systems outside the ColdFusion server that serves the component. Because Web services are consumed remotely, your must set the `access` level to `remote`.

✦ `output="no"` is required to suppress all direct output from the Web service, because the only way to return data to a consumer is through a formal `Return` value. This is necessary for providing WSDL with the data-typing metadata that it needs to specify the `output` interface of the Web service.

✦ `required="yes"` is technically not necessary in the *definition* of a Web-service method, but all arguments of the input interface to a Web-service method are strictly required as it is invoked. If you do not pass an optional argument, the Web service throws an error.

✦ `XMLFormat()` should always be used to return XML-formatted values from dynamic data. If you don't do so, your XML-based Web-service output throws an error if the data contains an angle bracket or other characters not easily contained in XML.

Other than these four points, your Web-service method is just the same as any other component function. You do have more potential caveats to work around in working with Web services, and we get to these in the section "Web-Service Details and Caveats," at the end of this chapter, but for now, you can move on to testing your new Web service.

Testing your Web service

Before you unleash your Web service on the civilized world, make sure that your Web service itself is indeed civilized by thoroughly testing it in a test harness.

Create a file named `TestHarness.cfm` and enter into it the code shown in Listing 25-2.

Listing 25-2: Harness for testing the validity of your Web service's XML result

```
<cfinvoke
    method="ListPartners"
    returnvariable="xmlPartners"
    webservice="http://localhost/com/WebService.cfc?wsdl">

    <cfinvokeargument name="zipFilter"
        value="3">
</cfinvoke>

<cfset xmlObj = XmlParse(xmlPartners)>

<cfdump var="#xmlObj#">
```

Notice the new `webservice` attribute of the `CFINVOKE` tag, which takes the place of the `Component` attribute that you see in Chapters 22 and 23. The fact that, in ColdFusion MX, all you need to do to consume a Web service is to switch a tag attribute and specify a URL is pretty amazing, but basically that's it!

By appending the `wsdl` attribute to the URL of the component that serves the Web service, you tell ColdFusion to automatically generate the WSDL description for the Web service, and the consumer uses this WSDL description to interface with the Web service.

Now run `TestHarness.cfm`. If you don't see output just like what's shown in Figure 25-1, go back and check your code. Notice that we have collapsed most of the Company elements in the figure for readability.

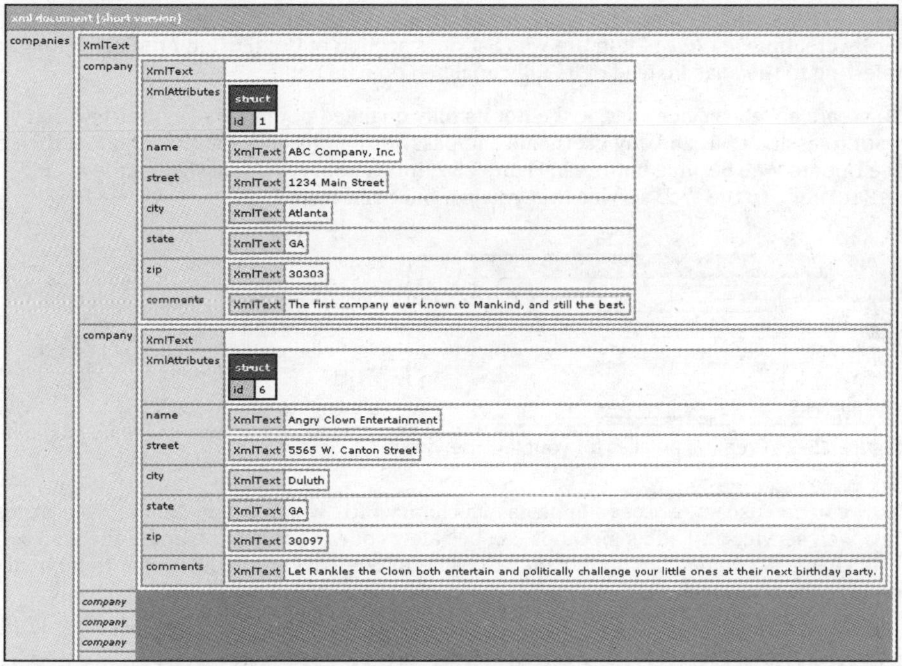

Figure 25-1: Checking the `CFDUMP` of the parsed XML object.

Edit the `Value` attribute of the `CFINVOKEARGUMENT` tag in the test harness to contain various values, including invalid ones such as peoples' names, and re-execute the harness to ensure that your Web service responds appropriately to all possible inputs that are accepted through the Web service's interface. Never publish a Web service that hasn't been thoroughly tested for all possible inputs.

After you've corrected any problems with your Web service and tested it thoroughly, the Web service is ready to be consumed.

Consuming Your First Web Service

Web-service publishers must fully consider how their services are to be consumed and are also responsible for documenting any recommendations, caveats, and so on for their consumers. In fact, a good idea is to create a complete *SDK*, or *Software Developer's Kit*, for your potential consumers so that they can easily integrate your Web service into their own Web sites for their own customers (whom, you hope, now also become your customers).

Although each platform has its own techniques for consuming Web services and displaying their results, we concentrate on a solution for remote ColdFusion MX-based systems because you can test these yourself. Because Web services almost always involve some element of display to the user, your best engineering solution for consuming them is most likely a custom tag, so that is the technique that you use in this chapter.

Creating an alias in ColdFusion Administrator

If you are consuming a remote Web service from ColdFusion MX, you can make your job easier by creating *an alias* to it in the Web Services section of ColdFusion Administrator and then referring to the alias instead of its fully qualified domain name.

To create a Web-service alias, just enter its fully qualified domain name, the alias that you want to assign to it, and any username and password required for authentication; then click the Update Web Service button. In Figure 25-2, for example, we're assigning the alias `wsPartners` to the Web service that you just built and tested.

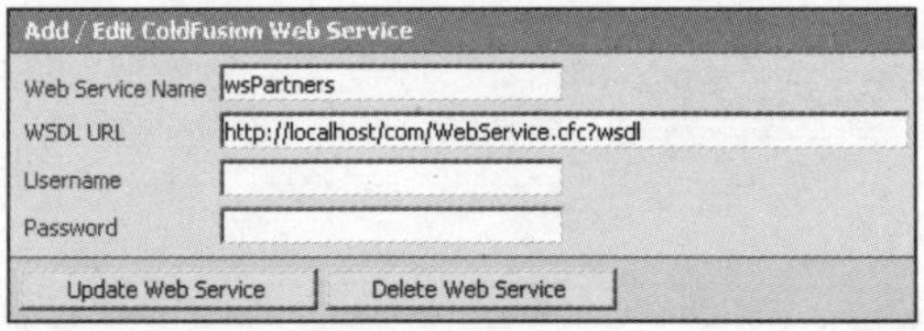

Figure 25-2: Creating an alias for your Web service.

Now you can use `wsPartners` in place of a clumsy URL, which means that all your access to this Web service and all its methods can be safely coded to this alias, and if the Web service URL changes, you need to update only the alias in ColdFusion Administrator to point all your code to the new location.

Implementing the consumer as a custom tag

In ColdFusion MX, you can separate business logic from display elements — even in custom tags that traditionally have combined the two — by calling a component method from the custom tag and then dedicating the remainder of the custom tag to displaying that data to the user. This example is going to show a really neat way to display XML-based data, which is something that you're going to need to get used to in consuming other Web services, as XML is the most common format for publishing Web-service results.

Create a file named `DisplayPartners.cfm` to contain the code in Listing 25-3.

Listing 25-3: Custom tag that consumes the Web service and transforms its XML result

```
<cfparam name="Attributes.zipFilter" type="String" default="">

<cfinvoke
    method="ListPartners"
    returnvariable="xmlPartners"
    webservice="wsPartners">
```

```
    <cfinvokeargument name="zipFilter"
        value="#Attributes.zipFilter#">
</cfinvoke>

<cffile action="READ"
    file="#ExpandPath('PartnerTransform.xsl')#"
    variable="xslPartners">

<div class="WSOutput">
    <h1>Here are the partners in your area:</h1>
    <cfoutput>#XmlTransform(xmlPartners, xslPartners)#</cfoutput>
</div>
```

Here's want this custom tag does:

✦ As with all custom tags, the first thing that you do is `CFPARAM` all attributes to ensure that they are castable to the correct data type and present as required. If an attribute isn't required, you provide a default value, but in this case, you're assigning a default because you must provide a `zipFilter` argument to the Web service regardless of whether a `zipFilter` attribute was passed to this custom tag.

✦ You are using the `wsPartners` alias that you create in the preceding section in the `CFINVOKE` tag, and you use this alias everywhere that you access this Web service in your code. Keep in mind that you can use any invocation method that you learn in Chapters 22 and 23 to invoke a Web service.

✦ By wrapping the output in a Web-service-specific *`div` container*, you can declare a style sheet specific to this `div` without affecting the rest of the Web site.

✦ And, most important, you transform the XML output from the Web service into displayable HTML content by using an *XSLT transformation*. This gives you the ultimate flexibility in controlling both the structure and format of the Web service's return data.

XSLT transformations are covered in detail in Chapter 30.

XSLT transformations are going to become a big part of your development life as you integrate more and more with external systems. If you really want to understand the details of Listing 25-4, refer to Chapter 30.

This custom tag effectively separates each major function into the best mechanism for providing that function and then aggregates the results of each function into a complete code module, as shown in the following table:

Function	*Mechanism*
Data services	Web services (components)
Content display	Custom tag
Data structuring	XSLT transformer
Formatting specifications	Cascading style sheet

Create a file named `PartnerTransform.xsl` to contain the code in Listing 25-4.

Listing 25-4: XSLT that performs the transformation

```
<?xml version='1.0'?>
<xsl:transform xmlns:xsl="http://www.w3.org/1999/XSL/Transform"
    version="1.0">

    <xsl:output omit-xml-declaration="yes"/>

    <xsl:template match="companies">
        <style>
        DIV.WSOutput H1 {
            font-family : Verdana, Arial, sans-serif;
            font-size : 18px;
            font-weight : bold;
        }
        DIV.WSOutput TH {
            font-family : Verdana, Arial, sans-serif;
            font-size : 11px;
            font-weight : bold;
            text-align : left;
            padding-right : 8px;
        }
        DIV.WSOutput TD {
            font-family : Verdana, Arial, sans-serif;
            font-size : 11px;
            padding-right : 8px;
        }
        DIV.WSOutput TD.comments {
            padding-right : 8px;
            padding-bottom : 12px;
            font-style : italic;
        }
        </style>

        <table width="600" border="0">
            <tr>
                <th>Partner Company</th>
                <th>Street Address</th>
                <th>City, State &amp; Zip Code</th>
            </tr>
            <xsl:apply-templates/>
        </table>
    </xsl:template>

    <xsl:template match="company">
        <tr>
            <td>
                <xsl:element name="a">
                    <xsl:attribute name="href">
```

```
http://www.ProductivityEnhancement.com/Ws.cfm?id=<xsl:value-of
select="@id"/>
                        </xsl:attribute>
                        <xsl:value-of select="name"/>
                    </xsl:element>
                </td>
                <td>
                    <xsl:value-of select="street"/>
                </td>
                <td>
                    <xsl:value-of select="city"/>,
                    <xsl:value-of select="state"/>
                    <xsl:text> </xsl:text>
                    <xsl:value-of select="zip"/>
                </td>
            </tr>
            <tr>
                <td colspan="3" class="comments">
                    <xsl:value-of select="comments"/>
                </td>
            </tr>
    </xsl:template>
</xsl:transform>
```

Here are the basics of what this transformer does (and please refer to Chapter 30 for details):

✦ For the root element `<companies>`, you output the cascading style sheet that you want to use for your HTML output. You could just as easily declare these `DIV`-specific styles in an external style sheet, but for easy integration into existing Web sites, you handle this by using an internal style sheet declared in the XSLT transformer itself. You also output the HTML for the table and cell headers.

✦ For each `<company>` element, you output a table row containing the partner's company information hyperlinked to an external Web site containing detailed data about each partner.

After your XSLT transformer is in place, all you need to do is call you custom tag, as follows:

```
<cf_DisplayPartners zipFilter="3">
```

The following HTML table shown in Figure 25-3 appears in its place.

Of course, after you deploy the custom tag, the `zipFilter` attribute receives its value from either a form post or a URL parameter, but you get the idea.

All in all, Web services are some pretty amazing stuff. The system that you just built is indeed a best practice approach for publishing and consuming Web services, as all functionality is correctly separated into its most appropriate mechanism, and each mechanism stands alone so that it may be modified as necessary.

If you want a bordered table with a totally different formatting, you simply change the definition of your cascading style sheet declared in your XSLT transformer, or you remove the internal style sheet entirely and declare those styles in an external style sheet. If you want to place a different heading before your table, you simple change it in the custom tag that displays the table. If, under certain circumstances, you want to use a different transformer altogether, you simply change which one you call from your custom tag.

Here are the partners in your area:

Partner Company	Street Address	City, State & Zip Code
ABC Company, Inc.	1234 Main Street	Atlanta, GA 30303
The first company ever known to Mankind, and still the best.		
Angry Clown Entertainment	5565 W. Canton Street	Duluth, GA 30097
Let Rankles the Clown both entertain and politically challenge your little ones at their next birthday party.		
Azure Productions	1087 Veritas Way	Duluth, GA 30096
Light and sound production for stage shows.		
Developers Anonymous	12 Recovery Way	Winter Haven, FL 33880-3453
Repeat: "I am a good person. I am not a machine. I have feelings, too. I will make some 'Me' time today. It's okay to stop refactoring my code. I will stop thinking in terms of pointers. I refuse to push what is important to me further down the stack. I will learn how to throw a baseball..."		
Star Trek Fan Club	1701 Getalife Lane	Orlando, FL 32801
It's not so bad living in mom's basement, really!		
The Very Big Corporation of America	One Corporate Boulevard	Norcross, GA 30071
Sooner or later, you'll be owned by us.		

Figure 25-3: The final result of consuming the Web service.

Web-Service Details and Caveats

Now to look at some of the details and "gotchas" that may crop up during Web-service development.

No spaces or special characters in URL

Your Web service throws an error on consumption if the URL contains any spaces or special characters. Typically, this crops up during only development, as you test from some subdirectory with spaces in its name.

Exception handling

If you remember back to Chapter 21, a thrown error should be handled as an exception to normal operations if such an error is the result of an expected alternative behavior. If, for example, a user inadvertently registers himself on a Web site a second time and throws a duplicate key error because his e-mail conflicts with the one that he already entered, the application should route him to an alternative interface that enables him to e-mail his password to himself or try to login by using his existing account rather than telling him that an error occurred.

Your Web service is implemented as a custom tag on the consumer side because it results in a display element that provides a portion of content for the Web page on which it is displayed. If the Web service throws an error, the entire custom tag cannot function as intended, but although this may be an error for the custom tag, the errored custom tag itself is considered an exception to that portion of the content for the entire Web page. For this reason, you need to catch any errors thrown by the Web service and handle them as an alternative display of `The web service is not available.`

Listing 25-5 is a retrofit of Listing 25-3, with exception handling and a little white-space suppression thrown in to boot.

Listing 25-5: Handling a Web service error as a "page-content exception"

```
<cfsetting enablecfoutputonly="Yes">
<cfparam name="Attributes.zipFilter" type="String" default="">

<cftry>
    <cfinvoke
        method="ListPartners"
        returnvariable="xmlPartners"
        webservice="wsPartners">

        <cfinvokeargument name="zipFilter"
            value="#Attributes.zipFilter#">
    </cfinvoke>

    <cffile action="READ"
        file="#ExpandPath('PartnerTransform.xsl')#"
        variable="xslPartners">

    <cfcatch type="Any">
        <cfoutput>The web service is not available.</cfoutput>
        <cfsetting enablecfoutputonly="No">
        <cfabort>
    </cfcatch>
</cftry>

<cfoutput>
<div class="WSOutput">
    <h1>Here are the partners in your area:</h1>
    #XmlTransform(xmlPartners, xslPartners)#
</div>
</cfoutput>

<cfsetting enablecfoutputonly="No">
```

This is one of the few legitimate uses of `CFCATCH type="Any"` that we have seen, because any error is truly an exception to the rest of the content on the Web page that contains it.

Authentication and authorization

So who gets to use your Web services? One way to secure your Web services to only certain parties is to require authentication and then check whether the user has been granted membership in one or more roles authorized to consume that Web service's methods.

The username and password that the consumer provides in defining a Web-service alias are passed to the Web service through the HTTP request header. If you don't declare the username and password in the definition of the alias, or if you don't use an alias at all, you can also provide them through the username and password attributes of the `CFINVOKE` tag.

See Chapter 40 for details on using the username and password passed during Web-service invocation to control access to your its methods. The same techniques that apply to component user authentication and authorization apply to Web service users as well.

Summary

In this chapter you've learned how to produce a web service from a ColdFusion component, how to consume this same component, and how to handle important details like exception handling and user authorization.

The capability to expose portions of your ColdFusion MX application to the rest of the world through Web services should start you thinking in a whole new direction. Everything from e-commerce to syndicated content is now easy to implement on remote systems, but you must put your mind even more toward separating data services from display of content, as the consumers of your Web services usually have their own ideas on how to display whatever you decide to publish. Yet another reason why you see Web-service content increasingly published as XML-based data is to conform to as wide a variety of remote systems as possible.

If your clients aren't already clamoring for Web services, they soon will be, so be ready. Practice what you've learned in this chapter, and shore up your XML skills in general — and XSLT, in particular — so that you can effectively integrate with virtually any remote system on the Internet.

✦ ✦ ✦

CHAPTER 26

Flash Remoting Services

In This Chapter

Understanding the "big picture" of Flash Remoting technology

Building a Flash movie for use with Flash Remoting

Using ColdFusion components, Web services, and templates to provide data to Flash Remoting

How ActionScript interacts with ColdFusion MX

Flash Remoting details and caveats to look out for

Advanced techniques for speeding up the retrieval of large queries

Flash Remoting is definitely the icing on the MX cake. Through the combination of the Flash Remoting Gateway that is built into ColdFusion MX Server and the new Flash MX authoring environment, developers can easily build high-performance scalable applications with attractive Flash interfaces. Those interfaces are much easier to build, too, thanks to the addition of Flash UI (user interface) components that encapsulate complex functionality into drag-and-drop interface elements.

You've probably heard some of the horror stories from Flash 4 and Flash 5 developers regarding the difficulty and bad performance of live data exchange between Flash and ColdFusion before the MX product line materialized. Believe them. Long strings of URL parameters, XML documents heavy-laden with markup characters, or WDDX packets needing deserialization were necessary to send data through ColdFusion to a Flash movie and back. It was messy, expensive, and the end result exhibited less than stellar performance.

The Flash Remoting Gateway eliminates all this trouble by exchanging data via a new *AMF*, or *Action Message Format*, which, because it's a binary data format, reduces the bandwidth (and time) required to transmit data by as much as 90 percent. This improvement, combined with the elimination of all serializing and deserializing of data, results in Flash Remoting applications that operate faster than normal Web applications.

Another big benefit to Flash Remoting applications is their inherent capability to combine multiple interface elements on the same "page" without resorting to complicated DHTML techniques or suffering browser-version incompatibilities.

Sound interesting? Then go ahead and begin!

How Flash Remoting Works

The best way for us to describe how Flash Remoting applications work is to have you read a comprehensive diagram that we built that shows each step in the process, along with a little of the code involved. Figure 26-1 gives you "the big picture" of Flash Remoting.

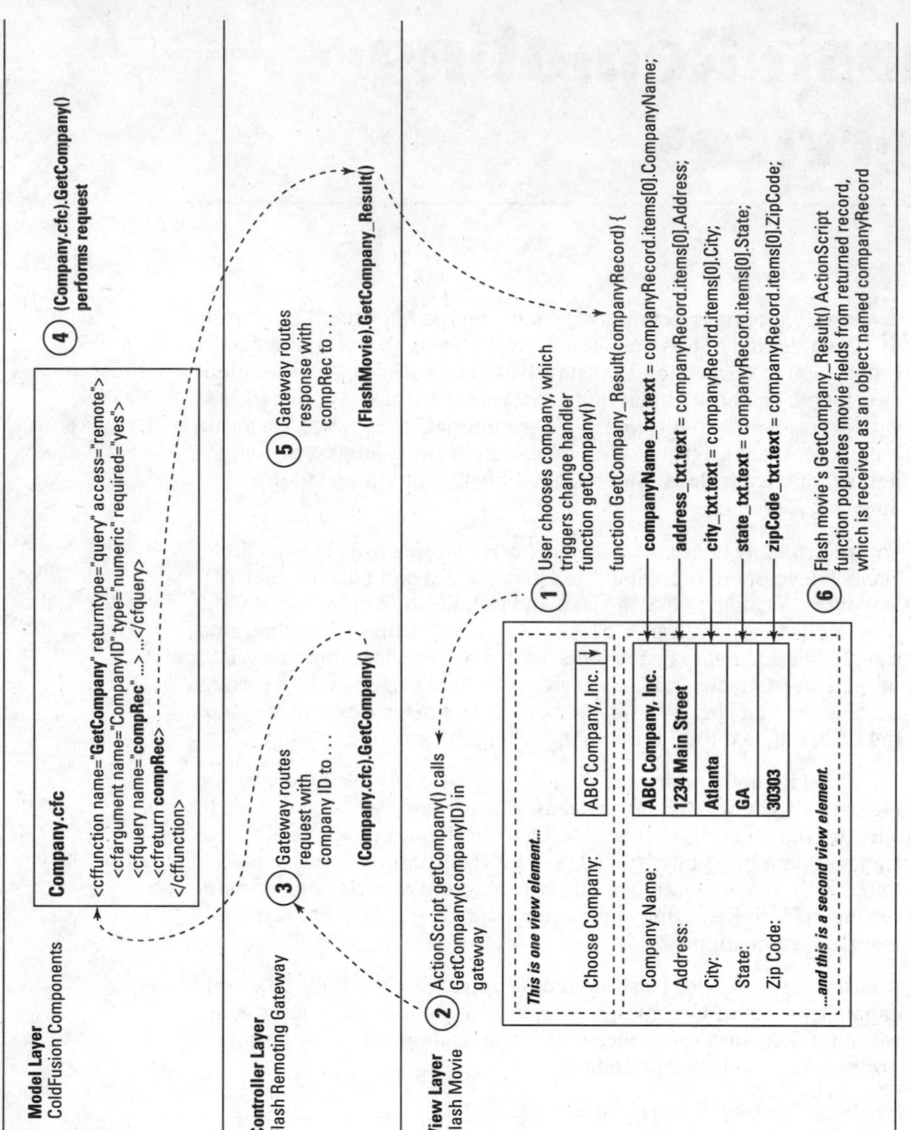

Figure 26-1: The big picture of how Flash Remoting works.

The following list breaks down the details, step by numbered step:

1. As the user chooses a different company from the Company combo box, his action triggers the combo box's change handler, which is the ActionScript function `getCompany()`.

2. The ActionScript function `getCompany()`, in turn, calls the `GetCompany()` function in the Flash Remoting Gateway, passing the `companyID` of the company currently selected in the combo box. This "function" is really just an interface into the real function that exists in the ColdFusion component.

Although it is not shown in Figure 26-1 for clarity's sake, as soon as the Flash movie is displayed in the user's browser, the movie initializes a connection with the Flash Remoting Gateway; then it creates an instance of the `Company.cfc` ColdFusion component. This instance gives the Flash Remoting Gateway access to the functions declared in the `Company` component, and it is from this instance that all outside function requests are made.

3. The Flash Remoting Gateway performs all necessary conversions from ActionScript data types to ColdFusion data types and then forwards the request, along with its converted arguments, to the ColdFusion component's `GetCompany()` function.

4. The ColdFusion component's `GetCompany()` function performs the request and then returns a query object named `compRec` back to the Flash Remoting Gateway.

5. The gateway again performs all necessary conversions from ColdFusion data types to ActionScript data types — in this case, from a ColdFusion query object to an ActionScript `RecordSet` object — before routing the resulting data returned from the function to an ActionScript function named `GetCompany_Result()` inside the Flash movie. This is called a *callback function*.

   Herein lies the reason why all Flash Remoting applications are true MVC (Model-View-Controller) architecture, as the Controller layer makes a final call back to the View layer after the Model layer has finished its request. A Flash movie screen may consist of multiple View elements; in this case, the combo box is one View element making a function call, and the collection of input fields is another View element receiving the callback function.

   The Controller (Flash Remoting Gateway) finds its callback function by looking for an ActionScript function with `_Result` appended to the name of the function making the original request.

6. The converted `compRec RecordSet` object is passed as the argument to the `GetCompany_Result()` callback function, where it is received as an object named `companyRecord` and is referred to by this name within the `GetCompany_Result()` function, which has the task of setting the values of the Flash movie fields to the values contained in the `companyRecord RecordSet` object.

And there you have it! All in all, the entire process is very straightforward, but you need to build a simple example and discuss some more details before you start deploying Flash Remoting applications in production.

What you need to install for this chapter

ColdFusion MX Server has the Flash Remoting Gateway already installed for you, but you also need to install the following:

- ✦ The Flash MX authoring tool
- ✦ A copy of the Flash Remoting Components

You can get both a free 30-day trial copy of Flash MX and a free full version of the Flash Remoting Components from `www.Macromedia.com`. After you have these installed, you can start building.

Building a Flash Remoting Application

So that you can get an idea of where you're going, Figure 26-2 shows what the finished Flash Remoting application that you're about to build looks like.

Choose Company ABC Company, Inc.
Company Name ABC Company, Inc.
Address 1234 Main Street
City Atlanta
State GA
Zip Code 30303
Update Company

Figure 26-2: The finished application.

After you launch the application, the Choose Company combo box fills with an alphabetical list of all companies in the database. After you choose a company, its data is retrieved from the database and displayed in the Flash movie's input fields. If you edit a value and click the Update Company button, that company's data is updated in the database, and the Choose Company combo box repopulates. If an error occurs while retrieving or manipulating data, an error message appears in red just above the Update Company button.

Not too complicated. In fact, we've kept everything very simple so that you can concentrate on the overall process rather than individual pieces of complicated code. If you're new to Flash, keeping a new authoring tool, a new language, and a new technology straight in your head is hard enough.

We only have a limited space in which to discuss Flash Remoting in this book, so we concentrate on getting the basics down and leave more elaborate instructions to books dedicated to Flash Remoting, such as "Complete Flash Remoting" by the very talented and wise Joey Lott (Wiley).

Building the ColdFusion component

You start your work with Flash Remoting by building what you're most familiar with at this point: ColdFusion components. Listing 26-1 shows the complete ColdFusion component for this application. Create a file named `Company.cfc` in your *`webroot`*`/com/flashremoting` directory, and enter into it the code shown in Listing 26-1.

Listing 26-1: The ColdFusion component used by the application

```
<cfcomponent>
    <cffunction name="GetCompany" returntype="query" access="remote">
        <cfargument name="CompanyID" type="numeric" required="yes">

        <cfset Var compRec = "">
        <cfquery name="compRec" datasource="#Request.MainDSN#">
            SELECT
                CompanyID,
```

```
                CompanyName,
                Address,
                City,
                State,
                ZipCode,
                Comments
            FROM
                Company
            WHERE
                CompanyID = #Arguments.CompanyID#
        </cfquery>

        <cfreturn compRec>
    </cffunction>

    <cffunction name="ListCompanies" returntype="query"
access="remote">
        <cfargument name="CompanyFilter" type="string" required="No"
default="">

        <cfset Var companyRecs = "">
        <cfquery name="companyRecs" datasource="#Request.MainDSN#">
            SELECT
                CompanyID,
                CompanyName,
                Address,
                City,
                State,
                ZipCode,
                Comments
            FROM
                Company
            <cfif Len(Trim(Arguments.CompanyFilter)) GT 0>
            WHERE
                CompanyName LIKE '#Trim(Arguments.CompanyFilter)#%'
            </cfif>
            ORDER BY
                CompanyName
        </cfquery>

        <cfreturn companyRecs>
    </cffunction>

    <cffunction name="UpdateCompany" returntype="void" access="remote">
        <cfargument name="CompanyID" type="numeric" required="Yes">
        <cfargument name="CompanyName" type="string" required="Yes">
        <cfargument name="Address" type="string" required="Yes">
        <cfargument name="City" type="string" required="Yes">
        <cfargument name="State" type="string" required="Yes">
        <cfargument name="ZipCode" type="string" required="Yes">
        <cfargument name="Comments" type="string" required="No">
```

Continued

Listing 26-1 *(continued)*

```
        <cfset Var updCompany = "">
        <cfquery name="updCompany" datasource="#Request.MainDSN#">
            UPDATE
                Company
            SET
                CompanyName = '#Trim(Arguments.CompanyName)#',
                Address = '#Trim(Arguments.Address)#',
                City = '#Trim(Arguments.City)#',
                State = '#Trim(Arguments.State)#',
                ZipCode = '#Trim(Arguments.ZipCode)#'
                <cfif IsDefined('Arguments.Comments')>
                    , Comments = '#Trim(Arguments.Comments)#'
                </cfif>
            WHERE
                CompanyID = #Arguments.CompanyID#
        </cfquery>

        <cfreturn>
    </cffunction>
</cfcomponent>
```

Pretty straightforward stuff, but we should mention a few important points, as follows:

- The first thing that you should notice is that all functions' `access` attributes are set to `remote`, just as you do in Chapter 25 with Web services. Basically, if it's accessed outside ColdFusion MX, the `access` level must be set to `remote`.
- In the `ListCompanies()` function, the `CompanyFilter` argument is optional, but it defaults to an empty string if the argument is not provided, so as the function executes, the `CompanyFilter` argument is always defined. Because your Flash application does not send the `CompanyFilter` argument, your code must test for its trimmed length rather than its declaration and then use it only if an actual value is passed.
- Similarly, your Flash application doesn't enable you to edit the `Company.Comments` column so `Comments` is an optional argument. You don't declare a default value for this argument because doing so overwrites the current contents of that column in updating the `Company` record, so here you test only whether it was passed.

Building the Flash movie

Now that the backend is built, you can work on the front-end. Launch Flash MX, create a new movie if one isn't already created for you, and then proceed with the instructions in the following sections.

Setup the Stage and Timeline

The *stage* is the place where everything that the user sees happens, and the *Timeline* coordinates when everything happens. After a Flash movie opens, it automatically starts playing, and a *playhead* begins to move across the Timeline. As the playhead moves through the frames in each Timeline layer, all the code in those frames is executed.

Although Flash movies can be scaled to almost any size, you still need to set the initial working size of the Stage to set the correct proportions. We suggest that you set your Stage size to the final size that you intend your movie to be for simplicity's sake, as we do.

We're also going to follow some conventional Flash wisdom here and have you create two layers in your Timeline: one for the form controls that you create on the Stage and one that just holds all the ActionScript code that you write. This is not strictly necessary, but it really helps organize your code and separate it from everything else.

To set the dimensions of the Flash Stage and set up the Timeline with two layers, follow these steps:

1. In the Properties palette, which enables you to interactively modify the properties of the currently selected object, click the Size button.

   The Size button always displays the current Stage size as its label.

2. Set the size of the Stage to 360w x 250h by editing the width and height fields and then clicking OK.

3. Double-click the name of the current layer in your Timeline (it is named Layer 1, and it is located in the upper left corner of your screen), type the name `components`, and press Enter.

4. To create the second layer, click the tiny page icon with the plus symbol in the lower-left corner of the Timeline. It is initially named Layer 2.

5. Double-click the name Layer 2, type the name `actions`, and press Enter.

6. Choose File ⇨ Save from the Flash menu bar and name your Flash movie `Company.fla`.

Now that the Stage and Timeline is configured the way that you want it, you can create the form controls.

Create the field labels

Three kinds of text objects are in Flash: `Static`, for plain text such as the field labels that you're about to create; *Dynamic*, for text that you can programmatically change the value of but can't manually enter; and *Input*, for data manually entered by a user.

To create the field labels for your application, follow these steps:

1. In Flash, select Frame 1 of the `components` layer by clicking the frame.

   You should always have Frame 1 of the `components` layer selected before you create, modify, or paste any form elements in your Flash movie. As you learn more about Flash and start programming its elements' behaviors, you see how organization in layers becomes very important, so you want to start with some good habits.

2. Select the text tool, which looks like a capital `A`, from the Tools palette.

3. Click the approximate location where you want the Choose Company label to appear.

   Refer to Figure 26-2 for guidance in placing the label.

4. Type Choose Company, click the solid-black pointer tool in the Tools palette, and drag the label into place.

5. Choose Static Text from the drop-down list in the Properties palette.

6. Repeat steps 2 through 5 for the other field labels, typing the correct text for each label.

Figure 26-3 shows the properties for a typical field label:

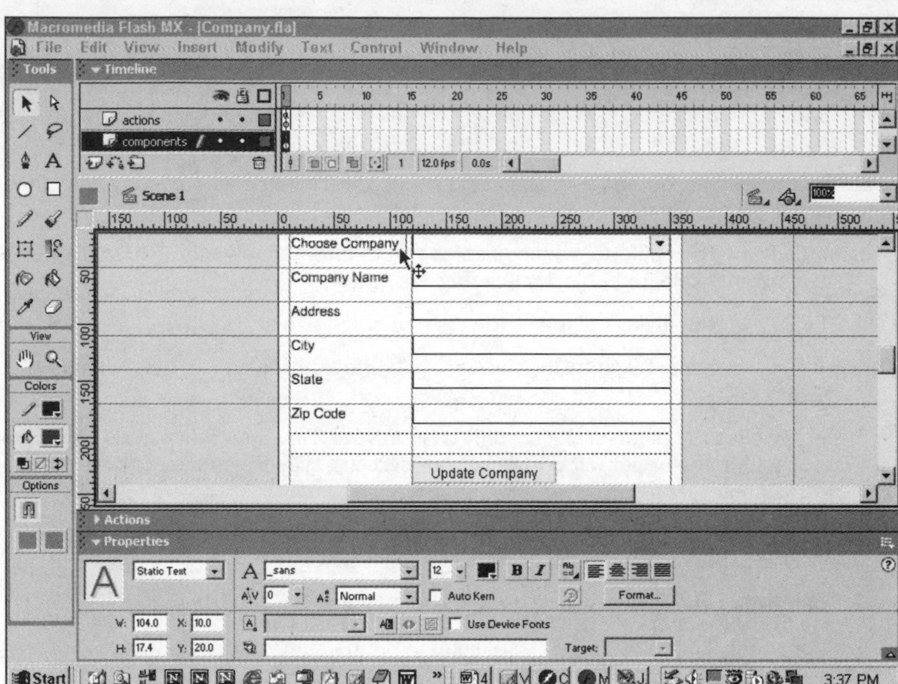

Figure 26-3: The properties of a typical field label.

Create the input fields

Continuing with text objects, it's time to create input fields.

To create the input fields for your application, follow these steps:

1. Select the text tool from the Tools palette again.
2. With the text object still selected, choose Input Text from the drop-down list in the Properties palette.
3. Click the approximate location where you want the Company Name field to appear and then drag the little white circle in the corner of the field to the right to give the field some width.
4. Type `companyName_txt` in the <Instance Name> field and then press Enter.

   Object names are case sensitive in Flash, so type everything exactly as you see it in this exercise.
5. Repeat steps 1 through 4 for the other input fields.

   Use these names for the fields:

   ```
   address_txt
   city_txt
   state_txt
   zipCode_txt
   ```

6. Roughly position the fields where they should appear on the form by dragging them with the solid pointer tool.

Figure 26-4 shows all the properties for a typical input field:

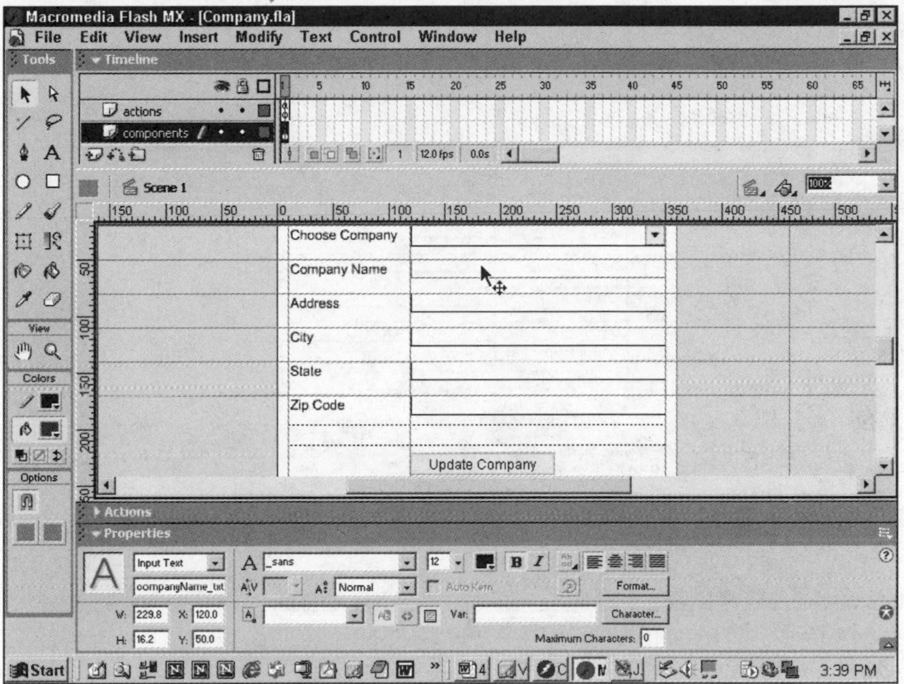

Figure 26-4: The properties of a typical input field.

Create the status message box

Our final text object is the status message box. You can't manually enter data into it, but you can programmatically change what it displays to the user.

To create the status message box, follow these steps:

1. Select the text tool from the Tools palette again.

   This time, you're going to use a different drawing technique.

2. Between the Zip Code field and the Update Company button, click and drag the text tool to draw a rectangle almost as wide as the Stage; then release the mouse button.

3. With the text object still selected, choose Dynamic Text from the drop-down list in the Properties palette.

4. Type `status_txt` in the <Instance Name> field and then press Enter.

5. Format the status message box with bold, red, centered type using the formatting controls in the Properties palette.

Figure 26-5 shows the properties for the status message box.

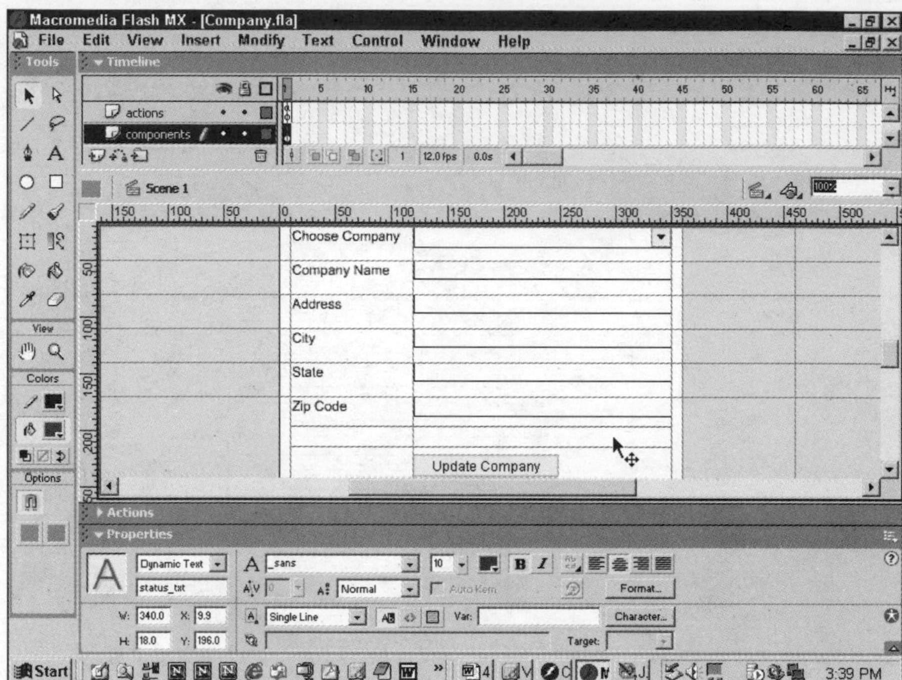

Figure 26-5: The properties of the status message box.

Create the Company combo box

Now that the basics are taken care of, it's onto Flash UI components.

To create the Choose Company combo box, follow these steps:

1. Choose Flash UI Components from the Components palette drop-down list.
2. Drag an instance of the `ComboBox` Component from the Components palette onto the Stage.
3. With the instance still selected, click the <Instance Name> field in the Properties palette, type `companyToShow_cb`, and press Enter.
4. Click to the right of the Change Handler item in the properties list of the Parameters tab as shown in Figure 26-6, type getCompany without any parentheses or punctuation, and press Enter.

   This means that, each time that you choose a different company in this combo box, the `getCompany()` ActionScript function is called.
5. The width of the combo box is probably too narrow, so enter a new width in the W (width) field and press Enter. Dial in the width that you want by adjusting the value of the W field and position the combo box where you want it by dragging it with the pointer tool.

Figure 26-6 shows the properties for the Choose Company combo box.

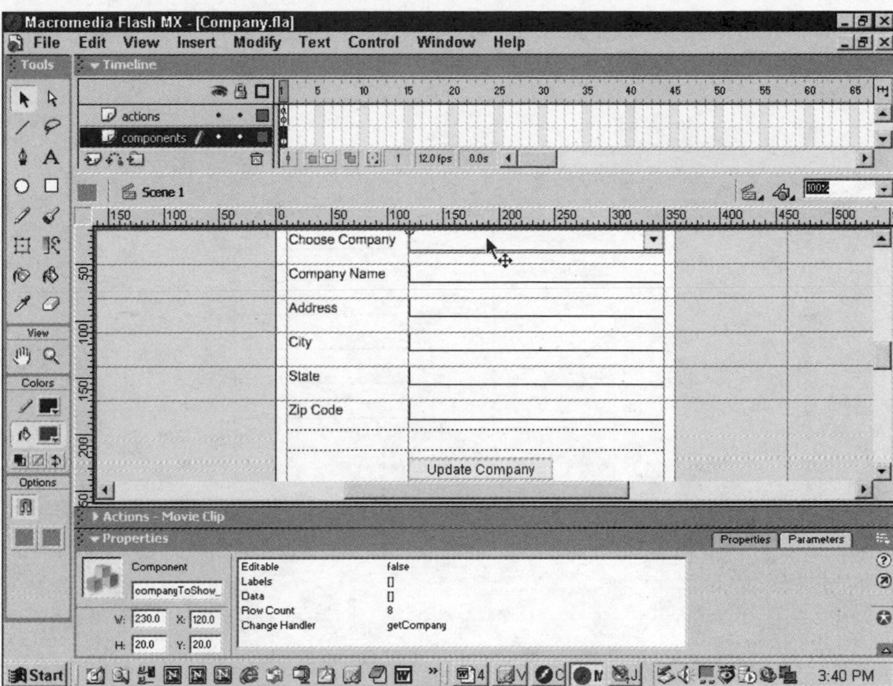

Figure 26-6: The properties of the Choose Company combo box.

Create the Update Company button

Our last form element to create is the Update Company button.

To create the Update Company button, follow these steps:

1. Drag an instance of the `PushButton` Component from the Components palette onto the Stage.
2. With the instance still selected, click the <Instance Name> field in the Properties palette, type `update_pb`, and press Enter.
3. Click to the right of the Click Handler item in the properties list of the Parameters tab and type `updateCompany` without any parentheses or punctuation; press Enter.

   This means that, each time that you click this button, the `updateCompany()` ActionScript function is called.
4. Click to the right of the Label item in the properties list of the Parameters tab and type `Update Company`; press Enter.
5. Drag the push button to its final position

Figure 26-7 shows the properties for Update Company button.

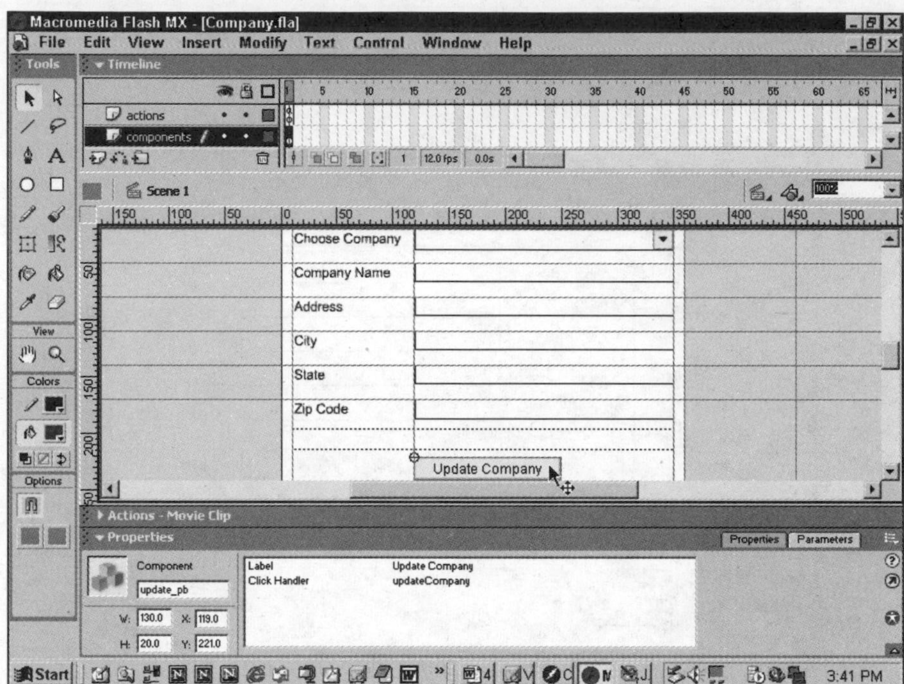

Figure 26-7: The properties of the Update Company button.

Later on, you may want to come back and set some guides on your Stage to help you position these form elements and maybe reformat text styles, but for now, push on to ActionScript.

Choose File ➪ Save from the Flash menu bar, and maybe take a little break. Can't? Too excited? Okay—onto the final piece of the Flash Remoting puzzle: ActionScript!

Building the ActionScript

The ActionScript that you're going to build can be placed in one frame for your convenience, then called from any other Flash object as needed. You can place code containing individual pieces of logic within specific objects in your Flash movie if you wish (which is useful when you are working with a team of other developers who have their own pieces of code), but keeping all your code in one place is probably the best way to start learning how to program with Flash MX.

Select Frame 1 of the `actions` layer before proceeding so that your code is easy to find, as shown in Figure 26-8.

Listing 26-2 shows the complete ActionScript for this application. Enter Listing 26-2 exactly as shown in Frame 1 of the `actions` layer. (Most of it is case sensitive, so treat all of it that way to be safe.) Then we can discuss it in detail.

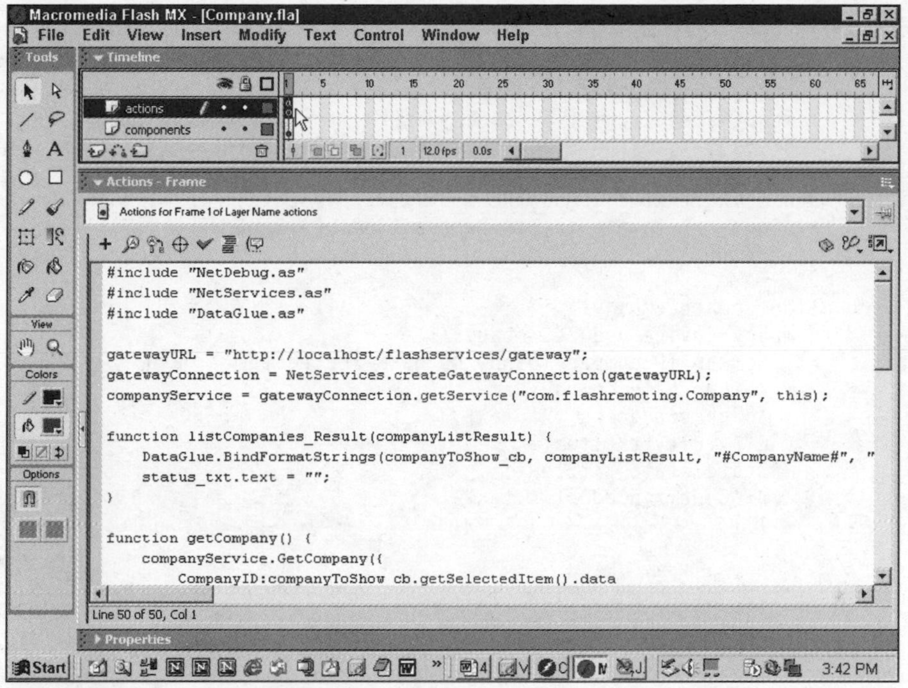

Figure 26-8: Enter all your ActionScript in this example into Frame 1 of the `actions` layer.

Listing 26-2: **The ActionScript used by the application**

```
#include "NetDebug.as"
#include "NetServices.as"
#include "DataGlue.as"

gatewayURL = "http://localhost/flashservices/gateway";
gatewayConnection = NetServices.createGatewayConnection(gatewayURL);
companyService =
gatewayConnection.getService("com.flashremoting.Company", this);

function listCompanies_Result(companyListResult) {
    DataGlue.BindFormatStrings(companyToShow_cb, companyListResult,
"#CompanyName#", "#CompanyID#");
    status_txt.text = "";
}

function getCompany() {
    companyService.GetCompany({
        CompanyID:companyToShow_cb.getSelectedItem().data
        });
}
```

Continued

Listing 26-2 *(continued)*

```
function getCompany_Result(companyRecord) {
    companyName_txt.text = companyRecord.items[0].CompanyName;
    address_txt.text = companyRecord.items[0].Address;
    city_txt.text = companyRecord.items[0].City;
    state_txt.text = companyRecord.items[0].State;
    zipCode_txt.text = companyRecord.items[0].ZipCode;
}

function updateCompany() {
    companyService.updateCompany({
        CompanyID:companyToShow_cb.getSelectedItem().data,
        CompanyName:companyName_txt.text,
        Address:address_txt.text,
        City:city_txt.text,
        State:state_txt.text,
        ZipCode:zipCode_txt.text
        });
}

function updateCompany_Result() {
    companyService.ListCompanies();
}

function updateCompany_Status() {
    status_txt.text = "An error occurred.";
}

companyService.listCompanies();

stop();
```

Let's take Listing 26-2 from the top and work our way down.

```
#include "NetDebug.as"
#include "NetServices.as"
#include "DataGlue.as"
```

These three `include` statements bring the ActionScript code from these script files into your script, so as you test and publish your Flash movie, the code from these external scripts isn't left behind. Notice that `include` statements do not end in semicolons.

`NetDebug.as` provides a very useful Flash debugger that you should absolutely love and rely on during Flash Remoting development. More on how to use it in the section "NetConnection Debugger." This line of code should be removed before production deployment.

`NetServices.as` provides extended Flash Remoting functionality and ease of use. Although it is technically not needed for Flash Remoting development per se, most developers we know use its extended methods as standard operating procedure (as do we).

`DataGlue.as` provides data-binding routines for Flash UI components, such as the Choose Company combo box that you created in the section "Create the Company combo box," earlier in this chapter. Its functions can be duplicated through a lot of extensive coding, so technically it is not absolutely necessary for Flash Remoting development, but trust us — you want to use DataGlue because, with it, you can bind a RecordSet object to a form control with a single function call, as follows:

```
gatewayURL = "http://localhost/flashservices/gateway";
gatewayConnection = NetServices.createGatewayConnection(gatewayURL);
```

If you are using ColdFusion MX Server with IIS or another Web server, your gatewayURL assignment is as shown. If your ColdFusion MX Server was installed with its own standalone Web server, you may need to address Port 8500 in the Flash Remoting Gateway URL, as follows:

```
gatewayURL = "http://localhost:8500/flashservices/gateway";
```

Either way, this is the virtual Web address of your Flash Remoting Gateway.

The gatewayConnection assignment creates an instance of the NetConnection object through which you instantiate instances of your ColdFusion components, as follows:

```
companyService =
gatewayConnection.getService("com.flashremoting.Company", this);
```

Now you can call methods of the Company component through the companyService instance, as you soon see.

As you learned in the section "How Flash Remoting Works," earlier in this chapter, callback functions are named by appending _Result to the name of the original calling function, so listCompanies_Result() is the callback function for the ListCompanies() function in the Company ColdFusion component:

```
function listCompanies_Result(companyListResult) {
    DataGlue.BindFormatStrings(companyToShow_cb, companyListResult,
"#CompanyName#", "#CompanyID#");
    status_txt.text = "";
}
```

The ColdFusion query object returned from the ListCompanies() ColdFusion component function is received by the listCompanies_Result ActionScript function as an ActionScript RecordSet object named companyListResult.

Then DataGlue's BindFormatStrings() function binds the companyToShow_cb combo box to the companyListResult RecordSet object, using the CompanyName column values as the display text in the combo box, and the CompanyID column values as their corresponding data values (similar to an HTML select menu), as follows:

```
function getCompany() {
    companyService.GetCompany({
        CompanyID:companyToShow_cb.getSelectedItem().data
        });
}

function getCompany_Result(companyRecord) {
    companyName_txt.text = companyRecord.items[0].CompanyName;
    address_txt.text = companyRecord.items[0].Address;
    city_txt.text = companyRecord.items[0].City;
    state_txt.text = companyRecord.items[0].State;
    zipCode_txt.text = companyRecord.items[0].ZipCode;
}
```

The getCompany() ActionScript function, which is called whenever the user chooses a different company in the Choose Company combo box, simply calls the GetCompany() ColdFusion component function in companyService, which is an instance of the Company ColdFusion component defined in the Flash Remoting Gateway. The argument to the GetCompany() ColdFusion function is the data value of the selected item in the companyToShow_cb (Choose Company) combo box. We are using named argument syntax here, where the name of the argument is followed by a colon and then by the value of the argument.

The callback function for getCompany()—getCompany_Result()—receives the returned RecordSet object containing a single record and internally refers to it as companyRecord. By using familiar dot notation, getCompany_Result() sets the values of the form fields in the Flash movie to those returned in the companyRecord object. Notice that you are setting the .text *attribute* of the object only, and not the entire object itself.

In a similar vein, updateCompany also uses named argument notation (our favorite method for clarity of code) to send the text attributes of the entry fields and the data attribute of the combo box (the currently selected companyID) to the UpdateCompany() ColdFusion function of the Company component. The callback function simply recalls listCompanies() to update the combo box's contents:

```
function updateCompany() {
    companyService.updateCompany({
        CompanyID:companyToShow_cb.getSelectedItem().data,
        CompanyName:companyName_txt.text,
        Address:address_txt.text,
        City:city_txt.text,
        State:state_txt.text,
        ZipCode:zipCode_txt.text
        });
}

function updateCompany_Result() {
    companyService.listCompanies();
}

function updateCompany_Status() {
    status_txt.text = "An error occurred.";
}
```

Here you see something new. Another automatic callback function is called if the original calling function throws an error. This error callback is named by appending _Status to the name of the original calling function.

Everything up to this point has either been establishing a connection, instantiating an object, or declaring functions that have yet to be called. But now you actually execute some code by calling the listCompanies() function of the companyServices instance of the Company ColdFusion component and then stopping the playhead by using the stop() action, which tells the Flash movie to stop playing. If this Flash movie contained multiple frames—as most of your production Flash movies will—and you don't tell the playhead to stop, it would keep running the entire time that your Flash movie was open:

```
companyService.listCompanies();

stop();
```

Choose File ➪ Save from the Flash menu bar, and you're done. Now to test your new baby!

Testing the application

Choose Control ➪ Test Movie from the menu bar and see what happens. Most likely, you find that you have a coding typo somewhere or maybe forgot to enter an instance name for one or more of your form objects, or did or forgot something else that prevents your Flash Remoting application from working. Don't worry—the NetConnection Debugger comes to your rescue!

Finally, a truly useful (and cool) debugger! To use it, just choose Window ➪ NetConnection Debugger from the menu bar and then Control ➪ Test Movie from the Flash menu bar, and reposition and resize the debugger window so that you don't obscure your view of the underlying Flash Remoting application that you're debugging.

If you see an error in the debugger right away, select it in the left list box and inspect its details on the right. Correct the problem and then try again. You may need to choose Window ➪ NetConnection Debugger again before testing the movie.

After you have all your initial errors debugged, your Flash Remoting application is ready to be put through the ringer. To test the error callback function, enter a very long value into the zip code field and then click the Update Company button. You should see a red error message in the status message box that you create in the section "Create the status message box," earlier in this chapter. By the way, you can restrict the number of characters that the user can enter into an input field through the Maximum Characters attribute in the input field's Properties palette.

See how everything works together? Are you getting a "feel" for the system in general. Good! Now to go further into the details and also learn what *not* to do.

Details and Caveats

We really wanted you to get your feet wet in the preceding sections of this chapter with a very simple Flash Remoting application before we dump a bunch of details on you. Learning is so much easier if you strip away all the details and focus just on the big stuff to begin with, but you need to know these important details and caveats before you start deploying Flash Remoting applications in a production environment.

Publishing your Flash movie

To publish your Flash movie, click an unpopulated area of the Stage and then click the Publish button in the Properties palette. A Publish Settings dialog box appears for you to specify the quality and size settings that you want to use. The defaults do well for now, so just click the dialog box's Publish button, click its OK button, and then open the `Company.html` file from the directory in which you saved your `Company.fla` Flash file. You now see your Flash Remoting application in live action!

Right-click anywhere off the Flash movie portion of the `Company.html` Web page, and choose View ➪ Source from your browser's menu bar. You can copy and paste this code, an example of which is shown in Listing 26-3, into your ColdFusion templates where you want to display the Flash movie. You can also open the `Company.html` file in your favorite editor.

Listing 26-3: Flash movie embedding code

```
<OBJECT classid="clsid:D27CDB6E-AE6D-11cf-96B8-444553540000"
    codebase="http://download.macromedia.com/pub/shockwave/cabs/flash/
swflash.cab#version=6,0,0,0"
    WIDTH="360"
    HEIGHT="250"
    id="Company"
    ALIGN="">

    <PARAM NAME=movie VALUE="Company.swf">
    <PARAM NAME=quality VALUE=high>
    <PARAM NAME=bgcolor VALUE=#FFFFFF>

    <EMBED src="Company.swf"
        quality=high
        bgcolor=#FFFFFF
        WIDTH="360"
        HEIGHT="250"
        NAME="Company"
        ALIGN=""
        TYPE="application/x-shockwave-flash"
        PLUGINSPAGE="http://www.macromedia.com/go/getflashplayer">
    </EMBED>
</OBJECT>
```

The advanced publishing options of Flash movies are beyond the scope of this book, but this shows you enough to make everything work very well. For more details, please refer to the *Flash MX Bible* by Robert Reinhardt and Snow Dowd (Wiley) or to your Flash documentation.

Using Flash Remoting with .cfm templates

In preceding sections of this chapter, you see ColdFusion components used to provide data services to the Flash Remoting Gateway, but you are not limited to components alone. You can also use plain ColdFusion templates to provide data for Flash Remoting, but the mechanism for returning data is necessarily different, as you have no formal "return" of data from a standard ColdFusion template.

To establish a Flash Remoting Gateway connection to a ColdFusion template, simply specify the directory containing the template as the service and use the file-name root of the template (that is, without the `.cfm` extension) as the name of the function that you're calling. So if you have a ColdFusion template named `GetCompanyList.cfm` inside *`webroot`*`/com/cfms`, you can call it from a Flash Remoting application as follows:

```
cfmService = gatewayConnection.getService("com.cfms", this);
cfmService.GetCompanyList();
```

If you want to send parameters to a ColdFusion template, just set them positionally in an ActionScript array, as follows:

```
Flash.Params = new Array();
Flash.Params[0] = 115;
Flash.Params[1] = "Razzmatazz Industries";
Flash.Params[2] = "35 Bowling Way";
Flash.Params[3] = "Atlanta";
```

`Flash.Params` is received by ColdFusion as a structure named Flash that's *containing* an array rather than as a plain array. You can access the parameters from within ColdFusion by using standard dot notation, as follows:

```
Flash.Params[1]
Flash.Params[2]
Flash.Params[3]
Flash.Params[4]
```

Notice that an "index shift" occurs because ActionScript arrays are zero-based (that is, they start at index 0) whereas ColdFusion arrays are one-based (that is, they start at index 1).

To send data from a ColdFusion template back to the Flash Remoting Gateway, you assign the return data to the `Result` variable in ColdFusion MX's new Flash scope. If you have a ColdFusion template that creates a query object named `myQuery` that you want to return to the Flash Remoting Gateway, for example, assign it to `Flash.Result`, as follows:

```
<cfset Flash.Result = myQuery>
```

The Flash Remoting Gateway takes whatever is set in `Flash.Result` and routes it to the appropriate callback method in your Flash movie, just as it would if it received data back from a ColdFusion component function.

Integrating Web services with Flash Remoting

To make your Flash Remoting application work from a Web service rather than a ColdFusion component, just replace the `webroot` subdirectory path with the full URL to the Web service's WSDL file, as follows:

```
wsdlURL = "http://www.mydomain.com/webservices/company.cfc?wsdl";
companyService = gatewayConnection.getService(wsdlURL, this);
```

Now you can call the Web service's functions by using the same syntax you're used to, as follows:

```
companyService.listCompanies();
```

You can reference any WSDL file on any platform. Where ColdFusion MX uses the URL to a CFC with a `wsdl` parameter tacked on, some systems have precreated WSDL files as follows:

```
wsdlURL = "http://www.yourdomain.com/ws/companysvc.wsdl";
companyService = gatewayConnection.getService(wsdlURL, this);
```

Regardless of the target platform or how the WSDL file is generated, as long as you can point to a valid WSDL file, the Flash Remoting Gateway can use it.

Creating paged data displays

If your Flash query returns thousands of records from ColdFusion, you probably want to start returning the first page of records to Flash as soon as they become available rather than wait for all of them. By setting the values of `Flash.Pagesize` in ColdFusion and calling `RecordSet.setDeliveryMode()` in ActionScript, you can make Flash Remoting handle large record sets in "pages."

ColdFusion controls the initial return of data by setting the value of `Flash.Pagesize` to the number of records to place in each "page," as follows:

```
<cfset Flash.Pagesize = 10>
```

If the query returned by the function call contains more than `Flash.Pagesize` number of records, the `RecordSet` becomes "pageable" by Flash Remoting (i.e., you can view one page of rows at a time, rather than all of them at once), and the first `Flash.Pagesize` number of records to be returned from the query are immediately returned to Flash Remoting while the remaining records continue to arrive in the background.

After ColdFusion makes its initial return to the Flash Remoting Gateway, the Flash movie must specify how the remainder of the data retrieval is to behave, and it does so through the `RecordSet` function `setDeliveryMode()`.

`setDeliveryMode()` has the following three settings:

- **`recordSet.setDeliveryMode("ondemand")`**: The default setting instructs the Gateway to stream more records as needed by the databound form control that requests them as, for example, a list box scrolls through its records.
- **`recordSet.setDeliveryMode("page", pageSize, pagesToPreFetch)`**: This setting instructs the Gateway to prefetch a number of pages of a specified size.
- **`recordSet.setDeliveryMode("fetchall", recordsInEachGroup)`**: This setting downloads a specific number of records in each group rather than a number of pages of a specific size.

Your Flash movie can test the current status of record retrieval through the use of the following additional `RecordSet` functions:

- **`recordSet.getNumberAvailable()`**: This function returns the number of records that have already been returned to the Flash movie.
- **`recordSet.isFullyPopulated()`**: This function returns `true` if all records have been received by the Flash movie; otherwise, it returns `false`.

`Flash.Pagesize` can control data returned from both standard ColdFusion templates and ColdFusion components.

Return numeric 1 or 0 rather than Boolean literal

Flash Remoting does a great job of data conversion between Flash and its remote platforms, but one conversion that it doesn't make is from ColdFusion's boolean literals `True` and `False` to Flash's version of `true` and `false`. For this reason, rewrite your ColdFusion functions that normally return a Boolean value to instead return a numeric `1` or `0` and your Flash Remoting applications can cast these values to their Boolean equivalents.

Securing Flash Remoting applications

To secure access to your Flash Remoting applications, use the `setCredentials()` function of the `NetConnection` object to set the username and password that are passed through the Flash Remoting Gateway to ColdFusion MX. Suppose, for example, that you modify the connection code from Listing 26-2 as follows:

```
gatewayURL = "http://localhost/flashservices/gateway";
gatewayConnection = NetServices.createGatewayConnection(gatewayURL);
gatewayConnection.setCredentials("lisa@churvis.com", "cutiepie");
companyService =
gatewayConnection.getService("com.flashremoting.Company", this);
```

ColdFusion creates two structure keys named `cflogin.name` and `cflogin.password` to contain `lisa@churvis.com` and `cutiepie`, respectively. In your ColdFusion code, you can now retrieve the user record based on `cflogin.name` (which contains `"lisa@churvis.com"`) and, if it's found, further test the retrieved password if it matches what was passed from Flash Remoting to `cflogin.password` (which contains `"cutiepie"`). If you get a complete match, you can then log in the Flash Remoting user by using ColdFusion MX's standard security mechanism, for example, as follows:

```
<cflogin>
    <cfloginuser name="#cflogin.name#"
        password="#cflogin.password#"
        roles="#ValueList(rolesQuery.RoleCode)#">
</cflogin>
```

`rolesQuery` is a ColdFusion query object with a `RoleCode` column that contains the names of the roles in which the authenticating user was granted membership.

Now if a Flash Remoting application attempts to call a component function or Web service that is secured by using the `roles` attribute of `CFFUNCTION`, the function throws an error if the Flash user is not authorized to have access, and the error callback function (`_Status`) is called instead of the standard callback function (`_Result`).

Summary

In this chapter you learned how to create a complete Flash Remoting application and how to handle various details such as role-based user authentication and authorization.

If you're not a Flash developer, now's the time to become one. Even if you're the typical coder-type who can't even draw a decent rectangle, you can team up with a designer-type who can, and the two of you can make beautiful music together.

For further details on coding Flash Remoting applications, download and read the PDF entitled "Using Flash Remoting MX with ColdFusion MX" from `www.Macromedia.com`. This document is an update that completely replaces Chapter 29 in your *Developing ColdFusion MX Applications with CFML* book, which is part of the standard ColdFusion MX documentation set. Among other things, this PDF shows additional methods for passing complex variables between ActionScript and ColdFusion.

We wish that we had more space to discuss Flash Remoting applications, as they are fast, scalable, relatively easy to create, and. most of all. *cool*, but to do justice to a deeper discussion of the topic would require its own book. Luckily, you will find such a book in *Complete Flash Remoting* by Joey Lott (Wiley).

✦ ✦ ✦

CHAPTER 27

Using Server-Side ActionScript

✦ ✦ ✦ ✦

In This Chapter

Understanding the scope and purpose of server-side ActionScript

Modifying client-side ActionScript to interface with server-side ActionScript

Performing queries, POSTs, and GETs by using server-side ActionScript

✦ ✦ ✦ ✦

Server-side ActionScript is another facet of Flash Remoting Services, but we wanted to split it out into its own chapter because we don't want you to confuse its purpose or its target developer audience.

Server-side ActionScript (SSAS) is similar in function to ColdFusion components in that a single server-side file that declares multiple functions can be instantiated as a service in the Flash Remoting Gateway, and a Flash movie may then call functions of this service through the Gateway. Although SSAS sounds at first like a direct replacement for ColdFusion components, it is not. SSAS has an extremely limited function set; in fact, it can perform only the equivalent of `CFQUERY` and `CFHTTP` calls, and even those are a bit cumbersome.

Most likely, this chapter is not for you, because SSAS was designed for Flash developers who need access to simple ColdFusion functionality. This chapter is included mainly for you to share with your Flash designer and developer associates so that they can perform these simple tasks by themselves. For anything more complicated, they need a ColdFusion developer such as you to implement their solutions by using the techniques that you learn in Chapter 26.

You should, however, learn the ins and outs of SSAS so that you can make informed decisions and correctly advise your clientele about the technology.

External ActionScripts as Data Providers

As you may remember from Chapter 26, the following code shows how you establish a Flash Remoting Gateway service between your Flash movie and a ColdFusion component:

```
gatewayURL =
"http://localhost/flashservices/gateway";
gatewayConnection =
NetServices.createGatewayConnection(gatewayURL);
companyService =
gatewayConnection.getService("com.flashremoting.Comp
any", this);
```

You can use SSAS files in the same way. Here's how it works: Whenever a service is requested, the Flash Remoting Gateway seeks out any file named either *servicename*.cfc or *servicename*.asr and establishes a service with the file that it finds.

If you declare similar functions in a SSAS file named CompanySS.asr and place it in the same directory as the Company.cfc component that you create in Chapter 26, for example, you simply change the service name from Company to CompanySS, as follows:

```
gatewayURL = "http://localhost/flashservices/gateway";
gatewayConnection = NetServices.createGatewayConnection(gatewayURL);
companyService =
gatewayConnection.getService("com.flashremoting.CompanySS", this);
```

The remainder of your syntax for calling SSAS functions and utilizing their results is almost identical to what you learn in Chapter 26.

To use SSAS with the Flash Remoting application that you build in Chapter 26, you need to make only the following two small changes to the ActionScript in Frame 1 of the actions layer:

✦ Change the service name from Company to CompanySS, as shown in the preceding code block.

✦ Change argument passing from named to positional syntax.

SSAS seems to balk at having named arguments passed to it, so this is another important caveat to consider in deciding whether to use SSAS, as optional arguments become a problem with positional syntax.

Listing 27-1 shows what the ActionScript in Frame 1 of the actions layer looks like after it's modified to work with SSAS.

Listing 27-1: Client-side ActionScript modified to work with server-side ActionScript

```
#include "NetDebug.as"
#include "NetServices.as"
#include "DataGlue.as"

gatewayURL = "http://localhost/flashservices/gateway";
gatewayConnection = NetServices.createGatewayConnection(gatewayURL);
companyService =
gatewayConnection.getService("com.flashremoting.CompanySS", this);

function listCompanies_Result(companyListResult) {
    DataGlue.BindFormatStrings(companyToShow_cb, companyListResult,
"#CompanyName#", "#CompanyID#");
    status_txt.text = "";
}

function getCompany() {
    companyService.GetCompany(companyToShow_cb.getSelectedItem().data);
}
```

```
function getCompany_Result(companyRecord) {
    companyName_txt.text = companyRecord.items[0].CompanyName;
    address_txt.text = companyRecord.items[0].Address;
    city_txt.text = companyRecord.items[0].City;
    state_txt.text = companyRecord.items[0].State;
    zipCode_txt.text = companyRecord.items[0].ZipCode;
}

function updateCompany() {
    companyService.updateCompany(
        companyToShow_cb.getSelectedItem().data,
        companyName_txt.text,
        address_txt.text,
        city_txt.text,
        state_txt.text,
        zipCode_txt.text
        );
}

function updateCompany_Result() {
    companyService.listCompanies();
}

function updateCompany_Status() {
    status_txt.text = "An error occurred.";
}

companyService.listCompanies();

stop();
```

Notice the switch from passing named arguments to passing positional arguments.

Now all you need to do is create a file named `CompanySS.asr` containing the code in Listing 27-2 and to place it in your *webroot*`/com/flashremoting/` directory.

Listing 27-2: Server-side ActionScript that duplicates the functionality of `Company.cfc`

```
function GetCompany(CompanyID) {
    var sqlString = "SELECT CompanyID, CompanyName, Address, City,
State, ZipCode, Comments FROM Company WHERE CompanyID = ";
    newSQL = sqlString.concat(CompanyID);
    selectData = CF.query({datasource:"CFMXBible", sql:newSQL});
    if (selectData) {
        return(selectData);
    } else {
        return null;
    }
}
```

Continued

Listing 27-2 *(continued)*

```
function listCompanies(companyFilter) {
    if (arguments.length > 0) {
        selectData = CF.query({datasource:"CFMXBible",
            sql:"SELECT CompanyID, CompanyName, Address, City, State,
ZipCode, Comments FROM Company WHERE CompanyName LIKE '" +
companyFilter + "%' ORDER BY CompanyName"});
    } else {
        selectData = CF.query({datasource:"CFMXBible",
            sql:"SELECT CompanyID, CompanyName, Address, City, State,
ZipCode, Comments FROM Company ORDER BY CompanyName"});
    }
    if (selectData) {
        return(selectData);
    } else {
        return null;
    }
}

function updateCompany (companyID, companyName, address, city, state,
zipCode, comments) {
    if (arguments.length = 7) {
        selectData = CF.query({datasource:"CFMXBible",
            sql:"UPDATE Company SET CompanyName = '" + companyName +
"', Address = '" + address + "', City = '" + city + "', State = '" +
state + "', ZipCode = '" + zipCode + "', Comments = '" + comments + "'
WHERE CompanyID = " + companyID});
    } else {
        selectData = CF.query({datasource:"CFMXBible",
            sql:"UPDATE Company SET CompanyName = '" + companyName +
"', Address = '" + address + "', City = '" + city + "', State = '" +
state + "', ZipCode = '" + zipCode + "' WHERE CompanyID = " +
companyID});
    }
        return;
}
```

Notice how this listing checks the number of arguments passed to the `listCompanies()` and `updateCompany()` functions. This is one of the only ways to check whether an optional argument (which must be the last argument in the list) is passed. We must formulate completely different SQL statements depending on whether or not the optional arguments are passed.

Now look at the code stew that we cooked up for the update statement in `updateCompany()`. *Yuck!* But that's what you must do because of the way that SSAS works. *Bon appetit!*

Anyway, give your repurposed Flash Remoting application a spin by choosing Control ⇨ Test Movie from the Flash menu bar. If you entered the code correctly, everything should work exactly as it did when it used the `Company.cfc` component. If not, check your code and use the NetConnection Debugger, as shown in Chapter 26.

Caution

Do not split SQL statements in SSAS on multiple lines as you often do in ColdFusion, as doing so throws an error.

Of importance to the more advanced Flash developers who may want to use SSAS is that the ColdFusion query object returned is automatically converted to an ActionScript `RecordSet` object. So after your Flash movie receives the `RecordSet` object, you may use any of the native methods available in ActionScript for manipulating `RecordSet` objects, such as `addItem()`, `removeItemAt()`, and so on.

External ActionScripts as Remote Agents

The only other functionality beside `CFQUERY` available to SSAS is the `CFHTTP` functionality found in ColdFusion, but a Flash movie is very limited as to what it can do with the results of a `CFHTTP` call.

The main reason why you would want to use SSAS's HTTP functionality is to `POST` data to an external server. Listing 27-3, for example, shows how you would `POST` to an external server and send its response data back to the Flash movie.

Listing 27-3: `CF.http` POST example

```
function postToURL (firstname, lastname) {
    var params = new Array();
    params[1] = {name:"firstname", type:"FormField", value:firstname};
    params[2] = {name:"lastname", type:"FormField", value:lastname};
    result = CF.http({method:"post",
        url:"http://localhost/com/flashremoting/ActionPage.cfm",
        params:params
        });
    return result.get("Filecontent");
}
```

The Flash movie's callback function now has full access to the data returned by the external server.

Caution

Pay special attention to white-space generation in performing HTTP calls, as white space becomes part of the HTTP response and, therefore, part of `result.get("Filecontent")`. If the `Application.cfm` file that is called as a part of the HTTP request does not contain any display elements (such as a graphical page header), wrap all its code within a `CFSILENT` tag pair. If the `Application.cfm` file does contain display elements, create a separate `Application.cfm` file for the directory containing your remotely accessed `POST` pages, include only functional (nondisplay) code in it, and wrap all its code in a `CFSILENT` tag pair.

Granted, the HTTP functionality of SSAS is very limited, but it's there if you need it.

Summary

In this chapter you learned how to make Flash Remoting applications with Server-Side ActionScript, and why SSAS is most likely not the way a professional ColdFusion developer would develop Flash Remoting applications.

Your first and best solution is to forego SSAS in favor of its stronger and more handsome brother, ColdFusion components. Think of all the functionality that you give up by moving away from the ColdFusion MX technology that you learn in this book!

If you're working with Flash designers who want to get started using a little ColdFusion, however, SSAS is perfect for them.

It may seem a bit funny, but we think that SSAS's biggest benefit is that it brings Flash developers and ColdFusion developers together in such a way that they often trade skill sets, and this natural "cross pollination" turns out a better quality development staff overall.

✦ ✦ ✦

P A R T

V

Integrating ColdFusion MX with Other Technologies

✦ ✦ ✦ ✦

In This Part

✦ ✦ ✦ ✦

CHAPTER 28

Integrating ColdFusion MX and Java

In This Chapter

Employing J2EE sessions

Calling JSP custom tags

Using applets

Leveraging the Java API by using CFOBJECT

Running JavaServer Pages and Servlets within CF MX

Exploring interactions between CFML and JSPs/Servlets

Calling Java CFX custom tags

Investigating other Java integration topics and learning more

Before you skip this chapter, thinking, "I don't know Java, so no point in reading on," please don't. Most of the opportunities for integrating ColdFusion and Java don't require that you have any Java language skills. That may seem hard to accept.

One of the great features of Java is a strong focus on reusability—the opportunity to develop code that can be reused by different programs and different developers. The converse is that you can use Java code developed by others. This extends to enabling CF developers to make use of many interesting Java integration points.

CF MX dramatically extends the Java integration capabilities that existed in CF 4.5.2 and CF 5. Even for developers still working in those releases, much of the information in this chapter still applies.

Of course, a Java developer can make even greater use of the integration possibilities, creating his own Java programs and taking advantage of still more Java and J2EE features. But non-Java developers also need to be aware of these integration opportunities.

Many aspects of using Java within ColdFusion don't require writing and compiling Java programs, and you have ways to employ the Java libraries, if you know what they are (as we explain later in this chapter), directly from within CFML.

We introduce in this chapter the many Java integration points by order of the features requiring the least Java language understanding and ending with those that require the most. Again, any of these can be used to even greater advantage by a developer with Java language skills. The topics that we address in this chapter are as follows:

Many, although not all, of these features are newly enabled or enhanced over those of earlier releases because of CF MX's underlying J2EE engine. We begin with those features that require the least amount of Java understanding.

Using J2EE Sessions

The first aspect integrating ColdFusion with Java doesn't really concern the Java language at all but *J2EE sessions*. This is an option that you can turn on or not and that comes to you by way of the underlying J2EE server that sits beneath CF MX.

One of the most powerful new features of CF MX is the fact that it's built to run atop a J2EE server. The underlying J2EE engine is Macromedia's JRun server. This is transparent to CF developers, and the fact that this integration is something that you needn't be concerned with is a testament to the engineering design achievement of CF MX. It does, however, open the doors to possibilities that simply weren't available prior to CF MX.

Just before this book went to print, Macromedia announced a new version of ColdFusion MX, called *ColdFusion MX for J2EE*, designed to be installed on an already existing J2EE server. Initially supported environments are IBM WebSphere, Sun One Server, and JRun (for customers who already own JRun), with support for BEA WebLogic to follow shortly thereafter (and likely available by the time that you read this chapter).

The differences between this new version and the basic ColdFusion MX should be relatively minor regarding the topics covered in this chapter. Still, you should explore the release notes for these products for compatibility issues that Macromedia identifies.

The *J2EE sessions* feature is simply an alternative to the built-in session support that's always been available in ColdFusion. But it adds several benefits, as follows:

- ✦ The session identifier used by J2EE sessions, `jsessionid`, is more secure.
- ✦ J2EE sessions are supported by a nonpersistent cookie, so sessions close whenever the browser closes.
- ✦ Sessions can be supported for browsers that do not permit persistent cookies.
- ✦ J2EE sessions can be shared with JSPs and servlets running under CF MX.

Unfortunately, some aspects of working with J2EE sessions can also cause trouble, particularly if the browser visitor doesn't support cookies. This is explained later in this chapter.

Enabling J2EE Sessions

J2EE sessions are easily enabled and require no changes in coding to use them. You find an option in the CF MX Administrator under the Server Settings heading, Memory Variables link. Select the Use J2EE Sessions check box. Although the screen doesn't say so, you need to restart the CF MX server before the change takes effect.

After J2EE sessions are enabled, they affect all code in all applications on the server that use `<cfapplication sessionmanagement="yes">`. No other change to the application code is necessary. This feature, by the way, works in both the Enterprise and Professional Editions of ColdFusion MX.

New SessionIDs

After enabling J2EE sessions and restarting the server, you notice (if you have server debugging displayed or use `<cfdump var="#session#">`, for example) that the values shown for session variables reflect new information. First, without J2EE sessions enabled, the value of the session variable `sessionid` may look as follows:

```
sessionid=_2704_73826960
```

This reflects a combination of the `cfid` and `cftoken`, which are the keys that have enabled session support prior to J2EE sessions. With J2EE sessions enabled, it instead appears in the following format:

```
sessionid=8030584681031438559214
```

This reflects a key change from using the old `cfid/cftoken` pair for supporting sessions to using a new single 22-digit number. We discuss the security benefits of that later in this chapter.

Second, you observe that the session variable `urltoken` also reflects new information. Without J2EE sessions, `urltoken` may look as follows:

```
urltoken=cfid=2704&cftoken=73826960
```

But with J2EE sessions enabled, it shows a new `jsessionid` value (rather than `sessionid`) appended to the end of the string, as in the following example:

```
urltoken=cfid=2704&cftoken=73826960&jsessionid=8030584681031438559214
```

This `urltoken` is formed as a query string, and it or `jsessionid` are used in supporting browsers that don't enable cookies. (You find more information about that later in this chapter.).

Finally, yet another difference is that, without J2EE sessions enabled, you also have `cfid` and `cftoken` variables in the session scope. But if you enable J2EE sessions, those no longer exist. It makes sense, because the `sessionid` is that 22-digit number. The `cfid` and `cftoken` still exist in the cookie scope, but be aware that, if you have code that refers to `session.cfid` or `session.cftoken`, that no longer works with J2EE sessions enabled.

Benefits of J2EE sessions

The change in format of the `urltoken` and `jsessionid` variables is key to enabling J2EE sessions, but it's not really an apparent benefit. Still, a couple aspects of the change are indeed beneficial.

First, the change to a 22-digit number for the `sessionid` has a security benefit. Sessions are generally supported by way of two cookie variables: `cfid` and `cftoken`. Sessions can also be supported by passing those variables on the query string in a URL (which, again, is the purpose of the `urltoken`). But the value of the `cfid` and `cftoken` variables being such small numbers makes them rather easy to guess.

If your J2EE sessions are using a much longer value for the `sessionid`, the chances are reduced that the `jsessionid` or `urltoken` values can be randomly guessed if presented as either cookie or URL variables.

Note

You can attain increased security regarding the simplicity of `cftoken` values, without enabling J2EE sessions, by using another new feature in CF MX that enables you to ask the server to generate more elaborate *UUIDs* (*universally unique identifiers*) for the `cftoken`. This is enabled in the CF Administrator, on the Server Settings page, by selecting the Use UUID for `cftoken` check box. As you do in enabling J2EE sessions, you need to restart the CF MX server for this change to take effect but do not need to change any code to benefit from the new feature.

Another, perhaps more valuable, benefit of J2EE sessions is the fact that the server creates a nonpersistent cookie that is sent to the browser for supporting sessions. By *nonpersistent*, we mean a cookie that is not stored on disk in the browser but instead is stored only in the browser's memory. That way, after the browser is closed, the cookie is lost, and that browser, therefore, no longer has any connection to that session. On the next visit by that user in a new browser window, he is given a new `jsessionid` by the server. (You need to understand some facets concerning when a browser is really considered "closed." See the section "When does a session end?" a little later in this chapter, for more information.)

These nonpersistent cookies are also sometimes referred to as *per-session* or *temporary* cookies. This leads to another benefit of using J2EE sessions to those organizations that can't use persistent cookies (such as the `cfid` and `cftoken` cookie values set by CF MX and earlier versions). These organizations can use J2EE sessions much more easily than they can CF-based sessions, because J2EE sessions use nonpersistent cookies. We should mention that you do have ways in all releases of CF to force the `cfid` and `cftoken` to become nonpersistent, as outlined in the Macromedia Technote at `www.macromedia.com/v1/Handlers/index.cfm?ID=21079&Method=Full`. But with J2EE sessions, you don't need to bother with that sort of "hack."

One final benefit of using J2EE sessions, which may not benefit all CF developers, is that using them enables the sharing of sessions and variables with JSP and servlet programs that also run in CF MX.

Challenges with J2EE sessions

While J2EE sessions represent a step forward in security and robustness, they leave some challenges to be dealt with. First, we must deal with the issue of when sessions end — a different proposition with ColdFusion MX. Second, we must find a way to provide applications that do not depend on cookies being enabled. This is particularly true with public sites.

When does a session end?

We mention in the section "Benefits of J2EE sessions," a bit earlier in this chapter, that understanding the "sessions terminate on browser close" notion that's enabled by J2EE sessions requires some further discussion. To clarify, the session closes (or, rather, the browser loses its nonpersistent cookie) after the last browser session that you opened is closed. In Netscape Navigator 4, for example, if you open multiple browser windows (by using the File ➪ New Navigator Window menu command or the Ctrl+N keystroke), those windows all share the same sessionid. Only after all these browser windows are closed us the session itself really "closed."

Technically, the session isn't really terminated — on the server at least — even after all browser windows are closed. The session continues to exist on the server until the server determines that the sessions must be timed out. But with the nonpersistent cookie now deleted, a new browser window that returns to the site is given a new `sessionid` and a new session.

In Internet Explorer, the question of whether one or many browser windows need to be closed to "close" the session depends on how the windows are opened. If they're opened by using the File ➪ New Window menu command or the Ctrl+N keystroke, those windows share a single `sessionid`. But if a new browser window is opened by using Start ➪ Programs ➪ Internet Explorer or by clicking an icon on the desktop or in your system tray's taskbar launcher, that new window gets its own `sessionid`. This has two ramifications: First, it means that you may be surprised to find that multiple IE windows *don't* share the same session. Further, you can have sessions for some windows that terminate after their browser windows closed while still keeping other IE windows—and their sessions—open. But, again, closing them all should "close" any sessions in which J2EE session variables are enabled. Be aware, however, that, if you ran the internal browser in ColdFusion Studio, doing so has created another instance of a browser window.

Challenges if cookies are not presented

Further challenges arise in respect to J2EE sessions if a visitor's browser doesn't support cookies. This problem doesn't involve only those browsers that are too old to support cookies but may also arise if organizations force users to disable cookie support in their browsers.

In such a case, you may be attempting to handle noncookie browsers by using the `session.cfid` and `session.cftoken` variables or the `session.urltoken` variable in either query strings or forms that you build and send to the browser. As we mention earlier in this chapter, with J2EE sessions, the `cfid` and `cftoken` variables no longer exist in the session scope. (They are still in the cookie scope—at least while the CFML is being executed—and in the client scope if client variables are enabled.)

You may think to use the `session.urltoken` variable that we mentioned, [GSL1]but on the built-in CF MX Web server, that doesn't persist your session. It doesn't pay attention to a `jsessionid` passed on the query string. Instead, being a Java Web server, it expects it to be passed in a different format.

Indeed, a new function is available to assist in doing just that sort of processing. The new `URLSessionFormat()` function is quite interesting, in that it appends the necessary `sessionid` variables to a URL if it detects that the browser requesting the page does not support cookies (or, more accurately, if it has not presented any cookies). An example may be as follows:

```
<cfoutput>
<a href="#urlsessionformat("mypage.cfm?id=123")#">link to mypage</a>
</cfoutput>
```

If the browser supports cookies (or, more accurately, cookies from this domain are presented by the browser as this page is executed), the result is simply as follows:

```
<a href="mypage.cfm?id=123">link to mypage</a>
```

But if the browser doesn't support cookies (or again, more accurately, cookies from this domain are *not* presented by the browser as this page is executed), the result depends on whether J2EE sessions are enabled. If they are not enabled, the result is as follows:

```
<a href="mypage.cfm?id=123&CFID=3004&CFTOKEN=98931500">link to
mypage</a>
```

But with J2EE sessions enabled, the result is as follows:

```
<a href="mypage.cfm;JSESSIONID=8030472831031469485864?id=123">link to
mypage</a>
```

Notice, however, that in the second case, the URL that is formed is not appending the `jsessionid` as a query string; instead, it's appending it immediately after the file name and extension, prefaced by a semicolon. That works fine for the built-in Web server that comes with CF MX (and other Java-based Web servers). But if you've integrated CF MX with Microsoft's Internet Information Server Web server, such a URL leads to a `404 File Not Found` error.

If you're using IIS with J2EE sessions, therefore, you should not use the URLSessionFormat() to support browsers with cookies disabled — at least until Macromedia (or Microsoft) addresses this issue. Instead, use code such as the following:

```
<cfoutput>
<a href="mypage.cfm?id=123<cfif cgi.http_cookie is
"">&#session.urltoken#</cfif>">link to mypage</a>
</cfoutput>
```

Unfortunately, you can't use this code fragment with the built-in CF MX Web server. It doesn't recognize the jsessionid that's being passed as a query string argument. It recognizes only a jsessionid being passed after the file name, prefaced by a semicolon.

Along the same lines, you face a similar problem in using the CFLOCATION tag. In this same sort of situation, where the tag's used in a page executed by a browser that doesn't present cookies, the tag creates a URL that includes the jsessionid following the file name and extension, prepended with a semicolon. That URL fails on IIS servers. Even using the addtoken="no" attribute with the tag doesn't change it.

What's worse, even if you are working on the CF MX Web server, consider what can happen if you use CFLOCATION to redirect control to a remote server that's running IIS. Again, if the browser executing the page does not support or present cookies, the URL that it generates fails. Again, perhaps Macromedia will eventually modify the tag so that the addtoken="no" attribute works to prevent this ;jsessionid string from getting appended to the file name if it's not desirable for it to be there.

Calling JSP Custom Tags

In ColdFusion MX, you can now use JSP custom tags — in the Enterprise Edition of CF MX, that is; unfortunately, this feature is not enabled in the Professional Edition. As are CF custom tags, JSP custom tags are a means by which JSP developers can add new functionality to their pages. What does that mean to you, as a CFML developer?

Well, as is the case with J2EE sessions, you don't need to know Java (nor even use or understand JSPs) to use JSP custom tags. They're very easy to use, and libraries with hundreds of them are available on the Internet for consumption by the JSP world — and now by CF developers as well.

Some solutions that you can use in your own CF development may already exist as JSP custom tags, and they are available to you in CF MX by following just a few simple steps. If you visit the Web site http://coldjava.hypermart.net/jsp.htm, for example, and view the calendar taglib link, you see a discussion of how to use a JSP custom tag to easily create a calendar for the current month by using the following line of code:

```
<%@ taglib uri="taglib.tld" prefix="cal" %>
<cal:Calendar />
```

Whoa! What's that? Well, it *is* JSP code. But we're going to show you how to use that same <cal:Calendar> custom tag in CFML, which is just as easy as using it in JSP. In fact, you can incorporate this JSP custom tag into your CF MX code in just five simple steps, which we describe in the following sections.

Locating JSP custom tags

The power of JSP custom tags is that, if someone else writes one, any JSP developer (and now CF developer) can use it. So if you can find one (or several of them), that's the first step. Besides the site that we mention in the preceding section, you can find other such repositories at the following URLs:

```
http://jsptags.com

http://jspin.com/home/tags

http://aewnet.com/root/webdev/jsp/jsptaglibs/

http://javashareware.com/CFScripts/jservlets.cfm

http://dotjonline.com

http://opensymphony.com

www.Jspsmart.com

http://javaskyline.com/dev.html

http://java.sun.com/products/jsp/jstl

http://jakarta.apache.org/taglibs/
```

Going back to the original calendar-tag example in the preceding section, if you read the rest of that Web page, you see that this particular custom tag has a lot more functionality and can display a calendar for a particular month, add hyperlinks for particular dates, and more.

Downloading a JSP custom tag into the correct CF MX directories

The key to using any JSP custom tag, whether for use in a JSP or CF page, is to download the *tag library* files that are offered for the tag. In this case, the tag is freely available via links at the bottom of the page. Notice the links to `caltag.jar` and `taglib.tld` (the latter of which actually links to a file named `taglib61.tld`).

Don't worry about what's in those files. They're simply the files that contain the Java code and descriptor information for using the custom tag. CF developers don't need to open the files or understand their contents. You just need to download these files into the correct directories for CF MX to use them. In case you're curious, a *JAR* file is a *J*ava *ar*chive file and a *TLD* file is a *t*ag-*l*ibrary *d*escription file.

So you want to download these files and place the JAR file in `CFusionMXCFusionMX/wwwroot/WEB-INF/lib` and place the TLD file (if any) in `CFusionMXCFusionMX/wwwroot/WEB-INF/`. Notice that the JAR file goes into the `lib` directory under `WEB-INF`, while the TLD file goes into `WEB-INF` itself. This may be your first observation of the `WEB-INF` directory, which CF MX installs automatically under `CFusionMX/wwwroot`. Even if you place your code in another *webroot*, perhaps under `IIS`, there this `CFusionMXCFusionMX/wwwroot/WEB-INF` is still there.

You may not have the authority to place these files in these directories, because they're global, administrative directories for the entire CF MX server. Ask your CF administrator for assistance if necessary.

Sometimes a TLD file not may be offered. You can still often use the custom tag with just the JAR. Still, notice also that the TLD file is sometimes stored within the JAR file. You can open a JAR file and extract the TLD by using any WinZip-type program.

After downloading the two files at our demonstration Web site, you should have the following:

```
CFusionMX/wwwroot/WEB-INF/taglib61.tld

CFusionMX/wwwroot/WEB-INF/lib/caltag.jar
```

You're almost ready to proceed, but we should add that the documentation for some JSP custom tags discuss changing a file called `web.xml`. Such a file is in the `CFusionMX/wwwroot/WEB-INF` directory, but you generally don't need to edit it to use JSP custom tags in CF MX.

Restart the CF MX Server

After placing a new custom tag library file into the appropriate CF MX directory, you'll need to restart the CF MX Server before attempting to use it. It may seem illogical to have to do so, but if you don't your attempts to use such a new JSP custom tag will result in:

```
"The type for attribute name of tag [tagname] could not be determined."
```

Use CFIMPORT and your JSP custom tag in CFML

You're finally ready to create your ColdFusion code to refer to the new custom tag. You may recall that your example in the section "Calling JSP Custom Tags," earlier in this chapter, was just the following two lines of JSP code:

```
<%@ taglib uri="taglib.tld" prefix="cal" %>
<cal:Calendar />
```

We said that your CF code would be equally simple, and indeed it is, as the following example shows:

```
<cfimport prefix="cal" taglib="/WEB-INF/taglib61.tld">
<cal:Calendar />
```

The difference lies just in the first line, where you now use the new CF MX tag `CFIMPORT`. Besides being a different tag than is used in the JSP example, `CFIMPORT` is also different in that the JSP example doesn't need to refer to the `/WEB-INF/` directory, but in CF MX, you do. And you can usually point to either the JAR or the TLD file. You could also write the `CFIMPORT` line as follows:

```
<cfimport prefix="cal" taglib="/WEB-INF/lib/caltag.jar">
```

Sometimes you find that you simply must point to the TLD to get the custom tag to work. You can even sometimes place the JAR file in the directory where you're calling the custom tag and leave off any directory path in the `TAGLIB` attribute. This technique can prove useful if you don't have access to the administrative directories, but it doesn't always work.

Getting back to the `CFIMPORT` tag, notice that you can also pick any value for the `PREFIX` attribute to use for referring to the custom tag. Notice, too, that this prefix is what's used in referring to the tag, as in the preceding example.

A given JSP custom-tag library may contain either multiple custom tags or various attributes to affect how the tag works. In the case of your `cal:Calendar` tag, you use only the most basic example. As documented at the taglib's Web site, different tags and attributes can do even more useful things.

Options are available, for example, to specify a specific month to display. You also have a means to create links on the calendar for a given day, using the `setLink` tag and its `day` attribute. Following is an example of the use of the `setLink` tag:

```
<cal:Calendar month="3" year="2002">

   <cal:setLink day="5">http://www.abc.com</cal:setLink>
   <cal:setLink day="15">http://www.def.com/</cal:setLink>
</cal:Calendar>
```

That's all there is to using a JSP custom tag with CF_MX!

(The ability to use JSP custom tags raises the possibility of not only reusing someone else's tags, but of creating your own. While that's outside the scope of this book, you'll find no shortage of books devoted to just this topic.)

Some challenges with using JSP custom tags

A couple of points about using JSP custom tags are worth particular mention. First, you may naturally come to wonder whether you can more easily reuse JSP custom tags by placing the `CFIMPORT` tag in an `Application.cfm` file or by referencing it by using a `CFINCLUDE`. Sadly, you can't do either.

The `CFIMPORT` tag must appear in the page that's using a custom tag. Admittedly, this makes reusing custom tags in multiple pages a little challenging. If you ever need to change something about the `CFIMPORT` tag, you need to change it in all pages that refer to the tag. And, as an aside, you have no default JSP custom tag location on CF MX server (as you do for CF custom tags), so you have no way to avoid using `CFIMPORT`.

Additionally, as you look at JSP custom-tag libraries at various Web sites, you may notice that not all JSP custom tags are particularly useful in CF. You have a very rich language in CFML. JSP, by comparison, is rather primitive. Many JSP custom tags simply provide functionality that CF already has, including functionality for:

- ✦ Database-manipulation tags
- ✦ `if/then` loop processing
- ✦ Form validation
- ✦ String manipulation
- ✦ Session and `form/url` variable processing

You also find many more custom tags that you don't really need. Indeed, the last two libraries that we mention in the section "Locating JSP custom tags," earlier in this chapter, are the Sun JSP Standard Tag (JSTL) Library (at `http://java.sun.com/products/jsp/jstl`) and the Jakarta Taglibs project (at `http://jakarta.apache.org/taglibs/`). Many of the tags that you find in these libraries offer redundant features that CF already has.

Examples of useful JSP custom tags

Although many available JSP custom tags may seem redundant to native features in CF, such tags still off many examples of things either that CF doesn't do or that perhaps the custom tag may do better. Such tags are worth looking into.

The following list describes a few parts of the JSTL libraries containing individual tags that you may wish to use in your applications:

✦ **Application Taglib:** Used to access information contained in the `ServletContext` scope for a Web application.

✦ **Cache Taglib:** Enables you to cache fragments of your JSP pages.

✦ **IO Taglib:** Used to perform HTTP `get` or `put` operations and to make XML-RPC and SOAP requests.

✦ **JMS Taglib:** Used to perform a variety of JMS-related operations, such as sending and receiving messages.

✦ **Mailer Taglib:** Used to send e-mail.

✦ **Scrape Taglib:** Used to *scrape*, or extract, content from Web documents.

✦ **XSL Taglib:** Used for transforming XML input sources by using XSL stylesheets.

✦ **Xtags Taglib:** Enables you to navigate, process, and style XML documents by using XSLT and XPath.

More information on each of the tags contained in these libararies is presented at `http://jakarta.apache.org/taglibs/doc/`.

And in the ColdJava tags suite, where you find the calendar custom tag we discussed in the "Use CFIMPORT and your JSP custom tag in CFML" section of this chapter, you may also find the following useful custom tags:

✦ **Button:** Creates HTML buttons that have confirmation dialog boxes.

✦ **Cache:** Supports dynamic caching of generated output.

✦ **Calendar:** Creates calendars.

✦ **Country:** Creates country select lists.

✦ **Delay:** Delays execution of the page.

✦ **Sessions Counter:** Calculates a number of active sessions.

✦ **Sessions Stats:** Collects statistics for sessions.

✦ **Smarttag:** Parses its own body, finding hyperlinks and mailtos and generating the appropriate code.

The tags in these collections are discussed at `http://coldjava.hypermart.net/jsp.htm`. And still many other useful tags can be found at the other sites that we list in the section "Locating JSP custom tags," earlier in this chapter.

Using Applets

As we continue presenting Java integration points, in the order of those requiring the least Java understanding, we shouldn't ignore *applets*, although applets may be perhaps hold the least interest to most CF developers. Applets are Java programs designed to run on the browser, usually bringing enhanced interface possibilities to make up for HTML's deficiencies. (Many, however, feel that Macromedia Flash provides a more effective opportunity for solving that problem.) The rest of the integration opportunities that we discuss in this chapter involve Java on the server.

Two aspects of using applets are specific to ColdFusion. Although any HTML sent to the browser can refer to an applet by using the HTML `APPLET` or new `OBJECT` tags, you can make using such applets in your CFML code easier by registering the applet with the ColdFusion Administrator (under the Extensions heading and the `Java Applets` link) and then by using `CFAPPLET`. See Chapter 55 for more information about the `CFAPPLET` tag and the ColdFusion documentation (in the online Help in CF Administrator) for information on registering applets in the Administrator.

Another facet of working with applets in ColdFusion comes by way of the built-in features of the `CFFORM` tag. It provides options for building various applet-based enhanced interfaces using ColdFusion-generated data. See the subtags of `CFFORM`, such as `CFGRID` (for building data grids), `CFTREE` (for building hierarchical tree controls), `CFSLIDER` (for building slider controls), and others. Even the `CFAPPLET` tag referred to in the preceding paragraph is technically a subtag of `CFFORM`.

Leveraging the Java API by Using CFOBJECT

The examples of Java integration that we have described in the preceding sections don't require any specific knowledge of Java language elements to use. That makes them compelling for those getting their first taste of Java integration. If you want to use Java most effectively, however, you need to "get your hands dirty" and start working with real Java elements. The remaining integration points involve a closer connection to Java itself. They still don't require that you write Java language statements, however, or learn how to compile Java classes.

Making use of the Java libraries

My copy of the Oxford English Dictionary has this as an example of the use of leverage: "It makes more sense to be able to leverage what we [public radio stations] do in a more effective way to our listeners" (Delano Lewis). I removed the duplicate use, but kept the first usage under the assumption that if it's good enough for the OED, it's probably good enough for our book. The first facet of working more closely with Java itself involves the fact that you can easily make use of any element of the Java API or application programming interface. Indeed, although writing Java programs involves learning the Java language, a great deal of it involves manipulating any of hundreds of built-in objects and their properties and methods.

Although you can't use Java-language statements within CFML, you can indeed work with the many built-in Java objects. Think of these objects as a vast subroutine library in which you can sometimes find additional tools, sources of information, and even the equivalent of functions (although Java calls them *methods*) that can provide functionality that may not be available within ColdFusion itself.

Dozens of libraries come built into Java, and each of them is documented in the Java 2 Platform API Specification, at http://java.sun.com/j2se/1.3/docs/api/index.html. Because the underlying Java Virtual Machine (JVM) for the current installation of ColdFusion MX is the 1.3.1 version, those docs reflect the nearly 100 libraries available to you from within CF MX.

But only a few of those libraries really are of interest to you in CF MX. Many of them are used for building applets (such as java.applet, java.awt), while some may have no apparent value (javax.sound). Others, however, may offer interesting possibilities, such as java.file, java.lang, java.net, java.util.zip. We don't have time to explore those in detail, but we can show you one example, and perhaps you can take it from there.

If you need to know the IP address for a given domain name, for example, you have no CF function to help with that, but if you explore the Java libraries, you see that a java.net library does indeed offer a solution. The InetAddress class has a couple useful methods in getByName and getHostAddress. Luckily, no great knowledge of Java programming is needed to work with the getByName and getHostAddress methods. The following code enables you to obtain the IP address for a given domain name. The key to making it work is either the CFOBJECT tag or its related CreateObject() function, both of which have existed in CFML for some time. Without further explanation, the following code reports the current IP address for the domain name "macromedia.com":

```
<cfobject action="create" class="java.net.InetAddress" type="java"
name="iaddress">
<cfoutput>
#iaddress.getByName("macromedia.com").getHostAddress()#
</cfoutput>
```

Only be aware that CF_MX will throw an error if the domain cannot be found or resolved into an IP address.

Although the CFOBJECT tag may be new to you and the apparent "functions" used within the CFOUTPUT may look unusual, the bottom line is that this is all CFML. None of this is Java, per se. You're just leveraging the Java libraries, whereby you can treat the methods in the libraries as functions in CFML. You find no getHostAddress function in CFML, but now you've enabled the equivalent by borrowing this functionality from the Java libraries.

You could also use the CreateObject() function within CFSCRIPT to achieve the same result, as follows:

```
<cfscript>
iaddrclass=createobject("java","java.net.InetAddress");
writeoutput(iaddrClass.getByName("macromedia.com").getHostAddress());
</cfscript>
```

You could certainly perform optimizations to this code. You could, for example, store the domain name in a variable, and you could persist the "created object" in the session scope to reuse it (testing for its existence and creating it only if it doesn't already exist and storing its functionality in a user-defined function), but the goal here is simply to demonstrate a simple example.

In working with Java objects this way, you may need to understand other issues, such as datatype and casting issues (and the available CF JavaCast() function), initialization and supporting multiple constructors, case-sensitivity issues, Java exception handling, dynamic class reloading, and more. With the capability demonstrated here, you can now explore Java books, articles, API references, and other resources to determine whether other possibilities are available. Built-in mechanisms in the Java API, for example, can create and read zip files, create and read text files, do math and string processing, provide access to properties of the underlying Java environment, and much more.

Accessing the Java API of third-party products and in-house Java objects

Although the preceding section discusses accessing the built-in Java libraries, you may also have installed on your server an application that provides its own Java API. It may consist of Java code that others have written within your organization, or you may have purchased a Java application that provides a Java API.

In either case, you can use this same basic approach that we describe in the preceding section to work with that API. Just study the documentation for the API and use `CFOBJECT` or `CreateObject()` to access it.

You do, however, face one difference in working with such code. To refer to any Java object within ColdFusion MX, you need to tell the ColdFusion Administrator where to locate that Java code. The subject of setting the `classpath` in the Administrator is also covered at the end of the chapter.

If the Java code that you want to access is written as a JavaServer Page, Servlet, JavaBean, or Enterprise Java Beans, and so on, see the remaining sections of this chapter for information.

Running JavaServer Pages and Servlets within CF MX

As we progress through the Java integration points in CF MX, we focused mostly on features that enable you to reuse the Java code that others have created. Although you can write your own JSP custom tag or Java class that you access via `CFOBJECT`, these would require substantial Java programming expertise as well as specialized knowledge about building either of them.

But CF MX enables yet another new opportunity, and this approach can prove more straightforward in getting started coding in Java. It's also another opportunity to benefit from the work of others.

JavaServer Pages (*JSPs*) and *Java Servlets* are alternative approaches to creating Web applications in a J2EE environment. Although CF developers (especially in CF MX) can generally do everything that a JSP or servlet developer can, you or your organization may still be interested in creating JSP and/or servlet templates and applications.

By using CF MX, you can place servlets and JSPs directly in the ColdFusion MX environment. (Unfortunately, support for JSPs is restricted to CF MX Enterprise.) You don't need to install a separate JSP/servlet engine such as Apache TomCat, JRun, IBM WebSphere, and so on because ColdFusion MX is built upon JRun (and the newer ColdFusion MX for J2EE runs on a number of J2EE environments).

Running JSPs within ColdFusion MX Enterprise

JSPs are one of two approaches available to Java developers for creating Web applications. They offer a tag-based approach to page development that's similar to CFML (although primitive by comparison in most respects). Still, you may want to take advantage of someone's JSP code or you may want to move all your JSPs into the CF MX environment. You can now do that.

In this book, we can't discuss the hows and whys of creating JSP pages. The focus is simply on how to use them within CF MX, assuming that you already know how to create them or find them written by others. But here's a simple example that you can try yourself just to see how things work.

A JSP template can be placed in the same directory as your ColdFusion code (in CF MX Enterprise). Save the following code in a file called `simple.jsp`:

```
<% for(int i=0;i<2;i++) { %>
Hello World!
<% } %>
```

Place it in the directory where your ColdFusion code resides. You may, for example, have installed ColdFusion so that your ColdFusion templates are in `c:\CFusionMX\wwwroot\`. If you place a file called `test.cfm` in this directory, you can run that file with the following URL: `http://localhost:8500/test.cfm` (perhaps changing `localhost:8500` to suit your environment).

Similarly, if you save this `simple.jsp` file in that same directory, you can now execute it (again, in CF MX Enterprise only) by using the following URL: `http://localhost:8500/simple.jsp`. The output of this code should be as follows:

```
Hello World! Hello World!
```

Of course, you can also place this code in a subdirectory of the Web-application directory and execute it by using a URL that includes the appropriate directory-path information.

As it does with its own templates, ColdFusion automatically detects and loads new or changed JSP pages. Try changing the value `2` in the first line of that example to another number; then save your template and refresh your browser to see that the change takes effect.

Be careful, however, as a JSP file name is case-sensitive. Make sure that you use the same case in the URL as you do in naming the file as you save it; otherwise, you may get a cryptic error such as the following:

```
Error Occurred While Processing Request
jrun__cfmxdemo__jsps__Simple2ejsp19 (wrong name:
jrun__cfmxdemo__jsps__simple2ejsp19)
```

This is the error that we got for using `Simple.jsp` (rather than `simple.jsp`) in the URL. (We happened to be running this code in a directory called `cfmxdemo/jsps`, so that's reflected in the listed file names as well.) Curiously, the CF MX engine seems capable of detecting the presence of a JSP by this name but in a different case. (Notice that it lists the lowercase version after `wrong name`.) If we instead used a URL of `ximple.jsp` and had no file of that name in any case, the CF_MX engine would have reported a `404 file not found` error. Maybe Macromedia can provide a friendlier error for such detected case-mismatch problems.

In the Professional Edition of CF MX, if you try to call a `.jsp` file, you get the following error, indicating that the feature is not supported:

```
A License Exception has been thrown
You tried to access a restricted feature for the Professional edition:
JSP
```

Of course, the preceding example is an incredibly simplistic example of a JSP page. Indeed, it's not a particularly well-written template because it includes Java code. A generally accepted rule in the Java development community is that JSPs should contain very little Java coding. We don't get into these details here. Just know that this simple example does enable you to demonstrate whether a JSP page works in ColdFusion.

Indeed, whenever a great deal of Java coding may be done in a JSP page, experienced Java developers recommend that you write a Java Servlet instead. And ColdFusion MX developers can do that as well, as the following section demonstrates. Plus they can use Java Servlets in both the Enterprise and Professional Editions of CF MX.

Running Java Servlets within ColdFusion MX, Professional or Enterprise

Java Servlets are the alternative (and original) means of creating Web applications for Java developers. They're written in pure Java language rather than by using tags, as in JSPs. Again this chapter can't offer a tutorial on writing servlets, but you should know that you can indeed place them within the CF MX server environment and execute them — if, of course, you know where to put them and the correct URL to use to execute them.

Whereas you can use JSPs within CF MX only in the Enterprise Edition, you may take advantage of Java servlets in either edition, although some of the documentation is unclear on whether this is within the licensing parameters of Professional. If you're running the Professional Edition of CF MX, contact Macromedia to ensure that your use of this feature is acceptable.

Running servlets is different from running JSPs in several ways. First, servlets are not stored in the same directory as your ColdFusion and JSP templates. You instead place them in the `wwwroot\WEB-INF\classes` directory, which already exists wherever ColdFusion MX is installed.

Second, if you run a servlet, you must use a special URL to access it, because it's not stored in the normal Web directory (and, normally, any files in the `WEB-INF` directory cannot be accessed directly via a URL request). Finally, you typically must compile a servlet from its `.java` source into a compiled `.class` file and place that `.class` file in the `WEB-INF\classes` directory.

Assume that you have a servlet called `SimpleServlet.class`. (Remember that the focus here is on how to use existing servlets within CF MX and not how to create or compile them.) After placing that `.class` file in the `WEB-INF\classes` directory, you may then execute it by using a special form of URL: `http://localhost:8500/servlet/SimpleServlet`.

Again, change the `localhost:8500` part of the URL to suit your domain name and port, if any. But the important distinction to notice is the use of `/servlet` between your domain name/port and the name of the servlet. This is a special designator that tells the CF MX server that you mean to execute a servlet, and so it knows to look in the `WEB-INF\classes` directory.

As with JSPs, the case of the servlet name on the URL must match the case of the actual `servlet.class` file (and, again, the error displayed for a mismatched case is slightly different from the error for naming a servlet class that doesn't exist in any case).

Detecting changes to servlets without a restart

By default, CF MX does not detect changes to (nor does it recompile) servlets. It detects a new servlet placed into the `WEB-INF\classes` directory, but to see a changed servlet, you must restart the server. In a development environment, of course, this could be an annoyance.

Fortunately, you can address this problem by reconfiguring ColdFusion MX to automatically reload changed servlets. Be aware that enabling this change is not recommended for production servers, as you incur a slight performance penalty in doing so.

You need to edit the `jrun-web.xml` file in the `WEB-INF` directory where ColdFusion is installed (the parent directory where you've been placing servlet classes). In that file, which already exists by default, you find a pair of `<jrun-web-app>` tags (or *elements* as they're referred to by XML adherents). Within those elements, add the following line:

```
<reload>true</reload>
```

After restarting the CF MX server, you find that, if you recompile changes to servlets, they are not displayed after you next refresh your browser.

Caution

Take great caution in editing the various XML configuration files in CF MX. Sometimes, a mistake may prevent the server from starting. Save a backup of any such file before changing it so that you can easily reverse the changes if needed. Also, this change may not apply in the newer ColdFusion MX For J2EE product if used on servers other than JRun.

Compiling servlets in CF MX — manually and automatically

This chapter presumes that you already know how to code the Java language statements to create a servlet and, further, that you know how to compile servlets. Those with experience from other servlet engines may know that you must make sure that the `servlet.jar` provided by the engine is included in the `classpath` in compiling. Where is that file in CF MX? It's in the `jrun\lib\ext` directory, where CF MX is installed.

So, again, without further elaboration, but for those who already understand how to use the Java compiler, the command to compile a servlet named `SimpleServlet` could look as follows:

```
javac SimpleServlet.java -classpath D:\CFusionMX\runtime\lib\jrun.jar
```

That's assuming, of course, that CF MX is installed in the `C:\CFusionMX`directory. (That's a single-line command, by the way, although it may not appear so in this book.) Then you can move the compiled `.class` file into the `WEB-INF\classes` directory to use it in CFMX. (If you need help in getting to the command line, in ensuring that the `javac` executable is in your path, in using the `javac` command, or in using its `-classpath` directive, consult any good book that describes how to use servlets such as *Java Servlet Programming Bible* [John Wiley & Sons, 2002] These issues are not unique to CF MX and are beyond the scope of this book.)

One very cool thing that is relatively unique to CF MX (or rather to the underlying JRun engine), however, is that you don't need to bother compiling servlets if you are changing them frequently. You can configure CF MX to automatically detect *and* compile changes to your Java Servlet source code. Again, this is a feature that should be enabled only in development environments.

In that same `jrun-web.xml` file and within that same `<jrun-web-app>` element described in the preceding section, add the following element:

```
<compile>true</compile>
```

(You must have both the `reload` and `compile` elements present to enable dynamic compilation.) After restarting the CF MX server, you find that any `.java` source files for a servlet that are placed in the `WEB-INF\classes` (or `WEB-INF\lib`) directory are automatically compiled if they're new or changed, whenever they are first called by a URL request.

Here's a trivial example that you can use to see how it works, in case you're new to working with servlets. Save the following as `SimpleServlet.java` in the `WEB-INF\classes` directory (and pay attention to the case of the file name):

```
import javax.servlet.*;
import javax.servlet.http.*;
import java.io.*;

public class SimpleServlet extends HttpServlet {
   public void doGet(HttpServletRequest req, HttpServletResponse resp)
      throws ServletException, IOException {
       resp.setContentType("text/html");
       PrintWriter out = resp.getWriter();
       out.println("<h1>Hello, from a simple servlet</h1>");
   }
}
```

Don't worry about what all this means if you're new to servlets. Notice, however, that the fourth line of code indicates `public class SimpleServlet` and that the word `SimpleServlet` must match the name and case of the `.java` file that you create. Again, if this code is placed in the `WEB-INF\classes` directory and the `compile` and `reload` elements are enabled as described before the example, CF MX automatically compiles this code as well as detects and recompiles it whenever you change the source file.

If you're concerned about naming conflicts with so many servlets being placed in the `WEB-INF\classes` directory, look in the Java `package` statement, whereby you can create a subdirectory of `WEB-INF\classes`, place your files there, specify that subdirectory name in the `package` statement, and then prefix the servlet name with `subdirectoryname.` notation on the URL.

Finally, those with experience in other servlet environments may know that creating servlet mappings (as an alternative to using the `\servlet` directive on a URL) is sometimes desirable. You can do that in CF MX as well (and also disable the `ServletInvoker`) by modifying the file `runtime\servers\default\SERVER-INF\default-web.xml`, under the directory where ColdFusion MX is installed on your server. To enable you to run your `SimpleServlet` by using an alternative URL mapping, such as `/Simple`, you add the following in between the `<web-app>` element tags in that `default-web.xml` file:

```
<servlet>
   <servlet-name>SimpleServlet</servlet-name>
   <servlet-class>SimpleServlet</servlet-class>
 </servlet>

<servlet-mapping>
   <servlet-name>SimpleServlet</servlet-name>
   <url-pattern>/Simple</url-pattern>
</servlet-mapping>
```

After restarting the CF MX server, you can now access the servlet by using the URL `http://localhost:8500/Simple` (changing the domain and port, as appropriate).

Interactions Between CFML and JSPs/Servlets

Besides the capability to create and run JSPs and Servlets, you may find that certain interactions between CFML and your JSPs and Servlets are also desirable. These programs can interact on a few levels. You can, for example, transfer control between one and another, include the output of one within another, and even share session, request, and/or application scope variables between them.

Part of that functionality is enabled by way of a new CFML function, `GetPageContext()`. This function exposes to CF developers the underlying `PageContext` object. This object exists when running any JSP page or Servlet. Since, technically, a CF template is converted to a servlet under the covers, the `PageContext` object is indeed available in CF MX templates. (You can access any Java library object if you know its published API.) The new function simply makes using the object's available properties and methods, including its available `include` and `forward` methods, easier.

Time and space don't permit a thorough discussion of this topic in this book, but fortunately, the CF MX documentation does cover the topic of interacting between CF and JSP/servlet templates.

Calling Java CFX Custom Tags

All the examples of Java integration in the preceding sections are components that you may reasonably find already existing and accessible from any Java Web-application environment. The focus was on how to make those readily accessible within the ColdFusion MX environment.

One final topic is quite specific to working with ColdFusion. Indeed, in releases 4.5 and 5, it was one of the primary ways that you may integrate ColdFusion and Java. *Java CFX custom tags* are similar to ColdFusion CFML custom tags in terms of how you use them — but they're written in Java.

Someone in your organization may already be (or may become interested in) writing Java CFX custom tags to perform some task that's not possible in CFML or to improve the performance of a repetitive task. CFX custom tags differ from other means of working with Java objects in that they can use and manipulate ColdFusion query objects, generate HTML, set variables on the page from which they're called, and more.

Of course, the new JSP and servlet integration possibilities can achieve nearly similar results and are far more standard. CFX custom tags are merely the oldest form of Java integration, so you may find existing CFX custom tags that you may want to use.

The term CFX is not related to CFMX at all. CFXs have existed for several releases of ColdFusion, and the *X* refers instead to the fact that these are extensions to the CF language. You can write them in C++ and Java.

In previous versions of ColdFusion, too, you needed to configure the ColdFusion Administrator to point to an available JVM installed on your server before you could use the techniques described in this and the following section. In CF MX, however, this step is handled automatically on installation. And you no longer need to configure an entry in the Administrator for the location of the `cfx jar` file. That value is automatically known to CF MX.

Again, our focus in this chapter is on how to use existing Java components rather than how to create such components, so we discuss how to call them within your code to effect a certain result.

Example Java CFX tags included in CF MX

Fortunately, you don't need to know how to create or compile Java CFX custom tags to work with them. A few examples come built into ColdFusion MX. In Windows systems, look in the directory `cfx\java\distrib\examples`, where ColdFusion MX is installed on your server. In Unix systems, look in `cfx/java/examples`.

You have five examples, as well as an `examples.html` file that briefly explains them and provides links so that you can easily view them. You work with the first and simplest, `HelloColdFusion`, in the following sections. It's a trivial example, but it demonstrates how Java CFX custom tags work.

Automatic compilation of Java CFX custom tags

The example tags that come in CF MX are the reason that you don't need to know how to create Java CFX custom tags. But we also said that you don't need to know how to compile them. Curious? In the same way that you don't need to compile Java code by telling CF_MX to compile it for you, you can tell CF_MX to compile and Java CFX custom tags. See the section "Compiling servlets in CFMX — manually and automatically," earlier in this chapter, for details on how to enable this feature.

If you do that (and then restart the server) and copy the `HelloColdFusion.java` file from the `examples` directory, CF MX automatically compiles it after you call it. This feature is very useful for testing and development. Be aware, however, that although CF MX can find any Java CFX custom tag in its defined `classpath` (see the following section), it compiles and loads only files in the `WEB-INF\classes` or `WEB-INF\lib` directories.

With Java programs, the name of the `.java` file must match the name of the public class definition in the source code. For example, Java source code with a public class definition of `public class Crocodopolis{}` must be saved in a file called `Crocodopolis.java`. In this example of a CFX, the source has a public-class name of `HelloColdFusion`, so you cannot rename the file or create another copy for any testing purposes without also renaming the internal public-class line of code.

Configuring the Administrator to enable Java CFX custom tags

One last step must be taken before you can call a Java CFX custom tag. Although ColdFusion custom tags don't require any administrative setup, CFX custom tags do. You must define the custom tag in the CF Administrator, indicating the name that it's to be known by within ColdFusion as well as the actual Java class name for the tag.

You find the option for controlling this by clicking the link `CFX Tags` in the Administrator, which you find under Extensions. Figure 28-1 shows the screen that you access as it may appear the first time that you visit that Administrator page. (The process of locating and opening the Administrator is discussed in Chapter 43.)

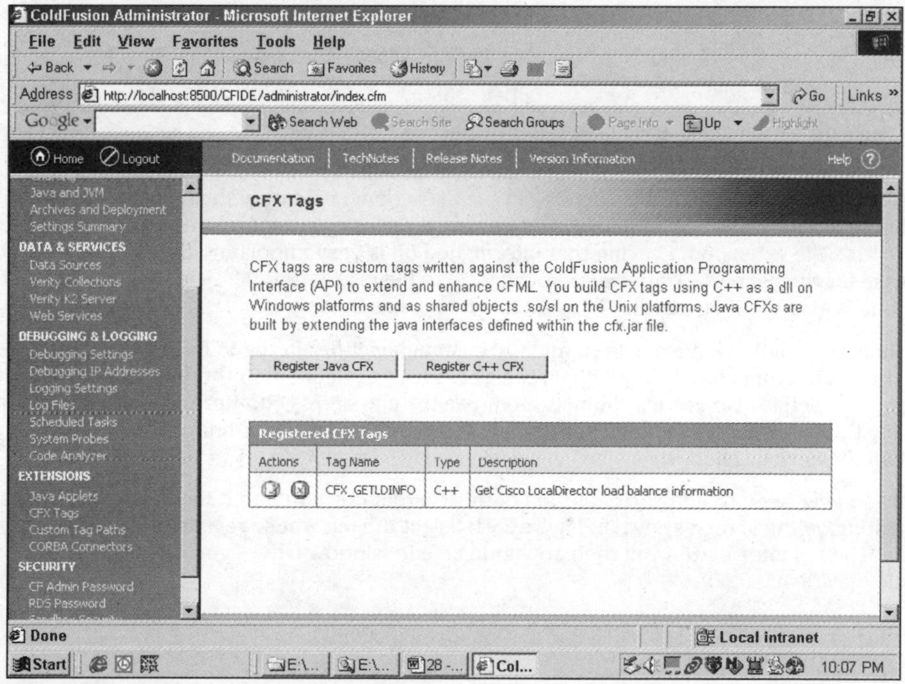

Figure 28-1: Administering CFX Custom Tags

From this page, click the Register Java CF" button for the screen on which you actually want to register a Java CFX custom tag. For the example that we are using, type in the dialog box that appears `cfx_HelloColdFusion` in the Tag Name field, `HelloColdFusion` in the Class Name field, and any optional Description in that field. Then click the Submit button, as shown in Figure 28-2.

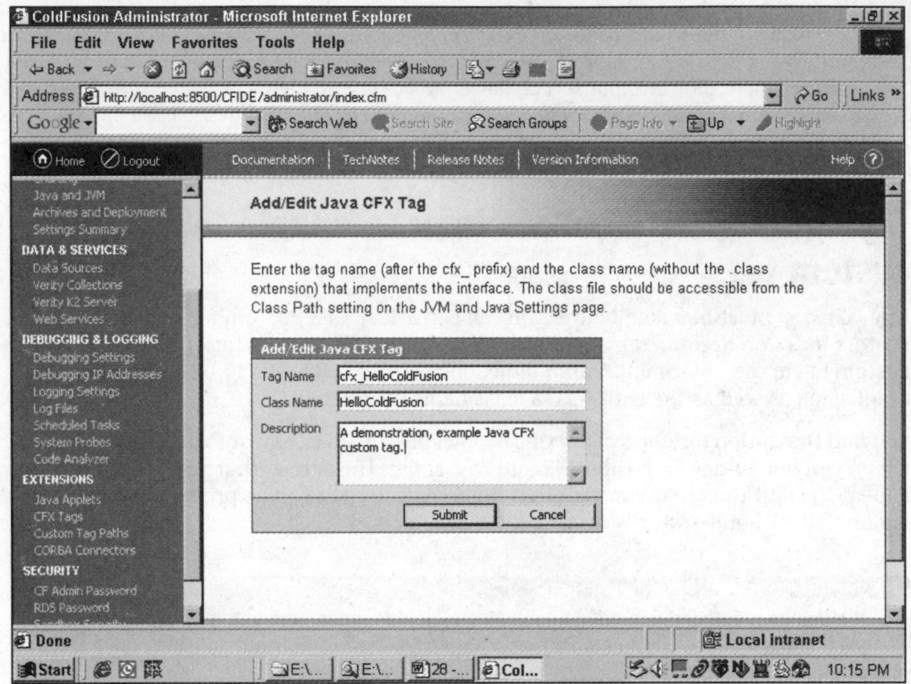

Figure 28-2: Registering cfx_HelloColdFusion

Notice that you are simply providing in the Class Name field only the name of the class that's holding the Java CFX custom tag, without any directory-path information and without any `.class` file extension. Leaving that information off is very important. Specifying the exact case for the file name of the custom-tag `.class` file is also critical. Using the incorrect case causes an error if an attempt is made to actually use the tag.

Similarly, ColdFusion expects to find the custom tag either in the `WEB-INF\classes` directory or in a directory that you specify in the `classpath` as defined on the Java and JVM settings page, which is also in the Administrator. (See the end of this chapter to learn more about setting the `classpath` in ColdFusion MX.) An error appears if you attempt to use the tag and ColdFusion can't find it.

If you ever need to edit the definition of this custom tag, you find it listed and available for editing on the screen shown in Figure 28-1. Select the tag whose registration you want to modify. The tag information will then appear in an edit window where you can make any needed changes.

Calling the Java CFX custom tag

With the Java CFX custom tag defined in the Administrator, you may now finally use the custom tag in your ColdFusion templates. The way that you call such a tag is similar to calling a regular ColdFusion custom tag, with just a slight difference. In the case of the example tag enabled in the preceding section, the simplest example of calling it would be as follows:

```
<cfx_HelloColdFusion>
```

This code causes execution of the example custom tag. (Again, it works only if you follow each of the steps that we discuss in the preceding sections.) It should display the following output:

```
Hello, null
```

Caution

Specifying the exact case of the class file name in defining the tag in the CF Administrator is important. Equally important is specifying the correct case in calling the custom tag as well. This is a change from behavior in CF5. In that version, whether the reference in `<CFX_tag-name>` matched the case of the actual definition in the Administrator didn't matter.

Of course, that's not a very friendly way to say, "Hello!" This custom tag is designed so that you can pass a name on the call to the tag, however, just as you can pass attributes on any ColdFusion custom tag. The designer of the custom tag defines and documents what attributes are supported. In the case of this example tag, if you add a `name` attribute, the value provided with that is also displayed, as in the following example:

```
<cfx_HelloColdFusion name="bob">
```

This code should render the following output:

```
Hello, bob
```

Much better. This is, of course, a trivial example of a Java CFX custom tag. The rest of the examples provided by Macromedia in the CF_MX distribution demonstrate much more interesting possibilities, including creating queries, doing file processing, generating graphics, and more.

Other Java Integration Topics (and Learning More)

One could write an entire book about integrating Java with CF MX. We could cover many more topics than are possible in this book. In regard to using `CFOBJECT` and `createobject()` with Java classes and objects, for example, you may also want to know more about the following topics:

- ✦ Working with JavaBeans
- ✦ Datatype conversion between CFML and Java
- ✦ Understanding `CFOBJECT` and its support of default and alternative constructors
- ✦ Case and `classpath` issues
- ✦ Handling Java exceptions in CFML code

Fortunately, these topics are covered in the Macromedia ColdFusion MX documentation. See the manual *Developing ColdFusion MX Applications with CFML*, Chapter 32, "Integrating J2EE and Java Elements in CFML Applications," and the section "Using Java Objects" in that chapter. The chapter also discusses some of the topics covered here, although we provide quite a bit of information here that's not documented well, if at all, in the CF MX manuals.

Some readers may be particularly interested in understanding how to integrate Enterprise JavaBeans (EJBs) with CF MX. We've tried to focus in this book on those aspects of Java integration that can be used with CF MX alone. CFMX is not an EJB Server, for example, so although you can integrate EJBs on another server, you can't do that with CF MX alone. But you can find brief coverage of the topic in the "Using Java Objects" section of the CF MX documentation mentioned in the preceding paragraph.

The Macromedia documents also cover how to work with Java CFX custom tags — especially how to create them and the kinds of features exposed by them. See Chapter 12, "Building Custom CFX API Tags," in the *Developing ColdFusion MX Applications with CFML* manual. It even includes a discussion of how to debug Java CFX tags, both within a Java IDE and by using special debugging methods. In the Macromedia CFML reference manual, Chapter 7, "ColdFusion Java CFX Reference," covers the details of the Java CFX API. Both manuals are available online, along with the rest of the ColdFusion MX documentation, at `http://livedocs.macromedia.com`.

Summary

In this chapter, we lean toward discussing features that are relatively easy to implement, even with just a modicum (or no) Java experience. The goal is to point you in the direction of integrating Java and CF MX. Along the way, we hope that you've discovered that quite a few useful benefits arise out of just the few integration points discussed in this chapter.

You may find additional coverage of Java topics at the Macromedia site at the following URL:

```
www.macromedia.com/desdev/mx/coldfusion/articles/java.html
```

There A few other topics are worth exploring on your own — topics that aren't covered in the CF MX manuals. Readers interested in learning more will find no lack of information available. These topics include using servlet filters and listeners and working with other J2EE features, such as JMS, JAAC, and more. Even developers with experience in working with these features can, however, better grasp how to implement them within CF MX by using the information that we provide in this chapter about configuring the underlying XML control files.

Java is a very large language and parts of Java are quite complicated, but these facts need not put ColdFusion developers off. In this chapter, we've shown relatively simple ways of using Java and CF_MX together and we hope to have inspired your own confidence for your forays into the rich world of Java.

✦ ✦ ✦

CHAPTER 29

Integrating COM

✦ ✦ ✦ ✦

In This Chapter

Creating COM objects and manipulating their properties

Inspecting COM classes and calling their methods

✦ ✦ ✦ ✦

COM (or *C*omponent *O*bject *M*odel) is a Microsoft technology that enables developers to write different parts of an application in different languages while enabling each part to communicate with the others through a common *interface* of properties and methods.

The front-end of your application, for example, can be written in ColdFusion and the business logic can be written as a *COM object* in C++. A COM object is compiled as either a DLL or EXE file.

The strength of using COM is that the ColdFusion developer doesn't need to know what the COM developer does and vice-versa; all either one needs is the published interface to the COM object. In fact, COM objects are often third-party components that you use to add extra functionality to your application; you didn't develop the COM object, so all you know is its interface and what it does.

This chapter shows you how to use COM and also shows you how to use a couple of these third-party objects in your application.

This chapter makes heavy use of CFSCRIPT. If you have not already read and understood all of Chapter 16, please do so before continuing with this chapter.

COM is only supported on Windows builds of ColdFusion MX. Because COM is a Windows-specific technology, do not attempt to use COM if you are running UNIX, Linux, or another version of ColdFusion MX Server. If you are running one of these other platforms, your best option is to find a Java object that does what you need.

Examples of Using COM

The only feature missing from ColdFusion MX's new XML functionality is the capability to validate an XML document against a Document Type Definition (DTD), which is necessary for building robust e-commerce systems based on XML. Luckily, Microsoft's XML parser can accomplish this task through COM with a surprisingly small amount of code, as shown in Listing 29-1.

Listing 29-1: Validating XML against a DTD

```
<cfobject type="COM"
          action="CREATE"
          class="MSXML2.DOMDocument"
          name="objXML">

<cfscript>
objXML.validateOnParse = False;
success = objXML.load("c:\hamlet.xml");
objError = objXML.validate();
</cfscript>

<cfoutput>#objError.errorCode#</cfoutput>
```

MSXML2.DOMDocument is part of Microsoft's MSXML 3.0 release. To find out more about MSXML and to download MSXML 3.0, go to www.microsoft.com/xml.

Congratulations; you've just used your first COM object! CFOBJECT creates the COM object, where MSXML2.DOMDocument is the name of the type or *class* of this new object, and "objXML" is the variable that contains the object.

After creating the object, you set the validateOnParse *property* to false, which tells the XML parser not to immediately validate the document. You then tell the COM object to load an XML file from disk by using the load() *method*; then you call the validate() method, which validates the XML document and returns an error object. You then output the error object's errorCode property to determine whether the validation was successful.

And that, in a nutshell, is COM. After creating a COM object, you can set *properties*, which are data elements belonging to that object, and you can call *methods*, which are functions operating on that object.

XML validation is by no means the only thing that you can do with a COM object. In the scenario for the next example, you have poorly-written HTML that you want to convert on the fly to XHTML. You can do so by using a COM object known as TidyCOM, as shown in Listing 29-2.

Listing 29-2: Using TidyCOM

```
<cfsavecontent variable="BadHTML">
<html>
<title>This is the title.

<body>
    <B>This is <i>some text.</b></I><P>
    <br>
    This is more.
</body>
</cfsavecontent>
```

```
<cfscript>
objTidy = CreateObject("COM", "TidyCOM.TidyObject");
objOpts = objTidy.Options;
objOpts.OutputXhtml = True;
objOpts.TidyMark = False;
objOpts.LogicalEmphasis = True;
objOpts.BreakBeforeBr = True;
objOpts.Indent = 2;
WriteOutput(objTidy.TidyMemToMem(BadHTML));
</cfscript>
```

TidyCOM is a COM-based wrapper for the HTML Tidy project. To obtain TidyCOM, go to http://perso.wanadoo.fr/ablavier/TidyCOM/, download it, and follow the installation instructions. To find out more about HTML Tidy, go to http://tidy.sourceforge.net/.

In this example, you create a variable named BadHTML by using CFSAVECONTENT, but BadHTML could just as easily have come from a form post.

Notice first that you're using a different method to create your COM object in this example; instead of using CFOBJECT, you're using a function named CreateObject(). This function returns the newly created COM object, which you're storing in a variable named objTidy. Figure 29-1 shows a graphical representation of objTidy.

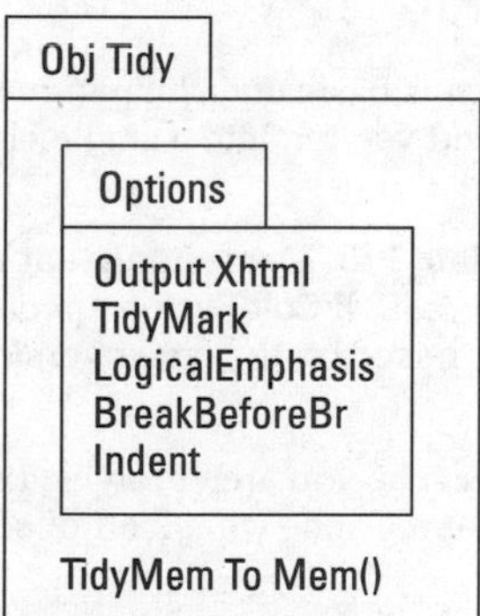

Figure 29-1: objTidy.

Notice that inside of objTidy is another COM object named Options. This Options object is a container for all the options that affect how TidyCOM does its job. Notice that the second line of the CFSCRIPT block creates a *reference* to this Options object so that you can modify its properties.

After setting some of TidyCOM's options, you call a method back in the original object that transforms the bad HTML into XHTML, which you then output by using WriteOutput().

This example is only slightly more complicated than the first one, because of its extra object, but notice that you're using exactly the same procedure as you did before: You create a COM object and then modify properties and called methods. The following sections go into much more detail about the mechanics of using COM, but keep in mind that COM boils down to just those three processes.

Creating a COM Object

Before you can use a COM object, ColdFusion must create one based on a *COM class*. You have a number of ways to do so, but the simplest way is by using the CFOBJECT tag as follows:

```
<cfobject type="COM"
          action="CREATE"
          class="MSXML2.DOMDocument"
          name="myCOMObject">
```

In the preceding call to CFOBJECT, you told ColdFusion the following four things:

1. You intend to create a COM object (in the type attribute).
2. You want to create a new COM object as opposed to connecting to one that already exists.
3. The COM *class* that you want to use for this new object is named "MSXML2.DOMDocument". This COM class defines the methods and properties that are attached to the new object. Thinking of the class as a "template" used to create the new object sometimes helps to understand what CFOBJECT does.

   The class name can be given in the following three different ways, from most specific to the easiest to use:

   - {F5078F32-C551-11D3-89B9-0000F81FE221}: Every COM object has an associated CLSID, or UUID, that uniquely identifies the COM class and version. Try to avoid using a CLSID if you can because telling at a glance what kind of COM object you're creating is nearly impossible.
   - MSXML2.DOMDocument.3.0: This is a ProgID, which is basically a human-readable form of the CLSID that combines the class name and version into a single class identifier.
   - MSXML2.DOMDocument: This is a version-independent ProgID, meaning that multiple versions of the same class can use the same ProgID. If ColdFusion encounters one of this type of ProgID, it creates a COM object based on the latest version of the class.

   Your best bet is to use a version-independent ProgID because you aren't relying on a specific version of the COM class, and you can also tell at a glance what kind of object you're creating.

4. After ColdFusion creates the COM object, the object is stored in a variable named myCOMObject.

CFOBJECT's action attribute can have one of two values: CREATE or CONNECT. CREATE, as you would expect, creates a new COM object based on the COM class name that you provided. CONNECT, on the other hand, instead uses an existing COM object already running on the system. Most developers use code such as the following:

```
<!--- Try to connect to the Word application object --->
<CFTRY>
    <!--- If it exists, connect to it --->
    <CFOBJECT
        ACTION="CONNECT"
        CLASS="Word.Application"
        NAME="objWord"
        TYPE="COM">
```

```
  <CFCATCH>
    <!--- The object doesn't exist, so create it --->
    <CFOBJECT
        ACTION="CREATE"
        CLASS="Word.Application"
        NAME="objWord"
        TYPE="COM">
  </CFCATCH>
</CFTRY>
```

This way, ColdFusion creates a new COM object only if one doesn't already exist instead of creating a new one on every request to this page.

Another attribute of `CFOBJECT` is named `context` and can be one of three values: `INPROC`, `LOCAL`, or `REMOTE`. `INPROC` means that the COM object is created inside ColdFusion Server's address space; these objects are usually made as DLLs. `LOCAL` means that the COM object is its own executable and it's running on the same machine as ColdFusion Server. (By the way, this is a case where you would use `action="CONNECT"` rather than `action="CREATE"` so that you don't have 50 executables running on your system at the same time.) `REMOTE` means that the COM object is its own executable but is executing on a different machine than ColdFusion Server.

But why would you want to call a COM object on a different machine? The idea is the same as putting ColdFusion on one machine and the database server on another. Because COM can be memory-intensive, for COM to be on a machine where it can't affect the overall performance of ColdFusion only makes sense.

To call an object remotely, you must do the following three things:

- ✦ Use a CLSID instead of a ProgID for the name of the class. Remote invocation doesn't understand ProgIDs such as `Word.Application`; instead, it understands a CLSID such as `{000209FF-0000-0000-C000-000000000046}`.
- ✦ Set the `context` to `REMOTE`.
- ✦ Add a `Server` attribute to `CFOBJECT` to tell the tag which server to connect to. The server can be specified in the following five different ways:

  `\\uncname`

  `uncname`

  `http://www.servername.com`

  `www.servername.com`

  `127.0.0.1`

In the following example you're connecting to a `Word.Application` object on a remote system by using a Universal Naming Convention (UNC) path:

```
<CFOBJECT
        ACTION="CONNECT"
        CLASS="{000209FF-0000-0000-C000-000000000046}"
        NAME="objWord"
        TYPE="COM"
        CONTEXT="REMOTE"
        SERVER="\\myothermachine">
```

UNC is an industry-standard way of naming computers and network shares; for CFOBJECT, the UNC is two backslashes followed by the name of the remote computer.

If you want to create an object by using CFSCRIPT, you can use CreateObject() as follows:

```
<cfscript>
objXML = CreateObject("COM", "MSXML2.DOMDocument");
</cfscript>
```

In the preceding line, you created a COM object based on the "MSXML2.DOMDocument" class using CreateObject() rather than CFOBJECT. The class name used with CreateObject() is just like the class name with CFOBJECT: You can use either a ProgID or a CLSID. Three more parameters to CreateObject() (although you only use two; the middle one is CORBA-specific) represent the context and Server attributes of CFOBJECT, as follows:

```
<cfscript>
objXML = CreateObject(
    "COM",
    "MSXML2.DOMDocument",
    "REMOTE",
    "",
    "\\myothermachine"
);
</cfscript>
```

Unfortunately, you have no way to *connect* to a COM object rather than to create a new one by using CreateObject().

Getting and Setting an Object's Properties

After you have created a COM object, you can set its properties and call its methods. *Properties* are the data stored with the object; for example, a Word Document object has a Title property, a Filename property, and many others. To read the value of a property, you *get* the property. Similarly, to set the value of a property, you *set* the property. Some properties support both operations, whereas others support only getting the property's value.

Setting a property uses what should be a familiar syntax to you, as follows:

```
<cfset myCOMObject.myPropertyName = "some value">
```

You access a COM object's properties in the same way that you access a structure's keys by using dot notation. The difference is that you can't create new properties in using COM objects as you can with structures. Getting a property from a COM object is just as easy as setting it, as the following example shows:

```
<cfoutput>#myCOMObject.myPropertyName#</cfoutput>
```

One concern in setting the value of a property is the value's type, because ColdFusion is not a type-safe language, and COM is. (When a language is *type-safe,* it means that variables are of a specific type, and all function calls and property assignments check the types of the incoming values.) To avoid any problems moving between the two, always do the following:

- ✦ If setting a numeric property, use Val() around the argument.
- ✦ If setting a date or date/time property, use one of the native ColdFusion functions that returns a date object, such as CreateDate() or CreateODBCDateTime().
- ✦ Trimming any value that you're putting in a string property is usually a good idea as well.

If a property is a read-only property, ColdFusion throws an error if you attempt to set it. Usually, a COM object's documentation tells you whether a property is read-only, and you see how to find out for yourself in the section "Interpreting method and property definitions," later in this chapter.

So far in this chapter, you've seen how to get and set simple strings, numbers, and dates. A property, however, isn't limited to a simple value. Remember how, in Listing 29-2, you create a *reference* to TidyCOM's Options object? Following is a snippet from that code:

```
<cfscript>
objTidy = CreateObject("COM", "TidyCOM.TidyObject");
objOpts = objTidy.Options;
objOpts.OutputXhtml = True;
</cfscript>
```

objTidy is the original COM object that you created. objOpts, on the other hand, is a reference to the Options object inside of objTidy, meaning that modifying a property of objOpts is the same as modifying a property of objTidy.Options. Essentially, objOpts and objTidy.Options are exactly the same thing, so modifying one always affects the other.

You may be wondering why we didn't just use the following:

```
objTidy.Options.OutputXhtml = True;
```

ColdFusion doesn't support accessing object properties more than one level deep at a time, so we must use these intermediate "reference" objects.

Calling an Object's Methods

Whereas *properties* store data in a COM object, *methods* perform a task on an object and possibly return some value. Calling the validate()method of an XML Document object, for example, validates the document, as follows:

```
objError = objXMLDoc.validate();
```

As you do properties, you access a method by using dot notation. The validate() method that we're using here returns an error object that you can use to determine whether the operation was successful.

The following line shows a method call that takes an argument:

```
success = objXMLDoc.load("c:\hamlet.xml");
```

You can see that, just as does a typical function, the method can take an argument and return a value; the only difference is the COM object name that appears in front of the method.

Some methods don't return a value; these methods, as shown in the following example, are known as *void methods*:

```
objXMLDoc.save("c:\hamlet-copy.xml");
```

In reality, however, you can use any method as a void method simply by ignoring the return value; for example, the call to load() earlier could have been written as follows:

```
objXMLDoc.load("c:\hamlet.xml");
```

The caveats about passing parameters to methods are the same as the caveats for setting the values of parameters we listed in the previous section — that is, always use Val() or a date function, always trim string arguments, and so on.

Advanced COM Concepts

The following section introduces OLEView, a utility that enables you to view the COM classes available on your system. Before we do that, however, we need to give you a tour of COM and the different players involved so that you can understand the terminology that OLEView uses. For the purposes of this section, we are going to use the TidyCOM library from Listing 29-2 as an example. To obtain `TidyCOM`, go to `http://perso.wanadoo.fr/ablavier/TidyCOM/`, download it, and follow the installation instructions. To find out more about HTML Tidy, go to `http://tidy.sourceforge.net/`.

Figure 29-2 shows COM's organizational model.

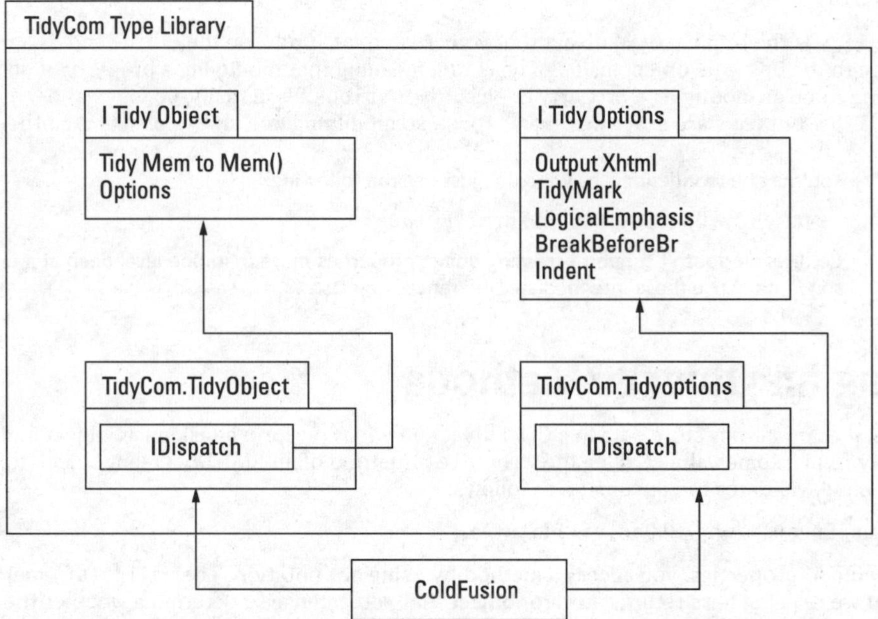

Figure 29-2: COM's organizational model.

A *type library* is COM's central organizational unit. This type library gathers together the interfaces, enumerations, and other objects defined for a given product. `TidyCOM`, for example, has a type library, as do Microsoft's XML parser, Microsoft Excel, TopStyle, Windows Media Player, or any other product with COM capabilities.

`TidyCOM`'s type library contains two *interfaces*, which are the mechanisms that COM uses to represent objects. `TidyCOM`'s interfaces are `ITidyObject` and `ITidyOptions`, and these interfaces define the methods and properties associated with a COM object. Notice, however, that in the figure, ColdFusion doesn't interact directly with `ITidyObject`. Instead, ColdFusion uses the `ProgID` `TidyCOM.TidyObject`, which acts as a kind of alias for `ITidyObject`.

`TidyCOM.TidyObject` wraps an interface named IDispatch, as does `TidyCOM.TidyOptions`. These `IDispatch` interfaces point back to `ITidyObject` and ITidyOptions, which is how ColdFusion knows what properties and methods are available for a given object. Every COM object has an `IDispatch` interface that binds the object to its associated interface within the type library. After an interface is bound to `IDispatch`, it's known as a *Dispinterface*. Remember these terms for the following section.

COM uses a programming language known as *IDL* (for *I*nterface *D*efinition *L*anguage) to describe interfaces, dispinterfaces, and libraries. You see small snippets of IDL in this chapter but only just enough to show what you need to know. Don't worry. You don't have yet *another* language to learn!

Inspecting COM classes, interfaces, and type libraries by Using OLEView

One of the benefits of COM is that every COM object is defined as part of the Windows Registry. OLEView is a utility from Microsoft that uses that registry information along with the information stored in type libraries to enable you to browse all the COM classes on your system. OLEView also gives information about a class's methods and properties as well as the CLSIDs and `ProgID`s available for each class.

You can get OLEView in either of the following two ways:

- ✦ OLEView is part of Microsoft Visual Studio's Developer Tools. If you have Visual Studio installed on your machine, you can access the tool from Programs ⇨ Microsoft Visual Studio ⇨ Microsoft Visual Studio Tools on the menu bar.
- ✦ If you don't have Visual Studio or didn't install the tools, you can get OLEView from Microsoft at `www.microsoft.com/com/resources/oleview.asp`.

After you launch OLEView, you are presented with a two-pane interface. The left pane is a tree control containing all the COM classes, interfaces, and libraries installed on your machine. The right pane changes depending on what's currently selected in the tree control on the left. The following discussion is not in the same order as the tree; instead, we take a more logical approach to the application.

You may want to use OLEView for any of the following three reasons:

- ✦ You are looking for the CLSID or `ProgID` for a specific object.
- ✦ You are looking for a library or class that contains the functionality that you need.
- ✦ You are looking for documentation on a specific class, interface, or type library.

The following sections take you through each process.

Finding a class's CLSID or ProgID

In the following example, you're going to find the `ProgID` for the `TidyCOM` class that you use in the section "Getting and Setting an Object's Properties," earlier in this chapter. (Yes, we know that you've already seen the `ProgID`, but this is a good way to show you the general method to use.) Just follow these steps:

1. Launch the OLEView Application and expand the Object Classes node in the tree on the right.
2. Look through the list of Component categories under the Object Classes node. If one of the categories describes what you're looking for, expand the category's node in the tree. (In this example, none of the categories describe the `TidyCOM` object so you need to expand the All Objects node to get a list of every registered object on the system.)

3. Look through the class nodes under the category you expanded to find the class you're looking for. Unfortunately, COM classes don't need to be named consistently, so start by assuming that the class name starts with either the name of the product or the name of the company. (In the case of `TidyCOM`, you luck out, because the name of the COM class that you're looking for is `TidyObject Class`.

4. After you find the class you're looking for, select its node in the tree control by clicking on it. You don't need to expand it.

5. Click the node to accesses information from the Registry in the right-hand pane. (Doing so also accesses information from other sources, but the extra information is hidden on other tabs and don't really affect this discussion.) Look through the Registry information for a key named `CLSID`. The first subkey under `CLSID` is the CLSID of the object. In this example, however, you're looking for the ProgID. `TidyObject` exposes both a ProgID (`TidyCOM.TidyObject.1`) and a version-independent ProgID (`TidyCOM.TidyObject`). Figure 29-3 shows the `TidyObject` class's Registry information as seen in OLEView.

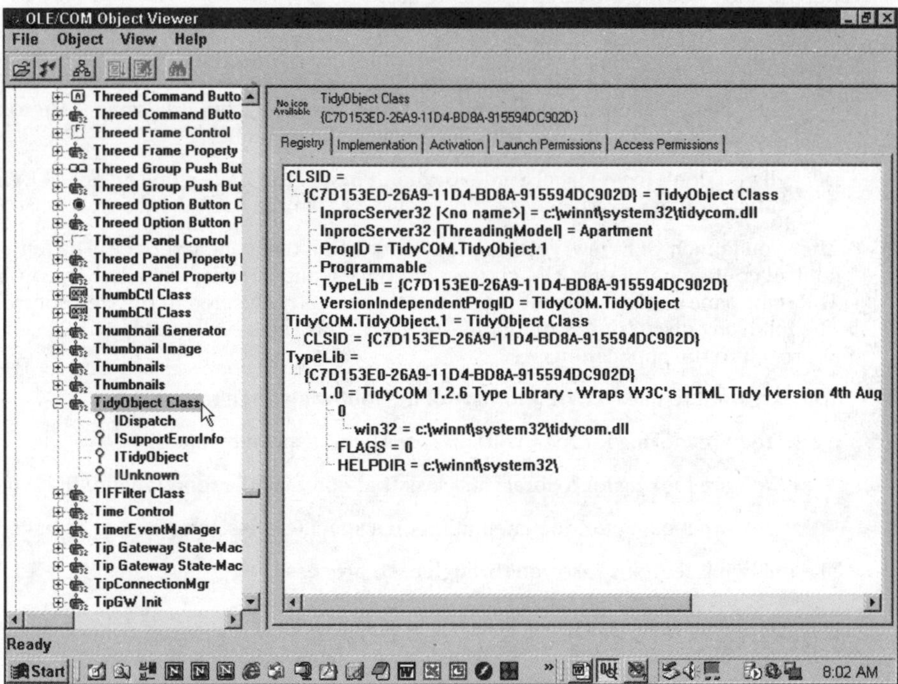

Figure 29-3: TidyCOM's registry information.

If no ProgID is given in the Registry information, you can use only the CLSID to create this object. If you can't find the object that you're looking for in the tree, it shouldn't be directly instantiated by `CFOBJECT`.

Finding a library or class containing certain functionality

Finding a library or class based on its functionality rather than its name is a more general process than what was laid out in the preceding section. Essentially, instead of following steps to find a specific piece of data, you're just browsing OLEView's tree to find something that catches your eye.

If you don't know exactly what you're looking for, the best option is probably to expand the Type Libraries node at the root of the tree and look carefully through the list of type libraries. Because the list of libraries is relatively small, finding what you're looking for should be easier than looking through a list of classes. If you were searching for TidyCOM on your system, you would just look in the list of libraries under the Type Libraries node in the tree control starting at the letter *T*. Clicking the name of a type library shows Registry information in the left-hand pane, but it's probably not going to be very useful to you. Double-clicking the type library's node opens the *library inspector window*, as we describe in the section "Finding documentation for a type library," later in this chapter.

Finding documentation for a class

If you follow the steps outlined in the section "Finding a class's CLSID or ProgID," earlier in this chapter, you arrive at a tree node describing a COM class. If you expand this node, you see a list of interfaces implemented by this class. Usually `IDispatch` is the only one you're concerned with. If you don't see `IDispatch` anywhere in the list of interfaces, *don't use the class!* You experience more problems than you can imagine if you try to use a COM object without an `IDispatch` interface from within ColdFusion.

Double-clicking the `IDispatch` interface under the class that you want to view opens a dialog box named *IDispatch Viewer* showing you how many type libraries implement this class (almost always 1) and a View TypeInfo button. Clicking this button launches a new window with two panes. Again, the right pane displays a tree, although this time, the tree describes the properties and methods of the current interface. The right pane this time is an IDL viewer showing the IDL for the node currently selected in the left pane. For information on interpreting the IDL for the various properties and methods that you see in this new window, see the section "Interpreting method and property definitions," later in the chapter.

Finding documentation for a type library

Double-clicking the name of a type library opens the library inspector window, which shows all the objects defined in the type library. Many types of objects are shown, but we describe in the following list only the sections of interest to ColdFusion developers:

✦ **Enums:** Often, in documentation for a COM object, you see example code such as the following:

```
myTidyObj.CharEncoding = ascii;
```

This is confusing, however, because `ascii` is not the name of a ColdFusion variable; rather, it is the name of an enumerated constant defined in the type library. These groups of enumerated constants are defined in this section of the library inspector. ColdFusion can't recognize these constant names, so you must use the library inspector to look up `ascii`, as shown in Figure 29-4.

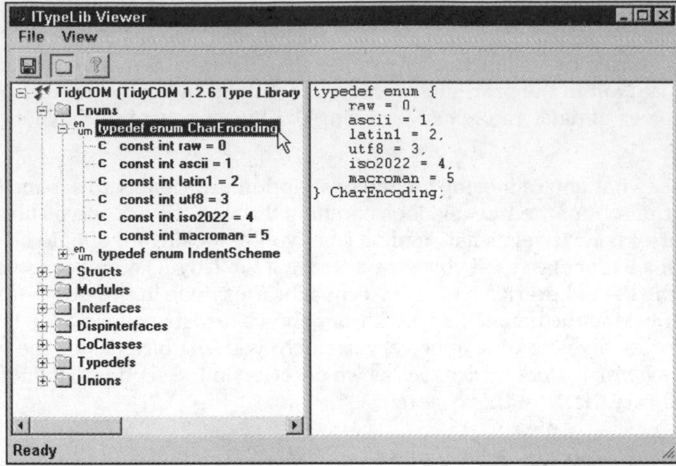

Figure 29-4: Viewing enumerated constants by using the library inspector.

You can see in the figure that the numeric equivalent to `ascii` is 1, so your ColdFusion code would look as follows:

```
myTidyObj.CharEncoding = 1;
```

✦ **Interfaces:** This is a list of all the interfaces implemented in this type library. Expanding one of these interfaces gives you a list of the properties and/or methods exposed by the interface; see the section "Interpreting method and property definitions," later in this chapter, for information on interpreting the property and method definitions.

✦ **Dispinterfaces:** Remember that, whenever an interface is bound to an object that implements `IDispatch`, it is known as a *dispinterface* and can be called by ColdFusion. As such, any of the interfaces listed in this section are callable by ColdFusion (although you must find the CLSID or `ProgID` first).

Finding documentation for an interface

If you know the name of an interface but you don't know the name of the associated type library or class, you can expand the Interfaces node in the OLEView tree to get a list of all the interfaces exposed by all the type libraries in the system. Double-clicking an interface accesses its CLSID (also called an *IID*) and a button to view the TypeInfo. Clicking this button opens the *interface inspector window*, showing you all the properties and/or methods exposed by this interface. See the following section for details on interpreting these methods and properties.

Interpreting method and property definitions

In inspecting the properties and methods of an interface, keep in mind that a COM developer can implement a property in two ways. The first, no longer common, is to clearly separate methods from properties, making the properties receptacles for data and the methods functions to work on those properties. The second method, which is much more prevalent and also more flexible, is to implement the properties as methods.

COM interfaces are defined in a language known as *IDL*, or *I*nterface *D*efinition *L*anguage. Implementing an old-style property in IDL looks as follows:

```
[id(0x0000008b), helpcontext(0x0001008b)]
BSTR Caption;
```

The `id` and `helpcontext` keywords assign numeric values to the property; `BSTR` is the type of the property (`BSTR` being the COM equivalent of a ColdFusion string); and `Caption` is the name of the property. As such, to assign a value to this property in ColdFusion, you would use the following syntax:

```
myCOMObject.Caption = "The new Caption";
```

This works, but you have no easy way to make this kind of property read-only. Worse is the fact that the `Caption` property can't have any intelligent logic attached to it because it's just a receptacle for data.

The way that most COM objects now define their properties is with IDL, as follows:

```
[id(0x0000008b), propget, helpcontext(0x0001008b)]
BSTR Caption();
[id(0x0000008b), propput, helpcontext(0x0001008b)]
void Caption([in] BSTR rhs);
```

Instead of defining an individual property named `Caption`, two methods are now named `Caption`, one (known as a *getter*) that takes no arguments but returns the current value and one (known as a *setter*) that returns nothing and sets the new value to whatever is passed in the `rhs` argument. Assigning a value to this kind of property uses the following syntax:

```
myCOMObject.Caption = "The new Caption";
```

Now wait! You're probably thinking that's the same syntax that you used in CFSCRIPT at the beginning of the chapter, and you're right. This change in the IDL is totally transparent to ColdFusion; notice the `propget` and `propput` keywords in the second snippet of IDL. Those keywords tell COM to treat these two functions as a transparent interface into the `Caption` property.

Interpreting explicit property definitions

If you open a Type Library and find no Interfaces in the library—only Disinterfaces—you likely have one of these old-style components. Expand the Dispinterface for the object that you want to inspect, and you should see the following four sections (although some may not appear in all cases):

- ✦ Constants
- ✦ Properties
- ✦ Methods
- ✦ Inherited Interfaces

Ignore the Inherited Interfaces node. As you may expect, constants, properties, and methods are all grouped under their appropriate headings. After you click one, its IDL snippet appears on the right-hand side, as shown in the following example, and interpreting these is usually pretty easy:

```
[id(0x0000008b), helpcontext(0x0001008b)]
VARIANT Caption;
```

That snippet defines a property named `Caption` with a type of `VARIANT`. `VARIANT` means that the property can hold data of any type.

Interpreting properties defined as methods

In searching for a new-style property, one thing to look for is two methods of the same name. The ITidyOptions interface, for example, has two methods named Doctype, as the following example shows:

```
[id(0x00000003), propget, helpstring("Doctype declaration")]
HRESULT Doctype([out, retval] BSTR* pVal);
[id(0x00000003), propput, helpstring("Doctype declaration")]
HRESULT Doctype([in] BSTR pVal);
```

The preceding definitions may seem confusing because both functions return a value—and both functions also take an argument! That's because the first method is a property getter, which you can tell because it has the propget keyword attached. You also know that the getter returns a BSTR (and remember that's the same as a ColdFusion string) because of the retval keyword attached to the BSTR* argument.

The second method is the property setter, which you can tell from the propput keyword. You also know that it takes a single BSTR argument that is to be the new value of the property.

The HRESULT return type from both methods is a new convention in COM programming. Every so-called "safe" COM object method must return an HRESULT, which is like a success flag. You can ignore HRESULT and assume that whichever argument is marked retval is the returned value.

What all this means is that the TidyOptions object has a property named Doctype that you can access by using the following syntax:

```
objOptions.Doctype = "My New Doctype value";
```

Notice that you cannot call either of these methods directly because they have been marked as a getter and setter pair, so COM handles the translation between the methods and the property.

Unfortunately, looking for two methods of the same name does not help you identify read-only properties, where you can read the property but not set it. The key to finding these is to look at all the methods of an interface; any methods marked with propget that have no corresponding propset method specify read-only properties. TotalWarnings in ITidyObject, for example, is a read-only property, as defined by its IDL:

```
[id(0x00000003), propget, helpstring("Number of warnings")]
HRESULT TotalWarnings([out, retval] long* pVal);
```

Notice that instead of BSTR, this property is defined as long, which is the IDL term for ColdFusion's integer type. Notice also that only the getter is present, meaning that you could refer to the property as follows:

```
<cfoutput>#objTidy.TotalWarnings#</cfoutput>
```

But setting the property would throw an error because there is no setter defined.

COM Caveats

COM has historically been difficult to integrate with ColdFusion. Before ColdFusion MX, COM was very memory intensive and contributed to a memory leak within ColdFusion Server. On the whole, however, COM was usually pretty stable.

With the release of ColdFusion MX, however, the situation has changed. Because MX is built on top of Java, it requires a Java-to-COM bridge that has the following two main faults:

✦ Establishing a COM connection takes longer in MX, so COM calls that used to take 50 milliseconds can now, in some cases, increase to two or three seconds per call.

✦ Some COM objects, most notably Microsoft Office objects, don't work very well with the Java-to-COM bridge, making it such that COM-based functionality that worked in ColdFusion 5 no longer works in ColdFusion MX.

Don't let those problems discourage you from using COM, however. The sheer amount of what you can do with COM, combined with Macromedia's continuing improvement in its support for COM, should be enough to convince you to use this technology if it's the best way to accomplish a task.

At this time, COM is only available on Windows operating systems, so servers operating on Unix-based operating systems can't use the techniques outlined in this chapter. There are COM port projects for other operating systems, but they may be unreliable and aren't supported by ColdFusion.

Summary

Most of the COM objects that you find on your machine are user-interface components that aren't usable from ColdFusion. Those few that do server-side functionality, however, are definitely gems. COM objects are also written to do backend business logic, as well as COM interfaces into some third-party shipping or banking services.

In this chapter you learned how to instantiate and use COM objects, set properties, and call methods. You also learned how to use OLEView to inspect the COM objects on your system to find out what you can do with COM, what objects are available, and how to use those objects.

By and large, most of what you do with COM probably revolves around Microsoft Office, which we have specifically steered clear from in this chapter for two reasons. First, getting Office to work correctly with the current release of ColdFusion MX is difficult and sometimes impossible (even after installing the CF MX Updater Version 1), and those problems would make the process difficult to explain. Second, CFComet, at `www.cfcomet.com/`, does a much better job of explaining Office COM than we could do in this space.

In short, COM is great technology for extending ColdFusion if you have an object that works correctly with ColdFusion. Always keep an eye out for functionality that you're implementing in ColdFusion that would be better implemented as a compiled object in COM.

✦ ✦ ✦

Integrating ColdFusion MX with XML and WDDX

✦ ✦ ✦ ✦

In This Chapter

Using WDDX

Exploring basic XML concepts

Using XML objects in ColdFusion

Understanding XPath

Building XSL transformations

✦ ✦ ✦ ✦

XML (e*X*tensible *M*arkup *L*anguage) is a hot topic in the Internet world. ColdFusion has historically lagged behind other languages in its support for XML, however, because before ColdFusion MX, the only way to use XML with ColdFusion was to integrate a third-party package such as Microsoft's COM-based parser. Because ColdFusion didn't have any native XML-handling capabilities, finding a purely XML-based application using ColdFusion was rare.

With the release of ColdFusion MX, the situation has reversed itself. The XML capabilities of MX are some of the easiest to use of any Web-programming language, enabling your development team to get XML-based applications developed quickly without a high learning curve.

This chapter covers the following five topics:

- How to use WDDX with ColdFusion and JavaScript
- Basic XML concepts
- Using XML objects within ColdFusion
- Using XPath to search XML objects
- Using XSL stylesheets to transform XML into HTML

Don't worry if some of these topics sound foreign to you. Everything should make sense by the time that you finish this chapter and then you should be ready to start building XML-based solutions by using ColdFusion.

Web Distributed Data Exchange (WDDX)

If you've been working in ColdFusion very long, you've probably heard about *WDDX*, or *W*eb *D*istributed *D*ata e*X*change. WDDX came about because ColdFusion needed a way to express complex variables such as structures and arrays in a way that any server or Web-application language could understand.

This chapter assumes that you are already familiar with arrays and structures, which are explained in Chapters 14 and 15. If you are not already familiar with these concepts, please read Chapters 14 and 15 before getting into this chapter.

To explain what we mean, you can use the following example of an array of employees. We created this array in ColdFusion by executing the following code:

```
<cfset arEmployees = ArrayNew(1)>
<cfset arEmployees[1] = StructNew()>
<cfset arEmployees[1].SSN = "123-45-6789">
<cfset arEmployees[1].Name = "David Churvis">
<cfset arEmployees[2] = StructNew()>
<cfset arEmployees[2].SSN = "312-54-9678">
<cfset arEmployees[2].Name = "Adam Churvis">
<cfset arEmployees[3] = StructNew()>
<cfset arEmployees[3].SSN = "231-45-8967">
<cfset arEmployees[3].Name = "Lisa Churvis">
```

To view this in a browser, you can use the CFDUMP tag to produce the output in Figure 30-1.

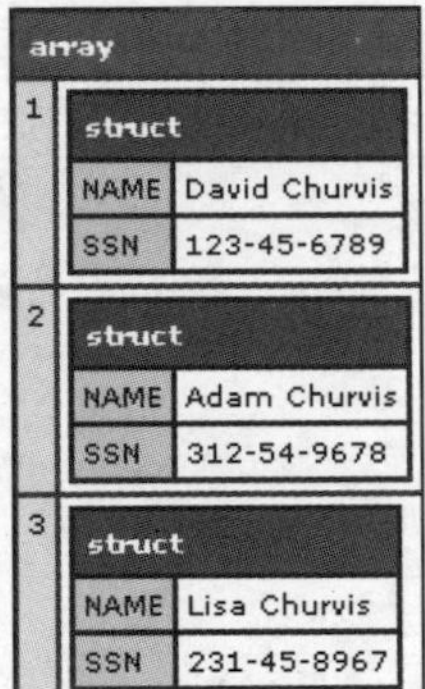

Figure 30-1: An array of employees as viewed through CFDUMP.

Now comes the problem. Instead of communicating with the user though CFDUMP and his Web browser, suppose that you want to communicate this array of employees to a different system across the Internet, such as another ColdFusion server or even an ASP or PHP server.

CFDUMP creates a string of HTML, but unfortunately, that doesn't serve your needs here. CFDUMP creates DHTML code that communicates a picture of the array to a user, but another Web server couldn't make heads or tails of the HTML produced by CFDUMP, because it is a graphical picture of an object rather than the object itself.

That's where WDDX comes in. Listing 30-1 shows this array of employees as expressed in WDDX.

Listing 30-1: A WDDX packet

```
<?xml version='1.0'?>
<wddxPacket version='1.0'>
  <header/>
  <data>
    <array length='3'>
      <struct>
        <var name='SSN'>
          <string>123-45-6789</string>
        </var>
        <var name='NAME'>
          <string>David Churvis</string>
        </var>
      </struct>
      <struct>
        <var name='SSN'>
          <string>312-54-9678</string>
        </var>
        <var name='NAME'>
          <string>Adam Churvis</string>
        </var>
      </struct>
      <struct>
        <var name='SSN'>
          <string>231-45-8967</string>
        </var>
        <var name='NAME'>
          <string>Lisa Churvis</string>
        </var>
      </struct>
    </array>
  </data>
</wddxPacket>
```

Now to analyze this packet. WDDX formally describes the structure and contents of the array by using a markup language similar to HTML. In fact, if you've ever output CFQUERY results in an HTML table, this example may look a little like *deja vu*.

The entire packet is surrounded by a <wddxPacket> element, which is always the root element of a WDDX packet. The <header> element does nothing right now but is required by a WDDX parser. Then comes the <data> element, which contains the real meat of the packet.

<array> describes the container for three array elements, each described by a <struct> tag, and each <struct> contains two <var> tags describing the keys of the structure. Finally, inside each <var> is a <string> tag describing the data type and value of the key in the structure.

The reason that WDDX goes into so much detail about the format of this object is that any WDDX-enabled language must be capable of parsing this packet and knowing exactly what kind of native object or objects to create from it. You could transmit the contents of Listing 30-1 to an ASP application (with the WDDX SDK installed), and ASP could understand and translate this WDDX packet into its equivalent of an array containing three *dictionaries* (the ASP equivalent of a ColdFusion *structure*).

Application Server Pages, or ASP, is a programming language from Microsoft that competes with ColdFusion. To facilitate communication between the two languages, the WDDX committee created a version of WDDX for ASP known as the WDDX SDK.

From this point on, we do not discuss using WDDX in other languages because this book is ColdFusion-specific and we want to concentrate on how ColdFusion uses WDDX. For information on using WDDX with other languages, go to `www.openwddx.org/`, which is the official site of the WDDX project.

The CFWDDX tag is the interface between ColdFusion and WDDX. In WDDX parlance, converting a complex object into WDDX is called serializing the object. Listing 30-2 uses CFWDDX to convert the array of employees into WDDX, outputs the resulting WDDX packet to the page (by using HTMLEditFormat so that you can see the WDDX tags in the browser), and then puts the WDDX into a client variable (more on this later in this section).

Listing 30-2: Serializing an array into WDDX

```
<cfset arEmployees = ArrayNew(1)>
<cfset arEmployees[1] = StructNew()>
<cfset arEmployees[1].SSN = "123-45-6789">
<cfset arEmployees[1].Name = "David Churvis">
<cfset arEmployees[2] = StructNew()>
<cfset arEmployees[2].SSN = "312-54-9678">
<cfset arEmployees[2].Name = "Adam Churvis">
<cfset arEmployees[3] = StructNew()>
<cfset arEmployees[3].SSN = "231-45-8967">
<cfset arEmployees[3].Name = "Lisa Churvis">

<cfwddx action="CFML2WDDX"
        input="#arEmployees#"
        output="WDDXPacket">

<cfoutput>
#HTMLEditFormat(WDDXPacket)#
</cfoutput>

<cfset Client.WDDXPacket = WDDXPacket>
```

Calling `CFWDDX` serialized `arEmployees` and put the resulting WDDX into `WDDXPacket`. The result of running this page is as shown in Figure 30-2.

```
<wddxPacket version='1.0'><header/><data><array length='3'><struct><var
name='SSN'><string>123-45-6789</string></var><var
name='NAME'><string>David Churvis</string></var></struct><struct><var
name='SSN'><string>312-54-9678</string></var><var
name='NAME'><string>Adam Churvis</string></var></struct><struct><var
name='SSN'><string>231-45-8967</string></var><var
name='NAME'><string>Lisa
Churvis</string></var></struct></array></data></wddxPacket>
```


Figure 30-2: The WDDX resulting from Listing 30-2.

You may notice that the XML is not nicely indented as in the packet that we show you in Listing 30-1; in fact, if you look closely, you should notice that no space at all lies between the tags. What we're showed you was a WDDX packet that we had tidied up to present to you, but in reality, WDDX parsers don't make the information so presentable.

You may also notice that we put the WDDX packet into a Client variable in the second listing. Chapter 12 mentions that you can't store a complex variable in the Client scope, and this is still true. You *can*, however, serialize a complex variable into WDDX and store the WDDX in a Client variable, because WDDX is just one long string.

Now that the array is stored as WDDX in a Client variable, you need a way to convert that WDDX back into an array so that your code can use it. Listing 30-3 shows how to *deserialize* the WDDX packet from the Client variable into an array.

Listing 30-3: **Transforming WDDX back into an array**

```
<cfwddx action="WDDX2CFML"
        input="#Client.WDDXPacket#"
        output="EmployeeArray">

<cfdump var="#EmployeeArray#">
```

Running Listing 30-3 produces the output shown in Figure 30-3.

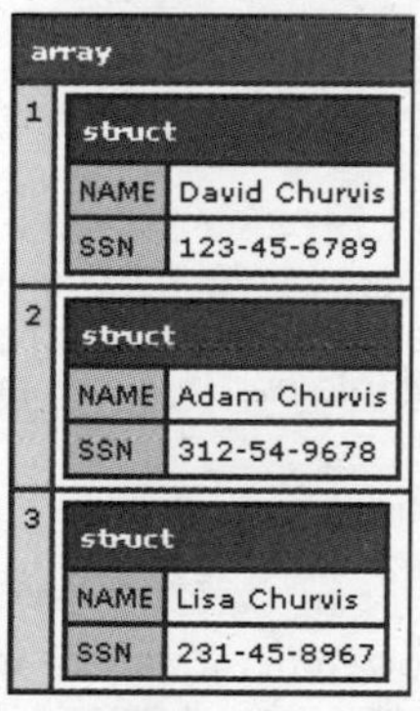

Figure 30-3: The array resulting from deserializing the WDDX packet.

Notice that, after deserializing the packet, you now have access to the values from the original structure. That's really all that using WDDX with ColdFusion involves. By the way, you just saw XML in action in both of the previous listings. WDDX is a data-centric flavor of XML that facilitates easy transfer of complex objects between disparate systems. Whenever we refer to "XML," we typically mean *generalized XML*, which is the generic technology on which specific flavors of XML are built.

What is XML?

WDDX was a great idea and worked very well but, unfortunately, didn't take off quite as well as Allaire and Macromedia had hoped. The reason is that WDDX is a great way to represent general data structure, but it is insufficient for representing the logical relationships between elements of data, something at which XML excels.

ColdFusion MX added native support for *generalized XML*. Listing 30-4 shows an XML document that represents a list of employees.

Listing 30-4: Generalized XML

```
<?xml version='1.0'?>
<employees>
  <employee>
    <ssn>123-45-6789</ssn>
    <name>David Churvis</name>
  </employee>
  <employee>
    <ssn>312-54-9678</ssn>
    <name>Adam Churvis</name>
  </employee>
  <employee>
    <ssn>231-45-8967</ssn>
    <name>Lisa Churvis</name>
  </employee>
</employees>
```

This XML packet, conceptually, carries the same information as the WDDX packet, but it is presented in a different way. Specifically, the XML packet is not concerned whether you use an array of employee structures or a structure containing arrays or anything such as that; instead, the XML states that a collection of `employees` contains multiple `employee` elements and that each employee has a `name` and an `ssn`.

Attributes vs. elements

Before we go into how ColdFusion uses XML, we should describe how XML formats its information. Listing 30-5 contrasts the two ways that you can specify an object's properties: *attributes* and *elements*.

Listing 30-5: An employee's ID *attribute* as opposed to his name *element*

```
<?xml version='1.0'?>
<employees>
  <employee id="1">
    <ssn>123-45-6789</ssn>
    <name>David Churvis</name>
  </employee>
  <employee id="2">
    <ssn>312-54-9678</ssn>
    <name>Adam Churvis</name>
  </employee>
  <employee id="3">
    <ssn>231-45-8967</ssn>
    <name>Lisa Churvis</name>
  </employee>
</employees>
```

The employee's ID is expressed as an *attribute* of the employee tag. On the other hand, the employee's `name` is expressed as an *element* inside the employee tag.

Now to answer the $64,000 question: Which is better? If you ask this question of five different developers, you probably get seven different answers. Following is the method that we use to decide:

1. If a piece of data has a structure of its own, it can't be an attribute because it requires subtags. The `line-item` in the following example could not be expressed as an attribute of `sales-order` because `line-item` has properties of its own:

```
<sales-order id="1">
  <line-item>
    <item-number>CAS30-BLK</item-number>
    <qty>3</qty>
  </line-item>
</sales-order>
```

2. If you have multiple occurrences of a piece of data, you don't express the data as an attribute but instead use elements, as in the following example:

```
<employee>
  <responsibility>Working</responsibility>
  <responsibility>Status Reports</responsibility>
  <responsibility>Making Coffee</responsibility>
</employee>
```

3. You must next determine whether the data is *descriptive data*, for which you use an element, or *metadata*, for which you use an attribute. The line between these two is maddening at times and can sometimes even seem a toss-up.

   Look at the difference between descriptive data and metadata this way: If data does nothing but describe other data (for example, the employee's ID from Listing 30-5), it's metadata, and you use an attribute. On the other hand, if data is descriptive but can stand on its own as a valid piece of data (as in the `ssn` or `name` from Listing 30-5), it's descriptive data, and you use an element.

Empty elements

The elements that you've seen in preceding sections have all contained content, as in the following example:

```
<ssn>123-45-6789</ssn>
```

Some elements in XML, however, just *are*; they don't contain any content of their own, as in the following example:

```
<header></header>
```

If an XML element contains no content, you can use the following shorthand notation that's easier to read than the long form:

```
<header/>
```

You see this syntax used often in XSL stylesheets in the section "Using XSL Transformations," later in this chapter.

XML documents vs. XML objects

You have two ways of working with XML. An XML *document* is just what you've seen so far in this chapter: a string containing a series of tags and their attributes and content that a human can read and understand. ColdFusion, however, doesn't use XML documents; ColdFusion works with XML *objects*, which are complex variables representing a hierarchy based on the structure of the XML document.

We rigidly follow the terms XML *document* and XML *object*; the two are not interchangeable. In the wide world of XML articles and documentation, however, the two terms are slightly muddied. XML documents are also referred to as *XML strings* or *XML files*, and XML objects are also referred to as *XML hierarchies*, *trees*, or most confusingly, *XML document objects*. In the context of this book, however, we never mix the two terms.

The easiest way to create an XML object in ColdFusion is to use the CFXML tag, as shown in Listing 30-6.

Listing 30-6: Creating an XML object by using CFXML

```
<cfxml variable="XmlObj">
<employees>
  <employee id="1">
    <ssn>123-45-6789</ssn>
    <name>David Churvis</name>
  </employee>
  <employee id="2">
    <ssn>312-54-9678</ssn>
    <name>Adam Churvis</name>
  </employee>
  <employee id="3">
    <ssn>231-45-8967</ssn>
    <name>Lisa Churvis</name>
  </employee>
```

```
</employees>
</cfxml>

<cfdump var="#XmlObj#">
```

Running Listing 30-6 produces the output shown in Figure 30-4.

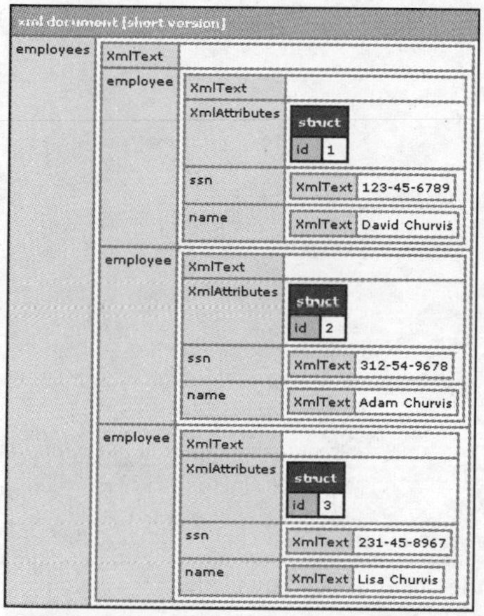

Figure 30-4: The XML object representing a collection of employees.

Notice that the XML document in between the `CFXML` tags was converted to an XML object that looks like a typical ColdFusion structure (except that you can have multiple keys named the same—we cover this difference in detail in the section "Accessing nodes," later in this chapter).

Another option if you have the XML content in a string variable is to use the `XmlParse()` function, as shown in Listing 30-7.

Listing 30-7: Creating an XML object by using `XmlParse`

```
<h1>XML Document</h1>

<cfsavecontent variable="XmlDoc">
<employees>
  <employee id="1">
    <ssn>123-45-6789</ssn>
    <name>David Churvis</name>
```

Continued

Listing 30-7 *(continued)*

```
    </employee>
    <employee id="2">
      <ssn>312-54-9678</ssn>
      <name>Adam Churvis</name>
    </employee>
    <employee id="3">
      <ssn>231-45-8967</ssn>
      <name>Lisa Churvis</name>
    </employee>
  </employees>
  </cfsavecontent>

  <cfoutput>#HTMLEditFormat(XmlDoc)#</cfoutput>

  <hr>

  <h1>XML Object</h1>

  <cfset XmlObj = XmlParse(XmlDoc)>

  <cfdump var="#XmlObj#">
```

Running Listing 30-7 produces the output shown in Figure 30-5.

Notice that you have an XML object just like the one produced by `CFXML`.

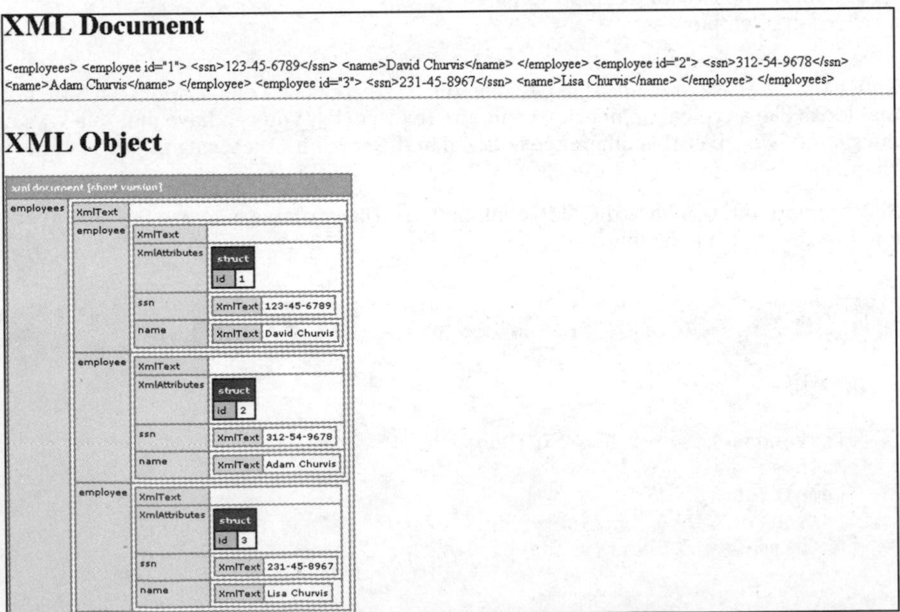

Figure 30-5: An XML document and its corresponding object.

Case sensitivity

According to standards, XML is case-sensitive. Most XML implementations, therefore, treat `<element>` and `<Element>` as two different things. By default, however, ColdFusion treats XML as case-insensitive; in other words, ColdFusion sees `<element>` and `<Element>` as the same thing. This difference can have far-reaching implications if you are communicating between ColdFusion and some other system, so use the guidelines:

✦ In using `CFXML`, `XmlParse()`, or `XmlNew()`, use the following forms of the tag or function:

```
<cfxml variable="XmlObj" casesensitive="True">
XmlParse(XmlDoc, True)
XmlNew(True)
```

✦ Always name your elements and attributes lowercase. If you look at the generalized XML that we use in this chapter, you see that we never use an uppercase element name or attribute name.

The code in this chapter doesn't follow the first guideline for brevity's sake, and we sometimes intercap our node names to make them more readable for the purpose of this book. Do notice, however, that we always pay careful attention to the case of an entity. In designing XML for production systems, always name items in lowercase unless your specifications compel you to do otherwise.

Accessing nodes

After you `CFDUMP` an XML object (take a look at Figure 20-4 again), you see what looks like a typical set of nested structures until you notice that multiple keys can have the same name and that every part of the structure has an `XmlText` item, leading to a kind of homogenous feel to the object.

Items in an XML object are called *nodes*. What's sometimes difficult to understand, however, is that every tag is a node, even if it contains just text. Attributes are another kind of node (although accessed differently—more on this topic later in this section).

To access the `name` node of the first employee of the XML object created in Listing 30-6, you would use the following syntax:

```
XmlObj.employees.employee[1].name
```

Much as with nested structures, you use dot notation to access nodes within an XML object. To follow the preceding notation, you're accessing the XML object and then the *root node*, which is named `employees`. (An XML document may have only one root node.) After I get to the `employees` node, notice (looking back to the XML document from Listing 30-7) that you have three `employee` nodes. You use array notation to access the first node (indexes start at one, as does a standard ColdFusion array) and then you find the `name` node of the first employee.

Dumping the `name` node produces the output shown in Figure 30-6.

It may seem strange, but accessing `XmlObj.employees.employee[1].name` doesn't give you the value of that node—`XmlObj.employees.employee[1].name` is the node itself. One of the most difficult things about using XML with ColdFusion is remembering to append `XmlText` to the end of your node references to get or set the value of a node, as in the following example:

```
XmlObj.employees.employee[1].name.XmlText
```

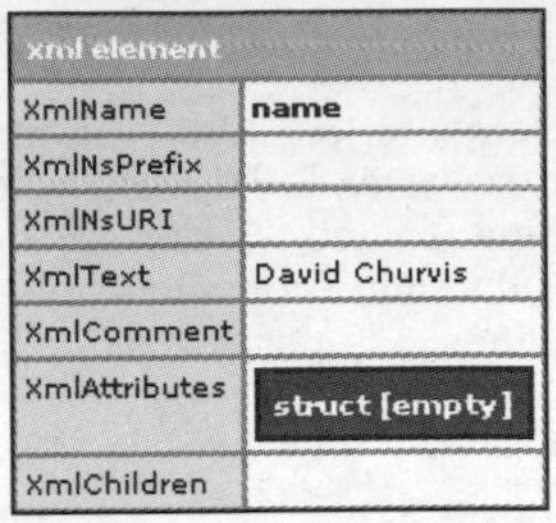

xml element	
XmlName	name
XmlNsPrefix	
XmlNsURI	
XmlText	David Churvis
XmlComment	
XmlAttributes	struct [empty]
XmlChildren	

Figure 30-6: The `name` node.

This method of accessing nodes is known as *short form*, where you use the node's name to access the node. If you don't know the name of the node ahead of time, however, you can use *long form* to access the node, as follows:

```
XmlObj.XmlRoot.XmlChildren[1].XmlChildren[2].XmlText
```

Long-form notation references nodes by their position relative to the root node rather than by a hierarchy of named nodes.

We prefer short-form notation wherever possible because it's easier to understand if you're familiar with the names of the XML nodes, and we're always familiar with the data structures that we're programming. And you can mix the two; in the following example, we're using both in the same node reference:

```
XmlObj.XmlRoot.employee[1].XmlChildren[2].XmlText
```

Accessing attributes is similar to accessing elements. A node may contain any number of attributes, which are simply key-value pairs. The collection of a node's attributes is contained in a structure named `XmlAttributes`, so you can use associative array notation to obtain the value of an attribute.

In the following code, for example, you're accessing the `id` attribute of the first `employee` element:

```
XmlObj.employees.employee[1].XmlAttributes["id"]
```

Make certain that you're familiar with the syntax for accessing XML nodes before continuing with this chapter.

Manipulating an XML object

The preceding section shows you how to access nodes in an XML object, but what about adding and modifying nodes? Functions for working with XML fall into two categories: *native XML functions* and *array and structure functions*.

XML functions

In the section "XML documents vs. XML objects," earlier in this chapter, you learn how to create a new XML object by using `CFXML` or `XmlParse()`, both of which use an existing XML document to create an XML object. You can also create a blank XML object by using `XmlNew()`, as follows:

```
<cfset NewXmlObj = XmlNew()>
```

After you have an XML object (regardless of how it was created), you can add elements to the object by using `XmlElemNew()`. Your first step in creating a completely new XML object is to create a root element, as follows:

```
<cfset NewRootElem = XmlElemNew(NewXmlObj, "myRootElement")>
```

After you *create* this root element, you *add* it to the XML object as follows:

```
<cfset NewXmlObj.XmlRoot = NewRootElem>
```

After you have a root element in your XML object, you can create child elements under the root. In the following example, you create a child element named myChildElement:

```
<cfset NewChildElem = XmlElemNew(NewXmlObj, "myChildElement")>
```

Then you add the child element to your XML object as follows:

```
<cfset NewXmlObj.myRootElement.XmlChildren[1] = NewChildElem>
```

Finally, you set the XmlText value of the child element to "Billy", as follows:

```
<cfset NewXmlObj.myRootElement.myChildElement.XmlText = "Billy">
```

As you would expect, you can get the value back out by using the same notation, as follows:

```
<cfoutput>#NewXmlObj.myRootElement.myChildElement.XmlText#</cfoutput>
```

You can get the XML from an object by using the ToString() function as follows:

```
<cfoutput>#ToString(NewXmlObj)#</cfoutput>
```

The output of ToString() looks as follows:

```
<?xml version="1.0" encoding="UTF-8"?>
<myRootElement><myChildElement>Billy</myChildElement></myRootElement>
```

Notice that as with WDDX, ToString() doesn't put any white space between tags.

Another native XML function—XmlChildPos()—helps if you have heterogeneous children (in other words, child elements of different names), as in Listing 30-8.

Listing 30-8: An XML packet with heterogeneous children

```
<?xml version="1.0" encoding="UTF-8"?>
<employee>
  <ssn>583-61-9274</ssn>
  <name>Herman Johnson</name>
  <responsibility>Programming</responsibility>
  <responsibility>Writing status reports</responsibility>
  <responsibility>Making coffee</responsibility>
  <responsibility>Sucking up to the boss</responsibility>
</employee>
```

Say that you want to add an element between the second and third responsibility elements. You know that you can access the third responsibility element as follows:

```
XmlObj.employee.responsibility[3]
```

But to add a new element, you need to know the location of the third responsibility element within <employee>'s XmlChildren array. You can get this index by using XmlChildPos(), as shown in Listing 30-9.

Listing 30-9: Adding another responsibility to the `employee` object

```
<cfxml variable="XmlObj">
<employee>
  <ssn>583-61-9274</ssn>
  <name>Herman Johnson</name>
  <responsibility>Programming</responsibility>
  <responsibility>Writing status reports</responsibility>
  <responsibility>Making coffee</responsibility>
  <responsibility>Sucking up to the boss</responsibility>
</employee>
</cfxml>

<cfdump var="#XmlObj#" label="Original Object">

<cfset ElemPos = XmlChildPos(XmlObj.employee, "responsibility", 3)>

<cfset NewElement = XmlElemNew(XmlObj, "responsibility")>
<cfset NewElement.XmlText = "Making copies">
<cfset success = ArrayInsertAt(XmlObj.employee.XmlChildren, ElemPos,
NewElement)>

<cfdump var="#XmlObj#" label="New Object">
```

Running Listing 30-9 produces the output shown in Figure 30-7.

Original Object - xml document [short version]

employee	XmlText	
	ssn	XmlText 583-61-9274
	name	XmlText Herman Johnson
	responsibility	XmlText Programming
	responsibility	XmlText Writing status reports
	responsibility	XmlText Making coffee
	responsibility	XmlText Sucking up to the boss

New Object - xml document [short version]

employee	XmlText	
	ssn	XmlText 583-61-9274
	name	XmlText Herman Johnson
	responsibility	XmlText Programming
	responsibility	XmlText Writing status reports
	responsibility	XmlText Making copies
	responsibility	XmlText Making coffee
	responsibility	XmlText Sucking up to the boss

Figure 30-7: Using `XmlChildPos()`.

The third `<responsibility>` node is also the fifth overall node under `<employee>`, so you use `XmlChildPos()` to translate the third `<responsibility>` into the fifth child. In other words, translate `responsibility[3]` to `XmlChildren[5]`.

Using array and structure functions with XML objects

Aside from the functions beginning with `Xml` that we describe in the preceding section, you can also use most of ColdFusion's array and structure functions with XML objects to modify elements and attributes.

The array functions always work over an `XmlChildren` array, and the structure functions always work over an `XmlAttributes` structure. If you want to delete the third child of the `employee` node, for example, you can use `ArrayDeleteAt()` as follows:

```
<cfset success = ArrayDeleteAt(XmlObj.employee.XmlChildren, 3)>
```

On the other hand, you can add an `ID` attribute to the employee node by using `StructInsert()` as follows:

```
<cfset success = StructInsert(XmlObj.employee.XmlAttributes, "id", 1)>
```

You can find a complete list of the array and structure functions that you can use with XML objects in *Developing Web Applications with ColdFusion*, which is part of the ColdFusion MX documentation set.

Creating XML from database content

XML is a useful data-interchange format, so the probability that you may create XML based on content from your database is only natural. Both Microsoft SQL Server and Oracle 9i have some manner of integrated XML capabilities, but these can be time-consuming and difficult to learn. A better solution for many developers is described in Listing 30-10, which creates an XML document based on the Company table and saves it to a file.

Listing 30-10: Marshalling database content into an XML format

```
<cfquery name="GetCompanies"
        datasource="#Request.MainDSN#">
SELECT
    CompanyID,
    CompanyName,
    Address,
    City,
    State,
    ZipCode,
    Comments
FROM
    Company
</cfquery>

<cfsavecontent variable="XMLDoc">
```

Continued

Listing 30-10 *(continued)*

```
<companies>
  <cfoutput query="GetCompanies">
  <company id="#CompanyID#">
    <name>#CompanyName#</name>
    <address>#Address#</address>
    <city>#City#</city>
    <state>#State#</state>
    <zipcode>#ZipCode#</zipcode>
    <comments>#Comments#</comments>
  </company>
  </cfoutput>
</companies>
</cfsavecontent>

<cffile action="WRITE"
        file="#ExpandPath('directory.xml')#"
        output="#XMLDoc#">
```

Running Listing 30-10 produces the following XML document file on disk:

```
<companies>
  <company id="13">
    <name>The Very Big Corporation of America</name>
    <address>5806 Glenn Hollow Lane</address>
    <city>Norcross</city>
    <state>GA</state>
    <zipcode>30071</zipcode>
    <comments>Sooner or later, you'll be owned by us.</comments>
  </company>
  <company id="14">
    <name>Ma's Homemade Pies</name>
    <address>5332 Courtland Court</address>
    <city>Abilene</city>
    <state>AL</state>
    <zipcode>29574</zipcode>
    <comments>The best homemade pies in the business!</comments>
  </company>
  <company id="15">
    <name>Shecky Records</name>
    <address>1548 High Point Freeway</address>
    <city>New York</city>
    <state>NY</state>
    <zipcode>00248</zipcode>
    <comments>What, me worry?</comments>
  </company>
</companies>
```

This method of putting database content into XML is a quick-and-dirty, yet surprisingly effective way of working with XML.

The Employee Directory

Listing 30-11 lists the XML file that is used for the XPath and XSL examples in the following sections of this chapter.

Listing 30-11: The XML file used for the remainder of this chapter (`empdirectory.xml`)

```
<?xml version="1.0"?>
<companies>
  <company id="13">
    <name>The Very Big Corporation of America</name>
    <comments>Sooner or later, you'll be owned by us.</comments>
    <rating>5</rating>
    <employees>
      <employee>
        <ssn>123-45-6789</ssn>
        <name>Churvis, Dave</name>
        <friend ssn="213-59-3005"/>
        <friend ssn="853-72-0192"/>
      </employee>
    </employees>
  </company>

  <company id="14">
    <name>Ma's Homemade Pies</name>
    <comments>The best homemade pies in the business!</comments>
    <rating>4</rating>
    <employees>
      <employee>
        <ssn>853-40-1954</ssn>
        <name>Johnson, Mabel</name>
        <friend ssn="853-40-1955"/>
        <friend ssn="853-72-0192"/>
      </employee>
      <employee>
        <ssn>853-40-1955</ssn>
        <name>Johnson, Penny</name>
        <friend ssn="853-40-1954"/>
        <friend ssn="853-72-0192"/>
      </employee>
      <employee>
        <ssn>853-72-0192</ssn>
        <name>Johnson, Mary Sue</name>
        <friend ssn="123-45-6789"/>
      </employee>
    </employees>
  </company>
```

Continued

Listing 30-11 *(continued)*

```
    <company id="15">
      <name>Shecky Records</name>
      <comments>What, me worry?</comments>
      <rating>6</rating>
      <employees>
        <employee>
          <ssn>213-59-3005</ssn>
          <name>Kaboom, Shecky</name>
          <friend ssn="123-45-6789"/>
        </employee>
        <employee>
          <ssn>385-10-2049</ssn>
          <name>Doe, John</name>
        </employee>
      </employees>
    </company>
  </companies>
```

We should explain what the <friend> element is. Every employee can have friends, and these are described by a `<friend>` element with an `ssn` attribute that matches the SSN of another employee in the document. This is used in the section "Using XSL Transformations," later in this chapter.

Using XPath to Search XML

Accessing the node of a large and complex XML object is impossible if you don't know exactly where the node is located. *XPath* is a query language for XML that enables you to find nodes within an arbitrarily complex XML object by using a flexible, intuitive syntax.

XPath is based on a directory-structure metaphor. To access the child node of a parent, you use a "parent/child" syntax, just as you would in a Web browser or file path. Listing 30-12, for example, reads the employee directory from an XML file and searches the document for `company name` nodes; then it outputs the results.

Listing 30-12: **Searching for company name nodes**

```
<cffile action="READ"
        file="#ExpandPath('empdirectory.xml')#"
        variable="XmlDoc">

<cfset XmlObj = XmlParse(XmlDoc)>
<cfset results = XmlSearch(XmlObj, "/companies/company/name")>

<cfdump var="#results#">
```

Notice the syntax of the search string. The path begins with `/`, meaning "start at the root of the document." From there, XPath selects the `companies` node, any nodes named `company` (of which you have three), and then the `name` node of each company node. Any node that matches that string is returned as an element in the array named `results`. Figure 30-8 shows the result of calling `XmlSearch()`.

array

1

xml element	
XmlName	**name**
XmlNsPrefix	
XmlNsURI	
XmlText	The Very Big Corporation of America
XmlComment	
XmlAttributes	struct [empty]
XmlChildren	

2

xml element	
XmlName	**name**
XmlNsPrefix	
XmlNsURI	
XmlText	Ma's Homemade Pies
XmlComment	
XmlAttributes	struct [empty]
XmlChildren	

3

xml element	
XmlName	**name**
XmlNsPrefix	
XmlNsURI	
XmlText	Shecky Records
XmlComment	
XmlAttributes	struct [empty]
XmlChildren	

Figure 30-8: The result of using `XmlSearch()` with `"/companies/company/name"`.

The result is an array of three XML elements, each corresponding to a company name.

Sometimes an XPath string beginning at the document root can get too long for effective development, especially in a deeply nested XML document such as the employee directory that we're using. Luckily, an XPath syntax is available that finds a node of a particular name anywhere within the document, as follows:

```
//name
```

If the XPath string begins with a double slash, XPath finds a matching node anywhere in the document. Searching on `//name` produces the result shown in Figure 30-9.

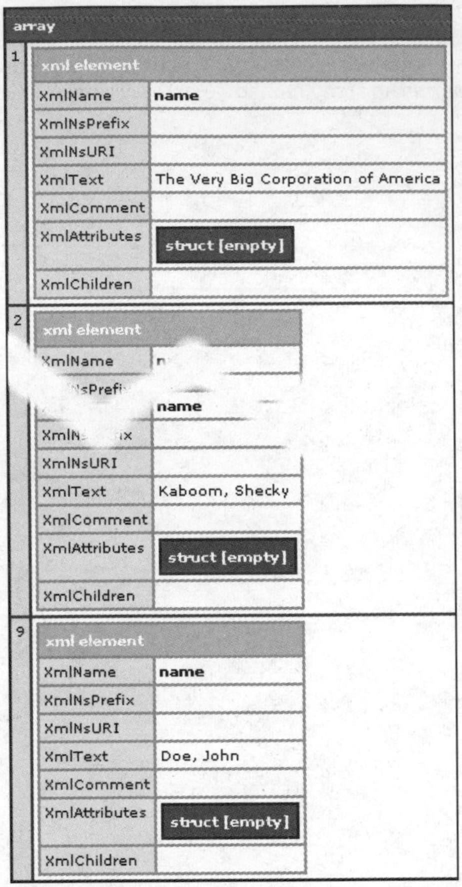

array

1	xml element	
	XmlName	name
	XmlNsPrefix	
	XmlNsURI	
	XmlText	The Very Big Corporation of America
	XmlComment	
	XmlAttributes	struct [empty]
	XmlChildren	

2	xml element	
	XmlName	name
	XmlNsPrefix	
	XmlNsURI	
	XmlText	Kaboom, Shecky
	XmlComment	
	XmlAttributes	struct [empty]
	XmlChildren	

9	xml element	
	XmlName	name
	XmlNsPrefix	
	XmlNsURI	
	XmlText	Doe, John
	XmlComment	
	XmlAttributes	struct [empty]
	XmlChildren	

Figure 30-9: The result of searching for `//name`.

What's going on here? Not only did `XmlSearch` return company names, but it returned employee names as well! Because using `//` means to find a matching node anywhere, and because both `company` and `employee` elements can have `name` elements underneath them, both types of `name` node are found.

To restrict the match so that it finds only company names, use the following syntax:

```
//company/name
```

Now XPath looks for `company` nodes regardless of where they are in the document and then selects the `name` node under each `company` node. Because XPath looks for `company` nodes before looking for `name` nodes, no employee names appear.

You can also restrict by the value of a tag attribute. If, for example, you want to find the company node with an `id` attribute of `13`, use the following syntax:

```
//company[@id = 13]
```

Whenever you see square brackets in an XPath expression, think "restriction," and whenever you see the @ symbol, think "attribute." In this case, you're telling XPath to find a `company` node anywhere in the XML document, but restrict the match to only those nodes with an `id` attribute with a value of `13`. Searching for this expression produces the result shown in Figure 30-10.

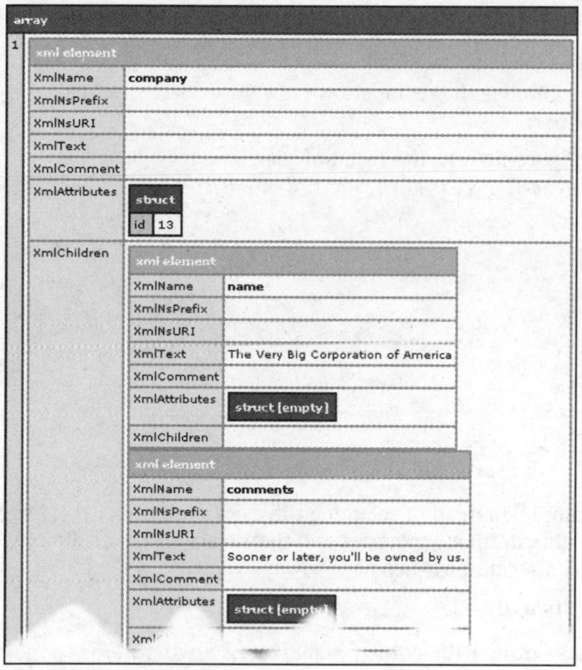

Figure 30-10: The result of searching for `//company[@id = 13]`.

Notice that only one `company` is returned, and that the company's `id` attribute is `13`.

You can also search based on a subelement of a node. You can, for example, search for the `employee` node with an `ssn` element's value of `"123-45-6789"` by using the following syntax:

```
//employee[ssn = "123-45-6789"]
```

XPath looks for `employee` nodes anywhere in the XML document and then restricts the found nodes to only those employees with an `ssn` element with a value of `"123-45-6789"`. Notice that since the `ssn` doesn't begin with an @ symbol, XPath looks for an *element* named `ssn` rather than an *attribute* named `ssn`.

You can also search based on a node's actual value by using XPath's dot operator, as in the following example:

```
//employee/ssn[. = "123-45-6789"]
```

Here's how XPath processes this statement:

1. XPath finds all `employee` elements anywhere in the XML document, regardless of their location.
2. XPath then finds all `ssn` elements directly underneath the `employee` nodes that it's already found.
3. XPath restricts the returned `ssn` elements to only those elements with a value of `"123-45-6789"`.

Running this search expression produces the result shown in Figure 30-11.

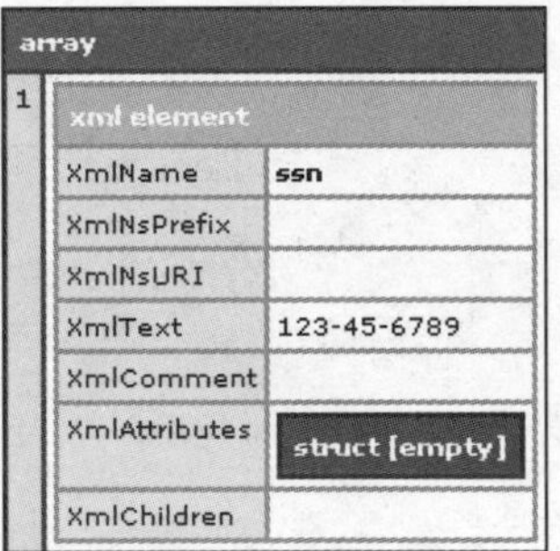

Figure 30-11: The result of searching for `//employee/ssn[. = "123-45-6789"]`.

Notice that, in the preceding example, instead of selecting the `employee` node, you inadvertently select the `ssn` node. To find matching `ssn` nodes and then reselect the containing `employee` node, you must use another new syntax, as follows:

```
//employee/ssn[. = "123-45-6789"]/..
```

Notice that, just as you would have done with a file system, you use two periods to move up one level in the hierarchy.

You can also use the following syntax to drill down further into a set of nodes:

```
//company[@id = 13]/employees/employee
```

XPath processes this expression as follows:

1. XPath searches for all `company` nodes anywhere in the XML document.
2. XPath restricts the set of `company` nodes to only the `company` with an `id` attribute with a value of `13`.
3. XPath then finds the `employees` node under the `company` found in Step 2.
4. Finally, XPath finds all `employee` nodes under the `employees` node found in Step 3.

Running that expression against the employee directory returns the output shown in Figure 30-12.

That's all the XPath that you need to know for now. What you've seen here is by no means a complete guide to XPath (as we haven't even touched on XPath functions, recursive descent, or node axes); this section is intended primarily as a guide to help you understand XSLT. To learn more about XPath, check out the XPath tutorial at `www.zvon.org`.

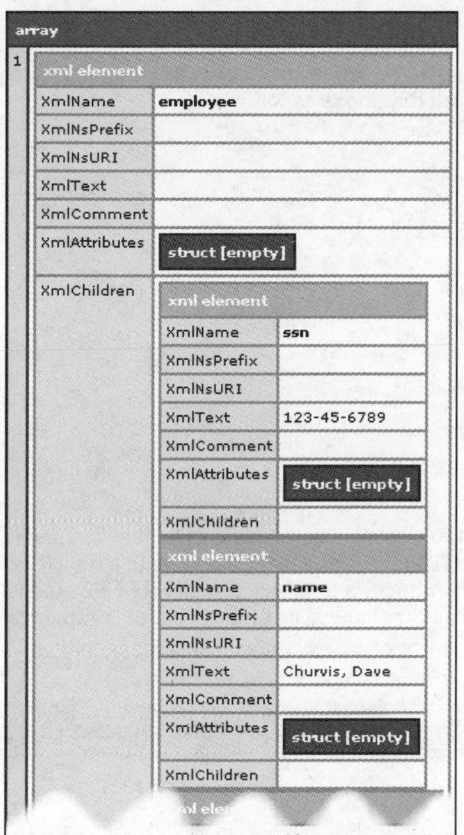

Figure 30-12: The result of searching for `//company[@id = 13]/employees/employee`.

Using XSL Transformations

XML's most powerful feature isn't its structured nature, its ease of use, or even the powerful XPath syntax that you see in the preceding section. The most powerful feature of XML is its capability to be transformed into any other language (anything from another XML format to HTML, to even source code such as C++ or Java). This is done by using another language named *XSLT*, which stands for e*X*tensible *S*tylesheet *L*anguage for *T*ransformations.

This chapter shows only how to transform XML into HTML, because that's likely most of what you do in ColdFusion.

Basic transformations

Look back at empdirectory.xml from Listing 30-11. You want to use the company data in empdirectory.xml to create a table structure that looks as follows:

```
<table>
  <tr>
    <td>13</td>
    <td>The Very Big Corporation of America</td>
  </tr>
  <tr>
    <td>14</td>
    <td>Ma's Homemade Pies</td>
  </tr>
  <tr>
    <td>15</td>
    <td>Shecky Records</td>
  </tr>
</table>
```

To transform empdirectory.xml into that table, you must create a *stylesheet* that tells ColdFusion how to translate pure XML into HTML, and you must also create a *transformer* that applies that stylesheet to the XML and produces a finished, transformed result. Listing 30-13 shows a stylesheet that transforms empdirectory.xml into the list of companies that we just showed you.

Listing 30-13: An XSL stylesheet to get a listing of companies

```
<xsl:transform
  version="1.0"
  xmlns:xsl="http://www.w3.org/1999/XSL/Transform">

<xsl:output omit-xml-declaration="yes"/>

<xsl:template match="companies">
  <table>
    <xsl:apply-templates/>
  </table>
</xsl:template>

<xsl:template match="company">
  <tr>
    <td>
      <xsl:value-of select="@id"/>
    </td>
    <td>
      <xsl:value-of select="name"/>
    </td>
  </tr>
</xsl:template>

</xsl:transform>
```

The xsl:transform element in Listing 30-13 is the same for every XSL stylesheet you build (until you get into some of the really advanced XSL out there, which is beyond the scope of this book). xsl:transform tells the XSL processor that this document is an XSL stylesheet and tells the processor what version of the standard is in use. The xsl:output in this case suppresses the output of the <?xml ...?> header that would ordinarily appear in the output buffer. The rest of these tags are described later in this section.

Save Listing 30-13 in a file named Listing30-13.xsl and put it in the same directory as Listing30-14.cfm.

Listing 30-14 is the transformer.

Listing 30-14: The code used to transform empdirectory.xml into a list of companies

```
<cffile action="READ"
        file="#ExpandPath('empdirectory.xml')#"
        variable="XmlDoc">

<cffile action="READ"
        file="#ExpandPath('Listing30-13.xsl')#"
        variable="XslDoc">

<cfoutput>#XmlTransform(XmlDoc, XslDoc)#</cfoutput>
```

Technically the transformer is the XmlTransform() function; the rest is just supporting code. Running Listing 30-14 produces the output shown in Figure 30-13.

13 The Very Big Corporation of America
14 Ma's Homemade Pies
15 Shecky Records

Figure 30-13: The result of a simple XSL transformation.

To transform XML according to a stylesheet, just use the XmlTransform() function, as shown in Listing 30-14. XmlTransform() returns the transformed XML—in this case, the finished HTML table. From this point forward in the chapter, we omit the ColdFusion code that performs the transformation and concentrate solely on the XSLT code.

Now go back to Listing 30-13 as we walk you through the XSLT process in the following list:

1. The transformer parses the XML document (empdirectory.xml) into an XML object so that ColdFusion can work with it. The transformation starts at the XML object's root node, which is named companies, as follows:

```
<companies>
  <company id="13">
    <name>The Very Big Corporation of America</name>
    <comments>Sooner or later, you'll be owned by us.</comments>
    . . .
```

```
   </company>

   <company id="14">
     . . .
   </company>

   <company id="15">
     . . .
   </company>
</companies>
```

2. The transformation looks in the XSL document to find an `<xsl:template>` tag with a `match` attribute that matches the name of the current node. In this case, the transformer finds the `<xsl:template match="companies">` tag, as in the following code:

   ```
   <xsl:template match="companies">
     <table>
       <xsl:apply-templates/>
     </table>
   </xsl:template>
   ```

3. The first thing inside the `<xsl:template>` is an opening `<table>` tag, so the transformer puts a `<table>` tag in the output buffer, as follows:

   ```
   <xsl:template match="companies">
     <table>
       <xsl:apply-templates/>
     </table>
   </xsl:template>
   ```

4. The next XSL tag is `<xsl:apply-templates>`, which tells the transformer to go back to the XML document and process all *the children* of the current node, as shown in the following code:

   The XSL Stylesheet:

   ```
   <xsl:template match="companies">
     <table>
       <xsl:apply-templates/>
     </table>
   </xsl:template>
   ```

   The XML:

   ```
   <companies>
     <company id="13">
     . . .
     </company>

     <company id="14">
     . . .
     </company>

     <company id="15">
     . . .
     </company>
   </companies>
   ```

5. The first node of <companies> is a <company id="13"> node, which becomes the current node. The transformer then tries to find an <xsl:template> tag that matches "company", as follows:

```
<xsl:template match="company">
  <tr>
    <td>
      <xsl:value-of select="@id"/>
    </td>
    <td>
      <xsl:value-of select="name"/>
    </td>
  </tr>
</xsl:template>
```

6. The transformer now begins executing the company template. The transformer puts a <tr> and a <td> into the output buffer, as follows:

```
<xsl:template match="company">
  <tr>
    <td>
      <xsl:value-of select="@id"/>
    </td>
    <td>
      <xsl:value-of select="name"/>
    </td>
  </tr>
</xsl:template>
```

7. The transformer now encounters <xsl:value-of>, which tells the transformer to execute an XPath search starting at the current node and put the value of the search into the output buffer. The XPath expression is "@id", which tells the transformer to find the id attribute of the current node, which in this case is 13. The transformer puts 13 into the output buffer, as follows:

```
<xsl:template match="company">
  <tr>
    <td>
      <xsl:value-of select="@id"/>
    </td>
    <td>
      <xsl:value-of select="name"/>
    </td>
  </tr>
</xsl:template>
```

8. The next tags after the <xsl:value-of> are </td> and <td>, which the transformer puts into the output buffer, as follows:

```
<xsl:template match="company">
  <tr>
    <td>
      <xsl:value-of select="@id"/>
    </td>
    <td>
```

```
        <xsl:value-of select="name"/>
      </td>
    </tr>
  </xsl:template>
```

9. Next comes another `<xsl:value-of>`, this time selecting the value of the `"name"` element inside the current node (in this case, `The Very Big Corporation of America`). The transformer puts the company name into the output buffer, as follows:

```
<xsl:template match="company">
  <tr>
    <td>
      <xsl:value-of select="@id"/>
    </td>
    <td>
      <xsl:value-of select="name"/>
    </td>
  </tr>
</xsl:template>
```

10. After processing the second `<xsl:value-of>`, the transformer puts the closing `</td>` and `</tr>` for this row into the output buffer and exits the current template, as follows:

```
<xsl:template match="company">
  <tr>
    <td>
      <xsl:value-of select="@id"/>
    </td>
    <td>
      <xsl:value-of select="name"/>
    </td>
  </tr>
</xsl:template>
```

11. Remember that the transformer is currently looping over the children of `<companies>`, so the transformer repeats Steps 5 through 10 two more times (because two more children are left to process), as follows:

```
<companies>
  <company id="13">
  . . .
  </company>

  <company id="14">
  . . .
  </company>

  <company id="15">
  . . .
  </company>
</companies>
```

12. After the transformer finishes looping over the child nodes of `<companies>`, the `<xsl:apply-templates>` tag originally called in Step 4 is now finished executing, so the transformer puts the ending `</table>` tag into the output buffer, as follows:

```
<xsl:template match="companies">
  <table>
    <xsl:apply-templates/>
  </table>
</xsl:template>
```

13. The output buffer is now filled with the completed instructions from the XSL stylesheet, so the contents of the output buffer become the return value of the `XmlTransform(XmlDoc, XslDoc)` function, as follows:

```
<table>
  <tr>
    <td>13</td>
    <td>The Very Big Corporation of America</td>
  </tr>
  <tr>
    <td>14</td>
    <td>Ma's Homemade Pies</td>
  </tr>
  <tr>
    <td>15</td>
    <td>Shecky Records</td>
  </tr>
</table>
```

The key thing to understand here is that the XML file drives the XSL transformation and not the other way around. One analogy that sometimes helps is to think of the templates in the XSL document as functions and the XML file as the code that calls those functions. Make sure that you understand Steps 1 through 12 before moving on, because from this point forward, we are only going to build on these concepts.

Next you're going to transform the XML in a different way. Instead of getting a list of companies, you're going to get a list of employees that looks as shown in Figure 30-14.

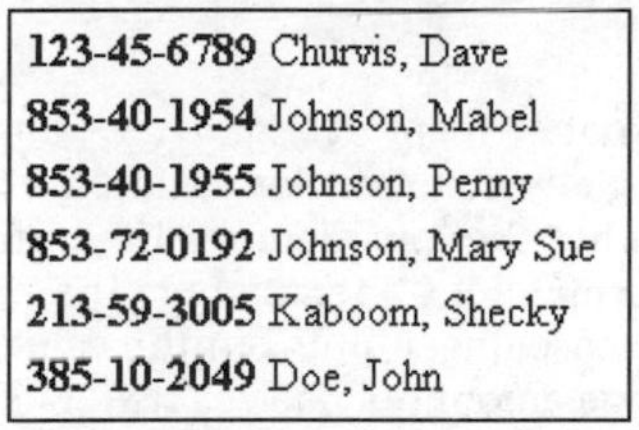

123-45-6789	Churvis, Dave
853-40-1954	Johnson, Mabel
853-40-1955	Johnson, Penny
853-72-0192	Johnson, Mary Sue
213-59-3005	Kaboom, Shecky
385-10-2049	Doe, John

Figure 30-14: The goal of the transformation described in Listing 30-15.

You may notice that no company information is listed here. Listing 30-15 shows the stylesheet that we used to produce the employee list.

Listing 30-15: A stylesheet to get a list of employees

```
<xsl:transform
  version="1.0"
  xmlns:xsl="http://www.w3.org/1999/XSL/Transform">

<xsl:output omit-xml-declaration="yes"/>

<xsl:template match="companies">
  <table>
    <xsl:apply-templates select="//employee"/>
  </table>
</xsl:template>

<xsl:template match="employee">
  <tr>
    <xsl:apply-templates/>
  </tr>
</xsl:template>

<xsl:template match="ssn">
  <td>
  <b>
    <xsl:value-of select="."/>
  </b>
  </td>
</xsl:template>

<xsl:template match="name">
  <td>
    <xsl:value-of select="."/>
  </td>
</xsl:template>

</xsl:transform>
```

Notice that, you again have a template that matches the root element <companies>, but you may be wondering why, because this listing is not showing any company information. The reason is simple: If you don't include a template that matches the root element, the transformer starts searching the document until it finds a node matching a template in the stylesheet. The problem is that, while the transformer is searching, it puts out the values of any nodes that it finds along the way, which puts out a large amount of useless text. Enabling the transformer to match the root node by including a template that matches the root node avoids this useless text altogether.

Because you're not including any company information in your list, you can't just use <xsl:apply-templates> as you did in Listing 30-13 because that would loop over <company> nodes rather than <employee> nodes. To skip <company> nodes, you use the optional select attribute of <xsl:apply-templates>, which tells the transformer to loop over all nodes matching "//employee", as follows:

```
<xsl:apply-templates select="//employee"/>
```

You want each employee element to resolve into a row in your HTML table, so the employee template puts out a table row and continues applying templates to the child elements of <employee>.

The last two templates in your XSL document match <ssn> and <name> elements. (Because you don't match <friend>, and <friend> has no content, <friend> elements are effectively ignored.) Both templates use <xsl:value-of select="."/>, which puts out the value of the current node (meaning the same node that matches the template).

Following is the HTML table that results from this transformation:

```
<table>
  <tr>
    <td>
      <b>123-45-6789</b>
    </td>
    <td>Churvis, Dave</td>
  </tr>
  <tr>
    <td>
      <b>853-40-1954</b>
    </td>
    <td>Johnson, Mabel</td>
  </tr>
  <tr>
    <td>
      <b>853-40-1955</b>
    </td>
    <td>Johnson, Penny</td>
  </tr>
  <tr>
    <td>
      <b>853-72-0192</b>
    </td>
    <td>Johnson, Mary Sue</td>
  </tr>
  <tr>
    <td>
      <b>213-59-3005</b>
    </td>
    <td>Kaboom, Shecky</td>
  </tr>
  <tr>
    <td>
      <b>385-10-2049</b>
    </td>
    <td>Doe, John</td>
  </tr>
</table>
```

Using if and choose statements

XSLT has two conditional execution tags: `<xsl:if>` and `<xsl:choose>`. `<xsl:if>` acts as a traditional `if` statement, and `<xsl:choose>` acts somewhat as a traditional switch/case statement.

In Listing 30-16, you go back to creating a list of companies, but you add a third column that tells whether a given company has more than one employee.

Listing 30-16: Using `<xsl:if>`

```
<xsl:transform
    version="1.0"
    xmlns:xsl="http://www.w3.org/1999/XSL/Transform">

<xsl:output omit-xml-declaration="yes"/>

<xsl:template match="companies">
  <table>
    <tr>
      <td>Name</td>
      <td>Comments</td>
      <td> </td>
    </tr>
    <xsl:apply-templates/>
  </table>
</xsl:template>

<xsl:template match="company">
  <tr>
    <td>
      <xsl:value-of select="name"/>
    </td>
    <td>
      <xsl:value-of select="comments"/>
    </td>
    <td>
      <xsl:if test="count(employees/employee) > 1">
        This company has multiple employees.
      </xsl:if>
      <xsl:if test="not(count(employees/employee) > 1)">
        This company does not have multiple employees.
      </xsl:if>
    </td>
  </tr>
</xsl:template>

</xsl:transform>
```

`count(employees/employee)` is an XPath function that gets the number of nodes of a particular type underneath the current node.

You may be surprised to learn that you have no `<xsl:else>`; instead, you must duplicate the condition in a second `<xsl:if>` tag and surround the second condition with `not()` as we do in Listing 30-16. Listing 30-16 produces the following HTML if run against `empdirectory.xml`:

```
<table>
  <tr>
    <td>Name</td>
    <td>Comments</td>
    <td></td>
  </tr>
  <tr>
    <td>The Very Big Corporation of America</td>
    <td>Sooner or later, you'll be owned by us.</td>
    <td>
      This company does not have multiple employees.
    </td>
  </tr>
  <tr>
    <td>Ma's Homemade Pies</td>
    <td>The best homemade pies in the business!</td>
    <td>
      This company has multiple employees.
    </td>
  </tr>
  <tr>
    <td>Shecky Records</td>
    <td>What, me worry?</td>
    <td>
      This company has multiple employees.
    </td>
  </tr>
</table>
```

We mention earlier in this section that `<xsl:choose>` is like a switch/case statement, but this is only partly true. As in a typical switch/case statement, `<xsl:choose>` follows one of many paths of execution; instead of evaluating a single expression, however, `<xsl:choose>` evaluates multiple expressions until it finds one that's true. Listing 30-17 shows an example of `<xsl:choose>` where you're converting from a numeric rating to a descriptive text rating.

Listing 30-17: Using `<xsl:choose>`

```
<xsl:transform
    version="1.0"
    xmlns:xsl="http://www.w3.org/1999/XSL/Transform">

<xsl:output omit-xml-declaration="yes"/>
```

Continued

Listing 30-17 *(continued)*

```
<xsl:template match="companies">
  <table>
    <tr>
      <th>Name</th>
      <th>Comments</th>
      <th>Rating</th>
    </tr>
    <xsl:apply-templates/>
  </table>
</xsl:template>
<xsl:template match="company">
  <tr>
    <td>
      <xsl:value-of select="name"/>
    </td>
    <td>
      <xsl:value-of select="comments"/>
    </td>
    <td>
      <xsl:choose>
        <xsl:when test="rating=1">Bad</xsl:when>
        <xsl:when test="rating=2">Poor</xsl:when>
        <xsl:when test="rating=3">Fair</xsl:when>
        <xsl:when test="rating=4">Good</xsl:when>
        <xsl:when test="rating=5">Superior</xsl:when>
        <xsl:otherwise>Rockin!</xsl:otherwise>
      </xsl:choose>
    </td>
  </tr>
</xsl:template>

</xsl:transform>
```

Running Listing 30-17 produces the following HTML:

```
<table>
  <tr>
    <th>Name</th>
    <th>Comments</th>
    <th>Rating</th>
  </tr>
  <tr>
    <td>The Very Big Corporation of America</td>
    <td>Sooner or later, you'll be owned by us.</td>
    <td>Superior</td>
  </tr>
  <tr>
    <td>Ma's Homemade Pies</td>
    <td>The best homemade pies in the business!</td>
    <td>Good</td>
```

```
    </tr>
    <tr>
      <td>Shecky Records</td>
      <td>What, me worry?</td>
      <td>Rockin!</td>
    </tr>
  </table>
```

You can almost think of `<xsl:choose>` as a series of `if/else-if/else` statements rather than as a switch/case statement.

Looping over nodes

You've already seen one form of looping over a set of nodes when you saw `xsl:apply-templates` in action. At times, however, you want finer control over the looping process, and for that you use `<xsl:for-each>`, as shown in Listing 30-18.

Listing 30-18: Looping over nodes by using `xsl:for-each`

```
<xsl:transform
    version="1.0"
    xmlns:xsl="http://www.w3.org/1999/XSL/Transform">

<xsl:output omit-xml-declaration="yes"/>

<xsl:template match="companies">
  <table>
    <tr>
      <th>SSN</th>
      <th>Name</th>
      <th>Friends</th>
    </tr>
    <xsl:apply-templates select="//employee"/>
  </table>
</xsl:template>

<xsl:template match="employee">
  <tr>
    <td>
      <xsl:value-of select="ssn"/>
    </td>
    <td>
      <xsl:value-of select="name"/>
    </td>
    <td>
      <xsl:for-each select="friend">
        <xsl:value-of select="@ssn"/><br/>
      </xsl:for-each>
    </td>
  </tr>
</xsl:template>

</xsl:transform>
```

Whenever the transformer encounters `<xsl:for-each>`, it selects all the `<friend>` elements under the current `<employee>` node. The transformer then loops over the selected elements, using `<xsl:value-of>` to extract the `SSN` attribute of each `friend` node and place the `SSN` in the table. The resulting HTML looks as follows:

```
<table>
  <tr>
    <th>SSN</th>
    <th>Name</th>
    <th>Friends</th>
  </tr>
  <tr>
    <td>123-45-6789</td>
    <td>Churvis, Dave</td>
    <td>
      213-59-3005<br />
      853-72-0192<br />
    </td>
  </tr>
  <tr>
    <td>853-40-1954</td>
    <td>Johnson, Mabel</td>
    <td>
      853-40-1955<br />
      853-72-0192<br />
    </td>
  </tr>
  <tr>
    <td>853-40-1955</td>
    <td>Johnson, Penny</td>
    <td>
      853-40-1954<br />
      853-72-0192<br />
    </td>
  </tr>
  <tr>
    <td>853-72-0192</td>
    <td>Johnson, Mary Sue</td>
    <td>
      123-45-6789<br />
    </td>
  </tr>
  <tr>
    <td>213-59-3005</td>
    <td>Kaboom, Shecky</td>
    <td>
      123-45-6789<br />
    </td>
  </tr>
  <tr>
    <td>385-10-2049</td>
    <td>Doe, John</td>
    <td></td>
  </tr>
</table>
```

The following section extends this example by replacing the friend's ssn with the friend's name.

Using named templates

We mention in the section "Basic transformations," earlier in this chapter that you can think of XSL templates as functions that are called by XML nodes. This section extends that metaphor even farther because named templates are very much like functions.

Listing 30-19 builds on Listing 30-18 by replacing the list of ssns with a list of names.

Listing 30-19: Using a named template to look up the name of a friend

```
<xsl:transform
    version="1.0"
    xmlns:xsl="http://www.w3.org/1999/XSL/Transform">

<xsl:output omit-xml-declaration="yes"/>

<xsl:template match="companies">
  <table>
    <tr>
      <th>SSN</th>
      <th>Name</th>
      <th>Friends</th>
    </tr>
    <xsl:apply-templates select="//employee"/>
  </table>
</xsl:template>

<xsl:template match="employee">
  <tr>
    <td>
      <xsl:value-of select="ssn"/>
    </td>
    <td>
      <xsl:value-of select="name"/>
    </td>
    <td>
      <xsl:for-each select="friend">
        <xsl:call-template name="GetFriend">
          <xsl:with-param name="ssn" select="@ssn"/>
        </xsl:call-template>
        <br/>
      </xsl:for-each>
    </td>
  </tr>
</xsl:template>
```

Continued

Listing 30-19 *(continued)*

```
<xsl:template name="GetFriend">
  <xsl:param name="ssn"/>

  <xsl:value-of select="//employee[ssn = $ssn]/name"/>
</xsl:template>

</xsl:transform>
```

What's going on here? Instead of using `<xsl:value-of>` to retrieve the `ssn`, you are calling a template to look up the name of the employee with that SSN. `<xsl:call-template>` tells the transformer to execute a specific template (in this case, `GetFriend`). `GetFriend` expects a parameter named `ssn`, and you pass the `ssn` by using `<xsl:with-param>`. Inside the template, you use `<xsl:value-of>` to look up the employee's name. (Notice the use of XPath; also notice that you're using `$ssn` to refer to the variable).

Using Listing 30-19 gives you the following HTML as output:

```
<table>
  <tr>
    <th>SSN</th>
    <th>Name</th>
    <th>Friends</th>
  </tr>
  <tr>
    <td>123-45-6789</td>
    <td>Churvis, Dave</td>
    <td>
      Kaboom, Shecky<br />
      Johnson, Mary Sue<br />
    </td>
  </tr>
  <tr>
    <td>853-40-1954</td>
    <td>Johnson, Mabel</td>
    <td>
      Johnson, Penny<br />
      Johnson, Mary Sue<br />
    </td>
  </tr>
  <tr>
    <td>853-40-1955</td>
    <td>Johnson, Penny</td>
    <td>
      Johnson, Mabel<br />
      Johnson, Mary Sue<br />
    </td>
  </tr>
  <tr>
    <td>853-72-0192</td>
    <td>Johnson, Mary Sue</td>
    <td>
```

```
        Churvis, Dave<br />
      </td>
    </tr>
    <tr>
      <td>213-59-3005</td>
      <td>Kaboom, Shecky</td>
      <td>
        Churvis, Dave<br />
      </td>
    </tr>
    <tr>
      <td>385-10-2049</td>
      <td>Doe, John</td>
      <td></td>
    </tr>
  </table>
```

Named templates are typically a rather advanced topic within XSL; what we've shown you here only scratches the surface of their power. Again, `www.zvon.org` is a great resource for learning more details about XML technologies.

Putting it all together: A complex transformation

The XSL stylesheets in this chapter all present one concept at a time. This is probably not very realistic, however, because you usually create complex content requiring a combination of multiple XSL techniques. Figure 30-15 shows a report that we want you to produce by using XSLT.

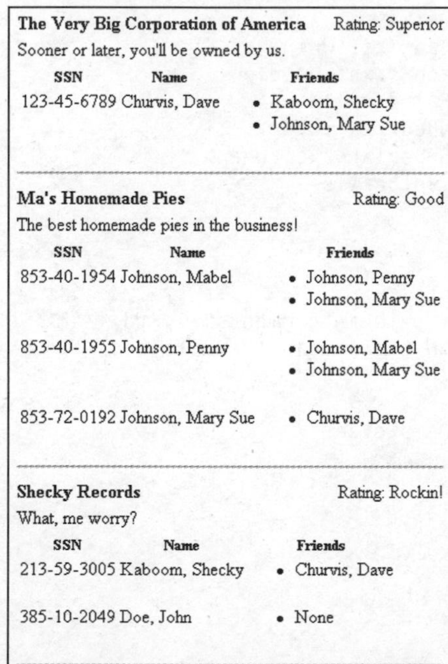

Figure 30-15: A report created with XSLT.

To produce this report, you create a stylesheet using all the concepts that we've presented in this chapter. Listing 30-20 uses inline comments to describe the action of this stylesheet.

Listing 30-20: A complex transformation

```
<xsl:transform
    version="1.0"
    xmlns:xsl="http://www.w3.org/1999/XSL/Transform">

<xsl:output omit-xml-declaration="yes"/>

<!-- This template matches the root node -->
<xsl:template match="companies">
  <table>
    <xsl:apply-templates/>
  </table>
</xsl:template>

<!-- Each company produces a section of the table with four rows -->
<xsl:template match="company">
  <!-- The first row is the company name and rating -->
  <tr>
    <td>
      <b><xsl:value-of select="name"/></b>
    </td>
    <td style="text-align: right;">
      Rating:
      <xsl:choose>
        <xsl:when test="rating=1">Bad</xsl:when>
        <xsl:when test="rating=2">Poor</xsl:when>
        <xsl:when test="rating=3">Fair</xsl:when>
        <xsl:when test="rating=4">Good</xsl:when>
        <xsl:when test="rating=5">Superior</xsl:when>
        <xsl:otherwise>Rockin!</xsl:otherwise>
      </xsl:choose>
    </td>
  </tr>
  <!-- The second row is the comments -->
  <tr><td colspan="2"><xsl:value-of select="comments"/></td></tr>
  <!-- The third row is a table with the company's employees -->
  <tr>
    <td colspan="2">
      <xsl:apply-templates select="employees"/>
    </td>
  </tr>
  <!-- The fourth row is a horizontal rule -->
  <tr>
    <td colspan="2"><hr/></td>
  </tr>
</xsl:template>

<!-- This template matches the employees node -->
<!--
```

```
This is much like the companies node; it shows the outer table tags and
a header row.
-->
<xsl:template match="employees">
  <table>
    <tr>
      <th><small>SSN</small></th>
      <th><small>Name</small></th>
      <th><small>Friends</small></th>
    </tr>
    <xsl:apply-templates/>
  </table>
</xsl:template>

<!-- This template displays a single employee row. -->
<xsl:template match="employee">
  <tr>
    <!-- The SSN and Name are simple element retrievals -->
    <td style="vertical-align: top;">
      <xsl:value-of select="ssn"/>
    </td>
    <td style="vertical-align: top;">
      <xsl:value-of select="name"/>
    </td>
    <td style="vertical-align: top;">
      <ul>
        <!-- if this employee has no friends, I output "None" -->
        <xsl:if test="count(friend) = 0">
        <li>None</li>
        </xsl:if>

        <!-- if this employee has friends, I put them out in a loop -->
        <xsl:if test="count(friend) > 0">
          <xsl:for-each select="friend">
            <li>
            <!-- I call GetFriend, passing the SSN attribute of the
current node -->
            <xsl:call-template name="GetFriend">
              <xsl:with-param name="ssn" select="@ssn"/>
            </xsl:call-template>
            </li>
          </xsl:for-each>
        </xsl:if>
      </ul>
    </td>
  </tr>
</xsl:template>

<!-- This is a named template that outputs the name of an employee
based on his SSN -->
<xsl:template name="GetFriend">
  <xsl:param name="ssn"/>
```

Continued

Listing 30-20 *(continued)*

```
    <xsl:value-of select="//employee[ssn = $ssn]/name"/>
  </xsl:template>

  </xsl:transform>
```

Executing Listing 30-20 produces the following HTML (see whether you can figure out where each part of the HTML comes from):

```
<table>
  <tr>
    <td><b>The Very Big Corporation of America</b></td>
    <td style="text-align: right;">Rating: Superior</td>
  </tr>
  <tr>
    <td colspan="2">Sooner or later, you'll be owned by us.</td>
  </tr>
  <tr>
    <td colspan="2">
      <table>
        <tr>
          <th><small>SSN</small></th>
          <th><small>Name</small></th>
          <th><small>Friends</small></th>
        </tr>
        <tr>
          <td style="vertical-align: top;">123-45-6789</td>
          <td style="vertical-align: top;">Churvis, Dave</td>
          <td style="vertical-align: top;">
            <ul>
              <li>Kaboom, Shecky</li>
              <li>Johnson, Mary Sue</li>
            </ul>
          </td>
        </tr>
      </table>
    </td>
  </tr>
  <tr><td colspan="2"><hr /></td></tr>

  <tr>
    <td><b>Ma&#39;s Homemade Pies</b></td>
    <td style="text-align: right;">Rating: Good</td>
  </tr>
  <tr>
    <td colspan="2">The best homemade pies in the business!</td>
  </tr>
  <tr>
    <td colspan="2">
      <table>
        <tr>
```

```
        <th><small>SSN</small></th>
        <th><small>Name</small></th>
        <th><small>Friends</small></th>
      </tr>
      <tr>
        <td style="vertical-align: top;">853-40-1954</td>
        <td style="vertical-align: top;">Johnson, Mabel</td>
        <td style="vertical-align: top;">
          <ul>
            <li>Johnson, Penny</li>
            <li>Johnson, Mary Sue</li>
          </ul>
        </td>
      </tr>
      <tr>
        <td style="vertical-align: top;">853-40-1955</td>
        <td style="vertical-align: top;">Johnson, Penny</td>
        <td style="vertical-align: top;">
          <ul>
            <li>Johnson, Mabel</li>
            <li>Johnson, Mary Sue</li>
          </ul>
        </td>
      </tr>
      <tr>
        <td style="vertical-align: top;">853-72-0192</td>
        <td style="vertical-align: top;">Johnson, Mary Sue</td>
        <td style="vertical-align: top;">
          <ul>
            <li>Churvis, Dave</li>
          </ul>
        </td>
      </tr>
    </table>
  </td>
</tr>
<tr><td colspan="2"><hr /></td></tr>

<tr>
  <td><b>Shecky Records</b></td>
  <td style="text-align: right;">Rating: Rockin!</td>
</tr>
<tr>
  <td colspan="2">What, me worry?</td>
</tr>
<tr>
  <td colspan="2">
    <table>
      <tr>
        <th><small>SSN</small></th>
        <th><small>Name</small></th>
        <th><small>Friends</small></th>
      </tr>
      <tr>
```

```
            <td style="vertical-align: top;">213-59-3005</td>
            <td style="vertical-align: top;">Kaboom, Shecky</td>
            <td style="vertical-align: top;">
              <ul>
                <li>Churvis, Dave</li>
              </ul>
            </td>
          </tr>
          <tr>
            <td style="vertical-align: top;">385-10-2049</td>
            <td style="vertical-align: top;">Doe, John</td>
            <td style="vertical-align: top;">
              <ul>
                <li>None</li>
              </ul>
            </td>
          </tr>
        </table>
      </td>
    </tr>
    <tr><td colspan="2"><hr /></td></tr>
  </table>
```

You can see that, by building on what you learn throughout this chapter, you can produce some pretty complicated stuff, but you may not believe that the report that we just showed you is small fry compared to what XSL can *really* do.

Summary

In this chapter you learn how to use WDDX to exchange data between requests in a consistent fashion, and how to serialize and deserialize data between CFML and WDDX. You also learn how to create XML documents, how to search those XML documents by using XPath, and finally, how to transform the XML into HTML by using XSLT.

XML is a hot topic in the Internet world for a reason. XML is such a flexible language (indeed, it stands for eXtensible Markup Language) that it can be used to describe *anything*. Just take a look at the XML Registry at `www.xml.org` to get a feel for the things that XML can describe, some of which are as follows:

- ✦ MathML is defined by the World Wide Web Consortium (W3C) as a way for mathematicians and scientists to communicate formulas using a clearly defined XML-based syntax.
- ✦ MusicXML enables you to use XML to define a musical score in a rigid and concise fashion.
- ✦ ebXML helps define Business-to-Business (B2B) transactions among disparate businesses.

These are just the first three formats that caught our eye; you find dozens more. Our purpose in showing these examples is to illustrate the many different kinds of information that can be stored in an XML format, meaning that XML's influence in the development world can't help but increase.

Start using XML now. If you haven't already done so, revisit Chapter 25 and make your own version of a Web service that produces XML and a consumer that transforms it into displayable HTML content.

✦ ✦ ✦

31 CHAPTER

Communicating via Mail, FTP, and HTTP

In This Chapter

Sending e-mail by using CFMAIL

Transferring files by using CFFTP

Connecting to other Web servers by using CFHTTP

At some point in creating a Web application, you're likely to want to communicate with other servers or other users. Three features in ColdFusion MX provide that capability: CFMAIL, CFFTP, and CFHTTP.

In this chapter, we introduce the basics of working with these features. They're not new to (nor updated too much for) ColdFusion MX, but they're important to understand, especially CFMAIL.

CFMAIL, enables you to send e-mail from within your application. This is a very powerful feature, and if you're familiar with mail merging in a word processor, the concept is similar. Briefly, just as you can use a CFOUTPUT loop to loop through a record set to display a report about a group of users, you can just as easily send a customized e-mail to each of them.

The second, CFFTP, is a tag that you may never use in your ColdFusion programming, but if you need it, it enables you to transfer files among servers. And perhaps your exposure to it in this chapter can help you remember it if you do find that you can use it.

The third feature, CFHTTP, is a really valuable feature that, in its simplest form, enables you to capture the output of another Web page programmatically. In other words, ColdFusion reads the web page for you and stores its resulting HTML in a variable. You can then break that apart to get some small portion of the page, store the output in a file on your system, or use it in any way that makes sense. The feature has additional uses, too, that often go unnoticed.

Each of these features opens the door to communicating with other servers. And if you need to do so, knowing that CF has the features to accomplish such tasks is very comforting.

Sending E-mail by Using CFMAIL

In the following sections, we explain how to use CFMAIL by starting with a very simple example of how to send a fixed message to a fixed user. CFMAIL is an incredibly flexible tag, however, that offers lots more functionality than many realize. We then expand the simple example into a much more dynamic one, changing it first to vary the to address, then the message content, then to send a single message to multiple recipients, and more.

The simplest CFMAIL

Say that you've got a web application that accepts registrations. A user has just filled in a form indicating interest in joining (or buying or whatever your service offers). You learned in Chapter 5 how to insert form data into a database, such as the user's contact information in this case. What if you want to send that user a confirmation e-mail to let him that know you got his registration? Perhaps you may also want to include some follow-up information or offer links to more information on your site.

This is one of the things that CFMAIL is made for. Sending an e-mail to someone is incredibly simple. But rather than compose the e-mail in your mail program, you compose it in your ColdFusion template, by using plain text that you enter between CFMAIL tags. Following is a very simple example of using CFMAIL:

```
<cfmail from="yourname@yourdomain.com" to="visitorname@
visitordomain.com" subject="Thanks for joining">

Thanks very much for joining our service. We welcome you to visit other
links on our site, including
http://www.yourdomain.com/somedir/somepage.cfm

If you require any assistance, don't hesitate to contact us at
yourname@yourdomain.com.

</cfmail>
```

Now, this example is incredibly simplistic. It assumes that you're creating a fixed message to be sent to a fixed user (visitorname@visitordomain.com). Notice a few characteristics about the CFMAIL tag. It has three required attributes: from, to, and subject. It has more options, too, as you will see in the next section and those that follow. These basic ones, however, are obvious.

After the template containing this tag is executed, the e-mail is generated by ColdFusion on your behalf and is sent to the address specified in the to field. It may not happen immediately, but it generally happens within moments.

How the e-mail is generated and sent in the background is something that we ignore for the moment. And you need to be aware that you usually can't get away with entering just any address for the from attribute. It most likely needs to include the domain name of the server from which you're sending the e-mail. You may not for example, get away with trying to send an e-mail with from="President@whitehouse.gov" in it. The same problem can trouble you if you make a typo in the from domain name. See the section "Behind the Scenes," later in this chapter, for an explanation of this and some other technical details that you may need to know.

Varying the TO address

The simple example in the preceding section gives you a taste of how CFMAIL works, but it really doesn't address the scenario that we describe in that section, where you create a mail message that can be reused for each of the users joining your site. We hard-coded the to value in that example, but you'd really want to vary the to address for each visitor.

Assume that we are executing this `CFMAIL` tag on a form action page that's processing a form that provides an input field called `email`. You then would have a variable on this page called `form.email`. You can easily use that, just as you may use a variable in any ColdFusion tag attribute.

In the example in the preceding section, you could change the `to="visitorname@ visitor-domain.com"` to `to="#form.email#"`. It's as simple as that. Now, whenever the page is executed, the e-mail is sent to the address specified by the user in the form.

Of course, performing some validation to make sure that the user did indeed provide an e-mail address or modifying that template to send the e-mail only if a value is entered would be helpful. See Chapter 20 for more information on implementing that sort of validation on the server or client.

Varying the message body

You could stop at this point in the example, but what if you want to vary not only the `to` address, but also the actual content of the message body? What if you want to display the person's name in the message that is sent to him? Again, assume that the input form has a field called `custname`, so you have an available variable called `form.custname`.

Using this variable is very easy if you realize that the `CFMAIL` tag works very much like a `CFOUTPUT` tag. If you want to refer to ColdFusion variables within the body of the message between the `CFMAIL` tags, you just use them as you would in text between `CFOUTPUT` tags. In other words, you simply wrap the variable in pound signs and place it wherever you want.

You could extend the first example in this chapter to include this change and the dynamically generated `to` address, as follows:

```
<cfmail from="yourname@yourdomain.com" to="#form.email#"
subject="Thanks for joining">

Dear #form.custname#,

Thanks very much for joining our service. We welcome you to visit other
links on our site, including
http://www.yourdomain.com/somedir/somepage.cfm

If you require any assistance, don't hesitate to contact us at
yourname@yourdomain.com.

</cfmail>
```

As this page is executed (after being called from a form containing the indicated `email` and `custname` fields), it generates an e-mail to the specific user, showing the user's name as, for example, `Dear John Doe`. Very nifty! Some of you can probably see how this feature works very much like mail merging in a word processor.

You can name any variables that you want, including those in the Variables (local), Session, Application, Client, or other scopes. Indeed, you can even refer to query result set variables, as the following section demonstrates.

Finally, know that you can also use a variable within the `subject` attribute if you want. Perhaps you may want to place the user's name in the `subject` as well, changing it to `subject="Thanks for joining, #form.custname#"`. You can also set the `from` address as a variable, although we don't do so in this chapter's example.

Sending a number of e-mails at once

The examples in the preceding sections presume that you are sending a single e-mail to a user who signed up on a registration page. What if you instead wanted to send an e-mail to all the users who had signed up? Or to all those who had signed up this week? Or to those who hadn't made a purchase in the past year? Or who lived in a certain state?

All these possibilities are very easy to accomplish if you consider that `CFMAIL` can be directed to send an e-mail to all the users in a given query result set. Notice, however, that we're *not* talking about putting your `CFMAIL` inside a `CFOUTPUT QUERY` loop (a mistake that newcomers frequently make).

We're saying that the `CFMAIL` tag has an available `QUERY` attribute, just like the `CFOUTPUT` tag. And just as that attribute causes the text (and variables) in within a `CFOUTPUT` tag pair to process once for each record, so, too, does it cause a single e-mail to be sent for each record.

Of course, one of the fields in the query result set needs to hold an e-mail address! Assume that you've performed a query that gets the name and e-mail address from a Registrants table, as in the following example:

```
<cfquery datasource="Customers" name="GetCustomers">
  SELECT Custname, Email FROM Registrants
  WHERE Email IS NOT Null
</cfquery>
```

Notice that this code adds a filter to ensure that you find only records that contain an e-mail address, because your intent is to send users e-mails. Of course, you could use still other filters in the `WHERE` clause to limit the results found so that they meet some intended criteria. But doing so wouldn't change the way that you'd code the `CFMAIL` tag.

By having a query result set named `GetCustomers` in that example, you can tell the `CFMAIL` to create an e-mail for each of the found customers. All you need to add is the `QUERY` attribute. Everything else about the preceding CFMAIL examples can remain the same, except that you change the variable references from form fields to `GetCustomers` fields, to refer to the query result set, as follows:

```
<cfmail from="yourname@yourdomain.com" query="GetCustomers"
to="#GetCustomers.Email#" subject="Thanks for joining,
#GetCustomers.Custname#">

Dear #GetCustomers.Custname#,

Thanks very much for joining our service. We welcome you to visit other
links on our site, including
http://www.yourdomain.com/somedir/somepage.cfm

If you require any assistance, don't hesitate to contact us at
yourname@yourdomain.com.

</cfmail>
```

Now you're rolling!

Sending a single message showing multiple records

The final example that we show you is one that we bet most developers don't realize is possible. Although you could use a query result set to send an e-mail for each record found, you could also use a query result set to send a single e-mail that shows all the records within the e-mail.

Assume that you need to send to your company CEO a list of how many registrants you have from each state. The SQL statement for that would use the GROUP clause to group records by department, and the COUNT aggregate function to return the number of records per department. (If you're not familiar with those features, refer to Chapter 9.) The following code shows how to do that:

```
<cfquery datasource="Customers" name="GetRegs">
   SELECT state, count(*) As numreg
   FROM registrants
   GROUP BY state
</cfquery>

<cfmail from="yourname@yourdomain.com" query="GetRegs"
to="boss@yourdomain.com" subject="Reg Report">

Following are the counts of registrants per state:
<cfoutput>
#state# - #numreg#
</cfoutput>
</cfmail>
```

Notice the embedded CFOUTPUT within the CFMAIL. That's very interesting, because we explained previously that CFMAIL acts like a CFOUTPUT. Why would you need another CFOUTPUT within CFMAIL?

And you may ask why the QUERY attribute doesn't cause multiple mails to be generated. What's happening is a subtle trick in CFMAIL. If the to attribute doesn't specify a query column name, CF assumes that you don't mean to create an e-mail for each record. Instead, it assumes that you mean to loop over the record set *within* the e-mail. And the way to do that is with the embedded CFOUTPUT, giving you maximum control over where and when the loop occurs.

Of course, if the database design held the state value as a numeric code to be looked up in another table, you'd need to add a join to support that. But you'd still end up with some column reflecting the state.

If you're familiar with the GROUP attribute of CFQUERY, you may not be surprised to learn that CFMAIL also supports that attribute. If you don't choose to GROUP records in the SQL and instead do an ORDER BY, you can then specify GROUP="state" in the CFMAIL tag. It may act in an unexpected manner, however: It sends a single message per GROUPed column (per state, in this example), and within the message body, the CFOUTPUT enables a loop over all the records for that GROUPed column.

Still more possibilities

In the preceding sections, we've shown you quite a number of possibilities with CFMAIL, but believe it or not, you have still more options. See Chapter 58 for all the available attributes. Some of them are easily recognized, such as cc and bcc (for sending e-mails to others at the same time). You can also specify multiple addresses for any of the to, cc, and bcc attributes. (Although be careful setting too many email addresses in each of these attributes — don't use this feature if the query-driven approach is more appropriate.)

And if a query can be used, you can also use the associated startrow and maxrows attributes to limit the number of records processed.

Sending attachments

Although the examples in the preceding sections all show simple text in the body of the message, you can also create HTML-formatted e-mails, which makes sense only if you're sending the mail to browsers that support such e-mails. To do so, simply add type="html" as an attribute on the CFMAIL.

You can also attach files to a message that you're sending. You have two approaches to this. The mimeattach attribute enables you to point to any file, and that file is included along with the text of the message as an attachment.

Going back to our simplest example, we could attach a file in that email as such:

```
<cfmail from="yourname@yourdomain.com" to="visitorname@
visitordomain.com" subject="Thanks for joining"
mimeattach="c:/somedir/somefile.ext">

Thanks very much for joining our service. We welcome you to visit other
links on our site, including
http://www.yourdomain.com/somedir/somepage.cfm

If you require any assistance, don't hesitate to contact us at
yourname@yourdomain.com.

</cfmail>
```

If you need to send multiple files, however, you need to use the newer CFMAILPARAM tag. See Chapter 58 for more about this tag, which would be specified between the opening and closing CFMAIL tag for a given message.

CFMAILPARAM can also be used to specify alternative mail headers to be sent with the message. This may seem an obscure subject, but an excellent example is adding an alternate reply-to, so that someone replying to this message would have the message returned to an address other than that specified in the from address.

Again, extending our simplest example, we could attach one or more files and also change the reply-to address as well using CFMAILPARAM as such:

```
<cfmail from="yourname@yourdomain.com" to="visitorname@
visitordomain.com" subject="Thanks for joining">

Thanks very much for joining our service. We welcome you to visit other
links on our site, including
http://www.yourdomain.com/somedir/somepage.cfm
```

```
If you require any assistance, don't hesitate to contact us
atyourname@yourdomain.com.
<cfmailparam name="Reply-To" value="othername@yourdomain.com">
<cfmailparam file="c:/somedir/somefile.ext">
<cfmailparam file="c:/somedir/someotherfile.ext">
</cfmail>
```

One other potential use of `CFMAILPARAM` is that, according to Macromedia Knowledge Base article 22923, some mail servers using SendMail may be set with header checking enabled. In that case, if you send a file without an attachment, you may find you need to add a `CFMAILPARAM` with `name="Mime-Version"` and `VALUE="1.0"`.

Behind the scenes

Before leaving the subject of `CFMAIL`, be aware that you may want to discuss a handful of topics with your mail administrator. ColdFusion doesn't actually know how to send mail. It needs a corresponding mail server — an SMTP (Simple Mail Transport Protocol) server — to handle the actual work. What the `CFMAIL` tag does is pass the generated e-mail to that mail server.

We don't indicate the mail server name or IP address in the examples in the preceding sections, because your CF administrator could possibly have specified it as a setting that's global to all ColdFusion templates on the server. This practice is very common. If the administrator has not done that or if you want to override that setting, the `CFMAIL` tag has an available `server` attribute.

Furthermore, because you may be generating a large number of e-mails in your `CFMAIL` request (especially query-driven ones), ColdFusion doesn't wait for all the e-mails to actually be sent out. That could otherwise force the template to take too long. Instead, ColdFusion automatically "spools" or copies the generated mail messages to a folder that it then passes to the SMTP server by using a background task.

A new feature in ColdFusion MX enables you to control that spooling behavior by using the `spoolenable` attribute. Setting it to `"no"`, which means don't do the default spooling, may save time in not needing to spool the messages to disk. Deciding which is faster is perhaps a balancing act.

Another aspect of understanding the role of the SMTP server is that, if for some reason ColdFusion cannot successfully move the mail from the spool to the mail server (it's down or the name that you provide is incorrect), the mail can't go through. Because the `CFMAIL` tag doesn't wait to confirm the success of the mailing, you have no way to provide feedback (an error message) to the user running the `CFMAIL` template.

Instead, such failed messages are stored in a folder where the ColdFusion Server is installed — in particular, the `\CFusionMX\Mail\UnDelivr` folder. This can be very unfortunate if the unavailability of the SMTP mail server is only temporary. All those e-mails now end up sitting in the `Undelivr` folder and are never sent. Some administrators have setup processes to copy any such messages back to the \CfusionMX\Mail\Spool\ directory on a regularly scheduled basis. (See Chapter 32 for more information on both `CFSCHEDULE` and `CFFILE`, which are key to such a solution.)

You also need to know that options in the ColdFusion Administrator can control the logging of certain error and status messages concerning mail handling, which may be written to log files in the `\CfusionMX\Logs` and `\CfusionMX\Mail\Log` files. It can be helpful to review these error and status messages if there are ever problems with the mailing process.

Finally, concerning the SMTP server, it's this server which may impose the restriction mentioned in the caution in the first section of this chapter. That is, the SMTP server may permit you to send out only e-mails that contain a `from` address in the same domain as that mail server (which, generally, is the domain of the Web site as well, although not always). A mail server may enable this restriction to prevent the server from being used for spamming purposes (where someone hides his true identity by using a fake domain name in their `from` address).

Other mail-handling possibilities

If you need to generate large volumes of e-mails from within ColdFusion or wish that the mail handling worked in some other ways, you should know that you indeed have alternatives to `CFMAIL`. Take a look at custom tags such as ActivMail (at `www.cfdev.com/activmail`) and alternative mail servers such as the InFusion Mail Server (at `www.coolfusion.com`).

In addition to creating one that sends e-mail, you can write a ColdFusion application that receives also e-mail. You can use `CFPOP` to retrieve e-mail from a given mail account, and the result is a list of messages (or the text of a given message) available as a query result set. See Chapter 58 for more information on `CFPOP`. A sample application, called the Crazy Cab Email Client, also demonstrates the use of `CFPOP` in a rather complete application. You may find it installed with your ColdFusion MX at
`http://<yourservername>/cfdocs/exampleapps/old/email/login.cfm`.

One last point: `CFPOP` can read only POP (Post Office Protocol) mail accounts, which are the most commonly used on the Internet. Some mail servers, however, use MAPI (Messaging Application Programming Interface)—including Microsoft Exchange servers. You cannot read such mail with CFPOP.

Because ColdFusion MX is built upon a Java foundation, you can also find value in using the available JavaMail API. See the resources available at
`http://java.sun.com/products/javamail/`.

Transferring Files by Using CFFTP

You may know that FTP (File Transfer Protocol) is used as a means to send files from one machine on the Internet to another. You may even use it frequently by way of an FTP client program to send files from your workstation to the remote server that hosts your ColdFusion applications.

But what if you need to send several files from your ColdFusion server to another server, perhaps to effect a backup of some critical files (something that you may schedule on a recurring basis by using `CFSCHEDULE`)? Or what if you have a business relationship that requires you to frequently download a set of files from a partner's server to your own? Finally, what if you want to programmatically manipulate the files on a remote server (deleting/moving/copying them)?

In these cases, the FTP protocol is a natural solution, but you probably don't want to use an FTP client to manually initiate this transfer if it's a recurring or event-driven activity. This is where the `CFFTP` tag comes in handy.

Like the `CFFILE` command that we mention in Chapter 32, the `CFFTP` command can be disabled by using the ColdFusion Administrator Resource/Sandbox Security features. See Chapter 40 for more information.

There are two styles of use of the `CFFTP` tag. A simple approach is useful in performing a single `get` or `put` operation to copy a file from or to a remote server. For some operations, however, such as in making several requests of the remote server, you want to use a "cached" connection. If you want to avoid specifying all the needed connection information (`username`, `password`, and `server` attributes) repeatedly, use the form that creates/uses a cached connection. Reusing a cached connection is also more efficient in performing multiple operations.

Be careful not to use the `CFFTP` tag for the wrong kind of operation. It's for server-to-server file transfers. If you want to send files from your browser client to the ColdFusion server, look at the `CFFILE action="upload"` operation described in Chapter 32. And to transfer files, especially those not HTML-formatted, from your server to a browser client, look at the information for the `CFCONTENT` tag, discussed in Chapter 56.

Connecting one time for file/directory operations

If you're just performing a single operation to copy a file to or from a remote server and your ColdFusion server or perhaps to delete or rename a file on a remote server, the operation is rather straightforward. You simply need to specify the connection information and describe the operation to be performed.

The connection information includes such obvious things as the domain name/IP address of the server to which you're connecting and the username and password to use to log in. These are specified in the `CFFTP`'s `server`, `username`, and `password` attributes, respectively.

You can perform several possible operations. See the Chapter 60 for more information on the available options for the `action` attribute. But for now, consider a simpler operation to copy a file from a remote server to the server that's running the template performing the `CFFTP` operation. An example may be as follows:

```
<cfftp action="getfile" server="yourdomain.com" username="yourid"
password="yourpw" remotefile="/remotepath/remotefilename"
localfile="/localpath/localfilename">
```

This code copies the `remotefilename` from the `remotepath` into the local server to be stored as `localfilename` in the `localpath`.

If you provide just a file name and no path (or a relative path) in the `localfile` attribute for an `action="getfile"`, the file may not end up getting placed in the directory where the template was executed, as you may expect. Instead, in our testing, it ended up in the `\CfusionMX\runtime\bin` directory! A relative path would become relative to that. So make sure that you specify a complete path for the `localfile`. To specify the current directory, you could use `localfile=" #getdirectoryfrompath(getcurrenttemplatepath())#/yourfilename"`.

If the file specified in `localfile` already exists, the FTP `get` operation fails. You can force it to overwrite the file by adding `failexists="no"`.

You can perform several other file operations (values for the `action` attribute) this way, including `putfile`, `rename`, `remove`, and `existsfile`.

And don't forget several directory operations as well, including `createdir`, `listdir`, `removedir`, and `existsdir`. (A few other directory operations, such as `changedir` and `getcurrentdir`, you are most likely to perform as part of a series of multiple operations, as we discuss in the following section.) Each of these variations may call for use of additional attributes. See Chapter 60 on `CFFTP` for more information.

Here's an example that's requesting a list of the files and directories in a given remote directory:

```
<cfftp action="listdir" server="yourdomain.com" username="yourid"
password="yourpw" directory="/remotepath/remotefilename"
name="GetResult">

<cfdump var="#GetResult#">
```

The resulting variable named in the `name` attribute (`GetResult`) is available to you as a query result set. You can use `CFOUTPUT query` to loop over it or `CFLOOP collection`. This example simply shows the use of `CFDUMP`, and its built-in formatting of output lists all the files and/or directories in the given remote directory. You can specify just a directory path in the `directory` attribute. You can also name a file or even a file pattern, such as `/remotepath/*.cfm`, which would list only `.cfm` files.

Finally, know that the results of any `CFFTP` operation are reflected in a set of variables of scope `CFFTP`. An example is `cfftp.returnvalue`. Others are `errorcode`, `errortext`, and `succeeded`. You can easily see them all by using `<cfdump var="#CFFTP#">` after the `CFFTP` operation.

Using "cached connections" for multiple operations

Some FTP processing may require that you perform multiple operations (perhaps to get a list of files or directories or change directories on the remote server and then `get` or `put` several different files). This would require specifying multiple `CFFTP` tags, each performing the desired action.

Although you could use the approach in the previous section and simply repeat the complete `CFFTP` connection information in each tag, this is poor programming practice. (A change in the connection information would require a change to all the tags.) It's also poor performing, because CF must open and close the FTP connection on each tag.

Fortunately, the ColdFusion engineers anticipated this problem and added a mechanism to enable you to create a connection once and then reuse it for multiple tags. The process is similar to the CFTP processing in the previous section, but instead of performing each desired remote `action` with all the necessary connection information, you would perform a single `CFFTP` with an `action="open"` and naming a `connection`, which you would then reuse for subsequent FTP operations on the same page.

By using this approach with the `listdir` code example in the preceding section, you can change that code as follows:

```
<cfftp action="open" server="yourdomain.com" username="yourid"
password="yourpw" connection="MyConn">

<cfftp action="existsdir" directory="/remotepath/" connection="MyConn">

<cfif cfftp.succeeded is "yes">
<cfftp action="listdir" connection="MyConn"
directory="/remotepath/remotefilename" name="GetResult">
<cfdump var="#GetResult#">
</cfif>
```

Notice that, after the first `CFFTP`, which opens a connection named `"MyConn"`, you can simply refer to that connection name in the remaining `CFFTP` operations. Notice, too, that this example uses an `action="existsdir"` to first test whether the named directory exists before trying to list its files and directories and then uses the available `cfftp.succeeded` variable to test the result. This is a benefit of using cached connections: You can perform several operations against the remote server to make sure that your desired results are achieved. The caching just makes the process more efficient.

Be careful in creating an `action="existsdir"`. If you mistakenly leave a combination directory path and file name in the `directory` attribute, the `succeeded` variable always returns `"no"`.

One final observation about using cached connections: The cached connection is closed after the template completes (or you use an `action="close"`). This may make sense in most cases, but what if you were doing several FTP operations across multiple pages (perhaps responding to a user filling out several forms in a row, indicating operations to be performed)? In such a case, wouldn't holding the cached connection over the multiple pages be sensible?

Fortunately, providing a value in the `connection` attribute that names a persistent variable, such as `session.MyConn`, is acceptable. You probably want to always use `IsDefined("session.MyConn")` to check whether the connection exists before using it this way. If it doesn't exist, you want to open the connection; otherwise, you'd proceed to use it, referring to the connection name as stored in the session scope. You could use the application scope as well, to cache the connection across multiple users. Just be careful to consider whether it's wise for multiple users to use the same login/password combination for their FTP operations.

Other useful FTP options

A few other options are available as attributes in working with `CFFTP`. First, some other error-handling attributes are available. If a `CFFTP` operation fails, it will fail silently (no ColdFusion error message) and simply return the `CFFTP`-scoped variables mentioned at the end of the section above, "Connecting one time for file/directory operations". The `stoponerror` attribute can change that behavior. The default is "`no`", but if it's set to `"yes"`, then a ColdFusion error will be triggered. This enables you to use `CFTRY/CFCATCH` processing to handle errors instead.

`timeout` and `retrycount` attributes are also available, which you can used to provide finer control over how the tag performs if you have connection problems.

In performing file and directory operations, tags are available to help you control how files are transferred (in text or binary more). See `asciiextensionlist` and `transfermode`, which are discussed in Chapter 60.

Finally, in making connections to a remote server, you may need to specifically enable *passive mode*, a feature required by some FTP servers. To enable it, specify `passive="yes"` in the CFTTP tag. (The default is `"no"`.) And if you need to specify a proxy server, the aptly named `proxyserver` attribute is the solution.

Connecting to Other Web Servers by Using CFHTTP

Have you ever needed (or wished that you could have) content that someone else has put on a Web site? Perhaps a partner company offers their product list on their site, and you wish to show those products for sale from within your site.

Or have you needed to find a way to programmatically submit a form to someone's site without actually filling out the form and submitting it? For instance, maybe you want to keep an eye on a page listing jobs in your area without having to fill out the form selecting location, job type, and salary range every time you visit it.

Or perhaps you want to test calling a page on your own site in an automated fashion (without needing to actually browse the page) and you need to simulate a browser passing some particular header ("user-agent" or "accept-encoding") or other values for what ColdFusion calls CGI variables.

All these operations become possible if you use ColdFusion's `CFHTTP` tag. In technical terms, it enables you to perform a `get` or `post` operation against any Web page, with an optional `CFHTTPPARAM` tag to enable specification of data to pass to a page.

Caution: Of course, like so many powerful tools, while there are legitimate uses of CFHTTP, you need to be careful not to violate copyright agreements or site usage policies in either retrieving or submitting information this way.

Still another, often untapped, capability of `CFHTTP` is that it not only can `get` Web pages, but if the page that you're "getting" is in a flat text file in a tabular format (such as a comma-separated value or a CSV file), the result of the `CFHTTP` operation can be treated as a query result set. Very nifty! It's an interesting alternative to using `CFFILE` to read the file into a single variable, as is discussed in Chapter 32.

We discuss each of these approaches of using CFHTTP in the following sections.

Note: The processes described here for requesting and processing the output of another Web page may seem a primitive means of transferring data from one server to another. Especially compared to approaches such as Web Services and WDDX, which we cover in Chapter 25 and Chapter 30, respectively.

These are far more effective ways to achieve similar results if the provider of the page chooses to present his data in such a machine-readable manner. But in working with a more traditional Web page or one that's not in your control, `CFHTTP` is a very handy alternative.

Grabbing someone else's Web page

The most common use of `CFHTTP` is to grab the output of some other Web page and make it available within your template as a variable that you can then manipulate. In effect, ColdFusion acts as a browser, but rather than showing the result on-screen, the result is held in memory in a variable.

What you choose to do with that variable is up to you. You can display it to the user (although then you're just acting as a needless middleman), or you could parse the variable (by using ColdFusion's many string-manipulation functions) and pull out just the part of the page that you're interested in. You may even just want to store the output to a file, perhaps for archival purposes. (We show a solution for that in the section, "Some other points about CFHTTP," later in this chapter.)

Say a co-worker has put up a report on the intranet that holds some data that you want to use. Maybe his report has several things in it, but you're interested only in this one portion of the report. Furthermore, the Web page on which the report appears is generated from something other than ColdFusion and perhaps comes from a database that you can't access. The output of the page is what you want your users to see.

But you don't want to just forward your users to that page, because it may have extraneous information that you don't need. You want to "grab" only that part of the Web page and show it to your users. How do you do it? That's just what `CFHTTP` was designed for.

Of course, this same capability can also be used to grab a Web page created by some third party, such as getting the stock reports from `quote.yahoo.com` or the weather from `weather.com`. Be careful: Copyright issues likely preclude your doing this legally, although it may be possible technically.

Assume that, at the page `http://ourdomain/somedir/acctreport.xyz`, is a report that you want to see. In this case, I'm referring to a page on our own site (ourdomain) but it could just as easily be on some other company's web site. You don't know what sort of application server serves up `.xyz` pages, but that really doesn't matter. Just as the output of a CF page is in HTML, in this case so, too, is the output of this `.xyz` page simply HTML. In fact, Figure 31-1 shows the output of that page.

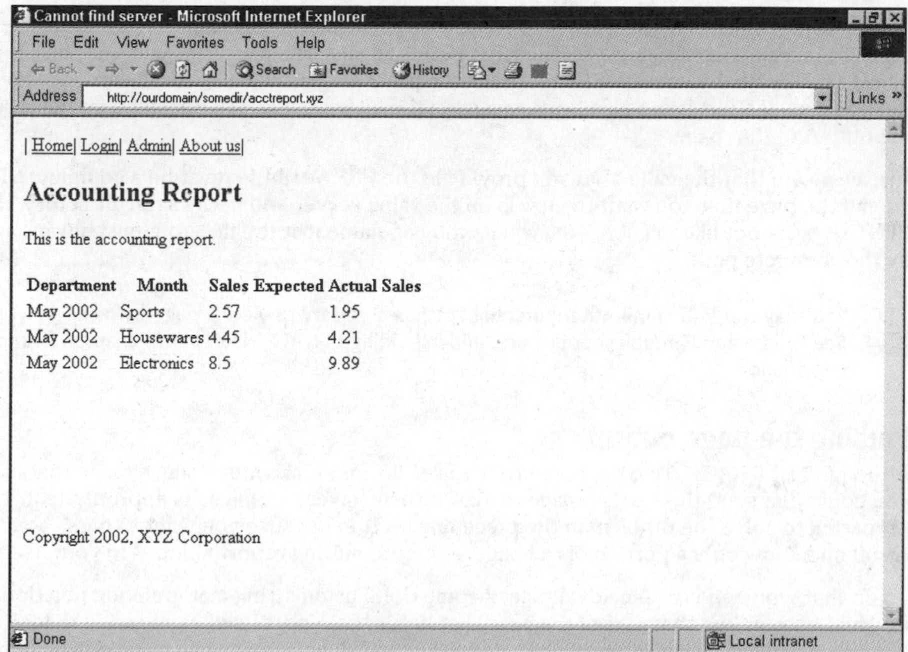

Figure 31-1: A report from another Web application server that we want to grab.

Again, you want to get just the actual report and not the navigational toolbar, the title or any other info that may appear on the page. And you don't just want to send users to this page. Not only may they be confused by the navigational links that don't apply to them, but the quality of the design certainly would clash with the efforts of your talented design team!

So you want to "grab" just a portion of the page. Indeed, you want to pull that page into ColdFusion so that you can decide what to do with it. That's what `CFHTTP` does if you use the following tag for that example:

```
<cfhttp template="http://ourdomain/somedir/acctreport.xyz">
```

Other attributes are possible (including the default `method="get"`), but this works for a basic page grab. Many developers, as they run this code for the first time, are surprised that their template creates no output (assuming that this tag is the only one in the template). The `CFHTTP` command doesn't create any output. Instead, it takes the HTML of the page that you've pointed it to and holds it in memory for you in the variable cfhttp.filecontent. You get to decide what to do with that variable.

You could, for testing purposes, just turn around and output it, as in the following code:

```
<cfoutput>#cfhttp.filecontent#</cfoutput>
```

What's important to remember is that what's in this variable is just the same HTML that users see if they open the URL (of the page you grabbed) in their own browsers. Indeed, you can accurately say that CFHTTP is acting as a browser for the user. But instead of always showing the output of the requested page, you get to decide what to do with the results in the cfhttp.filecontent.

We show some alternative things to do with that content in the next section. For now, demonstrating for yourself how this works may help to reinforce the point.

Create a template containing a CFHTTP that points to any Web page that you want and then display its results by using the CFOUTPUT in the preceding example. It can be an .htm file, a .cfm file, a .asp file. It can also be any page on the Internet. CFHTTP doesn't care. All it sees is the output of that page.

Just be aware that the value that you provide in the URL attribute must be a complete URL. Even if the page that you want to view is on the same server and in the same directory, this CFHTTP tag is not like CFLOCATION, where you can name just the file. You must always specify the complete path.

You may run into some other potential gotchas if you try to view a page by using CFHTTP. See the section, "Troubleshooting and understanding CFHTTP," later in this chapter, for more information.

Parsing the page output

Although just CFOUTPUTing the result to the user doesn't make much sense (as in that case, you could just send them to the page to view it themselves), doing so is appropriate in preparing to solve the problem in the preceding section because you want to parse apart the result and show only a portion of the page—the accounting report alone—to your users.

To do that, you need to take advantage of some ColdFusion string-manipulation functions to find and extract just that part of the page that holds the report itself. If you were to look at the page from the preceding section in a browser and use a View ➪ Source menu command (in IE or View ➪ Page Source in Netscape), you would see the following HTML:

```
| <a href="home.xyz">Home</a>| <a href="login.xyz">Login</a>| <a
href="admin.xyz">Admin</a>| <a href="aboutus.xyz">About us</a>|
<p>
<h2>Accounting Report</h2>
This is the accounting report.
<p>
<table>
<th>Department</th><th>Month</th><th>Sales Expected</th><th>Actual
Sales</th>
<tr>
   <td>May 2002</td>
   <td>Sports</td>
   <td>2.57</td>
   <td>1.95</td>
</tr>
```

```
<tr>
    <td>May 2002</td>
    <td>Housewares</td>
    <td>4.45</td>
    <td>4.21</td>
</tr>
<tr>
    <td>May 2002</td>
    <td>Electronics</td>
    <td>8.5</td>
    <td>9.89</td>
</tr>
</table>
<p> </p><p> </p><p> </p>
Copyright 2002, XYZ Corporation
```

Clearly, the report that you want is basically all the data within the pair of `<table>` tags. That's helpful, because in ColdFusion has mechanisms that make extracting just that part of a page rather simple.

Start by first making even more clear the fact that the results in the `cfhttp.filecontent` variable are indeed that same string of HTML that you see in the preceding example. More to the point, the capability to view the string of HTML within that example — or in any variable that you may create to hold a subset of it — would prove most helpful. Replace the `CFOUTPUT` from the preceding section with the following:

```
<cfoutput> #HTMLCodeFormat(cfhttp.filecontent)#</cfoutput>
```

Now, as you run your template, instead of seeing the display of the page as rendered by the browser, you instead see the HTML used to render that display. Indeed, you're viewing the same HTML that you'd see if you use the View ⇨ Source menu command, but it's appearing in the browser instead of in some View Source window or another editor.

This use of the HTMLCodeFormat function is useful because it enables you to see, as you're working with variables containing HTML strings, the actual HTML statements within those variable without needing to resort to a View ⇨ Source command.

If you're curious, what the `HTMLCodeFormat()` (and the related `HTMLEditFormat()` function) is really doing is converting the HTML string within the variable so that it uses the HTML character-code equivalents for displaying HTML on-screen. It converts any <, for example, to `<` and any > to `>`. You don't need to worry about that. The function does it for you.

So, knowing now that the `cfhttp.filecontent` variable holds that string of HTML that you saw at the start of this section, you can now use other ColdFusion functions to extract just the data within the `<table>`.

Literally dozens of string-manipulation functions that can prove useful in this sort of exercise are available to you. Just a few are `Find()`, `FindNoCase()`, `Left()`, `Len()`, `Mid()`, `REFnd()`, `REFindNoCase()`, `RemoveChars()`, `Replace()`, `ReplaceNoCase()`, `REReplace()`, `REReplaceNoCase()`, and `Right()`. You have still others as well. You should acquaint yourself with all the string-manipulation functions. Whenever they're appropriate, they can save you a lot of trouble. (Several list-processing functions can also prove useful in this sort of exercise.)

In the current example, you want to use a combination of FindNoCase(), RemoveChars() and Len() functions. Following is the code that you want to use, followed by an explanation:

```
<cfhttp template="http://ourdomain/somedir/acctreport.xyz">
<cfset startstring = cfhttp.filecontent>
<cfset tablestart = FindNoCase("<table>", startstring)>
<cfset tempstring = RemoveChars(startstring,1, tablestart-1)>
<cfset tableend = FindNoCase("</table>", tempstring)>
<cfset tempstring = RemoveChars(tempstring,tableend+8,len(tempstring))>
<cfoutput>#tempstring#</cfoutput>
```

This ability to parse a page's output is really quite simple if you understand the functions, and the capability to do this so easily is pretty powerful. Your first step after the CFHTTP is to copy the cfhttp.filecontent variable into another variable, startstring. Because you're referring to it several times, some developershave asserted that this assignment of cfhttp.filecontent to another variable has a slight performance benefit. We're not sure about that, but it does reduce the complexity of the variable name that you're going to be referring to a couple times later in that code.

Next, you want to find the location in the string where your table begins, which is just what the Find() and FindNoCase() functions do. FindNoCase() performs a case-insensitive search, which can prove helpful if you fail to notice and match the case of the strings that you're searching with and matching against. The result of this function is a number indicating where the <table> tag begins in the startstring (the cfhttp.filecontent). You assign that to a variable called tablestart.

Next, you use the RemoveChars() function to remove everything from the start of the string to the <table> tag. Given a string, that function removes from it the characters, from a given starting point to a given ending point. For this example, the starting point is the beginning of the string (as you don't want to keep anything from the start of the string to the <table> tag), and the ending point is the tablestart value, the location that you just determined in the prior statement as being where the <table> tag begins. So the RemoveChars() removes everything up to table tag.

One thing in the preceding step may need explaining: The point at which the <table> tag begins in the string is actually the point of the opening bracket of that tag. You don't want to remove that, so notice that the code subtracts 1 from the tablestart where you use it in the RemoveChars() function.

If the table were all that remained on this page, you'd be done. The tempstring would hold the table that you want. But in the preceding example, you may have noticed some footer information on the page. In this case, it's some copyright info. Again, you should *never* remove such a copyright notice from information obtained from a third-party site (and maybe we should still show it in this example), but assume, for convenience's sake, that it's some other sort of information, such as more navigational links. You don't want that to appear in your extracted table, so you need to remove it as well.

You simply repeat the process of identifying some text that will be removed, this time finding in the tempstring the location of the closing </table> tag. As before, you use RemoveChars() to remove from that string everything from that point (the location of the closing </table> tag) to the end, although you again need to adjust the location where the removal should start so that you do not clip off the </table> tag itself, by adding 8 (the length of the </table> tag itself) to the start location. The ending location is the end of the string, which is computed by using the len(tempstring) function. That's it!

You now have in the tempstring the table and nothing but the table. You could choose to show that to your users in this same page, perhaps surrounding it with some explanation or at least using CFINCLUDE to include your own navigational headers or other page elements that you always show on your pages. Or you could store it in a database. Really—you can now do anything that you want with the table.

Some may wonder why we use those intermediate variables to hold the values in parsing that string. Doing so just makes debugging easier and looks a little cleaner than using one long set of embedded functions. Printing out the string (or variable values) along the way is also useful to make sure that you're on the right track. Using the <cfdump var="#variables#"> tag, which displays the values of all local variables defined at that point, is also handy.

The ability to view the Variables scope with CFDUMP is new in CFMX. . See Chapter 48 for more information on CFDUMP.

Some other points about CFHTTP

The CFHTTP tag has more attributes than just the url attribute we've seen so far. Some are quite interesting.

The CFHTTP operation that we describe in the preceding section stores its HTML result in a variable called cfhttp.filecontent. But what if your goal in using the CFHTTP is simply to save the HTML to a file? Maybe you want to create an archive of some page. Although you can use CFFILE to write out the content of that variable, another way is much easier. If you specify a PATH attribute in the CFHTTP, it doesn't create the variable. Instead, it writes the file (using the filename as specified in the URL) to the specified directory on your server. If you want to specify a name, you also have an available NAME attribute.

You also get some new features for CFHTTP in CF MX. One of them, firstrowasheaders, we discuss in the section "Reading a flat tabular file as a query result set," later in this chapter. Another is the charset attribute, which is useful for supporting alternative-language character sets. Still another involves ColdFusion's use of the Sun JSSE library, which enables 128-bit encryption for Secure Sockets Layer (SSL).

Still other attributes are explained in the following section on troubleshooting.

Troubleshooting and understanding CFHTTP

As we mention in the section above, "Grabbing Someone Else's Web Page", one of the most common mistakes used by beginning or infrequent users of CFHTTP is the failure to specify a complete path for the URL. (People are just so used to using only the file name in all sorts of other tags such as CFLOCATION or even <form action> and <a href>.) It's just something that you must remember.

But sometimes you get an error from CFHTTP such as Connection failure. You may be stumped as to how to proceed.

Actually, you may get a "connection failure" during a CFHTTP for at least two reasons. The first is that a CF page that you're requesting contains a compilation or runtime error. As of CF 5 (and CFMX), if a ColdFusion page contains an error, ColdFusion generates not only the HTML error page that you're used to seeing (see Chapter 21 for more information), but it also now generates a 500 response status code. That causes this "connection failure".

We talk about handling status codes later in this section, but for now, know that if you try to use CFHTTP get the content of a ColdFusion page that itself contains an error, you will get this Connection failure message. Try running the page in a regular browser to see whether any CF error messages are displayed. If so, correct them and then try the CFHTTP again.

Still, you may find that you get this `Connection failure` even though you specify a URL that you know works: You've put the same URL in your browser and it responds as expected. What then? This is the second most common problem to trip up users of `CFHTTP`.

If the page that you're trying to access is on a Web server that has implemented security and authentication, meaning that you must provide a username and password to access the file, you must specify them (the `username` and `password` attributes) in the `CFHTTP` tag.

> **Note** These attributes are not to be used to respond to an application-specific login form that may be implemented to provide login security for the page in question (where the username prompt is created by a simple HTML form). In that case, the `username/password` attributes of CFHTTP cannot provide the needed authentication. You can possibly cause such a form to be filled out by using the information in the following section, "Submitting a form without submitting the form."

The problem with web server security authentication is that you may forget that a page requires authentication, and so the page works fine in the browser but gets the `Connection failure` message if you use `CFHTTP`.

> The way browsers work is that, after the first time you visit a secured site and provide a username and password, you're not prompted again. The authentication is remembered. So although you may not see a prompt in your browser when you visit the page (because you visited it earlier in that browser and logged in then), if you open another browser and visit the URL that you're trying to `CFHTTP` to, you may see the prompt, thus reminding you that you do indeed need to provide authentication information when you visit that page.

If you are required to provide Web-server authentication to run the page, you need to specify the `username` and `password` attributes on the `CFHTTP`, providing the authentication information expected by the Web server. Remember that the `CFHTTP` is acting as an agent on your behalf inside the ColdFusion server. It doesn't know about any authentication that you may have performed in your own browser. And even though your browser can often remember that authentication was performed from page to page, the `CFHTTP` requires you to always specify the necessary values.

> Be aware as well that if the Web server implementing the authentication and requiring a username and password has implemented what's called *digest authentication* or *integrated windows authentication*, `CFHTTP` can't participate in that sort of authentication. Your only choice is to change the authentication on the Web server to basic authentication, if not simply allowing anonymous access.

In Chapter 32, we point out that a scheduled task can also fail for similar reasons. Because the CF scheduler actually uses `CFHTTP` under the covers, these points about errors and authentication are worth remembering for both processes.

You may need to provide a few other attributes to get around apparent problems with the `CFHTTP` tag. If you need to specify a proxy server or port or a specific user agent to run a page, see the available `proxyserver`, `proxyport`, and `useragent` attributes, as discussed in the reference for CFHTTP in Chapter 55.

Similarly, if the page that you attempt to access takes too long to execute, you may want to force the `CFHTTP` request to be abandoned. A `timeout` attribute is available for that purpose. Indeed, you probably should always set a `timeout` to prevent waiting too long for a long-running request, perhaps resulting from a problem on the server of the page that you're requesting.

In terms of handling errors, you may want to know that, to use CFTRY/CFCATCH handling to better manage CFHTTP problems, you can choose to enable the throwonerror attribute. Otherwise, CFHTTP reports an error in the cfhttp.filecontent variable. It may also offer additional information in the cfhttp.statuscode variable.

Finally, to solve some other problems (or for those with an interest in understanding or controlling some other underlying features of the CFHTTP request process), you may want to look into the available redirect, mimetype, and resolveurl attributes and the available cfhttp.header and cfhttp.responseheader result variables. Again, these are discussed in Chapter 55.

One final potential problem is a very real one in working with CFHTTP: If changes are made to the page that you're grabbing data from (or in the next section that you're posting data to) – for example, changes in page layout, and so on – all your well-crafted string parsing may suddenly fail. The result is simply that you don't get the output that you expect. This is a real risk to working with CFHTTP, but it's a small price to pay if using CFHTTP to grab the page output provides a solution that may not otherwise be possible at all.

Submitting a form without submitting the form

Although the section "Grabbing someone else's Web page," earlier in this chapter, discusses performing a CFHTTP process to "grab" or get a Web page, you can also use CFHTTP to do the opposite—to pass to or post information to another Web page. As we mentioned at the start of this section on CFHTTP, you may use this method to, in effect, submit a filled-out form to a form action page without really needing to fill out the form on-screen.

This process involves passing to the form action page whatever data it needs that the filled-out form would have passed to it. It's an interesting feature that can provide some valuable benefits in the right circumstances.

Say, for example, that you knew that another page on your site offers some search result that you'd be interested in capturing for reuse. Let's assume you don't have access to either the source code for the page nor the database it gets it data from, so you can't just grab the code or connect to the database directly. The only access to the data is through this form.

How can you use CFHTTP to perform the search that you want? Not perhaps as you may think. You don't somehow CFHTTP to the form itself and fill it out. That approach just doesn't work. Instead, you can write a CFHTTP request that acts similar to the form itself. As you know, a form is simply a Web page with several fields in it (created by using input, select, textarea and other tags) that enable someone to fill in data to pass to an action page.

All you need to do with the CFHTTP is recreate all the necessary fields that are passed by the form to the action page and "submit" those in a new form of CFHTTP by using method="post". (The default method="get" did not need to be specified in the CFHTTP examples we've seen so far in this chapter.)

Furthermore, you name each of the necessary form fields in a relatively new CFHTTPPARAM tag that is specified within a pair of CFHTTP tags. (Again, in the previous examples we've seen, no closing </cfhttp> tag was needed.)

So the first step in submitting a form without actually submitting the form is to view the page that's holding the form containing the fields that we will want to submit using CFHTTP. Literally, use a View ➪ Source command in your browser to display the form's underlying HTML. Look for all the input, select, and textarea tags that may exist on the form. Don't forget hidden fields (where input type="hidden").

Say, for example, that the page `http://ourdomain/somedir/searchform.xyz` presents a form, with an action of `searchresult.xyz`, that offers the following input fields:

```
<input type="text" name="Search1">
<input type="hidden" name="DB" value="SomeDB">
<input type="submit" name="Search" value="Find It">
```

What the preceding code means is that, although the user types his search value into a single form field named `"Search1"`, there is a hidden field named `"db"` with a value of `"somedb"` that the user doesn't see and also a Submit button that has both an internal `name` (`"Search"`) and a `value` (`"Find it"`) that appears on the Submit button.

All these form fields are important to inventory, because you need to pass each of these to the action page if you're going to simulate the form submission. The action page may look for each of these to be present. Passing in only the `text` and `hidden` fields may not be enough for the action page to process the form correctly. If a page has `textarea` or `select` controls, you'd need to account for these, too.

Assuming the form fields in the preceding example, you can now construct a `CFHTTP` to request this page. You want to run the form's action page (not the form page), and you need to turn that into a complete URL. You also want to provide a CFHTTPPARAM tag for each of the three input fields. In this simple example, assume that you want to pass the value `"some data"` as input for the `"Search1"` field, as follows:

```
<cfhttp url="http://ourdomain/somedir/searchresult.xyz" method="Post">
<cfhttpparam type="FormField" name="search1" value="Some data">
<cfhttpparam type="FormField" name="db" value="SomeDB">
<cfhttpparam type="FormField" name="search" value="Find it">
</cfhttp>
```

This is really cool stuff. If you run this page, the `CFHTTP` proceeds to execute the search result page, presenting the necessary form fields that it would have presented if it were called from `searchform.xyz`.

Now the `cfhttp.filecontent` variable holds the output of the search result page, and again, you can do anything that you want with it, including parsing it, writing it to a file, and so on. Even just passing it for display to the user may not be too trivial a response: You may save the user from needing to fill in the form when all he really wants is the output.

But you're not finished. There could be other challenges in how the form action page processes its form data that could break your attempt to CFHTTP to it. The designers of the action page that you're calling may have written it so that it can be called only from the form page itself. Typically, they may be looking for the CGI variable `http_referer` to be equal to the URL of the form page on their own server. But when using CFHTTP, the value of that variable will instead reflect the URL of the server doing the `CFHTTP`—your server.

To solve this problem—and indeed any problem where a CGI variable needs to be "spoofed" or mimicked to process a form's action page—you can use another form of `CFHTTPPARAM` with a `type="cgi"` to pass the needed CGI variable.

Beware, however, that the ColdFusion variable `cgi.http_referer` is actually a renaming of the underlying HTTP header variable,called simply as `referrer`, which is passed to the page. (The typo in `referer` is an error in the HTTP specification.) Therefore, if you're going to override that value, you need to use the actual HTTP header name rather than the representation ColdFusion creates. The values are listed at `http://www.w3.org/Protocols/HTTP/HTRQ_Headers.html`.

You could, for example, add the following code along with the other CFHTTPPARAM tags that we specified in the previous CFHTTP example:

```
<cfhttpparam type="cgi" name="referer"
value="http://ourdomain/somedir/searchform.xyz">
```

Of course, the value we'd want to provide would typically the URL of the form where we found the input fields (notice it's searchform.xyz in our example), on the assumption that the form action page is expecting input to come from that referring page.

Very useful! Otherwise we may not have been able to perform the CFHTTP processing against that action page, yet it's such a simple solution. In fact, you can provide as many of these CFHTTPPARAM tags as you need within a CFHTTP to create not only CGI variables but others as well. Supported values of the type attribute include cookie and url (query string) fields. In fact, you can even pass a file to be uploaded (as we discuss in the CFFILE section of Chapter 32) by using type="file".

Finally, don't forget that, in the section on troubleshooting CFHTTP, earlier in this chapter, we also mentioned the available useragent attribute that may prove useful in trying to "convince" a page you want to run that the browser you're simulating is something other than what CFHTTP reports by default: "ColdFusion".

Unfortunately, as much as it might be useful to use CFHTTPPARAM for any kind of CFHTTP request (meaning get operations), it can only be used within a CFHTTP using action="post".

Before leaving the subject of using CFHTTP in this way, we should point out that many available custom tags in the Macromedia Developer's Exchange are written to use this very feature of submitting on your behalf to form action pages. You'll find tags to extract stock quotes, weather reports, and more. Whether they're all operating within the licensing restrictions of the servers that they're "grabbing" data from is another question. Some do gets and some do posts. They're all worth looking at for more examples of using CFHTTP in clever ways.

Reading a flat tabular file as a query result set

This final section on CFHTTP examines the use of this tag in a way that many even experienced CF developers have missed. It's just not as obvious as the two examples that we describe in the preceding sections.

You've explored in preceding sections how to "grab" a page that you can otherwise view in a Web browser, and you've seen that you can either store it in a file on your server and/or parse it by processing the available cfhttp.filecontent variable. And you saw that it contained the HTML that would be presented to a browser viewing that page.

But what if the page that you want to process (perhaps existing on another server — or not) is not an HTML file but rather just a simple text file. Or perhaps, more likely, it's a *flat tabular* file such as a CSV or tab-delimited file? Such files can be created as the output of a process to export data from certain databases and even from mainframe enterprise-information systems.

Again, as mentioned at the opening of this section on CFHTTP, Web services, XML, and/or WDDX are all possibly more effective means of performing server-to-server transfer of data. But if you must work with simple flat files, this is a cool feature.

If you want to process such a file, and it is on your local file system, you'd probably think of using `CFFILE` to read it and process the resulting variable as a big long string. That's okay, but such a file is very tedious to parse. And if the file is on a remote server, you may even think to use `CFFTP` to pull it down and, again, use `CFFILE` to parse it.

`CFHTTP`, however, has a special mechanism in it that can not only read such a tabular data file (whether local or remote), but also turn the result into a query result set.

Though all the previous examples of CFHTTP create a `cfhttp.filecontent` result that you'd need to parse, if you instead use the `name` attribute, `CFHTTP` indeed reads the given file and produces in the named variable a result set that you can treat just as if it were a `CFQUERY`.

To see it work, assume that a file of CSV data is available at `http://ourdomain/somedir/somefile.txt`, with data that looks as follows:

```
id,fname,lname,deptid,salary,city,state
1,"Bob","Smith",1,100000,"Nashua","NH"
2,"Jan","Carlson",1,75000,"Newton","MA"
3,"Joe","Johnson",3,56000,"Providence","RI"
5,"Larry","David",2,38750,"Derry","NH"
6,"Jim","Jones",2,110000,"Newton","MA"
7,"Carolyn","Dawn",1,103780,"Sharon","MA"
```

This is a fairly typical example of a CSV file. Notice that each line has some data, separated, or *delimited*, by commas. And if one of those values is a string, it's enclosed in, or *qualified by*, double quotes. (ColdFusion can handle files with other delimiters and qualifiers, as you'll see later in this section.) Notice, too, that the first line acts as a *header*, providing a name for each of the data elements on a row.

With this sort of file at that given location, reading it in by using a CFHTTP and converting it to a ColdFusion query result set is very easy, as in the following example:

```
<cfhttp url=http://ourdomain/somedir/somefile.txt  name="GetData">
```

The value provided for the `name` attribute can be anything that is valid for a ColdFusion variable. Indeed, the result of running this query is that you now have a query result set named `GetData` which has columns corresponding to the names in the `header`; you can, therefore, follow it with a `CFOUTPUT query` loop (or a `CFDUMP` or any tag that works with query result sets). The following example shows how you may output the `name` and `city` for each record in the text file:

```
<cfoutput query="GetData">
   #fname# #lname# - #city#<br>
</cfoutput>
```

See how you can not only treat the `GetData` variable as a query result set, but of course can also treat each of those data names from the first row's header as column names? And, again, you can use this form of the CFHTTP tag for local as well as remote files.

What if the file that you are reading doesn't have a header row naming the column names? Or what if you want to override those names? In either case, you can use the available `columns` attribute and provide a comma-delimited list of values to use as the column names for the generated query result set.

If the file has no row of headers, you also want to use the `firstrowwasheaders="no"` attribute, which is newly available in CF MX.

What if the file that you are reading doesn't use commas for delimiters and double quotes for the qualifier of strings? No problem. `delimiter` and `textqualifier` attributes are available. If tabs are separating or delimiting each value, for example, you can add `delimiter="→|"`. To enter a value between the quote marks, you simply press the Tab key in your editor.

You face a few potential gotchas in working with CSV files in this manner. First, all rows must have the same number of values. You can't have a row that contains an extra column of data; nor can you attempt to represent a `NULL` value by leaving an empty string between the delimiters (displaying two commas in a row). Furthermore, no space can come after the delimiter (the comma). Any of these problems cause ColdFusion to complain with a message that may be misleading: `Incorrect number of columns in row.`

Before closing this discussion concerning reading a flat tabular file as a query result set, you have one more useful application of this technique to consider. In the preceding example, the file that you were reading was simply a static text file. It could just as well be a dynamic page served by ColdFusion or some other server in that CSV or other tabular format. The `CFHTTP` process doesn't really care whether the file is generated by a server or is a static file. The point is, don't feel that if you want to make a page available for this sort of remote processing by a CFHTTP retrieving it, you have to create a static file. You can simply serve up the dynamic, perhaps database-generated content, in a tabular format.

You need to be aware of just a couple tricks in order to make that happen. If the `.cfm` page would generate ColdFusion debugging output, that output causes the `CFHTTP` conversion to a query to fail. It expects nothing but tabular (CSV, or whatever format you've described) data, and the debugging info isn't tabular. The solution is to add `<cfsetting showdebugoutput="no">` to the top of the page which is generating the tabular output (not the page doing the CFHTTP). This will stop it sending the debugging output.

You may also find that you need to add a `<cfcontent type="text/plain">` to that page creating the tabular output, to make sure that the Web server creates the file as a text MIME type. This may not prove necessary, but forewarned is forearmed.

Finally, in concluding this chapter, we should mention that you may want to connect to still one other sort of "other server." We've shown you in this chapter how to connect to mail, FTP, and Web servers, but we don't have room to cover the topic of connecting to LDAP servers. If you are interested in connecting to such servers, you should investigate the `CFLDAP` tag that we discuss in chapter 62. You also find coverage of how to use this tag in the ColdFusion documentation.

Summary

We've seen that there are several ways to interact with remote servers. First, `CFMAIL` processing allows us to send mail from within a ColdFusion application. We also learned about several variations on `CFMAIL` processing, including varying just the `to`, `from`, or `subject` fields, or the message body itself, or creating multiple emails from a query result set. We also learned that we can refer to a query result within the body of a mail message.

It may seem a little odd to consider CFMAIL in a chapter that also covers `CFFTP` and `CFHTTP`, but technically the `CFMAIL` does cause transmission of a file to a remote server.

`CFFTP` processing is useful when you need to either send files to a remote server or retrieve them from one. It's suitable when you have appropriate `FTP` access to that remote server. We learned that there is a caching version of `CFFTP` processing, which is useful when we are performing several operations in a single FTP processing session.

If instead you need to retrieve a file from a remote server via HTTP rather than FTP, that's one use of CFHTTP. We learned that we can extract a CSV or other tabular-formatted file and retrieve it into ColdFusion as a query result set. That's not a feature that many know about. More typically, it's used to "grab" the HTML output of a web page and pull that into a variable within our ColdFusion template. From there we saw that we could parse the HTML to select and perhaps display just some portion of the page. Finally, we also saw that we could use CFHTTP to simulate submission of a form, in particular by use of the CFHTTPPARAM tag.

✦ ✦ ✦

Extending Your ColdFusion MX Applications

P A R T

VI

✦ ✦ ✦ ✦

In This Part

✦ ✦ ✦ ✦

CHAPTER 32

Adding Useful ColdFusion MX Features to Your Application

In this chapter, we introduce some features in ColdFusion that you may consider using to enhance your application. They're not new to ColdFusion MX, but they're certainly classics, and they're often misunderstood (or plain missed) by many CF developers.

Each may involve some coordination with the CF Administrator, but we cover what you need to know so that you can effectively address any considerations that they may raise.

The first, `CFSCHEDULE`, enables you to create automation processes that execute at scheduled intervals. This can prove very useful if you have some process that needs to run repeatedly or at some point in the future. We discuss both setting up and using the scheduling features.

The second, `CFFILE`, is one of the richest of all CF tags in that it can perform many different functions, which can be broken into three broad areas. As suggested by its name, it enables the manipulation of files on the CF server. In one respect, it enables the processing of files as a whole (moving them, deleting them, and so on). In another respect, it enables you to read from and write to files. Finally, it also enables you to upload files from the client via a special HTTP form feature. We discuss each of these.

The third feature, *Verity Indexing*, enables you to create a searchable library of files on your server, which can be especially useful if you have a large number of HTML documents, word-processing files, spreadsheets, presentations, and Acrobat PDF files, to name just a few. The process of creating, populating, and searching an *index* of such files is quite straightforward and may be one of the under-utilized features in CF. We show you the basics and point you to other resources to learn still more, including how to leverage the Verity index capability to add more power to database searching as well.

✦ ✦ ✦ ✦

In This Chapter

Running unattended tasks by using `CFSCHEDULE` or the Administrator Scheduled Task facility

Reading, writing, manipulating, and uploading files by using `CFFILE`

Creating searchable file libraries or query results by using Verity Indexing

Running Unattended Tasks by Using CFSCHEDULE or the Administrator Scheduled Task Page

Have you ever wanted to execute some part of your application in an automated fashion, such that it occurs after some length of time or at some recurring point in a business cycle? Maybe you want to archive the records of customers who haven't placed an order in the past 12 months or you want to send an e-mail to members whose expiration date is approaching. You may also want to set up a scheduled task to repopulate a Verity index each day or week. (We discuss Verity indexes in the section "Creating Searchable File Libraries or Query Results by Using Verity Indexing," later in this chapter.)

The good news is that, if you have a ColdFusion template that performs some desired processing to be executed in an unattended, perhaps repeated manner, you can indeed schedule it by using the `CFSCHEDULE` tag. You can also use the Scheduled Tasks feature available in the ColdFusion Administrator, if you have access to that.

The feature can execute any available URL — it's really not limited to just CF pages nor even to those only on your own server. You can also choose to store any HTML output from the execution of the scheduled task for later viewing. This could prove handy if you need to create a report from a Web page for a user who doesn't have access to the application.

This scheduled-task feature was originally used by many to create static output of dynamic pages that may be visited by a large number of users but that contained content that didn't change often. Rather than point users to the dynamic CFML-generated page, they would use the scheduled-task capability to create a separate HTML file and then point users to that HTML file.

This rather tedious process is obviated by the `CFCACHE` tag. (See the ColdFusion documentation for more information on that tag.) The documentation for the scheduler, however, still refers to this outmoded process as one of the uses for the feature, without mentioning `CFCACHE`. Certainly, if for some reason you can't use the `CFCACHE` tag, knowing that this scheduled-task feature is available is useful.

The scheduled-task feature in ColdFusion is separate from a similar capability that may be available in your operating system. Windows has its own notion of *scheduled tasks,* and Unix has `chron` jobs. Although these features are generally used to execute some sort of system command or batch file on a scheduled basis, they may not be available to you as a developer. They're also not designed to execute CF templates (although they can indeed do that, but discussing that feature is beyond the scope of this book).

Remember, too, that the CF Scheduled Task feature enables you to execute a Web page, that is, any URL that can be called from the server that's hosting ColdFusion. An operating-system scheduler, on the other hand, generally just executes locally available commands.

Adding a scheduled task

You can set up a scheduled task either in the ColdFusion Administrator (if you have access to it) or by using the `CFSCHEDULE` tag (if it isn't disabled by the CF Administrator). We look briefly at each method in this and the following section.

Although many readers do not have access to the CF Administrator pages, we show the use of that interface first. In the following section, we show how to set up and manage a scheduled task by using the tag-based approach. Each is capable of the same results.

Figure 32-1 shows the Administrator's interface for the scheduler. After you first open the Administrator, the scheduler interface is listed (curiously) in the left navigational toolbar, under `Debugging & Logging`, as `Scheduled Tasks`. The page that this link takes you to offers a form where you can add, edit, or delete tasks.

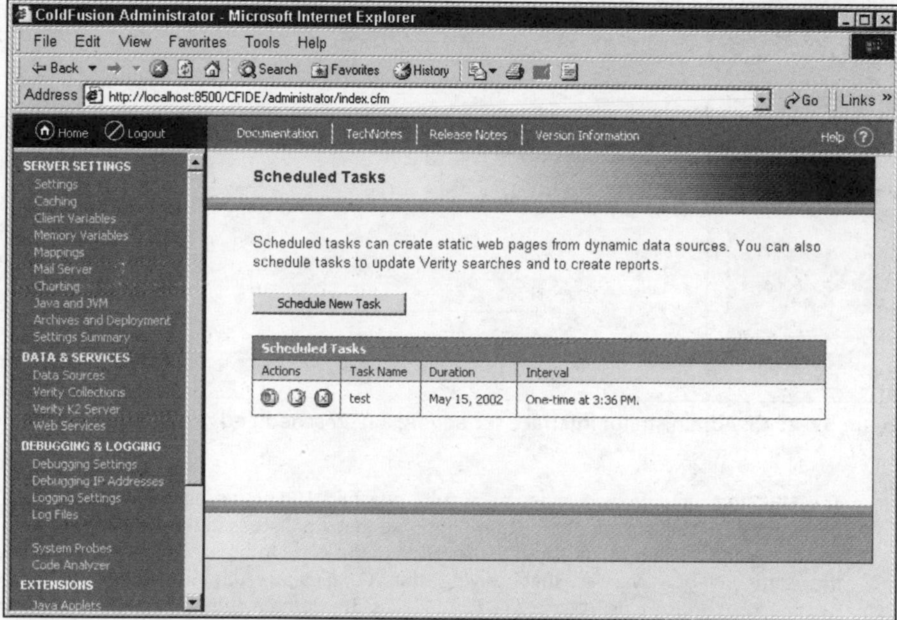

Figure 32-1: CF Administrator's interface for scheduled tasks.

To create a new task, click the Schedule New Task button. Figure 32-2 shows the form that appears for creating a new task, where you indicate which template you want to run, when you want to run it, how often, and several other characteristics that may be necessary.

The figure doesn't show all available fields on the form, but if you scroll down in the Administrator, you see them all. We discuss the most important ones in this section. See the online Help available within the Administrator for the others.

The Task Name field is where you just type a simple phrase of your choosing to label the task. Notice that it's *not* the URL of the actual page to be executed, as a field for that information comes further down on the form. The minimum information required to add a new task goes into the Duration fields (Start Date and an optional End Date), the Frequency options (choosing among One-time, Recurring, or Daily Every to indicate how often and when to run the task), and the URL field (the page to be executed).

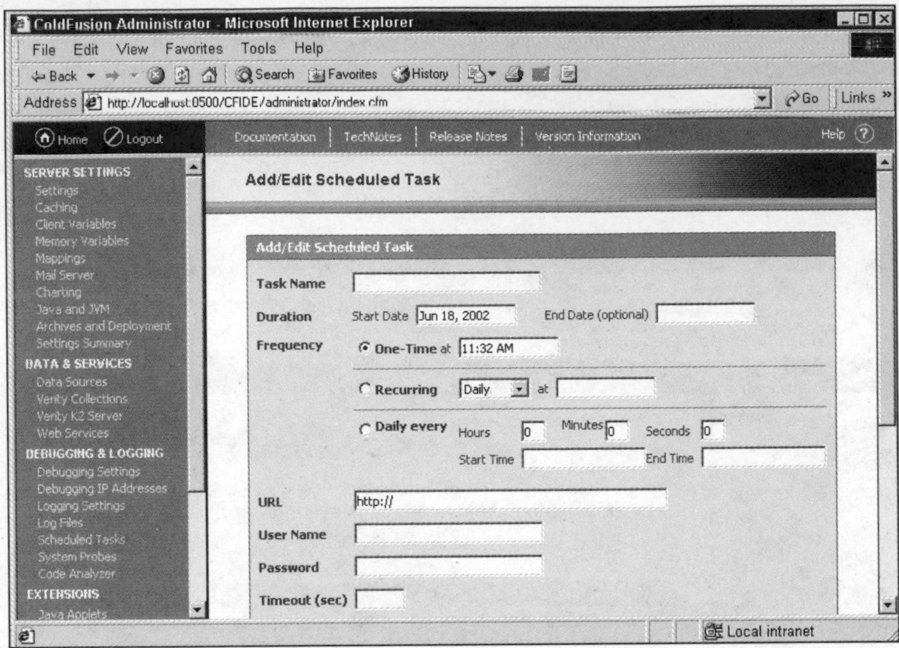

Figure 32-2: CF Administrator interface for adding a new scheduled task.

The URL that you provide must be a fully qualified URL (starting with `http://`). The Administrator interface and the `CFSCHEDULE` tag that we discuss in the following section do not make any presumptions about the location of the code to be executed. If the code is on the same Web server as that serving this ColdFusion Administrator, you can use `http://localhost` or `http://127.0.0.1` as the domain (before the rest of the URL). Indeed, this suggests that you can use the scheduler to execute any URL at all, including those on some other server on the network.

You may be required to provide additional information about the execution of the task. If the URL that you're executing requires Web-server authentication (a login and password), for example, you need to provide that here, as well in the available User Name and Password fields.

Failure to provide a URL in the URL field may cause more confusion for scheduling tasks than any other problem. You may assert that you can browse the URL in your browser without providing a username/password. First, however, you need to realize that the scheduling facility is executing the URL on your behalf as if it were the client. (It runs the equivalent of a `CFHTTP` request on your behalf.) So although you may find you can browse the URL without an authentication prompt, that may be because you provided such authentication earlier in your current browser session. Naturally, that has no effect on the scheduler that's running the task. If a page to be executed requires authentication, you must provide a username and password for the scheduled task.

Also, and more troubling for some, you must take into account the fact that the scheduler (and indeed `CFHTTP`) can't perform anything other than basic (plain-text) Web-server authentication. If the URL that you want to execute calls for *digest authentication* or *integrated Windows authentication* on IIS, you *cannot* execute that URL with a scheduled task.

Other information that you may want to provide for a new task (not shown in Figure 32-2) includes any needed proxy server information and an optional timeout that you may want to provide to cause a long-running scheduled task to give up if it may take too long to execute.

And if you're interested in retaining the output from the task, you have an option to publish the output to a path/filename of your choosing. That section also offers a resolve-URL option that, like CFHTTP, can convert relative URLs found in the HTML output of the requested page into absolute ones.

Using the CFSCHEDULE tag to add a task

Because most developers can't access the ColdFusion Administrator, a CFSCHEDULE tag is availablethat can perform all the same functions of the Administrator interface. Each of the options listed on the figures in the preceding section are available for the CFSCHEDULE tag via similarly named attributes (using the attribute action="update", which either adds or updates a scheduled task).

The following code provides an example of how to use the CFSCHEDULE tag to schedule a task called DeleteExpiredMembers so that it runs a template at www.somedomain.com/members/DeleteExpired.cfm at 12:10 p.m. starting 6/28/2002 and continuing on a monthly basis for an indefinite duration (because no enddate is provided). The output of that template is to be written to the file D:\inetpub\wwwroot\members\deletelog.txt, as the following example shows:

```
<cfschedule action="update" task="DeleteExpiredMembers"
operation="httprequest"
url="http://www.somedomain.com/members/DeleteExpired.cfm"
startdate="6/28/2002" starttime="12:10pm" interval="monthly"
resolveurl="no" publish="yes" file="deletelog.txt"
path="D:\inetpub\wwwroot\members\">
```

Again, as we mention in the preceding section, you need to provide a complete URL even if the code that you're executing is on the same server as ColdFusion MX.

Be aware that use of the CFSCHEDULE tag itself can be disabled in the ColdFusion Administrator so that it can't be used in any templates on the server. See Chapter 44 for more information.

Finally, you can update or delete (or run immediately) any scheduled task, either from the Administrator interface, as shown in Figure 32-1, or from the CFSCHEDULE tag. See Chapter 47 for more information.

Reading, Writing, Manipulating, and Uploading Files by Using CFFILE

It is common that ColdFusion developers will need to perform some sort of file processing (reading and writing) or file manipulation (move, copy, delete, and so on). If you need to read the contents of a file, want to create (or append to) a file to hold some sort of text, or need to manipulate files on the ColdFusion Server, you want to know about the CFFILE tag.

Another very different kind of capability is enabled via CFFILE, and its one that has no correlation to typical file processing. If you've ever wanted to create a process whereby visitors to your site could upload files from their local machines to your ColdFusion server, you should be happy to know that you can do that by using CFFILE. This kind of capability can be used to send photos of people on a membership site or of houses on a real estate site. It can also be used to upload a user's resume in its native word-processing format. This third capability is much more involved than the first two, so we're going to discuss the simpler processes first.

Reading/writing files on the server

Although the ColdFusion markup language (CFML) is a full-featured language with many capabilties of traditional languages (flow control, conditional expressions, rich variables and data structures), you need to keep in mind that it's primarily a language for creating Web pages dynamically. As such, the capability to read and write files isn't exactly a top priority for most Web developers. Indeed, you may often be better off resorting to some other language that may be better suited to the task.

Still, in certain instances, reading in a file's contents by using CFML may make sense. Perhaps you're processing a *CSV (comma-separated value)* file, for example, that you extracted from another program or database. Or maybe you're given an XML file. (See Chapter 30 for more information on XML.) Using CFFILE is one way that you could read the contents of such a file into ColdFusion's memory to process it as a simple variable.

Better tools than CFFILE may be available for processing CSV and other regularly delimited files. See the Chapter 55 for more information on the CFHTTP tag's available name attribute, which enables it to read a CSV file and convert it into a ColdFusion query result set. (See the entry on the delimiter and textqualifier attributes for information about defining something other than the default comma as a delimiter and using something other than double quotes as the text qualifier.) The Java libraries underlying CF MX also enable you to use Java to process such files. For more information, see the Macromedia TechNote at www.macromedia.com/handlers/index.cfm?ID=22250.

Reading a file on the server

If you need or want to read a file's contents into a ColdFusion variable, the CFFILE tag offers a very simple mechanism to do so. To read the contents of a file named test.txt in the directory c:\temp\ so that they are stored in a ColdFusion variable named holdfile, for example, the tag you would use is as follows:

```
<cffile action="read" file="C:\TEMP\TEST.TXT" variable="holdfile">
```

This code reads the entire file into the single variable. From there, you can do with it whatever you want, including using the variable in a CFQUERY tag to insert the contents into a database. More likely, you may want to manipulate the contents now in the variable by using any of ColdFusion's many string-manipulation functions, such as paragraphformat(), or find().

If you try to output the variable's value to the screen by using CFOUTPUT, make sure that the file contents are not pure text (but are HTML). If they're plain text, the browser ignores white spaces between words and lines of text, and it also ignores line breaks and carriage returns, causing the file to appear compressed into one large block of text. You can improve the appearance in that case by using the ColdFusion formatting function, paragraphformat().

The following code sample reads the contents of the CF server's `application.log` (one of CF's many administrative log files) and displays it on-screen. Notice the use of the `paragraphformat()` function to enhance the appearance of the output, as follows:

```
<cffile action="read" file="C:\CFusionMX\logs\application.log"
variable="getlog">
<cfoutput>#paragraphformat(getlog)#</cfoutput>
```

Unless the CF Administrator takes steps to change installation defaults, the `CFFILE` tag can be used to read, write, move, and so on any file on any drive accessible to the ColdFusion Server (or accessible to the user under which the server is running in environments that provide such process authorization). See the section, "Possible tag restrictions," later in this chapter, for more information.

Reading a binary file

If the contents of the file that you want to read are binary in nature (an image or a word-processing file format), you want to use `action="readbinary"`. You can still read the contents into a ColdFusion variable, but you can't use CFOUTPUT to display the value, because `CFOUTPUT` can display only data that can be converted to a string-data format. You can store the data into a database column or write it to another file (by using `CFFILE action="write"`, as we discuss in the next section).

Writing to a file on the server

Just as you can read an entire file's contents to a ColdFusion variable, you can perform the reverse action as well, writing a variable (or any string, really) to a text file.

As an example, the file that you read into ColdFusion in the section, "Reading a file on the server," can be written out to another path/name as follows:

```
<cffile action="write" file="c:\temp\testoutput.txt" output="#getlog#"
addnewline="no">
```

Of course, for this code to execute, you need a variable called `getlog` to be defined before the tag executes. And if the file named in the `FILE` attribute doesn't already exist, it is created.

Additional attributes are available to the tag that aren't needed but may be useful, including the option to specify file attributes (`readonly`, `hidden`, and so on) for the file created, an option to specify the mode that sets permissions on Unix platforms and is ignored in Windows, and an option to indicate whether a newline character is written to the file after the specified contents in the `output` attribute. See Chapter 60 in the Language Reference for more information.

Before leaving the discussion of writing to files, you should also know ColdFusion's `append` action (as in `action="append"`). The attributes for this are the same as for the `write` action; the difference is that the data written to the named file by using `append` is added at the end of the file, if one already exists (otherwise, a file is created). This option can be particularly useful for creating log files or writing other sorts of output files.

You have a better way to create log files than by using `write` or `append`. Release 5 of ColdFusion introduced a new `CFLOG` tag that is much more capable and straightforward to use, especially for writing to the standard administrative CF log files.

Manipulating files on the server

Maybe you're not interested in reading or writing files. You just need to manage and manipulate files on the ColdFusion server (or on a drive that it can access). CFFILE's second major category of actions is to provide just that sort of capability.

The actions move, rename, copy, and delete do just what their names suggest. The first three of these all share the following attributes:

- source: Describes the full path to the name of the file to be acted on.
- destination: Describes the full path of the directory to which the action is directed.
- attributes: Again, describes the intended file attributes (readonly, hidden, and so on) to apply against the destination file.

Again, see Chapter 60 for more information or the details of these attributes. Following is an example of moving the file testoutput.txt from the c:\temp directory to the d:\temp directory:

```
<cffile action="move" source="c:\temp\testoutput.txt"
destination="d:\temp\testoutput.txt">
```

You can leave off the file name (specifying only a directory path) in the destination attribute for action="move" and action="copy".

Finally, to delete a file, simply specify the full path to the file you want to remove and the action= "delete".

Although we don't discuss it in any detail in this chapter, you should also become familiar with the CFDIRECTORY tag, which enables you to list directories and files within a directory, as well as create, rename, and delete directories. See Chapter 60 for more information.

Uploading files from browser to server

The final of the three major groupings of CFFILE capabilities is quite different from the previous two. Whereas they simply manipulate (or read/write) files on the ColdFusion server, CFFILE action="upload" is the key to enabling the creation of Web interfaces where your visitors can upload files from their workstations to your server. As we mentioned in the section, "Reading, Writing, Manipulating, and Uploading Files by Using CFFILE," the possible uses of this capability are limited only by your imagination: Use it, for example, to enable the uploading of photos, documents, and more.

In general, the best thing to do with such an upoaded file is to store it as a file of the same format on the server. Some may want to store it in a database, but that generally is not the best choice. If the application is simply to make the file available to other users on a Web site (whether presenting the pictures for display or providing a link to download resumes, for example), all that you really need to do is store the file on the server and then store the *name* of the file in the database. We show you an example of this later in this chapter.

Whereas the previous uses of the CFFILE tag have just a couple or a few attributes to choose from, the "UPLOAD" action offers up to six other possible attributes : filefield, destination, nameconflict, accept, attributes, and mode. It also creates a set of result variables that can be used to determine the result of the upload process. Finally, unlike the other uses of the CFFILE tag, this one really works only in conjunction with a form that's passing data to the template that's executing the tag.

Requesting the file from the browser user

Before discussing the CFFILE tag any further, you need to take a look at an example form that may be used to send such file contents to the server. The following example shows a form that, in addition to the normal request for information about a member's name and e-mail address, also gives the member the option of uploading a photo of himself:

```
<h2>Update Your Membership Profile</h2>
<form action="uploadaction.cfm"  enctype="multipart/form-data"
method="post">
Name: <input type="text" name="name"><br>
Email: <input type="text" name="email"><p>
Enter the complete path and filename of any photo of yourself that
you'd like to upload:<br>
<input type="file" name="photo" size="45"><br>
(Or use the browse button to locate the file on your workstation.)
<p>
<input type="submit" value"Upload">
</form>
```

This code offers a couple possibly unusual characteristics. First, notice the use of enctype="multipart/form-data" on the FORM tag. Normally, you don't specify any such enctype attribute (and although you may not realize it, the form would be processed with a default value of "application/x-www-form-urlencoded"). You must specify this alternative value for the enctype attribute in performing file uploads.

The second unusual thing is the <input type= "file"> tag. This tage does several things: For one, it creates an input field where the user can type the name of a file. But the user may be better off using an operating-system dialog box to find and select the desired file, and that's the next thing that this tag does. Look at the output that results from use of this form and how it appears, as shown in Figure 32-3.

Notice that the <input type="file"> tag has caused the browser to display a Browse button for the user. This happens automatically (as long as the browser recognizes the <input type= "file"> tag, which is recognized by Netscape Navigator 3 or later and Internet Explorer 4 or later).

The user can now fill in the rest of the form and either type a location and file name for a photo or use the Browse button to open a dialog box (provided by the operating system of his workstation) to locate the file on his workstation. Of course, the user doesn't need to do either unless your application requires him to. (In other words, nothing in the HTML requires that the Photo field in the form shown in Figure 32-3 be filled in.)

After the user submits the form, the action page (as specified in the <form action attribute) receives the form submission and can access all the form fields (Name and Email, in the example in the figure) just as it normally can. At this point, you can store the member's profile information (name, e-mail) in a database record. The next question is what to do with this uploaded photo.

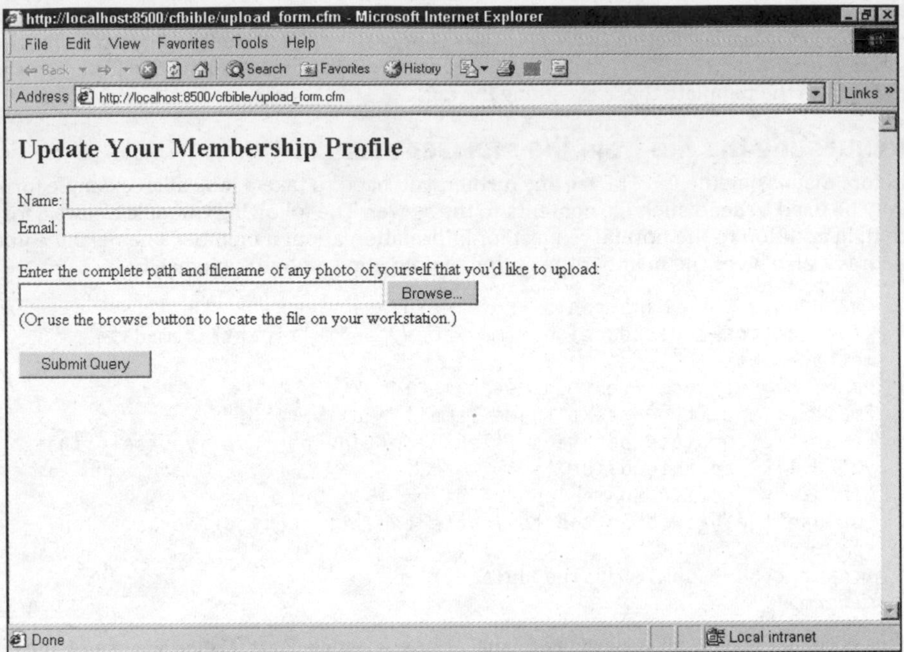

Figure 32-3: An HTML form using the `<input type= "file">` tag.

Processing the uploaded file on the server

The action page contains a field called Photo with a value that, if output to the screen or viewed in the available debugging output, simply shows the name of the file. How do you get the file itself, and what do you do with it? This Photo field involves more than just the name of the file.

As we explain in the section "Uploading files from browser to server," earlier in this chapter, although the idea of storing the uploaded file in a database may seem tempting, the more practical approach is to simply store the file on the server and then store the *name of the file, as its known on the server*, in a database field. The field where you store this name can be just another field in the record that's holding the member profile information in the example in the preceding section (name, e-mail), perhaps as just another text field called Photofile. The field just needs to be long enough to hold the name of the file.

But is the name of the file the same as it was as the user sent it? And where exactly is it to be stored after the upload? That's where the `<cffile action="upload">` tag comes into play. Its purpose is to take a form field that's holding a file name that someone uploaded from a browser (actually, the posted multipart form data containing the file contents that are loaded into a temporary file on the server) and store it in a location on the server with a file name of your choosing.

The following tag is the simplest version of `action="upload"` that can store the Photo field from this example to a directory on the server called `c:\CFusionMX\wwwroot\members`:

```
<cffile action="upload" filefield="photo"
destination="c:\CFusionMX\wwwroot\members\">
```

Notice that this code uses a new `filefield` attribute, which holds the name of the form field that was used to store the name of the file. Notice that this is *not* the name of the file that someone's uploading, but the name of the field that's holding that file name.

Although the value of the `filefield` is indeed the name of a ColdFusion form field, we don't refer to it here as `form.photo` nor do we specify it by placing pound signs around it, as in `#photo#`, otherwise you will encounter unexpected results.

See the discussion of other `CFFILE` processing capabilities in the section "Manipulating files on the server," earlier in this chapter, for more information about the `destination` attribute as well as the available `attributes` and `mode` attributes.

File name conflicts and alternatives

The simple example in the preceding section would store the name of the file exactly as it is named on the client's machine (although it would now be stored on the specified directory on the server). The problem is, what if another client submits another photo with the same name? You have no control over what people call files on their workstations, and making them rename it for uploading to the server is tedious and possibly unacceptable.

The `CFFILE` tag offers a solution in its `nameconflict` attribute. If not specified, it defaults to a value of `error`, which means that if the `CFFILE` tries to store a file on the server directory and another file of the same name is already there, the `CFFILE` tag fails. Although you could anticipate that error and handle it by using `CFTRY/CFCATCH` processing (see Chapter 21 for more information), and you can also use several result variables to determine what sort of problem occurred, using any of serveral alternative values for the `nameconflict` attribute may make more sense in preventing the problem.

First, you can use `nameconflict="skip"`, although it may not prove very useful. It doesn't generate an error if a conflict arises, but it also doesn't store the file on the server in such a case. Next, you can try `nameconflict="overwrite"`, which simply replaces the current file on the server with the newer one of the same name. For some applications, this approach is appropriate, such as a case where the client is naming the files in such a way that they're unique to him, but a different version is being uploaded which should always replace any previous one.

The final alternative, and one that probably makes the most sense for an application such as your member-photo upload process, is `nameconflict="makeunique"`. This option *automatically generates a unique file name* for the file stored on the server. As we mention later in this chapter, several variables are available for use after executing this form of the `CFFILE` tag, and one of those, serverfile, holds the name of the file as generated by the server. You learn more about those variables later in this chapter. For now, just know that a variable called `cffile.serverfile`, which holds the file name (and extension), is available. The name may be in a format such as `ACF181.ext`—with `.ext` the extension of the original file, which is preserved.

Controlling the types of files that can be uploaded

One other attribute available for the `CFFILE action="upload"` is the `accept` attribute, which enables you to control (or, to be more accurate, reject) any attempts to upload file formats that you're not prepared to accept.

The type specified in the value of the `accept` attribute is a comma-separated list of MIME types. If you want to permit GIF and JPG formatted images, for example, you can specify the example tag from the preceding sections (with the option to make file names unique) as follows:

```
<cffile action="upload" filefield="photo"
destination="c:\CFusionMX\wwwroot\members\"
accept="image/gif,image/jpeg">
```

The MIME type for the file that's uploaded is determined and passed to the server from the browser. Generally, browsers determine the MIME type from the file extension, but this is browser-specific. If the server receives a file of a type that's not expected, the CFFILE tag generates a ColdFusion error. Again, you may want to test such code within a CFTRY/CFCATCH error-handling routine, which is covered in Chapter 21, "Handling Exceptions."

Notice that no mechanism is available to limit the file uploaded in any other way, including, most noticeably, its size. You have no means of detecting the size before proceeding with the CFFILE tag to store the file, but you can indeed check the size of the file after its stored on the server by using the variable cffile.filesize. You can also delete the file if you detect that it's an excessively large one, for example, by using the CFFILE Action= "delete".

Available upload status variables

We mention a couple of the available variables that report on the status of an attempted CFFILE action= "upload". You can find a table of them in the Macromedia ColdFusion CFML Reference Manual's covereage of the CFFILE tag, under the usage section for action="upload".

These variables all begin with the cffile. prefix, and the most important ones are cffile.serverfile (the name of the file stored on the server) and cffile.filesize (the size of the file in bytes as stored on the server).

Note: Before ColdFusion5, these variables were referred to by the prefix file. instead of cffile.. Although you may see code that with older form of reference, it's formally deprecated and should be modified.

Other interesting cffile variables tell you more about the file as it existed on the client (its location, name, extension, size, and type), the file as it is now on the server (its location, name, and extension), as well as its creation and modification date/time, whether the process overwrote a previous file, and, if so, details about the file that it overwrote, including its name and size.

Possible tag restrictions

Again, as with all the file actions described in preceding sections of this chapter, you face an important security issue: Unless the CF Administrator has taken steps to change installation defaults, the CFFILE tag can be used to upload a file to any directory on any drive that's accessible to the ColdFusion server (or to the user under whose name the server is running in environments that provide such process authorization).

Because of the potential for abuse (for example, users reading/writing to system files that they shouldn't, reading/writing to files belonging to other CF developers on the server that they shouldn't, or uploading files into directories that they shouldn't), an option in the ColdFusion Administrator can disable the CFFILE tag entirely.

Unfortunately, this restriction is very broad, meaning that it applies to any use of the tag by any developer on the server attempting any of the three categories of CFFILE processing. It can't ne restricted to permit file uploads but prevent the reading of files. It also can't be set to permit some people to do things while restricting others nor to permit actions against only specific directories (perhaps for specific users).

Such restrictions aren't impossible. ColdFusion does offer a form of security that can be implemented, called *sandbox security*, which can achieve all of these objectives. (See Chapter 44 for more on various forms of security available in ColdFusion, including sandbox security.)

Unfortunately, most shops may be slow to implement sandbox security. It's a new feature, and its previous implementation in CF5 and earlier was especially challenging. The new CF MX approach is much simpler. Still, it's no small effort to set up, defining which resources (files, directories, tags, functions, datasources, and so on) that code in a given directory can access. So some shops simply disable the CFFILE tag (along with several related ones, also discussed in Chapter 44).

As such, you have little choice if your site has restricted the CFFILE tag but to persuade the administrator to implement sandbox security. You do have one other alternative, again discussed later in this book and unknown to many: The *unsecured tags directory*, which does permit the execution of otherwise restricted tags. This approach is discussed in a February 2002 ColdFusion Developer's Journal (*CFDJ*) article, "Unlocking Restricted Use of CFFILE, CFCONTENT, and More," by Charlie Arehart.

Creating Searchable File Libraries or Query Results by Using Verity Indexing

One of the many things that set ColdFusion apart from other scripting environments is that it comes bundled with additional tools that you would otherwise need to purchase. One of the most interesting of these is the *Verity Indexing* capability.

Verity is a company that was known for its file-indexing technology before the Web became popular, and its tool provides a means to perform a full-text search through a set of files so that you can find all references to a given term (or a more complex search expression, which we discuss later in this chapter). It's much more than "just a Web search engine."

ColdFusion 5 introduces a greatly enhanced version of the Verity search engine, called the Verity K2 Server. We discuss both the new and earlier versions of the engine in the following sections, as both are still supported. Everything that we discuss about using Verity Indexes applies to the new K2 Server as well. Setting up K2 Server is discussed in the new Macromedia ColdFusion MX manual, *Working with Verity Tools*.

Three forms of indexing

You may want to perform at least three forms of indexing by using the Verity tools.

The first — and the one for which Verity indexing has been used the longest — is searching against all the files in a given directory to find those that match some desired search criteria. This form of searching (and indexing) can prove very useful to organizations with the equivalent of an electronic library on their servers.

Verity can index more than 45 native file formats, including the following:

- ✦ Word-processing files (including MS Word, MS Works, WordPerfect, Lotus AmiPro/WordPro and others)
- ✦ Spreadsheets (MS Excel, MS Works, Lotus 1-2-3, Corel QuattroPro, and others)
- ✦ Presentation files (MS PowerPoint, Lotus FreeLance, and Corel Presentations)
- ✦ Acrobat PDF files, flat text files, RTF files, Unicode files, and more

You face a potential challenge in using this form of indexing and searching documents. Although Verity can index and search directories that include your CFM templates, this first mechanism processes only the source code of your template—not its output—on execution. This can cause real confusion, because your intention may be to index the output of the pages, not the source code. The next form of indexing, Web spidering, addresses that challenge.

The second form of indexing is what some may think of more commonly as a Web search engine. Verity refers to it as the *Verity Spider* feature. In this approach, the indexing engine is directed not to simply read and index all the files in a given directory, but instead is directed to start at a given URL on a Web site and then follow all the links on the page (and the links that the next page leads to). In this manner, it indeed processes the output of your CF templates.

The Verity Spider is a subject beyond the scope of this chapter but is covered in the ColdFusion documentation manual, *Working with Verity Tools*. But the process of searching an index created that way will be the same as that which we will cover in this chapter.

The Verity Spider capability is something that most CF developers, even experienced ones, don't know much, if anything, about. Since it was a feature only introduced to us in CF 5, and the enhanced documentation is newly made available in CF MX, it will take time for it to become popular. Again, you're learning about something that many others may never have heard of. Go look into it!

Finally, the third approach to using indexing is another that may surprise some folks. Verity can do more then index and search files, you can also use it to index-search against query result sets. You can take the result of a `CFQUERY`, for example, and store those results in a Verity index.

Why would you want to do that? Verity indexes are optimized for retrieval and not only may be faster (especially for text searches, as compared to a `LIKE` clause in a SQL `SELECT` statement), but also permit more complex search criteria, including proximity searching and much more.

And in addition to `CFQUERY` result sets, it can also index any other result set from tags that produce query-like results. `CFSTOREDPROC` is an obvious one, but others include `CFPOP` and `CFLDAP`. Again, we don't have room in this chapter to cover this use of indexing (although, again, the search process is similar). See the ColdFusion documentation manual *Developing ColdFusion MX Applications with CFML*— in particular, the section "Working with record sets" in Chapter 24, "Building a Search Interface."

For more information about extended features of the Verity Indexing capability, including internationalization, localization, and complex search criteria expressions, see the ColdFusion MX documentation.

In this chapter, we just get you started on the simple process of creating, populating, and searching a Verity Index based on a set of files. If you want to see an already existing example of using Verity indexing, the online documentation provided on installation of ColdFusion Server or Studio is completely searchable and is driven by a Verity Index.

But if you're interested in creating searchable indexes of your own, you can proceed with the next three steps in the following sections.

Creating a Verity Index (collection)

The first step in enabling a search facility against some files is to create a Verity Index—or what Verity calls a *collection*. The actual implementation of this file (which is actually a set of files and directories) is not really your concern as developers (or even administrators). You just need to execute a simple, one-time step to create the collection.

Just as you see in the case of the Scheduled Task page which we describe in the section "Adding a scheduled task," earlier in this chapter, ColdFusion offers both a menu-driven interface for doing creating a Verity collection, through use of the ColdFusion Administrator, and a tag-based interface, through use of the `CFCOLLECTION` attribute. In this chapter, we discuss only the tag-based approach, because many developers can't access the Administrator. (And the Administrator interface now provides online Help to assist those interested in learning that approach.)

The CFCOLLECTION tag

The `CFCOLLECTION` tag is a pretty simple tag that can be used to create a new collection. The Administrator interface accepts the same basic information: the collection's name, the location where the underlying collection support files are stored (which is not related at all to the files that you're going to be indexing), and a choice of language, with English the default.

As for where to place the underlying collection support files that it creates, the Administrator interface shows a default value of `C:\CFusionMX\verity\collections`. That's a typical place to store them, but you may place the files anywhere that you want. This is important to know if, for some reason, security constraints preclude you (or the `CFCOLLECTION` tag acting on your behalf) from writing to that default directory.

To create a collection named `"test"`, stored in the `C:\CFusionMX\verity\collections` directory, using the English language, you can use the following code:

```
<cfcollection action="create" collection="test"
path=" C:\CFusionMX\verity\collections\">
```

Assuming no errors occur, the result is an empty collection, ready for you to populate, or *index*.

Populating (indexing) a Verity collection

After you create a collection, the next step is to populate it—or what ColdFusion refers to as *indexing the collection*. Again, both an Administrator and a tag-based interface are possible. We focus on use of the `CFINDEX` tag.

To populate the newly created collection, you need to tell Verity where to look for files to use to populate the index. You can name the directory path and indicate whether you want it to recursively look through any subdirectories under that.

Again, the idea of having Verity "spider" through your site and process the *output* of your ColdFusion templates is an entirely different subject, covered in the Verity documentation, as described in the section "Three forms of indexing," earlier in this chapter.

You also can indicate which file types (extensions) you are interested in searching. This can prove useful in keeping Verity from indexing files that shouldn't be searched (or found, to put it another way) by end users. On the other hand, if you do mean to index other types of documents (such as text files, PDF files, word-processing documents, and so on), you need to indicate that. To index files that have no extension at all, you specify `*.` in the list.

You can also define a `urlpath` (or "return URL" on the administrator interface). This is used to cause the search results created (by later use of the `CFSEARCH` tag) to return the found file name, prepending it with a given URL prefix. This way, as the file name appears on-screen, it can be presented as a hyperlink that can locate the file. You see the use of that in the section "Searching a Verity Collection," later in this chapter.

The CFINDEX tag

Most of the attributes of the `CFINDEX` tag are rather self-explanatory, although a couple are less clear. It can also do more than the Administrator interface enables you to do.

Following is a simple example that indexes the `"test"` collection that you create in the section "The `CFCOLLECTION` tag," earlier in this chapter, so that the collection looks at files in the `c:\CFusionMX\wwwroot\members\` directory and recurses through any directories below that one. Finally, it stores with each index entry the URL prefix *`http://www.somedomain.com/members/`*, for use as the search results are later displayed, as follows:

```
<cfindex collection="test" action="update" type="path"
key="c:\CfusionMX\wwwroot\members\" recurse="yes"
urlpath="http://www.somedomain.com/members/">
```

Notice that you need to specify an `action` of `"update"`, to index the collection. Other values for `action` also are possible, which we discuss later in this chapter. And to specify the path to be indexed, you use the less-than-obvious `key` attribute and must also specify `type="path"`. This has to do with other uses of the `CFINDEX` tag, so just be aware that, to perform this simple action of populating an index based on the contents in files in a given path, you need this form of the tag. The `urlpath` attribute indicates the URL to be prefixed to the file name in any search results.

Unlike the situation that we discuss in the section "Adding a scheduled task," earlier in this chapter, regarding the scheduler, you almost certainly do *not* want to specify `localhost` or `127.0.0.1` for the domain in a production application. If the search results are displayed to end users, the hyperlinks shown need to send them to the server holding these pages (your ColdFusion server). If you mistakenly specify `localhost` in that situation, the end users' browsers end up trying to look for the files on their *own* local computers. Of course, if you're setting up a collection for your own use, using `localhost` is perfectly acceptable. Not providing any domain at all is also acceptable. See the section "Available Search Result Columns," later in this chapter, for more information.

An `extensions` attribute is also available, although you don't need it if you're willing to accept the default file types (HTM, HTML, CFM, and CFML files). Similarly, a `language` attribute exists that you needn't bother specifying if you're happy with the default value of English.

Additional capabilities of the CFINDEX tag

If you read the section in the Macromedia's ColdFusion documentation *CFML Reference* regarding the `CFINDEX` tag, you may be overwhelmed trying to find the attributes that you need to perform a simple index population based on a set of files as we describe in the section, "Populating (indexing) a Verity collection."

You see in the previous sections that several values are actually available for `action`. (These relate to managing Verity collections and are discussed later in this chapter.) Other values are also appropriate for the `key` attribute, as are two additional values for the `type` attribute.

Finally, you can also perform both `delete` and `refresh` actions by using `CFINDEX`. And really quite a bit more is going on whenever you run an `update` action than may be obvious at first. We cover each of these topics in the section "Managing individual records or groups of records in a collection," later in this chapter.

Updating a collection on a recurring basis

As we mention in the section "Adding a scheduled task," earlier in this chapter, setting up a scheduled task to perform an update to an index on a recurring basis is certainly reasonable. Creating a template to perform the desired `CFINDEX action="update"` is, in fact, a simple matter. An example can be found in the previous section, "The CFINDEX tag".

Searching a Verity collection

The final step in working with Verity collections is, of course, the payoff for the work that you've done to this point in creating a mechanism to search the index. This is where the `CFSEARCH` tag comes into play. Unlike in the two steps that we describe in the preceding sections, no equivalent Administrator interface for searching a Verity collection is available. You need to create a template to perform the search and display the search results.

Most likely, you present a form for a user to fill out requesting the search criteria, and mechanisms to enable users to enter either simple or more complex search expressions are available. Providing users with just a template that runs a search with fixed criteria or criteria that can be determined from some other source (perhaps a database query or data passed to the template) instead of a form is certainly possible as well.

In either case, you nearly always display the search results on a browser. The `CFSEARCH` tag creates its results in the form of a query result with special columns that you can display (or manipulate any way that you want, including storing them in a database if that makes sense, sending them in an e-mail, and so on).

As we discuss in the section "Populating (indexing) a Verity collection," earlier in this chapter, about storing a URL during the process of indexing file contents, you can also cause the results display to present the user with a hyperlink so that clicking a particular search result in the browser links him to the found document.

The actual process of searching a collection can be as simple as using the following `CFSEARCH` tag, which searches for all results in the index named `"test"` and holds them in a result set named `"result"`:

```
<cfsearch collection="test" name="result">
```

You can later process that result set just as you can any CFQUERY result set, including referring to it in a CFOUTPUT query loop. Of course, you most likely want to provide some sort of search criteria to help the user find only certain desired results, and we cover how to do so in the section "Providing CFSEARCH criteria," later in this chapter. For now, this search simply returns all the items found in the index. You also need a little more information on how to process the search results.

But before getting to that, we just need to mention a couple other things about the CFSEARCH tag. CFSEARCH has a language attribute that defaults to English. Perhaps more useful, you can also search multiple collections at once by using this tag. Simply specify the names of each collection that you want to search in the collection attribute as a comma-separated list of values.

And just as you do with the CFQUERY tag, you have a maxrows attribute in CFSEARCH. (This attribute limits how many results return; if you omit it in all rows are returned.) You also have a startrow attribute (which defaults to 1).

Before we discuss the capabilities in providing search criteria — because the preceding example indeed finds results — we first need to tell you how to display search results. Later, in the section "Providing CFSEARCH criteria," we refine the search to find only particular results.

Available search result columns

The result of the CFSEARCH tag is the equivalent of a query result set that you can process just as you can any query result set. A CFOUTPUT query loop is the obvious choice for this purpose, although others are also possible. Still, if you're to treat the CFSEARCH tag as you do a query, you need to know what columns are available in the query.

The CFSEARCH result returns the following result columns, some of which are relevant only to collections based on query results, which we cover later in the chapter:

✦ SCORE: Returns the relevancy score (number indicating how closely the document matched the criteria) of the document based on the search criteria. If no criteria are provided, it returns the empty string.

✦ SUMMARY: Returns the contents of an automatic summary about the search result (document or query result) that's generated during the indexing process. The default summarization selects the best three matching sentences, up to a maximum of 500 characters.

✦ URL: This column is useful only if the collection is an index of file contents. If it's an index of query results, this returns an empty string. Otherwise, this returns the indexed file name in a format appropriate for use as a URL (using forward slashes), with the path beginning relative to the location from which the indexing operation began. If any urlpath is specified in the CFINDEX tag or Administrator interface used to create the collection, it's prepended to the result. If no urlpath is specified, the path is returned without a leading slash, which makes it suitable for use as a relative URL. If the indexing operation took place in a different directory then the current files, you may need to provide an appropriate prefix in displaying it to help the user find the correct directory.

✦ KEY: If the collection is an index of file contents, this returns the complete path to the indexed file. Otherwise, it returns the value of the key attribute if the collection holds an index of query results.

✦ TITLE: If the collection is an index of file contents, this returns the value within HTML <title> tags in both HTML and CFML documents, if any, as well as the titles of PDF and MS Office documents. Otherwise, it returns whatever is placed in the title attribute in the CFINDEX operation (which, in an index of query results, may be the value of a column named in title). If no title is provided in the title attribute on an index of query results, CFSEARCH returns CF_TITLE.

✦ **CUSTOM1 and CUSTOM2: Return whatever is placed in the CUSTOM1 and CUSTOM2 attributes of the CFINDEX operation used to populate the collection. This column is useful only if the collection is an index of query results, because these attributes are ignored in a CFINDEX that you use to index file contents.**

✦ **CURRENTROW: Returns a number indicating the relative position of the current result in the result set, starting from 1 to the number total number of results returned. This typically appears during CFOUTPUT query loop processing and does not represent any sort of internal record number for the result.**

The most useful result columns depend on whether you're showing the results of a search against a collection populated from file contents or from a query result. The SCORE and SUMMARY are almost always useful. For a collection of file results, the URL holds the file name as a URL, and the TITLE holds any title found, while the KEY holds the full path to the file. For a collection of query results, the KEY, TITLE, and CUSTOM1/CUSTOM2 tags are more relevant.

Finally, three columns are returned that really relate to the search result as a whole rather than to each record in the result set. The first two are the same as those provided with the results of a CFQUERY, as the following list shows:

✦ **RECORDCOUNT: Returns the number of results, or *hits*.**

✦ **COLUMNLIST: Returns a list of the column names returned within the result set.**

✦ **RECORDSSEARCHED: Returns the number of records searched.**

Caution

Curiously, the RECORDSSEARCHED value returns an empty string if no records are found.

Following is an example of a set of statements to present the SCORE, URL, and TITLE result columns from an index of file contents. You may notice in the following code the use of a trick to change the color of every other pair of result rows. We are using the mod operator to check if the currentrow of the query is even or odd; if it is even then we color the row white, otherwise we color the row silver.

```
<cfsearch collection="test" name="result">

<cfoutput>
Records Searched: #result.recordssearched#<br>
Records Found: #result.recordcount# <br>
Columns Returned: #result.columnlist#
</cfoutput>
<p>

<table border="0" cellspacing="0" cellpadding="0">
<th>Count</th><th>Score</th><th>URL</th><th>Title</th>
<cfoutput query="result">
   <tr bgcolor="#iif(currentrow mod 2,de("silver"),de("white"))#">
<td>#currentrow#</td>
   <td>#score#</td>
   <td><a href="#url#">#url#</a></td>
   <td>#title#</td>
   </tr>
</cfoutput>
</table>
```

In this particular example, because the CFSEARCH tag has no criteria attribute, the SCORE result is empty. You may find displaying the SUMMARY column useful as well, which can be done simply by adding another cell (a pair of TD tags) after displaying the TITLE cell.

If this example were a search against a collection of query results rather than file contents, you'd also want to display the KEY, TITLE, and possibly CUSTOM1/CUSTOM2 columns rather than the URL column.

As of CF5, you can achieve nearly the same result as the HTML table above looping over the result set and printing all the search-result columns with alternating colors for the rows, by using the new CFDUMP tag. In the preceding example, try `<cfdump var="#result#">` instead of the HTML table. Be aware, however, that it doesn't provide the means to show the URL as a hyperlink nor to limit which columns are displayed. You can use the tag to dump to the screen the results of any complex ColdFusion variable, including CFQUERY result sets, structures, all current session variables for a user, and so on.

Providing CFSEARCH criteria

In the preceding sections, you execute a CFSEARCH with no search criteria, which simply finds all records in the collection. That's not typical. Instead, you normally want to pass the some search criteria to the tag, whether input gathered from a user or built from some other programmatic process.

On the simplest level, you can specify a criteria attribute, in which you provide the words or words with which you want to search. These are known as *simple queries* and permit the criteria to be simple, comma-delimited strings and to use wildcard characters. If multiple words are separated by commas, the comma is treated as a logical or. If commas are omitted, the query expression is treated as a phrase. A simple query can also contain and, not, or or operators.

An example to find records with the words (or matching stems of) *Java* and *data* but not *Oracle* may appear as follows:

```
<cfsearch collection="test" name="result" criteria="java and data not
oracle">
```

If the search criteria provided is all in lowercase letters, the search is case-insensitive and searches not only for the words provided, but also words that derive from those terms. So entering *data* returns documents that contain such terms as *data*, *database*, *datasource*, and so on (as these terms all have the same stem). Each document's relevance score is based on the density of the search term (or those matching its stem) in the searched documents. The more frequent the occurrence of a word (or its stem matches) in a document, the higher is that document's score.

You can prevent such stemming by surrounding a word or phrase with double quotation marks.

If you're testing this capability to use quotation marks in a search by typing this sort of quoted string into the criteria attribute directly, you must surround the string with two sets of double quotation marks, because the entire criteria value must be surrounded by quotation marks. So if you want to use "data" as the criteria, your CFSEARCH tag would require `criteria="""data"""`, with two double quotes on either side of data, and you would add another pair quotation marks around the attribute value as shown above. If the data is passed from a form input field, however, ColdFusion handles the string just as it's typed by the user ("data"), so you would use `criteria="#formfieldname#"`.

You may notice a `type` attribute for `CFSEARCH`, with a value of either `"simple"` or `"explicit"`. If you leave it off, the default is `"simple"` which leads to the behavior. Using `"explicit"` for queries is generally unnecessary, and its use is explained in the ColdFusion documentation.

Regardless of whether you're conducting a simple or explicit query, you can do much more than simply search for a word or set of words. The Verity search engine accepts more complex types of operators to modify the criteria, including the following:

✦ Word operators (including evidence operators such as `stem`, `wildcard`, and `word`)

✦ Proximity operators (including `near`, `paragraph`, `phrase`, and `sentence`)

✦ Concept-based operators (`and`, `or`, and `accrue`)

✦ Document field operators (meaning searches against the search-result fields `TITLE`, `KEY`, `URL`, `CUSTOM1`, and `CUSTOM2`), which can include relational or comparison operators such as =, <, >, and so on for numeric and date comparisons; and `contains`, `matches`, `starts`, `ends`, and `substring` for text comparisons)

✦ Scoring operators (to manipulate the relevancy score, including `yesno`, `product`, `sum`, and `complement`)

The `criteria` expression also has capabilities to provide four kinds of modifiers, six kinds of wildcards, and several special characters.

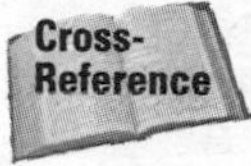

We don't have time to explain all these possibilities, but you should know that the capabilities are there. The ColdFusion MX documentation *Developing ColdFusion MX Applications with CFML* has a rather thorough discussion of each of these. A Macromedia Knowledge Base article is also available on narrowing the use of field searches; its URL is presented at the end of this chapter.

Whenever you use these operators, you need to surround them with brackets (whether using them in a simple or explicit query). An example to find results where *Java* and *data* (or their stem matches) occur in the same sentence would be as follows:

```
<cfsearch collection="test" name="result" criteria="java <sentence>
data">
```

Don't worry about the brackets within the string that occurs inside the brackets of the `CFSEARCH` tag. The search engine processes the bracketed criteria.

Summary

This chapter covers quite a bit of ground and, along the way, identifies a good bit of information that may be new to you (and to many experienced developers). The following list summarizes what you learn in this chapter:

✦ The `CFSCHEDULE` tag and the Administrator Scheduled Task page is a powerful feature that enables you to run unattended and/or recurring tasks. It's great for running processes to manage recurrent database operations (such as deleting expired members), sending off e-mail on a recurring basis (perhaps driven by a database query), and even managing the maintenance of Verity Index collections.

✦ The `CFFILE` tag is a true Swiss Army knife among ColdFusion tags, offering three broad areas of capability: reading and writing the contents of files, manipulating files, and uploading files from the client to the server.

- The Verity Index feature (the tags CFCOLLECTION, CFINDEX, and CFSEARCH, as well as the Administrator interface for related maintenance operations) offers a powerful mechanism for creating searchable file libraries. It also can be used to create indexes on query results, with greatly improved search capabilities and possible performance improvements over a standard SQL SELECT clause.

Those these are three classic features that, although not new or particularly different in ColdFusion MX from their versions in ColdFusion 5, take your applications to a new dimension if they're understood completely and used effectively. They also can provide valuable solutions to common needs that your clients have.

✦ ✦ ✦

Charting Data with ColdFusion MX

In This Chapter

Creating charts from both explicit data points and databases

Exploring a sampling of chart types

Charting multiple data series

Charting in ColdFusion has historically been very difficult. Before Version 5, the only way to chart data from ColdFusion was to use COM, CF_Excel, or some other external system to create a chart in Microsoft Excel. ColdFusion 5 introduced `CFGRAPH`, but it wasn't always satisfactory.

ColdFusion MX introduces the new `CFCHART` tag, a dramatic improvement over `CFGRAPH`. You can now have multiple series of data and you can display a much wider range of chart types. This chapter shows you how to use `CFCHART` and its related tags and ends with a real-world stock charting application.

Creating a Chart

Listing 33-1 shows a simple bar graph displaying the revenue figures for Stan Cox Industries' R&D department over five years' time.

Listing 33-1: A chart with five data points

```
<cfchart
        format="png"
        scalefrom="0"
        scaleto="10000000">
    <cfchartseries
            type="bar"
            serieslabel="R & D"
            seriescolor="##0000FF">
        <cfchartdata item="1997" value="1094756">
        <cfchartdata item="1998" value="2884755">
        <cfchartdata item="1999" value="6119385">
        <cfchartdata item="2000" value="8994864">
        <cfchartdata item="2001" value="9785773">
    </cfchartseries>
</cfchart>
```

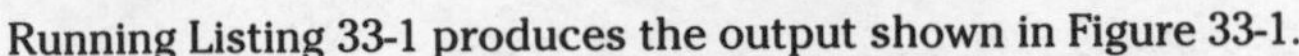

Running Listing 33-1 produces the output shown in Figure 33-1.

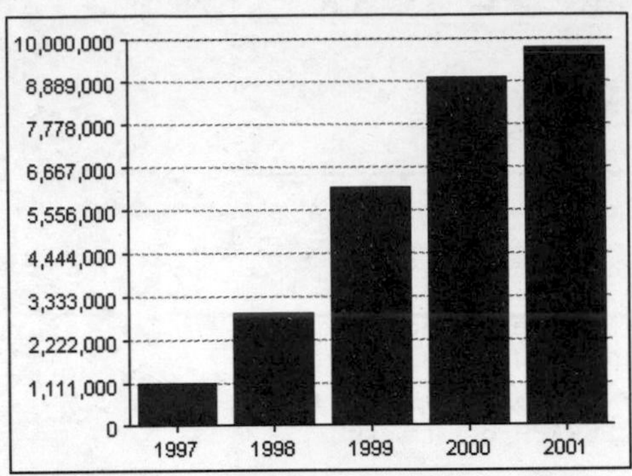

Figure 33-1: Revenues for R&D.

The R&D chart consists of a single *series* containing five data points. A series is a concrete set of data representing a single thing—in this case, the R&D department. If you wanted to graph Advertising along with R&D, you would add a second series to your chart, as in Listing 33-2.

Listing 33-2: A chart with two series

```
<cfchart
        format="png"
        scalefrom="0"
        scaleto="10000000">
    <cfchartseries
                type="bar"
                serieslabel="Advertising"
                seriescolor="##FF0000">
        <cfchartdata item="1997" value="882635">
        <cfchartdata item="1998" value="1672634">
        <cfchartdata item="1999" value="4098173">
        <cfchartdata item="2000" value="6782743">
        <cfchartdata item="2001" value="8674662">
    </cfchartseries>
    <cfchartseries
                type="bar"
                serieslabel="R & D"
                seriescolor="##0000FF">
        <cfchartdata item="1997" value="1094756">
        <cfchartdata item="1998" value="2884755">
        <cfchartdata item="1999" value="6119385">
        <cfchartdata item="2000" value="8994864">
        <cfchartdata item="2001" value="9785773">
    </cfchartseries>
</cfchart>
```

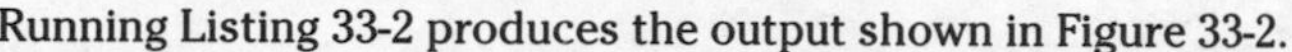

Running Listing 33-2 produces the output shown in Figure 33-2.

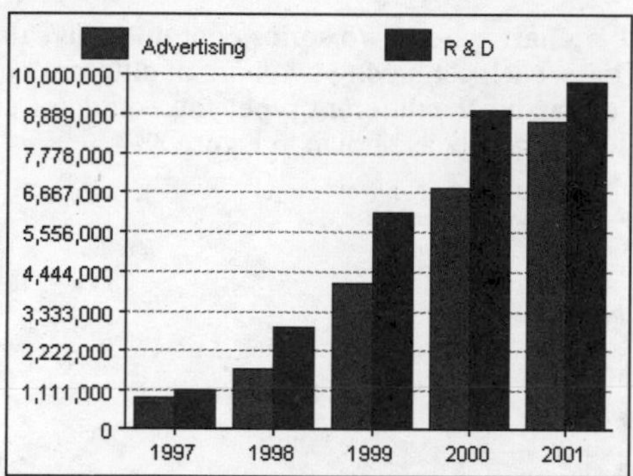

Figure 33-2: Adding a second series to the chart.

You can see from these examples that `CFCHART` controls the container for the displayed chart and that `CFCHARTSERIES` controls what the data looks like.

One of the neat things about `CFCHART` is that it can also produce three-dimensional charts, as in Figure 33-3.

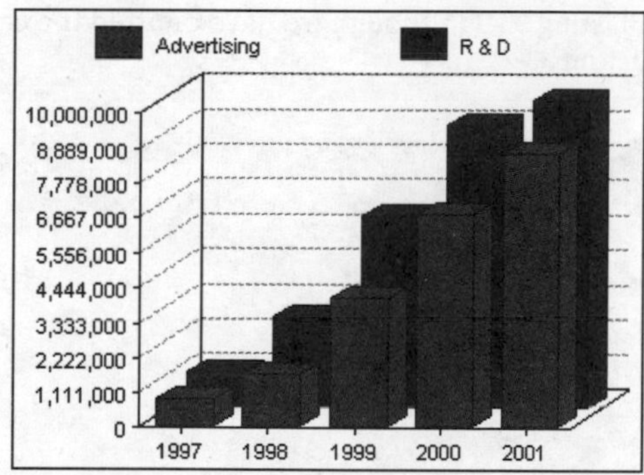

Figure 33-3: The revenue chart shown in 3-D.

All you need to do to make the chart 3-D is to add another attribute in your call to `CFCHART`, as follows:

```
<cfchart
        format="png"
        scalefrom="0"
        scaleto="10000000"
        show3d="Yes">
...
</cfchart>
```

`CFCHART` takes many more attributes than what you see here, but the others are beyond the scope of this chapter. Chapter 59 does a thorough job of explaining the others.

Types of Chart Series

In the preceding section, you see a typical bar chart, where two series containing five data points each are represented by five sets of bars, each set having two bars of different colors. If you're using CFCHART, however, each series can be of a different type; you could, for example, make R&D a bar graph and Advertising a line graph, as shown in Figure 33-4.

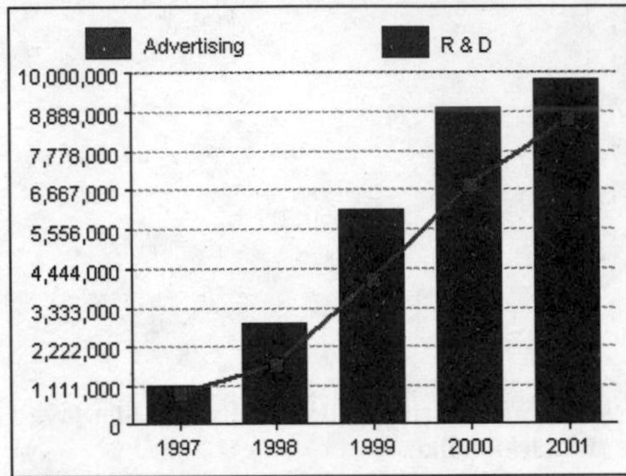

Figure 33-4: Two series of different types in the same chart.

Figure 33-4 was generated with the code in Listing 33-3 (although we have omitted the calls to CFCHARTDATA, as they are the same as in Listing 33-2).

Listing 33-3: Two different types of series

```
<cfchart
        format="png"
        scalefrom="0"
        scaleto="10000000">
    <cfchartseries
                type="line"
                serieslabel="Advertising"
                seriescolor="##FF0000">
    ...
    </cfchartseries>
    <cfchartseries
                type="bar"
                serieslabel="R & D"
                seriescolor="##0000FF">
    ...
    </cfchartseries>
</cfchart>
```

Ten types of series are available, and all look rather different from each other. The following sections show you each type in detail through a series of figures showing the 2-D and 3-D representations of each type side by side.

Scatter

A *scatter chart* is also referred to as a *scatter plot* or *scatter graph*. Data points in a scatter chart are represented by single points or markers on the chart, as shown in Figure 33-5.

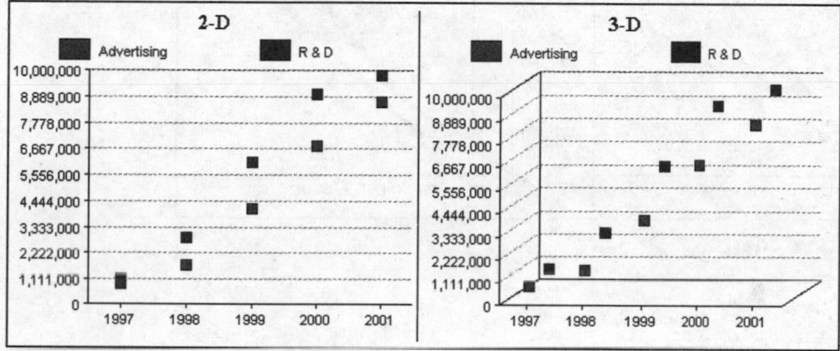

Figure 33-5: Scatter charts.

Notice that the 3-D version can be rather misleading and probably should not be used unless you have another series represented by a different type shown along with the scatter chart.

Line

A *line chart* plots a point at each data point and then draws a line connecting each dot to the next one. Figure 33-6 shows both a 2-D and a 3-D line chart.

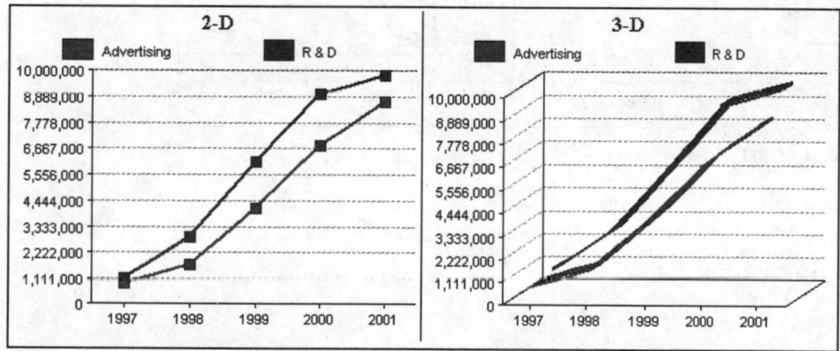

Figure 33-6: Line charts.

Curve

A *curve chart* is very similar to a line chart, but instead of drawing a straight line between data points, CFCHART draws a curved line connecting all the points, as shown in Figure 33-7.

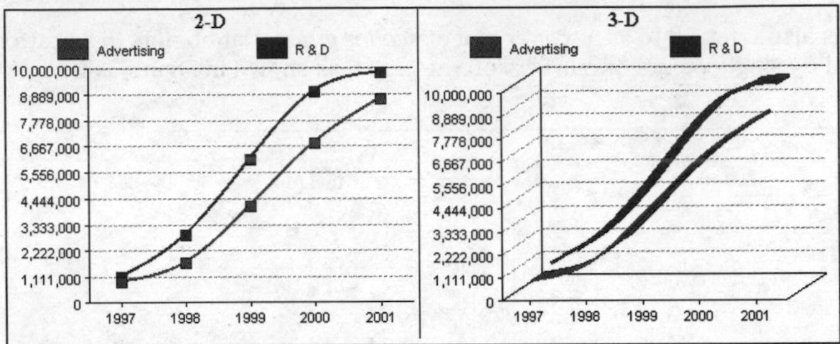

Figure 33-7: Curve charts.

Step

A *step chart* is also similar to a line chart, except that every line in the chart is parallel to an axis, as shown in Figure 33-8.

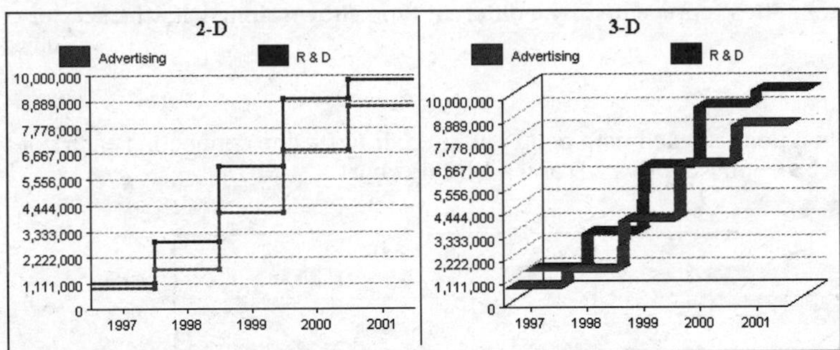

Figure 33-8: Step charts.

Area

An *area chart* is a line chart that's been filled from the line to the x-axis, as shown in Figure 33-9.

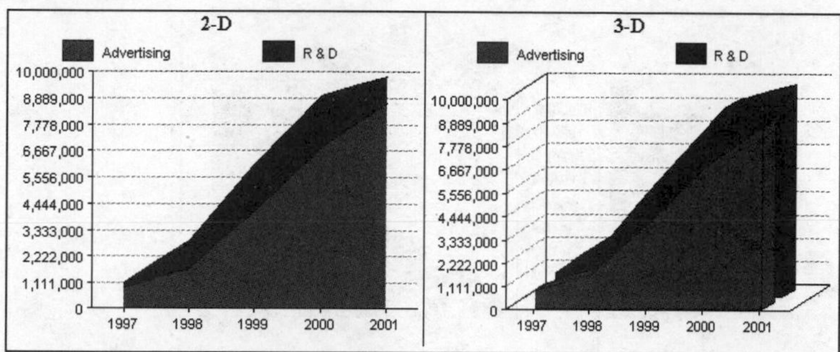

Figure 33-9: Area charts.

Bar

A *bar chart* shows just that: a bar representing each data point from the zero-point of the y-axis to the data point. In 3-D mode, a bar chart is represented as a rectangular "tower." Figure 33-10 shows the bar chart in action.

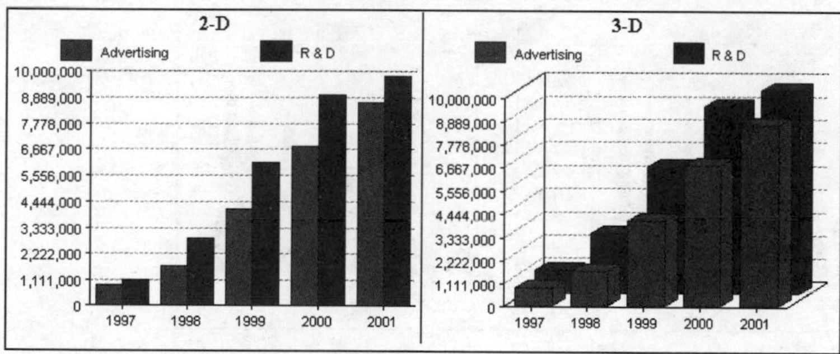

Figure 33-10: Bar charts.

Cylinder

In 2-D mode, a *cylinder chart* looks exactly like a bar chart. In 3-D mode, however, the cylinder chart uses cylinders instead of rectangular towers, as shown in Figure 33-11.

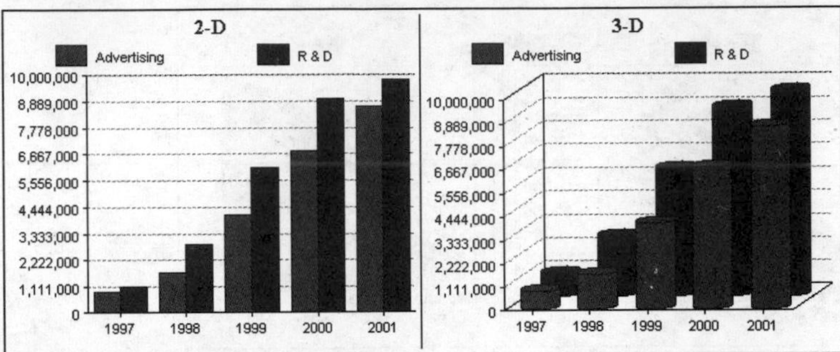

Figure 33-11: Cylinder charts.

Cone

A *cone chart* is like a cylinder chart except that it uses a cone instead of a cylinder in 3-D mode (see Figure 33-12).

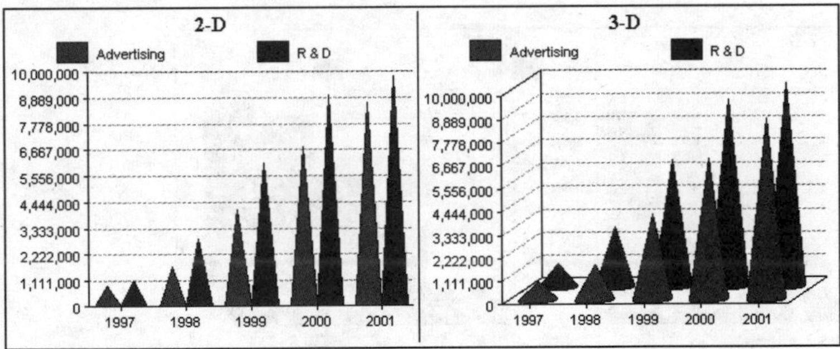

Figure 33-12: Cone charts.

Pyramid

A *pyramid chart* is like a cylinder chart except that it uses a pyramid instead of a cylinder in 3-D mode, as shown in Figure 33-13.

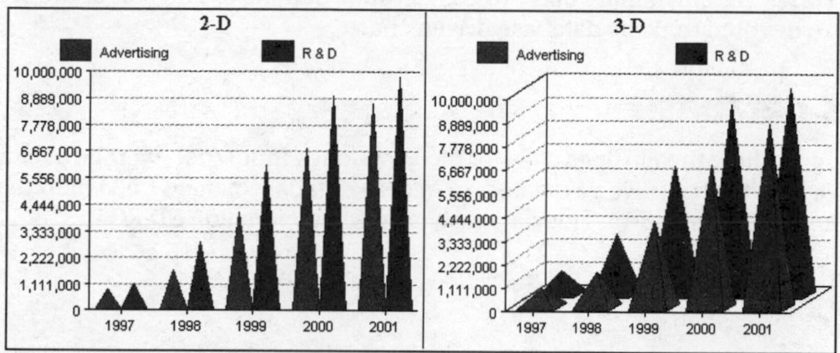

Figure 33-13: Pyramid charts.

Pie

A *pie chart* is different from the other nine types. A pie chart can have only a single series, and it represents fractions of a whole rather than individual data points. Figure 33-14 shows advertising revenue as a pie chart.

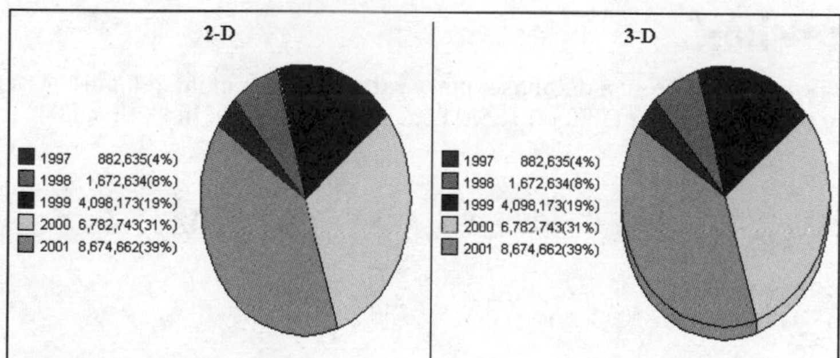

Figure 33-14: A pie chart.

The entire circle represents all of the revenue made from 1997-2001, and each slice of the pie is proportional to how much each year contributed to the total five-year revenue stream. Note that you can also "explode" pie slices by setting `pieslicestyle="sliced"` in the `CFCHART` tag.

Creating a Chart from the Database

You've already seen in the section "Creating a chart" how to create a chart by using manually plotted data points, but that's probably not going to happen very often in the real world. Your data points and series are much more likely to come from a database. The rest of the sections in this chapter are devoted to using database-driven charts.

The stocks database

Our chart is going to show the closing values of the Dow Jones Industrial Average over a six-month period. For this purpose, we've created an Access database named Ch33.mdb that is structured as shown in Figure 33-15. This database is on the companion CD-ROM.

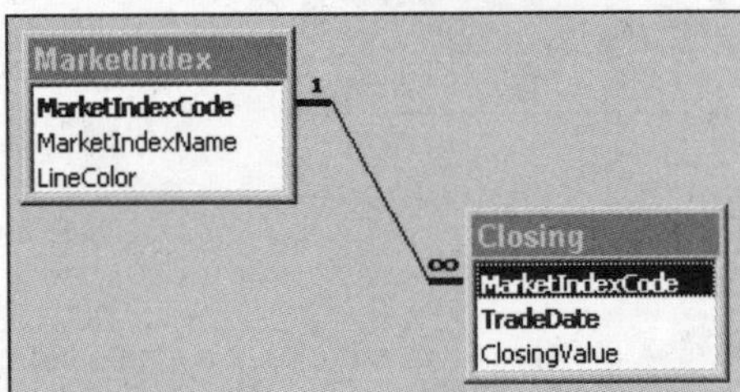

Figure 33-15: A stocks database.

Creating the chart

Because our data points come from a database query rather than manual CFCHARTDATA tags, we must use three new attributes of CFCHARTSERIES, as shown in bold in Listing 33-4.

Listing 33-4: Using a query as the source for data points

```
<cfquery name="GetDJIAData"
              datasource="Ch33">
SELECT
    MONTH(TradeDate) & '/' & DAY(TradeDate) & '/' & YEAR(TradeDate) AS
StringDate,
    ClosingValue
FROM
    Closing
WHERE
    MarketIndexCode = 'DJIA' AND
    TradeDate >= #CreateODBCDate('1/1/2002')# AND
    TradeDate <= #CreateODBCDate('6/30/2002')#
ORDER BY
    TradeDate
</cfquery>
```

```
<cfchart
        format="png"
        chartheight="400"
        chartwidth="600">
    <cfchartseries
                type="line"
                query="GetDJIAData"
                itemcolumn="StringDate"
                valuecolumn="ClosingValue"
                serieslabel="Dow Jones Industrial Index"
                seriescolor="##0000FF"
                markerstyle="none"></cfchartseries>
</cfchart>
```

Running Listing 33-4 produces the output shown in Figure 33-16.

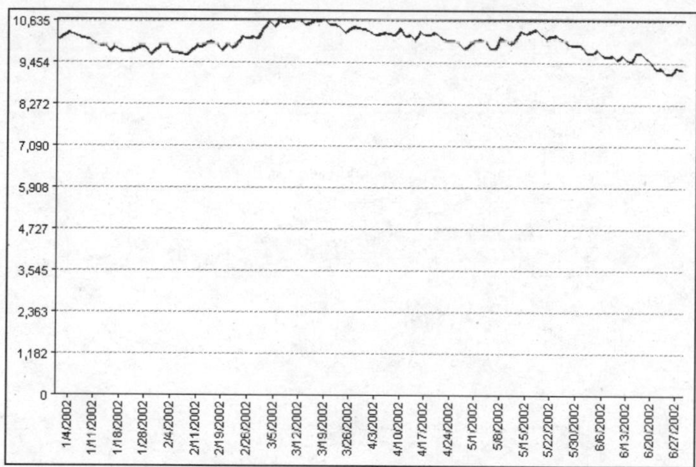

Figure 33-16: A database-driven chart.

`Query` is the name of the database query containing the data points of the chart. `ItemColumn` specifies the query column whose values become the X-axis of the chart, and `ValueColumn` specifies the query column whose values become the Y-axis of the chart.

You want to notice a few things about Listing 33-4. First, notice that the query assembles the date as a string rather than selecting the date directly. We do so because we want the chart labels to show dates and not values such as `{ts '1-1-2000 0:00:00'}`, which is ColdFusion's standard date format. Notice, too, that the `Query`, `ItemColumn`, and `ValueColumn` attributes of `CFCHARTSERIES` don't have pound signs around them. Placing pound signs around CFCHARTSERIES attributes is a common mistake you should not repeat.

Summary

In this chapter you've learned how to use ColdFusion MX's new charting tags to create both manually-plotted and database-driven charts of various types. ColdFusion's charting capabilities have greatly improved with the MX release. Certainly, the embedded charting engine isn't nearly as complete as those in other products on the market, such as ChartFX or Microsoft Excel, simply because those products were *made* for charting, but `CFCHART` presents an easy way to include excellent charts on your site.

This chapter has given a brief overview of ColdFusion's charting capabilities. To get a full appreciation of what's possible, play around with `CFCHART` and its attributes, all of which are covered in Chapter 59. See also Chapters 43 and 44 for information about charting settings in ColdFusion Administrator that may affect your charting applications' scalability.

✦ ✦ ✦

Leveraging Nifty Custom Tags

✦ ✦ ✦ ✦

In This Chapter

Finding custom tags and the Macromedia Developer's Exchange

Working with `CFLIB.org` and `CFCZone.org`

Implementing some of these resources

✦ ✦ ✦ ✦

Before you start implementing something on your site, you should check to make sure that someone else hasn't already implemented it for you. The ColdFusion developer community is unique in that so many people are willing to share their solutions with other developers, so make sure that you use the community as a resource.

The resources listed in this chapter are the most comprehensive sites devoted to code exchanges, but these are by no means the only sites that you should use. Almost all the ColdFusion User Group Web sites have some kind of code exchange where you can acquire code that you've seen at recent meetings, and many other sites distribute custom tags, components, and functions.

Where to Find Custom Tags

The Macromedia Developer's Exchange, at `http://devex.macromedia.com`, is the best place to find custom tags. Macromedia runs it, but almost all the many thousands of submissions are from the ColdFusion community. The best part is that the Developer's Exchange offers more than just custom tags. You can also find entire ColdFusion applications, Java applets, and ColdFusion Studio add-ins. (Note that some are freeware, but others are shareware or commercial licenses.) This section concentrates only on custom tags, but be aware that the Exchange has so much more.

Of course, a book this size can't cover all the thousands of custom tags available on the Exchange. We describe in the following sections five of the most popular and most useful custom tags that we found there just to give you an example of the kinds of tags that are available on the Exchange.

When using the Macromedia Developer's Exchange, always check the developer's website before using any tags you download. Some developers, when they release new versions of their tags, update their personal site but forget to update the Exchange. Most entries in the Exchange are accompanied by a link to the developer's personal site.

CF_MsMenu

CF_MsMenu is a family of custom tags that displays a menu bar at the top of the page, as shown in Figure 34-1.

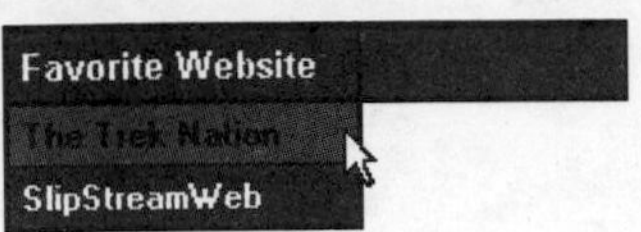

Figure 34-1: CF_MsMenu's menu bar.

That menu is easy to implement by adding the following code to your page:

```
<cf_MsMenu name="Favorite Website" jsdir="/mydir">
    <cf_MsMenuItem
        item="The Trek Nation"
        link="http://www.treknation.com">

    <cf_MsMenuItem
        item="SlipStreamWeb"
        link="http://www.slipstreamweb.com">
</cf_MsMenu>
<cf_MsMenuClose>
```

You call CF_MsMenu and CF_MsMenuClose to define the menu bar and CF_MsMenuItem to define the individual menu items. Other attributes of this tag describe the colors used in the menu bar, and the author provides documentation for the tag in the tag's header comments.

The only thing that this tag is missing is submenus, but submenus aren't always necessary.

CF_MsMenu works with Internet Explorer 5 and later versions and with Netscape 4. It does not work in Netscape 6.

CF_DHTMLMenu

CF_DHTMLMenu creates a different kind of menu than CF_MsMenu provides. Whereas CF_MsMenu gives you a menu bar across the top of the page, CF_DHTMLMenu displays a pop-up menu whenever you move your mouse over a link, as shown in Figure 34-2.

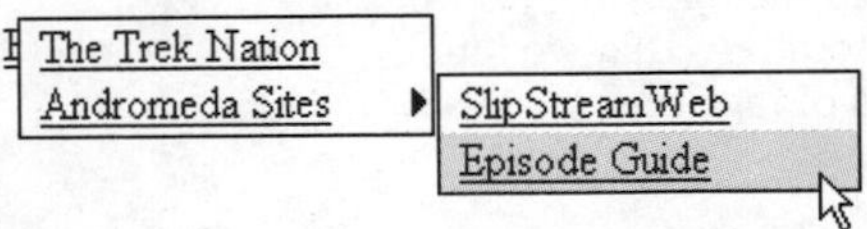

Figure 34-2: CF_DHTMLMenu's pop-up menu.

As you can see, CF_DHTMLMenu provides for submenus as well as regular items.

CF_DHTMLMenu is easy to use on your page, as the following code shows:

```
<cf_dhtmlmenu caption="Favorite Web Site"
        arrow="yes"
        left="15"
        scriptdir="/mydir"
        showrow="yes"
        top="15">

    <cf_dhtmlmenuitem
        caption="The Trek Nation"
        url="http://www.treknation.com">

    <cf_dhtmlmenusubmenu caption="Andromeda Sites">
        <cf_dhtmlmenuitem
            caption="SlipStreamWeb" url="http://www.slipstreamweb.com">
        <cf_dhtmlmenuitem
            caption="Episode Guide" url="http://www.st-hypertext.com">
    </cf_dhtmlmenusubmenu>
</cf_dhtmlmenu>
```

The preceding example is the code used to create the popup menu shown in Figure 34-2.

What's also nice is that these tags come with tag editors, although they may need some tweaking. (For some reason, the editor for CF_DHTMLMenu produces invalid code.)

The only bad part about CF_DHTMLMenu is that the menu is rigged to always pop up in exactly the same place, regardless of where you roll over the link, so you need to manage your page's layout very carefully.

The choice between CF_MsMenu and CF_DHTMLMenu is ultimately a choice between which one you like better — each is useful under different circumstances.

CF_TwoSelectsRelated

Say that you have a database of *Star Trek* shows and characters. You want to have two select menus, one containing the list of shows and the other containing a list of characters. After you select the name of a different show, you want the list of characters to automatically update to display only those characters involved in the show that you select. This interactivity is shown in Figures 34-3 and 34-4.

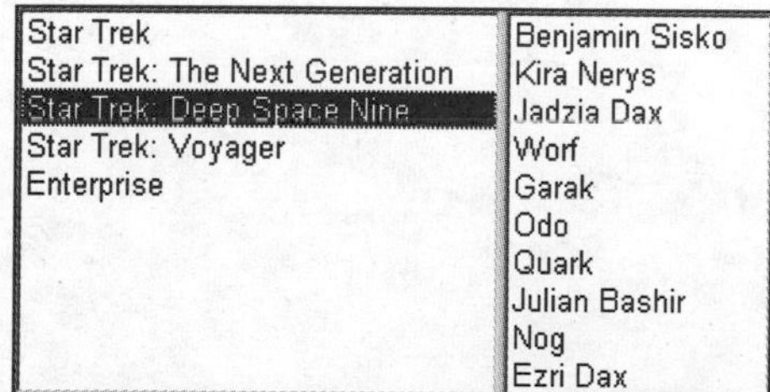

Figure 34-3: The list of characters that appears if *Star Trek: Deep Space Nine* is selected.

Figure 34-4: The list of characters that appears if *Star Trek: Voyager* is selected.

Normally, coding a system such as this would take a lot of effort and knowledge of JavaScript. By using `CF_TwoSelectsRelated`, however, the code is as simple as a `CFQUERY` and the call to the tag, as shown in Listing 34-1.

Listing 34-1: Using `CF_TwoSelectsRelated`

```
<cfquery name="GetCharacters"
         datasource="StarTrekDSN">
SELECT
    s.ShowID,
    s.ShowName,
    c.CharacterID,
    c.CharacterName
FROM
    Show s INNER JOIN Character c
        ON s.ShowID = c.ShowID
ORDER BY
    s.ShowID,
    c.Rating
</cfquery>

<form name="MyForm" action="ChooseCharacter.cfm" method="post">
<CF_TwoSelectsRelated
    QUERY="GetCharacters"
    NAME1="ShowID"
    NAME2="CharacterID"
    DISPLAY1="ShowName"
    DISPLAY2="CharacterName"
    VALUE1="ShowID"
    VALUE2="CharacterID"
    SIZE1="10"
    SIZE2="10"
    AUTOSELECTFIRST="No">
</form>
```

The custom tag takes care of all the interaction between the select menus. All you need to do is to provide it with the query that got the data from the database.

CF_TwoSelectsRelated doesn't come with a tag editor, but the included documentation file is excellent. It is extensible enough for most of what even an advanced developer would need and is a good tag to use for all but the most extreme circumstances.

Where to Find User-Defined Functions

The Developer's Exchange has been around since even before the Allaire/Macromedia merger, so it's had time to accumulate custom tags and gain popularity. *User-defined functions*, on the other hand, are a much newer technology, and you probably can't find that many on the Developer's Exchange.

Enter www.cflib.org, created by Raymond Camden and Rob Brooks-Bilson as a function-specific alternative to the Macromedia Developer's Exchange. The site is devoted to exchanging user-defined functions, all created by members of the community.

cflib.org has a truly huge number of functions, ranging from sorely needed additions to the ColdFusion language (such as DateTimeFormat()) to functions that are almost silly (ChineseZodiac()). These functions are arranged in 12 different libraries. The following sections show some of the highlights of cflib.org's most useful tags and functions.

CFMLLib

Before ColdFusion MX, the problem with using CFSCRIPT everywhere in your application was that you couldn't call ColdFusion tags from CFSCRIPT. In ColdFusion MX, however, that's changed. True, you can't *directly* call a ColdFusion tag, but you *can* use CFFUNCTION to wrap a ColdFusion tag and then call the function from CFSCRIPT.

CFMLLib presents a set of CFFUNCTION wrappers for tags such as CFWDDX, CFABORT, CFLOCATION, and many more so that you can call them from CFSCRIPT. CFMLLib is available only for ColdFusion MX.

Execute()

Execute() enables you to call CFEXECUTE from within a CFSCRIPT block and returns the output of the called program. In a scheduling application, for example, you could do something such as the following:

```
<cfscript>
progOutput = Execute("c:\winnt\system32\at.exe", "", 20);
... process progOutput with CFSCRIPT...
</script>
```

Granted, you could do the same thing in CFML, but the point is that now you can use CFSCRIPT to do it if you prefer.

Dump()

Dump() calls CFDUMP from within a CFSCRIPT block; this is a big help to debugging. You can call Dump() during the following loop, for example, to look at exactly what kind of object is inside your array:

```
<cfscript>
for(i = 1; i LTE ArrayLen(myArray); i = i + 1) {
    Dump(myArray[i]);
}
</cfscript>
```

CFDUMP is invaluable when programming with complex objects, and Dump() now makes it accessible to CFSCRIPT.

DataManipulationLib

This library is geared towards manipulating variables of all types, but the most useful functions in the library work with complex variables such as structures and arrays. The functions included in DataManipulationLib can be seen as extensions to ColdFusion's internal library of functions.

ArrayOfStructsSort()

ArrayOfStructsSort() is like an easier-to-use version of StructSort(). StructSort() returns an array of structure keys sorted by their values, whereas ArrayOfStructsSort() returns the actual array itself sorted by the value of a certain key. Run, for example, the following code:

```
<cfinclude template="ArrayOfStructsSort.cfm">

<cfset OldArray = ArrayNew(1)>
<cfset OldArray [1] = StructNew()>
<cfset OldArray [1]["Name"] = "Bartholomew">
<cfset OldArray [1]["Age"] = 17>
<cfset OldArray [2] = StructNew()>
<cfset OldArray [2]["Name"] = "David">
<cfset OldArray [2]["Age"] = 19>
<cfset OldArray [3] = StructNew()>
<cfset OldArray [3]["Name"] = "Carol">
<cfset OldArray [3]["Age"] = 8>
<cfset OldArray [4] = StructNew()>
<cfset OldArray [4]["Name"] = "Annie">
<cfset OldArray [4]["Age"] = 10>

<cfset NewArray = ArrayOfStructsSort(OldArray, "Age", "asc",
"numeric")>

<cfdump var="#OldArray#" label="Old Array">
<cfdump var="#NewArray#" label="New Array">
```

This code produces the output shown in Figure 34-5.

ListToStruct()

ListToStruct() converts a list of key-value pairs into an equivalent structure of key-value pairs. Suppose, for example, that you run the following code:

```
<cfset myList = "aKey=1,bKey=2,cKey=3">
<cfset myStruct = ListToStruct(myList)>
<cfdump var="#myStruct#">
```

This code produces the output shown in Figure 34-6.

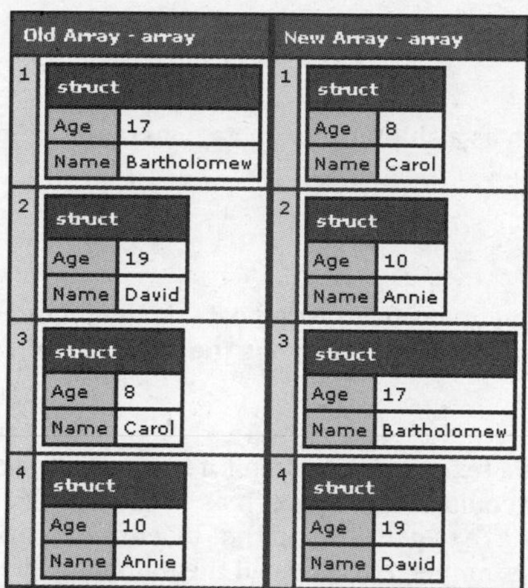

Figure 34-5: The result of running `ArrayOfStructsSort()` on an array of structures.

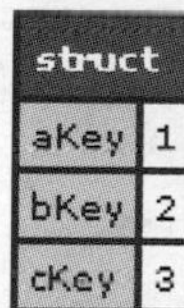

Figure 34-6: The result of running `ListToStruct()`.

DateLib

ColdFusion offers many different functions for working with dates, but some things just aren't internal. The functions in this library are extensions to ColdFusion's internal date functions.

DateTimeFormat()

`DateTimeFormat()` calls both `DateFormat()` and `TimeFormat()` on an object at the same time. Take, for example, the following line of code:

```
<cfoutput>#DateTimeFormat(Now(), "m/d/yyyy", "H:mm:ss")#</cfoutput>
```

It produces the following output:

```
11/16/2002 17:01:55
```

`DateTimeFormat()` is what we like to call "syntactical sugar." The task at hand can be accomplished without this function, but calling one function is more convenient than calling two.

BusinessDaysAdd()

The one kind of interval that `DateAdd()` is missing is *business days*; as in "What day is two business days from now?" That's what `BusinessDaysAdd()` does. Call, for example the following code:

```
<cfset LastFriday = "6 September 2002">
<cfset NextBDay = BusinessDaysAdd(LastFriday, 1)>
<cfoutput>#DateFormat(NextBDay, "dddd, d mmmm yyyy")#</cfoutput>
```

This code produces the following output:

```
Monday, 9 September 2002
```

This function would be useful for something such as a shipping estimate, where the number of business days is important rather than the number of calendar days.

StrLib

StrLib contains various functions for transforming or verifying string data. Many functions are in this library, but the two in the following sections seem to be among the most useful.

SafeText()

Whenever you enable a user to enter HTML into a text area and submit it to your site, you're opening yourself up to a security hole. The user could enter tags such as `SCRIPT` or `OBJECT` that could execute potentially harmful code. `SafeText` gets around that by either escaping all harmful tags or removing them entirely. Say, for example, that you call the following line:

```
<cfoutput>#SafeText("This is text with a <SCRIPT> in it.")#</cfoutput>
```

This code would provide the following output:

```
This is text with a &lt;SCRIPT&gt; in it.
```

On the other hand, call the following line (notice the extra parameter after the text):

```
<cfoutput>#SafeText("This is text with a <SCRIPT> in it.", 1)#</cfoutput>
```

This code would produce the following output:

```
This is text with a  in it.
```

Always use `SafeText()` in accepting HTML input from your users.

CreateGUID()

ColdFusion has a function named `CreateUUID()` that returns a large, globally unique number in hexadecimal format that looks as follows:

```
557996CB-D263-A64A-95E20541383EC9DF
```

The only problem is that most other systems recognize UUIDs only if they have an extra dash in them, which is what `CreateGUID()` returns, as follows:

```
557996CB-D263-A64A-95E2-0541383EC9DF
```

Always use `CreateGUID()` if you're passing one of these identifiers to Microsoft SQL Server or another product that recognizes only valid UUIDs

MathLib

ColdFusion has an impressive set of math and trig functions available, but some things are a royal pain to do, such as rounding a number to a set number of places or finding odd trigonometric ratios. MathLib offers functions to do just about anything connected with math, including functions for statistical analysis and complex numbers.

RoundIt()

`RoundIt()` rounds a number to a specified number of decimal places. Call, for example, the following line:

```
<cfoutput>#RoundIt(6.666666666667, 5)#</cfoutput>
```

This code would give you the following output:

```
6.66667
```

RoundSigFig()

`RoundSigFig()` rounds a number to a specific number of significant figures. Say, for example, that you call the following:

```
<cfoutput>#RoundSigFig(10.5660, 3)#</cfoutput>
```

This code would provide the following output:

```
10.6
```

These functions are mostly used in scientific calculations as a more accurate substitute for gross rounding.

Where to Find ColdFusion Components

ColdFusion Components are the real newbies to the ColdFusion Community. As of the time of this writing, no sites online exclusively distribute ColdFusion Components. That being said, the Macromedia Developer's Exchange does have a few components, but they are mixed in with the custom tags and tend to be difficult to find.

Very promising, however, is `www.cfczone.org`, a sister site to `cflib.org`. `cfczone.org` is run by Raymond Camden and Rob Brooks-Bilson and promises to be every bit as good as `cflib.org`. No components were available at the time of writing, but we've been assured that excellent components should become available there soon.

Summary

In this chapter, we've taken you on a tour of the ColdFusion community. We would like to stress, however, that this is just a tour, and by no means does this chapter cover the full breadth and depth of what the community has to offer. You can find many sites beyond those listed here, but so many are out there that we would need a much bigger book to mention them all.

The best resource that you're likely ever to find is a ColdFusion User Group near you. You can find a list of these on Macromedia's Web site at `www.macromedia.com/usergroups/`, or you can search for "ColdFusion User Group" online. User groups are located in most of the 50 states, and quite a few are overseas as well. The user groups are great places to network, learn a little ColdFusion, and learn about your fellow developers. The user-group sites also tend to distribute excellent code relating to recent meetings.

The mailing lists from House of Fusion (at `www.houseoffusion.com`) are probably the best community resource that you can find. They are well trafficked, and you can get answers to your questions almost immediately.

The next chapter discusses nifty tools that you can use to help the process of developing your ColdFusion applications.

✦ ✦ ✦

Tools to Enhance the Development Environment

✦ ✦ ✦ ✦

In This Chapter

Tools for manually and automatically creating ColdFusion code

Database design and generation tools

Load-testing and test-data generation tools

WYSIWYG HTML editing controls

Mind mapping and site planning tools

✦ ✦ ✦ ✦

The best developer is a "creatively lazy" developer. That may sound strange, but it's true, because creatively lazy developers would rather find a tool to do their work for them than do the work themselves, and development tools help to get the work done faster.

This chapter covers 16 products in the following six categories:

- ✦ Integrated Development Environments (IDEs)
- ✦ Database-design tools
- ✦ Load-testing tools
- ✦ Code generators
- ✦ WYSIWYG HTML editors
- ✦ Outlining tools

Before you stop reading this chapter saying, "I use Notepad, and that's good enough for me," consider that using these tools can not only speed up the development process, but in the case of the load-testing tools, may also end up saving your site.

Integrated Development Environments

Integrated Development Environments, or *IDEs*, are the workhorses of the development process. They are coding environments that include helpful visual assistants that help you do a better job. They also usually include some manner of project or site management to help control the files in your project.

These tools are by no means exclusive of each other. We use all three of them on a regular basis, because all of them serve a different purpose. HomeSite+ is our main coding environment, but we do all our visual site design in Dreamweaver MX, and we use TopStyle to edit our styles and also to edit any XHTML on our site.

ColdFusion Studio/HomeSite+

Most ColdFusion developers use ColdFusion Studio or its replacement, HomeSite+. Unfortunately, most developers consider it only as a better version of NotePad that color-codes their tags and includes a file manager; they don't realize that HomeSite+ can do so much more.

If HomeSite+ is used correctly, the simple mistakes that many developers make can be avoided entirely. One of the best features in HomSite+ is its Tag editors, which can help you write syntactically valid CFML code. To access a tag editor, all you need to do is right-click the tag that you want to edit, choose `Edit Current Tag`, and the tag editor opens, giving you a form to fill out that automatically generates the correct call to the tag.

If you prefer not to use the tag editors, you can use *tag insight*, which gives you a list of the available attributes of the tag that you are currently editing as you edit it. You also can use *function insight*, which shows you the syntax of a ColdFusion function call as you code it. Tag insight and function insight are features of HomeSite+.

To assist even further in your development, HomeSite+ includes an integrated Help system that organizes the ColdFusion documentation (as well as an HTML reference and quite a few other books) into a tree format where you can click the name of an article and have it appear in the main editing window. What's even better is that you can switch back and forth from editor to Help and the Help window keeps your place.

For the speed coders in the crowd, HomeSite+ includes two features that enable you to quickly churn out large blocks of code with only a few keystrokes. *Code Templates* enable you to define a block of code and assign it a mnemonic keyword. After you type the keyword and press Ctrl+J, the keyword expands into the full snippet, with the cursor at the point in the code where you defined in the template.

HomeSite+ also includes *snippets*, which enables you wrap a snippet of code around code that already exists in your template. You can assign keyboard shortcuts to these snippets, so repeating long passages of code is a simple matter of selecting the code that you want to surround and then using a quick keyboard shortcut to add your snippet.

HomeSite+ is highly extensible as well. The tag editors that we mention earlier in this section are defined in a language called *Visual Tools Markup Language* (*VTML*), which is easy to understand and modify, so you can change the included tag editors around if you want. You can also script HomeSite+ by using JavaScript or VBScript with the *Visual Tools Object Model* (*VTOM*). What's even better is that these extensibility options are very well documented in the integrated Help system.

We've scratched only the surface of HomeSite's features in this section. It also includes a visual SQL Builder, a Regular-Expression-based Search and Replace feature, an image-map editor, and many more features. We would need a review five times this size to cover them all. All told, HomeSite+ is currently the best ColdFusion editor on the market.

HomeSite+ is bundled with Dreamweaver MX, and Macromedia no longer sells ColdFusion Studio, so if you're used to ColdFusion Studio, you will need to upgrade to HomeSite+.

TopStyle

TopStyle 3.0 has a totally different focus than earlier versions of the editor; it is now a capable HTML and XHTML editor as well as an excellent stylesheet editor. Nick Bradbury, the man who originally wrote HomeSite and ColdFusion Studio, wrote TopStyle, so the philosophies behind all three products are similar: a good coding environment with great visual assistants.

TopStyle's strong points have always been its editing interface and editing assistants, and these features are improved in Version 3.0. You can now edit HTML/XHTML as well as Cascading Style Sheets (CSS), and TopStyle does an excellent job with both. Although TopStyle doesn't have tag editors such as HomeSite+, it uses a *tag inspector*, which shows a list of all a tag's attributes and their current values whenever you move the cursor into a tag.

TopStyle's stylesheet editor is the best on the market, offering a nice hybrid between manual code editing and a visual assistant that acts much like the tag inspector. After you move the cursor into a selector, all the available rules appear in the Style Inspector (which is a pane to the right of the main coding area), with intelligent drop-down menus that show you all the options available for each rule. In addition, the color picker you use to fill in color values in your CSS rules is fantastic.

TopStyle also helps developers keep track of which browsers use which styles by giving a readout below the Style Inspector showing how well each browser and CSS standard supports the current selected rule.

Moving back to the HTML arena, one of TopStyle's biggest innovations is its new hyperlinking capability, whereby you can click on a class name used in your HTML code and have TopStyle automatically take you to the definition of that class. This is a great boon to developers who must manage a lot of styles and may occasionally get lost.

TopStyle has also made a leap forward with its treatment of XHTML. TopStyle 3.0 is the first editor that we've seen where you can easily edit directly in XHTML and still have the visual editing tools of a standard HTML editing program. If you're working in XHTML mode, TopStyle automatically closes tags that need to be closed, putting out `<br />` tags where you may have forgotten the closing slash, and so on.

TopStyle has also improved its preview capability. If you are editing a ColdFusion template, you can set up TopStyle to have the preview show the actual template in action by running it against a ColdFusion Server.

That TopStyle's only drawback is that it leaves us wanting more is a good thing because everything about the editor is excellent. The only problem is that right now TopStyle can recognize ColdFusion tags and ASP and PHP blocks and color them accordingly, but the tags' attributes don't appear in the Tag Inspector, so you are essentially coding blind. TopStyle's beautiful interface and easy-to-use environment make it a great tool, and it would probably be our editor of choice if it supported CFML.

TopStyle 3.0 is available from Bradbury Software, at `www.bradsoft.com`.

Dreamweaver MX

Dreamweaver MX is Macromedia's IDE of choice. It has always been primarily a visual design and layout tool, but with the MX release, it is now a capable coding environment (although still miles away from HomeSite+). Macromedia has gone to great lengths to woo both designer and developer alike to Dreamweaver MX.

Dreamweaver's strength is its design environment. Everything is exposed through palettes, but in MX, you can now dock these palettes to the side of the screen and hide and show them at will. Another nice addition is that the palettes no longer overlap with the main editing window.

Another great aspect of Dreamweaver's design environment is its Layout View feature, which enables you to draw tables and cells exactly the way that you want, without any concern for how many cells or rows are in your table.

Dreamweaver also has a neat template feature, where you can use a template to create new pages, and if you update the template, it automatically updates the dependent pages. Unfortunately, using this feature limits your capability to effectively work outside of Dreamweaver because Dreamweaver expects to maintain complete control over your project, and if you change something Dreamweaver wasn't expecting you to change, there may be problems.

One way that Dreamweaver is attempting to be more than just a "design tool" is with the introduction of Server Behaviors. Although Server Behaviors were originally introduced in a previous version, Dreamweaver MX has improved them. Unfortunately, Server Behaviors are still not quite right for an advanced developer.

Server Behaviors enable you to create an interface into your application server without using any code. You choose an item on a menu, and it's inserted into your document. To get a list of items, for example, you create a Recordset server behavior, create a table on your page, choose a row from that table, and click Repeat Region. The code that the Server Behaviors produce is clean and easy to understand, and they certainly go a long way toward getting your site ready.

For an advanced developer, Server Behaviors don't take you where you need to go, and as soon as you start modifying them, Dreamweaver has a hard time understanding what's happening in your page. For a novice developer, however, Server Behaviors are definitely a good way to get a site made quickly. In addition, Server Behaviors enable you to use the Live Data view, where you can see your page working against the data in your database while you're designing it.

Clearly, design and layout are Dreamweaver's strong points. The coding environment, however, while certainly capable, is no match for the capabilities of HomeSite+. The tag editors exposed by Dreamweaver aren't as good as those available in HomeSite+. The customizability of the environment is there, but it's not quite as good as in HomeSite+ either. The documentation's content is better in Dreamweaver, but the Help system is better in HomeSite+. The good news is that HomeSite+ is bundled with Dreamweaver MX, so you don't need to choose one over the other; just use them both.

Another area that Dreamweaver shines is its tutorials. These take you through the major features of Dreamweaver at an easy pace but without leaving out any important details.

By far the best feature of Dreamweaver is its extensibility. You can add new server behaviors that can be as simple or complex as you need. You can script Dreamweaver with JavaScript by using its JavaScript API. But for the *really* hard-core programmer, you can actually program interfaces into other languages such as C++ or Visual Basic by using DLL-based extensions. In addition, Macromedia's Extension Manager makes installing and managing these extensions a breeze.

Ultimately, Dreamweaver MX is an excellent tool for designers and developers alike. It enables designers to build sites with some functionality, and it enables developers to visually design their pages. As time goes on, Macromedia is likely to improve Dreamweaver to the point that it is a great tool for coding as well, at which point it should become the IDE of choice for anyone who works with ColdFusion.

Dreamweaver MX is available from Macromedia at `www.macromedia.com/software/`. It is also available as part of Studio MX. Dreamweaver MX comes bundled with HomeSite+.

Database-Design Tools

The database is at the heart of most ColdFusion applications, but many developers tend to give their database design short shrift. Both Microsoft SQL Server and Access give you "diagrammers," where you can create tables and columns and define relationships, but this is no substitute for a database-design tool, which enables you to design your database *logically*, considering your business process's *entities* and *attributes* before considering your database's tables and columns.

Embarcadero ER/Studio 5.5

We must admit that ER/Studio is what we've been using for years, mostly because it's one of the best database-design tools on the market. It's geared toward the average developer, so it's easy to understand and work with. Embarcadero has gone to great lengths to make ER/Studio easy to use and understand; for example, Version 5.5 is a complete rewrite intended to address the issues that people have had with it in the past.

One of ER/Studio's great strengths is the number of database platforms that it supports — more than 30. In addition, you can design for more than one platform at a time. Because your design takes place in the *logical* model, where you are unconcerned with specific type constraints or syntax, you can design a database that fits your application's needs without worrying about any of your database platform's oddities.

Only after you turn the logical model into one or more *physical* models, which represent the actual types and objects used in your database platform of choice, must you worry about database-specific issues. In this way, you can concentrate on database *design*, and ER/Studio turns that into database *development*. What's good is that, after you make a change to the logical model, you can click Merge With Physical Model on the toolbar to automatically update the physical models.

ER/Studio's diagramming environment is easy to use and enables you to design your database in layers, first considering the entities to include in your diagram, then the attributes, and then the datatypes, and so on.

What also helps ER/Studio's diagramming is the AutoLayout feature, which automatically arranges the entities or tables in your diagram according to one of six different algorithms. This feature especially comes in handy if you use ER/Studio's reverse-engineering capability, in which you can point ER/Studio to a database and have it bring in the database's entire schema.

After you've designed your database, you can generate an SQL script that you can immediately run against your database server to create your new database. The entire process of designing and creating your database is drastically shortened. In addition, changing your design and regenerating your script takes but a matter of a few moments.

The only bad part about ER/Studio is that some of its interface can be difficult to use at times. Copying an object when you were only attempting to move it is all too easy, and copying attributes from one table to another is difficult. These interface problems are minor, however, and you get used to them after a while.

ER/Studio saves its files in a proprietary DM1 format, but what's really nice is that you can export your model to either an XML DTD or an XMLSchema document. Although the usefulness of this feature is somewhat limited because XML is not the ideal format for storing relational data, it does show that ER/Studio is rather forward thinking in its philosophy.

Another great thing about ER/Studio is that it can export an image of the data model in BMP, JPEG, or EMF format, enabling you to share the model with others in your team without needing another license to ER/Studio.

One of ER/Studio's coolest features is its reporting engine. You can generate an RTF report that describes every aspect of the database in a huge amount of detail, but this report gets very long rather quickly. The other option is to generate an HTML report, which contains the same information as the RTF version but in a more usable format. In addition, you can deploy the HTML version somewhere on your internal network, or even on your Web site, and then everyone can access the model and all its information.

Also worth noting is the documentation, which is well written and concise, as well as its internal scripting language that can be used to automate some tasks.

All told, ER/Studio is an excellent modeling tool for mere mortals and developers who don't want to spend their time being Database Administrators (DBAs).

ER/Studio is available from Embarcadero at `www.embarcadero.com/products/erstudio/`.

AllFusion ERwin Data Modeler

Erwin, from Computer Associates, has always been the granddaddy of database-design products. It's certainly been around for a while, and Computer Associates isn't exactly a small company. Recently, CA made ERwin part of it's AllFusion family of life-cycle management products, which also includes its business-process modeling software, its project-planning suite, and a large number of other products.

At its core, ERwin does things similar to ER/Studio. It has both logical and physical models, and the design elements are similar. What's nice is that changing something in the logical model automatically updates the physical model(s) so that they are always in sync, which ER/Studio doesn't do.

ERwin also has a reverse-engineering feature much like ER/Studio's, although ERwin can also compare an existing model to what's currently in the database to find out what's changed—something that ER/Studio doesn't have.

One thing that ERwin is lacking is an auto-layout feature similar to ER/Studio's, and ERwin tends to be slower than ER/Studio in many cases.

ERwin's chief flaw is its interface, which tends to be rather confusing. Where ER/Studio clearly enables you to assign the physical model's target platform while creating the model, for example, ERwin's equivalent feature doesn't seem to work, and you must instead choose the database a second time. The script generation interface is also more difficult to use and doesn't have the same wizard-based interface.

ERwin's generated SQL is also difficult to understand, because ERwin tends to break single-line statements across multiple lines with comments in between some parts. On the plus side, however, many more options are available in generating SQL, enabling you to include `CREATE` and `DROP` statements in a much easier way than in ER/Studio.

ERwin also has a much more extensible and comprehensive reporting interface than ER/Studio. In addition to RTF and HTML-based reports, you can also create CSV reports. What's nice is that the RTF reports included with ERwin are better looking than ER/Studio's (although I still prefer ER/Studio's HTML report). ERwin also enables you to create your own reporting packages and script them by using ERwin's internal scripting language. This feature can be difficult to use, however, because it has very little documentation.

In short, ERwin is made for a DBA who knows exactly what he's doing. For those of us who are just ColdFusion developers, however, ER/Studio is probably a safer bet.

ERwin is available from Computer Associates at `www.ca.com`. Choose Application Life Cycle Management from the Products menu on their home page and look for AllFusion ERwin Data Modeler.

Load-Testing Tools

You never know whether your ColdFusion application is viable for a high-volume production environment until it is thoroughly load-tested with professionally designed test scenarios running in commercial grade load-testing software. Period. No substitute is acceptable.

And forget about getting together with two of your best friends to bang on your app all at once to see whether it breaks. If you think that MBJJ testing (Me, Bubba, and Jimmy-Joe) in any way simulates a multi-user environment, you're wrong: All that simultaneous frantic keyboard banging is seen by your Web server, ColdFusion, and database server as nice, lazy individual worker threads moseying along at a snail's pace, miles from one another without any request queuing or a care in the world. If your hardware and software saw such piddly activity as anything other than something to laugh at, your production servers would be crashing every two minutes. Load happens only under extreme conditions, and extreme for you never translates into extreme for your systems.

Empirix e-TEST Suite 6.5

e-TEST Suite is the most capable, yet easy-to-use load-testing software suite in the world. By using e-TEST Suite, you can record every detail of various users' Web-browsing sessions and mix and match them into comprehensive "test scenarios" that replicate simultaneous user activity. You then replace user-entered form-field values from these various sessions with external testing data sets, specify how much "think time" (if any) your user actions have between page requests, and specify how many virtual users you want to run the test against and how rapidly you want to "ramp up" to that number of users. You can even distribute the load test between multiple machines on your network for an even more accurate test.

You can fully automate your load tests through e-TEST's built-in VBA (Visual Basic for Applications) environment, which is very straightforward to anyone who has used any flavor of VBA, JScript, or VBScript. VBA enables e-TEST Suite to do virtually anything that you would ever want it to, so developers with advanced testing needs can take heart.

After you click the Execute Test button, stand back for the fireworks. You see as never before exactly how your ColdFusion application operates under load. We hope that you have a robust exception-handling framework in place, because you're most likely going to throw errors that you've never dreamed of. And we hope that you don't have any questionable coding techniques in place such as `SELECT MAX(ID)` because these are most likely also to fail under heavy load and start putting Ms. McReady's line items on Mr. Darwish's sales order.

These are things that you don't want to find out about after deployment. In fact, at Productivity Enhancement, we use load testing during initial "proof-of-concept" work to indeed prove that an engineering concept works under load. We also thoroughly test critical blocks of code with test harnesses under full load to determine whether they can deploy before we complete a module and then load-test the module as a whole. Since employing e-TEST Suite in our everyday development efforts, we have never had a load-based failure in an application under the most extreme conditions.

e-TEST Suite doesn't stop there, however. You can also graph resource usage during the test and discover whether you're storing too much in Session variables and, thereby, choking RAM, for example. This is a very common problem for most ColdFusion developers, and one that you can learn to engineer around with the help of e-TEST Suite. You need to see only once the various metrics such as memory paging to disk and available memory go out of whack after hitting 10 users — and watch the entire system continuously peg the CPU at 20 users — to convince you that rigorous load testing has helped you avert absolute disaster. You can even monitor your database server's metrics during the test to see how it's fairing against the multi-user onslaught.

e-TEST Suite is currently in Version 6.5, which adds even-better Flash application support and streaming media testing, a welcome addition to all ColdFusion MX developers who have taken the joyful plunge into developing Flash MX Remoting applications. Version 6.5 introduces a slew of new features and functionality, so rather than list them here, we invite you to visit `Empirix.com` and download a fully functioning trial copy. The guys at Empirix are even willing to schedule a "fast-track" telephone training session at a time that's convenient for you.

If you are going to be a truly professional ColdFusion developer, you must employ rigorous formal load testing in your development efforts, and we are convinced, after our own very thorough search for the right load-testing tool, that e-TEST Suite is the very best solution. We've invested our own time and money into e-TEST Suite, and we would do it again. We only wish that we had purchased e-TEST Suite much, much sooner.

e-TEST Suite is available from `www.empirix.com`.

Quest DataFactory 5.2

DataFactory 5.2, from Quest Software, quickly and easily generates accurate production-scale test data for even the most complex relational database designs on virtually any database platform. Testing with data of sufficient quantity and quality is critically important to obtaining accurate load-testing metrics and validating your application's user interface.

If your Web application isn't load tested against a database populated with the same scale of data that you'd have in production, all your load testing is a waste of time. This results from many reasons, not the least of which is the fact that, in absence of large-scale data sets, database servers often perform table scans to read data because entire tables easily fit into server memory. The indexes that you are trying to tune, therefore, are most likely never accessed during tests, which totally invalidates the most critical of your database's performance metrics, such as join performance.

Even more important than index design is the structure of the database itself. Denormalization should be performed only if you have an absolutely compelling reason to do so, and then only to the smallest extent possible. Observing performance under load with production-scale data is the only way to make an informed decision about where to denormalize your database structure, if at all. For information on denormalizing your database, see Chapter 8.

With respect to user-interface design, Web artists and developers often neglect to take the scale of data being presented to the user into consideration and sometimes make wrong interface decisions because of this failure.

DataFactory ensures that initial interface design takes into consideration the actual scale of data presented to the user. A browser's select menu, for instance, should not contain a large number of items; otherwise, the browser renders slowly at best or not at all at worst. Using DataFactory early in the development process tells engineers how much data their interfaces must expose and lets those engineers more effectively choose the proper interface elements as a result.

We've been using DataFactory religiously for quite a while now to our great benefit. At less than $600 (US), it was a no-brainer. Our Return on Investment (ROI) was less than one day, as evidenced by our very first load test against a large news service site that we were building. (Return on Investment means how long it takes for the product to pay for itself.)

First, a database trace analysis showed that we could almost double the speed of the most critical and heavily used function of the site by eliminating one of the existing database indexes and creating a new one with an unusual collection of columns that we could not have guessed during initial design. Second, we discovered that one of the search criteria that our client wanted on his site could have brought the system to its knees many times a day by retrieving tens of thousands of rows under certain conditions.

Three quick adjustments later, the site was FLB (Fast Like Bunny) under load. It would have been technically impossible to discover these potential problems before deployment without the production-scale test data that we could generate in a matter of minutes by using DataFactory.

You can (and should) take DataFactory for a test-drive at `www.quest.com`.

Code Generators

Building a Web site from scratch is a time-consuming product that most of us want to avoid. Code generators give you a head start on your Web site by generating some of the code for you.

The products reviewed in the following sections fulfill different needs. CommerceBlocks provides a way to quickly generate the administrative side of your application, which you can then easily modify, while CodeCharge and CodeCharge Studio focus more on generating your entire Web site.

CommerceBlocks

CommerceBlocks 2.1 enables you to build the entire administrative interface for your application in a matter of minutes. You point it to your relational database, and CommerceBlocks reads it in and builds an entire hierarchy of your database's tables, columns, and relationships.

As soon as you read the database structure, you can click Generate, and the interfaces are all built for you. By default, every table is given a search page, a list, and separate Add, View, Edit, and Delete forms. In addition, CommerceBlocks automatically detects any auto-incrementing keys and treats them accordingly whenever adding or editing a record.

You can save the database structure into a project file (CommerceBlocks uses a proprietary CBP file format), and at that point, you can modify many aspects of the project. You can change field and table labels, and you can give each table a meaningful description. You can change the type of control used for a column or change how a particular column is validated.

You can also define sort orders for each table by using a neat little chooser interface. What's also nice is that, in any interface in CommerceBlocks, you can display information from both the main table and any of its parent tables; in other words, you could display both an employee's name and the name of the company he works for in the same list.

CommerceBlocks generates code that's rather simple to understand. That all the generated code contains comments describing exactly what's going on and that it's well-written, clean, and concise code helps.

Another way that CommerceBlocks assists you is in its innovative LiveHelp feature. Wherever you are in the application, the bottom pane shows a Help document describing the interface.

CommerceBlocks does have some faults. Chief among these is its database support. It was built primarily for Microsoft Access and Microsoft SQL Server, and it can also perform well for Oracle. Other database platforms, however, can cause errors while CommerceBlocks reads the database structure. Some interface elements also don't seem quite right. The generated code can be a little confusing at times, too, but it is still some of the best-generated code on the market.

Ultimately, CommerceBlocks 2.1 is an excellent tool for developers who want to get a jump start on their projects and don't want to get locked into one way of doing things. CommerceBlocks is easy to use, and understanding and modifying the generated code so that it fits in well to your application is very easy, too.

You can get CommerceBlocks from Productivity Enhancement by going to `www.commerceblocks.com`.

CodeCharge

CodeCharge is a Rapid Application Development (RAD) tool for Web applications. It can generate rather capable applications in many different programming languages, including CFML, ASP, and PHP. It enables you to get a pretty nice-looking site up in a much shorter time than ordinary.

CodeCharge has an excellent tutorial that takes you through the process of building an entire application. The tutorial takes a few hours to complete, but after you're done, you feel very comfortable with the product. The beauty of CodeCharge is its capability to enable you to build complicated applications visually with only a minimum of extra code.

Creating a master-detail form in which you can view a sales order and all of its line items at the same time, for example, is a simple process of pointing CodeCharge to your database, creating the pages used to access this master-detail information, and then literally dropping the master and detail forms onto your page. CodeCharge works in terms of *pages* and *forms*, enabling you to be flexible on the pages that you create. CodeCharge's included library of themes makes the generated pages look beautiful.

The main problem with CodeCharge is the code that it generates. It is nearly impossible to understand and even more impossible to modify. In short, if you need any kind of advanced functionality, steer clear of CodeCharge, because it cannot help you. The security model is also severely limited and rather difficult to use.

In a nutshell, CodeCharge is good for someone who needs *a* site up and running quickly and has no need to modify any code. For an advanced or even intermediate developer, however, you can often achieve similar or better results by coding the application by hand.

CodeCharge is available from YesSoftware at `www.codecharge.com`.

CodeCharge Studio

CodeCharge Studio is a step up from CodeCharge. Studio combines CodeCharge's site-building and -generation capabilities with a powerful code-editing environment and Application Builder.

The new code editor is very nice. It has a good default color scheme, and it uses a nice approach to tag editing. The integrated Help system is also one of the better ones that we've seen.

The focus of CodeCharge Studio is much the same as that of CodeCharge itself. The idea is that you can create a site easily and get it up and running quickly. In practice, however, this task is much more difficult in CodeCharge Studio than it is in CodeCharge. The interfaces are not as intuitive, and, in fact, the integrated Help system isn't available in those interfaces where it's most needed.

CodeCharge Studio also seems to have its fair share of bugs. The generated code is still difficult to understand (perhaps even more so than it was in CodeCharge).

Also, the tutorial provided with CodeCharge Studio is nothing like the wonderful tutorial provided with CodeCharge. The Studio tutorial broke our installation and we ended up needing to reinstall. What's nice, however, is that Studio provides you with an Application Builder to help you get your site up and running. In practice, however, this Application Builder is severely limited and can be more a hindrance than a help.

All told, the current version of CodeCharge Studio (version 1.07) is not as good as CodeCharge. We have a feeling, however, that the next version may address some of these inconsistencies and make it a better product.

CodeCharge Studio is available from YesSoftware at `www.codecharge.com`.

WYSIWYG HTML Editors

At times, you want a user able to enter formatted content without needing to know HTML. The products that we describe in the following sections all provide a *WYSIWYG* (*W*hat *Y*ou *S*ee *Is* *W*hat *Y*ou *G*et) interface in which they can lay out, format, and author their content visually without needing to know HTML code.

Note that the reviewed editors are ActiveX controls, so they will only work with Internet Explorer running Windows. Some companies do provide versions for other browser platforms, but these may be very different in their design and usage.

soEditor

soEditor, from SiteObjects, is a WYSIWYG editor with a simple, clean interface. It's easy to install (as you merely unzip the support files and move the soEditor custom tag wherever you need it), and it's also easy to use; a single line of code places soEditor on your form, as follows:

```
<cf_soEditor_pro
      form="myForm"
      field="myEditor"
      scriptpath="/soeditor/pro">
```

Most WYSIWYG editors have an image manager, which enables you to add an image to your content. soEditor has one, and it's a very good one too. soEditor also has a native stylesheet-handling capability; you point soEditor to your stylesheet, and it determines the styles available and uses them in the editor space. A bug is in Version 2.1, however, that makes removing a style impossible after you've applied the style to text. And soEditor's interface seems to flicker (refresh the interface repeatedly, causing annoying flashes in the interface) quite a bit, although this is a minor quibble.

In short, soEditor is a good, simple interface if you don't plan on integrating the editor with your site's style sheets. At the time of writing, a new version (2.5) is coming out that fixes all accumulated bugs and that apparently adds some interesting new features. You can obtain soEditor from SiteObjects at `www.siteobjects.com`.

eWebEditPro

eWebEditPro 2.6, from Ektron, is a very different beast from soEditor. Whereas soEditor focuses on being simple and easy to use, eWebEditPro is feature-laden but at the price of being slightly more difficult to use.

One of eWebEditPro's key features is its adherence to standards, such as XHTML and Section 508 compliance. The XHTML capability is nice (although it does require using a separate configuration utility and can slow down the editing interface), and the Section 508 compliance enables handicapped users better access to eWebEditPro's features.

eWebEditPro also has the capability to filter out invalid characters (characters that are not valid within an HTML document) as you are pasting from Word HTML, which is nice if you edit your content in Word before submitting it to your Web site.

eWebEditPro has a much more capable style sheet-handling feature than soEditor does. The only byproduct of removing styles from a page by using eWebEditPro is that, occasionally, an extra set of `DIV` tags turns up in your HTML. These `DIV` tags, however, do not affect your content's format in any way, and this bug is apparently in the process of being fixed at the time of writing.

As is soEditor, eWebEditPro is easy to place on your page, as follows:

```
<CF_eWebEditPro2
    Name="myEditor"
    Width="100%"
    Height="75%"
    Value="#variables.editorValue#">
```

What's also nice is that, if the user's browser doesn't support eWebEditPro, the tag automatically replaces the WYSIWYG editor with a simple text area so that the user can always enter *something*. eWebEditPro also gives you very granular control over the buttons and controls available to a user by way of a large number of extra attributes passed to the custom tag call.

The only bad part about eWebEditPro is its image manager. The image manager is very difficult to use and is nowhere near as streamlined as those of soEditor or ActivEdit (see the following section). This is probably because eWebEditPro was made to work with a number of different languages and, as such, could not rely on ColdFusion's file-handling capabilities. A knowledge-base article on `www.ektron.com`, however, addresses this shortcoming and can alleviate this problem.

In short, eWebEditPro is the heavyweight of the WYSIWYG editors. It uses an installer and includes a configuration wizard to run on the Web server to configure exactly how eWebEditPro acts. It's a good product to use if you're willing to put in the extra time necessary to really make it shine.

eWebEditPro is available at www.ektron.com.

ActivEdit

ActivEdit, from cfdev.com, is really the best of both worlds — it offers good features and is very easy to use. ActivEdit is really closer to soEditor in terms of its interface, and that works to its advantage.

As you do the other editors, you include ActivEdit on your page with a single tag call, as follows:

```
<cf_activedit
    inc="../inc/"
    fieldname="myEditor"
    upload="1"
    imageurl="http://localhost/mysite/images/"
    width="580"
    border="0px"
    imagepath="c:\inetpub\wwwroot\mysite\images\">
</cf_activedit>
```

ActivEdit's image manager is the best of the three that we've reviewed in this section. Seeing what you're going to include in your content is easy, as is very uploading a new image, (because ActivEdit has a version specifically written for ColdFusion, it uses CFFILE to manage its upload). The only problem is that ActivEdit doesn't include the height and width attributes in the image tag that it creates — you must specifically edit the image properties to put the height and width in.

ActivEdit is highly customizable, not only through its custom tag attributes, but also through its JavaScript API, which enables you to control the editing environment through a series of JavaScript objects.

Another area where ActivEdit shines is its table editor, which has no equal in the other two products. Just as in Microsoft Word, you can drag a table out to a specific number of rows and columns rather than needing to manually enter the number.

The only area where ActivEdit really lacks is in its stylesheet-handling capability. ActivEdit can't automatically parse a stylesheet to find what styles are available, and you also have no way to remove a style after it's been applied. You can, however, point ActivEdit to your site's stylesheet and have the editing window use those styles.

ActivEdit 3 introduced a Java applet version of the editor, in case you are concerned with cross-platform use. Unfortunately, the Java applet is slow and doesn't have many of the features of the standard ActiveX version.

ActivEdit is probably the best of the bunch of WYSIWYG editors and is recommended for just about anyone who needs a content-editing solution.

ActivEdit is available from www.cfdev.com.

Outlining and Mind-Mapping Tools

Before a contractor builds a house, he must have a blueprint or the entire structure falls. The same is true of software development; if you immediately start coding without any idea of what the site must do, the project fails. The tools in the following sections help you organize your thoughts into a coherent plan for your site development (a *mind map*) and can also help you uncover holes in the site plan.

Microsoft Word's outliner

Almost everyone has used Microsoft Word's outlining feature at some time. We used it to organize our thoughts for this book. Simply put, the Word outliner is a way to organize your thoughts in a sequential, hierarchical fashion.

In Word parlance, you organize *nodes* of text into *headings* and *body items*, which form the outline's *hierarchy*. What's nice about Word is that it's good for quickly jotting notes and adding text. To rearrange headings, you can use Tab and Shift+Tab to move headings in and out, and you can easily click and drag nodes from one place in an outline to another.

Word does have some interface quirks, however. Copying or moving a node from one place to another is downright infuriating; many users tend to accidentally put it in the wrong place or to end up with an extra node where they don't want one.

Word is also not very good at visualizing the relationship between nodes. Although you can see the outline hierarchically, seeing the outline in more of a "map" format is sometimes nice, which is where the other products in this section come in to play.

Microsoft Word is usually your best bet for writing an outline simply because almost everyone either has Microsoft Word or has the capability to read a Word document. For most of what you do, Word should be sufficient.

Word is part of Microsoft Office and can be found at `www.microsoft.com/office/`.

MindMapper

MindMapper takes a different approach to outlining than Microsoft Word. Whereas Word views its nodes as a vertically oriented tree and separates headings from body text, MindMapper views the outline as a map. MindMapper shows a more free-flowing outline, where the different nodes form a tree around the center, and the nodes exhibit no sequential order.

The good thing is that you can import and export directly between MindMapper and outlines in Microsoft Word, Project, or PowerPoint, so switching between MindMapper and the Microsoft product where you are directly using the outline is easy. You can also export your mind maps as XML or one of many other formats, for that matter.

Other good interface features include the product's excellent keyboard control and its hyperlinking feature, where you can link individual nodes either to other mind maps or to Web pages. Of course, you do find some interface quirks. You can't place nodes exactly where you want, and rearranging nodes in the hierarchy can become confusing. You also can't collapse tree branches to view a smaller outline.

MindMapper is an excellent outlining tool that is good if you want a more graphical representation of the nodes in your outline.

MindMapper is available from `www.mindmapper.com`.

Visual Mind

Visual Mind is remarkably similar to MindMapper. The difference is in certain differences in interface that ultimately make Visual Mind a better product.

Unlike MindMapper, Visual Mind enables you to expand and collapse nodes in your map, just as you can in a regular outliner. You can also specify that you want to look at a node's children from one to nine levels deep. Another improvement is that to attaching and detaching icons to nodes is easy in Visual Mind.

As does MindMapper, Visual Mind also enables you to save your files in a number of different formats, including HTML, RTF, BMP, or even XML. It also has good keyboard navigation and can import outlines from Microsoft Word, Project, or PowerPoint. Visual Mind also has a neat feature where you can deploy a mind map online by using an ActiveX control.

Visual Mind is in many ways a superior product to MindMapper, but ultimately, the choice comes down to a personal decision as to which interface you prefer.

Visual Mind is available from `www.visual-mind.com`.

Summary

A ColdFusion developer cannot be efficient without using tools of some kind. In this chapter we review some of the more popular tools, and we give you our opinion as to which ones are worth using and which ones aren't. Of course, our opinion is just that: an opinion. Ultimately, you must make your own choices based on your own reviews of the software that you want to use.

In our typical development cycle, we use Dreamweaver MX to do our site layout and HomeSite+ to develop our code. We use ER/Studio for the database design. We generally outline our ideas in Microsoft Word, and we use CommerceBlocks to generate code. When we need to use a content-management system, we make the decision each that time a project comes along, because every project calls for a different solution.

Then again, we know of people who don't use any of the same tools that we do (except maybe ColdFusion Studio), and they are perfectly happy with *their* style of doing things. We've found the most efficient work environment for us, but who says that the same setup works for anyone else? The bottom line is that you should choose whatever works for you, but stick with it from that point on.

✦ ✦ ✦

ColdFusion MX Development Practices

PART

VII

✦ ✦ ✦ ✦

In This Part

✦ ✦ ✦ ✦

Documenting Your Code

✦ ✦ ✦ ✦

In This Chapter

Creating a practical documentation strategy

Knowing when documentation helps and when it hurts

Working with CFML, HTML, JavaScript, and SQL comments and external documents

✦ ✦ ✦ ✦

Sometimes more debates seem to arise over documenting code than are over the code itself. Over the years (don't ask how many), we have observed that developers break down into the following three distinct camps regarding documentation:

- Hardliners ("You must document everything!")
- Minimalists ("Less is more.")
- Mavericks ("We don't need no stinking documentation!")

In this chapter, we discuss a little theory, go over the mechanics, and then come up with a practical and balanced approach to documentation that you can actually sustain in your daily development efforts.

The True Goals of Documentation

The true goals of documentation are as follows:

- To establish what your monster application should do.
- To remind you what you were doing as you originally coded that monster seven months ago.
- To bring new developers up to speed on the monster as quickly as possible.

To illustrate why both hardliners and mavericks miss these goals, imagine the following two scenarios as if you were the new developer just brought into a development team.

Scenario 1: You are presented with 324 total pages of documentation containing fold-out diagrams and flowcharts of all types, a 37-page "overview of the application," a 5-page "mission statement" written by the ambitious middle manager who envisioned the thing in the first place, tons of formal coding style definitions, and 211 pages of heavily commented code listings. *Bon appetit!*

Scenario 2: You are handed a 137-page dump of uncommented code as you are shown your new desk.

Clearly, neither of these approaches is going to work in actual practice, so the answer must lie somewhere in between, with the minimalists. Listing 36-1 shows an example of minimalist code documentation.

Listing 36-1: A brief example of minimalist-documented code

```
<!--- Run daily reports for all active companies --->
<cfset companyIDList = ValueList(activeCompanies.CompanyID)>
<cfloop
    index="iHoldCompanyIDDuringEachLoop"
    list="#companyIDList#">

    <cfinvoke
        component="Company"
        method="CalculateDailyReport"
        returnvariable="resultCode"
        CompanyID="#iHoldCompanyIDDuringEachLoop#">

    <!--- Positive resultCode is warning, negative is error --->
    <cfif resultCode GT 0>
        <cflog text="Warning #resultCode# when calculating daily report
        for CompanyID #iHoldCompanyIDDuringEachLoop#"
           file="CorporateApp"
           type="Warning">
    <cfelseif resultCode LT 0>
        <cfthrow message="The daily report failed for CompanyID
        #iHoldCompanyIDDuringEachLoop#"
           type="DailyReportError"
           errorcode="#resultCode#">
    </cfif>

</cfloop>
```

Does Listing 36-1 really need any more documenting than this? If such additional documentation existed, would you read it? Would you *need* to read it?

The minimalist approach treats code as though it were meat and comments as fat: You should include only enough fat to make the meat palatable; any more is unhealthy. Following are other cooking analogies that are also applicable:

✦ A good chef doesn't rely on fat alone to create flavor; he makes all his ingredients do as much "double duty" as possible. He uses the solidified meat drippings sticking to the bottom of his roasting pan, for example, into a finished sauce by simply adding stock and a little fat.

  In plain English, your code should document itself as much as possible by using obvious variable and object names, regardless of how long they become. If your code reads as Listing 36-1 does, it needs only a little bit of commenting (fat) to "bring everything together."

✦ The greater the chef, the more assistance he needs to create his masterpieces. Do you really think that the world's greatest chef peels and juliennes his own carrots, or does he have a team of assistant chefs do these things for him so that he can concentrate on more important matters?

You're probably using only a small percentage of your IDE's (Integrated Development Environment) capabilities, so learn and implement every trick and technique that makes sense. Chapter 41 shows you how to effectively use combinations of useful CF Studio productivity tools that you've probably never used before to make your code faster to write and easier to document. Use something else to do the dirty work for you.

✦ Have you ever seen a professional chef's recipe? Even the most complicated professional recipes can be expressed in a surprising economy of words because of the common knowledge that every chef already has. Veal Oscar, for example, consists of escallops, lump crab warmed in court bouillon, simmered peeled asparagus, and béarnaise; for a novice, the instructions to create the very same dish take up multiple pages.

Which is better, a variable named `bearnaiseSauce` with no comment or a variable named `theSauce` with the comment `A classic bàarnaise sauce, consisting of Hollandaise sauce and shredded tarragon leaves`? Just as your grandpappy told you, "Make your words plain, and you don't need to explain them later."

✦ Although it technically has nothing to do with taste, the overall visual presentation of the finished dish adds to the delight of the meal as a whole.

Simple touches such as consistently indenting your code so that you can match enclosing structures such as `if` statements and loops; blank lines and indenting to delineate blocks of code with specific purposes; and consistent capitalization go a long way toward one's ability to easily "digest" a listing of code.

Unfortunately, you can't document a complete application in code alone. It all starts outside the IDE with some form of external documentation.

External Documentation

An application is a collection of software that supports business processes, so starting out by documenting those processes makes sense. But how? Rational Unified Process? Unified Modeling Language (UML)? Visio diagrams? Microsoft Word? A paper napkin?

Believe it or not, we prefer the paper napkin! Perhaps we should explain. . . .

No matter how much head nodding and "Yeah, I understand that" that you may get back from your client, he just doesn't understand the UML diagrams that you're going over with him. Don't believe us? Have him draw one for you, and you see what we mean.

At the other end of the extreme, a series of plain flowcharts similar to the ones that you drew in fifth grade are easy to understand by even the most code-phobic clients, but these don't really work either, because they don't translate into Web pages, code modules, or other elements that you and your client envision about the application that you're designing.

One of your authors came up with a documentation technique some years ago that his company (Productivity Enhancement) and clients could both easily understand and that closely translates into Web pages and code modules in the finished product. (It's a small but important part of something that we call the *Practical Lightweight Universal Methodology — PLUM*, for short — which you're likely to be hearing more about someday soon.) Here's how it works:

1. List and formally name all the processes that the application supports. (We typically use Microsoft Word's outlining feature for this task.)
2. Create a list of all the actors that are involved in the whole of the business. (An *actor* can be a job title, a department, a payment gateway, a trading partner's B2B server—anything that "does something" in a business process.)
3. For each process, label an 11" x 17" (ledger-sized) piece of white paper with the name of the process and place it over a gridded surface so that a faint image of the grid squares shows through the paper. (We place the paper longways—landscape—in front of us.)
4. List down the left side those actors that are involved in that process and draw "swim lanes" across the page to visually separate each actor. These are called swim lanes because they are analogous to the marked lanes in a swimming pool within which each swimmer must confine himself. In the case of this chart, the "swimmers" are the actors that are involved in the processes your application supports.
5. List across the top from left to right the sequence of named phases that the process goes through during its entire life cycle, making sure that you account for things such as retiring matured process data to a data warehouse. (We also assign an integer code to each named phase, progressing from left to right in multiples of ten.)
6. Draw a tenth-grade flowchart but superimpose each task and decision box in the appropriate intersection of actor (who is doing it) and phase (at what point in the process is it done). Assign a short, yet descriptive name to each task or decision box in the flowchart.

   The result so far is a quick first draft of what is known as a *deployment chart* that clearly describes the business process in terms of workflow, resources, and life cycle. An abbreviated example of a deployment chart is shown in Figure 36-1. We have omitted the box names because the type would be too small to read; we're trying only to give you a general idea of how a deployment chart appears. (Beginning to get a little excited? Read on. . . .)
7. For each task or decision box in the deployment chart, label a separate piece of letter-sized white paper with the name of that task.
8. Draw boxes to represent the sequence of form submissions, hyperlinks, and so on that make up each finite step in the task and sketch a quick representation of the user interface of each step.
9. Give a short, yet descriptive name to each box and then draw arrows between the boxes to show progression.
10. Go over everything with the client, who normally can clearly follow the pencil sketch better than most can the prettiest multicolored UML diagram that lots of money can buy. Concentrate on exceptions to the normal process flow and sketch those in, too, which sometimes results in you discovering new actors that are involved under certain circumstances, special processes, and so on.

    After this step is done, you typically have a collection of heavily marked-up pencil diagrams and crowded task boxes (which is why I sketch these on ledger-size paper to begin with).

11. Redraw the diagrams to look nicer and then create the application's directory hierarchy, naming a separate directory for each process (the name coming directly from the name of the deployment chart that documents the process.)

12. Create blank templates named for each step in each task by using the format `TasknameStepname.cfm`, again taking these names directly from the diagrams already drawn and labeled in step 8.

13. The actors listed down the left side directly map to individual roles in ColdFusion MX's new role-based security mechanism. You can easily restrict access to only authorized users by simply testing whether the logged-in user was granted membership in the appropriate role for each task. Make a note of each role required by this process so you can create these roles in your database when the application is deployed.

14. The named phases across the top of a deployment chart are assigned progressive numeric values, so add a `Phase` attribute to the parent entity that will store the data related to each phase in the database.

    Now that you have a named template for every step of every task within every process in your application, you can concentrate on encapsulating your business logic into ColdFusion components, which directly fit the role-based framework defined in the diagrams.

15. Because the components are entity-centric rather than instance-centric, add a class method named `List<Entity>Status()` to each component. You will program this method in each entity's component to produce a sorted status list of all the rows in that entity's table, based on the value of its `Phase` attribute.

The end result of these steps is a complete, organized foundation upon which to build your completed ColdFusion MX application, all built upon the simple concept of a deployment chart like the one shown in Figure 36-1.

Using deployment charts for external documentation also greatly assists process analysis. If you see too many phases in a process diagram or if its workflow "ping pongs" between actors in a given phase, you're looking at a bottleneck of some sort. We love the revelations that our clients have after they see what they're really doing for the first time: "No wonder things take so long!" You may be surprised at how quickly your client can sometimes resolve his process problems with a deployment chart in hand. You may even end up with your client drawing revisions for you—and who better?

You can incorporate copies of your charts into your actual development contract with your client as well as use them as the application's external documentation. Now, whenever you add a new developer to the team, he can get a very quick read on the entire application, its directory structure, and every template involved at every step of every process. Now that's making the most of your documentation efforts!

So no, we don't really prefer a paper *napkin*, but we do prefer paper and a #2 pencil. We own just about every expensive drawing and charting tool on the market, including some very specialized process diagramming tools, but we can still generate a pencil-and-paper chart in less than a quarter of the time that doing the same thing in software takes.

We're perfectly happy to present hand-drawn diagrams to our clients and have them copied in our legal contracts. Experienced clients not only understand, but they also prefer it that way. After all, someone must pay for all that electronic diagramming labor, and it pushes the delivery date.

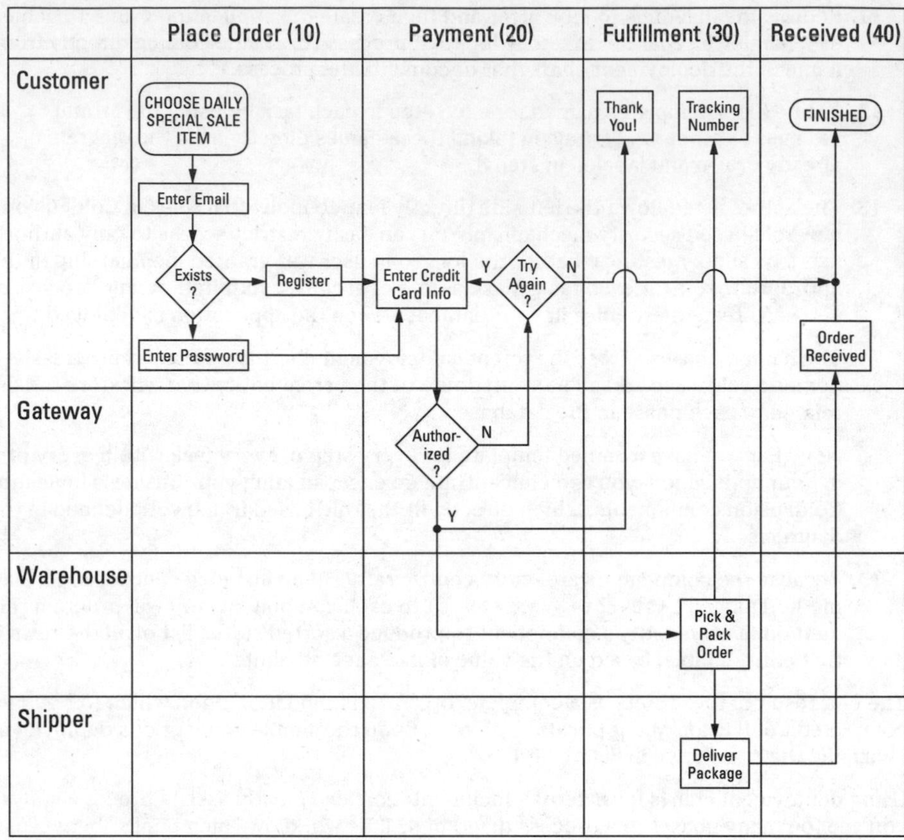

Figure 36-1: A finished deployment chart.

Internal Documentation

If external documentation shows your application through binoculars, *internal documentation* (comments in the code) shows it through a microscope.

Internal documentation should not try to describe what is outside a piece of code — only what is inside. External documentation's job is to show how everything relates together in the application. And your comments shouldn't try to teach the reader how to program, so don't explain the basics. If he's not a professional chef, don't let him into the kitchen!

Have your internal documentation explain only those parts of your code that really need explaining. If your external documentation does its job, and if you write your code by using the techniques and principles that we've shown you, you need only minimal internal documentation.

CFML comments

CFML comments are stripped out by ColdFusion Server, and white space is left in their place, so the resulting HTML sent to your Web server for delivery to the user's browser contains a bit of bloat from this white space. You can control this by using the ColdFusion tags and techniques that we discuss in this book. The main thing is that you can't see any of your CFML comments by viewing source in your browser if, for some reason, you want to see whether certain parts of your application are processing correctly or you want to see exactly where an error occurred in a loop.

CFML comments open with a left-angle bracket, an exclamation point, and three hyphens; they close with three more hyphens and a right angle bracket, as follows:

```
<!--- This is a CFML comment. --->
```

CFML comments can span multiple lines, too, as the following example shows:

```
<!---
This is a very long CFML comment that describes a complicated piece of
code and therefore requires more than a single line of text.
--->
```

If you still code by using ColdFusion Studio 5, make sure that you implement the F5 Yellow Comments trick in Chapter 41 to make your CFML comments easy to read and write.

HTML comments

HTML comments *do* pass through ColdFusion Server unchanged, so they are returned to your Web server and then to your browser. By strategically placing descriptive HTML comments inside loops, If tests, Switch statements, and in template headers, you can trace the exact path of code execution by choosing View ➪ Source in your browser.

You can place both single-line and multiline HTML comments in your code, just as you can with CFML comments. The only difference is that HTML comments have two hyphens rather than three, as the following examples show:

```
<!-- This is an HTML comment. -->

<!--
This is a very long HTML comment that describes a complicated piece
of code and therefore requires more than a single line of text.
-->
```

Make sure that you either convert your HTML comments to CFML comments or remove them before deployment, as you don't want end users learning about the internals of your code.

SQL comments

Documenting your SQL statements makes sense, because the database does most of your application's heavy lifting and is therefore a critical part of your enterprise that deserves its own documentation.

The following comment forms work with Microsoft SQL Server, which is the most common database server used with ColdFusion. Your database server's commenting requirements may differ.

Single-line comments can be embedded in `CFQUERY` calls as follows:

```
-- Never break a single-line SQL comment onto a second line
```

Multiline comments are embedded as follows:

```
/* If you need to create multiline comments in your SQL,
just enclose the lines of comments like this */
```

Both of these comment formats can also be used directly in stored procedures created directly in the database itself.

JavaScript comments

Multiline JavaScript comments work just as do multiline SQL comments, as follows:

```
/* If you need to create multiline comments in your JavaScript,
just enclose the lines of comments like this */
```

Single-line comments are different, however, as the following example shows:

```
// This is a single line comment in JavaScript
```

Remember that all JavaScript comments flow through to your browser and are, therefore, visible if you use the View ➪ Source command to view them in your browser.

XML considerations

Don't embed a pair of hyphens in an XML or XHTML comment. Doing so throws a parsing error. XML is documented with plain HTML comments. See Chapter 30 for details.

Documenting changes

We prefer to briefly document code changes directly where they appear in the code rather than group them in the header. That way, we don't need to read documentation in one place, go hunting for comments in the code, and then look back and forth between comment and code trying to interpret what the comment really means.

To assist us in finding all our changes, we religiously use source-code version control (see Chapter 39), and we also encode our change comments as follows:

```
<!--- [CHANGE 03/26/02] Now sorts by descending sale date --->
```

We can find all changes in our application by doing an Extended Find on `[CHANGE`, or we can just find all the changes in a single code template by comparing the current version against the previous version.

Personally, we don't find a need to document *fixes* unless they have some effect on code elsewhere in the application. Ask yourself, "What valuable decision could a developer make by reading this comment?" Don't distract readers from useful comments by filling your code with useless information.

Summary

In this chapter you've learned a new and practical way to document your code, and also a method for integrating documentation with design. The early coupling of these two disciplines ensures that your documentation won't get short shrift. But even the best documentation won't do any good unless it's easily digested. If all your rules and coding formats don't fit on a single page of paper and can't be memorized in ten minutes, you have too many rules and none of them are likely to be followed.

You've heard a lot of blasphemy against so-called "conventional wisdom" here, but don't be afraid to agree with us. If what we've said here makes perfect sense to you, it's because our approach is a sane and logical one. Vendors probably don't like this approach because it doesn't require you to spend money on vendors' tools, books, or training to make it work.

If your code still isn't understandable with this lightweight documentation approach, or if your code just seems too hard to document, take a second look at the code itself.

✦ ✦ ✦

Fusebox Basics

✦ ✦ ✦ ✦

In This Chapter

A brief history of Fusebox

How circuits, fuses, and fuseactions form the Fusebox framework

How the problem of complexity is tackled using a hub-and-spoke architecture

How the Fusebox core files work

How to create a simple Fusebox application

✦ ✦ ✦ ✦

In this chapter, you'll learn about a web application framework called Fusebox. Fusebox is by far the most popular framework for building ColdFusion applications and the success developers have had with it has caused it to be adopted by PHP, Java, and Lasso programmers — with work underway for a .NET version.

Why is Fusebox so popular? Building any application — web or otherwise — is hard work. As Fred Brooks noted a quarter of a century ago, the difficulty in building software is that software is, by its very nature, complex. Frameworks exist to mediate the complexity of building software. Fusebox is so popular simply because it has been so successful in this mission.

Frameworks, though, impose their own learning curves. It is an irony that before a developer can make use of a framework to reduce the difficulty of building software, he or she must first overcome the difficulty of learning that framework. In this chapter, we explain the basic concepts of Fusebox and provide you with a simple example of building a Fusebox application. This chapter will prepare you for Chapter 38, "Advanced Fusebox".

A Brief Fusebox Glossary

Throughout the following two chapters, we use some new terms. Although jargon is efficient in collapsing phrases down to a key word or two, it can also be confusing. You should find referring to this glossary of terms useful throughout this and the following chapter.

Adalon: A tool for visually architecting Fusebox applications (at `www.synthis.com`).

circuit: A directory in which the `FBX_Switch.cfm` file handles related *fuseactions*. A `ShoppingCart` circuit, for example, may handle such fuseactions as `addItem`, `removeItem`, and `display`. Usually, the *fuses* that fulfill a circuit's fuseactions are physically located in the same circuit.

circuit alias: The unique name given to each *circuit* in a Fusebox application. Circuit aliases enable you to uniquely identify circuits that have the same name, such as `MyApp/Users` and `MyApp/Admin/Users`. In a compound fuseaction, the first portion of the fuseaction is the circuit alias (for example, in `Cart.addItem`, `Cart` refers to the circuit alias).

compound fuseaction: A distinction made between Fusebox 2-style *fuseactions* (for example, `addItemToCart`) and Fusebox 3-style fuseactions, which are made up (compounded) of a circuit alias and a fuseaction request, separated by dot notation (for example, `Cart.addItem`).

core files: Files that create the foundation of a Fusebox application. They include the following:

- `FBX_Fusebox30_CFnn.cfm` (where *nn* refers to the version of the ColdFusion server to be used)
- `FBX_Circuits.cfm`
- `FBX_Settings.cfm`
- `FBX_Layouts.cfm`
- `FBX_Switch.cfm`
- `FBX_SaveContent.cfm`

DevNotes: (Part of FliP.) A simple threaded messaging system that sits at the bottom of each prototype page and enables users and developers to converse about the project.

FLiP (*Fusebox Lifecycle Process*): A methodology often used with Fusebox applications that stresses the use of wireframes, prototypes, DevNotes, test harnesses, and QuerySims. FLiP is not covered in this book.

fuse: A code file, typically small, discrete, and well focused in its scope. Fuses are the means of carrying out fuseactions.

fuseaction: A request made of a Fusebox application to perform an action. Similar to a method in object-oriented frameworks.

fuseaction path: The list of circuits traversed from the home circuit to the target circuit. An example would be `MyApp/Admin/Users` (assuming that the compound fuseaction was `Users.`*`foo`*.

fuseaction request: In a compound fuseaction, the second portion of the fuseaction is called the fuseaction request (for example, in `Cart.addItem`, `addItem` refers to the fuseaction request).

Fusebox: An architectural framework for building Web applications implemented by a set of core files available from `www.fusebox.org`.

Fusebox API: The variables provided by a Fusebox application, such as `Fusebox.isCustomTag` and `Fusebox.fuseaction`.

Fusedoc: A documentation system for each fuse that provides a "work order" for a fuse, detailing its responsibilities and input/output variables.

home circuit: The top-level *circuit* to which all fuseactions are directed; the first item in the fuseaction path (for example, `MyApp` in the fuseaction path `MyApp/Admin/Users`).

prototype: An exact replica of what becomes the finished application that is written prior to any architecting or coding. Its purpose is to provide a method of communicating with clients and among developers to determine the full scope of the application to be built.

nested circuits: Circuits that physically reside underneath other circuits, such as `Admin/Users`. These are often used to model parent-child relationships.

nested layouts: A system for applying circuit-wide processing of code run after any fuses are executed; often used to create header/footers, global navigation, and so on.

QuerySim: A custom tag that returns a recordset. Useful in writing and testing code before database queries are complete.

`self`: Variable given to the default page in a Fusebox application; a shortcut that is equivalent to the value of `cgi.script_name`. Used in referring back to the fusebox: `<form action="#self#?fuseaction=#XFA.submitForm#">`.

target circuit: The final circuit charged with handling the fuseaction request; the last item in the fuseaction path (for example, `Users` in the fuseaction path `MyApp/Admin/Users`).

test harness: (Used in FliP.) The use of a separate file that sets the variables (and otherwise creates the environment) needed to unit test a single fuse.

wireframe: (Used in FliP.) A simple, text-only, clickable representation of the application used at the beginning of the FLiP process.

XFAs (exit fuseactions): Variables provided to a fuse that replace hard-coded values for possible fuseactions. The following hard-coded values, for example, may be found in a menu of choices:

```
<a href="index.cfm?fuseaction=Cart.display">View Cart</a>

<a href="index.cfm?fuseaction=Products.new">New items</a>

<a href="index.cfm?fuseaction=Account.edit">Edit your account</a>
```

These values would be replaced by XFAs, as follows:

```
<a href="index.cfm?fuseaction=#XFA.viewCart#">View Cart</a>

<a href="index.cfm?fuseaction=#XFA.newStuff#">New items</a>

<a href="index.cfm?fuseaction=#XFA.editAccount#">Edit your account</a>
```

XFAs are resolved at runtime.

What is Fusebox?

You may have heard about Fusebox but been unsure about exactly what it is. If so, you're in good company. While many developers have adopted it enthusiastically, some have remained on the sidelines — perhaps worried over adding one more thing to the ever-growing list of things to be mastered. Luckily, learning Fusebox is quite simple. You're likely to recognize some of your own best practices in Fusebox., which makes sense: Fusebox was created not by a vendor but by developers looking to solve real-world problems.

A brief history of Fusebox

Rewind to 1998 — eons ago in "Internet time." Several developers are using the `cf-talk` e-mail list hosted by `HouseOfFusion.com` to discuss common problems in developing Web applications. The group includes Steve Nelson, Robi Sen, Joshua Cyr, Michael Dinowitz, and Gabe Roffman. As is the case with all such discussions, it begins with, "Wouldn't it be nice . . .?"

The group actively encourages freewheeling thinking. New people with new ideas are invited to participate. What emerges is an idea for an architectural framework to deal with some of these common problems. The group's members, realizing that something concrete has come out of their late-night discussions, casts about for a name for this new framework. "Because we're all working in ColdFusion," says Steve Nelson, "why don't we call it something like Fusebox?"

In the normal course of things, Fusebox would have been an interesting idea laid aside and forgotten in the crush of daily business, but such was not the case *this* time. Other developers, frustrated by a set of problems repeatedly cropping up in each new project, heard about Fusebox and began adopting it.

As ideas began to emerge and Fusebox began to evolve, it became less clear what someone meant when they said "Fusebox". Which of the many ideas that together constituted "Fusebox" were they talking about?

That both an "early" Fusebox and a "later" Fusebox were developed seems clear now. *Fusebox 1* was the name given to the original version of Fusebox. In 2000, Steve Nelson and Craig Girard published *Fusebox: Methodology and Techniques*, documenting the new ideas that had been adopted by the burgeoning Fusebox community. This provided a reference marker, and the ideas laid forth in the book became known as *Fusebox 2*.

About this time, Hal Helms and a group of developers began exploring the use of Fusebox in large-scale, complex Web applications. Again, new ideas emerged, and a version of Fusebox for large-scale applications, dubbed *Extended Fusebox*, or *XFB*, arose. XFB incorporated both a Fusebox architectural framework and a set of methodological best practices. The question, "What is Fusebox?" had no clear answer. Was one talking about Fusebox 1, Fusebox 2, or XFB? Fusebox, the architectural framework, or Fusebox, the methodology?

Understanding that such confusion was unhelpful to current Fusebox adopters — and bafflingly confusing for people new to Fusebox — a decision was made to use the architectural components of XFB as a base for a unified Fusebox. During much of 2001, a group of developers set about harmonizing and integrating the various versions, culminating in the release of *Fusebox 3* at the second annual Fusebox conference in October of 2001.

An architectural framework of a methodology?

Coinciding with the release of Fusebox 3, the methodological components that were widely adopted within the Fusebox community were given their own name: The *Fusebox Lifecycle Process*. *FLiP*, to use its common acronym, places great emphasis on creating a common understanding between client and architect about exactly what is to be built before any architecture, database design, or code is created.

In this book, whenever we speak of *Fusebox*, we are referring to the architectural framework released as Fusebox 3. Although FLiP works very nicely with Fusebox, the two are independent of each other; FLiP can be used with architectures other than Fusebox, and Fusebox can be built by using methodologies other than FLiP.

Readers interested in learning more about FLiP may find online resources at `www.halhelms.com`, `www.secretagents.com`, `www.techspedition.com`, and in the book, *Fusebox: Developing ColdFusion Applications*, by Jeff Peters and Nat Papovich and published in June 2002 by New Riders Publishing.

Exploring the Fusebox architectural framework

An architectural framework for software defines the components or building blocks that make up software applications. Fusebox is an architectural framework for creating Web applications and consists of a set of prewritten core files (available from `www.fusebox.org`) and application-specific code written by application developers that utilizes these core files.

Although understanding the parts of Fusebox is vital to using the framework, real success begins with the understanding that a Fusebox application is best thought of as a single entity that responds to requests called *fuseactions*. These fuseactions may be initiated by a user by means such as choosing menu items, clicking buttons or by typing a URL into the user's Web browser that includes a fuseaction name/value pair — for example `www.halhelms.com?fuseaction=training.details`. New fuseactions can also be initiated by code requesting a new fuseaction, as shown in Listing 37-1.

Listing 37-1: Code requesting a new fuseaction

```
<cfif ValidatedUser.recordCount EQ "1">
   <cflocation url="index.cfm?fuseaction=User.welcome" />
<cfelse>
   <cflocation url="index.cfm?fuseaction=Login.badLogin" />
</cfif>
```

In fact, everything that an application can do — from logging a user in to showing new products, to processing a credit card (to use the case of an e-commerce application) — must have a corresponding fuseaction. After one fuseaction is done, any new action that's necessary must begin with a new fuseaction.

Although the totality of an application can be defined by the fuseactions handled by the application, any one fuseaction works best if it is small in scope and discrete in nature. One can see that, in a large application, the number of fuseactions may be quite large — easily in the hundreds or thousands. Managing such a large number of fuseactions calls for adopting the strategy recommended by Machiavelli: *Divide et impera* — divide and conquer.

In the case of Fusebox, such a strategy involves finding a reasoned approach to grouping fuseactions into smaller clusters, known as *circuits*. These circuits can be either at the same level (in sibling fashion) or may be nested in parent-child arrangement.

Figure 37-1 shows a simple Fusebox architecture, where all circuits are at the same level, forming a *hub-and-spoke architecture*.

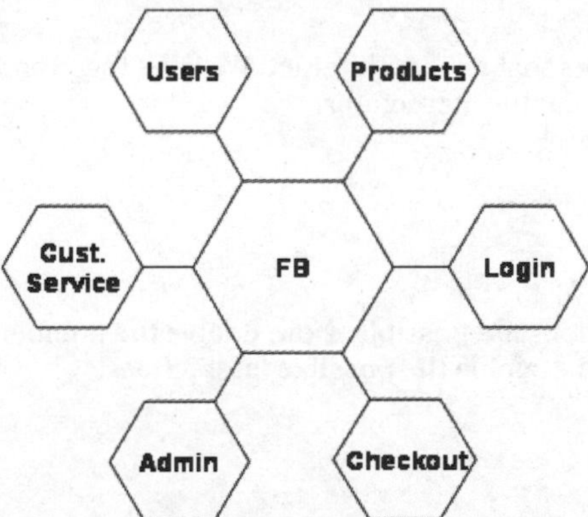

Figure 37-1: The Fusebox architecture as a hub-and-spoke arrangement.

Do we need Fusebox?

While Fusebox has thousands of fans, it also has a few, vocal critics. Some of them find that it simply doesn't solve the problems they have. Of course, no framework can be all things to all people and such a reasoned judgment is valid. Others, though, seem to have adapted the words of the bandito in Mel Brook's movie, "Blazing Saddles", arguing: "Framework? We don't need no stinkin' framework!" Still others have based their business model on keeping the issue of code architecture a secret — effectively tieing up both client and developer alike. But good reasons exist for adopting a framework.

The case for agreement on an architectural framework

Web applications typically require a more diverse set of skills than is needed in more traditional development. In creating a client-server application, for example, the user interface is normally designed by developers working in the same language as the application logic. Build a Java application, for example, and you're probably going to use the Java Swing components for a user interface.

Web development casts a wider net, and a typical application may use the services of graphics artists, HTML coders, JavaScript coders, application-logic developers, and database specialists. Although few people would urge us back to the "good old days" of pre-Web development, such a diverse set of Web developers (who are often working in separate locations) does present the problem of *complexity*.

Only recently have Web developers begun to understand that complexity (and its cousin, chaos) have much greater effects than has been commonly assumed. Such effects are examples of the law of unintended consequences. A town tries to alleviate a congested highway by adding a parallel road, but the new road encourages new businesses to spring up along it, thereby increasing the number of commuters and adding to, rather than subtracting from, the overall traffic. The town has fallen victim to the law of unintended consequences. (I'm indebted to Cory Doctorow for this excellent example.)

You're probably familiar with results that are at variance with your intentions. A special case of this general law applies if your intentions are good and the unintended results are ill. In such cases, we can offer the observation that "no good deed goes unpunished." Less well known has been how complexity increases the chances for unintended consequences — specifically failure of a system — to occur.

Consider a system with only three components that need to interact. We label these components A, B, and C. Following are the possible unique interactions:

- ✦ A_B
- ✦ A_C
- ✦ B_C

For three components, three distinct interactions are possible. Now, double the number of interactive components to six, as follows, and examine the possible interactions:

- ✦ A_B
- ✦ A_C
- ✦ A_D
- ✦ A_E

- A _ F
- B _ C
- B _ D
- B _ E
- B _ F
- C _ D
- C _ E
- C _ F
- D _ E
- D _ F
- E _ F

Doubling the number of independent, interactive components *quintuples* the number of possible interactions. The system has gone from a small number of "moving parts" to one five times more prone to break down, because a system with more components has far more chances for any one of these interactions to fail. This is true whether the components are mechanical or — as in the case of Web development — people. In both cases, complexity undermines the system's stability.

Now, take the same number of components — six — and rearrange them so that, instead of interacting with each other, they interact with a single, central point that we call *FB*, as shown in Figure 37-2.

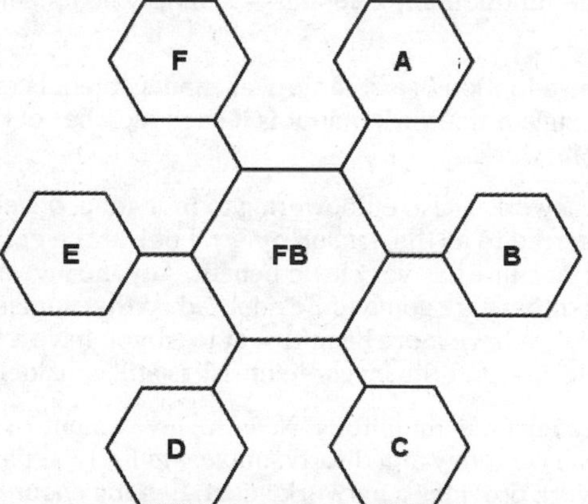

Figure 37-2: Rearranging components into a hub-and-spoke pattern.

Following is a listing of all possible unique interactions:

- FB _ A
- FB _ B
- FB _ C

✦ FB_D

✦ FB_E

✦ FB_F

We add a component, FB, yet reduce the complexity to less than half of its original. The difference becomes even more marked with more components; complexity has been tamed.

In the 1960s, United Airlines announced that it would employ a hub-and-spoke pattern for managing its flights. Instead of flying directly from one city to another, a plane would fly from its origin to a central hub. Then another plane would transfer passengers from that hub to the planned destination. This was done amid outcries that such a system would never work—that it would be unwieldy, duplicative, and inefficient. Today, of course, virtually every airline has adopted the hub-and-spoke arrangement.

Fusebox provides a similar hub-and-spoke design pattern with similar beneficial results. Instead of individuals needing to manage multiple interactions with a large number of other people, Fusebox provides a central architecture that is far more easily managed. This has proven very successful, both in building an application and—perhaps more important—in maintaining it.

The argument for agreement on an application architecture makes sense for a number of other reasons and transcends the choice of the architecture chosen. Such an agreement is likely to enable individuals to collaborate on a project far more easily in the same way that a common human language greatly eases communication and collaboration.

And the adoption of a common architectural framework based on a well-published and accepted standard can also provide a competitive advantage to the adopting group, as clients and prospects are often more willing to choose a vendor that has adopted a standard practice. Such adoption provides insurance for them in case that a sole vendor is not responsive to their future needs or—as in the case of the "dot-bomb" explosion—is simply no longer in business.

Individual developers, too, benefit from the adoption of a standard, as management is more likely to invest in tools and training for a single framework than it is if each member of the development team has no such uniting framework.

Learning to work with an architectural framework is also empowering to individual developers in managing their careers. This is often referred to as the *network effect*. Look at the case of the adoption of fax machines. A single fax machine has very little benefit. Anyone investing in one is simply gambling that, at some point, others are going to be adopted so that someone is there to communicate with. A few fax machines have more benefit—at least you have a better chance that you can use faxes to communicate—but the investment risk is still considerable.

The real benefit accrues after fax machines become ubiquitous. Now the investment risk is actually negative—*not* owning one puts the company at a disadvantage. Similarly, separate companies agreeing on a standard framework provides a network effect, helping ensure that individuals who invest the effort and time to develop expertise in that framework benefit because they can transfer that expertise from one company to another. At the very least, such ease of mobility helps developers in negotiating with their current employers.

The case for Fusebox

If you accept the arguments for adoption of a single architectural framework, the question remains, "Why adopt Fusebox?" Fusebox deserves your consideration for several reasons. First, Fusebox is a standard developed by a community of developers. This stands in contrast to other standards that are primarily vendor-driven.

Although such vendor sponsorship tells you nothing about the technical merits of the standard itself, you do need to understand that the motivations of developers and vendors are very different. Developers endorse a standard mostly because they find that it helps them solve problems in their daily jobs. Vendors are more likely to see the control of a standard as a valuable asset in locking developers in to a specific product or product line.

From its inception, Fusebox has been the work of developers whose allegiance is based solely on the degree to which Fusebox empowers them and makes their tasks easier. Fusebox has evolved from a loose collection of good ideas to a robust, powerful architectural framework. Features were added only because the Fusebox community found them to be helpful.

Innovation around a standard is strongly encouraged within the Fusebox community. Realizing that good ideas come from the entire developer base rather than from a few individuals, the Fusebox community has created a specification for the core files and a reference implementation but encourages others to try out new ideas while supporting the existing standard. This has led to Fusebox core-file innovations, such as more powerful exception handling (see `www.fusium.com`) and an entirely new set of powerful features (go to `www.techspedition.com`).

Such innovation around a stable core helps assure the community that Fusebox continues to be responsive to new needs. A Fusebox standards committee determines the features and *API* (*application programming interface*) that any "Fusebox-compliant" set of core files must support. Innovators are then encouraged to submit their ideas to the standards committee for consideration for formal adoption in a future Fusebox version.

Vendors are now beginning to support Fusebox, offering tools for handling aspects of documentation and testing (see `www.grokfusebox.com`) and online training (at `www.secretagents.com`) as well as a powerful, visual, integrated-development environment (see `www.synthis.com`). Additionally, books and instructor-led training are available (at, for example, `www.halhelms.com` and `www.techspedition.com`).

Finally, Fusebox enjoys an extremely active online community, with e-mail lists and forums that provide free help. Users find that their questions are barely posted before answers are posted. "Newbies" are warmly welcomed; indeed, the online Fusebox community has developed such a culture of helpfulness and friendliness that it draws in even non-Fuseboxers.

Fusebox Components

One appealing aspect of Fusebox is the low barrier to entry. While some frameworks exist that are very powerful and yet quite complex (particularly true in a language such as Java), the concepts behind Fusebox are simple and straightforward as are the code assets that provide the framework. This section will introduce you to those components and show how each fits together to make the Fusebox framework.

Fusebox terms

A Fusebox application can best be thought of as a single entity that responds to different action requests, known as *fuseactions*. In this section, you see how a Fusebox application fulfills these requests.

In addition to a fuseaction, a Fusebox application has two other main conceptual components: *circuits* and *fuses*. A circuit is a logical grouping of related fuseactions and is represented as a file directory or folder. Figure 37-3 shows the directory/circuit structure for the application shown in Figure 37-1.

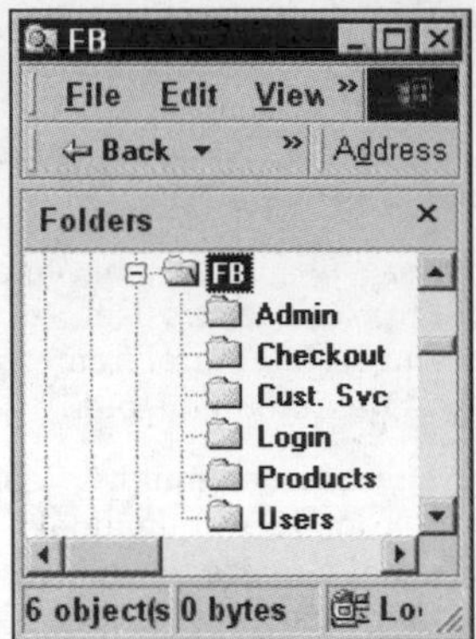

Figure 37-3: Circuits map to file directories.

Circuit names must be unique across a Fusebox application, but directory names may not be, as shown by the presence of two Users directories in Figure 37-4.

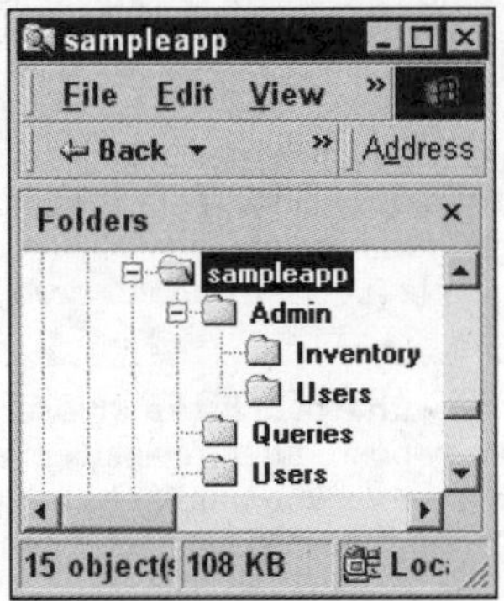

Figure 37-4: Similarly named directories (Users) within a single Fusebox application.

For this reason, circuits are given aliases, and these aliases are declared in one of the core Fusebox files, `FBX_Circuits.cfm`.

The third main conceptual component of Fusebox is the *fuse*. A fuse is an application-specific code file that performs some discrete function. Fuses are written by application developers and are used by the Fusebox framework to fulfill a fuseaction request.

The application architect determines what tasks a fuseaction must carry out and then apportions these tasks to one or more fuses. The mapping of fuses to fuseactions is done in another of the core files, `FBX_Switch.cfm`. Each circuit has its own `FBX_Switch.cfm`, file and each of these files handles the fuseaction-to-use mappings for that circuit alone.

Listing 37-2 is a portion of an `FBX_Switch.cfm` file for a `Login` circuit.

Listing 37-2: Mapping fuses to fuseactions

```
<cfswitch expression="#Fusebox.fuseaction#">

   <cfcase value="login">
      <cfinclude template="dsp_LoginForm.cfm" />
   </cfcase>

   <cfcase value="validateLogin">
      <cfinclude template="qry_ValidatedUser.cfm" />
      <cfinclude template="act_Validate.cfm" />
   </cfcase>

</cfswitch>
```

In the code shown in Listing 37-2, the fuseaction, `login`, requires only a single fuse, `dsp_LoginForm.cfm`. In the only other fuseaction shown, `validateLogin`, two fuses are used.

One of the most obvious features of Fusebox is the prefixes given to fuse names. The prefixes provide an indication of the type of work done by the fuse, as shown in table 37-1.

Table 37-1: Common Fuse Prefixes

Prefix	*Type of functionality*
`dsp_`	*Display files* are used to display information to the `user.` `dsp_` files would be used for such purposes as getting information from users through forms, displaying listings and details of items, and displaying the contents of a shopping cart.
`act_`	*Action files* perform behind-the-scenes processing, providing that the application `logic.` `act_` files are used for such purposes as processing form information previously filled out and adding or removing items from an array of structures used for a shopping cart.
`qry_`	*Query files* handle all interactions with databases. Some Fuseboxers restrict their use to return record sets, opting to place `UPDATE`, `DELETE`, and `INSERT` statements into `act_` files.
`lay_`	*Layout files* are used to provide common elements to a Web application, such as bread crumbs and navigation.

The use of these prefixes constitutes an unofficial but widely adopted practice. Fuseboxers find that the use of prefixes tells them the general nature of an individual fuse and serves to group fuses of the same general types together. Since the list is not official, you can add any new prefixes you find helpful.

Figure 37-5 shows a single circuit/directory with all fuses highlighted. The other files appearing in the circuit are core files.

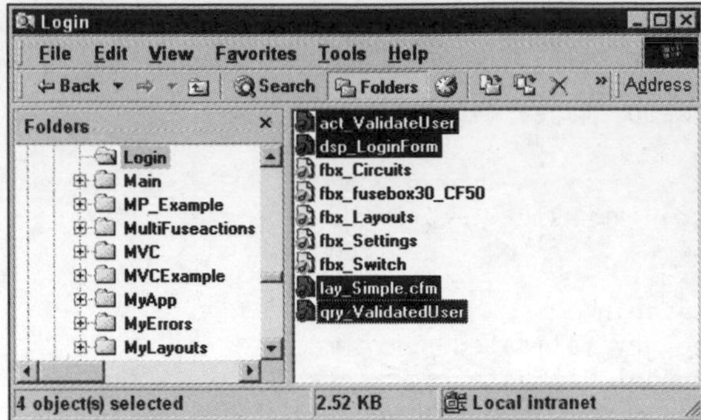

Figure 37-5: Login circuit, showing different fuse types.

The Fusebox core files

If you read any of the literature associated with Fusebox or talk with Fuseboxers, you hear the recurring expression *the fusebox*, as used in such phrases as "Then we return to the fusebox," and "Next, a new fuseaction is sent to the fusebox." What fusebox is being referred to? Where is this fusebox?

In fact, *the fusebox* is not a specific file (you have no `fusebox.cfm`, for example) but signifies the framework produced by the interaction of the core Fusebox files. Each core file has a specific purpose and each falls into one of three categories: *must change*, *may change*, and *may not change*. Table 37-2 lists the core files.

Table 37-2: Core Fusebox Files

File	*Category*	*Purpose*
`FBX_Fusebox30_CF`*`nn`*`.cfm`	May not change	This is the chief of the core Fusebox files and is responsible for calling each of the other core files as needed. Notice the use of *nn* in the file name, indicating that separate versions of the core file exist for the following ColdFusion server versions: Windows 4.0 Windows 4.5 Unix/Linux 4.5 Windows 5.0 Unix/Linux 5.0 This file is required in the Fusebox application root directory, referred to as the *home circuit*, and must be included by the default ColdFusion page (usually `index.cfm`).

File	Category	Purpose
FBX_Circuits.cfm	Must change	Circuit names must be unique across an application, although directory names need not be (refer to Figure 37-4). A *circuit alias* is the unique name given to a circuit. That alias is then mapped to a physical directory in this file. This file is required in the home circuit.
FBX_Settings.cfm	May change	This file enables code to be run that is specific to a circuit and its descendant circuits (in the case of nested circuits). FBX_Settings.cfm runs prior to any fuses and is useful for setting common or global variables. Each circuit may use this file if desired. In the case of nested circuits, the FBX_Settings.cfm files are included, beginning at the home circuit and working down through any intermediary circuits until the target circuit is reached. In the case of variable naming conflicts as would occur if a circuit, Parent, and a circuit, Child, both set the value of a variable, the value set by the child overrides that of the parent. FBX_Settings.cfm takes the place of Application.cfm, which is traditionally used as a global preprocessing file. The reasons for this are discussed in Chapter 38. This file must be included in the home circuit, where it must – at minimum – specify a value for the variable attributes.defaultfuseaction. It can be used by other circuits as well.
FBX_Switch.cfm	Must change	This file provides a mapping for fuseactions with fuses, effectively answering the question, "What does *this* fuseaction do?" The file is usually implemented as a <cfswitch> statement with individual fuseactions shown as <cfcase> blocks. Although standards lag behind new product version introductions, you may see future versions of ColdFusion implementing the same functionality contained in this file as a ColdFusion component (CFC). This file must be in every circuit that handles fuseaction requests.

Continued

Table 37-2 *(continued)*

File	*Category*	*Purpose*
`FBX_Layouts.cfm`	Must change	This file is responsible only for pointing to layouts files to be used by an individual circuit. As such, if this file is contained in a circuit, it must produce values for the variables `Fusebox.layoutFile` (the specific layout file to be used) and `Fusebox.layoutDir` (a relative path from the current circuit to the file specified in `Fusebox.layoutFile`). This file is optional, but must be used wherever the use of nested layouts is desired.

Creating a Hello World Fusebox Application

So far, you've viewed only the bones that make up a Fusebox application. In this section, you put muscles, ligaments, and sinews together to create a very simple Fusebox application that implements the Hello, World application used in many language tutorials. The application in this section has only two circuits: a main circuit, `Home`, and a single child circuit, `World`. Both circuits have a single fuseaction. Through building a complete Fusebox application—albeit a simple one—you can learn more about how to build real-world applications. In chapter 38, you add to your knowledge of Fusebox and put together a larger application.

Marking up the prototype

Taking a page from the FLiP methodology, you start with a prototype. Your prototype reflects the simplicity of the application itself, consisting of only two pages, as shown in Figures 37-6 and 37-7.

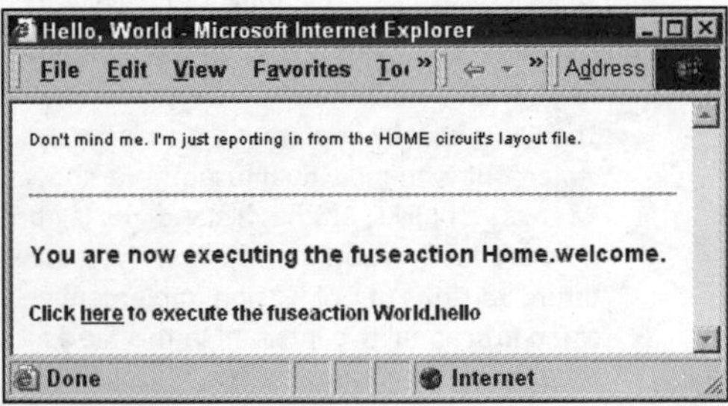

Figure 37-6: Prototype of Hello World application: page 1.

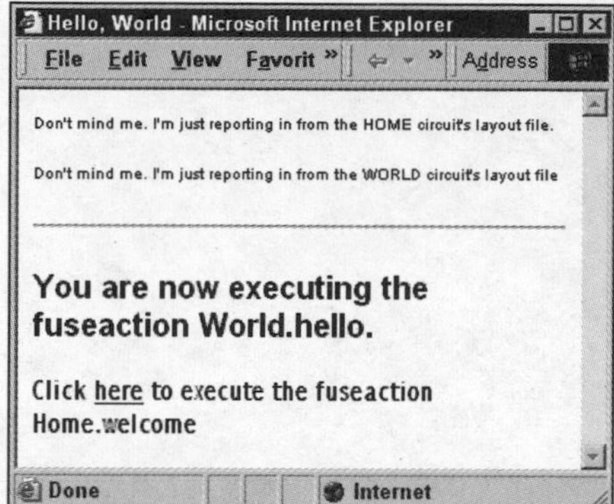

Figure 37-7: Prototype of Hello World application: page 2.

You begin by printing out the prototype pages so that they can be marked up. You then identify any *exit points* on a page, circling these on the page. An *exit po*int is any means by which a new fuseaction may be requested and is so called because it causes the user to *exit* the current page. Exit points are typically links or form submissions. Each page in the prototype has only one exit point — the link `here`.

These exit points are akin to events in other languages. In Fusebox, you assign names to these exit points, which are reflected on your marked-up prototype pages. These exit point names are not, however, fuseactions — not yet, at least. For now, they are simply descriptive names given to events by which a new fuseaction is requested.

You also mark up the prototype for any dynamic data that needs to be accounted for. This is data that is determined at runtime and includes such things as user names, product descriptions, and shopping-cart contents. Such dynamic data is marked with a square outline, and a variable name is decided on. To distinguish names for dynamic data and those for exit points, you use an `XFA.` prefix for exit points, as shown in Figure 37-8 and Figure 37-9.

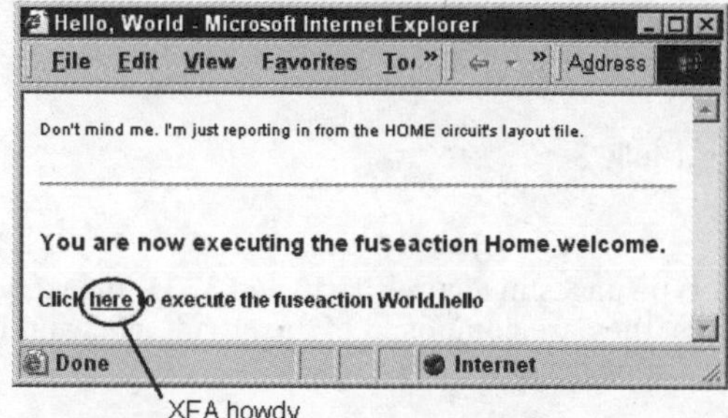

Figure 37-8: Marked-up Hello World prototype page 1.

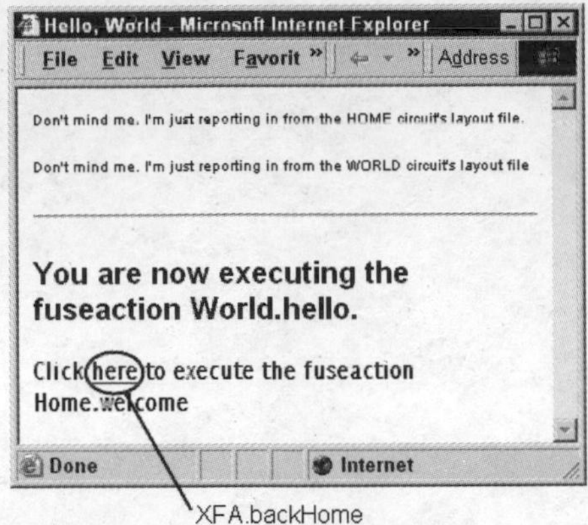

Figure 37-9: Marked-up Hello World prototype page 2.

Identifying exit points, fuseactions, and circuits

The text on both pages tells you the name of the fuseactions that are executed by clicking the appropriate links. In a real application, you would determine the actual fuseaction names after the prototype was fully marked up. By using this information, you can provide values for the XFAs already identified, as shown in Figures 37-10 and 37-11.

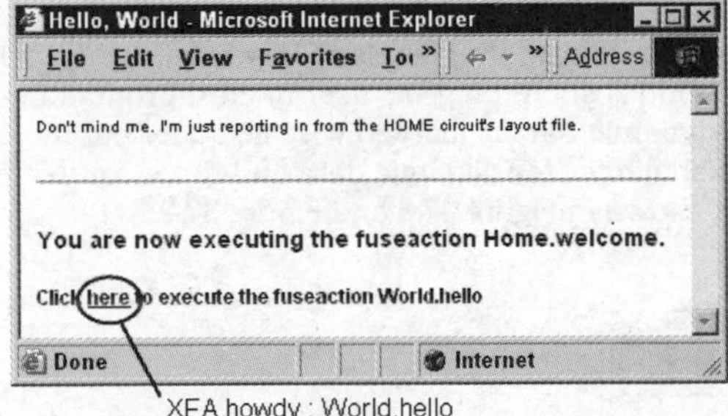

Figure 37-10: Hello World prototype page 1 fully marked up.

As you can see from the marked up prototype pages in Figures 37-10 and 37-11, fuseactions in Fusebox 3 are *compound* in nature—that is, they are composed of the circuit alias and the actual fuseaction request, separated by a dot or period.

Figure 37-11: Hello World prototype page 2 fully marked up.

At this point, you have identified the information shown in the following table about our first Fusebox application.

Circuit	*Request*
Home	Welcome
World	Hello

Identifying fuses

Next, you come to the point of determining exactly what tasks each fuseaction must accomplish — and what fuses perform these tasks. Both fuseactions do nothing more than display a page, as shown in the prototype. Each page can easily be created from a single display fuse, as shown in the following table.

Circuit	*Request*	*Fuse(s)*
Home	Welcome	`dsp_Welcome.cfm`
World	Hello	`dsp_Hello.cfm`

You can now create the directory framework for your application and drop the required core files into each directory, as shown in Figure 37-12.

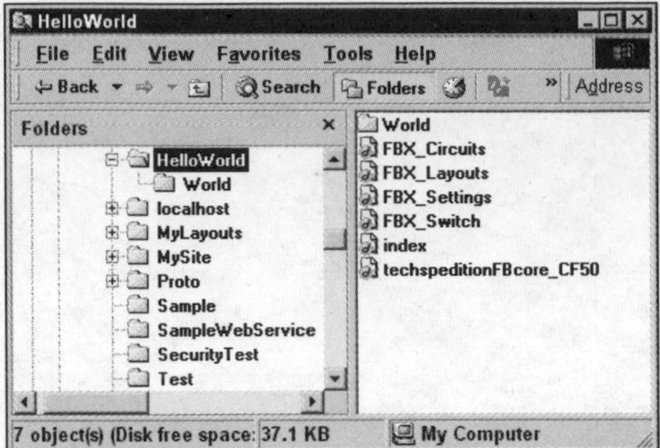

Figure 37-12: The circuit/directory framework for Hello World.

Mapping circuits to directories

Before you create the fuses themselves, you need to finish the setup work for your Fusebox application.

You must create circuit-to-directory mappings in the `FBX_Circuits.cfm` file in your home circuit. Listing 37-3 shows the file as downloaded from `www.fusebox.org`.

Listing 37-3: [`FBX_Circuits.cfm` skeleton]

```
<!---
<fusedoc fuse="FBX_Circuits.cfm">
   <responsibilities>
      I define the Circuits structure used with Fusebox 3.0.
   </responsibilities>
   <io>
      <out>
         <string name="fusebox.circuits.*" comments="set a variable for
each circuit name" />
      </out>
   </io>
</fusedoc>
--->

<!---Fusebox circuit code below in the syntax
Fusebox.Circuits.circuit_alias="relative/directory/path/from/applicatio
n/root --->
<cfscript>
   Fusebox.Circuits.???='???';
</cfscript>
```

The first part of the file is a comment beginning with `<fusedoc>` and ending in `</fusedoc>`. This is a standardized documentation scheme known as *Fusedoc*, about which you learn more in chapter 38. Notice, however, that the second comment indicates the syntax to be used for this circuit-to-directory mapping, and you have dummy code provided inside the `<cfscript>` tags that must be filled in and extended.

Using the table in the preceding section as a guide, you can change the model code provided as part of the core file to what you see in Listing 37-4.

Listing 37-4: [Code section of `FBX_Circuits.cfm`]

```
<cfscript>
   Fusebox.Circuits.Home='HelloWorld';
   Fusebox.Circuits.World='HelloWorld/World';
</cfscript>
```

With that completed, you can save `FBX_Circuits.cfm` to the `HelloWorld` directory (only the home circuit requires the `FBX_Circuits.cfm` file) and continue.

Setting a default fuseaction

Because a user of your HelloWorld application does not know to specify a fuseaction, you must provide a default fuseaction. This is done in the home circuit's `FBX_Settings.cfm file`, another of the core Fusebox files, as shown in Listing 37-5.

Listing 37-5: `FBX_Settings.cfm`

```
<cfparam name="attributes.defaultfuseaction" default="Home.welcome" />
```

In Chapter 38, you learn the reason for the `attributes.` prefix.

Mapping fuses to fuseactions

The last setup task prior to actually writing fuses is making the fuseaction-to-fuse mappings in each circuit's `FBX_Switch.cfm` file. Listing 37-6 shows the file as downloaded from `www.fusebox.org`.

Listing 37-6: `FBX_Switch.cfm` skeleton

```
<!---
<fusedoc fuse="FBX_Switch.cfm">
   <responsibilities>
      I am the cfswitch statement that handles the fuseaction,
delegating work to various fuses.
   </responsibilities>
   <io>
      <out>
         <string name="fusebox.fuseaction" />
```

Continued

Listing 37-6 *(continued)*

```
            <structure name="fusebox.circuit" />
         </out>
      </io>
   </fusedoc>
   --->
   <cfswitch expression="#fusebox.fuseaction#">

   <cfcase value="???">

   </cfcase>

   <!--- Default Execution --->
   <cfdefaultcase>
      <cfoutput>
         I received a fuseaction called #fusebox.fuseaction# that circuit
   #fusebox.circuit# doesn't have a handler for.
      </cfoutput>
   </cfdefaultcase>

   </cfswitch>
```

Again, don't worry about the Fusedoc; you get to that Chapter 38.

The `<cfdefaultcase>` code block is very useful, as it traps any fuseaction for which no mapping exists — something that you're likely to encounter both in the early stages of writing a Fusebox application and whenever misspelled fuseactions are presented to the fusebox. If such an event occurs, you see the message shown in Figure 37-13 in your browser.

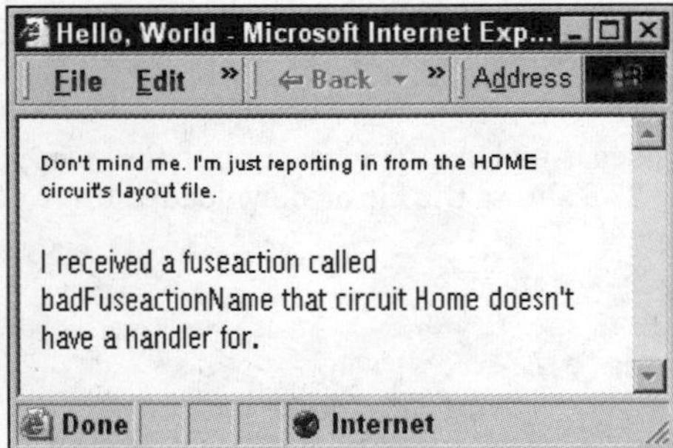

Figure 37-13: Executing a missing fuseaction request.

Listings 37-7 and 37-8 are the `FBX_Switch.cfm` files in the two circuits.

Listing 37-7: WelcomeHome/FBX_Switch.cfm

```
<cfswitch expression="#Fusebox.fuseaction#">
   <cfcase value="welcome">
      <cfset XFA.howdy = "World.hello" />
      <cfinclude template="dsp_Welcome.cfm" />
   </cfcase>
</cfswitch>
```

Listing 37-8: WelcomeHome/World/FBX_Switch.cfm

```
<cfswitch expression="#Fusebox.fuseaction#">
   <cfcase value="hello">
      <cfset XFA.backHome = "Home.welcome" />
      <cfinclude template="dsp_Hello.cfm" />
   </cfcase>
</cfswitch>
```

Notice that you set the values for the XFAs for each page in these listings. In chapter 38, you see why using variables rather than hard-coded values makes your code stronger and more maintainable, as well as enabling easier code reuse.

Setting the default page to include the Fusebox core file

All fuseactions are sent to the fusebox — that framework created by the interaction of the Fusebox core files. You need to make sure that the default page served up by the Web browser (usually `index.cfm`) points to the fusebox by including the core Fusebox file, as shown in Listing 37-9

Listing 37-9: Default page (index.cfm) in the home circuit

```
<cfinclude template="FBX_Fusebox30_CF50.cfm" />
```

Writing the fuses

Now, you get to write your fuses — although you don't have not much to them — in Listings 37-10 and 37-11

Listing 37-10: HelloWorld/dsp_Welcome.cfm

```
<title>Hello, World</title>
<h2>You are now executing the fuseaction Home.welcome.</h2>
<cfoutput>

<h3>Click <a href="index.cfm?fuseaction=#XFA.backHome#">here</a> to
execute the fuseaction World.hello</h3>

</cfoutput>
```

Listing 37-11: HelloWorld/World/dsp_Hello.cfm

```
<h2>You are now executing the fuseaction World.hello.</h2>
<cfoutput>

<h3>Click <a href="index.cfm?fuseaction=#XFA.howdy#">here</a> to
execute the fuseaction Home.welcome</h3>

</cfoutput>
```

Trying out HelloWorld

Now to try out your work. Execute the `index.cfm` file in a browser, and the default fuseaction, `Home.welcome` executes, as shown in Figure 37-14.

Figure 37-14: The opening screen from the HelloWorld application.

Click the single exit point on the page and the other fuseaction, `World.hello`, executes, as shown in Figure 37-15.

Figure 37-15: The opening screen from the HelloWorld application.

If you've been following along with these listings and figures, your code should be working, but astute readers may reflect that the output from their screens is different than that from the prototype pages shown in Figures 37-6 and 37-7. Specifically, the headers beginning with `Don't mind me` are missing. For that—and to go deeper into Fusebox—you must go on to the next chapter, Chapter 38.

Summary

Fusebox is a very popular and powerful framework for building web applications. Created *by* developers *for* developers, it can help manage the complexity that grows exponentially with the size of an application. Fusebox uses a hub-and-spoke architecture that neatly divides up an application into discrete pieces that can be worked on by separate developers—or separate teams of developers, if needed.

The framework itself is free and is well supported by a very active community. Fusebox is even portable across several languages. Building Fusebox applications is quite straightforward, as we hope the tutorial has shown you, but before you adopt Fusebox for your next job, you'll want to read about the advanced Fusebox concepts covered in Chapter 38.

✦ ✦ ✦

CHAPTER 38

Advanced Fusebox

✦ ✦ ✦ ✦

In This Chapter

Examining Fusebox more deeply

Learning how to approach and build a larger Fusebox application

✦ ✦ ✦ ✦

In the last chapter, we introduced key Fusebox concepts and terms, providing a glossary of terms at the beginning of the chapter. We then showed you how to build the obligatory Hello World application. In this chapter, you look at some of the more powerful aspects of Fusebox, including exit fuseactions (XFAs), Fusedocs, nested circuits, and nested layouts. You conclude the chapter by building a sample Fusebox application.

Exit Fuseactions (XFAs)

One of the design goals set for Fusebox 3 was enhanced code reusability on both the small scale (fuses) and the large scale (circuits). One of the biggest enemies to such reuse is the prevalence of hard-coded values in code. You can see this easily enough by looking at some code that is maximally *un*reusable, as shown in the code snippet below.

```
<h2> Hi, my name is Hal Helms. </h2>
```

The obvious way to make this code reusable is to replace the hard-coded name with variables, as shown in the next code snippet.

```
<h2> Hi, my name is <cfoutput>#firstName#
#lastName#</cfoutput>. </h2>
```

Anyone wanting to use this code now must supply the value of `firstName` and `lastName` before using it. In Fusebox code, actions are performed by making a request of the fusebox. If you are to code for reuse, you must *not* hard-code those fuseactions, unlike what you see in Listing 38-1.

Listing 38-1: Hard-coded fuseactions

```
<cfif ValidatedUser.recordCount>
   <cflocation url="index.cfm?fuseaction=Home.welcome">
<cfelse>
   <cflocation url="index.cfm?fuseaction=Login.badLogin">
</cfif>
```

The solution is to replace the hard-coded fuseaction values with variables, as shown in Listing 38-2. Fusebox uses a structure called *XFA* (for exit fuseaction) to hold these variables and the keys in this structure are known as *exit fuseactions*.

Listing 38-2: Code reworked to use XFAs

```
<cfif ValidatedUser.recordCount>
   <cflocation url="index.cfm?fuseaction=#XFA.successfulLogin#">
<cfelse>
   <cflocation url="index.cfm?fuseaction=#XFA.failedLogin#">
</cfif>
```

Anyone wishing to use this code can do so by providing the values for the variables, `XFA.successfulLogin` and `XFA.failedLogin`.

We often think of reusing code from one application to another, but code can also be reused in different contexts of the same application. Take the example shown in Listing 38-4. This code may be used in validating a login.

You can probably see that different applications may define `XFA.successfulLogin` differently. One application, for example, may send the validated user off to see a listing of new products, while another application takes the user to a menu of choices. That's code reuse across multiple applications.

An example of code reuse within the same application occurs whenever you, as the architect of a single application, use the same code to send a validated user to two separate places, depending on the context in which they were validated.

Say that you are writing an e-commerce site. You want users to log into the site as soon as they first arrive. If they do, you can tailor the experience for them, starting by executing the fuseaction, `Products.recommended`. Of course, you don't insist that people log in initially, lest users resent the requirement and leave for a friendlier climate.

But say that your user sees something that she wants to buy. She places the item in her shopping cart and begins to check out. Now, she really *must* log in. But where do you want to send her? Not back to `Products.recommended` but to `Checkout.getUserInfo`.

If fuseaction values were hard-coded, you would need to place conditional code in the fuse itself: In context A, send the user here; in context B, send the user there. Code is quickly cluttered up with `<cfif>`s, and you have no assurance that, later, you aren't going to need *more* conditional code to account for presently unforeseen conditions.

XFAs provide a very nice solution, because the value of the fuseactions is not decided until runtime. By using XFAs, either you can have separate fuseactions, as in Listing 38-3, or you can use a single fuseaction that accepts a parameter, as shown in Listing 38-4. Which solution is used depends, in large part, on the individual architect's philosophical preferences.

Listing 38-3: Using separate fuseactions

```
<cfcase value="validateLogin">
   <cfinclude template="qry_ValidatedUser.cfm">
   <cfset XFA.success="Products.recommended">
   <cfset XFA.failure="Login.badLogin">
   <cfinclude template="act_Validate.cfm">
</cfcase>

<cfcase value="validateLoginInCheckout">
   <cfinclude template="qry_ValidatedUser.cfm">
   <cfset XFA.success="Checkout.getUserInfo">
   <cfset XFA.failure="Login.badLogin">
   <cfinclude template="act_Validate.cfm">
</cfcase>
```

Listing 38-4: Using one fuseaction that accepts a return argument

```
<cfcase value="validateLogin">
   <cfinclude template="qry_ValidatedUser.cfm">
   <cfset XFA.success="#attributes.return#">
   <cfset XFA.failure="Login.badLogin">
   <cfinclude template="act_Validate.cfm">
</cfcase>
```

The idea of eliminating hard-coded values is central to writing code that can more easily be reused and maintained. XFAs help Fusebox developers achieve these goals, but you can do more to purge your code of hard-coded values.

You know that all action returns to the fusebox — each new request being processed by the home circuit's `FBX_Fusebox_CF30_nn.cfm` file. This is usually implemented by calling `index.cfm` and providing it with a new fuseaction request. Examples are shown in Listing 38-5.

Listing 38-5: Different ways of making new fuseaction requests

```
<cflocation url="index.cfm?fuseaction=#XFA.success#">

<a href="index.cfm?fuseaction=#XFA.productDetails#
```

Continued

Listing 38-5 *(continued)*

```
&productID=#attributes.itemID#>Click here for more details</a>

<script>
   document.href.location='index.cfm?fuseaction=#XFA.newUser#';
</script>

<META HTTP-EQUIV=Refresh CONTENT="10;
URL=http://www.halhelms.com/index.cfm?fuseaction=#XFA.training#">
```

Each of these different methods for initiating a fuseaction request admirably uses XFAs, but still has a hard-coded value: `index.cfm`. That may well be the default page on the system that you're currently working on, but what if the code is ported to a system that uses another default page—perhaps `default.cfm`? If you don't want hard-coded values for fuseaction names, why should you tolerate it here?

One solution, adopted by many Fuseboxers, is to use *an alias* to indicate the default page. This alias is a variable called `self` that can be set to whatever is appropriate to the environment. The entry to the `FBX_Settings.cfm` file shown in the following code snippet establishes the value for `self`.

```
<cfparam name="self" default="#cgi.script_name#" type="string">
```

Because the value is set by using `<cfparam>` rather than `<cfset>`, you can safely add this snippet into each circuit's `FBX_Settings.cfm` file.

Documenting Fuses

Fuses, as we discuss in Chapter 37 are the individual code files used by the core Fusebox files to perform actions; they're the workhorses of Fusebox.

Indeed, fuses are little different from code files used by other architectures—with two differences: Fuses rely on XFAs, and each fuse begins with an XML documentation system known as *Fusedoc*.

You know that you should document our code, having heard this mantra from your earliest days as coders. Although everyone is quick to point out that you *should* document your code, however, almost no one has any specific advice on *how* to achieve this. Such nonprescriptive advice is of little practical value, and programmer comments often tilt between the trivial and the oblique.

Fusedoc tells you exactly how to document your code. The fundamental rule of a Fusedoc is that a Fusedoc is responsible for telling a coder all the information necessary to write the code for the fuse.

A DTD (Document Type Definition) is available at `www.halhelms.com`. (If you use ColdFusion Studio as your code editor, you can find tag editors at `www.fusebox.org` that make writing Fusedocs much easier.)

Open a fuse, and the first thing that you see is the Fusedoc. It's an XML document that sits atop the page. Listing 38-6 shows the entire code for a fuse used to validate a user login.

Listing 38-6: Code for act_Validate.cfm

```
<!---
<fusedoc
   fuse="act_Validate.cfm"
   language="ColdFusion"
   version="2.0">
   <responsibilities>
      I determine the next fuseaction based on whether the user was
validated or not. If ValidatedUser returns any rows, I return to the FB
with XFA.success; else XFA.failure.
   </responsibilities>
   <properties>
      <history
         author="hal helms"
         date="4 July 2002"
         role="Architect" />
      <property name="complexity" value="1" />
   </properties>
   <io>
      <in>
         <string name="self" />
         <recordset name="ValidatedUser">
            <string name="userID" />
            <string name="firstName" />
            <string name="lastName" />
            <number name="userPermissions" precision="integer" />
         </recordset>
         <structure name="XFA">
            <string name="success" />
            <string name="failure" />
         </structure>
      </in>
      <out>
         <structure
            name="CurrentUser"
            scope="session"
            optional="true"
            oncondition="on XFA.success">
            <string
               name="userID"
               passthrough="ValidatedUser.userID" />
            <string
               name="firstName"
               passthrough="ValidatedUser.firstName" />
            <string
               name="lastName"
               passthrough="ValidatedUser.lastName" />
            <number
               name="userPermissions"
```

Continued

Listing 38-6 (continued)

```
                precision="integer"
                passthrough="ValidatedUser.userPermissions" />
          </structure>
          <string name="fuseaction" scope="formorurl" />
       </out>
    </io>
</fusedoc>
--->
<cfif ValidatedUser.recordCount>
   <cfset str = StructNew()>
   <cfset str.userID = ValidatedUser.userID>
   <cfset str.firstName = ValidatedUser.firstName>
   <cfset str.lastName = ValidatedUser.lastName>
   <cfset str.userPermissions = ValidatedUser.userPermissions>

   <cflock
      scope="session"
      timeout="5"
      type="exclusive">
      <cfset Session.CurrentUser = Duplicate( str )>
   </cflock>

   <cflocation url="index.cfm?fuseaction=#XFA.success#">

<cfelse>
   <cflocation url="index.cfm?fuseaction=#XFA.failure#">
</cfif>
```

To give you a sense of how Fusedocs work, though, the following steps dissect the Fusedoc for the fuse shown in Listing 38-6.

1. A Fusedoc is wrapped in ColdFusion comments so that it is stripped out prior to being sent to the browser. The information contained in the Fusedoc is for the coder, not for the end user, and exposing it could raise security concerns.

2. All XML documents have a single root element. In Fusedoc, the root element is `<fusedoc>`.

3. You have three subelements to `<fusedoc>`. They are `<responsibilities>`, `<properties>`, and `<io>` (for **i**nput/**o**utput). The only mandatory element is `<responsibilities>`.

4. The `<responsibilities>` element indicates to the coder the fuse's purpose—why does the fuse exist? It is written in the first person and should be stated as plainly as possible without duplicating information better left to the `<io>` section.

   In this example, the coder is told what the fuse is to do: Determine the next fuseaction to be taken.

5. The <properties> section is something of a catch-all. It is made to be as flexible as possible, enabling each development shop to adapt it to its own use. It has three possible sub-elements, <property>, <note>, and <history>, all of which are optional.

   The <property> can be any name/value pair that the architect wants to define. We use it here to define a "complexity" rating to divide fuses among coders of different skill levels.

6. The <io> section provides the coder information about variables that are being sent into the fuse or that the coder needs to be aware of (the <in> subelement) and those the coder needs to set (the <out> subelement).

7. We discuss using the alias, self, for the default page. In the example in the listing, the first <in> element is a <string>, self, that sets the value for this alias.

```
<string name="self" />
```

8. Because the Fusedoc is written in XML, elements that are not paired must have the closing slash. Although each data element (<string>, <number>, <array>, and so on) has a scope attribute, the default is set to variables, making specifying the scope of local variables unnecessary.

9. In the example in the listing, the user is said to be validated if a query previously run (and available to this fuse) returns any rows. The following example shows how to specify an incoming recordset:

```
<recordset name="ValidatedUser">
    <string name="userID" />
    <string name="firstName" />
    <string name="lastName" />
    <number
        name="userPermissions"
        precision="integer" />
</recordset>
```

10. Two XFAs are used by (and therefore must be sent into) the fuse. Because all XFAs are part of a structure, showing the entire structure sent into the fuse is easiest, as in the following example:

```
<structure name="XFA">
    <string name="success" />
    <string name="failure" />
</structure>
```

11. How XFAs are represented in the Fusedoc is often an initial source of confusion. Many coders assume that XFAs should be *outgoing* variables. Thinking of XFAs as *fuseaction candidates*, all coming into the fuse and vying for "election" to the one spot open for an outgoing *fuseaction*, may help you understand what's actually happening here. Or, to put things more succinctly, XFAs always come *into* a fuse; only one is selected and goes *out of* the fuse as a fuseaction.

12. The <out> section is of particular interest to the coder, as it shows what that programmer is responsible for setting. The first element specified to be set by the coder is a structure, CurrentUser, as the following example shows:

```
<structure
   name="CurrentUser"
   scope="session"
   optional="true"
   oncondition="on XFA.success">
   <string
      name="userID"
      passthrough="ValidatedUser.userID" />
   <string
      name="firstName"
      passthrough="ValidatedUser.firstName" />
   <string
      name="lastName"
      passthrough="ValidatedUser.lastName" />
   <number
      name="userPermissions"
      precision="integer"
      passthrough="ValidatedUser.userPermissions" />
</structure>
<string name="fuseaction" scope="formorurl" />
```

13. The `optional` attribute is set to `true`, indicating that this variable may or may not be set. To find out the conditions under which it should be written, you refer to the `oncondition` attribute, which tells you that it should be set only in the case where `XFA.success` is chosen.

14. Notice, too, the use of the `passthrough` attribute in the structure, `CurrentUser`. This attribute is used to tell the coder that the value for an element should be used *without change* from another element. Here, the structure is intended to be an exact copy of the recordset returned.

15. Finally, you must tell the coder that a variable, `fuseaction`, must be set as either a form or a URL variable. This is shown by setting the value of the `scope` attribute to `formorurl`.

Fusedoc is a very effective way of documenting an individual fuse. In fact, it is used to best effect if the Fusedoc is written *before* the application code is. Rather than documenting your code, you code your documentation. If used in this way, Fusedocs act as what is sometimes called a *program definition language*, or *PDL*.

Fusedocs are used not only by Fuseboxers, but also by other developers who want a standard method of documentation that supports both the creation and maintenance of code assets. Equipped with a Fusedoc and the accompanying prototype code, a coder knowing little of the application can make a significant contribution to a software development project. Experienced project managers recognize how valuable—and rare—such a capability is.

Nested Circuits

You know from Chapter 37 that all program actions begin as action requests—fuseactions—which are sent to the Fusebox core file, `FBX_Fusebox30_CFnn.cfm`. One of the jobs of this core file is to decipher the *circuit alias* part of a compound fuseaction.

In a compound fuseaction such as `Products.checkInventory`, the core file reads the circuit alias (`Products`, in this case) and, by using the `FBX_Circuits.cfm` file, determines which circuit the *fuseaction request*, `checkInventory`, belongs to. It then creates a *fuseaction path* beginning with the home circuit and traversing the circuits needed to arrive at the target circuit.

In the case shown in Figure 38-1, the fuseaction path for `Products.checkInventory` is `MyApp/Admin/Products`. The core file uses this information to include the `FBX_Settings.cfm` files for each circuit in the fuseaction path, from home circuit down to target circuit. This mechanism provides for a type of inheritance, as variables set (or code run) in `FBX_Settings.cfm` files farther up the fuseaction path (closer to the home circuit) bear on those farther down.

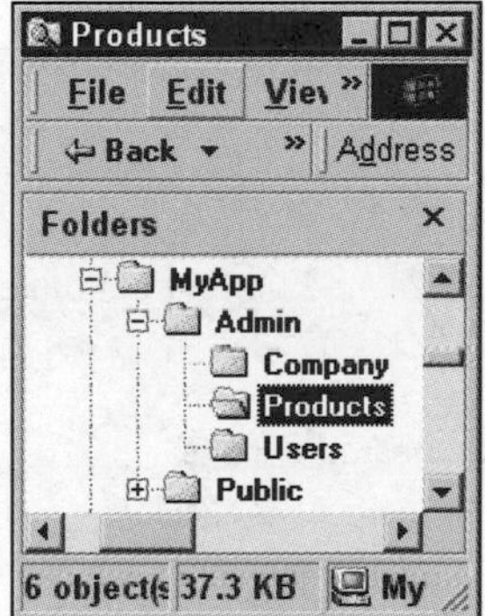

Figure 38-1: A Fusebox application's directory structure.

You also know from Chapter 37 that circuits are ways of creating logical groupings of fuseactions and associated fuses. Although no rule exists for determining the identity or scope of circuits, common sense is usually a reliable guide; people usually place fuseactions related to creating, editing, or deleting a product into a circuit called `Products`.

Circuits are often chosen to model a real-world entity. If you were dealing with various workers, for example, you may create a circuit called `Employee`. That's often sufficient, but on certain occasions, circuits should exist as separate entities but be dependently related. These are often known as *is-a* or *type-of* relationships.

By using this `Employee` example, you may find that an employee is best thought of as a *type of* person. In that case, you could decide to create a `Person` circuit that acts as a parent to `Employee`. Such dependent or parent-child relationships are modeled as *nested circuits* in Fusebox. Figure 38-2 shows a simple `Person-Employee` nested relationship.

Figure 38-2: A simple parent-child relationship modeled as a nested circuit.

Now, say that you want to model independent consultants. Because an independent consultant is a type of person, you create a subcircuit called `IndependentConsultant`, as shown in Figure 38-3.

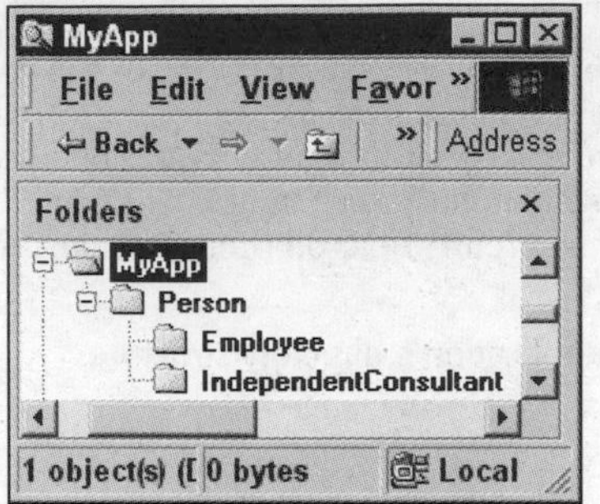

Figure 38-3: Further modeling parent-child relationships.

You can go even farther, creating `HourlyWorker`, `SalariedWorker`, and `ContractWorker` circuits — all as subcircuits to `Employee`, as shown in Figure 38-4.

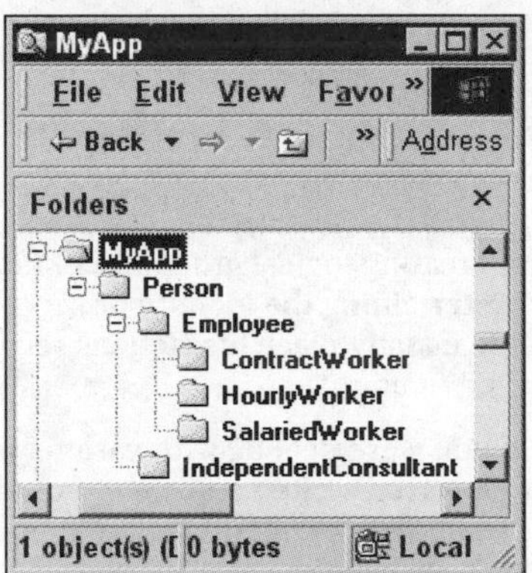

Figure 38-4: More complex nested circuits.

The appeal to such an approach is not only logical consistency, but also the capability to determine behavior common to siblings and abstract it into an ancestor circuit. Creating a new worker, for example, entails certain common tasks, whether that worker belongs to `HourlyWorker`, `SalariedWorker`, or `ContractWorker`. Common behavior may include adding the new worker to a database, ordering a package of "Welcome to the Company" materials sent to the worker's home, and so on.

Rather than duplicating this code across three circuits, abstracting the behavior "upward" makes more sense: Take the common behavior and assign it to a fuseaction called `new` in the `Employee` circuit, leaving the individual differences to be handled by each subcircuit. For its part, the `Employee` circuit may ask the `Person` circuit to first create a new person before proceeding, as shown in Figure 38-5.

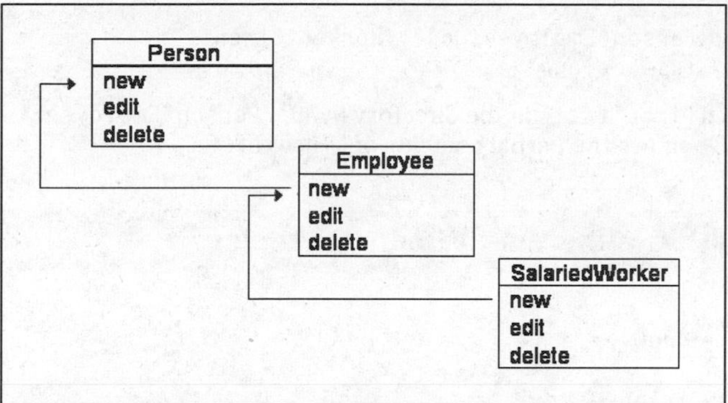

Figure 38-5: Distributed functionality across circuits.

Such partitioning of functionality among related circuits can be done in a number of ways. Prior to ColdFusion MX, the most common way was by calling the Fusebox application as though it were a custom tag, by using the `cfmodule tag`. Listing 38-7 shows the code block for the fuseaction `SalariedWorker.new`.

Listing 38-7: **Calling the fusebox as a custom tag**

```
<cfcase value="new">
   <cfmodule
      template="#Fusebox.rootPath##self#"
      fuseaction="Employee.new"
      returnAs="employeeID">
   <cfinclude template="dsp_SalariedWorker.cfm">
</cfcase>
```

This code is placed in the `FBX_Switch.cfm` file for the circuit, `SalariedWorker`. After the fuseaction, `Employee.new`, is executed, `Employee's FBX_Switch.cfm` itself makes a call to the fusebox by using `the cfmodule tag`—this time requesting the fuseaction, `Person.new`. But the code for `SalariedWorker.new` doesn't need to know about this recursive call. The original fuseaction (`SalariedWorker.new`) makes a single request and expects to get back an employee ID, having specified the variable name for the employee ID by using the `returnAs` attribute.

In ColdFusion MX, you have a more capable mechanism available to you—*ColdFusion components* (*CFCs*). Here, we discuss one way of using CFCs with Fusebox. (There is wide anticipation of a "Fusebox MX" version that will be released at some point. For updates on this, see `www.halhelms.com`.)

We use the `SalariedEmployee` circuit to show how to call the entire fusebox as a custom tag, so the following snippet uses `HourlyEmployee` to illustrate how to use CFCs to achieve the same results.

```
<cfinvoke
   component="MyApp.Person.Employee.HourlyWorker.Circuit"
   method="#Fusebox.fuseaction#">
```

This code calls a file called `Circuit.cfc` in the directory `MyApp/Person/Employee/HourlyWorker`. Listing 38-8 shows the partial contents of `Circuit.cfc`.

Listing 38-8: Circuit.cfc in the HourlyEmployee circuit

```
<cfcomponent>
   <cffunction name="new">
      <cfinvoke
         component="MyApp.Circuit"
         method="doFuseaction"
         returnVariable="employeeID"
         fuseaction="Employee.new">
      <cfinclude template="dsp_HourlyWorker.cfm">
   </cffunction>
   ...
</cfcomponent>
```

This calls the `Circuit.cfc` file in the home circuit, as shown in Listing 38-9.

Listing 38-9: Circuit.cfc in the MyApp circuit

```
<cfcomponent output="yes">
   <cffunction name="doFuseaction" access="remote">
      <cfargument
         name="fuseaction"
         type="string"
         required="true">
      <cfset attributes.fuseaction = arguments.fuseaction>
      <cfinclude template="FBX_Fusebox30_CF50.cfm">
      <cfparam name="returnValue" type="string" default="NULL">
      <cfreturn returnValue>
   </cffunction>
</cfcomponent>
```

This CFC has a single `<cffunction>`, called `doFuseaction`. It expects an argument, `fuseaction`, to be passed into it. It uses the value of `arguments.fuseaction` to set a variable, `attributes.fuseaction`. The core file is then `include`d and the value of `returnValue` is returned. If `returnValue` is not set during the course of executing the fuseaction, the string, `NULL` is returned. In the case of `HourlyWorker.new`, however, the expected `returnValue` is set as a result of calling `Employee.new`.

Recursively Calling the Fusebox

Because a user can't be expected to type a URL that includes the appropriate fuseaction, the architect must specify a default fuseaction to be used if none is provided. This is usually done in the `FBX_Settings.cfm` file of the home circuit. Astute readers may have noticed that, in the example provided in the Chapter 37 the default fuseaction set in the home circuit belonged to the *attributes* scope (as shown in Listing 37-5).

This may seem odd, as the attributes scope is used only with custom tag calls. Refer back to Listing 38-7, however, and you see that you call the fusebox as a custom tag through a `<cfmodule>` call. Something slightly odd is happening: You are calling the fusebox from within the fusebox—that is, you are calling it *recursively*.

The following two code snippets show two different ways of making a request for the fuseaction, `Products.checkInventory`. The first snippet is the one used in the normal course of things.

```
<form action="#self#" method="post">
   <input type="hidden" name="fuseaction" value="World.hello">
```

The second snippet shows the fusebox being called from within the fusebox—a sometimes-confusing state of affairs known as recursion.

```
<cfmodule template="#Fusebox.rootPath##self#" fuseaction="World.hello">
```

If the fusebox is called normally, as the first snippet shows, the variable, `fusebox` (along with any other variables similarly passed), belongs either to the URL scope or to the form scope. On the other hand, if the fusebox is called recursively, these variables are automatically placed into the attributes scope.

This creates a problem for the core files—how do they know in what scope to look? The core Fusebox file, `FBX_Fusebox30_CFnn.cfm`, solves this problem by automatically copying both form and URL variables into the attributes scope. This neat bit of alchemy enables developers to treat all variables passed from a previous page as belonging to the attributes scope, regardless of what scope they began life in. Variables that are not passed from previous pages, on the other hand—such as XFAs—are best set in the local variables scope.

Nested Layouts

Screens of information can often be decomposed into portions that are specific to an individual fuseaction, portions common to a general section of the site—an administrative portion, for example—and others that are global across all actions on a site, as shown in Figure 38-6.

Nested layouts is a powerful Fusebox 3 feature that makes dealing with these different types of content easy. As a fuseaction executes, the fusebox builds a fuseaction path that begins with the home circuit and includes all circuits down to and including the target circuit. Then, from top to target, the fusebox includes the `FBX_Settings.cfm` files in each of the circuits in the fuseaction path. After this is completed, the code associated with the specific fuseaction is run.

Nested layouts work almost exactly the same—but *in reverse*. After the fuse-specific code is run, the fusebox uses the fuseaction path to include the `FBX_Layouts.cfm` files in each of the circuits in the fuseaction path in reverse order, from target circuit up to and including the home circuit.

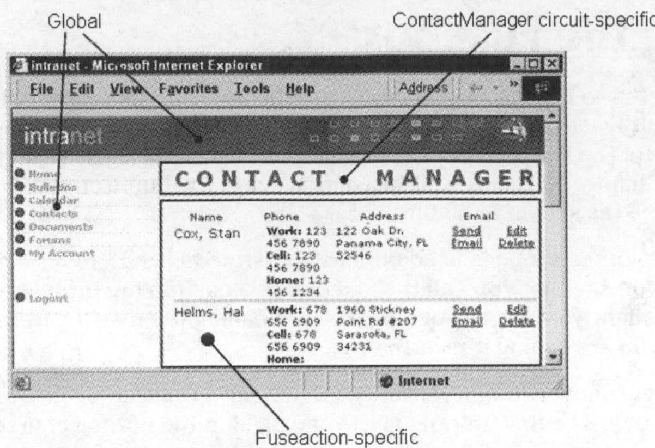

Figure 38-6: Screen blocked out for nested layouts.

Each circuit can, therefore, apply its own contribution to the whole, "building up" the page piece by piece until, after all layouts are applied, the finished screen is produced. You may think of nested layouts as *circuit-level code applied after the fuseaction-specific code is executed.* Thinking of nested Russian dolls may be also prove helpful. At the center is the content generated by the fuseaction. Each circuit in the fuseaction path is enabled to wrap that content in a layout (although the circuit is under no obligation to do so). After each circuit is done, the newly added-to content and all subsequent layouts are passed upward to the next circuit for another possible layout. This continues for all circuits in the reversed circuit path.

This "reverse wrapping" is possible because, within the core Fusebox file, `FBX_Fusebox30_CFnn.cfm`, the code is wrapped in a `<cfsavecontent></cfsavecontent>` tag set. This remarkably helpful tag ensures that the code within its province is not output to the screen, but rather saved to a variable[1], `Fusebox.layout`. The structure, Fusebox, is automatically created by the core Fusebox code and provides a number of useful publicly available variables. You've already used the Fusebox structure in FBX_Switch.cfm. There, the <cfswitch> expression attribute is set to Fusebox.fuseaction.

An example may help: Say that the screen shown in Figure 38-6 was produced by calling the fuseaction, `ContactManager.main`. Further, say that Figure 38-7 reflects the directory/circuit structure of the application.

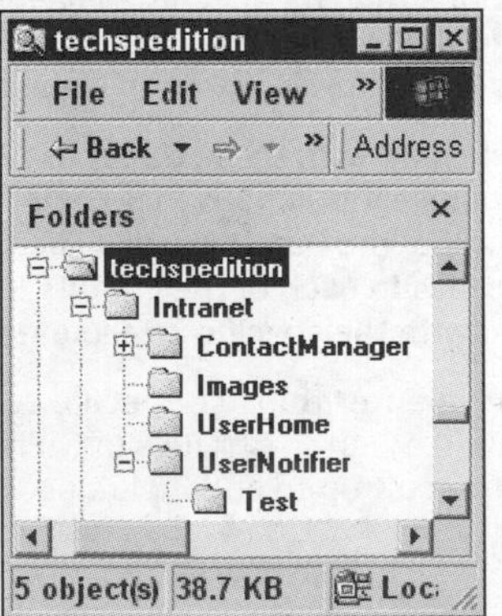

Figure 38-7: Directory structure of intranet application.

The fuseaction path generated by a call to `ContactManager.main` is `techspedition/Intranet/ContactManager`. After the code specified in the `FBX_Switch.cfm` file of `ContactManager` runs, the results of that code is saved to the variable, `Fusebox.layout`— not output to the screen (because of the wrapping `<cfsavecontent>` tags). At this point, the variable, Fusebox.layout, would (if output) look as shown in Figure 38-8.

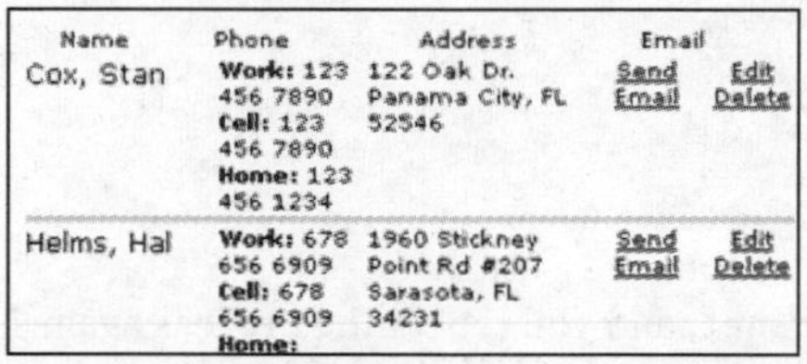

Name	Phone	Address	Email	
Cox, Stan	**Work:** 123 456 7890 **Cell:** 123 456 7890 **Home:** 123 456 1234	122 Oak Dr. Panama City, FL 32546	Send Email	Edit Delete
Helms, Hal	**Work:** 678 656 6909 **Cell:** 678 656 6909 **Home:**	1960 Stickney Point Rd #207 Sarasota, FL 34231	Send Email	Edit Delete

Figure 38-8: Fuseaction results prior to apply layouts.

Next, the fusebox checks to determine whether the *last* circuit in the fuseaction path, `ContactManger`, has a layout file to apply. If the architect wants to use a layout for a circuit, he does so inside that circuit's `FBX_Layouts.cfm` file. This file's only responsibilities are to set a value for `Fusebox.layoutFile` and `Fusebox.layoutDir`. `Fusebox.layoutFile` points to a layout file to use, while `Fusebox.layoutDir` indicates whether that file is to be found in a subdirectory to the circuit. The following snippet shows the contents of `FBX_Layouts.cfm`.

```
<cfset Fusebox.layoutFile="lay_Title.cfm">
<cfset Fusebox.layoutDir="">
```

The above code shows that `ContactManager` applies a layout file called `lay_Title.cfm` to the previously generated contents. Those contents were saved to the variable, `Fusebox.layout` (as shown in Figure 38-8). Now, a layout is applied to `Fusebox.layout`, and the result of that operation, as shown in Figure 38-9, becomes the new value of `Fusebox.layout`.

A layout file must, at bare minimum, output the contents of `Fusebox.layout`. Not to do so would cause any previously generated content (as shown in Figure 38-9 in the example) to be lost. The contents of `lay_Title.cfm` are only a little more complex than is absolutely necessary and are shown in Listing 38-10.

Listing 38-10: lay_Title.cfm in ContactManager circuit

```
<cfoutput>
   <div align="center">
      <h1>
         C O N T A C T       M A N A G E R
      </h1>
   </div>
   #fusebox.layout#
</cfoutput>
```

The code in listing 38-10 executes whenever any fuseaction in `ContactManager` (or any of its subcircuits) is called. After the code executes, the contents of `Fusebox.layout` is changed to incorporate the applied layout. If `Fusebox.layout` were to be output, it would look like what's shown in Figure 38-9—but you're not ready to output it yet.

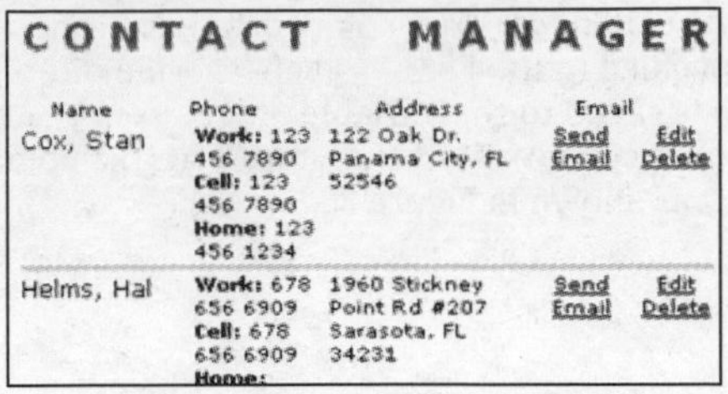

Figure 38-9: ContactManager layout code applied.

The next circuit up the fuseaction path is `Intranet`, and you repeat the process again. The core Fusebox file looks for the presence of `FBX_Layouts.cfm` file in the `Intranet` circuit. The contents of this file are as shown in Listing 38-11.

Listing 38-11: FBX_Layouts.cfm in Intranet circuit

```
<cfoutput>
<table class="header" cellpadding="0" cellspacing="0" bgcolor="006699"
border="0">
   <tr>
      <td class="topbottomborder">
         <img
            src="#fusebox.rootpath##imagesdir#intranet_logo.gif"
            width="133"
            height="36"
            border="0"
            alt="intranet logo">
      </td>
      <td class="topbottomborder" width="100%"> </td>
      <td class="topbottomborder">
         <img
            src="#fusebox.rootpath##imagesdir#top_graphic.jpg"
            width="377"
            height="36"
            border="0"
            alt="">
      </td>
   </tr>
</table>

<table>
   <tr>
      <td valign="top" class="grayrightborder">
         <img
            src="#fusebox.rootpath##imagesdir#arrow.gif"
            width="9"
            height="9"
            border="0"
            alt="home">
```

```
        <a class="orange2bluebold"
href="#self#?fuseaction=#XFA.welcome#">
           Home
        </a><br>
        <img
           src="#fusebox.rootpath##imagesdir#dotted_line.gif"
           width="139"
           height="1"
           border="0" alt=""><br>
        <img
           src="#fusebox.rootpath##imagesdir#arrow.gif"
           width="9"
           height="9"
           border="0"
           alt="bulletins">
        <a class="orange2bluebold"
href="#self#?fuseaction=#XFA.bulletins#">
           Bulletins
        </a><br>
        <img
           src="#fusebox.rootpath##imagesdir#dotted_line.gif"
           width="139"
           height="1"
           border="0"
           alt=""><br>
        <img
           src="#fusebox.rootpath##imagesdir#arrow.gif"
           width="9"
           height="9"
           border="0"
           alt="calendar">
        <a class="orange2bluebold"
href="#self#?fuseaction=#XFA.calendar#">
           Calendar
        </a><br>
        <img
           src="#fusebox.rootpath##imagesdir#dotted_line.gif"
           width="139"
           height="1"
           border="0"
           alt=""><br>
        <img
           src="#fusebox.rootpath##imagesdir#arrow.gif"
           width="9"
           height="9"
           border="0"
           alt="contacts">
        <a class="orange2bluebold"
href="#self#?fuseaction=#XFA.contacts#">
           Contacts
        </a><br>
        <img
```

Continued

Listing 38-11 (continued)

```
            src="#fusebox.rootpath##imagesdir#dotted_line.gif"
            width="139"
            height="1"
            border="0"
            alt=""><br>
         <img
            src="#fusebox.rootpath##imagesdir#arrow.gif"
            width="9"
            height="9"
            border="0"
            alt="documents">
         <a class="orange2bluebold"
href="#self#?fuseaction=#XFA.documents#">
            Documents</a><br>
         <img
            src="#fusebox.rootpath##imagesdir#dotted_line.gif"
            width="139"
            height="1"
            border="0"
            alt=""><br>
         <img
            src="#fusebox.rootpath##imagesdir#arrow.gif"
            width="9"
            height="9"
            border="0"
            alt="forums">
         <a class="orange2bluebold"
href="#self#?fuseaction=#XFA.forums#">
            Forums
         </a><br>
         <img
            src="#fusebox.rootpath##imagesdir#dotted_line.gif"
            width="139"
            height="1"
            border="0"
            alt=""><br>
         <img
            src="#fusebox.rootpath##imagesdir#arrow.gif"
            width="9"
            height="9"
            border="0"
            alt="MyAccount">
         <a class="orange2bluebold"
href="#self#?fuseaction=#XFA.myaccount#">
            My Account
         </a><br>
         <img
            src="#fusebox.rootpath##imagesdir#dotted_line.gif"
            width="139"
            height="1"
```

```
                border="0"
                alt=""><br>
            <P></P>
            <img
                src="#fusebox.rootpath##imagesdir#dotted_line.gif"
                width="139"
                height="1"
                border="0"
                alt="">
            <img
                src="#fusebox.rootpath##imagesdir#arrow.gif"
                width="9"
                height="9"
                border="0"
                alt="login/logout">
            <a class="orange2bluebold"
href="#self#?fuseaction=#XFA.security#">
                Logout
            </a><br>
            <img
                src="#fusebox.rootpath##imagesdir#dotted_line.gif"
                width="139"
                height="1"
                border="0"
                alt="">
        </td>
        <td valign="top" class="grayrightborder"></td>
        <td valign="top" class="content">
            <!-- ********* START CONTENT AREA ********* -->
            #fusebox.layout#
            <!-- ********** END CONTENT AREA ********** -->
        </td>
    </tr>
</table>

<table width="100%" class="topborder">
    <tr>
        <td align="center" class="bluestripe">
            <a class="white2bluebold"
href="#self#?fuseaction=#XFA.copyright#">
                &copy;copyright  2001,2002
            </a> 
            <a href="http://www.techspeditions.com"
class="white2bluebold">
                Techspedition, Inc.
            </a>  All Rights Reserved. 
        </td>
    </tr>
</table>

</cfoutput>
```

This code is executed whenever any fuseaction in Intranet (or any of its subcircuits) is called. Although the code looks rather dense, most of the complexity involves images and styles to be applied. Almost lost in the midst of it is the following code that carries over the previously generated content:

```
<!-- ********* START CONTENT AREA ********* -->
#fusebox.layout#
<!-- ********** END CONTENT AREA ********** -->
```

The results of applying this layout are then saved into Fusebox.layout, overwriting the previous contents, and the process repeats again, this time with the home circuit, techspedition. Now, layouts need to be applied. The code for FBX_Layouts.cfm is shown in Listing 38-12.

Listing 38-12: FBX_Layouts.cfm in techspedition circuit

```
<cfoutput>
   <html>
      <head>
         <title>intranet</title>
         <link rel="stylesheet" type="text/css" media="screen"
href="#fusebox.rootpath#stylesheet_web.css">
         <link rel="stylesheet" type="text/css" media="print"
href="#fusebox.rootpath#stylesheet_print.css">
      </head>
      <body bgcolor="ffffff">
         #Fusebox.layout#
      </body>
   </html>
</cfoutput>
```

The last layout to be applied provides the tags needed for valid HTML and points to the stylesheets to be used. This code is used whenever any fuseaction in techspedition or any of its subcircuits is called.

After the final layout is applied within the fuseaction path, the core file automatically outputs the variable, Fusebox.layout. Indeed, this is why the Hello World application, which had no layout files, worked. The value of Fusebox.layout, produced by the code called by the FBX_Switch.cfm file, is automatically output to the screen.

Nested layouts can be used in much more complex ways, but the basics remain the same. The advantage of using nested layouts is a better separation between content and layout. In practice, the layout files are often handled by graphics designers and HTML layout specialists, while the fuseaction-specific code is attended to by programmers.

12 Steps to a Fusebox Program

In both this chapter and the preceding one (Chapter 37), you've been exposed to many different terms and concepts. With so many new ideas to assimilate, you may be wondering exactly where to start. In this section, we provide you a series of 12 steps to follow when creating a

Fusebox application. One of the features people notice about Fusebox and the Fusebox community is the insistence on *not* writing code until we fully understand what the client wants, and one of the "great truths" of Fusebox is that clients can't tell you what they want until they see it. That leads us directly into the first of our twelve steps—the prototype.

Begin with a prototype

Attempts to make users define functional requirements may sound reasonable but very often fail in practice. An HTML prototype provides the user with the capability to "see" the application before it's built.

Mark up the prototype

Once the prototype has been agreed on (or "frozen"), print out the pages and, with two different colored highlighters, mark up the individual pages, looking for *exit points* (which become XFAs) and *variables* (either incoming or outgoing). Determine the names for XFAs along with any incoming or outgoing variables and write these on the page.

Next, decide on what parts of the page are specific to the fuseaction being called and what should belong to a layout file. Figure 38-10 shows a marked up prototype page. (The layout/content breakdown was already done in Figure 38-6.)

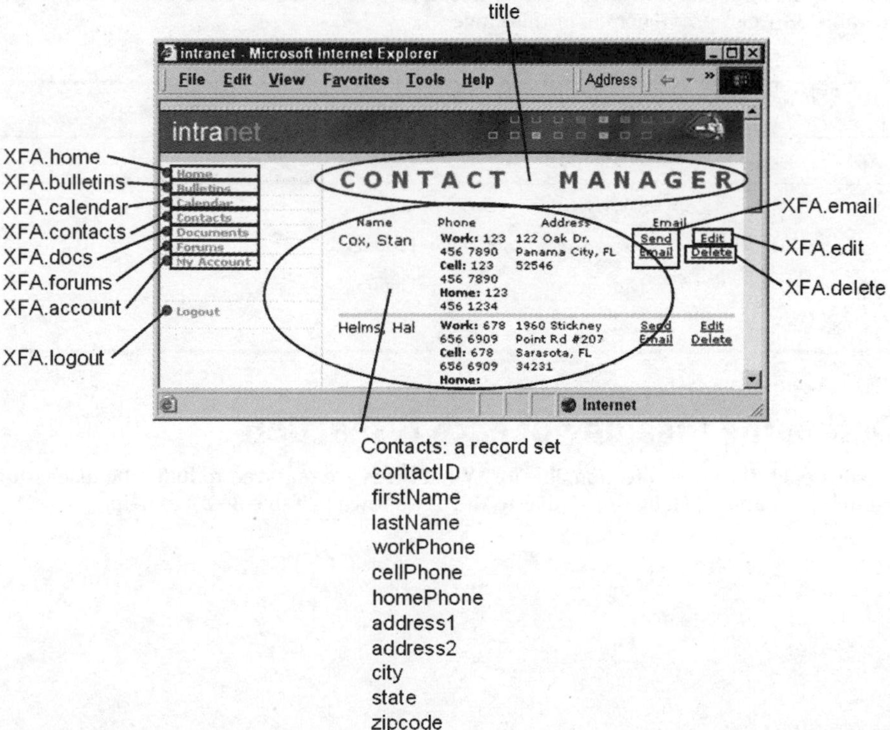

Figure 38-10: Marked-up prototype.

Identify all fuseactions

You should now have marked-up prototype pages, complete with XFAs. Next, you need to identify all the fuseactions required for your Fusebox application (including the ones needed to display each of your prototype pages). Some fuseactions match up with XFAs that you've marked up on your prototype. You may discover that others are necessary for the application to perform fully, but you could not identify them on the prototype page.

A login page, for example, may have defined `XFA.submitForm`. From this, you can determine that the fuseaction should be `Login.validateLogin`. You also, however, need to establish the fuseactions necessary for validating a user login. Although you have no prototype page for this, you must still identify the XFAs required and the fuseactions associated with them.

Separate fuseactions into circuits

You should separate your fuseactions into distinct circuits for your own mental health. The Fusebox code will work fine if you were to have a single, monolithic circuit with hundreds of fuseactions, but you (or the person maintaining your application) will greatly benefit from organizing your code into separate circuits. One way to approach this task is to take a "first cut" at identifying fuseactions without trying to determine which circuits these fuseactions should belong to. If you find that you have a list that includes `addItemToCart`, `removeItemFromCart`, `displayCart`, and `clearCart`, you probably want a circuit called `Cart`. In the end, you need to provide a circuit for every fuseaction. Creating a table similar to Table 38-1 can prove helpful at this stage.

Table 38-1: XFAs, Fuseactions, and Circuits

XFA	*Fuseaction*	*Circuit*
`login`	`login`	Login
`successfulLogin`	`recommendations`	Product
`failedLogin`	`badLogin`	Login
`newAccount`	`new`	User

Define the meaning of each fuseaction

What is each fuseaction responsible for? What fuses are required to fulfill the fuseaction request? Creating a structure similar to the one shown in Table 38-2 can help.

Table 38-2: Fuseactions, Fuses

Fuseaction	*Fuse*	*Responsibilities*
`Login.login`	`dsp_Login.cfm`	I display a login form to the user.
`Login.validateLogin`	`qry_ValidatedUser.cfm`	I return a recordset of user info by matching the username and password sent to me against a database of registered users.
	`act_Validate.cfm`	I receive a recordset called `ValidatedUsed`. If any rows are returned, I create a `CurrentUser` structure of user info and then call `XFA.successfulLogin`; otherwise, I call `XFA.failedLogin`.

After you've created this table, you can begin to write the `cfcase` statements (or create a CFC file) in each circuit's `FBX_Switch.cfm` file to handle the various fuseactions.

Define layout files

Now, determine what parts of the application are set in layout files? Will you have one layout file or multiple ones, spread across several circuits? What will you name the various layout files?

Write layout files

Having identified the layout files, create them. As we mention in the section "Nested Layouts," earlier in this chapter, this work is often done by graphics artists and HTML specialists, freeing up programmers for other tasks.

Determine the contents of the FBX_Settings.cfm files

What setup variables does your application require? If you're using a database, you may want to create a variable to hold the `datasource` attribute—something such as `request.dsn`. All your queries then use that variable in their `datasource` attribute. Since variables set in ancestor circuits are inherited by descendant circuits, you should place any variables that should have more global exposure higher "up" the circuits tree.

Write Fusedocs

Start by using your individual prototype pages, on top of which you write the Fusedoc. Use the variable names that you fixed on during the prototype markup phase. The responsibilities that you wrote in defining your fuseactions should be directly transferable to the `<responsibilities>` element in your Fusedoc.

Write fuses

The Fusedoc that you write in the preceding section should form a contract or work order, telling you exactly what each fuse is responsible for. If your Fusedocs and prototype are done well, any competent programmer can complete the fuses without knowing any more about the application than what the Fusedocs reveal.

Test your fuses

A fuse is designed to run in the context of a Fusebox application and, as such, can't simply be run. Unit-testing fuses before any attempt is made to integrate them into the application, however, is imperative. To accomplish this task, you need to create test harnesses for each fuse.

A *test harness* is a code file that creates the environment in which the fuse to be tested can run. Fusedocs reveal the variables needed. Listing 38-6 gives the Fusedoc and code for `act_Validate.cfm`. From this code, you can create the test harness shown in Listing 38-13.

Listing 38-13: tst_act_Validate.cfm

```
<cfset self="Test.cfm">
<cf_QuerySim>
   ValidatedUser
   userID,firstName,lastName,userPermissions
   100|Stan|Cox|13
</cf_QuerySim>
<cfset XFA.success="success">
<cfset XFA.failure="failure">
<cfinclude template="act_Validate.cfm">
```

This code can now be run to test `act_Validate.cfm`. Notice the use of the custom tag `QuerySim.cfm`. This custom tag creates a recordset "on the fly," without the need to connect to a database and is ideal for use in testing environments. (You can download the code for this tag at `www.halhelms.com`.)

Notice, too, that the variable, `self`, is set to `Test.cfm`, a file that does nothing more than call a wonderful custom tag, `Debug.cfm`, written by Dan Switzer. This custom tag returns a wealth of information that's very useful in debugging code. (`Debug.cfm` is available from `www.pengoworks.com`.)

Integrate and test

One of the nice features of Fusebox is its capability to enable incremental testing. Because circuits are built to run in either standalone or nested mode, you can test whole circuits to ensure that the fuses work together as planned. The `FBX_Switch.cfm` skeleton file, available at `www.fusebox.org`, responds to unknown fuseactions by displaying a message on-screen stating that the called fuseaction is not yet implemented — a situation preferable to getting `File Not Found` errors.

You may decide that, until your fuses are ready to run, you want to alter the fuseaction handling code in the FBX_Switch.cfm files so that fuseactions not ready for testing are not found by the Fusebox. Listing 38-14 shows a partial FBX_Switch.cfm in which the handler for the fuseaction request, deleteUser, is temporarily disabled by prefixing the fuseaction with an underscore.

Listing 38-14: Disabling a fuseaction handler in FBX_Switch.cfm

```
<cfswitch expression="#Fusebox.fuseaction#">
   <cfcase value="newUser">
      <cfinclude template="qry_NewUser.cfm">
      <cflocation url="#self#?fuseaction=Admin.main">
   </cfcase>
   <cfcase value="_deleteUser">
      <cfinclude template="qry_DeleteUser.cfm">
      <cflocation url="#self#?fuseaction=Admin.main">
   </cfcase>
</cfswitch>
```

Adalon

Recently, a new tool for visually designing Fusebox applications has come onto the scene. Created by Synthis Corporation (at www.synthis.com), *Adalon* has some very sophisticated features, including the following:

- Visual sitemapping/wireframing
- Business-process modeling and design
- Web-services support
- Customizable reporting and documentation
- Automated creation of core Fusebox files
- Visual Fusedocs

One of Adalon's most interesting features is the capability to generate Fusebox code for ColdFusion Fusebox, J2EE Fusebox, and PHP Fusebox. Developers who work extensively with Fusebox — particularly in a team or corporate environment — may want to investigate the product further. An evaluation copy is included on the accompanying CD.

Sample Code: A Small Fusebox Application

Many developers say that they learn best by seeing code. In this section, we present a complete — albeit small — application for handling users. It includes the common "CRUD" functions: create, read, update, and delete. We begin with the prototype, already marked up, as shown in Figure 38-11.

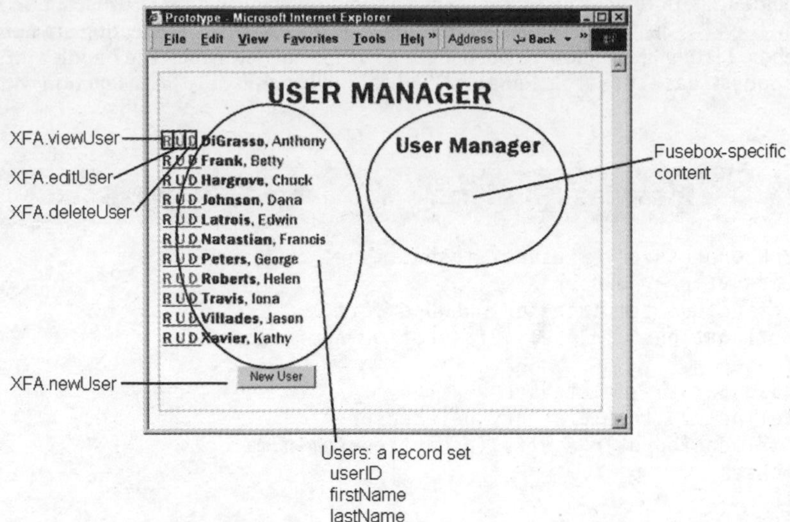

Figure 38-11: Main screen.

Notice the area marked *Fusebox-specific content*. The output of specific fuseactions goes here; everything else on-screen is a layout.

Because the layout portion marked up on the screen in Figure 38-12 doesn't change for this small application, you can disregard the layout portion and mark up only the fuseaction-specific content portion, as shown in Figure 38-13.

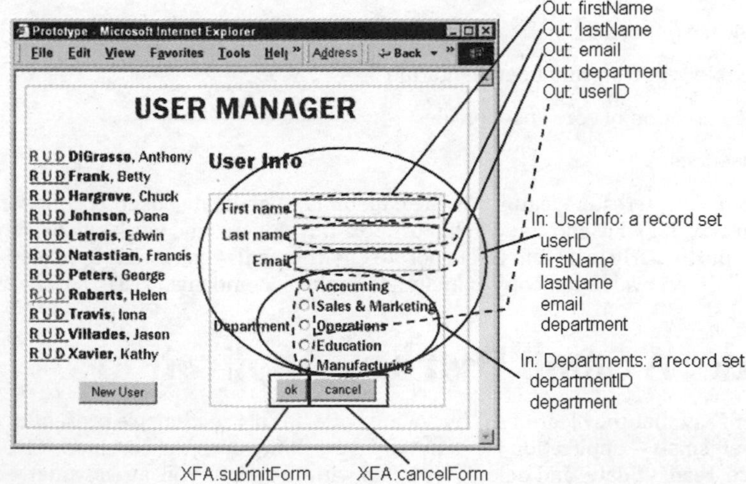

Figure 38-12: New user screen.

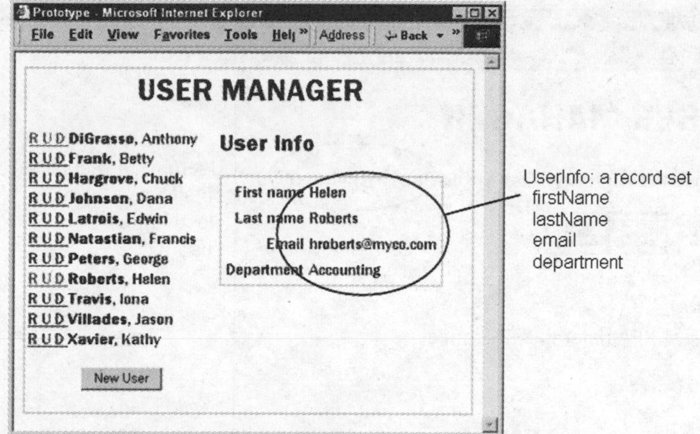

Figure 38-13: View user screen.

No XFAs are needed on this screen.

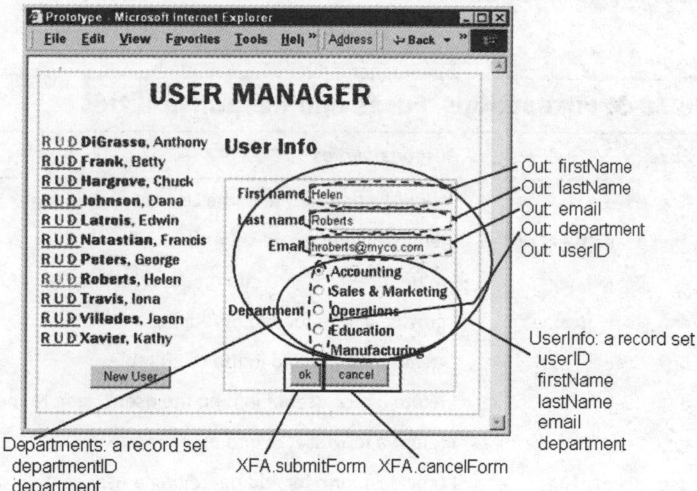

Figure 38-14: Edit user screen.

Notice that outgoing variables have dotted outlines in Figure 38-14. You may find that using different colors makes differentiating between outgoing and incoming variables easier.

With the prototype marked up, you're ready to identify the fuseactions and circuits needed. Because this is so small an application, you use only a single circuit that is aliased as `Users`. The fuseactions, fuses and their responsibilities are presented together in Table 38-3.

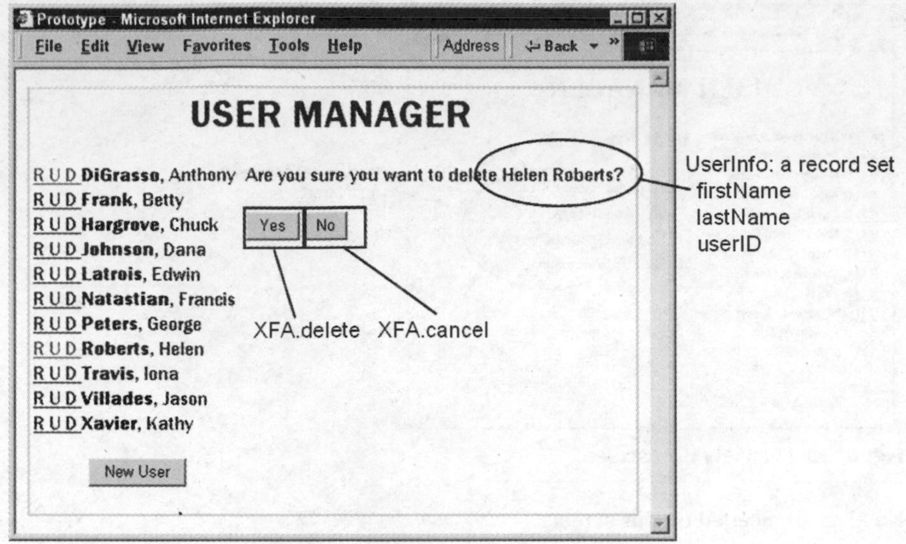

Figure 38-15: Delete confirmation screen.

Table 38-3: Fuseactions, Fuses and Responsibilities

Fuseaction	*Fuse*	*Responsibilities*
`Users.main`	`dsp_Main`	I tell users that they're in the Used Manager app.
`Users.new`	`qry_BlankUserInfo`	I return a blank record set of User info
	`qry_Departments`	I return a recordset of info on departments.
	`dsp_UserInfo`	I provide a form for adding/editing a user.
`Users.doNew`	`qry_Create`	I create a new record in the USER table.
`Users.edit`	`qry_UserInfo`	I return a recordset of info on the userID sent to me.
	`qry_Departments`	I return a recordset of info on departments.
	`dsp_UserInfo`	I provide a form for adding/editing a user.
`Users.doEdit`	`qry_Update`	I update the database with the info passed to me.
`Users.read`	`qry_UserInfo`	I return a recordset of info on the userID sent to me.
	`qry_Departments`	I return a recordset of info on departments.
	`dsp_Read`	I display information based on UserInfo passed to me.
`Users.delete`	`qry_UserInfo`	I return a recordset of info on the userID sent to me.
	`dsp_ConfirmDelete`	I ask the user whether he is sure about deleting the user.
`Users.doDelete`	`qry_Delete`	I remove a record from the database based on userID passed to me.

You need only a single layout file, `lay_UserManager.cfm`, as shown in Listing 38-15.

Listing 38-15: lay_UserManager.cfm

```
<!---
<fusedoc
   fuse="lay_UserManager.cfm"
   language="ColdFusion"
   version="2.0">
   <responsibilities>
      I provide a list of users with CRUD links.
   </responsibilities>
   <properties>
      <history
         author="hal helms"
         email="hal.helms@teamallaire.com">
   </properties>
   <io>
      <in>
         <string name="self" />
         <structure name="XFA">
            <string name="viewUser" />
            <string name="editUser" />
            <string name="deleteUser" />
            <string name="newUser" />
         </structure>
         <recordset name="Users">
            <string name="firstName" />
            <string name="lastName" />
            <string name="userID" />
         </recordset>
         <string name="Fusebox.layout" />
      </in>
      <out>
         <string name="fuseaction" scope="formorurl" />
         <string name="userID" scope="formorurl" oncondition="on
XFA.editUser, XFA.deleteUser, XFA.viewUser" optional="true" />
      </out>
   </io>
</fusedoc>
--->
<cfinclude template="qry_Users.cfm">
<html>
<head>
   <style>
      .tb {
         border-width: thin;
         border-color: Silver;
         border-style: solid;
```

Continued

Listing 38-15 *(continued)*

```
			padding: 4px;
		}
		.lbl{
			text-align: right;
		}
	</style>
	<title>Prototype</title>
</head>
<body>
<cfoutput>
<table class="tb" width="100%" align="center">
	<tr>
		<td colspan="2" align="center">
			<h1>USER MANAGER</h1>
		</td>
	</tr>
	<tr>
		<td valign="top">
			<cfloop query="Users">
				<a href="#self#?fuseaction=#XFA.viewUser#&userID=#userID#">
					R
				</a>
				<a href="#self#?fuseaction=#XFA.editUser#&userID=#userID#">
					U
				</a>
				<a
href="#self#?fuseaction=#XFA.deleteUser#&userID=#userID#">
					D
				</a><b> #LastName#</b>, #firstName#<br>
			</cfloop>

			<div align="center">
				<form action="#self#?fuseaction=#XFA.newUser#"
method="post">
					<input type="Submit" value="New User">
				</form>
			</div>
		</td>
		<td valign="top">
			#Fusebox.layout#
		</td>
	</tr>
</table>
</cfoutput>
</body>
</html>
```

Until now, you've been setting XFAs in the `<cfcase>` blocks for individual fuseactions, but here you now access XFAs on a more global level. Listing 38-16 shows how XFAs are set (and a query needed by `lay_UserManager.cfm` is called) in the circuit's `FBX_Settings.cfm` file.

Listing 38-16: FBX_Settings.cfm

```
<!---
<fusedoc fuse="FBX_Settings.cfm">
   <responsibilities>
      I set up the environment settings for this circuit. If this
settings file is being inherited, then you can use CFSET to override a
value set in a parent circuit or CFPARAM to a accept a value set by a
parent circuit.
   </responsibilities>
</fusedoc>
--->

<cfparam name="attributes.fuseaction" default="Users.main" />
<cfparam name="self" default="index.cfm" />
<cfset request.dsn="Users">
<cfset XFA.newUser="Users.new">
<cfset XFA.editUser="Users.edit">
<cfset XFA.deleteUser="Users.delete">
<cfset XFA.viewUser="Users.read">
```

The `FBX_Switch.cfm` is the physical output determining the meaning of each fuseaction, as shown in Listing 38-17.

Listing 38-17: FBX_Switch.cfm

```
<!---
<fusedoc fuse="FBX_Switch.cfm">
   <responsibilities>
      I am the cfswitch statement that handles the fuseaction,
delegating work to various fuses.
   </responsibilities>
   <io>
      <out>
         <string name="fusebox.fuseaction" />
         <string name="fusebox.circuit" />
      </out>
   </io>
</fusedoc>
--->
```

Continued

Listing 38-17 *(continued)*

```
<cfswitch expression="#fusebox.fuseaction#">

   <cfcase value="main">
      <cfinclude template="dsp_Main.cfm">
   </cfcase>

   <cfcase value="delete">
      <cfinclude template="qry_UserInfo.cfm">
      <cfset XFA.delete="Users.doDelete">
      <cfset XFA.cancel="Users.main">
      <cfinclude template="dsp_ConfirmDelete.cfm">
   </cfcase>

   <cfcase value="doDelete">
      <cfinclude template="qry_Delete.cfm">
      <cflocation url="#self#?fuseaction=Users.main">
   </cfcase>

   <cfcase value="edit">
      <cfinclude template="qry_UserInfo.cfm">
      <cfinclude template="qry_Departments.cfm">
      <cfset XFA.submitForm="Users.doEdit">
      <cfset XFA.cancelForm="Users.main">
      <cfinclude template="dsp_UserInfo.cfm">
   </cfcase>

   <cfcase value="doEdit">
      <cfinclude template="qry_Update.cfm">
      <cflocation url="#self#?fuseaction=Users.main">
   </cfcase>

   <cfcase value="read">
      <cfinclude template="qry_UserInfo.cfm">
      <cfinclude template="qry_Departments.cfm">
      <cfinclude template="dsp_Read.cfm">
   </cfcase>

   <cfcase value="new">
      <cfinclude template="qry_BlankUserInfo.cfm">
      <cfinclude template="qry_Departments.cfm">
      <cfset XFA.submitForm="Users.doNew">
      <cfset XFA.cancelForm="Users.main">
      <cfinclude template="dsp_UserInfo.cfm">
   </cfcase>

   <cfcase value="doNew">
      <cfinclude template="qry_Create.cfm">
      <cflocation url="#self#?fuseaction=Users.main">
```

```
    </cfcase>

    <cfdefaultcase>
        <cfoutput>
            I received a fuseaction called #fusebox.fuseaction# that
circuit #fusebox.circuit# doesn't have a handler for.
        </cfoutput>
    </cfdefaultcase>

</cfswitch>
```

Next, in the same order as they appear in the FBX_Switch.cfm file, are the fuses for this application. Notice that QuerySims is used in place of <cfquery> calls. This enables coding to be done before the database is finalized. Prior to production, the QuerySims should be commented out and replaced with calls either to <cfquery> or <cfstoredproc>.

We'll start with the main page of the application, shown in Listing 38-18.

Listing 38-18: **dsp_Main.cfm**

```
<!---
<fusedoc
    fuse="dsp_Main.cfm"
    language="ColdFusion"
    version="2.0">
    <responsibilities>
        I let the user know they're in the Used Manager app
    </responsibilities>
    <properties>
        <history author="hal helms" email="hal.helms@teamallaire.com">
    </properties>
</fusedoc>
--->

<h3>User Manager</h3>
```

Next, Listing 38-19 provides the query needed to get user information.

Listing 38-19: **qry_UserInfo.cfm**

```
<!---
<fusedoc
    fuse="qry_UserInfo.cfm"
    language="ColdFusion"
    version="2.0">
    <responsibilities>
```

Continued

Listing 38-19 *(continued)*

```
      I return a record set of info on the userID sent to me
   </responsibilities>
   <properties>
      <history author="hal helms" email="hal.helms@teamallaire.com">
   </properties>
   <io>
      <in>
         <string name="userID" scope="attributes" />
         <string name="dsn" scope="request" />
      </in>
      <out>
         <recordset name="UserInfo">
            <string name="userID" />
            <string name="firstName" />
            <string name="lastName" />
            <string name="email" />
            <number name="department" precision="integer" />
         </recordset>
      </out>
   </io>
</fusedoc>
--->

<cf_QuerySim>
   UserInfo
   userID,firstName,lastName,email,department
   800|Helen|Roberts|hroberts@myco.com|10
</cf_QuerySim>
```

Listing 38-20 provides the code to confirm a user deletion.

Listing 38-20: dsp_ConfirmDelete.cfm

```
<!---
<fusedoc
   fuse="dsp_ConfirmDelete.cfm"
   language="ColdFusion"
   version="2.0">
   <responsibilities>
      I ask the user if s/he is sure about deleting the user.
   </responsibilities>
   <properties>
      <history author="hal helms" email="hal.helms@teamallaire.com">
   </properties>
   <io>
      <in>
         <string name="self" />
```

```
         <structure name="XFA">
            <string name="delete" />
            <string name="cancel" />
         </structure>
         <recordset name="UserInfo">
            <string name="userID" />
            <string name="firstName" />
            <string name="lastName" />
            <string name="email" />
            <number name="department" precision="integer" />
         </recordset>
      </in>
      <out>
         <string name="fuseaction" scope="formorurl" />
         <string name="userID" passthrough="UserInfo.userID"
scope="formorurl" />
      </out>
   </io>
</fusedoc>
--->

<cfoutput>
Are you sure you want to delete #UserInfo.firstName#
#UserInfo.lastName#?<br>
<br>
<form action="#self#" method="post" name="MyForm">
   <input type="Hidden" name="fuseaction" value="#XFA.delete#">
   <input type="Hidden" name="userID" value="#UserInfo.userID#">
   <input type="Submit" value=" Yes "> <input type="button" value=" No
"
onclick="javascript:document.MyForm.fuseaction.value='#XFA.cancel#';doc
ument.MyForm.submit();">
</form>
</cfoutput>
```

Listing 38-21 provides the code to delete a user from the database. Note that since we're using QuerySims, the actual SQL is not provided, a comment forming a placeholder until we're ready to insert the actual code.

Listing 38-21: qry_Delete.cfm

```
<!---
<fusedoc
   fuse="qry_Delete.cfm"
   language="ColdFusion"
   version="2.0">
   <responsibilities>
```

Continued

Listing 38-21 *(continued)*

```
      I remove a record from the database based on userID passed to me
   </responsibilities>
   <properties>
      <history author="hal helms" email="hal.helms@teamallaire.com">
   </properties>
   <io>
      <in>
         <string name="userID" scope="attributes" />
         <string name="dsn" scope="request" />
      </in>
   </io>
</fusedoc>
--->

<!-- cfquery here -->
```

Listing 38-22 uses a QuerySim to return information about departments.

Listing 38-22: qry_Departments.cfm

```
<!---
<fusedoc
   fuse="qry_Departments.cfm"
   language="ColdFusion"
   version="2.0">
   <responsibilities>
      I return a record set of info on departments
   </responsibilities>
   <properties>
      <history author="hal helms" email="hal.helms@teamallaire.com">
   </properties>
   <io>
      <in>
         <string name="dsn" scope="request" />
      </in>
      <out>
         <recordset name="Departments">
            <string name="departmentID" />
            <string name="department" />
         </recordset>
      </out>
   </io>
</fusedoc>
--->

<cf_QuerySim>
```

```
    Departments
    departmentID,department
    10|Accounting
    20|Sales & Marketing
    30|Operations
    40|Education
    50|Manufacturing
</cf_QuerySim>
```

A QuerySim is ideal if you want a recordset with contents that seldom change, if at all. In that case, you have no need to incur the performance penalty of connecting to a database; QuerySims are simpler and faster. Situations may include company departments, states or provinces, and so on.

Listing 38-23 provides the code needed to display information about a user.

Listing 38-23: dsp_UserInfo.cfm

```
<!---
<fusedoc
   fuse="dsp_UserInfo.cfm"
   language="ColdFusion"
   version="2.0">
   <responsibilities>
      I provide a form for adding/editing a user
   </responsibilities>
   <properties>
      <history author="hal helms" email="hal.helms@teamallaire.com">
   </properties>
   <io>
      <in>
         <string name="self" />
         <recordset name="UserInfo">
            <string name="userID" />
            <string name="firstName" />
            <string name="lastName" />
            <string name="email" />
            <number name="department" precision="integer" />
         </recordset>
         <recordset name="Departments">
            <string name="departmentID" />
            <string name="department" />
         </recordset>
         <structure name="XFA">
            <string name="submitForm" />
            <string name="cancelForm" />
         </structure>
      </in>
```

Continued

Listing 38-23 *(continued)*

```
      <out>
         <string name="fuseaction" scope="formorurl" />
         <string name="userID" passthrough="UserInfo.userID" />
         <string name="firstName" />
         <string name="lastName" />
         <string name="email" />
         <string name="department" />
      </out>
   </io>
</fusedoc>
--->

<h2>User Info</h2>

<cfoutput>
<form action="#self#" method="post" name="MyForm">
   <input type="Hidden" name="fuseaction" value="#XFA.submitForm#">
   <input type="Hidden" name="userID" value="#UserInfo.userID#">
<table class="tb">
   <tr>
      <td align="right">First name</td>
      <td><input type="Text" name="firstName"
value="#UserInfo.firstName#"></td>
   </tr>
   <tr>
      <td align="right">Last name</td>
      <td><input type="Text" name="lastName"
value="#UserInfo.lastName#"></td>
   </tr>
   <tr>
      <td align="right">Email</td>
      <td><input type="Text" name="lastName"
value="#UserInfo.email#"></td>
   </tr>
   <tr>
      <td align="right">Department</td>
      <td>
         <cfloop query="Departments">
            <input type="Radio" name="department"
value="#departmentID#" <cfif departmentID EQ UserInfo.department>
checked</cfif>> #department#<br>
         </cfloop>
      </td>
   </tr>
   <tr>
      <td align="center" colspan="2">
         <input type="Submit" value=" ok ">
```

```
        <input type="Button" value=" cancel "
onclick="javascript:document.MyForm.fuseaction.value='#XFA.cancelForm#'
;document.MyForm.submit();">
      </td>
    </tr>
</table>

</form>
</cfoutput>
```

Programmers commonly use the same form for editing and adding, usually needing to use conditional code to do so. Another method is to have one form always populate its fields from the contents of a recordset—that is, the form is always editing data.

If the form is to be used to actually edit a record, the recordset called returns appropriate values, but if the form is to be used to add a record, a blank recordset is created and used. This makes the code simpler and easier to read.

Listing 38-24 is nothing more than a Fusedoc and a comment, waiting until the database has been finalized to have the <cfquery> added to it.

Listing 38-24: qry_Update.cfm

```
<!---
<fusedoc
   fuse="qry_Update.cfm"
   language="ColdFusion"
   version="2.0">
   <responsibilities>
      I update the database with the info passed to me
   </responsibilities>
   <properties>
      <history author="hal helms" email="hal.helms@teamallaire.com">
   </properties>
   <io>
      <in>
         <string name="dsn" scope="request" />
         <string name="userID" />
         <string name="firstName" />
         <string name="lastName" />
         <string name="email" />
         <string name="department" />
      </in>
   </io>
</fusedoc>
--->

<!-- cfquery here  -->
```

The next code, Listing 38-25, is a display file of user information.

Listing 38-25: dsp_Read.cfm

```
<!---
<fusedoc
   fuse="dsp_Read.cfm"
   language="ColdFusion"
   version="2.0">
   <responsibilities>
      I display information based on UserInfo passed to me.
   </responsibilities>
   <properties>
      <history author="hal helms" email="hal.helms@teamallaire.com">
   </properties>
   <io>
      <in>
         <recordset name="UserInfo">
            <string name="userID" />
            <string name="firstName" />
            <string name="lastName" />
            <string name="email" />
            <number name="department" precision="integer" />
         </recordset>
         <recordset name="Departments">
            <string name="departmentID" />
            <string name="department" />
         </recordset>
      </in>
   </io>
</fusedoc>
--->

<h2>User Info</h2>

<cfoutput>
<table class="tb" cellspacing="4">
   <tr>
      <td class="lbl">First name</td>
      <td>#UserInfo.firstName#</td>
   </tr>
   <tr>
      <td class="lbl">Last name</td>
      <td>#UserInfo.lastName#</td>
   </tr>
   <tr>
      <td class="lbl">Email</td>
      <td>#UserInfo.email#</td>
   </tr>
```

```
   <tr>
      <td class="lbl">Department</td>
         <cfquery dbtype="query" name="MyDepartment">
            SELECT department FROM Departments WHERE departmentID =
#UserInfo.department#
         </cfquery>
      <td>
         #MyDepartment.department#<br>
      </td>
   </tr>
</table>

</cfoutput>
```

Listing 38-26 uses a QuerySim to return an empty recordset.

Listing 38-26: qry_BlankUserInfo.cfm

```
<!---
<fusedoc
   fuse="qry_BlankUserInfo.cfm"
   language="ColdFusion"
   version="2.0">
   <responsibilities>
      I return a blank record set of User info
   </responsibilities>
   <properties>
      <history author="hal helms" email="hal.helms@teamallaire.com">
   </properties>
   <io>
      <out>
         <recordset name="UserInfo">
            <string name="userID" />
            <string name="firstName" />
            <string name="lastName" />
            <string name="email" />
            <number name="department" precision="integer" />
         </recordset>
      </out>
   </io>
</fusedoc>
--->

<cf_QuerySim>
   UserInfo
   userID,firstName,lastName,email,department
</cf_QuerySim>
```

You can create a record set with no rows either by calling a `QuerySim` with no row data or by calling a `<cfquery>` with a `WHERE` condition that is never true, as follows:

```
SELECT * FROM User WHERE 0 = 1
```

Listing 38-27: qry_Create.cfm

```
<!---
<fusedoc
   fuse="qry_Create.cfm"
   language="ColdFusion"
   version="2.0">
   <responsibilities>
      I create a new record in the USER table
   </responsibilities>
   <properties>
      <history author="hal helms" email="hal.helms@teamallaire.com">
   </properties>
   <io>
      <in>
         <string name="firstName" />
         <string name="lastName" />
         <string name="email" />
         <string name="department" />
         <string name="dsn" scope="request" />
      </in>
   </io>
</fusedoc>
--->

<!-- cfquery here -->
```

Summary

This chapter and the preceding chapter cover a good deal of information. If Fusebox is new to you, we advise you to take it slowly. Try to create the simple user manager application that begins in the "Sample Code" A Small Fusebox Application" of this chapter on your own, using the code listings only if you get stuck. In a short while, what now seems foreign and odd should seem quite natural, and you may find yourself joining with thousands of other developers who have found that Fusebox makes coding simpler, more successful, and more fun. (If you really are stuck, you can download the complete application at `www.halhelms.com`.)

✦ ✦ ✦

Handling Source-Code Version Control

✦ ✦ ✦ ✦

In This Chapter

Understanding why you need source-code control

Adding files to the source code repository

Checking files in and out and getting other developers' files

Rolling back to earlier file versions

✦ ✦ ✦ ✦

Say that you've spent four days coding a template when your boss comes in and tells you that the project guidelines have changed. As a result of this change, you must put things back to the way that they were yesterday before proceeding in a new direction — and how exactly do you effectively backtrack without causing more problems? Or say that you work with three other developers on a project and all of you are mistakenly working on the same file — whose modifications are applied if all of you hit Save at the same time?

Source-code control is one of the more underused development practices, and that's unfortunate because it could alleviate both problems mentioned in the preceding paragraph, along with many more. This chapter shows you how to effectively use source-code control on your projects.

What Is Source-Code Control?

Source-code control is based around the idea of having a central repository and management interface for your source code. Because everything that happens to your source code is managed and time-stamped through this central interface, getting a report of everything that's happened to your source code and when it happened is an easy matter. (This particular report is discussed later in this chapter in the section named "Viewing a file's version history.")

Source-code control also helps multiple developers avoid stepping on each other's toes. As only one person can work on a given file at a time, avoiding the problem of one developer overwriting another's code becomes easy if you use source-code control.

This chapter uses Microsoft Visual SourceSafe (VSS), which is our preferred source-code control program. VSS's user interface is shown in Figure 39-1.

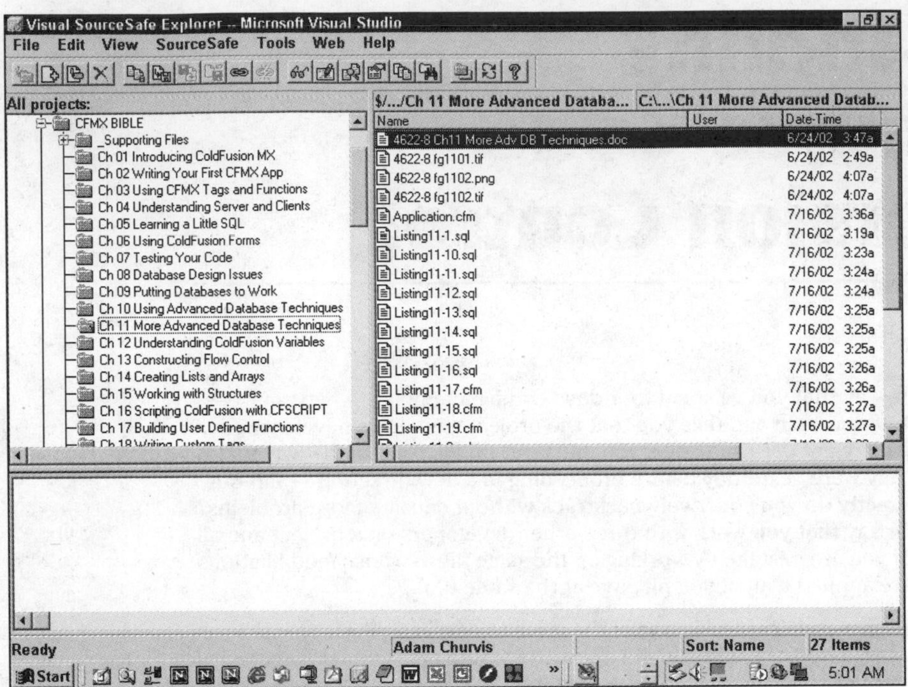

Figure 39-1: Microsoft Visual SourceSafe.

You can find out more about Visual SourceSafe from `http://msdn.microsoft.com/ssafe/`. This URL also provides a link to download a copy.

Other such programs are available, such as PVCS from Merant, but VSS seems to be the most stable and simplest to use and maintain. Because most source-code control systems use the same ideas, however, using the same plan laid out in this chapter with programs other than Visual Source Safe shouldn't be difficult.

Source-Code Control Concepts

Source-code control forces you to do your development in a slightly different way than you did before, with the biggest change being that you must keep much more careful track of what you're doing whenever you modify a template. You must also be very diligent about using the source-code control system, because one slip-up could cause a problem. (Don't let this warning discourage you, however. Using source control is an easy habit to get into and is well worth the effort.)

The repository and working directory

The heart of the source-code control system is the *source-code repository*. All source code is maintained in a central location, which is considered the authority on the current state of the code base. The repository is usually maintained in a folder on a central file server, preferably one that can be accessed by a Web server so that anyone can browse the central server to see the current state of the Web site. All files in the repository are set as read-only at all times. (This is managed by the source-code control application. Don't *touch* a single file in this directory unless you do so through source control.)

If you want to modify a source file, you don't modify it in the repository. Every developer has a *working directory*, where he does his work. This working directory usually contains a copy of all the files from the repository. Just as you should be able to browse the central repository to see the current state of the Web site, each developer should be able to browse his working directory to see the current state of what he's developing.

The idea of having the central repository separate from each developer's working directory is that each developer can be working on a different part of the application in his working directory, but what's in the central repository is always reflective of the last generally stable state of the application.

Setting up source-code control

Setting up Visual SourceSafe is a two-step process. First, run the VSS installer on your file server. After it asks which type of setup you want to perform, choose `Server`. After you've installed the VSS server, run the installer on all the developer machines, choosing `Client` whenever the installer asks what kind of install to perform.

If you don't have a separate file server, you can install both the client and server versions on your development machine. We would, however, still recommend that you have a separate repository and working directory so that you always have a backup copy of your source code.

Adding files to the repository

Before you can use source-code control, you must add files to the repository. Any kind of file may be added because source control is not ColdFusion-specific (or even code-specific for that matter). To add files to your source repository, choose your project in Visual SourceSafe and click the Add button in the toolbar. If you've set a working directory for this project, the Add File To dialog box defaults to showing files in the working directory, as shown in Figure 39-2.

Figure 39-2: The Add Files dialog box.

If you haven't already set a working directory, the Add Files dialog box shows an internal system directory, so you will need to navigate to the directory containing your source code.

You can add one of two things to source control: either a set of files or a single directory and all its subdirectories, as follows:

- ✦ If adding a set of files, simply choose whatever files you want to add to your project.
- ✦ If adding a directory, choose the directory that you want to add. SourceSafe automatically creates subprojects for this directory and any of its subdirectories.

After you click the Add button in the Add Files dialog, you get a dialog box that asks you to give the file a comment, as shown in Figure 39-3.

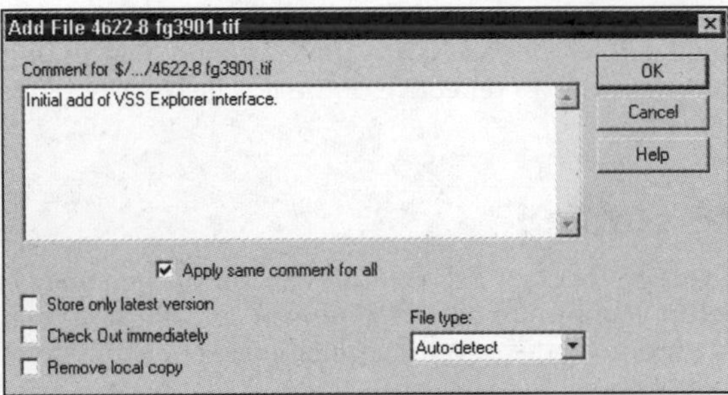

Figure 39-3: The Add File dialog box.

This comment shows up as the first entry in the file's history summary, which we discuss in the section "Viewing a file's version history," later in this chapter. If no working directory is set for the current project, you can also set the current folder as your working directory.

What files should be placed in the repository

Just about any file in your application is a candidate for being placed in source-code control. Of course you would place your ColdFusion code in source-code control. You should also place images in source-code control. You may also want to consider placing your application's supporting files, such as notes documents, database diagrams, SQL scripts, and so on in source control.

Anything that is routinely overwritten or changed by some ColdFusion process, on the other hand, should *never* be placed in source control. If one of your ColdFusion templates creates a text file every time that it's run, for example, don't place the text file in source control—just the ColdFusion template. You see in the next section how these overwritten files negatively affect your source-code control setup if they are included in the repository.

Checking in and out

After you have templates in the repository, you can start modifying them. By default, all your source code is *checked in*, meaning that no one can modify it. To modify a template, you must first *check out* the template, which copies the file from the repository to your local machine and sets the local copy as not read-only. You are then free to open the local copy and make modifications.

Never change the read-only flag on a file if it is in source control. Changing this flag can cause serious problems in your project and can ultimately lead to the failure of source control and possibly even lead to lost code. Let source control handle these flags for you and you're just fine.

On a side note, the read-only flag is the reason that you don't want to include constantly overwritten files in your source-code repository. If you run a ColdFusion process that overwrites this read-only file in your working directory, the replacement template is no longer read-only. Even the fact that the template changed can interfere with source control's processing of the template.

Whenever you check a file out, SourceSafe gives you the option to make a quick note as to what you are going to do in this check-out session. If you are checking out the file to fix a bug, for example, say so as you check it out. You see how this becomes useful in the section "Viewing a file's version history," later in this chapter.

After you finish modifying a file and have tested it in your working folder to make sure that it's stable, check it back in. As you check in a file, SourceSafe compares your version of the file to the version stored in the repository and makes a *delta file*, which is a binary map of the difference between the two files. It stores this delta file in its internal database and then copies your version of the file to the repository, setting both your file and the file in the repository to read-only. Both the current version of the file and the previous version, therefore, are accessible. In fact, every version of the file is always accessible, because SourceSafe keeps all these delta files.

Whenever you check in a file, SourceSafe gives you the option of including a history comment. By default, it's the same comment that you entered as you checked out the file. Be *very* explicit as to what you changed as you write this comment. Everything that you changed in that check-out session should be included in the history comment.

This brings us to our next point: Always make your check out sessions as short as you can. By checking your source code back in every time that you have a stable file, you can keep these history comments brief and be absolutely sure that you didn't miss anything.

Viewing a file's version history

To view a file's revision history, go into Visual SourceSafe, expand the project hierarchy until you get to your source code, right-click the name of the file that you want to inspect, and choose Show History from the pop-up menu. SourceSafe opens the History dialog box showing every check-in point since the time that the file was added to source control. It tells you who checked it in, when it occurred, and the precise action taken, as shown in Figure 39-4.

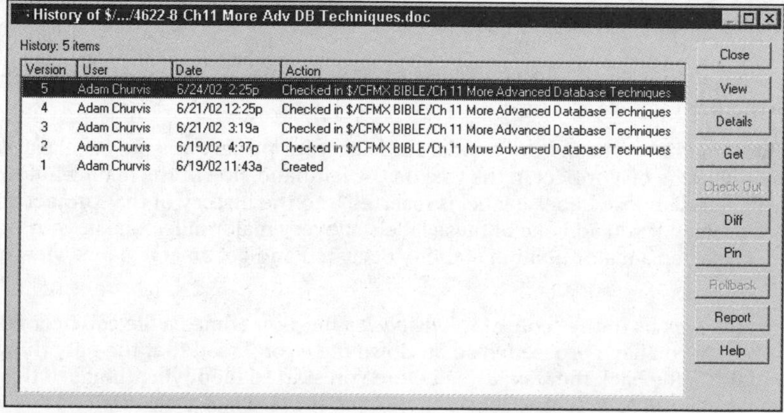

Figure 39-4: History dialog box.

To find out what happened in a specific version, you can do one of the following two things:

- ✦ Click Details to see the comment made for that particular check-in session.
- ✦ Click Diff to see the differences between the version in your working folder and the selected version in the list.

For ColdFusion files, Diff is one of the most useful tools that you're likely to ever use, as the plain-text format of `.cfm` files enables VSS to perform a character-by-character comparison of the contents of both files and produce a detailed report of the differences, as shown in Figure 39-5.

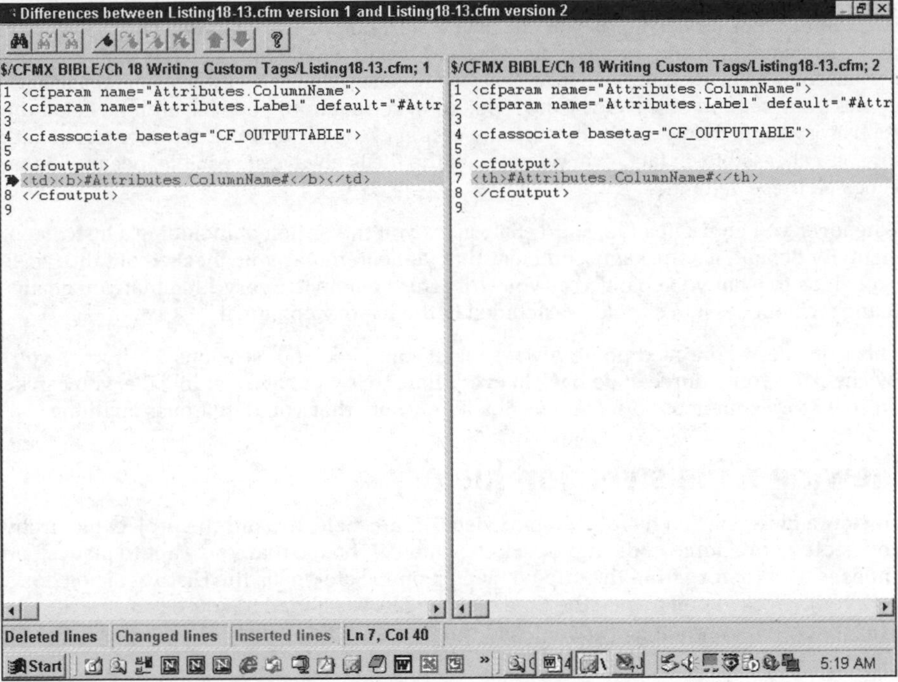

Figure 39-5: A Visual SourceSafe Diff(erences) report.

If the two files that you're comparing by using the Diff button are in a binary format, VSS can tell you only whether they are identical.

Another useful thing that you can do is to add a label to your project at a major milestone. If you right-click the name of a project in the tree on the left-hand side of the main window in Visual SourceSafe and choose Label, a label is inserted into the history of that project and all the files in that project. If you add one of these labels at every major milestone in your project, you can easily see when a major point of stability occurred and get an at-a-glance view of the history.

And that subject brings us to the topic of *rolling back* a file. Sometimes a file can become so massively broken or you have proceeded so far down the wrong road that the only thing that you can do is put the file back the way it was before you started modifying things. If this situation occurs, you can *roll back* to the last stable version (or to a label, if you want) and work on the file from that point forward.

To roll back a file, open the version history for the file or project that you want to roll back. Select the version or label to which you want to roll back in the list of file versions, and click the Rollback button. Doing so reverts to that version of the file and removes any history items that occurred between then and now.

Be *very* careful in rolling back a file! Because of the nature of the rollback operation, it is irreversible, and if used carelessly, it can destroy days, weeks, or even months of your hard work. Always triple-check what you're doing before rolling back a file.

Other source-control operations

We've mentioned that you should be able to browse your project from your working directory. Just browsing the file that you currently have checked out, however, is usually not very useful. *Getting* a file or project means that you take a copy of whatever's currently in the repository, leaving the read-only flag set. You want to get the entire project before every development session so that you are sure that you have the most recent code for the entire project in your working directory. To do this, right-click the name of the project or file that you want to get in the main SourceSafe window and choose Get Latest Version from the pop-up menu.

A time may come when you check something out, start modifying it, and then realize that it was correct the way that it was before. To revert to the way that the file was before you checked it out, right-click the file that you're working with in the main SourceSafe window and choose Undo Check Out from the pop-up menu. This action reverts the file back to the way that it was before you checked it out and checks the file back in. Be careful in using this feature, however, because none of the modifications that you made after checking the file out takes effect if you undo the checkout.

As you get deeper into your projects and source-control usage, you may come across the terms *branching*, *pinning*, and *merging*. These topics are beyond the scope of this chapter and involve running multiple versions of your site at the same time. Visual Source Safe's documentation goes into these topics in more detail than we can cover here.

Summary

In this chapter you learn how to use Visual SourceSafe to handle your source code control. In addition to the standard operations of checking in, checking out, and rolling back, you also learn how to use more advanced operations such as viewing a version history or labeling a project.

After reading this chapter, you probably have one of the following two reactions:

✦ "Wow! Gee whiz! I didn't know that source code control existed and now I'm going to use it for every single thing I do!"

✦ "That's a lot of work just to modify some source code. Only two developers are on my team — I think that our communication skills are good enough that we don't need source control."

We assure you that the first reaction is more appropriate. Even a single-developer shop can benefit from the use of source-code control because of the habits that it gets you into, as well as its capability to roll back a file if you go too far down the wrong road. Using source control on even the smallest projects is a good habit to get into.

✦ ✦ ✦

Integrating Security

✦ ✦ ✦ ✦

In This Chapter

✦ ✦ ✦ ✦

Throughout the book you've seen how easily you can create applications by using ColdFusion — for example, those designed for presenting and/or updating critical information in your organization's databases. Forgetting that you need to protect those applications and ensure that only authorized users can access them, however, can also prove all too easy.

You may want to secure your site so that it's accessible only by users who log in, or *authenticate* themselves. Or maybe even logged-in users shouldn't see a portion of your site (such as an administrative module) or even just one or a set of pages (such as a membership-information update process or some premium content) unless they're also specifically *authorized* to do so.

These two subjects, *authentication* and *authorization*, are separate matters, although people often focus only on the first. In this chapter, we discuss how to enable both types of security in your application. More important, we discuss them in the context of the new `CFLOGIN` and related tags provided in CF MX.

Authenticating Users: Login Processing

In traditional web application authentication, a user who tries to access a restricted site, portion, or page is prompted to log in by entering a username (or perhaps simply an e-mail address) and a password. From there, the remainder of the user's attempts to access restricted pages should also ensure that that user has indeed gone through that authentication process and, further, that if he doesn't use the site for some time period, his "authenticated" status is revoked.

Prior to CF MX, CF developers were left to devise their own strategies for performing authentication and tracking a user's authenticated status. For developer familiar with that approach, the use of session variables imposed some limitations. These limitations have been addressed and an easier process of authenticating introduced in CF MX with the new `CFLOGIN` and related tags.

And if you're familiar with the previously available notion of Advanced Security from ColdFusion 4 and 5, as well as its available `CFAUTHENTICATE` tag and `IsAuthenticated()` function, among others, you also need to know that those elements are no longer supported in ColdFusion MX. The good news, however, is that the `CFLOGIN` approach does add useful new features to make up for some of that loss.

We introduce this new mechanism slowly in this chapter, building on steps that lead to a complete authentication system by the time that we're finished. This is not just for newcomers to ColdFusion, but also developers with experience in using the old approaches to authentication. We've seen too many discussions of this new approach to authentication that offer only a single example and a couple paragraphs of explanation.

Maybe the assumption in such cases is that any CF developer can take that ball and run with it, but as we've explored these features, we've learned that an awful lot about the fact that how they work isn't obvious and isn't documented. By walking through this process slowly, we hope to share with you some observations in a way that makes sense as you're learning each aspect of the new feature.

Assume for the moment that you have created a directory called `secured` in which to place templates that users can't access unless they are authenticated, or `logged in`. How nice if that were all that you needed to do? It is possible. You just need to take a couple more steps, as we shall see.

Go ahead and create a new directory named `secured` under the directory where your ColdFusion code is placed (use Windows Explorer or whatever tool you use to create directories). There's nothing special about that directory name, but it serves as an apt example for these purposes. In that directory, create an Application.cfm. You learn in Chapters 2 and 19 that this special file is one that gets executed any time that a ColdFusion template is requested by the user; it's an excellent place, therefore, to put authentication code that makes sure that the user is authenticated before enabling him to continue.

CFLOGIN in action

The new `CFLOGIN` tag takes some getting used to for both new and experienced CF developers. It's used to surround code that performs the actual authentication process. More than that, it's smart enough to execute that code only if the user is *not* already authenticated. Finally, it creates a special set of indicators for ColdFusion to track that the user is authenticated, and these new indicators are *not* session variables.

First, look at a very simple example. It's not one that you would really use, but it helps demonstrate the process. In the `secured` directory that you've created, in the new Application.cfm file, place just the following lines:

```
<cflogin>
   not logged in<br>
</cflogin>
```

Now place another file called `test.cfm` in the `secured` directory containing the following code:

```
<cfoutput>#timeformat(now(),"hh:mm:ss tt")#</cfoutput>
```

If you run the `test.cfm` template, you should see output similar to the following:

```
not logged in
02:46:37 PM
```

This display shows that you're running the code inside the `CFLOGIN` tag (showing `not logged in`) and the current time in minutes and seconds. You take advantage of that time display in the next section. If you refresh the page, you notice that the same output is displayed (but with the time changing, of course).

Running this example shows that the code inside the CFLOGIN tag is continuing to execute. That may seem confusing if you expect CFLOGIN to log you in. But that's not what it does. Again, it runs code whenever you are *not* logged in.

What makes CF consider the user logged in? That's the purpose of the CFLOGINUSER tag.

The CFLOGINUSER tag in action

The CFLOGINUSER tag is used to tell ColdFusion that a user is authenticated with a given username and password. It doesn't actually do the authentication itself, however, which is also confusing at first. You are required to perform the actual checking (as well as cause the user to be prompted for values). You see how to do both of those things in the sections, "Prompting for Username and Password" and "Validating Username and Password." But you first need to concentrate on the simplest functionality of the CFLOGINUSER tag in conjunction with CFLOGIN. It has some very interesting aspects, as we will now see.

Change the code in the Application.cfm to the following:

```
<cflogin>
   not logged in<br>
   <!--- assume we've prompted the user for username and password
      and the values were bsmith and bpw--->
   <cfloginuser name="bsmith" password="bpw" roles="">
   now logged in<br>
</cflogin>
<cfoutput>#timeformat(now(),"hh:mm:ss tt")#</cfoutput>
```

The comment reflects the fact that you're assuming that the user is authenticated already and has provided the username and password values of bsmith and bpw respectively. But notice the new CFLOGINUSER tag. By using that tag, you provide the values that the user has entered, which are hard-coded in this example. A roles attribute also is required, but we hold off discussing that now, so you're leaving it empty in this example.

Now, when you save this file and run the test.cfm template, you see the following output the first time:

```
not logged in
now logged in
03:10:11 PM
```

What's happened here? You've obviously executed code inside the CFLOGIN tag because you're still shown as not logged in (which was output just before the CFLOGINUSER), but then you see the indication now logged in (which was output just after the CFLOGINUSER). Then you see the output from your test.cfm page as usual. But you don't see any apparent result from the CFLOGIN tag. Has anything really happened?

If you refresh the test.cfm page, you will see that, although the time changes to show that you are seeing new page output, you no longer see the messages that were displayed within the CFLOGIN tag; instead, you see only the following:

```
03:10:21 PM
```

Indeed, this output shows that the code inside the CFLOGIN tag is no longer running. CF now considers you to be logged in, or *authenticated*. And whenever code in this secured directory causes the Application.cfm template to execute, the code in CFLOGIN no longer runs, at least until the user logs out. We discuss a few ways that the user can become logged out in the next section, later in this chapter.

But did you notice that you've done nothing to track the logged-in status? ColdFusion is tracking it for you. That's one of the other powerful new features of CFLOGIN.

Before leaving the subject of CFLOGIN tag processing, you may want to know about one other attribute of the tag that may prove interesting to some. CookieDomain is useful in working in a clustered environment (where a user may be load-balanced to a new machine after logging in). Because the CFLOGIN process uses cookies, and cookies are by default sent back only to the server that sets them, this attribute enables you to indicate the higher-level domain to which all machines in the cluster belong. So if you used it on machines named *server1.yourdomain.com* and *server2.yourdomain.com*, you'd set CookieDomain to yourdomain.com so that all servers could share the authentication cookie.

Logout Processing

You may naturally wonder how long ColdFusion considers a user to be logged in or how you may intentionally log them out. Most authentication systems are designed so that, if a user doesn't use the system for some specified period of time, that user is considered logged out whenever he does return. The CFLOGIN process is no different.

But what may surprise many is that CFLOGIN does not use sessions to track the authentication status of a user. So the user is not logged out after his ColdFusion session ends. This can be an advantage, but it can also prove confusing if you expect ColdFusion to log them out when the session ends. This matter is discussed further in the next section.

Similarly new and different is the fact that you can also now manually log the user out by using the CFLOGOUT tag, which is discussed in "Logout using CFLOGOUT."

Finally, still another benefit of this change from using sessions to track authentication status is a powerful new feature: The user is logged out after closing his browser. (This is not related to the use of J2EE sessions, however, where—as you learn in Chapter 28—ColdFusion closes a session after the user's browser closes.) This feature will be discussed in "Logout by browser close."

Logout time specified by CFLOGIN idletimeout setting

The first and perhaps simplest approach to how a user is logged out comes into play if the user hasn't visited your site for some specified time. Just as developers in previous releases relied on ColdFusion session variables and their built-in timeout, so, too, can CFLOGIN users rely on a built-in timeout. But it's not based on sessions.

The CFLOGIN tag has an available attribute, idletimeout, which accepts a number of seconds to use for the timeout time. If not specified, it defaults to 30 minutes (1,800 seconds).

For those not familiar with session timeouts, here's the idea behind timeouts of either kind: If a user visits a page on your site, imagine that a clock starts on the server. If the user visits again within the timeout time, the clock gets reset and the user gets another interval of the specified time, during which he is considered active.

But if a user returns to your site after that specified time interval has passed since the last visit, the server considers that user to no longer be active. In the case of session variables, the user's session on the server is removed and that user no longer has any session variables accessible when they run code on the server.

In the case of the CFLOGIN timeout, the user's *authenticated status* is removed, and the next time that the user executes code that runs a CFLOGIN statement, that code inside the tag executes. (And as you learn in "Prompting for Username and Password," you present the user with a means to provide a username and password and then authenticate that user against some repository of usernames and passwords.)

If you want to demonstrate this, change the example CFLOGIN in the Application.cfm file in the section "CFLOGIN in action," earlier in this chapter, to specify a short idletimeout, such as 10 seconds, as in the following example:

```
<cflogin idletimeout="10">
```

Then save this changed Application.cfm and refresh your test.cfm template. Because this process causes the new code to execute, it starts your 10-second interval. (The code inside the CFLOGIN tag doesn't execute on this first execution unless the previously set time interval—the default of 30 minutes—had already passed since you last ran test.cfm.)

Now if you wait more than 10 seconds before refreshing the page, you see that the code inside the CFLOGIN tag does run, indicating that CF considers you to no longer be authenticated. The CFLOGIN code executes again and you've now been given another 10 seconds to return to the site before being logged out again.

We've noticed in our testing that the server isn't quite accurate to the second, so you may need to wait upward of 10 seconds beyond your stated idletimeout time for the server to consider you no longer authenticated. Of course, in the real world, a difference of so few seconds is trivial and not worth worrying about.

Ten seconds is also a ridiculously short time, and we're using it only for demo purposes. In a real application, you'd want to choose a number that's typical of your and your users' expectations of how long they can remain inactive (between visits to your site) before they're automatically logged off. Even as much as an hour or a few hours may make sense for your application.

New Feature

A very important point to note again, however, is that this login status is no longer tied to session timeouts. You may be reluctant to set sessions to timeout after such a long interval. The session scope often contains variables and possibly query result sets, and so on. Storing sessions for too long can consume a good deal of system memory, especially if multiplied by the number of active sessions.

CFLOGIN timeout tracking is not based on sessions. You are also, therefore, no longer forced to set a logout timeframe that's within the Administrator's Max Session Timeout value, which is another means to limit the effect of too many active sessions. This is a great new feature that has not been widely heralded (or perhaps not understood).

You face a potential complication with the idletimeout attribute. We discuss in the section "Prompting for Username and Password," later in this chapter, that you have four alternatives for prompting the user for a username and password. The idletimeout may seem to work only for simple login forms (and not for forms using j_username or basic authentication). These concepts are explained in that section. The problem has more to do with the fact that a special cflogin structure continues to exist within CFLOGIN tests even after a timeout occurs. (More about this in the section that section.)

Logout using CFLOGOUT

Although the concept of an `idletimeout` may be adequate for your needs in creating an authentication system, offering the user a means to log out intentionally may also be desirable. Consider, for example, a secure application in a workplace or a public application that may be used by multiple users. You should enable the user to manually log out in case he wants to walk away from his terminal. Leaving it to timeout may not be sufficient in case they want to leave and not have users who follow have access to your site with them logged in.

Fortunately, you have a solution in the new `CFLOGOUT` tag. It's quite simple, and takes no attributes. It simply logs the user out. What does that mean to your code? It means that, the next time that the user runs a `CFLOGIN` tag and its code, that code executes.

You need to consider how to enable the user to choose to log out. A simple example may be to add a form or hyperlink to your application so that a logout option appears on any secured pages (or, alternatively, by placing it on any page whenever the user is logged in).

The `Application.cfm` file is, as always, one possible place to put such code, both to display the logout option and to perform a test to determine whether the user has chosen to take that option. You may change your Application.cfm as follows (the bolded lines reflect what's changed versions the earlier version of this file we created earlier in this chapter):

```
<cfif isdefined("form.logout")>
   <cflogout>
</cfif>

<cflogin idletimeout="20">
   not logged in<br>
   <!--- assume we've prompted the user for username and password
      and the values were bsmith and bpw--->
   <cfloginuser name="bsmith" password="bpw" roles="">
   now logged in<br>
</cflogin>

<!--- GetAuthUser() returns the empty string if not logged in --->
<cfif GetAuthUser() is not "">
   <form method="post">
   <input type="submit" name="logout" value="Logout">
   </form>
</cfif>
<cfoutput>#timeformat(now(),"hh:mm:ss tt")#</cfoutput>
```

This example is using a new function in CF MX, called `GetAuthUser()`. Its purpose is to enable you to access the username that the user enters on logging in after you've used `CFLOGINUSER`. This saves you from needing to store the username in a session variable or the like. One other way to use it is for determining whether the user has indeed logged in. If not, the `GetAuthUser()` returns an empty string.

Note that the `GetAuthUser()`function will only return a value if it's used on a page that's executed a `CFLOGIN` tag, or if it's been executed (as in this case) in the `Application.cfm`. An exception to this rule will be if you use the approach to authentication in "Using declarative basic authentication." There we will see that `GetAuthUser()` returns the authenticated username even though we don't use a `CFLOGIN` tag at all.

As the code's comments above show, we're using it to assist in testing whether the user is logged in. The newly added code says that, if the user is indeed already logged in (that is, if `GetAuthUser()` returns a value, because it returns the username from `CFLOGIN` if the user is logged in), then the user should be shown a Logout button.

Note

> You may notice that this form is not using any `action` attribute. This ability to leave off the `action` is an interesting feature of HTML that works very well in this case. It causes the form to submit back to the page in which it appears. CF developers have long used complicated scripts to rebuild the URL of the page being requested. The `action` attribute doesn't seem necessary, unless in logging the user out you also want to send them to some different page. As long as you send them to a page in this directory (so that the `CFLOGOUT` we're about to discuss is executed), it will be ok to provide a value in the `action`.

Now you can look at the code at the top of the file. That's what actually performs the `CFLOGOUT` command if it detects that the user has come back to this page having submitted that logout form—that is, if the page detects a form submission with a field named `logout`. Notice that the form at the bottom of the previous listing offers `logout` as the `name` of the `submit` button in the form displayed to the user while he is logged in.

If you save this code into your Application.cfm and run the `test.cfm` program with this code in place, clicking the Logout button will show output from within the `CFLOGIN` tag that indicates that the user is no longer logged in.

The order in which those new lines of code are placed is important. `CFLOGOUT`, if it happens at all, should take place at the top, because you want to cause the following `CFLOGIN` to detect that they've been logged out and cause a new login.

> Continuing the discussion from the previous note, this code is presuming that after logging them out we want to remain in this directory and show them a new login prompt. If you wanted instead to send them to another page on logout, you could add a `CFLOCATION` tag here to send them to the desired page, or simply provide a display showing that they've logged out and offering a link to elsewhere, or provide some other means to direct them to a new page.

As for the placement of the Logout form and button using the approach described in this chapter and assuming that we want the `Application.cfm` to show the logout button, you also don't want to show it until after the `CFLOGIN/CFLOGINUSER` processing takes place (and, even then, only if the user has indeed logged in, as is the case if `GetAuthUser()` is not empty).

> In our testing, using `CFLOGOUT` this doesn't appear to function as expected if you're using basic authentication, as we discuss in the section "Prompting for Username and Password," later in this chapter.

Logout by browser close

Finally, something that may amaze and delight many developers is that this new form of authentication based on CFLOGINworks in a way that ColdFusion sessions don't. After users closes their browsers (that is, all instances of the browser), they find that ColdFusion considers them logged out.

This feature is very helpful for public internet terminals or other kiosk-style applications, where you want to know that, after a browser is closed, no way exists for another user to follow the first and still be logged in to the previous user's session on your site (as was the case with CF session-based login processing in previous releases).

This is a direct result of the fact that CF MX login processing does not use sessions to track the user's authentication status. CF MX uses a new non-persistent cookie instead of the persistent cookies used by CF sessions (`cfid` and `cftoken`). (You can learn more about those two special CF-generated cookies in Chapter 19.)

Because a user can open multiple windows that may all share the same nonresistant cookies, whenever we say that the login is terminated after the browser is closed, the safest thing to say is that it's actually terminated *after all windows of a given browser* are closed.

Indeed, a benefit of the new `CFLOGIN` process is that it does not require support of sessions at all. You may have noticed that, in the examples so far in this chapter, you haven't used a `CFAPPLICATION` tag (which you use to enable sessions) in the Application.cfm file. You can use one if you really want, and this new login processing is certainly compatible with sessions. They just are not related to each other.

This means the new `CFLOGIN` approach is especially well suited to environments with any of the following constraints:

- Persistent cookies (such as those used to support sessions) are not allowed at all
- Session timeouts defined in the application are too short for login timeouts
- Setting the session timeout higher to sustain longer login timeouts would burden server memory with too many sessions
- Attempts to set the session timeout higher is constrained by the maximum session timeout defined in the administrator and the maximum will not be increased
- Sessions are not desirable at all, such as high load or load balanced sites

Indeed, because the `CFLOGIN` `idletimeout` value is not related to `CFAPPLICATION`'s `sessiontimeout` timeframe, you can face synchronization issues if you enable those values to differ from one another. If `idletimeout` exceeds SESSIONTIMEOUT, the user can remain logged in but lose his sessions. This could be confusing to them and to you as a developer if you don't anticipate it in your code.

Prompting for Username and Password

Throughout the simple examples in the preceding sections, you take a significant shortcut and simply use a hard-coded username and password as you execute the `CFLOGINUSER` tag. Clearly, that's not the way that we would code this in a real application. Instead, you would want to cause the user to be prompted to provide a username and password.

Because the `CFLOGIN` tag executes its code only if the user is not logged in (or becomes logged out), that's where (and when) you want to cause the user to be prompted. You may notice that we keep saying, "cause the user to be prompted." You may wonder why we don't simply say, "present the user with a login form." That's because the user can actually be prompted in several ways, and only two of them involve your writing an actual form.

Still another issue is that of actually using the presented username and password to determine whether they are valid values. We hold that discussion for the section "Proceeding based on success or failure of authentication." For the examples in the next few sections, you focus only on the form and, therefore, will just put the entered username and password into the `CFLOGINUSER` tag without really evaluating if they are to be considered valid.

Prompting by using a simple form

Perhaps the simplest approach (although not the only one to consider) is to present the user with a form that you write, which you then process, both tasks occurring within the CFLOGIN tags. Following is an example form:

```
Please Login
<form method="post">
Username: <input type="text" name="username"><br>
Password: <input type="password" name="password"><br>
<input type="submit" value="Login" name="login">
</form>
```

This is a simple form using fields named "username" and "password". You could put this form directly into your CFLOGIN tags, but storing it in a file (such as login_form.cfm) and then using CFINCLUDE within the CFLOGIN tag (in the Application.cfm that we've been refining) to present the form to the user instead proves helpful later. An example of this is shown as follows (and, again, remember that you're not doing any real authentication with the username and password but are instead passing it right to the CFLOGINUSER tag for now):

```
<cflogin>
   <cfif not isdefined("form.login")>
      <cfinclude template="login_form.cfm">
      <cfabort>
   <cfelse>
      <!--- would validate username/password here --->
      <cfloginuser name="#form.username#"
password="#form.password#" roles="">
   </cfif>
</cflogin>
```

This example may look a little confusing for those new to ColdFusion form processing. You want to decide whether to show the user the form or process it, based on whether you are in fact receiving a request to process it. Because you create on the form a submit button with the name login, a form.login field is available to your template if the user has submitted the form. If no form.login field exists, you haven't yet sent the user the form and must now send it to the user—and stop processing any further parts of this Application.cfm or any page that was called whenever CFLOGIN detected that the user was not logged in.

Otherwise, if you do have a form.login field, you then want to validate the form's username and password fields, however you may do so. Again, in these simple examples, you're just passing the username and password to the CFLOGINUSER tag and not really validating them.

Note

You may notice that, again, you're not using an action attribute in the form itself, shown at the start of this section. In our testing, this not having an action causes submission of the page to transfer control to the page that itself showed the form, without any need for you to specify an action attribute and build the URL to point the page back to itself manually. In fact, if the page being called was called with a query string included, this approach of leaving off the action even causes the form action page to receive the query string that was passed into the page when the form was shown. And this behavior will remain if the form is redisplayed because of failed logins, as will be described later in "Proceeding based on success or failure of authentication." This behavior works out quite well for this sort of processing and, in our testing, works fine in both IE and Netscape Navigator (tested in 5.5 and 4.73 respectively).

Finally, in both this example and the one in the following section, adding JavaScript validation to ensure that the user provides a username and password would certainly prove helpful. See the discussions in Chapter 20 on how to use `CFFORM` and `CFINPUT` to achieve that goal.

Using JavaScript to place the cursor *focus* on the username field as the form loads may also be helpful. (See the article "Getting Focus(ed)—And a Quick JavaScript Overview," by Charlie Arehart, in the June 2000 issue of the *ColdFusion Developer's Journal* for more information on that technique. It's available at `http://www.syscon.com/coldfusion/article.cfm?id=122`.)

As you work with forms to perform login processing, be aware whenever you're testing to observe timeout issues that, if you simply refresh a page that's just been logged in to by using a form, the refresh causes the form data to be reposted. Even if the timeout time passed while you looked at the page, the refresh with the reposting presents the form fields necessary to reauthenticate. The code in Application.cfm detects this as a form submission, and you never actually see the form presented. It may lead you to think that no timeout is occurring. This is just a side effect of trying to run simple tests. The problem doesn't occur (nor would it matter if it did) in the real world.

A good work-around for this problem in simple testing is to add a hyperlink to your `test.cfm` page that calls itself. You use that link to test calling the page over and over to see what happens if is a timeout occurs.

Using special form variables: j_username and j_password

You may see examples in the ColdFusion documentation that use a form with the field names `j_username` and `j_password`. These are actually special names, and they are tied to the underlying J2EE server heritage in CF MX. If a form with these fields is presented, it causes creation of a special structure called `cflogin`, with the keys `name` and `password` (it is *not* `cflogin.username`.). You don't need to use that structure. (You see its value in the section, "Using programmatic basic authentication.") You can just use the form fields as you do in the example in "Prompting by using a simple form."

But if you want to use the special `cflogin` structure, you can use the following code in your Application.cfm file. It presumes that the `login_form.cfm` that you're *including* is using `j_username` and `j_password` as its form fields:

```
<cflogin>
   <cfif not isdefined("cflogin.name")>
      <cfinclude template="login_form.cfm">
      <cfabort>
   <cfelse>
      <!--- would validate username/password here --->
   <cfloginuser name="#form.j_username#"
Password="#form.j_password#" roles="">
   </cfif>
</cflogin>
```

Notice that the difference in the second line of this example (compared to that in "Prompting by using a simple form") is that you're not referring to the form fields `form.j_username` (or even `form.login`) to test for the form submission, although you could. Instead, you're referring to `cflogin.name`. This (and `cflogin.password`) is a special variable that is created only by this type of username/password prompting (as well as in the next two types that we discuss).

Note

The variable is accessible only within the processing of CFLOGIN tags. If you attempt to refer to the structure outside the tags (or by using the earlier simple form example), the cflogin structure seems not to exist.

Caution

We've noticed a quirk in using this j_username approach, however. This cflogin structure is not removed after the login process times out. If you use code such as that of the preceding example, the user never seems to be logged out after a timeout. That is, you never see a request to log in again. This has been identified as a bug. A work-around is available for the following test:

```
<cfif not isdefined("cflogin.name")>
```

You must replace that line with the following:

```
<cfif GetAuthUser() is "" and not isdefined("form.login")>
```

This code indeed causes the login page to appear after a timeout (as well as after a CFLOGOUT or on the first visit in a new browser session).

Another challenge that flows from this unexpected behavior is that, because the cflogin structure doesn't get erased on a timeout, it also continues to hold the previous login values even after a new login takes place, at least until the CFLOGINUSER takes place. This is important to note when you perform testing of the input values against a database or such. You should use form.j_username and form.j_password, just as the code in the previous listing does for the CFLOGINUSER tag to get around this problem. We can only hope for now that these bugs get addressed in future updates.

You may wonder, with the challenges in the caution, what is the value of the j_username approach. We would argue that there is none. Until these bugs are addressed, just using the simpler login form in the preceding section is probably easier and will give you far greater control over the login and logout process.

Using programmatic basic authentication

Did you know that you don't actually need to build a login form at all to perform authentication? Web browsers have a built-in means to prompt the user for a username and password if the Web application sends information that tells the browser to do so. This feature is often referred to as *basic authentication*, and it's not a feature unique to ColdFusion at all.

Note

The feature described in this and the next section may work only as described with the built-in web server in CFMX. If you are using an integrated web server like IIS or Apache, it may indeed work, or it may fail or seem that user never authenticates (because the cflogin structure is never populated). This has been noticed with the combination of IIS 5.1 and Internet Explorer 6. Getting it to work may require additional actions. This has been raised as bug 49304. But it does indeed work with the built-in web server in ColdFusion MX.

You have two different ways to perform this type of authentication: one programmatically and one declaratively. In the programmatic approach, you write code in your application to tell the browser to prompt the user for a username and password, and the browser opens a window for the user to respond to. This isn't an HTML form prompt as we've seen to this point, so no form fields are available to use for authentication testing. But just as occurs in the approach using j_username that we describe in the preceding section, the basic-authentication login process creates a cflogin structure holding the username and password entered.

And as occurs in each of the two previously described approaches (in "Prompting by using a simple form" and "Using special form variables: j_username and j_password"), you get to decide how to proceed with the resulting values that the user enters. This will be discussed in "Validating Username and Password."

Here's another simplistic example of code that you may use in Application.cfm. It doesn't do any real authentication yet. It just passes whatever value is entered in the CFLOGINUSER tag. Notice that the following example does use a few tags and functions that we have not used in the previous approaches to authentication:

```
<cflogin>
   <cfif not isdefined("cflogin")>
       <cfsetting enablecfoutputonly="yes" showdebugoutput="no">
       <cfheader statuscode="401">
       <cfheader name="WWW-Authenticate"
value='Basic realm="SecuredApp"'>
       <cfoutput>Not authorized</cfoutput>
      <cfabort>
   <cfelse>
      <!--- would validate username/password here --->
      <cfloginuser name="#cflogin.name#"
Password="#cflogin.password#" roles="">
   </cfif>
</cflogin>
```

This code is basically indicating that, if the cflogin structure doesn't already exist (and it doesn't until the user logs in successfully—or, rather, until your code runs the CFLOGINUSER tag), CF should send some browser standard headers including a Statuscode 401 using CFHEADER that tell the browser to open the basic-authentication login window. In CF MX, the values that the user enters are placed in the cflogin structure, after the user responds to the prompt; therefore, the CFELSE code is executed and the CFLOGINUSER tag is performed. We discuss in the section "Validating Username and Password," later in this chapter, how you may perform authentication on the username and password that the user enters.

Caution

See the Caution in the preceding section about how the cflogin scope is not cleared on a timeout. The same applies here.

A further caution is that trying to perform a logout in the Application.cfm file, as we discuss in previous sections, can prove challenging. The attempt to log out triggers a new authentication prompt, but then the reply to that prompt still acts as a form submission, thus triggering the logout again, leaving you in a loop where you cannot log in.

Closing a browser causes the logout most effectively.

Using declarative basic authentication

Yet another approach to basic authentication is through configuring some descriptor files within ColdFusion MX. In this approach, no code in your program indicates how to perform login processing, and the usernames and passwords used for authentication are not stored in a database or other file that your application accesses. Instead, the server uses the declared security controls to determine how to handle authentication.

Each Web server has its own way of declaring that a directory (or perhaps a directory or file pointed to by a URL) is to be secured this way. You should explore your own Web server documents for more information if you want to use a similar declarative approach as enabled by that web server.

In the case of the built-in Web server that comes with ColdFusion MX, the configuration requires changes to the `wwwroot\WEB-INF\web.xml` and `runtime\servers\default\SERVER-INF\jrun-users.xml` files.

To test this approach, you can create a new directory called `securedweb` (under `[cfusion-home]\wwwroot`). Then you can change your `web.xml` file to add the following code:

```
<login-config>
   <auth-method>BASIC</auth-method>
   <realm-name>Test</realm-name>
</login-config>

<security-constraint>
  <web-resource-collection>
     <web-resource-name>Test Application</web-resource-name>
     <url-pattern>/securedweb/*</url-pattern>
     <http-method>GET</http-method>
     <http-method>POST</http-method>
     <description>Test Resource</description>
  </web-resource-collection>
  <auth-constraint>
     <role-name>reg-users</role-name>
     <description>Reg users only</description>
  </auth-constraint>
</security-constraint>
```

As you should with any change to the XML configuration files, make sure that you save a backup of the original file in case you experience any problems. Some mistaken entries can prevent the server from starting at all.

The `<login-config>` elements (XML tags are referred to generally as *elements*) indicate that the server uses basic authentication for any applications using this declarative security. (You can have only one `<login-config>` declaration for the entire CFMX server.)

The `<web-resource-collection>` elements further declare that any attempts to access templates via the URL `/securedweb/` (whether `gets` or `posts`) need to be authenticated. And the `<auth-constraint>` elements indicate further that only users having the `reg-users` role are permitted access.

Where would ColdFusion find usernames and roles? CF MX (that is, the underlying JRun engine) is preconfigured to look for usernames and passwords in the `runtime\servers\default\SERVER-INF\jrun-users.xml` file. The following example shows some entries that can be used to test this declarative basic authentication approach:

```
<user>
   <user-name>testuser</user-name>
   <password>testpw</password>
</user>

<user>
   <user-name>anotheruser</user-name>
   <password>otherpw</password>
</user>

<role>
   <role-name>reg-users</role-name>
```

```
        <user-name>testuser</user-name>
        <user-name>anotheruser</user-name>
    </role>
```

This code names two username/password pairs and also indicates that both are defined within the reg-users role. You can have multiple role declarations. You can learn more about the XML configuration files in the JRun documentation, at http://livedocs.macromedia.com, and especially the descriptor file documentation at http://livedocs.macromedia.com/jrun4docs/descriptordocs/index.html. The ColdFusion manuals don't currently explain these configuration possibilities.

With these changes in place and after a restart, whenever any code in the named directory (/securedweb) is executed, the server now automatically causes the browser to prompt the user for authentication, using the basic-authentication prompt that we describe in the preceding section.

You don't need any specific support for authentication in the Application.cfm, because the Web server configuration applies to the entire directory (as defined in the example XML file earlier in this section). Indeed, this approach could be made to apply to any of several or in fact all directories on the server, by way of value entered for the *pattern* in the <url-pattern>*pattern*</url-pattern> element discussed at the start of this section.

You don't even need to use the CFLOGIN tag to make the username available via the GetAuthUser() function (and to make the role available in IsUserInRole()), as we discuss in the section "Authorizing Users: Permissions Control," later in this chapter. They're already populated automatically by ColdFusion after the login.

As with the programmatic basic authentication that we discuss in the preceding section, this approach has some quirks that make working with the CFLOGOUT and idletimeout features for controlling user logout troublesome. Closing a browser causes the logout most effectively.

If you're running under IIS, Apache, or another Web server, you may have still other different configuration features for causing a form of declarative authentication to work with that server. In those cases, just realize that the communication is between the browser and the Web server, so by the time that your code is executed in ColdFusion, the user is already authenticated. It's even possible that CFMX may detect that authorized state and populate the cflogin structure. If so, you could proceed to use the information in the remainder of this chapter.

Validating Username and Password

The discussion of declarative basic authentication in the preceding section indicates that that particular approach automatically looks up the username and password in configuration files built into the Web server. That was getting a little ahead of things, because in the first three approaches (using a simple form, using a form with j_username, and programmatic basic authentication) that we discuss in this chapter, we don't specify how to actually authenticate the user. In each of those cases, we leave the situation as follows:

```
<!--- would validate username/password here --->
```

What do you actually do for that step? It depends on your application, as well as which of the other three styles of login prompt you chose to use. So focus first on the bigger picture question: Where do you look up usernames and passwords anyway?

Authenticating against a database

For many developers, the simplest solution is to perform authentication (that is, looking up a given username and password) against a database table — either one that already exists in the environment or one that they create for the purpose of holding username and password values for legitimate users.

Still other developers may already have a database containing information about their users (members, customers, employees) and can add authentication support simply by adding username, password, and perhaps other fields to an existing table.

There is a database installed with CFMX called CompanyInfo, with a corresponding LoginInfo table. If you'd like to use that as an example and need to create the datasource, the database is installed in `[cfusion-home]\db\company.mdb`.

Assume that, for now, you want to authenticate against the table called LoginInfo in the CompanyInfo datasource. If we use the forms we created in the section "Prompting by using a simple form" above, then we will have form fields called `form.username` and `form.password` presented after the user submits the form. (If you were following along in the section "Using special form variables: j_username and j_password" or have used the approach offered in "Using programmatic basic authentication," then instead use the `cflogin.name` and cflogin.`password` fields).

To perform authentication against this database, you can use a query such as the following:

```
<cfquery datasource="CompanyInfo" name="GetLogin">
   SELECT UserID FROM LoginInfo
   WHERE UserID='#form.username#'
AND Password='#form.password#'
</cfquery>
```

If you were to run the test.cfm we had developed in "CFLOGIN in action" earlier in the chapter, you would now be expected to provide values that are found in this sample CompanyInfo database. One of the records includes a value of username with `bobz` who has a password of `ads10`.

But how do we in fact test that the user has given us those expected values, or that whatever values they give us cause us to find a corresponding record in the database?

The next step is to decide whether the values presented are a valid username/password pair. We continue with that in "Proceeding based on success or failure of authentication," after we take a moment in the next section to address another form of authentication that some may prefer.

Authenticating against an OS/LDAP repository

Rather than authenticate against a database table, you may work in an environment with an available repository for usernames and passwords that is used to control access to all resources on the server. Rather than create a new table of usernames and passwords in any database, you may prefer (or be expected) to use that. Examples include an LDAP (lightweight directory access protocol) server or a Windows NT domain.

For those who need to use such a repository for authentication, an article addressing several approaches to doing that is available from Macromedia; called "Security Best Practices: Authenticating And Authorizing Against NT Domains with ColdFusion MX," it's available at `www.macromedia.com/desdev/mx/coldfusion/articles/ntdomain.html`. Despite the title of the article, it also discusses authenticating against an LDAP server.

Proceeding based on success or failure of authentication

To continue processing the form from the discussions in "Authenticating against a database" and complete the login process, you want to perform the desired authentication and then decide how the user is to proceed based on success or failure.

The first step is deciding whether the username and password passed are valid. Going back to the CFQUERY that we discuss in that section and the continued presumption that we're using the simple login form with username and password from "Prompting by using a simple form," you may use the following code in an Application.cfm:

```
<cfif isdefined("form.logout")>
   <cflogout>
</cfif>

<cflogin>
   <cfif not isdefined("form.login")>
      <cfinclude template="login_form.cfm">
      <cfabort>
   <cfelse>
      <!--- validate username/password here --->
      <cfquery datasource="CompanyInfo" name="GetLogin">
      SELECT UserID FROM LoginInfo
      WHERE UserID='#form.username#'
         AND Password='#form.password#'
      </cfquery>
      <cfif getlogin.recordcount is 0>
         Invalid username/password. Try again.
         <cfinclude template="login_form.cfm">
         <cfabort>
      </cfif>
      <cfloginuser name="#form.username#"
password="#form.password#" roles="">
   </cfif>
</cflogin>

<!--- GetAuthUser() returns the empty string if not logged in --->
<cfif GetAuthUser() is not "">
   <form method="post">
   <input type="submit" name="logout" value="Logout">
   </form>
</cfif>
```

The significant lines are those added after the comment validate username/password here. You just add a CFQUERY and a CFIF test, which we will explain next. The rest of the page is the same as before. Again, if you're using any of the other forms of authentication (j_username forms or basic authentication), the process is similar, but the incoming pair of username and password values is in cflogin.username and cflogin.password, respectively.

ColdFusion queries always return a query variable called recordcount. In this case, getlogin.recordcount is available that indicates how many records are found.

If the query fails to return any records (that is, recordcount is 0), you know that the user provided an invalid username/password pair, and you should display the login form again and stop processing. Otherwise, the login is successful, and the flow of control of the program can proceed with the CFLOGINUSER. It's that simple.

Control then also flow out of the `Application.cfm` to whatever page was being executed that triggered the `Application.cfm` and when they were detected to not be logged in.

It took us quite a while to get to this point of 30 lines or so of code in this sample `Application.cfm`. I hope you can appreciate, however, that much of the process is simply not obvious, even to (and perhaps especially to) experienced CF developers. The details are also given short shrift in the documentation and many other articles and books.

Authorizing Users: Permissions Control

You could consider the subject of application security to be complete, now that you can cause the user to log in, be authenticated, and be logged out. For many applications, that's enough security.

But what if knowing only that someone can access your application is not enough? What if you need to track what rights a person has to perform various actions in your application? The first step, which we have covered throughout this chapter, is authentication—who a user is. Now we want to cover authorization—what the user gets to do.

Of course, a simple way to track whether a person has the "right" to perform an action could be to test result of `GetAuthUser()` against some sort of list, as in the following example:

```
<cfif listfind("bobz,sallyp,marys",GetAuthUser())>
<!--- ok to do something --->
</cfif>
```

The value of roles

The problem with the approach in the preceding section is that it soon gets messy. You must change the code whenever a new person is added to the list of authorized users. Indeed, the fact that an "authorized list" even exists suggests an alternative solution to the problem. This group of people is deemed a group that's permitted to do something. Maybe, for example, this group has the capability to view proprietary sales details for the company.

Another way to look at things is to suggest that these users have a *role* to play and that they belong to that designated role. For this example group, you could consider them in Sales and declare a Sales role in the system.

This way, if you could simply ask whether the person belonged to that role, you'd get the same result. That's the way that `CFLOGIN` authorization processing works.

The first question is where to store the roles that each person belongs to. Why not in the same place where usernames and passwords are stored? Another question is how do we track the user's role throughout the application? We answer these questions in the next (and final) three sections.

Where to store and how to track a user's role(s)

Recall the CompanyInfo database from the section "Authenticating against a database," earlier in this chapter. In addition to having username and password columns, the LoginInfo table also has a column called Roles that tracks what roles individuals belong to. In that CompanyInfo database, the column is designed to hold a comma-separated list of roles to which individuals belong. (It would be better to design the database to have roles in a one-to-many table rather than all held in a single column per user, but that's not something we'll fix here.)

To obtain the user's roles, you can change just one line in your Application.cfm file, changing the CFQUERY to the following:

```
<cfquery datasource="CompanyInfo" name="GetLogin">
   SELECT Roles FROM LoginInfo
   WHERE UserID='#form.username#'
   AND Password='#form.password#'
</cfquery>
```

Again, this is presuming we've used the simple form of prompting the user for username/password as in "Prompting by using a simple form." If you are using the j_username or programmatic basic authentication approaches described earlier in this chapter, you'll want to use the cflogin.name and cflogin.password fields instead of form.username and form.password, both in that code and the CFLOGINUSER explained next.

Notice the simple change from SELECT UserID to SELECT Roles. It didn't really matter before that you were selecting any column in particular, because you were simply using SELECT to determine whether any records existed at all for the given username and password. Now, however, by selecting the Roles column, you receive in return the very comma-separated list of roles to which each person belongs.

You may recall from the section, "Authenticating against a database," that this table has a test record for the username bobz. His roles in the database are "Employes,Sales". (That typo of Employes is in the database.)

Now you have a query result showing the roles that a person belongs to. This is useful as long as you're on the page doing the CFLOGIN process, but what about after you leave this page? Query result sets don't last beyond the end of a page. How can you recall on later pages that a given user belongs to a given role? You pass it to the CFLOGINUSER tag.

In the earlier section, "The CFLOGINUSER tag in action," we introduced the CFLOGINUSER tag and mentioned that it has a roles attribute, which we ignored at the time. Now you can start to see its purpose. You want to assign the roles for this user, as obtained from a database in this example, into this roles attribute. So you must change your CFLOGINUSER tag, for this simple form example, to the following:

```
<cfloginuser name="#form.username#" password="#form.password#"
roles="#GetLogin.Roles#">
```

Testing for authorization: IsUserInRole()

We now know how to retrieve the role(s) a user belongs to during the login process, and the CFLOGINUSER has caused the role to be stored internally in ColdFusion's memory somewhere. How then do we later refer back to that role designation in other pages of the application?

Is there perhaps a cflogin.roles variable we can test? Unfortunately, there is none. It's also useful to recall that we also learned (in the section "Using special form variables: j_username and j_password") that the cflogin variables are available only inside the CFLOGIN tag itself anyway. So how do we ask ColdFusion what role a user is in?

CF MX adds a new function, IsUserInRole(), but rather than use it to ask what role(s) a user may belong to, you instead use it to ask whether the user is in a given role. In the example offered at the opening of this section, "Authorizing Users: Permissions Control," we suggested you might test the username against a list of authorized users. Instead, we can now show you that you use the IsUserInRole() function to refer to some role that such users may belong to. Recall that, in the section "The value of roles," we propose a "Sales" role, so you can change the test for authorization as follows:

```
<cfif IsUserInRole("Sales")>
<!--- ok to do something --->
</cfif>
```

Isn't that a lot cleaner than tracking authorization by username? Now, if you want to add new people to the Sales role, you don't need to change the program but instead simply can assign them to that role in the `Roles` field of the database.

Use of roles in CFFUNCTION

Roles can be used in one other place in ColdFusionMX: the `CFFUNCTION` tag, meaning in ColdFusion components and user-defined functions. By using the `roles` attribute of `CFFUNCTION`, you can define the role(s) to which a person must belong to execute the method, as in the following example:

```
<cffunction name="somemethod" roles="Sales">
  ...
</cffunction>
```

Now, this method can be executed only by a user who is both authenticated (by using `CFLOGINUSER`) and authorized (is indicated by belonging to the named roles).

Some cautions about using roles in CFMX

Be careful when working with roles. There are a few issues that can easily complicate your attempts to use them.

First, be aware that roles are case-sensitive. If a user is in a `Sales` role but you test for `IsUserInRole("sales")`, the test does not match. Similarly, the testing performed by the `roles` attribute in CFFUNCTION is also case-sensitive.

Second, handling multiple roles can be especially tricky. If you want to ensure that the user belongs to multiple roles, or any of several roles, you can do that, but you must be very careful.

Consider that you might want to enable users to perform some task in some part of your application only if they are in *both* the `Sales` and `Manager` roles. With the `IsUserInRole` function, you wold perform this test as:

```
<cfif IsUserInRole("Sales,Manager")>
<!--- ok to do something --->
</cfif>
```

The user must belong to both roles.

But it's very easy to intend or interpret that to mean the user is expected to be in either role. That's not the way things work.

Going back to our test record from the section, "Where to store and how to track a user's role(s)", the test record for `bobz` is assigned to `Sales` and `Employes` (sic) but not `Manager`, so he can't execute the restricted code in that previous code fragment.

On the other hand, if you really want to test whether the user is in *either* one role or another, the proper test would be as follows:

```
<cfif IsUserInRole("Sales") or IsUserInRole("Manager")>
<!--- ok to do something --->
</cfif>
```

With the `roles` attribute of `CFFUNCTION`, you could also list both roles as in:

```
<cffunction name="somemethod" roles="Sales,Manager">
```

But there's an unfortunate inconsistency with testing multiple roles here. Whereas with the `IsUserInRole` function, the user must belong to both roles, with `CFFUNCTION`'s `roles` attribute, they can belong to either of the named roles. Indeed, it would seem there is no way with `CFFUNCTION`'s `roles` attribute to require the user belong to all the listed roles. They can belong to any one and will be permitted to execute the function or component method.

Finally, in working with these lists of roles, both in listing them in the `IsUserInRole()` function and `roles` attribute of `CFFUNCTION` as well as in storing them in the database, be aware that these are treated by ColdFusion MX as regular lists. CF list values are sensitive to spaces as well. So testing `IsUserInRole("Sales, Manager")`, where you leave a space before `Manager`, will not be a successful match in the example we're been working with, even if the person belongs to both roles. ColdFusion treats them as the roles `Sales` and `" Manager"` (`Manager` with a space before it.)

Summary

We have seen that there are two broad categories of security in ColdFusion, when it comes to controlling how users log into and use our applications.

The first is authentication: checking their login information against some resource. We saw that ColdFusion MX adds new features to support this process, in the form of `CFLOGIN` and `CFLOGINUSER` tag, the `cflogin` structure and `GetAuthUser()` function.

We also saw that the `CFLOGIN` process offers a few ways to prompt the use for their login, and these can bring new advantages over the more traditional way that developers would prompt users for login information. Another key difference with `CFLOGIN` is that the timeout for logins is now no longer tied to session timeouts (or even the use of sessions at all) and the login status terminates when the browser is closed. These differences can have substantial benefit in some situations.

The second category of security in processing logins is authorization: checking their designated role membership against that expected for a resource. We saw that the `CFLOGINUSER` tag has a `roles` attribute to track the role for a logged in user, and the `IsUserInRole()` function and the `roles` attribute of `CFFUNCTION` which are used to test the user's role during application processing.

Along the way, you've learned of many subtleties and challenges and are now far ahead of other developers who rely solely on the documentation for learning.

✦ ✦ ✦

ColdFusion Studio and HomeSite+ Tips and Tricks

✦ ✦ ✦ ✦

In This Chapter

Coding faster, easier, and better

Using combinations of IDE configuration techniques

✦ ✦ ✦ ✦

You're probably wondering why we're covering ColdFusion Studio 5/HomeSite+ in this chapter rather than Dreamweaver MX. Although Dreamweaver MX is an amazing product — we use it ourselves for visual Web-page layout — most diehard ColdFusion developers that we know still write code in ColdFusion Studio because Studio gives you more control over the documents you create. We're probably going to use it far into the future because there is simply nothing better on the market right now.

So we're going to cover our favorite tips and tricks for ColdFusion Studio 5. If you follow along and combine all the little (and not so little) techniques that we show you here, you can write better code faster and with less effort. It may be the only time in your life that you get to enjoy all three points of the Golden Triangle (Good-Fast-Cheap) at the same time, so don't pass up this opportunity.

Macromedia has replaced ColdFusion Studio 5 with a product named HomeSite+, which is a direct replacement for Studio. The tips and tricks in this chapter also apply to HomeSite+.

Updating ColdFusion Studio for MX

If you use ColdFusion Studio instead of HomeSite+ (which comes only with Dreamweaver MX), you should update it with the new MX tag definitions. At the time of this book's printing, the updater can be downloaded from the following Web address:

```
http://www.macromedia.com/software/coldfusionstudio/
productinfo/resources/tag_updaters/
```

Tricks for Faster Coding

The following sections describe the habits that we've fallen into over the years, and they've served us well.

F5 yellow comments

Mike Nimer from (then) Allaire showed us F5 yellow comments at a ColdFusion User Group meeting back in ColdFusion Version 3 days. He said that we wouldn't believe him, but if we did this one trick, we would start writing twice as many comments in our code and we could actually read them afterward. The default comment display format was light-gray italic type, and you needed to hand-code comments, so nobody commented their code.

We didn't believe him (nobody did), but he was actually understating things. We comment *all* our code as a matter of habit now, and our development efforts have benefited as a result. Give it a try! Just follow these steps:

1. Choose Options ⇨ Settings from the ColdFusion Studio menu bar.
2. Expand the Editor node in the tree on the left-hand side of the Settings dialog box and choose the Color Coding node underneath the node you just expanded.
3. Select either HTML or HTML Full Tag in the list of color coding schemes, depending on which one has extensions attached, and click the Edit Scheme button.
4. Select Comments in the list box on the left-hand side of the Edit Color Scheme dialog and deselect all five check boxes on the right-hand side.
5. Click the Foreground color swatch; the Color dialog appears. Make the foreground black, then click OK.
6. Click the Background color swatch; the Color dialog appears again. This time, choose the yellow color in the second row of the second column. The RGB values should read `255,255,0`. You should see the equivalent of what's shown in Figure 41-1. Click OK.
7. Click OK in the Edit Color Scheme dialog box, then click Apply in the Settings dialog box to return to ColdFusion Studio.
8. Choose Options ⇨ Customize from the ColdFusion Studio menu bar.
9. Switch to the Keyboard Shortcuts tab in the Customize dialog that appears.
10. Scroll down in the list of commands until you find ColdFusion Comment and select it from the list.
11. Click the keyboard shortcut field and press the F5 key. Click Apply and then click Close.

Now go to a blank window, press your F5 key (this begins your comment for you), and just start typing (notice that the comment has a yellow background and black text). Cool, huh?

Customized tag editors

Tag editors in ColdFusion Studio enable you to write your code more quickly by filling in dialog boxes rather than manually typing in tag names, attribute names, and other easily misspelled code. Unfortunately, most developers we've spoken with have never used their tag editors, and some didn't even know they existed. We started using them in daily development to ensure that we didn't miss (or misspell) an attribute, but after we learned that we could customize the tag editors' behavior, we continued to use them even more to speed our coding.

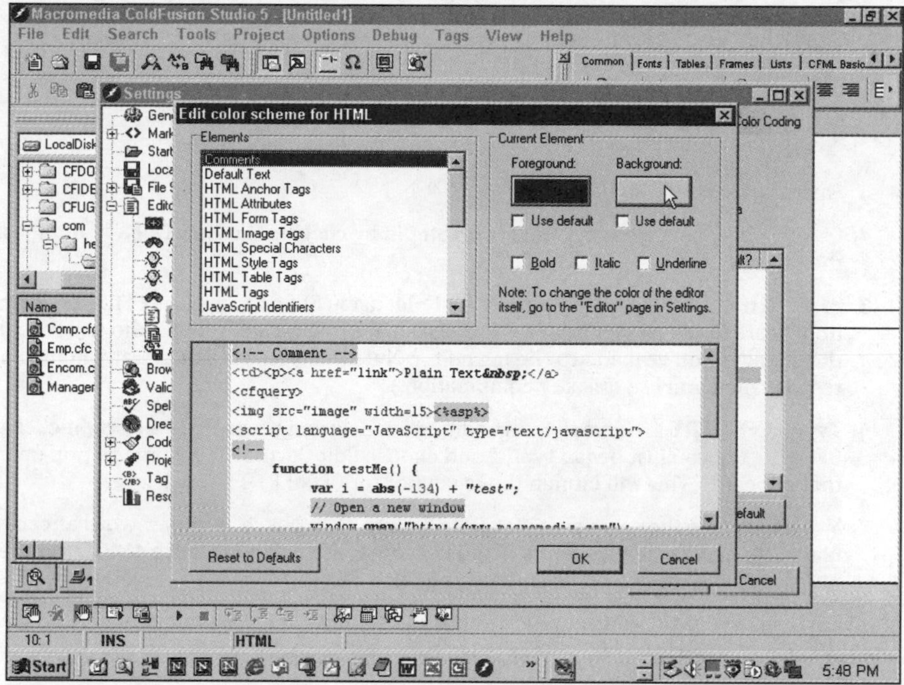

Figure 41-1: Enhancing ColdFusion Studio's color scheme with F5 yellow comments.

You can customize tag editors in many ways, but the most popular involve adding default values to the attributes generated by the editor and modifying a generated tag's multiline indenting format. Everything is controlled through a language called *Virtual Tools Markup Language*, or *VTML* for short. Follow these steps to give it a whirl:

1. For a typical installation, tag editors are located inside `c:\Program Files\Macromedia\ColdFusion Studio 5\Extensions\TagDefs\CFML\`. so go into this directory and open `cfquery.vtm`.

   Note that if you have applied the ColdFusion MX tag updaters, this file may be marked as read-only; unset the read-only flag on this file by right-clicking the file and choosing Properties, unchecking the Read Only check box, then clicking OK, before continuing.

2. Look for the following lines of code:

```
<CONTROL NAME="txtDataSource" TYPE="TextBox" ANCHOR="lblDataSource"
CORNER="NE" WIDTH="160"/>
. . .
<CONTROL NAME="txtUsername" TYPE="TextBox" ANCHOR="lblUsername"
CORNER="NE" WIDTH="MAXIMUM"/>
. . .
<CONTROL NAME="txtPassword" TYPE="TextBox" ANCHOR="lblPassword"
CORNER="NE" WIDTH="MAXIMUM"/>
```

   Change those lines to look as follows:

```
<CONTROL NAME="txtDataSource" TYPE="TextBox" ANCHOR="lblDataSource"
CORNER="NE" WIDTH="160" value="#Request.MainDSN#"/>
```

```
. . .
<CONTROL NAME="txtUsername" TYPE="TextBox" ANCHOR="lblUsername"
CORNER="NE" WIDTH="MAXIMUM" value="#Request.UserName#"/>
. . .
<CONTROL NAME="txtPassword" TYPE="TextBox" ANCHOR="lblPassword"
CORNER="NE" WIDTH="MAXIMUM" value="#Request.Password#"/>
```

3. Save `cfquery.vtm` and close it.
4. Create a new document in ColdFusion Studio by clicking the New Document button on the toolbar.
5. Press Ctrl+Alt+Shift+C anywhere in the ColdFusion Studio interface. (This key combination clears ColdFusion Studio's VTML cache, making it such that Studio will recognize the changes you've made to the tag editor. Note that you will not see any immediate results when you use this key combination.)
6. Type **<CFQUERY** in the main code editing window and press Ctrl-F4 or right-click the `CFQUERY` tag you just began typing and choose Edit Current Tag from the pop-up menu that appears. (This will launch the tag editor for `CFQUERY`.)
7. You should see the new values for Data Source, User Name, and Password already populated in their respective fields in the tag editor, as shown in Figure 41-2. Enter the query name in the Query Name field and click OK.

If you customize your tag editors to automatically supply your most commonly used values, and if you start to use your tag editors religiously, you can code faster and with fewer errors.

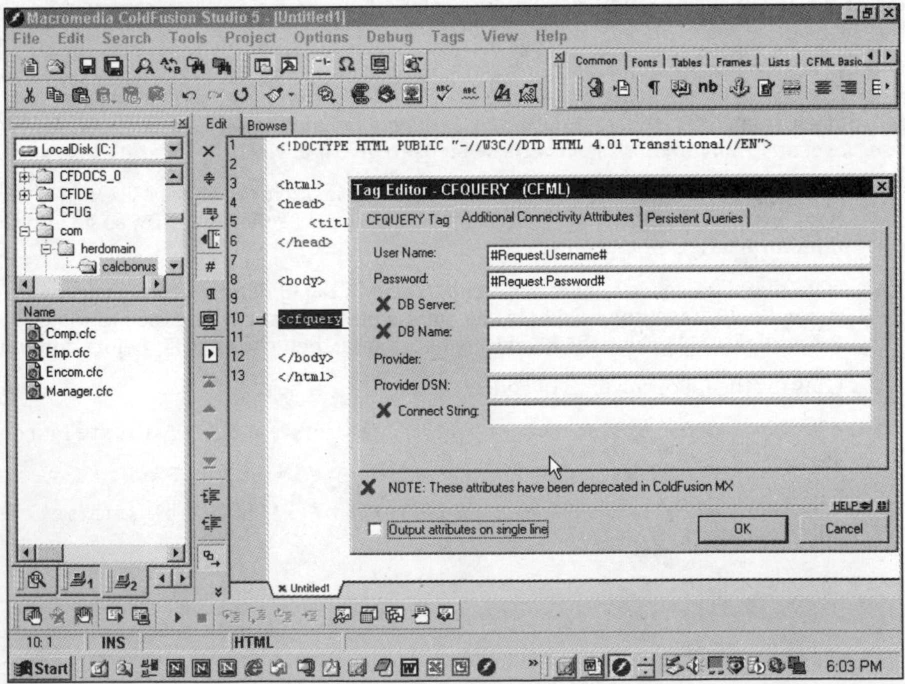

Figure 41-2: Customized CFQUERY Tag Editor with default values.

Default template

Do all your code pages have a common header? If they do, don't tell us that you create the header every time that you create a new page. You can let Studio create the header every time for you by following these steps to create a new default template:

1. Create the page that you want to serve as the new default template by using the New Document button on ColdFusion Studio's toolbar, type the code that will appear in the default template, and save the new document on your local drive.
2. Choose Options ➪ Settings from the ColdFusion Studio menu bar.
3. Select the Locations node in the tree on the left-hand side of the Settings dialog that appears.
4. In the Default Template section of the right-hand side of the Settings dialog, enter the full path and file name of the file that you just created (or use the browse button to choose the file as shown in Figure 41-3), and click OK.
5. After you press Ctrl+N, your new default page should appear in the main code editing window.

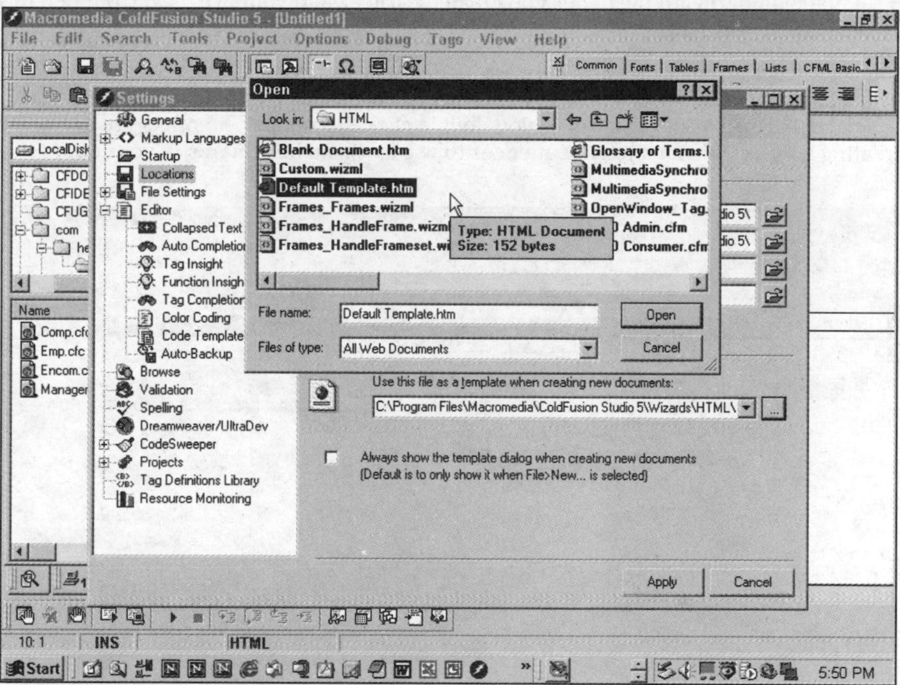

Figure 41-3: Selecting a new default template in ColdFusion Studio.

Snippets

A *snippet* is a named block of code that is split into top and bottom halves so that it can wrap around other code. To create a snippet, follow these steps:

1. Switch to the Snippets tab of the resource pane.

2. If a folder isn't already in the snippets panel, right-click anywhere in the snippets panel and choose Create Folder from the pop-up menu. Give the folder a name.
3. Right-click the folder that now appears in the snippets panel and choose Add Snippet from the pop-up menu. This opens the Snippet dialog.
4. Type a descriptive name for the snippet in the Description field of the Snippet dialog.
5. In the Start Text field of the Snippet dialog, type the complete opening tag to a `CFQUERY` call, as follows:

```
<cfquery name="" datasource="#Request.MainDSN#" . . .>
(blank line)
```

6. In the End Text field, type the following:

```
(blank line)
</cfquery>
```

7. After your Snippet dialog box looks like what's shown in Figure 41-4, click OK.
8. Type an SQL statement into a new document and select the SQL statement you just typed. Double-click the snippet that you just created (it should appear in the snippets panel underneath the folder you created earlier), and your SQL is surrounded by the `CFQUERY` tag pair.

You can create a snippet for any purpose, and you don't need to create a split snippet that wraps around code; you can just fill in the Start Text or End Text field, and the snippet appears wherever your cursor is as you double-click the snippet. Snippets are useful for creating large visible character sequences to use as visual bookmarks in your code.

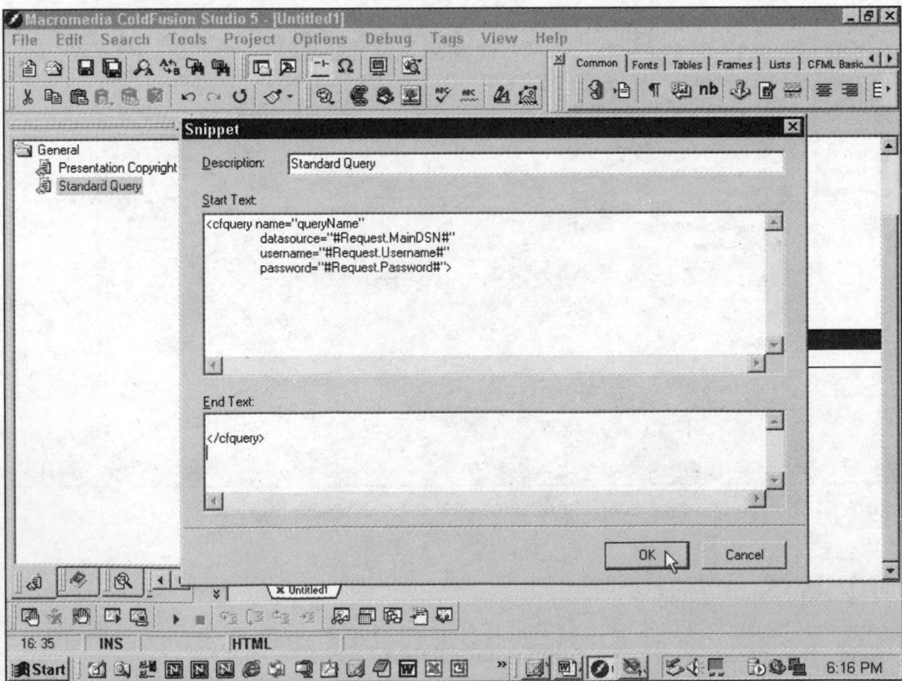

Figure 41-4: Creating a code snippet in the Snippet dialog box.

If you don't want your snippet code to butt against your selected code when you insert the snippet into your code, make sure that you end your top half and start your bottom half with blank lines. If you do want your snippet to wrap right up to the very start and end of your selected code, omit the blank lines.

Snippet shortcuts

Snippets are fast, but they're even faster if you assign shortcuts to them by following these steps:

1. Choose Options ⇨ Customize from the ColdFusion Studio menu bar; this opens the Customize dialog box.
2. Switch to the Snippet Shortcuts tab, as shown in Figure 41-5.
3. Select a snippet from the tree of snippets and assign it a keyboard shortcut by typing the shortcut into the field below the tree of snippets.
4. Click OK. Now if you use the keyboard shortcut that you just assigned, the snippet is inserted into your document at the insertion point or wraps around selected code.

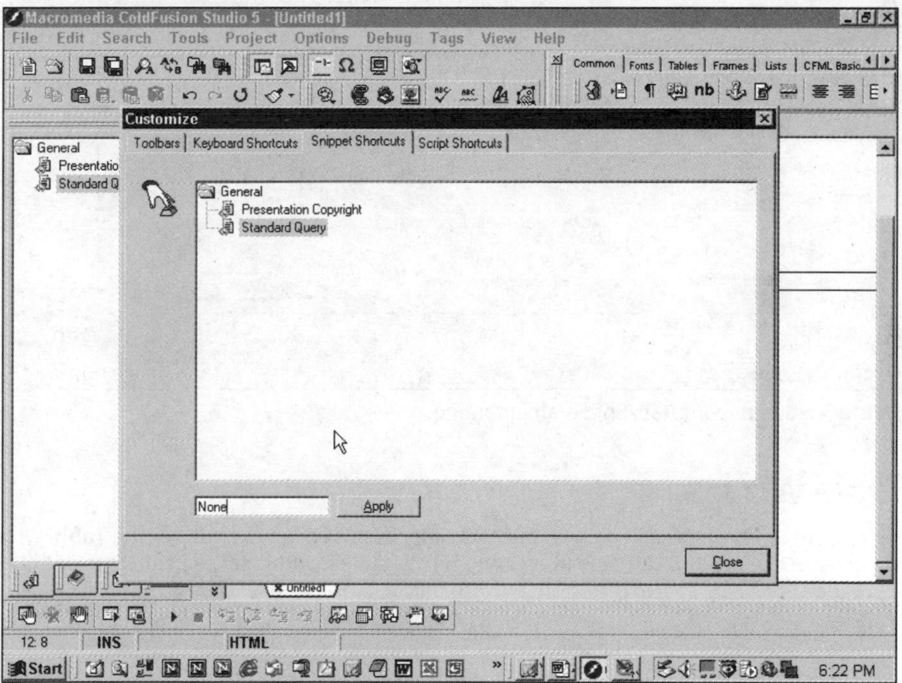

Figure 41-5: Assigning a shortcut to a snippet.

Tab/Shift+Tab indenting

If you've been programming in other languages, you've probably gotten used to indenting and outdenting your code by selecting an entire block and pressing either Tab to indent or Shift+Tab to outdent. ColdFusion studio finally added this capability in Version 4.5, but you must enable it by following these steps:

1. Choose Options ➪ Settings from the ColdFusion Studio menu bar to open the Settings dialog box.
2. Select the Editor node in the tree on the left.
3. Scroll to the bottom of the Options checklist and select the Tab/Shift+Tab Performs Block Indent/Unindent check box, as shown in Figure 41-6.
4. Click Apply.

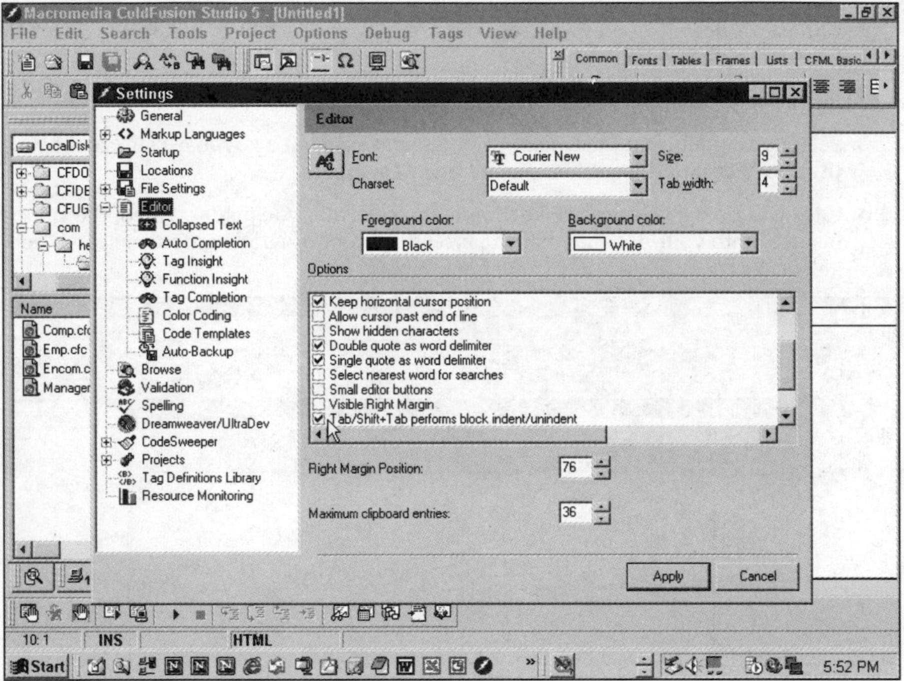

Figure 41-6: Enabling Tab/Shift+Tab indenting.

Table Wizard

We're constantly surprised by how many developers have never heard of the Table Wizard! We use it 99 percent of the time in creating HTML tables, and it saves us dozens of hours of lost labor per year. To use the Table Wizard, follow these steps:

1. Click the Tables tab of your QuickBar.
2. Click the Table Wizard icon in the QuickBar to launch the Table Wizard. (It's usually on the far left of the tab.)
3. Lay out the rows and columns of your table and their spans by using the + and – buttons in the Table Design area of the Table Wizard, as shown in Figure 41-7. Click the Next button when you have partitioned the table cells how you want.
4. Specify your table-formatting properties, then click Next.

5. Fill out cell content by clicking individual cells and filling in the form at the bottom of the last page of the wizard.

6. Click Finish.

Now you can just drag-and-drop content into your preformatted table cells. You can create nested tables by placing your cursor in a table cell and running the Table Wizard again. Using the Table Wizard saves you tons of time, as you never need to debug broken table markup.

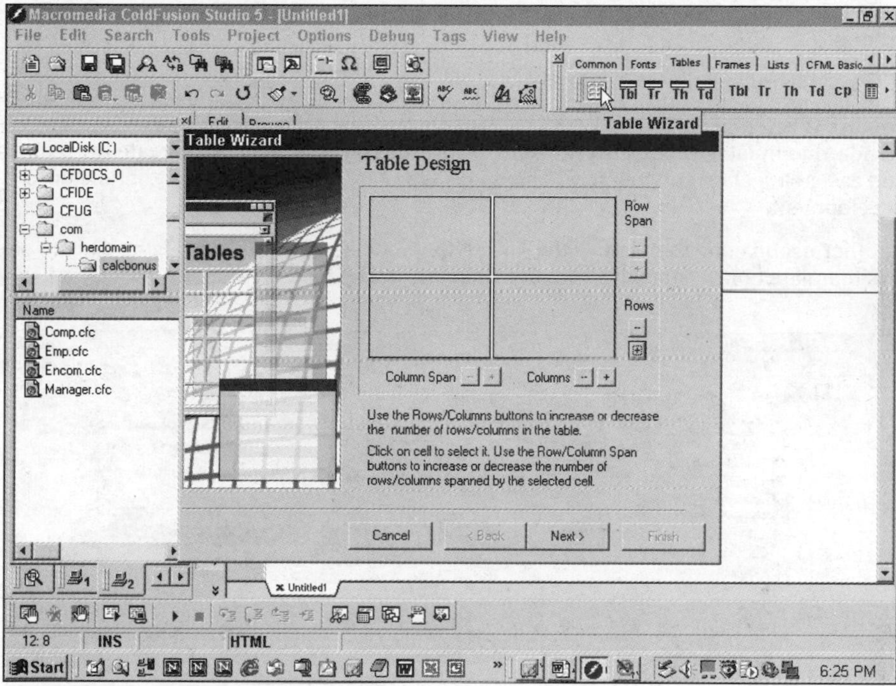

Figure 41-7: Using the Table Wizard.

Code templates

Remember the F5 yellow comments trick from the section of that name, earlier in this chapter? It's cool enough that you can create readable yellow comments with a single keystroke, but the really cool part is preplacing your cursor exactly where you want to start typing. You can create your own versions of this trick by using *code templates*; just follow these steps:

1. Choose Options ⇨ Settings from the ColdFusion Studio menu bar to launch the Settings dialog.

2. Expand the Editor node in the tree on the left-hand side of the Settings dialog box and choose the Code Templates node underneath the node you just expanded.

3. Click the Add button; this launches the Add Code Template dialog.

4. In the Keyword field, enter **a**, and enter **Author Line** in the Description field. In the Value field, type the following:

```
<!--- Author: | --->
```

Notice the placement of the pipe character |. This is where your cursor is positioned immediately after invoking this code template.

5. Click OK, then click Apply.
6. Type **a** in a new document.
7. Press Ctrl+J, and the keyword is expanded into the full author comment template you just created.

An even more useful code template is one that creates a `CFOUTPUT` tag and pound signs, as follows:

```
<cfoutput>#|#</cfoutput>
```

You use this template by typing O+Ctrl+J. (Note that the preceding template is not one of the standard templates provided with ColdFusion Studio; you will need to create the template and assign it a shortcut yourself.) This single template has saved us a lot of time during development.

Another useful code template—the JavaScript block—is as shown in Figure 41-8. (Note that this template comes standard with ColdFusion Studio.)

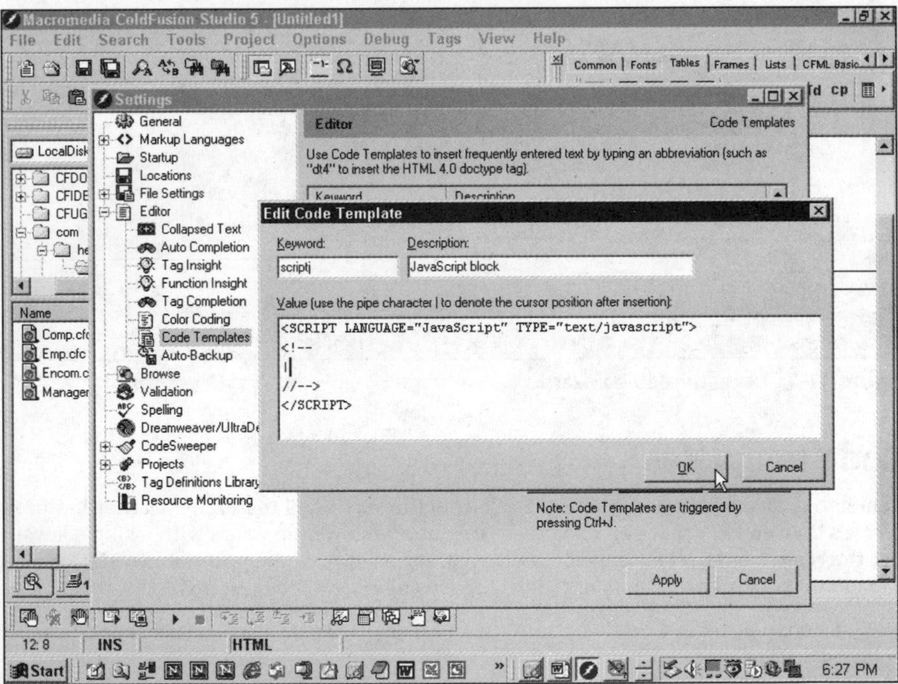

Figure 41-8: Creating code templates.

Keyboard shortcuts

Tired of reaching for a menu command? Afraid of mice? Use a keyboard shortcut instead by following these steps:

1. Choose Options ⇨ Customize from the ColdFusion Studio menu bar to open the Customize dialog box.
2. Switch to the Keyboard Shortcuts tab.
3. Select from the list that appears the command with the keyboard shortcut that you want to change or assign, as shown in Figure 41-9.
4. In the field below the main list box, type the keyboard shortcut that you want to associate with this command and click Apply.
5. Click Close.

Click somewhere in your document and press the key sequence for your shortcut to appear.

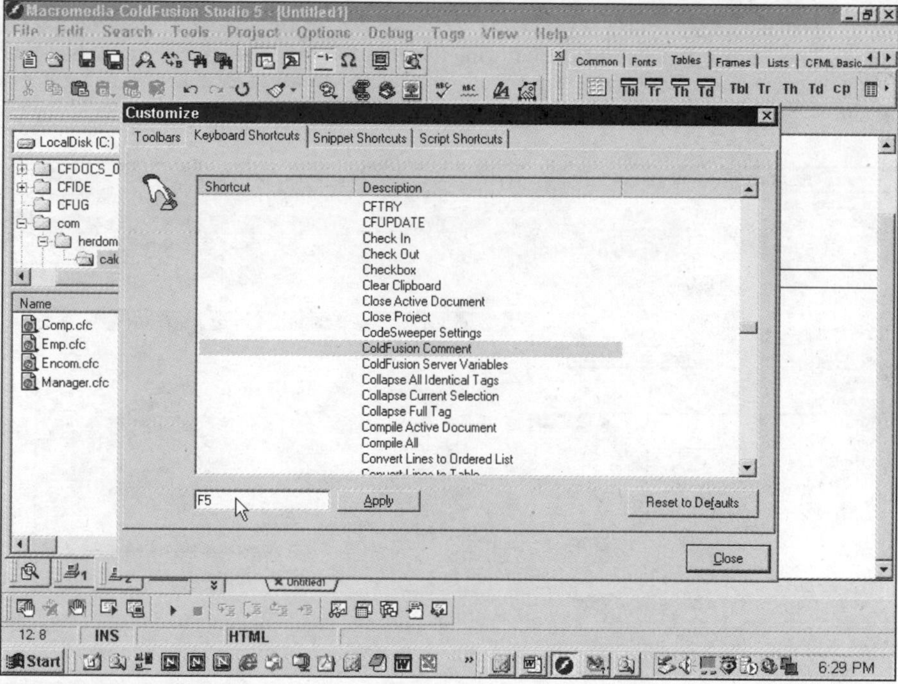

Figure 41-9: Assigning keyboard shortcuts.

Custom toolbars

Do you have a particular set of snippets, tricks, commands, and so on that you constantly use but must click-click-click just to get to them? You can create a single custom toolbar to contain most of what you need by following these steps:

1. Choose Options ⇨ Customize from the ColdFusion Studio menu bar to open the Customize dialog.

2. To add or delete a toolbar or toolbar button, take the following actions:
   - To add a custom toolbar, click the Add Toolbar button on the right-hand side of the Customize dialog. The Add Toolbar dialog appears, prompting you for the name of the new toolbar. After entering the name of the new toolbar, click OK, then make sure that the new toolbar has a check mark beside it in the Visible Toolbars list on the bottom right-hand side of the Customize dialog.
   - To delete a toolbar, click the Delete Toolbar button on the right-hand side of the Customize dialog.
   - To add a toolbar button, click the Add Custom Button in the center of the Customize dialog and specify the button's action in the Custom Toolbutton dialog box that appears, as shown in Figure 41-10. Click OK when you're finished configuring the new toolbar button.
   - To remove a toolbar button, click the toolbar button in the Customize dialog and drag the button off the toolbar.
3. Click Close on the Customize dialog when you are finished customizing your toolbars.

These instructions are rather abbreviated because you can do so many things with a custom toolbar. The details presented to you during the creation process are easy to understand after you know how to approach the general process of creating toolbars by using the preceding simple steps.

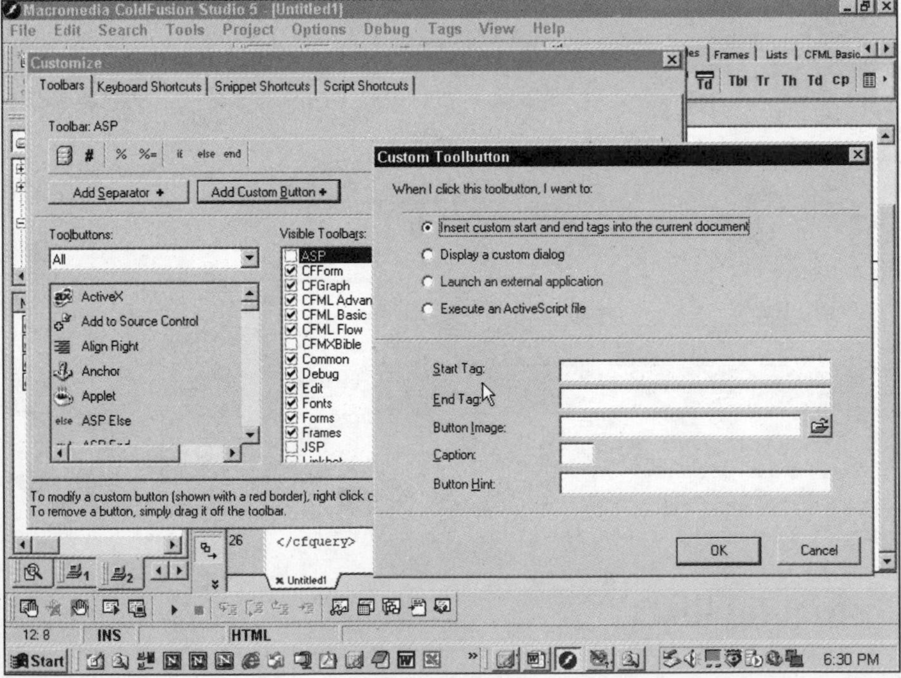

Figure 41-10: Using the Custom Toolbutton dialog box to add a button to a custom toolbar.

Outlining the current line of code

Lose your place in your code? Can't find your cursor? Making ColdFusion Studio add a black border around the current line of code can help; just follow these steps:

1. Choose Options ➪ Settings from the CF Studio menu bar to launch the Settings dialog.
2. Select the Editor node in the tree on the left-hand side of the Settings dialog.
3. Select Outline Current Line; it should be near the top of the scrolling checklist.
4. Click Apply.

Now, whenever you code, your current line of code is bordered in black.

Tag completion customization

Suppose that you upgrade to the new ColdFusion MX tag editors and tag definitions, but you find that you still must manually type that `</cffunction>` closing tag every time. Fear not! You can customize how CF Studio completes tags by following these steps:

1. Choose Options ➪ Settings from the ColdFusion Studio menu bar to launch the Settings dialog box.
2. Expand the Editor node in the tree on the left-hand side of the Settings dialog box and choose the Color Coding node underneath the node you just expanded.
3. Click the Add button in the Settings dialog box to add a new tag to the list of tags to be automatically completed, as shown in Figure 41-11. Type **CFFUNCTION** in the dialog box and click OK.

Now type `<CFFUNCTION>` in a new document, and you see the closing tag automatically appear after the opening tag you just typed.

Development mappings

How many hours a year do you waste by editing code in Studio, switching to a browser, typing the URL and pressing Enter, switching back to Studio, and so on? Development Mappings let you use ColdFusion Studio's internal browser to test the code you write; just follow these steps:

1. Choose Debug ➪ Development Mappings from the ColdFusion Studio menu bar to launch the Development Mappings window.
2. Select the RDS server for which you want to create a mapping from the RDS Server drop-down list.
3. Click the Add button to launch the Add RDS Server Mapping dialog and enter the path information according to the on-screen instructions.
4. Click OK on both dialogs and go back to editing your code.

After you finish editing your code and you think that it should work, just click the Browse tab above the main editing window (and probably the green Refresh double-arrow button in the Browse tab), and you see the effects of your code, as if you were in a browser embedded directly into CF Studio. This trick saves you a lot of time.

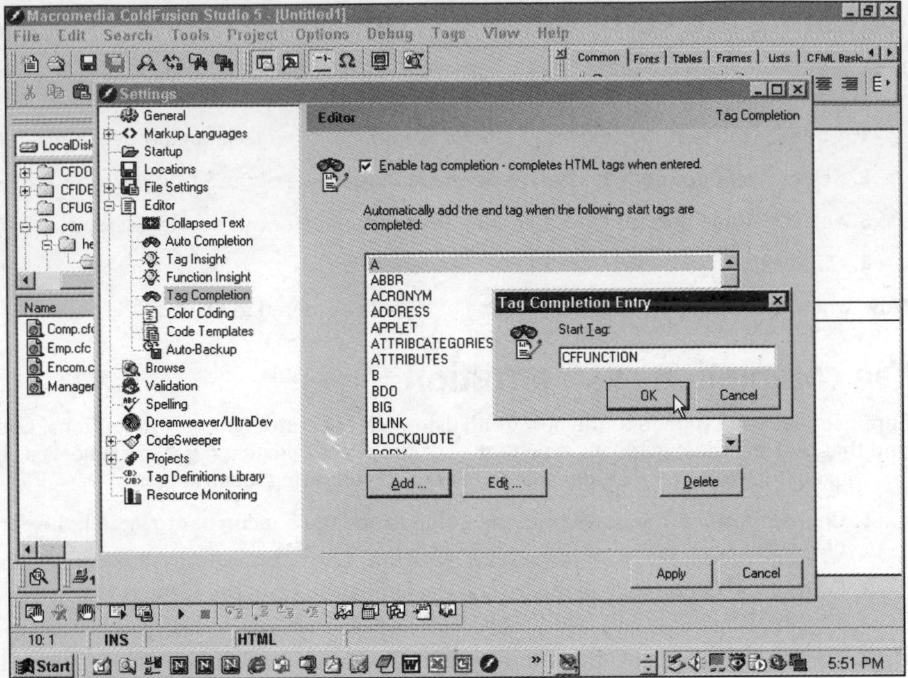

Figure 41-11: Adding a tag to Studio's automatic tag completion.

Split document window

So, that tight little page of code ballooned worse than Bubba at a church picnic, and now you're trying to make the top half of your 457 lines of code work with the bottom half, but you're tired of scrolling. Well, you can look at both parts at the same time by telling ColdFusion to split the document window. How? Just follow these steps:

1. Choose Options ➪ Split Current Document from the ColdFusion menu bar to split the window.
2. Choose Options ➪ Split Current Document from the menu bar again to remove the split.

Bookmarks

Still working in the big stack of code, and you're concentrating on three specific areas of your code that you want to quickly dash to as needed? You can't use Go To Line Number because you're still editing your code, and the line numbers constantly change? What's the solution? Try setting a *bookmark* by following these steps:

1. To set or remove a bookmark, click anywhere on the line of code that you want to bookmark and choose Edit ➪ Toggle Bookmark from the ColdFusion Studio menu bar.
2. To navigate between bookmarks, choose Edit ➪ Go to next Bookmark from the menu bar.

Bookmarks are not saved with your templates; they are only temporary, lasting only while you keep them open in Studio.

Thumbnails

Thumbnails are a nice little feature for working with collections of graphics, because you can preview an image before you place the image in your document. To enable thumbnails, follow these steps:

1. Open a document in a directory containing image files and click the Thumbnails toolbar button. This will display the Thumbnails panel underneath the main editing window.

2. Click and drag one of the thumbnails from the list of images in the Thumbnails panel onto the page where you want it to go.

Make sure that you save the page before you drag the image onto it. CF Studio needs to know where the template is on disk so that it can calculate a path to the graphic.

Tricks for Easier Coding

Sure, easier coding is also faster coding, but the tricks in the following sections are more focused on making things easier.

You may find that some of these tricks are better handled in other ways. We don't use the Query Builder anymore, for example, because we don't need its assistance in building complicated SQL, and we want to use a slightly different syntax than Query Builder uses. Many developers, however, find Query Builder a godsend for assisting them in tackling complicated SQL statements.

Query Builder

To build a query by using the Query Builder, follow these steps:

1. Choose Tools ➪ SQL Builder. (The terms SQL Builder and Query Builder are completely synonymous.)

2. Select the RDS server and database and click New Query. This will launch the Query Builder and a dialog containing a list of the tables in the database you selected.

2. Select the table you want to put in your query and click the Select button. If you want to add any additional tables to your query, click the Add Tables toolbar icon in Query Builder and choose the additional tables.

3. All the tables in your query appear as containers with a row for every column in the table. To create a join between two tables, drag the parent table's primary key column to the child table's foreign key column.

4. To make a join an outer join, right-click the join and choose which table will be the outer table from the pop-up menu.

5. Drag the columns that you want in the new query's result set from the tables in the diagram to the column labeled Column in the list of columns below.

6. Select which columns to sort by and in which direction they are to be sorted, as shown in Figure 41-12.

7. Enter the criteria for your `WHERE` clause in the Criteria column in the list of columns below.

8. Click the Close button in the Query Builder toolbar (it looks like a red X); click Yes after you're prompted to save; and give your query a name when you are prompted to do so.

9. After you're prompted whether you want to insert the query into your template, click Yes, and your query appears in your template.

You can also access the `query builder` from within the `CFQUERY` Tag Editor.

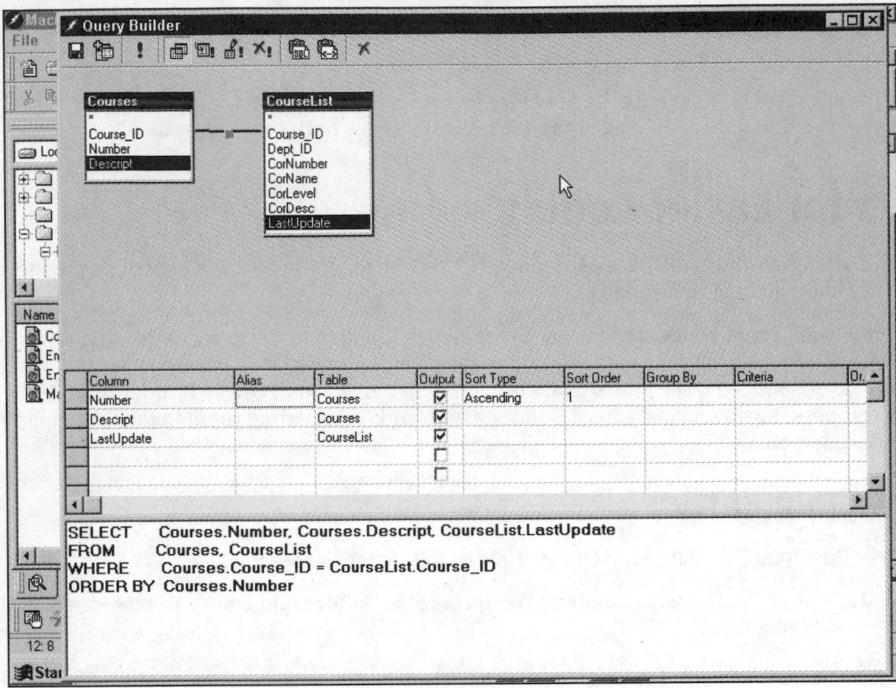

Figure 41-12: Building an inner join by using the Query Builder.

Style Editor

Can't remember all the syntax used by cascading style sheets? No problem—just follow these steps to use the CF Studio Style Editor:

1. Right-click *between* opening and closing `<style>` tags and choose Edit Style Block from the pop-up menu that appears.

2. Use the controls in the Style Editor to create the style definitions that you want. To add a selector, for example, click the Selector icon to the right of the Cancel button in the toolbar and then either create your selector using the New Selector window, as shown in Figure 41-13, and click OK.

3. After you finish editing the block, click Done in the Style Editor window (which closes the Style Editor) and then save your template in ColdFusion Studio.

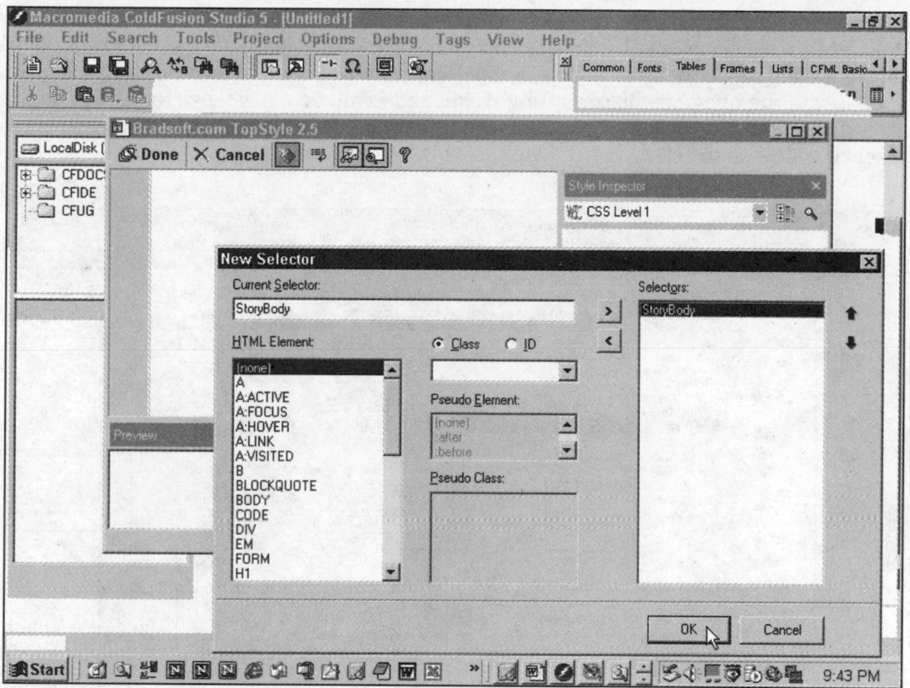

Figure 41-13: Creating a new selector in the Style Editor.

Color coding

For some developers, F5 yellow comments are only the beginning. We've seen some pretty outrageous uses of custom color coding in CF Studio, but many of them are clear and easy to focus on the code at hand. Stay away from bright or garish colors, and use highly visible colors (such as the yellow that we use for comment backgrounds) only sparingly, where your attention is truly needed. To edit ColdFusion Studio's color coding schemes, follow these steps:

1. Choose Options ⇨ Settings from the CF Studio menu bar to open the Settings dialog.
2. Expand the Editor node in the tree on the left-hand side of the Settings dialog box and choose the Color Coding node underneath the node you just expanded.
3. Select the color scheme of the language that you want to change and click the Edit button, which launches the Edit Color Scheme dialog.
4. Select the language element that you want to colorize in the list box on the left-hand side of the Edit Color Scheme dialog, as shown in Figure 41-14.
5. Click on either the Foreground or Background color swatches and select the new color from the palette, and then click OK.
6. Click OK again to exit the Settings Dialog.

Just do yourself a favor: Don't make your code look like an over-decorated Christmas tree! Make your code crisp but plain; make comments draw attention; and use different colors for different elements only if you have a compelling reason to do so. Form tags, for example, are often lost in the quagmire of formatting HTML and CFML on a page, but form tags really should stick out, because they are absolutely central to an application's functionality, so they deserve a little contrast.

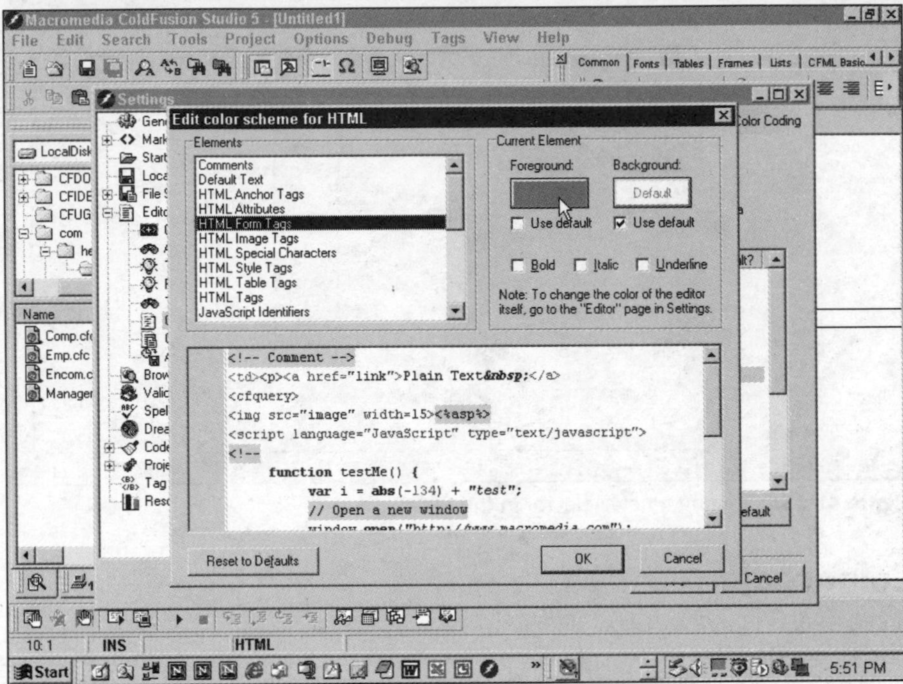

Figure 41-14: Editing ColdFusion's color-coding scheme.

Image Map Builder

No one in his right mind codes image maps by hand. To make the process of slicing an image up into hotspots and target areas, try the Image Map Builder built into CF Studio by following these steps:

1. Insert an image into your document in ColdFusion Studio. (You should be familiar with using images in ColdFusion Studio and with image maps in general before you attempt to use the Image Map Builder.)
2. Either choose Tools ➪ New Image Map from the CF Studio menu bar or right-click an existing `AREA` tag and choose Edit Image Map from the pop-up menu.
3. Select the image in the dialog that appears and type the name of the map you wish to insert, if you're prompted for a name.
4. Draw hotspots on the map by using the Rectangle, Circle, or Polygon tools.
5. After you draw an area, the `AREA` tag editor appears; use the editor to assign the area a hyperlink, as shown in Figure 41-15. Click OK when you're finished.

6. To edit the default hyperlink (this is where the map will take the user if he clicks on an area that's not a hotspot), choose Options ➪ Edit Default Area from the Image Map Editor menu bar.

7. Choose File ➪ Save and then File ➪ Exit in the Image Map Editor's menu bar to return to ColdFusion Studio, and the `MAP` and `AREA` tags appear in your document.

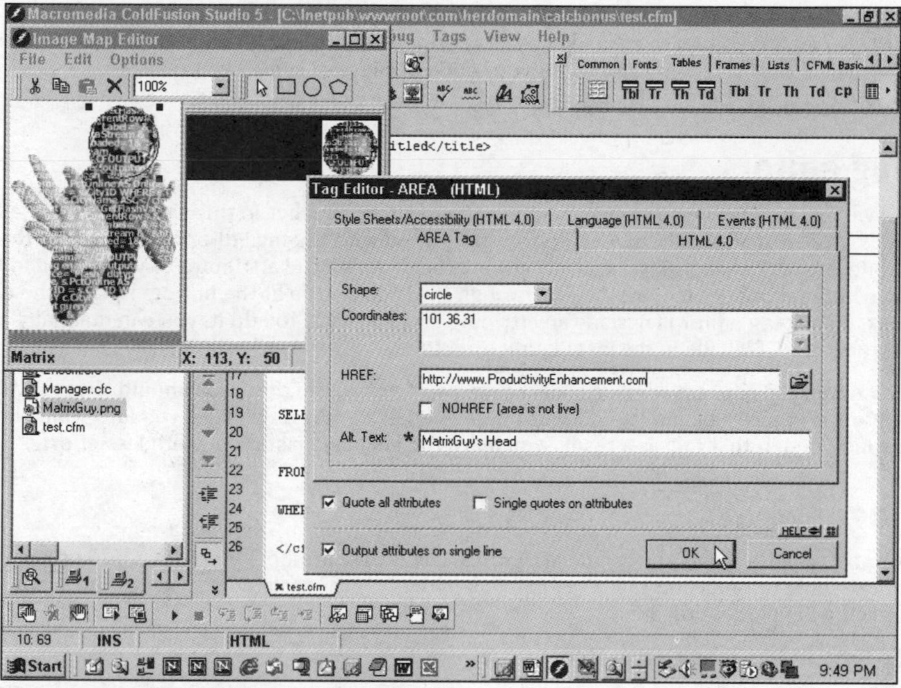

Figure 41-15: Using the Image Map Editor.

Right-clicking a code selection

We came on this trick just playing around one day. (We don't get out much.) If you select a block of content in CF Studio's main editing window and right-click it, you get a pop-up Selection submenu containing the following commands:

- ✦ Convert Lines to Ordered List
- ✦ Convert Lines to Unordered List
- ✦ Convert Lines to Table
- ✦ Add Line Breaks `<br>`
- ✦ Strip Tags
- ✦ Strip Outermost Tags
- ✦ Convert to Uppercase
- ✦ Convert to Lowercase

These commands are great for working with HTML and text pasted from other sources. We can't tell you how many times we've used the Strip Tags and Convert Lines to Ordered List commands to instantly create a numbered list out of text imported from somewhere.

Tips for Better Coding

Better coding is error-free coding, and that's the focus of this section. You may feel uncomfortable at first using assistants such as tag editors and the Expression Builder, but if you find yourself doing "ready-fire-aim!" with your code because of syntax errors, you should seriously consider trying these tools that we describe in the following sections.

Tag editors

As we mention in the section "Customized tag editors," earlier in this chapter, if you right-click a CF tag (or press Ctrl+F4), you are presented with the tag editor dialog box for that tag, if one exists. These editors typically contain fields for all the attributes of your tag, and they also contain online Help for the tag through the Help button at the bottom right of the dialog box. If your tag editor is missing an attribute and you want to add it, you can manually add it to the tag's VTML file in the installation directory.

Tag editors produce error-free code, so we use them all the time. You should always use tag editors if you're a beginning ColdFusion developer, as the editor clues you into what should be included in that tag; as a result, you learn the language faster and with less effort.

Tag Insight

As you type ColdFusion tags and attributes, *Tag Insight* prompts you with a pop-up menu of chooseable options and can be a great "fill-in-the-blanks" assistant, no matter how experienced a developer you are.

To turn on Tag Insight, follow these steps:

1. Choose Options ➪ Settings from the ColdFusion Studio menu bar to open the Settings dialog box.
2. Expand the Editor node in the tree on the left-hand side of the Settings dialog box and choose the Tag Insight node underneath the node you just expanded.
3. Select the Enable Tag Insight check box, as shown in Figure 41-16.
4. Click Apply.

Now click anywhere in a new document and type **<cfquery** plus a space; then wait a second. You get a pop-up menu with a selection of attributes from which to choose. Choose one, press your right-arrow key to move past any enclosing quotation marks, and press your spacebar again to open tag insight again.

We use this assistant to this day, mainly because we can configure how long a delay we want between pressing our spacebar and displaying tag insight. Just decrease the delay as you get faster coding, and tag insight adapts to your speed.

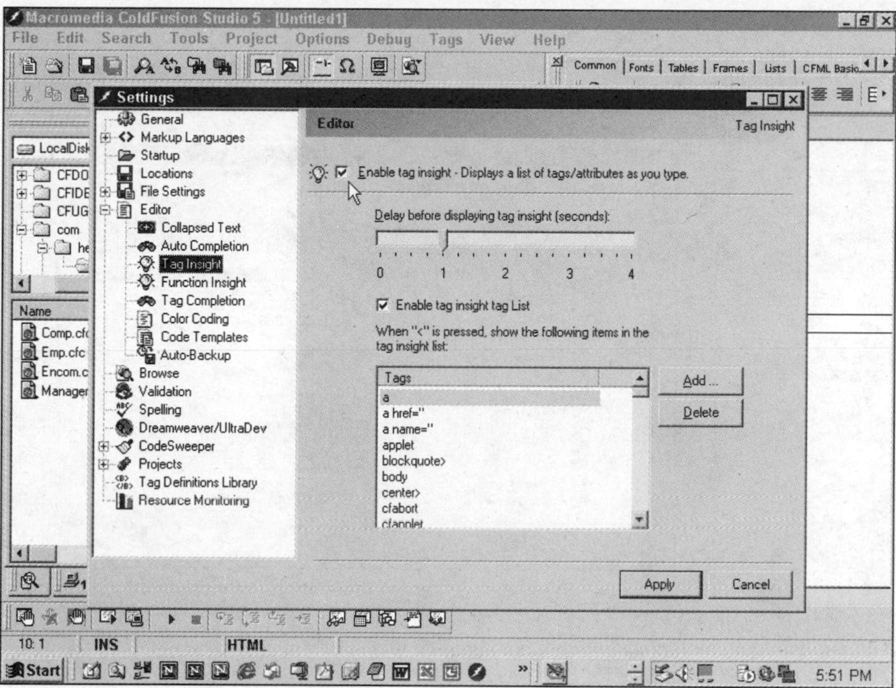

Figure 41-16: Configuring Tag Insight.

Expression Builder

The expression Builder is like a tag editor for a function. If we forget the syntax for a function, we don't look it up in online Help or the printed documentation; we invoke the Expression Builder — and you can, too, by following these steps:

1. Choose Tools ⇨ Insert Expression from the ColdFusion Studio menu bar, which launches the Expression Builder dialog.
2. To add a function to the expression, locate the category where it belongs in the category tree and double-click the function name in the list of functions on the right-hand side of the Expression Builder dialog to make the function appear in the field at the top of the Expression Builder where you assemble the expression.
3. Select the argument placeholders in the field at the top of the Expression Builder and replace the placeholders with actual values, as shown in Figure 41-17.
4. To add an operator to the expression, click one of the operator buttons at the top of the Expression Builder dialog box.
5. Click Finish to place the finished expression in your ColdFusion page.

You can build an expression containing a single function or a complicated calculation involving many functions.

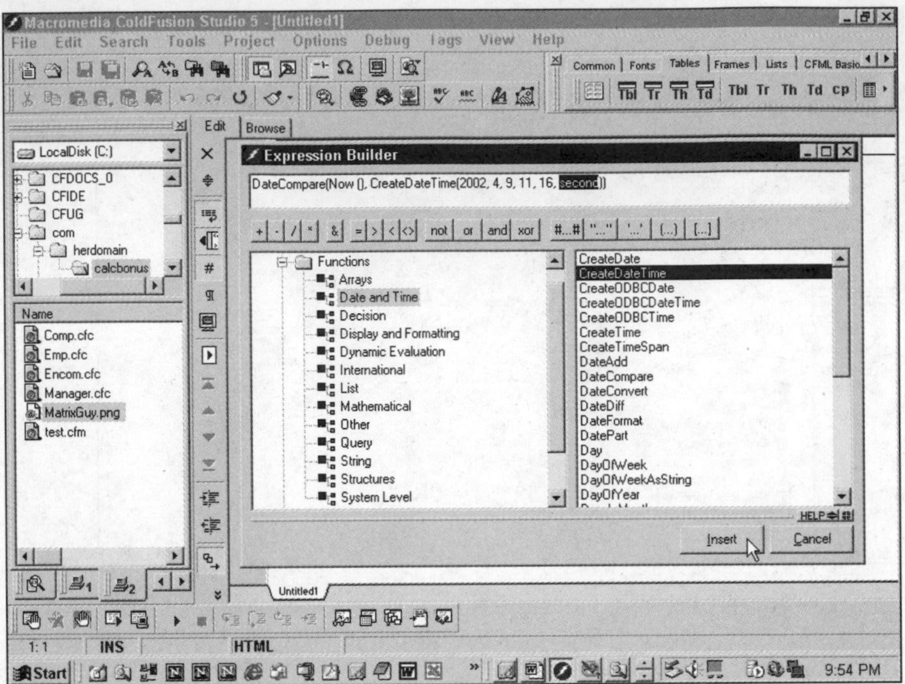

Figure 41-17: Using the Expression Builder to add a call to DateCompare() to our code.

Function Insight

Function Insight works exactly the same as tag insight. To enable Function Insight, follow these steps:

1. Choose Options ⇨ Settings from the CF Studio menu bar to launch the Settings dialog box.
2. Expand the Editor node in the tree on the left-hand side of the Settings dialog box and choose the Function Insight node underneath the node you just expanded.
3. Select the Enable Function Insight check box, as shown in Figure 41-18.
4. Click Apply.

Click anywhere in a new document, type the name of a function plus the open parenthesis, and wait a second. You get a pop-up menu with a selection of argument forms from which to choose. Choose one, press Enter, and then replace the argument placeholders with actual values.

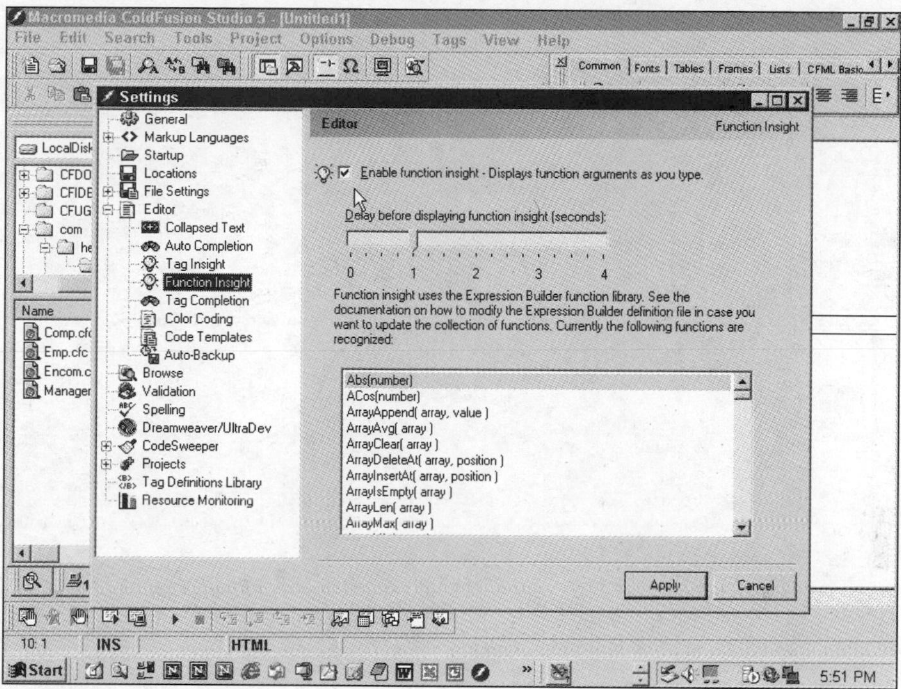

Figure 41-18: Configuring Function Insight.

Summary

The tips and tricks in this chapter are not secrets. They've been right in front of you the whole time, but until you see them all working together, these tricks seem to be little ways to waste a lot of time.

Only if you use these tricks *together* do you realize the true increase in coding speed and quality that we claim you can enjoy, so take an hour to set everything up as we've shown you, take a second hour to get your feet wet with these new techniques, and then take a third hour to add more comprehensive snippets, default templates, code templates, and customized tag editors. The three hours that you spend reworking your workspace pay you off with faster production of high-quality, readable code from now on.

✦ ✦ ✦

CHAPTER 42

Testing and Performance

In This Chapter

Testing Web applications

Measuring performance

Performance tuning

Learning more about testing and performance

Preceding chapters of this book have taken you a long way in covering the many realms and aspects of ColdFusion development. Indeed, the fact that ColdFusion is an incredibly easy, yet rich development platform should be clear to you by now.

Some have argued that this is the product's Achilles' Heel. Because it's so simple and easy to learn and because they can create applications so quickly, many developers may also ignore certain aspects of quality assurance for the application.

In this chapter, we send you on your way with a series of insights that can help make your applications run as effectively as possible. This chapter, however, is about more than just raw performance tuning and testing. Indeed, that's only one part of what we cover in this chapter.

Many developers often ignore several aspects of Web-application testing — all to their own peril. Running an application yourself to confirm that it's ready for production is not enough. We introduce you to several forms of testing, ranging from those that confirm the quality of your HTML (simple but important) to those that confirm the quality of your CFML code and those that check the overall interactions of all parts of your application.

In addition to knowing what tests you can perform, discovering which programs can benefit from testing and improving may also prove helpful. How can you measure quality and performance in your application and the ColdFusion server? We show you several forms of measurement to use.

Probably the most important aspect of measuring your application involves its performance. An application that works well with a few visitors can bog down with only a few more. And what if you need to support thousands of users? CF can certainly handle the load, but success is often more about the choices you make as a developer or administrator.

You can do many things to increase the performance of your application, and only some of them relate to your CFML code. A host of other aspects concern how you develop and deploy your application, including SQL coding, database design, administration configuration settings, and more.

This chapter can scratch only the surface of most of these topics, so it concludes by pointing out resources for further learning.

Web-Application Testing

Preceding chapters of this book give you all the skills that you need to create a ColdFusion Web application. But are you sure that you're ready to crank out production code? Indeed, are you sure that your code is production ready? How do you think that it may perform — not only in terms of raw numbers of transactions per second, but also in simpler ways, such as how it works for customers.

You can't simply trust that, because the application runs okay for you, it works just fine for everyone. Potential browser issues may crop up as a result of HTML choices that you've made, the application's use of JavaScript, accessibility and usability issues, and much more. You may even discover problems in the CFML coding choices that you've made. (Remembering all the best coding practices can often prove difficult.)

Add to those problems unanticipated errors in such areas as the database and the server on which you're hosting the application or unexpected load increases, and you can quickly see that you need to work a little harder to make sure that the code really runs well in production.

Whether you're a lone code-slinger or part of a large team, you need to know about testing. Many CF developers, however, are not aware of the options that may already be available to them without cost or much effort. In the following sections, we organize such options into the following three categories:

✦ HTML-oriented testing

✦ CFML code testing

✦ Application integration testing

We're not talking about performance tuning yet, covering that instead in the latter half of this chapter. Despite assumptions of many, there's more to web application testing than just performance.

HTML-oriented testing

Did you know that you can perform at least 13 different kinds of tests against the HTML produced by your ColdFusion applications, ranging from HTML syntax validation to link checking, to testing cookie support and JavaScript error detection? CF developers who don't recognize the importance of these kinds of tests often dismiss them. Indeed, although you may be tempted to skip this section and proceed to the section "CFML Code Testing," later in this chapter, taking a few minutes to become familiar with the possibilities is well worth your time.

We'll cover the following in this section:

HTML validation

Cascading Style Sheet validation

JavaScript validation

Link checking

Spell-checking

Document weight (download time) testing

Browser-size testing

Accessibility testing

Testing for disabled JavaScript

Testing for disabled cookie support

Testing for JavaScript errors

Testing for browser caching issues

Search-engine compatibility and site-link popularity

Before looking into each of those, you should understand the difference between tools that run on your workstation (what I call "local testing tools") and tools that are web-based tools where an external resource performs evaluation of your program. Each has its place in your toolkit, and you may be surprised to learn what's available. First, let's discuss some differences between local and web-based testing tools.

Local testing tools

Several tools are available to aid with testing from your workstation, and many of them are free. Indeed, editors like Macromedia's Dreamweaver MX, ColdFusion Studio, and HomeSite+ all include features to perform such validation and testing.

A problem arises, however, in using editors such as these to perform HTML-oriented testing. Their testing tools are designed for performing tests against HTML source files. But in Web applications created by using ColdFusion, for instance, the source file is a combination of CFML and HTML, so that can confuse the testing tools, reporting errors that may not exist—or failing to catch errors that may exist—only when the file is executed from a browser.

Indeed, the important HTML to be tested is that which is shown to the user who is browsing the page. Such HTML is often generated dynamically, and therefore, it is the output of your application that must be tested, rather than the source. The testing features in editors don't typically process the output of your pages. This doesn't means such editors are not useful—just challenging.

Note

How could you test the output of your page in an editor like those mentioned? One solution is to use the web-based tools discussed in the next section. But it is possible to apply local testing tools and editors to the output of your dynamic pages.

Simply run a page to be tested in your browser and view its HTML source code (by choosing View ⇨ Source from the menu bar in Internet Explorer and View ⇨ Page Source in Netscape). Copy that HTML into the clipboard (by using Ctrl+A to select all, and Ctrl+C to copy it to the clipboard). Open a new blank page in the editor and then paste the copied HTML into the editor (by pressing Ctrl+V). Now you can run the editor's testing tools, as discussed in the remainder of this section. Dreamweaver MX requires that you save such a file first before testing it, however, which can complicate matters sometimes.

In this first half of the chapter, we'll show examples of using Dreamweaver MX, which is Macromedia's now-preferred editor for web application developers. A trial edition has been included on the CD accompanying this book.

Because many developers may still be using the older ColdFusion Studio and HomeSite products, or the HomeSite+ product included on the Dreamweaver CD, I'll also provide instructions for using the features where they exist in those tools as well.

Note

HomeSite+ can be found on the CD you receive when you purchase Dreamweaver from Macromedia. It's not installed automatically, nor is it offered on the installation menu when installing Dreamweaver. It also cannot be downloaded from Macromedia, not even as a trial (and therefore not on the book's CD). It's basically HomeSite 5 with features of ColdFusion Studio added, and it's worth installing along with Dreamweaver MX.

Besides the features within editors, there are other local testing tools that you can download and install. I will refer you to some of these throughout this section.

Web-based testing tools

Rather than install and run testing tools on your workstation, or to get around their limitations for testing the output of your applications, you should consider web-based testing tools. These are generally very easy to use, are most often free, and perform many of the same tests as those offered by local testing tools.

You simply visit the URL of the testing tool (I provide the URLs of several throughout this section) and point the tool to a page on your site to be tested. The tool executes the page on your server (and, therefore, is looking at the resulting HTML of the page) and achieves the same result as the local-testing tools but without you needing to copy/paste the HTML into an editor.

Several such tools are available, including the W3C HTML Validation Service (a free tool at `http://validator.w3.org`), Dr. Watson (a free tool at `http://watson.addy.com/`), the CSE online HTML validator (http://www.htmlvalidator.com/), and NetMechanic (a commercial service with trial versions at `www.netmechanic.com/`). Netscape's Web Site Garage has been discontinued. Do a search on **"html validation"** in your favorite search engine to find more.

Note

If your Web application runs inside a firewall, you may think that these Web-based tools are unusable. Can you make available (outside the firewall) a copy of the code to be tested? Or, just as in using the testing tools in the editors, can you copy/paste the output of a page to be tested into a file that can itself be placed outside the firewall? If so, you can still use these Web-based tools.

The following sections look at the various kinds of tests available to you.

HTML validation

Is your HTML valid? Have you perhaps left off a closing tag here or there? Or used some HTML that's nonstandard? Such practices can cause your page to render incorrectly in some browsers. Indeed, it may appear correct on your own browser but fail to load at all on others.

Both editors have mechanisms to validate HTML. In Dreamweaver MX, you would choose File ⇨ Check Page ⇨ Validate Markup (or press Shift+F6) while editing a file. Figure 42-1 shows an example of the errors that appear for a page within the ColdFusion Example applications.

Note

The page being edited in Figure 42-1 is simply a file from the online example applications that are installed, as an option, with ColdFusion MX. In fact, this particular file is part of several complete example applications that came with earlier releases of ColdFusion and still remain in the `exampleapps` directory in CF MX. If you have not installed the documentation and/or example applications, simply open any file that you have which is mostly HTML and follow along with the demonstrations of editor testing features.

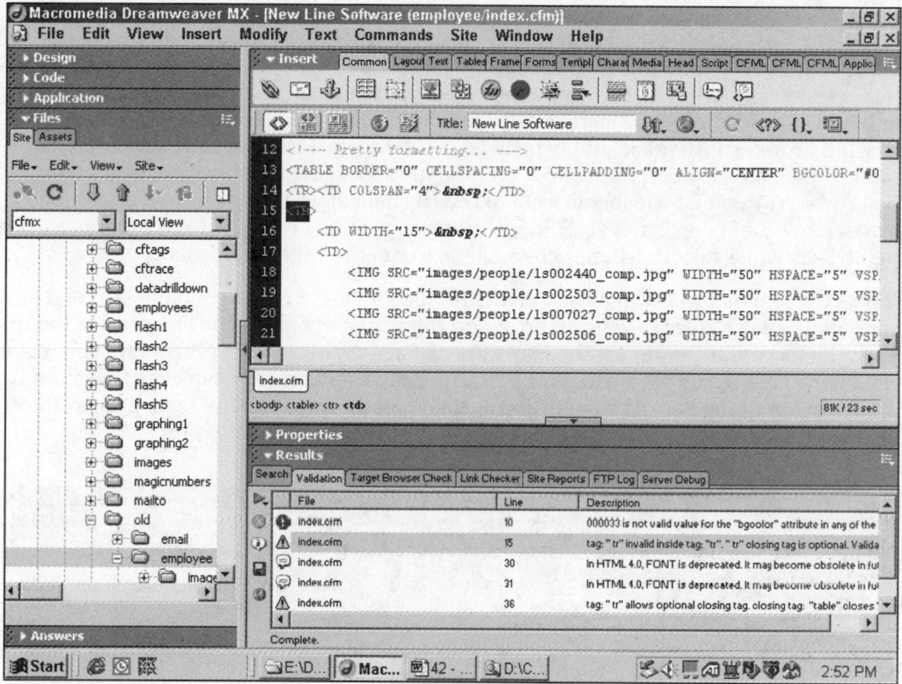

Figure 42-1: Validate Markup option in Dreamweaver MX.

In Figure 42-1, the lower portion of the screen, which Dreamweaver labels the `Results` panel in gray, has opened to its `Validation` tab which shows any validation errors found. This page contains a few HTML syntax errors, and a very useful feature is that if you select (by double-clicking) an error in the page, such as is shown here selecting the second line's error `tag "tr" invalid inside tag: "tr"`, you'll notice that the upper portion of the editor display will jump to the line of code containing that error.

This particular example reflects a simple but all too easily missed mistake—improperly nested table tags, such as `<tr>`, in the HTML code. You might miss such mistakes by simply trusting your eyes to catch this sort of mistake, so you see how the validation tool can catch such errors quickly and efficiently.

After correcting the mistake, you can run the validation test again either of two ways. First, you could use the command or keystroke (Shift+F6) given previously to execute the test. But now that the `Results` panel's `Validation` tab is already open, you can also click the green triangle shown in the top left corner of that `Results` panel. This not only allows you to re-run the test, but upon clicking it you're given the option to validate the current document, selected files, or the entire site, as well as to modify settings that control several options that determine how your HTML validation works.

Remember that, if you want to test the output of a ColdFusion page rather than its source code, you want to use the View ⇨ Source or equivalent command in a browser while viewing that page's output; then copy/paste that source code into Dreamweaver, save it, and validate it. If you have ColdFusion debugging turned on, you'll likely want to remove the HTML at the bottom of the page, which held the debugging output, before running the test.

Dreamweaver MX also offers the File ➪ Check Page ➪ Check Target Browsers command that focuses on browser-specific support concerns. In other words, rather than just test for generic HTML validation errors, this feature lets you target the rules and features of specific browsers. This is especially helpful when you want to test your page or site for how well it will perform on browsers you don't have installed of don't use often. The feature doesn't launch the selected browser. Instead, it simply tests your code against the rules Dreamweaver has for that browser. As shown in Figure 42-2, on executing the command you are prompted to select the browser(s) against which you wish to test. By default, the dialogue opens with one browser selected (see Figure 42-2). To select more than one browser to test, press and hold the Ctrl key while selecting them. Press `Check` to run the validation tests.

The `Results` panel will display any errors (in the `Target Browser Check` tab) and again you can double-click a row showing an error and the editor will show the line of code in error. To rerun the tests you can repeat the File ➪ Check Page ➪ Check Target Browsers command, but again because the `Results` panel is open after running a test, you can click the green triangle at the top left of the `Results` panel and again choose now to run the tests against the current file, the entire site, or selected folders.

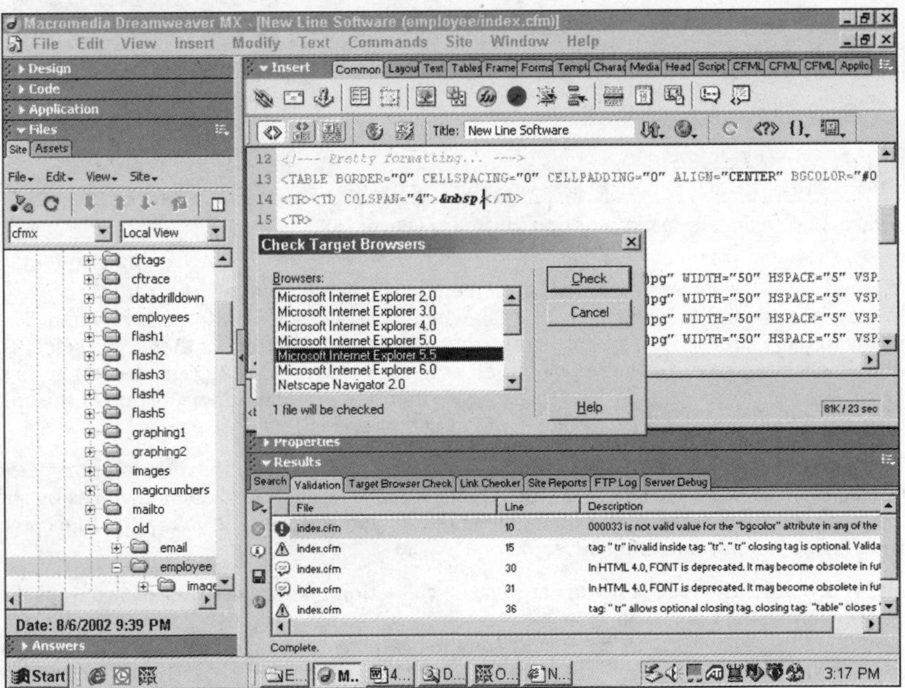

Figure 42-2: Check Target Browsers in Dreamweaver MX.

If you're using HomeSite+ or ColdFusion Studio, you can use the Tools ➪ Validate Document command to do much the same sort of validation. (But you don't need to save the file before validating it, which is useful in validating output that you've copied/pasted from a browser.)

Each of the Web-based tools that we list in the preceding section offers HTML validation as well.

Dreamweaver MX offers still more options for HTML validation, which you can access by choosing Site ⇨ Reports from the menu bar to open the Reports dialog box. The dialog box's options, shown in Figure 42-3, enable you to check for any of several possible errors: combinable nested font tags, accessibility, missing Alt text, redundant nested tags, removable empty tags, and untitled documents. In that dialogue, you can also choose to apply the selected tests to either the current document, selected files, or the entire site.

After choosing `Run`, the results of the test are shown in the Results pane at the bottom of the screen, this time in the `Site Reports` tab.

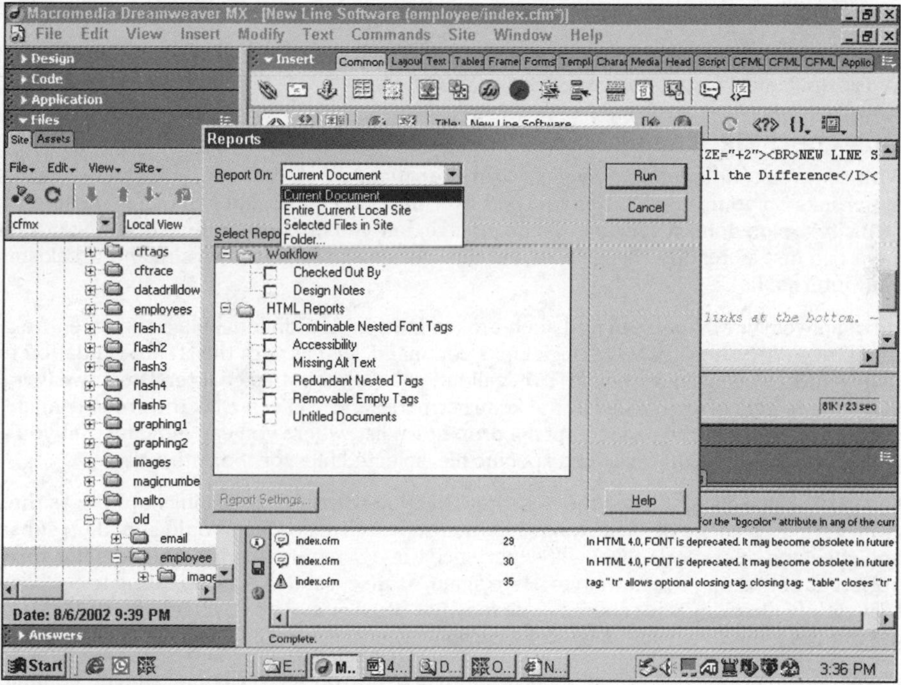

Figure 42-3: Site Reports in Dreamweaver MX.

Cascading Style Sheet validation

Just as you want to validate your HTML, you should also validate your Cascading Style Sheets (CSS). While HomeSite+/ColdFusion Studio includes TopStyle Lite, which is a CSS editor, and Dreamweaver MX offers an evaluation version on its CD, TopStyle Lite is not a CSS validator. The TopStyle Pro product, available at `http://www.bradsoft.com/topstyle/index.asp`, includes an automatic mechanism to link to the W3C online CSS validator. But you can use that online tool yourself at `http://jigsaw.w3.org/css-validator/`. On the page you will be shown at that address, choose the link to validate by URL (meaning you can provide a web page for it to validate) and provide the URL for a page on your site. The tool will report on the validity, and any errors or warnings in your use, of CSS on the page.

JavaScript validation

If you're using JavaScript code in your application, you will want to make sure that code is valid. While neither Dreamweaver nor Studio/HomeSite+ offer any tools that can test the syntax of your scripts, there is at least one web-based tool that can validate JavaScript syntax. The "JavaScript Lint" page at `http://www.crockford.com/javascript/jslint.html` offers a text area where you can paste in JavaScript code to check its validity.

The fact that you must copy/paste the tool rather than point it to your page is an annoyance, but more important is that it's simply checking if the code would compile. It's not testing whether it would execute when browsed. For instance, it doesn't detect if variables are referenced that are not yet defined, though that would cause an error at runtime.

We'll cover other aspects of JavaScript testing later in the sections, "Testing for disabled JavaScript" and "Testing for JavaScript errors."

Link checking

With the Web (and undoubtedly your own site) changing all the time, you can't expect all the hyperlinks on your pages to remain valid over time. Of course, links to pages outside your own site are obvious suspects for such change, but you or another developer in your environment can just as readily change files and directories within your own site and break some of your internal links.

In Dreamweaver MX, you can find such broken links in an individual file or on an entire site by using the File ➪ Check Page ➪ Check Links command. Just as with the HTML-validation process that we describe in the section "HTML validation," earlier in this chapter, Dreamweaver displays the results of such a test in the `Results` pane, and you can click the green triangle in the upper left corner of the pane to open a drop-down list, where you can indicate that you want to perform link checking against a specific file, selected files, or the entire site.

You may notice a slight delay the first time that you use this Check Links option, as the program gathers a cache of all file names in the project. (This cache should speed up subsequent link-checking operations.) You will experience the delay only the first time you use this option after starting Dreamweaver. Here again, as discussed in "Local testing tools," beware that simply checking your source code may not be as complete as checking the HTML output of your file after its execution by ColdFusion.

If you're using HomeSite+/ColdFusion Studio, use the Tools ➪ Verify Links menu command for this same link-checking purpose.

Finally, each of the Web-based tools that we list in the section "Web-based testing tools," earlier in this chapter, offers link-checking validation as well.

Spell-checking

Another easily forgotten test involves ensuring that you don't have typographical and spelling mistakes on your pages. Everyone makes such mistakes, and Web pages often contain as much text as a letter or document. Typos can easily creep in, but testing for them is also easy.

In DreamWeaver MX, use the Text ➪ Check Spelling menu command. In HomeSite+/ColdFusion Studio, use the Tools ➪ Spell Check menu command.

The Web-based tools that listed in "Web-based testing tools" can also perform spell checking.

Of course, since we've talked about copy/pasting HTML output to an editor, it's reasonable to point out that you could also spell check your HTML by cutting and pasting it to a word processor (such as Microsoft Word), doing the spell check (Tools ⇨ Spelling and Grammar) and correction there, then copy/pasting the code back into your editor.

Document weight (download time) testing

Because many developers work on their sites locally (with a ColdFusion server on their workstation or within their network) or have high-speed lines if working remotely, they often don't notice that the Web pages they design (or have ColdFusion generate dynamically) may be very large in terms of the amount of text, images, JavaScript, and other web page elements that they contain.

For users visiting your site, who must await downloads of the page across the network and who may not have such high-speed lines, you need to consider the "weight" of your pages or, more precisely, the relative time that such pages take to download for various connection speeds.

Dreamweaver MX constantly displays (in the right side of the status bar, just under the source code shown in the editing window) the estimated document size and estimated download time for the current page. (You can see this information in any of the figures in preceding sections of this chapter — about halfway up the figure, on the right side.) More than just evaluating the page in terms of its HTML source code, Dreamweaver goes further in considering the size of all dependent files, such as images and media files (as in those referenced by `img src` tags). This addition of the size of dependent files in calculating the weight of the page is powerful! In fact, if you remove a line of code containing an `img src` tag, you see that removal immediately reflected in a reduction of the download size/time.

Again, however, you must consider whether the page is generating still more HTML dynamically. Conversely, the value computed presumes that the user needs to download all the page's components (images, JavaScript source files if any, and so on). Keep in mind that, after a user downloads these components, they are not generally downloaded again because the user's browser caches them. Still, the information computing their total weight can prove useful. If a page's weight shows that it takes more than eight seconds to download, you should consider redesigning the page to reduce its overall weight.

How does Dreamweaver determine the speed at which it estimates that downloads of the page would take place? That's an option that you can control, by choosing Edit ⇨ Preferences ⇨ Status Bar from the menu bar. The display you will be shown is very simple to understand. The default speed is 28.8K per second, which may not be representative of your true audience.

If you're using HomeSite+/ColdFusion Studio, you can achieve nearly the same result of determining the document's weight with the Tools ⇨ Document Weight menu command. The resulting dialog box shows both the size of the file (and its dependencies) as well as estimated download times, although it's present to estimate times only for 14K, 28K, and 56K connections, and you cannot change the values.

Finally, the Web-based tools can also perform document weight testing. In addition, it's worth noting that most of the load testing tools discussed in the later section, "Load-testing," also have bandwidth- or data rate-throttling mechanisms to simulate testing your applications with different simulated bandwidth rates.

The tests that we describe in the next several sections evaluate how your coding designs may work with various settings that visitors to your site may use in their browser and browser-environment configurations. These types of problems are easier to miss because, unless you hear people complaining about them, you may never realize that an issue exists — but better that you detect these problems before a user does. For every user who does complain, many, many more may simply "walk away" from your site.

Browser-size testing

Many developers don't realize that, although a design may look great on their 19-inch monitors, the same design may look terrible on a smaller monitor and/or at a lower resolution. Choices such as how wide to make a `TEXTAREA` (via its `cols` attribute) or a `TABLE` (via its `width` attribute) can often make a page unviewable to some visitors without their having to scroll to the right in their browsers. This situation can prove disastrous, as most users find scrolling horizontally quite undesirable.

Although you may not find tools to tell you what choices to make, tools do exist to help you see what a page looks like at different resolutions.

In order to use the Dreamweaver MX feature for this test, you need to understand that Dreamweaver MX offers two modes of viewing your pages: `Code View` and `Design View`. You can choose each from the `View` command in the menu bar. `Code View` shows your raw HTML/CFML code, while `Design View` shows your page in a WYSIWYG (What You See Is What You Get) display which is generally only suitable for pure HTML.

Still, while in `Design View`, you have two ways to see how your page will appear at different resolutions. First, the status bar shows the current size dimensions in width and height just to the left of the document weight indicator discussed in "Document weight (download time) testing." If you resize the page in Design view, that status bar indicator will change to reflect the current size of the page in pixels.

How do you resize the page in Dreamweaver? You can't resize the window if the document is maximized in the Dreamweaver display. You can change this with the Window ➪ Cascade menu command. You can then resize the entire Dreamweaver window by dragging its corners and observing how (while in Design View) the dimensions in the status bar's size indicator change at the same time. You can use that to set the screen to any size to see how the page would appear at different widths and heights.

Rather than select random sizes, you can also select a designated setting, such as 640 x 480 or 800 x 600. Again, while in Design View, if you left-click that aforementioned status-bar size indicator, a drop-down list of options is displayed showing different window sizes. Click one to see the page at that size. See an example in Figure 42-4.

By left clicking one of the options displayed, the window will be sized to the selected dimensions. To return to a maximized display of the document, double-click the blue title bar at the top of the code display.

If you try to select that size indicator and find the options grayed out and not selectable, the problem is that you're viewing the document maximized. Again, you need to change the document from being "maximized" as described earlier in this section. And, again, the size indicator only appears in the status bar if you are in `Design View`.

A very similar feature is available in HomeSite+/ColdFusion Studio, although it works only while in you're the Internal Browser mode (which you access by pressing F12 or by choosing the View ➪ Toggle Edit/Browse menu command). If you get an error trying to use the Internal Browse feature, see the chapter "Configuring Browsers and Servers" in the HomeSite+ or ColdFusion Studio manual.

While you're browsing a page internally, an option is offered within a set of tools represented by icons that appear just above the browsed page. The Browser Size icon looks like two crossed arrows. Clicking that icon displays alternative sizes in which the page can appear. After you finish your testing, make sure that you reset it to the option `Fit To Window`.

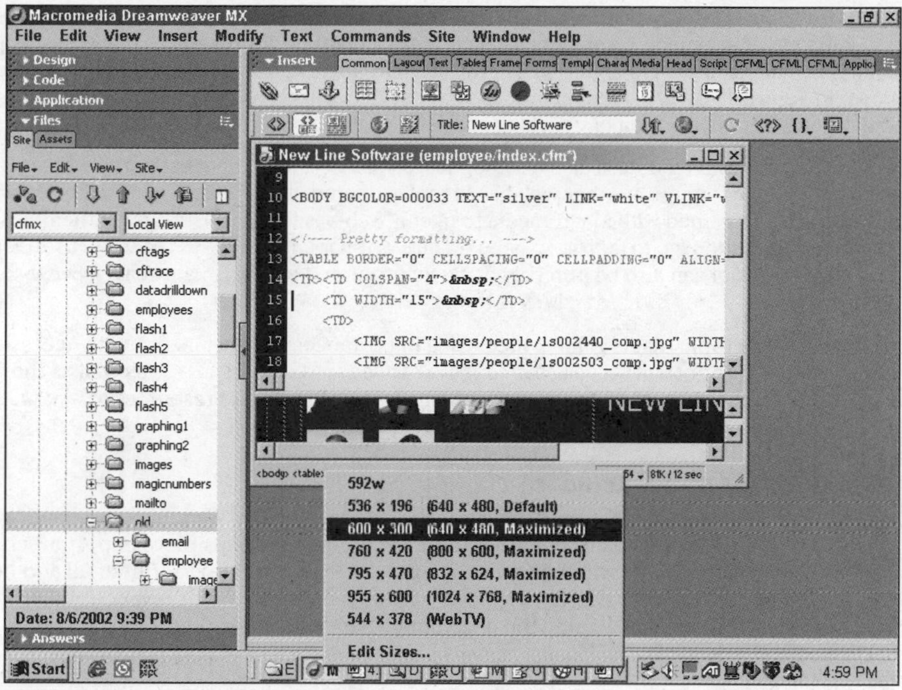

Figure 42-4: Menu of window sizes.

Finally, certain Web-based tools can perform similar testing, including the unusual and powerful Browser Photo service, at `www.netmechanic.com/browser-index.htm`. Here, for a fee, you can have snapshots of your page provided at different resolutions and on different browsers and browser versions. Still another tool is the shareware tool, BrowserSizer, which you can find at `http://www.applythis.com/browsersizer/`.

Accessibility testing

Accessibility testing continues the theme of considering your browser visitor's needs. Disabled visitors (those who are vision impaired, color-blind, deaf, and so on) can face substantial challenges in visiting Web sites that don't accommodate their rather unique needs. Too many sites ignore those needs. For many developers, federal law has mandated accommodating this audience. Section 508 of the Federal Rehabilitation Act requires that Federal agencies must make their information technology accessible to people with disabilities. (Several resources are provided at the end of this section that provide more explanation of accessibility, the Section 508 law, and how to make sites meet the law's requirements.)

Most existing Web sites require only minor modifications to make them accessible to the estimated 750 million people worldwide who have disabilities that would challenge their obtaining information from web site. Even agencies and organizations not covered by the law are choosing to follow those guidelines to ensure that their sites are as widely accessible as possible.

Some of the modifications can be beneficial to all users: media files should be labeled with text tags so that screen readers used by the visually impaired can communicate what's in a picture, for instance. This also benefits users who have chosen to disable image downloads. There are many other examples.

Fortunately, accessibility testing is built into Dreamweaver MX, via the File ➪ Check Page ➪ Check Accessibility menu command. This command displays its results in the `Results` panel, much like what is shown in Figure 42-1. The Site ➪ Reports feature, whose dialogue box is shown in Figure 42-3, also offers an `accessibility` checkbox which performs the same tests, although it offers the option of checking against selected files or the entire site.

Web-based tools and resources also exist for accessibility testing, the most notable being Bobby at `www.cast.org/bobby`. Another web-based tool is offered at `www.usable.net`. The organizers of that site have teamed with Macromedia to offer a Web-based demonstration of their LIFT tool. For more information, go to `www.macromedia.com/macromedia/accessibility/usablenet.html`. The LIFT tool can also be purchased and incorporated within Dreamweaver. See `www.usablenet.com/lift_dw/lift_dw.html`.

Accessibility is a topic that is gaining increasing importance. See the Macromedia Accessibility resource at `www.macromedia.com/macromedia/accessibility/tools/`, as well as those at `www.microsoft.com/enable/` and a very complete list of tools and resources at `www.w3.org/WAI/ER/existingtools.html`.

Testing for disabled JavaScript

JavaScript testing is another area of concern to some developers. We touched on one facet in the section, "JavaScript validation" earlier in this chapter. A perhaps more important challenge is simply determining whether a visitor's browser supports JavaScript at all and how your site responds if it does not. Seeing what your page looks like with JavaScript disabled can prove very helpful in designing the page (and a wise precaution).

This subject shouldn't just be dismissed as one limited to users of older browsers that don't support JavaScript. Users may also disable JavaScript in their browsers for security reasons, while some organizations require that all their users disable it. Their having JavaScript disabled can wreak havoc on your application if you are using JavaScript for enhanced interfaces.

If you're developing an application for an intranet or some other controlled environment, where a certain browser can be mandated (or perhaps just for the administrative portion of a site), this point is perhaps moot. Otherwise, you should be wary of using JavaScript too much in public sites.

Macromedia is promoting Macromedia Flash as a new way to achieve many of the kinds of enhanced interfaces that were previously available only by using dynamic HTML, JavaScript, and the like. A significant benefit is that the Flash player is available for nearly every browser and operating system, making it a much more uniform and widely acceptable approach.

That the use of JavaScript can add measurably to the quality of the user experience is undeniable, but if the browser doesn't support it, JavaScript doesn't add anything at all and it detracts from the site if you have not anticipated the problem.

Of course, one solution is to code the site to respond to varying levels of JavaScript support. You can find several tools and code samples that test whether (and even which release of) JavaScript is supported by a browser when executing a page on your site. See the JavaScript sniffer from WebReference at `www.webreference.com/tools/browser/javascript.html` or the Browserawk tool at `www.cyscape.com/`. That's not really what I mean by testing for JavaScript support.

The point of this section is more to discuss how your application supports cookies being disabled. Both Netscape and Internet Explorer offer options for disabling JavaScript temporarily, which you as a developer should do occasionally while browsing your site to experience it as a user would with JavaScript disabled.

In Internet Explorer 5 and 6, for example, use Tools ⇨ Internet Options. From there, choose the `Security` tab, then the `Internet` (or `Local Intranet`) option in "Select a Web Content zone." If you're testing an application on a local web server (using `localhost` or `127.0.0.1` as the domain in URL), select Local Intranet. After choosing either of those, click the `Custom Level` option on that same dialogue under `Security level for this zone`. You'll be presented a dialogue with a long list of options. Find the one labeled Scripting, then the sub-option for Active Scripting. There, select Disable. Figure 42-5 shows how your screen may appear after following all these steps. After pressing `OK`, when you visit pages in the zone you selected, any JavaScript present on the page will not be executed.

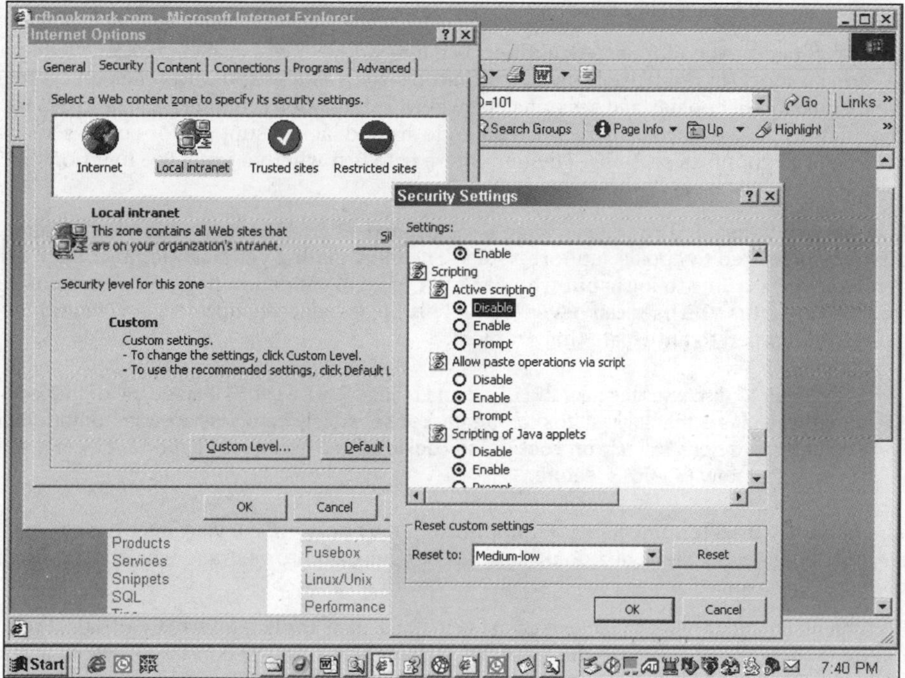

Figure 42-5: Disabling JavaScript in IE 5 and 6.

In Netscape Navigator 4.7, use Edit ⇨ Preferences and choose the `Advanced` category in the dialogue presented. From there, uncheck `Enable JavaScript` to disable the use of scripts in the browser.

Netscape 7 requires just one more steps. Use Edit ⇨ Preferences and choose the `Advanced` category then the `Scripts & Plugins` subcategory. From there, uncheck the checkbox next to `Navigator` in the `Enable JavaScript for` area.

After disabling JavaScript, visit your site to see how it responds as you access its various pages. Unfortunately, this test is something that you simply must do manually. After your testing, of course, make sure that you turn JavaScript back on so that you can enjoy normal visits to your and other sites.

One direct example of where the lack of JavaScript support in a browser can impact ColdFusion developers is if you have chosen to use the client-side validation features of `CFFORM`, as discussed in Chapter 20. This would be a good opportunity to go try the sample code there and see how, with JavaScript disabled in the browser, the client-side validation is ignored. That chapter discusses ways you can handle that problem. This is just one of many examples of how browsers not supporting JavaScript, whether intentionally or by mistake, can be problematic, and further reason why it's in your interest to test your application to see how it works with JavaScript disabled.

Testing for disabled cookie support

Closely related to the disabled JavaScript problem is the issue of testing how your application runs if a visitor's browser has disabled support cookies. Again, the problem may not lie simply with older browsers, but with organizations and individuals who have chosen to disable cookies for security reasons.

This problem is even more important because many developers don't consider the fact that session support (in ColdFusion, as well as in tools such as ASP and JSP) relies on cookies. See the discussion of cookies and sessions elsewhere in this book (chapters 2, 4, and 12) for more information. As we discuss there, you can code around lack of support for cookies so that a browser still supports sessions. The point here is to test whether your site functions properly if cookies are disabled.

Cookies being disabled can cause some very strange errors that may not be immediately obvious as related to cookie-support issues. The most glaring yet disappointing such error involves users trying to log in but who can't. If the login validation page sets a session to track login status, the user can never log in if his browser don't support cookies and the site isn't programmed to anticipate this problem.

Note Chapter 40 discusses the new `CFLOGIN` and related `CFLOGINUSER` tags. One of the features of these tags is that login status can be tracked separately from session state. Unfortunately, that feature does still rely on cookies, so cookie support is equally important even if you're using that new `CFLOGIN` feature.

The best way to determine how your application may perform if a visitor's browser does not support cookies is to turn off cookie support in your own browser and visit the application's pages.

To turn off the capability to receive cookies in IE 5.5, use Tools ➪ Internet Options. From the dialogue then opened, choose the `Security` tab and (as discussed in the previous section) choose either `Internet` (or `Local Intranet`), then the Custom Level button, which opens a new window. There, find the `Cookies` section. Refer to Figure 42-5, which shows an interface similar to the one in which these changes can be made. Options available include causing Internet Explorer to enable, disable, or prompt the user whether to enable each cookie set by a visited web page.

In IE 6, the feature is moved to Tools ➪ Internet Options and a new `Privacy` option which offers a sliding bar to set a range of cookie-control options.

Note Internet Explorer 5.5 and 6 enable you to control either of two specific kinds of cookies: *persistent cookies* that are stored on your computer and *non-persistent* cookies which are not stored (called `per-session` in IE 5 and simply `session` in IE 6, where they are controlled under an Advanced button). This persistence distinction is important. By default, the cookies that ColdFusion creates in support of sessions are *persistent* ones that are stored on the browser's disk. The new J2EE session-variables support discussed in Chapter 28, however, are *nonpersistent* ones stored in memory that are removed when the browser is closed. Make sure that you disable the correct kind of cookie to adequately simulate user experience against your site when testing features that use each kind of cookie.

In Netscape Navigator 4.7, you can disable cookies by using Edit ⇨ Preferences and selecting the `Advanced` category then choosing the `Cookies` subcategory to make similar selections to IE. In Netscape 7 it's controlled by Edit ⇨ Preferences and the `Privacy & Security` category, then choose the `Cookies` subcategory to make selections. Again, in each version you can indicate whether to enable, disable, or prompt the user to enable cookies. Neither version of Netscape enables separate controls for persistent versus per session cookies.

But both versions of Netscape and IE 6 offer an option that IE 5.5 does not: You can separately restrict whether to accept only cookies that are sent from the server that's presenting the page (referred to as the *originating server* in Netscape), or whether to allow cookies sent from other servers (called *third-party* cookies in IE 6). If your pages cause sending of cookies from another server, be aware of the option to disable these type of cookies which you also need to test.

Although the browser feature to disable cookie support prevents the receipt of cookies after it's disabled, be aware that disabling this feature doesn't turn off the browser's capability to *send* cookies to your server. This is an easily missed facet of this sort of testing. For instance, you may already have cookies set in your browser that are sent to your server whenever you visit a page. Turning off cookie support won't stop the browser sending those cookies, so you may be confused in testing because you're still sending cookies to the server. To most effectively perform this cookie-support testing, you must clear any cookies already set for your application that are currently stored in your browser. See your browser's Help for assistance in clearing cookies. Be careful to delete only cookies related to your application, if possible.

And make sure that you re-enable cookies after you finish testing so that you can browse your and other sites normally.

Testing for JavaScript errors

Still another matter in working with JavaScript on your site is simply becoming aware of errors that your JavaScript code is generating. By default, modern browsers (both IE and Netscape) hide JavaScript errors that occur. Although that may approach be desirable for end users, it's a very unfortunate one for developers. We should be sure to have JavaScript errors displayed when testing our own sites.

To enable the display of JavaScript errors in IE 5.5 and IE 6, use Tools ⇨ Internet Options then choose the `Advanced` tab then select the `Browsing` category under `Settings` and from there choose the option, `Display a Notification About Every Script Error`.

Netscape's has another approach, which may be considered an improvement or an annoyance. There doesn't seem a way to easily cause the browser to show every JavaScript error. Instead, JavaScript errors are held for display only if you enable the `JavaScript console`, by entering `javascript:` on the browser address line. Netscape 7 also offers the menu option, Tools ⇨ Web Development ⇨ JavaScript console. For Netscape 4.x and earlier browsers, see the Netscape Client-side JavaScript Guide at `http://developer.netscape.com/docs/manuals/js/client/jsguide/console.htm#1045065` for more details on controlling display of the console whenever errors occur.

Of course, enabling the display of JavaScript errors exposes you to errors that occur on pages on other sites that you visit. This is an annoyance but a rather small price to pay to ensure that you can detect any errors occurring on your own site.

Testing for browser caching issues

Still another form of testing that you need to perform, to determine how your code may respond to different browser configurations, is testing for browser caching issues. In other words, how well does your application run under different browser settings for page caching and refreshing? Did you even know that you can choose how a browser caches and refreshes its cached version of your site's HTML output? More important, are you aware that there are coding practices you can use that can influence how a browser caches your pages?

All browsers attempt to improve the browsing experience of their users by caching pages whenever users visit them. This way, if the user returns to the page soon afterward, the browser need not return to the host server to obtain the page (as well as its graphics, any JavaScript stored in files, and so on).

But how long does a browser wait before it considers the cached version of a page "stale"? When does it make a new request to the host server for the latest copy? A certain browser setting controls this interval, and you can use it perform some additional testing of your application.

Both major browsers (IE and Navigator) make general assumptions about how best to cache pages and perform refreshes. But you can, as a test, override those assumptions and force a browser to refresh the cache (revisit the server) on every visit or perhaps only once per session (since the browser started)—or never (which is, of course, not very useful for general purposes).

Since you can't know what settings your visitors may enable, it pays to determine how your site responds to the various settings. Again, later in this section, we'll offer a sidebar to discuss some of the coding options that can influence how your page should direct the page caching mechanisms in the browser. But here's how to simulate different user-settable configurations.

In Internet Explorer 5.5 and 6, use Tools ➪ Internet Options and from the `General` tab select the `Settings` button under `Temporary Internet Files`. There, in the option `Check for Newer Versions of Stored Pages`, you can select among the options offered ranging from `Every Visit` to `Never`. The default is `Automatically`. (Unlike the settings for cookies and JavaScript, where you can distinguish `local intranet` from `internet` sites, this setting applies to all types of sites.)

In Netscape Navigator 4.7, use Edit ➪ Preferences and choose the `Advanced` category, then the `Cache` subcategory. From there, choose an option for `Document in Cache is Compared to Network`. The choices are similar to IE, ranging from `Once per Session` (the default) to `Never`. Navigator 4.7 offers no `Automatically` choice. Netscape 7 uses virtually the same command options to open the dialogue but it does offer an additional choice of `when the page is out of date`, which is the default.

Forcing the browser to refresh the cache on every visit is an expensive proposition, although doing so may very well be justified if the page contains data for which the user wants the latest version all the time.

Just consider the cost of a user enabling the `Every Time` option (supported in all the listed browsers): Not only are the browser and the user's network connection performing extra work and not benefiting from the usefulness of caching, but your server and its network connection are also burdened by the fact that users may be making page requests to your server more frequently (than they would if the browser normally served them pages from the cache).

This cost is why the default setting in each browser is not to refresh on every page. But this approach also has a downside: What if the page that the user is requesting is indeed a dynamically generated one? Have you ever observed a situation where you know that data has changed in a database on the server, but a page built from that database is not reflecting the update? This is what happens if the browser uses a cached version of the page.

Some browsers try to solve the problem to a degree by not caching form action pages, so that a refresh of those is generally going to get the latest version, but many database-generated pages are not the result of form submissions.

The caching situation poses a conundrum. The best choice for all users and all servers is not always clear. We certainly can't expect that every user will have settings enabled to refresh their cache frequently. And the browser's defaults differ by browser and even version. Finally, settings such as `automatically` and when the `page is out of date` are vague and unclear as to what their impact will be.

Although this section has focused on the effect of caching in the browser, there's yet another location between the browser and your server where caching may take place: a proxy. A proxy server may cache results on behalf of all users in a local network (or perhaps on an entire internet service provider network), and the proxy caching may take place regardless of the user's browser settings.

The point of raising all these caching issues is to suggest that you need to test the effect your site's appearance to users with different cache/refresh settings. The effect of different settings may not be readily apparent, but it's an effort that's certainly worth taking. Given the challenge, and while this chapter is supposed to be about testing, it may help to also take a look at some choices you can make as a programmer in how you cause the browser to cache a page's output.

How You Can Influence Browser Caching in Code

Forcing the user to (or hoping they will) set their browser to refresh a page frequently is unrealistic. And with a proxy server possibly caching on their behalf as well, it may be better to instead code your application (or parts of it) to inform the browser and/or proxy how to cache your pages. There are defined mechanisms for doing this, and for handling both browser and proxy caching.

You can either tell the browser and/or proxy never to cache the page or, perhaps, to cache it only for a very short time (minutes or seconds). Then again, perhaps the data does not change frequently at all, so you may want to tell the browser to freely cache it for an extended period of time (a time you set, or a time you leave the browser or cache to determine).

How you do you accomplish this task? It's not a feature of ColdFusion, although certain CF tags can facilitate the process. Certain Web specifications exist regarding browser caching and when a browser can consider cached data to be stale. A Web page can either set `META` tags within the HTML that's sent to a page, or it can use HTTP header codes, which can also be interpreted by proxies, to indicate how to control caching. Indeed, the available options include settings with terms such as `Cache-Control` and `Expires`. An example of setting such a `META` tag follows:

```
<meta http-equiv="pragma" content="no-cache">
```

Unfortunately, the web standard specifications for handling caching have changed and generally improved over time, and different releases of different browsers implement different levels of support for these cache controlling settings (to be shown in a moment). Some browsers ignore some of the existing settings, and proxies may also step in to perform or ignore cache settings. So developers have put together a sort of "kitchen-sink" approach to indicating a range of settings in order to prevent a browser from caching a page at all, as shown in the following example:

```
<cfset slastmod = dateformat(now(), "dd mmm yyyy")
   & " " & timeformat(now(), "hh:mm:ss") & " GMT-5">
<cfheader name="pragma" value="no-cache">
```

Continued

Continued

```
<cfheader name="cache-control"
   value="no-cache, no-store, must-revalidate">
<cfheader name="last-modified" value="#sLastMod#">
<cfheader name="expires" value=" Sun, 06 Nov 1994 08:49:37 GMT ">
<meta http-equiv="expires"
   content="Mon, 26 Jul 1997 05:00:00 EST">
<meta http-equiv="pragma" content="no-cache">
<meta http-equiv="cache-control"
   content="no-cache, no-store, must-revalidate">
<meta http-equiv="last-modified"
   content="<cfoutput>#sLastMod#</cfoutput>">
```

Each of these set a different form of cache controlling settings for the browser, in the hopes that any browser or cache will respect at least on of the directives and not cache the page. One approach for using this effectively is to place this code in a file and use the `CFINCLUDE` tag wherever it's needed. Again, don't overuse this form of forcing the browser to not cache the page, as this forces a page to refresh whenever any browser visits the page, which is an expensive and possibly time-consuming operation for them and for your server.

A way to test the effectiveness of the page for any given browser and/or proxy combination is to have these settings in place as you visit a page that shows, say, the current time (outputting the result of the `Now()` function). Then use the browser's Back button to return to a previous page and use the Forward button to return to the page under consideration. If the time changes without you needing to do a manual page refresh, the page's cached version is being refreshed.

Of course, the only way to determine whether this is working on various browser and/or proxy combinations is to find such combinations or people using them and have them run such a test. Otherwise, you can take consolation in the fact that you've at least tried to achieve an improvement that could benefit a large number of your users, if not all of them.

If the goal of preventing caching is to protect sensitive information on your site, such as to prevent users backing up after they've logged out, then it may not be sufficient to simply hope you solved the problem for even a large number of visitors. Unfortunately, this is an area where there are no complete solutions, it seems.

There is still one more solution worth trying: Many have found that if they generate a unique URL for every page (and even a unique URL for subsequent presentations of the page to the same user), then browsers and proxies should consider pages with different URLs to be different pages and therefore never find them in their cache. This approach is useful only if you are creating links to a page. In that case, consider using the CF function `CreateUUID()`, such as with the following two examples of code. They demonstrate transferring control to a `test.cfm` page, passing a query string that holds a long random string of values for an offered `clientid` variable (there's nothing special about that variable name):

```
<a href="test.cfm?cacheid=#createuuid()#">test.cfm</a>

<cflocation url="test2.cfm?cacheid=#createuuid()#">
```

Finally, just as we warned you to remember to reset the disabled JavaScript and cookie settings in the two previous sections for when you resume normal development of your site and browsing your sites and others', the same applies when changing the cache-refresh settings.

Indeed, don't be lulled into the benefit of using the `Every Time` setting because it saves you needing to refresh the browser. For instance, you may have noticed that whenever you're browsing pages in the internal browser of HomeSite+/ColdFusion Studio, you need to refresh the page to see the latest version you've created. Setting `Every Time` for your browser cache setting may facilitate development, but as this section has discussed, it's not the default setting for most visitors.

Worse, in such a situation you may not even notice that you have a problem in that the average user is seeing stale data on a page generated from changed dynamic data while you always see the latest data. The better solution is to keep your browser set to its defaults (like most users) and instead use coding techniques offered in the previous sidebar, "How You Can Influence Browser Caching in Code," to tell the browser not to cache the page.

Search-engine compatibility and site-link popularity

A final pair of tests involves only search engines and their success in finding your site. First, a feature at the Dr. Watson site (`http://watson.addy.com/`, which we mentioned in "Web-based testing tools" earlier in this chapter), helps identify design choices (such as the use of `META` tags) that can help search engines more easily reach and index your site. Visit the site, provide the URL for a page you want to test, and choose "Check Search engine compatibility."

The Dr. Watson site also helps you discover how well your site has been indexed by popular search engines (or by AltaVista, at least), by choosing"check site link popularity."

Still another useful tool for determining your site's popularity is available from Google. Perform a search in Google (at `http://www.google.com`) with the search criteria being `link:`*`siteURL`*, where you replace your site's domain name for *siteURL*.

Each of these testing tools can prove useful in gauging how successfully visitors using different search engines can find your site.

CFML-code testing

All the tests that we describe in the preceding sections of this chapter can evaluate your code from an HTML perspective, but because you're writing your code in ColdFusion Markup Language, or CFML, you also face potential challenges in that aspect of your coding.

Can your CFML be tested as well as your HTML? Yes it can. Sadly, the choices are much more limited. Indeed, you may not even be able to use the tool offered in this section because it's a feature that Macromedia has chosen to enable only as a tool available inside the CF Administrator.

CF MX offers a new Compatibility Analyzer that can prove very useful not only for migration testing (it's main purpose) but even just for CFML syntax checking. If you've installed your own copy of ColdFusion MX, then you likely have access to the Administrator on your workstation, so you could benefit from this tool for testing just your own code.

Why may you need a syntax checker, especially if your code is compiled as it's first executed and you can view the errors simply by running the program? Well, consider that you're about to release some code. You may find that trying to run a given template in isolation may generate a runtime error if the code does not contain needed variables (such as session variables). ColdFusion programs are usually highly dependent on previously executed templates within the application. So you may be disinclined to try to run such a page. Or perhaps you have several pages that you've edited that you would want to test.

If you could test just the syntax without actually running the code, you can perhaps identify code that would never work, even at runtime. At a minimum, before turning the code over to production (or uploading it to the live server), you should ensure that you've not introduced any CFML-syntax errors if you can't run the code yourself. The Compatibility Analyzer can help you test for such a possibility. The location for the Compatibility Analyzer in CF MX is as follows:

```
http://[server]/CFIDE/administrator/analyzer/index.cfm
```

Replace *[server]* with the domain name and port (if needed) for your CF server location. Figure 42-6 shows the interface for the Compatibility Analyzer. (The URL in the figure differs from what you type only because CF does a redirect to take you into the proper framed interface of the Administrator.) From there, enter a complete file path for the code to be tested. By default, the Compatibility Analyzer tests code not only in the named directory but its subdirectories as well.

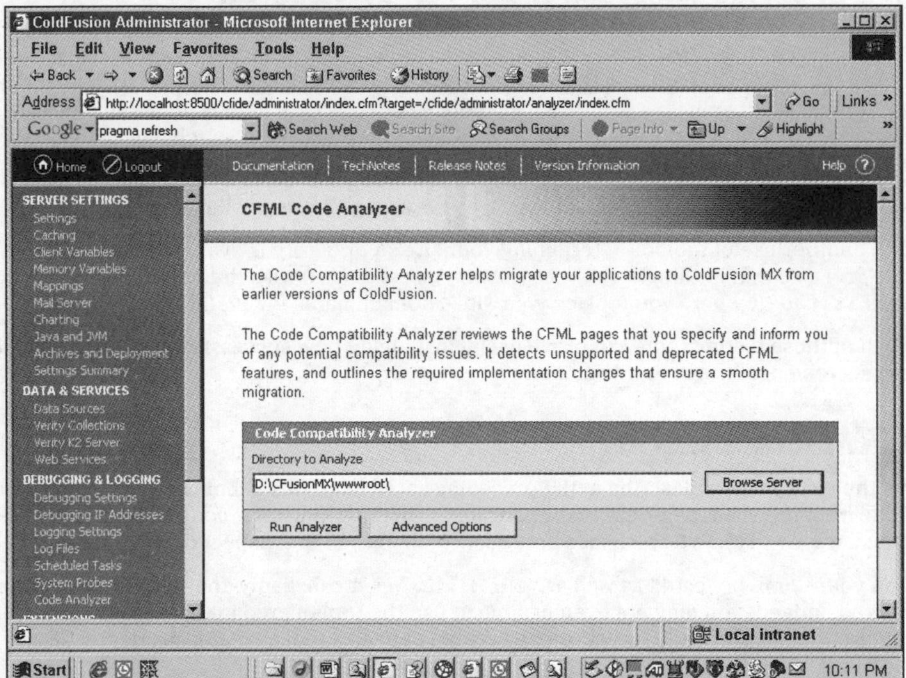
ColdFusion Administrator - Microsoft Internet Explorer
File Edit View Favorites Tools Help
Address http://localhost:8500/cfide/administrator/index.cfm?target=/cfide/administrator/analyzer/index.cfm
CFML Code Analyzer
The Code Compatibility Analyzer helps migrate your applications to ColdFusion MX from earlier versions of ColdFusion.
The Code Compatibility Analyzer reviews the CFML pages that you specify and inform you of any potential compatibility issues. It detects unsupported and deprecated CFML features, and outlines the required implementation changes that ensure a smooth migration.
Code Compatibility Analyzer
Directory to Analyze
D:\CFusionMX\wwwroot\
Browse Server
Run Analyzer
Advanced Options

Figure 42-6: ColdFusion MX Compatibility Analyzer.

It may seem shocking that that's it for CFML code testing. Other environments have more robust tools, including profiling tools, more straightforward syntax and code analysis tools, etc. Sadly, there really aren't any other tools that exist to perform CFML code testing. (There was a web-based tool called STOMP at `http://www.secretagents.com`, but the tool seems no longer to be available.)

While the chapter to this point has otherwise focused on HTML, there are still several elements of testing that can apply to you (and are more coding-oriented than those above), as will be discussed in the remaining sections.

Application-integration testing

Although the first two types of tests that we discuss in the preceding sections of this chapter (HTML testing and CFML-code testing) can be run against the static HTML output or CFML source code of your application, another group of tests focus on how the application works together as a whole (including its HTML, JavaScript, CFML, and so on), at execution times, in both reasonable and unexpected situations. This sort of testing includes the following components, which will be discussed further in this section:

- ✦ Data validation/`bounds` checking. (Does your code handle unexpected input well? What are the extents of the valid ranges that it will accept? What if users enter values out of expected bounds?)
- ✦ Functionality testing. (Does the code work as expected?)
- ✦ Security testing, (Can only authenticated, authorized activities take place?)
- ✦ Regression/functional/smoke testing. (Does the code produce the expected result if you run it after performing code changes?)
- ✦ Performance/load/stress testing. (Can the code sustain a large load?)
- ✦ Concurrency testing. (Do problems arise if multiple users access the code or a single user opens multiple browsers?)
- ✦ Site monitoring. (Is the site up? Is anyone aware if it goes down?)
- ✦ Server-integration testing. (Are the related servers also up and running?)

The first three are tests that really can't be automated. You simply need to create a set of manual tests (run-throughs of the code) that ensure that everything works as expected (and that unexpected things are handled appropriately). Most important, you need to make sure that the code does what the user expects.

Still, although the creation of such tests can't easily be automated, you can indeed record the execution of your tests and then play back the tests in a repetitive manner so that you can detect whether code that worked at one point in your development can now no longer pass the recorded tests.

Several tools are available to assist you with this sort of recording and playback of Web applications. Predominant companies with tools in this space include the following:

- ✦ Empirix, at `www.empirix.com` (formerly RSW Software)
- ✦ Mercury-Interactive, at `www.mercuryinteractive.com`
- ✦ Segue, at `www.segue.com`

Each of these companies' tools are mature (and relatively expensive) but of substantial value for the benefit that they provide. A few smaller, relatively new companies also offer tools, but with a much lower price (or free), as the following list identifies:

- ✦ Microsoft Web Application Stress, at `http://webtool.rte.microsoft.com/`
- ✦ OpenDemand, at `www.opendemand.com`
- ✦ EValid, at `www.soft.com/eValid/`
- ✦ Paessler Webserver Stress Tool, at `www.paessler.com/WebStress/webstress.htm`

✦ OpenSta, at `www.opensta.org`

✦ JMeter, at `http://jakarta.apache.org/jmeter/`

Most of the tools in this arena work as easily as a VCR, enabling you to literally hit a Record button to start watching as you run through your application, while the tool tracks all your links taken, data entered, and even JavaScript or Flash events fired (in the better tools). The recorded scenarios can then be played back repeatedly with relatively little effort and interaction. In fact, most tools include features that enable you to change the input values entered for the tests as you rerun them so each run uses new data. This is typically enabled by directing the test tool to extract data from a database or flat file.

These automated testing tools are often dismissed as either too expensive or perhaps too much work for a given project, but the cost and effort can be justified in the testing time that's saved (or facilitated). The good news is that some vendors are making available limited virtual user (but nonexpiring) trial versions, such as that offered by OpenDemand, and it and other of the less prominent load testing tools are relatively inexpensive but often feature-rich.

These tools can be used for several of the forms of testing that we described at the beginning of this section and, in some more detail in the following sections.

Regression testing

The fourth item in the list in the preceding section is *regression testing*. The point with this test is that you're trying to determine whether solved problems remain solved or whether your code has *regressed* to a non-functioning point.

Going back to the original premise of testing in development, if you've made a change in some code that lies deep in a set of pages that the browser must traverse through (perhaps to order multiple items on a shopping cart and then delete one, for example) before reaching the page you want to test, such automated testing tools as described in the previous section can make it easy to retrace those steps as often as you want.

Indeed, it becomes a nice baseline to have a script that runs through your site or a section that you're working on, so that at regular intervals (hours, days, weeks as appropriate) you can rerun the script to make sure that nothing's been broken by your changes. Of course, if the changes are intentional and would break the script because the script is now out of date, this is an area where better tools help you modify the script without having to re-record the entire test scenario.

Load-testing

Further, most of the tools described in the section "Application-integration testing" also enable the recorded, data-driven regression tests to be used for the fifth type of testing that we mention in the list in that section: *load testing*. This answers the following question: Can the code (and environment) scale, meaning accept and sustain an increasing load without failing?

This area of testing may be where these tools really shine, because although regression testing can prove a bit cumbersome (dealing with a constantly changing code bases), load testing is more straightforward: You record the tests, make them data-driven, and then use the tool's capability to create "virtual users" that mimic many (perhaps thousands) of users hitting your site.

And the better of these tools do more than simply bang on a single page—instead, they run through the same sort of multipage execution that works the way a user really would. The tests are limited only by your creativity and the time that you can put into creating the tests. Although some tools use scripting languages to create tests, which are powerful but can prove cumbersome to learn, all the tools offer the record/playback approach, which is simpler.

Concurrency testing

Even if you don't think that your site needs to support thousands (or even hundreds) of concurrent users, make sure that you consider using some form of load-testing tool to determine what happens if even more than just one or a few users visit your site. Many an application is brought to its knees by problems with sessions that are unexpectedly shared among multiple users. *Concurrency testing* can catch this sort of problem. And it not only tests for multiple users accessing the code, but even just a single user opening multiple browsers. Using even the simplest of freeware tool to simulate multiple users visiting the site may reveal unexpected problems.

Site monitoring

Another form of integration testing that we list earlier is *site monitoring*, which can also be facilitated using the recorded scripts/scenarios from the testing tools we've been describing in this section on "Application-integration testing."

Site monitoring tells you about the ongoing state of the application after it's in production, asking the simple questions: Is the site up? Is anyone aware if it goes down? Did changes break the site?

Most of the aforementioned Web-application testing tool-makers offer ways in which their tool can be set up to perform long-term monitoring of your applications. Other players in the market who can also provide tools for this task include `freshwater.com` and `tracert.com`, as well as several others. Some of these tools merely provide a mechanism to ping your site (or a given page) to ensure that the site is up and e-mail you if it goes down, while others are more elaborate in their testing and reporting.

The Enterprise edition of CF MX offers yet another approach to site monitoring with its system-probes mechanism within the Administrator. (See Chapter 43 for a brief discussion of probes, and the ColdFusion MX manual *Administering ColdFusion MX* for more details.)

Server-integration testing

Finally, a CF project usually exists within the context of several other servers providing related services. Still more opportunities for testing your application are available in this area, including testing the availability and performance of the Web server (and cluster, if any), the physical hardware running the ColdFusion server, the particular database (and database server, if any), the mail server, the ftp server, and so on. It may be possible to use some of the tools listed at the opening of this section, but I raise this point simply so you don't forget to consider these cross-server integration issues as you develop a testing plan.

We could discuss other forms of testing as well, such as usability, documentation, installation, configuration, reliability/recovery, end-to-end, unit, white/gray/black-box and so on. See the many resources that we offer in the section "Resources For Learning More," near the end of this chapter, for more information on these and all the forms of testing that we discuss in this chapter.

Performance Measurement

Perhaps a flip side of testing is measurement — in particular, *performance measurement*. How well is the application performing? You can measure the performance of your application by several means, and performance can also be evaluated on several levels. Indeed, beyond such measurements within your ColdFusion application, you also face matters of measurement for the entire ColdFusion server. The next few sections deal with measuring ColdFusion performance.

You also must deal with measurement concerns involving your web server, database server, the server on which ColdFusion is running, and perhaps other issues, such as your network and other servers. We can't take the time to detail all those possibilities, plus it would be difficult with so many possible different configurations that our readers may have. There will be plenty of resources available to assist with the broader issue of server and operating system performance measurement, and we leave it to the reader to find those resources or seek assistance in measuring the non-ColdFusion aspects of their particular environment.

But a discussion of ColdFusion-specific performance measurement is very appropriate and would in fact be harder to find discussed in general performance measurement and tuning books, to the following section focuses on that.

ColdFusion performance measurement

Several forms of measurement are available within your ColdFusion application and the ColdFusion server. The following sections focus first on the measurements that you can perform on or within your template.

ColdFusion debugging information

Perhaps the simplest form of measurement is provided automatically in ColdFusion's debugging information. Debugging information is enabled in the ColdFusion Administrator by clicking the link for Debugging Settings in the left navigational toolbar and then checking the Enable Debugging check box, as shown in Figure 42-7. Be sure to click the Submit Changes button on the top right of the administrator screen (which does not appear in the figure). This will enable debugging. We'll discuss in a moment how to actually see debugging in the output of your templates.

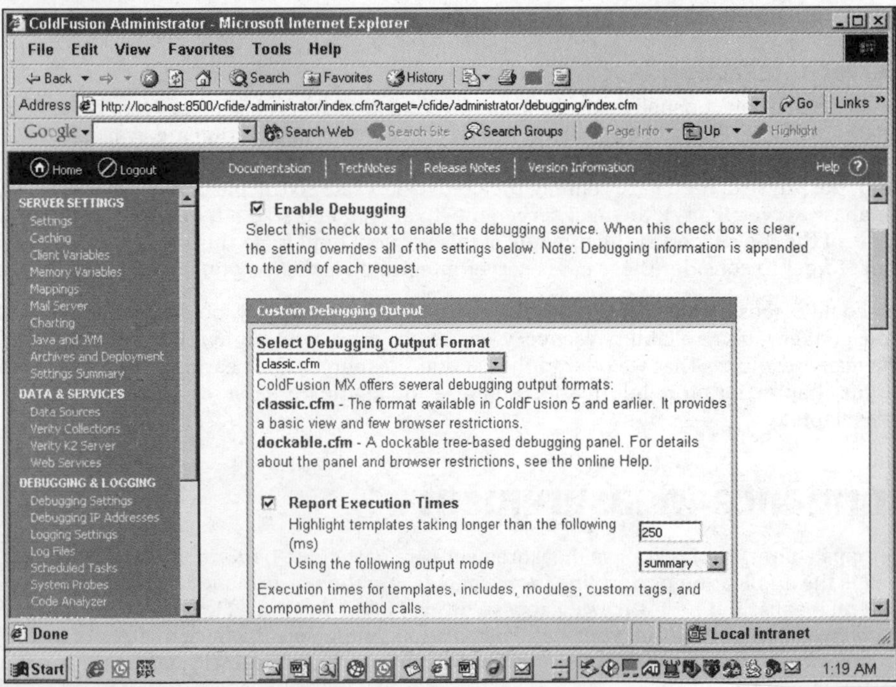

Figure 42-7: ColdFusion Administrator Debugging Settings.

Enabling the debugging option is generally appropriate only in a development environment, because some of the information provided — such as the physical path to a CF template or the datasource names and table and column names used in your queries — could be used by hackers or other unauthorized users. There may also be a modest performance penalty of displaying and gathering the debugging information. Still, the debugging information is invaluable in many circumstances.

Viewing debugging output

After you enable the debugging output in the Administrator as described in the previous section, it will then appear at the bottom of the output in your browser whenever the page is executed. It displays such measurement information as how long code takes to compile, how long queries take to execute, and so on. See the example shown in Figure 42-8.

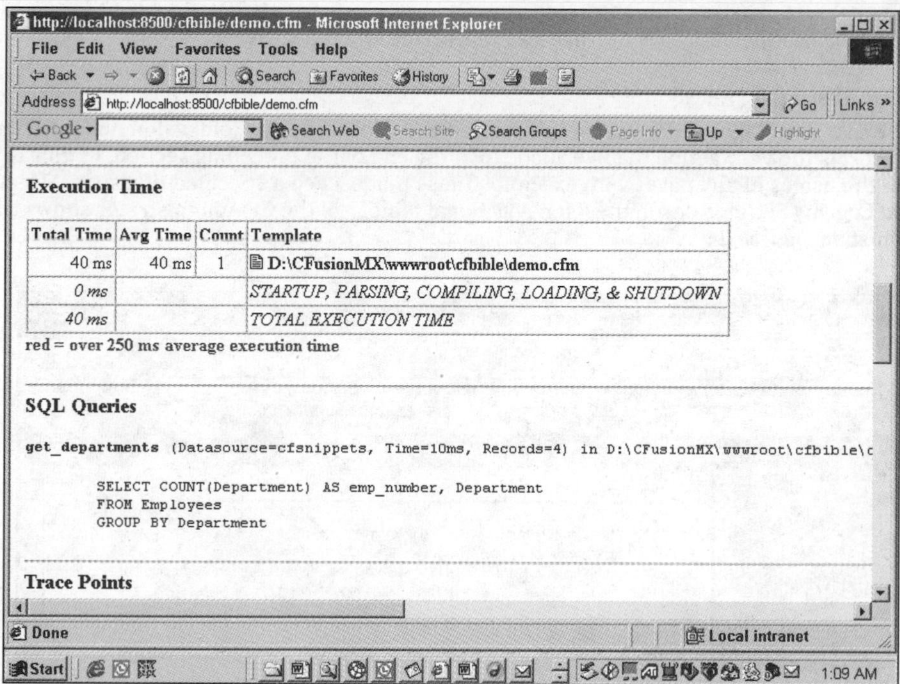

Figure 42-8: ColdFusion Debugging output, including measurements.

Notice that this figure shows both the time that a template took to run (as well as to start up and compile), and it also shows the time that any queries on the page took to run (such as the `get_departments` query on this page).

With these basic measurements, you can begin to understand the performance and bottlenecks in your applications. Notice as well that, if the page includes any files or if an `Application.cfm` is executed before the program that's executing, the performance information for those pages is shown as well.

While the debugging information will by default display at the bottom of the page (assuming debugging is enabled), it's possible to cause an alternative form of display. If the Administrator changes the `Debugging Settings` page (see Figure 42-7) to select `dockable.cfm` option for `Select Debugging Output Format`, debugging information instead shows up in a new browser window that changes to reflect whatever CF page you've most recently browsed.

Finally, one other new feature in CF MX can also assist in focusing on performance trouble spots. Notice in Figure 42-8 that, at the bottom of the table showing the time for executing parts of the page, it also reads as follows:

```
red = over 250 ms average execution time
```

This information indicates if any part of the execution of one of the pages displayed had exceeded 250 milliseconds, in which case it would appear in this table in red. You can change the timeframe for that in the Report Execution Times area of the Debugging Settings page (refer to Figure 42-7).

With all this debugging (and some metric) information, you can start to focus on specific aspects of your application that deserve attention. The approach to obtaining this information is imperfect, in that you must be viewing the debugging info of the page to see that measurement information. A better solution would be to instead ask CF to highlight for you any pages run on the entire server that exceed a preferred time-span.

Log slow pages

The Log Slow Pages Taking Longer than x Seconds option in the ColdFusion Administrator performs the very action that we allude to at the end of the preceding section, writing to a log file the names of any pages with execution times that exceed a specified timespan. Selecting the Logging Settings link in the left navigational toolbar of the CF Administrator shows the screen in Figure 42-9.

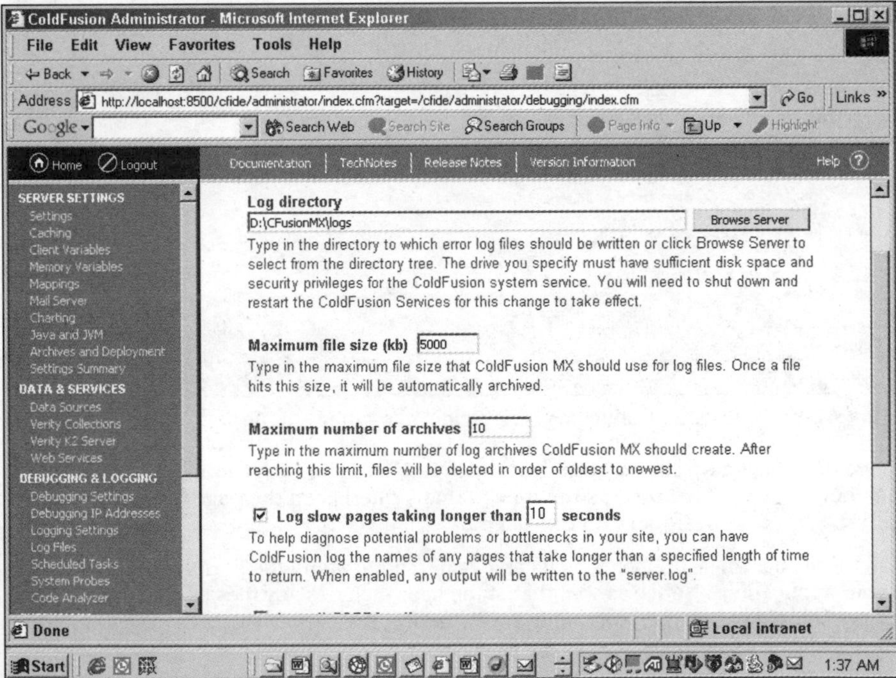

Figure 42-9: Log Slow Pages setting in the administrator.

With this setting enabled, if the execution time of any CF templates exceeds the specified timespan (10 seconds in Figure 42-9), an entry is written to the `server.log` file (in the directory also specified on that screen for the Log Directory option). The log-file entry may appear in a format similar to the following example:

```
"Warning","web-0","09/02/02","16:23:48",,"Thread: web-0, processing
template: D:\CFusionMX\wwwroot\CFIDE\administrator\index.cfm, completed
in 22 seconds, exceeding the 10 second warning limit"
```

In this example, an attempt to use the Administrator itself caused an execution time of 22 seconds for some reason. Any such long-running tasks may be good candidates for performance tuning, as discussed later in "Performance Tuning." Indeed, you may want to set this `Log Slow Pages` value to a low enough value that you find a few example templates to tune.

Be careful, however, about focusing only on the longest-running templates. If something runs for a long time but only very infrequently, that may not be as important (nor use as many resources) as a template that run in less time but is executed far more often. This setting and log file are but one of several tools in your ColdFusion performance measurement toolkit.

New CFTRACE tag

Although the two performance-measurement tools that we describe in the preceding sections are useful for measuring the *total* execution time of your templates, you may be interested in knowing how much time is spent performing some *segment* of your template.

Until CF MX, if you wanted to track the elapsed time between two points in your code, you needed to use the `GetTickCount()` function to set temporary variables to note the start time and end time around some task and then compute and report the difference between the two.

Now, this process is much simpler if you use the new `CFTRACE` tag. `CFTRACE` is discussed further in Chapter 59, but it can be used very simply to track performance of a segment of code, reporting the time that code takes to execute.

Simply surround any code to be timed with `CFTRACE` tags (not paired opening/closing tags but simply a pair of opening tags) as in the following example:

```
<cftrace>
<!--- some code to be timed --->
<cftrace>
```

By default, this tag create reports of the time taken executing the code between the tags, placing that report in the debugging information at the bottom of the executed page's output (if that's enabled in the ColdFusion Administrator). The following is a sample of the output that might be shown there:

```
Trace Points
 [10:36:44.044 D:\CFusionMX\wwwroot\cfbible\demo.cfm
@ line: 9] [10 ms (1st trace)] -
 [10:36:44.044 D:\CFusionMX\wwwroot\cfbible\demo.cfm
@ line: 18] [30 ms (20 ms)] -
```

This segment from the debugging output, labeled `Trace Points` shows an entry for each time that the CFTRACE was executed. Notice that the second entry concludes with the indication `(20 ms)` that tells us the code fragment took 20 milliseconds to execute. The `CFTRACE` tag, used this way, simply reports the time interval between the start of the template and the first `CFTRACE` (indicated as `1st trace` in that output fragment), then the time between subsequent `CFTRACEs`.

Although you can also use the `inline="yes"` attribute to cause the tracing information to appear within the output of the page (where the `CFTRACE` occurs) in addition to the debugging output, the "inline" version of information does not calculate the time difference between invocations of the CFTRACE.

The same information is also automatically written to a log file — the `logs\cftrace.log` file in the ColdFusion MX installation directory — in the following format:

```
"Information","web-183","09/20/02","10:36:44","TEST","[10 ms (1st
trace)] [D:\CFusionMX\wwwroot\cfbible\demo.cfm @ line: 9] - "
"Information","web-183","09/20/02","10:36:44","TEST","[30 ms (20)]
[D:\CFusionMX\wwwroot\cfbible\demo.cfm @ line: 18] -
```

As Chapter 59 of this book explains, `CFTRACE` offers various ways to help make other aspects of debugging simpler. For instance, you can use the `type` and `category` attributes to group related traces, and the `text` and `var` attributes enable you to specify additional information to appear along with the trace (a message with the text or value of the value of the named variable, respectively).

For the `var` attribute, a couple matters deserve clarification. First, the attribute expects the name of a variable — in other words, a name without pound signs. Furthermore, if the variable named is a complex variable (such as a query or structure), the information appearing in the debugging output and log file lists only the variable name and number of elements in the complex variable object; it does not show the contents of the variable. If you specify `inline="yes"`, however, it shows the output in the form of `CFDUMP` output. See chapters 7 and 48 for more information on CFDUMP and how it's output appears for complex variables.

CFStat utility

Finally, besides simply measuring the total time (or even the time of a segment) of running a CF template, another important thing that you need to know is how the entire ColdFusion server is performing while your applications are running (and even if they are not). Such real-time performance metrics, especially if analyzed over time, can be key in understanding the nature of certain performance bottlenecks.

Although several operating system features also monitor system-level real-time statistics — for example, the Windows Performance Monitor — the CFStat utility doesn't require that you run that tool to view these statistics.

For ColdFusion to write to the needed statistics, you must check the `Enable Performance Monitor` checkbox, which you also find on the Debugging Settings page of the CF Administrator. After you enable it, you must restart the server for the option to take effect.

With the performance monitor option enabled, you can then execute the CFStat utility from the command line. In Windows NT/2000/XP, you can access the command line by using the Start ⇨ Run ⇨ cmd menu command. In Windows 95/98/ME, use Start ⇨ Run ⇨ Command. If ColdFusion MX is installed in the `d:\cfusionmx` directory, issue the following commands:

```
d:
cd \cfusionmx\bin\
```

Then, to run the CFStat utility, simply type `cfstat` at the command line. The output may appear as shown in Figure 42-10.

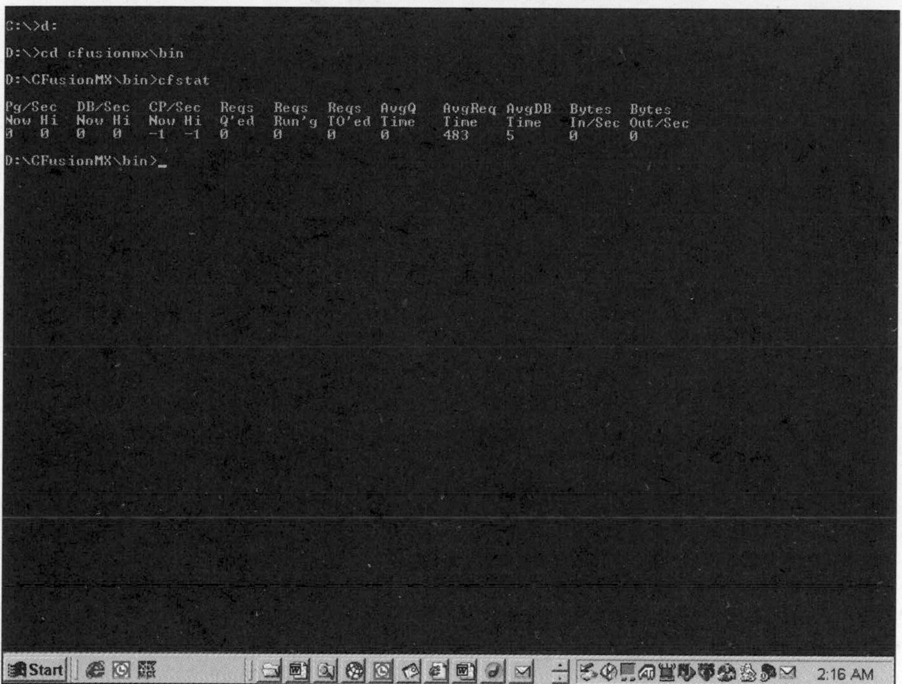

Figure 42-10: CFStat command line output.

The statistics displayed are described in Table 42-1.

Table 42-1

Metric Abbreviation	*Metric Name*	*Description*
Pg/Sec	Page hits per second	The number of ColdFusion pages processed per second. You can reduce this by moving static content to HTML pages.
DB/Sec	Database accesses per second	The number of database accesses per second made by ColdFusion. Any difference in complexity and resource load between calls is ignored.
CP/Sec	Cache pops per second	The number of ColdFusion template cache pops per second. A *cache pop* occurs whenever ColdFusion ejects a cached template from the template cache to make room for a new template.
Reqs Q'ed	Number of queued requests	The number of requests that are currently waiting for ColdFusion to process them. Lower values, which you can achieve with efficient CFML, are better.

Continued

Table 42-1: *(continued)*

Metric Abbreviation	*Metric Name*	*Description*
Reqs Run'g	Number of running requests	The number of requests that ColdFusion is currently actively processing.
Reqs TO'ed	Number of timed out requests	The total number of ColdFusion requests that have timed out. Lower values, which you can achieve by aggressive caching and removing unnecessary dynamic operations and third-party events, are better.
AvgQ Time	Average queue time	A running average of the time, in milliseconds, that requests spend waiting for ColdFusion to process them. Lower values, which you can achieve with efficient CFML and enhanced caching, are better.
AvgReq Time	Average request time	A running average of the time, in milliseconds, that ColdFusion spends to process a request (including queued time). Lower values, which you can achieve with efficient CFML, are better.
AvgDB Time	Average database transaction time	A running average of the time ColdFusion spends on database-related processing of ColdFusion requests.
Bytes In/Sec	Bytes incoming per second	The number of bytes ColdFusion read in the last second (not an average).
Bytes Out/Sec	Bytes outgoing per second	The number of bytes ColdFusion wrote in the last second (not an average).

The information in the third column of Table 42-1 offers some insights into performance-tuning opportunities based on the values displayed by CFStat. Finally, the `cfstat` command offers a couple arguments that change how it works, including displaying the output automatically every few seconds. Simply enter the command `cfstat /?` to see those options.

As useful as observing this information in real time may be, viewing the ColdFusion performance statistics in some sort of repository that tracks the information over time may also prove helpful, as is the case with the option in "Log slow pages" to display long-running requests to a log file. You can set up your operating system's performance-monitoring tools, such as the Windows Performance Monitor, to enable them to create log files, warnings, and more, all of which, however, are beyond the scope of this book.

Performance Tuning

After learning about many ways to test and measure ColdFusion applications, as you do in preceding sections of this chapter, you may find a discussion about a variety of common performance-tuning opportunities helpful now. The sections that follow offer some general guidelines about such opportunities. You may, however, be aware of some exceptions and variations to what we describe in these sections, depending on circumstances. We recommend that you test any alternatives for your own environment to determine their value.

The tuning opportunities that we discuss range from changes that you can make in your code to changes that you can make in your database (in terms of selection, design, configuration, and SQL coding), to changes that you can make in your CF administrator or in the configuration of the server, which could, of course, affect the entire server.

CF-coding tuning opportunities

Many readers may expect this section to launch into discussions of certain classic CF tuning arguments, such as whether to use CFOUTPUT around an entire page or each variable, whether to worry about over-use of pound signs or the Evaluate() function, the asserted importance of prefixing all variable references, or using CFSCRIPT wherever possible. In our experience, these issues may not be that all important compared to many others that we discuss.

Caching with CFCACHE

Do you think you may have ColdFusion pages on your site aren't really that dynamic? Maybe you've enabled a CFINCLUDE of headers and footers, for example. You're asking ColdFusion to process this page each time a visitor comes to the site.

We don't have enough room to explain the caching process and CFCACHE in particular completely. See Chapter 59 or the Macromedia *CFML Reference* for more information. Just know that, if you simply place a CFCACHE tag on a page, ColdFusion automatically creates a static HTML version of the page and serves that version to users who visit the page from now on. The process of creating the cached HTML and serving it up to subsequent visitors is transparent to them and to you as a developer (outside using the CFCACHE tag on the page).

Of course, you may prefer to specify a timespan that is allowed to pass before the server refreshes the cached version of the page. Using the new timespan attribute, which is used with the CreateTimeSpan function as in the following example, does that:

```
<cfcache timespan="#CreateTimeSpan(0,8,0,0)#">
```

This code sets the cache to be flushed whenever a visitor returns to the site any time beyond eight hours after the first user's visit causes it to be cached. These visitors can be the same or different users. (CF5 and earlier versions had a timeout attribute, which is now deprecated).

Of course, you may want to flush the cache sooner than that, and you can do so by using the action="flush" attribute of the CFCACHE tag. See Chapter 59 for the details of how to use that option.

Another new characteristic of the tag is that the default action for caching now takes place on both the client and server. It's also capable of caching different result sets based on session state and the new CFLOGIN structure, as discussed in Chapter 40.

Finally, the CFCACHE tag is smart enough to consider visits to the page using different URLs to create/use different cached results. In other words, if one visit to the page presents a query string of ?id=5, that will create a different cached result than ?id=6, as indeed you'd hope it would. See the other resources mentioned for more details on the tag.

Caching by using CFSAVECONTENT

Some find that the CFCACHE tag involves a little too much brute force in that it's typically used to cache an entire page. What if only some part of the page is dynamic, but the rest can be cached? If you use CFCACHE, you seem to be stuck caching the entire page. Many came to realize, however, that the CFSAVECONTENT tag, introduced in CF5, offered a solution. For more information about this solution, see "Simple Caching Techniques with CFSAVECONTENT", at www.macromedia.com/v1/handlers/index.cfm?ID=21422.

Be careful about enabling Client variables

The `Application.cfm` file, because it executes before every execution of every page in the directory or directories under its influence, is a powerful opportunity in ColdFusion. Settings implemented here affect an entire application. In terms of bang for your buck, if you can make an effective improvement here, it can have a multiplying effect in improving performance for the entire application. Some opportunities for improvement may not be readily apparent.

If your `CFAPPLICATION` tag is set to `clientmanagement="yes"`, for example, a couple small but possibly substantial issues may be hurting you.

First, the location where Client variables are stored is something that you can set by using the `CFAPPLICATION` tag's `clientstorage` attribute. If you don't set it, you get the default setting for the entire server. As installed, CF defaults to writing Client variables to the Registry. Although the administrator may change that default, if he or she doesn't and you don't choose a value in `CFAPPLICATION` for the `clientstorage` attribute, you end up storing data in the registry.

The registry isn't the most scalable solution for writing Client variable data for all the visitors to your (and possibly others') CF applications. It may not perform well with a large number of concurrent users writing to it, and it can grow to a size that could break the Registry and compromise the integrity of the entire server.

Instead, you can choose to store Client variables in a database or in your browser visitors' cookies. You should carefully consider which choice you make. Each has its benefits and detriments. See chapters 4 and 46 for more information.

But a more substantial problem occurs if you're not really using Client variables at all but still have them enabled as we just described. Enabling Client variables may seem innocuous if you're doing nothing with them, but by default, ColdFusion also tracks information about each user's visit to your site and stores that information (last visit, hit count) in the Client-variable store. Again, this could be the registry if the defaults in the Administrator and the `CFAPPLICATION` tag are in effect. That's needless overhead if you're not really using Client variables. Consider turning them off if that's the case.

These are just a few CF-coding issues that may be worth considering. We're not done offering CF tuning tips. It's just that the remainder of them are related to database processing. To be honest, far more challenge and wasted resources are likely to come from matters related to database processing, as we discuss in the following sections.

Database selection/design/indexing

Many consultants and developers recognize that database processing is usually the largest contributor to poor performance in a Web application. Several aspects of database processing are worth investigating, many of which again have nothing to do with actual coding.

Database optimization starts with choosing the right DBMS for the job, proceeds to good database design, includes the correct use of indexing, and finally involves using your DBMS options to test and tune your SQL and DB design. These are generic topics that apply to many development environments other than ColdFusion.

See the section "Database-tuning resources," near the end of this chapter, for many documents and Web sites that can assist you with this aspect of tuning.

Database-coding tuning opportunities

Sticking with the discussion of opportunities for tuning in your ColdFusion code, you need to be aware of a few important coding practices. Your main goal should be to avoid unnecessary database I/O (interactivity), and also avoid doing in ColdFusion anything that you can do in the database. Databases are designed and optimized to perform data analysis and manipulation. Many developers fall into a trap of performing extensive string manipulation, calculations, and record matching in CF code, which would be better performed in SQL.

Again, see the section "Database-tuning resources," for pointers to information on learning more about SQL and what the language can do. It's a subject about which many CF developers could stand to learn a good deal more.

Cfqueryparam tag

The `CFQUERYPARAM` tag is a subtag of `CFQUERY`. Many developers never use it, or they know of it only as a security-related feature. Instead, it is indeed a performance-tuning opportunity. See Chapter 52 for more information. The most important tuning aspect of the tag is that it creates what are called *bind parameters* in the SQL that are passed to the database, which can dramatically improve performance in most DBMSes in most instances. Chapter 52 has examples of how to use this tag.

Just be aware of an issue in specifying Date/Time data types in the `cfsqltype` attribute of this tag. Instead of using `cf_sql_date`, which may seem perfectly normal, you may find using `cf_sql_timestamp` to be more appropriate. Just be aware of the two choices. One or the other will work for your combination of database and data being passed by way of the tag.

CachedWithin attribute of CFQUERY

If your visitors are repeatedly calling one or more pages that perform queries producing results that don't change often, you should seriously consider using the `cachedwithin` attribute of `CFQUERY`. This attribute causes ColdFusion to store the query result set in memory and reuse it for a timespan specified in the `cachdwithin` attribute. This caching of the data, and its reuse and reduction in the performance of database i/o, can lead to tremendous savings in resources and also speeds the execution of pages benefiting from the cached result. Again, see Chapter 52 for more information on this tag and also the related `cachedafter` attribute, which may have value in some situations.

Avoid SELECT *

The recommendation to avoid `SELECT *` in SQL may seem either obvious or not worth bothering about, depending on your experience with databases, but asking the database to return all columns in a query (with `SELECT *`) is usually a potential performance-tuning opportunity if you're not using all the columns in the query. Simply put, if you don't need all the columns to perform your intended output processing, you're wasting resources asking for all the columns.

Consider that you're asking the DBMS to retrieve all columns from all the records found, bringing them over the network connection from the database server to ColdFusion (or through an in-memory process from a local database on the same server), and then filling ColdFusion's memory with all the columns. If you then use only a small number of the columns, you may have wasted a great deal of effort (all the worse if you're not using the caching features mentioned the preceding section).

Consider too that some poorly designed tables have many, many columns, and the cost of this simple recommendation starts to grow exponentially.

Using Count(*) to count records

Many CF developers who want a count of all records in a table or those that meet a certain criteria may perform a simple `CFQUERY` containing a `SELECT` statement (such as `SELECT *`) to find the records. Then they refer to the special CF variable *queryname*.`recordcount` to determine the number of records found.

This approach of selecting records to be counted this way is acceptable only so as long as you are also using all the records (and columns) that you've retrieved for some purpose. Even if you avoid the `SELECT *` (see the tip in the preceding section), you may still have wasted tremendous resources gathering one or more columns and all the selected records.

If all you want is that count of the number of records found, using any features in the database for providing that more succinctly is far better.

For instance, the `SELECT count(*)` statement in SQL is designed specifically to retrieve and return just the `recordcount` for records that meet whatever other `WHERE` clause criteria (if any) that may be provided. In most databases, this syntax results in a very quick retrieval of just that record count with minimal I/O. Be aware, however, that some DBMS's may still perform an inefficient retrieval to answer that `SELECT` statement.

See the manuals for your DBMS for more details about how your DBMS processes `count(*)`. And any introductory SQL reference or manual will generally provide for more information on using the count() aggregate function. The next section recommends a very good one for CF developers.

See Ben Forta's *Teach Yourself SQL in 10 Minutes*

We know that listing a reference to a book may seem a strange "tuning opportunity," but we really feel that many CF developers have only a passing understanding of the least amount of SQL that they need to know to just get by. Improving your SQL skills can help improve the performance of your applications. It's usually very easy to use after you know the solutions.

The problem is that many CF developers never learn these solutions. Ben Forta's *Teach Yourself SQL in 10 Minutes* does a great job of distilling the "least that you need to know" in working with basic SQL operations. Yet it also quickly moves past the basics into intermediate and (for some) rather advanced operations. Topics covered in the book that are worth learning include the use of aggregate functions (including the `count(*)` clause referred to in the preceding section), the use of inner and outer joins and unions, considering subqueries (in both `SELECT` and `WHERE` clauses), and so much more.

Consider the effect of CFTRANSACTION's isolation level

Use of isolation levels in `CFTRANSACTION` (and in database processing in general) is a topic that many developers don't seem to fully understand. If you're using the `CFTRANSACTION` tag to indicate that a series of database update operations should be executed in total or not at all, you need to understand the *isolation level* of the transaction.

This level is a setting that you can control by using the `Isolation` attribute of `CFTRANSACTION`. If you don't specify this level, however, you leave yourself at the whim of the DBMS and/or database designer, each of which may provide a default value if you don't indicate one.

The concept of isolation levels isn't unique to ColdFusion. Again, any good reference on SQL and database processing should explain the concept adequately. Learn about it and make a conscious, correct decision. Finally, while we're mentioning `CFTRANSACTION`, be careful not to use it if it's not really needed. Considerable overhead is involved in managing transactions.

`CFTRANSACTION` is covered further in chapters 10 and 52.

Consider stored procedures for faster execution

If your DBMS supports the feature known generically as stored procedures, you should seriously consider using them. These are discussed in Chapter 10. For many reasons, they can increase the performance of your SQL operations. The SQL book by Ben Forta that we mention in the section before last also does a good job explaining the benefits.

Even if you're using a database such as Microsoft Access, which doesn't support true stored procedures, you can at least approximate them, as described in an October 1999 *ColdFusion Developers Journal* article "Stored Procedures in Access? Yes indeed!" by Charles Arehart, at `http://www.sys-con.com/coldfusion/article.cfm?id=51`.

Datasource configuration

Many developers and administrators make the mistaken assumption that there's nothing more to defining a datasource in ColdFusion than mapping a datasource name to a physical database name in the Administrator (a process discussed in Chapter 9).

What they often miss are several available options under the "Show Advanced Settings" button on that datasource configuration screen in the CF Administrator. There are many alternatives presented there, but two that could have a performance impact are:

- `Maintain Connections` – this option controls whether ColdFusion should keep a connection to a database once obtained. While the conventional wisdom is that you should maintain connections to improve performance, there have been documented instances where in some situations it is more effective to disable this option. See Macromedia TechNote at `http://www.macromedia.com/v1/Handlers/index.cfm?ID=1540&Method=Full`
- `Limit Connections` – this option controls how many connections can be made to this datasource by multiple concurrently running users.

These two settings are ones where you must determine for yourself the balance of setting the value either too high or too low. Use either a load testing tool, as discussed in the section "Load-testing", or consider making the change in a testing environment and observe the performance impact while your application is tested.

Be aware, too, that if you're using specific usernames and passwords within your `CFQUERY` tags, doing so causes new connections to be created for each user. If you can avoid that, you generally get better performance.

Also, for more information on database connections, see the Macromedia TechNote "How Are Database Connections Handled in ColdFusion?" at `http://www.macromedia.com/v1/Handlers/index.cfm?ID=22128&Method=Full`.

Still another choice to be made during datasource configuration is the type of database driver connection to be used. While it may seem obvious (since in CFMX most driver names match the database names), just be aware that in the Enterprise edition of CFMX you have the choice of Native drivers for Oracle, DB2, Informix, and Sybase.

CF Administrator settings

We simply don't have room in this single chapter to address in detail each of the options in the ColdFusion Administrator that may prove fruitful in providing an opportunity for tuning performance. But because many CF developers either never have access to the Administrator interface or, in case they may, can make only suggestions to their administrators, we want to just mention in this section a few topics worth your further consideration.

We leave it to you to investigate in further detail the options that we mention in the following list:

- ✦ Tune the `Limit simultaneous requests` option on the `Server Settings` page.
- ✦ Tune the `Template cache` size and consider enabling the `Trusted cache` option, on the `Caching` page.
- ✦ Tune the `Limit the maximum number of cached queries on the server to x` option, also on the `Caching` page.
- ✦ Disable the `Enable Performance Monitoring`, `Enable CFSTAT` and `Enable Robust Exception Information` options in the Debug Settings page if you're not benefiting from their output.
- ✦ Consider the effect of storing Client variables in the registry versus in a database (see the discussion above in "Be careful about enabling Client variables").
- ✦ Consider raising or lowering the`Timeout Requests after (n) Seconds` on the `Server Settings` page (see the Macromedia Technotes listed in the next section for more information).
- ✦ Consider the impact of setting the `Enable Whitespace Management` option on the `Server Settings` page.
- ✦ Consider the effect of enabling Application and Session variables.
- ✦ Consider the effect of setting the default and maximum Application and Session timeouts.
- ✦ Consider the effect of enabling J2EE sessions.
- ✦ Consider the effect of tuning the `Connection Timeout` and Spool Interval settings for mail processing on the `Mail Server` page.
- ✦ Consider configuring the `Mail Server` setting on that page to an IP address rather than a domain name.
- ✦ Consider the options on the `Charting` page, including the options for `Cache Type` (disk or memory), `Maximum number of images in cache`, `Maximum Number of charting threads`, and `Disk cache lLocation`.
- ✦ Consider the effect of which Java Virtual Machine is selected, how it's configured, and the `Initial` and `Maximum Memory Size` in the `Java and JVM` page.
- ✦ Beware the new `Logging Settings` page options, which specify a `Maximum file size` for log files and then initiates the process of rolling them off to archives until the `Maximum number of archives` is reached, at which point the oldest archives are deleted. This default behavior may not be expected by users familiar with previous releases of CFMX where log files could grow to enormous sizes and who may not notice they are now losing old, rolled off logs.
- ✦ As we discuss in the section " Log slow pages," earlier in this chapter, enable the `Log Slow Pages` option to monitor pages taking excessive time to process.
- ✦ Ensure that scheduled tasks are not running more often than necessary. For instance, someone might mistakenly (or intentionally) setup a scheduled task to run every minute, or every 5 or 20 or 60 minutes. The point is, make sure that the scheduled task isn't running any more often than needed.
- ✦ Similarly, with probes set on the `System Probes` page, ensure there are not an excessive number of them and that they're not running more often than really needed.

Resources For Learning More

As we note at the outset of this chapter, we have little chance of adequately exploring the topics of testing and performance in this chapter. To compensate, we now conclude the chapter with the following sections, listing a wide range of resources that can help you learn more about these topics.

ColdFusion tuning resources

Macromedia has offered several resources in the form of technotes, whitepapers, and briefs that attempt to address common concerns of CF developers and administrators regarding performance:

- ✦ CF MX Performance Brief (`www.macromedia.com/software/coldfusion/whitepapers/pdf/cfmx_performance_brief.pdf`)
- ✦ ColdFusion 5 Performance Brief (`www.macromedia.com/software/coldfusion/whitepapers/pdf/cfmx_performance_brief.pdf`)
- ✦ Macromedia Knowledge Base/TechNotes (`www.macromedia.com/v1/support/knowledgebase/searchform.cfm`)—see 922 (somewhat dated), 566, 8627 (detailed tuning ideas), 12,970 (general load-testing guidelines), 11,773
- ✦ CFMX manual *Using ClusterCats,* Chapter 2, "Creating Scalable and Highly Available Web Sites"

There are some other resources that are related to ColdFusion tuning available from other publishers:

- ✦ *Optimizing ColdFusion*, by Chris Cortes, (published by Osborne/McGraw-Hill), which was written for CF 5 and may have many ideas that are still relevant in CFMX
- ✦ "E-Testing: Debugging Your Projects," by Charlie Arehart, *ColdFusion Developers Journal*, October 2001 (`www.sys-con.com/coldfusion/article.cfm?id=349`)
- ✦ "Toward Better CF Server Administration—Part 1: Performance," by Charlie Arehart, published in *Cold Fusion Developers Journal*, January 2002 (`http://www.sys-con.com/coldfusion/article.cfm?id=387`)

Web-application testing resources

Because Web application testing really isn't specific to ColdFusion, many resources can prove helpful. The following sections describe several such resources.

Online Articles

The first group of resources includes articles that appear on various web sites:

- ✦ "Stranger in a Strange Land: Bringing Quality Assurance to a Web Startup," by Lisa Crispin (`www.stickyminds.com/docs_index/XUS247559file1.doc`)
- ✦ "Understanding Performance Testing" (`msdn.microsoft.com/library/en-us/dnduwon/html/d5dplyover.asp`)
- ✦ "Web-Site Monitoring Derails Problems," by Billie Shea (`www.informationweek.com/805/webdev.htm`)

Books

A few good books on Web-application testing are. Again, they are generic but still valuable. Following are just a few:

- *Testing Applications on the Web: Test Planning for Internet-Based Systems*, by Hung Quoc Nguyen (published by Wiley, 2000)
- *The Web Testing Handbook*, by Steven Splaine (published by Software Quality Engineering Pub, 2001)
- *Automated Software Testing: Introduction, Management, and Performance*, by Elfriede Dustin, *et al*
- *Software Test Automation: Effective Use of Test Execution Tools*, by Dorothy Graham, et al
- *Surviving the Challenges of Software Testing*, by William E. Perry, *et al*

Perhaps on par with any book in size and value is an informative and contemporary thesis, "Web Application Testing", by Jesper Ryden and Par Svensson, at `http://www.stickyminds.com/getfile.asp?ot=XML&id=2671&fn=XUS512798file1%2Ezip`.

Portal and information resource Web sites

Many Web sites offer useful resources in the area of Web-application testing , but some of the more prominent ones include the following:

- QAForums (`www.qaforums.com/`)
- Software Quality Engineering (`www.sqe.com/`)
- Sticky Minds (`www.stickyminds.com/`)
- Software QA Test Resource Center (`www.softwareqatest.com/`)
- QA City (`www.qacity.com`)
- Keynote Systems (`www.keynote.com/services/html/product_lib.html`)
- Mercury Interactive (`www-svca.mercuryinteractive.com/resources/library/`)

Performance-tuning resources

As is the case for Web-application testing, many resources are available for performance tuning, especially in regard to database tuning. Although a number of the following resources are Microsoft specific, many of the suggestions may be more generically valuable:

- "Performance Tuning", including a walkthrough of using PerfMon (`www.15seconds.com/issue/971127.htm`)
- "The Art and Science of Web Server Tuning with Internet Information Services 5.0 "(`www.microsoft.com/windows2000/techinfo/administration/web/tuning.asp`)
- "Server Performance and Scalability Killers" (`http://msdn.microsoft.com/library/default.asp?URL=/library/en-us/dniis/html/tencom.asp`)
- "Improving ASP Application Performance" "(`http://msdn.microsoft.com/library/default.asp?url=/library/en-us/dnserv/html/server03272000.asp`)
- "15 Seconds Performance Section" (`www.15seconds.com/focus/Performance.htm`)

✦ "Server Performance Optimization on Microsoft's Web Site", (www.microsoft.com/technet/treeview/default.asp?url=/technet/prodtechnol/iis/maintain/optimize/serverop.asp)

Database-tuning resources

Many resources are available for database tuning, and most developers working with Enterprise-class databases already have the luxury of ample resources (both human and intellectual) to assist them. So the list in the following section may lean toward the Microsoft world, especially low-end databases where clients may be seeking to eek out the most possible performance before moving to a larger, more scalable DBMS. SQL Server resources follow in the section by that name.

Access/ODBC resources

Despite many asserting that Microsoft Access is ill-suited to production use, the fact is that many developers still use it by choice or by force. In fact, despite the frequent assertion by some that "even Microsoft says not to use it in production," there are a surprising number of articles and white papers showing performance tuning of Access databases from the company:

✦ "Using Microsoft Jet with IIS"—recommends OLE database over ODBC (http://support.microsoft.com/default.aspx?scid=KB;EN-US;Q222135)

✦ "How to Improve the Performance of Your MDAC Application" (www.microsoft.com/technet/treeview/default.asp?url=/technet/prodtechnol/sscomm/reskit/mdacapp.asp)

✦ "How to Optimize Microsoft Access When Using ODBC Data Sources" (http://support.microsoft.com/default.aspx?scid=KB;EN-US;Q209091)

✦ "Improve Performance of Applications Using Jet 4.0" (http://support.microsoft.com/default.aspx?scid=KB;EN-US;Q240434)

✦ "Speed Up Apps that Use the Microsoft Access ODBC Driver" (http://support.microsoft.com/default.aspx?scid=KB;EN-US;Q126131)

✦ "How to Enable ODBC Connection Pooling Performance Counters" (http://support.microsoft.com/default.aspx?scid=KB;EN-US;Q216950)

✦ "ODBC Connection Pooling Counters in Performance Monitor and ADO" (http://support.microsoft.com/default.aspx?scid=KB;EN-US;Q245543)

SQL Server resources

As would be expected, there are many more articles and resources about SQL Server:

✦ "MS SQL Server Diagnostics" (www.microsoft.com/technet/treeview/default.asp?url=/technet/prodtechnol/sql/proddocs/diag/75528frt.asp)

✦ "Database Performance Tuning Strategies" (www.eweek.com/article2/0,3959,12410,00.asp)

✦ SearchDatabase.com's "SQL Server Performance and Tuning Tips" (http://searchdatabase.techtarget.com/bestWebLinks/0,289521,sid13_tax286880,00.html)

✦ "Microsoft SQL Server Performance Tuning and Optimization" (www.sql-server-performance.com/)

- "Tips for Performance Tuning SQL Server's Configuration Settings" (www.sql-server-performance.com/sql_server_configuration_settings.asp)
- "Performance Tuning for SQL Server Developers" (www.sql-server-performance.com/developers_tuning_tutorial.asp)
- "How to Take Advantage of SQL Server 2000 Performance Tuning Tools" (www.sql-server-performance.com/sql_2000_tools_tutorial.asp)
- "SQL Server ODBC Driver Performance Analysis Tools"—dated but still interesting (http://support.microsoft.com/default.aspx?scid=KB;EN-US;Q157802)

Summary

This has been a big chapter, because testing and performance are really expansive topics. Indeed, we've had to struggle to keep the chapter within reasonable page limits in the context of other chapters in the book. But the goal was to bring to your attention many of the available resources, tools, and techniques that could contribute to your improving the effectiveness and performance of your applications.

We started with a discussion of many forms of testing, especially evaluating the effectiveness of the HTML we generate since the result of our ColdFusion pages is almost always HTML shown to the user.

An important point made there is that while our favorite editing tools, like Dreamweaver and HomeSite+, may offer a surprising number of features to evaluate the HTML in our source code, the challenge with ColdFusion-generated HTML is that it's not really available to be evaluated until the program executes. We offered the tip of copy/pasting the output of the page back into the editor to do such testing, and we also pointed to several web-based services that can perform a wide range of tests (including CSS, usability, and many other forms) against your page output.

Beyond just HTML, we also discussed disabling JavaScript and cookie support as well as options for reconfiguring your browser cache settings, all to simulate what your end users may experience. We also discussed how you might be able to solve browser caching problems with how you code your application.

We then discussed the broader issue of application testing in the context our server environment, with particular focus on load testing tools and the value and process of performing such tests. But it's not enough to just generate load: you need to have the means to monitor the environment while you're stressing it, and we discussed several forms of measurement and monitoring available in CFMX.

Once you've got the means to stress your environment and measure the effectiveness of your code and environment, then it's time to consider alternatives for tuning, and we discussed several options for tuning ColdFusion, the Administrator, your code, your database connection, and more.

Finally, admitting that this single chapter can't do justice to the broad range of topics associated with testing and tuning, we concluded with dozens of resources for you to consider and evaluate. Here's hoping that the information presented in the chapter or made known to you through the references will help you make your application and environment run at higher levels of efficiency and effectiveness.

✦ ✦ ✦

ColdFusion MX Administration

PART VIII

In This Part

An Overview of ColdFusion MX Administrator

In This Chapter

ColdFusion Administrator settings

Configuring datasources and understanding how they differ from earlier versions

Archiving and deployment

Logging and scheduling

Extending ColdFusion

ColdFusion Administrator is the central management console for ColdFusion Server. Many aspects of how ColdFusion operates can be controlled from the Administrator — everything from how ColdFusion connects to a database to how much memory ColdFusion can use.

This chapter does not go into great detail about the Administrator; the intent is to cover only those things that the average developer needs to know. The next chapter goes into configuration details for those who want to tune and tweak ColdFusion Server.

The headings in this chapter correspond to the sections and links within ColdFusion Administrator. You can follow along with the chapter by logging in to ColdFusion Administrator and following the links on the left of the ColdFusion Administrator interface.

Server Settings

The links in the Server Settings section of ColdFusion Administrator's navigation bar describe how ColdFusion Server's internals work — everything from request timeouts to server mappings to Java and JVM settings. These settings are typically set up at the beginning of the server's life and rarely need to be modified if correctly set.

Settings

The Settings page of ColdFusion Administrator describes the most general aspects of how ColdFusion works. It is shown in Figure 43-1:

The settings on this page may seem very general, but don't treat them trivially. Three of these settings have a huge effect on how your server responds under load; one can help prevent your URLs from being easily hacked and yet another directly figures into your exception handling framework.

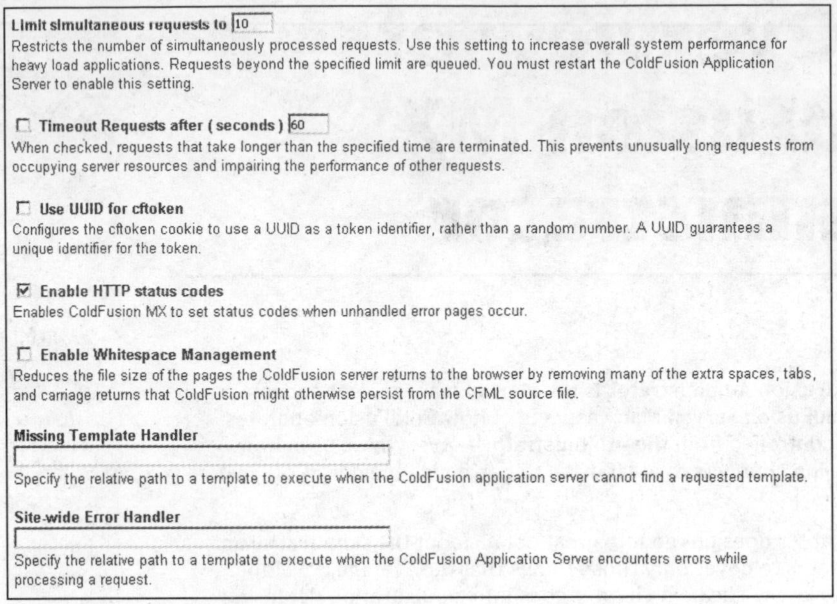

Limit simultaneous requests to 10
Restricts the number of simultaneously processed requests. Use this setting to increase overall system performance for heavy load applications. Requests beyond the specified limit are queued. You must restart the ColdFusion Application Server to enable this setting.

☐ **Timeout Requests after (seconds)** 60
When checked, requests that take longer than the specified time are terminated. This prevents unusually long requests from occupying server resources and impairing the performance of other requests.

☐ **Use UUID for cftoken**
Configures the cftoken cookie to use a UUID as a token identifier, rather than a random number. A UUID guarantees a unique identifier for the token.

☑ **Enable HTTP status codes**
Enables ColdFusion MX to set status codes when unhandled error pages occur.

☐ **Enable Whitespace Management**
Reduces the file size of the pages the ColdFusion server returns to the browser by removing many of the extra spaces, tabs, and carriage returns that ColdFusion might otherwise persist from the CFML source file.

Missing Template Handler
Specify the relative path to a template to execute when the ColdFusion application server cannot find a requested template.

Site-wide Error Handler
Specify the relative path to a template to execute when the ColdFusion Application Server encounters errors while processing a request.

Figure 43-1: The Settings page.

The settings on this page are as follows:

- **Limit Simultaneous Requests To:** The maximum number of requests that ColdFusion can handle at a given time. If you set this parameter to ten, for example, ColdFusion simultaneously handles up to ten requests. If more than ten requests present themselves to ColdFusion Server simultaneously, ten are picked up by worker threads and the remaining requests are queued. The combination of this value and the request time-out value that we discuss in the next paragraph significantly affect the performance of ColdFusion Server. (See Chapter 44 for more details.)
- **Timeout Requests After *x* Seconds:** If this option is selected, ColdFusion aborts any page requests that take longer than the specified number of seconds and tell the user that an error occurred. You can override this behavior on a page-by-page basis by using `<cfsetting RequestTimeout="(number of seconds)">`.
- **Use UUID For `CFTOKEN`:** By default, ColdFusion uses an eight-digit number for the value of `CFTOKEN`. Enabling this option makes ColdFusion use a modified UUID for `CFTOKEN`, which prevents any user from hacking into another user's session by manipulating the `CFTOKEN` value in his browser's URL. (The following chapter discusses this option in more detail.)
- **Enable HTTP Status Codes:** If this option is disabled, ColdFusion sends an HTTP status code of 200 (success) along with every page that it sends to your browser, even if an error occurs. Enabling this option means that ColdFusion sends a status code of 500 if an error is on the page. Enabling this option has a few disadvantages, as follows:
  - Whenever some browsers (such as IE 6) come across a page with a code other than 200, they sometimes opt to show a "friendly error page," which in reality completely masks the error. This feature can be turned off but is a major nuisance.

- If you call a page by using `CFHTTP` and the called page returns an error code of 500, `CFHTTP` reports a "connection failure" but doesn't report the actual error message.
- Some load testing products report `Internal Server Error` if they receive a 500-error code, possibly misleading your testing team.

We almost always leave this option disabled because it serves no purpose for our development efforts.

✦ **Enable Whitespace Management:** This option strips extraneous white space from all content generated by ColdFusion pages. This applies even to `CFMAIL` messages, which may affect the formatting you've set up. This option also requires additional processing time for every ColdFusion template in your application. We always prefer to leave this option off and use explicit `CFPROCESSINGDIRECTIVE` calls to suppress white space.

✦ **Missing Template Handler:** Normally, if the user requests a page that doesn't exist, your Web server shows him a 404-error page. If the user requests a *ColdFusion* template that doesn't exist, however, ColdFusion redirects him to the template specified here. If none is given, ColdFusion shows the user the default 404 error message.

✦ **Site-Wide Error Handler:** This feature is described in Chapter 21. The template specified in this field must begin with a forward slash and describe a path beginning at your Web server's Web root.

Caching

The Caching page in ColdFusion Administrator controls how ColdFusion caches pages and queries to relieve some of the burden off of the application server. This page is shown in Figure 43-2:

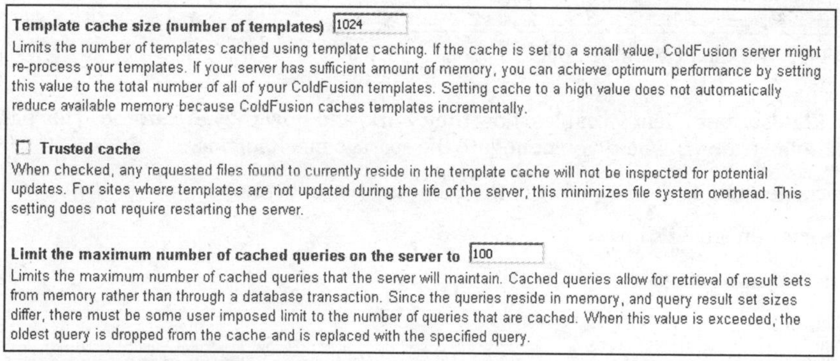

Template cache size (number of templates) 1024

Limits the number of templates cached using template caching. If the cache is set to a small value, ColdFusion server might re-process your templates. If your server has sufficient amount of memory, you can achieve optimum performance by setting this value to the total number of all of your ColdFusion templates. Setting cache to a high value does not automatically reduce available memory because ColdFusion caches templates incrementally.

☐ **Trusted cache**

When checked, any requested files found to currently reside in the template cache will not be inspected for potential updates. For sites where templates are not updated during the life of the server, this minimizes file system overhead. This setting does not require restarting the server.

Limit the maximum number of cached queries on the server to 100

Limits the maximum number of cached queries that the server will maintain. Cached queries allow for retrieval of result sets from memory rather than through a database transaction. Since the queries reside in memory, and query result set sizes differ, there must be some user imposed limit to the number of queries that are cached. When this value is exceeded, the oldest query is dropped from the cache and is replaced with the specified query.

Figure 43-2: The Caching page.

Caching enables ColdFusion to store often-used resources in memory, which speeds access to those resources. The settings on the Caching page tell ColdFusion how to cache templates and queries; chart caching is configured elsewhere. These settings are described in greater detail in the following chapter, but here's a quick breakdown:

✦ **Template Cache Size (Number of Templates):** This option tells ColdFusion the maximum number of templates that it may cache in memory. For information on setting this parameter, see the following chapter.

✦ **Trusted Cache:** If this option is enabled, ColdFusion never checks the disk for changes to the source code if a template is cached in memory. Never turn this option on unless you are running a production server where the code does not change very often, as you must cycle ColdFusion Server to enable any changes to your code.

✦ **Limit the Maximum Number of Cached Queries on the Server to:** If you cache a query, ColdFusion places the results of that query in memory, so you must carefully weigh performance increase against available memory. Setting this parameter can be tricky, so read the following chapter for information on setting this value.

Client Variables

The Client Variables page in ColdFusion Administrator controls how ColdFusion stores its client variables. This page is shown in Figure 43-3:

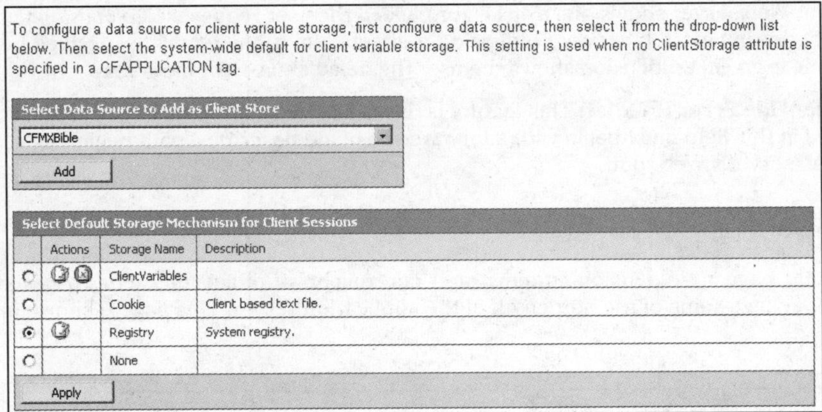

Figure 43-3: The Client Variables page.

Chapter 12 describes client variables, how they work, and how they are stored. This page of the CF Administrator is where you configure the storage mechanisms.

Client variables can be stored in one of the following three locations:

✦ Cookies on a user's browser

✦ The Windows Registry

✦ A database

By default, only cookies and the Registry are preconfigured as storage mechanisms, but a database works for storing Client variables on a clustered system.

Never store client variables in the same database that stores your application data. Create a separate database and datasource for your Client variables. It's generally a bad idea to have two separate, concurrent processes (in this case, your application and ColdFusion's client variables) accessing the same database at the same time.

To configure a datasource as a client storage mechanism, choose the datasource in the drop-down list at the top of the page and click Add. You are taken to a page where you are presented with the following four options:

✦ **Description:** This should be a brief description of the datasource. Something witty such as **Stores client variables for the ABC application** does just fine.

✦ **Create Client Database Tables:** If this option is enabled as you submit this form, ColdFusion creates two tables named `CDATA` and `CGLOBAL` in the datasource that you selected to hold the client variables. If the datasource already contains these two tables, don't enable this option.

✦ **Purge Data for Clients that Remain Unvisited for *x* Days:** If you enable this option, ColdFusion checks once a day for expired clients and removes any that haven't been visited for more than the specified number of days. (The default is 90.) We strongly recommend enabling this option and making the timeout rather short (only one day for most of the sites that we create). If you don't purge unvisited clients, the client datastore becomes bloated and runs more and more slowly as time goes on.

✦ **Disable Global Client Variable Updates:** If global client variable updates are enabled, ColdFusion automatically maintains two client variables named `Client.LastVisit` and `Client.HitCount`. `Client.LastVisit` tells when the client last visited a page on the site, and `Client.HitCount` is the number of page hits the client has made since the `CFID` and `CFTOKEN` were issued. If you select this option, however, these variables are not updated. If you don't use these values in your application, *by all means* disable global client variable updates so that every page hit in your application doesn't generate a taxing call to the database.

After you add a datasource as a client variable store, it appears in the list at the bottom of the page. A radio button is next to each variable store, denoting which is the default. We always set our default to be a datasource, and we never permit client variables in our Registry.

Memory Variables

The Memory Variables page controls how ColdFusion handles Session and Application variables; it is shown in Figure 43-4:

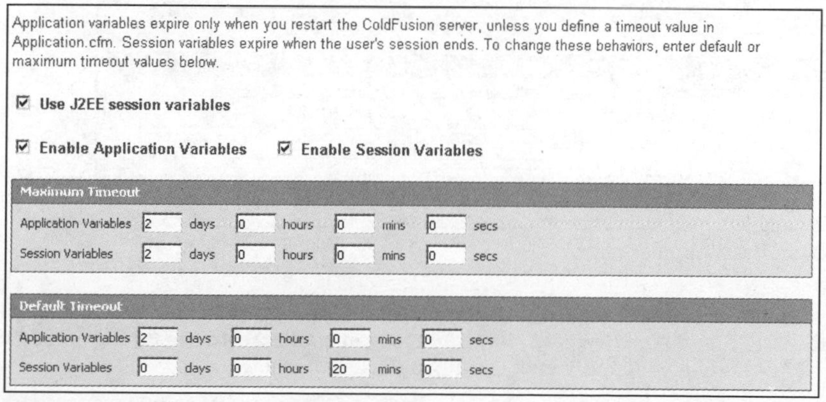

Application variables expire only when you restart the ColdFusion server, unless you define a timeout value in Application.cfm. Session variables expire when the user's session ends. To change these behaviors, enter default or maximum timeout values below.

☑ Use J2EE session variables

☑ Enable Application Variables ☑ Enable Session Variables

Maximum Timeout								
Application Variables	2	days	0	hours	0	mins	0	secs
Session Variables	2	days	0	hours	0	mins	0	secs

Default Timeout								
Application Variables	2	days	0	hours	0	mins	0	secs
Session Variables	0	days	0	hours	20	mins	0	secs

Figure 43-4: The Memory Variables page.

This page defines how ColdFusion uses Session and Application variables, as follows:

✦ **Use J2EE Session Variables:** Enabling this option tells ColdFusion to use J2EE session management rather than ColdFusion's own session-management mechanism. This option is typically used if you're sharing variables with JSP applications. (See Chapter 28 for complete details.)

✦ **Enable Application Variables:** If this option isn't selected, no application on your server may use Application variables.

✦ **Enable Session Variables:** If this option isn't selected, no application on your server may use Session variables. Even if this option is selected, you must also enable session management in each ColdFusion application via `<CFAPPLICATION SessionManagement="Yes">` to use Session variables in it.

✦ **Maximum Timeout:** These values represent the maximum possible timeouts for Session and Application variables for all applications on your server. If `CFAPPLICATION` attempts to set a timeout higher than the maximum values, ColdFusion uses these maximums rather than the value defined in `CFAPPLICATION`.

✦ **Default Timeout:** If no Session or Application timeouts are defined in a call to `CFAPPLICATION`, these default timeout values are used.

Mappings

The Mappings page in ColdFusion Administrator describes the mappings available to ColdFusion applications. This page is shown in Figure 43-5:

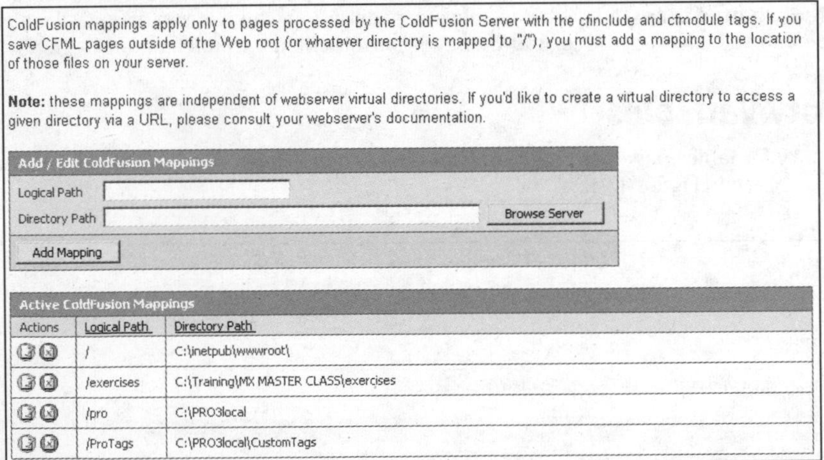

Figure 43-5: The Mappings page.

Mappings assign aliases to directories on your server. If you stored all of your custom tags in `c:\mywebsite\common\customtags`, for example, you could create a mapping named `ct` such that anywhere in your application, you could use the following:

```
<cfmodule template="/ct/customtag.cfm">
```

You can use this code instead of needing to use a relative path such as the following:

```
<cfmodule template="../../common/customtags/customtag.cfm">
```

The Mappings page in ColdFusion Administrator has two sections. The first section is where you add or edit a mapping, and the second shows you which mappings are currently active.

To add a mapping, use the Add/Edit ColdFusion mappings section. If you want a mapping named `/ct` that maps to `c:\mywebsite\common\customtags`, enter `/ct` in the Logical Path field and the disk path in the Directory Path field and click the Add Mapping button.

Mail Server

The Mail Server page of ColdFusion Administrator controls how ColdFusion sends mail with `CFMAIL` (note that these settings do not affect `CFPOP`, however). The Mail Server page is shown in Figure 43-6:

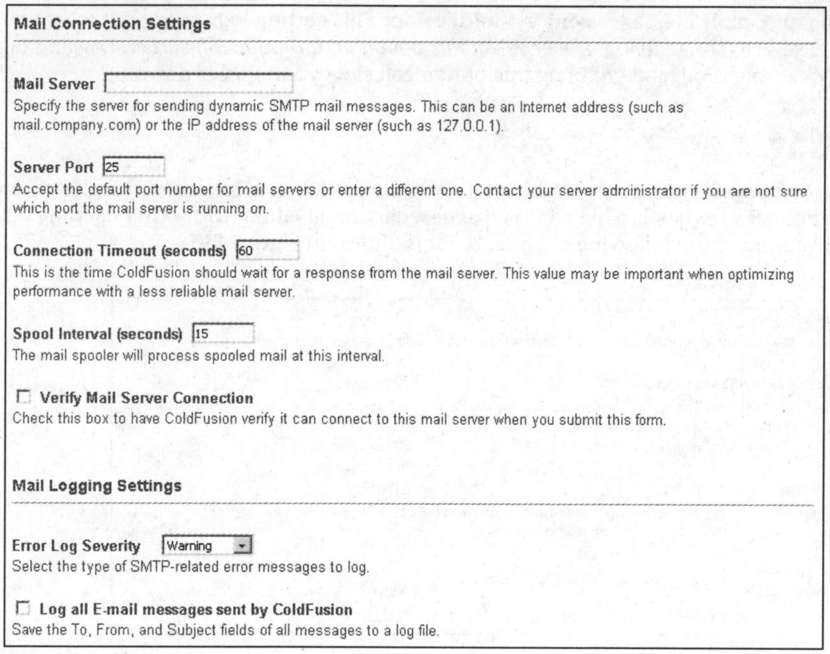

Mail Connection Settings

Mail Server [ ]
Specify the server for sending dynamic SMTP mail messages. This can be an Internet address (such as mail.company.com) or the IP address of the mail server (such as 127.0.0.1).

Server Port [25]
Accept the default port number for mail servers or enter a different one. Contact your server administrator if you are not sure which port the mail server is running on.

Connection Timeout (seconds) [60]
This is the time ColdFusion should wait for a response from the mail server. This value may be important when optimizing performance with a less reliable mail server.

Spool Interval (seconds) [15]
The mail spooler will process spooled mail at this interval.

☐ **Verify Mail Server Connection**
Check this box to have ColdFusion verify it can connect to this mail server when you submit this form.

Mail Logging Settings

Error Log Severity [Warning]
Select the type of SMTP-related error messages to log.

☐ **Log all E-mail messages sent by ColdFusion**
Save the To, From, and Subject fields of all messages to a log file.

Figure 43-6: The Mail Server page.

This page has two sections — one for connection settings and one for logging settings — as the following two sections describe.

Mail Connection Settings

Following are the options in the Mail Connection Settings section of the Mail Server page:

- ✦ **Mail Server:** The name or IP address of the default mail server that ColdFusion is to use if none is defined in a call to CFMAIL. This is the address of an SMTP server and not a POP server.
- ✦ **Server Port:** Defines the default port for interacting with a mail server. This defaults to 25.

✦ **Connection Timeout:** The number of seconds that ColdFusion waits while connecting to a remote mail server before throwing an error or recording an entry in the mail log.

✦ **Spool Interval:** This parameter controls the number of seconds that ColdFusion Server waits before rechecking its outgoing mail queue for new mail waiting to be sent.

✦ **Verify Mail Server Connection:** If this option is enabled, whenever you submit this page in the Administrator, ColdFusion attempts to connect to your default mail server to make sure that the correct connection can be made. This is a temporary test for your convenience; after you submit the page, this setting automatically is disabled again.

Mail Logging Settings

Following are the options in the Mail Logging Settings section of the Mail Server page:

✦ **Error Log Severity:** Whenever ColdFusion logs a mail error to the error log, it records this level of severity. The default is Warning, which should be sufficient for most purposes

✦ **Log all E-mail messages sent by ColdFusion:** This setting logs every outgoing mail message to the mail log. *Never select this option on a production server!* Logging takes processing time, and enabling this option can slow your server down.

Charting

The Charting page of ColdFusion Administrator tells ColdFusion how to cache charts and handle CFCHART requests. This page is discussed in detail, along with other caching options, at the beginning of the following chapter, but it is shown in Figure 43-7:

Cache type Disk Cache
Charts can be cached either in memory or to disk. In memory caching is faster, but more memory intensive.

Maximum number of images in cache 50
You can specify the maximum number of charts to store in the cache. After the cache is full, if a new chart is generated, then the oldest chart in the cache will be discarded. Caching of charts allows multiple requests for the same chart to be much faster, as the chart is only generated once.

Maximum Number of charting threads 4
Specify the maximum number of chart requests that can be processed concurrently. The minimum number is 1 and the maximum is 5. The higher the number the more memory intensive.

Disk cache location
C:\CFusionMX\charting\cache Browse Server
When caching to disk, specify the directory in which to store the generated charts.

Figure 43-7: The Charting page.

Java and JVM

The settings in the Java and JVM page of ColdFusion Administrator affect how ColdFusion interacts with the Java Virtual Machine (JVM) on top of which ColdFusion MX runs. This page is shown in Figure 43-8:

Don't modify the settings on this page unless you have a compelling reason to do so. Configuring these settings is discussed in the following chapter.

Java and JVM settings control the way ColdFusion starts the Java Virtual Machine when it starts. You can control settings like what classpaths are used and how memory is allocated as well as add custom command line arguments. Changing these settings requires restarting ColdFusion. If you enter an incorrect setting, ColdFusion may not restart properly.

Backups of the jvm.config file are created when you hit the submit button. You can use this backup to restore from a critical change.

Java Virtual Machine Path

C:/CFusionMX/runtime/jre [Browse Server]

Specify the location of the Java Virtual Machine.

Initial Memory Size (MB) **Maximum Memory Size (MB)** 512

The Memory Size settings determines the memory range to be used by ColdFusion server.

Class Path

Specify any additional class paths for the JVM. Separate multiple directories with commas.

JVM Arguments

Specify any specific JVM initialization options separated by space(s).

Figure 43-8: The Java and JVM page.

Archives and Deployment

The Archives and Deployment page in ColdFusion Administrator lets you set up ColdFusion Archives, which let you easily deploy code and settings across multiple ColdFusion Servers. This page is shown in Figure 43-9:

Deploy an Existing Archive

[Browse Server]

[Deploy]

ColdFusion MX lets developers define applications for organizing work, archiving files, and migrating and deploying sites. You can create and store ColdFusion Archive definitions to archive, migrate, or re-deploy applications at a later date.

Create New Archive

Archive Name

[Create]

Current Archive Definition List

Actions	Archive Name
	Archive Test

Figure 43-9: The Archives and Deployment page.

ColdFusion Archives are available only in ColdFusion MX Enterprise.

Whenever you are using ColdFusion clustering, making certain that all the machines in the cluster have the same code installed can prove difficult, and making certain that all the machines in the cluster have the same settings is even more difficult. ColdFusion Archives enable you to package your source code and server settings into a single CAR file and deploy that one file to all servers in your cluster. The archiving feature is also useful for single-server deployments, because you can archive your application after successfully testing it in your staging environment and then deploy it to your production server.

Archiving and deploying involve the following three steps:

1. Create/Edit the archive. (This step sets up the archive process.)
2. Build the archive. (This step actually populates the archive with code and settings.)
3. Deploy the archive.

These three steps are all performed from the `Archives and Deployment` link in the Settings section of ColdFusion Administrator's navigation bar. The following sections describe these three steps.

Creating a new archive

The first step in creating a new archive is to enter the name of the archive and click Create, which adds a new empty archive to the list of existing archives and launches the Archive Wizard, which takes you through the process of setting up the archive. You can leave this wizard and come back at any time by clicking the leftmost icon next to the archive's name in the list of archives.

Building an archive

This step uses the information that you used in creating the archive to create a CAR file containing all the files and settings needed to deploy the site. This CAR file is in the same format as a JAR or ZIP file, so you can open it by using WinZip to inspect its contents. To build the archive, click the middle icon next to the name of the archive that you want to build and follow the steps in the Build Wizard that appears.

Deploying an archive

After ColdFusion finishes creating the CAR file, deploy the CAR file to all your remote servers. Log in to ColdFusion Administrator on your remote server and go to the Archives and Deployment page. In the Deploy an Existing Archive section, enter the path to the archive file and click Deploy, which launches the Deployment Wizard. Follow the instructions in the Deployment Wizard, and all the files and settings are correctly deployed. Repeat this step for every server in your cluster.

Settings Summary

The Settings Summary page in ColdFusion Administrator provides a birds-eye view of all the settings in ColdFusion Administrator. Figure 43-10 shows a portion of this page:

This page of the Administrator is just a summary of all the settings in the Administrator. Nothing is set here, but saving or printing a copy of this report for your records can prove useful.

Server Settings	
General Settings	
Simultaneous request limit	10
Timeout requests	No
Request time limit	60
Use UUID for cftoken	No
Enable whitespace management	No
Missing template handler	
Site-wide error handler	
Caching	
Template cache size	1024
Enable trusted cache	No
Cached query limit	100
Client Variables	
Default client variable store	Registry
Client Stores	
Cookie	
Type	COOKIE
Description	Client based text file.
Purge data after time limit	YES
Time limit	10
Disable global updates	NO
Registry	
Type	REGISTRY
Description	System registry.
Purge data after time limit	YES
Time limit	90
Disable global updates	NO
ClientVariables	
Type	JDBC

Figure 43-10: The Settings Summary page.

Data & Services

This section of the Administrator controls how ColdFusion exchanges data with other systems, whether they are databases, Verity collections, or Web services.

Data Sources

The Data Sources page of ColdFusion Administrator is where you configure ColdFusion's database connections. From it, you can add a new data source or edit, verify, or delete an existing datasource. This page is shown in Figure 43-11:

If you are coming from ColdFusion 5 or earlier versions, disregard everything that you know about datasources because they are totally different now. In ColdFusion 5 and earlier, datasources came in two flavors: *Open Database Connectivity (ODBC)* and *Native Connections*. ODBC connections were simple to set up and use, and they were defined as part of the operating system. Native Connections were slightly more difficult to set up and use (although usually more reliable and scalable) and were ColdFusion-specific.

ColdFusion MX uses neither ODBC nor Native Connections but, instead, uses JDBC, Java's preferred method for connecting to databases.

JDBC doesn't stand for anything, although some people think that JDBC means Java DataBase Connectivity. Really, it's just a way of saying that Java has something that parallels ODBC.

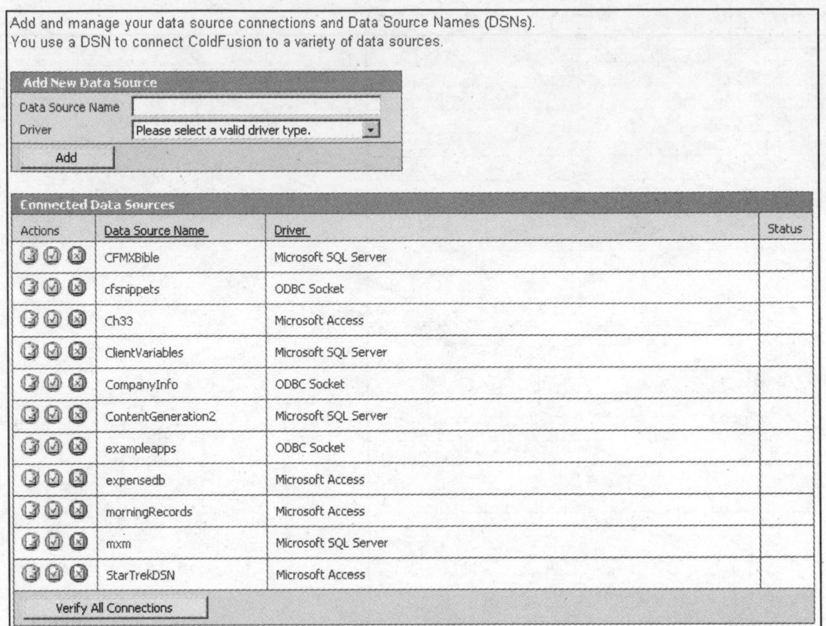

Figure 43-11: The Data Sources page.

To connect to a database through JDBC, you must have a database driver that translates JDBC calls into requests that the target database server understands. You have four JDBC driver types (1 through 4), the best-performing being Type 4. ColdFusion Enterprise ships with both Type 3 and Type 4 database drivers, but ColdFusion Professional's Type 4 drivers are restricted to SQL Server and MySQL only.

You may be wondering how we can say that no more ODBC datasources are available for ColdFusion when it has an ODBC Socket driver type. ColdFusion's ODBC Socket driver enables ColdFusion to use an existing ODBC datasource to connect to a database — but at the expense of scalability. Technically, the ODBC Socket driver is a Type 3 driver, but it takes a big performance hit by tunneling through ODBC to connect with your database. You should use the ODBC Socket driver only if you can't obtain a Type 4 driver for your database platform or, at least, a Type 3 driver that makes a non-ODBC connection with your database. Always use a pure JDBC driver if possible.

Choosing a JDBC driver

Before you can define a datasource, you must give it a name and choose a JDBC driver type. Table 43-1 describes the driver types offered by ColdFusion.

Table 43-1: JDBC Database Drivers Available in ColdFusion MX

Driver	*Description*
DB2 Universal Database	Available with ColdFusion MX Enterprise only. Connects to IBM DB2 databases. This is a Type 4 driver.
Informix	Available with ColdFusion MX Enterprise only. Connects to Informix databases. This is a Type 4 driver.

Driver	*Description*
Microsoft Access	Available with all versions of ColdFusion MX. Connects to a Microsoft Access database. This is a Type 3 driver.
Microsoft SQL Server	Available with all versions of ColdFusion MX. Connects to a Microsoft SQL Server database. This is a Type 4 driver.
MySQL	Available with all versions of ColdFusion MX. Connects to a MySQL database. This is a Type 4 driver.
ODBC Socket	Available with all versions of ColdFusion MX. Connects to an ODBC datasource defined on the server machine. Use this option only if ColdFusion doesn't have a native JDBC database driver for your database platform, because the native JDBC drivers are much more reliable. This is a type 3 driver.
Oracle	Available with ColdFusion MX Enterprise only. Connects to an Oracle database. This is a Type 4 driver.
Sybase	Available with ColdFusion MX Enterprise only. Connects to a Sybase database. This is a Type 4 driver.
Other	Connects to a database by using a JDBC driver not available through ColdFusion MX. Using this option implies using a JDBC URL and connection string during the setup process. This can use any driver type.

If you click Add after entering the datasource name and driver type, you are taken to a page to configure the connection settings for the chosen database type. These settings differ between drivers; for example, a Microsoft SQL Server datasource has a `Port` parameter, but an Access datasource does not. Conversely, Access datasources have a `filename` parameter, where SQL Server doesn't. The exact setting simply depends on what the database driver needs to connect to the target database. The following chapter covers datasource configuration details.

Defining a new Microsoft SQL Server datasource

We're going to show you in this section how to set up a SQL Server datasource within ColdFusion Administrator. If you want to follow along, log in to ColdFusion Administrator and click Data Sources under Data & Services on the left-hand panel. Then just follow these steps:

1. In the Add New Data Source section, as shown in Figure 43-12, enter the name of the new datasource — in this example, **CFMXBibleExample** — in the Data Source Name field and select Microsoft SQL Server from the Driver drop-down list as the driver type; then click Add.

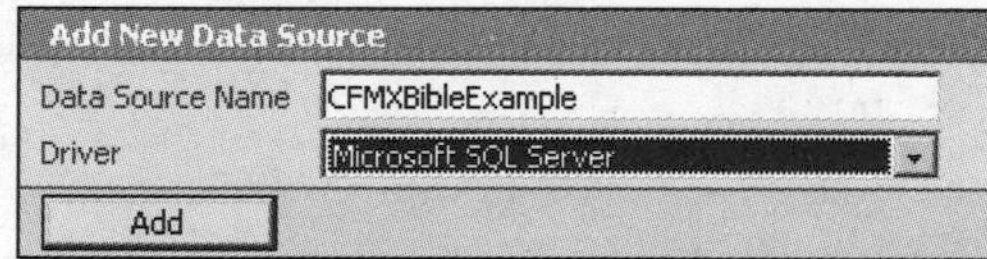

Figure 43-12: Filling out the new datasource's name and driver type.

2. For this example, we previously created a database named `CFMXDatabase` in SQL Server Enterprise Manager, as shown in Figure 43-13. (Note that you would replace CFMXDatabase with your own SQL Server database. Setting up this database is beyond the scope of this book, as it has more to do with SQL Server administration than ColdFusion.)

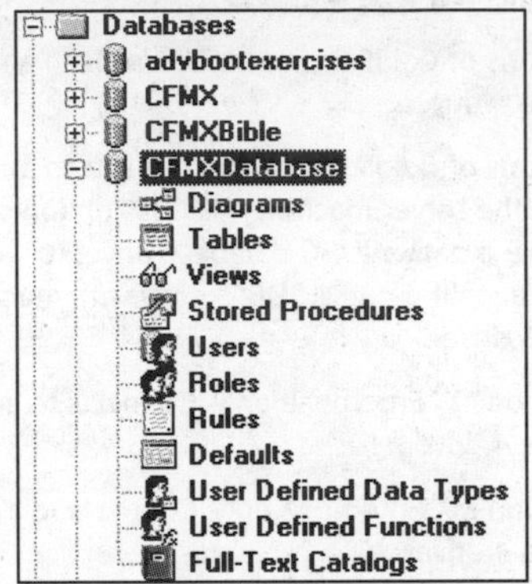

Figure 43-13: The database in SQL Server Enterprise Manager.

3. In ColdFusion Administrator, enter **CFMXDatabase** (or the name of your own SQL Server database) in the Database field and **127.0.0.1** in the Server field. For the username and password, of course, use whatever you set up for this purpose. (In this example, we enter CFMXUser and the CFMXUser's password.) Keep the default port of `1443` and enter a brief description. After you finish, the form looks as shown in Figure 43-14 (with your own database name, username and password, of course).

Microsoft SQL Server Data Source : CFMXBibleExample

CF Data Source Name: CFMXBibleExample
Database: CFMXDatabase
Server: 127.0.0.1 Port: 1433
Username: CFMXUser
Password: ****************
Description: This is an example data source for The ColdFusion MX Bible.

Show Advanced Settings | Submit | Cancel

Figure 43-14: The datasource settings form.

4. Click Submit, and you're taken back to the list of datasources, where the new datasource now appears with an "ok" beside it.

And that's it. Now, simply referring to `CFMXBibleExample` in your `CFQUERY` and `CFSTOREDPROC` tags gives you access to the CFMXDatabase database.

Most datasource setups are about the same, although some target databases that require a different set of parameters from those shown for SQL Server. The Oracle driver, for example, communicates with an Oracle database by using a different set of parameters, as you see in the following section.

Defining a new Oracle datasource

The process of setting up an Oracle datasource is similar to the one that we describe in the preceding section for SQL Server, but Oracle requires different connection parameters. Just as you do with SQL Server, you start by clicking the `Data Sources` link under Data & Services on the left-hand panel of Administrator. (***Note:*** The Oracle driver is available only with ColdFusion MX Enterprise.) Then just follow these steps:

1. In the Add New Data Source section, enter the name of the new datasource (in this example, we're calling it `CFMXBibleOracle`) and choose Oracle as the driver type; then click Add.

   Our Oracle installation in this example has a SID (Service ID) named `CFMXServer` and a user named `CFMXUser`. Note that administering Oracle is beyond the scope of this book; the database, username, and password used in this example should be replaced with your own values.

2. In ColdFusion Administrator, enter **CFMXServer** in the SID Name field and **CFMXUser** in the Username field. Then enter the password, leave the default port of `1521`, enter a brief description, and click Submit.

The built-in Type 4 Oracle driver supports multiple result sets returned from Oracle packages. See Listing 10-24 in Chapter 10 for a very scalable way to accomplish this task.

Verity Collections

The Verity Collections page of ColdFusion Administrator (shown in Figure 43-15) enables you to manage your Verity collections. Here you can create new collections, or you can index, repair, optimize, purge, or delete an existing collection without resorting to writing code.

This section assumes that you are familiar with Verity and its terminology. If you are not, please read the Verity section of Chapter 32.

To create a new collection, just enter the name of the collection, the collection's language, and the name of the directory where you want the collection to be created. The default is *cf_root*`\verity\collections`.

To index a collection, click the Index Collection icon next to the name of the collection that you want to index. (This icon is the farthest left.) The indexing utility in Administrator gives you the capability to do only a *path* index; if you want to use *file* or *custom* indexing you must use a manually coded call to `CFINDEX`.

Occasionally, a collection may become unstable and start producing incorrect results. If this happens, try repairing the collection. (The icon that you click to start this task is the second from the left.) Repairing the collection may take a long time, so don't rush it, and especially don't try to do anything else with the collection until Administrator is finished.

Optimizing a collection makes it run faster. To optimize a collection, click the middle icon next to the name of the collection. Optimizing the collection may take a few minutes.

The fourth icon from the left purges the collection, removing all entries from the collection but leaving the empty collection intact. The last icon, next to the collection name, deletes the collection entirely.

The bottom section of this Administrator page shows all collections currently available from an attached Verity K2 Server. No actions may be performed in this section, because K2 Collections are managed through an INI file as part of the setup process for Verity K2 Server.

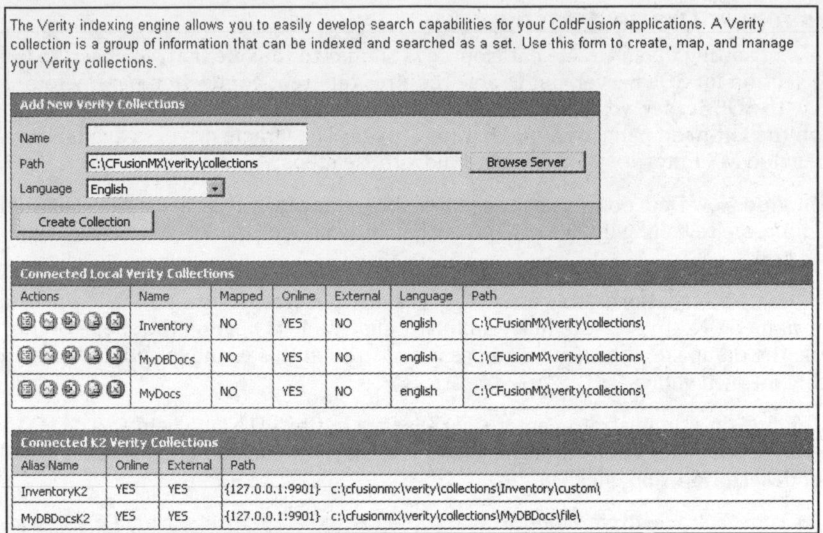

Figure 43-15: The Verity Collections page.

Verity K2 Server

The Verity K2 Server page of ColdFusion Administrator manages ColdFusion's connection to Verity K2 Server, the standalone server software that ships with ColdFusion as a high-performance alternative to ColdFusion Server's built-in Verity routines. This page is shown in Figure 43-16:

Add Verity K2 Server

K2 Server Host Name	127.0.0.1
K2 Server Port	9901

Connect

Connected Verity Collections

Actions	Name	Port	Online	Broker	Doc Count	Doc Count Limit
	127.0.0.1	9901	YES	NO	4	10000

Connected Verity K2 Collections

Alias Name	Online	External	Path
InventoryK2	YES	YES	{127.0.0.1:9901} c:\cfusionmx\verity\collections\Inventory\custom\
MyDBDocsK2	YES	YES	{127.0.0.1:9901} c:\cfusionmx\verity\collections\MyDBDocs\file\

Figure 43-16: The Verity K2 Server page.

The Add Verity K2 Server section of the page is where you tell ColdFusion which K2 Server to connect to. You just need to specify the name (or IP address) and port number of the server where Verity K2 is running in the appropriate fields.

Connected Verity Collections is a misnomer; it should be called Connected Verity Server. This section of the page tells you which K2 Server is currently connected to the ColdFusion Server and whether the K2 Server is online. You can disconnect from the K2 Server by clicking the red X next to the server name.

The Connected Verity K2 Collections section tells you which collections the K2 Server exposes. You can't do anything to maintain or modify these collections, because they are managed by K2 Server's INI file.

Web Services

The Web Services page of ColdFusion Administrator (shown in Figure 43-17) is where you manage ColdFusion's connections to Web services. This form has two sections: Add / Edit ColdFusion Web Service and Active ColdFusion Web Services.

ColdFusion lets you map names to your web service URLs.

Add / Edit ColdFusion Web Service

Web Service Name

WSDL URL

Username

Password

Add Web Service

Active ColdFusion Web Serivces

Actions	Web Service Name	WSDL URL
	http://localhost/presentation/webservices/GetEmployees.cfc?wsdl	http://localhost/presentation/webservices/GetEmployees.cfc?wsdl
	http://localhost/mxmaster/webservices/lecture/employee.cfc?wsdl	http://localhost/mxmaster/webservices/lecture/employee.cfc?wsdl
	http://localhost/presentation/webservices/employee.cfc?wsdl	http://localhost/presentation/webservices/employee.cfc?wsdl
	wsGetEmployees	http://localhost/presentation/webservices/GetEmployees.cfc?wsdl

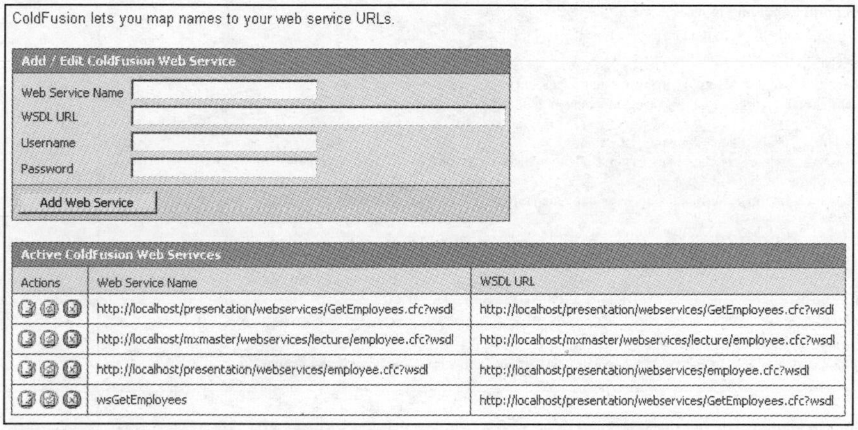

Figure 43-17: The Web Services page.

The Add / Edit ColdFusion Web Service is where you set up the Web-service URLs and the usernames and passwords that they require. You can assign a name to a Web-service URL here and use the name as an alias in the `Webservice` attribute of your `CFINVOKE` tags. The username and password are passed to the Web service's basic authentication mechanism after a request for service is made.

Active ColdFusion Web Services describes the Web services to which ColdFusion is currently subscribed. Each one can be edited, refreshed, or deleted. Refreshing a Web-service connection releases it from ColdFusion's cache, reestablishes the WSDL interface to that Web service, and keeps the Web service's name unchanged, whereas removing a Web service permanently removes its name.

Debugging & Logging

This section of Administrator is focused more on debugging code than on configuring ColdFusion Server. From here, you can configure debugging output, view log files, and set up system probes. This section also includes scheduled tasks and a tool to analyze existing ColdFusion code to help determine incompatibilities with ColdFusion MX. The following sections describe each of these settings.

Debugging Settings

The Debugging Settings page of ColdFusion Administrator is where you turn on debugging and manage other performance monitoring settings. This page is shown in Figure 43-18:

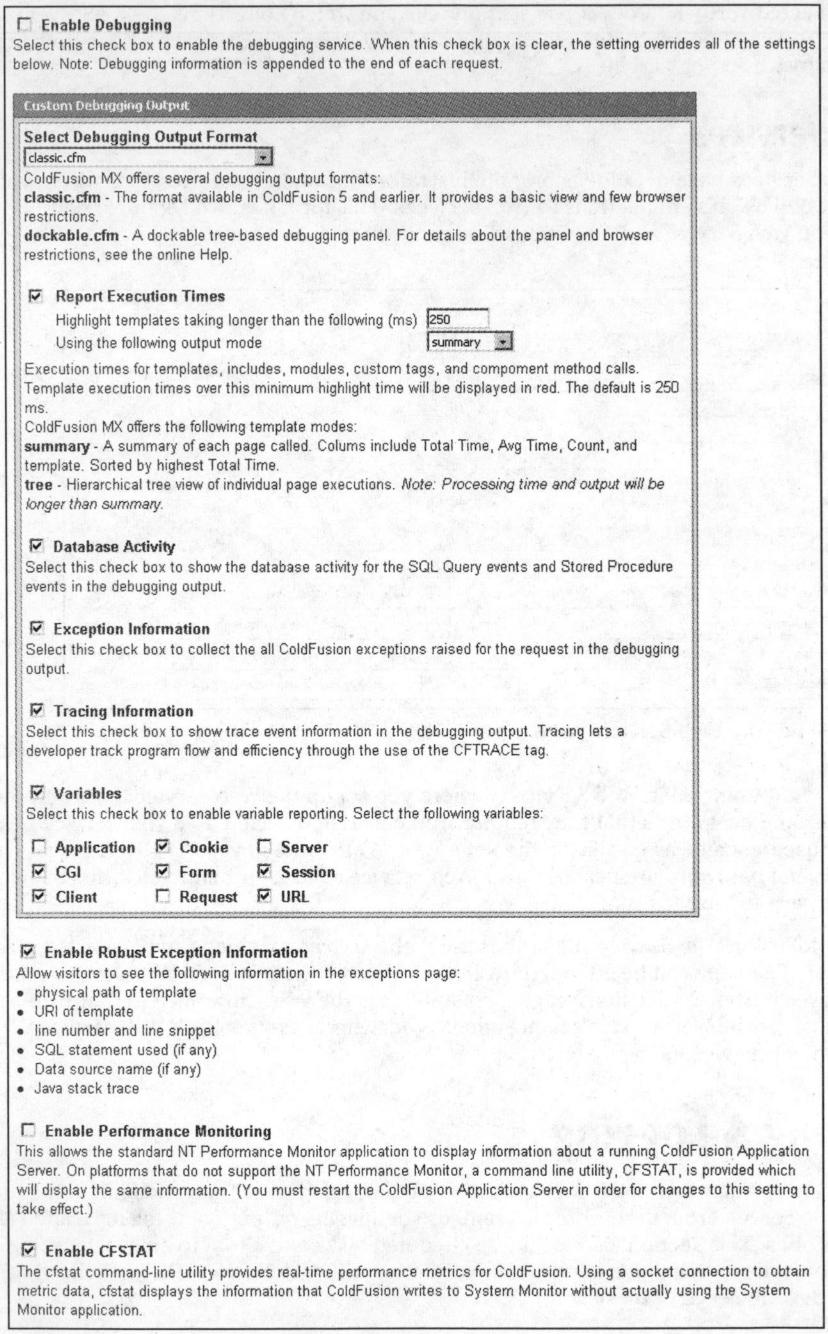

☐ **Enable Debugging**
Select this check box to enable the debugging service. When this check box is clear, the setting overrides all of the settings below. Note: Debugging information is appended to the end of each request.

Custom Debugging Output

Select Debugging Output Format
classic.cfm
ColdFusion MX offers several debugging output formats:
classic.cfm - The format available in ColdFusion 5 and earlier. It provides a basic view and few browser restrictions.
dockable.cfm - A dockable tree-based debugging panel. For details about the panel and browser restrictions, see the online Help.

☑ **Report Execution Times**
Highlight templates taking longer than the following (ms) 250
Using the following output mode summary
Execution times for templates, includes, modules, custom tags, and compoment method calls. Template execution times over this minimum highlight time will be displayed in red. The default is 250 ms.
ColdFusion MX offers the following template modes:
summary - A summary of each page called. Colums include Total Time, Avg Time, Count, and template. Sorted by highest Total Time.
tree - Hierarchical tree view of individual page executions. *Note: Processing time and output will be longer than summary.*

☑ **Database Activity**
Select this check box to show the database activity for the SQL Query events and Stored Procedure events in the debugging output.

☑ **Exception Information**
Select this check box to collect the all ColdFusion exceptions raised for the request in the debugging output.

☑ **Tracing Information**
Select this check box to show trace event information in the debugging output. Tracing lets a developer track program flow and efficiency through the use of the CFTRACE tag.

☑ **Variables**
Select this check box to enable variable reporting. Select the following variables:

☐ **Application** ☑ **Cookie** ☐ **Server**
☑ **CGI** ☑ **Form** ☑ **Session**
☑ **Client** ☐ **Request** ☑ **URL**

☑ **Enable Robust Exception Information**
Allow visitors to see the following information in the exceptions page:
- physical path of template
- URI of template
- line number and line snippet
- SQL statement used (if any)
- Data source name (if any)
- Java stack trace

☐ **Enable Performance Monitoring**
This allows the standard NT Performance Monitor application to display information about a running ColdFusion Application Server. On platforms that do not support the NT Performance Monitor, a command line utility, CFSTAT, is provided which will display the same information. (You must restart the ColdFusion Application Server in order for changes to this setting to take effect.)

☑ **Enable CFSTAT**
The cfstat command-line utility provides real-time performance metrics for ColdFusion. Using a socket connection to obtain metric data, cfstat displays the information that ColdFusion writes to System Monitor without actually using the System Monitor application.

Figure 43-18: The Debugging Settings page.

Following are the four major settings on this page, each of which is described in the four sections that follow:

- ✦ Enable Debugging
- ✦ Enable Robust Exception Information
- ✦ Enable Performance Monitoring
- ✦ Enable CFSTAT

Enable Debugging

This check box also controls all the options in the Custom Debugging Output section. If this check box is disabled, no debugging output is shown regardless of the settings in the Custom Debugging Output section.

Enable Robust Exception Information

Normally, ColdFusion's default error message shows you only the error message and detail. If this option is selected, ColdFusion includes the following extra information along with the error message:

- ✦ Physical path of template
- ✦ URI of template
- ✦ Line number and line snippet
- ✦ SQL statement used (if any)
- ✦ Data source name (if any)
- ✦ Java stack trace

Enable Performance Monitoring

If this option is enabled, ColdFusion Server publishes its performance metric data so that Windows Performance Monitor can process it. Among the many metrics published are the following:

- ✦ Running Requests
- ✦ Queued Requests
- ✦ Page Hits/sec
- ✦ DB Hits/sec

Always enable this option if you're load-testing your application. If your load-testing suite is a great one, such as e-TEST Suite from Empirix, it can parallel this data with the other performance metrics from your application and its supporting database servers and Web servers. Do make sure that you keep this option off in production environments, however, because publishing these metrics causes a performance hit.

Enable CFSTAT

If your platform doesn't support the Windows Performance Monitor, you can use a command-line utility named `CFSTAT` to get the same information exposed to the Performance Monitor. Leave this option disabled unless you need it; as happens with the Performance Monitor, enabling this option causes a performance hit.

Debugging IP Addresses

The Debugging IP Addresses page of ColdFusion Administrator tells ColdFusion what IP addresses are allowed to receive debugging information. This page is shown in Figure 43-19:

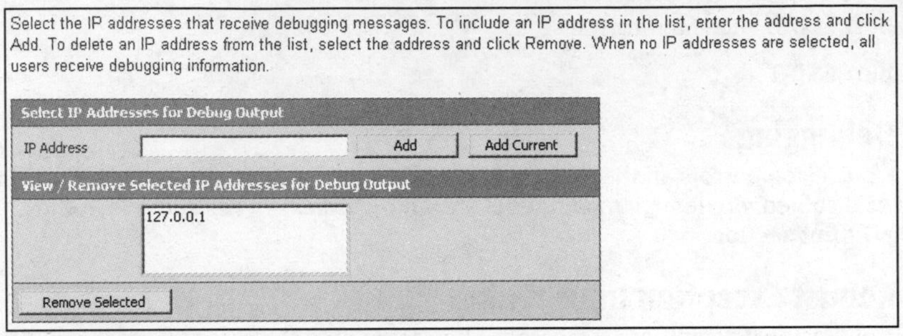

Select the IP addresses that receive debugging messages. To include an IP address in the list, enter the address and click Add. To delete an IP address from the list, select the address and click Remove. When no IP addresses are selected, all users receive debugging information.

Select IP Addresses for Debug Output

IP Address [ ] Add | Add Current

View / Remove Selected IP Addresses for Debug Output

127.0.0.1

Remove Selected

Figure 43-19: The Debugging IP Addresses page.

You may want to restrict debugging information to a single IP address (usually 127.0.0.1), meaning that only users accessing ColdFusion from a certain location may see debugging information. Restricting this list to only those addresses of developers' machines is usually a good idea.

Logging Settings

The Logging Settings page of ColdFusion Administrator (shown in Figure 43-20) tells ColdFusion where and how log entries should be stored.

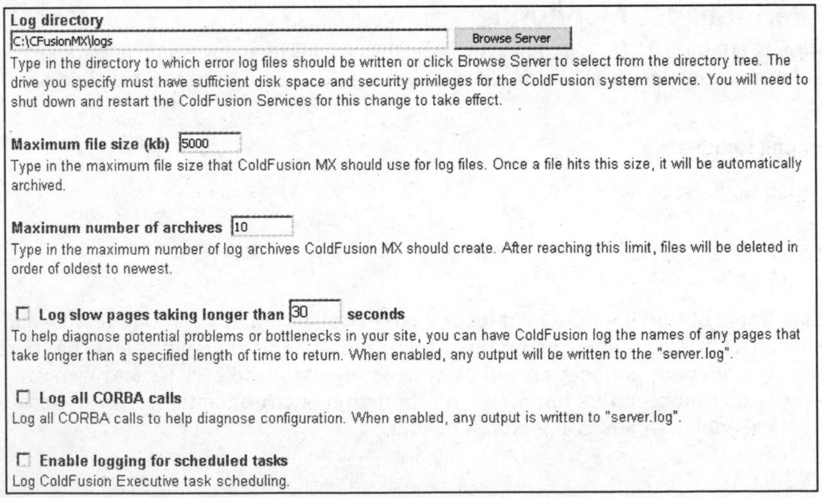

Log directory

C:\CFusionMX\logs | Browse Server

Type in the directory to which error log files should be written or click Browse Server to select from the directory tree. The drive you specify must have sufficient disk space and security privileges for the ColdFusion system service. You will need to shut down and restart the ColdFusion Services for this change to take effect.

Maximum file size (kb) 5000

Type in the maximum file size that ColdFusion MX should use for log files. Once a file hits this size, it will be automatically archived.

Maximum number of archives 10

Type in the maximum number of log archives ColdFusion MX should create. After reaching this limit, files will be deleted in order of oldest to newest.

☐ **Log slow pages taking longer than** 30 **seconds**

To help diagnose potential problems or bottlenecks in your site, you can have ColdFusion log the names of any pages that take longer than a specified length of time to return. When enabled, any output will be written to the "server.log".

☐ **Log all CORBA calls**

Log all CORBA calls to help diagnose configuration. When enabled, any output is written to "server.log".

☐ **Enable logging for scheduled tasks**

Log ColdFusion Executive task scheduling.

Figure 43-20: The Logging Settings page.

You've probably never paid much attention to this page, but it is one of the more important pages in ColdFusion Administrator. From here, you can turn on the logging of slow pages and scheduled tasks, which helps you discover performance bottlenecks and related problems. This page offers the following options:

✦ **Log Directory:** This directory is where ColdFusion stores its log files. to Changing this value from the default probably isn't a good idea. Most tools assume that the ColdFusion log files are in this directory, and you shouldn't have any reason to change its location.

✦ **Maximum File Size:** This size limit is specified in kilobytes. After the log reaches this size, it is automatically archived. See the next section for details on how these archives are stored.

✦ **Maximum Number of Archives:** After this number of archives is reached, the oldest is automatically deleted.

✦ **Log Slow Pages Taking Longer than *x* Seconds:** By default, this option is disabled. Enable this feature to discover any potential bottlenecks in your system.

✦ **Log All CORBA Calls:** Enabling this option is probably not a good idea if your site is very CORBA-intensive, but it can be a useful debugging tool because you can use the log files to inspect every call to a CORBA object.

✦ **Enable Logging for Scheduled Tasks:** If this option is on, all scheduled tasks are logged as they are executed.

Log Files

The Log Files page of ColdFusion Administrator lets you search, view, download, archive, or delete ColdFusion's log files. This page is shown in Figure 43-21:

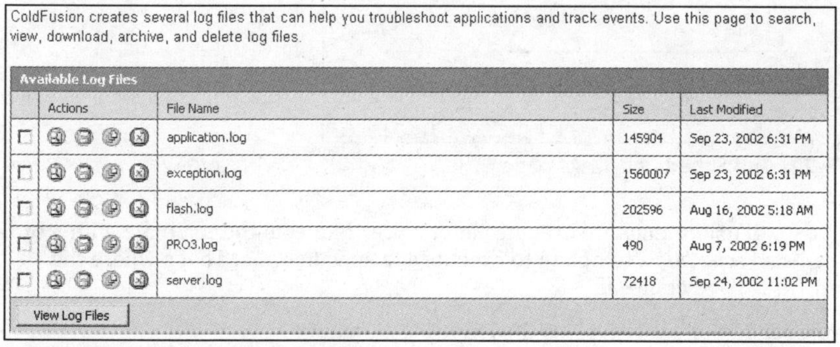

ColdFusion creates several log files that can help you troubleshoot applications and track events. Use this page to search, view, download, archive, and delete log files.

Available Log Files

	Actions	File Name	Size	Last Modified
☐		application.log	145904	Sep 23, 2002 6:31 PM
☐		exception.log	1560007	Sep 23, 2002 6:31 PM
☐		flash.log	202596	Aug 16, 2002 5:18 AM
☐		PRO3.log	490	Aug 7, 2002 6:19 PM
☐		server.log	72418	Sep 24, 2002 11:02 PM

View Log Files

Figure 43-21: The Log Files page.

This page enables you to keep track of ColdFusion's log files by using a slick graphical interface. This feature is enabled only for ColdFusion MX Enterprise; if you are using Professional, your only option is to open the log files and view them in a text editor or build a custom application to view them. Next to each log file are icons for the following four actions (These are listed from left to right):

- **Search/View:** This icon takes you to the log-file viewer, where you can search the log files or browse through them to look at all the messages.
- **Download:** This option downloads the log file to your machine for offsite analysis.
- **Archive:** This option copies the log file to an archive file and clears the original log. The archive file is named `logfilename.log.x`, where `x` is the number of the log file, with `1` the most recent.
- **Delete:** This option deletes the log file entirely.

Scheduled Tasks

The Scheduled Tasks page of ColdFusion Administrator tells ColdFusion when and how to execute certain ColdFusion templates on a schedule. This page is shown in Figure 43-22:

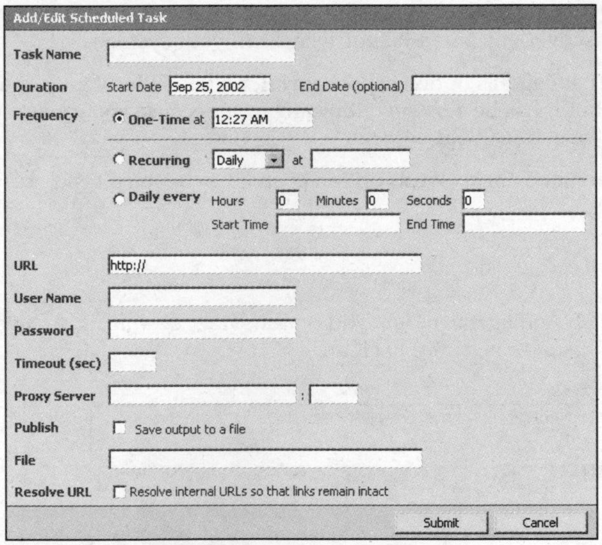

Figure 43-22: The Scheduled Tasks page.

Normally, a ColdFusion template executes after a user requests the template with a browser. But you can also *schedule* a template to execute at a specific time. That's where the Scheduled Tasks page comes in.

Setting up a scheduled task involves the following parameters:

- **Task Name:** Enter an easily identifiable name for the task in this field, as you use this name to refer to the task in your scheduled-tasks logs.
- **Duration:** This setting consists of a Start Date and an optional End Date. Some confusion surrounds these values, because some people think that ColdFusion begins the request on the start date and ends the request on the end date. This is not the case; the value that you enter in the Start Date field is when ColdFusion starts *scheduling* the task, and the value in the End Date field is when ColdFusion stops scheduling the task.

- **Frequency:** You can select among the following three types of scheduling frequency:
  - **One Time:** As the name indicates, this task is executed only once, at the specified time.
  - **Recurring:** You can execute the task once a day, once a week, or once a month, at the specified time. If the task recurs daily, the task is executed every day at the specified time. If the task recurs weekly, the task executes on the same day of the week as the start date, at the specified time. If the task recurs monthly, the task executes on the same day of the month as the start date, at the specified time.
  - **Daily every:** This option may seem confusing because you have a Daily option for Recurring, but they do two different things. *This* Daily executes the task over a repeating interval; you could, for example, execute a task every hour from 12 a.m. to 12 p.m. The Start Time and End Time in this section indicate the time of the first execution and the time when execution stops for the given day, respectively.
- **URL:** As you've probably guessed, this field is where you enter the URL of the template that's to execute. This value cannot be an `https://` URL, as `CFSCHEDULE` currently does not support SSL.
- **Username** and **Password:** Use these parameters if the page requires basic authentication.
- **Timeout (sec):** Enter here the number of seconds to wait for a response from the server before considering the task "failed" and throwing an error.
- **Proxy Server:** If a proxy server is used, specify its address and port number here.
- **Publish:** If this option is enabled, the output from the scheduled task is saved to the file named in the File field.
- **File:** See the previous option for information.
- **Resolve URL:** If Publish is enabled, all links in the scheduled task's output are resolved into a fully qualified URL before the content is written to the file.

System Probes

The System Probes page of ColdFusion Administrator (shown in Figure 43-23) tells ColdFusion when and how to execute system probes to diagnose the health of your ColdFusion Server.

System probes check the "heartbeat" of your ColdFusion server and report back to you if the heartbeat cannot be detected. A *system probe* is a template that ColdFusion executes at a regular interval, much as it does a scheduled task. The difference is that, every time that ColdFusion executes a probe, it does the following two things:

- ColdFusion marks the probe as either successful or failed depending on the result of executing the probe — more on this later in this section.
- If the probe fails, ColdFusion sends an e-mail to the site administrator telling him that the probe failed and exactly how it failed.

The following three things cause a probe to fail:

- ColdFusion cannot connect to the probe template to execute it, either because the page does not exist or the Web server is down

✦ ColdFusion does not receive a 200-success code from the probe template. See the Enable HTTP Status Codes option in the section "Settings" earlier in this chapter, for more information.

✦ The probe constraint defined within Administrator fails. You can set up the probe so that it looks for a particular string or regular expression within the output returned from the probe and fails depending on whether the string is found.

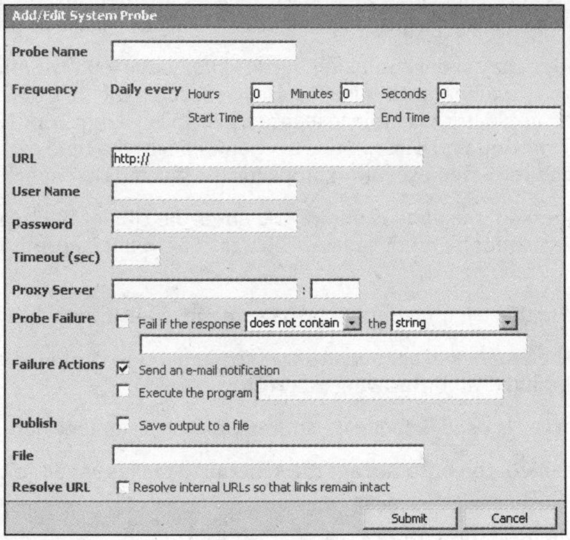

Figure 43-23: The System Probes page.

If the probe does fail, you can e-mail the site administrator and/or execute an external program.

Code Analyzer

The Code Analyzer was included with ColdFusion MX as an assistant to developers upgrading from earlier versions of ColdFusion. It can find code that results in an error in MX, such as the old Oracle `maxrows` technique and problems using `QueryNew()`. You point the Cold Analyzer to the directory containing your source code by entering its path in the Directory to Analyze field, and the Code Analyzer parses and analyzes all your code. This page is shown in Figure 43-24:

Unfortunately, the Code Analyzer can't detect all the problems with your code, so don't just run a quick report and tell your client, "We're good to go" because you probably have lots of detailed migration work to do. The only real way to analyze your code for migration is to first perform this basic Code Analyzer run-through, resolve any issues that it spots, and then perform full formal regression and load tests on the code that is running on an MX staging server.

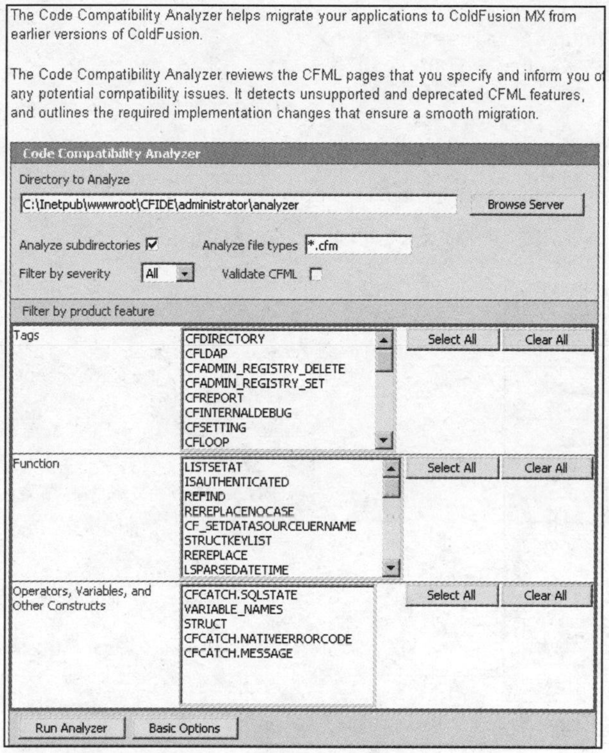

Figure 43-24: The Code Analyzer page.

Extensions

The links in the `Extensions` section of ColdFusion Administrator enable you to extend ColdFusion's capabilities through other technologies, such as Java, C++, and CORBA.

Java Applets

The Java Applets page of ColdFusion Administrator (shown in Figure 43-25) sets up applets that ColdFusion Server can use with `CFAPPLET`.

This page is where you register the applets that you can use with `CFAPPLET` so that you don't need to write code such as the following:

```
<applet name="TickerApplet" code="sText"
codebase="http://localhost/classes/" width="350" height="20"
hspace="20">
    <param name="background" value="000000">
    <param name="data" value="http://localhost/ticker.txt">
    <param name="defaultMessage" value="Please wait...">
    <param name="defaultURL" value="http://localhost/index.cfm">
```

```
      <param name="font" value="Arial">
      <param name="foreground" value="FFFFFF">
      <param name="frame" value="_blankLoad">
      <param name="highlite" value="FF0000">
      <param name="pause" value="2">
      <param name="refresh" value="2">
      <param name="size" value="12">
      <param name="wait" value="3000">
   </applet>
```

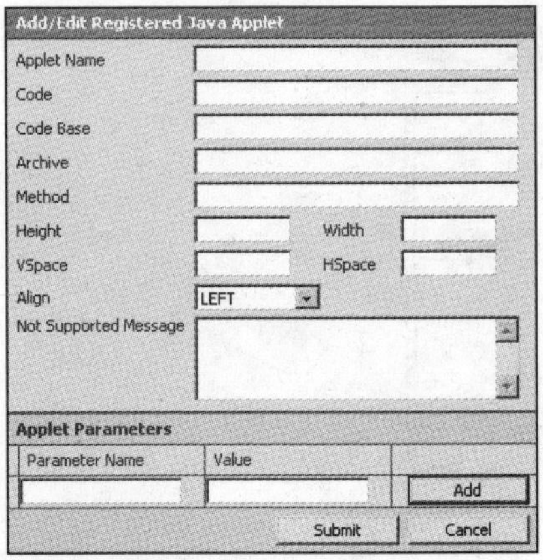

Figure 43-25: The Java Applets page.

Instead, by using this option, you can write the same code as follows:

```
<cfapplet appletsource="Ticker" name="TickerApplet">
```

From the main page, you can register a new applet or modify an existing registration. Both options take you to the applet configuration page, which contains the following options:

✦ **Applet Name:** This field is where you enter a short alias for your applet.

✦ **Code:** This field is where you enter is the name of the `.class` file without the extension. Don't specify a path.

✦ **Code Path:** This field is for the URL of the directory containing the `.class` file or for the JAR file containing the `.class` file.

✦ **Archive:** If the `.class` file is stored in a JAR file, this filed is where you enter the name of the JAR file. Otherwise, leave this field blank.

✦ **Method:** If the applet is intended for use as a form control, the applet should expose a method that returns a single string; ColdFusion uses this string as the field value that is submitted to the action page. This field contains the name of the method that returns this single string value.

✦ **Height:** The default height of the applet goes in this field.

✦ **Width:** The default width of the applet goes in this field.

✦ **VSpace:** The default amount of space above and below the applet when the applet is rendered in a user's browser goes in this field.

- ✦ **HSpace:** The default amount of space to the left and right of the applet when the applet is rendered in a user's browser goes in this field.
- ✦ **Align:** The default alignment of the applet goes in this field.
- ✦ **Not Supported Message:** If the user's browser doesn't support Java, he sees the message that you enter in this instead of the applet itself.
- ✦ **Applet Parameters:** These fields are for any default parameters that should be passed to the applet.

If your code calls `CFAPPLET` by using one or more of the parameters in these last fields, the parameters given in the `CFAPPLET` tag take precedence over the configurations you setup in ColdFusion Administrator.

CFX Tags

This page enables you to register CFX tags, which are custom tags written in Java or C++ instead of CFML. The setup parameters for each type of tag are different, so we discuss them separately in the following sections.

C++ CFX Tags

C++ tags are easier to set up than their Java counterparts. After you click Register C++ CFX or edit an existing one, you see the interface shown in Figure 43-26:

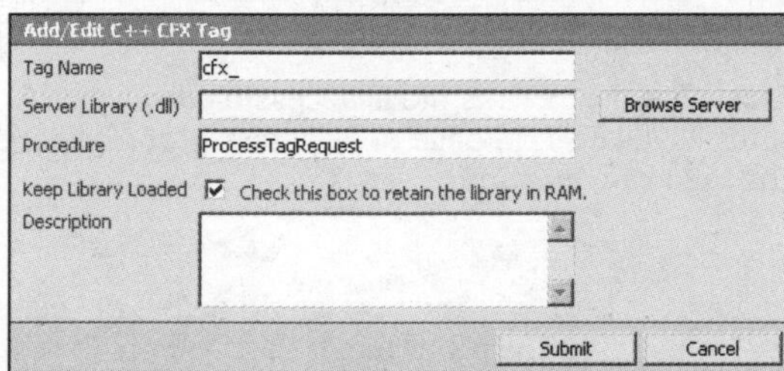

Figure 43-26: The C++ CFX Tags page.

The C++ CFX Tag registration page contains the following five parameters:

- ✦ **Tag Name:** Must begin with CFX_. This is the name of the tag referenced in your ColdFusion code.
- ✦ **Server Library (.dll):** This is the full path and file name of the tag's DLL.
- ✦ **Procedure:** This is the name of the function to call within the DLL after the CFX tag is called. This is almost always `ProcessTagRequest` unless the same DLL is used for multiple CFX tags.
- ✦ **Keep Library Loaded:** If this option is enabled, ColdFusion does not release the DLL after calling the tag the first time so that ColdFusion doesn't need to allocate memory for the tag more than once. This has the side effect of locking the DLL until the ColdFusion Server service is cycled, so disable this option during development but enable it during production.
- ✦ **Description:** A short description of the tag.

Java CFX Tags

Java CFX Tags use fewer parameters than their C++ counterparts, but the setup process is more extensive. The interface for creating a Java CFX tag is shown in Figure 43-27:

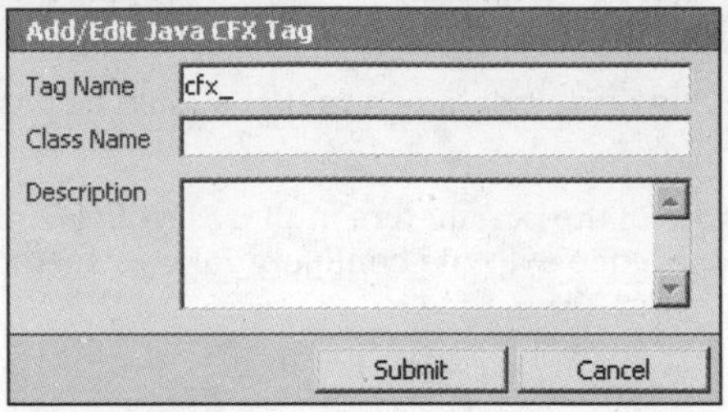

Figure 43-27: The Java CFX Tags page.

As for C++ CFX tags, the process begins on the CFX Tags page of Administrator. After you click Register Java CFX or edit an existing one, you must supply the following three parameters:

✦ **Tag Name:** Must begin with `CFX_`. This is the name of the tag referenced in your ColdFusion code.

✦ **Class Name:** The name of the Java class to invoke. This class name must be accessible from the Java `classpath` defined in the Java and JVM settings.

✦ **Description:** A short description of the tag.

After you register the tag, you must ensure that the `.class` file is accessible from ColdFusion's `classpath`, as defined on the Java and JVM page of Administrator. Suppose, for example, that if your `.class` file is at the following location:

```
c:\classes\myTag.class
```

ColdFusion's `classpath` must then include `c:\classes\`, and you would define the class name on the registration page as `myTag`. Suppose, on the other hand, that your `.class` file is stored in the following location:

```
c:\classes\cf\customtags\myTag.class
```

If so, and if `c:\classes` is defined on the `classpath`, you would define the class name as follows:

```
cf.customtags.myTag
```

A best practice is to create a single directory to contain all your Java class files and to place this directory in your classpath.

Custom Tag Paths

The Custom Tag Paths page of ColdFusion Administrator (shown in Figure 43-28) is where you tell ColdFusion how to find commonly-used custom tags.

By default, only one shared custom tag directory (located at *cf_root*/`CustomTags`) is defined for ColdFusion Server. You can use this page, however, to add additional shared tag paths.

For information on using custom tags and how these shared paths are used, see Chapter 18.

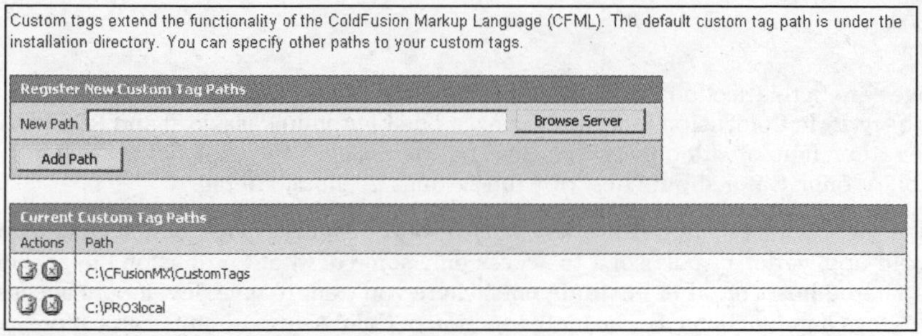

Custom tags extend the functionality of the ColdFusion Markup Language (CFML). The default custom tag path is under the installation directory. You can specify other paths to your custom tags.

Register New Custom Tag Paths

New Path [ ] Browse Server

Add Path

Current Custom Tag Paths

Actions	Path
	C:\CFusionMX\CustomTags
	C:\PRO3local

Figure 43-28: The Custom Tag Paths page.

CORBA Connectors

In this section, we'll discuss CORBA Connectors. Figure 43-29 shows the CORBA Connectors Page.

Edit CORBA Connector:
ColdFusion dynamically loads the ORB Java libraries using a connector. You can add a connector and specify the location of the library. Each of these connectors depends on the vendor's runtime library. You can also specify the ORB initialization options via a property file.

Note: Changes to the connector setting will be reflected after the server is restarted.

CORBA Connector

ORB Name
ORB Class Name
Classpath — Browse Server
ORB Property File — Browse Server

Submit Cancel

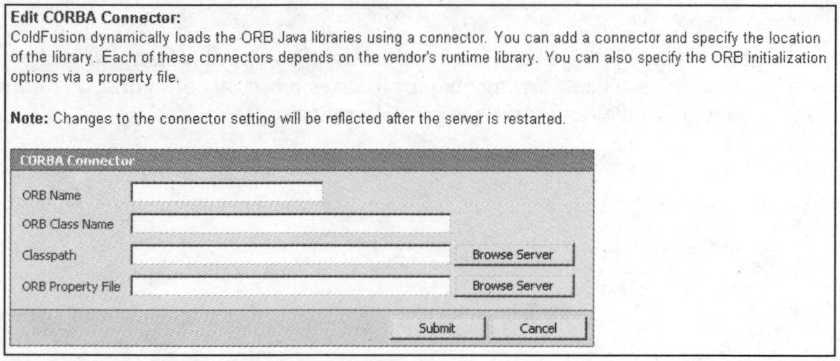

Figure 43-29: The CORBA Connectors page.

This page is where you set up CORBA connectors for use with Borland's VisiBroker. To get to this page in ColdFusion Administrator, click `CORBA Connectors` in the Extensions section of ColdFusion Administrator's navigation bar. To set up the VisiBroker connector, follow these steps:

1. Click Register CORBA Connector.
2. Enter a name for the connector in the ORB Name field. (We use **VisiBroker**.)
3. Enter `coldfusion.runtime.corba.VisibrokerConnector` in the ORB Class Name field.
4. Leave the Classpath field blank and enter *`cf_root`*`/lib/vbjorb.properties` in the ORB Property File field (replacing *`cf_root`* with the root of your ColdFusion installation).
5. Click Submit.
6. Open vbjorb.properties inside of C:\CFusionMX\lib and edit the `SVCnameroot` property so that ColdFusion can find the root. (This assumes that you are familiar with CORBA.)

Restart ColdFusion Server after adding the CORBA connection.

Security

Three pages are in this section: *CF Admin Password*, *RDS Password*, and *Sandbox Security* (or *Resource Security* in ColdFusion MX Professional). The CF Admin Password and RDS Password pages are rather simple, with only two settings on each page—the explanatory text in ColdFusion Administrator should describe the settings in enough detail.

The heavyweight in this section is the Sandbox/Resource Security page, which enables you to restrict your application or parts of it to access only some of what ColdFusion offers. This is useful for shared hosts or other environments where you want to give developers access to only "safe" tags and functions. Because this section of ColdFusion Administrator more involves the issue of server configuration than administrative settings, it is discussed in detail in the following chapter.

Summary

In this chapter you learn the basics of how to use ColdFusion Administrator. Every setting is covered, and you learn some details about setting up ColdFusion Server for best performance.

This chapter is intended only as a general overview of ColdFusion Administrator and to describe some of its options. The following chapter focuses more on configuration details, sandbox/resource security measures, and better performance.

✦ ✦ ✦

Configuration Tips and Tricks

In This Chapter

Tuning for performance

Shoring up security

Exploring advanced datasource-configuration options

Tuning the JVM

The preceding chapter gave you an overview of the settings in ColdFusion Administrator, but some things warrant more discussion, such as caching settings and sandbox security. This chapter is geared more toward configuration for performance and security and is intended for someone already familiar with the basics of ColdFusion Administration.

Choosing the Number of Simultaneous Request Threads

How many simultaneous request threads should you choose? This question is one of the most common that's asked about ColdFusion tuning and configuration. Unfortunately, we can give you no hard-and-fast answer. Whether this number should be five, fifty, or something in between (or even more) can be determined only by a formal load test of your application using a commercial-grade testing suite. (Refer to Chapter 43 for a discussion of what request threads are.)

To determine this optimum number of simultaneous requests, follow these steps (This assumes you are already in the Settings page of ColdFusion Administrator):

1. Start with five simultaneous requests (*request threads*) and run a comprehensive test scenario at high load.
2. Double the number of request threads to 10 and rerun the same test scenario at the same load.
3. Compare the full compliment of performance metrics recorded in your test, but pay particular attention to minimum, maximum, and average response times and the standard deviation for response times. Keep your eye on RAM and CPU usage to determine whether you get a nonlinear jump in values.
4. Double the number of request threads to 20 and rerun everything else exactly the same as before.

   How do your metrics look now? Are they still responding in a fairly linear fashion with a fast response time?

5. If so, keep this cycle up, doubling the number of threads with each retest and recheck of your metrics. Keep the cycle up until response times become erratic (that is, the standard deviation grows very large) or slow or your RAM and CPU usage jump sharply. After this jump happens, you want to back off in the opposite direction, as described in Step 6.
6. In ramping down, start by taking the difference between the first "failed" setting for the number of simultaneous requests and the previous run, dividing that difference by two and adding it to the previous run's value. If the previous run used 20 threads and the first failed run used 40, for example, the next run should use 30, calculated as 20 + ((40 - 20) / 2).
7. If this "ramped-down" test yields successful performance metrics, scale it back up by half. In the example in the preceding step, this new value would be 35, calculated as 30 + ((40 - 30) / 2).
8. Continue ramping back and forth (aka *hopscotching*) until your test performance metrics yield the best results.

But believe it or not, you're not finished! The number of simultaneous request threads is only one setting that affects and is affected by many other settings in ColdFusion MX, your Web server, your database server, and even your operating system and hardware. In reality, all these factors must be balanced like the old Chinese Spinning Plate Trick—not an easy thing to do even with the best of training.

A general guideline, however, is that you don't want to set this number too low or requests queue up and negatively affect the performance of your site, and you don't want to set this number too high because that uses up too many resources on your server and causes memory to constantly page to disk, which also negatively affects performance.

Caching

Developers frequently ask how many templates they should set ColdFusion to cache in RAM. The simple answer is "as many as possible." The more templates that ColdFusion can store in its cache, the less ColdFusion must access the hard drive to execute code. If memory is at a premium on your server, however, you should probably scale this number back to give ColdFusion room to breathe.

In an ideal environment, you would take the total number of ColdFusion templates in your Web site, multiply that number by 1.25, and then use that as the size of your template cache. This formula makes sure that you have room for all your templates in the cache and also gives you a little breathing room in case you add more templates.

Cache size in ColdFusion MX is a different unit of measure from earlier versions of ColdFusion Server, which measured cache size in kilobytes. ColdFusion MX measures the cache size in the number of templates instead.

You can also speed up the cache even more by turning on the *Trusted Cache* feature. (Trusted Cache is available in the Caching page of ColdFusion Administrator.) This option tells ColdFusion to "trust" whatever is already cached and not to waste a single millisecond checking to determine whether a file has been updated. We always turn on this option on our production servers, and we always turn it off on our development servers. A side-effect of enabling this option is that you must restart the ColdFusion service for ColdFusion to recognize changes to the source code.

Chart caching

ColdFusion MX also adds options for caching charts (generated by calls to `CFCHART`). First, you can specify whether the chart cache is stored in memory or on disk (with disk caching the default). If you have the RAM to spare, use in-memory caching to speed your server's performance. If, on the other hand, you either don't have much RAM or you do a *lot* of charting, choose disk caching to save memory.

Choosing the maximum number of images in the cache differs depending on whether you're doing disk caching or memory caching. If using memory caching, keep this number relatively low so that you don't end up using all your memory for chart caching. If using disk caching, make this number as high as feasible because you are limited only by the amount of free space on your hard drive.

Query caching

Query caching is another one of those parameters that you can't truly set until you load-test your application by using a commercial-grade load-testing tool *and* production-scale test data. (This parameter is set on the Caching page of ColdFusion Adminstrator.) You can't tell how large or varied your queries may be until you perform such a test, and these two factors (variance and scale) completely dominate the number of queries that you should set ColdFusion Server to cache in its memory.

You should set this parameter only after you set parameters for JVM memory usage, template cache size, and simultaneous requests — in that order. Start with a very low number such as five and run a high load-test scenario with the maximum number of virtual users that you expect your system to handle (a very important test, especially if you exhaust a lot of your memory through heavy use of the Session scope). Your watchpoints are response timings (minimum, maximum, average, and standard deviation) and available physical memory.

If you adjust this parameter, but your application's response time doesn't improve significantly, make sure that you are making effective use of query caching in your code.

If you do receive a significant benefit from increasing the number of cached queries, use the hopscotching method that we describe in the section "Choosing the Number of Simultaneous Request Threads," earlier in this chapter, to balance available physical memory with response times. If you do so, you eventually set the right number. Remember that a large standard deviation on response times indicates erratic behavior, so back off if you see this value jump sharply.

Using a UUID For CFTOKEN

Using a UUID for `CFTOKEN` is a security precaution. (You can find this option on the Settings page of ColdFusion Administrator.) By default, ColdFusion uses an eight-digit random number for the value of `CFTOKEN`, making it relatively easy to guess. Enabling this option makes ColdFusion use a UUID with a random 12-digit hexadecimal number prepended as `CFTOKEN`. This modified UUID is impossible to guess, removing any possibility of a user hacking into another user's session by manipulating the values of `CFID` and `CFTOKEN` in URL.

It's always a good idea to use a UUID for `CFTOKEN`. It's usually not a concern on development servers (although it certainly won't hurt), but on a production server, always consider enabling this option.

Using J2EE Session Variables

By default, ColdFusion MX doesn't use J2EE session management and opts instead to identify a user's Session variables through the combination of `CFID` and `CFTOKEN` sent by each of his browser requests. Enabling J2EE Session variables makes ColdFusion forego `CFID` and `CFTOKEN` for session management purposes and instead use J2EE's native session-management mechanism. (You can find this option in the Memory Variables page of ColdFusion Administrator.)

With J2EE Session variables enabled, your ColdFusion MX application can share Session, Application, and Request variables with JSP pages and other J2EE applications running on the same server.

For more information on J2EE session management, see Chapter 19. (You must restart ColdFusion server for this setting to take effect.)

Datasources

If you're using a database server rather than a file-based database such as Microsoft Access, you want to use an IP address rather than a host name or computer name in specifying your database server. Using the host name requires ColdFusion to perform a DNS lookup before connecting to the database server, and using a computer name means doing a network lookup. Using an IP address enables ColdFusion to connect to the database server directly.

After setting up and verifying your datasource with a correct username and password to make sure that you can connect to your database, edit the datasource definition and remove the username and password. (See the Data Sources section in Chapter 43 for information on verifying and editing datasources.) Instead, store the username and password in Request variables defined in `Application.cfm` or a similar mechanism and pass them in every call to `CFQUERY` and `CFSTOREDPROC`. Doing so takes the username and password out of ColdFusion MX's XML properties files and puts the connection information in `Application.cfm` templates, which are easier to secure.

A datasource's connection settings define how ColdFusion connects to the database server and which database it uses. You also have advanced settings, however, that, if used correctly, can really enhance your application's performance. Table 44-1 describes these advanced settings:

Table 44-1: Advanced Datasource Parameters

Parameter Name	*Description*
Connection String	If a database driver accepts connection strings, you can provide any additional connection parameters in the form of a connection string provided in this parameter.
Limit Connections	If this option is enabled, ColdFusion limits the number of simultaneous database requests according to the number provided in the setting for Restrict Connections To.
Restrict Connections To	See the description of the preceding parameter for information.
Maintain Connections	If this parameter is enabled, ColdFusion connects to the datasource once for a given client instead of reconnecting on every request. See Timeout (min) and Interval (min) for more information.

Parameter Name	Description
Timeout (min)	If you are maintaining connections and the time between a client's requests is greater than this number of minutes, ColdFusion expires the cached connection.
Interval (min)	If you are maintaining connections, ColdFusion checks every *x* number of minutes for expired connections.
Disable Connections	If this option is enabled, no application can use this datasource.
Login Timeout (sec)	In connecting to a database, ColdFusion waits this number of seconds before timing out the attempt and throwing an error.
CLOB	Enabling this option enables ColdFusion to retrieve the entire contents of a CLOB field (meaning a Memo field in Access or a Text field in Microsoft SQL Server). Don't enable this parameter unless you are absolutely sure that you need it, as this option causes a large performance hit.
BLOB	Enabling this option enables ColdFusion to retrieve the entire contents of a BLOB field (meaning an Image field in Microsoft SQL Server). Don't enable this parameter unless you are absolutely sure that you need it, as this option causes a large performance hit.
Long Text Buffer	If CLOB retrieval is disabled, ColdFusion retrieves a maximum of this number of characters from a CLOB, Memo, or Text field and truncates the rest. The default is 64,000 characters.
Blob Buffer	If BLOB retrieval is disabled, ColdFusion retrieves a maximum of this number of bytes from a BLOB or Image field and truncates the rest. The default is 64,000 bytes.
Allowed SQL	This set of check boxes enables you to choose the SQL statements that can be executed through this datasource, enabling you to restrict what applications can do.
Select Method	This option exists only for SQL Server and Sybase datasources. The value can be either Direct, meaning to use a standard client-side retrieval (fine for nearly all users), or Cursor, meaning to use a server-side cursor (only for advanced developers). Don't change this option unless you have a compelling reason to do so.
Trusted Connection	This option exists only for ODBC socket datasources. A trusted connection implies that, instead of using a username and password to access a database, the connection uses the name of the currently logged in user to connect. Using a Trusted Connection implies a Windows network and currently works only for Microsoft SQL Server.

Java and JVM Settings

The Java and JVM settings section of Administrator tells ColdFusion how to use the Java Virtual Machine (JVM). Naturally, these settings are rather sensitive and the defaults should be acceptable for most users. Modify these settings only if you have a compelling reason to do so.

The Java Virtual Machine path tells ColdFusion where to find the Java Virtual Machine DLL (`jvm.dll` on Windows or `jvm.so` on Solaris). Don't modify this parameter unless the JVM location changes.

Adjusting the Initial Memory Size and Maximum Memory upward is probably a good idea if you have the RAM to do so. The default maximum is 512MB, but don't set the maximum any lower than 32MB because ColdFusion may not be able to start up again. These settings control how much memory Java can allocate to ColdFusion.

Our suggestion is to leave the Initial Memory Size value blank so that the JVM is unrestricted during ColdFusion startup, but explicitly specify a Maximum Memory value as large as your hardware, operating system, and other software requirements enable. One good indicator for how much you can safely increase the Maximum Memory value is the Available Physical Memory value that you should be measuring during your load tests. Consider increasing your JVM's Maximum Memory value if you still have RAM to spare during your load tests.

The Classpath setting tells Java where to look for Java classes. This is a comma-delimited list of directories, JAR files, and/or ZIP files where ColdFusion looks for Java `.class` files. The only reason that you would need to modify this parameter is if you are using a custom Java extension such as a Java-based CFX custom tag or JSP tag library.

Sandbox and Resource Security

Sandbox/Resource Security is probably one of the best new features in the MX release of ColdFusion Server. Before MX, ColdFusion Server used a tool called Advanced Security that was notoriously unreliable and difficult to use — so much so that it is no longer supported in ColdFusion MX. Because it is built on Java, MX can make use of J2EE Sandbox Security, which is easy to use and configure and works remarkably well.

We should note the difference between *Sandbox security* and *Resource security*. The two are often used interchangeably, but they really shouldn't be. Sandbox Security is available only in ColdFusion MX Enterprise and enables you to define different security settings for different directories on your server. ColdFusion MX Professional offers a version known as Resource Security, which enables you define similar security settings, but they apply for the entire server. This chapter describes Enterprise's Sandbox Security; Resource Security is virtually identical.

To access Sandbox Security, log in to ColdFusion Administrator and click the Sandbox Security link at the bottom of the left bar. Before you can use Sandbox Security, you must enable it by selecting the check box on the main Sandbox Security page. Restart the ColdFusion Application Server service after enabling Sandbox Security.

To define a security sandbox, choose the directory containing the files that you want to secure in the Add Security Sandbox section. You can either create a new sandbox or copy an existing one by using the drop-down list. After you click Add, the new sandbox appears in the list of active sandboxes. Click Edit to modify the security settings.

Five pages in the Sandbox Security editor correspond to the five resources that you can restrict: Data Sources, CF Tags, CF Functions, Files and Directories, and Servers and Ports. The following sections describe each of these pages.

Data Sources

The first page of the Sandbox Security editor enables you to choose the datasources that the application that runs in a sandbox directory can access. The data sources are presented in a familiar *chooser* interface, where you have a list of Enabled Data Sources, a list of Disabled Data Sources, and buttons to move data sources between the two lists, as shown in Figure 44-1.

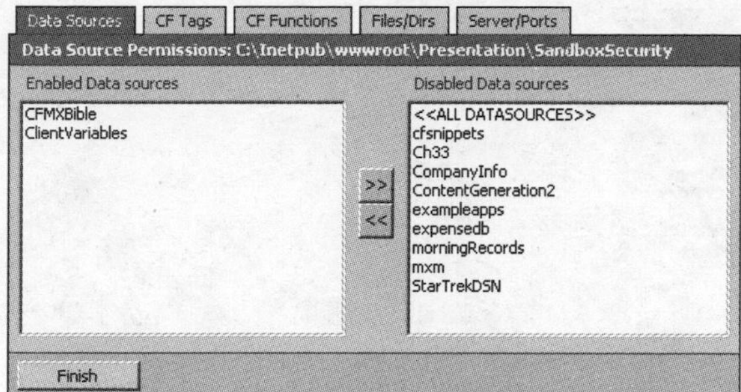

Figure 44-1: The Data Sources page of the Sandbox Security editor.

`<<ALL DATASOURCES>>` may seem rather confusing; after all, not all datasources must be on the same side of the chooser interface. Think of `<<ALL DATASOURCES>>` as a placeholder for new datasources; if `<<ALL DATASOURCES>>` is disabled, any new datasources created after the sandbox is configured are also disabled.

CF Tags

The second page of the Sandbox Security editor enables you to disable access to ColdFusion Tags that may be dangerous, such as `CFOBJECT` or CFREGISTRY. As is the Data Sources page, the CF Tags are presented in a chooser, as shown in Figure 44-2.

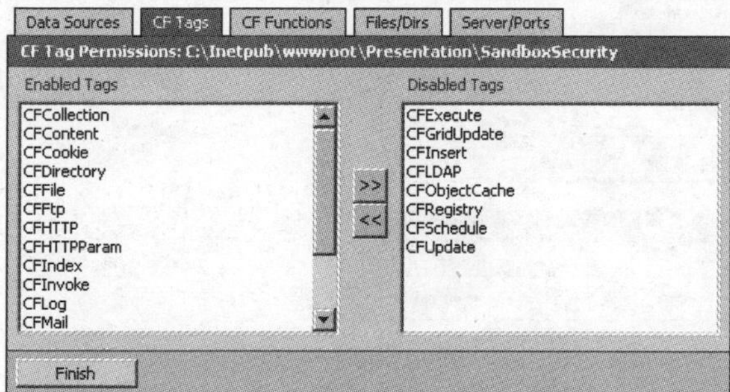

Figure 44-2: The CF Tags page of the Sandbox Security editor.

Always disable tags that aren't to be used in a particular application, because they tend to present a security hole. Make sure that you don't enable `CFOBJECT` unless really necessary, because `CFOBJECT` can invoke destructive code through a COM or Java object on your server. If you use CFCs, however, you may need to enable `CFOBJECT`.

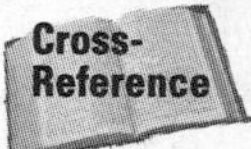

Part IV of this book describes CFCs, or ColdFusion Components, in detail.

CF Functions

The CF Functions page is similar to the CF Tags page, but it enables you to disable functions rather than tags, as shown in Figure 44-3.

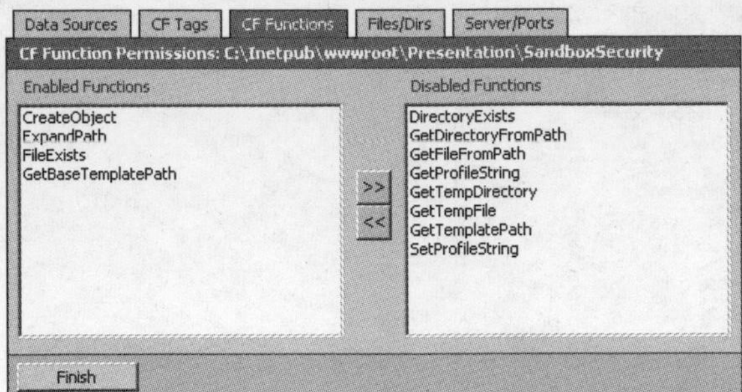

Figure 44-3: The CF Functions page of the Sandbox Security editor.

Disable `CreateObject()` unless you're sure that it's going to be used, such as to instantiate ColdFusion components.

Files and Directories

The Files and Directories page enables you to granularly control who can access what files on your system. By default, code in a sandbox can access files in the sandbox directory and its subdirectories but cannot access any files outside the sandbox.

The Files and Directories page interface is shown in Figure 44-4.

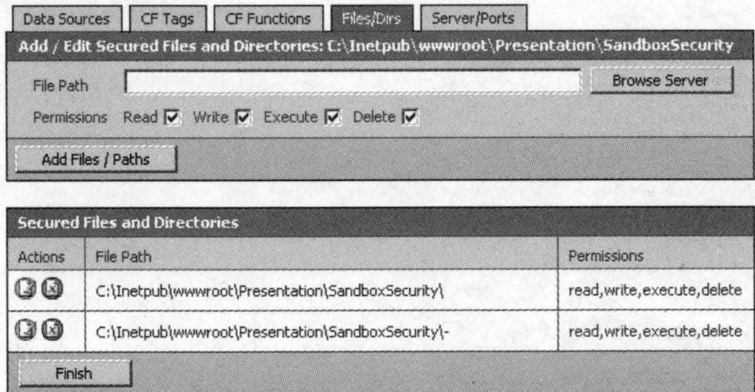

Figure 44-4: The Files and Directories page of the Sandbox Security editor.

To grant the sandbox permissions on a directory that isn't already part of the current sandbox, follow these steps:

1. Enter the path to the file or directory or choose the path by using the Browse Server button. To grant permissions on a directory and all files and subfolders in that directory, put a `/*` after the directory name. To grant permissions on a directory and *recursively* apply those permissions to all files and subfolders of the directory, no matter how deeply nested, put a `/-` after the directory name.

2. Choose the permissions to enable for that directory. Be especially careful of enabling both write and execute access on the same directory, as this could lead to malicious programs getting executed on your server.

3. Click Add Files / Paths.

Use the same basic technique to edit existing permissions by first clicking the item that you want to edit in the Secured Files and Directories list and then editing the permissions and clicking Edit Files / Paths.

Servers and Ports

The last page of the Sandbox Security editor enables you to restrict an application's access to outside resources. This page's interface is similar to the one used for Files and Directories, and is shown in Figure 44-5.

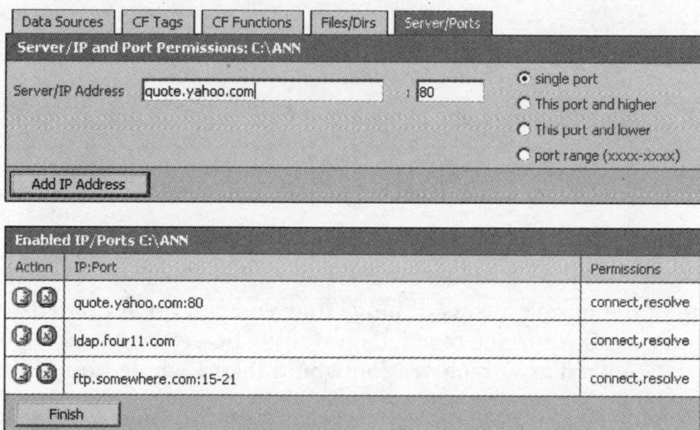

Figure 44-5: The Servers and Ports page of the Sandbox Security editor.

To give an example, say that the application in the sandbox that you're configuring uses the following calls to outside systems:

✦ `CFHTTP` to `quote.yahoo.com` on port 80

✦ `CFLDAP` to `ldap.four11.com` on any port

✦ `CFFTP` with ftp.*somewhere*.com on any port between 15 and 21

These three servers are the only ones that this sandbox should have access to, because you certainly don't want some rogue developer establishing a `CFFTP` session with `ftp.wegotviruses.com` and infecting the entire server!

As an example of using the Servers and Ports, follow these steps to configure the three server and port configurations from the preceding list:

1. Enter `quote.yahoo.com` in the Server/IP Address field and `80` in the Port field and then click Add IP Address.

2. Put `ldap.four11.com` in the Server/IP Address field but leave the Port field blank (because you don't want to restrict by port) and then click Add IP Address again.

3. Put `ftp.`*`somewhere`*`.com` in the Server/IP Address field. In the Port field, enter `15-21` and, before clicking Add IP Address, select the Port Range radio button next to the Port field to tell ColdFusion that you are entering a range rather than a single port number.

Table 44-2 describes the standard ports used with ColdFusion's Internet Protocol tags.

Table 44-2: Standard Port Assignments for ColdFusion's Networking Tags

Tag	*Standard Port (see www.iana.org/assignments/port-numbers for a list of all standard port assignments)*
`CFFTP`	21
`CFHTTP`	80
`CFHTTP` using SSL	443
`CFLDAP`	389
`CFMAIL`	25
`CFPOP`	110

Summary

This chapter shows you some of the more advanced things that you can do in ColdFusion Administrator. It has scratched only the surface of what's possible, however; to show you everything that can be done in ColdFusion Administration would take a whole book by itself.

We have specifically avoided giving advice such as "set this parameter to this number" or "always set your configuration this way" because everyone's server is different, and no parameter can be set in isolation from the others. As we state near the end of the section "Choosing the Number of Simultaneous Request Threads," earlier in this chapter . . .

"[Each parameter] is only one setting that affects and is affected by many other settings in ColdFusion MX, your Web server, your database server, and even your operating system and hardware. In reality, all these factors must be balanced like the old Chinese Spinning Plate Trick—not an easy thing to do even with the best of training."

The only way to verify your settings is as a complete server configuration rather than an individual setting—and then only in a production environment. The only way to estimate your configuration in advance of deploying to your production environment is by using a commercial-grade load-testing tool. Anything else is just guessing, and guessing is never good enough.

After you have everything tuned to perfection, you can use ColdFusion's Archive and Deploy feature to ensure that your settings are deployed along with your application. (Note that Archive and Deploy is only available in ColdFusion MX Enterprise.)

✦ ✦ ✦

ColdFusion MX Language Reference

P A R T

✦ ✦ ✦ ✦

In This Part

✦ ✦ ✦ ✦

CHAPTER 45

Introduction to the Language Reference

✦ ✦ ✦ ✦

We've always found the language references in most computer books to be useless wastes of space. They are typically abbreviated to the point of being cryptic; they give no real examples of how the language is used; and they are organized alphabetically. Either that or they are nothing more than mirrors of the standard references that you receive with the software.

Until writing one ourselves we didn't understand why language guides turn out that way. If we wrote the kind of language reference for ColdFusion MX that we really want to, it would have a page count larger than the entire *ColdFusion MX Bible* that you are reading now. That approach doesn't work for the publisher, who has a realistic page count within which to work; nor does it work for the printer, who can physically bind only so many pages into a single book; nor does it work for you, the reader, who doesn't want to spend more than $100 for a book about ColdFusion MX.

We were told to keep the language reference relatively brief because of these page limits. So we can't show example code for tags, as Macromedia's 738-page *CFML Reference* does. Our mandate is to impart as much practical knowledge as is possible in a very small space. Here goes. . . .

How This Language Reference is Organized

We decided to do things differently from all other ColdFusion references in organizing this language reference. We've turned it into a solutions-oriented guide to the CF MX language, designed to work hand-in-hand with the language implementation techniques detailed in Part III, "The ColdFusion MX Language." This language reference shows language syntax and important usage notes, and Part III describes how everything fits together in the real world.

First, we grouped all tags and functions into their most familiar categories according to how they are thought of in real-world development. Macromedia, for example, categorizes `DateFormat()` as a display function and `Now()` as a date function. Putting these functions into separate categories may be true technically, but don't you really consider both these functions to be date-related? We do, and so do many new ColdFusion developers struggling to learn the language, so we have grouped all functions that are most commonly used to work with dates and date-related issues under a common heading.

Second, we didn't separate tags from functions. Why do this? Wouldn't discussing `QueryNew()` alongside `CFQUERY` make better sense than separating them? We think so. Now, whenever you have a language-related question about working with databases or the queries that they produce, you just flip to Chapter 52, and all the tags and functions that you need are right there in one place. Seeing all the tags and functions related to a specific topic together can often inspire you to intelligently solve a problem by using tags and functions that you never before considered.

We didn't, however, do away with alphabetizing tags and functions for quick reference. As in the case in traditional references, we include separate alphabetical listings of tags and functions in the following sections so that you can quickly find the reference for a specific item. We also separate tags and functions into their own alphabetical groups within each topic-specific section in each chapter.

How to read the listings

Keep the following points in mind in reading through the language reference:

✦ To avoid confusion, if a tag or function has multiple forms of use, each is listed with only the attributes used in that form.

✦ If an attribute is required, its name appears in boldface.

✦ If an attribute accepts one of a specific set of values, each is shown separated by a pipe character | and the default value is listed first. Each specific value is listed in all caps.

✦ We sometimes use long variable names that precisely describe their contents and purpose.

✦ We group related attributes in order to show how they work together.

✦ We explicitly show where pound signs are needed around variables and where they are not. You use pound signs one way in looping over a collection, for example, and another way in looping over a query object. (See the listing for `CFLOOP` in Chapter 49 for details.)

✦ We sometimes use actual values in place of variables if the resulting description is more clear and straightforward. The value of the `applicationTimeout` attribute of the `CFAPPLICATION` tag, for example, is simply `#CreateTimeSpan(2,0,0,0)#` rather than `#CreateTimeSpan(days, hours, minutes, seconds)#`, because the former is very close to what you may typically use, and we're not trying to explain how `CreateTimeSpan()` works.

✦ In listing a function, we boldface the data type returned.

✦ We list only those tags and functions that are operable in ColdFusion MX.

We hope that you like your Language Reference!

Alphabetical Listing of Tags

The following alphabetical listing of tags will help you quickly find the reference for a tag whose name you already know. Just find the tag in the following list and go to the chapter shown to the right of the tag. Each chapter separates tags and functions into separate groups that are alphabetically listed. Some chapters are broken into topic-specific sections, where each section is separately alphabetized.

CFABORT (Ch. 49)
CFAPPLET (Ch. 55, Java, COM, and CORBA)
CFAPPLICATION (Ch. 46)
CFARGUMENT (Ch. 63)
CFASSOCIATE (Ch. 53)
CFBREAK (Ch. 49)
CFCACHE (Ch. 47, General)
CFCASE (Ch. 49)
CFCATCH (Ch. 50)
CFCHART (Ch. 59, Charting)
CFCHARTDATA (Ch. 59, Charting)
CFCHARTSERIES (Ch. 59, Charting)
CFCOL (Ch. 52)
CFCOLLECTION (Ch. 57)
CFCOMPONENT (Ch. 63)
CFCONTENT (Ch. 60, On the Client (User's) Computer)
CFCOOKIE (Ch. 48, General)
CFDEFAULTCASE (Ch. 49)
CFDIRECTORY (Ch. 60, On ColdFusion Server)
CFDUMP (Ch. 48, General)
CFELSE (Ch. 49)
CFELSEIF (Ch. 49)
CFERROR (Ch. 50)
CFEXECUTE (Ch. 55, Operating System)
CFEXIT (Ch. 53)
CFFILE (Ch. 60, On ColdFusion Server)
CFFLUSH (Ch. 56, Server Output)
CFFORM (Ch. 51)
CFFTP (Ch. 60, On an FTP Server)
CFFUNCTION (Ch. 63)
CFGRAPH (Ch. 59, Charting)
CFGRAPHDATA (Ch. 59, Charting)
CFGRID (Ch. 51)
CFGRIDCOLUMN (Ch. 51)
CFGRIDROW (Ch. 51)
CFGRIDUPDATE (Ch. 51)
CFHEADER (Ch. 47, General)
CFHTMLHEAD (Ch. 56, Server Output)
CFHTTP (Ch. 55, Web Servers)
CFHTTPPARAM (Ch. 55, Web Servers)
CFIF (Ch. 49)
CFIMPORT (Ch. 55, Java, COM, and CORBA)
CFINCLUDE (Ch. 47, General)
CFINDEX (Ch. 57)
CFINPUT (Ch. 51)
CFINSERT (Ch. 52)
CFINVOKE (Ch. 63)
CFINVOKEARGUMENT (Ch. 63)
CFLDAP (Ch. 62, Authentication and Authorization)
CFLOCATION (Ch. 49)
CFLOCK (Ch. 48, General)
CFLOG (Ch. 59, Logging)
CFLOGIN (Ch. 62, Authentication and Authorization)
CFLOGINUSER (Ch. 62, Authentication and Authorization)
CFLOGOUT (Ch. 62, Authentication and Authorization)
CFLOOP (Ch. 49)
CFMAIL (Ch. 58)
CFMAILPARAM (Ch. 58)
CFMODULE (Ch. 53)
CFOBJECT (Ch. 55, Java, COM, and CORBA; and Ch. 63)
CFOBJECTCACHE (Ch. 52)
CFOUTPUT (Ch. 47, General & Ch. 52)
CFPARAM (Ch. 48, General)
CFPOP (Ch. 58)
CFPROCESSINGDIRECTIVE (Ch. 56, Whitespace)
CFPROCPARAM (Ch. 52)
CFPROCRESULT (Ch. 52)
CFPROPERTY (Ch. 63)
CFQUERY (Ch. 52)
CFQUERYPARAM (Ch. 52)
CFREGISTRY (Ch. 61)
CFREPORT (Ch. 59, Reporting)
CFRETHROW (Ch. 50)
CFRETURN (Ch. 63)
CFSAVECONTENT (Ch. 56, Server Output)
CFSCHEDULE (Ch. 47, General)
CFSCRIPT (Ch. 54)
CFSEARCH (Ch. 57)
CFSELECT (Ch. 51)
CFSERVLET (Ch. 55, Java, COM, and CORBA)
CFSERVLETPARAM (Ch. 55, Java, COM, and CORBA)
CFSET (Ch. 48, General)
CFSETTING (Ch. 56, Whitespace)
CFSILENT (Ch. 56, Whitespace)
CFSLIDER (Ch. 51)
CFSTOREDPROC (Ch. 52)
CFSWITCH (Ch. 49)
CFTABLE (Ch. 52)
CFTEXTINPUT (Ch. 51)
CFTHROW (Ch. 50)
CFTRACE (Ch. 59, Logging)
CFTRANSACTION (Ch. 52)
CFTREE (Ch. 51)
CFTREEITEM (Ch. 51)
CFTRY (Ch. 50)
CFUPDATE (Ch. 52)
CFWDDX (Ch. 55, WDDX)
CFXML (Ch. 55, XML)

Alphabetical Listing of Functions

The following alphabetical listing of functions will help you quickly find the reference for a function whose name you already know. Just find the function in the following list and go to the chapter shown to the right of the function. Each chapter separates tags and functions into separate groups that are alphabetically listed. Some chapters are broken into topic-specific sections, where each section is separately alphabetized.

Abs() (Ch. 48, Basic Math)
ACos() (Ch. 48, Geometry and Trigonometry)
ArrayAppend() (Ch. 48, Arrays)
ArrayAvg() (Ch. 48, Arrays)
ArrayClear() (Ch. 48, Arrays)
ArrayDeleteAt() (Ch. 48, Arrays)
ArrayInsertAt() (Ch. 48, Arrays)
ArrayIsEmpty() (Ch. 48, Arrays)
ArrayLen() (Ch. 48, Arrays)
ArrayMax() (Ch. 48, Arrays)
ArrayMin() (Ch. 48, Arrays)
ArrayNew() (Ch. 48, Arrays)
ArrayPrepend() (Ch. 48, Arrays)
ArrayResize() (Ch. 48, Arrays)
ArraySet() (Ch. 48, Arrays)
ArraySort() (Ch. 48, Arrays)
ArraySum() (Ch. 48, Arrays)
ArraySwap() (Ch. 48, Arrays)
ArrayToList() (Ch. 48, Arrays)
Asc() (Ch. 48, ASCII)
ASin() (Ch. 48, Geometry and Trigonometry)
Atn() (Ch. 48, Geometry and Trigonometry)
BitAnd() (Ch. 48, Binary Data)
BitMaskClear() (Ch. 48, Binary Data)
BitMaskRead() (Ch. 48, Binary Data)
BitMaskSet() (Ch. 48, Binary Data)
BitNot() (Ch. 48, Binary Data)
BitOr() (Ch. 48, Binary Data)
BitSHLN() (Ch. 48, Binary Data)
BitSHRN() (Ch. 48, Binary Data)
BitXor() (Ch. 48, Binary Data)
Ceiling() (Ch. 48, Numbers)
Chr() (Ch. 48, ASCII)
CJustify() (Ch. 48, Strings)
Compare() (Ch. 48, Strings)
CompareNoCase() (Ch. 48, Strings)
Cos() (Ch. 48, Geometry and Trigonometry)
CreateDate() (Ch. 48, Dates and Times)
CreateDateTime() (Ch. 48, Dates and Times)
CreateObject() (Ch. 55, Java, COM, and CORBA; and Ch. 63)
CreateODBCDate() (Ch. 48, Dates and Times)
CreateODBCDateTime() (Ch. 48, Dates and Times)
CreateODBCTime() (Ch. 48, Dates and Times)
CreateTime() (Ch. 48, Dates and Times)
CreateTimeSpan() (Ch. 48, Dates and Times)
CreateUUID() (Ch. 48, General)
DateAdd() (Ch. 48, Dates and Times)
DateCompare() (Ch. 48, Dates and Times)
DateConvert() (Ch. 48, Dates and Times)
DateDiff() (Ch. 48, Dates and Times)
DateFormat() (Ch. 48, Dates and Times)
DatePart() (Ch. 48, Dates and Times)
Day() (Ch. 48, Dates and Times)
DayOfWeek() (Ch. 48, Dates and Times)
DayOfWeekAsString() (Ch. 48, Dates and Times)
DayOfYear() (Ch. 48, Dates and Times)
DaysInMonth() (Ch. 48, Dates and Times)
DaysInYear() (Ch. 48, Dates and Times)
DE() (Ch. 48, General)
DecimalFormat() (Ch. 48, Numbers)
DecrementValue() (Ch. 48, General)
Decrypt() (Ch. 62, Encryption)
DeleteClientVariable() (Ch. 48, General)
DirectoryExists() (Ch. 60, On ColdFusion Server)
DollarFormat() (Ch. 48, Numbers)
Duplicate() (Ch. 48, Structures)
Encrypt() (Ch. 62, Encryption)
Evaluate() (Ch. 48, General)
Exp() (Ch. 48, Geometry and Trigonometry)
ExpandPath() (Ch. 60, On ColdFusion Server)

FileExists() (Ch. 60, On ColdFusion Server)
Find() (Ch. 48, Strings)
FindNoCase() (Ch. 48, Strings)
FindOneOf() (Ch. 48, Strings)
FirstDayOfMonth() (Ch. 48, Dates and Times)
Fix() (Ch. 48, Numbers)
FormatBaseN() (Ch. 48, Numbers)
GetAuthUser() (Ch. 62, Authentication and Authorization)
GetBaseTagData() (Ch. 53)
GetBaseTagList() (Ch. 53)
GetBaseTemplatePath() (Ch. 60, On ColdFusion Server)
GetClientVariablesList() (Ch. 48, General)
GetCurrentTemplatePath() (Ch. 60, On ColdFusion Server)
GetDirectoryFromPath() (Ch. 60, On ColdFusion Server)
GetException() (Ch. 50)
GetFileFromPath() (Ch. 60, On ColdFusion Server)
GetFunctionList() (Ch. 47, System)
GetHttpRequestData() (Ch. 55, Web Servers)
GetHttpTimeString() (Ch. 48, Dates and Times)
GetK2ServerDocCount() (Ch. 57)
GetK2ServerDocCountLimit() (Ch. 57)
GetLocale() (Ch. 47, System)
GetMetaData() (Ch. 63)
GetMetricData() (Ch. 47, System)
GetPageContext() (Ch. 47, System)
GetProfileSections() (Ch. 47, System)
GetProfileString() (Ch. 47, System)
GetTempDirectory() (Ch. 60, On ColdFusion Server)
GetTempFile() (Ch. 60, On ColdFusion Server)
GetTemplatePath() (Ch. 60, On ColdFusion Server)
GetTickCount() (Ch. 48, Dates and Times)
GetTimeZoneInfo() (Ch. 48, Dates and Times)
GetToken() (Ch. 48, Lists)
Hash() (Ch. 62, Encryption)
Hour() (Ch. 48, Dates and Times)
HTMLCodeFormat() (Ch. 56, Server Output)
HTMLEditFormat() (Ch. 56, Server Output)
IIf() (Ch. 48, General)
IncrementValue() (Ch. 48, General)
InputBaseN() (Ch. 48, Numbers)
Insert() (Ch. 48, Strings)
Int() (Ch. 48, Numbers)
IsArray() (Ch. 48, Arrays)
IsBinary() (Ch. 48, Binary Data)
IsBoolean() (Ch. 48, General)
IsCustomFunction() (Ch. 54)
IsDate() (Ch. 48, Dates and Times)
IsDebugMode() (Ch. 47, System)
IsDefined() (Ch. 48, General)
IsK2ServerABroker() (Ch. 57)
IsK2ServerDocCountExceeded() (Ch. 57)
IsK2ServerOnline() (Ch. 57)
IsLeapYear() (Ch. 48, Dates and Times)
IsNumeric() (Ch. 48, Numbers)
IsNumericDate() (Ch. 48, Dates and Times)
IsObject() (Ch. 48, General)
IsQuery() (Ch. 52)
IsSimpleValue() (Ch. 48, General)
IsStruct() (Ch. 48, Structures)
IsUserInRole() (Ch. 62, Authentication and Authorization)
IsWDDX() (Ch. 55, WDDX)
IsXmlDoc() (Ch. 55, XML)
IsXMLElem() (Ch. 55, XML)
IsXMLRoot() (Ch. 55, XML)
JavaCast() (Ch. 55, Java, COM, and CORBA)
JSStringFormat() (Ch. 48, Strings)
LCase() (Ch. 48, Strings)
Left() (Ch. 48, Strings)
Len() (Ch. 48, Strings)
ListAppend() (Ch. 48, Lists)
ListChangeDelims() (Ch. 48, Lists)
ListContains() (Ch. 48, Lists)
ListContainsNoCase() (Ch. 48, Lists)
ListDeleteAt() (Ch. 48, Lists)
ListFind() (Ch. 48, Lists)
ListFindNoCase() (Ch. 48, Lists)
ListFirst() (Ch. 48, Lists)
ListGetAt() (Ch. 48, Lists)
ListInsertAt() (Ch. 48, Lists)
ListLast() (Ch. 48, Lists)
ListLen() (Ch. 48, Lists)
ListPrepend() (Ch. 48, Lists)
ListQualify() (Ch. 48, Lists)
ListRest() (Ch. 48, Lists)
ListSetAt() (Ch. 48, Lists)
ListSort() (Ch. 48, Lists)
ListToArray() (Ch. 48, Lists)

ToBinary() (Ch. 48, Binary Data)
ToString() (Ch. 48, Strings)
Trim() (Ch. 48, Strings)
UCase() (Ch. 48, Strings)
URLDecode() (Ch. 48, General)
URLEncodedFormat() (Ch. 48, General)
URLSessionFormat() (Ch. 46)
Val() (Ch. 48, Numbers)
ValueList() (Ch. 48, Lists)
Week() (Ch. 48, Dates and Times)
WriteOutput() (Ch. 54)
XmlChildPos() (Ch. 55, XML)
XmlElemNew() (Ch. 55, XML)
XmlFormat() (Ch. 55, XML)
XmlNew() (Ch. 55, XML)
XmlParse() (Ch. 55, XML)
XmlSearch() (Ch. 55, XML)
XmlTransform() (Ch. 55, XML)
Year() (Ch. 48, Dates and Times)
YesNoFormat() (Ch. 48, Strings)

✦ ✦ ✦

Designing Your Application Framework

<CFAPPLICATION>

Defines the application space of a ColdFusion application, selectively enables session and client management, and determines the behavior of cookies.

<CFAPPLICATION	
name = "applicationName"	If only Client variables are used in the application, the ***name*** attribute is optional.
applicationTimeout = #CreateTimeSpan(2,0,0,0)#	Lifespan of Application variables. Defaults to the value specified in ColdFusion Administrator.
clientManagement = "NO | YES"	Enables Client variables.
clientStorage = "REGISTRY | dataSourceName | COOKIE"	If set to COOKIE, Client variables fail on computers that disable cookies.
sessionManagement = "NO | YES"	Enables Session variables.
sessionTimeout = #CreateTimeSpan(0,0,20,0)#	Lifespan of Session variables. Defaults to the value specified in ColdFusion Administrator.
setClientCookies = "YES | NO"	Sends CFID and CFTOKEN cookies to browser.
setDomainCookies = "NO | YES">	Required if the application runs on a cluster.

URLSessionFormat()

Returns a URL containing the client and session data if cookies are turned off.

URLSessionFormat(
    "DestinationPage.cfm")

✦ ✦ ✦

General Use Tags and Functions

General

<CFCACHE>

Stores the static HTML generated by a ColdFusion template in a temporary file on the server and retrieves it instead of the requested ColdFusion template during the specified time span. Judicious use of CFCACHE on ColdFusion templates that generate latent content can greatly increase the overall performance of ColdFusion applications.

```
<CFCACHE
    action = "CACHE                              Both Client- and Server-side caching.
      | FLUSH                                    Flushes the cache.
      | CLIENTCACHE                              Client-side caching only.
      | SERVERCACHE                              Server-side caching only.
      | OPTIMAL"                                 Same as CACHE.
    directory = "#absolutePathToDirectory#"
    timespan = "#CreateTimeSpan(1,0,0,0)#"
    expireURL = "*/report.cfm*"
    userName = "#userName#"
    password = "#password#"
    port = "80"
    protocol = "http:// | https://">
```

<CFHEADER>

Generates custom HTTP response headers and returns them to the client browser. Can also be used to change the HTTP status code. Cannot be called after a CFFLUSH.

If creating a response header:

```
<CFHEADER
    name = "#headerName#"
    value = "#headerValue#">
```

If changing the HTTP status code:

```
<CFHEADER
    statusCode = "#statusCode#"
    statusText = "#statusText#">
```

Cross References

CFCONTENT	Changes the Content-Type header of the current request.

<CFINCLUDE>

Tells ColdFusion to include the CFML contained in an external template into the calling template.

```
<CFINCLUDE
    template = "IncludedTemplate.cfm">
```

Cross References

CFMODULE	Calls a template as a custom tag.
CFINVOKE	Calls a function in either the current template or in a component.

<CFOUTPUT>

Instructs ColdFusion to evaluate expressions between the opening and closing CFOUTPUT tags. NOTE: The form of CFOUTPUT that outputs database queries is covered in Chapter 52.

```
<CFOUTPUT>
    #someVariable#
</CFOUTPUT>
```

<CFSCHEDULE>

Schedules tasks to run from ColdFusion Server. Also enables scheduled tasks to be run on demand and deleted if no longer needed.

Schedule some general task to run:

```
<CFSCHEDULE
    action = "update"
    task = "Task Name"
    operation = "HTTPRequest"
    url = "http://www.mydomain.com/page.cfm"
    startDate = "1/1/2003"
    startTime = "12:30 PM"
    interval = "numberOfSeconds        Default is 3600 seconds, or one hour.
     | ONCE                            Task will execute one time and will then be deleted.
     | DAILY                           Task will execute once a day at the specified start time.
     | WEEKLY                          Task will execute once a week on the same day as startDate at the specified
                                       start time.
     | MONTHLY"                        Task will execute once a month on the same day of the month as startDate at
                                       the specified start time.
```

```
    file = "FileToOutput.htm"
    path = "c:\inetpub\wwwroot\OutputDirectory"
    publish = "NO | YES"
    endDate = "4/1/2003"
    endTime = "3:00 AM"
    requestTimeout = "#timeOutInSeconds#"
    username = "#userName#"
    password = "#password#"
    resolveURL = "NO | YES"
    proxyServer = "proxyServer"
    port = "80"
    proxyPort = "80">
```

Publish the dynamic content of a ColdFusion template as static HTML files:

```
<CFSCHEDULE
    action = "update"
    task = "Create Daily News"
    operation = "HTTPRequest"
    url = "http://www.mydomain.com/DailyNews.cfm"
    publish = "Yes"
    file = "DailyNews.htm"
    path = "c:\inetpub\wwwroot\mydomain"
    startDate = "1/1/2003"
    startTime = "12:00 AM"
    interval = "numberOfSeconds      Default is 3600 seconds, or one hour.
      | ONCE                         Task will execute one time and will then be deleted.
      | DAILY                        Task will execute once a day at the specified start time.
      | WEEKLY                       Task will execute once a week on the same day as startDate at the specified
                                     start time.
      | MONTHLY"                     Task will execute once a month on the same day of the month as startDate at the
                                     specified start time.
    requestTimeout = "#timeOutInSeconds#"
    resolveURL = "Yes">
```

Run a scheduled task immediately:

```
<CFSCHEDULE
    action = "run"
    task = "Task Name">
```

Delete a task:

```
<CFSCHEDULE
    action = "delete"
    task = "Task Name">
```

System

GetFunctionList()

Returns a **structure** containing keys that name every available ColdFusion function.

GetFunctionList()

GetLocale()

Returns a **string** containing the currently set locale.

GetLocale()

GetMetricData()

Returns a **structure** containing metric data when mode is PERF_MONITOR; otherwise returns an **integer**.

GetMetricData(	
"PERF_MONITOR	Returns Performance Monitor data.
| SIMPLE_LOAD	Returns overall server load.
| PREV_REQ_TIME	Returns milliseconds required to process load.
| AVG_REQ_TIME")	Returns average request processing time.

Application Notes

The arguments to this function are enumerated constants, not variables.

GetPageContext()

Returns the current **Java PageContext object**.

GetPageContext()

GetProfileSections()

Returns a **structure** containing keys named for each INI section. The value of each key is a comma-delimited list containing the names of the entries in that section. An example filePath value is shown here.

GetProfileSections(	
filePath)	"C:\myDir\filename.ini"

GetProfileString()

Returns a **string** containing the INI file entry from a specific section of the specified INI file. If the example data shown to the right of each attribute is substituted, GetProfileString() returns the value of the entry Frequency in the section JobsToRun stored in the file C:\myDir\filename.ini.

GetProfileString(	
filePath,	"C:\myDir\filename.ini"
sectionName,	"JobsToRun"
entryName)	"Frequency"

IsDebugMode()

Returns a **logical** TRUE if debugging mode is on and FALSE if not.

IsDebugMode()

SetEncoding()

This is a **Void** function; it returns nothing. Sets the character encoding of the variables in the specified scope. This is used when incoming form or URL variables are in a character set other than Latin-1 (ISO-8859-1)

SetEncoding(

ScopeName,	"URL | Form"
characterSet)	See www.w3.org/international/o-chaset-lang.html

SetLocale()

Returns a **string** containing the *current* locale – not the new locale to which you are setting ColdFusion Server. The locale is set to the new locale after `SetLocale()` is called, such that `GetLocale()` returns the new locale if called immediately after `SetLocale()`. If the example localeCode value is used, `SetLocale()` sets the current locale to U.S. English.

SetLocale(

localeCode)	"English (US)". For other possible values, see Macromedia's ***CFML Language Reference***.

SetProfileString()

Returns an empty **string** if successful; returns an error message if unsuccessful. If the example data shown to the right of each attribute is substituted, `SetProfileString()` sets the value of the entry `Frequency` in the section `JobsToRun` stored in the file `C:\myDir\filename.ini` to `12` and returns zero if successful.

SetProfileString(

filePath,	"C:\myDir\filename.ini"
sectionName,	"JobsToRun"
entryName,	"Frequency"
value)	12

✦ ✦ ✦

Working with Variables

General

<CFCOOKIE>

Sets variables in the Cookie scope (browser cookies).

```
<CFCOOKIE
    name = "visitorEmail"             Sets a browser cookie named "visitorEmail".
    value = "#Client.Email#"
    expires = "01/01/2003             Expires on January 1, 2003.
      | 10                            Expires in ten days.
      | NOW                           Expires cookie immediately (and deletes it from the browser).
      | NEVER"                        Cookie never expires.
    secure = "NO | YES"
    path = "/subpath"
    domain = ".mydomain.com">
```

<CFDUMP>

Displays both simple and complex objects in a human-readable format. Mainly used for testing and debugging.

```
<CFDUMP
    var = "#variableName#"
    expand = "YES | NO"
    label = "This appears at the top of the dump">
```

<CFLOCK>

Preserves the integrity of shared memory objects by synchronizing access to them via a series of locks. A `READONLY` lock enables multiple process threads to read an object in shared memory while preventing any updates to the object's memory space. An `EXCLUSIVE` lock's purpose is to enable the safe creation or update of an object in shared memory space, so it prevents all other process threads from reading from or writing to the object's memory space until such creation or update is finished.

To synchronize a specific collection of memory-based objects:

```
<CFLOCK
    timeout = "timeOutInSeconds"
    name = "iAmTheNameOfTheLock"
    throwOnTimeout = "YES | NO"
    type = "EXCLUSIVE | READONLY">
    ...
</CFLOCK>
```

To synchronize all memory-based objects in an entire scope:

```
<CFLOCK
    timeout = "#timeOutInSeconds#"
    scope = "SERVER | APPLICATION | SESSION"
    throwOnTimeout = "YES | NO"
    type = "EXCLUSIVE | READONLY">
    ...
</CFLOCK>
```

<CFPARAM>

Creates a variable if it doesn't already exist. Optionally assigns a default value and tests for correct data type.

```
<CFPARAM
    name = "variableName"
    default = "value"
    type = "ANY
      | ARRAY
      | BINARY
      | BOOLEAN
      | DATE
      | NUMERIC
      | QUERY
      | STRING
      | STRUCT
      | UUID
      | VARIABLENAME">
```

If ***default*** is not specified and the variable specified by ***Name*** does not exist, this tag will throw an error.

If ***type*** is specified and the variable specified by ***Name*** is not of the correct type, this tag will throw an error.

<CFSET>

Defines a variable and assigns a value to it.

```
<CFSET
    variableName = expression>
```

Cross References

`SetVariable()`	An alternative syntax for setting variables

CreateUUID()

Returns a **UUID** (or Universally Unique IDentifier). A UUID is a 35-character long hexadecimal representation of a 128-bit random number and is guaranteed to be unique across every machine in the world.

```
CreateUUID()
```

DE()

Returns *string* as a **string** correctly escaped so that it is preserved intact for use in the `Iif()` and `Evaluate()` functions.

```
DE(
    "string")
```

Cross References

`Evaluate()`	Evaluates a string expression.
`IIf()`	Conditionally returns one of two expressions depending on a condition.

DecrementValue()

Returns a **number** containing *value* decremented by 1.

```
DecrementValue(
    value)
```

DeleteClientVariable()

Returns **TRUE** if the client variable *variableName* is successfully deleted; otherwise, returns **FALSE**.

DeleteClientVariable("**variableName**")	Deletes the Client variable named Client.variableName. variableName must be enclosed in double quotes.

Evaluate()

Returns the **last result** of evaluating a series of *stringExpressions*, where the result of each expression is available for evaluation of later expressions in the series.

```
Evaluate(
    stringExpression1,
    stringExpression2,
    stringExpressionN...)
```

Cross References

`DE()`	"Delays" evaluation such that a string will be unmodified by a call to Evaluate().
`IIf()`	Conditionally returns one of two expressions depending on a condition.

GetClientVariablesList()

Returns a **comma-delimited list** containing writable Client variable names.

```
GetClientVariablesList()
```

IIf()

Returns the **evaluation** of either the *expressionToEvaluateIfTrue* or *expressionToEvaluateIfFalse*, depending on whether the result of *condition* was `TRUE` or `FALSE`, respectively.

```
IIf(
    condition,
    "expressionToEvaluateIfTrue",
    "expressionToEvaluateIfFalse")
```

Cross References

`DE()`	"Delays" evaluation such that a string will be unmodified by a call to Evaluate().
`Evaluate()`	Evaluates an expression.

IncrementValue()

Returns a **number** that is *value* incremented by 1.

```
IncrementValue(
    value)
```

IsBoolean()

Returns **Yes** if *value* is or can be converted to Boolean value; otherwise, **No**.

```
IsBoolean(
    value)
```

IsDefined()

Returns **Yes** if *variableName* exists; otherwise, **No.**

IsDefined(
    "variableName") — *variableName* is enclosed in double quotes.

IsObject()

Returns **Yes** if *value* is an object; otherwise, **No.**

IsObject(
    value)

IsSimpleValue()

Returns **Yes** if *value* is a simple data type (meaning not a COM object, Java object, CORBA object, structure, array, or query); otherwise, **No.**

IsSimpleValue(
    value)

ParameterExists()

Deprecated. Use `IsDefined()` instead.

SetVariable()

Returns the **new value** of the evaluated variable *name*. No longer required; use `CFSET` instead.

SetVariable(
    name,
    value)

Cross References

`CFSET`	The preferred syntax for setting variables

URLDecode()

Returns the **decoded string** contained in *URLEncodedString* as plain text.

URLDecode(
    URLEncodedString,
    charset) — See www.w3.org/international/o-chaset-lang.html for possible values.

URLEncodedFormat()

Returns the **URL-encoded string** version of *string*.

URLEncodedFormat(
string,
charset) See www.w3.org/international/o-chaset-lang.html for possible values.

Strings

CJustify()

Returns a **string** that is *length* characters long and that contains *string* centered within the return value.

CJustify(
string,
length)

Compare()

Returns **-1** if *string1* is less than *string2*, **0** if *string1* and *string2* are equal, and **1** if *string1* is greater than *string2*, according to a case-sensitive comparison of the two strings.

Compare(
string1,
string2)

CompareNoCase()

Returns **-1** if *string1* is less than *string2*, **0** if *string1* and *string2* are equal, and **1** if *string1* is greater than *string2*, according to a case-insensitive comparison of the two strings.

CompareNoCase(
string1,
string2)

Find()

Returns an **integer** containing the first found position of *substring* in *string* (zero, if not found), searching from *start* position, based on a case-sensitive search.

Find(
substring,
string,
Start) Defaults to 1.

FindNoCase()

Returns an **integer** containing the first found position of *substring* in *string* (zero, if not found), searching from *start* position, based on a case-insensitive search.

FindNoCase(
substring,
string,
Start) Defaults to 1.

FindOneOf()

Returns an **integer** containing the first found position of any single character in *set* that occurs inside *string* (zero, if not found), searching from *start* position, based on a case-sensitive search.

FindOneOf(
set,
String,
start) Defaults to 1.

Insert()

Returns a **string** containing *substring* inserted into *string* at *position*.

Insert(
substring,
string,
position)

JSStringFormat()

Returns a **string** that contains *string* correctly escaped for safe use in javascript functions.

JSStringFormat(
string)

LCase()

Returns a **string** containing *string* converted to all lowercase characters.

LCase(
string)

Left()

Returns a **string** containing the first *count* characters of *string*.

Left(
string,
count)

Len()

Returns an **integer** containing the length of *stringOrBinaryObject*.

Len(
    stringOrBinaryObject)

LJustify()

Returns a **string** that is *length* characters long and that contains *string* left-justified within the return value.

LJustify(
    string,
    length)   If *length* is less than the length of *string*, *string* will be returned unmodified.

LTrim()

Returns a **string** containing *string* with all leading spaces removed.

LTrim(
    string)

Mid()

Returns a **string** that is *count* characters long starting from position *start* in *string*.

Mid(
    string,
    start,
    count)

REFind()

If *returnSubexpressions* is `TRUE`, returns a **structure** containing two arrays named `len` and `pos` that contain the lengths and positions of each case-sensitive match. If *returnSubexpressions* is `FALSE`, returns an **integer** containing the position of the case-sensitive match, or zero if no match.

REFind(
    regularExpression,
    string,
    start,   Defaults to 1.
    returnSubexpressions)   "FALSE | TRUE".

REFindNoCase()

If *returnSubexpressions* is `TRUE`, returns a **structure** containing two arrays named `len` and `pos` that contain the lengths and positions of each case-insensitive match. If *returnSubexpressions* is `FALSE`, returns an **integer** containing the position of the case-insensitive match, or zero if no match.

```
REFindNoCase(
    regularExpression,
    string,
    start,                      Defaults to 1.
    returnSubexpressions)       "FALSE | TRUE".
```

RemoveChars()

Returns a **string** containing *string* with *count* characters removed starting from position *start*.

```
RemoveChars(
    string,
    start,
    count)
```

RepeatString()

Returns a **string** containing *string* repeated *count* times.

```
RepeatString(
    string,
    count)
```

Replace()

Returns a **string** containing the case-sensitive result of *substring1* being replaced by *substring2* inside *string*. The *scope* parameter describes whether all occurrences or only the first occurrence of *substring*1 is replaced.

```
Replace(
    string,
    substring1,
    substring2,
    scope)                      "ONE | ALL"
```

ReplaceList()

Returns a **string** containing *string* after it has had all occurrences of the elements of *list1* replaced by the corresponding elements of *list2*.

```
ReplaceList(
    string,
    list1,
    list2)
```

ReplaceNoCase()

Returns a **string** containing the case-insensitive result of *substring1* being replaced by *substring2* inside *string*. The *scope* parameter describes whether all occurrences or only the first occurrence of *substring*1 is replaced.

ReplaceNoCase(
string,
substring1,
substring2,
scope) "ONE | ALL".

REReplace()

Returns a **string** containing *string* after the text matched by a case-sensitive *regularExpression* is replaced by *substring*. The *scope* parameter describes whether all occurrences or only the first occurrence of *substring*1 is replaced.

REReplace(
string,
regularExpression,
substring,
scope) "ONE | ALL".

REReplaceNoCase()

Returns a **string** containing *string* after the text matched by a case-insensitive *regularExpression* is replaced by *substring*. The *scope* parameter describes whether all occurrences or only the first occurrence of *substring*1 is replaced.

REReplaceNoCase(
string,
regularExpression,
substring,
scope) "ONE | ALL".

Reverse()

Returns a **string** containing *string* in reverse character order.

Reverse(
string)

Right()

Returns a **string** containing the rightmost *count* characters of *string*.

Right(
string,
count)

RJustify()

Returns a **string** that is *length* characters long and that contains *string* right-justified within the return value.

RJustify(
    string,
    length)

RTrim()

Returns a **string** containing *string* with all trailing spaces removed.

RTrim(
    string)

SpanExcluding()

Returns a **string** containing the leading characters of *string* up to the first character contained in *set* as a case-sensitive match.

SpanExcluding(
    string,
    set)

SpanIncluding()

Returns a **string** containing the leading characters of *string* up to the first character not contained in *set* as a case-sensitive match.

SpanIncluding(
    string,
    set)

ToString()

Returns a **string** containing *value* converted to a string according to the type of *encoding* specified.

ToString(
    value,
    encoding) — "US-ASCII | ISO-8859-1 | UTF-8 | UTF-16": defaults to the encoding set for the page in which the function is called.

Trim()

Returns a **string** containing *string* with both leading and trailing spaces removed.

Trim(
    string)

UCase()

Returns a **string** containing *string* converted to all uppercase characters.

UCase(
    string)

YesNoFormat()

Returns a **string** containing either `Yes` for a non-zero *value* or `No` for a *value* of zero.

YesNoFormat(
  value)

Numbers

Ceiling()

Returns the **integer** that is closest to but greater than *value*.

Ceiling(
  number)

DecimalFormat()

Returns the **string** equivalent of *number* formatted with commas separating thousands, two decimal places, and a leading hyphen if *number* is negative.

DecimalFormat(
  number)

DollarFormat()

Returns the **string** equivalent of *number* formatted with a dollar sign, commas separating thousands, two decimal places, and enclosing parentheses if *number* is negative.

DollarFormat(
  number)

Fix()

If *number* is greater than or equal to zero, returns the closest **integer** less than *number*. If *number* is less than zero, returns the closest **integer** greater than *number*.

Fix(
  number)

FormatBaseN()

Returns a **string** containing *number* in base 10 converted to base *radix*.

FormatBaseN(
 number,
 radix)

InputBaseN()

Returns a **string** containing *number* in base *radix* converted to base 10.

InputBaseN(
 string,
 radix)

Int()

Returns a **string** containing the closest integer smaller than *number*.

Int(
 number)

IsNumeric()

Returns **Yes** if *string* can be converted to a number; otherwise **No**.

IsNumeric(
 string)

LSCurrencyFormat()

Returns a **string** containing *number* formatted according to a location *type*.

LSCurrencyFormat(
 number,
 type) LOCAL | INTERNATIONAL | NONE

LSEuroCurrencyFormat()

Returns a **string** containing *number* formatted with the Euro symbol or sign according to a location *type*.

LSEuroCurrencyFormat(
 number,
 type) LOCAL | INTERNATIONAL | NONE

LSIsCurrency()

Returns **Yes** if the current locale setting is that of a Euro Zone country and *string* is in a valid currency format; otherwise, **No**.

LSIsCurrency(
  string)

LSIsNumeric()

Returns **Yes** if *string* can be formatted in the current locale format; otherwise, **No**.

LSIsNumeric(
  string)

LSNumberFormat()

Returns a **string** containing *number* formatted according to the current locale and the pattern specified by *mask*.

LSNumberFormat(
  number,
  mask) See Allowed Mask Elements below.

Allowed Mask Elements

- _ (underscore): digit placeholder
- 9: same as underscore, but shows decimal places more clearly
- . (dot): placeholder for a decimal point or locale-specific symbol
- 0: pads with zeros
- ( ): if number is negative, surrounds the number with parentheses
- +: puts a plus sign before a positive number and a minus sign before a negative number
- -: puts a space before a positive number and a minus sign before a positive number
- , (comma): separates every third character with a comma or locale-specific symbol
- L or C: left- or center-justifies the number within the mask; must be the first character in the mask string
- $: precedes number with dollar sign or locale-specific symbol; must be the first character in the mask string
- ^ (caret): separates the right- and left-hand sides of the format mask

LSParseCurrency()

Returns a **number** containing the numeric equivalent of *string* according to the current locale.

LSParseCurrency(
  string)

LSParseEuroCurrency()

Returns a **number** containing the numeric equivalent of a *string* containing the Euro symbol or sign, according to the current locale.

LSParseEuroCurrency(
    string)

LSParseNumber()

Returns a **number** containing the numeric equivalent of *string* formatted according to the current locale.

LSParseNumber(
    string)

NumberFormat()

Returns a **string** containing *number* formatted according to the pattern specified in *mask*.

NumberFormat(
    number,
    mask)   See Allowed Mask Elements under LSNumberFormat(). Note that no locale-specific symbols will be used when using NumberFormat().

Cross References

`DecimalFormat()`	Formats a number as a decimal number.
`DollarFormat()`	Formats a number like a dollar amount.
`LSCurrencyFormat()`	Formats a number as a locale-specific currency amount.
`LSEuroCurrencyFormat()`	Formats a number as a locale-specific currency amount, using the Euro currency symbol for locales that use the Euro.
`LSNumberFormat()`	Formats a number using locale-specific symbols in place of the generic symbols used in the format mask.

Round()

Returns an **integer** containing *number* rounded to the closest integer.

Round(
    number)

Val()

Returns a **number** containing the numeric equivalent of *string*; if *string* cannot be converted to a number, returns zero.

Val(
    string)

Dates and Times

CreateDate()

Returns a **date/time object** with the time value always specified as `00:00:00`.

CreateDate(
 year,
 month,
 day)

CreateDateTime()

Returns a **date/time object** with an accurate time value.

CreateDateTime(
 year,
 month,
 day,
 hour,
 minute,
 second)

CreateODBCDate()

Returns an **ODBC date object**.

CreateODBCDate(
 date)

CreateODBCDateTime()

Returns an **ODBC date/time object**.

CreateODBCDateTime(
 date)

CreateODBCTime()

Returns an **ODBC time object**.

CreateODBCTime(
 date)

CreateTime()

Returns a **time object**, which is a date/time object with the date value always specified as `December 30, 1899`.

```
CreateTime(
    hour,
    minute,
    second)
```

CreateTimeSpan()

Returns a **numeric date** equivalent to the *days*, *hours*, *minutes*, and *seconds* specified.

```
CreateTimeSpan(
    days,
    hours,
    minutes,
    seconds)
```

DateAdd()

Returns a **date/time object** containing *date* after its value has been increased by *number* of *datePart*.

```
DateAdd(
    datePart,
    number,
    date)                    See Allowed Date Parts under DatePart().
```

DateCompare()

Returns **-1** if *datetime1* is less than *datetime2*, **0** if *datetime1* and *datetime2* are equal, or **1** if *datetime1* is greater than *datetime2,* according to the degree of *precision* specified.

```
DateCompare(
    datetime1,
    datetime2,
    precision)               See Allowed Date Comparison Precisions below.
```

Allowed Date Comparison Precisions

- s: precise to the second; this is the default.
- n: precise to the minute.
- h: precise to the hour.
- d: precise to the day.
- m: precise to the month.
- yyyy: precise to the year.

DateConvert()

Returns a **date/time object** containing *date* converted to either from Coordinated Universal Time (UTC) to local time or from local time to UTC time, depending on *conversionType*.

```
DateConvert(
    conversionType,          "LOCAL2UTC | UTC2LOCAL".
    date)
```

DateDiff()

Returns a **number** containing the difference between *datetime1* and *datetime2* measured in *datePart*.

```
DateDiff(
    datePart,                See Allowed Date Parts under DatePart().
    datetime1,
    datetime2)
```

DateFormat()

Returns a **string** containing *date* formatted according to the pattern specified in *mask*.

```
DateFormat(
    date,
    mask)                    See Allowed Mask Elements below.
```

Allowed Mask Elements

- d: Day of the month with no leading zero for single-digit days.
- dd: Day of the month with a leading zero for single-digit days.
- ddd: Day of the week as a three-letter abbreviation.
- dddd: Day of the week spelled out.
- m: Month with no leading zero for single-digit months.
- mm: Month with a leading zero for single-digit months.
- mmm: Month as a three-letter abbreviation.
- mmmm: Month spelled out.
- y: Year as its last two digits with no leading zero for a single-digit year.
- yy: Year as its last two digits.
- yyyy: Year as four digits.
- gg: Period/Era. Ignored. Reserved for future use.
- short: Java standard short date format.
- medium: Java standard medium date format.
- long: Java standard long date format.
- full: Java standard full date format.
- Default mask is "dd-mmm-yy".

DatePart()

Returns an **integer** containing the *datePart* of *date*.

```
DatePart(
    datePart,                See Allowed Date Parts below.
    date)
```

Allowed Date Parts

- yyyy: Year
- q: Quarter
- m: Month
- y: Day of year
- d: Day of month
- w: Day of week
- ww: Week of year
- h: Hour
- n: Minute
- s: Second

Day()

Returns an **integer** containing the ordinal for the day of the month in which *date* occurs (1 to 31).

```
Day(
    date)
```

DayOfWeek()

Returns an **integer** containing the ordinal for the day of the week in which *date* occurs (1 to 7).

```
DayOfWeek(
    date)
```

DayOfWeekAsString()

Returns a **string** containing the name of the day of the week represented by the ordinal *dayOfWeek*.

```
DayOfWeekAsString(
    dayOfWeek)
```

DayOfYear()

Returns an **integer** containing the ordinal for the day of the year in which *date* occurs (1 to 366).

```
DayOfYear(
    date)
```

DaysInMonth()

Returns an **integer** containing the number of days in the month in which *date* occurs (1 to 31).

DaysInMonth(
    date)

DaysInYear()

Returns an **integer** containing the number of days in the year in which *date* occurs (1 to 366).

DaysInYear(
    date)

FirstDayOfMonth()

Returns an **integer** containing the ordinal (in the year) of the first day of the month in which *date* occurs.

FirstDayOfMonth(
    date)

GetHttpTimeString()

Returns a **string** containing *datetime* converted to UTC and displayed in the HTTP standard format.

GetHttpTimeString(
    datetime)

GetTickCount()

Returns an **integer** containing the number of milliseconds the server computer has been running since its most recent boot.

GetTickCount()

GetTimeZoneInfo()

Returns a **structure** containing keys representing the offset of local time in seconds from UTC (`utcTotalOffset`), the offset in whole hours of local time from UTC (`utcHourOffset`), the offset in whole minutes beyond the offset in hours (`utcMinuteOffset`), and whether or not Daylight Savings Time is set on the server computer (`isDTCOn`).

GetTimeZoneInfo()

Hour()

Returns an **integer** containing the ordinal of the hour in which *datetime* occurs (0 to 23).

Hour(
    datetime)

IsDate()

Returns **Yes** if *string* can be converted to a date/time value; otherwise, **No**.

IsDate(
    string)

IsLeapYear()

Returns **Yes** if *year* is a leap year; otherwise, **No**.

IsLeapYear(
    year)

IsNumericDate()

Returns **Yes** if *number* is the numeric equivalent of a date/time object; otherwise, **No**.

IsNumericDate(
    number)

LSDateFormat()

Returns a **string** containing *date* formatted according to the locale-specific pattern specified in *mask*.

LSDateFormat(
    date,
    mask) See Allowed Mask Elements under DateFormat().

LSIsDate()

Returns **Yes** if *string* can be converted to a locale-specific date/time value; otherwise, **No**.

LSIsDate(
    string)

LSParseDateTime()

Returns a **date/time object** containing the converted value of *string* if supplied in a locale-specific format.

LSParseDateTime(
    string)

LSTimeFormat()

Returns a **string** containing *time* formatted according to the pattern of the locale-specific *mask*.

LSTimeFormat(
time,
mask) — See Allowed Mask Elements under TimeFormat().

Minute()

Returns an **integer** containing the ordinal minute within the hour in which *datetime* occurs (0 to 59).

Minute(
datetime)

Month()

Returns an **integer** containing the ordinal month within the year in which *datetime* occurs (1 to 12).

Month(
date)

MonthAsString()

Returns a **string** containing the name of the month represented by the ordinal *monthNumber*, from 1 to 12.

MonthAsString(
monthNumber)

Now()

Returns a **date/time object** containing the current date and time as set on the server.

Now()

ParseDateTime()

Returns a **date/time object** containing the converted value of *string* according to the specified *conversionType*.

ParseDateTime(
string,
conversionType) — "POP | STANDARD": if POP, will convert the date to a POP-standard UTC date.

Quarter()

Returns an **integer** containing the ordinal quarter in the year in which *datetime* occurs (1 to 4).

Quarter(
 datetime)

Second()

Returns an **integer** containing the ordinal second in the minute in which *datetime* occurs (0 to 59).

Second(
 datetime)

TimeFormat()

Returns a **string** containing *time* formatted according to the pattern in *mask*.

TimeFormat(
 time,
 mask) See Allowed Mask Options below.

Allowed Mask Options

- h: Hours on a 12-hour clock with no leading zero for single-digit hours.
- hh: Hours on a 12-hour clock with a leading zero for single-digit hours.
- H: Hours on a 24-hour clock with no leading zero for single-digit hours.
- HH: Hours on a 24-hour clock with a leading zero for single-digit hours.
- m: Minutes with no leading zero for single-digit minutes.
- mm: Minutes with a leading zero for single-digit minutes.
- s: Seconds with no leading zero for single-digit seconds.
- ss: Seconds with a leading zero for single-digit seconds.
- t: Single-character period marker, either A or P.
- tt: Double-character period marker, either AM or PM.
- short: Java standard short time format.
- medium: Java standard medium time format.
- long: Java standard long time format.
- full: Java standard full time format.
- Default mask is "hh:mm tt".

Week()

Returns an **integer** containing the ordinal week of the year in which *datetime* occurs (1 to 53).

Week(
 datetime)

Year()

Returns an **integer** containing the year in which *datetime* occurs.

Year(
    datetime)

Lists

Note that for all of the list functions except `GetToken()`, the default delimiter is a comma. The default delimiters for `GetToken()` are spaces, newlines, and tabs.

GetToken()

Returns a **string** containing the token found at position *index* of *string* if using one or more of the *delimiters* to separate tokens.

GetToken(
    string,
    index,
    delimiters)

Unlike the other List functions, GetToken() uses spaces, newlines, and tabs as its default set of delimiters.

ListAppend()

Returns a **list** containing *originalList* with *value* added to the end of it by using *delimiter* as the list delimiter.

ListAppend(
    originalList,
    value,
    delimiter)

ListChangeDelims()

Returns a **list** containing *originalList* with any of its *oldDelimiters* replaced by the *newDelimiter* character.

ListChangeDelims(
    originalList,
    newDelimiter,
    oldDelimiters)

ListContains()

Returns an **integer** containing the index of the first *list* element that contains *substring* with a case-sensitive match; otherwise, zero.

ListContains(
    list,
    substring,
    delimiters)

ListContainsNoCase()

Returns an **integer** containing the index of the first *list* element that contains *substring* with a case-insensitive match; otherwise zero.

ListContainsNoCase(
    list,
    substring,
    delimiters)

ListDeleteAt()

Returns a **list** containing *originalList* with the element at position *index* deleted.

ListDeleteAt(
    originalList,
    index,
    delimiters)

ListFind()

Returns an **integer** containing the index of the first *list* element equal to *value* with a case-sensitive match.

ListFind(
    list,
    value,
    delimiters)

ListFindNoCase()

Returns an **integer** containing the index of the first *list* element equal to *value* with a case-insensitive match.

ListFindNoCase(
    list,
    value,
    delimiters)

ListFirst()

Returns a **string** containing the first element of *list*.

ListFirst(
    list,
    delimiters)

ListGetAt()

Returns a **string** containing the element at position *index* in *list*.

ListGetAt(
 list,
 index,
 delimiters)

ListInsertAt()

Returns a **list** containing *originalList* with *value* inserted at position *index*.

ListInsertAt(
 originalList,
 index,
 value,
 delimiters)

ListLast()

Returns a **string** containing the last element in *list*.

ListLast(
 list,
 delimiters)

ListLen()

Returns an **integer** containing the number of elements in *list*.

ListLen(
 list,
 delimiters)

ListPrepend()

Returns a **list** containing *originalList* with *value* added to the beginning of it using *delimiter* as the list delimiter.

ListPrepend(
 originalList,
 value,
 delimiter)

ListQualify()

Returns a **list** containing *originalList* with its elements surrounded by *qualifier*. If *whichElements* is `ALL` then all elements are qualified. If *whichElements* is `CHAR` then only elements containing alphabetic characters are qualified.

```
ListQualify(
    originalList,
    qualifier,
    delimiters,
    whichElements)                "ALL | CHAR".
```

ListRest()

Returns a **list** containing *originalList* with its first element removed.

```
ListRest(
    originalList,
    delimiters)
```

ListSetAt()

Returns a **list** containing *originalList* with the element at position *index* set to *value*.

```
ListSetAt(
    originalList,
    index,
    value,
    delimiters)
```

ListSort()

Returns a **list** containing *originalList* sorted in *sortOrder*. If *sortType* is `TEXT`, the sort is case-sensitive. If *sortType* is `TEXTNOCASE`, the sort is case-insensitive. If *sortType* is `NUMERIC`, the sort is strictly numeric.

```
ListSort(
    originalList,
    sortType,                     "NUMERIC | TEXT | TEXTNOCASE".
    sortOrder,                    "ASC | DESC".
    delimiters)
```

ListToArray()

Returns an **array** containing the elements of *list*.

```
ListToArray(
    list,
    delimiters)
```

ListValueCount()

Returns an **integer** containing the number of times *value* occurs in *list* according to a case-sensitive match.

```
ListValueCount(
    list,
    value,
    delimiters)
```

ListValueCountNoCase()

Returns an **integer** containing the number of times *value* occurs in *list* according to a case-insensitive match.

```
ListValueCountNoCase(
    list,
    value,
    delimiters)
```

QuotedValueList()

Returns a **list** containing the values in column *columnName* of query *queryName* surrounded by single quotes.

```
QuotedValueList(
    queryName.columnName,
    delimiters)
```

ValueList()

Returns a **list** containing the values in column *columnName* of query *queryName*.

```
ValueList(
    QueryName.columnName,
    delimiters)
```

Arrays

ArrayAppend()

Returns **Yes** if adding *value* to the end of *array* is successful; otherwise, **No**.

```
ArrayAppend(
    array,
    value)
```

ArrayAvg()

Returns a **number** containing the average value of all elements in *array*.

```
ArrayAvg(
    array)
```

ArrayClear()

Returns **Yes** if successfully deletes all data from *array*; otherwise, **No**.

ArrayClear(
  array)

ArrayDeleteAt()

Returns **Yes** if successfully deletes the element at position *index* in *array*; otherwise, **No**.

ArrayDeleteAt(
  array,
  index)

ArrayInsertAt()

Returns **Yes** if successfully inserts the element at position *index* in *array*; otherwise, **No**.

ArrayInsertAt(
  array,
  index,
  value)

ArrayIsEmpty()

Returns **Yes** if *array* is empty; otherwise, **No**.

ArrayIsEmpty(
  array)

ArrayLen()

Returns an **integer** containing the number of elements in *array*.

ArrayLen(
  array)

ArrayMax()

Returns an **integer** containing the maximum numeric value in *array*, or zero if *array* is empty. Throws an error if one or more values in *array* are non-numeric.

ArrayMax(
  array)

ArrayMin()

Returns an **integer** containing the minimum numeric value in *array*, or zero if *array* is empty. Throws an error if one or more values in *array* are non-numeric.

```
ArrayMin(
    array)
```

ArrayNew()

Returns an **empty array** of dimension *dimensions*.

```
ArrayNew(
    dimensions)
```

ArrayPrepend()

Returns **Yes** if successfully adds *value* as a new element to the beginning of *array*; otherwise, **No.**

```
ArrayPrepend(
    array,
    value)
```

ArrayResize()

Returns **Yes** if successfully sets the minimum size of *array* to *minimumSize* elements; otherwise, **No.**

```
ArrayResize(
    array,
    minimumSize)
```

ArraySet()

Returns **Yes** if successfully sets the range of elements in *array* from position *startPosition* to position *endPosition* to *value*; otherwise, **No.**

```
ArraySet(
    array,
    startPosition,
    endPosition,
    value)
```

ArraySort()

Returns **Yes** if successfully sorts *array* in order *sortOrder*; otherwise, **No.** If *sortType* is `TEXT`, the sort is case-sensitive. If *sortType* is `TEXTNOCASE`, the sort is case-insensitive. If *sortType* is `NUMERIC`, the sort is strictly numeric.

ArraySort(
array,
sortType, "NUMERIC | TEXT | TEXTNOCASE".
sortOrder) "ASC | DESC".

ArraySum()

Returns an **integer** containing the sum of all elements in *array*, or zero if *array* is empty. Throws an error if all elements of *array* are not numeric.

ArraySum(
array)

ArraySwap()

Returns **Yes** if successfully swaps the values in *array* at positions *index1* and *index2*; otherwise, **No**.

ArraySwap(
array,
index1,
index2)

ArrayToList()

Returns a **list** containing the elements of *array* delimited by *delimiter*.

ArrayToList(
array,
delimiter)

IsArray()

Returns **Yes** if *value* is an array; otherwise, **No**. Also tests whether array is of dimension *dimension*, if supplied.

IsArray(
value,
dimension) Defaults to 1.

Structures

Duplicate()

Returns a **deep copy** of *variableName*. No referential connection exists between *variableName* and its duplicate returned from this function, so setting a value in the deep copy has no effect on the corresponding value in *variableName*.

Duplicate(
    variableName)

IsStruct()

Returns **Yes** if *value* is a structure; otherwise, **No**.

IsStruct(
    value)

StructAppend()

Returns **Yes** if successfully appends the keys from *structure2* to *structure1*; otherwise, **No**. If *overwrite* is `YES` or `TRUE`, keys in *structure2* overwrite similarly named keys in *structure1*.

StructAppend(
    structure1,
    structure2,
    overWrite) YES | NO

StructClear()

Returns **Yes** if successfully removes all data from *structure*.

StructClear(
    structure)

StructCopy()

Returns a **structure** containing a copy of *structure*. If you set the value of a key in a nested structure within the copy, the value in the corresponding key in the original structure is changed as well.

StructCopy(
    structure)

StructCount()

Returns an **integer** containing the number of keys in *structure*.

StructCount(
    structure)

StructDelete()

Returns a **structure** containing *structure* with key *keyName* deleted.

StructDelete(
    structure,
    keyName,
    indicateNotExisting) NO | YES

StructFind()

Returns the **value** of *key* in *structure*.

StructFind(
  structure,
  key)

StructFindKey()

Returns an **array** containing structures that in turn contain three keys: `owner`, which contains *keyName*'s enclosing structure; `path`, which contains the dot-path to *keyName* within its enclosing structure; and `value`, which contains *keyName*'s value. If scope is `ALL`, the array contains all matching keys. If scope is `ONE`, the array contains only the first matching key.

StructFindKey(	
top,	
keyName,	
scope)	ONE | ALL

StructFindValue()

Returns an **array** containing structures that in turn contain three keys: `owner`, which contains the found *value*'s enclosing structure; `path`, which contains the dot-path to the found *value* within its enclosing structure; and `key`, which contains the found value's key name. If scope is `ALL`, the array contains all matching values. If scope is `ONE`, the array contains only the first matching value.

StructFindValue(	
top,	
value,	
scope)	ONE | ALL

StructGet()

Returns an **alias** to the variable at *dotPath*.

StructGet(
  dotPath)

StructInsert()

Returns **Yes** if successfully inserts the *key-value* pair into *structure*; otherwise, **No**. If *overWrite* is `YES` or `TRUE` and *key* already exists, its *value* is overwritten. If *overwrite* is `NO` or `FALSE` and *key* already exists, an error is thrown.

StructInsert(
structure,
key,
value,
overWrite) NO | YES.

StructIsEmpty()

Returns **Yes** if *structure* is empty.

StructIsEmpty(
structure)

StructKeyArray()

Returns an **array** containing the names of keys in *structure*.

StructKeyArray(
structure)

StructKeyExists()

Returns **Yes** if key *keyName* exists in *structure*; otherwise, **No**.

StructKeyExists(
structure,
keyName)

StructKeyList()

Returns a **list** containing the names of keys in *structure* delimited by *delimiter*.

StructKeyList(
structure,
delimiter)

StructNew()

Returns an **empty structure**.

StructNew()

StructSort()

Returns an **array** containing the names of keys at the top level of *structure* sorted in *sortOrder* according to the values of the keys at *dotPath*. *sortType* can be `NUMERIC`, `TEXT`, or `TEXTNOCASE`.

StructSort(
structure,
sortType, "NUMERIC | TEXT | TEXTNOCASE".

```
    sortOrder,                    "ASC | DESC".
    dotPath)
```

StructUpdate()

Returns **Yes** if successfully updates key *keyName* in *structure* with *value*; otherwise, **No.**

```
StructUpdate(
    structure,
    keyName,
    value)
```

Query Objects

We thought referencing query objects in Chapter 52 a better course, as the functions that manipulate query objects are most often used in conjunction with the tags that create them.

ASCII

Asc()

Returns a **number** containing the ASCII value of the first character of *string*.

```
Asc(
    string)
```

Chr()

Returns a **string** containing the character represented by the ASCII value *number.*

```
Chr(
    number)
```

Basic Math

Abs()

Returns a **number** containing the absolute value of *number*.

```
Abs(
    number)
```

Max()

Returns a **number** containing the greater of *number1* and *number2*.

```
Max(
    number1,
    number2)
```

Min()

Returns a **number** containing the lesser of *number1* and *number2*.

```
Min(
    number1,
    number2)
```

Rand()

Returns a **number** containing a random decimal value between 0 and 1.

```
Rand()
```

Randomize()

Returns a **number** between 0 and 1 based on *seedNumber*. The sole purpose of this function is to seed the Random Number Generator immediately before calling the `Rand()` function.

```
Randomize(
    seedNumber)
```

RandRange()

Returns a **random integer** between the values of *minimumValue* and *maximumValue*.

```
RandRange(
    minimumValue,
    maximumValue)
```

Sgn()

Returns **1** if *number* is positive, **0** if *number* is zero, or **-1** if *number* is negative.

```
Sgn(
    number)
```

Sqr()

Returns a **number** containing the square root of *number*.

```
Sqr(
    number)
```

Binary Data

BitAnd()

Returns an **integer** containing the bitwise AND of *number1* and *number2*.

BitAnd(
    number1,
    number2)

BitMaskClear()

Returns an **integer** containing *number* cleared of *length* bits starting at position *start*.

BitMaskClear(
    number,
    start,
    length)

BitMaskRead()

Returns an **integer** containing *length* bits from *number* starting at position *start*.

BitMaskRead(
    number,
    start,
    length)

BitMaskSet()

Returns an **integer** containing *number* bitwise masked with *mask* for *length* bits starting at position *start*.

BitMaskSet(
    number,
    mask,
    start,
    length)

BitNot()

Returns an **integer** containing the bitwise NOT of *number*.

BitNot(
    number)

BitOr()

Returns an **integer** containing the bitwise OR of *number1* and *number2*.

BitOr(
number1,
number2)

BitSHLN()

Returns an **integer** containing the bits of *number* shifted left *count* positions, with any bits shifted out of range discarded rather than rotated to the tail end of the bitstream.

BitSHLN(
number,
count)

BitSHRN()

Returns an **integer** containing the bits of *number* shifted right *count* positions, with any bits shifted out of range discarded rather than rotated to the tail end of the bitstream.

BitSHRN(
number,
count)

BitXor()

Returns an **integer** containing the bitwise XOR (exclusive OR) of *number1* and *number2*.

BitXor(
number1,
number2)

IsBinary()

Returns **Yes** if *value* is in binary form; otherwise, **No**.

IsBinary(
value)

ToBase64()

Returns a **string** containing the Base64 representation of *value* according to the *encoding* used.

ToBase64(

value,	A string or binary object
encoding)	"US-ASCII | ISO-8859-1 | UTF-8 | UTF-16": defaults to the encoding set for the page in which the function is called.

ToBinary()

Returns a **binary** representation of *value.*

ToBinary(
value) Either a Base64-encoded string or a binary object. Passing a binary object validates it; passing a Base64 string converts it.

Geometry and Trigonometry

ACos()

Returns a **number** containing the arccosine of *number,* measured in radians.

ACos(
number)

ASin()

Returns a **number** containing the arcsine of *number,* measured in radians.

ASin(
number)

Atn()

Returns a **number** containing the arctangent of *number,* measured in radians.

Atn(
number)

Cos()

Returns a **number** containing the cosine of *angle* in radians.

Cos(
angle)

Exp()

Returns a **number** containing the constant e rasied to the power of *number*.

Exp(
number)

Log()

Returns a **number** containing the natural logarithm of *number*.

```
Log(
    number)
```

Log10()

Returns a **number** containing the logarithm of *number* raised to base 10.

```
Log10(
    number)
```

Pi()

Returns the constant **Pi** accurate to 14 decimal places.

```
Pi()
```

Sin()

Returns a **number** containing the sine of *angle* in radians.

```
Sin(
    angle)
```

Tan()

Returns a **number** containing the tangent of *angle* in radians.

```
Tan(
    angle)
```

✦ ✦ ✦

Flow Control

CFML

<CFABORT>

Immediately halts execution of the current template and returns everything processed up to the position of the `CFABORT` tag.

<CFABORT
showError = "#errorMessage#">

<CFBREAK>

Breaks out of a `CFLOOP`.

<CFBREAK>

<CFCASE>

Control passes to the CFML within the body of a `CFCASE` tag pair if its value matches the result of the expression in the enclosing `CFSWITCH` tag. Used only inside a `CFSWITCH` tag pair.

<CFCASE

value = "value">	Must be a constant value or a list of constant values. The list is comma-delimited if the ***delimiters*** attribute is not specified.
delimiters = ",;|"	The delimiters used to separate items in the ***value*** attribute. ***value*** is delimited by commas, semicolons, and pipe characters in this example.

. . .

</CFCASE>

Cross References

CFSWITCH	Defines the expression used to match CFCASE tags.
CFDEFAULTCASE	Control passes here if present and no matching CFCASE.

<CFDEFAULTCASE>

Control passes to the CFML within the body of a `CFDEFAULTCASE` tag pair if the result of the expression in the enclosing `CFSWITCH` tag matches no value in any `CFCASE` tag. Used only inside a `CFSWITCH` tag pair.

```
<CFDEFAULTCASE>
    ...
</CFDEFAULTCASE>
```

Cross References

`CFSWITCH`	Defines the expression used to match CFCASE tags.
`CFCASE`	Control passes here if value matches result of CFSWITCH expression.

<CFELSE>

Defines the boundary of CFML to execute if the *testExpression* of a `CFIF` tag evaluates to `FALSE`. Used only inside a `CFIF` tag pair.

```
<cfif
    testExpression>
    ...
    <CFELSE>
    <!--- CFML to execute if testExpression is FALSE --->
</cfif>
```

Cross References

`CFIF`	Defines the initial test expression to evaluate.
`CFELSEIF`	Defines additional test expressions.

<CFELSEIF>

Defines an additional conditional test to perform inside a `CFIF` tag body. Multiple `CFELSEIF` tests may be performed, but only the first *testExpression* that evaluates to `TRUE` is executed. Used only inside a `CFIF` tag pair.

```
<cfif
    testExpression>
    ...
    <CFELSEIF testExpression2>
    ...
    <cfelse>
    ...
</cfif>
```

Cross References

`CFIF`	Defines the initial test expression to evaluate.
`CFELSE`	Defines the boundary of CFML to execute if test expression is `FALSE`.

<CFIF>

Evaluates *testExpression* and, if the result of *testExpression* is `TRUE`, executes the CFML within the body of the `CFIF` tag pair. If a `CFELSE` tag is nested within the body of the `CFIF` tag and the result of *testExpression* is `FALSE`, only the CFML following the `CFELSE` tag executes. Additional conditions may be tested within the same construct by using the `CFELSEIF` tag.

```
<CFIF
    testExpression>
    ...
    <cfelseif testExpression2>
    ...
    <cfelse>
    ...
</CFIF>
```

Cross References

`CFELSE`	Defines the boundary of CFML to execute if the test expression is `FALSE`.
`CFELSEIF`	Defines additional test expressions.
`CFSWITCH`	A better way to control flow for multiple test expression results.

<CFLOCATION>

Stops template execution and performs a client-side redirect to another ColdFusion template or HTML web page.

```
<CFLOCATION
    url = "#urlOfTemplate#"
    addToken = "YES | NO">
```

<CFLOOP>

Executes the block of code contained between its opening and closing tags either a specified number of times, once for each element in an object, or while a condition is true.

A For loop executes a specified number of times:

```
<CFLOOP
    index = "iWillContainTheCurrentLoopCount"
    from = "#indexStartingValue#"
    to = "#indexEndingValue#"
    step = "1">
    ...
```

index starts with the value of ***from,*** gets incremented by the value of ***step*** on each iteration, and looping continues through the value of ***to.***

Step increment is 1 in this example. Negative value decrements ***index***.

```
</CFLOOP>
```

Application Notes

- *index* variable does not need to be defined prior to using it in CFLOOP.
- Use only integers for *from, to,* and *step.*
- Don't modify the values of either *from* or *to* from within the loop, as they are evaluated only once.

A Conditional loop executes while a condition is True:

```
<CFLOOP
    condition = "ThisValue GTE ThatValue">
    . . .
</CFLOOP>
```

Application Notes

- Condition uses same operators as `CFIF: EQ, NEQ, LT, LTE, GT, GTE`, and so on.
- Condition is evaluated each time that the loop iterates.

A Query loop executes for each record in a query object:

```
<CFLOOP
    query = "queryName"
    startRow = "#firstRowToLoopOver#"
    endRow = "#lastRowToLoopOver#">
    . . .
</CFLOOP>
```

A List loop executes for each element in a list:

```
<CFLOOP
    list = "#listName#"
    index = "iWillContainTheCurrentListItem"
    delimiters = ",;|">
    . . .
</CFLOOP>
```

index contains the value of the current ***list*** item each time that the loop iterates.

Commas, semicolons, and pipes are delimiters in this example.

A Collection loop executes for each element in a structure or COM object:

```
<CFLOOP
    collection = "#collectionName#"
    item = "iWillContainTheCurrentKeyName">
    . . .
</CFLOOP>
```

Cross References

`CFBREAK`	Breaks out of a loop.

<CFSWITCH>

Evaluates *expression* and passes control to the `CFCASE` tag whose *value* matches the result of *expression*. If no matching `CFCASE`, control passes to the `CFDEFAULTCASE` tag if one is present.

```
<CFSWITCH
    expression = "#expression#">
    <cfcase value = "value1">...</cfcase>
    <cfcase value = "value2">...</cfcase>
    <cfdefaultcase>...</cfdefaultcase>
</CFSWITCH>
```

Cross References

`CFCASE`	Control passes here if value matches result of `CFSWITCH` expression.
`CFDEFAULTCASE`	Control passes here if present and no matching `CFCASE`.

ColdFusion Scripting

break

Ends a `while`, `do-while`, or `for` loop, passing control to the next statement after the body of the loop. Also signifies the end of a `case` inside of a `switch` block.

```
break;
```

Cross References

`continue`	Begins the next iteration of a loop rather than ending the loop entirely
`for`	A kind of `CFSCRIPT` loop.
`switch`	Executes code based on the value of an expression
`while`	A kind of `CFSCRIPT` loop.

case

Signifies a case label inside of a switch statement. If *testValue* matches *expression*, `CFSCRIPT` will execute everything beginning with the statement after the case label until the next break statement. If the block is not terminated with break, execution will pass to the statements following the next case label.

```
switch(
    expression) {
    case testValue:
```

testValue must be a constant expression. ***testValue*** does not behave like CFCASE's ***value*** attribute in that it will not treat a comma-delimited list as a set of multiple values. See the second case label in this example for more information.

```
    ...
    break;
```
break ends the case block; execution will pass to the end of the body of the switch statement.

```
    case testValue2:
    case testValue3:
```
Because there are two case labels next to each other, CFSCRIPT will execute the block of code between this case label and the next break statement if ***expression*** matches either ***testValue2*** or ***testValue3***.

```
    ...
    break;
}
```

Cross References

`break`	Ends a `case` section and passes control to the end of the `switch` body.
`default`	Begins the `default` case section.
`switch`	Defines the initial expression used to choose which `case` label to run.

continue

Ends the current iteration of a `while`, `do-while`, or `for` loop and begins the next iteration. Evaluates the loop condition and passes control to the first statement inside the loop body.

```
continue;
```

Cross References

`break`	Ends a loop entirely.
`for`	A kind of `CFSCRIPT` loop.
`while`	A kind of `CFSCRIPT` loop.

default

Signifies the default case label inside of a switch statement. If case label matches the value of *expression*, `CFSCRIPT` executes everything beginning with the statement after the default label until the next break statement. If the statement is not terminated with break, execution will pass to the statements following the next case label.

```
switch(
    expression) {
    ... case labels ...
    default:
    ...
    break;
}
```

Cross References

`break`	Ends a `case` section and passes control to the end of the `switch` body.
`case`	Defines a `case` label within a `switch` statement.
`switch`	Defines the initial expression used to choose which `case` label to run.

else

Defines the body of code to execute if *testExpression* evaluates to `FALSE`. Valid only after the body of an `if` statement.

```
if(
    testExpression) {
    ...
    }
    else {
    ...
}
```

Cross References

`if`	Defines the initial test expression to evaluate.

for

Executes the block of code following the `for` statement (the *body* of the statement) either a specified number of times, or once for each item in a collection.

A for loop that executes a specified number of times

```
for(
    counter = start;
    counter <= end;
    counter = counter + 1) {
    ...
}
```

counter = start;	***start*** is usually one or zero. This initialization section of the for statement executes before the loop begins.
counter <= end;	The condition section of the for statement is a condition, much like ***testExpression*** in an if statement. The condition is tested before each iteration of the loop body; if the condition returns FALSE, the body of the loop isn't executed and execution passes to the first statement after the loop body. If the condition returns TRUE, the loop body is executed again.
counter = counter + 1) {	The increment section of the for statement executes after the body of the loop and before the condition is re-evaluated.

A for loop that executes once for every item in a collection

```
for(
    iWillContainTheCurrentKeyName
    in
    collectionName) {
    ...
}
```

Cross References

`break`	Ends a loop entirely.
`continue`	Begins the next iteration of a loop rather than ending the loop entirely.
`while`	A different kind of `CFSCRIPT` loop.

if

Evaluates *testExpression* and, if the result of *testExpression* is `TRUE`, executes the `CFSCRIPT` within the block after the `if` statement (the *body* of the `if` statement). If an `else` statement occurs after the body of the `if` statement and the result of *testExpression* is `FALSE`, only the body of the `else` statement executes. Additional conditions may be tested using the `else` and `if` keywords together.

```
if(
    testExpression) {
    ...
    }
    else if(testExpression2) {
    ...
    }
    else {
    ...
}
```

Cross References

`else`	Defines the block of code to be executed if test expression is `FALSE`.

switch

Evaluates *expression* and passes control to the `case` label that matches *expression*. If none of the `case` labels' values match, control passes to the `default` label.

```
switch(
    expression) {
    case testValue:
    ...
    break;
    case testValue2:
    case testValue3:
    ...
    break;
    default:
    ...
    break;
}
```

Cross References

`break`	Ends a `case` section and passes control to the end of the `switch` body.
`case`	Defines a `case` label within a `switch` statement.
`default`	Begins the `default` case section.

while

Executes the body of the loop while a given condition is `TRUE`. (See the attribute notes for information on how the loop body is defined.) Available in two forms: `while` and `do-while`. `While` loops test the loop condition *before* the body of the loop is executed; as such, if the loop condition is `FALSE` before the loop starts, the loop body will never execute. `Do-While` loops test the loop condition *after* the body of the loop is executed; as such, the loop body will always execute at least once.

A While Loop

```
while(
    condition) {
    ...
}
```

In a while loop, the loop body is the block of code after the ***while*** statement.

A Do-While Loop

```
do {
    ...
    }
    while(condition)
```

In a do-while loop, the loop body is the block of code between the ***do*** and ***while*** keywords.

Cross References

`break`	Ends a loop entirely.
`continue`	Begins the next iteration of a loop rather than ending the loop entirely.
`for`	A different kind of `CFSCRIPT` loop.

✦ ✦ ✦

Exception Handling

<CFCATCH>

Specifies a type of error to catch and handle as an exception. If a `CFCATCH` tag catches an error, it executes the CFML contained within its opening and closing tags rather than permitting the error to be thrown. Used within the `CFTRY` tag.

<CFCATCH	
type = "ANY	catches any and all exceptions of any type.
| DATABASE	catches errors thrown by the database.
| TEMPLATE	catches page errors from CFMODULE (but not CF_), CFERROR, and CFINCLUDE.
| SECURITY	catches security-related errors.
| OBJECT	catches errors thrown in CFOBJECT or CreateObject() calls.
| MISSINGINCLUDE	catches errors thrown from attempting to CFINCLUDE a missing template.
| EXPRESSION	catches errors thrown from faulty expressions, such as dividing by zero.
| LOCK	catches locking exceptions, such as the incapability to acquire a lock within the specified timeout period.
| SEARCHENGINE	catches Verity-related errors.
| APPLICATION	catches errors thrown at the application level, such as component faults.
| customType	catches specific custom errors defined by the developer.
| advancedType">	catches the advanced exception specified by this value.
...	
</CFCATCH>	

Cross References

`CFRETHROW`	"Re-throws" a caught exception as an error.
`CFTHROW`	Throws a custom exception.
`CFTRY`	Defines a block of code that may throw an error.

<CFERROR>

Installs a custom error template that handles errors not caught by a `CFTRY/CFCATCH` construct. If `Type="EXCEPTION"` the error template may contain CFML. Because `CFERROR` persists only as long as a single request, it is most often placed in either an `Application.cfm` template or a settings template that is included via `CFINCLUDE` by `Application.cfm`.

```
<CFERROR
    type = "REQUEST
     | VALIDATION
     | EXCEPTION"
    template = "/ErrorPage.cfm"
    mailto = "webmaster@mydomain.com"
    exception = "exceptionType">              Required if Type="EXCEPTION".
```

<CFRETHROW>

Rethrows a caught exception to the next higher level of exception handling, if any. Used to delegate a specific exception to an outside handler. Must be contained within a CFCATCH tag pair.

```
<CFRETHROW>
```

Cross References

CFCATCH	Catches an error thrown from a CFTRY block.
CFTHROW	Throws a custom exception.
CFTRY	Defines a block of code that may throw an error.

<CFTHROW>

Throws a custom exception designed by the developer so that it can be caught and handled by a specific CFCATCH tag pair.

```
<CFTHROW
    type = "APPLICATION
     | customType"
    message = "I am the short description"
    detail = "I am the lengthy detail"
    errorCode = "customCodeNumber"
    extendedInfo = "additionalErrorCode"
    object = "javaExceptionObject">
```

Cross References

CFCATCH	Catches an error thrown from a CFTRY block.
CFRETHROW	"Re-throws" a caught exception as an error.
CFTRY	Defines a block of code that may throw an error.

<CFTRY>

Creates the exception handling mechanism for testing specific blocks of CFML. Any error — regardless of which errors may or may not be caught by CFCATCH tags — thrown by a block of code wrapped in a pair of CFTRY tags halts the execution of that block and routes processing to the CFCATCH calls preceding the closing CFTRY tag.

```
<CFTRY>
    <cfthrow type="exceptionType" . . .>
    <cfcatch type="exceptionType">
      <cfrethrow>
    </cfcatch>
</CFTRY>
```

Cross References

`CFCATCH`	Catches an error thrown from a `CFTRY` block.
`CFRETHROW`	"Re-throws" a caught exception as an error.
`CFTHROW`	Throws a custom exception.

GetException()

Returns a **Java exception object** containing the exception object inside *javaObject*.

```
GetException(
    javaObject)
```

ColdFusion Scripting

catch

Catches an exception thrown from inside the body of a `try` statement. Must occur immediately after the body of the `try` statement.

```
try {
    . . .
    }
    catch(
    exceptionType                         corresponds to CFCATCH's Type attribute.
    nameOfExceptionInfoStructure) {       do not enclose the name in quotes; this is not a string but rather the name
                                          of an object that will contain the information about the exception.
    . . .
}
```

Cross References

`try`	Defines the block of code that may throw an exception.

try

Defines a block of code that may throw an error that can then be caught by a `catch` statement. The body of the `try` statement must be immediately followed by one or more `catch` statements.

```
try {
    ...
    }
    catch(
    exceptionType
    nameOfExceptionInfoStructure) {
    ...
}
```

If any of the code in the try body throws an error, the error will be immediately passed to the catch statements.

Cross References

`catch` Defines one or more blocks of code that can catch an error.

✦ ✦ ✦

Forms

<CFFORM>

Creates an intelligent HTML form containing a library of JavaScript validation functions and an `onSubmit` call that triggers client-side validation of the data entered into its form controls.

```
<CFFORM
    name = "iAmTheNameOfTheForm"
    action = "ActionPage.cfm"
    preserveData = "NO | YES"                    If YES and form submits to itself, submitted values populate controls.
    onSubmit = "return javascriptFunction();"    This function runs after validation functions.
    target = "windowName"
    encType = "application/x-www-form-urlencoded
      | multipart/form-data"                     Use this value for a form that uploads files.
    passThrough = "style=""font-weight:bold;"""  Notice how escaping works here.
    codeBase = "alternateJRElocation"
    archive = "alternateCFJavaClassesLocation"
    scriptSrc = "alternateJSFileLocation">
```

<CFGRID>

Places a Java-based grid control on a `CFFORM`. The grid control is populated with either a query or a combination of `CFGRIDCOLUMN` and `CFGRIDROW` tags.

```
<CFGRID
    name = "EmployeeGrid"        This name is used by the Java applet and ColdFusion to identify the data (if
                                 any) submitted from this grid control.
    height = "500"               Makes this grid 500 pixels tall.
    width = "300"                Makes this grid 300 pixels wide.
    autoWidth = "NO | YES"       NO = columns set to equal widths; YES = columns squeezed/expanded to fit
                                 grid width.
    vSpace = "10"                Puts 10 pixels of whitespace above and below this grid.
    hSpace = "10"                Puts 10 pixels of whitespace to the left and right of this grid.
```

align = "TOP | LEFT | BOTTOM | BASELINE | TEXTTOP | ABSBOTTOM | MIDDLE | ABSMIDDLE | RIGHT"	
query = "getEmployees"	Populates this grid control with the columns and rows of the getEmployees query object.
insert = "NO | YES"	YES = user can insert rows if ***selectMode*** = EDIT.
delete = "NO | YES"	YES = user can delete rows if ***selectMode*** = EDIT.
sort = "NO | YES"	YES = sort buttons display on grid.
font = "Arial"	Displays columns in the Arial font.
fontsize = "10"	Displays columns in 10-point size.
italic = "NO | YES"	
bold = "NO | YES"	
textColor = "Black"	
href = "EmpHomePage"	The EmpHomePage column of the getEmployees query object contains the URL to which each row is linked.
hrefkey = "AdditionalKeyValue"	The AdditionalKeyValue column of the getEmployees query object contains a key value that will be appended to the HREF value to form a complete URL.
appendKey = "YES | NO"	YES = appends CFGRIDKEY= and the value of the cell clicked by the user to the URL.
target = "windowName"	The HREF appears in the frame or window named the same as this attribute. If not specified, the HREF appears in the current window.
highlightHref = "YES | NO"	If YES, all cells that have an HREF will have their contents underlined as does a typical HTML link.
onValidate = "validateGrid();"	At the moment the form is submitted it will call this JavaScript function, which returns TRUE or FALSE.
onError = "gridError();"	If the ***onValidate*** function returns FALSE, the form is not submitted and this function is called.
gridDataAlign = "LEFT | RIGHT | CENTER"	Text alignment within grid cells.
gridLines = "YES | NO"	
rowHeight = "12"	Row height, in pixels.
rowHeaders = "YES | NO"	
rowHeaderAlign = "LEFT | RIGHT | CENTER"	
rowHeaderFont = "Arial"	
rowHeaderFontSize = "12"	
rowHeaderItalic = "NO |YES "	
rowHeaderBold = "NO | YES"	
rowHeaderTextColor = "Black"	
bgColor = "White"	
selectColor = "Yellow"	If a cell is selected, it is outlined in this color.
selectMode = "BROWSE	The user cannot select a cell.
| SINGLE	The user can select a single cell.
| ROW	The user can select an entire row.

```
    | COLUMN                                  The user can select an entire column.
    | EDIT"                                   The user can edit the grid's data; after the form is submitted, you can use
                                              CFGRIDUPDATE to update the database with any changes.
  maxRows = "100"                             Maximum number of rows displayed from query.
  notSupported = "messageIfNoJava"
  pictureBar = "NO | YES"                     If YES, grid uses images for the Insert, Delete, and Sort buttons.
  insertButton = "Insert"                     Text of the Insert button.
  deleteButton = "Delete"                     Text of the Delete button.
  sortAscendingButton = "A -> Z"              Text of the Sort Ascending button.
  sortDescendingButton = "Z -> A">            Text of the Sort Descending button.
  . . .
</CFGRID>
```

Cross References

CFGRIDCOLUMN	Describes a column in the grid.
CFGRIDROW	Describes a row of data in the grid.
CFGRIDUPDATE	Updates a database by using the data from an editable grid.

<CFGRIDCOLUMN>

Describes a column within a CFGRID control. Can be populated either with data from a database query or by using manual CFGRIDROW tags.

```
<CFGRIDCOLUMN
  name = "EmployeeName"                       Name of the grid column. If the grid has a query attribute, the column name
                                              must match one in the query.
  header = "Employee Name"                    Applies only if CFGRID's colHeaders attribute is YES.
  width = "100"
  font = "Arial"
  fontSize = "12"
  italic = "YES | NO"
  bold = "YES | NO"
  textColor = "Black"
  bgColor = "White"
  href = "EmpHomePage"                        Page to link to if the user selects a cell in this column. If this attribute
                                              matches a column in CFGRID's query, the column value is used; otherwise,
                                              the literal text is used.
  hrefKey = "AdditionalKeyValue"              Query column to use for CFGRIDKEY value if you don't want to use the cell
                                              contents.
  target = "windowName"
  select = "YES | NO"                         If YES, the user can select cells in this column. If NO, the user cannot select
                                              or edit cells in this column. Does not apply if CFGRID's SelectMode is ROW
                                              or BROWSE.
  display = "YES | NO"                        If NO, this column is hidden.
  type = "IMAGE                               The value of this column is the name of an image, which is put in the cell
                                              rather than the specified value.
    | NUMERIC                                 The user can sort grid data by number.
    | BOOLEAN                                 This column is displayed as a column of check boxes.
    | STRING_NOCASE"                          The user can sort grid data as text without regard to case.
```

headerFont = "Arial"
headerFontSize = "12"
headerItalic = "NO | YES"
headerBold = "NO | YES "
headerTextColor = "Black"
dataAlign = "LEFT | RIGHT | CENTER" — Sets the text alignment within cells.
headerAlign = "LEFT | RIGHT | CENTER"
numberFormat = "___,___.__" — The mask to use to format numeric values.
values = "listOfDropDownItemValues" — If CFGRID's ***SelectMode*** = EDIT, this attribute makes this column's cells act the same as drop-down lists. Values is a comma-delimited list of option values, and valuesDisplay is a comma-delimited list of option text.
valuesDisplay = "listOfDropDownItemText"
valuesDelimiter = "dropDownListDelimiter"> — If you'd rather not use a comma as the values delimiter, specify a different one here.

Cross References

`CFGRID` — Describes the grid containing this column.

<CFGRIDROW>

Describes a row of data in a `CFGRID` control.

<CFGRIDROW
data = "123-45-6789,Charles,Jones"> — A comma-delimited list of row data. Escape commas by doubling them.

Cross References

`CFGRID` — Describes the grid containing this row.

<CFGRIDUPDATE>

Updates a database with the contents of a `CFGRID` control with a *Select* attribute of `EDIT`. Given the grid name, performs all necessary create, update, and delete operations.

<CFGRIDUPDATE
grid = "EmployeeGrid" The name of the `CFGRID` performing this update. Notice that is uses no pound signs.
dataSource = "dataSourceName"
tableName = "Employee"
userName = "userName"
password = "password"
tableOwner = "ownerName" — If the owner of the table that you're updating is not the default user, specify the owner here.
tableQualifier = "databaseName" — If you are updating a table in a different database than the default, specify the database name here.
keyOnly = "NO | YES"> — If YES, the updates will match their target rows only by key rather than by all columns.

Application Notes

- The grid associated with this `CFGRIDUPDATE` must have its *SelectMode* set to `EDIT`.

Cross References

`CFGRID`	The grid from which this update gets its data.

<CFINPUT>

Creates an input control inside of a `CFFORM`. Can be used to create text input fields, radio buttons, check boxes, and password-input fields. All other types must use standard HTML `INPUT` tag.

```
<CFINPUT
    name = "Salary"                      Name of the form control.
    type = "TEXT                         Creates a text-input field.
      | RADIO                            Creates a radio button.
      | CHECKBOX                         Creates a check box.
      | PASSWORD"                        Creates a password-input field.
    value = "#InitialValue#"
    required = "YES | NO"
    range = "1,1000000"                  If the value that the user enters is not between 1 and 1000000 at the
                                         moment when the form is submitted, he will see a JavaScript alert.
    validate = "DATE
      | EURODATE
      | TIME
      | FLOAT
      | INTEGER
      | TELEPHONE
      | ZIPCODE
      | CREDITCARD
      | SOCIAL_SECURITY_NUMBER
      | REGULAR_EXPRESSION"
    pattern = "regularExpression"        If Validate is REGULAR_EXPRESSION, this pattern is used. it must be
                                         compatible with JavaScript's RegEx syntax and you must omit the leading
                                         and trailing slashes.
    onValidate = "javascriptFunction();"
    message = "messageToShowIfValidationFails"
    onError = "javascriptFunction();"
    size = "22"                          The size of the input field.
    maxLength = "20"                     The maximum number of characters allowed in the input field.
    checked = "NO | YES"                 Valid only for check boxes and radio buttons.
    passThrough = "style=""font-weight:bold;""">   This value will be placed inside the HTML INPUT tag created by this call
                                         to CFINPUT. Notice that we escape double quotes here by doubling
                                         them.
```

Cross References

CFFORM	The containing form for the input control.

<CFSELECT>

Creates a select menu within a CFFORM. Menu options can be created either from a database query or by manually coding OPTION tags inside the CFSELECT tag.

```
<CFSELECT
    name = "Department"  The name of the select menu.
    required = "NO | YES"  Applies only if size is 2 or greater.
    message = "Please select a department."
    onError = "javascriptFunction();"
    size = "1"                          If 1, represents a drop-down select menu. If greater, represents a list box.
    multiple = "NO | YES"               If YES, user can select multiple items at once.
    query = "GetDepartments"            CFSELECT generates an option for every row in this query.
    selected = "#CurrentDepartment#"    Currently selected item.
    value = "DepartmentID"              The name of the column in Query that represents option values. Note
                                        that this attribute is required if query is specified.
    display = "DepartmentName"          The name of the column in Query that represents option text. Note that
                                        this attribute is required if query is specified.
    passThrough = "style=""font-weight:bold;""">
    ...
</CFSELECT>
```

Cross References

CFFORM	The containing form for this select menu.

<CFSLIDER>

Creates a Java-based slider control on a CFFORM. After the form is submitted the action page receives a form variable that contains the position of the slider's thumb button.

```
<CFSLIDER
    name = "Salary"
    label = "Employee Salary: %value% per year"  The label shown on the slider control. %value% is replaced with the
                                                 current value of the slider's thumb button. If %value% is not put in the
                                                 label, the value is appended onto the end of the label.
    refreshLabel = "YES | NO"                    If NO, label does not receive current value of slider's thumb button.
    range = "0,1000000"                          Minimum and Maximum values of slider control. Represent far left and
                                                 right values of slider.
    scale = "1000"                               Thumb button stops only at intervals of this number.
    value = "#CurrentSalary#"
    onValidate = "javascriptFunction();"
    message = "messageToShowIfValidationFails"
    onError = "javascriptFunction();"
    height = "40"
```

```
     width = "300"
     vSpace = "10"                    vertical spacing around the top and bottom of the slider control, in pixels.
     hSpace = "10"                    horizontal spacing around the left and right of the slider control, in pixels.
     align = "TOP
       | LEFT
       | BOTTOM
       | BASELINE
       | TEXTTOP
       | ABSBOTTOM
       | MIDDLE
       | ABSMIDDLE
       | RIGHT"
     tickMarkMajor = "NO | YES"       Shows tick marks at each interval specified by scale.
     tickMarkMinor = "NO | YES"       Shows smaller tick marks in between the tick marks at major intervals.
     tickMarkImages = "listOfImageURLS"  You can show images at the slider's tick marks by specifying their names
                                      in a list.
     tickMarkLabels = "NO             Does not show tick mark values.
       | YES                          Shows values underneath each tick mark.
       | listOfLabelText"             A list of special values; lists element 1 under the first tick mark, element 2
                                      under the second, and so on.
     lookAndFeel = "MOTIF | WINDOWS | METAL"
     vertical = "NO | YES"
     bgColor = "White"
     textColor = "Black"
     font = "Arial"
     fontSize = "10"
     italic = "NO | YES"
     bold = "NO | YES"
     notSupported = "messageIfNoJava">  Show this message in HTML if the user's browser does not support Java.
```

Cross References

`CFFORM`	The containing form for this slider control.

<CFTEXTINPUT>

Creates a Java-based text input control on a `CFFORM`.

```
<CFTEXTINPUT
     name = "EmployeeName"            The name of the input field.
     value = "#CurrentName#"
     required = "NO | YES"
     range = "1,100000"
     validate = "DATE
       | EURODATE
       | TIME
       | FLOAT
       | INTEGER
       | TELEPHONE
       | ZIPCODE
```

| CREDITCARD
| SOCIAL_SECURITY_NUMBER
| REGULAR_EXPRESSION"

Attribute	Description
pattern = "regularExpression"	If Validate is REGULAR_EXPRESSION, this pattern is used. It must be compatible with JavaScript's RegEx syntax, and you must omit the leading and trailing slashes.
onValidate = "javascriptFunction();"	
message = "messageToShowIfValidationFails"	
onError = "javascriptFunction();"	
size = "40"	Number of characters the user can enter before displaying a horizontal scrollbar.
font = "Arial"	
fontSize = "10"	
italic = "NO | YES"	
bold = "NO | YES"	
height = "20"	
width = "300"	
vSpace = "10"	
hSpace = "10"	
align = "TOP | LEFT | BOTTOM | BASELINE | TEXTTOP | ABSBOTTOM | MIDDLE | ABSMIDDLE | RIGHT"	
bgColor = "White"	
textColor = "Black"	
maxLength = "40"	Maximum number of characters the user can enter in this field.
notSupported = "messageIfNoJava">	Show this message in HTML if the user's browser does not support Java.

Cross References

CFFORM	The container for this text-input control.

<CFTREE>

Creates a Java-based tree control on a CFFORM. Data is added to the tree by using the CFTREEITEM tag.

<CFTREE

Attribute	Description
name = "LocationTree"	Name of the tree control.
required = "YES | NO"	If YES, the user must select an item in the tree control before submitting the form.
delimiter = "\"	Delimiter for path components. After form is submitted, Form.LocationTree.path contains all the nodes leading up to the one selected by the user, separated by this delimiter.

```
completePath = "NO | YES"                    If YES, includes the root element in Form.LocationTree.path; if NO, does
                                             not include the root element.
appendKey = "YES | NO"
highlightHref = "YES | NO"
onValidate = "javascriptFunction();"
message = "messageToShowIfValidationFails"
onError = "javascriptFunction();"
lookAndFeel = "MOTIF | WINDOWS | METAL"
font = "Arial"
fontSize = "10"
italic = "NO | YES"
bold = "NO | YES"
height = "350"
width = "300"
vSpace = "10"
hSpace = "10"
align = "TOP
  | LEFT
  | BOTTOM
  | BASELINE
  | TEXTTOP
  | ABSBOTTOM
  | MIDDLE
  | ABSMIDDLE
  | RIGHT"
border = "YES | NO"
hScroll = "YES | NO"
vscroll = "YES | NO"
notSupported = "messageIfNoJava">
```

Cross References

CFFORM	The container for this tree control.
CFTREEITEM	Describes the items inside the tree control.

<CFTREEITEM>

Describes data inside a CFTREE control. Can be acquired from a query object or manually specified. Query objects should usually be pre-sorted with CF_MAKE_TREE or CFX_MAKE_TREE, both of which are available from the Macromedia Developer's Exchange on Macromedia.com.

```
<CFTREEITEM
    value = "#ItemValue#"                    The value of this item. Can be either a literal value, as here, or a column
                                             name if using the query attribute.
    display = "#ItemText#"                   The text of this item. Can be a literal value or a query column.
    parent = "#ParentItemvalue#"             The value of this item's parent. Omit this attribute if this item has no
                                             parent.
    img = "nameOfItemImage"
    imgOpen = "nameOfItemImageWhenSelected"
```

href = "EmpLocationURL"	The URL to send the user to after he chooses this tree item.
target = "windowName"	
query = "GetLocations"	A query used to generate items at the current level.
queryAsRoot = "NO	
| YES	Makes the ***query*** name the root item of the tree.
| nameOfRootItem"	Names the root item something specific.
expand = "YES | NO">	If NO, the tree item cannot be expanded.

Cross References

CFTREE	**The tree control containing this tree item.**

✦ ✦ ✦

Databases and Queries

<CFCOL>

Describes a column within a CFTABLE.

```
<CFCOL
    text = "#ColumnText#"
    header = "Column Header Text"
    width = "20"
    align = "left">
```

text = "#ColumnText#"	Usually a column from the query used for CFTABLE.
header = "Column Header Text"	The ***header*** attribute is not required; this is in conflict with the documentation.
width = "20"	If CFTABLE uses the ***htmlTable*** attribute, this width is the percentage of the full table width this column takes up. If CFTABLE does not use ***htmlTable***, this is the maximum number of characters shown for any value in this column.
align = "left">	

Cross References

CFTABLE	The table containing this column.

<CFINSERT>

Inserts a record into a database by using data from the form scope without using SQL.

```
<CFINSERT
    dataSource = "#MainDSN#"
    tableName = "tableToUpdate"
    tableOwner = "dbo"
    tableQualifier = "databaseName"
    userName = "#Username#"
    password = "#Password#"
    formFields = "listOfFormFields">
```

dataSource = "#MainDSN#"	
tableName = "tableToUpdate"	
tableOwner = "dbo"	
tableQualifier = "databaseName"	
userName = "#Username#"	
password = "#Password#"	
formFields = "listOfFormFields">	Does not include key fields. Key fields must be present in the Form scope, however. If this attribute is not included, ColdFusion uses all fields in the Form scope.

Cross References

CFUPDATE	Updates data in the same manner as CFINSERT.
CFQUERY	Runs an actual SQL query against the database.

<CFOBJECTCACHE>

Clears the query cache, which destroys all currently cached queries on the server. Use this tag to cause all queries to refresh from the database the next time they are executed.

```
<CFOBJECTCACHE
    action = "clear">
```

<CFOUTPUT>

Outputs data, either simple expressions or the results of a complex query object.

<CFOUTPUT	
query = "queryName"	The name of a query to output. If this attribute is specified, the body of the CFOUTPUT tag will run once for each record in the ***query*** object.
group = "groupColumn"	Column name by which to group output.
groupCaseSensitive = "YES | NO"	
startRow = "1"	
maxRows = "100">	
...	
</CFOUTPUT>	

Cross References

CFLOOP	Loops over a query but doesn't necessarily output data.
CFQUERY	Performs a query against a database.
WriteOutput()	Outputs page content from within a CFSCRIPT block.

<CFPROCPARAM>

Describes a stored procedure parameter. Must be inside a CFSTOREDPROC tag.

Input Parameter:

<CFPROCPARAM	
type = "IN"	
value = "#ParameterValue#"	The value to pass into the database.
dbVarName = "dbSpecifiedVarName"	Database-specified parameter name. Though ignored by ColdFusion MX, it is still useful for documenting the tag's purpose.
CFSQLTYPE = "CF_SQL_BIGINT	
| CF_SQL_BIT	
| CF_SQL_BLOB	
| CF_SQL_CHAR	
| CF_SQL_CLOB	
| CF_SQL_DATE	
| CF_SQL_DECIMAL	
| CF_SQL_DOUBLE	
| CF_SQL_FLOAT	
| CF_SQL_IDSTAMP	

| CF_SQL_INTEGER	
| CF_SQL_LONGVARCHAR	
| CF_SQL_MONEY	
| CF_SQL_MONEY4	
| CF_SQL_NUMERIC	
| CF_SQL_REAL	
| CF_SQL_REFCURSOR	
| CF_SQL_SMALLINT	
| CF_SQL_TIME	
| CF_SQL_TIMESTAMP	
| CF_SQL_TINYINT	
| CF_SQL_VARCHAR"	
MaxLength = "20"	Maximum number of characters in the input value.
Scale = "2"	Maximum number of decimal places (numeric types only).
Null = "NO | YES">	If YES, NULL is passed as this parameter's value; value attribute is ignored.

InOut Parameter:

<CFPROCPARAM	
type = "INOUT"	
value = "#InputValue#"	The value to pass to the database.
dbVarName = "dbSpecifiedVarName"	Database-specified parameter name. Though ignored by ColdFusion MX, it is still useful for documenting the tag's purpose.
variable = "VariableToContainOutputValue"	This ***variable*** contains the value returned from the database for this parameter.
CFSQLTYPE = "CF_SQL_BIGINT	
| CF_SQL_BIT	
| CF_SQL_BLOB	
| CF_SQL_CHAR	
| CF_SQL_CLOB	
| CF_SQL_DATE	
| CF_SQL_DECIMAL	
| CF_SQL_DOUBLE	
| CF_SQL_FLOAT	
| CF_SQL_IDSTAMP	
| CF_SQL_INTEGER	
| CF_SQL_LONGVARCHAR	
| CF_SQL_MONEY	
| CF_SQL_MONEY4	
| CF_SQL_NUMERIC	
| CF_SQL_REAL	
| CF_SQL_REFCURSOR	
| CF_SQL_SMALLINT	
| CF_SQL_TIME	
| CF_SQL_TIMESTAMP	
| CF_SQL_TINYINT	
| CF_SQL_VARCHAR"	
MaxLength = "20"	Maximum number of characters in the input value.
Scale = "2"	Maximum number of decimal places (numeric types only).
Null = "NO | YES">	If YES, NULL is passed as this parameter's value; ***value*** attribute is ignored.

Output Parameter:

```
<CFPROCPARAM
    type = "OUT"
    variable = "VariableToContainOutputValue"   This variable will contain the value returned from the database for this parameter.
    dbVarName = "dbSpecifiedVarName"            Database-specified parameter name. Though ignored by ColdFusion MX, it is still useful for documenting the tag's purpose.
    CFSQLTYPE = "CF_SQL_BIGINT
     | CF_SQL_BIT
     | CF_SQL_BLOB
     | CF_SQL_CHAR
     | CF_SQL_CLOB
     | CF_SQL_DATE
     | CF_SQL_DECIMAL
     | CF_SQL_DOUBLE
     | CF_SQL_FLOAT
     | CF_SQL_IDSTAMP
     | CF_SQL_INTEGER
     | CF_SQL_LONGVARCHAR
     | CF_SQL_MONEY
     | CF_SQL_MONEY4
     | CF_SQL_NUMERIC
     | CF_SQL_REAL
     | CF_SQL_REFCURSOR
     | CF_SQL_SMALLINT
     | CF_SQL_TIME
     | CF_SQL_TIMESTAMP
     | CF_SQL_TINYINT
     | CF_SQL_VARCHAR"
    MaxLength = "20"                            Maximum number of characters in the input value.
    Scale = "2"                                 Maximum number of decimal places (numeric types only).
    Null = "NO | YES">                          If YES, NULL is passed as this parameter's value; value attribute is ignored.
```

Cross References

CFSTOREDPROC	Executes a stored procedure against a database.

<CFPROCRESULT>

Describes a result set from a stored procedure. Must exist within a `CFSTOREDPROC` tag (though not all `CFSTOREDPROC` tags will contain a `CFPROCRESULT`).

```
<CFPROCRESULT
    name = "NameOfQueryObjectToBeCreated"   A query object of this name will be created.
    resultSet = "1"                         First resultset in the procedure is 1, second is 2, and so on.
    maxRows = "100">
```

Cross References

CFSTOREDPROC	The procedure to which this tag passes parameters.

<CFQUERY>

Executes a SQL query against a database or a query of queries against another query object.

Executing a query against a database:

```
<CFQUERY
    name = "queryObjectName"                      Name of the query object that will be created.
    dataSource = "#MainDSN#"
    userName = "#Username#"
    password = "#Password#"
    maxRows = "100"                               The maximum number of rows to retrieve from the database.
    blockFactor = "1"                             Number of rows to retrieve from the database with each internal fetch
                                                  made by the database driver. Can be from 1 to 100.
    timeOut = "30"
    cachedAfter = "April 16, 1999"                If this query was last run after April 16, 1999, cached data is used.
                                                  Otherwise, the query is re-run.
    cachedWithin = "#CreateTimeSpan(1,0,0,0)#">   If this query's cached data is older than one day, it is re-run; otherwise,
                                                  the cached data is used.
    ...
</CFQUERY>
```

Executing a query of queries:

```
<CFQUERY
    name = "queryObjectName"
    dbType = "query"
    >
    ...
</CFQUERY>
```

Cross References

CFINSERT	Inserts data into a database without using SQL.
CFLOOP	Loops over a query without necessarily producing output.
CFOUTPUT	Outputs data from a query.
CFQUERYPARAM	Defines a parameter for this query.
CFSTOREDPROC	Executes a stored procedure against a database.
CFUPDATE	Updates data in a database without using SQL.

<CFQUERYPARAM>

Defines a database bind parameter for a CFQUERY statement. Note that the CFQUERYPARAM tag can only be nested within a CFQUERY tag. CFQUERYPARAM cannot be used with cached queries.

```
<CFQUERYPARAM
    value = "#valueToPass#"
    CFSQLTYPE = "CF_SQL_BIGINT
     | CF_SQL_BIT
     | CF_SQL_BLOB
     | CF_SQL_CHAR
     | CF_SQL_CLOB
     | CF_SQL_DATE
     | CF_SQL_DECIMAL
     | CF_SQL_DOUBLE
     | CF_SQL_FLOAT
     | CF_SQL_IDSTAMP
     | CF_SQL_INTEGER
     | CF_SQL_LONGVARCHAR
     | CF_SQL_MONEY
     | CF_SQL_MONEY4
     | CF_SQL_NUMERIC
     | CF_SQL_REAL
     | CF_SQL_REFCURSOR
     | CF_SQL_SMALLINT
     | CF_SQL_TIME
     | CF_SQL_TIMESTAMP
     | CF_SQL_TINYINT
     | CF_SQL_VARCHAR"
    MaxLength = "20"                    Maximum number of characters in the input value.
    Scale = "2"                         Maximum number of decimal places (numeric types only). Default is zero.
    Null = "NO | YES"                   If YES, NULL is passed as this parameter's value; value attribute is ignored.
    List = "NO | YES"                   If YES, the value attribute represents a delimited list.
    Separator = "listDelimiter">        The delimiter for individual items within the value attribute.
```

<CFSTOREDPROC>

Executes a stored procedure against a database.

```
<CFSTOREDPROC
    procedure = "procedureName"
    dataSource = "#MainDSN#"
    userName = "#Username#"
    password = "#Password#"
    blockFactor = "1"                   Number of rows to retrieve from the database at a given time. Can be from
                                        1 to 100.
    debug = "NO | YES"                  If YES, lists debug information at end of request.
    returnCode = "NO | YES">            If YES, and the procedure returns an integer, the returned value is available in
                                        CFSTOREDPROC.StatusCode.
```

Cross References

`CFPROCPARAM`	Defines parameters for this procedure call.
`CFPROCRESULT`	Defines result sets from this procedure call.

<CFTABLE>

Generates an HTML or text-based table based on a query.

<CFTABLE	
query = "queryName"	The name of the ***query*** with the data that generates this table.
maxRows = "100"	
colSpacing = "2"	Number of spaces between columns.
headerLines = "2"	Number of lines to use for header.
StartRow = "1"	
HTMLTable = "YES"	If this attribute is included, regardless of its value, this tag generates an HTML table. If it is omitted, CFTABLE generates a text-based table.
Border = "YES"	Include this attribute only for HTML tables. It's value is ignored; if you include this attribute CFTABLE puts a border around the table.
ColHeaders = "YES">	If you include this attribute, CFTABLE will include a header row. To use this attribute you must also use the CFCOL ***header*** attribute.

Cross References

CFCOL	Defines a column for this table.
CFOUTPUT	Outputs data from a query; lets you granularly define your table's format.

<CFTRANSACTION>

Wraps one or more database operations in a "transactional envelope," meaning that if one query in the body of the `CFTRANSACTION` tag fails, all queries are rolled back as if they had never occurred in the first place.

<CFTRANSACTION	
action = "BEGIN	Begins a transactional block. The end of the block is the ending </CFTRANSACTION> tag.
| COMMIT	Commits an open transaction. This is nested inside of a CFTRANSACTION with Action = Begin.
| ROLLBACK"	Rolls back an open transaction. This is nested inside of a CFTRANSACTION with Action = Begin.
isolation = "READ_UNCOMMITTED	ODBC Lock Isolation Level. Read Chapter 10 for more information.
| READ_COMMITTED	
| REPEATABLE_READ	
| SERIALIZABLE">	

<CFUPDATE>

Updates a record in a database by using data from the Form scope without using SQL.

<CFINSERT
  dataSource = "#MainDSN#"
  tableName = "tableToUpdate"
  tableOwner = "dbo"
  tableQualifier = "databaseName"

userName = "#Username#"
password = "#Password#"
formFields = "listOfFormFields"> — Does not include key fields. Key fields must be present in the Form scope, however. If this attribute is not included, ColdFusion uses all fields in the Form scope.

Cross References

CFINSERT	Inserts data into a database in the same manner as CFUPDATE.
CFQUERY	Runs an actual SQL query against the database.

IsQuery()

Returns **TRUE** if *value* represents a query object, **FALSE** otherwise.

IsQuery(
Value)

PreserveSingleQuotes()

Returns ***variable*** without escaping single quotes. Used only in CFQUERY operations; CFQUERY automatically escapes single quotes unless you use this function.

PreserveSingleQuotes(
Variable)

QueryAddColumn()

Returns **a number** representing the new number of columns in the query. Adds a column to a query object.

QueryAddColumn(

query,	The query object to which the column will be added.
columnName,	The name of the column to add.
array)	The array containing the values that will populate the query column.

QueryAddRow()

Returns **the number** of rows in the query after adding new rows.

QueryAddRow(

query,	The query object to which the row will be added.
numberOfRows)	The number of rows to add to ***query***.

QueryNew()

Returns a newly created **query object**.

QueryNew(

columnList)	The list of columns to be created in the new query.

QuerySetCell()

Sets the value of a specific cell in a *query* object.

QuerySetCell(

query,	The query object to modify.
columnName,	The name of the column containing the cell to be modified.
value,	The value to set in the cell at the intersection of ***columnName*** and ***rowNumber***.
rowNumber)	The row number containing the cell to modify – defaults to the last row in the query.

CHAPTER 53

Custom Tags

<CFASSOCIATE>

Associates a child tag with its parent by creating an entry in the parent tag's ThisTag scope. See Chapter 18 for more details.

<CFASSOCIATE	
baseTag = "CF_MYTAGNAME"	The name of the tag with which you want to associate this child. Even if calling by CFMODULE, use CF_ notation.
dataCollection = "AssocAttribs">	The name of the array in which this tag's attributes are stored. Each call to CFASSOCIATE creates an element in this array; the element's value is a structure containing all of the current custom tag's attributes. If ***dataCollection*** is not specified, it defaults to AssocAttribs.

Application Notes

- Macromedia's CFML Language Reference erroneously refers to *dataCollection* as a structure. It is not a structure; it is an array *containing* structures.

Cross References

`GetBaseTagData()`	Gets tag data from the parent tag.

<CFEXIT>

Controls process flow within custom tags.

<CFEXIT	
method = "exittag	Aborts processing of the currently executing custom tag
| exittemplate	Exits the template containing the currently executing custom tag.
| loop">	Re-executes the body of the currently executing custom tag.

<CFMODULE>

Calls a custom tag. A more efficient alternative to using the `CF_` tag call syntax.

Calling a tag by its template:

<CFMODULE	
template = "relative/path/to/tag.cfm | /mapping/to/tag.cfm"	
attributeCollection = "#structure#"	All the keys inside ***structure*** become variables in the custom tag's Attributes scope.
...>	Any extra attributes are passed to the custom tag in the Attributes scope.

Calling a tag by its name:

<CFMODULE

name = "myTags.tag"	Calls C:\CFusionMX\CustomTags\myTags\Tag.cfm
attributeCollection = "#structure#"	All the keys inside structure will become variables in the custom tag's Attributes scope.
...>	Any extra attributes are passed to the custom tag in the Attributes scope.

Cross References

CFIMPORT	Imports a custom tag library; alternative to CFMODULE.
CFINVOKE	Invokes a custom function.

GetBaseTagData()

Returns a **structure** containing a parent tag's variables, including its Attributes scope.

GetBaseTagData(

tagName,	The name of the tag with which you want to associate this child. Even if calling by CFMODULE, use CF_ notation.
instanceNumber)	If multiple occurrences of ***tagName*** are in this tag's parent hierarchy, you can use ***instanceNumber*** to tell GetBaseTagData() how many levels to skip before getting tag data. By default, this argument is 1, meaning that it retrieves the closest ancestor.

Cross References

CFASSOCIATE	Associates a child tag with its parent tag.

GetBaseTagList()

Returns a **comma-delimited list** of this tag's ancestors.

GetBaseTagList()

✦ ✦ ✦

ColdFusion Scripting

<CFSCRIPT>

Defines a block of CFSCRIPT code.

```
<CFSCRIPT>
    . . .
</CFSCRIPT>
```

IsCustomFunction()

Returns **Yes** if *functionName* represents a user-defined function or one created by using CFFUNCTION; returns **No** otherwise.

```
IsCustomFunction(
    "functionName")
```

WriteOutput()

Returns **Yes**. Writes *string* to the page. Used within CFSCRIPT to write content to the page without needing to interrupt the CFSCRIPT block. Essentially, WriteOutput() is the equivalent of CFOUTPUT within a CFSCRIPT block.

```
WriteOutput(
    string)
```

Cross References

CFOUTPUT	CFML-based alternative to WriteOutput()

✦ ✦ ✦

Working with Systems Outside ColdFusion

XML

<CFXML>

Creates an XML document object, given well-formed XML. ColdFusion processes the tag content and creates an XML object out of it. The tag content cannot contain the `<?xml ?>` header.

<CFXML
  variable = "nameOfXMLObjectToCreate"
  caseSensitive = "NO | YES"> — If YES, CFXML treats tags with different case names as different types of elements. Defaults to NO.
  ...
</CFXML>

IsXmlDoc()

Returns **TRUE** if *object* is an XML document object; **FALSE** otherwise.

IsXmlDoc(
  object)

IsXMLElem()

Returns **TRUE** if *object* is an XML document element; **FALSE** otherwise.

IsXMLElem(
  object)

IsXMLRoot()

Returns **TRUE** if *object* is the root of an XML document object; **FALSE** otherwise.

IsXMLRoot(
object)

XmlChildPos()

Returns an **integer** containing the position of the *index*ed element named the same as *childName* in *xmlelement*'s `XMLChildren` array.

XmlChildPos(	
xmlelement,	An XML document object element.
childName,	The name of a child of ***xmlelement***.
index)	The ***index***th occurrence of ***childname*** inside ***xmlelement***.

XmlElemNew()

Returns a new **element** created inside of *xmlObject*. After creating the element, it must be assigned to a specific position in the document object.

XmlElemNew(	
xmlObject,	The XML document object.
childName)	The name of the new child.

Application Notes

- `XmlElemNew()` creates a new element in a document object, but the element does not have a home yet. You must explicitly specify where the new element is in the hierarchy before it is truly part of the document object.

XmlFormat()

Returns a **string** escaped so that it may be used inside an XML element. Replaces any special characters with their XML-safe equivalents.

XmlFormat(
string)

XmlNew()

Returns a new **XML document object**.

XmlNew(	
caseSensitive)	"NO | YES": If YES, CFXML treats tags with different case names as different types of elements. Defaults to NO.

XmlParse()

Returns an **XML document object** created by parsing the XML inside *xmlString*.

XmlParse(
 xmlString, The XML string to parse.
 caseSensitive) "NO | YES": If YES, CFXML treats tags with different case names as different types of elements. Defaults to NO.

XmlSearch()

Returns an **array** containing all the elements inside *xmlObject* that match *xPathString*.

XmlSearch(
 xmlObject, The XML document object to search.
 xPathString) An XPath expression to apply to the document object.

XmlTransform()

Returns a **string** containing the XML resulting from applying the XSLT inside *xslString* to either *xmlString* or *xmlObject*.

An XML String:

XmlTransform(
 xmlString, The XML source document to transform.
 xslString) The XSL stylesheet to apply to the source.

An object representing an XML document:

XmlTransform(
 xmlObject, The XML document object to transform.
 xslString) The XSL stylesheet to apply to the source.

WDDX

<CFWDDX>

Converts ColdFusion and JavaScript objects to and from WDDX (Web Development Data exchange, a data-centric flavor of XML).

To serialize a ColdFusion variable into WDDX:

<CFWDDX
 action = "CFML2WDDX"
 input = "#coldFusionObject#"
 output = "nameOfVariableToContainWDDX" This variable contains the WDDX that describes the variable passed in ***input***. If you omit this attribute, CFWDDX outputs the serialized WDDX to the HTML stream.
 useTimeZoneInfo = "YES | NO"> If YES, ColdFusion includes time-zone information in any date-time values inside the packet.

To deserialize WDDX into a ColdFusion variable:

```
<CFWDDX
    action = "WDDX2CFML"
    input = "#wddxPacket#"
    output = "nameOfColdFusionVariableToCreate"
    validate = "YES | NO">
```

validate: If YES, ColdFusion validates the WDDX packet before deserializing and throws an error if the packet is invalid.

To convert a ColdFusion variable to a JavaScript object:

```
<CFWDDX
    action = "CFML2JS"
    input = "#coldFusionObject#"
    topLevelVariable = "nameOfJSVariable"
    output = "nameOfVariableToContainJavaScript">
```

topLevelVariable: This is the name of the JavaScript variable that this tag creates.

output: This variable contains JavaScript code that creates the WDDX object. If you omit this attribute, the JavaScript is just output to the HTML stream.

To deserialize WDDX into a JavaScript object:

```
<CFWDDX
    action = "WDDX2JS"
    input = "#wddxPacket#"
    topLevelVariable = "nameOfJSVariable"
    output = "nameOfVariableToContainJavaScript"
    validate = "YES | NO">
```

topLevelVariable: The name of the JavaScript variable that this tag creates.

output: This variable contains JavaScript code that creates the WDDX object. If you omit this attribute, the JavaScript is just output to the HTML stream.

validate: If YES, ColdFusion validates the WDDX packet before deserializing and throws an error if the packet is invalid.

IsWDDX()

Returns **TRUE** if *value* represents a valid WDDX packet, and **FALSE** otherwise.

```
IsWDDX(
    value)
```

Web Servers

<CFHTTP>

Requests a page from a remote server by using HTTP. Can also create a query object from a delimited text file on a remote machine.

In getting data from a remote server:

Syntax	Notes
<CFHTTP	
url = "URLOfPageToCall"	
method = "GET"	Any request parameters must be passed as part of the URL.
port = "80"	
userName = "userNameForBasicAuthorization"	
password = "passwordForBasicAuthorization"	
path = "PathToDirectoryToStoreResults"	You can save the results of the request by specifying ***path*** and ***file***. If these attributes aren't given, the output is available in CFHTTP.FileContent.
file = "NameOfFileToStoreResults"	
resolveURL = "YES | NO"	Modifies any URLs in the returned page content such that they include the full server and port so that all links remain functional.
proxyServer = "NameOrIPOfProxyServer"	
proxyPort = "portNumber"	
userAgent = "customRequestUserAgent"	To put a custom value in the HTTP user agent for the request, specify this attribute.
throwOnError = "YES | NO"	If YES, any HTTP error causes CFHTTP to throw a ColdFusion error. Default is NO.
redirect = "YES | NO"	If YES, ColdFusion follows up to four request redirections. If NO, ColdFusion treats a redirect as an error.
timeOut = "60"	
charSet = "UTF-8	
| ISO-8859-1	
| UTF-16	
| US-ASCII	
| UTF-16LE	
| UTF-16BE	
| otherCharacterSet">	

In posting data to a remote server:

Syntax	Notes
<CFHTTP	
url = "URLOfPageToCall"	
method = "POST"	
port = "80"	
userName = "userNameForBasicAuthorization"	
password = "passwordForBasicAuthorization"	
path = "PathToDirectoryToStoreResults"	You can save the results of the request by specifying ***path*** and ***file***. If these attributes aren't given, the output is available in CFHTTP.FileContent.
file = "NameOfFileToStoreResults"	
resolveURL = "YES | NO"	Modifies any URLs in the returned page content such that they include the full server and port so that all links remain functional
proxyServer = "NameOrIPOfProxyServer"	
proxyPort = "portNumber"	

userAgent = "customRequestUserAgent"
To put a custom value in the HTTP user agent for the request, specify this attribute.

throwOnError = "YES | NO"
If YES, any HTTP error causes CFHTTP to throw a ColdFusion error. Default is NO.

redirect = "YES | NO"
If YES, ColdFusion follows up to four request redirections. If NO, ColdFusion treats a redirect as an error.

timeOut = "60"
charSet = "UTF-8
| ISO-8859-1
| UTF-16
| US-ASCII
| UTF-16LE
| UTF-16BE
| otherCharacterSet">
...
POST operations must have at least one CFHTTPPARAM tag.

</CFHTTP>

In creating a query object from a text file:

<CFHTTP
url = "URLOfPageToCall"
name = "nameOfConstructedQuery"
This variable contains the query constructed from the data retrieved by CFHTTP.

delimiter = "queryDelimiter"
The delimiter that appears between each column.

textQualifier = "queryValueQualifier"
The qualifier that surrounds the values of each field.

columns = "column1,column2,column3"
The names of the query columns, if ***firstRowAsHeaders*** is NO.

firstRowAsHeaders = "YES | NO"
If YES, the first row of the retrieved data file contains the column names.

method = "GET | POST"
port = "80"
userName = "userNameForBasicAuthorization"
password = "passwordForBasicAuthorization"
path = "PathToDirectoryToStoreResults"
file = "NameOfFileToStoreResults"
resolveURL = "YES | NO"
proxyServer = "NameOrIPOfProxyServer"
proxyPort = "portNumber"
userAgent = "customRequestUserAgent"
throwOnError = "YES | NO"
redirect = "YES | NO"
timeOut = "60"
charSet = "UTF-8
| ISO-8859-1
| UTF-16
| US-ASCII

```
        | UTF-16LE
        | UTF-16BE
        | otherCharacterSet">
```

Cross References

CFHTTPPARAM	Describes the parameters to be passed to the called page. (POSTs only).

<CFHTTPPARAM>

Describes a parameter to pass during a POST made by using CFHTTP.

```
<CFHTTPPARAM
    name = "nameOfParam"
    type = "URL
        | FORMFIELD
        | COOKIE
        | CGI
        | FILE"
    value = "#valueToSend#"
    file = "fullPathToFileToSend">
```

Cross References

CFHTTP	Defines the HTTP request.

GetHttpRequestData()

Returns a **structure** containing the HTTP headers in effect for the current HTTP request.

```
GetHttpRequestData()
```

Java, COM, and CORBA

<CFAPPLET>

Places a registered Java applet on the page. Any applet referenced by using CFAPPLET must be registered in ColdFusion Administrator.

```
<CFAPPLET
    appletSource = "nameOfRegisteredApplet"
    name = "nameOfFormVariable"          Applies only if the method was supplied as the applet was registered
                                         with ColdFusion Administrator.
    height = "300"
    width = "400"
    vSpace = "10"
```

hSpace = "10"	
align = "TOP	
	LEFT	
	BOTTOM	
	BASELINE	
	TEXTTOP	
	ABSBOTTOM	
	MIDDLE	
	ABSMIDDLE	
	RIGHT"	
notSupported = "messageIfNoJava"	
...	Any additional parameters become applet parameters.
>	

Cross References

CFFORM	Describes the form containing this applet.

<CFIMPORT>

Imports a custom tag library and assigns it a tag prefix. Can import JSP custom tags based on a JAR or TLD file; can also import ColdFusion custom tags if given the name of a directory.

<CFIMPORT	
taglib = "/taglib.jar	The URL path of a JAR file to import as a tag library. Should be located inside the webroot; must also be located on the classpath in ColdFusion Administrator.
	/taglib.tld	The URL path of a Tag Library Description XML file describing the tag library to import.
	/directoryContainingCFMLCustomTags"	The URL path to a directory containing ColdFusion custom tags.
prefix = "tagPrefix">	The imported tags can be called by using the prefix specified here.

<CFOBJECT>

Instantiates a COM, CORBA, Java, component, or web service object.

To instantiate a COM object:

<CFOBJECT	
action = "CREATE	Creates a new instance of the COM object.
	CONNECT"	Connects to an existing instance of the COM object.
class = "ProgIDOfCOMClass	
	NameOfCOMClass"	
name = "nameOfNewObject"	Specifies the name of the variable that will contain the COM object.
type = "COM"	
context = "INPROC	In-process object.
	LOCAL	Out-of-process but on this machine.
	REMOTE"	Calls a DCOM object on a remote machine.
server = "NameOfRemoteServer">	Required if ***context*** is REMOTE.

To instantiate a component object:

<CFOBJECT
 name = "nameOfNewObject"
 component = "nameOfComponent">

To instantiate a CORBA object:

<CFOBJECT

context = "IOR	Use the Interoperable Object Reference (IOR) to access the CORBA server.
| NAMESERVICE"	Use a naming service to access the CORBA server. Valid only with a VisiBroker ORB (Object Request Broker).
class = "NameOfServiceOrClass"	If context is IOR, this attribute contains the path to a file containing the string IOR. If the context is NAMESERVICE, this is the naming context for a naming service.
name = "nameOfNewObject"	
type = "CORBA"	
locale = "argumentsToVisiBrokerORB">	If the ORB needs any extra arguments, pass them in this attribute. Valid only for VisiBroker ORBs.

To instantiate a Java or EJB (Enterprise JavaBean) object:

<CFOBJECT
 action = "CREATE"
 class = "nameOfJavaClass"
 name = "nameOfNewObject"
 type = "JAVA">

To instantiate a web service object:

<CFOBJECT
 webService = "mappedServiceName
 | URLToWSDLFile"
 name = "nameOfNewObject">

Cross References

`CreateObject()`	Instantiates an object inside of `CFSCRIPT`.

<CFSERVLET>

Deprecated.

<CFSERVLETPARAM>

Deprecated.

CreateObject()

Returns a new COM, CORBA, Java, component, or web service **object**. Equivalent to `CFOBJECT` but can be used inside `CFSCRIPT`.

To instantiate a COM object:

CreateObject(
- **"COM"**,
- **class**, — Can be either a ProgID or ProgName.
- **context**, — INPROC, LOCAL, or REMOTE.
- **server**) — Server name if ***context*** is REMOTE.

To instantiate a component object:

CreateObject(
- **"component"**, — The literal string "component".
- **componentName**)

To instantiate a CORBA object:

CreateObject(
- **"CORBA"**,
- **context**, — IOR or NAMESERVICE.
- **class**, — Class name or IOR file.
- **locale**) — Extra arguments for a VisiBroker ORB.

To instantiate a Java or EJB object:

CreateObject(
- **"Java"**,
- **class**)

To instantiate a web service object:

CreateObject(
- **"webservice"**,
- **wsdlURL**)

Cross References

`CFOBJECT`	Instantiates an object by using CFML.

JavaCast()

Returns a **java-compatible value** given a ColdFusion variable

JavaCast(
- **type**, — Boolean, int, long, double, or string.
- **variable**) — ColdFusion variable to cast.

Operating System

<CFEXECUTE>

Executes an external application or batch file.

<CFEXECUTE	
name = "C:\dir\myapp.exe	Executes a Windows .EXE file.
| C:\dir\mybatchfile.bat	Executes a Windows batch file.
| home/dir/myapp"	Executes a UNIX command.
arguments = "executableArguments"	
outputFile = "fullPathOfOutputFile"	To redirect output to a file instead of just showing it on the page, use this attribute. If you use the Windows file-redirect operator (>) in your batch file, however, this attribute has no effect.
timeOut = "30">	Maximum amount of time in seconds that this CFEXECUTE call may take. Setting this to 0 makes the executable run asynchronously, also called "non-blocking mode".
. . .	
</CFEXECUTE>	

✦ ✦ ✦

CHAPTER 56

Controlling Server Output and Whitespace

Server Output

<CFFLUSH>

Flushes or "pushes" page content to the browser so that the browser can begin rendering a web page before receiving all of the content.

```
<CFFLUSH
    interval = "128">
```

If ***interval*** is specified, content is flushed to the browser whenever this number of bytes of output is accumulated. Omitting this output just flushes whatever has accumulated since the last flush operation.

Application Notes

- There are several tags that cannot be called after you call CFFLUSH: CFCONTENT, CFCOOKIE, CFFORM, CFHEADER, CFHTMLHEAD, and CFLOCATION.

<CFHTMLHEAD>

Adds text to the current page's HTML HEAD section. Cannot be called after CFFLUSH.

```
<CFHTMLHEAD
    text = "textToPutInHTMLHeadSection">
```

<CFSAVECONTENT>

Saves the tag's content into a variable named after *nameOfVariableToCreate*. Does not output the tag's content to the page.

```
<CFSAVECONTENT
    variable = "nameOfVariableToCreate">
    . . .
</CFSAVECONTENT>
```

HTMLCodeFormat()

Returns a **string** surrounded with <PRE> tags and all HTML tags escaped such that any HTML source may be put out the page as actual content, as in a code example.

HTMLCodeFormat(
    string,
    version) -1, 2.0, or 3.2. Version of HTML to escape for. -1 indicates latest version.

HTMLEditFormat()

Returns a **string** with all HTML tags replaced by their HTML-safe equivalents so that the returned string may be used as a tag attribute or safely output to a page.

HTMLEditFormat(
    string,
    version) -1, 2.0, or 3.2. Version of HTML to escape for. -1 indicates latest version.

ParagraphFormat()

Returns a **string** with single carriage returns replaced by spaces and blank lines replaced by <P> tags.

ParagraphFormat(
    string)

StripCR()

Returns a **string** with all carriage returns removed.

StripCR(
    string)

White Space

<CFPROCESSINGDIRECTIVE>

Tells ColdFusion to strip extraneous white space from a block of code; can also be used to specify page encoding.

To specify page encoding:
<CFPROCESSINGDIRECTIVE
    pageEncoding = "JavaEncodingType">

To suppress whitespace:

```
<CFPROCESSINGDIRECTIVE
    suppressWhitespace = "YES | NO">
    ...
</CFPROCESSINGDIRECTIVE>
```

<CFSETTING>

Controls certain aspects of how a page is processed.

`<CFSETTING`	
`enableCFOutputOnly = "YES | NO"`	If YES, only text within a CFOUTPUT tag or WriteOutput() function is output to the page.
`showDebugOutput = "YES | NO"`	If NO, debug output is not shown after a request finishes. Applies only if debugging information is currently enabled in ColdFusion Administrator.
`requestTimeOut = "1800">`	In this example, if the request does not finish executing within 1,800 milliseconds, an error is thrown and the request is flagged as a long-running request.

<CFSILENT>

Suppresses all output such that nothing between the opening and closing `CFSILENT` tags is output to the page.

```
<CFSILENT>
    ...
</CFSILENT>
```

✦ ✦ ✦

Verity

<CFCOLLECTION>

Used to manage Verity collections. Can create a new collection; map a new name to an existing collection; repair, delete, or optimize an existing collection; or list all current collections. See Chapter 32 for details on Verity collections.

To list all collections:

```
<CFCOLLECTION
    action = "LIST"
    name = "NameOfQueryToCreate">     CFCOLLECTION creates a query object with this name.
```

To repair, delete, or optimize a collection:

```
<CFCOLLECTION
    action = "REPAIR                  Repairs a collection.
      | DELETE                        Deletes a collection.
      | OPTIMIZE"                     Optimizes a collection.
    collection = "NameOfCollection">
```

To create a new collection:

```
<CFCOLLECTION
    action = "CREATE"
    collection = "NameOfCollection"
    path = "PathToCollectionDirectory"   The path to the directory where the collection directory is created. If this value
                                         is "c:\verity", for example, CFCOLLECTION creates a directory named
                                         "c:\verity\NameOfCollection".
    language = "collectionLanguage">
```

Cross References

CFINDEX	Indexes data in a collection.
CFSEARCH	Searches a collection.

<CFINDEX>

Used to add or remove entries from a Verity collection. Entries can be specified one at a time or can be retrieved from a query object.

To update or refresh a collection:

<CFINDEX	
action = "UPDATE	Adds and updates entries in the collection, but does not remove any.
| REFRESH"	Purges the collection before adding entries.
collection = "nameOfCollection"	
key = "KeyOfEntry"	If ***type*** = PATH, ***key*** is the directory to index. If ***type*** = FILE, ***key*** is the name of the file to index. If ***type*** = CUSTOM, key is the primary key of the record to index.
type = "PATH	Indexes directories.
| FILE	Indexes individual files.
| CUSTOM"	Indexes custom data, usually from a query.
title = "TitleOfEntry"	Applies to CUSTOM and FILE types. Title of the entry to be created.
body = "TextToIndex"	Applies to CUSTOM type. Body of the entry being created.
custom1 = "customData"	
custom2 = "customData"	
URLpath = "URLToPrependToFilename"	Applies to PATH and FILE types. This path is prepended onto the file name to create a URL that the user can use to access the indexed file.
extensions = "ExtensionsToIndex"	Applies only to PATH type. Verity indexes only files of these extensions. Default is ".htm, .html, .cfm, .cfml".
query = "NameOfQuery"	The name of a ***query*** to populate index data. If ***query*** is provided, the ***key, title, body, custom1, custom2,*** and ***URLpath*** attributes can point to query columns rather than literal text. Verity creates an entry in the collection for every row in the query.
recurse = "NO |YES"	If YES, Verity adds entries for subdirectories of the directory specified in ***key***. Applies only to the PATH type.
language = "collectionLanguage">	

Application Notes

- If the Query attribute is given, Verity checks the values of the *key, title, body, custom1, custom2,* and *URLpath* attributes against the columns of the query. If the attribute value matches, Verity uses the query column; otherwise, Verity uses literal text. You can use this literal text technique to put a specific hard-coded value in a given field even if you are getting data from a query.

To delete an entry from a collection:

<CFINDEX	
action = "DELETE"	
collection = "nameOfCollection"	
key = "KeyOfEntry">	Specifies the ***key*** of the entry to delete.

To purge all keys from a collection:

<CFINDEX
action = "PURGE"
collection = "nameOfCollection">

Cross References

CFCOLLECTION	Manages a collection.

<CFSEARCH>

Used to search a Verity collection.

<CFSEARCH
collection = "nameOfCollection"
name = "nameOfQueryToCreate" — Verity will create a query with this name containing the results of the search.
type = "SIMPLE — Verity automatically applies the STEM and MANY operators to the search.
| EXPLICIT" — Verity will not automatically apply any operators to the search.
criteria = "searchCriteria"
maxRows = "100"
startRow = "1"
language = "collectionLanguage">

GetK2ServerDocCount()

Returns the **number** of documents currently searchable by the Verity K2 Server. See Chapter 32 for details about Verity K2 Server.

GetK2ServerDocCount()

GetK2ServerDocCountLimit()

Returns the maximum **number** of documents that the K2Server and the current installation of ColdFusion MX can handle: 10,000 for Developer; 125,000 for Professional; and 250,000 for Evaluation and Enterprise.

GetK2ServerDocCountLimit()

IsK2ServerABroker()

Returns **TRUE** if the current K2 Server is a K2 Broker, and **FALSE** otherwise.

IsK2ServerABroker()

IsK2ServerDocCountExceeded()

Returns **TRUE** if the collections being managed by the K2 Server exceed the current limit for the current edition of ColdFusion MX and **FALSE** otherwise.

IsK2ServerDocCountExceeded()

IsK2ServerOnline()

Returns **TRUE** if the connected K2 Server is current online and **FALSE** otherwise.

```
IsK2ServerOnline()
```

✦ ✦ ✦

Mail

<CFMAIL>

Sends an e-mail message to a given address. Can send either HTML or plain-text mail.

<CFMAIL	
to = "addressToSendMessageTo"	
from = "addressToSendMessageFrom"	
subject = "subjectOfMessage"	
cc = "copiedAddresses"	Mail is copied to these addresses, given in a comma-delimited list.
bcc = "blindCopiedAddresses"	Mail is copied to these addresses, but recipients cannot see any of these addresses in the mail headers.
type = "HTML"	Omit this attribute for plain-text messages, and include it to send HTML-encoded messages.
maxRows = "100"	
mimeAttach = "PathOfAttachedFile"	To attach a single file, specify the full path here.
query = "nameOfQueryToGenerateMessages"	
group = "columnToGroupBy"	
groupCaseSensitive = "YES | NO"	
startRow = "1"	
server = "addressOfSMTPServer"	If not specified, uses the default mail server as specified in ColdFusion Administrator.
port = "25"	
mailerID = "IDToSendInXMailerHeader"	
timeOut = "-1 | numberOfSeconds"	
spoolEnable = "YES | NO">	YES saves a copy of the message until it is sent; NO does not save a copy of the message.

Cross References

CFMAILPARAM	Describes a mail header or attachment for this mail message.
CFPOP	Retrieves mail from a POP server.

<CFMAILPARAM>

Specifies a mail header or attachment for a call to `CFMAIL`. The *name* and *file* attributes are mutually exclusive.

To include a message header:

```
<CFMAILPARAM
    name = "nameOfHeader"
    value = "valueOfHeader">
```

To attach a file:

```
<CFMAILPARAM
    file = "FullPathToFile">
```

Cross References

`CFMAIL`	Describes the mail message being sent.

<CFPOP>

Retrieves e-mail messages from a POP server. Can also be used to delete a given message.

To retrieve headers or full messages from a POP Server:

```
<CFPOP
    server = "addressOfPOPServer"
    action = "GETHEADERONLY                 Retrieves only message headers from the POP server.
      | GETALL"                             Retrieves all message content, including attachments.
    name = "nameOfQueryToCreate"
    port = "110"
    userName = "userNameofPOPAccount"
    password = "passwordOfPOPAccount"
    timeOut = "60"
    maxRows = "100"
    startRow = "1"
    attachmentPath = "directoryForAttachments"     Attachments are saved into this directory.
    generateUniqueFilenames = "YES | NO">          If YES, attachments are given unique file names so that they don't
                                                   conflict with one another.
```

To delete messages from a POP server based on their message numbers:

```
<CFPOP
    server = "addressOfPOPServer"
    action = "DELETE"
    messageNumber = "messageNumberToDelete"    CFPOP deletes this message from the POP server. Be careful, as this
                                               technique deletes the message based on its ordinal position rather
                                               than its Unique Identifier (UID).
```

```
    port = "110"
    userName = "userNameofPOPAccount"
    password = "passwordOfPOPAccount"
    timeOut = "60">
```

To delete messages from a POP server based on their UIDs:

```
<CFPOP
    server = "addressOfPOPServer"
    action = "DELETE"
    uid = "messageUIDToDelete"
    port = "110"
    userName = "userNameofPOPAccount"
    password = "passwordOfPOPAccount"
    timeOut = "60">
```

CFPOP deletes the message containing this UID from the POP server. If the message does not exist, CFPOP does not throw an error.

Application Notes

- Always delete messages by UID rather than message number.

Cross References

CFMAIL	Sends a mail message through SMTP.

✦ ✦ ✦

Charting, Reporting, and Logging

Charting

<CFCHART>

Defines the container and scale for chart data. Always contains at least one `CFCHARTSERIES` tag.

<CFCHART	
format = "FLASH | JPG | PNG"	
chartHeight = "240"	
chartWidth = "320"	
scaleFrom = "0"	Y-Axis minimum value. If larger than the smallest data point, CFCHART ignores this value and chooses the smaller point.
scaleTo = "10000"	Y-Axis maximum value. If smaller than the largest data point, CFCHART ignores this value and chooses the larger point.
showXGridLines = "YES | NO"	
showYGridLines = "YES | NO"	
gridLines = "numberOfYAxisGridlines"	
seriesPlacement = "DEFAULT | CLUSTER | STACKED | PERCENT"	
foregroundColor = "Black"	
dataBackgroundColor = "White"	
borderBackgroundColor = "White"	
showBorder = "YES | NO"	
font = "ARIAL | TIMES | COURIER | ARIALUNICODEMS"	Use ArialUnicodeMS for a double-byte character set on UNIX or a double-byte character set with Flash.
fontSize = "10"	
fontBold = "NO | YES"	
fontItalic = "NO | YES"	

```
    labelFormat = "NUMBER                     Format for Y-Axis labels.
      | CURRENCY | PERCENT | DATE"
    xAxisTitle = "titleOfXAxis"
    yAxisTitle = "titleOfYAxis"
    sortXAxis = "YES | NO"
    show3D = "YES | NO"
    xOffset = "0.1"                           Amount of horizontal rotation. -1 is 90 degrees left, and 1 is 90 degrees
                                              right.
    yOffset = "0.1"                           Amount of vertical rotation. -1 is 90 degrees down, and 1 is 90 degrees up.
    rotated = "YES | NO"                      YES rotates chart 90 degrees.
    showLegend = "YES | NO"
    tipStyle = "MOUSEDOWN
      | MOUSEOVER
      | OFF"
    tipBGColor = "White"
    showMarkers = "YES | NO"
    markerSize = "6"
    pieSliceStyle = "SOLID
      | SLICED"
    url = "URLOfPageToOpen
      | javascript:javascriptFunction();"
    name = "nameOfBinaryVariableToCreate">
    ...
</CFCHART>
```

Cross References

CFCHARTSERIES	A series of data within this chart.

<CFCHARTDATA>

Defines an individual data point within a chart series. Always found inside of a CFCHARTSERIES tag.

```
<CFCHARTDATA
    value = "valueOfDataPoint"                Placement on the X-Axis.
    item = "nameOfDataPoint">                 Placement on the Y-Axis.
```

Cross References

CFCHARTSERIES	The series containing this data point.

<CFCHARTSERIES>

Defines a series of chart data points. Each series can have a different color, style, and method of display.

```
<CFCHARTSERIES
    type = "BAR
      | LINE
      | PYRAMID
      | AREA
      | CONE
      | CURVE
      | CYLINDER
      | STEP
      | SCATTER
      | PIE"
    query = "nameOfQuery"                        Query used to populate series data.
    itemColumn = "columnForXAxisValues"
    valueColumn = "columnForYAxisValues"
    seriesLabel = "Human-Readable Series Name"
    seriesColor = "Black"
    paintStyle = "PLAIN
      | RAISE
      | SHADE
      | LIGHT"
    markerStyle = "RECTANGLE
      | TRIANGLE
      | DIAMOND
      | CIRCLE
      | LETTER
      | MCROSS
      | SNOW
      | RCROSS"
    colorList = "listOfPieSliceColors">          Used for PIE type. This is a list of colors used to color each pie slice.
    . . .
</CFCHARTSERIES>
```

Cross References

CFCHART	The chart containing this series.
CFCHARTDATA	Data points within this series.

<CFGRAPH>

Deprecated. Use CFCHART and CFCHARTSERIES instead.

<CFGRAPHDATA>

Deprecated. Use CFCHARTDATA instead.

Reporting

<CFREPORT>

Calls a Crystal Reports file.

```
<CFREPORT
    report = "pathToCrystalReportsFile"
    dataSource = "#MainDSN#"
    type = "STANDARD
      | NETSCAPE
      | MICROSOFT"
```

Not valid with Crystal Reports 8.0.

```
    timeOut = "20"
    orderBy = "orderColumns"
    userName = "#Username#"
    password = "#Password#"
    formula = "reportFormulas"
    >
    ...
</CFREPORT>
```

Logging

<CFLOG>

Adds an entry to a ColdFusion MX log file.

```
<CFLOG
    text = "messageText"
    log = "APPLICATION
      | SCHEDULER"
    file = "LogFileName"
```

The name of the log file without the extension; for example, a value of "MyLog" would put the log entry in a file named "MyLog.log". If neither ***log*** nor ***file*** are specified, the log entry is written to application.log.

```
    type = "INFORMATION
      | WARNING
      | ERROR
      | FATAL INFORMATION"
    application = "YES | NO">
```

If YES, adds the application name to the log entry.

<CFTRACE>

Displays and logs debugging data. Appears in the debug information at the end of the page, and also generates an entry in the ColdFusion log file named cftrace.log.

```
<CFTRACE
    abort = "YES | NO"                       If YES, aborts page processing after calling CFTRACE.
    category = "traceGroup"
    inline = "YES | NO"                      If YES, displays trace code along with trace summary.
    text = "traceInformation"
    type = "INFORMATION
      | WARNING
      | ERROR
      | FATAL INFORMATION"
    var = "variableNameToDisplay"            If specified, displays the contents of the passed variable.
    >
    . . .
</CFTRACE>
```

✦ ✦ ✦

CHAPTER 60

Files and Directories

On ColdFusion Server

<CFDIRECTORY>

Performs an action on a directory on ColdFusion Server. Can be used to list directory contents or to create, delete, or rename a given directory.

To list the contents of a directory:

<CFDIRECTORY
 action = "LIST"
 directory = "c:\mydir\"
 name = "nameOfQuery" — ColdFusion creates a query with this name to contain data about the directory contents.
 filter = "*.cfm" — Only one filter may be applied at a time.
 sort = "dateLastModified DESC">

Columns in the Returned Query Object

- Name
- Size: The size of the file in bytes.
- Type: "File" or "Dir".
- DateLastModified
- Attributes
- Mode

Application Notes

- ColdFusion MX no longer returns rows for "." and ".." in the returned query object.

To create a new directory:

<CFDIRECTORY
 action = "CREATE"
 directory = "c:\mydir\"
 mode = "UnixPermissionDescriptor">

To delete a directory:

<CFDIRECTORY
    action = "DELETE" — This action fails if the directory is not empty.
    directory = "c:\mydir\">

To rename a directory:

<CFDIRECTORY
    action = "RENAME"
    directory = "c:\mydir\"
    newDirectory = "c:\mynewdir\">

Application Notes

- You cannot rename a directory if the directory isn't empty.

Cross References

`CFFILE`	Operates on files within a directory.
`DirectoryExists()`	Tests to determine whether a given directory exists.

<CFFILE>

Performs file operations on files located on ColdFusion server. The possible operations are:

- Upload a file
- Move a file
- Rename a file
- Copy a file
- Delete a file
- Read a file containing text content
- Read a file containing binary content
- Write a file
- Append text to the end of a file containing text content

Upload a file:

<CFFILE	
action = "UPLOAD"	
fileField = "nameOfFileInputField"	Notice that the field name is not in pound signs.
destination = "c:\mydir\	If specifying only a directory, the name of the file is the same as the name of the file on the client's computer.
| c:\mydir\myfile.ext"	You can rename a file by giving the file name at the end of the path.
nameConflict = "ERROR	If the file being uploaded has the same name as one that already exists in the target location, CFFILE throws an error.
| SKIP	If the file being uploaded has the same name as one that already exists in the target location, the file is not uploaded.
| OVERWRITE	If the file being uploaded has the same name as one that already exists in the target location, the pre existing file is overwritten.
| MAKEUNIQUE"	If the file being uploaded has the same name as one that already exists in the target location, the new file is given a unique name. The new name is available in CFFILE.ServerFile.

```
    accept = "image/jpg, image/gif"              A comma-delimited list of MIME types that the server accepts.
    mode = "UnixPermissionDescriptor"
    attributes = "READONLY
      | HIDDEN
      | NORMAL
      | commaDelimitedList">
```

Application Notes

- When uploading a file, the form that submits the file to the server must use `enctype="multipart/form-data"`.

Move a file:

```
<CFFILE
    action = "MOVE"
    source = "c:\mydir\myfile.ext"
    destination = "c:\myotherdir\               File is be named the same as the source but moved to a different directory.
      | c:\mydir\myotherfile.ext"               File is renamed and moved.
    mode = "UnixPermissionDescriptor"
    attributes = "READONLY
      | HIDDEN
      | NORMAL
      | commaDelimitedList"
    charSet = "UTF-8
      | ISO-8859-1
      | UTF-16
      | US-ASCII
      | UTF-16LE
      | UTF-16BE
      | otherCharacterSet">
```

Rename a file:

```
<CFFILE
    action = "RENAME"
    source = "c:\mydir\myfile.ext"
    destination = "c:\mydir\mynewfile.ext"
    mode = "UnixPermissionDescriptor"
    attributes = "READONLY
      | HIDDEN
      | NORMAL
      | commaDelimitedList">
```

Copy a file:

```
<CFFILE
    action = "COPY"
    source = "c:\mydir\myfile.ext"
    destination = "c:\mydir\mynewfile.ext       File is renamed and copied.
      | c:\myotherdir\"                         File is copied to a different location and named the same as the original file.
    mode = "UnixPermissionDescriptor"
```

```
    attributes = "READONLY
      | HIDDEN
      | NORMAL
      | commaDelimitedList">
```

Delete a file:

```
<CFFILE
    action = "DELETE"
    file = "c:\mydir\myfile.ext">
```

Read a file containing text content:

```
<CFFILE
    action = "READ"
    file = "c:\mydir\myfile.ext"
    variable = "nameOfVariableToCreate"      This variable is a standard string.
    charSet = "UTF-8
      | ISO-8859-1
      | UTF-16
      | US-ASCII
      | UTF-16LE
      | UTF-16BE
      | otherCharacterSet">
```

Read a file containing binary content:

```
<CFFILE
    action = "READBINARY"
    file = "c:\mydir\myfile.ext"
    variable = "nameOfVariableTocreate">     This variable is a ByteArray.  You can use it as the argument to ToString() or
                                             ToBase64().
```

Write a file:

```
<CFFILE
    action = "WRITE"
    file = "c:\mydir\myfile.ext"             If this file does not exist, it is created automatically.
    output = "#FileContent#"                 Content to write to file.
    mode = "UnixPermissionDescriptor"
    addNewLine = "YES | NO"                  If YES, a newline (carriage return/line feed) is tacked on to the end of the
                                             output.
    attributes = "READONLY
      | HIDDEN
      | NORMAL
      | commaDelimitedList"
    charSet = "UTF-8
      | ISO-8859-1
      | UTF-16
      | US-ASCII
      | UTF-16LE
      | UTF-16BE
      | otherCharacterSet">
```

Append text to the end of a file containing text content:

```
<CFFILE
    action = "APPEND"
    file = "c:\mydir\myfile.ext"              If this file does not exist it is created automatically.
    output = "#NewContent#"                   Content to append to end of file.
    addNewLine = "YES | NO"                   If YES, a newline (carriage return/line feed) is tacked on to the end of the
                                              output.
    attributes = "READONLY
     | HIDDEN
     | NORMAL
     | commaDelimitedList"
    mode = "UnixPermissionDescriptor"
    charSet = "UTF-8
     | ISO-8859-1
     | UTF-16
     | US-ASCII
     | UTF-16LE
     | UTF-16BE
     | otherCharacterSet ">
```

Cross References

`CFDIRECTORY`	Performs operations on directories.
`FileExists()`	Tests to determine whether a given file exists.

DirectoryExists()

Returns **TRUE** if *absolutePath* describes a valid directory; **FALSE** otherwise.

```
DirectoryExists(
    absolutePath)
```

ExpandPath()

Returns **a full disk path** given a path relative to the current template.

```
ExpandPath(
    relativePath)
```

FileExists()

Returns **TRUE** if *absolutePath* describes a valid file; **FALSE** otherwise.

```
FileExists(
    absolutePath)
```

GetBaseTemplatePath()

Returns **the full disk path** of the file at the root of the current request.

GetBaseTemplatePath()

Cross References

`GetCurrentTemplatePath()`

GetCurrentTemplatePath()

Returns **the full disk path** of the file in which this function is called.

GetCurrentTemplatePath()

Cross References

`GetBaseTemplatePath()`

GetDirectoryFromPath()

Returns **the directory portion** of *absolutePathToFile*.

GetDirectoryFromPath(
absolutePathToFile)

GetFileFromPath()

Returns **the file name** from *absolutePathToFile*.

GetFileFromPath(
absolutePathToFile)

GetTempDirectory()

Returns **the disk path** of ColdFusion's temporary files directory.

GetTempDirectory()

GetTempFile()

Returns **the name of a temporary file** inside *directoryName*. Uses *filePrefix* as the first three characters of the temporary file name.

GetTempFile(
directoryName,
filePrefix)

If ***filePrefix*** is more than three characters long, ColdFusion uses only the first three characters.

GetTemplatePath()

Deprecated. Use GetBaseTemplatePath() instead.

On the Client (User's) Computer

<CFCONTENT>

Changes the MIME type of the current request. Can optionally return a file along with the request. Useful for serving binary or secured files located outside the web root. Cannot be called after `CFFLUSH`.

```
<CFCONTENT
    type = "mime-type/mime-sub-type"      MIME type to which to change this request.
    deleteFile = "YES | NO"               If YES, file specified in file attribute is deleted after delivering it to the user.
    file = "c:\mydir\myfile.ext"          Name of the file to make up this request's content.
    reset = "YES | NO">                   If YES, all output to this point is cleared.
```

Application Notes

- At least one of the *type, file,* or *reset* attributes must be specified.
- *file* and *reset* are mutually exclusive.

On an FTP Server

<CFFTP>

Manages an FTP connection between ColdFusion Server and a remote FTP server.

Connect to an FTP server:

```
<CFFTP
    action = "OPEN"
    server = "ftp.servername.com"
    userName = "#ftpuserName#"
    password = "#ftppassword#"
    connection = "nameOfConnectionForReuse"   A connection name. You can reuse this connection throughout your code if
                                              you want to perform multiple FTP actions without needing to reconnect
                                              every time.
    proxyServer = "ftp.proxyservername.com"
    port = "21"
    timeOut = "20"
    retryCount = "5"
    stopOnError = "NO | YES"                  If NO, an error is not thrown if something goes wrong during the FTP
                                              session.
    passive = "NO | YES">                     YES enables passive transfer mode.
```

Close the connection to an FTP server:

```
<CFFTP
    action = "CLOSE"
    connection = "nameOfConnectionForReuse">
```

Change to a different directory on the FTP server, reconnecting each time:

```
<CFFTP
    action = "CHANGEDIR"
    directory = "relativePathToNewDirectory"    Uses forward slashes: "subdir/subsubdir".
    server = "ftp.servername.com"
    userName = "#ftpuserName#"
    password = "#ftppassword#"
    proxyServer = "ftp.proxyservername.com"
    port = "21"
    timeOut = "20"
    retryCount = "5"
    stopOnError = "NO | YES"
    passive = "NO | YES">
```

Change to a different directory on the FTP server by using a cached connection:

```
<CFFTP
    action = "CHANGEDIR"
    directory = "relativePathToNewDirectory"    Uses forward slashes: "subdir/subsubdir".
    connection = "nameOfConnectionForReuse"     The name of a connection established by using CFFTP action =
                                                "OPEN".
    timeOut = "20"
    retryCount = "5"
    stopOnError = "NO | YES"
    passive = "NO | YES">
```

Create a directory on the FTP server, reconnecting each time:

```
<CFFTP
    action = "CREATEDIR"
    directory = "nameOfNewDirectory"
    server = "ftp.servername.com"
    userName = "#ftpuserName#"
    password = "#ftppassword#"
    proxyServer = "ftp.proxyservername.com"
    port = "21"
    timeOut = "20"
    retryCount = "5"
    stopOnError = "NO | YES"
    passive = "NO | YES">
```

Create a directory on the FTP server by using a cached connection:

```
<CFFTP
    action = "CREATEDIR"
    directory = "nameOfNewDirectory"
    connection = "nameOfConnectionForReuse"     The name of a connection established by using CFFTP action =
                                                "OPEN".
    timeOut = "20"
    retryCount = "5"
    stopOnError = "NO | YES"
    passive = "NO | YES">
```

List the contents of a directory on the FTP server, reconnecting each time:

<CFFTP
action = "LISTDIR"
name = "nameOfQueryToCreate"
directory = "LeaveBlankOrRelativePath" — Leave blank to use working directory; otherwise give a relative path (by using forward slashes).
server = "ftp.servername.com"
userName = "#ftpuserName#"
password = "#ftppassword#"
proxyServer = "ftp.proxyservername.com"
port = "21"
timeOut = "20"
retryCount = "5"
stopOnError = "NO | YES"
passive = "NO | YES">

List the contents of a directory on the FTP server by using a cached connection:

<CFFTP
action = "LISTDIR"
name = "nameOfQueryToCreate"
directory = "LeaveBlankOrRelativePath" — Leave blank to use working directory; otherwise give a relative path (by using forward slashes).
connection = "nameOfConnectionForReuse" — The name of a connection established by using CFFTP action = "OPEN".
timeOut = "20"
retryCount = "5"
stopOnError = "NO | YES"
passive = "NO | YES">

Delete a directory on the FTP server, reconnecting each time:

<CFFTP
action = "REMOVEDIR"
directory = "nameOfDirectoryToDelete" — The call fails if the directory is not empty.
server = "ftp.servername.com"
userName = "#ftpuserName#"
password = "#ftppassword#"
proxyServer = "ftp.proxyservername.com"
port = "21"
timeOut = "20"
retryCount = "5"
stopOnError = "NO | YES"
passive = "NO | YES">

Delete a directory on the FTP server by using a cached connection:

<CFFTP
action = "REMOVEDIR"
directory = "nameOfDirectoryToDelete" — The call fails if the directory is not empty.

connection = "nameOfConnectionForReuse"	The name of a connection established by using CFFTP action = "OPEN".
timeOut = "20"	
retryCount = "5"	
stopOnError = "NO | YES"	
passive = "NO | YES">	

Copy a file from an FTP server to ColdFusion Server, reconnecting each time:

<CFFTP	
action = "GETFILE"	
localFile = "c:\mydir\myfile.ext"	The file to download.
remoteFile = "myfile.ext	Downloads a file in the working directory.
| relativePath/myFile.ext"	Downloads a file in a different directory by using a relative path from the working directory.
server = "ftp.servername.com"	
userName = "#ftpuserName#"	
password = "#ftppassword#"	
proxyServer = "ftp.proxyservername.com"	
port = "21"	
timeOut = "20"	
retryCount = "5"	
stopOnError = "NO | YES"	
passive = "NO | YES"	
ASCIIExtensionList = "txt;htm;html;cfm;cfml"	A list of extensions that are considered ASCII files. If the ***TransferMode*** = AUTO and the file name ends with one of these extensions, it is transferred as ASCII.
transferMode = "AUTO | ASCII | BINARY"	
failIfExists = "YES | NO">	If YES and the file already exists locally, the call fails. If NO, the pre-existing file is overwritten.

Copy a file from an FTP server to ColdFusion Server by using a cached connection:

<CFFTP	
action = "GETFILE"	
localFile = "c:\mydir\myfile.ext"	The file to download.
remoteFile = "myfile.ext	Downloads a file in the working directory.
| relativePath/myFile.ext"	Downloads a file in a different directory by using a relative path from the working directory.
connection = "nameOfConnectionForReuse"	The name of a connection established by using CFFTP action = "OPEN".
timeOut = "20"	
retryCount = "5"	
stopOnError = "NO | YES"	
passive = "NO | YES"	
ASCIIExtensionList = "txt;htm;html;cfm;cfml"	A list of extensions that are considered ASCII files. If the ***TransferMode*** = AUTO and the file name ends with one of these extensions, it is transferred as ASCII.

transferMode = "AUTO
| ASCII
| BINARY"
failIfExists = "YES | NO"> — If YES, if the file already exists locally, the call fails. If NO, the pre-existing file is overwritten.

Copy a file from ColdFusion Server to an FTP server, reconnecting each time:

<CFFTP
action = "PUTFILE"
localFile = "c:\mydir\myfile.ext" — The file to upload.
remoteFile = "myfile.ext — Uploads a file to the working directory.
| relativePath/myFile.ext" — Uploads a file to a different directory by using a relative path from the working directory.
server = "ftp.servername.com"
userName = "#ftpuserName#"
password = "#ftppassword#"
proxyServer = "ftp.proxyservername.com"
port = "21"
timeOut = "20"
retryCount = "5"
stopOnError = "NO | YES"
passive = "NO | YES"
ASCIIExtensionList = "txt;htm;html;cfm;cfml" — A list of extensions that are considered ASCII files. If the ***TransferMode*** = AUTO and the file name ends with one of these extensions, it is transferred as ASCII.
transferMode = "AUTO
| ASCII
| BINARY">

Copy a file from ColdFusion Server to an FTP server by using a cached connection:

<CFFTP
action = "PUTFILE"
localFile = "c:\mydir\myfile.ext" — The file to upload.
remoteFile = "myfile.ext — Uploads a file to the working directory.
| relativePath/myFile.ext" — Uploads a file to a different directory by using a relative path from the working directory.
connection = "nameOfConnectionForReuse" — The name of a connection established by using CFFTP action = "OPEN".
timeOut = "20"
retryCount = "5"
stopOnError = "NO | YES"
passive = "NO | YES"
ASCIIExtensionList = "txt;htm;html;cfm;cfml" — A list of extensions that are considered ASCII files. If the ***TransferMode*** = AUTO and the file name ends with one of these extensions, it is transferred as ASCII.
transferMode = "AUTO
| ASCII
| BINARY">

Rename a file on the FTP server, reconnecting each time:

<CFFTP	
action = "RENAME"	
existing = "myfile.ext	The name of a file in the working directory.
| relativePath/myFile.ext"	The name of and relative path to a file in a different directory.
new = "mynewfile.ext	Renames a file in the working directory.
| relativePath/myNewFile.ext"	Moves a file to a different directory.
server = "ftp.servername.com"	
userName = "#ftpuserName#"	
password = "#ftppassword#"	
proxyServer = "ftp.proxyservername.com"	
port = "21"	
timeOut = "20"	
retryCount = "5"	
stopOnError = "NO | YES"	
passive = "NO | YES">	

Rename a file on the FTP server by using a cached connection:

<CFFTP	
action = "RENAME"	
existing = "myfile.ext	The name of a file in the working directory.
| relativePath/myFile.ext"	The name of and relative path to a file in a different directory.
new = "mynewfile.ext	Renames a file in the working directory.
| relativePath/myNewFile.ext"	Moves a file to a different directory.
connection = "nameOfConnectionForReuse"	The name of a connection established by using CFFTP action = "OPEN".
timeOut = "20"	
retryCount = "5"	
stopOnError = "NO | YES"	
passive = "NO | YES">	

Remove a file from the FTP server, reconnecting each time:

<CFFTP	
action = "REMOVE"	
item = "myfile.ext	The name of a file to remove from the working directory.
| relativePath/myfile.ext"	The name of and relative path to a file in a different directory.
server = "ftp.servername.com"	
userName = "#ftpuserName#"	
password = "#ftppassword#"	
proxyServer = "ftp.proxyservername.com"	
port = "21"	
timeOut = "20"	
retryCount = "5"	
stopOnError = "NO | YES"	
passive = "NO | YES">	

Remove a file from the FTP server by using a cached connection:

```
<CFFTP
    action = "REMOVE"
    item = "myfile.ext                      The name of a file to remove from the working directory
     | relativePath/myfile.ext"             The name of and relative path to a file in a different directory.
    connection = "nameOfConnectionForReuse"  The name of a connection established by using CFFTP action =
                                             "OPEN".
    timeOut = "20"
    retryCount = "5"
    stopOnError = "NO | YES"
    passive = "NO | YES">
```

Get the name of the current directory on the FTP server, reconnecting each time:

```
<CFFTP
    action = "GETCURRENTDIR"
    server = "ftp.servername.com"
    userName = "#ftpuserName#"
    password = "#ftppassword#"
    proxyServer = "ftp.proxyservername.com"
    port = "21"
    timeOut = "20"
    retryCount = "5"
    stopOnError = "NO | YES"
    passive = "NO | YES">
```

Application Notes

- `CFFTP.returnValue` contains the path of the working directory after calling this tag.

Get the name of the current directory on the FTP server by using a cached connection:

```
<CFFTP
    action = "GETCURRENTDIR"
    connection = "nameOfConnectionForReuse"  The name of a connection established by using CFFTP action =
                                             "OPEN".
    timeOut = "20"
    retryCount = "5"
    stopOnError = "NO | YES"
    passive = "NO | YES">
```

Application Notes

- `CFFTP.returnValue` contains the path of the working directory after calling this tag.

Get the current URL to the current directory on the FTP server, reconnecting each time:

```
<CFFTP
    action = "GETCURRENTURL"
    server = "ftp.servername.com"
    userName = "#ftpuserName#"
```

password = "#ftppassword#"
proxyServer = "ftp.proxyservername.com"
port = "21"
timeOut = "20"
retryCount = "5"
stopOnError = "NO | YES"
passive = "NO | YES">

Application Notes

- `CFFTP.returnValue` contains the current URL of the FTP server after calling this tag.

Get the current URL to the current directory on the FTP server by using a cached connection:

<CFFTP
action = "GETCURRENTURL"
connection = "nameOfConnectionForReuse" — The name of a connection established by using CFFTP action = "OPEN".
timeOut = "20"
retryCount = "5"
stopOnError = "NO | YES"
passive = "NO | YES">

Application Notes

- `CFFTP.returnValue` contains the current URL of the FTP server after calling this tag.

Determine whether or not a specified item exists on the FTP server, reconnecting each time:

<CFFTP
action = "EXISTS"
item = "myfile.ext — A file in the working directory.
| mydir — A subdirectory of the working directory.
| relativePathToFileOrDir" — A relative path to a file or directory in another location.
server = "ftp.servername.com"
userName = "#ftpuserName#"
password = "#ftppassword#"
proxyServer = "ftp.proxyservername.com"
port = "21"
timeOut = "20"
retryCount = "5"
stopOnError = "NO | YES"
passive = "NO | YES">

Application Notes

- `CFFTP.returnValue` contains `YES` or `NO` depending on whether the given item exists.

Determine whether or not a specified item exists on the FTP server by using a cached connection:

```
<CFFTP
    action = "EXISTS"
    item = "myfile.ext                        A file in the working directory.
     | mydir                                 A subdirectory of the working directory.
     | relativePathToFileOrDir"              A relative path to a file or directory in another location.
    connection = "nameOfConnectionForReuse"  The name of a connection established by using CFFTP action =
                                             "OPEN".
    timeOut = "20"
    retryCount = "5"
    stopOnError = "NO | YES"
    passive = "NO | YES">
```

Application Notes

- `CFFTP.returnValue` **contains** `YES` **or** `NO` **depending on whether the given item exists.**

Determine whether a specified file exists on the FTP server, reconnecting each time:

```
<CFFTP
    action = "EXISTSFILE"
    remoteFile = "myfile.ext                 A file in the working directory.
     | relativePath/myfile.ext"              A relative path to a file in another location.
    server = "ftp.servername.com"
    userName = "#ftpuserName#"
    password = "#ftppassword#"
    proxyServer = "ftp.proxyservername.com"
    port = "21"
    timeOut = "20"
    retryCount = "5"
    stopOnError = "NO | YES"
    passive = "NO | YES">
```

Application Notes

- `CFFTP.returnValue` **contains** `YES` **or** `NO` **depending on whether the given item exists.**

Determine whether a specified file exists on the FTP server by using a cached connection:

```
<CFFTP
    action = "EXISTSFILE"
    remoteFile = "myfile.ext                 A file in the working directory.
     | relativePath/myfile.ext"              A relative path to a file in another location.
    connection = "nameOfConnectionForReuse"  The name of a connection established with CFFTP action = "OPEN".
    timeOut = "20"
    retryCount = "5"
    stopOnError = "NO | YES"
    passive = "NO | YES">
```

Application Notes

* CFFTP.returnValue contains YES or NO depending on whether the given item exists.

Determine whether a specified directory exists on the FTP server, reconnecting each time:

```
<CFFTP
    action = "EXISTSDIR"
    directory = "mydir                       A subdirectory of the working directory.
     | relativePath/mydir"                   A relative path to a directory in another location.
    server = "ftp.servername.com"
    userName = "#ftpuserName#"
    password = "#ftppassword#"
    proxyServer = "ftp.proxyservername.com"
    port = "21"
    timeOut = "20"
    retryCount = "5"
    stopOnError = "NO | YES"
    passive = "NO | YES">
```

Application Notes

* CFFTP.returnValue contains YES or NO depending on whether the given item exists.

Determine whether a specified directory exists on the FTP server by using a cached connection:

```
<CFFTP
    action = "EXISTSDIR"
    directory = "mydir                       A subdirectory of the working directory.
     | relativePath/mydir"                   A relative path to a directory in another location.
    connection = "nameOfConnectionForReuse"  The name of a connection established with CFFTP action = "OPEN".
    timeOut = "20"
    retryCount = "5"
    stopOnError = "NO | YES"
    passive = "NO | YES">
```

Application Notes

* CFFTP.returnValue contains YES or NO depending on whether the given item exists.

✦ ✦ ✦

CHAPTER 61

The Registry

<CFREGISTRY>

Manages keys in the Windows registry. This tag is deprecated on Unix platforms. Note that ColdFusion server-specific information that was stored in the registry in ColdFusion 5 and earlier releases is likely no longer in the registry in ColdFusion MX. In ColdFusion MX, this information is often stored in XML files under the ColdFusion installation root.

Return all Registry keys and values in a branch:

<CFREGISTRY	
action = "GETALL"	
branch = "HKEY_LOCAL_MACHINE\key\key\key"	The branch with keys and/or values that you want to retrieve.
name = "nameOfQueryToCreate"	CFREGISTRY creates a query with this name.
type = "STRING	Retrieves only STRING values.
| DWORD	Retrieves only DWORD values.
| KEY	Retrieves only KEYs.
| ANY"	Retrieves all KEYs and values.
sort = "entry asc, value desc, type desc">	

Return a single Registry value and store it in a variable:

<CFREGISTRY	
action = "GET"	
branch = "HKEY_LOCAL_MACHINE\key\key\key"	The branch containing the value that you want to retrieve.
entry = "nameOfEntry"	The name of the value that you want to retrieve.
variable = "nameOfVariableToCreate"	The name of the variable that stores the returned value.
type = "STRING	Retrieves a STRING value.
| DWORD	Retrieves a DWORD value.
| KEY">	Retrieves a KEY's default value.

Add or update a Registry key:

<CFREGISTRY	
action = "SET"	
branch = "HKEY_LOCAL_MACHINE\key\key\key"	The branch containing the KEY or value that you want to create or update.
entry = "nameOfEntry"	Name of the KEY or value to create.
type = "STRING	Creates or updates a STRING value (default).
| DWORD	Creates or updates a DWORD value.
| KEY"	Creates a new KEY.
value = "valueOfNewEntry">	***value*** to set. Omit this attribute for a KEY.

Delete a Registry key:

```
<CFREGISTRY
    action = "DELETE"
    branch = "HKEY_LOCAL_MACHINE\key\key\key">    KEY to delete. Also deletes any associated subkeys.
```

Delete a Registry value:

```
<CFREGISTRY
    action = "DELETE"
    branch = "HKEY_LOCAL_MACHINE\key\key\key"    KEY containing the value to delete.
    entry = "nameOfEntry">                       Name of the value to delete.
```

✦ ✦ ✦

Security

Authentication and Authorization

<CFLDAP>

Retrieves and modifies data on an LDAP authentication server.

To retrieve entries from an LDAP server:

```
<CFLDAP
    server = "nameOrIPOfLDAPServer"
    name = "nameOfQueryToCreate"
    start = "nameOfFirstEntryForSearch"
    attributes = "listOfLDAPFieldsToGet"
    port = "389"
    username = "usernameForBasicAuthorization"
    password = "passwordForBasicAuthorization"
    action = "QUERY"
    timeOut = "60"
    maxRows = "100"
    scope = "ONELEVEL          Restricts the search to the level below the start attribute.
      | BASE               Restricts the query to only the start attribute.
      | SUBTREE"           Returns start and all subentries below it.
    filter = "(sn = Smith)"  An LDAP search string. Refer to "Developing ColdFusion MX Applications
                             with CFML" in the ColdFusion MX Documentation Set for more information.
    sort = "listOfLDAPFieldsToSortBy"
    sortControl = "NOCASE
      | ASC
      | DESC
      | combinationOfOthers"
    startRow = "1"
    rebind = "YES | NO"
    referral = "numberOfHopsAllowed"
    secure = "CFSSL_BASIC"
    separator = "attributeValueDelimiter"     Character that separates multiple attribute values from one another.
    delimiter = "nameValuePairDelimiter">     Character that separates multiple attributes from one another.
```

To add or modify an entry on an LDAP server:

```
<CFLDAP
    server = "nameOrIPOfLDAPServer"
    dn = "distingushedName"                      Distinguished name of the entry that you are adding or modifying.
    action = "ADD                                Adds a new entry.
     | MODIFY                                    Modifies attributes of an existing entry.
     | MODIFYDN"                                 Modifies the distinguished name of an existing entry.
    attributes = "listOfLDAPFieldsToModify"
    port = "389"
    username = "usernameForBasicAuthorization"
    password = "passwordForBasicAuthorization"
    timeOut = "60"
    modifyType = "ADD                            If an attribute already exists for an entry, appends the new value to the
                                                 current value.
     | DELETE                                    If an attribute already exists on an entry, skips the new value.
     | REPLACE"                                  If an attribute already exists on an entry, replaces the current value with the
                                                 new value.
    rebind = "YES | NO"
    referral = "numberOfHopsAllowed"
    secure = "CFSSL_BASIC"
    separator = "attributeValueDelimiter"
    delimiter = "nameValuePairDelimiter">
```

To delete an entry from an LDAP server:

```
<CFLDAP
    server = "nameOrIPOfLDAPServer"
    dn = "distingushedName"                      The name of the entry to delete.
    port = "389"
    username = "usernameForBasicAuthorization"
    password = "passwordForBasicAuthorization"
    action = "DELETE"
    timeOut = "60"
    rebind = "YES | NO"
    referral = "numberOfHopsAllowed"
    secure = "CFSSL_BASIC">
```

<CFLOGIN>

Surrounds login and authentication code. The content of the `CFLOGIN` tag executes only if no user is currently logged in.

```
<CFLOGIN
    idleTimeOut = "1800"                         Number of seconds before user's session expires.
    applicationToken = "specialTokenName"
    cookieDomain = ".mydomain.com"               To use domain-level cookies, specify this attribute.
    >
    ...
</CFLOGIN>
```

<CFLOGINUSER>

Authenticates a user. Tells ColdFusion what the current user's name, password, and roles are. Must be called inside a CFLOGIN tag.

```
<CFLOGINUSER
    name = "userNameToAuthenticate"
    password = "passwordToAuthenticate"
    roles = "listOfAttachedRoles">
```

Do not put spaces between the commas; "ADMIN,MYROLE" is different from "ADMIN, MYROLE". ***roles*** is case-sensitive as well, so "ADMIN,MYROLE" is different from "Admin,MyRole".

<CFLOGOUT>

Unauthenticates a user. Removes the current user's name and roles from the current session.

```
<CFLOGOUT>
```

GetAuthUser()

Returns **the name** of the current authenticated user or a blank string if none.

```
GetAuthUser()
```

IsUserInRole()

Returns **TRUE** if the current user's list of roles contains *roleName*.

```
IsUserInRole(
    "roleName")
```

Encryption

Decrypt()

Returns **a string** that is the result of decrypting *encryptedString* by using the specified *encryptionKey*.

```
Decrypt(
    encryptedString,
    encryptionKey)
```

Encrypt()

Returns **a string** that is the result of encrypting *clearTextString* using the specified *encryptionKey*.

Encrypt(
clearTextString,
encryptionKey)

Hash()

Returns **an MD5 hash** of *clearTextString*. This hashed value cannot be decrypted.

Hash(
clearTextString)

✦ ✦ ✦

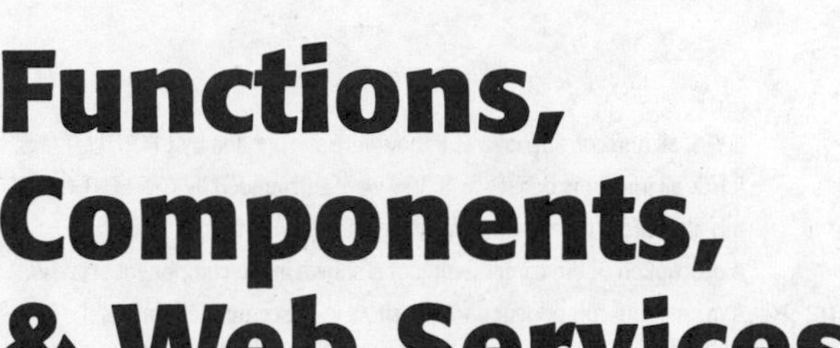

Functions, Components, & Web Services

<CFARGUMENT>

Describes an argument to a function created by using CFFUNCTION.

<CFARGUMENT	
name = "nameOfArgument"	The name of the function argument. Must be a valid variable name. This attribute is required if you use its containing component as a web service.
type = "ANY	
| ARRAY	
| BINARY	
| BOOLEAN	
| DATE	
| DATE	
| GUID	
| NUMERIC	Notice that it is NUMERIC, not NUMBER.
| QUERY	
| STRING	
| STRUCT	
| UUID	
| VARIABLENAME	
| nameOfComponent"	If the ***type*** attribute is not one of the standard types, ColdFusion assumes that it is the name of a component.
required = "NO | YES"	If YES, the argument must be supplied whenever invoking the function.
default = "argumentValueIfNotSupplied"	To use the ***default*** attribute, ***required*** must be NO.
hint = "documentationHint"	A description of the argument that is shown in the component browser.
displayName = "Human-Readable Name">	A meaningful argument name to show in the component browser.

Cross References

CFFUNCTION Creates a custom function.

<CFCOMPONENT>

Wraps function and property definitions to make them part of a ColdFusion component.

<CFCOMPONENT	
extends = "componentName"	
output = "YES	If YES, all functions behave as if they were surrounded by CFOUTPUT tags.
| NO"	If NO, all functions behave as if they were surrounded by CFSILENT tags. If this attribute is not specified, you see no special output behavior.
hint = "documentationHint"	A description of the component that is shown in the component browser.
displayName = "Human-Readable Name">	A meaningful component name to show in the component browser.
. . .	
</CFCOMPONENT>	

Cross References

CFFUNCTION	Defines a component method.
CFINVOKE	Calls a component method.

<CFFUNCTION>

Defines a user-defined function, or a component method if used in conjunction with CFCOMPONENT.

<CFFUNCTION	
name = "nameOfFunction"	
returnType = "ANY	The type of expression or variable this function will return.
| ARRAY	
| BINARY	
| BOOLEAN	
| DATE	
| DATE	
| GUID	
| NUMERIC	
| QUERY	
| STRING	
| STRUCT	
| UUID	
| VARIABLENAME	
| VOID	VOID means that the function does not return a value.
| nameOfComponent"	
roles = "ADMIN,CLERK,MANAGER"	A comma-delimited list of the roles that can access this function. Applies only to functions used as part of a component definition.
access = "PRIVATE	Access applies only to functions used as part of a component definition. PRIVATE indicates that only functions within the same component can call this function.
| PACKAGE	Indicates that only components within the same component package as this one can call this function.
| PUBLIC	Indicates that any ColdFusion routine can call this function.
| REMOTE"	Indicates that this function is available if this component is being used as a web service; can also be used by Flash Remoting. See Chapters 25 and 26 for details.

output = "YES | NO" — If yes, all functions behave as if they were surrounded with CFOUTPUT tags. If no, all functions behave as if they were surrounded with CFSILENT tags. If this attribute is not specified, there is no special output behavior.
hint = "documentationHint"
displayName = "Human-Readable Name">
...
</CFFUNCTION>

Cross References

CFARGUMENT	Defines a function argument.
CFCOMPONENT	Defines a component.
CFINVOKE	Calls a custom function.

<CFINVOKE>

Invokes a user-defined function or a component method. If invoking a component method and the component does not already exist, automatically instantiates and destroys an instance of that component.

As a method of a component:

<CFINVOKE

component = "componentName	Passing the name of a component to ***component*** instantiates a component object, calls the method, and then immediately destroys the object.
| #componentVariable#"	Passing an object to ***component*** invokes the method on that object.
method = "methodName"	
returnVariable = "nameOfReturnedVariable"	The name of the variable that contains the value returned from the function.
argumentCollection = "#structure#"	All the keys in structure are incorporated into the Arguments scope inside the function call.
...	Any additional attributes of the CFINVOKE tag become members of the Arguments scope inside the function.

>

As a local method within a component, or if calling a UDF defined in the current page:

<CFINVOKE

method = "functionName"	The name of the function to call.
returnVariable = "nameOfReturnedVariable"	The name of the variable that contains the value returned from the function.
argumentCollection = "#structure#"	All the keys in structure are incorporated into the Arguments scope inside the function call.
...	Any additional attributes of the CFINVOKE tag become members of the Arguments scope inside the function.

>

As a method of a web service:

<CFINVOKE

webService = "mappedServiceName	The name of a web service mapped inside ColdFusion Administrator.
| URLToWSDLFile"	The URL of a web service's WSDL file (for ColdFusion, that means http://server/file.cfc?wsdl).
method = "methodName"	
userName = "userNameForBasicAuthentication"	
password = "passwordForBasicAuthentication"	
returnVariable = "nameOfReturnedVariable"	The name of the variable that contains the value returned from the function.
argumentCollection = "#structure#"	All the keys in structure are incorporated into the Arguments scope inside the function call.
...	Any additional attributes of the CFINVOKE tag become members of the Arguments scope inside the function.

>

Cross References

CFCOMPONENT	Defines a ColdFusion component.
CFFUNCTION	Defines a function or component method.
CFINVOKEARGUMENT	Describes the arguments to pass to this function call.

<CFINVOKEARGUMENT>

Describes an argument to be passed to a call to CFINVOKE. Must be located inside of a CFINVOKE tag.

<CFINVOKEARGUMENT

name = "argumentName"	The name of the argument that you're passing. To pass arguments by position rather than name, leave this attribute blank.
value = "valueToPass">	The value of this function argument.

Cross References

CFINVOKE	Calls a custom function or component method.

<CFOBJECT>

Instantiates a COM, CORBA, Java, component, or web service object.

To instantiate a COM object:

<CFOBJECT

action = "CREATE	Creates a new instance of the COM object.
| CONNECT"	Connects to an existing instance of the COM object.
class = "ProgIDOfCOMClass	
| NameOfCOMClass"	
name = "nameOfNewObject"	Specifies the name of the variable that contains the COM object.
type = "COM"	

context = "INPROC	In-process object.
| LOCAL	Out-of-process but on this machine.
| REMOTE"	Calls a DCOM object on a remote machine.
server = "NameOfRemoteServer">	Required if ***context*** is REMOTE.

To instantiate a component object:

<CFOBJECT
name = "nameOfNewObject"
component = "nameOfComponent">

To instantiate a CORBA object:

<CFOBJECT

context = "IOR	Uses the Interoperable Object Reference (IOR) to access the CORBA server.
| NAMESERVICE"	Use a naming service to access the CORBA server. Valid only with a VisiBroker ORB (Object Request Broker).
class = "NameOfServiceOrClass"	If context is IOR, this attribute contains the path to a file containing the string IOR. If the context is NAMESERVICE, this is the naming context for a naming service.
name = "nameOfNewObject"	
type = "CORBA"	
locale = "argumentsToVisiBrokerORB">	If the ORB needs any extra arguments, pass them in this attribute. Valid only for VisiBroker ORBs.

To instantiate a Java or EJB object:

<CFOBJECT
action = "CREATE"
class = "nameOfJavaClass"
name = "nameOfNewObject"
type = "JAVA">

To instantiate a web service object:

<CFOBJECT
webService = "mappedServiceName
| URLToWSDLFile"
name = "nameOfNewObject">

Cross References

`CreateObject()` **Instantiates an object inside of** `CFSCRIPT`.

<CFPROPERTY>

Describes a property of a component.

<CFPROPERTY
name = "propertyName"
type = "ANY
| ARRAY

```
        | BINARY
        | BOOLEAN
        | DATE
        | DATE
        | GUID
        | NUMERIC
        | QUERY
        | STRING
        | STRUCT
        | UUID
        | VARIABLENAME
        | nameOfComponent"
    displayName = "Human-Readable Name"    Used in component documentation.
    hint = "documentationHint"             Used in component documentation.
    required = "NO | YES"                  Only for component documentation – has no relevance to your code.
    default = "defaultValue">              Only for component documentation – has no relevance to your code.
```

Cross References

`CFCOMPONENT`	Defines a ColdFusion component.

<CFRETURN>

Can be used inside only CFFUNCTION. Returns an expression to the routine that called the current function.

```
<CFRETURN
    expression>
```

Cross References

`CFFUNCTION`	Defines a function or component method.

CreateObject()

Returns a new COM, CORBA, Java, component, or web service **object**. Equivalent to `CFOBJECT` but can be used inside of `CFSCRIPT`.

To instantiate a component object:

```
CreateObject(
    "component",          The literal string "component".
    "componentName")      The name of the component.
```

To instantiate a web service object:

```
CreateObject(
    "webservice",
    wsdlURL)
```

Application Notes

- The complete syntax reference for `CreateObject()` is detailed in Chapter 55.

Cross References

`CFOBJECT`	Instantiates an object by using CFML.

GetMetaData()

Returns a **structure** containing information about the methods and properties of a given component.

GetMetaData(	
object)	A ColdFusion component object.

✦ ✦ ✦

What's on the CD-ROM

This appendix provides you with information on the contents of the CD that accompanies this book. For the latest and greatest information, please refer to the ReadMe file located at the root of the CD. Here is what you will find:

- ✦ System requirements
- ✦ Using the CD with Windows
- ✦ What's on the CD
- ✦ Troubleshooting notes

System Requirements

Make sure that your computer meets the minimum system requirements listed in this section. If your computer doesn't match most of these requirements, you may have a problem using the contents of the CD.

For Windows 98, Windows 2000, Windows NT4 (with SP6a or later), or Windows XP:

- ✦ PC with a Pentium II processor running at 300 Mhz or faster
- ✦ At least 128 MB of total RAM installed on your computer; for best performance, we recommend at least 256 MB
- ✦ At least 400 MB of free disk space to install ColdFusion Server; other products may require more
- ✦ A CD-ROM drive

Using the CD with Windows

To install the items from the CD to your hard drive, follow these steps:

1. Insert the CD into your computer's CD-ROM drive.
2. A window appears displaying the following options: Install, Browse, eBook, Links and Exit. Choose the option that best describes what you intend to do, as follows:

   Install: Gives you the option to install the supplied software and/or the author-created samples on the CD-ROM.

Browse: Enables you to view the contents of the CD-ROM in its directory structure.

eBook: Enables you to view an electronic version of the book.

Links: Opens a hyperlinked page of Web sites.

Exit: Closes the Autorun window.

If you do not have Autorun enabled or if the Autorun window does not appear, follow these steps to access the CD:

1. Click Start ⇨ Run.
2. In the dialog box that appears, type ***d*:\setup.exe**, where *d* is the letter of your CD-ROM drive, and click OK. This action opens the Autorun window described in the preceding set of steps.
3. Choose the Install, Browse, eBook, Links, or Exit option from the menu. (See the list following Step 2 in the preceding set of steps for a description of these options.)

What's on the CD

The following sections provide a summary of the software and other materials that you find on the CD.

Author-created materials

All author-created material from the book, including code listings and samples, are on the CD in the folder named `Author`. Inside this folder are folders labeled for each chapter of the book. (Chapter 2's files, for example, are located in a folder named `Ch02`, and so on.) Each folder contains files corresponding to the setup files and/or numbered listings in each chapter. If you find no folder for a given chapter, that chapter has no listings or setup files.

Another option is to use the self-extractor available on the CD to copy the chapter files from the CD to your hard drive. This self-extractor also provides a shortcut to these files from your Start menu. The files appear on your hard drive with the same hierarchy as the files on the CD.

Applications

This section describes the applications and tools provided on the CD to help make your development process a little easier.

Shareware programs are fully functional, trial versions of copyrighted programs. If you like particular programs, register with their authors for a nominal fee and receive licenses, enhanced versions, and technical support. *Freeware programs* are copyrighted games, applications, and utilities that are free for personal use. Unlike shareware, these programs do not require a fee or provide technical support. *GNU software* is governed by its own license, which is included inside the folder of the GNU product. See the GNU license for more details.

Trial, demo, or evaluation versions are usually limited either by time or functionality (such as no capability to save projects). Some trial versions are very sensitive to system date changes. If you alter your computer's date, the programs "time out" and are no longer functional.

Acrobat Reader 5.0, from Adobe Systems, Inc.

Freeware for Windows. Adobe Acrobat Reader enables you to read and search all the PDF documents provided on the CD. For more information, see `www.adobe.com`.

Adalon Developer Edition 2.5, from Synthis Corporation

Trial version for Windows. Adalon enables you to quickly build a Fusebox-specific framework and set of documentation to help get your application up and running that much faster. For more information, see `www.synthis.com`.

ColdFusion Server MX, from Macromedia

Thirty-day trial version for Windows. ColdFusion MX is a server-side scripting environment that enables you to quickly build Enterprise-level applications. After 30 days this trial version will revert to a two-user server (the machine on which ColdFusion Server MX is installed, plus one additional machine on your network). For more information, see `www.macromedia.com`.

CommerceBlocks v2.1, from Productivity Enhancement

Fifteen-day trial version for Windows. CommerceBlocks is a code generation tool that enables you to quickly and easily create an administrative interface into your relational database by using ColdFusion. For more information, see `www.commerceblocks.com`.

DataFactory 5.2, from Quest Software

Trial version for Windows. The most important part of effectively testing your ColdFusion application is making sure that the data you test against is of the same scale as the data that is to go in your production database. DataFactory enables you to populate your test database with data from many different data files to ensure a correct testing cycle. For more information, see `www.quest.com/datafactory`.

LoRCAT 1.0, from Productivity Enhancement

Fifteen-day trial version for Windows. LoRCAT helps improve your site's performance by stripping all extraneous white space from your code, thus reducing the amount of white space that must be delivered to and processed by the user's browser. LoRCAT also helps you locate "trouble spots" in your application with its reporting interface. For more information, see `www.ProductivityEnhancement.com`.

qForms 1.5, from PengoWorks

GNU software for all platforms. qForms is a JavaScript API that makes implementing complex form validation and field interaction easier by using simplified JavaScript that hides cross-platform and cross-browser compatibility issues. For more information, see `www.pengoworks.com`.

SourceOffSite 3.5.3, from SourceGear Corporation

Thirty-day, 10-user demo version for Windows. SourceOffSite enables you to access your Microsoft Visual SourceSafe database across the Internet. It is endorsed by Microsoft and contains features such as data compression and cryptography. For more information, see `www.sourcegear.com`.

Stored Procedure Wizard, from Productivity Enhancement

Freeware for Windows. This program is a wizard that integrates with Macromedia's ColdFusion Studio or HomeSite+ IDEs and that enables you to easily generate a Transact/SQL shell for a stored procedure as well as the ColdFusion code necessary to call the stored procedure. For more information, see `www.ProductivityEnhancement.com`.

eBook version of the ColdFusion MX Bible

For your convenience, we have included the contents of this book in PDF format on the CD so that you can read and search the book content by using the Adobe Acrobat Reader (also included on the CD). You cannot print the PDF, however, and it should not be distributed to anyone who doesn't already own the ColdFusion MX Bible.

Troubleshooting

If you have difficulty installing or using any of the materials on the companion CD, try the following solutions:

- **Turn off any anti-virus software that you may have running:** Installers sometimes mimic virus activity and can make your computer incorrectly believe that it is under attack by a virus. (Make sure that you turn the anti-virus software back on later.)
- **Close all running programs:** The more programs that you're running, the less memory is available to other programs. Installers also typically update files and programs; if you keep other programs running, installation may not work correctly.
- **Reference the ReadMe:** Please refer to the ReadMe file located at the root of the CD-ROM for the latest product information at the time of publication.
- **Refer to the documentation provided with a specific tool:** If you are having difficulty with a specific tool provided on the CD, check that tool's documentation to help diagnose and/or fix your problem.

If you still have trouble with the CD, please call the Customer Care phone number: (800) 762-2974. Outside the United States, call 1 (317) 572-3994. You can also contact Customer Service by e-mail at `techsupdum@wiley.com`. Wiley Publishing, Inc. provides technical support only for installation and other general quality-control items; for technical support on the applications themselves, consult the program's vendor or author.

✦ ✦ ✦

Index

Continued

Continued

B

C

Continued

Continued

Continued

Continued

Continued

F

Continued

Continued

G

H

I

Continued

K

L

Continued

M

N

O

Q

Continued

R

Continued

S

Continued

Continued

T

Continued

V

Continued

W

X

Continued

Z

Wiley Publishing, Inc.
End-User License Agreement

READ THIS. You should carefully read these terms and conditions before opening the software packet(s) included with this book "Book". This is a license agreement "Agreement" between you and Wiley Publishing, Inc."WPI". By opening the accompanying software packet(s), you acknowledge that you have read and accept the following terms and conditions. If you do not agree and do not want to be bound by such terms and conditions, promptly return the Book and the unopened software packet(s) to the place you obtained them for a full refund.

1. **License Grant.** WPI grants to you (either an individual or entity) a nonexclusive license to use one copy of the enclosed software program(s) (collectively, the "Software" solely for your own personal or non-commercial purposes on a single computer (whether a standard computer or a workstation component of a multi-user network). The Software is in use on a computer when it is loaded into temporary memory (RAM) or installed into permanent memory (hard disk, CD-ROM, or other storage device). WPI reserves all rights not expressly granted herein.
2. **Ownership.** WPI is the owner of all right, title, and interest, including copyright, in and to the compilation of the Software recorded on the disk(s) or CD-ROM "Software Media". Copyright to the individual programs recorded on the Software Media is owned by the author or other authorized copyright ownerof each program. Ownership of the Software and all proprietary rights relatingthereto remain with WPI and its licensers.
3. **Restrictions On Use and Transfer.** (a) You may only (i) make one copy of the Software for backup or archival purposes, or (ii) transfer the Software to a single hard disk, provided that you keep the original for backup or archival purposes. You may not (i) rent or lease the Software, (ii) copy or reproduce the Software through a LAN or other network system or through any computer subscriber system or bulletin- board system, or (iii) modify, adapt, or create derivative works based on the Software. (b) You may not reverse engineer, decompile, or disassemble the Software. You may transfer the Software and user documentation on a permanent basis, provided that the transferee agrees to accept the terms and conditions of this Agreement and you retain no copies. If the Software is an update or has been updated, any transfer must include the most recent update and all prior versions.
4. **Restrictions on Use of Individual Programs.** You must follow the individual requirements and restrictions detailed for each individual program in the About the CD-ROM appendix of this Book. These limitations are also contained in the individual license agreements recorded on the Software Media. These limitations may include a requirement that after using the program for a specified period of time, the user must pay a registration fee or discontinue use. By opening the Software packet(s), you will be agreeing to abide by the licenses and restrictions for these individual programs that are detailed in the About the CD-ROM appendix and on the Software Media. None of the material on this Software Media or listed in this Book may ever be redistributed, in original or modified form, for commercialpurposes.

5. **Limited Warranty.** (a) WPI warrants that the Software and Software Media are free from defects in materials and workmanship under normal use for a period of sixty (60) days from the date of purchase of this Book. If WPI receives notification within the warranty period of defects in materials or workmanship, WPI will replace the defective Software Media. (b) WPI AND THE AUTHOR OF THE BOOK DISCLAIM ALL OTHER WARRANTIES, EXPRESS OR IMPLIED, INCLUDING WITHOUT LIMITATION IMPLIED WARRANTIES OF MERCHANTABILITY AND FITNESS FOR A PARTICULAR PURPOSE, WITH RESPECT TO THE SOFTWARE, THE PROGRAMS, THE SOURCE CODE CONTAINED THEREIN, AND/OR THE TECHNIQUES DESCRIBED IN THIS BOOK. WPI DOES NOT WARRANT THAT THE FUNCTIONS CONTAINED IN THE SOFTWARE WILL MEET YOUR REQUIREMENTS OR THAT THE OPERATION OF THE SOFTWARE WILL BE ERROR FREE. (c) This limited warranty gives you specific legal rights, andyou may have other rights that vary from jurisdiction to jurisdiction.
6. **Remedies.** (a) WPI's entire liability and your exclusive remedy for defects in materials and workmanship shall be limited to replacement of the Software Media, which may be returned to WPI with a copy of your receipt at the following address: Software Media Fulfillment Department, Attn.: *ColdFusion MX Bible*, Wiley Publishing, Inc., 10475 Crosspoint Blvd., Indianapolis, IN 46256, or call 1-800-762-2974. Please allow four to six weeks for delivery. This Limited Warranty is void if failure of the Software Media has resulted from accident, abuse, or misapplication. Any replacement Software Media will be warranted for the remainder of the original warranty period or thirty (30) days, whichever is longer. (b) In no event shall WPI or the author be liable for any damages whatsoever (including without limitation damages for loss of business profits, business interruption, loss of business information, or any other pecuniary loss) arising from the use of or inability to use the Book or the Software, even if WPI has been advised of the possibility of such damages. (c) Because some jurisdictions do not allow the exclusion or limitation of liability for consequential or incidental damages, the above limitation or exclusion may not apply to you.
7. **U.S. Government Restricted Rights.** Use, duplication, or disclosure of the Software for or on behalf of the United States of America, its agencies and/or instrumentalities "U.S. Government" is subject to restrictions as stated in paragraph (c)(1)(ii) of the Rights in Technical Data and Computer Software clause of DFARS 252.227-7013, or subparagraphs (c) (1) and (2) of the Commercial Computer Software - Restricted Rights clause at FAR 52.227-19, and in similar clauses in the NASA FAR supplement, as applicable.
8. **General.** This Agreement constitutes the entire understanding of the parties and revokes and supersedes all prior agreements, oral or written, between them and may not be modified or amended except in a writing signed by both parties hereto that specifically refers to this Agreement. This Agreement shall take precedence over any other documents that may be in conflict herewith. If any one or more provisions contained in this Agreement are held by any court or tribunal to be invalid, illegal, or otherwise unenforceable, each and every other provision shall remain in full force and effect.